taste of home

Best LOVED Recipes

taste of home
BOOKS

taste of home Reader's Digest

A TASTE OF HOME/READER'S DIGEST BOOK
© 2012 Reiman Media Group, LLC
5400 S. 60th St., Greendale WI 53129

EDITORIAL
Editor-in-Chief: **CATHERINE CASSIDY**

Executive Editor, Print and Digital Books: **STEPHEN C. GEORGE**
Creative Director: **HOWARD GREENBERG**
Editorial Services Manager: **KERRI BALLIET**

Editor: **JANET BRIGGS**
Associate Creative Director: **EDWIN ROBLES JR.**
Art Director: **RUDY KROCHALK**
Content Production Manager: **JULIE WAGNER**
Project Layout Designers: **HOLLY PATCH, CATHERINE FLETCHER**
Copy Chief: **DEB WARLAUMONT MULVEY**
Copy Editors: **ALYSSE GEAR, DULCIE SHOENER, MARY C. HANSON**
Project Proofreaders: **BARBARA SCHUETZ, JEAN DAL PORTO, VALERIE BERG PHILLIPS**
Project Indexer: **JULIE KASTELLO**
Recipe Content Manager: **COLLEEN KING**
Recipe Testing & Editing: **TASTE OF HOME TEST KITCHEN**
Food Photography: **TASTE OF HOME PHOTO STUDIO**
Executive Assistant: **MARIE BRANNON**
Editorial Assistants: **MARILYN ICZKOWSKI, VICTORIA SOUKUP JENSEN**

BUSINESS
Vice President, Publisher: **JAN STUDIN, JAN_STUDIN@RD.COM**
Regional Account Director: **DONNA LINDSKOG, DONNA_LINDSKOG@RD.COM**
Eastern Account Director: **JENNIFER DIETZ**
Midwest & Western Account Director: **JACKIE FALLON**
Midwest Account Manager: **LORNA PHILLIPS**
Western Account Manager: **JOEL MILLIKIN**
Michigan Sales Representative: **LINDA C. DONALDSON**

Corporate Integrated Sales Director: **STEVE SOTTILE**
Vice President, Digital Sales and Development: **DAN MEEHAN**
Digital Sales Planner: **TIM BAARDA**

General Manager, Taste of Home Cooking Schools: **ERIN PUARIEA**

Direct Response: **KATHERINE ZITO, DAVID GELLER ASSOCIATES**

Executive Director, Brand Marketing: **LEAH WEST**
Associate Marketing Managers: **BETSY CONNORS, EMILY MOORE**

Vice President, Creative Director: **PAUL LIVORNESE**
Public Relations Manager: **HEIDI FRANK**

Vice President, Magazine Marketing: **DAVE FIEGEL**

READER'S DIGEST NORTH AMERICA
President: **DAN LAGANI**

President, Canada: **TONY CIOFFI**
President, Books and Home Entertaining: **HAROLD CLARKE**
Chief Financial Officer: **HOWARD HALLIGAN**
Vice President, General Manager, Reader's Digest Media: **MARILYNN JACOBS**
Chief Marketing Officer: **RENEE JORDAN**
Vice President, Chief Sales Officer: **MARK JOSEPHSON**
Vice President, General Manager, RD Milwaukee: **LISA KARPINSKI**
Vice President, Chief Strategy Officer: **JACQUELINE MAJERS LACHMAN**
Vice President, Marketing and Creative Services: **ELIZABETH TIGHE**
Vice President, Chief Content Officer: **LIZ VACCARIELLO**

THE READER'S DIGEST ASSOCIATION, INC.
President and Chief Executive Officer: **ROBERT E. GUTH**

For other **TASTE OF HOME BOOKS** and products, visit us at TASTEOFHOME.COM.

For more **READER'S DIGEST** products and information, visit **RD.COM** (in the United States) or **RD.CA** (in Canada).

International Standard Book Number: **(10): 0-89821-991-4**
International Standard Book Number: **(13): 978-0-89821-991-3**
Library of Congress Control Number: **2011937237**

COVER PHOTOGRAPHY
Photographers: **JIM WIELAND, GRACE NATOLI SHELDON**
Food Styling Manager: **SARAH THOMPSON**
Food Stylist: **KAITLYN BESASIE**
Set Styling Manager: **STEPHANIE MARCHESE**
Set Stylist: **PAM STASNEY**

PICTURED ON FRONT COVER (left to right): Meaty Spinach Manicotti, pg. 648; Sour Cream Chocolate Cake, pg. 171; Champagne-Basted Turkey, pg. 730.
PICTURED ON SPINE: Texas-Style Beef Brisket, pg. 656.
PICTURED ON BACK COVER (top to bottom): Southwestern Omelet, pg. 133; Chocolate Raspberry Cheesecake, pg. 376; Chicken Satay, pg. 15.
PICTURED ON BACK FLAP: Turkey Potpies, pg. 739.

Printed in China.
13 5 7 9 10 8 6 4 2

TABLE *of* CONTENTS

Think about your favorite dishes—your own family's creations, the ones you grew up with, the stuff of legends, the ones everyone loves. Now call to mind the faces and stories behind each of those memorable dishes. Right there, my friends, is the magic of food.

> **"What I love so much about *Taste of Home* is that we celebrate the folks who make each recipe come to life."**

The most popular recipes are always wed to at least one wonderful story, and the best loved have a namesake, a person, attached right to them. They say that people make the place. Well, people make the food, too, in more ways than just cooking it. What I love so much about *Taste of Home* is that we celebrate the folks who make each recipe come to life.

And that's exactly what makes this book so special. It's not just great recipes, and not just award-winning recipes. These are our best loved recipes. The ones that conjure up heavenly aromas, that bring you back to Sunday dinner tables, summer picnics and holiday parties, that call vividly to mind the special cooks who made them. The ones that make you close your eyes, smile and say, "*Mmmm!*"

Food is most nourishing when there's a history of love baked right into the crust, caramelized into the casserole, simmered into the sauce. In this beautiful book, as well as in *Taste of Home* magazine, on our website and even in technology that has yet to appear on kitchen counters, we will always share with you the name of the special home cook who has been generous and proud enough to share a best loved recipe, a personal story, a moment in time with us. That your loved ones have been enchanted enough with a dish to turn it into family legend in your recipe collection is, in the end, the magic of food. And it's what *Taste of Home* is all about.

Enjoy!

Catherine Cassidy
Editor-in-Chief
Taste of Home

❧ GOOD RECIPES, GREAT STORIES ❧

Celebrating 20 Years of *Taste of Home*

The recipe was simple: Create a magazine devoted to delicious home-cooked food, packed with recipes submitted by readers. Share the recipes with others—and share the stories, cooking hints and tips of the folks who submitted them. Mix and serve.

So the call went out to 1,400 home cooks across North America and nearly all of them responded, sending in their best, tastiest, most treasured recipes for the first issue.

But all good recipes need a great name, and the editors cooking up this new magazine didn't have one. They batted around titles like *Home Cooking, What's Cooking, Dinner Bell,* and many others that didn't quite fit.

In the end, it was one of those home cooks who saved the day. Responding to our earliest requests for ideas to shape the magazine, Janet Siciak of Bernard, Massachusetts, wrote: "You want the title of your magazine to conjure up the kind of expectant anticipation you get when you're offered a peek into a dear friend's heirloom recipe collection; a title that suggests food that is...a taste of home."

From its humble origins 20 years ago, *Taste of Home* has become one of America's most popular—and most trusted—names in home cooking. What started as one bimonthly publication has evolved into a family of magazines, special issues, annuals, cookbooks and digital editions. Those first 1,400 home cooks who sent in the handwritten recipes that filled our early issues have been joined by a reading audience numbered in the millions, and they submit almost 100,000 recipes a year, covering a range of tastes and styles as broad as the American palate.

Our staff has grown too, from a few editors trying out recipes in their own homes to a diverse team of cooking professionals who prepare up to 100 different recipes per week in our three Test Kitchens. We've recruited our most dedicated readers from throughout the U.S. and Canada to form our 1,000-strong network of Field Editors—the largest of its kind. These folks deserve a special shout-out. After all, our Field Editors are volunteers from all walks of life. These are busy people—nurses, farmers, teachers, dietitians, caterers, secretaries, stay-at-home moms—who still selflessly dedicate their time and energy to support *Taste of Home*. As you might expect, they provide recipes, tips and ideas for the magazine as well as the forums on tasteofhome.com. But these Field Editors also serve as our cheerleaders and goodwill ambassadors, promoting *Taste of Home* in their communities in a variety of ways, from chatting about the magazine at the hairdresser to conducting cooking demonstrations for women's groups or at community centers and libraries. They even get calls at home from people seeking cooking advice. Over the years, many Field Editors have become local celebrities, appearing on television and radio, or writing blogs and columns in local newspapers.

But some things haven't changed. Our recipes, whether sent to us by text, via email or on handwritten cards, are still and always real food from real home cooks. Our staffers, whether working in the Test Kitchen or in their home kitchens, still check every recipe to make sure it's simple, delicious, and uses ingredients you can find at your local supermarket. And no matter how much *Taste of Home* has grown, we've never forgotten that we're part of a community—a group of like-minded home cooks of all ages and backgrounds who share kitchen secrets, stories, glimpses into their homes and lives—and, of course, great recipes for delicious food made with care and love. Without them, you wouldn't be holding this book, the ultimate collection of *Taste of Home's* most beloved entrees, sides, desserts and more.

Best *of the* Best Loved

Since day one, *Taste of Home* has selected only the very best of the tens of thousands of recipes submitted every year both by readers and Field Editors across North America. So believe us when we say: It wasn't easy picking the recipes you'll find here.

From submission to publication, all our recipes go through numerous reviews and tests. First, we look at the basics: Are the directions clear and simple? Are the ingredients readily available in the average grocery store or farmers market—and, in the rare cases when they aren't, can we suggest reasonable substitutes? Most importantly, does the recipe work? It has to: We guarantee that every recipe we feature—including the ones in this book—will look, smell and taste as delicious in your kitchen as it does in ours.

Beyond that, we look for other qualities, factors that make a recipe uniquely worthy of *Taste of Home*. It might be a recipe that offers a fresh take on a classic, or a dish that uses traditional ethnic or regional ingredients in an interesting (and flavorful) way. Knowing that most households have at least one picky eater at the table, we always keep an eye out for recipes that add a "yum" factor to foods normally rejected by finicky palates. Good recipes often come with great stories, so we pay attention when a reader shares the entree that impressed the prickly in-laws, the last-minute entry that won the bake-off, or the surprise side dish that introduced a dubious child to his new favorite food. And we admit it: We have a particular soft spot for secret family recipes, and the home cooks who trust us to do them justice, and to share them with others.

You'll find all of the above in the 26 chapters that comprise this collection, the absolute best recipes we've ever published, based on editors' picks, reader reviews and feedback from our community on tasteofhome.com. You'll even find many of those comments sprinkled throughout the book. For each recipe listed, we've included the year it was originally published, the reader who submitted it, and short tips, facts, or stories the submitter shared with us. The top 100 favorite recipes, based on ratings from our readers, are highlighted with:

Of course, as you cook and bake your way through this book, we expect you to pick your personal favorites. And if you have a beloved recipe of your own, we hope you'll share it with us—it's as simple as visiting tasteofhome.com/submit. You'll be joining a conversation—and a community—that's been going strong for the past 20 years. And all it takes is a single, simple recipe.

~ APPETIZERS ~

[2011]

CARAMELIZED FENNEL TARTS

yield: 2 dozen ∞ prep: 45 min.
bake: 15 min.

(Pictured on page 36)

*I love fennel cooked in every way, but think it is
really amazing when sauteed until golden, then
baked on delicious puff pastry!*

—Lisa Speer, Palm Beach, Florida

---

  2 medium fennel bulbs, quartered and
     thinly sliced
  2 tablespoons olive oil
1-1/2 teaspoons minced fresh thyme *or*
     1/2 teaspoon dried thyme
  1 teaspoon balsamic vinegar
1/4 teaspoon salt
1/8 teaspoon pepper
  1 package (17.3 ounces) frozen puff
     pastry, thawed

---

1. In a large skillet, saute fennel in oil
   until softened. Reduce the heat to
   medium-low; cook, uncovered, for
   40 minutes or until deep golden
   brown, stirring occasionally. Stir in
   thyme, vinegar, salt and pepper.

2. Unfold each puff pastry sheet onto an
   ungreased baking sheet. Using a knife,
   score 1 in. from the edges of each
   pastry. Spread the fennel mixture to
   within 1/2 in. of edges.

3. Bake at 400° for 12-15 minutes or until
   pastry is golden brown. Cut each tart
   into 12 pieces.

[1996]

APPETIZER MEATBALLS

yield: about 3 dozen ∞ prep: 15 min.
bake: 50 min.

*These tasty meatballs are a perennial favorite
at our Christmas parties.*

—Pat Waymire
  Yellow Springs, Ohio, Field Editor

---

  1 egg, lightly beaten
1/2 cup soft bread crumbs
1/4 cup 2% milk
1/3 cup finely chopped onion
  1 teaspoon salt
1/2 teaspoon Worcestershire sauce
  1 pound ground beef
SAUCE:
1/2 cup ketchup
1/2 cup chopped onion
1/3 cup sugar
1/3 cup vinegar
  1 tablespoon Worcestershire sauce
1/8 teaspoon pepper

TOP 100 RECIPE

---

1. In a small bowl, combine the egg,
   bread crumbs, milk, onion, salt and
   Worcestershire sauce. Crumble beef
   over mixture and mix well. Shape into
   1-in. balls.

2. In a large skillet over medium heat,
   brown meatballs; drain. Place in a
   2-1/2-qt. baking dish. Combine the
   sauce ingredients. Pour over meatballs.
   Bake, uncovered, at 350° for 50-60
   minutes or until meatballs are no
   longer pink.

[2012]

BEEF TENDERLOIN & PUMPERNICKEL CROSTINI

yield: 3 dozen ∾ prep: 20 min.
bake: 30 min. + standing

The horseradish sauce wakes up the flavor of roast beef in this crowd-pleasing canape. The watercress garnish will give it a peppery bite.

—*Sharon Tipton, Winter Garden, Florida*

---

  1 tablespoon olive oil
  1 beef tenderloin roast (2 pounds)
  1 teaspoon salt, *divided*
1/2 teaspoon coarsely ground pepper
  1 cup (8 ounces) sour cream
1/4 cup prepared horseradish
  2 tablespoons lemon juice
1/4 teaspoon paprika
 18 slices pumpernickel bread, halved
  3 tablespoons butter, melted
  1 bunch watercress

---

1. Rub oil over tenderloin; sprinkle with 3/4 teaspoon salt and pepper. In a large skillet, brown beef on all sides. Place on a rack in a shallow roasting pan.

2. Bake, uncovered, at 425° for 25-35 minutes or until meat reaches desired doneness (for medium-rare, a thermometer should read 145°; medium, 160°; well-done, 170°). Let the meat stand for 10 minutes before slicing thinly.

3. In a small bowl, combine sour cream, horseradish, lemon juice, paprika and remaining salt. Chill until serving.

4. Brush both sides of bread with butter; place on baking sheets. Bake at 425° for 4-6 minutes or until the bread is toasted, turning once.

5. Spread with sauce; top with beef. Garnish with watercress sprigs.

[2002]

COCONUT FRIED SHRIMP

yield: 4 servings ∾ prep/total time: 20 min.

These crisp and crunchy shrimp make a tempting appetizer or a fun change-of-pace main dish. The coconut coating adds a little sweetness and the tangy orange marmalade and honey sauce is wonderful for dipping. It's impossible to stop munching these once you start!

—*Ann Atchison, O'Fallon, Missouri*

1-1/4 cups all-purpose flour
1-1/4 cups cornstarch
6-1/2 teaspoons baking powder
  1/2 teaspoon salt
  1/4 teaspoon Cajun seasoning
1-1/2 cups cold water
  1/2 teaspoon canola oil
2-1/2 cups flaked coconut
    1 pound uncooked large shrimp, peeled and deveined
Additional oil for deep-fat frying
    1 cup orange marmalade
  1/4 cup honey

---

1. In a large bowl, combine the first five ingredients. Stir in water and oil until smooth. Place coconut in another bowl. Dip shrimp into batter, then coat with coconut.

2. In an electric skillet or deep-fat fryer, heat oil to 375°. Fry shrimp, a few at a time, for 3 minutes or until golden brown. Drain on paper towels.

3. In a small saucepan, heat marmalade and honey; stir until blended. Serve with shrimp.

Editor's Note: Fry only two to three shrimp at a time or the temperature of the oil will lower and the shrimp will not be crisp.

COCONUT FRIED SHRIMP

"We were blown away with this recipe! My husband loves coconut so I knew he would like this. I have tried other coconut shrimp recipes, but this one had a thicker batter, which stayed on and held the coconut. I fried the shrimp in a fryer on the stove and I could not have asked it to be any better. Will definitely use again and often."
—*gypsy11110*

[2011]

MEDITERRANEAN NACHOS

yield: 12 servings ∞ **prep: 30 min.+ standing**
cook: 15 min.

Try this healthy and nutritious alternative to regular nachos. The beauty of this recipe is that I can prep all the veggies and make the dressing in the morning, then store each separately in the refrigerator. Later in the day, all I need to do is make the meat mixture and pita chips.

—*Zaza Fullman-Kasl, Ventura, California*

2	medium cucumbers, peeled, seeded and grated
1-1/2	teaspoons salt, *divided*
1/2	teaspoon ground cumin
1/2	teaspoon ground coriander
1/2	teaspoon paprika
3/4	teaspoon pepper, *divided*
6	whole pita breads (6 inches)

Cooking spray

1	pound ground lamb *or* beef
2	garlic cloves, minced
1	teaspoon cornstarch
1/2	cup beef broth
2	cups plain Greek yogurt
2	tablespoons lemon juice
1/4	teaspoon grated lemon peel
2	cups torn romaine
2	medium tomatoes, seeded and chopped
1/2	cup pitted Greek olives, sliced
4	green onions, thinly sliced
1/2	cup crumbled feta cheese

1. In a colander set over a bowl, toss cucumbers with 1/2 teaspoon salt. Let stand for 30 minutes. Squeeze and pat dry. Set aside. In a small bowl, combine the cumin, coriander, paprika, 1/2 teaspoon pepper and 1/2 teaspoon salt; set aside.

2. Cut each pita into eight wedges; arrange in a single layer on ungreased baking sheets. Spritz both sides of pitas with cooking spray; sprinkle with 3/4 teaspoon seasoning mixture. Broil 3-4 in. from the heat for 3-4 minutes on each side or until golden brown. Cool on wire racks.

3. In a large skillet, cook lamb and remaining seasoning mix over medium heat until lamb is no longer pink. Add garlic; cook 1 minute longer. Drain. Combine the cornstarch and broth until smooth; gradually stir into the pan. Bring to a boil; cook and stir for 2 minutes or until thickened.

4. In a small bowl, combine the yogurt, lemon juice, lemon peel, cucumbers and remaining salt and pepper. Arrange pita wedges on a serving platter. Layer with lettuce, lamb mixture, tomatoes, olives, onions and cheese. Serve immediately with cucumber sauce.

[1993]

BLT BITES

yield: 16-20 appetizer servings ∞ **prep: 25 min. + chilling**
(Pictured on page 34)

These quick hors d'oeuvres may be mini, but their bacon and tomato flavor is full size. I serve them at parties, brunches and picnics, and they're always a hit. Even my kids love them.

—*Kellie Remmen, Detroit Lakes, Minnesota*

16	to 20 cherry tomatoes
1	pound sliced bacon, cooked and crumbled
1/2	cup mayonnaise
1/3	cup chopped green onions
3	tablespoons grated Parmesan cheese
2	tablespoons snipped fresh parsley

1. Cut a thin slice off of each tomato top. Scoop out and discard pulp. Invert tomatoes on a paper towel to drain.

2. In a small bowl, combine the remaining ingredients. Spoon into tomatoes. Refrigerate for several hours before serving.

[2001]

CHICKEN QUESADILLAS WITH HOMEMADE TORTILLAS

yield: 14 quesadillas
prep/total time: 30 min.

Tender homemade tortillas make this savory snack extra-special.

—Linda Miller, Klamath Falls, Oregon

4	cups all-purpose flour
1-1/2	teaspoons salt
1/2	teaspoon baking powder
1	cup shortening
1-1/4	cups warm water
1	cup *each* shredded cheddar, part-skim mozzarella and pepper Jack cheese
2	cups diced cooked chicken
1	cup sliced green onions
1	cup sliced ripe olives
1	can (4 ounces) chopped green chilies, drained

Salsa and sour cream

---

1. In a large bowl, combine the flour, salt and baking powder. Cut in shortening until crumbly. Add enough warm water, stirring, until mixture forms a ball. Let stand for 10 minutes. Divide into 28 portions.

2. On a lightly floured surface, roll each portion into a 7-in. circle. Cook on a lightly greased griddle for 1-1/2 to 2 minutes on each side, breaking any bubbles with a toothpick if necessary. Keep warm.

3. In a bowl, combine cheeses. For each quesadilla, place a tortilla on griddle; sprinkle with about 2 tablespoons cheese mixture, 2 tablespoons chicken, 1 tablespoon onions, 1 tablespoon olives and 1 teaspoon chilies. Top with 1 tablespoon cheese mixture and another tortilla.

4. Cook for 30-60 seconds; turn and cook 30 seconds longer or until cheese is melted. Cut into wedges. Serve with salsa and sour cream.

[1999]

MINI CORN DOGS

yield: 2 dozen ∞ prep/total time: 30 min.

(*Pictured on page 36*)

Summertime means county fairs and corn dogs! I make my own by wrapping cornmeal dough around mini hot dogs. The young and young at heart love them.

—Geralyn Harrington
Floral Park, New York

1-2/3	cups all-purpose flour
1/3	cup cornmeal
3	teaspoons baking powder
1	teaspoon salt
3	tablespoons cold butter
1	tablespoon shortening
1	egg
3/4	cup 2% milk
24	miniature hot dogs

HONEY MUSTARD SAUCE:

1/3	cup honey
1/3	cup prepared mustard
1	tablespoon molasses

---

1. In a large bowl, combine the first four ingredients. Cut in the butter and shortening until mixture resembles coarse crumbs. Beat egg and milk; stir into the dry ingredients until a soft dough forms.

2. Turn onto a lightly floured surface; knead 6-8 times or until smooth. Roll out to 1/4-in. thickness. Cut with a 2-1/4-in. biscuit cutter. Fold each dough circle over a hot dog and press edges to seal (dough will be sticky). Place on greased baking sheets.

3. Bake at 450° for 10-12 minutes or until golden brown. In a small bowl, combine sauce ingredients. Serve with corn dogs.

MINI CORN DOGS

"This is a great recipe!!! Super easy, mixed the dough in my food processor and I used turkey dogs to make it a little healthier :) The sauce is fantastic too!!"
—twinklestar241

[2001]

PORK EGG ROLLS

yield: 8 egg rolls ∞ prep: 25 min.
cook: 20 min.

I take these egg rolls and their tasty sweet-and-sour sauce to every family gathering.

—*Jody Minke, Hugo, Minnesota*

- 1/2 pound ground pork
- 3/4 cup shredded cabbage
- 1/2 cup chopped celery
- 4 green onions, sliced
- 3 tablespoons canola oil
- 1/2 cup salad shrimp, chopped
- 1/2 cup water chestnuts, chopped
- 1/2 cup canned bean sprouts, chopped
- 1 garlic clove, minced
- 2 to 3 tablespoons reduced-sodium soy sauce
- 1 teaspoon sugar
- 8 refrigerated egg roll wrappers
  Oil for frying
  SWEET-AND-SOUR SAUCE:
- 1 cup sugar
- 2 tablespoons cornstarch
- 1 teaspoon seasoned salt
- 1/2 cup white vinegar
- 1/2 cup water
- 1 tablespoon maraschino cherry juice, optional
- 1 teaspoon Worcestershire sauce

1. In a large skillet, cook pork over medium heat until no longer pink; drain. Remove pork with a slotted spoon and set aside.

2. In the same skillet, stir-fry cabbage, celery and onions in oil until crisp-tender. Add shrimp, water chestnuts, bean sprouts, garlic, soy sauce, sugar and reserved pork; stir-fry 4 minutes longer or until liquid has evaporated. Remove from the heat.

3. Position one egg roll wrapper with a corner facing you. Spoon 1/3 cup filling on the bottom third of wrapper.

Fold a bottom corner over filling; fold sides over filling toward the center. Moisten top corner with water; roll up tightly to seal. Repeat with remaining wrappers and filling.

4. In an electric skillet, heat 1 in. of oil to 375°. Fry egg rolls for 1-2 minutes on each side or until golden brown. Drain on paper towels.

5. For sauce, combine sugar, cornstarch and seasoned salt in a saucepan; gradually add remaining ingredients. Bring to a boil; cook and stir for 2 minutes or until thickened. Serve with egg rolls.

[2003]

RANCH HAM ROLL-UPS

yield: about 7-1/2 dozen
prep: 15 min. + chilling
(*Pictured on page 34*)

These pretty pinwheel appetizers are easy to make and fun to nibble, with a yummy cream cheese filling that's layered with ham.

—*Charlie Clutts, New Tazewell, Tennessee*

- 2 packages (8 ounces each) cream cheese, softened
- 1 envelope ranch salad dressing mix
- 3 green onions, chopped
- 11 flour tortillas (8 inches)
- 22 thin slices deli ham

1. In a small bowl, beat cream cheese and salad dressing mix until smooth. Stir in onions. Spread about 3 tablespoons over each tortilla; top each with two ham slices.

2. Roll up tightly and wrap in plastic wrap. Refrigerate until firm. Unwrap and cut into 3/4-in. slices.

[2010]

TAPAS MEATBALLS WITH ORANGE GLAZE

yield: 16 meatballs ∽ prep: 25 min.
bake: 20 min.

Crisp on the outside, moist on the inside, these baked cheese-stuffed appetizers are drizzled with a tangy, irresistible glaze.

—Bonnie Stallings
    Martinsburg, West Virginia, Field Editor

---

  1 egg, lightly beaten
1/4 cup ketchup
  1 small onion, finely chopped
1/2 cup soft bread crumbs
1/4 cup minced fresh parsley
  3 teaspoons paprika
  2 garlic cloves, minced
1/2 teaspoon salt
1/2 teaspoon pepper
  1 pound lean ground beef (90% lean)
2-1/2 ounces feta cheese, cut into sixteen 1/2-in. cubes

GLAZE:
  1 jar (12 ounces) orange marmalade
1/4 cup orange juice
  3 green onions, chopped, *divided*
  1 jalapeno pepper, seeded and chopped

---

1. In a large bowl, combine the first nine ingredients. Crumble the beef over the mixture and mix well. Divide into 16 portions; flatten. Top each with a cheese cube; form beef mixture around cheese into meatballs.

2. Place on a greased rack in a shallow baking pan. Bake, uncovered, at 400° for 20-25 minutes or until no longer pink.

3. In a small saucepan, heat the marmalade, orange juice, half of the green onions and the jalapeno.

4. Place meatballs in a serving dish; pour glaze over the top and gently stir to coat. Garnish with the remaining green onions.

Editor's Note: Wear disposable gloves when cutting hot peppers; the oils can burn skin. Avoid touching your face.

[2006]

SPICY SHRIMP

yield: 6 servings ∽ prep/total time: 30 min.

I think my shrimp recipe is unique, and it's easy to prepare.

—Bob Gebhardt, Wausau, Wisconsin

---

  6 bacon strips, diced
1-1/2 teaspoons chili powder
  1 cup butter, cubed
  2 tablespoons seafood seasoning
  2 tablespoons Dijon mustard
  1 teaspoon pepper
1/2 to 1 teaspoon Louisiana-style hot sauce
1/4 teaspoon *each* dried basil, oregano and thyme
  2 garlic cloves, minced
1-1/2 pounds uncooked shell-on medium shrimp

---

1. In a large skillet, cook bacon over medium heat until partially cooked but not crisp; drain. Stir in the butter, seafood seasoning, mustard, chili powder, pepper, hot sauce, basil, oregano and thyme. Cook over low heat for 5 minutes. Add the garlic; cook 1 minute longer.

2. Place the shrimp in an ungreased 13-in. x 9-in. baking dish. Add sauce and stir to coat. Bake, uncovered, at 375° for 20-25 minutes or until the shrimp turn pink, stirring twice.

SPICY SHRIMP

"Really great shrimp. The thing I love about this recipe is how versatile it is! To make it even spicier (I've got spicehounds in my household), I substituted cayenne pepper for black pepper and marinated the shrimp for a couple of hours in a 'brine' made up of chopped garlic, jalapenos and jalapeno juice. The result was outstanding! Make sure to serve this with something to sop up the sauce! (Rice or French bread!) Thank you, Bob!"

—Sarah_Marie_Bee

[2011]

TOMATO-HERB FOCACCIA
yield: 1 loaf (12 pieces)
prep: 30 min. + rising ∽ **bake: 20 min.**

With its medley of herbs and tomatoes, this rustic bread will liven up any occasion, from a family meal to a game day get-together. And it won't last long.

—*Janet Miller, Indianapolis, Indiana*

---

    1 package (1/4 ounce) active dry yeast
    1 cup warm water (110° to 115°)
    2 tablespoons olive oil, *divided*
1-1/2 teaspoons salt
    1 teaspoon sugar
    1 teaspoon garlic powder
    1 teaspoon *each* dried oregano, thyme and rosemary, crushed
  1/2 teaspoon dried basil
Dash pepper
    2 to 2-1/2 cups all-purpose flour
    2 plum tomatoes, thinly sliced
  1/4 cup shredded part-skim mozzarella cheese
    1 tablespoon grated Parmesan cheese

---

1. In a large bowl, dissolve yeast in warm water. Add 1 tablespoon oil, salt, sugar, garlic powder, herbs, pepper and 1-1/2 cups flour. Beat until smooth. Stir in enough remaining flour to form a soft dough (dough will be sticky).

2. Turn onto a floured surface; knead until smooth and elastic, about 6-8 minutes. Place in a greased bowl, turning once to grease the top. Cover and let rise in a warm place until doubled, about 1 hour.

3. Punch dough down. Cover and let rest for 10 minutes. Shape into a 13-in. x 9-in. rectangle; place on a greased baking sheet. Cover and let rise until doubled, about 30 minutes. With fingertips, make several dimples over top of dough.

4. Brush dough with remaining oil; arrange tomatoes over the top. Sprinkle with cheeses. Bake at 400° for 20-25 minutes or until golden brown. Remove to a wire rack.

[2007]

ZUCCHINI FETA BRUSCHETTA
yield: 3 dozen
prep: 30 min. + chilling ∽ **cook: 15 min.**
(Pictured on page 35)

I make this bruschetta with tomatoes, zucchini, garlic and basil fresh from the garden. I took it to a family gathering and everybody loved it.

—*Tootie Ann Webber, Lupton, Michigan*

---

    1 large tomato, seeded and chopped
    1 medium zucchini, finely chopped
    4 green onions, thinly sliced
    2 tablespoons minced fresh basil
    4 to 6 garlic cloves, minced
    2 tablespoons lemon juice
    2 tablespoons olive oil
  3/4 teaspoon salt
  1/4 teaspoon pepper
  1/2 cup crumbled feta cheese
    1 loaf (1 pound) unsliced Italian bread
  1/4 to 1/3 cup butter, softened

---

1. In a large bowl, combine the tomato, zucchini, onions, basil and garlic. In a small bowl, whisk the lemon juice, oil, salt and pepper. Pour over the tomato mixture and toss to coat. Stir in the cheese. Cover and refrigerate for at least 1 hour.

2. Cut bread into 18 slices; spread butter on both sides. In a large skillet or griddle, toast bread on both sides or until lightly browned. Cut each slice in half; use a slotted spoon to top each with tomato mixture.

TOMATO-HERB FOCACCIA

"I made this with my 8-year-old daughter and it was FANTASTIC!"
—*tamarachronister*

[2005]

CHICKEN SATAY
yield: 8 servings (1 cup sauce)
prep: 15 min. + marinating   ∽   grill: 5 min.

(Pictured on page 36)

These golden skewered chicken snacks are marinated and grilled, then served with a zesty Thai-style peanut butter sauce.

—*Sue Gronholz*
Beaver Dam, Wisconsin, Field Editor

>   2   **pounds boneless skinless**
>   **chicken breasts**
>   1/2   **cup 2% milk**
>   6   **garlic cloves, minced**
>   1   **tablespoon brown sugar**
>   1   **tablespoon** *each* **ground coriander,**
>   **ground turmeric and ground cumin**
>   1   **teaspoon salt**
>   1   **teaspoon white pepper**
>   1/8   **teaspoon coconut extract**
>
> **PEANUT BUTTER SAUCE:**
>   1/3   **cup peanut butter**
>   1/3   **cup 2% milk**
>   2   **green onions, chopped**
>   1   **small jalapeno pepper, seeded and**
>   **finely chopped**
>   2   **to 3 tablespoons lime juice**
>   2   **tablespoons reduced-sodium**
>   **soy sauce**
>   1   **garlic clove, minced**
>   1   **teaspoon sugar**
>   1   **teaspoon minced fresh cilantro**
>   1   **teaspoon minced fresh gingerroot**
>   1/8   **teaspoon coconut extract**

1. Flatten chicken to 1/4-in. thickness; cut lengthwise into 1-in.-wide strips. In a large resealable plastic bag, combine milk, garlic, brown sugar, seasonings and extract. Add the chicken; seal bag and turn to coat. Refrigerate for 8 hours or overnight.

2. In a small bowl, whisk the sauce ingredients until blended. Cover and refrigerate until serving. Drain and discard marinade. Thread two chicken strips onto each metal or soaked wooden skewer.

3. Grill, uncovered, over medium-hot heat for 2-3 minutes on each side or until chicken juices run clear. Serve with peanut butter sauce.

Editor's Note: Wear disposable gloves when cutting hot peppers; the oils can burn skin. Avoid touching your face.

[1998]

BAKED POTATO SKINS
yield: 8 servings   ∽   prep/total time: 20 min.

Both crisp and hearty, this snack is one that my family requests often.

—*Trish Perrin, Keizer, Oregon*

>   4   **large baking potatoes, baked**
>   3   **tablespoons canola oil**
>   1   **tablespoon grated Parmesan cheese**
>   1/2   **teaspoon salt**
>   1/4   **teaspoon garlic powder**
>   1/4   **teaspoon paprika**
>   1/8   **teaspoon pepper**
>   8   **bacon strips, cooked and crumbled**
> 1-1/2   **cups (6 ounces) shredded**
>   **cheddar cheese**
>   1/2   **cup sour cream**
>   4   **green onions, sliced**

1. Cut potatoes in half lengthwise; scoop out pulp, leaving a 1/4-in. shell (save pulp for another use). Place potato skins on a greased baking sheet.

2. In a small bowl, combine the oil, Parmesan cheese, salt, garlic powder, paprika and pepper; brush over both sides of skins.

3. Bake at 475° for 7 minutes on each side or until crisp. Sprinkle bacon and cheddar cheese inside skins. Bake 2 minutes longer or until the cheese is melted. Top with sour cream and onions. Serve immediately.

BAKED POTATO SKINS

"AWESOME! These tasted better than the ones at the store! I will use less salt in the spread as they were a little too salty. I can't wait to make them again!"
—*jennifer32*

CHEESY SAUSAGE STROMBOLI

[2000]

CHEESY SAUSAGE STROMBOLI

yield: 2 loaves (16 slices each)
prep: 30 min. + rising   bake: 20 min.

I've had a hundred requests for this recipe over the years. Perfect for brunch or as an evening snack, this sausage-filled bread is not tricky to make...and I never have to worry about storing leftovers!

—Vada McRoberts, Silver Lake, Kansas

5 cups all-purpose flour
2 tablespoons sugar
2 teaspoons salt
2 packages (1/4 ounce each) active dry yeast
1-1/2 cups warm water (120° to 130°)
1/2 cup warm 2% milk (120° to 130°)
2 tablespoons butter, melted
2 pounds bulk pork sausage
4 cups (16 ounces) shredded part-skim mozzarella cheese
3 eggs
1 teaspoon minced fresh basil *or* 1/4 teaspoon dried basil
2 tablespoons grated Parmesan cheese

1. In a large bowl, combine the flour, sugar, salt and yeast. Add the water, milk and butter; beat on low until well combined.

2. Turn onto a well-floured surface; knead until smooth and elastic, about 6-8 minutes. Place in a greased bowl, turning once to grease top. Cover and let rise in a warm place until doubled, about 1 hour.

3. Meanwhile, in a large skillet, cook the sausage until no longer pink; drain and cool. Stir in the mozzarella, 2 eggs and basil; set aside.

4. Punch dough down; divide in half. Roll one portion of dough into a 15-in. x 10-in. rectangle on a greased baking sheet. Spoon half of the sausage mixture lengthwise down one side of rectangle to within 1 in. of edges.

5. Fold dough over filling; pinch edges to seal. Cut four diagonal slits on top of stromboli. Repeat with remaining dough and filling. Beat remaining egg; brush over loaves. Sprinkle with Parmesan cheese. Cover and let rise until doubled, about 45 minutes.

6. Bake at 375° for 20-25 minutes or until golden brown. Slice; serve warm.

[2000]

CHEESY OLIVE SNACKS

yield: about 4 dozen
prep/total time: 15 min.
(Pictured on page 35)

Olive lovers will snap up these appetizers. They're easy—the topping can be made ahead, and they're in the oven for only seven minutes.

—Dorothy Anderson
Ottawa, Kansas, Former Field Editor

1 cup (4 ounces) shredded part-skim mozzarella cheese
1 cup (4 ounces) shredded cheddar cheese
1 can (4-1/4 ounces) chopped ripe olives, drained
1/2 cup mayonnaise
1/3 cup chopped green onions
Triscuit crackers

1. In a large bowl, combine the first five ingredients. Spread on crackers. Place on an ungreased baking sheet. Bake at 375° for 7 minutes. Serve immediately.

[2011]

CRISPY PUB RINGS

**yield: 4 servings • prep: 40 min.
cook: 5 min./batch**

I created this recipe for a beer-tasting party we hosted (my husband brews his own), and they were a hit. Try it when you entertain or on those nights when you want homemade take-out food.

—Jennifer Rodriguez, West Jordan, Utah

- 1/2 **cup sour cream**
- 1/2 **cup mayonnaise**
- 1/2 **cup crumbled blue cheese**
- 2 **green onions, finely chopped**
- 1 **tablespoon dried parsley flakes**
- 1 **garlic clove, minced**
- 1/2 **teaspoon hot pepper sauce**
- 1/4 **teaspoon garlic salt**

RINGS:
- 1-1/4 **cups all-purpose flour**
- 1 **teaspoon salt**
- 1 **teaspoon baking powder**
- 1 **egg**
- 1 **cup 2% milk**
- 1-1/2 **teaspoons hot pepper sauce**
- 1 **garlic clove, minced**
- 3/4 **cup dry bread crumbs**
- 1 **teaspoon garlic powder**
- 1 **teaspoon seasoned salt**
- 1 **large sweet onion, sliced and separated into rings**

Oil for deep-fat frying

1. In a small bowl, combine the first eight ingredients; chill until serving.

2. In a large shallow bowl, combine the flour, salt and baking powder. In another shallow bowl, whisk the egg, milk, pepper sauce and minced garlic. In a third bowl, combine the bread crumbs, garlic powder and seasoned salt. Coat onions in flour mixture, dip in egg mixture, then roll in crumbs.

3. In a deep fryer or electric skillet, heat oil to 375°. Drop onion rings, a few at a time, into hot oil. Fry for 2-3 minutes or until golden brown. Drain on paper towels. Serve with sauce.

[2007]

HOT CRAB PINWHEELS

**yield: 3 dozen • prep: 15 min. + chilling
bake: 10 min.**

I got the recipe for these crabmeat bites from a friend. What amazed me most is that my husband, who hates seafood, couldn't stop eating them.

—Kitti Boesel, Woodbridge, Virginia

- 1 **package (8 ounces) reduced-fat cream cheese**
- 1 **can (6 ounces) crabmeat, drained, flaked and cartilage removed**
- 3/4 **cup finely chopped sweet red pepper**
- 1/2 **cup shredded reduced-fat cheddar cheese**
- 2 **green onions, finely chopped**
- 3 **tablespoons minced fresh parsley**
- 1/4 **to 1/2 teaspoon cayenne pepper**
- 6 **flour tortillas (6 inches)**

1. In a large bowl, beat cream cheese until smooth. Stir in the crab, red pepper, cheese, onions, parsley and cayenne. Spread 1/3 cupful over one side of each tortilla; roll up tightly. Wrap in plastic wrap and refrigerate for at least 2 hours.

2. Cut and discard ends of roll-ups. Cut each into six slices. Place on baking sheets coated with cooking spray. Bake at 350° for 10 minutes or until bubbly. Serve warm.

HOT CRAB PINWHEELS

"I've also found that the crab spread makes a great hot dip when served with Triscuits or Club crackers."
—kldudley

ITALIAN STUFFED MUSHROOMS

*"*Easy to make and so delicious! Fed them to my Bunco group and they absolutely loved the flavor. I had to make a dozen copies of the recipe for them. This will be my tradition when it's my turn for hosting the game.*"*
—donitalouise

[1994]

ITALIAN STUFFED MUSHROOMS

yield: 15 servings ∞ prep: 30 min.
bake: 15 min.

(Pictured on page 37)

Every year during the holidays, I use this delicious recipe that I got from my brother. These appealing mushrooms get their hearty flavor from the ham, bacon and cheese.

—*Virginia Slater*
West Sunbury, Pennsylvania
Former Field Editor

4	bacon strips, diced
30	large fresh mushrooms
1	cup onion and garlic salad croutons, crushed
1	cup (4 ounces) shredded part-skim mozzarella cheese
1	medium tomato, finely chopped
1/4	pound ground fully cooked ham
1/4	cup grated Parmesan cheese
2	tablespoons minced fresh parsley
1-1/2	teaspoons minced fresh oregano *or* 1/2 teaspoon dried oregano

---

1. In a large skillet, cook the bacon over medium heat until the bacon is crisp. Using a slotted spoon, remove the bacon to paper towels; drain, reserving 1 tablespoon drippings.

2. Remove stems from mushrooms; set caps aside. Finely chop half of stems (save remaining for another use). Add chopped stems to drippings with bacon; saute for 2-3 minutes. Remove from the heat. Stir in remaining ingredients.

3. Firmly stuff crouton mixture into mushroom caps. Place in a greased 15-in. x 10-in. x 1-in. baking pan. Bake at 425° for 12-15 minutes or until mushrooms are tender.

[2001]

SWEET SAUSAGE ROLLS

yield: 2 dozen ∞ prep: 25 min.
bake: 15 min.

It's hard to stop eating these savory sausage rolls, which are bathed in a sweet, nutty glaze.

—*Lori Cabuno, Canfield, Ohio*

1	tube (8 ounces) refrigerated crescent rolls
24	miniature smoked sausage links
1/2	cup butter, melted
1/2	cup chopped nuts
3	tablespoons honey
3	tablespoons brown sugar

---

1. Unroll crescent dough and separate into triangles; cut each lengthwise into three triangles. Place a sausage on the long end and roll up tightly; set aside.

2. Combine remaining ingredients in an 11-in. x 7-in. baking dish. Arrange sausage rolls, seam side down, in dish. Bake, uncovered, at 400° for 15-20 minutes or until golden brown.

PREPARE MUSHROOMS FOR STUFFING

To prepare mushrooms for stuffing, hold the mushroom cap in one hand and grab the stem with the other hand. Twist to snap off the stem; place caps on a greased baking sheet. Mince or finely chop stems.

[1999]

GROUND BEEF SNACK QUICHES

yield: 1-1/2 dozen   **prep: 15 min.**
bake: 20 min.

A hearty appetizer like these meaty mini quiches is the perfect start for a meal. Try making them with bacon, ham, ground pork or sausage, too.

—Stacy Atkinson, Rugby, North Dakota

- 1/4 **pound ground beef**
- 1/8 **to 1/4 teaspoon garlic powder**
- 1/8 **teaspoon pepper**
- 1 **cup biscuit/baking mix**
- 1/4 **cup cornmeal**
- 1/4 **cup cold butter, cubed**
- 2 **to 3 tablespoons boiling water**
- 1 **egg**
- 1/2 **cup half-and-half cream**
- 1 **tablespoon chopped green onion**
- 1 **tablespoon chopped sweet red pepper**
- 1/8 **to 1/4 teaspoon salt**
- 1/8 **to 1/4 teaspoon cayenne pepper**
- 1/2 **cup finely shredded cheddar cheese**

---

1. In a large saucepan over medium heat, cook the beef, garlic powder and pepper until meat is no longer pink; drain and set aside.

2. Meanwhile, in a small bowl, combine biscuit mix and cornmeal; cut in butter. Add enough water to form a soft dough.

3. Press onto the bottom and up the sides of greased miniature muffin cups. Place teaspoonfuls of beef mixture into each shell.

4. In a small bowl, combine the egg, cream, onion, red pepper, salt and cayenne; pour over beef mixture. Sprinkle with cheese.

5. Bake at 375° for 20 minutes or until a knife inserted near the center of a quiche comes out clean.

[2012]

SUN-DRIED TOMATO & GOAT CHEESE BITES

yield: 20 appetizers
prep/total time: 30 min.

I play Bunco once a month and one of my fellow players brought this for us to snack on. I thought these mini tarts were so delectable that I requested the recipe. I've since made them for my yearly Christmas party and they are always a smash.

—Jean Wysocki
Rancho Santa Margarita, California

- 1 **tube (12 ounces) refrigerated buttermilk biscuits, separated into 10 biscuits**
- 1/2 **cup mayonnaise**
- 1/2 **cup crumbled goat cheese**
- 1/4 **cup chopped oil-packed sun-dried tomatoes**
- 1 **teaspoon dried minced onion**
- 1 **teaspoon pesto sauce mix**
- 1 **tablespoon grated Parmesan cheese**

---

1. Separate each biscuit into two layers; press each into an ungreased miniature muffin cup.

2. In a small bowl, combine mayonnaise, goat cheese, tomatoes, onion and pesto sauce mix; place a scant 2 teaspoonfuls in each cup. Sprinkle with Parmesan cheese. Bake at 375° for 10-15 minutes or until golden brown. Serve warm.

GROUND BEEF SNACK QUICHES

"I've made these mini quiches for many years, getting the recipe from a *Taste of Home* magazine years ago. My family really likes them. I make them in advance and then freeze them. It takes just a few minutes to reheat them. I also made them as one of my New Year Eve's snacks. I especially like the cornmeal crust. It gives a crunchy, nutty texture."
—mscooky

ROASTED VEGETABLE TURKEY PINWHEELS

[2008]

ROASTED VEGETABLE TURKEY PINWHEELS

yield: 64 appetizers
prep: 45 min. + chilling

These are always popular and I especially like being able to make them ahead of time. I make a double batch of the veggie cream cheese to use on crackers and bagels.

—*Kristin Andrews, Gresham, Oregon*

2	medium yellow summer squash, cut into 1/2-inch slices
1	large sweet yellow pepper, cut into 1-inch pieces
1	large sweet red pepper, cut into 1-inch pieces
2	large carrots, cut into 1/2-inch slices
3	garlic cloves, peeled
2	tablespoons olive oil
2	packages (8 ounces each) cream cheese, cubed
1/2	teaspoon salt
1/2	teaspoon pepper
8	flavored tortillas of your choice (10 inches), room temperature
1	pound thinly sliced deli turkey
4	cups torn Bibb or Boston lettuce

1. Place the vegetables and garlic in a 15-in. x 10-in. x 1-in. baking pan coated with cooking spray. Drizzle with oil; toss to coat. Bake, uncovered, at 425° for 25-30 minutes or until lightly browned and tender; stir once. Cool slightly.

2. Place vegetables, cream cheese, salt and pepper in a food processor; cover and process until blended. Transfer to a large bowl; cover and refrigerate for 2-3 hours or until thickened.

3. Spread 1/2 cup cream cheese mixture over each tortilla; layer with turkey and lettuce. Roll up tightly; wrap each in plastic wrap. Refrigerate for at least 1 hour. Unwrap; cut each into eight slices.

[1998]

SAVORY PARTY BREAD

yield: 6-8 servings
prep/total time: 30 min.

(*Pictured on page 38*)

You won't be able to stop nibbling on warm pieces of this cheesy, oniony bread. The sliced loaf fans out for a fun presentation.

—*Kay Daly, Raleigh, North Carolina*

1	unsliced round loaf (1 pound) sourdough bread
1	pound Monterey Jack cheese, sliced
1/2	cup butter, melted
1/2	cup chopped green onions
2	to 3 teaspoons poppy seeds

1. Cut the bread lengthwise and widthwise without cutting through the bottom crust. Insert cheese between cuts. Combine butter, onions and poppy seeds; drizzle over the bread. Wrap in foil; place on a baking sheet.

2. Bake at 350° for 15 minutes. Unwrap; bake 10 minutes longer or until the cheese is melted.

MAKE-AHEAD SAVORY PARTY BREAD

The bread for Savory Party Bread can be sliced and filled a day ahead. Right before company comes, melt the butter and add the green onions and poppy seeds.

—*Taste of Home Cooking Experts*

[2006]

PROSCIUTTO CHICKEN KABOBS

yield: 12 appetizers
prep: 30 min. + marinating ∽ **grill: 10 min.**

(*Pictured on page 39*)

Everyone will think you spent hours preparing these simple and very clever grilled wraps served with a guacamole-like dip. Basil gives the chicken a lovely fresh herb flavor.

—*Elaine Sweet, Dallas, Texas*

3/4   cup five-cheese Italian salad dressing
1/4   cup lime juice
  2   teaspoons marinade for chicken
1/2   pound boneless skinless chicken breasts, cut into 3-inch x 1/2-inch strips
 12   thin slices prosciutto
 24   fresh basil leaves
AVOCADO DIP:
  2   medium ripe avocados, peeled
1/4   cup minced fresh cilantro
  2   green onions, chopped
  2   tablespoons lime juice
  2   tablespoons mayonnaise
1-1/2 teaspoons prepared horseradish
  1   garlic clove, minced
1/4   teaspoon salt

---

1. In a large resealable plastic bag, combine the salad dressing, lime juice and marinade for chicken; add chicken. Seal bag and turn to coat; refrigerate for 1 hour.

2. Drain and discard marinade. Fold prosciutto slices in half; top each with two basil leaves and a chicken strip. Roll up jelly-roll style, starting with a short side. Thread onto metal or soaked wooden skewers.

3. Grill, covered, over medium heat or broil 4 in. from the heat for 5 minutes on each side or until the chicken is no longer pink.

4. Meanwhile, in a small bowl, mash the avocados. Stir in the cilantro, onions, lime juice, mayonnaise, horseradish, garlic and salt. Serve with kabobs.

Editor's Note: This recipe was tested with Lea & Perrins Marinade for Chicken.

[2004]

SMOKY JALAPENOS

yield: 14 appetizers ∽ **prep: 25 min.**
bake: 20 min.

When I make these excellent appetizers, there are no leftovers. They can also be made with mild banana peppers or yellow chili peppers. I got this recipe from my brother, Larry.

—*Melinda Strable, Ankeny, Iowa*

---

 14   jalapeno peppers
  4   ounces cream cheese, softened
 14   miniature smoked sausages
  7   bacon strips

---

1. Cut a lengthwise slit in each pepper; remove seeds and membranes. Spread a teaspoonful of cream cheese into each pepper; stuff each with a sausage.

2. Cut the bacon strips in half widthwise; cook in a microwave or skillet until bacon is partially cooked. Wrap a bacon piece around each pepper; secure with a toothpick.

3. Place in an ungreased 13-in. x 9-in. baking dish. Bake, uncovered, at 350° for 20 minutes for spicy flavor, 30 minutes for medium and 40 minutes for mild.

Editor's Note: Wear disposable gloves when cutting hot peppers; the oils can burn skin. Avoid touching your face.

PROSCIUTTO CHICKEN KABOBS

"Oh my...these are the most amazing appies..the dip is the jewel in the crown. Made them for my girlfriend's birthday...the only problem is there wasn't more. Double the recipe!!!!"
—*Okanagan Girl*

STUFFED BABY RED POTATOES

"These are so delicious and cute. I used a good shredded Parm from Costco, it added great flavor. Everyone loved them. I served them as a side dish to bourbon salmon and Caesar salad (to use the shredded Parm again). I will definitely make these again!"
—*wolfenlion*

[2009]

STUFFED BABY RED POTATOES

yield: 2 dozen ∽ prep: 45 min.
bake: 15 min.

(*Pictured on page 39*)

This recipe just says "party"! The ingredients are basic, but the finished appetizer looks like you worked a lot harder than you did.

—*Carole Bess White, Portland, Oregon*

24	small red potatoes (about 2-1/2 pounds)
1/4	cup butter, cubed
1/2	cup shredded Parmesan cheese, *divided*
1/2	cup crumbled cooked bacon, *divided*
2/3	cup sour cream
1	egg, lightly beaten
1/2	teaspoon salt
1/8	teaspoon pepper
1/8	teaspoon paprika

1. Scrub the potatoes; place in a large saucepan and cover with water. Bring to a boil. Reduce heat; cover and cook for 15-20 minutes or until potatoes are tender. Drain.

2. When cool enough to handle, cut a thin slice off the top of each potato. Scoop out pulp, leaving a thin shell. (Cut thin slices from potato bottoms to level if necessary.)

3. In a large bowl, mash the potato tops and pulp with butter. Set aside 2 tablespoons each of cheese and bacon for garnish; add remaining cheese and bacon to potatoes. Stir in the sour cream, egg, salt and pepper. Spoon mixture into potato shells. Top with remaining cheese and bacon; sprinkle with paprika.

4. Place in an ungreased 15-in. x 10-in. x 1-in. baking pan. Bake at 375° for 12-18 minutes or until heated through.

[2003]

SESAME CHICKEN BITES

yield: 8-10 servings
prep/total time: 30 min.

So tender and tasty, these chicken appetizers are enhanced by a honey-mustard dipping sauce. I used to spend several days creating hors d'oeuvres for our holiday open house, and these bites were among the favorites.

—*Kathy Green, Layton, New Jersey*

1/2	cup dry bread crumbs
1/4	cup sesame seeds
2	teaspoons minced fresh parsley
1/2	cup mayonnaise
1	teaspoon onion powder
1	teaspoon ground mustard
1/4	teaspoon pepper
1	pound boneless skinless chicken breasts, cut into 1-inch cubes
2	to 4 tablespoons canola oil

HONEY-MUSTARD SAUCE:

3/4	cup mayonnaise
4-1/2	teaspoons honey
1-1/2	teaspoons Dijon mustard

1. In a large resealable plastic bag, combine the bread crumbs, sesame seeds and parsley; set aside.

2. In a small bowl, combine mayonnaise, onion powder, mustard and pepper. Coat chicken in mayonnaise mixture, then add to crumb mixture, a few pieces at a time; shake to coat.

3. In a large skillet, saute chicken in oil in batches until no longer pink, adding additional oil as needed. In a small bowl, combine the sauce ingredients. Serve with chicken.

[2011]

WONTON POT STICKERS WITH SOY REDUCTION

yield: about 3-1/2 dozen (3/4 cup sauce)
prep: 45 min. + freezing ∞ **cook: 15 min./batch**

(Pictured on page 39)

This is one of the first recipes I created that really took off with friends and family. I found I could make a large batch of 45 dumplings, freeze them, and pull out as many as I need at a moment's notice. Freeze overnight laid out in layers before combining in a large freezer bag; separate multiple layers with waxed paper.

—*Michael Angelo, Spring, Texas*

- 1/2 cup mirin (sweet rice wine)
- 1/2 cup balsamic vinegar
- 1/4 cup reduced-sodium soy sauce
- 2 fresh basil leaves

POT STICKERS:
- 1-1/2 cups finely chopped bok choy
- 2 tablespoons minced fresh cilantro
- 1 tablespoon minced fresh gingerroot
- 1 tablespoon chopped green onion
- 1 tablespoon oyster sauce
- 3/4 teaspoon toasted sesame oil
- 1 pound ground pork
- 45 wonton wrappers

ADDITIONAL INGREDIENT:
- 1/4 cup toasted sesame oil

---

1. In a small saucepan, combine the mirin, balsamic vinegar and soy sauce. Bring to a boil; cook until liquid is reduced by half, about 15 minutes. Add basil; cover and steep for 2 minutes. Remove basil and discard. Cool sauce and transfer to a freezer container.

2. For pot stickers, combine the first six ingredients in a large bowl. Crumble pork over mixture and mix well.

3. Place about 1 tablespoon pork mixture in the center of each wonton wrapper. (Keep remaining wrappers covered with a damp paper towel until ready to use.) Moisten edges with water. Fold one corner diagonally over filling and press edges to seal.

4. Place on a waxed paper-lined 15-in. x 10-in. x 1-in. baking sheet; freeze until firm. Transfer to resealable plastic freezer bags. May be frozen for up to 3 months.

5. To use pot stickers: Thaw sauce in the refrigerator overnight. Arrange a fourth of the pot stickers 1 in. apart in a greased steamer; place in a large saucepan over 1 in. of water. Bring to a boil; cover and steam for 12-14 minutes or until a thermometer inserted into filling reads 160°. Repeat with remaining pot stickers.

6. In a large skillet, cook pot stickers in oil in batches over medium-high heat for 1-2 minutes on each side or until golden brown.

[2002]

BACON-WRAPPED WATER CHESTNUTS

yield: 32 appetizers ∞ **prep: 10 min.** ∞ **bake: 50 min.**

My husband and I do lots of entertaining and always start off with appetizers like these tempting morsels.

—*Midge Scurlock, Creston, Iowa, Field Editor*

- 8 bacon strips
- 2 cans (8 ounces each) whole water chestnuts, drained
- 3/4 cup ketchup
- 1 jar (2-1/2 ounces) strained peach baby food
- 1/4 cup sugar
- Dash salt

---

1. Cut bacon strips in half lengthwise and then in half widthwise. Wrap each bacon piece around a water chestnut; secure with a toothpick.

2. Place in an ungreased 13-in. x 9-in. baking dish. Bake, uncovered, at 350° for 25 minutes, turning once; drain if necessary.

3. In a small bowl, combine the remaining ingredients. Drizzle over water chestnuts. Bake 25-35 minutes longer or until bacon is crisp. Serve warm.

BEST DEVILED EGGS

[2005]

CHEDDAR SHRIMP NACHOS

yield: 4 dozen ⁓ prep/total time: 20 min.

These fun finger foods in tortilla chip scoops are just the thing for cold-weather gatherings.

—Lisa Feld
Grafton, Wisconsin, Field Editor

3/4	pound cooked medium shrimp, peeled and deveined, chopped
1-1/2	cups (6 ounces) shredded cheddar cheese
1	can (4 ounces) chopped green chilies, drained
1/3	cup chopped green onions
1/4	cup sliced ripe olives, drained
1/2	cup mayonnaise
1/4	teaspoon ground cumin
48	tortilla chip scoops

1. In a large bowl, combine the shrimp, cheese, chilies, onions and olives. Combine mayonnaise and cumin; add to shrimp mixture and toss to coat.

2. Drop by tablespoonfuls into tortilla scoops. Place on ungreased baking sheets. Bake at 350° for 5-10 minutes or until cheese is melted. Serve warm.

[2002]

GARLIC TOMATO BRUSCHETTA

yield: 12 servings ⁓ prep: 30 min. + chilling

(Pictured on page 38)

My bruschetta makes a crispy complement to Italian entrees. I started with my grandmother's recipe and added fresh tomatoes.

—Jean Franzoni, Rutland, Vermont

1/4	cup olive oil
3	tablespoons chopped fresh basil
3	to 4 garlic cloves, minced
1/2	teaspoon salt
1/4	teaspoon pepper
4	medium tomatoes, diced
2	tablespoons grated Parmesan cheese
1	loaf (1 pound) unsliced French bread

1. In a large bowl, combine the oil, basil, garlic, salt and pepper. Add tomatoes and toss gently. Sprinkle with cheese. Refrigerate for at least 1 hour.

2. Bring the tomato mixture to room temperature before serving. Cut bread into 24 slices; toast under broiler until lightly browned. Top with tomato mixture. Serve immediately.

[1996]

BEST DEVILED EGGS

yield: 2 dozen ⁓ prep/total time: 15 min.

Herbs lend zest to these deviled eggs, which make a fine accompaniment to any menu.

—Jesse & Anne Foust
Bluefield, West Virginia
Former Field Editors

12	hard-cooked eggs
1/2	cup mayonnaise
1	teaspoon dried parsley flakes
1/2	teaspoon minced chives
1/2	teaspoon ground mustard
1/2	teaspoon dill weed
1/4	teaspoon salt
1/4	teaspoon paprika
1/8	teaspoon pepper
1/8	teaspoon garlic powder
2	tablespoons 2% milk

Fresh parsley
Additional paprika

1. Slice eggs in half lengthwise; remove yolks and set whites aside. In a small bowl, mash yolks. Add the next 10 ingredients; mix well. Stuff or pipe into egg whites. Garnish with parsley and paprika. Refrigerate until serving.

[1997]

PADYSAURUS PIZZA POCKETS

yield: 1 dozen ∞ prep: 40 min.
bake: 20 min.

Stuffed with a pizza-style filling, these special sandwiches surprise you with a burst of flavor in every bite. They were popular with the preschool set when our son had a birthday party with a dinosaur theme, but you can be sure adults will love them, too!

—Robin Werner
Brush Prairie, Washington

- 1 package (1/4 ounce) active dry yeast
- 1 cup warm water (110° to 115°)
- 1 tablespoon sugar
- 1 tablespoon butter, melted
- 1 teaspoon salt
- 3 to 3-1/4 cups all-purpose flour
- 1 can (8 ounces) pizza sauce, *divided*
- 12 slices pepperoni
- 1 package (2-1/2 ounces) thinly sliced deli pastrami, chopped
- 1 package (2-1/2 ounces) thinly sliced deli ham, chopped
- 3/4 cup shredded part-skim mozzarella cheese
- 1 egg, lightly beaten

1. In a large bowl, dissolve yeast in warm water. Add the sugar, butter, salt and 2-1/4 cups flour. Beat until smooth. Stir in enough remaining flour to form a soft dough.

2. Turn onto a floured surface; knead until smooth and elastic, about 6-8 minutes. Roll dough into a 14-in. x 10-in. rectangle. Cut with a 3-in. round cookie cutter. Reroll scraps to cut a total of 24 circles. Place 1 teaspoon pizza sauce and a slice of pepperoni in the centers of 12 circles.

3. Combine the pastrami, ham and cheese; place equal amounts over pepperoni. Top each with 1/2 teaspoon pizza sauce. Cover with remaining circles; press edges with a fork to seal.

4. Place on greased baking sheets. Brush with egg. Bake at 400° for 20-25 minutes or until golden brown. Warm remaining pizza sauce; serve with pizza pockets.

[1994]

MINI HAMBURGERS

yield: 40 servings ∞ prep: 15 min.
bake: 25 min.

These hearty snacks are perfect for Sunday afternoon football games and teen parties. The mini buns are actually store-purchased pan dinner rolls, which are available everywhere.

—Judy Lewis, Sterling Heights, Michigan

- 1/2 cup chopped onion
- 1 tablespoon butter
- 1 egg, lightly beaten
- 1/4 teaspoon seasoned salt
- 1/4 teaspoon ground sage
- 1/4 teaspoon salt
- 1/8 teaspoon pepper
- 1 pound lean ground beef (90% lean) *or* ground beef
- 40 mini rolls, split
- 8 ounces process American cheese slices, cut into 1-1/2-inch squares, optional
- 40 dill pickle slices, optional

1. In a large skillet, saute onion in butter. Transfer to large bowl; add egg and seasonings. Crumble beef over mixture and mix well. Spread over bottom halves of the rolls; replace tops. Place on baking sheets; cover with foil.

2. Bake at 350° for 20 minutes or until a thermometer reads 160° and juices run clear. If desired, place a cheese square and pickle on each hamburger; replace tops and foil and return to the oven for 5 minutes.

PADYSAURUS PIZZA POCKETS

"These are great. I was looking for something to take to the football game for my family of 6. These are great to throw into a cooler and everyone can grab what they want."
—Daltonfamily01

ZESTY CHICKEN WINGS

[2003]

SWEET 'N' SOUR MEATBALLS

yield: 8 servings ∞ **prep: 30 min.**
bake: 40 min.

(Pictured on page 33)

When we entertain friends for Sunday dinner, I frequently serve these tangy meatballs. My guests loves the distinctive sauce, but they're often surprised when I tell them that it's made with gingersnaps.

—*Melody Mellinger*
Myerstown, Pennsylvania, Field Editor

---

    3 eggs
    1 medium onion, chopped
1-1/2 cups dry bread crumbs
    1 teaspoon salt
    2 pounds ground beef
    2 tablespoons canola oil
SAUCE:
3-1/2 cups tomato juice
    1 cup packed brown sugar
   10 gingersnaps, finely crushed
  1/4 cup white vinegar
    1 teaspoon onion salt

---

1. In a large bowl, combine eggs, onion, bread crumbs and salt. Crumble beef over mixture and mix well. Shape into 1-1/2-in. balls.

2. In a large skillet, brown meatballs in batches in oil. Transfer to a greased 13-in. x 9-in. baking dish.

3. In a large saucepan, combine the sauce ingredients. Bring to a boil over medium heat, stirring until the cookie crumbs are dissolved. Pour sauce over the meatballs.

4. Bake meatballs, uncovered, at 350° for 40-45 minutes or until the meat is no longer pink.

[2000]

ZESTY CHICKEN WINGS

yield: 10-12 servings ∞ **prep: 30 min.**
bake: 50 min.

These spicy barbecue wings are easy to make. I fix a double batch since my family thinks they're great. You should see them disappear!

—*Joan Rose, Langley, British Columbia*

  1/2 cup corn syrup
  1/2 cup ketchup
  1/4 cup cider vinegar
  1/4 cup Worcestershire sauce
  1/4 cup Dijon mustard
    1 small onion, chopped
    3 garlic cloves, minced
    1 tablespoon chili powder
   16 chicken wings (about 3 pounds)

---

1. In a large saucepan, combine the first eight ingredients. Bring to a boil. Reduce heat; simmer, uncovered, for 15-20 minutes or until thickened.

2. Meanwhile, cut chicken wings into three sections; discard wing tips. Place wings in a well-greased 15-in. x 10-in. x 1-in. baking pan.

3. Bake at 375° for 30 minutes, turning once. Brush with sauce. Bake wings 20-25 minutes longer, turning and basting once, or until chicken juices run clear. Serve with additional sauce if desired.

[2010]

MAMMA'S CAPONATA

yield: 6 cups 〜 prep: 30 min.
cook: 40 min.

Great as an appetizer, but you can easily turn this into a meal. Instead of topping bread, serve over warm pasta.

—*Georgette Stubin, Canton, Michigan*

---

1 large eggplant, peeled and chopped
1/4 cup plus 2 tablespoons olive oil, *divided*
2 medium onions, chopped
2 celery ribs, chopped
2 cans (14-1/2 ounces *each*) diced tomatoes, undrained
1/3 cup chopped ripe olives
1/4 cup red wine vinegar
2 tablespoons sugar
2 tablespoons capers, drained
1/2 teaspoon salt
1/2 teaspoon pepper
French bread baguettes, sliced and toasted

---

1. In a Dutch oven, saute eggplant in 1/4 cup oil until tender. Remove from the pan and set aside. In the same pan, saute onions and celery in remaining oil until tender. Stir in tomatoes and eggplant. Bring to a boil. Reduce heat; simmer, uncovered, for 15 minutes.

2. Add the olives, vinegar, sugar, capers, salt and pepper. Return to a boil. Reduce the heat; simmer, uncovered, for 20 minutes or until thickened. Serve warm or at room temperature with baguettes.

[2007]

BAKED BRIE WITH ROASTED GARLIC

yield: 8 servings 〜 prep: 35 min. + cooling
bake: 45 min.

The garlic is mellow and sweet in this recipe. It never fails to get compliments when I serve it as a first course.

—*Lara Pennell, Mauldin, South Carolina*

---

1 whole garlic bulb
1-1/2 teaspoons plus 1 tablespoon olive oil, *divided*
1 tablespoon minced fresh rosemary *or* 1 teaspoon dried rosemary, crushed
1 round loaf (1 pound) sourdough bread
1 round (8 ounces) Brie cheese
1 loaf (10-1/2 ounces) French bread baguette, sliced and toasted
Red and green grapes

---

1. Remove papery outer skin from garlic (do not peel or separate cloves). Cut top off bulb. Brush with 1-1/2 teaspoons oil; sprinkle with rosemary. Wrap in heavy-duty foil. Bake at 425° for 30-35 minutes or until softened.

2. Meanwhile, cut the top fourth off the loaf of bread; carefully hollow out enough of the bottom of the bread so cheese will fit. Cube removed bread; set aside. Place cheese in bread.

3. Cool garlic for 10-15 minutes. Reduce heat to 375°. Squeeze softened garlic into a bowl and mash with a fork; spread over cheese. Replace the bread top; brush outside of bread with the remaining oil. Wrap the loaf in heavy-duty foil.

4. Bake for 45-50 minutes or until the cheese is melted. Serve with toasted baguette, grapes and the reserved bread cubes.

BAKED BRIE WITH ROASTED GARLIC

❝This is a standby for holiday gatherings. It never fails to please. I serve it with sliced pears in addition to the bread. ❞
— *Emproper*

BUFFALO CHICKEN DIP

[2007]

BUFFALO CHICKEN DIP

yield: about 2 cups
prep/total time: 30 min.

This is a great dip my family loves for football parties and holidays. Everywhere I take it, people ask for the recipe.

—*Peggy Foster, Florence, Kentucky*

1 package (8 ounces) cream cheese, softened
1 can (10 ounces) chunk white chicken, drained
1/2 cup buffalo wing sauce
1/2 cup ranch salad dressing
2 cups (8 ounces) shredded Colby-Monterey Jack cheese
Tortilla chips

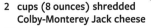

1. Spread the cream cheese into an ungreased shallow 1-qt. baking dish. Layer with the chicken, buffalo wing sauce and ranch dressing. Sprinkle with the cheese.

2. Bake, uncovered, at 350° for 20-25 minutes or until the cheese is melted. Serve warm with tortilla chips.

BUFFALO CHICKEN DIP

"I do not like hot sauce, but my family does. I made this for a NYE (New Year's Eve) party and it was a big hit. Used a mini Crock-Pot and it was very easy and the texture was good. I added a bit more cheese, and that made it thick and yummy."
—*eye_lady*

[1997]

FESTIVE HAM 'N' CHEESE SPREAD

yield: about 4 cups
prep/total time: 15 min.

(*Pictured on page 35*)

My family goes wild over hearty yet mild spread. Now they refuse to eat any cheese spread from the store.

—*Cara Flora, Olathe, Colorado*

2 packages (8 ounces *each*) cream cheese, softened
1/2 cup sour cream
2 tablespoons onion soup mix
1 cup chopped fully cooked ham
1 cup (4 ounces) shredded Swiss *or* cheddar cheese

1/4 cup minced fresh parsley
Assorted crackers

1. In a large bowl, beat cream cheese, sour cream and soup mix until blended. Stir in ham and cheese.

2. Form cheese mixture into a ball or spoon into a plastic wrap-lined mold. Roll in ball in parsley. Refrigerate until serving. Serve with crackers.

[1995]

SPINACH DIP IN A BREAD BOWL

yield: 10-15 servings
prep: 15 min. + chilling

(*Pictured on page 40*)

When we get together with friends, I like to prepare this creamy dip. It's a crowd-pleaser.

—*Janelle Lee*
Appleton, Wisconsin, Field Editor

2 cups (16 ounces) sour cream
1 envelope (1 ounce) ranch salad dressing mix
1 package (10 ounces) frozen chopped spinach, thawed and well drained
1/4 cup chopped onion
3/4 teaspoon dried basil
1/2 teaspoon dried oregano
1 round loaf of bread (1 pound)
Raw vegetables

1. In a large bowl, combine first six ingredients. Chill for at least 1 hour. Cut a 1-1/2-in. slice off the top of the loaf; set aside. Hollow out the bottom part, leaving a thick shell. Cut the slice from the top of the loaf and the bread from inside into bite-size pieces.

2. Fill shell with dip; set on a large platter. Arrange bread pieces and vegetables around it and serve immediately.

[2004]

BRIE IN PUFF PASTRY

yield: 8-10 servings
prep/total time: 30 min.

This rich, stylish appetizer adds an elegant touch to any party.

—*Marion Lowery*
Medford, Oregon, Former Field Editor

- 1 sheet frozen puff pastry, thawed
- 1/4 cup apricot jam
- 1 round (13.2 ounces) Brie cheese
- 1 egg
- 1 tablespoon water
Apple slices

1. Roll puff pastry into a 14-in. square. Spread jam into a 4-1/2-in. circle in center of pastry; place cheese over jam. Fold pastry around cheese; trim excess dough. Pinch edges to seal. Place seam side down on ungreased baking sheet. Beat the egg and water; brush over pastry.

2. Cut the trimmed pastry pieces into decorative shapes and place on top; brush with egg mixture if desired. Bake at 400° for 20-25 minutes or until puffed and golden brown. Serve warm with apple slices.

[1993]

TAFFY APPLE DIP

yield: 6 servings　　**prep/total time: 10 min.**

My mother-in-law gave me this recipe. It's simple to make, and it tastes like the real thing!

—*Sue Gronholz*
Beaver Dam, Wisconsin, Field Editor

- 1 package (8 ounces) cream cheese, softened
- 3/4 cup packed brown sugar
- 1 tablespoon vanilla extract
- 1/2 cup chopped peanuts
- 6 apples, cut into wedges

1. In a small bowl, beat the cream cheese, brown sugar and vanilla until smooth. Spread mixture on a small serving plate; top with nuts. Serve with the apple wedges.

[2004]

SMOKY SESAME CHEESE LOG

yield: 1 cheese log
prep: 15 min. + chilling

We love the bacon flavor in this cheesy mixture. Served with wheat or sesame crackers, this deliciously different appetizer is delish!

—*Katie Sloan*
Charlotte, North Carolina, Field Editor

- 2 packages (8 ounces each) cream cheese, softened
- 1 cup (4 ounces) shredded Monterey Jack cheese
- 1/2 cup crumbled cooked bacon
- 2 tablespoons sesame seeds, toasted
- 2 tablespoons Worcestershire sauce
- 1 teaspoon Liquid Smoke, optional
TOPPING:
- 1/2 cup crumbled cooked bacon
- 1/2 cup sesame seeds, toasted
- 1 tablespoon minced chives
Assorted fresh vegetables *or* crackers

1. In a large bowl, beat the first five ingredients until blended. Add Liquid Smoke if desired. Shape mixture into a log. Cover and refrigerate for 8 hours or overnight.

2. For topping, combine the bacon, sesame seeds and chives; roll cheese log in topping. Serve with vegetables or crackers.

BRIE IN PUFF PASTRY

"This is my favorite way to prepare baked Brie. I've tried several other recipes, but ultimately, I keep coming back to this one. I love the mild sweet flavor along with the savory cheese and puff pastry. I always receive great compliments when I prepare this for parties."
—*nataliemd*

[2003]

CHOCOLATE FONDUE
yield: 2-1/2 cups
prep: 15 min. ∽ **cook: 30 min.**

This creamy, delectable dip is a chocolate lover's dream. You'll want to sample it with a variety of dippers, including strawberries, banana chunks and cake cubes.

—*Jane Shapton, Irvine, California*

1-1/2 cups sugar
1-1/4 cups water
1/4 cup light corn syrup
1 cup baking cocoa
1/2 cup heavy whipping cream
5 ounces semisweet chocolate, chopped
Strawberries, banana chunks, apple slices *or* angel food cake cubes

1. In a small saucepan, bring sugar, water and corn syrup to a boil. Reduce heat; simmer, uncovered, for 20 minutes, stirring frequently.

2. In a small bowl, combine cocoa, cream and half of the syrup mixture until smooth; return to the pan. Bring to a boil, stirring constantly. Reduce heat; simmer, uncovered, for 5 minutes. Stir in chopped chocolate until melted. Serve warm with fruit or cake for dipping. Refrigerate leftovers.

[2009]

MEXICAN SALSA
yield: 3-1/2 cups ∽ **prep: 40 min.**

In the summertime, I love to make this zippy salsa with fresh tomatoes and peppers from my garden. When my tomatoes are gone, I use canned, and it is still a great salsa.

—*Roger Stenman, Batavia, Illinois*

3 jalapeno peppers
1 medium onion, quartered
1 garlic clove, halved
2 cans (one 28 ounces, one 14-1/2 ounces) whole tomatoes, drained

4 fresh cilantro sprigs
1/2 teaspoon salt
Tortilla chips

1. Heat a small ungreased cast-iron skillet over high heat. With a small sharp knife, pierce jalapenos; add to hot skillet. Cook for 15-20 minutes or until peppers are blistered and blackened, turning occasionally.

2. Immediately place the jalapenos in a small bowl; cover and let stand for 20 minutes. Peel off and discard charred skins. Remove stems and seeds.

3. Place onion and garlic in a food processor; cover and pulse four times. Add the tomatoes, cilantro, salt and jalapenos. Cover and process until desired consistency. Chill until serving. Serve with chips.

Editor's Note: Wear disposable gloves when cutting hot peppers; the oils can burn skin. Avoid touching your face.

[2010]

HOMEMADE GUACAMOLE
yield: 2 cups ∽ **prep/total time: 10 min.**
(*Pictured on page 36*)

My daughters sometimes call this dip "five-finger guacamole" to remember that it is only made with five ingredients.

—*Nanette Hilton, Las Vegas, Nevada*

3 medium ripe avocados, peeled
1/4 cup finely chopped onion
1/4 cup minced fresh cilantro
2 tablespoons lime juice
1/8 teaspoon salt
Tortilla chips

1. In a small bowl, mash avocado with a fork. Stir in the onion, cilantro, lime juice and salt. Refrigerate until serving. Serve with chips.

HOMEMADE GUACAMOLE

"LOVED the fact that this is so simple and that the flavor of the avocado is not overpowered by any other ingredients! Love chunky avocado and lime! Reminds me of Chipotle!"
—*Tella2010*

[2008]

CORN 'N' BLACK BEAN SALSA

yield: 11 cups ∞ **prep: 45 min.**

I'm a high school football coach who also likes to cook and garden. This hearty salsa is a hit with my family and friends.

—*Mike Bass, Alvin, Texas*

- 2 cans (15-1/4 ounces *each*) whole kernel corn, drained
- 2 cans (15 ounces *each*) black beans, rinsed and drained
- 8 plum tomatoes, seeded and chopped
- 1 medium red onion, chopped
- 3/4 cup minced fresh cilantro
- 4 jalapeno peppers, seeded and chopped
- 1/4 cup lime juice
- 1/2 teaspoon salt

Tortilla chips

1. In a very large bowl, combine the first eight ingredients. Cover; refrigerate until serving. Serve with tortilla chips.

Editor's Note: Wear disposable gloves when cutting hot peppers; the oils can burn skin. Avoid touching your face.

[2006]

FRESH PEACH MANGO SALSA

yield: 4 cups ∞ **prep/total time: 20 min.**

This colorful, freshly made salsa tastes wonderful with tortilla chips and on fish tacos. The garlic and veggies nicely complement the peach and mango flavors.

—*Marina Castle*
  La Crescenta, California, Field Editor

1-1/2 cups chopped fresh tomatoes
  3/4 cup chopped peeled fresh peaches
  1/2 cup chopped red onion
  1/2 cup chopped sweet yellow pepper
  1/2 cup chopped peeled mango

- 2 tablespoons chopped seeded jalapeno pepper
- 3 garlic cloves, minced
- 1-1/2 teaspoons lime juice
- 1/2 teaspoon minced fresh cilantro

Tortilla chips

1. In a large bowl, combine the first nine ingredients. Cover and refrigerate until serving. Serve with tortilla chips.

Editor's Note: Wear disposable gloves when cutting hot peppers; the oils can burn skin. Avoid touching your face.

[2008]

NO-BONES CHICKEN WING DIP

yield: 6-1/2 cups
prep: 15 min. ∞ **bake: 25 min.**

This hot party dip delivers the delicious flavor of the chicken wings we love to snack on—without the mess or bones.

—*Shirley Gawlik, Oakfield, New York*

- 1 package (8 ounces) cream cheese, softened
- 2 cups (16 ounces) sour cream
- 1 cup blue cheese salad dressing
- 1/2 cup buffalo wing sauce
- 2-1/2 cups shredded cooked chicken
- 2 cups (8 ounces) provolone cheese

Baby carrots, celery ribs and crackers

1. In a large bowl, beat the cream cheese, sour cream, salad dressing and buffalo wing sauce until blended. Stir in the chicken and provolone cheese.

2. Transfer to a greased 2-qt. baking dish. Cover and bake the dip at 350° for 25-30 minutes or until hot and bubbly. Serve dip warm with carrots, celery and crackers.

FRESH PEACH MANGO SALSA

❝ I love this salsa. I sometimes make it with just peach or mango depending on what's available or on sale. I also often leave out the bell pepper. Fresh squeezed lime juice makes it even better. ❞
—*deajoh*

CREAMY TACO DIP

❝I only use reduced fat cream cheese and sour cream. For the salsa part, I mix half salsa, half taco sauce and use the refried beans that have jalapenos. Delicious!❞

—scrapo

[2008]

COWBOY BEEF DIP

yield: 3 cups ⁓ prep: 20 min.
cook: 25 min.

(Pictured on page 34)

A group of us in a foods class developed this recipe for the North Dakota State Beef Bash Competition in 1995. We won the contest, and now my family requests this dip for all our special gatherings!

—*Jessica Klym, Killdeer, North Dakota*

- 1 **pound ground beef**
- 4 **tablespoons chopped onion,** *divided*
- 3 **tablespoons chopped sweet red pepper,** *divided*
- 2 **tablespoons chopped green pepper,** *divided*
- 1 **can (10-3/4 ounces) condensed nacho cheese soup, undiluted**
- 1/2 **cup salsa**
- 4 **tablespoons sliced ripe olives,** *divided*
- 4 **tablespoons sliced pimiento-stuffed olives,** *divided*
- 2 **tablespoons chopped green chilies**
- 1 **teaspoon chopped seeded jalapeno pepper**
- 1/4 **teaspoon dried oregano**
- 1/4 **teaspoon pepper**
- 1/4 **cup shredded cheddar cheese**
- 2 **tablespoons sour cream**
- 2 **to 3 teaspoons minced fresh parsley**

Tortilla chips

1. In a large skillet, cook beef, 3 tablespoons onion, 2 tablespoons red pepper and 1 tablespoon green pepper over medium heat until meat is no longer pink; drain. Stir in the soup, salsa, 3 tablespoons ripe olives, 3 tablespoons pimiento-stuffed olives, chilies, jalapeno, oregano and pepper. Bring to a boil. Reduce heat; simmer, uncovered, for 5 minutes.

2. Transfer to a serving dish. Top with the cheese, sour cream and parsley; sprinkle with the remaining onion, peppers and olives. Serve with the tortilla chips.

Editor's Note: Wear disposable gloves when cutting hot peppers; the oils can burn skin. Avoid touching your face.

[1996]

CREAMY TACO DIP

yield: 20 servings ⁓ prep/total time: 15 min.

You'll know this snack is a hit at your next gathering when you come home with an empty dish!

—*Denise Smith*
Lusk, Wyoming, Field Editor

- 1 **package (8 ounces) fat-free cream cheese, softened**
- 1/2 **cup (4 ounces) fat-free sour cream**
- 1/2 **cup taco sauce**
- 1 **teaspoons ground cumin**
- 1 **can (15 ounces) fat-free refried beans**
- 1 **cup shredded lettuce**
- 1 **cup (4 ounces) shredded fat-free cheddar cheese**
- 1 **medium tomato, diced**
- 1/4 **cup chopped ripe olives**
- 1/4 **cup chopped green chilies**

Tortilla chips

1. In a large bowl, beat cream cheese and sour cream until smooth. Stir in taco sauce and cumin; set aside.

2. Spread the refried beans over the bottom on a serving platter or 13-in. x 9-in. dish. Spread the cream cheese mixture over the beans, leaving about 1 in. uncovered around the edges. Top with lettuce, cheese, tomato, olives and chilies. Serve with tortilla chips.

SWEET 'N' SOUR MEATBALLS, page 26

RANCH HAM ROLL-UPS, page 12

COWBOY BEEF DIP, page 32

BLT BITES, page 10

CHEESY OLIVE SNACKS, page 16

FESTIVE HAM 'N' CHEESE SPREAD, page 28

ZUCCHINI FETA BRUSCHETTA, page 14

MINI CORN DOGS, page 11

CARAMELIZED FENNEL TARTS, page 8

CHICKEN SATAY, page 15

HOMEMADE GUACAMOLE, page 30

ITALIAN STUFFED MUSHROOMS, page 18

SANTA FE CHEESECAKE, page 42

SAVORY PARTY BREAD, page 20

GARLIC TOMATO BRUSCHETTA, page 24

WONTON POT STICKERS WITH SOY REDUCTION, page 23

PROSCIUTTO CHICKEN KABOBS, page 21

STUFFED BABY RED POTATOES, page 22

SPINACH DIP IN A BREAD BOWL, page 28

[2003]

WARM BACON
CHEESE SPREAD

**yield: 4 cups   prep: 15 min.
bake: 1 hour**

*My friends threaten not to come by unless this
dip is on the menu! The rich spread bakes right
in the bread bowl and goes well with almost
any dipper. Plus, cleanup is a breeze.*

**—Nicole Marcotte
Smithers, British Columbia**

- 1 round loaf (1 pound) sourdough
  bread
- 1 package (8 ounces) cream cheese,
  softened
- 1-1/2 cups (12 ounces) sour cream
- 2 cups (8 ounces) shredded cheddar
  cheese
- 1-1/2 teaspoons Worcestershire sauce
- 3/4 pound sliced bacon, cooked and
  crumbled
- 1/2 cup chopped green onions
- **Assorted crackers**

1. Cut the top fourth off the loaf of
bread; carefully hollow out the bottom,
leaving a 1-in. shell. Cut the removed
bread and top of loaf into cubes; set
cubes aside.

2. In a large bowl, beat cream cheese
until fluffy. Add the sour cream,
cheddar cheese and Worcestershire
sauce until blended; stir in the bacon
and onions.

3. Spoon into bread shell. Wrap in a
piece of heavy-duty foil (about 24 in. x
17 in.). Bake at 325° for 1 hour or until
heated through. Serve with crackers
and reserved bread cubes.

[2008]

LUSCIOUS LEMON
FRUIT DIP

**yield: 5 cups
prep/total time: 20 min.**

*One of the treats served at my bridal shower
was this creamy dip. It received such raves that
I just had to get the recipe. Now I bring it to the
showers I attend.*

—Deb Ceman, Wauwatosa, Wisconsin

- 2 cups sugar
- 2/3 cup cornstarch
- 1 cup cold water
- 4 egg, lightly beaten
- 2/3 cup lemon juice
- 2 teaspoons vanilla extract
- 2 cups heavy whipping cream, whipped
- **Assorted fresh fruit**

TOP 100 RECIPE

1. In a large heavy saucepan, combine the
sugar and cornstarch. Gradually whisk
in water until smooth. Cook and stir
over medium-high heat until thickened
and bubbly. Reduce heat; cook and stir
2 minutes longer. Remove from the heat.

2. Stir a small amount of hot mixture into
the eggs; return all to the pan, stirring
constantly. Bring to a gentle boil; cook
and stir 2 minutes longer. Remove from
the heat. Gently stir in the lemon juice
and vanilla.

3. Transfer to a large bowl. Cool to room
temperature without stirring. Cover
surface of mixture with waxed paper;
refrigerate until cooled. Fold in the
whipped cream. Serve with fresh fruit.

LUSCIOUS LEMON
FRUIT DIP

*"I've been making this dip
for YEARS and never tire of
it (nor do my guests—
because they always
request it)."*
—*sharonkaym48*

FAVORITE SNACK MIX

[2005]

SANTA FE CHEESECAKE

yield: 16-20 servings ∞ **prep: 25 min.**
bake: 30 min.-+ chilling

(Pictured on page 38)

All of my favorite Southwestern ingredients are combined in this savory cheesecake. It looks and tastes fantastic!

—Jean Ecos
Hartland, Wisconsin, Field Editor

- 1 cup crushed tortilla chips
- 3 tablespoons butter, melted
- 2 packages (8 ounces *each*) cream cheese, softened
- 2 eggs, lightly beaten
- 2 cups (8 ounces) shredded Monterey Jack cheese
- 1 can (4 ounces) chopped green chilies, drained
- 1 cup (8 ounces) sour cream
- 1 cup chopped sweet yellow pepper
- 1/2 cup chopped green onions
- 1/3 cup chopped tomato

---

1. In a small bowl, combine tortilla chips and butter; press onto the bottom of a greased 9-in. springform pan. Place on a baking sheet. Bake crust at 325° for 15 minutes or until lightly browned.

2. In a large bowl, beat cream cheese until smooth. Add eggs; beat on low speed just until combined. Stir in Monterey Jack cheese and chilies; pour into crust.

3. Place pan on a baking sheet. Bake for 30-35 minutes or until center is almost set. Cool cheesecake on a wire rack for 10 minutes. Spread the sour cream over cheesecake. Carefully run a knife around edge of pan to loosen; cool for 1 hour. Refrigerate overnight.

4. Remove the sides of pan. Garnish with the yellow pepper, onions and tomato. Refrigerate leftovers.

[1995]

FAVORITE SNACK MIX

yield: about 14 cups ∞ **prep: 10 min.**
bake: 15 min./batch + cooling

For a great change of pace from the usual mix, try this recipe. It's almost impossible to stop eating this sweet and salty snack.

—Carol Allen, McLeansboro, Illinois

- 6 cups Crispix
- 1 can (10 ounces) mixed nuts
- 1 package (10 ounces) pretzel sticks
- 3/4 cup butter, cubed
- 3/4 cup packed brown sugar

---

1. In a large bowl, combine the cereal, nuts and pretzels. In a small saucepan over low heat, melt butter. Add brown sugar; cook and stir until dissolved. Pour over cereal mixture; stir to coat.

2. Place a third on a greased 15-in. x 10-in. x 1-in. baking pan. Bake at 325° for 8 minutes; stir and bake 6 minutes longer. Spread on waxed paper to cool. Repeat with remaining mixture. Store in airtight containers.

[1996]

SWEET POTATO CHIPS

yield: 5 servings ∞ **prep: 10 min. + soaking**
cook: 10 min.

My husband never cared for sweet potatoes until he married me. I tell him it must be my cooking! He can't resist dipping into a bowl of these crunchy chips.

—Janelle Lee
Appleton, Wisconsin, Field Editor

- 1 pound sweet potatoes, peeled and thinly sliced
- Oil for deep-fat frying
- Salt to taste

---

1. Soak potatoes in 2 qt. ice water for 1 hour; drain and pat dry. In an electric

skillet or deep fryer, heat oil to 375°. Fry potatoes, seven or eight slices at a time, 1-2 minutes or until golden brown on both sides, turning once. Drain on paper towels; sprinkle with salt.

[2001]

CAYENNE PRETZELS

yield: 3 quarts ∞ **prep: 10 min.** ∞ **bake: 1-1/4 hours**

These well-seasoned pretzels were a huge hit at my daughter's graduation party. The longer they sit, the spicier they seem to get!

—*Gayle Zebo, Warren, Pennsylvania*

- 1 cup canola oil
- 1 envelope ranch salad dressing mix
- 1 teaspoon garlic salt
- 1 teaspoon cayenne pepper
- 1 pound (12 cups) pretzel sticks

1. In a small bowl, combine oil, dressing mix, garlic salt and cayenne. Divide pretzels between two ungreased 15-in. x 10-in. x 1-in. baking pans. Pour oil mixture over pretzels; stir to coat. Bake at 200° for 1-1/4 to 1-1/2 hours or until golden brown; stir occasionally. Cool completely. Store in an airtight container.

[2011]

BANANAS FOSTER CRUNCH MIX

yield: 2-1/2 quarts ∞ **prep: 10 min.**
cook: 5 min. + cooling

Bananas Foster is one of my favorite desserts, so I thought a crunchy, snackable version would be good—and it is.

—*David Dahlman, Chatsworth, California*

- 3 cups Honey Nut Chex
- 3 cups Cinnamon Chex
- 2-1/4 cups pecan halves
- 1-1/2 cups dried banana chips
- 1/3 cup butter, cubed
- 1/3 cup packed brown sugar
- 1/2 teaspoon ground cinnamon
- 1/2 teaspoon banana extract
- 1/2 teaspoon rum extract

1. In a large microwave-safe bowl, combine first four ingredients. In a small microwave-safe bowl, microwave butter, brown sugar and cinnamon, uncovered, on high for 2 minutes; stir once. Stir in extracts. Pour over cereal mixture; toss to coat. Cook mix, uncovered, on high for 3 minutes; stir at 1-minute intervals. Spread onto waxed paper to cool. Store in an airtight container.

Editor's Note: This was tested in a 1,100-watt microwave.

[2010]

CARAMEL CORN WITH NUTS

yield: 2-1/2 quarts ∞ **prep: 20 min.** ∞ **bake: 45 min.**

Homemade caramel corn far surpasses anything you can buy. Adding nuts makes it extra special. I like to double the recipe so I have plenty to give as gifts.

—*Karen Scaglione, Nanuet, New York*

- 10 cups popped popcorn
- 1 cup packed brown sugar
- 1/2 cup butter, cubed
- 1/4 cup dark corn syrup
- 1/4 teaspoon salt
- 1/4 teaspoon baking soda
- 1/2 cup mixed nuts

1. Place popcorn in a large bowl; set aside.

2. In a large heavy saucepan, combine the brown sugar, butter, corn syrup and salt. Cook over medium heat, stirring occasionally, until mixture comes to a rolling boil. Cook and stir until candy thermometer reads 238° (soft-ball stage). Remove from the heat; stir in baking soda (mixture will foam). Quickly pour over popcorn and mix well; stir in nuts.

3. Transfer to two greased 13-in. x 9-in. baking pans. Bake at 200° for 45 minutes, stirring once. Remove from pans and place on waxed paper to cool. Break into clusters. Store in airtight containers.

Editor's Note: We recommend that you test your candy thermometer before each use by bringing water to a boil; the thermometer should read 212°. Adjust your recipe temperature up or down based on your test.

ASPARAGUS BEEF STIR-FRY

❝Best stir fry I've ever made—Yummy!❞
—MelodyMahala

[2007]

ASPARAGUS BEEF STIR-FRY

yield: 4 servings ∽ prep/total time: 30 min.

(Pictured on page 73)

I love filet mignon, but not its price! While at the supermarket, I picked up a more affordable beef cut. I brought it home and came up with this recipe. Now I cook it once a week, plus my husband loves taking the leftovers to work.

—Linda Flynn, Ellicott City, Maryland

---

1 pound beef tenderloin roast, cubed
1 green onion, sliced
1/2 teaspoon salt
1/4 teaspoon pepper
1 tablespoon canola oil
2 garlic cloves, minced
1 pound fresh asparagus, trimmed and cut into 2-inch pieces
1/2 pound sliced fresh mushrooms
1/4 cup butter, cubed
1 tablespoon reduced-sodium soy sauce
1-1/2 teaspoons lemon juice
Hot cooked rice

---

1. In a wok or large skillet, stir-fry the beef, onion, salt and pepper in oil for 3-5 minutes. Add garlic; cook 1 minute longer. Remove and keep warm.

2. In the same pan, stir-fry asparagus and mushrooms in butter until asparagus is tender. Return beef mixture to the pan. Stir in soy sauce and lemon juice; heat through. Serve with rice.

[2009]

MUSHROOM-BLUE CHEESE TENDERLOIN

yield: 10 servings (1-1/2 cups sauce)
prep: 10 min. + marinating
bake: 45 min. + standing

(Pictured on page 79)

This is a simple entree that tastes fabulous. I usually double the mushroom-blue cheese sauce, because it always disappears very fast.

—Eric Schoen, Lincoln, Nebraska

---

1 cup reduced-sodium soy sauce
3/4 cup Worcestershire sauce
1 beef tenderloin roast (3-1/2 to 4 pounds)
4 garlic cloves, minced
1 tablespoon coarsely ground pepper
1 can (10-1/2 ounces) condensed beef broth, undiluted
SAUCE:
1/2 pound sliced fresh mushrooms
1/2 cup butter, cubed
2 garlic cloves, minced
1 cup (4 ounces) crumbled blue cheese
1 tablespoon Worcestershire sauce
1/4 teaspoon caraway seeds
4 green onions, chopped

---

1. In a large resealable plastic bag, combine soy sauce and Worcestershire sauce. Add the beef; seal bag and turn to coat. Refrigerate for 2 hours, turning the beef occasionally.

2. Drain and discard marinade. Rub the beef with garlic and pepper; place in a shallow roasting pan. Add broth to the pan. Bake, uncovered, at 425° for 45-55 minutes or until meat reaches

desired doneness (for medium-rare, a thermometer should read 145°; medium, 160°; well-done, 170°). Let stand for 10 minutes before slicing.

3. Meanwhile, in a small saucepan, saute the mushrooms in butter until tender. Add the garlic; cook 1 minute longer. Add the cheese, Worcestershire sauce and caraway seeds; cook and stir over low heat until the cheese is melted. Stir in the onions; heat through. Serve sauce with beef.

[2011]

HERBED ITALIAN RIB ROAST

yield: 10 servings ∞ prep: 30 min.
bake: 1-3/4 hours + standing

This amazing recipe has been a favorite in my family for years. I like to roast twice as many vegetables so I can make a quick, full-flavored hash with the leftovers.

—Lily Julow
Gainesville, Florida, Field Editor

- 1 bone-in beef rib roast (4 to 5 pounds)
- 2 pounds Yukon gold potatoes, peeled and quartered
- 1 pound parsnips, quartered
- 1 pound carrots, quartered
- 2 large onions, cut into wedges
- 1/2 cup butter, melted
- 2 tablespoons dried rosemary, crushed
- 2 tablespoons dried oregano
- 1 teaspoon salt
- 1/4 teaspoon pepper

1. Place the roast in a large shallow roasting pan. Bake, uncovered, at 350° for 45 minutes.

2. In a large bowl, combine the potatoes, parsnips, carrots and onions. Drizzle with butter; toss to coat. Spoon vegetables around roast; sprinkle with the rosemary, oregano, salt and pepper. Bake 1 to 1-1/4 hours longer or until

meat reaches desired doneness (for medium-rare, a thermometer should read 145°; medium, 160°; well-done, 170°), stirring vegetables occasionally. Let stand for 10 minutes before slicing.

[2002]

GLAZED CORNED BEEF

yield: 12 servings ∞ prep: 3 hours
bake: 25 min. + standing

I serve this delicious entree at St. Patrick's Day celebrations. The meat is so tender and tasty topped with a simple tangy glaze. Leftovers make excellent Reuben sandwiches.

—Perlene Hoekema
Lynden, Washington, Field Editor

- 1 corned beef brisket with spice packet (3 to 4 pounds), trimmed
- 1 medium onion, sliced
- 1 celery rib, sliced
- 1/4 cup butter, cubed
- 1 cup packed brown sugar
- 2/3 cup ketchup
- 1/3 cup white vinegar
- 2 tablespoons prepared mustard
- 2 teaspoons prepared horseradish

1. Place corned beef and contents of seasoning packet in a Dutch oven; cover with water. Add onion and celery; bring to a boil. Reduce heat; cover and simmer for 2-1/2 hours or until meat is tender.

2. Drain and discard the liquid and vegetables. Place the beef on a greased rack in a shallow roasting pan and set aside.

3. In a small saucepan, melt butter over medium heat. Stir in the remaining ingredients. Cook and stir until sugar is dissolved. Brush over beef.

4. Bake, uncovered, at 350° for 25 minutes. Let stand for 10 minutes before slicing.

GLAZED CORNED BEEF

"My entire family loves the way this corned beef comes out. We end up making it for more than just St. Patrick's Day. The sauce is also great on ham."
—dotchi

PRIME RIB WITH HORSERADISH SAUCE

"Great recipe! Will pass on to friends and family. Cooking instructions couldn't have been more precise. Did add garlic, rosemary and thyme along with the pepper. Thank you TOH (Taste of Home)!"
—luv2cookalot

[2010]

BEEF ROAST AU POIVRE WITH CARAMELIZED ONIONS

yield: 6 servings ⚬ prep: 30 min. + chilling ⚬ bake: 1 hour + standing

(Pictured on page 76)

This beef roast with crushed peppercorns is elegant, delicious and perfect for company. The aroma in your kitchen while it's cooking will be out of this world!
—*Elaine Sweet, Dallas, Texas*

　2　tablespoons *or* 1/4 cup whole black peppercorns
　3　dried chipotle chilies, stems removed
　1　tablespoon coriander seeds
　1　tablespoon dried minced onion
　1　tablespoon dried thyme
1-1/2　teaspoons salt
　1　teaspoon dried orange peel
　3　tablespoons steak sauce
　1　beef tri-tip roast (2 to 3 pounds)
ONIONS:
　4　large onions, thinly sliced
　3　tablespoons olive oil
1/2　cup chardonnay *or* other white wine
　2　teaspoons dried thyme
1/2　teaspoon pepper
1/8　teaspoon salt
　2　tablespoons minced fresh parsley

---

1. Place peppercorns, chilies and coriander in a blender. Cover and process until coarsely ground. Stir in the onion, thyme, salt and orange peel.

2. Rub steak sauce and seasoning mixture over roast; cover and refrigerate for 8 hours or overnight.

3. Place the roast on a rack in a shallow roasting pan. Bake roast, uncovered, at 425° for 1 to 1-1/2 hours or until meat reaches desired doneness (for medium-rare, a thermometer should read 145°; medium, 160°; well-done, 170°).

4. Meanwhile, in a large skillet, cook onions in oil over low heat for 30-35 minutes or until golden brown, stirring frequently. Stir in wine and bring to a boil. Reduce heat; cook and stir for 1-2 minutes or until liquid is evaporated. Stir in the thyme, pepper and salt.

5. Transfer meat to a warm serving platter. Let stand for 10 minutes before slicing. Sprinkle with parsley. Serve with onions.

[2006]

PRIME RIB WITH HORSERADISH SAUCE

yield: 6-8 servings **prep: 5 min.**
bake: 3 hours

(*Pictured on page 78*)

We invite friends over for dinner to ring in the New Year. A menu featuring tender prime rib is festive, yet simple to prepare. A pepper rub and mild horseradish sauce complement the beef's great flavor.

—*Paula Zsiray, Logan, Utah, Field Editor*

- 1 bone-in beef rib roast (4 to 6 pounds)
- 1 tablespoon olive oil
- 1 to 2 teaspoons coarsely ground pepper

HORSERADISH SAUCE:

- 1 cup (8 ounces) sour cream
- 3 to 4 tablespoons prepared horseradish
- 1 teaspoon coarsely ground pepper
- 1/8 teaspoon Worcestershire sauce

1. Brush roast with oil; rub with pepper. Place roast, fat side up, on a rack in a shallow roasting pan. Bake, uncovered, at 450° for 15 minutes.

2. Reduce heat to 325°. Bake for 2-3/4 hours or until meat reaches desired doneness (for medium-rare, a thermometer should read 145°; medium, 160°; well-done, 170°), basting with pan drippings every 30 minutes.

3. Let stand for 10-15 minutes before slicing. Meanwhile, in a small bowl, combine the sauce ingredients. Serve with beef.

[2008]

POT ROAST WITH GRAVY

yield: 10 servings **prep: 30 min.**
cook: 7-1/2 hours

(*Pictured on page 75*)

My family loves this tangy, slow-cooked beef roast with gravy. We always hope for leftovers, which I then turn into a tasty sandwich spread.

—*Deborah Dailey, Vancouver, Washington*

- 1 beef rump roast *or* bottom round roast (5 pounds)
- 6 tablespoons balsamic vinegar, *divided*
- 1 teaspoon salt
- 1/2 teaspoon garlic powder
- 1/4 teaspoon pepper
- 2 tablespoons canola oil
- 3 garlic cloves, minced
- 4 bay leaves
- 1 large onion, thinly sliced
- 3 teaspoons beef bouillon granules
- 1/2 cup boiling water
- 1 can (10-3/4 ounces) condensed cream of mushroom soup, undiluted
- 4 to 5 tablespoons cornstarch
- 1/4 cup cold water

1. Cut roast in half; rub with 2 tablespoons vinegar. Combine salt, garlic powder and pepper; rub over meat. In a large skillet, brown roast in oil on all sides. Transfer to a 5-qt. slow cooker.

2. Add the garlic, bay leaves and onion over roast. In a small bowl, dissolve bouillon in boiling water; stir in soup and remaining vinegar. Slowly pour over roast. Cover and cook on low for 6-8 hours or until meat is tender.

3. Remove the roast; keep warm. Discard bay leaves. Whisk the cornstarch and cold water until smooth; stir into cooking juices.

4. Cover and cook on high for 30 minutes or until gravy is thickened. Slice roast; return to slow cooker and heat through.

POT ROAST WITH GRAVY

“We made this last night and there were no leftovers. My hubby and I compete to see who is the better cook and he conceded his loss last night. I think the vinegar makes it smell so good, I couldn't wait for dinner!”
—*mariekelly*

MIXED GRILL KABOBS

[2002]

MIXED GRILL KABOBS

yield: 10-12 servings
prep: 20 min. + marinating ∞ **grill: 15 min.**

(Pictured on page 76)

These hearty kabobs combine beef and sausage, two of my favorite foods. Both the meat and vegetables are marinated, which makes this skewered meal extra flavorful.

—*Glenda Adams, Vanndale, Arkansas*

- 3 cups pineapple juice
- 1 cup cider vinegar
- 1 cup canola oil
- 1/4 cup sugar
- 1/4 cup reduced-sodium soy sauce
- 1 tablespoon browning sauce, optional
- 1/2 teaspoon garlic powder
- 1/4 teaspoon lemon-pepper seasoning
- 2 pounds beef tenderloin, cut into 1-inch cubes
- 1 pound smoked kielbasa *or* Polish sausage, cut into 1-inch chunks
- 3 to 4 medium tomatoes, quartered
- 3 to 4 medium green peppers, quartered
- 1 jar (4-1/2 ounces) whole mushrooms, drained
- 5 medium onions, quartered

1. In a small bowl, combine the first eight ingredients. Pour half into a large resealable plastic bag; add meat. Seal bag and turn to coat. Pour remaining marinade into another large resealable plastic bag; add vegetables. Seal bag and turn to coat. Refrigerate meat and vegetables overnight.

2. Drain and discard the marinade. Alternately thread the beef, sausage and vegetables onto metal or soaked wooden skewers.

3. Grill, covered, over medium-hot heat for 6-8 minutes. Turn kabobs; cook 6-8 minutes longer or until beef reaches desired doneness.

[1996]

HERBED POT ROAST

yield: 8 servings ∞ **prep: 25 min.**
bake: 3 hours

I prepare this delicious main dish several times a month. The herbs give the beef an excellent taste. Adding the onion, carrots and potatoes makes this a meal-in-one dish. My husband, Jack, a real meat-and-potatoes man, even enjoys the leftovers, which isn't always the case with other dishes.

—*Christel McKinley, East Liverpool, Ohio*

- 1 boneless beef rump *or* chuck roast (3 to 3-1/2 pounds)
- 1 tablespoon canola oil
- 1 teaspoon salt
- 1 teaspoon dried marjoram
- 1 teaspoon dried thyme
- 1/2 teaspoon dried oregano
- 1/2 teaspoon garlic powder
- 1/2 teaspoon pepper
- 1 can (10-1/2 ounces) condensed beef broth, undiluted
- 8 medium carrots, cut into thirds
- 8 medium potatoes, peeled and quartered
- 1 large onion, quartered
- 1 cup water

1. In a Dutch oven over medium heat, brown roast in oil on all sides. Combine seasonings; sprinkle over meat. Add broth and bring to a boil.

2. Cover and bake at 325° for 2 hours, basting occasionally. Add the carrots, potatoes, onion and water.

3. Cover and bake for 1 hour longer or until beef and vegetables are tender. Thicken pan juices for gravy if desired.

[2010]

GENROSE'S STUFFED BEEF TENDERLOIN

yield: 16 servings ∽ **prep:** 30 min.
bake: 50 min. + standing

We've belonged to the same supper club for 45 years. This flavorful, elegant stuffed tenderloin may just steal the show!

—Katie Whitworth, Lexington, Kentucky

---

5 bacon strips
1/2 pound sliced fresh mushrooms
1 medium onion, chopped
1 tablespoon butter
2 cups seasoned stuffing cubes
1/4 cup chicken broth
1/4 teaspoon salt
1/4 teaspoon garlic salt
1/4 teaspoon pepper
1 beef tenderloin (5 pounds)

TOP 100 RECIPE

---

1. In a large skillet, cook bacon over medium heat until partially cooked but not crisp. Remove to paper towels to drain; keep warm.

2. In the same skillet, saute mushrooms and onion in butter until tender. Stir in the stuffing cubes, broth, salt, garlic salt and pepper.

3. Make a lengthwise slit down the center of tenderloin to within 1/2 in. of bottom. Open meat so it lies flat. Mound stuffing over the center. Bring up sides of tenderloin; tie at 2-in. intervals with kitchen string. Place on a rack in a shallow roasting pan. Arrange bacon over the top.

4. Bake, uncovered, at 425° for 50-80 minutes or the until meat reaches desired doneness (for medium-rare, a thermometer should read 145°; medium, 160°; well-done, 170°). Cover loosely with foil if top browns too quickly. Remove the meat to a serving platter. Cover and let stand for 10 minutes before slicing.

[2011]

PANHANDLE BEEF BRISKET

yield: 16 servings (2 cups sauce)
prep: 40 min. ∽ **bake:** 3 hours

This tender, Texas-style brisket, paired nicely with a savory sauce, is a superb dinner for cooler weather.

—Laurel Leslie, Sonora, California

2-1/4 cups ketchup
1-1/2 cups beef broth
1 large onion, chopped
1/2 cup packed brown sugar
1/2 cup white wine vinegar
2 tablespoons chili powder
2 tablespoons Worcestershire sauce
3 garlic cloves, minced
1/4 teaspoon cayenne pepper
1 fresh beef brisket (5 to 7 pounds), trimmed
2 tablespoons Liquid Smoke, optional

---

1. In a large saucepan, combine the first nine ingredients. Bring to a boil, stirring constantly. Reduce heat; simmer, uncovered, for 30 minutes, stirring occasionally. Remove from the heat. Remove 2 cups sauce to a bowl; cover and refrigerate for serving.

2. Place brisket in a shallow roasting pan; brush with Liquid Smoke if desired. Pour remaining sauce over meat. Cover and bake at 325° for 3 hours or until meat is tender.

3. Let stand for 5 minutes. Heat reserved sauce. Thinly slice meat across the grain. Serve sauce with meat.

Editor's Note: This is a fresh beef brisket, not corned beef.

GENROSE'S STUFFED BEEF TENDERLOIN

"I made the original recipe as-is and a second one using a pork tenderloin, omitting the onion and adding 1 thinly sliced Granny Smith apple. I made two sauces: one made with whole cranberry sauce and sweet red wine and the second with hot apple cider and a little of the drippings and cornstarch to thicken. Both were the talk of the event. HIGH praise for Genrose; hope you submit more recipes."
—alleytt

[1997]

DIJON SIRLOIN TIPS

yield: 4 servings ∾ prep: 20 min. ∾ bake: 1 hour

I received this recipe years ago and have put it to excellent use ever since. This beef and mushroom dish is such a hit with our family that it has become a tradition for birthdays and Christmas.

—*Janelle Lee, Appleton, Wisconsin, Field Editor*

1	beef top sirloin steak (1-1/4 pounds), cubed
2	tablespoons butter
1	tablespoon canola oil
3	cups sliced fresh mushrooms
1	garlic clove, minced
1/2	cup beef broth
1/4	cup white wine vinegar
1-1/2	teaspoons reduced-sodium soy sauce
2	teaspoons Dijon mustard
2	teaspoons cornstarch
1/2	cup heavy whipping cream

Hot cooked noodles
Chopped fresh parsley, optional

1. In a large skillet, brown meat in butter and oil; transfer to a 2-qt. baking dish. In the same skillet, saute mushrooms until tender, about 3 minutes. Add garlic; cook 1 minute longer. Pour mushroom mixture and drippings over meat. Cover and bake at 325° for 1 hour or until beef is tender.

2. In a skillet, combine the broth, vinegar and soy sauce; bring to a boil. Boil for 2 minutes; set aside. Combine mustard, cornstarch and cream; stir into broth mixture. Bring to a boil; cook and stir for 2 minutes or until thickened.

3. Drain juices from baking dish into broth mixture. Cook over medium heat until thickened and bubbly, stirring constantly. Add beef mixture. Serve with noodles. Garnish with parsley if desired.

DIJON SIRLOIN TIPS

❝This recipe is delicious! Easy to make and elegant enough to serve to special guests. The meat is always tender and flavorful! Thank you Janelle for a great recipe!❞
—*jillea*

MINCING FRESH GARLIC

To mince fresh garlic, crush a garlic clove with the blade of a chef's knife. Peel away skin. Mince as directed.

[2001]

MARINATED BEEF FONDUE

**yield: 12-16 servings
prep: 15 min. + marinating
cook: 5 min./batch**

Guests will enjoy cooking their own serving of this boldly seasoned meat. It goes so wonderfully with the tasty dipping sauces.

—DeEtta Rasmussen
Fort Madison, Iowa, Former Field Editor

- 3/4 cup reduced-sodium soy sauce
- 1/4 cup Worcestershire sauce
- 2 garlic cloves, minced
- 2-1/2 pounds beef tenderloin, cut into 1-inch cubes
- 2-1/2 pounds pork tenderloin, cut into 1-inch cubes

HORSERADISH SAUCE:
- 1 cup (8 ounces) sour cream
- 3 tablespoons prepared horseradish
- 1 tablespoon chopped onion
- 1 teaspoon white vinegar
- 1/2 teaspoon salt
- 1/4 teaspoon pepper

BARBECUE SAUCE:
- 1 can (8 ounces) tomato sauce
- 1/3 cup steak sauce
- 2 tablespoons brown sugar
- 6 to 9 cups peanut oil *or* 6 to 9 cups canola oil

1. In a large resealable plastic bag, combine the soy sauce, Worcestershire sauce and garlic; add meat. Seal the bag and turn to coat; refrigerate for 4 hours, turning occasionally.

2. Meanwhile, in a small bowl, combine the horseradish sauce ingredients; cover and refrigerate. In another bowl, combine the tomato sauce, steak sauce and brown sugar; cover and refrigerate.

3. Drain and discard marinade. Pat meat dry with paper towels. Using one fondue pot for every six people, heat 2-3 cups oil in each pot to 375°. Use fondue forks to cook meat in oil until it reaches desired doneness. Serve with horseradish and barbecue sauces.

Editor's Note: You can use additional beef tenderloin for the pork tenderloin.

[1998]

GARLIC SWISS STEAK

**yield: 6 servings   prep: 20 min.
bake: 1-1/2 hours**

This favorite beef entree was perfect when our four children were at home. It was simple for me to fix this budget-stretcher, and the kids loved it.

—Patricia Hooks, Greenville, Texas

- 1-1/2 pounds bone-in beef round steak
- 1/3 cup all-purpose flour
- 1 teaspoon salt
- 1/2 teaspoon pepper
- 2 tablespoons canola oil
- 1 can (14-1/2 ounces) stewed tomatoes
- 1 small onion, chopped
- 1/2 medium green pepper, chopped
- 2 garlic cloves, minced

1. Cut steak into serving-size pieces; discard bone. Combine the flour, salt and pepper; pound to 1/4-in. thickness. In a large skillet over medium heat, brown steak on both sides in oil.

2. Transfer to a greased 13-in. x 9-in. baking dish. Combine the tomatoes, onion, green pepper and garlic; pour over steak. Cover and bake at 350° for 1-1/2 hours or until meat is tender.

GARLIC SWISS STEAK

"This was fabulous! It was so quick to throw together and then let it cook itself. The flavors were wonderful! It will become a regular in our household. Would be great for company too."
—craigsuem

[1994]

SLOW-COOKED PEPPER STEAK

yield: 6 servings ∽ prep: 10 min.
cook: 6-1/2 hours

(Pictured on page 77)

After a long day in our greenhouse raising bedding plants for sale, I appreciate coming in to this hearty beef dish for supper.

—Sue Gronholz
Beaver Dam, Wisconsin, Field Editor

1-1/2	pounds beef top round steak
2	tablespoons canola oil
1	cup chopped onion
1/4	cup reduced-sodium soy sauce
1	garlic clove, minced
1	teaspoon sugar
1/2	teaspoon salt
1/4	teaspoon ground ginger
1/4	teaspoon pepper
4	medium tomatoes, cut into wedges *or* 1 can (14-1/2 ounces) diced tomatoes, undrained
1	large green pepper, cut into strips
1	tablespoon cornstarch
1/2	cup cold water

Hot cooked noodles *or* rice

1. Cut beef into 3-in. x 1-in. strips. In a large skillet, brown beef in oil. Transfer to a 3-qt. slow cooker. Combine the onion, soy sauce, garlic, sugar, salt, ginger and pepper; pour over beef. Cover and cook on low for 5-6 hours or until meat is tender. Add tomatoes and green pepper; cook on low 1 hour longer or until vegetables are tender.

2. Combine cornstarch and cold water until smooth; gradually stir into slow cooker. Cover and cook on high for 20-30 minutes until thickened. Serve with noodles or rice.

SLOW-COOKED PEPPER STEAK

"This is the best recipe ever. My son is a very picky eater and he loves this. We put it over mashed potatoes and add veggies. It's quick and fast."
—katiem65

[1996]

FABULOUS FAJITAS

yield: 6-8 servings ∽ prep: 20 min.
cook: 3-1/2 hours

I've enjoyed cooking since I was a girl growing up in the Southwest. When friends call to ask me for new recipes to try, I suggest these flavorful fajitas. It's wonderful to put the beef in the slow cooker before church and come home to a hot delicious main dish.

—Janie Reitz, Rochester, Minnesota

1-1/2	pounds beef top sirloin steak, cut into thin strips
2	tablespoons canola oil
2	tablespoons lemon juice
1	garlic clove, minced
1-1/2	teaspoons ground cumin
1	teaspoon seasoned salt
1/2	teaspoon chili powder
1/4	to 1/2 teaspoon crushed red pepper flakes
1	large green pepper, julienned
1	large onion, julienned
6	to 8 flour tortillas (8 inches)

Shredded cheddar cheese, salsa, sour cream, lettuce and tomatoes, optional

1. In a large skillet, brown steak in oil over medium heat. Place steak and drippings in a 3-qt. slow cooker. Stir in the lemon juice, garlic, cumin, salt, chili powder and red pepper flakes.

2. Cover and cook on high for 2-3 hours or until meat is almost tender. Add green pepper and onion; cover and cook for 1 hour or until meat and vegetables are tender.

3. Warm tortillas according to package directions; spoon beef and vegetables down the center of tortillas. Top each with cheese, salsa, sour cream, lettuce and tomatoes if desired.

[1996]

COUNTRY-FRIED STEAKS

yield: 4 servings ∾ **prep/total time: 30 min.**

This down-home recipe reminds me of my mother, who was raised in the South. It calls for cubed steak instead of round steak, so there's no need to pound the meat. I just dip and coat the beef, then cook it in my cast-iron skillet.

—*Bonnie Malloy, Norwood, Pennsylvania*

---

    5 tablespoons all-purpose flour, *divided*
  1/4 cup cornmeal
  1/2 teaspoon salt
  1/4 teaspoon pepper
    4 beef cubed steaks (4 ounces *each*)
    1 egg white
    1 teaspoon water
    2 tablespoons canola oil, *divided*
GRAVY:
    1 tablespoon butter
    2 tablespoons all-purpose flour
1-1/2 cups 2% milk
    1 teaspoon beef bouillon granules
  1/2 teaspoon dried marjoram
  1/4 teaspoon dried thyme
  1/8 teaspoon pepper

---

1. Combine 3 tablespoons flour, cornmeal, salt and pepper; set aside. Coat steaks with remaining flour. Beat egg white and water; dip steaks, then dredge in cornmeal mixture.

2. In a large skillet, cook two steaks in 1 tablespoon oil over medium-high heat for 5-7 minutes on each side or until crisp, lightly browned and cooked to desired doneness. Remove steaks and keep warm. Repeat with the remaining oil and steaks.

3. Meanwhile, for gravy, melt butter in a small saucepan; stir in flour until smooth. Gradually add milk. Bring to a boil over medium heat; cook and stir for 2 minutes or until thickened. Reduce heat to medium-low. Add the

bouillon, marjoram, thyme and pepper; simmer, uncovered, for 4-5 minutes, stirring occasionally. Serve with steaks.

[2003]

BREADED SIRLOIN

yield: 8 servings ∾ **prep/total time: 25 min.**

Looking for a fabulous weeknight dinner? Look no further than this recipe. It is easy to prep and cooks quickly.

—*Sandra Lee Pippin, Aurora, Colorado*

---

    2 eggs
  1/2 cup 2% milk
    1 cup seasoned bread crumbs
    3 tablespoons grated Parmesan cheese
    2 tablespoons minced fresh parsley
    2 garlic cloves, minced
  1/4 teaspoon salt
  1/8 teaspoon pepper
    2 pounds beef top sirloin steak (1-1/2 inches thick), cut into eight pieces
  1/4 cup canola oil
    4 medium ripe tomatoes, sliced
    8 slices part-skim mozzarella cheese
Lemon wedges

---

1. In a shallow bowl, whisk the eggs and milk. In another shallow bowl, combine the bread crumbs, Parmesan cheese, parsley, garlic, salt and pepper. Dip the steak in the egg mixture, then roll in crumb mixture.

2. In a large skillet over medium-high heat, cook the steaks in oil in batches for 2-3 minutes on each side or until the meat is no longer pink. Drain on paper towels.

3. Transfer to an ungreased baking sheet. Top beef with tomato and cheese slices. Broil 4-6 in. from the heat for 1-2 minutes or until cheese is melted. Serve with lemon.

COUNTRY-FRIED STEAKS

❝I have made this recipe many times for me and my husband (I only use two cubed steaks then) and we love it. The gravy is awesome too. When my father-in-law made chicken-fried steaks his way, I made this gravy and everyone loved it. Will definitely keep making this recipe again and again and again.❞

—*k8blujay*

TANGY BEEF STROGANOFF

❝Love this recipe! My kids gag at the sight of mushrooms so I use about three times the amount called for in the recipe in wide variety and cut them in half. Then, just before adding the sour cream, I set aside their portion and take out the mushrooms. The kids love the flavor and my husband and I enjoy the extra mushrooms.❞

—*meehankkb*

[2012]

RANCHERO GRILLED STEAK WRAPS

yield: 4 servings ∞ prep: 25 min.
grill: 10 min.

Flat iron steak is a lean cut of beef, so take care not to overcook it. The ancho chili-mayonnaise sauce gives the meat a nice smoky flavor.

—*Patricia Harmon, Baden, Pennsylvania*

- 2 dried ancho chilies
- 2 cups boiling water
- 3/4 cup reduced-fat mayonnaise
- 2 tablespoons minced fresh cilantro
- 1 tablespoon lime juice
- 1 garlic clove, minced
- 1 teaspoon honey
- 1 beef flat iron steak *or* top sirloin steak (1 pound)

Salt and pepper to taste
- 4 fat-free flour tortillas (8 inches), warmed
- 1 medium ripe avocado, peeled and diced
- 1 cup (4 ounces) shredded reduced-fat Mexican cheese blend
- 1 cup torn romaine
- 1/2 cup chopped tomatoes
- 1/4 cup chopped red onion

1. Place the chilies in a small bowl. Cover with the boiling water; let stand for 5 minutes. Drain. Remove stems, seeds and skins. Finely chop; place in a small bowl. Stir in mayonnaise, cilantro, lime juice, garlic and honey; set aside.

2. Season the steak with salt and pepper to taste. Grill, covered, over medium heat for 4-5 minutes on each side or until meat reaches desired doneness (for medium-rare, a thermometer should read 145°; medium, 160°; well-done, 170°).

3. Spread 3 tablespoons of ancho mayonnaise over each tortilla. Thinly slice steak across the grain; divide

evenly among tortillas. Top with avocado, cheese, romaine, tomatoes and onion. Roll up.

[1997]

TANGY BEEF STROGANOFF

yield: 4 servings ∞ prep/total time: 25 min.

Your family and friends will think you spent all day in the kitchen when they taste their first bite of this fantastic stroganoff.

—*Rita Farmer, Greendale, Wisconsin*

- 1 pound beef top sirloin steak
- 1/4 cup butter
- 1/2 pound mushrooms, sliced
- 1/2 cup sliced onion
- 1 garlic clove, minced
- 2 tablespoons all-purpose flour
- 1 cup water
- 1 tablespoon lemon juice
- 1 tablespoon red wine vinegar
- 2 teaspoons beef bouillon granules
- 1/2 teaspoon salt
- 1/4 teaspoon pepper
- 1 cup (8 ounces) sour cream

Hot cooked noodles
Paprika and chopped fresh parsley

1. Cut beef into 1/8-in. thick strips. In a large skillet over medium-high heat, cook beef in butter until no longer pink. Remove with a slotted spoon and keep warm.

2. In pan juices, cook mushrooms and onion until tender. Add garlic; cook 1 minute longer. Stir in flour. Add the water, lemon juice, vinegar, bouillon, salt and pepper; bring to a boil. Cook and stir for 2 minutes or until thickened. Stir in the sour cream and beef; heat through (do not boil). Serve with noodles. Garnish with the paprika and parsley.

[2004]

THAI BEEF STIR-FRY

yield: 6 servings ∞ **prep: 20 min.** ∞ **cook: 20 min.**

A distinctive peanut sauce complements this colorful combination of tender sirloin strips, cauliflower, carrots, broccoli and mushrooms. I like to dish it up over spaghetti, but you could also use fried noodles.

—*Janice Fehr, Austin, Manitoba*

1/2	cup packed brown sugar
2	tablespoons cornstarch
2	cups beef broth
1/3	cup reduced-sodium soy sauce
1	teaspoon onion powder
1	teaspoon garlic powder
1	teaspoon ground ginger
1/4	teaspoon hot pepper sauce
2	pounds boneless beef sirloin steak, cut into thin strips
6	tablespoons olive oil, *divided*
2	cups fresh cauliflowerets
1-1/2	cups julienned carrots
4	cups fresh broccoli florets
2	cups sliced fresh mushrooms
1/4	cup peanut butter

Hot cooked spaghetti

1/2	cup chopped peanuts

---

1. In a small bowl, combine the first eight ingredients until smooth; set aside. In a large skillet or wok, stir-fry beef in 3 tablespoons oil until meat is no longer pink. Remove and keep warm.

2. In the same skillet, stir-fry cauliflower and carrots in remaining oil for 5 minutes. Add broccoli; stir-fry for 7 minutes. Add mushrooms; stir-fry 6-8 minutes longer or until the vegetables are crisp-tender.

3. Stir broth mixture and add to the pan. Bring to a boil; cook and stir for 2 minutes or until thickened. Reduce heat; add beef and peanut butter. Cook and stir over medium heat until peanut butter is blended. Serve with spaghetti. Sprinkle with peanuts.

THAI BEEF STIR-FRY

"This was incredible! I turned up the heat by adding a little more hot sauce. Definitely will make this again."
—*sswade*

[1996]

PARTY BEEF CASSEROLE

yield: 6-8 servings ∞ prep: 30 min.
bake: 1-3/4 hours

Round steak is economical and delicious. That's why I was thrilled to find the recipe for this comforting meal-in-one casserole. With a salad and rolls, it's an inexpensive, hearty dinner.

—*Kelly Hardgrave, Hartman, Arkansas*

- 3 tablespoons all-purpose flour
- 1 teaspoon salt
- 1/2 teaspoon pepper
- 2 pounds beef top round steak, cut into 1/2-inch cubes
- 2 tablespoons canola oil
- 1 cup water
- 1/2 cup beef broth
- 1 garlic clove, minced
- 1 tablespoon dried minced onion
- 1/2 teaspoon dried thyme
- 1/4 teaspoon dried rosemary, crushed
- 2 cups sliced fresh mushrooms
- 2 cups frozen peas, thawed
- 3 cups mashed potatoes (with added milk and butter)
- 1 tablespoon butter, melted

Paprika

---

1. In a large resealable plastic bag, combine the flour, salt and pepper; add the beef in batches; shake to coat. In a large skillet, cook beef over medium heat in oil until meat is no longer pink. Place beef and drippings in a greased shallow 2-1/2-qt. baking dish.

2. In the same skillet, add water, broth, garlic, onion, thyme and rosemary; bring to a boil. Simmer, uncovered, for 5 minutes; stir in mushrooms. Pour over meat; stir to coat.

3. Cover and bake at 350° for 1-1/2 to 1-3/4 hours or until beef is tender. Sprinkle peas over meat. Spread the potatoes evenly over top. Brush with butter; sprinkle with paprika. Cover and bake 15-20 minutes longer.

[1999]

STEAK DIANE

yield: 4 servings ∞ prep/total time: 15 min.

When I want to provide a memorable supper but don't want to spend hours in the kitchen, this is the recipe I rely on. I've used it many times on holidays or other occasions for a quick, impressive main dish. We relish the savory sauce poured over the steaks.

—*Phoebe Carre, Mullica Hill, New Jersey*

- 4 beef ribeye steaks (1/2 inch thick and 8 ounces *each*)
- 1/4 teaspoon pepper
- 1/8 teaspoon salt
- 2 tablespoons finely chopped green onion
- 1/2 teaspoon ground mustard
- 4 tablespoons butter, *divided*
- 1 tablespoon lemon juice
- 1-1/2 teaspoons Worcestershire sauce
- 1 tablespoon minced fresh parsley
- 1 tablespoon minced chives

---

1. Sprinkle steaks on both sides with pepper and salt; set aside. In a large skillet, cook the onion and mustard in 2 tablespoons butter for 1 minute. Add the steaks; cook for 2-5 minutes on each side or until the meat reaches desired doneness (for medium-rare, a thermometer should read 145°; medium 160°; well-done 170°).

2. Remove steaks to a serving platter and keep warm. In the same skillet, add the lemon juice, Worcestershire sauce and remaining butter; cook and stir for 2 minutes or until thickened. Add the parsley and chives. Serve with steaks.

[2009]

GINGERED BEEF STIR-FRY

yield: 4 servings
prep: 20 min. + marinating ∞ **cook: 20 min.**

A friend who owns a bed-and-breakfast in Maryland shared this recipe with me. It's a delicious and different way to serve asparagus.

—Sonja Blow, Nixa, Missouri, Field Editor

- 3 tablespoons reduced-sodium soy sauce, *divided*
- 1 tablespoon sherry
- 1/4 teaspoon minced fresh gingerroot *or* dash ground ginger
- 1/2 pound beef flank steak, cut into thin strips
- 1 teaspoon cornstarch
- 1/2 cup beef broth
- 1-1/2 teaspoons hoisin sauce
- 1/8 teaspoon sugar
- 2 tablespoons canola oil, *divided*
- 2 pounds fresh asparagus, trimmed and cut into 1-inch pieces
- 1 garlic clove, minced
- 3 cups hot cooked rice

---

1. In a large resealable plastic bag, combine 2 tablespoons soy sauce, sherry and ginger; add the beef. Seal bag and turn to coat; refrigerate for 30 minutes.

2. In a small bowl, combine cornstarch, broth, hoisin sauce, sugar and the remaining soy sauce until smooth; set aside.

3. In a large skillet or wok, stir-fry beef in 1 tablespoon oil until no longer pink. Remove and set aside. Stir-fry the asparagus in the remaining oil until crisp-tender. Add the garlic; cook 1 minute longer.

4. Stir cornstarch mixture and add to the pan. Bring to a boil; cook and stir for 2 minutes or until thickened. Return beef to the pan; heat through. Serve with rice.

[2011]

MERLOT FILET MIGNON

yield: 2 servings ∞ **prep/total time: 20 min.**

(Pictured on page 80)

If you don't want to spend much time in the kitchen, turn to this beef recipe. It's not only easy to make, but it is elegant and will impress your guests.

—Jauneen Hosking, Waterford, Wisconsin

- 2 beef tenderloin steaks (8 ounces each)
- 3 tablespoons butter, *divided*
- 1 tablespoon olive oil
- 1 cup merlot
- 2 tablespoons heavy whipping cream
- 1/8 teaspoon salt

---

1. In a small skillet, cook the steaks in 1 tablespoon butter and oil over medium heat for 4-6 minutes on each side or until the meat reaches desired doneness (for medium-rare, a thermometer should read 145°; medium, 160°; well-done, 170°). Remove and keep warm.

2. In the same skillet, add wine, stirring to loosen browned bits from pan. Bring to a boil; cook until liquid is reduced to 1/4 cup. Add the cream, salt and remaining butter; bring to a boil. Cook and stir for 1-2 minutes or until slightly thickened and butter is melted. Serve with steaks.

GINGERED BEEF STIR-FRY

❝AWESOME!!! I substituted boneless pork chops for the beef and topped with sesame seeds and diced green onions. This was very easy and excellent!❞
—*motomom36*

[1993]

CORNISH PASTIES

yield: 4 servings ❧ prep: 30 min. ❧ bake: 50 min.

(Pictured on page 76)

Years ago, when bakeries in my Midwestern hometown made pasties, people scrambled to get there before they were all gone. Now I make my own...filled with meat, potatoes and vegetables, they make a complete meal and are great for picnics or potlucks.

—*Gayle Lewis, Yucaipa, California*

FILLING:

- 1 pound beef top round steak, cut into 1/2-inch pieces
- 2 to 3 medium potatoes, peeled and cut into 1/2-inch cubes
- 1 cup chopped carrots
- 1/2 cup finely chopped onion
- 2 tablespoons minced fresh parsley
- 1 teaspoon salt
- 1/2 teaspoon pepper
- 1/4 cup butter, melted

PASTRY:

- 3 cups all-purpose flour
- 1 teaspoon salt
- 1 cup shortening
- 8 to 9 tablespoons ice water
- 1 egg, lightly beaten, optional

1. In a large bowl, combine the round steak, potatoes, carrots, onion, parsley, salt and pepper. Add butter and toss to coat; set aside.

2. For pastry, combine flour and salt in a large bowl. Cut in shortening until mixture forms pea-size crumbs. Sprinkle with water, 1 tablespoon at a time. Toss lightly with a fork until dough forms a ball. Do not overmix.

3. Divide dough into fourths. Roll out one portion into a 9-in. circle; transfer to a greased baking sheet. Mound about 1-1/4 cups of meat filling on half of circle. Moisten edges with water; fold dough over mixture and press edges with fork to seal. Repeat with remaining pastry and filling.

4. Cut slits in top of each pasty. Brush with beaten egg if desired. Bake at 375° for 50-60 minutes or until golden brown.

CORNISH PASTIES

❝Well I tell everyone this was excellent. This was a great meal. Easy to make when you use any premade dough. Thank you for the recipe!❞
—*teddie28*

[2004]

CUBED STEAKS PARMIGIANA
yield: 4 servings ∾ **prep: 20 min.
bake: 40 min.**

*Are you tired of chicken-fried steak? This
recipe dresses up cubed steaks Italian-style
with cheese, tomato sauce, basil and oregano.
My husband and I like this main dish with a
side of fettuccine Alfredo.*

—*Sarah Befort, Hays, Kansas*

- 3 tablespoons all-purpose flour
- 1/2 teaspoon salt
- 1/4 teaspoon pepper
- 2 eggs
- 3 tablespoons water
- 1/3 cup finely crushed saltines
- 1/3 cup grated Parmesan cheese
- 1/2 teaspoon dried basil
- 4 beef cubed steaks (4 ounces *each*)
- 3 tablespoons canola oil
- 1-1/4 cups tomato sauce
- 2-1/4 teaspoons sugar
- 1/2 teaspoon dried oregano, *divided*
- 1/4 teaspoon garlic powder
- 4 slices part-skim mozzarella cheese
- 1/3 cup shredded Parmesan cheese

1. In a shallow bowl, combine the flour,
salt and pepper. In another bowl, beat
eggs and water. Place cracker crumbs,
grated Parmesan cheese and basil in a
third bowl.

2. Coat steaks with flour mixture, then
dip in egg mixture and coat with
crumb mixture. In a large skillet,
brown steaks in oil for 2-3 minutes on
each side.

3. Arrange steaks in a greased 13-in. x
9-in. baking dish. Bake, uncovered,
at 375° for 25 minutes or until
thermometer reads 160°. Combine
the tomato sauce, sugar, 1/4 teaspoon
oregano and garlic powder; spoon over
steaks. Bake 10 minutes longer.

4. Top each steak with mozzarella
cheese; sprinkle with shredded
Parmesan cheese and remaining
oregano. Bake 2-3 minutes longer or
until cheese is melted.

[2007]

MARINATED FLANK STEAK
**yield: 8 servings
prep: 10 min. + marinating
grill: 15 min. + standing**

*An Asian-style marinade flavors this tender
grilled steak. It's an ideal summer entree, but
you can enjoy it year-round...just broil it
indoors instead.*

—*Isabel Fowler
Anchorage, Alaska, Former Field Editor*

- 1 beef flank steak (2 pounds)
- 1/2 cup canola oil
- 1/2 cup reduced-sodium soy sauce
- 1/4 cup red wine vinegar
- 2 tablespoons water
- 2 teaspoons brown sugar
- 2 teaspoons minced fresh gingerroot
- 2 garlic cloves, minced
- 1/4 teaspoon pepper

1. Score surface of the steak, making
diamond shapes 1/2 in. deep. In a large
resealable plastic bag, combine the
remaining ingredients; add steak. Seal
bag and turn to coat; refrigerate for at
least 2 hours, turning occasionally.

2. Drain and discard marinade. Grill
steak, covered, over medium heat
for 6-8 minutes on each side or until
meat reaches desired doneness
(for medium-rare, a thermometer
should read 145°; medium, 160°;
well-done, 170°). Let the steak stand
for 10 minutes. To serve, thinly slice
across the grain.

CUBED STEAKS PARMIGIANA

"This has become one of my
husbands favorites (and
mine)! I love the flavor of
the tomato sauce and I
make sure to really pound
out my meat thin. My
mouth waters when I think
of this recipe! Sometimes,
if I am in a hurry, I have
substituted Italian bread
crumbs and then mixed in
the Parm cheese. That way
I am not scrabbling through
my spices ."
—Hotcookie2

[2012]

BEEF AND MUSHROOM POTPIES

yield: 4 servings ❧ **prep: 40 min.** ❧ **bake: 20 min.**

All the world loves a good potpie with its flaky crust draped over a hearty package of meat, vegetables and gravy. The very idea is a comfort, but the prep is another story. So skip the homemade pie dough step and let a package of crescent rolls fill in.

—*Macey Allen, Green Forest, Arkansas*

1-1/2 cups cubed peeled potatoes
   1 pound beef top sirloin steak, cut into 1/4-inch pieces
   2 tablespoons olive oil, *divided*
   1 large red onion, chopped
   2 cups sliced fresh mushrooms
   1 cup frozen sliced carrots
   1 cup frozen peas
   2 tablespoons ketchup
   1 teaspoon pepper
   1 tablespoon cornstarch
   1 cup sour cream
   1 cup beef gravy
   1 tube (8 ounces) refrigerated crescent rolls

1. Place potatoes in a microwave-safe dish; cover with water. Cover and microwave on high for 7-8 minutes or until tender; drain and set aside.

2. In a large skillet, saute beef in 1 tablespoon oil in batches until no longer pink. Remove and set aside.

3. In the same pan, saute onion and mushrooms in remaining oil until tender; add the carrots, peas, ketchup and pepper. Combine the cornstarch, sour cream and gravy until blended; stir into pan and heat through. Stir in potatoes and beef. Divide mixture between four greased 16 oz. ramekins.

4. Remove crescent roll dough from tube, but do not unroll; cut dough into 16 slices. Cut each slice in half. Arrange seven pieces, curved sides out, around the edge of each ramekin. Press dough slightly to secure in place. Place remaining pieces on the center of each ramekin. Place ramekins on a baking sheet.

5. Bake at 375° for 17-20 minutes or until filling is bubbly and crusts are golden brown.

[2004]

SANTA FE STRIP STEAKS

yield: 4 servings ❧ **prep/total time: 25 min.**

We love Southwestern flavor, and this recipe certainly provides it.
—*Joan Hallford, North Richland Hills, Texas, Field Editor*

1/2 cup chopped onion
   1 tablespoon olive oil
   2 cans (4 ounces *each*) chopped green chilies
1/2 cup fresh cilantro leaves
   1 jalapeno pepper, seeded
   2 teaspoons red currant jelly
   1 teaspoon chicken bouillon granules
   1 teaspoon Worcestershire sauce
   1 garlic clove, peeled
1/2 teaspoon seasoned salt
1/4 teaspoon dried oregano
   4 boneless beef top loin steaks (1 inch thick and 8 ounces *each*)
Salt and pepper to taste
1/2 cup shredded Monterey Jack cheese, optional

1. In a small saucepan, saute onion in oil until tender. Transfer to a blender. Add the green chilies, cilantro, jalapeno, jelly, bouillon, Worcestershire sauce, garlic, seasoned salt and oregano; cover and process until smooth. Return mixture to saucepan. Bring to a boil. Reduce heat; simmer, uncovered, for 10 minutes or until heated through. Set aside and keep warm

2. Sprinkle steaks with salt and pepper. Broil 4-6 in. from heat for 4-8 minutes on each side or until meat reaches desired doneness (for medium-rare, a thermometer should read 145°; medium, 160°; well-done, 170°).

3. Serve steaks with green chili sauce and sprinkle with cheese if desired.

Editor's Note: Steaks may also be grilled, covered, over medium heat. Top loin steak may be labeled as strip steak, Kansas City steak, New York strip steak, ambassador steak or boneless club steak. When cutting hot peppers, disposable gloves are recommended. Avoid touching your face.

[2009]

THAI STEAK SKEWERS

yield: 16 skewers (1-1/3 cups sauce)
prep: 20 min. + marinating ∽ grill: 10 min.

With one bite of these slightly spicy kabobs, you'll feel like you took a trip to the orient. Combining peanut butter and coconut milk creates a combination sure to wow everyone. There's no doubt you'll want seconds!

—*Amy Frye, Goodyear, Arizona*

- 1/4 cup packed brown sugar
- 2 tablespoons lime juice
- 2 tablespoons reduced-sodium soy sauce
- 1 tablespoon curry powder
- 1 teaspoon lemon juice
- 1 can (13.66 ounces) coconut milk, *divided*
- 1-1/2 teaspoons crushed red pepper flakes, *divided*
- 2 pounds beef top sirloin steak, cut into 1/4-inch slices
- 2 medium limes, halved and thinly sliced, optional
- 1/4 cup creamy peanut butter
- 1 tablespoon chopped salted peanuts

1. In a large resealable plastic bag, combine the brown sugar, lime juice, soy sauce, curry powder, lemon juice, 1/4 cup coconut milk and 1 teaspoon pepper flakes; add the steak. Seal the bag and turn to coat. Refrigerate for 2-4 hours.

2. Drain and discard marinade. Thread the beef onto 16 metal or soaked wooden skewers, alternately threading beef with lime slices if desired. Grill the skewers covered, over medium-hot heat for 6-8 minutes or until meat reaches desired doneness, turning occasionally.

3. Meanwhile, in a small saucepan, combine the peanut butter, remaining coconut milk and pepper flakes. Cook and stir over medium heat until blended. Transfer to a small bowl; sprinkle with peanuts. Serve with steak skewers.

[2011]

GARLIC-MUSHROOM RIBEYES

yield: 4 servings ∽ prep/total time: 25 min.

It's easy to dress up ribeyes with mushrooms and garlic for a special steak dinner. This recipe gives a stovetop method, but you can grill the steaks if you prefer.

—*Kelly Ward-Hartman*
Cape Coral, Florida, Field Editor

- 4 beef ribeye steaks (1 inch thick and 8 ounces *each*)
- 1/4 teaspoon pepper
- 1/8 teaspoon salt
- 4 tablespoons butter, *divided*
- 4 to 8 garlic cloves, peeled and sliced
- 1 pound sliced fresh mushrooms
- 3 tablespoons beef broth

1. Sprinkle the steaks with pepper and salt. In a large skillet, saute steaks for 2 minutes on each side in 1 tablespoon butter or until the meat reaches desired doneness (for medium-rare, a thermometer should read 145°; medium, 160°; well-done, 170°). Remove and keep warm.

2. In the same skillet, cook the garlic in 1 tablespoon butter for 1 minute. Remove garlic and set aside. Add the mushrooms to skillet; saute in the remaining butter for 5 minutes or until tender. Stir in the broth. Bring to a boil; cook and stir over high heat until liquid is absorbed. Add reserved garlic. Serve with steaks.

THAI STEAK SKEWERS

"Well to be honest, the kids thought there was too much of a lime taste, and my boyfriend didn't like the dipping sauce, but I'm writing this review—I loved everything about this and couldn't give it anything less than a top rating! Very packed with flavor and the dip gives such a unique taste to every bite. I liked the dip so much I poured a little on my rice and enjoyed it in a new way!"
—*Tommypoo*

[2006]

ZIPPY PEANUT STEAK KABOBS

yield: 8 servings

prep: 40 min. + marinating   grill: 10 min.

(Pictured on page 73)

If you like your kabobs with a kick, you're sure to savor these meaty skewers seasoned with habanero pepper sauce. Sometimes I substitute chicken for the beef.

—*Sheri Nutter, Oneida, Kentucky*

3/4	cup packed brown sugar
3/4	cup water
1	cup chunky peanut butter
1	cup reduced-sodium soy sauce
3/4	cup honey barbecue sauce
1/3	cup canola oil
1	to 2 tablespoons habanero pepper sauce
3	garlic cloves, minced
2	pounds beef top sirloin steak, cut into thin strips
2	teaspoons ground ginger
1	fresh pineapple, cut into 1-inch cubes
2	large sweet red peppers, cut into 1-inch pieces

Hot cooked jasmine rice

---

1. In a small saucepan, combine brown sugar and water. Cook and stir over low heat until sugar is completely dissolved. Remove from the heat. Whisk in peanut butter until blended. Stir in the soy sauce, barbecue sauce, oil, pepper sauce and garlic.

2. Pour 3 cups of the marinade into a large resealable plastic bag; add beef. Seal bag and turn to coat; refrigerate for 4 hours. Cover and refrigerate remaining marinade until serving.

3. Drain and discard marinade. Sprinkle ginger over pineapple. On 16 metal or soaked wooden skewers, alternately thread beef, pineapple and red peppers.

4. Grill, covered, over medium heat for 5-7 minutes on each side or until the meat reaches desired doneness. Serve with the rice and reserved marinade for dipping.

[2000]

OLD-WORLD BEEF ROULADEN

yield: 6 servings   prep: 30 min. cook: 1-1/2 hours

(Pictured on page 74)

Until I went to kindergarten, we spoke German in our home and practiced many old-world customs. We always enjoyed the food of our homeland. Mom usually prepared this for my birthday dinner.

—*Helga Schlape*
Florham Park, New Jersey
Former Field Editor

3	pounds beef top round steak (1/2 inch thick)
1/2	teaspoon salt
1/4	teaspoon pepper
6	bacon strips
3	whole dill pickles, halved lengthwise
2	tablespoons canola oil
2	cups water
1	medium onion, chopped
2	tablespoons minced fresh parsley
2	teaspoons beef bouillon granules, optional
1/4	cup all-purpose flour
1/2	cup cold water
1/2	teaspoon browning sauce, optional

---

1. Cut steak into six serving-size pieces; pound to 1/4-in. thickness. Sprinkle with salt and pepper. Place a bacon strip down the center of each piece; arrange a pickle half on one edge. Roll up and secure with a toothpick.

2. In a large skillet, heat oil over medium-high heat. Brown beef on all sides. Add

if desired. Bring to a boil. Reduce heat; cover and simmer for 1-1/2 to 2 hours or until the meat is tender. Remove meat to a serving platter and keep warm.

3. For gravy, skim fat from drippings. Combine flour, water and browning sauce if desired; stir into drippings. Bring to a boil; cook and stir for 2 minutes or until thickened. Serve with beef.

[2010]

CASHEW CURRIED BEEF

yield: 5 servings ∞ **prep: 20 min.** ∞ **cook: 20 min.**

(Pictured on page 75)

This recipe is a favorite with my whole family. The ingredients are a wonderful mix of sweet, salty and spicy.

—*Jennifer Fridgen, East Grand Forks, Minnesota*

- 1 **pound beef top sirloin steak, thinly sliced**
- 2 **tablespoons canola oil,** *divided*
- 1 **can (13.66 ounces) coconut milk,** *divided*
- 1 **tablespoon red curry paste**
- 2 **tablespoons packed brown sugar**
- 2 **tablespoons fish** *or* **soy sauce**
- 8 **cups chopped bok choy**
- 1 **small sweet red pepper, sliced**
- 1/2 **cup salted cashews**
- 1/2 **cup minced fresh cilantro**

Hot cooked brown rice

1. In a large skillet, saute beef in 1 tablespoon oil until no longer pink. Remove from skillet and set aside.

2. Spoon 1/2 cup cream from top of coconut milk and place in the pan. Add remaining oil; bring to a boil. Add curry paste; cook and stir for 5 minutes or until oil separates from coconut milk mixture.

3. Stir in the brown sugar, fish sauce and remaining coconut milk. Bring to a boil. Reduce heat; simmer, uncovered, for 5 minutes or until slightly thickened. Add bok choy and red pepper; return to a boil. Cook and stir 2-3 minutes longer or until vegetables are tender.

4. Stir in the cashews, cilantro and beef; heat through. Serve with rice.

Editor's Note: This recipe was tested with regular (full-fat) coconut milk. Light coconut milk contains less cream.

CASHEW CURRIED BEEF

"My whole family loved this. We were pleasantly surprised at how flavorful this dish was as well as how easy it is to make. The only change I made was to use light coconut milk. We will definitely be making this again."

—*Ann Kashian*

BARBECUED BEEF SHORT RIBS

yield: 10 servings   prep: 5 min. + marinating   bake: 2-1/4 hours

These sweet-spicy barbecue ribs are always a hit. I've also used the sauce on pork ribs with excellent results.

—*Paula Zsiray, Logan, Utah, Field Editor*

1	cup sugar
1/2	cup packed brown sugar
2	tablespoons salt
2	tablespoons garlic powder
2	tablespoons paprika
2	teaspoons pepper
1/4	teaspoon cayenne pepper
7	pounds bone-in beef short ribs

SAUCE:

1	small onion, finely chopped
2	teaspoons canola oil
1-1/2	cups water
1	cup ketchup
1	can (6 ounces) tomato paste
2	tablespoons brown sugar

Pepper to taste

1. In a large bowl, combine the first seven ingredients; rub over ribs. Place in two large resealable plastic bags; seal and refrigerate overnight.

2. Line two 15-in. x 10-in. x 1-in. baking pans with foil; grease the foil. Place ribs in prepared pans. Bake, uncovered, at 325° for 2 hours or until meat is tender.

3. Meanwhile, in a large saucepan, saute onion in oil until tender. Stir in the water, ketchup, tomato paste, brown sugar and pepper. Bring to a boil. Reduce heat; cover and simmer for 1 hour.

4. Remove ribs from the oven. Grill ribs, covered, over indirect medium heat for 20 minutes, turning and basting frequently with sauce.

BARBECUED BEEF SHORT RIBS

"I made this a while ago using short ribs and was on here (Taste of Home website) trying to find this recipe for pork baby back ribs for dinner tomorrow. I am so glad I found it! It's one of those recipes you remember! The rub was outstanding and so simple."

—*Hotcookie2*

ABOUT SHORT RIBS

Beef short ribs come from the chuck section. This less-tender cut contains layers of fat, meat and bone. The ribs require slow, long cooking and/or moist heat to tenderize them.

—*Taste of Home Cooking Experts*

[2009]

LOADED VEGETABLE BEEF STEW

yield: 12 servings (1-1/3 cups each)
prep: 40 min. ∞ cook: 8-1/2 hours

(Pictured on page 80)

I first had this dish during a trip to Argentina a few years ago. It inspired me to re-create it at home. It turned out so well, I wrote "Yum!" on the recipe card!

—*Kari Caven, Post Falls, Idaho*

- 8 bacon strips, diced
- 3 pounds beef stew meat, cut into 1-inch cubes
- 6 medium carrots, cut into 1-inch pieces
- 6 medium tomatoes, peeled and cut into wedges
- 4 medium potatoes, peeled and cubed
- 3 cups cubed peeled butternut squash
- 2 medium green peppers, chopped
- 2 teaspoons dried thyme
- 2 garlic cloves, minced
- 2 cans (14-1/2 ounces each) beef broth
- 6 cups chopped cabbage
- 1/2 teaspoon pepper

1. In a large skillet, cook the bacon over medium heat until crisp. Using a slotted spoon, remove to paper towels to drain. In the drippings, brown the beef in batches. Refrigerate the bacon until serving.

2. In a 5-qt. slow cooker, combine the carrots, tomatoes, potatoes, squash, green peppers, thyme and garlic. Top with beef. Pour broth over the top. Cover and cook on low for 8-10 hours.

3. Stir in cabbage and pepper. Cover and cook on high for 30 minutes or until the cabbage is tender. Sprinkle each serving with bacon.

[1995]

BEEF BARLEY STEW

yield: 8 servings ∞ prep: 15 min.
cook: 1-1/2 hours

(Pictured on page 79)

I like barley, so I knew I had to try this recipe when I ran across it in a newspaper some years ago. It's nice to have a tasty, filling dish that's lower in fat.

—*June Formanek, Belle Plaine, Iowa*

- 1-1/2 pounds beef stew meat, cut into 1/2-inch cubes
- 1 tablespoon canola oil
- 1 medium onion, chopped
- 3 cans (14-1/2 ounces each) beef broth
- 1 cup medium pearl barley
- 1 teaspoon dried thyme
- 1/2 teaspoon dried marjoram
- 1/4 teaspoon dried rosemary, crushed
- 1/4 teaspoon pepper
- 4 medium carrots, sliced
- 2 tablespoons chopped fresh parsley

1. In a large saucepan or Dutch oven, brown meat in oil in batches. Remove and set aside. In the same pan, saute onion until crisp-tender. Add the broth, barley, seasonings and beef; bring to a boil. Reduce heat; cover and simmer for 1 hour.

2. Add carrots; bring to a boil. Reduce heat; cover and simmer 30-40 minutes or until meat and carrots are tender. Add parsley just before serving.

LOADED VEGETABLE BEEF STEW

"Only change I made was to substitute a can of petite diced tomatoes (undrained) for the tomatoes. This dish should rate 10 stars! I was told to throw out my other beef stew recipes and only keep this one! It is really awesome!"
—*Wingslady*

[2011]

MUSHROOM BEEF STEW

yield: 9 servings ∞ prep: 45 min. ∞ cook: 1-1/2 hours

Weeknight supper or company entree, this very hearty, flavorful stew is excellent for any meal, and I think the flavor improves after freezing. Don't leave off the blue cheese...it adds a little zing. Warm crusty bread with garlic butter completes this dish.

—*Nancy Latulippe, Simcoe, Ontario*

1 carton (32 ounces) beef broth
1 ounce dried mixed mushrooms
1/4 cup all-purpose flour
1 teaspoon salt
1 teaspoon pepper
1 boneless beef chuck roast (2 pounds), cubed
3 tablespoons canola oil
1 pound whole baby portobello mushrooms
5 medium carrots, chopped
1 large onion, chopped
3 garlic cloves, minced
3 teaspoons minced fresh rosemary *or* 1 teaspoon dried rosemary, crushed
ADDITIONAL INGREDIENTS:
2 tablespoons cornstarch
2 tablespoons water
Hot cooked egg noodles, optional
1/4 cup crumbled blue cheese

1. In a large saucepan, bring broth and mushrooms to a boil. Remove from the heat; let stand 15-20 minutes or until mushrooms are softened. Using a slotted spoon, remove mushrooms; finely chop. Strain remaining broth through a fine mesh strainer. Set aside the mushrooms and broth.

2. In a large resealable plastic bag, combine the flour, salt and pepper; set aside 1 tablespoon for sauce. Add beef, a few pieces at a time, to the remaining flour mixture and shake to coat.

3. In a Dutch oven, brown beef in oil in batches. Add the portobello mushrooms, carrots and onion; saute until onion is tender. Add the garlic, rosemary and rehydrated mushrooms; cook 1 minute longer. Stir in reserved flour mixture until blended; gradually add mushroom broth.

4. Bring to a boil. Reduce heat; cover and simmer for 1-1/2 to 2 hours or until the beef is tender. Cool the stew; transfer to freezer containers. Cover and freeze for up to 6 months.

To use frozen stew: Thaw in the refrigerator overnight. Place in a Dutch oven; bring to a boil. Combine cornstarch and water until smooth; gradually stir into the pan. Return to a boil; cook and stir for 2 minutes or until thickened. Serve with egg noodles if desired; top with blue cheese.

[1993]

HERBED BEEF STEW

yield: 10-12 servings ∞ prep: 15 min. ∞ cook: 2-1/2 hours

This stew looks as terrific as it tastes! Flavored with a variety of herbs and chock-full of vegetables, this recipe lists salt as an option, making it ideal for family members and friends who must restrict sodium.

—*Marlene Severson, Everson, Washington*

2 pounds beef stew meat, cut into 1-inch cubes
2 tablespoons canola oil
3 cups water
1 large onion, chopped
2 teaspoons pepper
1 to 2 teaspoons salt, optional
1-1/2 teaspoons garlic powder
1 teaspoon rosemary, crushed
1 teaspoon dried oregano
1 teaspoon dried basil
1 teaspoon ground marjoram
2 bay leaves
1 can (6 ounces) tomato paste
2 cups cubed peeled potatoes
2 cups sliced carrots
1 large green pepper, chopped
1 package (9 ounces) frozen cut green beans
1 package (10 ounces) frozen corn
1/4 pound mushrooms, sliced
3 medium tomatoes, chopped

1. In a Dutch oven, brown meat in oil. Add the water, onion, seasonings and tomato paste. Cover and simmer for 1-1/2 hours or until meat is tender.

2. Stir in potatoes, carrots and green pepper; simmer 30 minutes. Add additional water if necessary. Stir in remaining ingredients; cover and simmer 20 minutes.

[1999]

GARLIC BEEF ENCHILADAS

yield: 5 servings ∞ **prep: 30 min.** ∞ **bake: 40 min.**

(Pictured on page 75)

Enchiladas are typically prepared with corn tortillas, but my husband, Jeff, and I prefer flour tortillas. I use them in this saucy casserole that has irresistible home-cooked flavor and a subtle kick.

—*Jennifer Standridge, Dallas, Georgia*

    1 pound ground beef
    1 medium onion, chopped
    2 tablespoons all-purpose flour
    1 tablespoon chili powder
    1 teaspoon salt
    1 teaspoon garlic powder
  1/2 teaspoon ground cumin
  1/4 teaspoon rubbed sage
    1 can (14-1/2 ounces) stewed tomatoes
SAUCE:
    4 to 6 garlic cloves, minced
  1/3 cup butter
  1/2 cup all-purpose flour
    1 can (14-1/2 ounces) beef broth
    1 can (15 ounces) tomato sauce
    1 to 2 tablespoons chili powder
    1 to 2 teaspoons ground cumin
    1 to 2 teaspoons rubbed sage
  1/2 teaspoon salt
   10 flour tortillas (6 inches), warmed
    2 cups (8 ounces) shredded Colby-Monterey Jack cheese

1. In a large saucepan, cook beef and onion over medium heat until meat is no longer pink; drain. Stir in flour and seasonings until blended. Stir in tomatoes; bring to a boil. Reduce heat; cover and simmer for 15 minutes.

2. Meanwhile, in another saucepan, saute garlic in butter for 1 minute or until tender. Stir in flour until blended. Gradually stir in broth; bring to a boil. Cook and stir for 2 minutes or until thickened. Stir in tomato sauce and seasonings; heat through.

3. Pour about 1-1/2 cups sauce into an ungreased 13-in. x 9-in. baking dish. Spread about 1/4 cup beef mixture down the center of each tortilla; top with 1-2 tablespoons cheese. Roll up tightly; place seam side down over sauce. Top with the remaining sauce.

4. Cover and bake at 350° for 30-35 minutes. Sprinkle with remaining cheese. Bake, uncovered, 10-15 minutes longer or until cheese is melted.

GARLIC BEEF ENCHILADAS

"Delicious! I didn't add any salt and used low-sodium broth and they turned out great! For the sauce I used 1 tsp of chili powder, cumin and sage and it still had enough kick for us. Will make again!"
—*nikschwid*

PIZZA CASSEROLE

"Quick, tasty casserole to put together. I only made one to make sure we liked it, but next time I'll make two!"
—*justmbeth*

[2003]

MOM'S TAMALE PIE

yield: 12 servings   **prep:** 25 min.
bake: 20 min.

I don't recall my mom ever using a recipe for her tamale pie, but I came up with this version that tastes very much like hers did. The grits add a Southern accent.

—*Waldine Guillott, DeQuincy, Louisiana*

2	pounds ground beef
1	large onion, chopped
1	large green pepper, chopped
1	can (15-1/4 ounces) whole kernel corn, undrained
1-1/2	cups chopped fresh tomatoes
5	tablespoons tomato paste
1	envelope chili seasoning
1-1/2	teaspoons sugar
1	teaspoon garlic powder
1	teaspoon dried basil
1	teaspoon dried oregano
6	cups cooked grits (prepared with butter and salt)
1-1/2	teaspoons chili powder, *divided*
1-1/2	cups (6 ounces) shredded cheddar cheese

1. In a large skillet, cook the beef, onion and green pepper over medium heat until meat is no longer pink; drain. Add the corn, tomatoes, tomato paste, chili seasoning, sugar, garlic powder, basil and oregano. Cook and stir until heated through; keep warm.

2. Spread half of the grits in a greased 3-qt. baking dish. Sprinkle with 1 teaspoon chili powder. Top with beef mixture and cheese. Pipe remaining grits around edge of dish; sprinkle with remaining chili powder.

3. Bake, uncovered, at 325° for 20-25 minutes or until cheese is melted. Let stand for 5 minutes before serving.

[2007]

PIZZA CASSEROLE

yield: 2 casseroles (8 servings each)
prep: 20 min.   **bake:** 30 min.

Friends and family love my new spin on pizza. Packed with cheeses, meats, and tomatoes, this hearty pasta dish will go fast!

—*Nancy Foust*
Stoneboro, Pennsylvania, Field Editor

3	cups uncooked spiral pasta
2	pounds ground beef
1	medium onion, chopped
2	cans (8 ounces *each*) mushroom stems and pieces, drained
1	can (15 ounces) tomato sauce
1	jar (14 ounces) pizza sauce
1	can (6 ounces) tomato paste
1/2	teaspoon sugar
1/2	teaspoon garlic powder
1/2	teaspoon onion powder
1/2	teaspoon dried oregano
4	cups (16 ounces) shredded part-skim mozzarella cheese, *divided*
1	package (3-1/2 ounces) sliced pepperoni
1/2	cup grated Parmesan cheese

1. Cook pasta according to package directions. Meanwhile, in a Dutch oven, cook beef and onion over medium heat until meat is no longer pink; drain. Stir in the mushrooms, tomato sauce, pizza sauce, tomato paste, sugar and seasonings. Drain pasta; stir into meat sauce.

2. Divide half of the mixture between two greased 11-in. x 7-in. baking dishes; sprinkle each with 1 cup mozzarella cheese. Repeat layers. Top each with pepperoni and Parmesan cheese.

3. Cover and bake at 350° for 20 minutes. Uncover; bake 10-15 minutes longer or until heated through.

[2007]

SPICY NACHO BAKE

yield: 2 casseroles (15 servings each)
prep: 1 hour ∞ bake: 20 min.

I made this hearty, layered Southwestern casserole for a dinner meeting once, and now, I'm asked to bring it every time we have a potluck. Everybody loves the ground beef and bean filling and crunchy, cheesy topping.

—Anita Wilson, Mansfield, Ohio

- 2 pounds ground beef
- 2 large onions, chopped
- 2 large green peppers, chopped
- 2 cans (28 ounces *each*) diced tomatoes, undrained
- 2 cans (16 ounces *each*) hot chili beans, undrained
- 2 cans (15 ounces *each*) black beans, rinsed and drained
- 2 cans (11 ounces *each*) whole kernel corn, drained
- 2 cans (8 ounces *each*) tomato sauce
- 2 envelopes taco seasoning
- 2 packages (13 ounces *each*) spicy nacho tortilla chips
- 4 cups (16 ounces) shredded cheddar cheese

1. In a Dutch oven, cook the beef, onions and green peppers over medium heat until meat is no longer pink; drain. Stir in the tomatoes, beans, corn, tomato sauce and taco seasoning. Bring to a boil. Reduce heat; simmer, uncovered, for 30 minutes (mixture will be thin).

2. In each of two greased 13-in. x 9-in. baking dishes, layer 5 cups of chips and 4-2/3 cups of meat mixture. Repeat layers. Top each with 4 cups of chips and 2 cups of cheese.

3. Bake, uncovered, at 350° for 20-25 minutes or until golden brown.

[2006]

BEEFY BAKED SPAGHETTI

yield: 12 servings ∞ prep: 20 min.
bake: 40 min.

This is a wonderful casserole for a potluck. Wherever I take it, people enjoy it, especially men. I use whatever cheese I have on hand, so try your favorite.

—Pat Walter
  Pine Island, Minnesota, Field Editor

- 1 package (16 ounces) spaghetti
- 1-1/2 pounds ground beef
- 1 medium onion, chopped
- 1/2 cup chopped green pepper
- 1 can (10-3/4 ounces) condensed cream of mushroom soup, undiluted
- 1 can (10-3/4 ounces) condensed tomato soup, undiluted
- 1 can (8 ounces) tomato sauce
- 1 cup water
- 2 tablespoons brown sugar
- 1 teaspoon salt
- 1 teaspoon dried basil
- 1 teaspoon dried oregano
- 1/2 teaspoon dried marjoram
- 1/2 teaspoon dried rosemary, crushed
- 1/8 teaspoon garlic salt
- 1 cup (4 ounces) shredded part-skim mozzarella cheese, *divided*

TOP 100 RECIPE

1. Break spaghetti in half; cook according to package directions. Meanwhile, in a Dutch oven, cook the beef, onion and green pepper over medium heat until meat is no longer pink; drain. Stir in the soups, tomato sauce, water, brown sugar and seasonings.

2. Drain spaghetti; stir into meat sauce. Add 1/2 cup cheese. Transfer to a greased 13-in. x 9-in. baking dish.

3. Cover and bake at 350° for 30 minutes. Uncover; sprinkle with the remaining cheese. Bake 10-15 minutes longer or until cheese is melted.

BEEFY BAKED SPAGHETTI

"Easy, creamy, very good. I didn't change a thing and will definitely keep this recipe."
—Paige17

[2010]

CREAM CHEESE AND SWISS LASAGNA

yield: 12 servings
prep: 40 min. + simmering
bake: 55 min. + standing

(Pictured on page 80)

I like to fix the chunky meat sauce for this dish the day before, so the flavors can blend. It serves 12, unless you have big eaters who will definitely want seconds.

—Betty Pearson, Edgewater, Maryland

1-1/2   pounds lean ground beef (90% lean)
1   pound bulk Italian sausage
1   medium onion, finely chopped
3   garlic cloves, minced
2   cans (15 ounces each) tomato sauce
1   can (14-1/2 ounces) Italian diced tomatoes, undrained
1   can (6 ounces) tomato paste
2   teaspoons dried oregano
1   teaspoon dried basil
1   teaspoon Italian seasoning
1/2   teaspoon sugar
1/2   teaspoon salt
1/4   teaspoon pepper
9   no-cook lasagna noodles
12   ounces cream cheese, softened
2   cups shredded part-skim mozzarella cheese, *divided*
2   cups shredded Parmesan cheese
2   cups shredded Swiss cheese

TOP 100 RECIPE

---

1. In a Dutch oven, cook the beef, sausage and onion over medium heat until meat is no longer pink. Add the garlic; cook 1 minute longer. Drain. Stir in the tomato sauce, tomatoes, tomato paste, oregano, basil, Italian seasoning, sugar, salt and pepper. Bring to a boil. Reduce heat; simmer, uncovered, for 30 minutes.

2. Spread 1 cup sauce in a greased 13-in. x 9-in. baking dish. Top with three noodles. Drop a third of the cream cheese by teaspoonfuls over the top. Sprinkle with 1/2 cup mozzarella and 2/3 cup each of Parmesan cheese and Swiss cheese; spoon a third of the remaining sauce over the top. Repeat with layers of noodles, cheeses and sauce twice (dish will be full). Place dish on a baking sheet.

3. Cover and bake at 350° for 45 minutes. Sprinkle with remaining mozzarella. Bake, uncovered, 10-15 minutes longer or until bubbly and cheese is melted. Let stand for 15 minutes before cutting.

[2005]

SPANISH RICE DINNER

yield: 4 servings ✦ prep/total time: 25 min.

(Pictured on page 76)

I discovered this recipe in our church cookbook, and after the first time I served it, my family decided it was a keeper. It reheats very well in the microwave.

—Jeri Dobrowski
Beach, North Dakota, Field Editor

---

1   pound ground beef
1-1/2   cups cooked long grain rice
1   can (14-1/2 ounces) stewed tomatoes
1   can (14-1/2 ounces) cut green beans, drained
1   tablespoon dried minced onion
1   tablespoon sugar
1   teaspoon salt
1   teaspoon Worcestershire sauce
1/2   teaspoon ground mustard
1/4   teaspoon garlic powder
1/8   teaspoon pepper
1/8   teaspoon hot pepper sauce

---

1. In a large skillet, cook beef over medium heat until no longer pink; drain. Stir in the remaining ingredients. Bring to a boil. Reduce heat; cover and simmer for 5-10 minutes or until heated through.

[2001]

TACO BRAID

yield: 12-16 servings
prep: 40 min. + rising ∽ **bake: 20 min.**

(*Pictured on page 80*)

This pretty braided sandwich loaf is a winner! My daughter entered the recipe in a state 4-H beef cooking contest and won a trip to the national competition. It seems to rate tops with most folks who taste it.

—*Lucile Proctor*
Panguitch, Utah, Field Editor

---

1   teaspoon active dry yeast
2   tablespoons sugar, *divided*
3/4 cup warm water (110° to 115°), *divided*
2   tablespoons butter, softened
2   tablespoons nonfat dry milk powder
1   egg, lightly beaten
1/2 teaspoon salt
2   cups all-purpose flour
FILLING:
1   pound lean ground beef (90% lean)
1/4 cup sliced fresh mushrooms
1   can (8 ounces) tomato sauce
2   tablespoons taco seasoning
1   egg, lightly beaten
1/2 cup shredded cheddar cheese
1/4 cup sliced ripe olives

---

1. In a large bowl, dissolve yeast and 1 teaspoon sugar in 1/2 cup water; let stand for 5 minutes. Add the butter, milk powder, egg, salt, remaining sugar and water and 1-1/2 cups flour. Beat until smooth. Stir in enough remaining flour to form a soft dough.

2. Turn onto a floured surface; knead until smooth and elastic, about 6-8 minutes. Place in a greased bowl, turning once to grease top. Cover and let rise in a warm place until doubled, about 1 hour.

3. In a large skillet, cook beef and mushrooms over medium heat until meat is no longer pink; drain. Stir in the tomato sauce and taco seasoning. Set aside 1 tablespoon beaten egg. Stir remaining egg into beef mixture. Cool completely.

4. Punch dough down. Turn onto a lightly floured surface; roll into a 15-in. x 12-in. rectangle. Place on a greased baking sheet. Spread filling lengthwise down center third of rectangle. Sprinkle with the cheese and olives.

5. On each long side, cut 1-in.-wide strips about 2-1/2 in. into center. Starting at one end, fold alternating strips at an angle across filling. Pinch ends to seal and tuck under. Cover and let rise for 30 minutes.

6. Brush with reserved egg. Bake at 350° for 20-25 minutes or until golden brown. Remove from pan to a wire rack to cool.

[2006]

TRADITIONAL MEAT LOAF

yield: 6 servings
prep: 15 min. ∽ **bake: 1 hour + standing**

(*Pictured on page 73*)

Topped with a sweet sauce, this meat loaf tastes so good that you might want to double the recipe so everyone can have a second helping. It also freezes well.

—*Gail Graham, Maple Ridge, British Columbia*

---

1   egg, lightly beaten
2/3 cup 2% milk
3   slices bread, crumbled
1   cup (4 ounces) shredded cheddar cheese
1   medium onion, chopped
1/2 cup finely shredded carrot
1   teaspoon salt
1/4 teaspoon pepper
1-1/2 pounds ground beef
1/4 cup packed brown sugar
1/4 cup ketchup
1   tablespoon prepared mustard

---

1. In a large bowl, combine the first eight ingredients. Crumble beef over mixture and mix well. Shape into a loaf. Place in a greased 9-in. x 5-in. loaf pan.

2. In a small bowl, combine the brown sugar, ketchup and mustard; spread over loaf. Bake at 350° for 60-75 minutes or until no pink remains and a thermometer reads 160°. Drain. Let meat loaf stand for 10 minutes before slicing.

BACON-TOPPED MEAT LOAF

"I've made this meat loaf many times over the past year or so. I think it's really very delicious (and so does everyone who has tasted it). However, I made one change in the recipe. Instead of 1/2 cup of chili sauce, I use 1/2 cup of barbecue sauce. YUM!"

—ronaynne

[1998]

SALISBURY STEAK WITH ONION GRAVY

yield: 6 servings ∞ prep: 10 min.
cook: 25 min.

These moist meat patties are simmered in a delicious gravy that starts with French onion soup. Let the egg noodles cook while you prepare the rest of the recipe, and dinner will be done in 30 minutes.

—Kim Kidd, New Freedom, Pennsylvania

1	egg
1	can (10-1/2 ounces) condensed French onion soup, undiluted, *divided*
1/2	cup dry bread crumbs
1/4	teaspoon salt
Pinch pepper	
1-1/2	pounds ground beef
1/4	cup water
1/4	cup ketchup
1	teaspoon Worcestershire sauce
1/2	teaspoon prepared mustard
1	tablespoon all-purpose flour
2	tablespoons cold water
6	cups hot cooked egg noodles
Chopped fresh parsley, optional	

1. In a large bowl, beat egg. Stir in 1/3 cup of soup, bread crumbs, salt and pepper. Crumble beef over mixture and mix well. Shape into six oval patties.

2. In a large skillet, brown patties over medium heat for 3-4 minutes on each side or until a thermometer reads 160° and juices run clear. Remove and set aside; drain. Add the water, ketchup, Worcestershire sauce, mustard and the remaining soup to skillet. Bring to a boil.

3. Return patties to the skillet. Reduce heat; cover and simmer for 15 minutes or until heated through. Combine flour and cold water until smooth. Stir into

pan. Bring to a boil; cook and stir for 2 minutes or until thickened. Serve patties and gravy with noodles. Garnish with parsley if desired.

[2001]

BACON-TOPPED MEAT LOAF

yield: 8 servings ∞ prep: 10 min.
bake: 70 min. + standing

My family loves meat loaf and this one in particular. I created the recipe after trying and adjusting many other recipes over the years. Cheddar cheese tucked inside and a flavorful bacon topping dress it up just right for Sunday dinner!

—Sue Call, Beech Grove, Indiana
Former Field Editor

1/2	cup chili sauce
2	eggs, lightly beaten
1	tablespoon Worcestershire sauce
1	medium onion, chopped
1	cup (4 ounces) shredded cheddar cheese
2/3	cup dry bread crumbs
1/2	teaspoon salt
1/4	teaspoon pepper
2	pounds lean ground beef (90% lean)
2	bacon strips, halved

1. In a large bowl, combine the first eight ingredients. Crumble the beef over mixture and mix well. Shape into a loaf in an ungreased 13-in. x 9-in. baking dish. Top with bacon.

2. Bake, uncovered, at 350° for 70-80 minutes or until meat is no longer pink and a thermometer reads 160°. Drain; let stand for 10 minutes before cutting.

TRADITIONAL MEAT LOAF, page 71

ASPARAGUS BEEF STIR-FRY, page 44

ZIPPY PEANUT STEAK KABOBS, page 62

OLD-WORLD BEEF ROULADEN, page 62

POT ROAST WITH GRAVY, page 47

CASHEW CURRIED BEEF, page 63

GARLIC BEEF ENCHILADAS, page 67

SPANISH RICE DINNER, page 70

MIXED GRILL KABOBS, page 48

CORNISH PASTIES, page 58

BEEF ROAST AU POIVRE WITH
CARAMELIZED ONIONS, page 46

SLOW-COOKED PEPPER STEAK, page 52

PRIME RIB WITH HORSERADISH SAUCE, page 47

MUSHROOM-BLUE CHEESE TENDERLOIN, page 44

TACO-FILLED PEPPERS, page 81

BEEF BARLEY STEW, page 65

CREAM CHEESE AND SWISS LASAGNA, page 70

MERLOT FILET MIGNON, page 57

LOADED VEGETABLE BEEF STEW, page 65

TACO BRAID, page 71

Taste of Home *Best Loved Recipes*

[1994]

TACO-FILLED PEPPERS

yield: 4 servings ∞ **prep/total time: 30 min.**

(*Pictured on page 79*)

With the refreshing vegetables and zippy beef and beans, these stuffed peppers stand out from any others. This tasty dish is so easy to make, I serve it often during summer and fall...much to my family's delight.

—*Nancy McDonald, Burns, Wyoming*

- 1 pound ground beef
- 1 envelope taco seasoning
- 3/4 cup canned kidney beans, rinsed and drained
- 1 cup salsa
- 4 medium green peppers
- 1 medium tomato, chopped
- 1/2 cup shredded cheddar cheese
- 1/2 cup sour cream

1. In a large skillet, cook beef over medium heat until no longer pink; drain. Stir in the taco seasoning, kidney beans and salsa. Bring to a boil; reduce heat and simmer for 5 minutes.

2. Cut peppers in half lengthwise; remove stems and discard seeds. In a stockpot, cook peppers in boiling water for 3-5 minutes. Drain and rinse in cold water.

3. Spoon about 1/2 cup meat mixture into each pepper half. Place in an ungreased 13-in. x 9-in. baking dish. Cover and bake at 350° for 15-20 minutes or until peppers are crisp-tender and filling is heated through. Top each with tomato and cheese. Serve with sour cream.

[2010]

COWBOY CASSEROLE

yield: 2 servings ∞ **prep: 15 min.**
bake: 20 min.

This quick and creamy Tater Tot bake is great comfort food, especially on a cold night.

—*Donna Donhauser, Remsen, New York*

- 1/2 pound lean ground beef (90% lean)
- 1 can (8-3/4 ounces) whole kernel corn, drained
- 2/3 cup condensed cream of chicken soup, undiluted
- 1/2 cup shredded cheddar cheese, *divided*
- 1/3 cup 2% milk
- 2 tablespoons sour cream
- 3/4 teaspoon onion powder
- 1/4 teaspoon pepper
- 2 cups frozen Tater Tots

1. In a large skillet, cook beef over medium heat until no longer pink. Stir in the corn, soup, 1/4 cup cheese, milk, sour cream, onion powder and pepper.

2. Place 1 cup Tater Tots in a greased 3-cup baking dish. Layer with beef mixture and remaining Tater Tots; sprinkle with remaining cheese. Bake, uncovered, at 375° for 20-25 minutes or until bubbly.

PARBOILING A PEPPER

Bring water to a boil in a Dutch oven or soup kettle. Cook seeded whole peppers until crisp-tender, about 2-3 minutes depending on the size of the pepper. Remove from the water with tongs and invert onto paper towels to drain before stuffing.

[2003]

SPINACH BEEF MACARONI BAKE

yield: 2 casseroles (12 servings each)
prep: 55 min. ∽ **bake: 25 min.**

This satisfying casserole is great for a family reunion or church supper. I've also made half the recipe for family gatherings. It's become a special favorite of my grandson-in-law and great-grandson, who often ask me to serve it when they're visiting.

—Lois Lauppe, Lahoma, Oklahoma

5-1/4 cups uncooked elbow macaroni
2-1/2 pounds ground beef
  2 large onions, chopped
  3 large carrots, shredded
  3 celery ribs, chopped
  2 cans (28 ounces *each*) Italian diced tomatoes, undrained
  4 teaspoons salt
  1 teaspoon garlic powder
  1 teaspoon pepper
1/2 teaspoon dried oregano
  2 packages (10 ounces *each*) frozen chopped spinach, thawed and squeezed dry
  1 cup grated Parmesan cheese

1. Cook macaroni according to package directions. Meanwhile, in a large Dutch oven, cook the beef, onions, carrots and celery over medium heat until meat is no longer pink; drain. Add the tomatoes, salt, garlic powder, pepper and oregano. Bring to a boil. Reduce heat; cover and simmer for 30 minutes or until vegetables are tender.

2. Drain the macaroni. Add macaroni and spinach to the beef mixture. Pour into two greased 3-qt. baking dishes. Sprinkle with cheese. Bake casserole, uncovered, at 350° for 25-30 minutes or until heated through.

[2000]

CINCINNATI CHILI

yield: 8 servings ∽ **prep: 20 min.**
cook: 1-3/4 hours

Cinnamon and cocoa give a rich brown color to this hearty chili. This dish will warm you up on a cold day.

—Edith Joyce, Parkman, Ohio

  1 pound ground beef
  1 pound ground pork
  4 medium onions, chopped
  6 garlic cloves, minced
  2 cans (16 ounces *each*) kidney beans, rinsed and drained
  1 can (28 ounces) crushed tomatoes
1/4 cup white vinegar
1/4 cup baking cocoa
  2 tablespoons chili powder
  2 tablespoons Worcestershire sauce
  4 teaspoons ground cinnamon
  3 teaspoons dried oregano
  2 teaspoons ground cumin
  2 teaspoons ground allspice
  2 teaspoons hot pepper sauce
  3 bay leaves
  1 teaspoon sugar
Salt and pepper to taste
Hot cooked spaghetti
Shredded cheddar cheese, sour cream, chopped tomatoes and green onions

1. In a Dutch oven, cook the beef, pork and onions over medium heat until meat is no longer pink. Add garlic; cook 1 minute longer. Drain. Add the beans, tomatoes, vinegar, cocoa and seasonings; bring to a boil. Reduce heat; cover and simmer for 1-1/2 hours or until heated through.

2. Discard bay leaves. Serve with spaghetti. Garnish with cheese, sour cream, tomatoes and onions.

[1998]
SAVORY MEAT PIE
yield: 6 servings ❧ **prep: 30 min.**
bake: 35 min.

A friend gave me this recipe after I had mentioned that my meat pies lacked punch. The pie has a delicious, distinctive flavor thanks to lots of seasonings. Flecks of carrots peek out of each neat slice. My family especially enjoys this dinner when the weather turns chilly.

—*Paula L'Hirondelle, Red Deer, Alberta*

- 2 medium potatoes, peeled and quartered
- 1 pound ground beef
- 3/4 cup sliced green onions
- 1 large carrot, finely chopped
- 1 garlic clove, minced
- 1/2 teaspoon dried thyme
- 1/2 teaspoon rubbed sage
- 1/2 teaspoon salt
- 1/2 teaspoon pepper
- 1/4 teaspoon celery salt

Pinch ground cinnamon
- 1/4 cup minced fresh parsley
- 1/4 cup chili sauce

Pastry for double-crust pie (9 inches)
- 1 tablespoon Dijon mustard
- 1 tablespoon 2% milk

1. In a saucepan, cook potatoes in boiling water until tender; mash and set aside.

2. Meanwhile, in a large skillet, brown beef until no longer pink; drain. Stir in the next nine ingredients. Simmer for 4-5 minutes. Stir in the potatoes, parsley and chili sauce; remove from the heat.

3. Place bottom pastry in a 9-in. pie plate; brush with mustard. Add the meat mixture. Top with remaining pastry; seal and flute edges. Cut slits in the top crust.

4. Brush with milk. Bake at 450° for 10 minutes. Reduce heat to 350°; bake 25 minutes longer or until crust is golden brown.

[1999]
CLASSIC CABBAGE ROLLS
yield: 4 servings ❧ **prep: 30 min.** ❧ **cook: 1-1/2 hours**

I've always enjoyed cabbage rolls but didn't make them since most methods were too complicated. This one is fairly simple and results in the best cabbage rolls. My husband requests them often. They're terrific to share at gatherings with our children and grandchildren.

—*Beverly Zehner, McMinnville, Oregon*

- 1 medium head cabbage
- 1-1/2 cups chopped onion, *divided*
- 1 tablespoon butter
- 2 cans (14-1/2 ounces *each*) Italian stewed tomatoes
- 4 garlic cloves, minced
- 2 tablespoons brown sugar
- 1-1/2 teaspoons salt, *divided*
- 1 cup cooked rice
- 1/4 cup ketchup
- 2 tablespoons Worcestershire sauce
- 1/4 teaspoon pepper
- 1 pound lean ground beef (90% lean)
- 1/4 pound bulk Italian sausage
- 1/2 cup V8 juice, optional

1. In a Dutch oven, cook the cabbage in boiling water for 10 minutes or until outer leaves are tender; drain. Rinse in cold water; drain. Remove eight large outer leaves (refrigerate remaining cabbage for another use); set aside.

2. In a saucepan, saute 1 cup onion in butter until tender. Add tomatoes, garlic, brown sugar and 1/2 teaspoon salt. Simmer for 15 minutes, stirring occasionally.

3. Meanwhile, in a large bowl, combine the rice, ketchup, Worcestershire sauce, pepper and remaining onion and salt. Crumble the beef and sausage over mixture and mix well.

4. Remove thick vein from cabbage leaves for easier rolling. Place about 1/2 cup meat mixture on each leaf; fold in sides. Starting at an unfolded edge, roll up leaf to completely enclose filling. Place seam side down in a skillet. Top with the sauce.

5. Cover and cook over medium-low heat for 1 hour. Add the V8 juice if desired. Reduce heat to low; cook 20 minutes longer or until rolls are heated through and a thermometer inserted in the filling reads 160°.

❧ BEVERAGES ❧

CINNAMON MOCHA COFFEE

❝I really enjoyed this coffee, but when making it, I used a medium-roasted coffee rather than dark-roasted, and the brand I used was Folger's Gourmet Selections Lively Colombian Medium Roast. I also cut the recipe in half, but did add about 3/4 to 1 teaspoon of the vanilla extract. Be sure this coffee is good and hot when serving, as the whipped cream will cool it down somewhat.
 For all those coffee lovers out there, I highly recommend this recipe. This is one coffee others will certainly enjoy. Thank you, Bernice, for sharing this recipe. It's a keeper!!❞
—*1DomesticGoddess*

[2006]

CINNAMON MOCHA COFFEE
yield: 6 servings ∾ **prep/total time: 20 min.**
(*Pictured on page 118*)

One snowy day, my neighbor called and invited me over to try a new drink she'd made. It was delicious! This spiced coffee is a lovely treat and would make a breakfast or brunch a real delight. Double the recipe to serve a larger group.

—*Bernice Morris*
 Marshfield, Missouri, Field Editor

1/2	cup ground dark roast coffee
1	tablespoon ground cinnamon
1/4	teaspoon ground nutmeg
5	cups water
1	cup 2% milk
1/3	cup chocolate syrup
1/4	cup packed brown sugar
1	teaspoon vanilla extract

Whipped cream, optional

1. In a bowl, combine coffee grounds, cinnamon and nutmeg; pour into a coffee filter of a drip coffeemaker. Add the water; brew according to manufacturer's directions.

2. In a large saucepan, combine the milk, chocolate syrup and brown sugar. Cook over low heat until the sugar is dissolved, stirring occasionally. Stir in vanilla and brewed coffee.

3. Ladle into mugs; garnish with whipped cream if desired.

[1997]

WHITE HOT CHOCOLATE
yield: 4 servings ∾ **prep/total time: 15 min.**

In winter, my family eagerly awaits the days when I make this luscious drink. It's creamy, smooth and soothing, with a hint of spice.

—*Debbi Smith*
 Crossett, Arkansas, Former Field Editor

3	cups half-and-half cream, *divided*
2/3	cup white baking chips
1	cinnamon stick (3 inches)
1/8	teaspoon ground nutmeg
1	teaspoon vanilla extract
1/4	teaspoon almond extract

Ground cinnamon, optional

1. In a large saucepan, combine 1/4 cup cream, white chips, cinnamon stick and nutmeg. Stir over low heat until chips are melted; discard cinnamon. Add remaining cream; stir until heated through. Remove from the heat; add extracts. Sprinkle each serving with ground cinnamon if desired.

[2004]

ORANGE JUICE SPRITZER
yield: 2 quarts ∾ **prep/total time: 5 min.**

This is a nice twist on regular orange juice, and we like that it's not overly sweet.

—*Michelle Krzmarzick*
 Redondo Beach, California

4	cups orange juice
1	liter ginger ale, chilled
1/4	cup maraschino cherry juice

Orange wedges and maraschino cherries, optional

1. In a 2-qt. container, combine the orange juice, ginger ale and cherry juice; stir well. Serve over ice. Garnish each glass with an orange wedge and cherry if desired.

[2004]

SIX-VEGETABLE JUICE

yield: 2 quarts
prep: 35 min. ∾ cook: 30 min. + chilling

Our family and friends enjoy my vegetable garden by the glassfuls. My husband likes spicy foods, and after one sip, he proclaimed this juice perfect. For more delicate palates, you can leave out the hot peppers.

—*Deborah Moyer*
Liberty, Pennsylvania, Field Editor

5	pounds ripe tomatoes, peeled and chopped
1/2	cup water
1/4	cup chopped green pepper
1/4	cup chopped carrot
1/4	cup chopped celery
1/4	cup lemon juice
2	tablespoons chopped onion
1	tablespoon salt
1	to 1-1/2 small serrano peppers

1. In a large Dutch oven or stockpot, combine the first eight ingredients. Remove stems and seeds if desired from peppers; add to tomato mixture. Bring to a boil; reduce heat. Cover and simmer for 30 minutes or until vegetables are tender. Cool.

2. Press mixture through a food mill or fine sieve. Refrigerate or freeze. Shake or stir juice well before serving.

Editor's Note: Wear disposable gloves when cutting hot peppers; the oils can burn skin. Avoid touching your face.

[1999]

ICY HOLIDAY PUNCH

yield: 32-36 servings (5-3/4 quarts)
prep: 10 min. + freezing

It's easy and convenient to prepare the base of this slushy punch ahead. Its rosy color makes it so pretty for Christmas. I've also made it with apricot gelatin for a bridal shower. This fun beverage makes any occasion a bit more special.

—*Margaret Matson, Metamora, Illinois*

1	package (6 ounces) cherry gelatin
3/4	cup sugar
2	cups boiling water
1	can (46 ounces) pineapple juice
6	cups cold water
2	liters ginger ale, chilled

1. In a 4-qt. freezer-proof container, dissolve gelatin and sugar in boiling water. Stir in pineapple juice and cold water. Cover and freeze overnight.

2. Remove from the freezer 2 hours before serving. Place in a punch bowl; stir in ginger ale just before serving.

SIX-VEGETABLE JUICE

"This is a fantastic recipe.... I've passed it along to many friends and family members. I cook my hot peppers (I use jalapenos because I grow them in my garden and have them on hand) with the vegetables, but pull them out before running the mixture through a food mill. ... Great over ice, made into a Bloody Mary, or in my favorite chili recipe! Thanks for a keeper of a recipe!!!"
—*kristel.stephany*

MAKING AN ICE RING

Fill a ring mold halfway with water. Freeze until solid. Top with your choice of fruit. Add lemon leaves if desired. Add enough water to almost cover fruit. Freeze until solid.

Unmold by wrapping the bottom of the mold with a hot, damp dishcloth. Turn out onto a baking sheet; place in punch bowl fruit side up.

RHUBARB SLUSH

[2008]

FRUIT SMOOTHIES

yield: 4 servings ∾ **prep/total time: 5 min.**

I served this delicious smoothie to my family at a Sunday gathering, and it was enjoyed by everyone.

—*Deb Doran, Temecula, California*

2 cups peach *or* apricot nectar
2 cups (16 ounces) plain yogurt
1 medium peach, peeled and sliced
6 frozen whole strawberries
2 teaspoons sugar
1/8 teaspoon ground cinnamon

1. In a blender, combine all ingredients; cover and process for 30-45 seconds or until blended. Pour into chilled glasses; serve immediately.

[2003]

TANGY PARTY PUNCH

yield: 8 quarts ∾ **prep/total time: 10 min.**

As social chair one year during college, I tried to come up with a more interesting beverage than the usual cranberry juice and lemon-lime soda. This pastel punch was always a hit at receptions and parties.

—*Jennifer Bangerter, Nixa, Missouri*

1 can (46 ounces) pineapple juice, chilled
1 can (46 ounces) orange juice, chilled
1 can (12 ounces) frozen limeade concentrate, thawed
1 can (12 ounces) frozen lemonade concentrate, thawed
3 liters ginger ale, chilled
1 pint *each* orange, lemon and lime sherbet

1. In a large punch bowl, combine the first four ingredients. Stir in ginger ale. Add scoops of sherbet. Serve immediately.

[2009]

RHUBARB SLUSH

yield: 22 servings (1 cup each)
prep: 40 min. + freezing

Sweet and refreshing, this pretty pink slush stores well in the freezer, so it's ideal to have on hand for summer guests. Just thaw and add ginger ale or lemon-lime soda. Mmmm!

—*Danielle Brandt, Ruthton, Minnesota*

8 cups diced fresh *or* frozen rhubarb
1 package (16 ounces) frozen unsweetened strawberries
3 cups sugar
8 cups water
1 package (3 ounces) strawberry gelatin
1/2 cup lemon juice
11 cups ginger ale, chilled
Rhubarb curls, optional

1. In a Dutch oven, bring the rhubarb, strawberries, sugar and water to a boil. Reduce heat; simmer, uncovered, for 5-8 minutes or until the rhubarb is tender. Press through a sieve; discard pulp. Stir in the gelatin and lemon juice until dissolved.

2. Transfer to a freezer container and freeze, stirring occasionally, until firm. May be frozen for up to 3 months.

3. To use frozen rhubarb mixture: In a punch bowl or several pitchers, combine equal amounts of rhubarb mixture and ginger ale. Or for one serving, combine 1/2 cup rhubarb mixture and 1/2 cup ginger ale in a glass. Garnish with rhubarb curls if desired. Serve immediately.

Editor's Note: If using frozen rhubarb, measure rhubarb while still frozen, then thaw completely. Drain in a colander, but do not press liquid out.

[2011]

BLUEBERRY THIRST QUENCHER

yield: 9 servings　∞　prep/total time: 5 min.

My adult-only quencher is a welcome change of pace from the usual lemonade- or orange-juice-based drinks. The eye-catching color makes for a very festive look.

—Peggy Foster, Florence, Kentucky

6　cups chilled blueberry juice cocktail
3　cups chilled lemon-lime soda
9　ounces blueberry-flavored vodka, chilled
Crushed ice
1　cup fresh blueberries
Sliced peeled mango, optional

1. In a large pitcher, combine the juice, soda and vodka. Serve over ice; garnish with blueberries and, if desired, mango.

[1993]

PINEAPPLE SMOOTHIE

yield: 5 servings　∞　prep/total time: 5 min.

I got this recipe over 30 years ago. I've tried several diabetic recipes, and this is one of the best.

—Margery Bryan
Moses Lake, Washington
Former Field Editor

1　can (20 ounces) unsweetened pineapple chunks, undrained
1　cup buttermilk
2　teaspoons vanilla extract
2　teaspoons sugar substitute
Mint leaves, optional

1. Drain pineapple, reserving 1/2 cup juice. Freeze pineapple chunks. Place the juice, buttermilk, vanilla, sugar substitute and frozen pineapple into a blender container. Beat until smooth. Pour into glasses and garnish with mint if desired. Serve immediately.

[1995]

AUNT FRANCES' LEMONADE

**yield: 12-16 servings (1 gallon)
prep/total time: 15 min.**

My sister and I spent a week each summer with our Aunt Frances, who always had this thirst-quenching lemonade in a stoneware crock in the refrigerator.

—Debbie Reinhart
New Cumberland, Pennsylvania

5　lemons
5　limes
5　oranges
3　quarts water
1-1/2　to 2 cups sugar
Ice cubes

1. Squeeze the juice from four of the lemons, limes and oranges; pour into a gallon container.

2. Thinly slice the remaining fruit and set aside for garnish. Add water and sugar to juice; mix well. Store in refrigerator. Serve over ice with fruit slices.

[1999]

CHERRY CRANBERRY SHAKES

yield: 3-1/2 cups　∞　prep/total time: 10 min.

My family has enjoyed this frothy pink drink for many years. The combination of cranberry juice and cherry soda is tongue-tingling.

—Gayle Lewis, Yucaipa, California

1　cup cranberry juice, chilled
1　cup cherry soda, chilled
1　tablespoon milk *or* half-and-half cream
3/4　teaspoon vanilla extract
1　cup vanilla ice cream, softened

1. In a blender, combine all ingredients; cover and process until smooth. Pour into chilled glasses; serve immediately.

AUNT FRANCES' LEMONADE

"My kids LOVE this. They often request it. The only suggestion I have is, if you have leftovers, remove the slices of fruit. Otherwise the lemonade becomes bitter from the peels."
—christmasbaby

[2006]

LEMONADE ICED TEA

yield: 12 servings (about 3 quarts)
prep: 15 min. + chilling

*I have always loved iced tea with lemon, and
this thirst-quencher just takes it one step
further. The lemonade gives this refreshing
drink a nice color, too.*

—*Gail Buss*
  Beverly Hills, Florida, Field Editor

  3   **quarts water**
  9   **individual tea bags**
3/4   **to 1-1/4 cups sugar**
  1   **can (12 ounces) frozen lemonade**
      concentrate, thawed
Ice cubes

1. In a Dutch oven, bring water to a boil.
Remove from the heat; add tea bags.
Cover and steep for 5 minutes. Discard
tea bags. Stir in sugar and lemonade
concentrate. Cover and refrigerate
until chilled. Serve over ice.

[2004]

CITRUS PUNCH

yield: 4 quarts   prep/total time: 10 min.

*For a crowd-pleasing addition to any party,
you can't go wrong with this punch. The mix of
lemonade and orange juice lends a fruity taste!*

—*Edie DeSpain, Logan, Utah, Field Editor*

  1   **can (12 ounces) frozen lemonade**
      concentrate, thawed
  1   **can (12 ounces) frozen orange juice**
      concentrate, thawed
  1   **cup sugar**
  1   **teaspoon vanilla extract**
  1   **teaspoon almond extract, optional**
  8   **cups cold water**
  2   **liters lemon-lime soda, chilled**

1. In two large pitchers or a large
punch bowl, combine the first six
ingredients. Gently stir in soda.
Serve in chilled glasses.

[2008]

VERY BERRY-LICIOUS SMOOTHIES

yield: 6 servings   prep/total time: 10 min.

*Four berry flavors combine in this cool,
colorful beverage. It's perfect to sip while
enjoying a lazy summer afternoon on the patio.*

—*Colleen Belbey, Warwick, Rhode Island*

      2   **cups cranberry juice**
      4   **cups frozen unsweetened**
          strawberries
      2   **cups frozen unsweetened raspberries**
1-1/2   **cups (12 ounces) blackberry yogurt**

1. In a blender, combine half of the
ingredients; cover and process until
blended. Pour into chilled glasses.
Repeat with remaining ingredients.
Serve immediately.

[2012]

MULLED RED CIDER

yield: 7 servings (3/4 cup each)
prep/total time: 20 min.

*Red wine gives a rosy glow to the warm apple
cider. The spices are a wonderful complement
to both the cider and wine.*

—*Steve Foy, Kirkwood, Missouri*

Cinnamon-sugar, optional
1-3/4   **cups apple cider *or* juice**
  1/2   **cup sugar**
    3   **cinnamon sticks (3 inches)**
    4   **whole cloves**
    1   **bottle (750 milliliters) dry red wine**

1. If desired, moisten the rims of seven
mugs with water. Sprinkle cinnamon-
sugar on a plate; dip rims in cinnamon-
sugar. Set mugs aside.

2. In a large saucepan, combine the cider,
sugar, cinnamon sticks and cloves.
Cook and stir over medium heat until
sugar is dissolved.

3. Add the wine and heat through. Remove from the heat. Cover and steep for 10 minutes; strain. Serve in prepared mugs.

[2007]

MOCK MINT JULEP

yield: 13 servings (about 3 quarts)
prep: 15 min. + standing

Here's an alcohol-free spin on this time-honored Southern beverage.

—Annette Grahl, Midway, Kentucky

2	cups cold water
1-1/2	cups sugar
3/4	cup lemon juice
6	mint sprigs
5	cups ice cubes
2-1/2	cups ginger ale, chilled

Lemon slices and additional mint, optional

1. In a large bowl, combine the water, sugar, lemon juice and mint. Let stand for at least 45 minutes. Strain and discard mint. Place ice cubes in two 2-qt. pitchers; add half of the lemon mixture and ginger ale to each. Garnish with lemon and mint if desired.

[2009]

SPICED CHAI MIX

yield: about 5 cups mix (26 servings)
prep/total time: 15 min.

One Christmas, my sister-in-law mixed up this drink for our family gathering. I asked for the recipe and have been enjoying its warm, spicy flavor ever since. It tastes great when you snuggle down with a warm blanket and a good book!

—Dee Falk, Stromsburg, Nebraska, Field Editor

3	cups nonfat dry milk powder
1-1/2	cups sugar
1	cup unsweetened instant tea
3/4	cup vanilla powdered nondairy creamer

1-1/2	teaspoons ground ginger
1-1/2	teaspoons ground cinnamon
1/2	teaspoon ground cardamom
1/2	teaspoon ground cloves

OPTIONAL GARNISH:
Whipped cream

1. In a food processor, combine all dry ingredients; cover and process until powdery. Store in an airtight container in a cool dry place for up to 6 months.

2. To prepare 1 serving: Dissolve 3 tablespoons of mix in 3/4 cup boiling water; stir well. Dollop with whipped cream if desired.

[2011]

TOPSY-TURVY SANGRIA

yield: 10 servings (3/4 cup each)
prep/total time: 10 min.

(Pictured on page 120)

I got this recipe from a friend a few years ago. It's perfect for relaxed get-togethers. It's even better if you make it the night before and let the flavors steep. But be careful—it goes down easy.

—Tracy Field, Bremerton, Washington

1	bottle (750 milliliters) merlot
1	cup sugar
1	cup orange liqueur
1/2	to 1 cup brandy
3	cups lemon-lime soda, chilled
1	cup sliced fresh strawberries
1	medium lemon, sliced
1	medium orange, sliced
1	medium peach, sliced

Ice cubes

1. In a pitcher, stir the wine, sugar, orange liqueur and brandy until sugar is dissolved. Stir in soda and fruit. Serve over ice.

TOPSY-TURVY SANGRIA

"Yum! I have been searching for a good recipe for sangria, and now I have finally found it. Fruity, sweet and delicious. You probably could make this with a white wine as well. Leave it to the good folks at *Taste of Home* for another winner of a recipe!"

—daisylight

HOMEMADE ORANGE REFRESHER

"My only change is to use Splenda to taste in place of sugar, as the concentrate is sweet enough. This makes for a refreshing treat on a warm night."
—meanmary5

[1994]

HOMEMADE ORANGE REFRESHER

yield: 4 servings   prep/total time: 10 min.

For a sweet garnish, dip the rim of each glass into orange juice and then in granulated white sugar. Allow to dry 1 hour before filling glasses.

—Iola Egle
Bella Vista, Arkansas, Field Editor

- 1 can (6 ounces) frozen orange juice concentrate, thawed
- 1/3 cup sugar
- 1/2 cup instant nonfat dry milk powder
- 2 teaspoons vanilla extract
- 3/4 cup cold water
- 10 to 12 ice cubes
- Orange slices and mint, optional

1. In a blender, combine the first five ingredients; cover and process on high until smooth. Add the ice cubes, a few at a time, blending until mixture is slushy. Serve in chilled glasses. Garnish with orange slices and mint if desired. Serve immediately.

[2011]

SUMMERTIME TEA

yield: 18 servings (3/4 cup each)
prep: 15 min + chilling

You can't have a summer gathering around here without this sweet tea to cool you down. It's wonderful for sipping while basking by the pool.

—Angela Lively
Baxter, Tennessee, Field Editor

- 14 cups water, *divided*
- 6 individual black tea bags
- 1-1/2 cups sugar
- 3/4 cup thawed frozen orange juice concentrate
- 3/4 cup thawed frozen lemonade concentrate

- 1 cup tequila, optional
- Fresh mint leaves and lemon or lime slices, optional

1. In a large saucepan, bring 4 cups water to a boil. Remove from the heat; add the tea bags. Cover and steep for 3-5 minutes. Discard tea bags.

2. Stir in the sugar, concentrates and remaining water. Add tequila if desired. Refrigerate until chilled. Garnish with mint and lemon if desired.

[2001]

BANANA PINEAPPLE SLUSH

yield: about 9-1/2 quarts
prep/total time: 10 min. + freezing

This sunny tropical slush refreshes on summer days and is perfect for brunches, showers, weddings and neighborhood parties.

—Beth Myers, Lewisburg, West Virginia

- 4 cups sugar
- 2 cups water
- 1 can (46 ounces) pineapple juice
- 3 cups orange juice
- 3/4 cup lemon juice
- 1/2 cup orange juice concentrate
- 8 medium ripe bananas, mashed
- 2 bottles (2 liters each) cream soda
- 3 cans (12 ounces each) lemon-lime soda

1. In a saucepan, bring sugar and water to a boil over medium heat; cool. Pour into a large freezer container; add juices, orange juice concentrate and bananas. Cover and freeze. To serve, thaw mixture until slushy; stir in cream soda and lemon-lime soda.

[1995]

ICED STRAWBERRY TEA

yield: 5 cups ∞ **prep: 10 min. + chilling**

Strawberry season here coincides with the first day of summer and the end of our school year. So it's no wonder that popular fruit is treasured in favorite recipes like this colorful tea.

—*Laurie Andrews, Milton, Ontario*

1 pint fresh strawberries
4 cups brewed tea, chilled
1/3 to 1/2 cup sugar
1/4 cup lemon juice
Ice cubes

1. Set aside five strawberries. Place the remaining strawberries in a blender; cover and puree. Strain into pitcher. Stir in the tea, sugar and lemon juice until sugar is dissolved. Chill.

2. Serve in chilled glasses over ice. Garnish with reserved berries.

[1999]

CHOCOLATE MALTS

yield: 2-1/2 cups ∞ **prep/total time: 10 min.**

I can whip up this decadent ice cream treat in just minutes. It's a favorite with kids of all ages, particularly after a day in the pool or for dessert after a hot, summer barbecue.

—*Marion Lowery
Medford, Oregon, Former Field Editor*

3/4 cup milk
1/2 cup caramel ice cream topping
2 cups chocolate ice cream, softened
3 tablespoons malted milk powder
2 tablespoons chopped pecans, optional
Grated chocolate, optional

1. In a blender, combine the first five ingredients; cover and process until blended. Pour into chilled glasses. Sprinkle with grated chocolate if desired. Serve immediately.

[1998]

MOCK CHAMPAGNE PUNCH

**yield: 16 (1/2-cup) servings
prep/total time: 10 min.**

Of all the punch recipes I've tried, I keep coming back to this pretty, nonalcoholic one.

—*Betty Claycomb
Alverton, Pennsylvania, Field Editor*

1 quart white grape juice, chilled
1 quart ginger ale, chilled
Strawberries and raspberries

1. Combine grape juice and ginger ale; pour into a punch bowl or glasses. Garnish with berries.

[2005]

RED CREAM SODA PUNCH

**yield: about 7 quarts
prep: 5 min. + chilling**

The bright coral color and sweet citrusy flavor make this fizzy punch a hit. Since it makes a lot, it is ideal for parties and large gatherings.

—*Naomi Cross
Owenton, Kentucky, Field Editor*

4 quarts cold water
2 cans (12 ounces each) frozen orange juice concentrate, thawed
1 can (12 ounces) frozen lemonade concentrate, thawed
1/2 cup sugar
1 bottle (2 liters) red cream soda, chilled

1. In a large punch bowl or several pitchers, combine water, concentrates and sugar; stir until sugar is dissolved. Refrigerate for 2 hours or until chilled. Just before serving, stir in cream soda.

Editor's Note: This recipe was tested with Barq's Red Cream Soda.

MOCK CHAMPAGNE PUNCH

"We go to bridal shows over the winter and we make this punch to showcase our champagne fountain. Everyone who tries it just loves it—it's always a hit!"
—*TNeifert*

[2010]

A.M. RUSH
ESPRESSO SMOOTHIE

yield: 1 serving ∾ **prep/total time: 10 min.**

(Pictured on page 117)

Want an early-morning pick-me-up that's good for you, too? Fruit and flaxseed give this sweet espresso a nutritious twist.

—*Aimee Wilson, Clovis, California*

1/2	cup cold fat-free milk
1	tablespoon vanilla flavoring syrup
1	cup ice cubes
1/2	medium banana, cut up
1	to 2 teaspoons instant espresso powder
1	teaspoon ground flaxseed
1	teaspoon baking cocoa

---

1. In a blender, combine all ingredients; cover and process for 1-2 minutes or until blended. Pour into a chilled glass; serve immediately.

Editor's Note: This recipe was tested with Torani brand flavoring syrup. Look for it in the coffee section.

[2003]

AUTUMN TEA

yield: 3 quarts ∾ **prep/total time: 15 min.**

I've been serving beverages made with various flavors of tea at gatherings, and people are always surprised by the results. This blend features flavors we associate with fall.

—*Sandy McKenzie, Braham, Minnesota*

5	individual tea bags
5	cups boiling water
5	cups unsweetened apple juice
2	cups cranberry juice
1/2	cup sugar
1/3	cup lemon juice
1/4	teaspoon pumpkin pie spice

---

1. Place the tea bags in a large heat-proof bowl; add boiling water. Cover and steep for 8 minutes. Discard tea bags. Add the remaining ingredients to tea; stir until sugar is dissolved. Serve warm or over ice.

[1995]

BANANA BRUNCH PUNCH

yield: 60-70 servings (10 quarts)
prep: 10 min. + freezing

A cold glass of refreshing punch really brightens a brunch. It's nice to serve a crisp beverage like this that's more spectacular than plain juice. With bananas, orange juice and lemonade, it can add tropical flair to a winter day.

—*Mary Anne McWhirter*
Pearland, Texas, Field Editor

6	medium ripe bananas
1	can (12 ounces) frozen orange juice concentrate, thawed
3/4	cup thawed lemonade concentrate
3	cups warm water, *divided*
2	cups sugar, *divided*
1	can (46 ounces) pineapple juice, chilled
3	bottles (2 liters each) lemon-lime soda, chilled

Orange slices, optional

---

1. In a blender or food processor, cover and process the bananas, orange juice and lemonade until smooth. Remove half of the mixture and set aside. Add 1-1/2 cups warm water and 1 cup sugar to blender; blend until smooth. Place in a large freezer container. Repeat with remaining banana mixture, water and sugar; add to container. Cover and freeze until solid.

2. Remove from freezer 1 hour before serving. Just before serving, place in a large punch bowl. Add pineapple juice and soda; stir until well blended. Garnish with orange slices if desired.

[2009]

LEMONY COOLER

yield: 8 servings (2 quarts)
prep: 15 min. + chilling

Everyone thinks I've gone to a lot of trouble when making this refreshing summer drink, but it's so easy! I also like to make my own pretty ice cubes by adding 1/2 cup lemon juice and a mint sprig to 4 cups water.

—*Bonnie Hawkins*
Elkhorn, Wisconsin, Field Editor

3 cups white grape juice
1/2 cup sugar
1/2 cup lemon juice
1 bottle (1 liter) club soda, chilled
Ice cubes
Assorted fresh fruit, optional

1. In a pitcher, combine the grape juice, sugar and lemon juice; stir until sugar is dissolved. Refrigerate until chilled.

2. Just before serving, stir in the club soda. Serve over ice. Garnish with fruit if desired.

[2011]

HOT BUTTERED RUM

yield: 7 servings (3-1/2 cups mix)
prep/total time: 15 min.

I received this recipe from a friend over 30 years ago, and I think of her when I stir up a batch of this delightful mix. It keeps well in the freezer.

—*Joyce Moynihan*
Lakeville, Minnesota, Field Editor

1 cup butter, softened
1/2 cup confectioners' sugar
1/2 cup packed brown sugar
2 cups vanilla ice cream, softened
1 teaspoon ground cinnamon
1 teaspoon ground nutmeg
EACH SERVING:
1/2 cup boiling water
1 to 3 tablespoons rum

1. In a large bowl, cream the butter and sugars until light and fluffy. Beat in the ice cream, cinnamon and nutmeg. Cover and store in the freezer.

2. For each serving, place 1/2 cup butter mixture in a mug; add boiling water and stir to dissolve. Stir in rum.

[2002]

TANGY STRAWBERRY PUNCH

yield: 35-40 servings (about 7-1/2 quarts)
prep: 10 min. + freezing

A fantastic summertime drink, this punch is tart and sweet. I like to serve it at showers, parties and other occasions. I find that kids really like it, too.

—*Shirley Hughes, Gadsden, Alabama*

2 cans (46 ounces *each*) unsweetened pineapple juice
2 quarts water
6 cups sugar
6 envelopes (.19 ounce *each*) unsweetened strawberry lemonade soft drink mix
2 liters ginger ale, chilled
1 can (8 ounces) crushed pineapple, optional

1. In a large container, combine the pineapple juice, water, sugar and drink mix. Stir until the sugar is dissolved. Freeze.

2. Remove from the freezer 1-2 hours before serving. Just before serving, stir in the ginger ale and, if desired, the crushed pineapple. Serve immediately.

LEMONY COOLER

"Love this!! The lemon juice brightens up the grape juice, and the club soda cuts the sweetness, making it sweet, tart and refreshing all at once." —*stephanie.milner*

∾ BREADS ∾

[2000]

HOME-STYLE YEAST BREAD

yield: 2 loaves (16 slices each)
prep: 25 min. + rising
bake: 30 min. + cooling

Everyone will like the light texture and slightly sweet taste of this homemade bread. The dough also makes heavenly rolls.

—Launa Shoemaker
  Landrum, South Carolina

2	packages (1/4 ounce each) active dry yeast
2	cups warm water (110° to 115°)
1/2	cup sugar
1/2	cup butter, melted
1-1/2	teaspoons salt
2	eggs
6	to 7 cups bread flour

---

1. In a bowl, dissolve yeast in warm water. Add sugar, butter, salt, eggs and 4 cups flour. Beat until smooth. Stir in enough remaining flour to form a firm dough.

2. Turn onto a floured surface; knead until smooth and elastic, about 6-8 minutes. Place in a greased bowl; turn once to grease top. Cover; let rise in a warm place until doubled, about 1 hour.

3. Punch dough down; turn onto a floured surface. Divide in half. Shape into loaves and place in two greased 9-in. x 5-in. loaf pans. Cover and let rise until doubled, about 45 minutes.

4. Bake at 350° for 30-35 minutes or until golden brown. Remove from pans to wire racks to cool.

[2010]

MOM'S ITALIAN BREAD

yield: 2 loaves (12 slices each)
prep: 30 min. + rising ∾ bake: 20 min. + cooling

(Pictured on page 116)

I think Mom used to bake at least four of these tender loaves at once and they never lasted long. I love it toasted, too.

—Linda Harrington
  Hudson, New Hampshire, Field Editor

1	package (1/4 ounce) active dry yeast
2	cups warm water (110° to 115°)
1	teaspoon sugar
2	teaspoons salt
5-1/2	cups all-purpose flour

TOP 100 RECIPE

---

1. In a large bowl, dissolve yeast in warm water. Add the sugar, salt and 3 cups flour. Beat on medium speed for 3 minutes. Stir in remaining flour to form a soft dough.

2. Turn onto a floured surface; knead until smooth and elastic, about 6-8 minutes. Place in a greased bowl; turn once to grease top. Cover and let rise in a warm place until doubled, about 1 hour.

3. Punch dough down. Turn onto a floured surface; divide in half. Shape each portion into a loaf. Place each loaf seam side down on a greased baking sheet. Cover and let rise until doubled, about 30 minutes. With a sharp knife, make four shallow slashes across top of each loaf.

4. Bake at 400° for 20-25 minutes or until golden brown. Remove from pans to wire racks to cool.

MOM'S ITALIAN BREAD

❝This recipe was excellent. I did use an egg wash and it turned out a beautiful golden brown. This recipe is very forgiving—I accidentally doubled the yeast and accidentally forgot to add any salt at all and it was still fine!!! Big hit—thanks :)❞
—meaghs

[2006]

BUTTERCUP YEAST BREAD

yield: 3 loaves (16 slices each)
prep: 40 min. + rising
bake: 35 min. + cooling

(*Pictured on page 117*)

People love the colorful slices of this delicious, fluffy bread even though they have a hard time guessing where the pretty orange tint comes from!

—*Kelly Kirby*
Westville, Nova Scotia, Field Editor

---

 3 packages (1/4 ounce *each*) active dry yeast
 1/2 cup warm water (110° to 115°)
 2 tablespoons sugar
 2-1/2 cups mashed cooked buttercup *or* butternut squash
 2 cups 2% milk
 2/3 cup packed brown sugar
 2/3 cup butter, softened
 2 eggs, lightly beaten
 3 teaspoons salt
 13 cups all-purpose flour

---

1. In a very large bowl, dissolve yeast in warm water. Add sugar; let stand for 5 minutes. Add squash, milk, brown sugar, butter, eggs and salt and about 6 cups flour. Beat on medium speed for 3 minutes. Stir in enough of the remaining flour to form a soft dough.

2. Turn dough onto a floured surface; knead until smooth and elastic, about 10 minutes. Place in a greased bowl, turning once to grease top. Cover and let rise in a warm place until doubled, about 1-1/4 hours.

3. Punch dough down. Divide into three pieces; shape into loaves. Place in three greased 9-in. x 5-in. loaf pans. Cover; let rise until doubled, about 45 minutes.

4. Bake at 350° for 35-40 minutes or until golden brown. Cool 10 minutes; remove from pans to wire racks to cool.

[1995]

HERBED PEASANT BREAD

yield: 1 loaf (16 slices)
prep: 30 min. + rising   bake: 25 min.

(*Pictured on page 118*)

The recipe for this beautiful, flavorful loaf came from our daughter-in-law, Karen. Everyone who enjoys a slice of this moist bread asks me for the recipe.

—*Ardath Effa, Villa Park, Illinois*

 1/2 cup chopped onion
 3 tablespoons butter
 1 cup warm 2% milk (110° to 115°) plus 2 tablespoons warm 2% milk (110° to 115°)
 1 tablespoon sugar
 1-1/2 teaspoons salt
 1/2 teaspoon dill weed
 1/2 teaspoon dried basil
 1/2 teaspoon dried rosemary, crushed
 1 package (1/4 ounce) active dry yeast
 3 to 3-1/2 cups all-purpose flour
Melted butter

---

1. In a large skillet, cook onion in butter over low heat until tender. Cool for 10 minutes.

2. Transfer to a large bowl. Add the milk, sugar, salt, herbs, yeast and 3 cups flour; beat until smooth. Stir in enough remaining flour to form a soft dough.

3. Turn onto a floured board; knead dough until smooth and elastic, about 6 to 8 minutes. Place in a greased bowl, turning once to grease top. Cover and let rise in a warm place until doubled, about 45 minutes.

4. Punch the dough down. Shape into a ball and place on a greased baking sheet. Cover and let rise until doubled, about 45 minutes.

5. Bake at 375° for 25-30 minutes. Remove to a wire rack; brush with the melted butter. Cool.

HERBED PEASANT BREAD

"I baked this yesterday morning to enter into our county fair. I won first place plus judges' choice over all the submitted entries in the fresh foods division at the fair. I can't say enough good about this bread...I wouldn't change a thing! I had never made it before this point in time. I was so pleased with the overall results. Thanks Ardath for submitting."
—*Halfways*

[2011]

CONFETTI FIESTA BRAIDS

yield: 2 loaves (20 slices each)
prep: 1 hour + rising
bake: 25 min. + cooling

(Pictured on page 113)

This bread is based on the winning recipe in a local contest I judged. I turned it into a double braid and added more peppers. It's not difficult and is well worth the effort. Plus, it smells glorious when baking!

—Fancheon Resler
Bluffton, Indiana, Field Editor

5-1/2 to 6-1/2 cups all-purpose flour
1 cup cornmeal
2 packages (1/4 ounce *each*) active dry yeast
1 tablespoon sugar
2 teaspoons salt
1 cup buttermilk
1/2 cup butter, cubed
1/2 cup finely chopped onion
2 eggs
1-1/2 cups (6 ounces) shredded cheddar cheese
1 can (8-1/4 ounces) cream-style corn
1/2 cup finely chopped sweet red, yellow *and/or* orange peppers
1/4 cup chopped seeded jalapeno peppers
1/4 cup butter, melted

1. In a large bowl, combine 4 cups flour, cornmeal, yeast, sugar and salt. In a small saucepan, heat the buttermilk, butter and onion to 120°-130°. Add to dry ingredients; beat just until moistened. Add eggs; beat until smooth. Stir in the cheese, corn and peppers. Stir in enough remaining flour to form a stiff dough.

2. Turn onto a floured surface; knead until smooth and elastic, about 6-8 minutes. Place in a greased bowl, turning once to grease the top. Cover and let rise in a warm place until doubled, about 1 hour.

3. Punch dough down. Turn onto a lightly floured surface; divide dough in half. Divide half of dough into two portions so that one portion is twice the size of the other; shape larger portion into three 16-in. ropes. Place on a greased baking sheet and braid; pinch ends to seal and tuck under.

4. Shape smaller portion into three 10-in. ropes. Braid on a lightly floured surface; tuck ends under. Brush bottom of braid with water and place over larger braid. Cover loaf and let rise until doubled, about 45 minutes. Repeat with remaining dough.

5. Bake at 350° for 25-30 minutes or until golden brown. Brush with melted butter. Cool on a wire rack. Refrigerate leftovers.

Editor's Note: Wear disposable gloves when cutting hot peppers; the oils can burn skin. Avoid touching your face. Warmed buttermilk will appear curdled.

CONFETTI FIESTA BRAIDS

"This delightful, savory bread is excellent with chili, soup or stew with southern flavor. Well worth the effort. Beautiful braids are quite easy!"
—KShoney

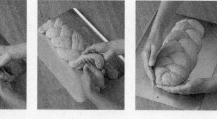

BRAIDING BREAD

1. Place three ropes almost touching on a baking sheet. Starting in the middle, loosely bring left rope under center rope. Bring the right rope under the new center rope and repeat until you reach the end.

2. Turn the pan and repeat braiding, bringing the ropes over instead of under.

3. Press each end to seal; tuck ends under.

[2005]
CHEESY ONION FOCACCIA
yield: 12 servings ∾ **prep: 1 hour + rising
bake: 15 min.**

*The pleasing onion flavor of this golden brown
loaf is enhanced by garlic and Italian seasoning.
With melted cheddar and Parmesan cheese on
top, this bread tastes best when served warm.*

—*Christina Romanyshyn, Granbury, Texas*

3/4	cup water (70° to 80°)
2	tablespoons olive oil
1	teaspoon salt
2	cups bread flour
1	tablespoon sugar
1-1/2	teaspoons active dry yeast
2	medium onions, sliced and quartered
1/4	cup butter
3	garlic cloves, minced
2	teaspoons Italian seasoning
1	cup (4 ounces) shredded cheddar cheese
2	tablespoons grated Parmesan cheese

1. In bread machine pan, place the first six ingredients in order suggested by manufacturer. Select dough setting (check dough after 5 minutes of mixing; add 1 to 2 tablespoons of water or flour if needed).

2. When the cycle is completed, turn dough onto a lightly greased 12-in. pizza pan; pat into a 10-in. circle. Cover and let rise in a warm place until doubled, about 30 minutes.

3. Meanwhile, in a large skillet, saute the onions in butter for 18-20 minutes or until golden brown. Add the garlic and Italian seasoning; cook for 1 minute longer.

4. Using the end of a wooden spoon handle, make deep indentations 1 in. apart in dough. Top with the onion mixture and cheeses. Bake at 400° for 15-18 minutes or until golden brown. Serve warm.

[2002]
MOLASSES OAT BREAD
yield: 3 loaves (12 slices each)
prep: 20 min. + rising ∾ **bake: 45 min.**

*This recipe has been passed down through my
family from my Swedish great-grandmother.
Last Christmas, my 78-year-old mom made
and distributed 25 of these loaves. The slightly
sweet bread receives high praise, even from my
children, who are picky eaters.*

—*Patricia Finch Kelly
Rindge, New Hampshire*

4	cups boiling water
2	cups old-fashioned oats
1	cup molasses
1/4	cup sugar
3	tablespoons canola oil
3	teaspoons salt
1	package (1/4 ounce) active dry yeast
9	to 10 cups all-purpose flour

1. In a large bowl, pour boiling water over the cereal. Add the molasses, sugar, oil and salt. Let stand until the mixture cools to 110°-115°, stirring occasionally. Stir in the yeast. Add 8 cups flour. Beat until smooth. Add enough remaining flour to form a soft dough.

2. Turn onto a floured surface; knead until smooth and elastic, about 6-8 minutes. Place dough in a greased bowl, turning once to grease the top. Cover and let rise in a warm place until doubled, about 1-1/2 hours.

3. Punch dough down and divide into thirds; shape into loaves. Place in three greased 9-in. x 5-in. loaf pans. Cover and let rise until doubled, about 1 hour.

4. Bake at 350° for 45-50 minutes or until golden brown. Remove from pans to wire racks to cool.

MOLASSES OAT BREAD

‟So good! I made this bread today—it's delicious! It reminds me of the bread they serve at our local Black Angus. I split the recipe in half and made four small round loaves on a cookie sheet. I also sprinkled a few oats on the top before baking. I enjoyed some right out the oven— great stuff!”
—*maggieaw*

[2010]

SUNFLOWER SEED & HONEY WHEAT BREAD

yield: 3 loaves (12 slices each) ∞ **prep: 40 min. + rising** ∞ **bake: 35 min.**

I've tried other bread recipes, but this one is a staple in our home. I won $50 in a bake-off with a loaf that I had stored in the freezer.

—**Mickey Turner, Grants Pass, Oregon, Field Editor**

2	packages (1/4 ounce each) active dry yeast
3-1/4	cups warm water (110° to 115°)
1/4	cup bread flour
1/3	cup canola oil
1/3	cup honey
3	teaspoons salt
6-1/2 to 7-1/2	cups whole wheat flour
1/2	cup sunflower kernels
3	tablespoons butter, melted

1. In a large bowl, dissolve yeast in warm water. Add the bread flour, oil, honey, salt and 4 cups whole wheat flour. Beat until smooth. Stir in sunflower kernels and enough remaining flour to form a firm dough.

2. Turn onto a floured surface; knead until smooth and elastic, about 6-8 minutes. Place in a greased bowl, turning once to grease the top. Cover and let rise in a warm place until doubled, about 1 hour.

3. Punch dough down; divide into three portions. Shape into loaves; place in three greased 8-in. x 4-in. loaf pans. Cover and let rise until doubled, about 30 minutes.

4. Bake at 350° for 35-40 minutes or until golden brown. Brush with melted butter. Remove from pans to wire racks to cool.

SUNFLOWER SEED & HONEY WHEAT BREAD

❝I made this bread (1/3 recipe) completely in my bread machine. I did add 1-1/4 teaspoons of vital wheat gluten; also, I added extra water (1-1/2 tablespoons). This is the first 100% wheat bread that turned out moist and light. There are only two of us and I make bread at least twice a week. This will be great to alternate with our usual multigrain.❞

—*jerber674*

STORING YEAST BREADS

Cool unsliced yeast bread completely before placing in an airtight container or resealable plastic bag. Yeast bread will stay fresh at room temperature for 2 to 3 days. Bread with cheese or other perishable ingredients should be stored in the refrigerator.

For longer storage, freeze bread in an airtight container or resealable freezer bag for up to 3 months.

—*Taste of Home Cooking Experts*

[1996]

WHOLESOME
WHEAT BREAD

yield: 2 loaves (16 slices each)
prep: 25 min. + rising ∾ bake: 55 min. + cooling

My sister and I were in 4-H, and Mom was our breads project leader for years. Because of that early training, fresh homemade bread like this is a staple in my own kitchen.

—*Karen Wingate, Coldwater, Kansas*

2 packages (1/4 ounce *each*) active dry yeast
2-1/4 cups warm water (110° to 115°)
3 tablespoons sugar
1/3 cup butter, softened
1/3 cup honey
1/2 cup nonfat dry milk powder
1 tablespoon salt
4-1/2 cups whole wheat flour
2-3/4 to 3-1/2 cups all-purpose flour

1. In a large bowl, dissolve yeast in water. Add the sugar, butter, honey, milk powder, salt and whole wheat flour; beat until smooth. Add enough of the all-purpose flour to form a soft dough.

2. Turn onto floured surface; knead until smooth and elastic, about 10 minutes. Place in a greased bowl, turning once to grease top. Cover and let rise in a warm place until doubled, about 1 hour.

3. Punch dough down. Shape dough into traditional loaves or divide into fourths and roll each portion into a 15-in. rope. Twist two ropes together. Place the dough in greased 9-in. x 5-in. loaf pans. Cover and let rise until doubled, about 30 minutes.

4. Bake at 375° for 25-30 minutes or until golden brown. Remove from pans to cool on wire racks.

[2005]

HONEY-OAT
CASSEROLE BREAD

yield: 1 loaf (12 wedges)
prep: 20 min. + rising ∾ bake: 35 min. + cooling

When you bake my bread, the appetizing aroma will fill your kitchen and you will impatiently wait for it to be cool enough to taste.

—*Beverly Sterling, Gasport, New York*

1 cup boiling water
1 cup quick-cooking oats
1/4 cup butter, softened
1/4 cup honey
1 teaspoon salt
1 package (1/4 ounce) active dry yeast
1/4 cup warm water (110° to 115°)
2 eggs
3-1/2 cups all-purpose flour

1. In a large bowl, pour boiling water over cereal. Add the butter, honey and salt. Let stand until mixture cools to 110°-115°, stirring occasionally.

2. In a large bowl, dissolve yeast in warm water. Add the eggs, oat mixture and 2 cups flour. Beat on medium speed for 2 minutes. Stir in enough remaining flour to form a soft dough (dough will be sticky). Cover and let rise in a warm place until doubled, about 55 minutes.

3. Punch dough down. Transfer to a greased 1-1/2-qt. round baking dish. Cover and let rise in a warm place until doubled, about 30 minutes.

4. Bake at 375° for 35-40 minutes or until golden brown. Cool for 10 minutes; remove from baking dish to a wire rack to cool. Cut into wedges.

HONEY-OAT CASSEROLE BREAD

"This is my family's favorite bread recipe. I've made it in loaf pans but think it turns out better in the round baking dish."
—*williekat2*

[2002]

WHOLE GRAIN LOAF

yield: 1 loaf (16 slices)
prep: 30 min. + rising ∞ bake: 25 min. + cooling

This flavorful bread is eye-catching and chock-full of nutrients. I baked this beautiful loaf on stage at the state fair and won Reserve Grand Champion.

—Nancy Means, Moline, Illinois, Former Field Editor

- 1 package (1/4 ounce) active dry yeast
- 1/2 cup warm water (110° to 115°)
- 1/2 cup 2% cottage cheese
- 1/4 cup honey
- 2 tablespoons canola oil
- 1 teaspoon salt
- 1 egg
- 2 to 2-1/2 cups all-purpose flour
- 1/2 cup whole wheat flour
- 1/4 cup rye flour
- 1/4 cup quick-cooking oats
- 1/4 cup toasted wheat germ
- Cornmeal
- 1 egg white
- 2 tablespoons cold water
- 1 tablespoon sesame seeds

1. In a large bowl, dissolve yeast in warm water. Add the cottage cheese, honey, oil, salt, egg and 1-1/2 cups all-purpose flour; beat until smooth. Stir in whole wheat and rye flours, oats, wheat germ and enough remaining all-purpose flour to make a soft dough.

2. Tun onto a floured surface; knead until smooth and elastic, about 8-10 minutes. Place in a greased bowl, turning once to grease the top. Cover and let rise in a warm place until doubled, about 75 minutes.

3. Punch dough down; let rest for 10 minutes. Shape into a ball. Place on a greased baking sheet sprinkled with cornmeal. Cover and let rise until doubled, about 30 minutes.

4. Beat egg white and cold water; brush over dough. Sprinkle with sesame seeds. Bake at 350° for 25-30 minutes or until golden brown. Remove from pan to cool on a wire rack.

[2001]

CINNAMON SWIRL BREAD

yield: 2 loaves (16 slices each) ∞ prep: 20 min. + rising
bake: 30 min.

(Pictured on page 118)

My aunt gave me the recipe for these pretty, rich-tasting loaves many years ago. I use my bread machine for the first step in the recipe.

—Peggy Burdick, Burlington, Michigan, Field Editor

- 1 cup warm 2% milk (70° to 80°)
- 1/4 cup water (70° to 80°)
- 2 eggs
- 1/4 cup butter, softened
- 1 teaspoon salt
- 1/4 cup sugar
- 5 cups bread flour
- 2-1/4 teaspoons active dry yeast
- **FILLING:**
- 2 tablespoons butter, melted
- 1/3 cup sugar
- 1 tablespoon ground cinnamon
- **GLAZE:**
- 1 cup confectioners' sugar
- 1/2 teaspoon vanilla extract
- 4 to 5 teaspoons milk

1. In bread machine pan, place the first eight ingredients in order suggested by manufacturer. Select dough setting (check dough after 5 minutes of mixing; add 1 to 2 tablespoons water or flour if needed).

2. When cycle is completed, turn dough onto a lightly floured surface; divide in half. Roll each portion into a 10-in. x 8-in. rectangle. Brush with butter. Combine sugar and cinnamon; sprinkle over dough.

3. Roll up tightly jelly-roll style, starting with a short side. Pinch seams and ends to seal. Place seam side down in two greased 9-in. x 5-in. loaf pans. Cover and let rise in a warm place until doubled, about 1 hour.

4. Bake at 350° for 25 minutes. Cover with foil; bake 5-10 minutes longer or until golden brown. Remove from pans to wire racks to cool completely.

5. In a large bowl, combine confectioners' sugar, vanilla and enough milk to achieve desired consistency; drizzle over warm loaves.

[2002]

POTATO PAN ROLLS

yield: 2-1/2 dozen ∾ **prep: 55 min. + rising**
bake: 20 min.

Beautiful color and light-as-a-feather texture make these rolls our family's favorite for holiday meals. I won a top award at a 4-H yeast bread competition with this recipe.

—LeAnne Hofferichter-Tieken
 Floresville, Texas

2	medium potatoes, peeled and quartered
1-1/2	cups water
2	packages (1/4 ounce each) active dry yeast
1	teaspoon sugar
1/2	cup butter, melted
1/2	cup honey
1/4	cup canola oil
2	eggs
2	teaspoons salt
6	to 7 cups all-purpose flour

---

1. In a large saucepan, bring potatoes and water to a boil. Reduce heat; cover and simmer for 15-20 minutes or until tender. Drain, reserving 1 cup cooking liquid; cool liquid to 110° to 115°. Mash potatoes; set aside 1 cup to cool to 110°-115° (save remaining potatoes for another use).

2. In a large bowl, dissolve yeast and sugar in reserved potato liquid; let stand for 5 minutes. Add reserved mashed potatoes, butter, honey, oil, eggs, salt and 1-1/2 cups flour; beat until smooth. Stir in enough remaining flour to form a soft dough.

3. Turn onto a floured surface; knead until smooth and elastic, about 6-8 minutes. Place in a greased bowl; turn once to grease top. Cover; let rise in a warm place until doubled, about 1 hour.

4. Punch dough down and turn onto a floured surface; divide into 30 pieces.

Shape each piece into a ball. Place 10 balls each in three greased 9-in. round baking pans. Cover and let rise until doubled, about 30 minutes.

5. Bake at 400° for 20-25 minutes or until golden brown. Remove from pans to wire racks to cool.

[1993]

ANGEL BISCUITS

yield: 2-1/2 dozen
prep: 20 min. + rising ∾ **bake: 10 min.**

Here's a recipe that combines both yeast bread and quick bread techniques to create a light, wonderful biscuit.

—Faye Hintz, Springfield, Missouri

2	packages (1/4 ounce each) active dry yeast
1/4	cup warm water (110° to 115°)
2	cups warm buttermilk (110° to 115°)
5	cups all-purpose flour
1/3	cup sugar
2	teaspoons salt
2	teaspoons baking powder
1	teaspoon baking soda
1	cup shortening

Melted butter

---

1. Dissolve yeast in warm water. Let stand for 5 minutes. Stir in buttermilk; set aside. In a large bowl, combine the flour, sugar, salt, baking powder and soda. Cut in shortening with a pastry blender until mixture resembles coarse meal. Stir in yeast mixture.

2. Turn out onto a lightly floured surface; knead lightly 3-4 times. Roll into a 1/2-in. thickness. Cut with a 2-1/2-in. biscuit cutter. Place on a lightly greased baking sheet. Cover and let rise in a warm place about 1-1/2 hours.

3. Bake at 450° for 8-10 minutes until golden brown. Lightly brush tops with melted butter. Serve warm.

ANGEL BISCUITS

"I've used a slightly different version for 25+ years. I usually divide into 2 portions. It will sit happily in the fridge overnight. I can make biscuits for dinner & roll out the rest for cinnamon rolls in the morning. I have also used the dough for pigs in a blanket & my version of piroshki."
—celiot

[1997]

PARKERHOUSE ROLLS

yield: 2-1/2 dozen ⌒ prep: 30 min. + rising ⌒ bake: 10 min.

(Pictured on page 115)

My mom is especially well-known for the delectable things she bakes, like these moist, golden rolls. When that basket comes around the table, we all automatically take two because one is just never enough.

—*Sandra Melnychenko, Grandview, Manitoba*

2	packages (1/4 ounce *each*) active dry yeast
1	teaspoon plus 6 tablespoons sugar, *divided*
1	cup warm water (110° to 115°), *divided*
1	cup warm 2% milk (110° to 115°)
2	teaspoons salt
1	egg
2	tablespoons plus 2 teaspoons canola oil
5-1/2	to 6 cups all-purpose flour
3	tablespoons butter, melted, optional

---

1. In a large bowl, dissolve yeast and 1 teaspoon sugar in 1/2 cup warm water; let stand for 5 minutes. Add the milk, salt, egg, oil, remaining sugar, water and 2 cups flour. Beat until smooth. Stir in enough remaining flour to make a soft dough.

2. Turn onto a floured surface; knead until smooth and elastic, about 6-8 minutes. Place in a greased bowl, turning once to grease the top. Cover and let rise in a warm place until doubled, about 45 minutes.

3. Punch dough down. Turn onto a lightly floured surface; divide in half. Roll out each piece to 1/3-in. or 1/2-in. thickness. Cut with a floured 2-1/2-in. biscuit cutter. Brush with butter if desired.

4. Make an off-center crease in each roll. Fold along crease so the large half is on top; press along folded edge. Place 2 in. apart on greased baking sheets. Cover and let rise until doubled, about 30 minutes.

5. Bake at 375° for 10-15 minutes or until golden brown. Remove from pans to wire racks to cool.

PARKERHOUSE ROLLS

❝I've made these rolls dozens of times now. Ever since we tried the recipe, this has been the one we use for Sunday dinner or anytime we want homemade rolls. My husband says they are exactly like the ones he remembers from his childhood. The only thing I do differently is make balls of dough instead of folding the cut circles. Works great like this!❞

—*Kensmoma*

SHAPING PARKERHOUSE ROLLS

Roll out to 1/2-in. thickness. Cut with a floured biscuit cutter. Brush with melted butter. Using the dull edge of a table knife, make an off-center crease in each roll. Fold along crease.

[2000]

CINNAMON LOVE KNOTS

yield: 3 dozen ❧ prep: 45 min. + rising bake: 15 min.

My sister-in-law and I enjoy these flavorful yeast rolls for breakfast, brunch or dessert.

—Marlene Fetter, Alpena, Michigan

- 2 packages (1/4 ounce each) active dry yeast
- 1/2 cup warm water (110° to 115°)
- 1/2 cup warm 2% milk (110° to 115°)
- 1/2 cup butter, softened
- 1/2 cup sugar
- 2 eggs, lightly beaten
- 1 teaspoon salt
- 4-1/2 to 5 cups all-purpose flour

TOPPING:
- 2 cups sugar
- 2 tablespoons ground cinnamon
- 3/4 cup butter, melted

1. In a large bowl, dissolve yeast in warm water. Add milk, butter, sugar, eggs and salt. Beat until smooth. Stir in enough flour to form a stiff dough.

2. Turn onto a floured surface; knead until smooth and elastic, about 6-8 minutes. Place in a greased bowl, turning once to grease top. Cover and let rise in a warm place until doubled, about 1-1/2 hours.

3. Punch dough down; divide into three portions. Cover two with plastic wrap. Shape one portion into 12 balls. Roll each ball into an 8-in. rope. Combine sugar and cinnamon. Dip rope into melted butter, then coat with the cinnamon-sugar. Tie into a knot. Tuck and pinch ends under and place on ungreased baking sheets. Repeat with remaining dough. Cover and let rise until doubled, about 30 minutes.

4. Bake at 375° for 12-14 minutes or until golden brown.

[1999]

OAT DINNER ROLLS

yield: 2 dozen ❧ prep: 30 min. + rising bake: 20 min.

These delicious homemade rolls make a delightful addition to any holiday or special-occasion meal.

—Patricia Rutherford
Winchester, Illinois, Field Editor

- 2-1/3 cups water, *divided*
- 1 cup quick-cooking oats
- 2/3 cup packed brown sugar
- 3 tablespoons butter
- 1-1/2 teaspoons salt
- 2 packages (1/4 ounce each) active dry yeast
- 5 to 5-3/4 cups all-purpose flour

1. In a large saucepan, bring 2 cups water to a boil. Stir in the oats; reduce heat. Simmer, uncovered, for 1 minute. Stir in the brown sugar, butter, salt and remaining water.

2. Transfer to a large bowl; let stand until mixture reaches 110°-115°. Stir in the yeast. Add 3 cups flour; beat well. Add enough of the remaining flour to form a soft dough.

3. Turn onto a floured surface; knead until smooth and elastic, about 6-8 minutes. Place in a greased bowl; turn once to grease the top. Cover and let rise in a warm place until doubled, about 1 hour.

4. Punch dough down; shape into 24 rolls. Place on greased baking sheets. Cover and let rise until doubled, about 30 minutes.

5. Bake at 350° for 20-25 minutes or until golden brown. Remove from pan and cool on wire racks.

OAT DINNER ROLLS

❝These are light and fluffy and also hearty at the same time. Just sweet enough with a good nutty aftertaste. I highly recommend them.❞
—colarc01

[1993]

WHOLE WHEAT REFRIGERATOR ROLLS

yield: 24 servings ∞ prep: 20 min. + rising
bake: 10 min.

(Pictured on page 119)

This roll recipe is easy and versatile. I like to mix up the dough beforehand and let it rise in the refrigerator.

—Sharon Mensing
Greenfield, Iowa, Field Editor

- 2 **packages (1/4 ounce each) active dry yeast**
- 2 **cups warm water (110° to 115°)**
- 1/2 **cup sugar**
- 1 **egg**
- 1/4 **cup canola oil**
- 2 **teaspoons salt**
- 4-1/2 **to 5 cups all-purpose flour, *divided***
- 2 **cups whole wheat flour**

---

1. In a large bowl, dissolve yeast in warm water. Add sugar, egg, oil, salt and 3 cups all-purpose flour. Beat on medium speed for 3 minutes. Stir in the whole wheat flour and enough remaining all-purpose flour to make a soft dough.

2. Turn out onto a lightly floured surface. Knead until smooth and elastic, about 6 to 8 minutes. Place in a greased bowl, turning once to grease the top. Cover and let rise until doubled or cover and refrigerate overnight.

3. Punch dough down; divide into 24 pieces. Shape each into a roll. Place on greased baking sheets for plain rolls or knots, or in greased muffin tins for cloverleaf rolls. Cover and let rise until doubled, about 1 hour for dough prepared the same day or 1-2 hours for refrigerated dough.

4. Bake at 375° for 10-12 minutes or until light golden brown. Serve warm. If desired, dough may be kept up to

4 days in the refrigerator. Punch the dough down daily.

[1998]

ONION MUSTARD BUNS

yield: 2 dozen ∞ prep: 25 min. + rising
bake: 20 min.

I'm an avid bread baker and was thrilled to find this recipe. It makes delectably different rolls that are a hit wherever I take them. The onion and mustard flavors go so well with ham or hamburgers and are special enough to serve alongside an elaborate main dish.

—Melodie Shumaker
Elizabethtown, Pennsylvania

- 1 **package (1/4 ounce) active dry yeast**
- 1/4 **cup warm water (110° to 115°)**
- 2 **cups warm 2% milk (110° to 115°)**
- 3 **tablespoons dried minced onion**
- 3 **tablespoons prepared mustard**
- 2 **tablespoons canola oil**
- 2 **tablespoons sugar**
- 1-1/2 **teaspoons salt**
- 6 **to 6-1/2 cups all-purpose flour**

---

1. In a large bowl, dissolve yeast in warm water. Add the milk, onion, mustard, oil, sugar, salt and 4 cups flour; beat until smooth. Add enough remaining flour to form a soft dough.

2. Turn out onto a floured surface; knead until smooth and elastic, about 6-8 minutes. Place in a greased bowl, turning once to grease the top. Cover and let rise in a warm place until doubled, about 1 hour.

3. Punch dough down; divide into 24 pieces. Flatten each piece into a 3-in. circle. Place 1 in. apart on greased baking sheets. Cover and let rise until doubled, about 45 minutes.

4. Bake at 350° for 20-25 minutes or until golden brown. Cool on wire racks.

WHOLE WHEAT REFRIGERATOR ROLLS

"We love these rolls. Easy to put together and very tasty. We love to be able to refrigerate the dough overnight on Saturdays and enjoy fresh-baked rolls on Sundays."

—prmom

[1994]

MAKE-AHEAD BUTTERHORNS

yield: 32 rolls   prep: 30 min. + rising
bake: 15 min. + freezing

*Mom loved to make these lightly sweet, golden
rolls. They're beautiful and impressive to serve
and have a wonderful, homemade taste that
makes them so unforgettable.*

—Bernice Morris
Marshfield, Missouri, Field Editor

---

  2   packages (1/4 ounce *each*) active
      dry yeast
1/3   cup warm water (110° to 115°)
  2   cups warm 2% milk (110° to 115°)
  1   cup shortening
  1   cup sugar
  6   eggs
  2   teaspoons salt
  9   cups all-purpose flour, *divided*
  3   to 4 tablespoons butter, melted

---

1. In a large bowl, dissolve yeast in warm water. Add the milk, shortening, sugar, eggs, salt and 4 cups flour; beat for 3 minutes or until smooth. Add enough remaining flour to form a soft dough.

2. Turn onto a floured surface; knead lightly. Place in a greased bowl, turning once to grease top. Cover and let rise in a warm place until doubled, about 2 hours.

3. Punch dough down; divided into four equal parts. Roll each into a 9-in. circle; brush with butter. Cut each circle into eight wedges. Roll up from the wide ends.

4. Place rolls place point side down on baking sheets; freeze. When frozen, place in freezer bags and seal. Store in freezer for up to 4 weeks.

5. Place on greased baking sheets; thaw 5 hours or until doubled in size. Bake at 375° for 12-15 minutes or until lightly browned. Remove from baking sheets; serve warm or cool on wire rack.

[2008]

PERFECT DINNER ROLLS

yield: 2 dozen   prep: 30 min. + rising
bake: 15 min.

*These rolls melt in your mouth. I enjoyed them as
a child, and I'm happy to make them for my kids
because I know I am making for them the same
delightful memories my mom made for me!*

—Gayleen Grote, Battleview, North Dakota

---

  1   tablespoon active dry yeast
2-1/4 cups warm water (110° to 115°)
1/3   cup sugar
1/3   cup shortening
1/4   cup powdered
      nondairy creamer
2-1/4 teaspoons salt
  6   to 7 cups bread flour

TOP 100 RECIPE

---

1. In a large bowl, dissolve the yeast in warm water. Add sugar, shortening, creamer, salt and 5 cups flour. Beat until smooth. Stir in enough remaining flour to form a soft dough (dough will be sticky).

2. Turn onto a floured surface; knead until smooth and elastic, about 6-8 minutes. Place in a bowl coated with cooking spray, turning once to coat the top. Cover and let rise in a warm place until doubled, about 1 hour.

3. Punch dough down. Turn onto a lightly floured surface; divide into 24 pieces. Shape each into a roll. Place 2 in. apart on baking sheets coated with cooking spray. Cover and let rise until doubled, about 30 minutes.

4. Bake at 350° for 12-15 minutes or until lightly browned. Remove from pans to wire racks.

MAKE-AHEAD BUTTERHORNS

"Great for any recipe that calls for croissant rolls from a can—but tastes much better. Everyone loves them. I find they are a bit large, so I divide the dough into 6 equal parts instead of 4, then into 8, so I get 48 rolls total."
—psychocoombs

[2006]

HONEY-OAT PAN ROLLS

yield: 2 dozen ∞ prep: 45 min. + rising
bake: 20 min.

These tender rolls are a welcome addition to any meal. Whole wheat flour and oats make them nutritious, too.

—Arlene Butler, Ogden, Utah, Field Editor

2-1/2 to 2-3/4 cups all-purpose flour
   3/4 **cup whole wheat flour**
   1/2 **cup old-fashioned oats**
     2 **packages (1/4 ounce *each*) active dry yeast**
     1 **teaspoon salt**
     1 **cup water**
   1/4 **cup honey**
     5 **tablespoons butter, *divided***
     1 **egg**

---

1. In a large bowl, combine 1 cup all-purpose flour, whole wheat flour, oats, yeast and salt. In a small saucepan, heat the water, honey and 4 tablespoons butter to 120°-130°. Add to the dry ingredients; beat just until moistened. Add egg; beat until well combined. Stir in enough remaining all-purpose flour to form a soft dough.

2. Turn onto a floured surface; knead until smooth and elastic, about 6-8 minutes. Place in a greased bowl, turning once to grease top. Cover and let rise in a warm place until doubled, about 1 hour.

3. Punch dough down. Turn onto a lightly floured surface; divide into 24 pieces. Shape each into a ball. Place in a greased 13-in. x 9-in. baking pan. Cover and let rise until doubled, about 30 minutes.

4. Bake at 375° for 20-22 minutes or until golden brown. Melt remaining butter; brush over rolls. Remove from pan to a wire rack.

HONEY-OAT PAN ROLLS

❝The rolls were very tasty (especially with some honey butter while they were still warm!)❞
—rharkless

[2002]

BUTTERMILK CHOCOLATE BREAD

yield: 1 loaf (16 slices, 1/2 cup butter)
prep: 20 min. ∞ bake: 55 min. + cooling

I serve this rich, cake-like bread and its creamy chocolate honey butter often at Christmastime. It makes a great brunch item, but it also goes well on a dinner buffet. With this recipe I won a "Best in Category" award in a local cooking contest.

—Patrice Bruwer-Miller
Wyoming, Michigan

1/2 **cup butter, softened**
  1 **cup sugar**
  2 **eggs**
1-1/2 **cups all-purpose flour**
1/2 **cup baking cocoa**
1/2 **teaspoon salt**
1/2 **teaspoon baking powder**
1/2 **teaspoon baking soda**
  1 **cup buttermilk**
1/3 **cup chopped pecans**
CHOCOLATE HONEY BUTTER:
1/2 **cup butter, softened**
  2 **tablespoons honey**
  2 **tablespoons chocolate syrup**

---

1. In a large bowl, cream butter and sugar until light and fluffy. Add eggs, one at a time, beating well after each addition. Combine the flour, cocoa, salt, baking powder and baking soda; add to the creamed mixture alternately with buttermilk just until moistened. Fold in pecans.

2. Pour into a greased 9-in. x 5-in. loaf pans. Bake at 350° for 55-60 minutes or until a toothpick inserted near the center comes out clean. Cool for 10 minutes before removing from pan to a wire rack.

3. In a small bowl, beat butter until fluffy. Beat in the honey and chocolate syrup. Serve with bread.

[1993]

CORN BREAD SQUARES

yield: 9 servings ∾ **prep/total time: 30 min.**

This inexpensive corn bread will disappear as fast as you can make it. It is fluffy and moist.

—Marcia Salisbury, Waukesha, Wisconsin

- 1 cup all-purpose flour
- 1 cup yellow cornmeal
- 1/4 cup sugar
- 2 teaspoons baking powder
- 3/4 teaspoon salt
- 2 eggs, lightly beaten
- 1 cup 2% milk
- 1/4 cup canola oil

1. In a large bowl, combine the flour, cornmeal, sugar, baking powder and salt. Add the eggs, milk and oil. Beat just until moistened.

2. Spoon into a greased 8-in. square baking pan. Bake at 400° for 20-25 minutes or until a toothpick inserted near the center comes out clean.

[2001]

WALNUT BANANA BREAD

yield: 1 loaf ∾ **prep: 15 min.**
bake: 65 min. + cooling

(Pictured on page 119)

Between Thanksgiving and Christmas, I bake 200 loaves of bread. This one is very popular.

—Douglas Jennings, Ottawa, Kansas

- 1/2 cup shortening
- 1 cup sugar
- 2 eggs
- 1 cup mashed ripe bananas (2 to 3 medium)
- 1 tablespoon 2% milk
- 2 cups all-purpose flour
- 1 teaspoon baking soda
- 1/4 teaspoon salt
- 1/2 cup chopped walnuts

1. In a large bowl, cream shortening and sugar until light and fluffy. Add eggs, one at a time, beating well after each addition. Beat in bananas and milk. Combine the flour, baking soda and salt; gradually add to creamed mixture just until moistened. Fold in nuts.

2. Pour into a greased 9-in. x 5-in. loaf pan. Bake at 325° for 65-70 minutes or until a toothpick inserted near the center comes out clean. Cool for 10 minutes before removing from pan to a wire rack.

[2005]

SPICED PEAR BREAD

yield: 4 mini loaves (6 slices each)
prep: 15 min. ∾ **bake: 50 min. + cooling**

My mom and I put up our own pears, so I always have plenty on hand when I want to make this wonderful bread. It's so moist and delicious that you'll want to have another slice or two!

—Rachel Barefoot, Linden, Michigan

- 3-1/4 cups all-purpose flour
- 1 cup sugar
- 3 teaspoons ground cinnamon
- 1 teaspoon baking powder
- 1 teaspoon baking soda
- 1 teaspoon ground cloves
- 1/2 teaspoon salt
- 3 eggs
- 3 cans (15-1/4 ounces each) sliced pears, drained and mashed
- 1/4 cup unsweetened applesauce
- 1/4 cup canola oil

1. In a large bowl, combine the first seven ingredients. In a small bowl, whisk the eggs, pears, applesauce and oil. Stir into dry ingredients just until moistened.

2. Pour into four 5-3/4-in. x 3-in. x 2-in. loaf pans coated with cooking spray. Bake at 350° for 50-60 minutes or until a toothpick inserted near the center comes out clean. Cool for 10 minutes; remove from pans to wire racks.

CORN BREAD SQUARES

❝It really was fluffy and moist, not crumbly. Had a nice taste to it—not too sweet, not too bland, just right. I had some left over from supper, and I'm pouring a glass of nice cold buttermilk and having it for dessert. Yum.❞
—savanna2

LEMON BREAD

"After years of looking, I finally found the perfect Lemon Bread recipe. I love the versatility of this bread. I have added frozen blueberries or raspberries, even poppy seeds with excellent results. This recipe is a definite keeper. One of my most-requested quick breads."
—erospert

[2009]

PINA COLADA
ZUCCHINI BREAD

yield: 3 loaves (12 slices each)
prep: 25 min. ∞ bake: 45 min. + cooling

At my husband's urging, I entered this recipe at the Pennsylvania Farm Show and won first place! I think you'll love the fluffy texture and tropical flavors.

—*Sharon Rydbom, Tipton, Pennsylvania*

4	cups all-purpose flour
3	cups sugar
2	teaspoons baking powder
1-1/2	teaspoons salt
1	teaspoon baking soda
4	eggs
1-1/2	cups canola oil
1	teaspoon *each* coconut, rum and vanilla extracts
3	cups shredded zucchini
1	cup canned crushed pineapple, drained
1/2	cup chopped walnuts *or* chopped pecans

1. Line the bottoms of three greased and floured 8-in. x 4-in. loaf pans with waxed paper and grease the paper; set aside.

2. In a large bowl, combine the flour, sugar, baking powder, salt and baking soda. In another bowl, whisk the eggs, oil and extracts. Stir into the dry ingredients just until moistened. Fold in the zucchini, pineapple and walnuts.

3. Transfer to prepared pans. Bake at 350° for 45-55 minutes or until a toothpick inserted near the center comes out clean. Cool for 10 minutes before removing from pans to wire racks. Gently remove waxed paper.

[1995]

LEMON BREAD

yield: 1 loaf (12 slices) ∞ prep: 10 min.
bake: 45 min. + cooling

(Pictured on page 114)

I frequently bake this sunshiny-sweet bread when I'm expecting company. It has a pound cake-like texture.

—*Kathy Scott*
Lingle, Wyoming, Field Editor

1/2	cup butter, softened
1	cup sugar
2	eggs
2	tablespoons lemon juice
1	tablespoon grated lemon peel
1-1/2	cups all-purpose flour
1	teaspoon baking powder
1/8	teaspoon salt
1/2	cup 2% milk
GLAZE:	
1/2	cup confectioners' sugar
2	tablespoons lemon juice

1. In a large bowl, cream butter and sugar until light and fluffy. Beat in the eggs, lemon juice and peel. Combine flour, baking powder and salt; gradually stir into creamed mixture alternately with milk, beating well after each addition.

2. Pour into a greased 8-in. x 4-in. loaf pan. Bake at 350° for 45 minutes or until a toothpick inserted near the center comes out clean.

3. Combine glaze ingredients. Remove bread from pan; immediately drizzle with the glaze. Cool on a wire rack. Serve warm.

[2009]

CHOCOLATE CHAI MINI LOAVES

yield: 3 mini loaves (6 slices each) ∾ **prep: 25 min.** ∾ **bake: 35 min. + cooling**

(Pictured on page 117)

This popular bread is irresistible. A friend of mine "complains" when I give her a loaf because she just can't help but eat the whole thing!

—Lisa Christensen, Poplar Grove, Illinois

2 ounces semisweet chocolate, chopped
1/2 cup water
1/2 cup butter, softened
1 cup packed brown sugar
2 eggs
1 teaspoon vanilla extract
1-1/2 cups all-purpose flour
3 tablespoons chai tea latte mix
1 teaspoon baking soda
1/2 teaspoon salt
1/2 cup sour cream

FROSTING:

1 cup confectioners' sugar
1 tablespoon butter, softened
1 tablespoon chai tea latte mix
1/2 teaspoon vanilla extract
4 to 5 teaspoons milk

1. In a microwave, melt chocolate with the water; stir until smooth. Cool slightly. In a large bowl, cream the butter and brown sugar until light and fluffy. Add eggs, one at a time, beating well after each addition. Beat in vanilla, then chocolate mixture.

2. Combine the flour, latte mix, baking soda and salt; add to creamed mixture alternately with sour cream.

3. Transfer to three greased 5-3/4-in. x 3-in. x 2-in. loaf pans. Bake at 350° for 35-40 minutes or until a toothpick inserted near the center comes out clean. Cool for 10 minutes before removing from pans to a wire rack to cool completely.

4. For frosting, combine the confectioners' sugar, butter, latte mix, vanilla and enough milk to achieve desired consistency. Frost tops of loaves.

Editor's Note: If you can not find chai tea latte mix, then try the Spiced Chai Mix on page 89.

CHOCOLATE CHAI MINI LOAVES

"Very delicious. I also thought it was more like cake than bread so I made 24 cupcakes instead. I suggest doubling the frosting recipe if you do cupcakes. They turned out great and were a hit at work. I will be making these again for sure."
—dramekers

BRANANA BREAD

"This is a yummy and good-for-you bread. I didn't have plain yogurt on hand, so I substituted half vanilla yogurt and half sour cream. I also sprinkled chopped walnuts on the top of the bread before I baked it. It turned out moist and keeps in the fridge well."
— amateur cook

[2010]

BRANANA BREAD
yield: 1 loaf (16 slices) ∞ prep: 20 min.
bake: 50 min. + cooling

Moist and delicious, this nutritious chocolate-chip banana bread is made with bran and flax.

—*Janet and Greta Podleski, Kitchener, Ontario*

1-1/2   cups all-purpose flour
1/2   cup wheat bran
1/3   cup granulated sugar
1/4   cup ground flaxseed *or* flaxmeal
1   teaspoon *each* baking powder and baking soda
1/2   teaspoon cinnamon
1/4   teaspoon salt
1-1/2   cups mashed ripe bananas
3/4   cup plain yogurt (2%)
2   eggs
2   tablespoons butter, melted
1   teaspoon vanilla extract
1/2   cup finely chopped walnuts
1/3   cup miniature semisweet chocolate chips

1. In a large bowl, combine dry ingredients.

2. In a small bowl, whisk the bananas, yogurt, eggs, butter and vanilla. Add yogurt mixture to dry ingredients and stir just until moistened. Fold in nuts and chocolate chips.

3. Spoon batter into a greased 9-in. x 5-in. pan. Bake for about 50 minutes, or until a toothpick inserted near the center comes out clean. Cool for 10 minutes before removing from pan to wire rack. Serve warm.

[2002]

ZUCCHINI BREAD
yield: 2 loaves (12 slices each)
prep: 15 min. ∞ bake: 55 min. + cooling
(Pictured on page 116)

I like this bread because it's lighter and fluffier than most zucchini breads. Plus it's a great way to put that abundant vegetable to good use!

—*Kevin Bruckerhoff, Columbia, Missouri*

2   cups sugar
1   cup canola oil
3   eggs
2   teaspoons vanilla extract
3   cups all-purpose flour
1   teaspoon salt
1   teaspoon baking soda
1   teaspoon ground cinnamon
1/4   teaspoon baking powder
2   cups shredded zucchini (about 2 medium)
1/2   cup chopped nuts
1   teaspoon grated lemon peel

1. In a large bowl, beat sugar, oil, eggs and vanilla until well blended. Combine the flour, salt, baking soda, cinnamon and baking powder; stir into sugar mixture just until moistened. Stir in the zucchini, nuts and lemon peel.

2. Transfer to two greased 8-in. x 4-in. loaf pans. Bake at 350° for 55-65 minutes or until a toothpick inserted near the center comes out clean. Cool for 10 minutes before removing from pans to wire racks to cool completely.

BRANANA BREAD TIP

The bananas must be very, very ripe (sweet!) for this banana bread as there's very little added sugar. Freeze your bananas as they become overripe and you will always be ready to throw together a banana loaf!

—*Janet and Greta Podleski*

[1997]

CRANBERRY NUT BREAD

yield: 1 loaf (16 slices) ∾ **prep: 15 min.
bake: 65 min. + cooling**

I created this bread years ago by combining a couple of recipes from my collection. There's a big burst of tart cranberry and lots of crunchy nuts in every piece. People also like the delicious hint of orange.

—Dawn Lowenstein, Hatboro, Pennsylvania

- 2 cups all-purpose flour
- 1 cup sugar
- 1-1/2 teaspoons baking powder
- 1 teaspoon salt
- 1/2 teaspoon baking soda
- 1/4 cup butter, cubed
- 1 egg
- 3/4 cup orange juice
- 1 tablespoon grated orange peel
- 1-1/2 cups fresh *or* frozen cranberries
- 1/2 cup chopped walnuts

1. In a large bowl, combine flour, sugar, baking powder, salt and baking soda. Cut in butter until mixture resembles coarse crumbs. In a small bowl, whisk the egg, orange juice and peel; stir into dry ingredients just until moistened. Fold in cranberries and walnuts.

2. Spoon batter into a greased and floured 8-in. x 4-in. loaf pan. Bake at 350° for 65-70 minutes or until a toothpick inserted near the center comes out clean. Cool for 10 minutes before removing from pan to a wire rack to cool completely.

[2007]

SWEET POTATO BREAD

yield: 1 loaf ∾ **prep: 15 min.
bake: 1 hour + cooling**

(*Pictured on page 117*)

This spicy quick bread gives me a true feeling of fall. My family isn't fond of traditional sweet potatoes, so I make this yummy bread instead.

**—Rebecca Cook Jones
Henderson, Nevada, Field Editor**

- 1-3/4 cups all-purpose flour
- 1-1/2 cups sugar
- 1 teaspoon baking soda
- 1 teaspoon ground cinnamon
- 1 teaspoon ground nutmeg
- 3/4 teaspoon salt
- 1/4 teaspoon ground allspice
- 1/4 teaspoon ground cloves
- 2 eggs
- 1-1/2 cups mashed sweet potatoes (about 2 medium)
- 1/2 cup canola oil
- 6 tablespoons orange juice
- 1/2 cup chopped pecans

1. In a large bowl, combine the first eight ingredients. In a small bowl, whisk the eggs, sweet potatoes, oil and orange juice. Stir into dry ingredients just until moistened. Fold in the pecans.

2. Transfer to a greased 9-in. x 5-in. loaf pan. Bake at 350° for 60-65 minutes or until a toothpick inserted near the center comes out clean. Cool for 10 minutes before removing from pan to a wire rack to cool completely.

CRANBERRY NUT BREAD

❝This recipe makes out-of-this-world delicious bread. I've added as much as 2 cups cranberries with excellent results. If you have not yet made this bread, do so. When my son was in the Army, I'd sent him several loaves to share with buddies and superiors. Thank you for sharing this recipe.❞
—Joscy

[2005]

ALMOND BERRY MUFFINS

yield: 1-1/2 dozen ∞ prep: 20 min.
bake: 20 min.

(Pictured on page 119)

I made these moist muffins to take to the office, and they were a hit. Sugared almonds give them a crunchy topping. When strawberries aren't in season, I use individual frozen cut strawberries directly from the freezer.

—Deborah Feinberg, Gulf Breeze, Florida

1-1/4	cups sliced almonds, *divided*
1	egg white, lightly beaten
1-1/2	cups sugar, *divided*
1/4	cup shortening
1/4	cup butter, softened
2	eggs
1	teaspoon vanilla extract
1/2	teaspoon almond extract
2	cups all-purpose flour
1	teaspoon baking powder
1/2	teaspoon salt
1/4	teaspoon baking soda
3/4	cup buttermilk
1-1/4	cups fresh strawberries, chopped

1. In a large bowl, combine 1 cup almonds and egg white. Add 1/2 cup sugar; toss to coat. Spoon into a greased 15-in. x 10-in. x 1-in. baking pan. Bake at 350° for 9-11 minutes or until golden brown, stirring occasionally.

2. In a large bowl, cream the shortening, butter and remaining sugar until light and fluffy. Add the eggs, one at a time, beating well after each addition. Beat in the extracts. Combine the flour, baking powder, salt and baking soda; add to the creamed mixture alternately with buttermilk just until moistened. Fold in the strawberries and remaining almonds.

3. Fill greased or paper-lined muffin cups two-thirds full. Sprinkle with sugared almonds. Bake at 350° for 20-25 minutes or until a toothpick inserted near center comes out clean. Cool 5 minutes; remove from pans to wire racks. Serve warm.

[2005]

SWEET POTATO BISCUITS

yield: 1-1/2 dozen ∞ prep: 25 min.
bake: 10 min.

Whoever said biscuits were boring never tasted these. We love their rich flavor. These tender treats are great with a meal or as a snack with honey butter.

—Katie Sloan, Charlotte, North Carolina, Field Editor

2	cups self-rising flour
1/4	cup packed brown sugar
1	teaspoon ground cinnamon
1	teaspoon ground ginger
7	tablespoons cold butter, *divided*
3	tablespoons shortening
1	cup mashed sweet potatoes
6	tablespoons 2% milk

1. In a bowl, combine the first four ingredients. Cut in 4 tablespoons butter and shortening until mixture resembles coarse crumbs.

2. In a small bowl, combine sweet potatoes and milk; stir into crumb mixture just until moistened. Turn onto a lightly floured surface; knead 10 times.

3. Pat or roll out the dough to 1/2-in. thickness; cut with a floured 2-1/2-in. biscuit cutter. Place 2 in. apart on ungreased baking sheets.

4. Melt remaining butter; brush over dough. Bake at 425° for 10-12 minutes or until golden brown. Remove from pans to wire racks. Serve warm.

Editor's Note: As a substitute for each cup of self-rising flour, place 1-1/2 teaspoons baking powder and 1/2 teaspoon salt in a measuring cup. Add all-purpose flour to measure 1 cup.

APRICOT SCONES, page 125

WHITE CHOCOLATE MACADAMIA MUFFINS, page 121

CONFETTI FIESTA BRAIDS, page 96

LEMON BREAD, page 108

PARKERHOUSE ROLLS, page 102

PARMESAN KNOTS, page 124

MOM'S ITALIAN BREAD, page 94

ZUCCHINI BREAD, page 110

CHOCOLATE CHAI MINI LOAVES, page 109

BUTTERCUP YEAST BREAD, page 95

A.M. RUSH ESPRESSO SMOOTHIE, page 92

SWEET POTATO BREAD, page 111

HERBED PEASANT BREAD, page 95

SOUR CREAM BISCUITS, page 122

CINNAMON MOCHA COFFEE, page 84

CINNAMON SWIRL BREAD, page 100

WALNUT BANANA BREAD, page 107

ALMOND BERRY MUFFINS, page 112

WHOLE WHEAT REFRIGERATOR ROLLS, page 104

TOPSY-TURVY SANGRIA, page 89

[1999]

GRANDMA'S POPOVERS
yield: 9 popovers ∾ prep: 10 min.
bake: 30 min.

Still warm from the oven, popovers are always a fun accompaniment to a homey meal. I was raised on these—my grandmother often made them for our Sunday dinners.

—Debbie Terenzini, Lusby, Maryland

1 cup all-purpose flour
1/8 teaspoon salt
3 eggs
1 cup 2% milk

1. In a large bowl, combine flour and salt. Beat eggs and milk; whisk into dry ingredients just until combined. Cover and let stand at room temperature for 45 minutes. Grease cups of a popover pan well with butter or oil; fill cups of two-thirds full with batter.

2. Bake at 450° for 15 minutes. Reduce heat to 350° (do not open oven door). Bake 15 minutes longer or until deep golden brown (do not underbake).

3. Run a table knife or small metal spatula round edges of cups to loosen if necessary. Immediately remove popovers from pan; prick with a small sharp knife to allow steam to escape. Serve immediately.

Editor's Note: You may use greased muffin tins instead of a popover pan. Fill every other cup two-thirds full with batter to avoid crowding the popovers; fill remaining cups with water. Bake at 450° for 15 minutes and 350° for 10 minutes. Yield: 9 popovers.

[2006]

WHITE CHOCOLATE MACADAMIA MUFFINS
yield: 1 dozen ∾ prep: 20 min.
bake: 15 min.

(Pictured on page 113)

I like making muffins because they are so versatile and everyone loves them. These sweet muffins remind me of one of my favorite cookies. They're real kid-pleasers.

—Lorie Roach, Buckatunna, Mississippi

1-3/4 cups all-purpose flour
3/4 cup sugar
2-1/2 teaspoons baking powder
1/2 teaspoon salt
1 egg
1/2 cup 2% milk
1/4 cup butter, melted
3/4 cup white baking chips
3/4 cup chopped macadamia nuts
GLAZE:
1/2 cup white baking chips
2 tablespoons heavy whipping cream

1. In a large bowl, combine flour, sugar, baking powder and salt. In another bowl, combine egg, milk and butter; stir into dry ingredients just until moistened. Fold in chips and nuts.

2. Fill paper-lined muffin cups two-thirds full. Bake at 400° for 15-18 minutes or until a toothpick inserted near the center comes out clean. Cool for 5 minutes before removing from pan to a wire rack.

3. For glaze, in a microwave, melt chips with cream; stir until smooth. Drizzle over warm muffins. Serve warm.

WHITE CHOCOLATE MACADAMIA MUFFINS

"These taste just like the cookie—IF you substitute brown sugar for the regular granulated."
—gontarzc

CRISSCROSS APPLE CROWNS

" These were amazing!! They are like mini apple pies! Very tasty and easy to make. This recipe is going in the favorites. "

—dstampp

[2010]

CRISSCROSS APPLE CROWNS

yield: 8 servings ∞ prep: 30 min.
bake: 20 min.

Wake 'em up on chilly mornings with the tempting aroma of apples and cinnamon filling the house. I love making these for breakfast. They're different and so easy.

—*Teresa Morris, Laurel, Delaware*

1-1/3 cups chopped peeled tart apples
1/3 cup chopped walnuts
1/3 cup raisins
1/2 cup sugar, *divided*
2 tablespoons all-purpose flour
2 teaspoons ground cinnamon, *divided*
Dash salt
1 package (16.3 ounces) large refrigerated flaky biscuits
2 teaspoons butter, melted

1. In a large microwave-safe bowl, combine the apples, walnuts, raisins, 3 tablespoons sugar, flour, 3/4 teaspoon cinnamon and salt. Microwave on high for 2-3 minutes or until almost tender.

2. Flatten each biscuit into a 5-in. circle. Combine the remaining sugar and cinnamon; sprinkle a rounded teaspoonful of sugar mixture over each. Top each with 1/4 cup apple mixture. Bring up edges to enclose mixture; pinch edges to seal.

3. Place seam side down in ungreased muffin cups. Brush tops with butter; sprinkle with remaining sugar mixture. With a sharp knife, cut an X in the top of each.

4. Bake at 350° for 18-22 minutes or until golden brown. Cool for 5 minutes before removing from the pan to a wire rack.

[2000]

MOIST BRAN MUFFINS

yield: 4 muffins ∞ prep/total time: 30 min.

These tender, slightly sweet muffins are a tasty way to round out any meal. The recipe makes a small quantity for a couple or a single person.

—*Mildred Ross, Badin, North Carolina*

1/2 cup All-Bran
1/2 cup 2% milk
2 tablespoons canola oil
1/2 cup all-purpose flour
2 tablespoons sugar
1 teaspoon baking powder
1/4 teaspoon salt

1. In a large bowl, combine the bran and milk; let stand for 5 minutes. Stir in oil. Combine remaining ingredients; stir into bran mixture just until moistened.

2. Fill greased or paper-lined muffin cups half full. Bake at 400° for 18-22 minutes or until a toothpick inserted near the center comes out clean. Cool for 5 minutes before removing from pan to a wire rack. Serve warm.

[1997]

SOUR CREAM BISCUITS

yield: 4 biscuits ∞ prep/total time: 30 min.
(*Pictured on page 118*)

Biscuit recipes that feed a few are hard to come by. I couldn't wait to try these.

—*Nell Jones, Smyrna, Georgia*

1 cup self-rising flour
1/4 teaspoon baking soda
3/4 cup sour cream
2 teaspoons canola oil

1. In a large bowl, combine flour and baking soda. Stir in sour cream and oil just until moistened. Turn onto a floured surface; knead 4-6 times. Roll

out to 3/4-in. thickness; cut with a
2-1/2-in. biscuit cutter.

2. Place on a greased baking sheet.
Lightly spray tops with cooking spray.
Bake at 425° for 10-12 minutes or until
golden brown.

Editor's Note: As a substitute for 1 cup of
self-rising flour, place 1-1/2 teaspoons baking
powder and 1/2 teaspoon salt in a measuring
cup. Add all-purpose flour to measure 1 cup.

[2003]

HAZELNUT CHIP SCONES
**yield: 16 scones ∞ prep: 20 min.
bake: 15 min.**

*When I made a friend's scone recipe, I didn't
have enough milk, so I used hazelnut-flavored
nondairy creamer and added chocolate chips.*

—Elisa Lochridge, Beaverton, Oregon

    4 cups all-purpose flour
    3 tablespoons sugar
    4 teaspoons baking powder
  1/2 teaspoon salt
  1/2 teaspoon cream of tartar
  3/4 cup cold butter, cold
    1 egg, *separated*
1-1/2 cups refrigerated hazelnut nondairy
       creamer *or* half-and-half cream
1-1/2 cups semisweet chocolate chips
Additional sugar
SPICED BUTTER:
  1/2 cup butter, softened
    3 tablespoons brown sugar
  1/4 teaspoon ground cinnamon
  1/4 teaspoon ground allspice
  1/8 teaspoon ground nutmeg

1. In a large bowl, combine the first five
ingredients; cut in the butter until
crumbly. In a small bowl, whisk egg
yolk and creamer; add to the dry
ingredients just until moistened. Fold
in chocolate chips.

2. Turn onto a floured surface; knead
10 times. Divide dough in half. Pat
each portion into a 7-in. circle; cut into
eight wedges. Separate wedges and
place on greased baking sheets.

3. Beat egg white; brush over the top.
Sprinkle with the additional sugar.
Bake at 425° for 15-18 minutes or until
golden brown.

4. Meanwhile, in a small bowl, combine
the spiced butter ingredients; beat
until smooth. Serve with warm scones.

[2005]

PECAN CORN MUFFINS
**yield: 16 muffins ∞ prep: 20 min.
bake: 15 min.**

*These dressed-up cornmeal muffins are chock-full
of chopped pecans. Served warm with jalapeno
pepper jelly, they make a zippy accompaniment.*

*—Shirley Glaab
Hattiesburg, Mississippi, Field Editor*

1-1/4 cups yellow cornmeal
    1 cup sugar
  3/4 cup all-purpose flour
    2 teaspoons baking powder
  1/4 teaspoon salt
    2 eggs, lightly beaten
    1 cup 2% milk
  1/2 cup butter, melted
    1 cup chopped pecans
Jalapeno pepper jelly

1. In a bowl, combine first five
ingredients. In a bowl, whisk eggs, milk
and butter; stir into dry ingredients
just until moistened. Fold in pecans.

2. Fill greased or paper-lined muffin cups
two-thirds full. Bake at 400° for 15-18
minutes or until a toothpick inserted
near center comes out clean. Cool for
5 minutes; remove from pans to wire
racks. Serve warm with pepper jelly.

HAZELNUT CHIP SCONES

"Delicious!!! I didn't have
hazelnut creamer on hand
so I just used the English
toffee creamer I had in the
fridge—they turned out
great! I like the fact that
they can be changed up by
just changing the flavor of
creamer or adding different
stir-ins (toffee chips, etc.)
I think I will be making
these quite a bit!"
—*joniotto*

[1996]

CHOCOLATE CHIP MINI-MUFFINS

**yield: about 3 dozen   prep: 15 min.
bake: 10 min. + cooling**

I bake a lot of different muffins, but I use this recipe the most. People just seem to enjoy the flavor.

—*Joanne Shew Chuk
St. Benedict, Saskatchewan*

1/2   **cup sugar**
1/4   **cup shortening**
1   **egg**
1/2   **cup 2% milk**
1/2   **teaspoon vanilla extract**
1   **cup all-purpose flour**
1/2   **teaspoon baking powder**
1/2   **teaspoon baking soda**
1/4   **teaspoon salt**
2/3   **cup miniature semisweet chocolate chips**

---

1. In a large bowl, cream the sugar and shortening until light and fluffy. Beat in egg; mix well. Beat in the milk and vanilla. Combine the flour, baking powder, baking soda and salt; add to butter mixture just until combined. Fold in chocolate chips.

2. Spoon about 1 tablespoon of batter into each greased or paper-lined mini-muffin cup. Bake at 375° for 10-13 minutes or until a toothpick inserted near the center comes out clean. Cool for 10 minutes before removing from the pan to a wire rack. Serve warm.

[2009]

PARMESAN KNOTS

**yield: 2-1/2 dozen
prep/total time: 15 min.**

(Pictured on page 115)

These novel knots are handy because they can be made ahead of time and reheated when needed.

—*Jane Paschke, University Park, Florida*

---

1   **tube (12 ounces) refrigerated buttermilk biscuits**
1/4   **cup canola oil**
3   **tablespoons grated Parmesan cheese**
1   **teaspoon garlic powder**
1   **teaspoon dried oregano**
1   **teaspoon dried parsley flakes**

---

1. Cut each biscuit into thirds. Roll each piece into a 3-in. rope and tie into a knot; tuck ends under.

2. Place 2 in. apart on a greased baking sheet. Bake at 400° for 8-10 minutes or until golden brown.

3. In a large bowl, combine the remaining ingredients; add the warm knots and gently toss to coat.

PARMESAN KNOTS

"I made these with dinner instead of garlic bread. Tossing them in a bowl instead of giving each knot individual attention is what made it so simple."
—*crash9875*

STORING MUFFINS, BISCUITS & SCONES

Store them in an airtight container at room temperature. If made with cheese, cream cheese or other perishable foods, they should be stored in the refrigerator. Muffins stay fresh for up to 3 days, biscuits and scones for 1 to 2 days.

—*Taste of Home Cooking Experts*

[2000]

APRICOT SCONES

yield: 16 scones (1 cup cream) ∞ prep: 20 min. ∞ bake: 15 min.

(Pictured on page 113)

Popular served with tea in Victorian days, scones are making a big comeback. Apricots and nuts are stirred into the batter for a delicious treat. I baked for a theme shower. Spread with Devonshire cream, they delighted the bride-to-be and guests.

—*Robin Fuhrman, Fond du Lac, Wisconsin*

DEVONSHIRE CREAM:
- 1 package (3 ounces) cream cheese, softened
- 1 tablespoon confectioners' sugar
- 1/2 teaspoon vanilla extract
- 1/4 to 1/3 cup heavy whipping cream

SCONES:
- 2 cups all-purpose flour
- 1/4 cup sugar
- 1 tablespoon baking powder
- 1/4 teaspoon salt
- 1/3 cup cold butter
- 1/2 cup chopped dried apricots
- 1/2 cup chopped pecans
- 1 teaspoon grated orange peel
- 1 cup plus 2 tablespoons heavy whipping cream, *divided*

Jam of your choice

1. For Devonshire cream, in a large bowl, beat the cream cheese, confectioners' sugar and vanilla until fluffy. Gradually beat in enough cream to achieve a spreading consistency. Cover and chill for at least 2 hours.

2. For scones, combine the dry ingredients in a large bowl. Cut in butter until mixture resembles fine crumbs. Add the apricots, pecans and orange peel. With a fork, rapidly stir in 1 cup whipping cream just until moistened.

3. Turn onto a floured surface; knead 5-6 times. Divide in half; shape each into a ball. Flatten each ball into a 6-in. circle; cut each circle into eight wedges. Place 1 in. apart on an ungreased baking sheet. Brush with the remaining whipping cream.

4. Bake at 375° for 13-15 minutes or until a toothpick inserted near the center comes out clean. Remove from pan to a wire rack. Serve warm with Devonshire cream and jam.

[1999]

CHERRY ALMOND MUFFINS

yield: 7 jumbo muffins or 14 regular muffins
prep: 20 min. ∞ bake: 30 min.

As a kid, I loved doughnuts filled with custard or jelly. So I decided to experiment and came up with this terrific treat. These fancy muffins are almost like a pastry with a creamy center and a nutty topping.

—*John Montgomery, Fortuna, California*

- 1-3/4 cups all-purpose flour
- 1/2 cup plus 1 tablespoon sugar
- 1/2 teaspoon baking powder
- 1/2 teaspoon baking soda
- 1/4 teaspoon salt
- 1/2 cup cold butter, cubed
- 1 egg
- 3/4 cup sour cream
- 1 teaspoon almond extract

TOPPING:
- 1/3 cup all-purpose flour
- 2 tablespoons sugar
- 2 tablespoons cold butter
- 1/3 cup chopped sliced almonds

FILLING:
- 1 package (8 ounces) cream cheese, softened
- 1 egg
- 1/4 cup sugar
- 1/2 teaspoon vanilla extract
- 3/4 cup cherry preserves, warmed

1. In a bowl, combine the first five ingredients. Cut in butter until mixture resembles coarse crumbs. Beat the egg, sour cream and extract until smooth; stir into dry ingredients just until moistened (batter will be thick).

2. Combine flour and sugar in a small bowl; cut in butter until crumbly. Stir in almonds; set aside. In a large bowl, beat cream cheese, egg, sugar and vanilla until smooth. In a saucepan over low heat, warm preserves.

3. Fill greased jumbo muffin cups half full with batter. Divide filling and preserves evenly among muffin cups; swirl. Cover with remaining batter. Sprinkle with topping.

4. Bake at 350° for 30-35 minutes or until a toothpick inserted in muffin comes out clean. Cool for 5 minutes before removing from pans to wire racks. Serve warm.

Editor's Note: For regular-size muffin cups, bake 20-25 minutes.

BLARNEY BREAKFAST BAKE

" Good! I used wheat bread for the bread cubes. The pepper jack cheese made it somewhat spicy. My 1-year-old would only have a few bites. My DH (dear husband) and I loved it though. I think for kids though, I would just omit the pepper jack and double the cheddar. "

—scrapo

[2008]

BLARNEY BREAKFAST BAKE

yield: 12 servings ∞ prep: 20 min.
bake: 50 min. + standing

Mom gave me this recipe and served it as an Irish brunch to the neighbors for St. Patrick's Day.

—Kerry Barnett-Amundson
Ocean Park, Washington

- 1 pound bulk pork sausage
- 1/2 pound sliced fresh mushrooms
- 1 large onion, chopped
- 10 eggs, lightly beaten
- 3 cups 2% milk
- 2 teaspoons ground mustard
- 1 teaspoon salt
- 1/2 teaspoon pepper
- 6 cups cubed day-old bread
- 1 cup chopped seeded tomatoes
- 1 cup (4 ounces) shredded pepper jack cheese
- 1 cup (4 ounces) shredded cheddar cheese

1. In a large skillet, cook the sausage, mushrooms and onion over medium heat until meat is no longer pink; drain. In a large bowl, whisk the eggs, milk, mustard, salt and pepper.

2. In a greased 13-in. x 9-in. baking dish, layer half of the bread cubes, tomatoes, cheeses and sausage mixture. Repeat layers. Pour egg mixture over the top.

3. Bake, uncovered, at 325° for 50-55 minutes or until a knife inserted near the center comes out clean. Let stand for 10 minutes before serving.

[2005]

CAMPER'S BREAKFAST HASH

yield: 8 servings ∞ prep/total time: 25 min.

When we go camping with family and friends, I'm always asked to make this hearty breakfast. It's a favorite at home, too.

—Linda Krivanek, Oak Creek, Wisconsin

- 1/4 cup butter, cubed
- 2 packages (20 ounces *each*) refrigerated shredded hash brown potatoes
- 1 package (7 ounces) brown-and-serve sausage links, cut into 1/2-inch pieces
- 1/4 cup chopped onion
- 1/4 cup chopped green pepper
- 12 eggs, lightly beaten

Salt and pepper to taste

- 1 cup (4 ounces) shredded cheddar cheese

1. In a large skillet, melt butter. Add the potatoes, sausage, onion and green pepper. Cook, uncovered, over medium heat for 10-15 minutes or until the potatoes are lightly browned, turning once.

2. Push potato mixture to the sides of pan. Pour eggs into center of pan. Cook and stir over medium heat until eggs are completely set. Season with salt and pepper. Reduce heat; stir eggs into potato mixture. Top with cheese; cover and cook for 1-2 minutes or until cheese is melted.

[2009]

SPIRAL OMELET SUPREME

yield: 8 servings ⌒ prep: 20 min.
bake: 20 min.

(Pictured on page 141)

You can substitute 2 cups of any combination of your favorite omelet fillings for the vegetables in this recipe. Use serrated knife for slicing it.

—*Debbie Morris, Hamilton, Ohio*

---

    4   ounces cream cheese, softened
    3/4 cup 2% milk
    1/4 cup plus 2 tablespoons grated
        Parmesan cheese, *divided*
    2   tablespoons all-purpose flour
    12 eggs
    1   large green pepper, chopped
    1   cup sliced fresh
        mushrooms
    1   small onion, chopped
    2   teaspoons canola oil
    1-1/2 cups (6 ounces) shredded part-skim
        mozzarella cheese
    1   plum tomato, seeded and chopped
    1-1/4 teaspoons Italian seasoning, *divided*

---

1. Line the bottom and sides of a greased 15-in. x 10-in. x 1-in. baking pan with parchment paper; grease the paper and set aside.

2. In a small bowl, beat the cream cheese and milk until smooth. Beat in 1/4 cup Parmesan cheese and flour until blended. In a large bowl, beat the eggs; add cream cheese mixture and mix well. Pour into prepared pan.

3. Bake at 375° for 20-25 minutes or until set. Meanwhile, in a large skillet, saute the pepper, mushrooms and onion in oil until crisp-tender. Keep warm.

4. Turn omelet onto a work surface; peel off the parchment paper. Sprinkle with the vegetable mixture, mozzarella cheese, tomato and 1 teaspoon Italian seasoning. Roll up jelly-roll style,

starting with a short side. Place on a serving platter. Sprinkle the omelet with the remaining Parmesan cheese and Italian seasoning.

[1993]

TOMATO QUICHE

yield: 6-8 servings ⌒ prep: 20 min.
bake: 50 min. + standing

(Pictured on page 138)

I first tried this recipe at a family gathering and loved it! It is a great meatless brunch dish, served hot or cold.

—*Heidi Anne Quinn
West Kingston, Rhode Island*

---

    1   cup chopped onion
    2   tablespoons butter
    4   large tomatoes, peeled, seeded,
        chopped and drained
    1   teaspoon salt
    1/4 teaspoon pepper
    1/4 teaspoon dried thyme
    2   cups (8 ounces) Monterey Jack
        cheese, *divided*
    1   unbaked pastry shell (10 inches)
    4   eggs
    1-1/2 cups half-and-half cream

---

1. In a large skillet, saute onion in butter until tender. Add the tomatoes, salt, pepper and thyme. Cook over medium-high heat until liquid is almost evaporated, about 10 to 15 minutes. Remove from the heat.

2. Sprinkle 1 cup cheese into bottom of pie shell. Cover with tomato mixture; sprinkle with remaining cheese.

3. In a small bowl, beat eggs until foamy. Beat in cream. Pour into pie shell.

4. Bake at 425° for 10 minutes. Reduce heat to 325°; bake 40 minutes longer or until top begins to brown and a knife inserted near the center comes out clean. Let stand for 10 minutes before cutting.

TOMATO QUICHE

"This was fabulous, got rave reviews from the gals at brunch. I did substitute whole milk for the cream because I forgot to buy cream and used 5 eggs instead of 4 in case the whole milk wouldn't let it set—and it came out perfect."
—*amcoffeebean*

[2006]

AVOCADO EGGS BENEDICT

yield: 6 servings ∞ **prep/total time: 20 min.**

(Pictured on page 144)

Fresh avocado slices and a special creamy sauce really dress up this classic egg dish. It's great for breakfast or brunch.

—*Jory Hilpipre, Eden Prairie, Minnesota*

- 1/2 cup butter
- 1/4 cup all-purpose flour
- 2 cups 2% milk
- 2 cups (8 ounces) shredded cheddar cheese
- 1 tablespoon grated Romano cheese
- 1/2 teaspoon salt
- 1/8 teaspoon garlic powder
- 1/8 teaspoon dried thyme
- 1/8 teaspoon *each* ground mustard, coriander and pepper
- 1 tablespoon white vinegar
- 6 eggs
- 6 slices Canadian bacon, warmed
- 1 large ripe avocado, peeled and sliced
- 3 English muffins, split and toasted

---

1. In a large saucepan, melt butter. Stir in flour until smooth; gradually add milk. Bring to a boil; cook and stir for 2 minutes or until thickened. Reduce heat; stir in cheeses and seasonings. Cook and stir until cheese is melted; keep warm.

2. Place 2-3 in. of water in a large skillet with high sides; add vinegar. Bring to a boil; reduce heat and simmer gently. Break cold eggs, one at a time, into a custard cup or saucer; holding the cup close to the surface of the water, slip each egg into water. Cook, uncovered, until whites are completely set and yolks begin to thicken (but are not hard), about 4 minutes.

3. Place Canadian bacon and avocado on each muffin half. With a slotted spoon, lift each egg out of the water and place over avocado. Top with cheese sauce.

[2010]

POTATO & RED ONION FRITTATA

yield: 4 servings ∞ **prep: 30 min. bake: 15 min.**

Frittata is an Italian classic perfect for any meal of the day, even a special-occasion brunch.

—*Maria Regakis*
Somerville, Massachusetts, Field Editor

- 1 large red onion, chopped
- 1/2 teaspoon minced fresh rosemary *or* 1/8 teaspoon dried rosemary, crushed
- 4 tablespoons butter, *divided*
- 1 garlic clove, minced
- 1/2 pound red potatoes (about 5 small), thinly sliced
- 6 eggs, lightly beaten
- 1/3 cup 2% milk
- 1/2 teaspoon salt
- 1/4 teaspoon pepper
- 1/2 cup shredded Gruyere *or* Swiss cheese

---

1. In a 10-in. ovenproof skillet, saute onion and rosemary in 1 tablespoon butter until tender. Add garlic; cook 1 minute longer. Remove from pan; set aside. In same skillet, cook potatoes in 2 tablespoons butter until tender and golden brown. Remove and keep warm.

2. In a large bowl, whisk the eggs, milk, salt and pepper. Stir in cheese and onion mixture. Melt remaining butter in the skillet; tilt pan to evenly coat. Add egg mixture. Bake at 350° for 8-10 minutes or until nearly set.

3. Top with the potatoes; bake for 3-5 minutes or until eggs are completely set. Let frittata stand for 5 minutes. Cut into wedges.

AVOCADO EGGS BENEDICT

"Great! I made it without the avocado, since I was just looking for a better sauce recipe than others I'd tried. It was a hit!"

—*Pinstripes*

[2009]

BEAR'S BREAKFAST BURRITOS

yield: 12 servings ∞ **prep: 45 min.** ∞ **cook: 15 min.**

My husband, Larry ("Bear"), makes his burritos for our church's Fourth of July taco booth. Everyone loves them and always asks when he is going to make more.

—*Larry & Sandy Kelley, Grangeville, Idaho*

2	packages (22-1/2 ounces *each*) frozen hash brown patties
15	eggs, lightly beaten
2	tablespoons chili powder
2	tablespoons garlic salt
1	tablespoon ground cumin
1/2	pound uncooked chorizo *or* bulk spicy pork sausage
6	jalapeno peppers, seeded and minced
1	large green pepper, chopped
1	large sweet red pepper, chopped
1	large onion, chopped
1	bunch green onions, chopped
3	cups salsa
12	flour tortillas (12 inches), warmed
4	cups (16 ounces) shredded Monterey Jack cheese

Sour cream, optional

---

1. Cook hash browns according to package directions; crumble and keep warm. In a large bowl, whisk the eggs, chili powder, garlic salt and cumin. Set aside.

2. Crumble chorizo into a large skillet; add the jalapenos, peppers and onions. Cook and stir over medium heat until meat is no longer pink; drain. Add reserved egg mixture; cook and stir over medium heat until eggs are set. Stir in salsa.

3. Spoon 1/2 cup hash browns and 1/2 cup egg mixture off center on each tortilla; sprinkle with 1/3 cup cheese. Fold sides and ends over filling and roll up. Wrap each burrito in waxed paper and foil. Serve warm with sour cream if desired. Cool remaining burritos to room temperature; freeze for up to 1 month.

4. To use frozen burritos: Remove foil and waxed paper. Place burritos 2 in. apart on an ungreased baking sheet. Bake, uncovered, at 350° for 50-55 minutes or until heated through.

Editor's Note: Wear disposable gloves when cutting hot peppers; the oils can burn skin. Avoid touching your face.

[2007]

GARDEN VEGETABLE QUICHE

yield: 6-8 servings ∞ **prep: 20 min.**
bake: 40 min. + standing

(Pictured on page 139)

Make your next brunch special with this fluffy, deep-dish quiche. Fresh rosemary enhances this delightful egg dish that's chock-full of savory garden ingredients. It cuts nicely, too.

—*Kristina Ledford, Indianapolis, Indiana*

1	frozen pie shell (9 inches)
1	small red onion, sliced
1/2	cup sliced fresh mushrooms
1/4	cup diced yellow summer squash
1	tablespoon butter
1/2	cup fresh baby spinach
3	garlic cloves, minced
1	cup (4 ounces) shredded Swiss cheese
4	eggs, lightly beaten
1-2/3	cups heavy whipping cream
1/2	teaspoon salt
1/2	teaspoon minced fresh rosemary
1/4	teaspoon pepper

---

1. Let pastry shell stand at room temperature for 10 minutes. Line unpricked pastry shell with a double thickness of heavy-duty foil. Bake pastry shell at 400° for 4 minutes. Remove foil; bake 4 minutes longer. Cool on a wire rack. Reduce heat to 350°.

2. In a large skillet, saute onion, mushrooms and squash in butter until tender. Add spinach and garlic; cook 1 minute longer. Spoon into crust; top with cheese.

3. In a large bowl, whisk the eggs, cream, salt, rosemary and pepper until blended; pour over cheese.

4. Cover edges of the crust loosely with foil. Bake for 40-45 minutes or until a knife inserted near the center comes out clean. Let quiche stand for 10 minutes before cutting.

[2002]

POTATO HAM OMELET PIE

yield: 8 servings ∞ prep: 45 min. ∞ bake: 30 min. + standing

(Pictured on page 142)

As a holiday kickoff, my family gets together in early December for a hearty brunch before going out to cut our Christmas trees. This flavorful breakfast pie, assembled in layers, was a big hit at last year's gathering.

—*Shelly Rynearson, Oconomowoc, Wisconsin*

1	package (17-1/4 ounces) frozen puff pastry, thawed
1/4	cup butter, cubed
3	cups sliced peeled red potatoes
1	cup thinly sliced onion
1/4	teaspoon salt
1/4	teaspoon pepper

OMELETS:

6	eggs, lightly beaten
1/4	cup minced fresh parsley
2	tablespoons water

Dash *each* salt and pepper

2 tablespoons butter, *divided*

FILLING:

2	cups (8 ounces) shredded cheddar cheese, *divided*
1-1/2	cups cubed fully cooked ham
1	egg, lightly beaten
1	tablespoon water

POTATO HAM OMELET PIE

"Time-consuming but worth the effort. I used a very thick slice of deli ham, cubed. Lots of rave reviews for this one! Thanks! "

—*ronayne*

1. On a lightly floured surface, roll each puff pastry sheet into a 12-in. square. Place one square in a 10-in. quiche dish; set dish and remaining pastry aside. In a large skillet, melt butter. Add potatoes, onion, salt and pepper; cover and cook for 10-12 minutes or until potatoes are tender and golden brown, stirring occasionally. Set aside.

2. In a large bowl, beat the eggs, parsley, water, salt and pepper. In a 10-in. skillet, melt 1 tablespoon butter; add half of the egg mixture. Cook over medium heat. As eggs set, lift edges, letting uncooked portion flow underneath. Continue cooking until set. Slide omelet onto a baking sheet. Repeat with remaining butter and egg mixture to make a second omelet.

3. Sprinkle 1 cup cheese over prepared pastry. Top with one omelet and half of the potato mixture. Layer with ham and the remaining potato mixture, cheese, omelet and puff pastry. Trim pastry to fit dish; seal and flute edges. In a small bowl, combine egg and water; brush over pastry. Bake at 375° for 30-35 minutes or until golden brown. Let stand for 10 minutes before serving.

[2005]

BRUNCH STRATA

yield: 2 casseroles (8 servings each)
prep: 45 min. ∞ bake: 35 min. + standing

(Pictured on page 139)

Ham, zucchini, mushrooms and cheese flavor this rich, hearty egg dish. It adds appeal to a breakfast or lunch buffet and cuts easily, too. Make sure you bring the recipe—everyone will want it.

—*Arlene Butler, Ogden, Utah, Field Editor*

- 3 cups sliced fresh mushrooms
- 3 cups chopped zucchini
- 2 cups cubed fully cooked ham
- 1-1/2 cups chopped onions
- 1-1/2 cups chopped green peppers
- 1/3 cup canola oil
- 2 garlic cloves, minced
- 2 packages (8 ounces *each*) cream cheese, softened
- 1/2 cup half-and-half cream
- 12 eggs, lightly beaten
- 4 cups cubed day-old bread
- 3 cups (12 ounces) shredded cheddar cheese
- 1 teaspoon salt
- 1/2 teaspoon pepper

---

1. In a large skillet, saute the mushrooms, zucchini, ham, onions, green peppers in oil until vegetables are tender. Add garlic; cook 1 minute longer. Drain and pat dry; set aside.

2. In a large bowl, beat cream cheese and cream until smooth. Beat in eggs. Stir in the bread, cheese, salt, pepper and vegetable mixture.

3. Pour into two greased 11-in. x 7-in. baking dishes. Bake, uncovered, at 350° for 35-40 minutes or until a knife inserted near the center comes out clean. Let stand for 10 minutes before serving.

[2003]

MEXICAN EGG CASSEROLE

yield: 8 servings ∞ prep: 15 min.
bake: 45 min.

Tomatoes and green chilies give color and zip to this very cheesy egg bake. It makes a hearty morning entree, or you can enjoy a square topped with salsa for lunch or supper.

—*Mary Steiner*
West Bend, Wisconsin, Field Editor

- 1/2 cup all-purpose flour
- 1 teaspoon baking powder
- 12 eggs, lightly beaten
- 4 cups (16 ounces) shredded Monterey Jack cheese, *divided*
- 2 cups (16 ounces) 4% cottage cheese
- 2 plum tomatoes, seeded and diced
- 1 can (4 ounces) chopped green chilies, drained
- 4 green onions, sliced
- 1/2 teaspoon hot pepper sauce
- 1 teaspoon dried oregano
- 2 tablespoons minced fresh cilantro
- 1/2 teaspoon salt
- 1/2 teaspoon pepper

Salsa, optional

---

1. In a large bowl, combine the flour and baking powder. Add the eggs, 3-1/2 cups Monterey Jack cheese, cottage cheese, tomatoes, chilies, onions, hot pepper sauce, oregano, cilantro, salt and pepper. Pour into a greased 13-in. x 9-in. baking dish. Sprinkle with the remaining Monterey Jack cheese.

2. Bake casserole, uncovered, at 400° for 15 minutes. Reduce heat to 350°; bake 30 minutes longer or until a knife inserted near the center comes out clean. Let stand for 5 minutes before cutting. Serve with salsa if desired.

BRUNCH STRATA

❝I have made this more times than I can count, always with the same results—requests for the recipe!❞
—*dianervt*

[2001]

BLT EGG BAKE

yield: 4 servings ∾ prep/total time: 30 min.

(*Pictured on page 138*)

BLT's are a favorite at my house, so I created this recipe to combine those flavors in a "dressier" dish. It was such a hit, I served it to my church ladies' group at a brunch I hosted. I received lots of compliments and wrote out the recipe many times that day.

—*Priscilla Detrick, Catoosa, Oklahoma*

1/4	cup mayonnaise
5	slices bread, toasted
4	slices process American cheese
12	bacon strips, cooked and crumbled
4	eggs
1	medium tomato, halved and sliced
2	tablespoons butter
2	tablespoons all-purpose flour
1/4	teaspoon salt
1/8	teaspoon pepper
1	cup 2% milk
1/2	cup shredded cheddar cheese
2	green onions, thinly sliced

Shredded lettuce

---

1. Spread mayonnaise on one side of each slice of toast and cut into small pieces. Arrange toast, mayonnaise side up, in a greased 8-in. square baking dish. Top with cheese slices and bacon.

2. In a large skillet, fry the eggs over medium heat until completely set; place over bacon. Top with tomato slices; set aside.

3. In a small saucepan, melt butter. Stir in the flour, salt and pepper until smooth. Gradually add milk. Bring to a boil; cook and stir for 2 minutes or until thickened.

4. Pour over tomatoes. Sprinkle with cheddar cheese and onions. Bake, uncovered, at 325° for 10 minutes. Cut in squares; serve with lettuce.

[2011]

ITALIAN BRUNCH TORTE

yield: 12 servings ∾ prep: 50 min.
bake 1 hour + standing

(*Pictured on page 142*)

We always serve this impressive layered breakfast bake with a salad of mixed greens and tomato wedges. It is one of our most requested dishes and can be served warm or cold.

—*Danny Diamond*
Farmington Hills, Michigan

2	tubes (8 ounces *each*) refrigerated crescent rolls, *divided*
1	package (6 ounces) fresh baby spinach
1	cup sliced fresh mushrooms
1	teaspoon olive oil
7	eggs
1	cup grated Parmesan cheese
2	teaspoons Italian seasoning
1/8	teaspoon pepper
1/2	pound thinly sliced deli ham
1/2	pound thinly sliced hard salami
1/2	pound sliced provolone cheese
2	jars (12 ounces *each*) roasted sweet red peppers, drained, sliced and patted dry

---

1. Place a greased 9-in. springform pan on a double thickness of heavy-duty foil (about 18 in. square). Securely wrap foil around pan. Separate one tube crescent dough into eight triangles; press onto bottom of prepared pan. Bake at 350° for 10-15 minutes or until set.

2. Meanwhile, in a large skillet over medium heat, cook spinach and mushrooms in oil until spinach is wilted. Place between two paper towels and blot to remove excess liquid. In a large bowl, whisk six eggs, Parmesan cheese, Italian seasoning and pepper.

3. Layer prepared crust with half of the ham, salami, provolone cheese, red

peppers, the spinach mixture and the egg mixture. Repeat the layers.

4. Separate remaining crescent dough; press triangles together to form a top crust. Place over casserole. Whisk remaining egg; brush over dough.

5. Bake, uncovered, at 350° for 1 to 1-1/4 hours or until a thermometer reads 160°. Cover loosely with foil if top browns too quickly. Carefully run a knife around edge of pan to loosen; remove sides of pan. Let stand for 20 minutes before slicing.

[1995]

SOUTHWESTERN OMELET

yield: 4 servings ∽ prep/total time: 20 min.

(Pictured on page 142)

Flavors of the Southwest spark the eggs in this dish. Hearty home-style food is popular in our small farming and timber community.

—*Patricia Collins, Imbler, Oregon, Former Field Editor*

1/2 cup chopped onion
1 jalapeno pepper, minced
1 tablespoon canola oil
6 eggs, lightly beaten
6 bacon strips, cooked and crumbled
1 small tomato, chopped
1 ripe avocado, cut into 1-inch slices
1 cup (4 ounces) shredded Monterey Jack cheese, *divided*
Salt and pepper to taste
Salsa, optional

1. In a large skillet, saute onion and jalapeno in oil until tender; remove with a slotted spoon and set aside. Pour eggs into the same skillet; cover and cook over low heat for 3-4 minutes.

2. Sprinkle with onion mixture, bacon, tomato, avocado and 1/2 cup cheese. Season with salt and pepper.

3. Fold omelet in half over filling. Cover and cook for 3-4 minutes or until eggs are set. Sprinkle with remaining cheese. Serve with salsa if desired.

Editor's Note: Wear disposable gloves when cutting hot peppers; the oils can burn skin. Avoid touching your face.

[2000]

BACON 'N' EGG LASAGNA

yield: 12 servings ∽ prep: 45 min.
bake: 35 min. + standing

My sister-in-law served this special lasagna for Easter breakfast one year, and our whole family loved the mix of bacon, eggs, noodles and cheese. Now I assemble it the night before and bake it in the morning for a terrific and hassle-free brunch entree.

—*Dianne Meyer, Graniteville, Vermont*

1 pound bacon strips, diced
1 large onion, chopped
1/3 cup all-purpose flour
1/2 to 1 teaspoon salt
1/4 teaspoon pepper
4 cups 2% milk
12 lasagna noodles, cooked and drained
12 hard-cooked eggs, sliced
2 cups (8 ounces) shredded Swiss cheese
1/3 cup grated Parmesan cheese
2 tablespoons minced fresh parsley

1. In a large skillet, cook bacon over medium heat until crisp. Using a slotted spoon, remove to paper towels. Drain, reserving 1/3 cup drippings. In the drippings, saute onion until tender. Stir in the flour, salt and pepper until blended. Gradually stir in milk. Bring to a boil; cook and stir for 2 minutes or until thickened. Remove from the heat.

2. Spread 1/2 cup sauce in a greased 13-in. x 9-in. baking dish. Layer with four noodles, a third of the eggs and bacon, Swiss cheese and white sauce. Repeat layers twice. Sprinkle with Parmesan cheese.

3. Bake, uncovered, at 350° for 35-40 minutes or until bubbly. Sprinkle with parsley. Let stand for 15 minutes before cutting.

[2010]

RAINBOW QUICHE

yield: 8 servings ∞ prep: 20 min.
bake: 45 min. + standing

With plenty of veggies and a creamy egg-cheese filling, this tasty quiche gets two thumbs up!

—*Lilith Fury-Thompson, Pittsburgh, Pennsylvania*

Pastry for single-crust pie (9 inches)
1-1/2 cups chopped fresh broccoli florets
   1 small onion, finely chopped
   1 cup sliced fresh mushrooms
   1 each small green, sweet red and orange peppers, finely chopped
   2 tablespoons butter
   1 cup chopped fresh spinach
   1 cup (4 ounces) shredded Mexican cheese blend
   6 eggs, lightly beaten
1-3/4 cups 2% milk
   1/2 teaspoon salt

1. Line a 9-in. deep-dish pie plate with pastry; trim and flute edges. In a large skillet, saute the broccoli, onion, mushrooms and peppers in butter until tender. Stir in spinach. Spoon into prepared crust; sprinkle with the cheese. In a large bowl, whisk the eggs, milk and salt; pour over cheese.

2. Bake at 350° for 45-55 minutes or until a knife inserted near center comes out clean. Let stand for 10 minutes before cutting.

[2006]

OMELET CASSEROLE FOR 60

yield: 60 servings ∞ prep: 35 min. ∞ bake: 40 min.

Not only is this dish simple to make, it's also perfect for a church breakfast or an afternoon brunch. The Swiss cheese and diced ham add nice flavor.

—*Renee Schwebach, Dumont, Minnesota, Field Editor*

   1 cup butter, melted
 100 eggs
2-1/2 quarts 2% milk
1-1/4 teaspoons white pepper
7-1/2 cups (30 ounces) shredded Swiss cheese
7-1/2 cups cubed fully cooked ham

1. Divide the butter among five 13-in. x 9-in. baking dishes; set aside. In a large bowl, beat 20 eggs, 2 cups milk and 1/4 teaspoon pepper until blended. Stir in 1-1/2 cups cheese and 1-1/2 cups ham; pour into one prepared dish. Repeat four times.

2. Bake, uncovered, at 350° for 40-45 minutes or until a knife inserted near the center comes out clean (cover with foil if the top browns too quickly). Let stand for 5 minutes before cutting.

[2004]

SPRING-AHEAD BRUNCH BAKE

yield: 8 servings ∞ prep: 20 min. + chilling ∞ bake: 35 min.

The great taste of this enchilada-style dish makes it popular with my family. The fact that it can be made ahead makes it popular with me.

—*Lois Jacobsen, Dallas, Wisconsin*

   2 cups sliced fresh mushrooms
   1/2 cup sliced green onions
   1/2 cup chopped green pepper
   2 tablespoons butter
   8 slices deli ham
   8 flour tortillas (7 inches), warmed
1-1/2 cups (6 ounces) shredded Swiss cheese
   1/2 cup shredded cheddar cheese
   1 tablespoon all-purpose flour
   4 eggs, lightly beaten
   2 cups 2% milk
   1/4 teaspoon garlic powder
   1/4 teaspoon salt
   1/8 teaspoon hot pepper sauce

1. In a large skillet, saute the mushrooms, onions and green pepper in butter until tender; set aside. Place one slice of ham on each tortilla. Top each with about 1/4 cup mushroom mixture. Combine cheeses; set aside 1/4 cup. Sprinkle remaining cheese over tortillas.

2. Roll up tortillas. Place seam side down in a greased 11-in. x 7-in. baking dish. In a large bowl, beat the flour, eggs, milk, garlic powder, salt and hot pepper sauce until blended.

3. Pour over tortillas. Sprinkle with reserved 1/4 cup cheese. Cover and refrigerate for at least 30 minutes.

4. Bake, uncovered, at 350° for 35-45 minutes or until set.

[2010]

PECAN APPLE PANCAKES

yield: 1-1/2 dozen ∞ **prep: 15 min.** ∞ **cook: 10 min./batch**

(Pictured on page 141)

Weekend breakfasts are a big deal here in Texas, and these sweet, well-spiced pancakes make any breakfast special. So put on your apron and invite the neighbors in!

—*Sharon Richardson, Dallas, Texas*

---

2 cups all-purpose flour
1 cup sugar
2 teaspoons baking powder
1 teaspoon baking soda
1 teaspoon ground cinnamon
1/2 teaspoon salt
1/2 teaspoon ground ginger
1/2 teaspoon ground mace
1/2 teaspoon ground cloves
2 eggs
1-3/4 cups buttermilk
3 tablespoons canola oil
1-3/4 cups shredded peeled apples
1/2 cup chopped pecans

---

1. In a large bowl, combine the first nine ingredients. In another bowl, combine the eggs, buttermilk and oil; stir into dry ingredients just until blended. Stir in apples and pecans.

2. Pour batter by 1/4 cupfuls onto a greased griddle over medium-low heat. Turn when bubbles form on top; cook until second side is golden brown.

PECAN APPLE PANCAKES

"I'm really not a pancake person, but these are so de-LISH! They smell and taste like Christmas. I think they're perfect just the way they are. It's a great combination of spices. My family and I love them with buttermilk syrup. Highly recommend this recipe."

— *kristinscotth*

WHEN TO FLIP PANCAKES

Turn pancakes over when edges become dry and bubbles that appear on top begin to pop.

[2003]

CHERRY CHEESE BLINTZES

yield: 9 servings ∾ **prep: 30 min. + chilling
bake: 10 min.**

(Pictured on page 141)

These elegant blintzes can be served as an attractive dessert or a brunch entree. The bright cherry sauce gives them a delightful flavor. I sometimes substitute other fruits, such as raspberries, blueberries or peaches.

—Jessica Vantrease, Anderson, Alaska

1-1/2   cups 2% milk
    3   eggs
    2   tablespoons butter, melted
  2/3   cup all-purpose flour
  1/2   teaspoon salt
FILLING:
    1   cup (8 ounces) 4% cottage cheese
    1   package (3 ounces) cream cheese, softened
  1/4   cup sugar
  1/2   teaspoon vanilla extract
CHERRY SAUCE:
    1   pound fresh *or* frozen pitted sweet cherries
  2/3   cup plus 1 tablespoon water, *divided*
  1/4   cup sugar
    1   tablespoon cornstarch

1. In a small bowl, combine the milk, eggs and butter. Combine flour and salt; add to milk mixture and mix well. Cover and refrigerate for 2 hours.

2. Heat a lightly greased 8-in. nonstick skillet; pour 2 tablespoons batter into the center of skillet. Lift and tilt pan to evenly coat bottom. Cook until top appears dry; turn and cook 15-20 seconds longer. Remove to a wire rack. Repeat with remaining batter. When cool, stack crepes with waxed paper or paper towels in between. Wrap in foil; refrigerate.

3. In a blender, process cottage cheese until smooth. Transfer to a small bowl; add cream cheese and beat until smooth. Beat in sugar and vanilla. Spread about 1 rounded tablespoonful onto each crepe. Fold opposite sides of crepe over filling, forming a little bundle.

4. Place seam side down in a greased 15-in. x 10-in. x 1-in. baking pan. Bake, uncovered, at 350° for 10 minutes or until heated through.

5. Meanwhile, in a large saucepan, bring cherries, 2/3 cup water and sugar to a boil over medium heat. Reduce heat; cover and simmer for 5 minutes or until heated through. Combine cornstarch and remaining water until smooth; stir into cherry mixture. Bring to a boil; cook and stir for 2 minutes or until thickened. Serve with crepes.

[2010]

ROLLED SWEDISH PANCAKES

yield: 1 dozen ∾ **prep/total time: 20 min.**

We love the hint of lemon wrapped inside these rich flavorful pancakes. While we use sour cream and cherry preserves , you can use your favorite flavor of preserves.

—Tami Escher, Dumont, Minnesota, Field Editor

  1/2   cup plus 1 tablespoon sugar, *divided*
    2   tablespoons grated lemon peel
1-1/2   cups all-purpose flour
  1/2   teaspoon salt
    8   eggs, lightly beaten
    3   cups 2% milk
    3   tablespoons butter, melted
Sour cream and cherry preserves

1. Combine 1/2 cup sugar and the lemon peel; set aside. In a large bowl, combine the flour, salt and remaining sugar. Beat the eggs, milk and butter; stir into dry ingredients and mix well.

2. Pour batter by 1/2 cupfuls onto a lightly greased hot griddle; turn when set and lightly browned. Cook 1 minute longer.

3. Immediately sprinkle each pancake with lemon sugar mixture; roll up and keep warm. Top with sour cream and preserves.

SOUR CREAM CARDAMOM WAFFLES, page 146

BLT EGG BAKE, page 132

TOMATO QUICHE, page 127

FRUIT 'N' NUT STOLLEN, page 153

BRUNCH STRATA, page 131

GARDEN VEGETABLE QUICHE, page 129

CHERRY COFFEE CAKE, page 151

CARAMEL-PECAN CINNAMON ROLLS, page 155

JAM 'N' CREAM FRENCH TOAST, page 147

OATMEAL BRULEE WITH GINGER CREAM, page 149

CHERRY CHEESE BLINTZES, page 136

PECAN APPLE PANCAKES, page 135

SPIRAL OMELET SUPREME, page 127

POTATO HAM OMELET PIE, page 130

SOUTHWESTERN OMELET, page 133

ITALIAN BRUNCH TORTE, page 132

BLUEBERRY SOUR CREAM COFFEE CAKE, page 151

OVERNIGHT CHERRY DANISH, page 154

AVOCADO EGGS BENEDICT, page 128

[2002]
APPLE-HONEY DUTCH BABY

yield: 4 servings ∾ **prep/total time: 30 min.**

I love to make this treat on Sunday morning. It's so impressive when it's served warm right out of the oven, and the honey and apple filling is yummy!

—Kathy Fleming, Lisle, Illinois

- 3/4 cup all-purpose flour
- 1 tablespoon sugar
- 3 eggs
- 3/4 cup 2% milk
- 2 tablespoons butter

TOPPING:
- 2 large apples, sliced
- 1 tablespoon butter
- 1/2 cup honey
- 2 to 3 teaspoons lemon juice
- 1/2 teaspoon ground cardamom
- 1 teaspoon cornstarch
- 2 teaspoons cold water

1. In a large bowl, whisk the flour, sugar, eggs and milk until smooth. Place butter in a 10-in. ovenproof skillet. Heat at 400° for 3-4 minutes or until melted; tilt pan to coat bottom and sides. Pour batter into hot skillet. Bake for 16-20 minutes or until edges are lightly browned.

2. Meanwhile, in a large saucepan, saute the apples in butter until lightly browned. Stir in the honey, lemon juice and cardamom. Combine the cornstarch and water until smooth; add to the apple mixture. Bring to a boil; cook and stir for 2 minutes or until thickened. Spoon into pancake. Serve immediately.

[2009]
BLUEBERRY CHEESECAKE FLAPJACKS

yield: 12 pancakes (3/4 cup topping)
prep: 30 min. ∾ **cook: 5 min./batch**

These flapjacks are so pretty, it's tempting to just gaze at them. But as good as they are to look at, they're even better to eat!

—Donna Cline, Pensacola, Florida

- 1 package (3 ounces) cream cheese, softened
- 3/4 cup whipped topping
- 1 cup all-purpose flour
- 1/2 cup graham cracker crumbs
- 1 tablespoon sugar
- 1 teaspoon baking powder
- 1/2 teaspoon baking soda
- 1/4 teaspoon salt
- 2 eggs, lightly beaten
- 1-1/4 cups buttermilk
- 1/4 cup butter, melted
- 1 cup fresh *or* frozen blueberries
- 3/4 cup maple syrup, warmed

Additional blueberries, optional

TOP 100 RECIPE

1. For topping, in a small bowl, beat cream cheese and whipped topping until smooth. Chill until serving.

2. In a large bowl, combine the flour, cracker crumbs, sugar, baking powder, baking soda and salt. Combine the eggs, buttermilk and butter; add to dry ingredients just until moistened. Fold in blueberries.

3. Pour batter by 1/4 cupfuls onto a greased hot griddle; turn when bubbles form on top. Cook until the second side is golden brown. Spread topping over pancakes. Top with warm syrup; sprinkle with additional blueberries if desired.

Editor's Note: If using frozen blueberries, use them without thawing to avoid discoloring the batter.

BLUEBERRY CHEESECAKE FLAPJACKS

"These pancakes were excellent. They had a good balance of sweetness and tanginess. I've made them several times, and they are always a hit!"
—KitKat204

[2000]

STRAWBERRY-TOPPED WAFFLES

yield: 6-8 waffles ⬥ prep/total time: 30 min.

Topped with a sweet strawberry sauce, these tender from-scratch waffles will make a breakfast or brunch truly special.

—*Sue Mackey*
Jackson, Wisconsin, Field Editor

---

  2 pints fresh strawberries
  5 tablespoons sugar, *divided*
  2 cups all-purpose flour
  2 teaspoons baking powder
1/2 teaspoon baking soda
1/2 teaspoon salt
  2 eggs
  2 cups (16 ounces) sour cream
  1 cup 2% milk
  3 tablespoons canola oil
Whipped topping *or* vanilla ice cream
Additional strawberries, optional

---

1. Process strawberries and 3 tablespoons of sugar in a food processor until coarsely chopped; set aside.

2. In a large bowl, combine flour, baking powder, baking soda, salt and remaining sugar. In another bowl, whisk the eggs, sour cream, milk and oil; stir into the dry ingredients just until combined.

3. Bake in a preheated waffle iron according to manufacturer's directions until golden brown. Serve with the strawberry topping, whipped topping and additional strawberries if desired.

[1997]

SOUR CREAM CARDAMOM WAFFLES

yield: 6 waffles (about 6-1/2 inches)
prep/total time: 25 min.

(Pictured on page 137)

Cardamom has such a delicate flavor. I've been making coffee cakes with this interesting spice for years, and now I found a use for it in waffles. More often than not, my family will request these waffles instead of plain ones.

—*Ruth Andrewson*
Leavenworth, Washington
Former Field Editor

---

  1 cup all-purpose flour
1/4 cup sugar
  1 teaspoon baking powder
  1 teaspoon ground cardamom
Dash salt
2/3 cup 2% milk
2/3 cup sour cream
1/4 cup butter, melted
  2 eggs, *separated*
Honey *or* syrup

---

1. In a bowl, combine flour, sugar, baking powder, cardamom and salt. In a small bowl, combine milk, sour cream, butter and egg yolks; stir into dry ingredients just until combined. Beat egg whites until stiff peaks form; fold into batter.

2. Bake in a preheated waffle iron according to manufacturer's directions until golden brown (waffles will be soft). Serve with honey or syrup.

EXTRA WAFFLES & PANCAKES

Don't throw away leftover waffles or pancakes. Freeze them in a single layer on a baking sheet and when frozen, transfer to freezer bags. Reheat them in the toaster oven for a quick weekday breakfast.

—*Taste of Home Cooking Experts*

[2005]

JAM 'N' CREAM FRENCH TOAST

yield: 1 serving ∾ **prep/total time: 10 min.**

(Pictured on page 140)

My grandmother used to make this for me when I was a child. You can experiment with other flavors of jam and bread.

—*B MacKinnon, Kodak, Tennessee*

2 tablespoons cream cheese, softened
2 thick slices cinnamon-raisin bread
2 tablespoons strawberry jam
1 egg
1 tablespoon butter
Maple syrup, optional

1. Spread cream cheese on one slice of bread. Spread jam on the other slice; place jam side down over the cream cheese. In a shallow bowl, beat egg. Dip both sides of bread into egg.

2. In a small skillet, melt butter; toast the bread for 3-4 minutes on each side or until golden brown. Serve with syrup if desired.

[2006]

SWEET CHERRY FRENCH TOAST

yield: 4 servings ∾ **prep: 15 min. + chilling** ∾ **bake: 10 min.**

You'll be delighted to serve this tasty brunch bake. The cherry topping and dollop of yogurt make each bite a special treat.

—*Elisa Lochridge, Beaverton, Oregon*

8 slices French bread (1 inch thick)
6 eggs, lightly beaten
1-1/2 cups 2% milk
1/3 cup maple syrup
2 tablespoons sugar
1 tablespoon grated orange peel
1/8 teaspoon salt
CHERRY TOPPING:
4 cups fresh *or* frozen pitted sweet cherries
1/2 cup orange juice
1 tablespoon sugar
4 teaspoons cornstarch
4 teaspoons cold water
Vanilla yogurt

1. Place the bread in a greased 15-in. x 10-in. x 1-in. baking pan. In a large bowl, whisk the eggs, milk, syrup, sugar, orange peel and salt. Pour over bread; turn to coat. Cover and refrigerate overnight. In another large bowl, combine the cherries, orange juice and sugar. Cover and refrigerate overnight.

2. Transfer bread slices to another greased 15-in. x 10-in. x 1-in. baking pan. Discard any remaining egg mixture. Bake at 400° for 7-9 minutes or until golden brown.

3. Meanwhile, in a small saucepan, combine cornstarch and water until smooth. Stir in the reserved cherry mixture. Bring to a boil; cook and stir for 2 minutes or until thickened. Serve over French toast; drizzle with yogurt.

[2000]

ORANGE-CINNAMON FRENCH TOAST

yield: 6 slices ∾ **prep/total time: 30 min.**

Everyone eats at the same time when you fix this tasty oven-baked French toast.

—*Bernice Smith, Sturgeon Lake, Minnesota*

2 to 4 tablespoons butter, melted
2 tablespoons honey
1/2 teaspoon ground cinnamon
3 eggs
1/2 cup orange juice
1/8 teaspoon salt, optional
6 slices bread
Additional honey, optional

1. In a small bowl, combine the butter, honey and cinnamon. Pour into a greased 13-in. x 9-in. baking pan; spread to coat bottom of pan.

2. In a shallow bowl, beat the eggs, orange juice and salt if desired. Dip bread into egg mixture and place in prepared pan.

3. Bake French toast at 400° for 15-20 minutes or until golden brown. Invert onto a serving platter; serve with honey if desired.

GLAZED FRUIT MEDLEY

"This is an AWESOME, refreshing summer side dish!! My family can not get enough. It's easy to make and great for potlucks!! I add cantaloupe and every other fruit that's in season. It's a must have in the ol' recipe file."

—hahymen

[2006]

TURKEY SAUSAGE PATTIES

yield: 6 patties ∾ prep: 10 min. + chilling
cook: 15 min.

Eat smart, starting with this homemade turkey sausage. If you like garlic, try substituting it for the sage.

—Janice Wuertzer, Dubuque, Iowa

- 1 small onion, finely chopped
- 1/4 cup dry bread crumbs
- 1 teaspoon rubbed sage
- 1/2 teaspoon salt
- 1/2 teaspoon paprika
- 1/4 teaspoon pepper
- 1 pound lean ground turkey
- 2 teaspoons canola oil

1. In a large bowl, combine the onion, bread crumbs, sage, salt, paprika and pepper. Crumble turkey over mixture and mix well. Shape into six patties. Cover and refrigerate for 2 hours.

2. In a large nonstick skillet over medium heat, cook patties in oil for 7 minutes on each side or until meat is no longer pink.

[2012]

BROWN SUGAR & BANANA OATMEAL

yield: 3 servings ∾ prep/total time: 15 min.

When it is nippy outside, oatmeal is just the thing to warm you up. It is one of my favorite breakfast foods. It's quick, easy, and good for you! I came up with this version by using some of the same ingredients from my favorite breakfast smoothie recipes.

—Jessi Rizzi, Odenton, Maryland

- 2 cups fat-free milk
- 1 cup quick-cooking oats
- 1 large ripe banana, sliced
- 2 teaspoons brown sugar
- 1 teaspoon honey
- 1/2 teaspoon ground cinnamon
Additional fat-free milk, optional

1. In a small saucepan, bring milk to a boil; stir in oats. Cook over medium heat for 1-2 minutes or until thickened, stirring occasionally.

2. Stir in the banana, brown sugar, honey and cinnamon. Divide among three serving bowls. Serve with additional milk if desired.

[2006]

GLAZED FRUIT MEDLEY

yield: 10 servings ∾ prep: 20 min. + chilling

The orange dressing on this salad complements the fresh fruit flavors beautifully. It's perfect for a spring or summer brunch.

—Karen Bourne
Magrath, Alberta, Field Editor

- 1 cup sugar
- 2 tablespoons cornstarch
- 2 cups orange juice
- 3 cups cubed honeydew
- 3 medium firm bananas, sliced
- 2 cups halved fresh strawberries
- 2 cups green grapes

1. In a small saucepan, combine the sugar, cornstarch and orange juice until smooth. Bring to a boil; cook and stir for 2 minutes or until thickened. Transfer to a small bowl. Cover and chill for 2 hours.

2. In a large serving bowl, combine the honeydew, bananas, strawberries and grapes. Drizzle with glaze; gently toss to coat.

[2009]

OATMEAL BRULEE WITH GINGER CREAM

yield: 4 servings ∞ prep: 30 min.
broil: 10 min.

(Pictured on page 141)

This is a lovely dish for a chilly morning. I adore the crispy, caramelized top and raspberry surprise at the bottom.

—Yvonne Starlin, Hermitage, Tennessee

GINGER CREAM:

- 1/2 cup heavy whipping cream
- 2 slices fresh gingerroot (about 3/4-inch diameter)
- 1 cinnamon stick (3 inches)
- 1 tablespoon grated orange peel
- 3 tablespoons maple syrup
- 1/8 teaspoon ground nutmeg

OATMEAL:

- 4 cups water
- 2 cups old-fashioned oats
- 1/4 cup chopped dried apricots
- 1/4 cup dried cherries, chopped
- 1/2 teaspoon salt
- 3 tablespoons brown sugar
- 2 tablespoons butter
- 1 cup fresh *or* frozen unsweetened raspberries, thawed
- 1/4 cup sugar

1. In a small saucepan, bring the cream, ginger, cinnamon and orange peel to a boil. Reduce heat; cover and simmer for 10 minutes. Remove from the heat; strain and discard the solids. Stir in syrup and nutmeg; set aside.

2. In a large saucepan over medium heat, bring water to a boil. Add the oats, apricots, cherries and salt; cook and stir for 5 minutes. Remove from the heat; stir in brown sugar and 1/4 cup ginger cream. Cover and let stand for 2 minutes.

3. Grease four 10-oz. ramekins with butter; add raspberries. Spoon in oatmeal; sprinkle with sugar. Place on a baking sheet. Broil 4-6 in. from heat for 7-9 minutes or until sugar is caramelized. Serve with remaining ginger cream.

[2010]

SUPER LOW-FAT GRANOLA CEREAL

yield: 9 cups ∞ prep: 15 min.
bake: 25 min. + cooling

Serve this delicious mix for breakfast with milk, or sprinkle it over yogurt. You can add chopped walnuts or pecans, but it will increase the calorie count.

—Kelly Kirby
Westville, Nova Scotia, Field Editor

- 8 cups old-fashioned oats
- 1 cup raisins
- 1/2 cup chopped dried apricots
- 1/2 cup dried cranberries
- 1-1/2 cups packed brown sugar
- 1/2 cup water
- 1 teaspoon salt
- 1 teaspoon maple flavoring
- 1 teaspoon vanilla extract
- 2% milk *or* reduced-fat plain yogurt

1. In a large bowl, combine the oats, raisins, apricots and cranberries; set aside. In a small saucepan, combine the brown sugar, water and salt. Cook and stir over medium heat for 3-4 minutes or until brown sugar is dissolved. Remove from the heat; stir in maple flavoring and vanilla. Pour over oat mixture; stir to coat.

2. Transfer to two greased 15-in. x 10-in. x 1-in. baking pans. Bake at 350° for 25-30 minutes or until crisp, stirring every 10 minutes. Cool completely on wire racks. Store granola in an airtight container. Serve with milk or yogurt.

SUPER LOW-FAT GRANOLA CEREAL

"No more buying granola for me! I was really impressed at the ease of this recipe & its delicious results—it's easy to substitute ingredients to your family's liking! I made this this not even 2 days ago, and it's almost gone!"
—Karli Gorsline

[1999]

ORANGE-GLAZED CRULLERS

yield: about 3 dozen ∽ **prep: 25 min. + rising**
cook: 20 min. + chilling

I enjoy preparing these lovely treats with my grandchildren. The make-ahead dough is handy for a gathering.

—*Muriel Lerdal, Humboldt, Iowa, Former Field Editor*

1 package (1/4 ounce) active dry yeast
1/4 cup warm water (110° to 115°)
3/4 cup warm 2% milk (110° to 115°)
1/2 cup butter, softened
2 eggs, lightly beaten
1/4 cup sugar
1 teaspoon salt
4 cups all-purpose flour
Oil for deep-fat frying
GLAZE:
2 cups confectioners' sugar
3 tablespoons orange juice
1 teaspoon grated orange peel

1. In a large bowl, dissolve yeast in water. Beat in the milk, butter, eggs, sugar, salt and 2 cups of flour. Beat until smooth. Stir in enough remaining flour to form a soft dough. Place in a greased bowl, turning once to grease top. Cover and refrigerate overnight.

2. Punch dough down; divide in half. Return one portion to the refrigerator. On a floured surface, roll out the second portion into an 18-in. x 9-in. rectangle; cut width-wise into 3/4-in. strips. Fold each strip in half lengthwise and then twist several times. Pinch the ends to seal.

3. Place on greased baking sheets. Repeat with the remaining dough. Cover and let rise until almost doubled, about 35-45 minutes.

4. In an electric skillet or deep-fat fryer, heat oil to 375°. Fry crullers, a few at a time, about 1 minute on each side or until golden brown, turning with a slotted spoon. Drain on paper towels. In a small bowl, combine glaze ingredients; brush over warm crullers.

[2010]

OLD-TIME CAKE DOUGHNUTS

yield: about 2 dozen ∽ **prep: 30 min. + chilling**
cook: 5 min./batch

This tender cake doughnut is a little piece of heaven at breakfast. For a variation, add 1 tablespoon dark rum for a richer flavor.

—*Alissa Stehr, Gau-Odernheim, Germany*

2 tablespoons unsalted butter, softened
1-1/2 cups sugar, *divided*
3 eggs
4 cups all-purpose flour
1 tablespoon baking powder
3 teaspoons ground cinnamon, *divided*
1/2 teaspoon salt
1/8 teaspoon ground nutmeg
3/4 cup 2% milk
Oil for deep-fat frying

(TOP 100 RECIPE)

1. In a large bowl, beat butter and 1 cup sugar until crumbly, about 2 minutes. Add eggs, one at a time, beating well after each addition.

2. Combine the flour, baking powder, 1 teaspoon cinnamon, salt and nutmeg; add to butter mixture alternately with milk, beating well after each addition. Cover and refrigerate for 2 hours.

3. Turn onto a heavily floured surface; pat dough to 1/4-in. thickness. Cut with a floured 2-1/2-in. doughnut cutter.

4. In an electric skillet or deep fryer, heat oil to 375°. Fry the doughnuts, a few at a time, until golden brown on both sides. Drain on paper towels.

5. Combine remaining sugar and cinnamon; roll warm doughnuts in mixture.

[2006]

BLUEBERRY SOUR CREAM COFFEE CAKE

yield: 10-12 servings ✎ prep: 25 min.
bake: 55 min. + cooling

(Pictured on page 142)

Holiday breakfasts would not be the same at our house without this delectable coffee cake. Whenever I take it anywhere, everyone raves about it and wants the recipe.

—Susan Walschlager, Anderson, Indiana

3/4 cup butter, softened
1-1/2 cups sugar
4 eggs
1 teaspoon vanilla extract
3 cups all-purpose flour
1-1/2 teaspoons baking powder
3/4 teaspoon baking soda
1/4 teaspoon salt
1 cup (8 ounces) sour cream
FILLING:
1/4 cup packed brown sugar
1 tablespoon all-purpose flour
1/2 teaspoon ground cinnamon
2 cups fresh *or* frozen blueberries
GLAZE:
1 cup confectioners' sugar
2 to 3 tablespoons 2% milk

1. In a large bowl, cream butter and sugar until light and fluffy. Add eggs, one at a time, beating well after each addition. Beat in vanilla. Combine the flour, baking powder, baking soda and salt; add to creamed mixture alternately with sour cream, beating well after each addition.

2. Spoon a third of the batter into a greased and floured 10-in. tube pan. Combine brown sugar, flour and cinnamon; sprinkle half over batter. Top with half of the berries. Repeat layers. Top with remaining batter.

3. Bake at 350° for 55-65 minutes or until a toothpick inserted near the center comes out clean. Cool for 10 minutes; remove from pan to a wire rack to cool completely. Combine glaze ingredients; drizzle over warm coffee cake.

Editor's Note: If using frozen blueberries, use them without thawing to avoid discoloring the batter.

[2006]

CHERRY COFFEE CAKE

yield: 12-16 servings ✎ prep: 25 min.
bake: 35 min. + cooling

(Pictured on page 139)

With its pretty layer of cherries and crunchy streusel topping, this coffee cake is great for breakfast. Or you can even serve it for dessert.

—Gail Buss, Beverly Hills, Florida

1 package (18-1/4 ounces) yellow cake mix, *divided*
1 cup all-purpose flour
1 package (1/4 ounce) active dry yeast
2/3 cup warm water (120° to 130°)
2 eggs, lightly beaten
1 can (21 ounces) cherry pie filling
1/3 cup cold butter, cubed
GLAZE:
1 cup confectioners' sugar
1 tablespoon corn syrup
1 to 2 tablespoons water

1. In a large bowl, combine 1-1/2 cups cake mix, flour, yeast and water until smooth. Stir in eggs until blended. Transfer to a greased 13-in. x 9-in. baking dish. Gently spoon pie filling over top.

2. In a small bowl, place remaining cake mix; cut in butter until crumbly. Sprinkle over filling.

3. Bake at 350° for 35-40 minutes or until lightly browned. Cool on a wire rack. Combine the confectioners' sugar, corn syrup and enough water to achieve desired consistency. Drizzle over warm coffee cake.

BLUEBERRY SOUR CREAM COFFEE CAKE

"I made this delicious, moist cake in a Bundt pan and loved it. I will definitely make this again, but I might try apples instead of blueberries in the fall."
—pepsikin

[2011]

CLASSIC LONG JOHNS

**yield: 2 dozen   prep: 30 min. + rising
cook: 5 min./batch + cooling**

*I came across the recipe for these wonderful raised doughnuts
many years ago. I remember Mom making some similar to these.
You can frost them with maple or chocolate glaze, then top with
chopped nuts, jimmies, toasted coconut or sprinkles.*

—Ann Sorgent, Fond du Lac, Wisconsin

- 2   packages (1/4 ounce each) active dry yeast
- 1/2 cup warm water (110° to 115°)
- 1/2 cup half-and-half cream
- 1/4 cup sugar
- 1/4 cup shortening
- 1   egg
- 1   teaspoon salt
- 1/2 teaspoon ground nutmeg
- 3   to 3-1/2 cups all-purpose flour
- Oil for deep-fat frying
- **MAPLE FROSTING:**
- 1/4 cup packed brown sugar
- 2   tablespoons butter
- 1   tablespoon half-and-half cream
- 1/8 teaspoon maple flavoring
- 1   cup confectioners' sugar
- **CHOCOLATE FROSTING:**
- 2   ounces semisweet chocolate, chopped
- 2   tablespoons butter
- 1   cup confectioners' sugar
- 2   tablespoons boiling water
- 1   teaspoon vanilla extract

---

1. In a large bowl, dissolve yeast in warm water. Add the
   cream, sugar, shortening, egg, salt, nutmeg and 3 cups
   flour. Beat until smooth. Stir in enough remaining
   flour to form a soft dough (dough will be sticky).

2. Turn onto a floured surface; knead until smooth and
   elastic, about 6-8 minutes. Place in a greased bowl,
   turning once to grease the top. Cover and let rise in a
   warm place until doubled, about 1 hour.

3. Punch dough down; divide in half. Turn onto a lightly
   floured surface; roll each half into a 12-in. x 6-in.

rectangle. Cut into 3-in. x 2-in. rectangles. Place on
greased baking sheets. Cover and let rise in a warm
place until doubled, about 30 minutes.

4. In an electric skillet or deep fryer, heat oil to 375°. Fry
   long johns, a few at a time, until golden brown on both
   sides. Drain on paper towels.

5. For maple frosting, combine brown sugar and butter
   in a small saucepan. Bring to a boil; cook and stir for
   2 minutes or until sugar is dissolved. Remove from the
   heat; stir in the cream and maple flavoring. Add the
   confectioners' sugar; beat for 1 minute or until
   smooth. Frost cooled long johns.

6. For chocolate frosting, in a microwave, melt chocolate
   and butter; stir until smooth. Stir in the remaining
   ingredients. Spread over cooled long johns; let stand
   until set.

[2010]

SOUR CREAM
COFFEE CAKE

**yield: 16 servings   prep: 40 min.
bake: 45 min. + cooling**

*This yummy cake is so moist, you won't even need the cup of
coffee! Make it for your next get-together—your guests will
thank you.*

—Kathleen Larimer, Dayton, Ohio

- 2/3 cup chopped pecans
- 2   tablespoons brown sugar
- 1-1/2 teaspoons ground cinnamon
- **BATTER:**
- 1   cup butter, softened
- 2   cups sugar
- 2   eggs
- 1/2 teaspoon vanilla extract
- 2   cups all-purpose flour
- 1   teaspoon baking powder
- 1/4 teaspoon baking soda
- 1/4 teaspoon salt
- 1   cup (8 ounces) sour cream
- Confectioners' sugar

1. In a small bowl, combine the pecans, brown sugar and cinnamon; set aside. In a large bowl, cream butter and sugar until light and fluffy. Add eggs, one at a time, beating well after each addition. Beat in vanilla. Combine the flour, baking powder, baking soda and salt; add to creamed mixture alternately with sour cream, beating well after each addition.

2. Pour half of the batter into a greased and floured 10-in. fluted tube pan; sprinkle with half of the pecan mixture. Gently top with remaining batter and the pecan mixture.

3. Bake at 350° for 45-50 minutes or until a toothpick inserted near the center comes out clean. Cool for 10 minutes before removing from pan to a wire rack to cool completely. Sprinkle with confectioners' sugar.

[2007]

FRUIT 'N' NUT STOLLEN

yield: 3 loaves (12 slices each)
prep: 40 min. + rising ∽ bake: 15 min.
(Pictured on page 138)

Making this stollen has become a tradition for our clan. Our family, friends and neighbors look forward to it every Christmas. We like it because it does not contain the usual candied fruits and citron called for in other stollens.
—*Rebekah Radewahn, Wauwatosa, Wisconsin*

4	to 4-1/2 cups all-purpose flour
1/4	cup sugar
3	teaspoons active dry yeast
1	teaspoon ground cardamom
1/2	teaspoon salt
1-1/4	cups 2% milk
1/2	cup plus 3 tablespoons butter, softened, *divided*
1	egg
1/4	cup *each* raisins and dried cranberries
1/4	cup *each* chopped dried pineapple and apricots
1/4	cup *each* chopped pecans, almonds, Brazil nuts and walnuts
1/2	teaspoon lemon extract

LEMON GLAZE:

1	cup confectioners' sugar
4-1/2	teaspoons lemon juice

1. In a large bowl, combine 2 cups flour, sugar, yeast, cardamom and salt. In a small saucepan, heat milk and 1/2 cup butter to 120°-130°. Add to dry ingredients; beat just until moistened. Add egg; beat until smooth. Stir in enough remaining flour to form a soft dough (dough will be sticky).

2. Turn onto a floured surface; knead until smooth and elastic, about 6-8 minutes. Place in a bowl coated with cooking spray, turning once to coat top. Cover and let rise in a warm place until doubled, about 1 hour. In a small bowl, combine the dried fruits, nuts and extract; set aside.

3. Punch dough down. Turn onto a lightly floured surface; knead fruit mixture into dough. Divide into thirds. Roll each portion into a 10-in. x 8-in. oval. Melt remaining butter; brush over dough. Fold a long side over to within 1 in. of opposite side; press edges lightly to seal. Place on baking sheets coated with cooking spray. Cover and let rise until doubled, about 45 minutes.

4. Bake at 375° for 14-16 minutes or until golden brown. Remove to wire racks. Combine glaze ingredients; drizzle over warm loaves.

CLASSIC STOLLEN

Stollen is a traditional German yeast bread that is studded with dried fruits. This rich bread is folded over to create an oval shape. It's typically served at Christmastime and is frequently topped with a confectioners' sugar glaze, and candied cherries.

—*Taste of Home Cooking Experts*

[2010]

OVERNIGHT CHERRY DANISH

yield: 3 dozen ⟳ **prep: 1-1/2 hours + rising** ⟳ **bake: 15 min. + cooling**

(Pictured on page 143)

These rolls with their cherry-filled centers melt in your mouth and put a touch of holiday color on your table. They store well, unfrosted, in the freezer.

—*Leann Sauder, Tremont, Illinois*

---

      2 packages (1/4 ounce each) active dry yeast
    1/2 cup warm 2% milk (110° to 115°)
      6 cups all-purpose flour
    1/3 cup sugar
      2 teaspoons salt
      1 cup cold butter, cubed
    1-1/2 cups warm half-and-half cream (110° to 115°)
      6 egg yolks, lightly beaten
      1 can (21 ounces) cherry pie filling

ICING:

      2 tablespoons butter, softened
      3 cups confectioners' sugar
    1/4 teaspoon vanilla extract
Dash salt
      4 to 5 tablespoons half-and-half cream

---

1. In a small bowl, dissolve yeast in warm milk. In a large bowl, combine the flour, sugar and salt. Cut in butter until crumbly. Add the yeast mixture, cream and egg yolks; stir until mixture forms a soft dough (dough will be sticky). Cover and refrigerate overnight.

2. Punch down dough; divide into quarters. Roll each portion into an 18-in. x 4-in. rectangle; cut into 1-in. x 4-in. strips.

3. Place two strips side by side; twist together. Shape into a ring; pinch ends together. Repeat with remaining strips. Place 2 in. apart on greased baking sheets. Cover and let rise in a warm place until doubled, about 45 minutes.

4. Using the end of a wooden spoon handle, make a 1/2-in.-deep indentation in the center of each roll. Fill each with about 1 tablespoon pie filling.

5. Bake at 350° for 14-16 minutes or until lightly browned. Remove from pans to wire racks to cool.

6. For icing, in a large bowl, beat butter until fluffy. Gradually beat in the confectioners' sugar, vanilla, salt and enough cream to achieve a drizzling consistency. Drizzle over warm rolls.

OVERNIGHT CHERRY DANISH

❝ I loved this recipe. Have been looking for something like this for years! I did add 8 oz. of cream cheese, softened, and 3/4 cup of powdered sugar, creamed them together and put this mixture in the hole before adding the cherries. It was great. ❞

—*nw1653*

[2004]

CARAMEL-PECAN CINNAMON ROLLS

yield: 15 servings ∽ **prep: 20 min. + rising** ∽ **bake: 30 min.**

(Pictured on page 140)

These irresistible rolls are perfect for an Easter brunch!
—*Lois Jacobsen, Dallas, Wisconsin*

        2   packages (1/4 ounce *each*) active dry yeast
        1   cup warm 2% milk (110° to 115°)
        2   eggs
        5   tablespoons butter, melted
    1/2   cup sugar
        1   teaspoon salt
        5   cups all-purpose flour
    CARAMEL SAUCE:
        1   cup butter, cubed
        2   cups packed brown sugar
    1/4   cup corn syrup
    1/2   to 3/4 cup chopped pecans
    FILLING:
        2   tablespoons butter, melted
    1/2   cup sugar
        1   teaspoon ground cinnamon

1. In a large bowl, dissolve yeast in warm milk. Add the eggs, butter, sugar, salt and 3 cups flour. Beat until smooth. Stir in enough of the remaining flour to form a soft dough.

2. Turn onto a lightly floured surface; knead until smooth and elastic, about 6-8 minutes. Place in a greased bowl, turning once to grease top. Cover and let rise in a warm place until doubled, about 1 hour.

3. Meanwhile, for sauce, melt butter in a large saucepan. Stir in brown sugar and corn syrup. Bring to a boil over medium heat for 2 minutes, stirring constantly. Pour into a greased 13-in. x 9-in. baking dish. Sprinkle with pecans; set aside.

4. Punch the dough down. Turn onto a floured surface. Roll into a 17-in. x 15-in. rectangle. Spread butter to within 1/2 in. of edges. Combine sugar and cinnamon; sprinkle over dough. Roll up jelly-roll style, starting with a long side; pinch seams to seal.

5. Cut into 15 slices. Place cut side down over caramel sauce. Cover; let rise until doubled, about 30 minutes.

6. Bake at 350° for 30-35 minutes or until golden brown. Let stand 5 minutes; invert onto a serving platter.

[2002]

JELLY DOUGHNUTS

yield: 16 doughnuts ∽ **prep: 30 min.**
cook: 10 min.

There's no need to run to the bakery for delicious jelly doughnuts! These sweet treats are lighter than air. I've been fixing them for my family for many years. They disappear almost as fast as I make them.

—*Kathy Westendorf, Westgate, Iowa*

        2   packages (1/4 ounce *each*) active dry yeast
    1/2   cup warm water (110° to 115°)
    1/2   cup warm 2% milk (110° to 115°)
    1/3   cup butter, softened
    1-1/3   cups sugar, *divided*
        3   egg yolks
        1   teaspoon salt
    3-3/4   cups all-purpose flour
        3   tablespoons jelly *or* jam
        1   egg white, lightly beaten
    Oil for deep-fat frying

1. In a large bowl, dissolve the yeast in warm water. Add the milk, butter, 1/3 cup sugar, egg yolks and salt; mix well. Stir in enough of the flour to form a soft dough (do not knead).

2. Place in a greased bowl, turning once to grease top. Cover and let rise in a warm place until doubled, about 1-1/2 hours.

3. Punch dough down. Turn onto a lightly floured surface; knead about 10 times. Divide dough in half.

4. Roll each portion of dough to 1/4-in. thickness; cut with a floured 2-1/2-in. round cutter. Place about 1/2 teaspoon jelly in the center of half of the circles; brush edges with egg white. Top with the remaining circles; press edges to seal tightly.

5. Place on greased baking sheet. Cover and let rise until doubled, about 1 hour.

6. In an electric skillet or deep-fat fryer, heat oil to 375°. Fry doughnuts, a few at a time, for 1-2 minutes on each side or until golden brown. Drain doughnuts on paper towels. Roll doughnuts in the remaining sugar while warm.

∽ CAKES ∽

[2003]

CHOCOLATE MINT LAYER CAKE

yield: 12 servings ∽ **prep: 35 min. + chilling**
bake: 25 min. + cooling

With its chocolate icing and minty whipped cream filling, this cake is a great way to end a meal.

—*Jean Portwine, Recluse, Wyoming*

CHOCOLATE MINT LAYER CAKE

"Excellent cake recipe, but instead of using peppermint extract, I used Andes mint chips and melted them into a mousse filling. Added just enough flavor to balance the cake."
—*Butterflyj76*

1/2 cup butter, softened
1-3/4 cups sugar
3 eggs
4 ounces unsweetened chocolate, melted and cooled
1 teaspoon vanilla extract
3/4 cup 2% milk
1/2 cup water
1-3/4 cups all-purpose flour
3/4 teaspoon baking soda
1/2 teaspoon salt
FILLING:
1 cup heavy whipping cream
3 tablespoons confectioners' sugar
1/8 teaspoon peppermint extract
3 to 4 drops green food coloring, optional
ICING:
1 cup (6 ounces) semisweet chocolate chips
1/4 cup butter, cubed
1/3 cup evaporated milk
1 teaspoon vanilla extract
1-1/2 cups confectioners' sugar

1. Line two greased 9-in. round baking pans with waxed paper. Grease and flour the paper; set aside.

2. In a large bowl, cream butter and sugar until light and fluffy. Beat in eggs, one at a time, beating well after each addition. Beat in chocolate and vanilla. Combine milk and water. Combine dry ingredients; add to creamed mixture alternately with milk mixture, beating well after each addition.

3. Pour into prepared pans. Bake at 350° for 24-28 minutes or until a toothpick inserted near the center comes out clean. Cool for 10 minutes; remove from pans to wire racks. Gently peel off waxed paper; cool completely.

4. For filling, in a small bowl, beat the cream until it begins to thicken. Add confectioners' sugar and extract; beat until stiff peaks form. Beat in food coloring if desired. Place one cake layer on a serving plate; spread with filling. Top with second layer.

5. For icing, in a microwave, melt chips and butter; stir until smooth. Cool slightly. Beat in evaporated milk and vanilla. Gradually beat in confectioners' sugar until smooth. Frost and decorate cake. Chill 2 hours before slicing.

[2002]

STRAWBERRY POKE CAKE

yield: 10-12 servings ∽ **prep: 20 min. + chilling**
bake: 25 min. + cooling

That classic spring treat—strawberry shortcake—takes on a wonderful new twist. Strawberry gelatin and strawberries liven up each pretty slice.

—*Mary Jo Griggs, West Bend, Wisconsin*

1 package (18-1/4 ounces) white cake mix
1-1/4 cups water

2 **eggs**

1/4 **cup canola oil**

2 **packages (10 ounces *each*) frozen sweetened sliced strawberries, thawed**

2 **packages (3 ounces *each*) strawberry gelatin**

1 **carton (12 ounces) frozen whipped topping, thawed, *divided***

Fresh strawberries, optional

1. In a large bowl, beat cake mix, water, eggs and oil; beat on low speed for 30 seconds. Beat on medium for 2 minutes.

2. Pour into two greased and floured 9-in. round baking pans. Bake at 350° for 25-35 minutes or until a toothpick inserted near the center comes out clean. Cool for 10 minutes before removing from pans to wire racks to cool completely.

3. Using a serrated knife, level top of each cake if necessary. Return layers, top side up, to two clean 9-in. round baking pans. Pierce cakes with a meat fork or wooden skewer at 1/2-in. intervals.

4. Drain juice from strawberries into a 2-cup measuring cup; refrigerate berries. Add water to juice to measure 2 cups; pour into a small saucepan. Bring to a boil; stir in gelatin until dissolved. Chill for 30 minutes. Gently spoon over each cake layer. Chill for 2-3 hours.

5. Dip bottom of one pan in warm water for 10 seconds. Invert cake onto a plate. Top with reserved strawberries and 1 cup whipped topping. Place the second cake layer over topping.

6. Frost cake with remaining whipped topping. Refrigerate for at least 1 hour. Serve with the fresh berries if desired. Refrigerate leftovers.

Editor's Note: This cake was tested with Pillsbury white cake mix.

[2001]

LIME CREAM TORTE
yield: 10-14 servings
prep: 20 min. + chilling
bake: 20 min. + cooling

This impressive-looking dessert is surprisingly simple to prepare. Light and refreshing, it's a super make-ahead treat. The flavor gets better as it sits in the refrigerator.

—Theresa Tometich, Coralville, Iowa

1 **package (18-1/4 ounces) butter recipe golden cake mix**

3 **eggs**

1/2 **cup butter, softened**

7 **tablespoons water**

3 **tablespoons lime juice**

FILLING:

1 **can (14 ounces) sweetened condensed milk**

1/2 **cup lime juice**

2 **cups heavy whipping cream, whipped**

Lime slices, optional

1. In a large bowl, combine the cake mix, eggs, butter, water and lime juice; beat on low speed for 30 seconds. Beat on medium for 2 minutes.

2. Pour into two greased and floured 9-in. round baking pans. Bake at 375° for 20-25 minutes or until a toothpick inserted near the center comes out clean. Cool for 10 minutes before removing from pans to wire racks.

3. In a large bowl, combine milk and lime juice. Fold in whipped cream. Cut each cake horizontally into two layers. Place the bottom layer on a serving plate; top with 1-1/4 cups filling. Repeat layers twice. Top with the remaining cake layer. Frost the top of cake with remaining filling.

4. Refrigerate for at least 1 hour. Serve with lime slices if desired.

LIME CREAM TORTE

"We love this cake. I make it all the time, but I use Key lime juice instead. It reminds us of past vacations."

—brbeltmt

[2005]

CHOCOLATE CARROT CAKE
yield: 12-16 servings ∽ prep: 35 min.
bake: 25 min. + cooling
(Pictured on page 184)

Finely shredding the carrots gives this cake an extra-nice texture. The walnuts sprinkled on top add crunch, but omit them if you prefer.

—*Pamela Brown, Williamsburg, Michigan*

3	cups finely shredded carrots
2	cups sugar
1-1/4	cups canola oil
4	eggs
2	cups all-purpose flour
1/2	cup baking cocoa
1	teaspoon baking soda
1/2	teaspoon salt

FROSTING:

1	package (8 ounces) cream cheese, softened
1/2	cup butter, softened
3-3/4	cups confectioners' sugar
1/4	cup baking cocoa
3	teaspoons vanilla extract
1/4	cup chopped walnuts
1/4	cup semisweet chocolate chips

1. Line two 9-in. round baking pans with waxed paper; grease the paper and set aside. In a large bowl, beat the carrots, sugar, oil and eggs until well blended. Combine the flour, cocoa, baking soda and salt; gradually beat into carrot mixture until blended.

2. Pour into prepared pans. Bake at 350° for 25-30 minutes or until a toothpick inserted near the center comes out clean. Cool for 10 minutes before removing from pans to wire racks. Gently peel off waxed paper; cool completely.

3. For frosting, in a large bowl, beat cream cheese and butter until fluffy. Beat in the confectioners' sugar, cocoa and vanilla until smooth.

4. Place bottom layer on a serving plate; top with half of the frosting. Repeat with remaining cake layer. Sprinkle with nuts and chocolate chips.

[1999]

STRAWBERRY MERINGUE CAKE
yield: 12-16 servings ∽ prep: 30 min.
bake: 35 min. + cooling

Guests say "Wow!" when I present this torte. Mashed berries add fresh flavor to the cream filling.

—*Dorothy Anderson, Ottawa, Kansas, Former Field Editor*

4	eggs, *separated*
1	package (18-1/4 ounces) yellow cake mix
1-1/3	cups orange juice
1-1/2	teaspoons grated orange peel
1/4	teaspoon cream of tartar
1	cup plus 1/4 cup sugar, *divided*
2	cups heavy whipping cream
2	pints fresh strawberries, *divided*

1. Let the egg whites stand at room temperature for 30 minutes.

2. In a large bowl, combine the cake mix, orange juice, egg yolks and orange peel; beat on low speed for 30 seconds. Beat on medium for 2 minutes. Pour into two greased and floured 9-in. round baking pans; set aside.

3. In a large bowl with clean beaters, beat the egg whites and cream of tartar on medium until soft peaks form. Gradually beat in 1 cup sugar, a tablespoon at a time, on high until stiff glossy peaks form. Spread meringue evenly over cake batter.

4. Bake at 350° for 35 minutes or until the meringue is lightly browned. Cool in pans on wire racks (meringue will crack).

5. Meanwhile, in a large bowl, beat cream until stiff peaks form. Mash 1/2 cup of strawberries with remaining sugar; fold into whipped cream.

6. Loosen edges of cakes from pans with a knife. Using two large spatulas, carefully remove one cake to a serving platter, meringue side up. Carefully spread with about two-thirds of the cream mixture. Slice the remaining berries; arrange half over cream mixture. Repeat layers. Store in the refrigerator.

[2001]

RASPBERRY WALNUT TORTE

yield: 16 servings ∽ **prep: 30 min.**
bake: 25 min. + cooling

I often serve this impressive cake for dinner parties or whenever a special dessert is called for. It's delicious and also very pretty.

—*Bonnie Malloy, Norwood, Pennsylvania*

1-1/2 cups heavy whipping cream
 3 eggs
1-1/2 cups sugar
 3 teaspoons vanilla extract
1-3/4 cups all-purpose flour
 1 cup ground walnuts, toasted
 2 teaspoons baking powder
1/2 teaspoon salt

FROSTING:
1-1/2 cups heavy whipping cream
 1 package (8 ounces) cream cheese, softened
 1 cup sugar
1/8 teaspoon salt
 1 teaspoon vanilla extract
 1 jar (12 ounces) raspberry preserves

1. In a small bowl, beat cream until stiff peaks form; set aside. In a large bowl, beat the eggs, sugar and vanilla until thick and pale yellow. Combine flour, walnuts, baking powder and salt; fold into egg mixture alternately with whipped cream.

2. Pour into two greased and floured 9-in. round baking pans. Bake at 350° for 25-30 minutes or until a toothpick inserted near the center comes out clean. Cool for 10 minutes before removing from pans to wire racks to cool completely.

3. For frosting, in a small bowl, beat the cream until stiff peaks form; set aside. In a large bowl, beat the cream cheese, sugar and salt until fluffy. Beat in vanilla. Fold in whipped cream.

4. Cut each cake horizontally into two layers. Place bottom layer on serving plate; spread with about 1/2 cup frosting. Top with the second cake layer; spread with half of the raspberry preserves. Repeat layers. Frost sides of cake with frosting.

5. Cut a small hole in the corner of a pastry or plastic bag; insert ribbon tip #47. Fill bag with remaining frosting; pipe a lattice design on top of cake. Using star tip #32, pipe stars around top and bottom edges of cake. Store in the refrigerator.

Editor's Note: Use of a coupler ring will allow you to easily change pastry tips for different designs.

RASPBERRY WALNUT TORTE

❝Really wonderful cake! Everyone who tasted this cake just loved it.❞
—*Nanykat*

SPLITTING CAKE LAYERS

Using a ruler, mark the center of the side of the cake with a toothpick. Continue inserting toothpicks around the cake. Using the toothpicks as a guide, cut the cake horizontally in half with a long serrated knife. Carefully remove the top half. Frost or fill the bottom half as recipe instructs and replace the top cut side down.

[2006]

HUMMINGBIRD CAKE

yield: 12-14 servings ∾ prep: 40 min.
bake: 25 min. + cooling

(Pictured on page 182)

This impressive cake is my dad's favorite, so I always make it for his birthday. It also makes a great Easter dessert and is lovely with a summer meal.

—*Nancy Zimmerman*
Cape May Court House, New Jersey
Field Editor

---

2 cups mashed ripe bananas
1-1/2 cups canola oil
3 eggs
1 can (8 ounces) unsweetened crushed pineapple, undrained
1-1/2 teaspoons vanilla extract
3 cups all-purpose flour
2 cups sugar
1 teaspoon salt
1 teaspoon baking soda
1 teaspoon ground cinnamon
1 cup chopped walnuts
PINEAPPLE FROSTING:
1/4 cup shortening
2 tablespoons butter, softened
1 teaspoon grated lemon peel
1/4 teaspoon salt
6 cups confectioners' sugar
1/2 cup unsweetened pineapple juice
2 teaspoons half-and-half cream
Chopped walnuts, optional

---

1. In a large bowl, beat the bananas, oil, eggs, pineapple and vanilla until well blended. In another bowl, combine the flour, sugar, salt, baking soda and cinnamon; gradually beat into banana mixture until blended. Stir in walnuts.

2. Pour into three greased and floured 9-in. round baking pans. Bake at 350° for 25-30 minutes or until a toothpick inserted near center comes out clean. Cool for 10 minutes; remove from pans to wire racks to cool completely.

HUMMINGBIRD CAKE

❝We found that putting this in the refrigerator overnight really sets it up. We love this cake and my husband makes it all the time. He just loves to bake. We first heard of this from his boss, and his mother made it for years. Just a good ol' Southern cake.❞
—*shygirl55*

3. For frosting, in a large bowl, beat the shortening, butter, lemon peel and salt until fluffy. Add confectioners' sugar alternately with pineapple juice. Beat in cream. Spread between layers and over top and sides of cake. Sprinkle with walnuts if desired.

[2010]

APRICOT ALMOND TORTE

yield: 12 servings ∾ prep: 45 min.
bake: 25 min. + cooling

(Pictured on page 181)

This pretty cake takes a bit of time, so I bake the layers ahead of time and assemble the day of serving, which is easier for entertaining.

—*Trisha Kruse, Eagle, Idaho, Field Editor*

---

3 eggs
1-1/2 cups sugar
1 teaspoon vanilla extract
1-3/4 cups all-purpose flour
1 cup ground almonds, toasted
2 teaspoons baking powder
1/2 teaspoon salt
1-1/2 cups heavy whipping cream, whipped
FROSTING:
1 package (8 ounces) cream cheese, softened
1 cup sugar
1/8 teaspoon salt
1 teaspoon almond extract
1-1/2 cups heavy whipping cream, whipped
1 jar (10 to 12 ounces) apricot preserves
1/2 cup slivered almonds, toasted

---

1. In a large bowl, beat the eggs, sugar and vanilla on high speed until thick and pale yellow. Combine the flour, almonds, baking powder and salt; gradually fold into the egg mixture alternately with the whipped cream.

2. Transfer to two greased and floured 9-in. round baking pans. Bake at 350° for 22-28 minutes or until a toothpick inserted near the center comes out clean. Cool for 10 minutes before removing from pans to wire racks to cool completely.

3. In a large bowl, beat the cream cheese, sugar and salt until smooth. Beat in extract. Fold in whipped cream.

4. Cut each cake horizontally into two layers. Place bottom layer on a serving plate; spread with 1 cup frosting. Top with another cake layer; spread with half of the preserves. Repeat layers. Frost sides of cake; decorate the top edge with remaining frosting. Sprinkle with almonds.

[2003]

STRAWBERRY HAZELNUT TORTE

yield: 10-12 servings ∞ prep: 45 min. + chilling bake: 30 min. + cooling

This beautiful dessert is a very big hit at parties. The tender meringues have a wonderful hazelnut flavor with layers of chocolate, whipped cream and berries. I got the recipe when we were in Israel for a few months in 1979. I had no cookbooks with me, and my hairdresser gave me an old Australian cookbook with this recipe in it. I made a few changes and this is the result.

—Phyllis Amboss
Pacific Palisades, California

4   egg whites
1   teaspoon white vinegar
1   teaspoon vanilla extract, *divided*
Dash salt
1-1/4   cups sugar
1/2   cup ground hazelnuts
6   ounces semisweet chocolate, chopped
1   teaspoon shortening

1-1/2   cups heavy whipping cream
1/3   cup confectioners' sugar
2-1/2   cups sliced fresh strawberries
Additional fresh strawberries, halved

1. Place egg whites in a large bowl; let stand at room temperature for 30 minutes. Line a baking sheet with parchment paper. Trace two 8-in. circles 1/2 in. apart on the paper and set aside.

2. Add vinegar, 1/2 teaspoon vanilla and salt to egg whites; beat until soft peaks form. Add sugar, 1 tablespoon at a time, beating until stiff peaks form. Spread over paper circles. Sprinkle with hazelnuts; cut through meringues with a knife to swirl nuts.

3. Bake at 375° for 30-35 minutes or until the meringue and nuts are lightly browned. Cool on baking sheet. When completely cool, remove meringues from paper and store in an airtight container. In a microwave, melt chocolate and shortening; stir until smooth. Cool to room temperature.

4. To assemble, place one meringue, flat side down, on a serving plate; spread with half of the melted chocolate. In a large bowl, beat cream until it begins to thicken. Add confectioners' sugar and remaining vanilla; beat until stiff peaks form. Spread half over chocolate layer. Arrange sliced strawberries over whipped cream.

5. Spread flat side of remaining meringue with melted chocolate. Place chocolate side down over the strawberries; spread with the remaining whipped cream. Refrigerate for up to 4 hours before serving. Garnish with the halved strawberries.

STRAWBERRY HAZELNUT TORTE

"This is an impressive dessert that looks fantastic and tastes incredible. I and several members of my family are gluten intolerant and this torte makes a great birthday "cake." I suggest following the recipe exactly. The first time I made it, I tried to cut corners by folding the hazelnuts into the meringue before forming it into circles. That did not work out. I thought it might be something else I did wrong, and so I folded them in again on the second try. WRONG! It only worked on the third try, in which I followed the directions. Huh. This is a keeper!"
—zooklayer

[2010]

CHOCOLATE BANANA CREAM CAKE

yield: 12 servings ～ prep: 40 min.
bake: 20 min. + cooling

(Pictured on page 183)

My inspiration for this cake came from my desire to create a dessert combining my father's love for cake, my mother's love for chocolate and my love for bananas. It's divine!

—*Susie Pattison, Dublin, Ohio*

---

2 eggs, *separated*
1/2 cup butter, softened
1-1/4 cups sugar
1-1/2 cups mashed ripe bananas (about 3 medium)
1/4 cup sour cream
2 teaspoons vanilla extract
1-1/2 cups all-purpose flour
1 teaspoon baking soda
1/4 teaspoon salt

FILLING/FROSTING:
1-1/2 cups cold 2% milk
1 package (3.4 ounces) instant banana cream pudding mix
1 can (16 ounces) chocolate frosting
2 medium firm bananas, sliced
3 tablespoons lemon juice

---

1. Place egg whites in a bowl; let stand at room temperature for 30 minutes. In large bowl, cream the butter and sugar until light and fluffy. Beat in egg yolks. Beat in bananas, sour cream and vanilla. Combine flour, baking soda and salt; add to creamed mixture and mix well.

2. In a small bowl with clean beaters, beat egg whites until stiff peaks form. Fold into batter. Transfer to two greased and floured 9-in. round baking pans. Bake at 350° for 20-25 minutes or until a toothpick inserted near the center comes out clean. Cool for 10 minutes before removing from pans to wire racks to cool completely.

3. For filling, in a small bowl, whisk milk and pudding mix for 2 minutes. Let stand for 2 minutes or until soft-set. Cover and refrigerate until chilled.

4. In a small bowl, beat frosting until light and fluffy. Place bananas in a small bowl; toss with lemon juice.

5. Place one cake layer on a serving plate; spread with 3 tablespoons frosting. Stir pudding; spread half over the frosting. Top with half of the bananas and the remaining cake layer. Repeat frosting, filling and banana layers. Frost sides and decorate top edge of cake with remaining frosting. Store in the refrigerator.

[2002]

PECAN TORTE

yield: 12-14 servings ～ prep: 40 min. + chilling
bake: 25 min. + cooling

Even though the holidays always seem to be more pie-oriented, this cake steals the show at our family celebrations. It tastes scrumptious!

—*Lois Thayer, Hutchinson, Kansas*

---

5 eggs, *separated*
3 cups finely chopped toasted pecans, *divided*
1/2 cup butter, softened
1/2 cup shortening
2 cups sugar
2 teaspoons vanilla extract
2 cups all-purpose flour
1 teaspoon baking soda
1 cup buttermilk
3/4 cup dark corn syrup

FILLING:
1/2 cup packed brown sugar
1/3 cup cornstarch
1/8 teaspoon salt
1-1/2 cups half-and-half cream
3/4 cup dark corn syrup
4 egg yolks, lightly beaten

  3 tablespoons butter, cubed
  1 teaspoon vanilla extract
1/2 cup coarsely chopped pecans

1. Place egg whites in a small bowl; let stand at room temperature for 30 minutes. Sprinkle 2/3 cup pecans each into three greased 9-in. round baking pans and set aside.

2. In a large bowl, cream the butter, shortening and sugar until light and fluffy. Add egg yolks, one at time, beating well after each addition. Beat in the vanilla. Combine the flour and baking soda; add to creamed mixture alternately with buttermilk, beating well after each addition. Stir in the remaining pecans.

3. In a small bowl with clean beaters, beat egg whites until stiff peaks form; fold into batter. Pour into prepared pans. Bake at 350° for 25-30 minutes or until a toothpick inserted near the center comes out clean. Cool for 10 minutes before removing from pans to wire racks. Brush with corn syrup; cool completely.

4. For filling, in a large heavy saucepan, combine the brown sugar, cornstarch and salt. Gradually stir in cream until smooth. Add the corn syrup. Bring to a boil over medium heat, stirring constantly; cook and stir for 1-2 minutes or until thickened. Remove from the heat.

5. Stir a small amount of hot filling into egg yolks; return all to the pan, stirring constantly. Bring to a gentle boil; cook and stir for 3 minutes. Remove from the heat; stir in butter and vanilla. Cover and refrigerate until cool, about 4 hours.

6. Place one cake layer, pecan side up, on a serving plate; spread with about 2/3 cup of the filling. Repeat the layers twice. Sprinkle with the chopped pecans. Refrigerate leftovers.

[2006]

MOCHA LAYER CAKE

yield: 14-16 servings ∾ prep: 40 min.
bake: 30 min. + cooling

Without a doubt, this is the best chocolate cake I've ever made. I share this decadent dessert with everyone I can!

—*Katherine DeLoach, Visalia, California*

    1 cup butter, softened
    3 cups packed brown sugar
    4 eggs
    3 teaspoons vanilla extract
    3 cups all-purpose flour
  3/4 cup baking cocoa
    3 teaspoons baking soda
  1/2 teaspoon salt
1-1/2 cups brewed coffee, cooled
1-1/3 cups sour cream
FROSTING:
   12 ounces cream cheese, softened
    6 tablespoons butter, softened
    6 ounces unsweetened chocolate, melted
    6 tablespoons brewed coffee
    2 teaspoons vanilla extract
4-1/2 to 5-1/2 cups confectioners' sugar

1. In a large bowl, cream butter and brown sugar until light and fluffy. Add eggs, one at a time, beating well after each addition. Beat in vanilla. Combine flour, cocoa, baking soda and salt; add to creamed mixture alternately with coffee and sour cream, beating well after each addition.

2. Pour into three greased and floured 9-in. round baking pans. Bake at 350° for 30-35 minutes or until a toothpick inserted near the center comes out clean. Cool for 10 minutes before removing from pans to wire racks to cool completely.

3. For frosting, in a large bowl, beat cream cheese and butter until fluffy. Beat in the chocolate, coffee and vanilla until blended. Gradually beat in confectioners' sugar. Spread between the layers and over top and sides of cake. Cover and refrigerate until serving.

[2007]

BLUE-RIBBON PEANUT BUTTER TORTE

yield: 14 servings ∞ prep: 55 min. + chilling
bake: 20 min. + cooling

This impressive three-layer torte will delight any peanut butter lover.

—*Carol Wilson, Ancho, New Mexico*

1/2	cup plus 2 tablespoons butter, softened
1/2	cup chunky peanut butter
2	cups packed brown sugar
4	eggs
1	teaspoon vanilla extract
2-1/2	cups all-purpose flour
1	teaspoon baking soda
1	teaspoon baking powder
1/2	teaspoon salt
1	cup buttermilk

CHOCOLATE FILLING:

2-1/4	cups heavy whipping cream
1/2	cup packed brown sugar
12	ounces bittersweet chocolate *or* semisweet chocolate, coarsely chopped
1/2	cup chunky peanut butter

CREAM CHEESE FROSTING:

12	ounces cream cheese, softened
6	tablespoons butter, softened
1	teaspoon vanilla extract
2	cups confectioners' sugar, *divided*
3/4	cup heavy whipping cream
2	Butterfinger candy bars (2.1 ounces each), coarsely chopped
1/3	cup honey-roasted peanuts, coarsely chopped

1. Grease three 9-in. round baking pans; set aside. In a bowl, cream butter, peanut butter and brown sugar until light and fluffy. Add eggs, one at a time, beating well after each addition. Beat in vanilla. Combine flour, baking soda, baking powder and salt; add to creamed mixture alternately with buttermilk, beating well after each addition.

2. Pour into prepared pans (pans will have a shallow fill). Bake at 350° for 17-20 minutes or until a toothpick inserted near the center comes out clean. Cool for 10 minutes before removing from pans to wire racks.

3. For filling, in a large heavy saucepan, bring cream and brown sugar to a boil over medium heat. Reduce heat; cover and simmer for 1-2 minutes or until sugar is dissolved. Remove from heat; stir in chocolate and peanut butter until blended. Transfer to a bowl; chill until mixture achieves spreading consistency.

4. For frosting, in a large bowl, beat cream cheese and butter until blended. Beat in vanilla. Gradually beat in 1-1/4 cups confectioners' sugar until light and fluffy. In a small bowl, beat cream and remaining confectioners' sugar until stiff peaks form; fold into cream cheese mixture.

5. Spread filling between layers. Frost top and sides of cake. Garnish with candy bars and peanuts. Store in refrigerator.

Editor's Note: Reduced-fat peanut butter is not recommended for this recipe.

[2009]

RASPBERRY CHOCOLATE CAKE

yield: 16 servings ∞ prep: 45 min. + standing
bake: 35 min. + cooling

(Pictured on page 179)

Whenever I make this cake, I get a ton of compliments. It's impressive, and the raspberry filling is just wonderful.

—*Marlene Sanders, Paradise, Texas*

3	cups sugar
2-3/4	cups all-purpose flour
1	cup baking cocoa
2	teaspoons baking soda
1-1/2	teaspoons salt

TOP 100 RECIPE

RASPBERRY CHOCOLATE CAKE

"This cake is absolutely delicious! Love the raspberry and chocolate. Omitted the shortening and used butter instead. Was to die for! My family does not like coffee either. You do not even taste the coffee. I brewed just regular coffee, not strong. It just enhances the chocolate flavor. Put it in, you will not even taste it!! Enjoy! "

—5100

3/4 teaspoon baking powder
1-1/4 cups buttermilk
3/4 cup canola oil
3 teaspoons vanilla extract
3 eggs
1-1/2 cups strong brewed coffee, room temperature
FILLING:
3 tablespoons all-purpose flour
6 tablespoons 2% milk
6 tablespoons shortening
3 tablespoons butter, softened
3 cups confectioners' sugar
2 tablespoons raspberry liqueur
1/4 teaspoon salt
2 drops red food coloring, optional
4 tablespoons seedless raspberry jam, melted
FROSTING:
1 package (8 ounces) cold cream cheese
1/3 cup butter, softened
1/2 cup baking cocoa
1 tablespoon raspberry liqueur
4 cups confectioners' sugar

1. Line three greased 9-in. round baking pans with waxed paper and grease paper; set aside. In a large bowl, combine the first six ingredients. Combine the buttermilk, oil and vanilla; add to the dry ingredients. Add eggs, one at a time, beating well after each addition; beat for 2 minutes. Gradually add coffee (batter will be thin).

2. Pour batter into prepared pans. Bake at 350° for 35-40 minutes or until a toothpick inserted near the center comes out clean. Cool for 10 minutes before removing from pans to wire racks. Gently peel off waxed paper; cool completely.

3. For filling, in a small saucepan, whisk together the flour and milk until smooth. Cook over medium heat for 1 minute or until thickened, stirring constantly. Remove from the heat and let stand until cool.

4. In a large bowl, cream shortening and butter until light and fluffy. Gradually add confectioners' sugar and mix well. Gradually add cooled milk mixture; beat for 4 minutes or until light and fluffy. Beat in liqueur, salt and food coloring if desired.

5. Level tops of cakes if necessary. Place one layer on a serving plate; spread with about 2 tablespoons jam. Place remaining layers on waxed paper; spread one of the remaining layers with remaining jam. Let stand for 30 minutes.

6. Spread 1/2 cup filling over cake on the plate to within 1/4 in. of edges. Top with the jam-covered cake, then spread with remaining filling. Top with the remaining cake layer.

7. In a large bowl, beat the cream cheese and butter until smooth. Beat in cocoa and liqueur. Gradually beat in confectioners' sugar until light and fluffy. Frost top and sides of cake. Store in the refrigerator.

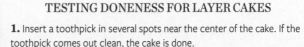

TESTING DONENESS FOR LAYER CAKES

1. Insert a toothpick in several spots near the center of the cake. If the toothpick comes out clean, the cake is done.

2. If the toothpick comes out with crumbs, the cake will need to bake a little longer.

[2007]

CHOCOLATE GANACHE CAKE

yield: 12-14 servings ∞ prep: 40 min. + chilling
bake: 20 min. + cooling

(Pictured on page 182)

Here's to that chocolate fix we all need. I use cream in both the filling and the glaze.

—Kathy Kittell, Lenexa, Kansas, Field Editor

3/4	cup butter, softened
1-1/2	cups sugar
1	egg
1	teaspoon vanilla extract
1	cup buttermilk
3/4	cup sour cream
2	cups all-purpose flour
2/3	cup baking cocoa
1	teaspoon baking soda
1/4	teaspoon salt

FILLING:

4	ounces semisweet chocolate, chopped
1	cup heavy whipping cream
1/2	teaspoon vanilla extract

GANACHE:

8	ounces semisweet chocolate, chopped
3/4	cup heavy whipping cream
1/4	cup butter, cubed

1. In a large bowl, cream butter and sugar until light and fluffy. Add egg and vanilla; beat for 2 minutes. Combine buttermilk and sour cream. Combine the flour, cocoa, baking soda and salt; add to creamed mixture alternately with buttermilk mixture, beating well after each addition.

2. Pour into two greased and waxed paper-lined 9-in. round baking pans. Bake at 350° for 20-25 minutes or until a toothpick inserted near center comes out clean. Cool 10 minutes; remove from pans to wire racks . Gently peel off waxed paper; cool completely.

3. For filling, in a heavy saucepan, melt chocolate with cream over low heat.

Remove from the heat; stir in vanilla. Transfer to a small bowl; chill until slightly thickened, stirring occasionally. Beat on medium speed until light and fluffy. Chill until mixture achieves spreading consistency.

4. For ganache, place chocolate in a bowl. In a saucepan, bring cream just to a boil. Pour over chocolate; add butter. Whisk until smooth. Chill until slightly thickened.

5. Place one cake layer on a serving plate; spread with filling. Top with remaining cake layer. Slowly pour ganache over top of cake. Store in the refrigerator.

[2004]

CHOCOLATE CHIFFON TORTE

yield: 12 servings ∞ prep: 40 min. + chilling
bake: 15 min. + cooling

This classic recipe is one I made often when we lived on the farm and I had lots of cream to use up.

—Iola Egle
Bella Vista, Arkansas, Field Editor

6	eggs, *separated*
2	cups cake flour
1-1/2	cups sugar
3	teaspoons baking powder
1/2	teaspoon salt
1/2	cup water
1/2	cup canola oil
2	ounces semisweet chocolate, melted and cooled
1/2	teaspoon cream of tartar

FILLING:

1-1/2	cups heavy whipping cream
1-1/4	cups semisweet chocolate chips
1/4	cup butter, cubed

FROSTING:

1	cup heavy whipping cream
1/2	cup confectioners' sugar
1	tablespoon baking cocoa

Chocolate curls

CHOCOLATE GANACHE CAKE

"The preparation takes a bit of time but it is worth it. This is the perfect cake for chocolate lovers."
—mbvanzante

1. In a large bowl, let eggs stand at room temperature for 30 minutes. Line three 9-in. round baking pans with waxed paper and grease the paper; set aside. .

2. In another large bowl, combine the flour, sugar, baking powder and salt. Whisk the water, oil, egg yolks and melted chocolate. Add to dry ingredients; beat until well blended. Using clean beaters, beat egg whites and cream of tartar until stiff peaks form; fold into batter.

3. Pour into prepared pans. Bake at 350° for 15-20 minutes or until a toothpick inserted near the center comes out clean. Cool for 10 minutes before removing from pans to wire racks to cool completely. Carefully remove waxed paper.

4. In a large saucepan, combine filling ingredients. Cook and stir over medium heat until mixture comes to a boil. Chill for 2 hours or until filling reaches spreading consistency, stirring occasionally. Beat with a mixer until fluffy.

5. Cut each cake horizontally into two layers. Place bottom layer on a serving plate; top with a fifth of the filling. Repeat layers.

6. For frosting, in a large bowl, beat cream, confectioners' sugar and cocoa until stiff peaks form. Spread over top and sides of cake. Garnish with chocolate curls. Store in the refrigerator.

[2001]

LEMON MERINGUE CAKE
**yield: 12-14 servings ∞ prep: 40 min.
bake: 25 min. + cooling**

This cake tastes just like lemon meringue pie! Fresh lemon flavor shines through in the custard filling between the layers and the light meringue frosting adds a fancy finish. It's not only a deliciously different dessert, but it's also a conversation piece!

—*Julie Courier, Macomb, Michigan*

- 1 package (18-1/4 ounces) lemon *or* yellow cake mix
- 3 eggs
- 1 cup water
- 1/3 cup canola oil

FILLING:
- 1 cup sugar
- 3 tablespoons cornstarch
- 1/4 teaspoon salt
- 1/2 cup water
- 1/4 cup lemon juice
- 4 egg yolks, lightly beaten
- 4 teaspoons butter
- 1 teaspoon grated lemon peel

MERINGUE:
- 4 egg whites
- 1/4 teaspoon cream of tartar
- 3/4 cup sugar

1. In a large bowl, combine cake mix, eggs, water and oil. Beat on low speed for 30 seconds. Beat on medium for 2 minutes.

2. Pour into two greased and floured 9-in. round baking pans. Bake at 350° for 25-30 minutes or until a toothpick inserted near the center comes out clean. Cool for 10 minutes before removing from pans to wire racks to cool completely.

3. For filling, in a large saucepan, combine the sugar, cornstarch and salt. Stir in water and juice until smooth. Cook and stir over medium-high heat until thickened and bubbly. Reduce heat to low; cook and stir for 2 minutes longer. Remove from the heat. Stir a small amount of hot filling into egg yolks; return all to the pan, stirring constantly. Bring to a gentle boil; cook and stir for 2 minutes. Remove from the heat; gently stir in butter and lemon peel. Cool completely.

4. For meringue, in a large bowl, beat egg whites and cream of tartar on medium speed until soft peaks form. Gradually beat in sugar, 1 tablespoon at a time, on high until stiff peaks form.

5. Cut each cake horizontally into two layers. Place bottom layer on an ovenproof serving plate; spread with a third of the filling. Repeat layers twice. Top with remaining cake layer.

6. Spread meringue over top and sides. Bake at 350° for 10-15 minutes or until meringue is lightly browned. Cool. Store in the refrigerator.

[1995]

"FISHY" RED VELVET CAKE

yield: 12-16 servings
prep: 30 min. + cooling
bake: 15 min. + cooling

Based on an old-fashioned recipe, this unusual vibrant red birthday cake will steal the show at your party.

—*Elizabeth LeBlanc, Bourg, Louisiana*

1	cup butter, softened
1-1/2	cups sugar
2	eggs
1	teaspoon vanilla extract
1	teaspoon butter flavoring
1	bottle (1 ounce) red food coloring, optional
2-1/2	cups cake flour
2	tablespoons baking cocoa
1	teaspoon baking soda
1	cup buttermilk
1	teaspoon vinegar

FLUFFY FROSTING:

1-1/2	cups 2% milk
1/2	cup all-purpose flour
1-1/2	cups butter, softened
1-1/2	cups sugar
1-1/2	teaspoons vanilla extract
1-1/2	teaspoons butter flavoring

Gummy fish and worms, optional

1. In a large bowl, cream butter and sugar until light and fluffy. Add eggs, one at a time, beating well after each addition. Beat in the vanilla, butter flavoring and food coloring if desired. Combine the flour, cocoa and baking soda. Combine buttermilk and vinegar. Add the flour mixture alternately with buttermilk mixture to creamed mixture, beating well after each addition.

2. Pour into three greased and floured 9-in. round baking pans. Bake at 350° for 15-20 minutes or until a toothpick inserted near center comes out clean. Cool for 10 minutes; remove from pans to wire racks to cool completely.

3. For frosting, whisk together milk and flour in a saucepan. Cook, over medium heat stirring constantly, for 5 minutes or until thickened. Cover and cool.

4. In a large bowl, cream butter and sugar until light and fluffy. Beat in vanilla and butter flavoring. Gradually add cooled milk mixture and beat 4 minutes or until light and fluffy. Frost cooled cake. Decorate with gummy fish and worms if desired.

[2006]

MERINGUE TORTE

yield: 16-18 servings ∾ **prep: 40 min**
bake: 30 min. + cooling

(Pictured on page 179)

My grandmother, who came here from Sweden when she was 21, used to make this cake for our birthdays, and it is still a family favorite.

—*Ruth Grover, Portland, Connecticut*

3/4	cup butter, softened
3/4	cup sugar
6	egg yolks
1	teaspoon vanilla extract
1-1/2	cups all-purpose flour
1-1/2	teaspoons baking powder
6	tablespoons 2% milk

MERINGUE:

6	egg whites
1-1/2	cups sugar
1/2	teaspoon vanilla extract
1/2	cup plus 3 tablespoons finely chopped walnuts, *divided*

FILLING:

2	cups heavy whipping cream
1/4	cup confectioners' sugar
2	cups fresh raspberries

1. In a large bowl, cream butter and sugar until light and fluffy. Add egg yolks, one at a time, beating well after each addition. Beat in vanilla. Combine flour and baking powder; add to the creamed mixture alternately with milk,

---

"FISHY" RED VELVET CAKE

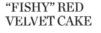

❝This cake went over great. The cake is dense yet fluffy, and the frosting is great. It's sweet but not heavy even though it has so much butter. It's the perfect amount for this three layer cake. I'll be making this for St. Patrick's day but using green instead of red. Highly recommend this for anyone to try.❞

—*jjam1303*

beating well after each addition. Pour into three parchment paper-lined 9-in. round baking pans; set aside.

2. In a large bowl and with clean beaters, beat egg whites on medium speed until foamy. Gradually beat in sugar, 1 tablespoon at a time, on high until stiff glossy peaks form and sugar is dissolved. Add vanilla. Fold in 1/2 cup nuts. Spread meringue evenly over cake batter; sprinkle with remaining nuts.

3. Bake at 325° for 30-35 minutes or until meringue is lightly browned. Cool on wire racks for 10 minutes (meringue will crack). Loosen edges of cakes from pans with a knife. Using two large spatulas, carefully remove one cake to a serving plate, meringue side up. Carefully remove remaining cakes, meringue side up, to wire racks.

4. In a large bowl, beat cream until it begins to thicken. Gradually add confectioners' sugar; beat until stiff peaks form. Carefully spread half of the filling over cake on serving plate; top with half of the raspberries. Repeat layers. Top with remaining cake. Store in the refrigerator.

[2003]

SOUR CREAM SPICE CAKE

yield: 12-16 servings ∽ prep: 35 min.
bake: 25 min. + cooling

This dense, old-fashioned dessert is rich in spices. Fluffy, sweet frosting makes a delectable contrast to the cake.

—*Edna Hoffman*
Hebron, Indiana, Field Editor

3 eggs, *separated*
1/2 cup butter, softened
1-1/2 cups packed brown sugar
1 teaspoon vanilla extract
1-3/4 cups cake flour
1-1/2 teaspoons ground allspice
1 teaspoon baking soda
1 teaspoon ground cinnamon
1 teaspoon ground cloves
1/2 teaspoon salt
1 cup (8 ounces) sour cream
FROSTING:
1 cup packed brown sugar
2 egg whites
1/3 cup water
1/4 teaspoon cream of tartar
1-1/2 teaspoons vanilla extract

1. In a small bowl, let egg whites stand at room temperature for 30 minutes. In a large bowl, cream butter and brown sugar until light and fluffy. Add egg yolks, one at a time, beating well after each addition. Beat in vanilla. Combine the dry ingredients; add to creamed mixture alternately with sour cream, beating well after each addition. With clean beaters, beat egg whites until stiff; gently fold into batter.

2. Pour into two greased and floured 9-in. round baking pans. Bake at 350° for 25-30 minutes or until a toothpick inserted near the center comes out clean. Cool for 10 minutes before removing from pans to wire racks.

3. For frosting, combine the brown sugar, egg whites, water and cream of tartar in a small heavy saucepan over low heat. With a hand mixer, beat on low speed for 1 minute. Continue beating on low over low heat until frosting reaches 160°, about 20 minutes.

4. Pour into a large bowl; add vanilla. Beat on high until stiff peaks form, about 7 minutes. Spread between layers and over top and sides of cake. Refrigerate leftovers.

SOUR CREAM SPICE CAKE

"I made this for my grandmother's birthday and everyone loved it, especially the frosting!"
—*cocoafevr*

[2002]

TIRAMISU TOFFEE TORTE
yield: 12-14 servings ∞ prep: 25 min. + chilling
bake: 25 min. + cooling

Tiramisu is Italian for pick-me-up, and this treat truly lives up to its name. It's worth every bit of effort to see my husband's eyes light up when I put a piece of this delicious torte in front of him.

—*Donna Gonda, North Canton, Ohio*

- 1 package (18-1/4 ounces) white cake mix
- 1 cup strong brewed coffee, room temperature
- 4 egg whites
- 4 Heath candy bars (1.4 ounces each), chopped

FROSTING:
- 4 ounces cream cheese, softened
- 2/3 cup sugar
- 1/3 cup chocolate syrup
- 2 teaspoons vanilla extract
- 2 cups heavy whipping cream
- 6 tablespoons strong brewed coffee, room temperature
- 1 Heath candy bar (1.4 ounces), chopped

1. Line two greased 9-in. round baking pans with waxed paper and grease paper; set aside. In a large bowl, combine cake mix, coffee and egg whites; beat on low speed for 30 seconds. Beat on medium for 2 minutes. Fold in candy bars.

2. Pour into prepared pans. Bake at 350° for 25-30 minutes or until a toothpick inserted near the center comes out clean. Cool for 10 minutes before removing to wire racks. Gently peel off waxed paper; cool completely.

3. For frosting, in a large bowl, beat the cream cheese and sugar until smooth. Beat in the chocolate syrup and vanilla. Add the whipping cream. Beat frosting on high speed until light and fluffy, about 5 minutes.

4. Cut each cake horizontally into two layers. Place bottom layer on a serving plate; drizzle with 2 tablespoons of the coffee. Spread with 3/4 cup frosting. Repeat twice. Top with the remaining cake layer. Frost top and sides of cake with remaining frosting. Refrigerate overnight. Garnish with chopped candy bar. Store in the refrigerator.

[2001]

TOFFEE-MOCHA CREAM TORTE
yield: 12-14 servings ∞ prep: 20 min. + cooling
bake: 20 min. + cooling

When you really want to impress someone, this scrumptious torte is just the thing to make! Instant coffee granules give the moist chocolate cake a mild mocha flavor...while the fluffy whipped cream layers, blended with brown sugar and crunchy toffee bits, are deliciously rich.

—*Lynn Rogers, Richfield, North Carolina*

- 1 cup butter, softened
- 2 cups sugar
- 2 eggs
- 1-1/2 teaspoons vanilla extract
- 2-2/3 cups all-purpose flour
- 3/4 cup baking cocoa
- 2 teaspoons baking soda
- 1/4 teaspoon salt
- 1 cup buttermilk
- 2 teaspoons instant coffee granules
- 1 cup boiling water

TOPPING:
- 1/2 teaspoon instant coffee granules
- 1 teaspoon hot water
- 2 cups heavy whipping cream
- 3 tablespoons light brown sugar
- 6 Heath candy bars (1.4 ounces each), crushed, *divided*

1. In a large bowl, cream butter and sugar until light and fluffy. Add eggs, one at a time, beating well after each addition. Beat in vanilla. Combine the flour, cocoa, baking soda and salt; add to the creamed mixture alternately with buttermilk, beating well after each addition. Dissolve coffee in water; stir into batter.

2. Pour into three greased and floured 9-in. round baking pans. Bake at 350° for 16-20 minutes or until a toothpick inserted near the center comes out clean. Cool for 10 minutes before removing from pans to wire racks to cool completely.

3. For topping, dissolve coffee in water in a large bowl; cool. Add cream and brown sugar. Beat until stiff peaks form. Place bottom cake layer on a serving plate; top with 1-1/3 cups of topping. Sprinkle with 1/2 cup of crushed candy bars. Repeat layers twice. Store in the refrigerator.

[1998]

SOUR CREAM CHOCOLATE CAKE

yield: 16 servings prep: 35 min.
bake: 30 min. + cooling

(Pictured on page 177)

This classic layer cake is still hard to beat for a Sunday dinner or birthday celebration.

—*Marsha Lawson, Pflugerville, Texas*

- 1 cup baking cocoa
- 1 cup boiling water
- 1 cup butter, softened
- 2-1/2 cups sugar
- 4 eggs
- 2 teaspoons vanilla extract
- 3 cups cake flour
- 2 teaspoons baking soda
- 1/2 teaspoon baking powder
- 1/2 teaspoon salt
- 1 cup (8 ounces) sour cream

FROSTING:
- 2 cups (12 ounces) semisweet chocolate chips
- 1/2 cup butter, cubed
- 1 cup (8 ounces) sour cream
- 1 teaspoon vanilla extract
- 4-1/2 to 5 cups confectioners' sugar

Chocolate ruffles, optional

1. Dissolve cocoa in boiling water; cool. In a large bowl, cream butter and sugar until light and fluffy. Add eggs, one at a time, beating well after each. Beat in vanilla. Combine the flour, baking soda, baking powder and salt; gradually add to creamed mixture alternately with sour cream, beating well after each addition. Add cocoa mixture and mix well.

2. Pour into three greased and floured 9-in. round baking pans. Bake at 350° for 30-35 minutes or until a

toothpick inserted near center comes out clean. Cool 10 minutes; remove from pans to wire racks to cool.

3. In a microwave, melt chocolate chips and butter; stir until smooth. Cool for 5 minutes. Transfer to a large bowl. Beat in the sour cream and vanilla. Add the confectioners' sugar; beat until light and fluffy. Spread between layers and over top and sides of cake. Garnish with chocolate ruffles if desired. Refrigerate.

[2008]

PEEPS SUNFLOWER CAKE

yield: 12 servings prep: 15 min.
bake: 30 min. + cooling

(Pictured on page 181)

The yellow peeps make eye-catching flower petals, and I carefully placed chocolate chips in a circular pattern to resemble the seeds in the middle of a sunflower. This cake is easy but looks quite impressive.

—*Bethany Eledge, Cleveland, Tennessee*

- 1 package (18-1/4 ounces) yellow cake mix
- 2 cans (16 ounces each) chocolate frosting
- 19 yellow chick Peeps candies
- 1-1/2 cups semisweet chocolate chips

TOP 100 RECIPE

1. Prepare and bake cake according to package directions, using two greased and waxed paper-lined 9-in. round baking pans. Cool for 10 minutes before removing from pans to wire racks. Gently peel off waxed paper; cool completely.

2. Level tops of cakes. Spread frosting between layers and over the top and sides of cake.

3. Without separating Peeps and curving slightly to fit, arrange chicks around edge of cake for sunflower petals. For sunflower seeds, arrange chocolate chips in center of cake.

HOW TO MAKE CHOCOLATE RUFFLES WITH A GIROLLE

Mount chocolate roll on girolle according to manufacturer's directions. Alternating between room temperature and refrigerator as needed to bring roll to correct temperature, rotate cutter over chocolate roll lightly, releasing ruffles in 3-to 4-in. pieces. Refrigerate ruffles until ready to arrange on frosted cake.

[2003]

PEACH POUND CAKE

yield: 12-16 servings ∞ **prep: 10 min.
bake: 1 hour + cooling**

*Our state grows excellent peaches, and this is
one recipe I'm quick to pull out when they are
in season. It's a tender, moist cake that receives
rave reviews wherever I take it.*

—Betty Jean Gosnell
   Inman, South Carolina

1 cup butter, softened
2 cups sugar
6 eggs
1 teaspoon almond extract
1 teaspoon vanilla extract
3 cups all-purpose flour
1/4 teaspoon baking soda
1/4 teaspoon salt
1/2 cup sour cream
2 cups diced fresh *or* frozen peaches
Confectioners' sugar

1. In a large bowl, cream butter and sugar
until light and fluffy. Add eggs, one at a
time, beating well after each addition.
Beat in extracts. Combine flour, baking
soda and salt; add to batter alternately
with sour cream, beating well after
each addition. Fold in the peaches.

2. Pour into a greased and floured 10-in.
fluted tube pan. Bake at 350° for 60-70
minutes or until a toothpick inserted
near the center comes out clean. Cool
cake for 10 minutes before removing
from pan to a wire rack to cool
completely. Dust with confectioners'
sugar if desired.

PEACH
POUND CAKE

"This is DEE-LISHUS! The next
time I do this, I'll use three
cups of diced peaches.
We like peaches."
—buyer1

[2007]

BUTTERMILK CAKE WITH
CARAMEL ICING

yield: 12-16 servings ∞ **prep: 35 min.
bake: 45 min. + cooling**

*This cake is so tender, it melts in your mouth!
It's been a favorite cake recipe of my family
since the 70s.*

—Anna Jean Allen
   West Liberty, Kentucky, Field Editor

1 cup butter, softened
2-1/3 cups sugar
3 eggs
1-1/2 teaspoons vanilla extract
3 cups all-purpose flour
1 teaspoon baking powder
1/2 teaspoon baking soda
1 cup buttermilk
ICING:
1/4 cup butter, cubed
1/2 cup packed brown sugar
1/3 cup heavy whipping cream
1 cup confectioners' sugar

1. In a large bowl, cream butter and sugar
until light and fluffy. Add eggs, one at a
time, beating well after each addition.
Beat in vanilla. Combine flour, baking
powder and baking soda; add to the
creamed mixture alternately with the
buttermilk, beating well after each
addition (batter will be thick).

2. Pour into a greased and floured 10-in.
fluted tube pan. Bake at 350° for 45-50
minutes or until a toothpick inserted
near the center comes out clean. Cool
for 10 minutes before removing from
pan to a wire rack to cool completely.

3. For icing, in a small saucepan, combine
the butter, brown sugar and cream.
Bring to a boil over medium heat,
stirring constantly. Remove from the
heat; cool for 5-10 minutes. Gradually
beat in confectioners' sugar until
smooth. Drizzle over cake.

[2004]

CRAN-ORANGE COCONUT CAKE

yield: 12-16 servings ∞ prep: 30 min.
bake: 50 min. + cooling

I am sharing this popular dessert as part of my Easter menu, but it's a recipe I use throughout the year. The Bundt cake serves a group and is always well-received at parties and potlucks.

—Marie Hattrup, Sparks, Nevada

- 1/2 cup dried cranberries
- 1/4 cup orange juice
- 1/2 cup chopped pecans
- 2 tablespoons grated orange peel
- 2 tablespoons brown sugar
- 3/4 cup butter, softened
- 1 cup sugar
- 4 eggs
- 1 teaspoon vanilla extract
- 2-2/3 cups all-purpose flour
- 1 teaspoon baking powder
- 1 teaspoon baking soda
- 1/4 teaspoon salt
- 1 cup plus 2 tablespoons sour cream
- 1-1/2 cups flaked coconut
  Confectioners' sugar

1. In a small saucepan, combine cranberries and orange juice. Cook over medium-high heat for 2-3 minutes or until juice is absorbed. Remove from the heat. When cool enough to handle, finely chop cranberries. Place in a small bowl; add pecans, orange peel and brown sugar. Set aside.

2. In a bowl, cream butter and sugar until light and fluffy. Beat in eggs, one at a time, beating well after each addition. Beat in vanilla. Combine dry ingredients; add to creamed mixture alternately with sour cream, beating well after each addition. Fold in coconut.

3. Spoon a third of the batter into a greased and floured 10-in. fluted tube pan. Spoon half of the cranberry mixture over batter. Repeat layers. Carefully spread remaining batter over cranberry mixture.

4. Bake at 325° for 50-60 minutes or until toothpick inserted near the center comes out clean. Cool for 10 minutes before removing from pan to a wire rack to cool completely. Dust with confectioners' sugar.

[2001]

CHOCOLATE CHIP POUND CAKE

yield: 12-14 servings ∞ prep: 15 min.
bake: 1 hour + cooling

My mom has been making this cake for over 30 years. Dotted with chips and topped with a chocolate glaze, it is absolutely divine.

—Michele Werts, Brookville, Ohio

- 1 cup butter, softened
- 2 cups sugar
- 4 eggs
- 1 teaspoon vanilla extract
- 4 cups all-purpose flour
- 4 teaspoons baking powder
- 1 teaspoon baking soda
- 2 cups (16 ounces) sour cream
- 2 cups (12 ounces) semisweet chocolate chips
  GLAZE:
- 1/4 cup semisweet chocolate chips
- 2 tablespoons butter
- 1-1/4 cups confectioners' sugar
- 3 tablespoons 2% milk
- 1/2 teaspoon vanilla extract

1. In a large bowl, cream butter and sugar until light and fluffy. Add eggs, one at a time, beating well after each addition. Beat in vanilla. Combine the flour, baking powder and baking soda; add to creamed mixture alternately with sour cream, beating well after each addition. Fold in chocolate chips.

2. Pour into a greased and floured 10-in. fluted tube pan. Bake at 350° for 60-65 minutes or until a toothpick inserted near the center comes out clean. Cool for 10 minutes before removing from pan to a wire rack to cool completely.

3. For glaze, in a microwave-safe bowl, melt chocolate chips and butter; stir until smooth. Whisk in the confectioners' sugar, milk and vanilla until smooth. Drizzle over cake.

[2003]

CHOCOLATE MACAROON CAKE

yield: 12-16 servings ∽ prep: 30 min.
bake: 55 min. + cooling

This cake is always popular with chocolate lovers, including my five children. I got the recipe from a dear friend more than 30 years ago.

—*Saburo Aburano, Ann Arbor, Michigan*

---

1   **egg white**
3   **tablespoons sugar**
2   **cups flaked coconut, finely chopped**
1   **tablespoon all-purpose flour**
CAKE BATTER:
4   **eggs,** *separated*
1-3/4 **cups sugar,** *divided*
1/2 **cup shortening**
1/2 **cup sour cream**
2   **teaspoons vanilla extract**
1/2 **cup cold brewed coffee**
1/4 **cup buttermilk**
2   **cups all-purpose flour**
1/2 **cup baking cocoa**
1   **teaspoon baking soda**
1   **teaspoon salt**
FROSTING:
1   **cup semisweet chocolate chips, melted and cooled**
3   **tablespoons butter, softened**
2   **cups confectioners' sugar**
5   **tablespoons 2% milk**

---

1. In a small bowl, beat egg white on medium speed until soft peaks form. Gradually beat in sugar, 1 tablespoon at a time, on high until stiff glossy peaks form and sugar is dissolved. Fold in coconut and flour; set aside.

2. In a large bowl, beat the egg whites on medium until soft peaks form. Gradually beat in 1/2 cup sugar, 1 tablespoon at a time, on high until stiff glossy peaks form and sugar is dissolved; set aside.

3. In another large bowl, cream the shortening and remaining sugar until light and fluffy. Beat in the egg yolks, one at a time, beating well after each addition. Beat in sour cream and vanilla. Combine coffee and buttermilk. Combine the flour, cocoa, baking soda and salt; add to creamed mixture alternately with coffee mixture, beating well after each addition. Fold in beaten egg whites.

4. Pour half of the batter into an ungreased 10-in. tube pan with removable bottom. Drop coconut filling by spoonfuls over batter. Top with remaining batter.

5. Bake at 350° for 55-60 minutes or until a toothpick inserted near the center comes out clean. Immediately invert cake onto a wire rack; cool completely, about 1 hour. Run a knife around side of pan and remove.

6. In a small bowl, beat frosting ingredients until smooth and creamy. Spread over the top and sides of cake.

[1996]

SWEET POTATO CAKE

yield: 8-10 servings ∽ prep: 10 min.
bake: 45 min. + cooling

This dessert is easy to prepare and makes an excellent snack cake or breakfast coffee cake.

—*Kathy Theriot, St. Martinville, Louisiana*

1-1/3 **cups sugar**
1   **cup cold mashed sweet potatoes (without added milk or butter)**
1/3 **cup shortening**
1/3 **cup water**
1   **egg**
1-2/3 **cups all-purpose flour**
1   **teaspoon salt**
1   **teaspoon baking soda**
1   **teaspoon ground cinnamon**
1/4 **teaspoon baking powder**
1/4 **teaspoon ground ginger**
2/3 **cup raisins**
1/3 **cup chopped pecans**
Confectioners' sugar

---

1. In a large bowl, beat the sugar, potatoes, shortening, water and egg. Combine dry ingredients; add to potato mixture and mix well. Stir in raisins and pecans. Pour into a greased 10-in. fluted tube pan.

2. Bake at 350° for 45-50 minutes or until a toothpick inserted near the center comes out clean. Cool for 10 minutes before removing from pan to a wire rack to cool completely. Dust with confectioners' sugar.

Editor's Note: An 11-in. x 7-in. baking pan can be used instead of a tube pan; bake for 30-35 minutes.

[2012]

ORANGE CRANBERRY POUND CAKE WITH VANILLA GLAZE

yield: 12 servings ∾ **prep: 25 min.**
bake: 50 min. + cooling

(*Pictured on page 180*)

For me, pound cake is both comforting and delicious. This buttery cake combines the tastes of both orange and cranberry and tops it off with a sweet vanilla glaze.

—*Angela Spengler, Clovis, New Mexico*

1-1/4	cups butter, softened
2-3/4	cups sugar
5	eggs
1	tablespoon grated orange peel
1	teaspoon orange extract
3	cups all-purpose flour
1	teaspoon baking powder
1/4	teaspoon salt
1	cup 2% milk
1/2	cup fresh *or* frozen cranberries, halved
1/2	cup chopped walnuts

GLAZE:

2	cups confectioners' sugar
1/3	cup butter, melted
2	teaspoons vanilla extract
2	to 3 tablespoons hot water

1. In a large bowl, cream butter and sugar until light and fluffy. Add eggs, one at a time, beating well after each addition. Beat in the orange peel and extract. Combine the flour, baking powder and salt; add to the creamed mixture alternately with milk. Beat just until combined. Fold in cranberries and nuts.

2. Transfer to a greased and floured 10-in. fluted tube pan. Bake at 350° for 50-60 minutes or until a toothpick inserted near the center comes out clean. Cool cake for 10 minutes before removing from pan to a wire rack to cool completely.

3. For glaze, in a small bowl, combine the confectioners' sugar, butter, vanilla and enough of the water to achieve desired consistency. Drizzle over cake.

[2009]

CREAM CHEESE POUND CAKE

yield: 16 servings ∾ **prep: 25 min**
bake: 1-1/4 hours + cooling

Fresh fruit and a dollop of whipped cream dress up this tender pound cake

—*Richard Hogg, Anderson, South Carolina*

1-1/2	cups butter, softened
1	package (8 ounces) cream cheese, softened
3	cups sugar
6	eggs
2	teaspoons vanilla extract
1	teaspoon lemon extract
3	cups all-purpose flour
1/2	teaspoon baking powder
1/4	teaspoon salt

Confectioners' sugar, sliced fresh strawberries and whipped cream, optional

1. In a large bowl, cream the butter, cream cheese and sugar until light and fluffy. Add eggs, one at a time, beating well after each addition. Beat in the extracts. Combine the flour, baking powder and salt; beat into creamed mixture until blended.

2. Pour into a greased and floured 10-in. fluted tube pan. Bake at 325° for 1-1/4 to 1-1/2 hours or until a toothpick inserted near center comes out clean.

3. Cool cake for 10 minutes before removing from pan to a wire rack to cool completely. Garnish with the confectioners' sugar, strawberries and whipped cream if desired.

CREAM CHEESE POUND CAKE

"This is one of the best pound cakes I've tried. The outside is crisp and the inside is dense and moist. My family loves it. I wanted a little more lemon taste so increased the lemon extract to one-and-a-half teaspoons the second time I made it. This one is a definite keeper."
—*dglong*

PEANUT BUTTER CHOCOLATE CAKE

[2002]

PEANUT BUTTER CHOCOLATE CAKE

yield: 24 servings ∞ prep: 15 min.
bake: 30 min.

Since chocolate and peanut butter are two of my granddaughters' favorite flavors, I fix this cake often. It's moist and scrumptious.

—*Elaine Medeiros, Wamego, Kansas*

1-1/2 cups sugar
1-1/2 cups water
  1/2 cup canola oil
4-1/2 teaspoons white vinegar
1-1/2 teaspoons vanilla extract
2-1/4 cups all-purpose flour
  1/3 cup baking cocoa
1-1/2 teaspoons baking soda
  1/2 teaspoon salt
PEANUT BUTTER BATTER:
    4 ounces cream cheese, softened
  1/4 cup creamy peanut butter
  1/3 cup plus 1 tablespoon sugar, *divided*
    1 egg
  1/8 teaspoon salt
  1/2 cup semisweet chocolate chips
  1/2 cup chopped pecans

1. In a large bowl, beat the sugar, water, oil, vinegar and vanilla. Combine the flour, cocoa, baking soda and salt; gradually beat into oil mixture. Pour into a greased 13-in. x 9-in. baking pan.

2. In another bowl, beat cream cheese, peanut butter, 1/3 cup sugar, egg and salt until smooth. Stir in chocolate chips.

3. Drop by tablespoonfuls over the cake batter; cut through batter with a knife to swirl peanut butter mixture. Sprinkle with pecans and remaining sugar.

4. Bake at 350° for 30-35 minutes or until a toothpick inserted near the center comes out clean. Cool on a wire rack before cutting. Refrigerate leftovers.

[1996]

MOM'S STRAWBERRY SHORTCAKE

yield: 9 servings ∞ prep: 20 min.
bake: 25 min. + cooling

When I was growing up, Mom sometimes experimented with different dessert recipes, but this tried-and-true spongy shortcake was always great just the way it was. It melted in my mouth!

—*Karen Wingate, Coldwater, Kansas*

    2 eggs
1-1/2 cup sugar, *divided*
    1 cup all-purpose flour
    1 teaspoon baking powder
  1/4 teaspoon salt
  1/2 cup 2% milk
    1 tablespoon butter
    1 teaspoon vanilla extract
    1 to 1-1/2 quarts fresh strawberries, sliced
Whipped cream
Mint leaves, optional

1. In a large bowl, beat eggs on medium speed for 3 minutes. Gradually add 1 cup sugar, beating until thick and pale yellow. Combine the flour, baking powder and salt; beat into the egg mixture. Heat milk and butter just until butter begins to melt. Beat into batter with vanilla (batter will be thin).

2. Pour into a greased 8-in. square baking pan. Bake at 350° for 25 minutes or until a toothpick inserted near the center comes out clean. Cool the cake for 10 minutes before removing from pan to a wire rack to cool completely.

3. Just before serving, cut cake into serving-size pieces; cut each slice in half horizontally. Combine the strawberries and remaining sugar. Spoon strawberries between the cake layers and over the top of each serving. Top with whipped cream; garnish with mint leaves if desired.

SOUR CREAM CHOCOLATE CAKE, page 171

PUMPKIN CUPCAKES, page 198

ORANGE SPONGE CAKE, page 202

MERINGUE TORTE, page 168

CLASSIC CARROT CAKE, page 188

RASPBERRY CHOCOLATE CAKE, page 164

PINK VELVET CUPCAKES, page 197

ORANGE CRANBERRY POUND CAKE WITH VANILLA GLAZE, page 175

LEMON TEA CAKES, page 196

APRICOT ALMOND TORTE, page 160

PEEPS SUNFLOWER CAKE, page 171

STRAWBERRY-MALLOW CAKE ROLL, page 202

CUPCAKE CONES, page 198

GERMAN CHOCOLATE CREAM CHEESE CAKE, page 192

HUMMINGBIRD CAKE, page 160

CHOCOLATE GANACHE CAKE, page 166

CHOCOLATE BANANA CREAM CAKE, page 162

UPSIDE-DOWN STRAWBERRY SHORTCAKE, page 189

CHOCOLATE CARROT CAKE, page 158

PICNIC CUPCAKES, page 197

LAZY DAISY CAKE, page 189

[1997]
GERMAN CHOCOLATE BIRTHDAY CAKE
yield: 12-15 servings ∽ **prep: 25 min.**
bake: 50 min. + cooling

Despite its name, this recipe didn't come from Germany. It refers to the type of chocolate called for. German chocolate is similar to milk chocolate and sweeter than regular baking chocolate.

—*Lisa Andis, Morristown, Indiana*

- 4 **eggs,** *separated*
- 4 **ounces German sweet chocolate, chopped**
- 1/2 **cup water**
- 1 **cup butter, softened**
- 2 **cups sugar**
- 1 **teaspoon vanilla extract**
- 2-1/2 **cups cake flour**
- 1 **teaspoon baking soda**
- 1/2 **teaspoon salt**
- 1 **cup buttermilk**

COCONUT-PECAN FROSTING
- 1 **cup evaporated milk**
- 1 **cup sugar**
- 3 **egg yolks, lightly beaten**
- 1/2 **cup butter, cubed**
- 1-1/3 **cups flaked coconut**
- 1 **cup chopped pecans**
- 1 **teaspoon vanilla extract**

1. Let eggs stand at room temperature for 30 minutes. Line a greased 13-in. x 9-in. baking pan with waxed paper. Grease and flour the paper; set aside.

2. In a microwave, melt chocolate with water; stir until smooth. Cool. In a large bowl, cream butter and sugar until light and fluffy. Add egg yolks, one at a time, beating well after each addition. Beat in chocolate mixture and vanilla. Combine the flour, baking soda and salt; add to creamed mixture alternately with buttermilk, beating well after each addition. In a small bowl with clean beaters, beat egg whites until stiff peaks form; fold into batter.

3. Spread batter evenly into prepared pan. Bake at 350° for 50-55 minutes or until a toothpick inserted near the center comes out clean. Cool for 10 minutes before inverting onto a wire rack. Gently peel off waxed paper; cool completely.

4. For frosting, in a heavy saucepan, combine milk, sugar, egg yolks and butter. Cook and stir over medium-low heat until thickened and a thermometer reads 160° or is thick enough to coat the back of a metal spoon.

5. Remove from the heat. Stir in the coconut, pecans and vanilla. Beat on high until frosting is cool and achieves spreading consistency. Place cake on a serving platter; frost top and sides of cake.

[1998]
PEACH UPSIDE-DOWN CAKE
yield: 6-8 servings ∽ **prep: 20 min.**
bake: 50 min. + cooling

Peaches and coconut give this variation a refreshing flavor that's especially nice for spring and summer.

—*Terri Holmgren, Swanville, Minnesota*

- 1/3 **cup butter, melted**
- 1/2 **cup packed brown sugar**
- 1 **can (29 ounces) peach halves**
- 1/4 **cup flaked coconut**
- 2 **eggs**
- 2/3 **cup sugar**
- 1/2 **teaspoon almond extract**
- 1 **cup all-purpose flour**
- 1 **teaspoon baking powder**
- 1/4 **teaspoon salt**

1. Pour butter into a 9-in. round baking pan; sprinkle with brown sugar. Drain the peaches, reserving 6 tablespoons of syrup. Arrange peach halves, cut side down, in a single layer over the sugar. Sprinkle the coconut around peaches; set aside.

2. In a large bowl, beat eggs until thick and lemon-colored, about 5 minutes; gradually beat in sugar. Add extract and reserved syrup. Combine flour, baking powder and salt; add to egg mixture and mix well.

3. Pour over peaches. Bake at 350° for 50-60 minutes or until a toothpick inserted near the center comes out clean. Cool for 10 minutes; invert cake onto a serving plate. Serve warm.

SPICY APPLESAUCE CAKE

"This is yet another *Taste of Home* recipe that I prepared and brought in to work and that my co-workers fell upon like starving wolves. I used a pint jar of my mom's homemade applesauce. It worked out great texture-wise, but because it's already well-seasoned with cinnamon I used a lighter hand with the cinnamon in the cake batter. Next time I think I'll go easier on the other spices as well if I use the homemade applesauce. However, if I were to use the jarred supermarket applesauce, I'd add the full teaspoon of cinnamon, nutmeg, allspice and cloves."

—*Aquarelle*

[1995]

SPICY APPLESAUCE CAKE

yield: 20-24 servings ∞ prep: 15 min.
bake: 35 min.

For a "picnic perfect" dessert, this moist delicious cake travels and slices very well. With chocolate chips, walnuts and raisins, it's a real crowd-pleaser.

—**Marian Platt**
Sequim, Washington, Field Editor

- 2 cups applesauce
- 1-1/2 cups sugar
- 1/2 cup shortening
- 2 eggs, lightly beaten
- 2 cups all-purpose flour
- 1 tablespoon baking cocoa
- 1-1/2 teaspoons baking soda
- 1 teaspoon salt
- 1 teaspoon *each* ground cinnamon, nutmeg, allspice and cloves
- 1 cup raisins
- 1/2 cup semisweet chocolate chips
- 1/2 cup chopped walnuts

TOPPING:
- 1/2 cup semisweet chocolate chips
- 1/2 cup chopped walnuts
- 2 tablespoons brown sugar

---

1. In a large bowl, beat the applesauce, sugar, shortening and eggs. Combine the flour, cocoa, baking soda, salt, cinnamon, nutmeg, allspice and cloves; gradually beat into applesauce mixture until blended. Stir in the raisins, chocolate chips and walnuts.

2. Pour into a greased 13-in. x 9-in. baking pan. Combine the topping ingredients and sprinkle over batter. Bake at 350° for 35-40 minutes or until a toothpick inserted near the center comes out clean. Cool on a wire rack.

[2000]

HAWAIIAN CAKE

yield: 12-15 servings ∞ prep: 15 min. + chilling
bake: 20 min. + cooling

Pairing pineapple with coconut lent a tropical flavor to the dessert served as the finale to our theme party. Shared by a former co-worker, this recipe has been in my file for over 20 years and never fails to delight those who try a piece.

—**JoAnn Fox, Johnson City, Tennessee**

- 1 package (18-1/4 ounces) yellow cake mix
- 1-1/4 cups cold 2% milk
- 1 package (3.4 ounces) instant vanilla pudding mix
- 1 can (20 ounces) crushed pineapple, drained
- 1 envelope whipped topping mix (Dream Whip)
- 1 package (3 ounces) cream cheese, softened
- 1/4 cup sugar
- 1/2 teaspoon vanilla extract
- 1/2 cup flaked coconut, toasted

---

1. Prepare and bake the cake according to package directions, using a greased 13-in. x 9-in. baking pan. Cool on a wire rack.

2. In a large bowl, whisk the milk and pudding mix for 2 minutes. Let stand for 2 minutes or until soft-set. Stir in pineapple. Spread over cake. Prepare whipped topping mix according to package directions; set aside.

3. In a bowl, beat cream cheese, sugar and vanilla until smooth. Beat in 1 cup whipped topping. Fold in remaining topping. Spread over the pudding. Sprinkle with coconut. Cover and refrigerate for 3 hours or overnight.

[2001]

MISSISSIPPI MUD CAKE
**yield: 16-20 servings ✎ prep: 20 min.
bake: 35 min. + cooling**

Make this tempting cake and you'll satisfy kids of all ages! A fudgy brownie-like base is topped with marshmallow creme and a nutty frosting. Your family will be very happy when you serve up big slices with glasses of cold milk or steaming mugs of coffee.

—Tammi Simpson, Greensburg, Kentucky

- 1 cup butter, softened
- 2 cups sugar
- 4 eggs
- 1-1/2 cups self-rising flour
- 1/2 cup baking cocoa
- 1 cup chopped pecans
- 1 jar (7 ounces) marshmallow creme

FROSTING:
- 1/2 cup butter, softened
- 3-3/4 cups confectioners' sugar
- 3 tablespoons baking cocoa
- 1 tablespoon vanilla extract
- 4 to 5 tablespoons 2% milk
- 1 cup chopped pecans

1. In a large bowl, cream butter and sugar until light and fluffy. Add eggs, one at a time, beating well after each addition. Combine flour and cocoa; gradually add to creamed mixture until blended. Fold in the pecans.

2. Transfer to a greased 13-in. x 9-in. baking pan. Bake at 350° for 35-40 minutes or until a toothpick inserted near the center comes out clean. Cool the cake for 3 minutes (cake will fall in the center). Spoon the marshmallow creme over cake; carefully spread to cover top. Cool completely.

3. For frosting, in a small bowl, cream the butter and confectioners' sugar until light and fluffy. Beat in the cocoa, vanilla and enough milk to achieve frosting consistency. Fold in pecans. Spread over marshmallow creme layer. Store in the refrigerator.

Editor's Note: As a substitute for 1-1/2 cups self-rising flour, place 2-1/4 teaspoons baking powder and 3/4 teaspoon salt in a measuring cup. Add all-purpose flour to measure 1 cup. Combine with an additional 1/2 cup all-purpose flour.

[2001]

PRALINE ICE CREAM CAKE
**yield: 15 servings ✎ prep: 20 min.
bake: 25 min. + cooling**

Melted ice cream is a key ingredient in this delectable golden cake. It's been a family favorite for years—we love the pecan praline flavor. It's also a joy to serve to company, since it's not tricky to fix but always wins rave reviews!

**—Joan Hallford
North Richland Hills, Texas, Field Editor**

- 1 cup packed brown sugar
- 1/2 cup sour cream
- 2 tablespoons plus 1/2 cup butter, *divided*
- 2 teaspoons cornstarch
- 1 teaspoon vanilla extract, *divided*
- 2 cups vanilla ice cream, softened
- 2 eggs
- 1-1/2 cups all-purpose flour
- 1 cup graham cracker crumbs
- 2/3 cup sugar
- 2-1/2 teaspoons baking powder
- 1/2 teaspoon salt
- 1/2 cup chopped pecans, toasted

Whipped cream, optional

1. In a heavy saucepan, combine the brown sugar, sour cream, 2 tablespoons butter and cornstarch. Cook and stir over medium heat until mixture comes to a boil. Remove from the heat.

2. Stir in 1/2 teaspoon of vanilla; set aside. Melt the remaining butter; place in a bowl. Add ice cream; stir to blend. Add eggs, one at a time, beating well after each addition; stir in the remaining vanilla. Combine flour, cracker crumbs, sugar, baking powder and salt; gradually add to ice cream mixture until combined.

3. Pour into a greased 13-in. x 9-in. baking pan. Drizzle with half of the praline sauce. Bake at 350° for 25-30 minutes or until a toothpick inserted near the center comes out clean. Cool on a wire rack.

4. Add pecans to remaining sauce; spoon over warm cake (sauce will not cover the entire cake top). Cool in pan. Serve with whipped cream if desired.

[2008]

CLASSIC CARROT CAKE

yield: 12 servings ∾ **prep: 30 min.**
bake: 35 min. + cooling

(Pictured on page 179)

I entered this yummy, moist cake in a Colorado Outfitters Association dessert contest, and it took first place!

—Cheri Eby, Gunnison, Colorado, Field Editor

1 **can (8 ounces) unsweetened crushed pineapple**
2 **cups shredded carrots**
4 **eggs**
1 **cup sugar**
1 **cup packed brown sugar**
1 **cup canola oil**
2 **cups all-purpose flour**
2 **teaspoons baking soda**
2 **teaspoons ground cinnamon**
1/4 **teaspoon salt**
3/4 **cup chopped walnuts**
FROSTING:
2 **packages (8 ounces *each*) cream cheese, softened**
1/4 **cup butter, softened**
2 **teaspoons vanilla extract**
1-1/2 **cups confectioners' sugar**

1. Drain the pineapple, reserving 2 tablespoons juice (discard remaining juice or save for another use). In a large bowl, beat the carrots, eggs, sugars, oil, pineapple and reserved juice until well blended. In a small bowl, combine the flour, baking soda, cinnamon and salt; gradually beat into pineapple mixture until blended. Stir in walnuts.

2. Transfer to a greased 13-in. x 9-in. baking dish. Bake at 350° for 35-40 minutes or until a toothpick inserted near the center comes out clean. Cool on a wire rack.

3. For frosting, in a large bowl, beat cream cheese and butter until smooth. Beat in vanilla. Gradually beat in confectioners' sugar until smooth. Spread over cake. Store in the refrigerator.

[2000]

RHUBARB CUSTARD CAKE

yield: 12-15 servings ∾ **prep: 10 min.**
bake: 40 min. + cooling

Rhubarb thrives in my northern garden and is one of the few crops the pesky moose don't bother! Of all the rhubarb desserts I've tried, this pudding cake is my number 1 choice. It has old-fashioned appeal but is so simple to prepare.

—Evelyn Gebhardt, Kasilof, Alaska, Former Field Editor

1 **package (18-1/4 ounces) yellow cake mix**
4 **cups chopped fresh *or* frozen rhubarb**
1 **cup sugar**
1 **cup heavy whipping cream**
Whipped cream and fresh mint, optional

1. Prepare cake batter according to package directions. Pour into a greased 13-in. x 9-in. baking dish. Sprinkle with rhubarb and sugar. Slowly pour cream over top.

2. Bake at 350° for 40-45 minutes or until golden brown. Cool the cake for 15 minutes before serving. Garnish with the whipped cream and mint if desired. Store in the refrigerator.

Editor's Note: If using frozen rhubarb, measure rhubarb while still frozen, then thaw completely. Drain in a colander, but do not press liquid out.

FROSTING TOO THICK OR THIN?

If your frosting is not the right consistency for spreading, it is easily fixed. If it's too thick, add milk a teaspoon at a time until it's the right consistency. If it's too thin, let it stand for 10 to 20 minutes; it may thicken up by itself. If it's still too thin, beat in some sifted confectioners' sugar until it is spreadable.

—Taste of Home Cooking Experts

[1995]

LAZY DAISY CAKE

yield: 16-20 servings   **prep: 25 min.**
bake: 35 min.

(*Pictured on page 184*)

We couldn't wait until Mom sliced this old-fashioned cake with its caramel-like frosting, loaded with chewy coconut. Even after one of Mom's delicious meals, one piece of this cake wasn't enough.

—*Darlis Wilfer*
West Bend, Wisconsin, Field Editor

  4 **eggs**
  2 **cups sugar**
  2 **teaspoons vanilla extract**
  2 **cups all-purpose flour**
  2 **teaspoons baking powder**
1/2 **teaspoon salt**
  1 **cup 2% milk**
1/4 **cup butter, cubed**
FROSTING:
1-1/2 **cups packed brown sugar**
3/4 **cup butter, melted**
1/2 **cup half-and-half cream**
  2 **cups flaked coconut**

1. In a large bowl, beat the eggs, sugar and vanilla until thick and pale yellow, about 4 minutes. Combine the flour, baking powder and salt; add to egg mixture and beat just until combined. In a saucepan, bring milk and butter to a boil, stirring constantly. Add to batter and beat until combined.

2. Pour into a greased 13-in. x 9-in. baking pan. Bake at 350° for 30-35 minutes or until a toothpick inserted near the center comes out clean.

3. Combine frosting ingredients; spread over warm cake. Broil 4 in. from heat until lightly browned, about 3-4 minutes.

[2000]

UPSIDE-DOWN STRAWBERRY SHORTCAKE

yield: 12-16 servings   **prep: 20 min.**
bake: 45 min.

(*Pictured on page 184*)

For a tasty twist at dessert time, this special spring shortcake dessert has a bountiful berry layer on the bottom. The tempting cake is a sweet our family has savored for years.

—*Debra Falkiner, St. Charles, Missouri*

  1 **cup miniature marshmallows**
  2 **packages (10 ounces each) frozen sweetened sliced strawberries**
  1 **package (3 ounces) strawberry gelatin**
1/2 **cup shortening**
1-1/2 **cups sugar**
  3 **eggs**
  1 **teaspoon vanilla extract**
2-1/4 **cups all-purpose flour**
  3 **teaspoons baking powder**
1/2 **teaspoon salt**
  1 **cup 2% milk**
Fresh strawberries and whipped cream

1. Sprinkle marshmallows evenly into a greased 13-in. x 9-in. baking dish; set aside. In a bowl, combine strawberries and gelatin powder; set aside.

2. In a large bowl, cream shortening and sugar until light and fluffy. Add eggs, one at a time, beating well after each addition. Beat in vanilla. Combine the flour, baking powder and salt; add to creamed mixture alternately with milk, beating well after each addition.

3. Pour batter over the marshmallows. Spoon strawberry mixture evenly over batter. Bake at 350° for 45-50 minutes or until a toothpick inserted near the center comes out clean. Cool on a wire rack. Cut into squares. Garnish with strawberries and whipped cream.

UPSIDE-DOWN STRAWBERRY SHORTCAKE

❝Delicious! This turned out better than I expected and was the perfect summer dessert. It would be good with whipped topping or ice cream, but it is wonderful on its own! I will make this again and again. It is easy and great enough for company! I am going to try it with blueberries next time.❞
—*gitrumm*

[2004]

CRANBERRY ZUCCHINI WEDGES

yield: 2 cakes (8 wedges each)
prep: 15 min.   bake: 30 min. + cooling

I try to slip zucchini into as many dishes as possible. These cake wedges have wonderful, unique flavor and a tender texture—and they're pretty, too.

—Redawna Kalynchuk, Sexsmith, Alberta, Field Editor

    1 can (20 ounces) pineapple chunks
    3 cups all-purpose flour
1-3/4 cups sugar
    1 teaspoon baking powder
    1 teaspoon baking soda
    1 teaspoon salt
    3 eggs
    1 cup canola oil
    2 teaspoons vanilla extract
    1 cup tightly packed shredded zucchini
    1 cup fresh *or* frozen cranberries, halved
  1/2 cup chopped walnuts
Confectioners' sugar

1. Drain the pineapple, reserving 1/3 cup juice (save remaining juice for another use). Place the pineapple and reserved juice in a blender; cover and process until smooth. Set aside.

2. In a large bowl, combine the flour, sugar, baking powder, baking soda and salt. In a small bowl, whisk the eggs, oil, vanilla, pineapple mixture; stir into the dry ingredients until blended. Fold in the zucchini, cranberries and walnuts.

3. Pour into two greased and floured 9-in. round baking pans. Bake at 350° for 30-35 minutes or until a toothpick inserted near the center comes out clean. Cool for 10 minutes before removing from pans to wire racks to cool completely.

4. Just before serving, dust with confectioners' sugar.

[2000]

CREAM CAKE DESSERT

yield: 16-20 servings   prep: 30 min.
bake: 30 min. + cooling

Folks really go for this light cake with fluffy cream filling. My son first tried this treat while in high school and asked me to get the recipe. I've used it countless times since for all sorts of occasions. It's easy to transport to a potluck because the cream is on the inside.

—Peggy Stott, Lomax, Iowa

    1 package (18-1/4 ounces) yellow cake mix
    1 package (3.4 ounces) instant vanilla pudding mix
  1/2 cup shortening
    1 cup water
    4 eggs
FILLING:
    5 tablespoons all-purpose flour
    1 cup 2% milk
  1/2 cup butter, softened
  1/2 cup shortening
    1 cup sugar
    1 teaspoon vanilla extract
  1/2 teaspoon salt
Fresh raspberries, optional

1. In a large bowl, beat the cake mix, dry pudding mix and shortening on low speed until crumbly. Add water and eggs; beat on low speed for 30 seconds. Beat on medium for 2 minutes. Pour into a greased and floured 13-in. x 9-in. baking pan.

2. Bake at 350° for 30-35 minutes or until a toothpick inserted near the center comes out clean. Cool for 10 minutes; invert onto a wire rack to cool completely.

3. Meanwhile, in a small saucepan, combine flour and milk until smooth. Bring to a boil; cook and stir for 2 minutes or until thickened. Cool completely.

4. In a large bowl, cream the butter, shortening and sugar until light and fluffy. Beat in the milk mixture, vanilla and salt until smooth.

5. Cut cake horizontally into two layers. Place bottom layer on a serving plate; top with the filling. Top with the remaining cake layer. Garnish with the raspberries if desired.

[1996]

SPICED PINEAPPLE UPSIDE-DOWN CAKE

**yield: 12 servings ∞ prep: 15 min.
bake: 40 min.**

Upside-down cakes, which have been around since the 1800's, were once called skillet cakes because they were cooked in cast-iron skillets on the stovetop.

—*Jennifer Sergesketter, Newburgh, Indiana*

- 1-1/3 cups butter, softened, *divided*
- 1 cup packed brown sugar
- 1 can (20 ounces) pineapple slices, drained
- 10 to 12 maraschino cherries
- 1/2 cup chopped pecans
- 1-1/2 cups sugar
- 2 eggs
- 1 teaspoon vanilla extract
- 2 cups all-purpose flour
- 2 teaspoons baking powder
- 1/2 teaspoon baking soda
- 1/2 teaspoon salt
- 1/2 teaspoon ground cinnamon
- 1/2 teaspoon ground nutmeg
- 1 cup buttermilk

1. In a saucepan, melt 2/3 cup of butter; stir in brown sugar. Spread in the bottom of an ungreased heavy 12-in. skillet or a 13-in. x 9-in. baking pan. Arrange pineapple in a single layer over sugar mixture; place a cherry in the center of each slice. Sprinkle with pecans and set aside.

2. In a large bowl, cream sugar and remaining butter until light and fluffy. Add eggs, one at a time, beating well after each addition. Beat in vanilla. Combine flour, baking powder, baking soda, salt, cinnamon and nutmeg; add alternately to batter with buttermilk, beating well after each addition.

3. Carefully pour over pineapple. Bake at 350° for 40 minutes for skillet (50-60 minutes for baking pan) or until a toothpick inserted near the center comes out clean. Immediately invert onto a serving platter. Serve warm.

[1994]

HOT FUDGE CAKE

**yield: 9 servings ∞ prep: 20 min.
bake: 35 min.**

Here's a wonderful way to top off a great meal.

—*Vera Reid
Laramie, Wyoming, Field Editor*

- 1 cup all-purpose flour
- 3/4 cup sugar
- 6 tablespoons baking cocoa, *divided*
- 2 teaspoons baking powder
- 1/4 teaspoon salt
- 1/2 cup 2% milk
- 2 tablespoons canola oil
- 1 teaspoon vanilla extract
- 1 cup packed brown sugar
- 1-3/4 cups hot water

Whipped cream *or* ice cream, optional

1. In a large bowl, combine the flour, sugar, 2 tablespoons cocoa, baking powder and salt. Stir in the milk, oil and vanilla until smooth.

2. Spread in an ungreased 9-in. square baking pan. Combine brown sugar and remaining cocoa; sprinkle over batter. Pour hot water over all; do not stir.

3. Bake at 350° for 35-40 minutes. Serve warm. Top with whipped cream or ice cream if desired.

SPICED PINEAPPLE UPSIDE-DOWN CAKE

❝What a great twist on an old fave! I found the spices to be really appealing in this recipe. I added a little extra cinnamon so the nutmeg wouldn't be overpowering. We loved this cake! Next time though, I think I will use a little less butter and sugar for the pineapple layer—it was a little too much for us.**❞**

—*Dizzaster*

[2004]

GERMAN CHOCOLATE
CREAM CHEESE CAKE

yield: 16 servings ∽ **prep: 15 min.**
bake: 1-1/4 hours + cooling

(Pictured on page 182)

My daughter requests this as her birthday cake, and I take it to potlucks, church dinners or any time the dessert is my responsibility.

—*Kathy Johnson, Lake City, South Dakota*

---

  1 package (18-1/4 ounces) German Chocolate cake mix
  2 packages (8 ounces *each*) cream cheese, softened
1-1/2 cups sugar
  4 eggs, lightly beaten
FROSTING:
  1 cup sugar
  1 cup evaporated milk
1/2 cup butter, cubed
  3 egg yolks, lightly beaten
  1 teaspoon vanilla extract
1-1/2 cups flaked coconut
  1 cup chopped pecans

---

1. Prepare cake batter according to package directions; set aside. In a small bowl, beat cream cheese and sugar until smooth. Add eggs; beat on low speed just until combined.

2. Pour half of the cake batter into a greased 13-in. x 9-in. baking dish. Gently pour cream cheese mixture over batter. Gently spoon remaining batter over top; spread to edge of pan.

3. Bake at 325° for 70-75 minutes or until a toothpick inserted near the center comes out clean. Cool on a wire rack for 1 hour.

4. For frosting, in a heavy saucepan, combine sugar, milk, butter and egg yolks. Cook and stir over medium-low heat until thickened and a thermometer reads 160° or is thick enough to coat the back of a metal spoon.

5. Remove from the heat. Stir in vanilla; fold in coconut and pecans. Cool until frosting reaches spreading consistency. Frost cooled cake. Refrigerate leftovers.

[2003]

ZUCCHINI CHIP
SNACK CAKE

yield: 12-15 servings ∽ **prep: 15 min.**
bake: 45 min.

Here's a mouthwatering dessert that is so rich, it doesn't need frosting. The shredded zucchini makes it especially moist. With a scoop of vanilla ice cream, this cake makes an unbeatable finale for any occasion.

—*Mared Metzgar Beling, Eagle River, Alaska*

1/2 cup butter, softened
1-3/4 cups sugar
  2 eggs
1/2 cup canola oil
  1 teaspoon vanilla extract
2-1/2 cups all-purpose flour
  2 tablespoons baking cocoa
  1 teaspoon baking soda
1/2 teaspoon baking powder
1/2 teaspoon ground cinnamon
1/2 teaspoon ground cloves
1/2 cup buttermilk
  2 cups shredded peeled zucchini
  2 cups (12 ounces) semisweet chocolate chips

---

1. In a large bowl, cream butter and sugar until light and fluffy. Add eggs, one at a time, beating well after each addition. Beat in oil and vanilla. Combine the dry ingredients; add to the creamed mixture alternately with buttermilk, beating well after each addition. Stir in the zucchini.

2. Pour into a greased 13-in. x 9-in. baking pan. Sprinkle with chocolate chips. Bake at 350° for 45-50 minutes or until a toothpick inserted near the center comes out clean. Cool on a wire rack.

[2007]

POPPY SEED CAKE

yield: 12-15 servings
prep: 20 min. + standing
bake: 25 min. + cooling

A sweet ending for my favorite meal, this moist cake is chock-full of poppy seeds. The cream cheese frosting adds the final touch!

—*Darlis Wilfer*
West Bend, Wisconsin, Field Editor

- 1/3 cup poppy seeds
- 1 cup 2% milk
- 4 egg whites
- 3/4 cup shortening
- 1-1/2 cups sugar
- 1 teaspoon vanilla extract
- 2 cups all-purpose flour
- 2 teaspoons baking powder

CREAM CHEESE FROSTING:

- 1 package (8 ounces) cream cheese, softened
- 1/2 cup butter, softened
- 1 teaspoon vanilla extract
- 2 cups confectioners' sugar

---

1. In a small bowl, soak poppy seeds in milk for 30 minutes. Place egg whites in a large bowl; let stand at room temperature for 30 minutes.

2. In a large bowl, cream shortening and sugar until light and fluffy. Beat in the vanilla. Mix flour and baking powder; add to creamed mixture alternately with poppy seed mixture, beating well after each addition. Using clean beater, beat whites until soft peaks form; fold into batter.

3. Pour into a greased 13-in. x 9-in. baking dish. Bake at 375° for 25-30 minutes or until a toothpick inserted near center comes out clean. Cool on a wire rack.

4. For frosting, in a large bowl, beat cream cheese, butter and vanilla until smooth. Gradually beat in confectioners' sugar. Spread over cake. Store in the refrigerator.

[2004]

COCONUT BLUEBERRY CAKE

yield: 12-15 servings ∞ **prep: 15 min.**
bake: 25 min. + cooling

We pick wild blueberries every summer and store plenty of them in the freezer. That way, we can enjoy this delicious coffee cake all year long.

—*Janis Plourde*
Smooth Rock Falls, Ontario, Field Editor

- 2 cups all-purpose flour
- 1 cup sugar
- 3 teaspoons baking powder
- 1/4 teaspoon salt
- 2 eggs
- 1 cup milk
- 1/2 cup canola oil
- 1-1/2 cups fresh or frozen blueberries
- 1 cup flaked coconut

LEMON SAUCE:

- 1/2 cup sugar
- 4-1/2 teaspoons cornstarch
- 1 teaspoon grated lemon peel
- 1 cup water
- 1 tablespoon butter
- 2 tablespoons lemon juice

---

1. In a bowl, combine dry ingredients. Beat the eggs, milk and oil; stir into the dry ingredients just until moistened. Fold in blueberries. Transfer to a greased 13-in. x 9-in. baking dish. Sprinkle with coconut. Bake at 375° for 22-24 minutes or until a toothpick inserted near the center comes out clean. Cool on a wire rack.

2. In a small saucepan, combine sugar, cornstarch and lemon peel. Gradually add water until blended. Bring to a boil; cook and stir for 2 minutes or until thickened. Remove from the heat; stir in butter and lemon juice. Cut cake into squares; drizzle with lemon sauce.

Editor's Note: If using frozen blueberries, use them without thawing to avoid discoloring the batter.

POPPY SEED CAKE

❝So good and moist! This is a staple when I need to bring dessert somewhere. The frosting is delicious as well.❞

—*hjwoodward*

IDAHO
POTATO CAKE

❝ Moist, fluffy and most of all YUMMY!!**❞**
—ray tice

[1993]

IDAHO POTATO CAKE

yield: 12-16 servings ∾ **prep: 15 min.**
bake: 40 min.

Potatoes in dessert? Many cooks never think of the possibility. But this delicious cake gets its moist texture from Idaho spuds. We raise them here on our farm, and our son has also developed and now markets potato ice cream!

—LaRene Reed, Idaho Falls, Idaho

1 cup butter, softened
2 cups sugar
2 eggs
1 cup cold mashed potatoes
1 teaspoon vanilla extract
2 cups all-purpose flour
1/4 cup baking cocoa
1 teaspoon baking soda
1 cup 2% milk
1 cup chopped nuts

1. In a large bowl, cream butter and sugar until light and fluffy. Add eggs, one at a time, beating well after each addition. Beat in potatoes and vanilla. Combine the flour, cocoa and baking soda; add alternately with milk, beating well after each addition. Stir in nuts.

2. Pour batter into a greased 13-in. x 9-in. baking pan. Bake at 350° for 40-45 minutes or until a toothpick inserted near the center comes out clean. Cool on a wire rack.

POTLUCK CAKES

Cakes baked in a 13-in. x 9-in. pan are so easy to take to potlucks... just cover the pan with foil. Precut the cake into uniform sizes just before serving.

—Taste of Home Cooking Experts

[2002]

CHOCOLATE OAT SNACK CAKE

yield: 12-16 servings ∾ **prep: 20 min.**
bake: 40 min.

A sprinkling of walnuts and chips tops this subtly sweet treat.

—Bonnie Spaulding
Litchfield, New Hampshire

1-3/4 cups boiling water
1 cup quick-cooking oats
1/2 cup butter, softened
1 cup sugar
1 cup packed brown sugar
2 eggs
1-3/4 cups all-purpose flour
2 tablespoons baking cocoa
1 teaspoon baking soda
1/2 teaspoon salt
1 package (11-1/2 ounces) milk chocolate chips, *divided*
1 cup chopped walnuts

1. In a small bowl, combine the water and oats; let stand for 10 minutes. Meanwhile, in a large bowl, cream the butter and sugars until light and fluffy. Add the eggs, one at a time, beating well after each addition. Beat in oat mixture. Combine the flour, cocoa, baking soda and salt; gradually add to creamed mixture and mix well. Stir in 1 cup chips.

2. Pour batter into a greased 13-in. x 9-in. baking pan. Sprinkle with the walnuts and remaining chips. Bake at 350° for 40-45 minutes or until a toothpick comes out clean. Cool on a wire rack.

[2007]

CHOCOLATE CREAM CHEESE CUPCAKES

**yield: 20 cupcakes ～ prep: 30 min.
bake: 25 min. + cooling**

I got the recipe for these moist filled cupcakes from a dear friend many, many years ago. I have made them many times for my family and for church functions. They're irresistible.

—*Vivian Morris, Cleburne, Texas*

1 package (8 ounces) cream cheese, softened
1-1/2 cups sugar, *divided*
1 egg
1 teaspoon salt, *divided*
1 cup (6 ounces) semisweet chocolate chips
1-1/2 cups all-purpose flour
1/4 cup baking cocoa
1 teaspoon baking soda
1 cup water
1/3 cup canola oil
1 tablespoon white vinegar
FROSTING:
3-3/4 cups confectioners' sugar
3 tablespoons baking cocoa
1/2 cup butter, melted
6 tablespoons milk
1 teaspoon vanilla extract
1/3 cup chopped pecans

1. For filling, in a small bowl, beat cream cheese and 1/2 cup sugar until smooth. Beat in egg and 1/2 teaspoon salt until combined. Fold in chocolate chips; set aside.

2. In a bowl, combine the flour, cocoa, baking soda, and remaining sugar and salt. In another bowl, whisk the water, oil and vinegar; stir into dry ingredients just until moistened.

3. Fill paper-lined muffin cups half full with batter. Drop filling by heaping tablespoonfuls into the center of each. Bake at 350° for 24-26 minutes or until a toothpick inserted in cake comes out clean. Cool for 10 minutes; remove from pans to wire racks to cool completely.

4. For frosting, in a large bowl, combine confectioners' sugar, cocoa, butter, milk and vanilla; beat until blended. Frost cupcakes; sprinkle with the pecans. Store in the refrigerator.

[2007]

CHIP LOVER'S CUPCAKES

**yield: 1-1/2 dozen ～ prep: 30 min.
bake: 20 min. + cooling**

Making chocolate chip cookies is a challenge with three teenagers who are always grabbing the dough to sample. Their love of cookie dough inspired the recipe for these cupcakes.

—*Donna Scully, Middletown, Delaware*

1 package (18-1/4 ounces) white cake mix
1/4 cup butter, softened
1/4 cup packed brown sugar
2 tablespoons sugar
1/3 cup all-purpose flour
1/4 cup confectioners' sugar
1/4 cup miniature semisweet chocolate chips
BUTTERCREAM FROSTING:
1/2 cup butter, softened
1/2 cup shortening
4-1/2 cups confectioners' sugar
4 tablespoons 2% milk, *divided*
1-1/2 teaspoons vanilla extract
1/4 cup baking cocoa
18 miniature chocolate chip cookies

1. Prepare cake batter according to package directions. For filling, in a large bowl, cream butter and sugars until light and fluffy. Gradually beat in the flour and confectioners' sugar until blended. Fold in the chocolate chips.

2. Fill paper-lined muffin cups half full with cake batter. Drop filling by tablespoonfuls into the center of each; cover with remaining batter.

3. Bake at 350° for 20-22 minutes or until a toothpick inserted in cake comes out clean. Cool for 10 minutes; remove from pans to wire racks to cool completely.

4. For frosting, in a large bowl, cream butter, shortening and confectioners' sugar until smooth. Beat in 3 tablespoons milk and vanilla until creamy. Set aside 1 cup frosting; frost cupcakes with remaining frosting.

5. Stir baking cocoa and remaining milk into reserved frosting. Cut a small hole in a corner of a pastry or plastic bag; insert star tip. Fill bag with the chocolate frosting. Pipe a rosette on top of each cupcake; garnish with a cookie.

[2002]

LEMON TEA CAKES

yield: 8-1/2 dozen ∾ prep: 30 min.
bake: 10 min./batch + cooling

(Pictured on page 180)

Whenever I serve these lovely, bite-size, glazed cakes, they get rave reviews...and I get requests for the recipe. Lemon and cream cheese make for a winning combination.

—*Charlene Crump, Montgomery, Alabama*

1-1/2 cups butter, softened
   1 package (8 ounces) cream cheese, softened
2-1/4 cups sugar
   6 eggs
   3 tablespoons lemon juice
   2 teaspoons lemon extract
   1 teaspoon vanilla extract
1-1/2 teaspoons grated lemon peel
   3 cups all-purpose flour
GLAZE:
5-1/4 cups confectioners' sugar
 1/2 cup plus 3 tablespoons 2% milk
3-1/2 teaspoons lemon extract

1. In a large bowl, cream the butter, cream cheese and sugar until light and fluffy. Add eggs, one at a time, beating well after each addition. Beat in the lemon juice, extracts and lemon peel. Add flour; beat just until moistened.

2. Fill greased miniature muffin cups two-thirds full. Bake at 325° for 10-15 minutes or until a toothpick inserted near the center comes out clean. Cool for 5 minutes before removing from pans to wire racks to cool completely.

3. In a small bowl, combine glaze ingredients. Dip tops of cakes into glaze; place on waxed paper to dry.

LEMON TEA CAKES

❝OH my ohhh so yummy! Made these for Easter— everyone loved them. Couldn't stop eating these little things! My hubby thinks they get more lemony over time...soo soo good.❞
—*kat83*

[2007]

SOUR CREAM CHOCOLATE CUPCAKES

yield: 2 dozen ∾ prep: 30 min.
bake: 20 min. + cooling

The sour cream is definitely the ingredient that gives these cupcakes their distinction.

—*Alicsa Mayer, Alta Vista, Kansas*

1/4 cup butter, cubed
   4 ounces unsweetened chocolate, chopped
   2 eggs
   2 cups sugar
   1 cup water
3/4 cup sour cream
   1 teaspoon vanilla extract
   2 cups all-purpose flour
   1 teaspoon baking soda
FROSTING:
1/2 cup butter, cubed
   4 ounces unsweetened chocolate, chopped
   4 cups confectioners' sugar
1/2 cup sour cream
   2 teaspoons vanilla extract

1. In a microwave, melt the butter and chocolate; stir until smooth. Cool for 10 minutes. In a bowl, beat eggs, sugar, water, sour cream and vanilla. Combine dry ingredients; add to egg mixture and mix well. Add chocolate mixture; beat on high speed for 2-3 minutes.

2. Fill paper-lined muffin cups two-thirds full. Bake at 350° for 18-20 minutes or until a toothpick inserted near center comes out clean. Cool for 10 minutes before removing from pans to wire racks to cool completely.

3. For frosting, in a microwave, melt butter and chocolate; stir until smooth. Cool for 10 minutes. With a portable mixer, beat in confectioners' sugar, sour cream and vanilla on low until smooth. Frost cupcakes. Store in the refrigerator.

[2007]

PINK VELVET CUPCAKES

yield: 2 dozen ∽ **prep: 30 min. + chilling**
bake: 25 min. + cooling

(Pictured on page 179)

*Pretty in pink, these cupcakes were a big
success at my daughter's princess-themed
birthday party!*

—Paulette Smith
Winston-Salem, North Carolina

1	cup butter, softened
1-1/4	cups sugar
1/8	teaspoon pink paste food coloring
3	eggs
1	teaspoon vanilla extract
2-1/2	cups all-purpose flour
1-1/2	teaspoons baking powder
1/4	teaspoon baking soda
1/4	teaspoon salt
1	cup buttermilk

WHITE CHOCOLATE GANACHE:

2	cups white baking chips
1/2	cup heavy whipping cream
1	tablespoon butter

Pink coarse sugar and edible glitter

1. In a large bowl, cream the butter, sugar and food coloring until light and fluffy. Add eggs, one at a time, beating well after each addition. Beat in the vanilla. Combine the flour, baking powder, baking soda and salt; add to creamed mixture alternately with buttermilk, beating well after each addition.

2. Fill paper-lined muffin cups two-thirds full. Bake at 350° for 23-27 minutes or until a toothpick inserted near the center comes out clean. Cool for 10 minutes before removing from pans to wire racks to cool completely.

3. Place white chips in a small bowl. In a saucepan, bring cream just to a boil. Pour over chips; whisk until smooth. Stir in butter. Transfer to a large bowl. Chill for 30 minutes, stirring once.

4. Beat on high speed for 2-3 minutes or until soft peaks form and frosting is light and fluffy. Cut a small hole in the corner of a pastry or plastic bag; insert #30 star tip. Fill the bag with frosting; frost the cupcakes. Sprinkle with the coarse sugar and edible glitter. Store in the refrigerator.

Editor's Note: Edible glitter is available from Wilton Industries. Call 800-794-5866 or visit wilton.com.

[1994]

PICNIC CUPCAKES

yield: 24 servings ∽ **prep: 20 min.**
bake: 20 min.

(Pictured on page 184)

*These moist cupcakes don't need frosting, so
they're perfect for a picnic or traveling. Kids
and adults love them!*

—Florence Leinweber
Endicott, Washington

1	package (18-1/4 ounces) chocolate *or yellow cake mix*

FILLING:

1	package (8 ounces) cream cheese, softened
1	egg, lightly beaten
1/3	cup sugar
1	cup (6 ounces) semisweet chocolate chips

1. Prepare cake mix batter according to package directions for cupcakes. Fill 24 paper-lined muffin cups two-thirds full.

2. In a small bowl, beat cream cheese, egg and sugar until smooth. Fold in chips.

3. Drop by tablespoonfuls into batter. Bake at 350° for 20 minutes or until a toothpick inserted in the cupcake comes out clean. Cool for 10 minutes before removing from pans to wire racks to cool completely.

PINK VELVET CUPCAKES

"Quite good—I never know why it's called velvet. I realize this is a play on the red velvet cake. But this turns out to be a flavorful, dense cake with the most scrumptious frosting I have ever eaten! Oh my... so good."
—*maggieaw*

[1997]

CUPCAKE CONES

yield: about 2 dozen ∾ prep: 15 min.
bake: 25 min.

(Pictured on page 182)

Children love this treat, which is not as messy as a piece of cake.

—*Mina Dyck*
Boissevain, Manitoba, Former Field Editor

- 1/3 cup butter, softened
- 1/2 cup creamy peanut butter
- 1-1/2 cups packed brown sugar
- 2 eggs
- 1 teaspoon vanilla extract
- 2 cups all-purpose flour
- 2-1/2 teaspoons baking powder
- 1/2 teaspoon salt
- 3/4 cup 2% milk
- 24 ice cream cake cones (about 3 inches tall)
- Frosting of your choice
- Sprinkles *or* chopped peanuts, optional

1. In a large bowl, cream the butter, peanut butter and brown sugar until light and fluffy. Beat in eggs and vanilla. Combine dry ingredients; add to creamed mixture alternately with milk, beating well after each addition.

2. Place ice cream cones in muffin cups. Spoon about 3 tablespoons batter into each cone, filling to 3/4 in. from top.

3. Bake at 350° for 25-30 minutes or until a toothpick inserted near the center of the cake comes out clean. Cool the cupcakes completely on wire racks. Frost and decorate as desired.

Editor's Note: Reduced-fat peanut butter is not recommended for this recipe.

[2008]

PUMPKIN CUPCAKES

yield: 16 cupcakes ∾ prep: 30 min.
bake: 20 min. + cooling

(Pictured on page 178)

A unique mix of pineapple and pumpkin creates a cupcake with mouthwatering flavor.

—*Mary Relyea, Canastota, New York*

- 2/3 cup shortening
- 2 eggs
- 3/4 cup maple syrup
- 1/2 cup 2% milk
- 1-1/2 cups all-purpose flour
- 1-1/4 teaspoons baking powder
- 1/2 teaspoon salt
- 1/2 teaspoon baking soda
- 1/2 teaspoon ground ginger
- 1/2 teaspoon ground allspice
- 1 cup canned pumpkin
- 1 can (8 ounces) crushed pineapple, drained
- 1 package (8 ounces) cream cheese, softened
- 1/4 cup butter, softened
- 1-1/2 cups confectioners' sugar

1. In a large bowl, beat shortening until light and fluffy. Add eggs, one at a time, beating well after each addition (mixture will appear curdled). Beat in syrup and milk. Combine the flour, baking powder, salt, baking soda, ginger and allspice; add to shortening mixture and beat just until moistened. Stir in pumpkin and pineapple.

2. Fill paper-lined muffin cups two-thirds full. Bake at 350° for 20-25 minutes or until a toothpick inserted near the center comes out clean. Cool for 10 minutes before removing from pans to a wire rack to cool completely.

3. For frosting, in a small bowl, beat the cream cheese and butter until fluffy. Add confectioners' sugar; beat until smooth. Frost cupcakes.

[2007]

APPLE BUTTER CAKE ROLL

**yield: 10 servings ∞ prep: 35 min.
bake: 15 min. + chilling**

This is a new take on a pumpkin roll. My spicy gingerbread cake might make you think back to Christmas at Grandma's.

—*Debbie White, Williamson, West Virginia, Field Editor*

---

3   eggs, *separated*
1   cup all-purpose flour, *divided*
2   tablespoons plus 1/2 cup sugar, *divided*
2   teaspoons ground cinnamon
1   teaspoon baking powder
1   teaspoon ground ginger
1   teaspoon ground cloves
1/4 teaspoon baking soda
1/4 cup butter, melted
1/4 cup molasses
2   tablespoons water
1   tablespoon confectioners' sugar
2   cups apple butter

---

1. Place egg whites in a small bowl; let stand at room temperature for 30 minutes. Line a greased 15-in. x 10-in. x 1-in. baking pan with waxed paper and grease the paper. Sprinkle paper with 1 tablespoon flour and 2 tablespoons sugar; set aside.

2. In a large bowl, combine remaining flour and sugar; add the cinnamon, baking powder, ginger, cloves and baking soda. In another bowl, whisk the egg yolks, butter, molasses and water. Add to dry ingredients and beat until blended. Using clean beaters, beat egg whites on medium speed until soft peaks form; fold into batter. Pour into prepared pan.

3. Bake at 375° for 12-14 minutes or until cake springs back when lightly touched. Cool for 5 minutes. Turn cake onto a kitchen towel dusted with confectioners' sugar. Peel off waxed paper. Roll up cake in towel jelly-roll style, starting with a short side. Cool completely on a wire rack.

4. Unroll cake; spread apple butter to within 1/2 in. of edges. Roll up again. Cover and chill for 1 hour before serving. Refrigerate leftovers.

Editor's Note: This recipe was tested with commercially prepared apple butter.

[2000]

GLAZED LEMON CHIFFON CAKE

**yield: 16 servings ∞ prep: 15 min.
bake: 45 min. + cooling**

It's a real treat to serve this delightful chiffon cake. It has a divine lemon flavor and is drizzled with sweet-tart lemon glaze.

—*Rebecca Baird, Salt Lake City, Utah, Field Editor*

---

1   cup egg whites (about 7)
1/2   cup fat-free evaporated milk
1/2   cup reduced-fat sour cream
1/4   cup lemon juice
2   tablespoons canola oil
2   teaspoons vanilla extract
1   teaspoon grated lemon peel
1   teaspoon lemon extract
2   cups cake flour
1-1/2 cups sugar
1   tablespoon baking powder
1/2   teaspoon salt
1/2   teaspoon cream of tartar
LEMON GLAZE:
1-3/4 cups confectioners' sugar
3   tablespoons lemon juice

---

1. Place egg whites in a large bowl; let stand at room temperature for 30 minutes. In another large bowl, combine the milk, sour cream, lemon juice, oil, vanilla, lemon peel and lemon extract. Sift together the flour, sugar, baking powder and salt; gradually beat into lemon mixture until smooth. With clean beaters, beat egg whites until foamy. Add cream of tartar; beat until stiff peaks form. Gently fold into the lemon mixture.

2. Gently spoon into an ungreased 10-in. tube pan with removable bottom. Cut through batter with a knife to remove air pockets

3. Bake on the lowest oven rack at 325° for 45-55 minutes or until cake springs back when lightly touched. Immediately invert pan; cool completely, about 1 hour.

4. Run a knife around sides and center tube of pan. Remove cake to a serving platter. Combine glaze ingredients; drizzle over cake.

[1998]

PUMPKIN CAKE ROLL
yield: 8-10 servings ⚯ prep: 25 min.
bake: 15 min.

This lovely cake is delicious—especially if you like cream cheese and pumpkin. It tastes so good in fall and makes a fancy dessert for Thanksgiving, too.

—*Elizabeth Montgomery, Allston, Massachusetts*

    3 eggs
    1 cup sugar
  2/3 cup canned pumpkin
    1 teaspoon lemon juice
  3/4 cup all-purpose flour
    2 teaspoons ground cinnamon
    1 teaspoon baking powder
  1/2 teaspoon salt
  1/4 teaspoon ground nutmeg
    1 cup finely chopped walnuts
    1 tablespoon confectioners' sugar
CREAM CHEESE FILLING:
    2 packages (3 ounces *each*) cream cheese, softened
    1 cup confectioners' sugar
  1/4 cup butter, softened
  1/2 teaspoon vanilla extract
Additional confectioners' sugar

1. In a large bowl, beat the eggs on high for 5 minutes until thick and lemon-colored. Gradually beat in sugar until thicker and pale yellow. Add pumpkin and lemon juice. Combine the flour, cinnamon, baking powder, salt and nutmeg; fold into pumpkin mixture.

2. Grease a 15-in. x 10-in. x 1-in. baking pan and line with waxed paper. Grease and flour paper. Spread batter into pan; sprinkle with nuts. Bake at 375° for 15 minutes or until cake springs back when lightly touched.

3. Immediately turn out onto a kitchen towel dusted with confectioners' sugar. Gently peel off paper and roll cake up in towel, starting with a short end. Cool.

4. Meanwhile, in a large bowl, beat the cream cheese, sugar, butter and vanilla until fluffy. Carefully unroll the cake. Spread filling over cake to within 1 in. of edges. Roll up again. Cover and chill until serving. Dust with confectioners' sugar.

[2011]

INCREDIBLE COCONUT CAKE
yield: 16 servings ⚯ prep: 35 min.
bake: 25 min. + chilling

I found this recipe in a newspaper many years ago and modified it to suit my taste. This is my all-time favorite cake, and my family and friends absolutely love it.

—*Lynne Bassler, Indiana, Pennsylvania*

    5 eggs, *separated*
    2 cups sugar
  1/2 cup butter, softened
  1/2 cup canola oil
    1 teaspoon coconut extract
  1/2 teaspoon vanilla extract
  1/4 teaspoon almond extract
2-1/4 cups cake flour
    1 teaspoon baking powder
  1/2 teaspoon baking soda
  1/4 teaspoon salt
    1 cup buttermilk
    2 cups flaked coconut, chopped
  1/4 teaspoon cream of tartar
FROSTING:
    2 packages (one 8 ounces, one 3 ounces) cream cheese, softened
  2/3 cup butter, softened
4-1/3 cups confectioners' sugar
1-1/4 teaspoons coconut extract
    2 cups flaked coconut, toasted

1. Place egg whites in a large bowl; let stand at room temperature for 30 minutes. In another large bowl, beat the sugar, butter and oil until light and fluffy. Add egg yolks, one at a time, beating well after each addition. Beat in extracts.

2. Combine flour, baking powder, baking soda and salt; add to creamed mixture alternately with buttermilk, beating well after each addition. Stir in coconut.

3. Add cream of tartar to egg whites; using clean beaters, beat until stiff peaks form. Gently fold into batter.

4. Transfer to three greased and floured 9-in. round baking pans. Bake at 325° for 25-30 minutes or until a toothpick inserted near the center comes out clean.

Cool the cake for 10 minutes before removing from pans to wire racks to cool completely.

5. For frosting, in a small bowl, beat the cream cheese and butter until fluffy. Add confectioners' sugar and extract; beat until smooth.

6. Place one cake layer on a serving plate; spread with 1/2 cup of the frosting and sprinkle with 1/3 cup coconut. Repeat. Top with remaining cake layer. Spread remaining frosting over top and sides of cake; sprinkle with the remaining coconut. Refrigerate for 2 hours before cutting. Store in the refrigerator.

[1998]

CHOCOLATE ANGEL CAKE

yield: 12-16 servings   prep: 25 min.
bake: 35 min. + cooling

When I first got married, I could barely boil water. My mother-in-law taught me her specialty of making the lightest angel food cakes ever. This chocolate version is an impressive treat. For many years, it was our son's birthday cake.

—*Joyce Shiffler, Colorado Springs, Colorado*

1-1/2   cups egg whites (about 10)
1-1/2   cups confectioners' sugar
   1   cup cake flour
  1/4   cup baking cocoa
1-1/2   teaspoons cream of tartar
  1/2   teaspoon salt
   1   cup sugar
FROSTING:
1-1/2   cups heavy whipping cream
  1/2   cup sugar
  1/4   cup baking cocoa
  1/2   teaspoon salt
  1/2   teaspoon vanilla extract
  Chocolate leaves, optional

1. Place the egg whites in a large bowl; let stand at room temperature for 30 minutes. Sift together confectioners' sugar, flour and cocoa three times and set aside.

2. Add cream of tartar and salt to egg whites; beat on medium speed until soft peaks form. Gradually add sugar, about 2 tablespoons at a time; beat on high until stiff glossy peaks form and sugar is dissolved. Gradually fold in flour mixture, about 1/2 cup at a time.

3. Spoon into an ungreased 10-in. tube pan. Carefully run a metal spatula or knife through the batter to remove air pockets. Bake on the lowest oven rack at 375° for 35-40 minutes or until lightly browned and entire top appears dry. Immediately invert the pan; cool completely, about 1 hour.

4. Run a knife around the side and center tube of the pan. Remove the cake to a serving plate.

5. In a large bowl, combine the first five frosting ingredients; cover and chill for 1 hour. Beat until stiff peaks form.

6. Spread over the top and sides of cake. Store in the refrigerator. Garnish with chocolate leaves if desired.

BEATING EGG WHITES

For best results, egg whites should be beaten in a clean, dry metal or glass bowl with clean, dry beaters. Any fat mixed in with the egg whites, from either specks of egg yolk or oil film on plastic bowl, will interfere with the whites reaching their maximum volume.
—*Taste of Home Cooking Experts*

CHOCOLATE ANGEL CAKE

"Great twist on the traditional angel food cake! I served it with a strawberry-raspberry sauce and whipped cream and everyone loved it!"
—*japrill*

[2008]

ORANGE SPONGE CAKE

yield: 12 servings ✎ prep: 40 min.
bake: 45 min. + cooling

(Pictured on page 178)

My dad requested this cake for his birthday every year. For a wedding present, my aunt Marilyn included this recipe in a family cookbook for me.

**—Amy Sauser
Omaha, Nebraska, Field Editor**

6 eggs, *separated*
1-1/3 cups cake flour
1-1/2 cups sugar, *divided*
1/4 teaspoon salt
1/2 cup orange juice
3 teaspoons grated orange peel
3/4 teaspoon cream of tartar
GLAZE:
1/3 cup butter, cubed
2 cups confectioners' sugar
3 to 5 teaspoons water
1-1/2 teaspoons vanilla extract

1. Place the egg whites in a large bowl; let stand at room temperature for 30 minutes. Sift the flour, 1/3 cup sugar and salt together twice; set aside.

2. In another bowl, beat egg yolks on high speed for 5 minutes or until thick and lemon-colored. Gradually beat in 2/3 cup sugar. Add orange juice and peel; beat 3 minutes longer. Gradually add flour mixture and mix well.

3. Add cream of tartar to egg whites; using clean beaters, beat on medium speed until soft peaks form. Gradually beat in remaining sugar, 1 tablespoon at a time, on high until stiff peaks form. Fold into batter.

4. Gently spoon into an ungreased 10-in. tube pan. Cut through batter with a knife to remove air pockets.

5. Bake on the lowest oven rack at 325° for 45-55 minutes or until cake springs back when lightly touched. Immediately invert pan; cool completely, about 1 hour.

6. Run a knife around sides and center tube of pan. Remove to a serving plate.

7. For glaze, melt the butter in a small saucepan; remove from the heat. Add confectioners' sugar, water and vanilla; stir until smooth. Pour over the cake, allowing it to drizzle down sides.

[2007]

STRAWBERRY-MALLOW CAKE ROLL

yield: 10 servings ✎ prep: 30 min.
bake: 10 min. + chilling

(Pictured on page 181)

This stunning cake roll is so much fun to make and present to guests.

—Susan Olsen, Huntley, Montana

4 eggs, *separated*
2/3 cup all-purpose flour
1 teaspoon baking powder
1/4 teaspoon salt
3/4 cup sugar, *divided*
1/2 teaspoon vanilla extract
1 tablespoon confectioners' sugar
2 cartons (8 ounces *each*) spreadable strawberry cream cheese
1 jar (7 ounces) marshmallow creme
3 cups sliced fresh strawberries, *divided*
Chocolate syrup, optional

1. Let eggs stand at room temperature for 30 minutes. Line a greased 15-in. x 10-in. x 1-in. baking pan with waxed paper and grease the paper; set aside.

2. Sift together flour, baking powder and salt; set aside. In a large bowl, beat egg yolks until slightly thickened. Gradually add 1/4 cup sugar, beating until thick and pale yellow. Beat in vanilla. Add dry ingredients and mix well.

ORANGE SPONGE CAKE

❝Definitely a 5-star recipe. I've never made a sponge cake and was a little hesitant, but it was easy and picture-perfect. Nice light orange flavor, and the glaze was outstanding. Thanks for sharing.❞
—rfkey13

3. In a small bowl using clean beaters, beat egg whites on medium speed until soft peaks form. Gradually beat in remaining sugar, about 2 tablespoons at a time, on high until stiff glossy peaks form and the sugar is dissolved. Fold a fourth of the egg whites into batter; fold in remaining whites.

4. Gently spoon into prepared pan. Bake at 375° for 10-12 minutes or until cake springs back when lightly touched. Cool for 5 minutes. Turn cake onto a kitchen towel dusted with confectioners' sugar. Gently peel off waxed paper. Roll up cake in the towel, starting with a short side. Cool completely on a wire rack.

5. In a small bowl, beat cream cheese and marshmallow creme. Unroll cake; spread cream cheese mixture to within 1/2 in. of edges. Top with 2-1/2 cups strawberries. Roll up again. Place seam side down on a platter. Refrigerate for at least 2 hours.

6. Just before serving, garnish with the remaining strawberries. Serve with chocolate syrup if desired. Refrigerate leftovers.

[1998]

MARBLE CHIFFON CAKE
yield: 12-14 servings   prep: 20 min.
bake: 70 min. + cooling

My cake won a blue ribbon for best chiffon cake at our county fair. The delicate-flavored orange cake has ribbons of chocolate cake swirled throughout.

—*Sharon Evans*
   Clear Lake, Iowa, Former Field Editor

7 **eggs**, *separated*
1/3 **cup baking cocoa**
1/4 **cup boiling water**
1-1/2 **cups plus 3 tablespoons sugar**, *divided*
1/2 **cup plus 2 tablespoons canola oil**, *divided*
2-1/4 **cups all-purpose flour**
1 **tablespoon baking powder**
1 **teaspoon salt**
3/4 **cup water**
1/2 **teaspoon cream of tartar**
2 **teaspoons grated orange peel**

ORANGE GLAZE:
2 **cups confectioners' sugar**
1/3 **cup butter, melted**
3 **to 4 tablespoons orange juice**
1/2 **teaspoon grated orange peel**

1. Let eggs stand at room temperature for 30 minutes. In a large bowl, whisk cocoa, boiling water, 3 tablespoons sugar and 2 tablespoons oil; cool and set aside.

2. In a large bowl, combine the flour, baking powder, salt and remaining sugar. In another bowl, whisk the egg yolks, water and remaining oil. Add to dry ingredients; beat until well blended. In another bowl using clean beaters, beat egg whites and cream of tartar until stiff peaks form; fold into batter.

3. Remove 2 cups of batter; stir into cocoa mixture. To the remaining batter, add orange peel. Alternately spoon the batters into an ungreased 10-in. tube pan. Swirl with a knife.

4. Gently spoon into an ungreased 10-in. tube pan. Cut through batter with a knife to remove air pockets. Bake on the lowest oven rack at 325° for 70-75 minutes or until cake springs back when lightly touched. Immediately invert pan; cool completely, about 1 hour.

5. Run a knife around side and center tube of pan. Remove cake to a serving plate.

6. For glaze, in a small bowl, combine the sugar, butter and enough orange juice to reach desired drizzling consistency. Add orange peel; drizzle over cake.

TESTING ANGEL FOOD, CHIFFON AND SPONGE CAKES FOR DONENESS

Foam cakes are done when the top springs back when touched with your finger and the cracks at the top of the cake look and feel dry.

CANDIES

CHOCOLATE PEANUT BUTTER CANDY

"These were super easy to make, and what a great taste. The combination of chocolate, peanut butter and salty crunch from the crackers is wonderful!"
—cbalbierz

[2007]

PECAN CARAMEL CLUSTERS

yield: about 2 pounds ✥ prep: 25 min. + chilling

A box of this mouthwatering homemade candy does an outstanding job of showing your affection on Valentine's Day or any time. These are delicious and so easy to make.

—Janice Price, Lexington, Kentucky

1 package (14 ounces) caramels
2 tablespoons water
2 tablespoons butter
2 cups coarsely chopped pecans
4 ounces white candy coating, coarsely chopped
4 ounces dark chocolate candy coating, coarsely chopped

1. In a microwave-safe bowl, combine the caramels, water and butter. Microwave, uncovered, on high for 3 to 3-1/2 minutes, stirring every 30 seconds. Stir in the pecans.

2. Drop by tablespoonfuls onto greased baking sheets. Freeze for 15-20 minutes or until set.

3. In a microwave-safe bowl, combine candy coatings. Microwave, uncovered, on high for 1-2 minutes, stirring every 15 seconds; stir until smooth. Dip the caramel clusters in coating; allow excess to drip off. Place on waxed paper-lined baking sheets. Chill until firm.

Editor's Note: This recipe was tested in a 1,100-watt microwave.

[2010]

CHOCOLATE PEANUT BUTTER CANDY

yield: 15 servings ✥ prep: 25 min. cook: 10 min. + standing

Tell the kids to roll up their sleeves and help make these crunchy, chocolaty bars. They're easy and will surely satisfy anyone's sweet tooth.

—Kathy Mitchell, Brookfield, Wisconsin

1-1/2 cups graham cracker crumbs
1 cup sugar
3/4 cup packed brown sugar
3/4 cup butter, cubed
1/3 cup 2% milk
2 sleeves butter-flavored crackers (about 80 crackers)
1 cup butterscotch chips
1 cup (6 ounces) semisweet chocolate chips
3/4 cup creamy peanut butter

1. In a saucepan, combine the cracker crumbs, sugars, butter and milk. Bring to a boil, stirring constantly; cook and stir 5 minutes longer.

2. Place a single layer of crackers in a greased 13-in. x 9-in. dish; top with half of crumb mixture. Repeat layers. Top with remaining crackers.

3. In a small saucepan, combine the butterscotch chips, chocolate chips and peanut butter. Cook and stir until smooth. Pour over the crackers. Let stand until set.

Editor's Note: This recipe was tested with Keebler Town House crackers.

[2005]

BUTTERSCOTCH HARD CANDY

**yield: 1-1/2 pounds ∞ prep: 10 min.
cook: 30 min. + cooling**

*I love making this classic butterscotch recipe.
We think these irresistible bites are better than
the store-bought variety...and around here they
sure don't last long!*

—*Darlene Smithers, Elkhart, Indiana*

- 1 teaspoon plus 1 cup butter, *divided*
- 2-1/2 cups sugar
- 3/4 cup water
- 1/2 cup light corn syrup
- 1/4 cup honey
- 1/2 teaspoon salt
- 1/2 teaspoon rum extract

---

1. Butter a 15-in. x 10-in. x 1-in. pan with 1 teaspoon butter; set aside. Cube remaining butter and set aside.

2. In a heavy saucepan, combine the sugar, water and corn syrup. Cover and bring to a boil over medium heat without stirring. Cook, uncovered, until a candy thermometer reads 270° (soft-crack stage). Add the honey, salt and remaining butter; stir constantly until the mixture reaches 300° (hard-crack stage).

3. Remove from the heat. Stir in the rum extract. Pour into prepared pan without scraping; do not spread. Cool for 1-2 minutes or until the candy is almost set. Score into 1-in. squares; cool completely. Break squares apart. Store in an airtight container.

Editor's Note: We recommend that you test your candy thermometer before each use by bringing water to a boil; the thermometer should read 212°. Adjust your recipe temperature up or down based on your test.

[2007]

ALMOND CRUNCH

**yield: 1 pound ∞ prep: 20 min.
bake: 15 min. + chilling**

*Once you start eating this taste-tempting treat,
you may not be able to stop! Matzo crackers
are topped with buttery caramel, chocolate and
slivered almonds, and then baked to perfection.*

—*Sharalyn Zander, Jacksonville, Alabama*

- 4 to 6 unsalted saltine matzo crackers
- 1 cup butter, cubed
- 1 cup packed brown sugar
- 3/4 cup semisweet chocolate chips
- 1 teaspoon shortening
- 1 cup slivered almonds, toasted

---

1. Line a 15-in. x 10-in. x 1-in. baking pan with foil; line the foil with parchment paper. Arrange the crackers in the pan; set aside.

2. In a large heavy saucepan over medium heat, melt the butter. Stir in the brown sugar. Bring to a boil; cook and stir for 3-4 minutes or until sugar is dissolved. Spread evenly over crackers.

3. Bake at 350° for 15-17 minutes (cover loosely with foil if the top browns too quickly). Cool on a wire rack for 5 minutes. Meanwhile, melt chocolate chips and shortening; stir mixture until smooth. Stir in almonds; spread over top. Cool for 1 hour.

4. Break candy into pieces. Cover and refrigerate for at least 2 hours or until set. Store in an airtight container.

ALMOND CRUNCH

❝Very good recipe. My husband loved it. I actually made it as a gift to give to the attorney I work for who is Jewish. He in turn gave some to his mother who raved about it and wanted the recipe too.❞
—*LegalSec*

[1996]

CANDY BAR FUDGE

yield: 2-3/4 pounds ∞ **prep: 20 min. + chilling**

I've made this chewy and chocolaty fudge many times. Packed with nuts and caramel, it's like a candy bar. Everyone who tries it loves it.

—*Lois Freeman, Oxford, Michigan*

- 1/2 cup butter
- 1/3 cup baking cocoa
- 1/4 cup packed brown sugar
- 1/4 cup milk
- 3-1/2 cups confectioners' sugar
- 1 teaspoon vanilla extract
- 30 caramels, unwrapped
- 1 tablespoon water
- 2 cups salted peanuts
- 1/2 cup semisweet chocolate chips
- 1/2 cup milk chocolate chips

1. In a microwave-safe bowl, combine the butter, cocoa, brown sugar and milk. Microwave on high until mixture boils, about 2 minutes. Stir in confectioners' sugar and vanilla. Pour into a greased 8-in. square dish.

2. In another microwave-safe bowl, heat caramels and water on high for 1-1/4 minutes or until melted. Stir in the peanuts; spread over chocolate layer. Microwave chocolate chips on high for 30 seconds or until melted; spread over caramel layer. Chill until firm.

Editor's Note: This recipe was tested in a 1,100-watt microwave.

CANDY BAR FUDGE

❝So simple, so nummy! I didn't have peanuts so I used chopped pecans. Reminded me of the turtles I make at Christmas—but so much easier! This is a keeper!❞
—*cherrylady*

[2005]

HINT-OF-BERRY BONBONS

yield: about 4-1/2 dozen
prep: 1-1/2 hours + chilling

You'll have a hard time eating just one of these scrumptious sweets. Inside the rich milk chocolate coating is a fudgy center with a hint of strawberry. Their white chocolate drizzle makes these bonbons even more special.

—*Brenda Hoffman, Stanton, Michigan*

- 1 package (8 ounces) cream cheese, softened
- 1 cup milk chocolate chips, melted and cooled
- 3/4 cup crushed vanilla wafers (about 25 wafers)
- 1/4 cup strawberry preserves
- 15 ounces milk chocolate candy coating, chopped
- 2 ounces white baking chocolate

1. In a large bowl, beat cream cheese until fluffy. Beat in melted chocolate chips. Stir in the wafer crumbs and preserves. Cover and refrigerate for 2 hours or until easy to handle.

2. Divide mixture in half. Return one portion to refrigerator. Shape remaining mixture into 1-in. balls. Place on a waxed paper-lined pan; refrigerate. Repeat with remaining mixture.

3. In a microwave, melt milk chocolate coating; stir until smooth. Dip balls in coating; allow excess to drip off. Place on waxed paper-lined baking sheets. Refrigerate until set.

4. Melt the white chocolate; stir until smooth. Transfer to a heavy-duty resealable plastic bag; cut a small hole in a corner of bag. Decorate candies with white chocolate. Store in an airtight container in the refrigerator.

[2009]

PEPPERMINT FUDGE

yield: 1-1/4 pounds ∞ **prep: 20 min. + chilling**

Three of the season's best flavors—nuts, chocolate and peppermint—combine in a delightful manner in this scrumptious fudge. The two distinct layers are eye-catching— another reason why this candy makes a great holiday gift.

—Connie Denmark, St. Joseph, Illinois

- 1-1/2 teaspoons butter, softened
- 2 ounces cream cheese, softened
- 2 cups confectioners' sugar
- 3 tablespoons baking cocoa
- 1 teaspoon 2% milk
- 1/2 teaspoon vanilla extract
- 1/4 cup chopped nuts

PEPPERMINT LAYER:

- 2 ounces cream cheese, softened
- 2 cups confectioners' sugar
- 1-1/2 teaspoons 2% milk
- 1/2 teaspoon peppermint extract
- 1/4 cup crushed peppermint candy

1. Line the bottom and sides of an 8-in. x 4-in. loaf pan with foil. Grease foil with 1-1/2 teaspoons butter; set aside.

2. In a small bowl, beat cream cheese until creamy. Gradually beat in the confectioners' sugar, cocoa, milk and vanilla until smooth. Stir in the nuts. Spread into prepared pan. Chill for 1 hour or until firm.

3. For peppermint layer, beat cream cheese in a small bowl until creamy. Gradually beat in the confectioners' sugar, milk and peppermint extract until smooth. Stir in peppermint candy. Spread evenly over chocolate layer. Chill for 1 hour or until firm.

4. Using foil, lift fudge from pan. Gently peel off foil. Cut into squares.

[1995]

CARAMEL MARSHMALLOW DELIGHTS

yield: 5-6 dozen ∞ **prep: 25 min. + chilling**

(Pictured on page 239)

Sweet and chewy, these yummy layered squares are a delectable treat.

—Susan Kerr, Crown Point, Indiana

- 1 package (10 ounces) crisp rice cereal
- 1 can (14 ounces) sweetened condensed milk
- 1/2 cup butter, cubed
- 1 package (14 ounces) caramels
- 1 package (16 ounces) large marshmallows

1. Place cereal in a large bowl; set aside. In a double boiler or metal bowl over simmering water, combine the milk, butter and caramels, stirring until smooth. Remove from the heat.

2. With a fork, quickly dip marshmallows into hot mixture; allow excess to drip off. Roll in cereal. Place on a foil-lined pan; chill 30 minutes. Remove from pan and refrigerate in an airtight container.

CANDY MAKING TIPS

Do not substitute or alter the basic ingredients.

Use deep, heavy-gauge saucepans so the candy mixtures won't boil over.

Use wooden spoons when preparing recipes with hot boiling sugar.

For best results, make candy that requires a candy thermometer or uses egg whites on days when the humidity is less than 60%.

—Taste of Home Cooking Experts

PEPPERMINT FUDGE

"Amazing! Used at cookie exchange and everyone wanted the recipe so I am making it again this year. I sprinkled some candy cane powder on the top too. Tastes just like...no... BETTER than Junior Mints! Make them small because they are very rich. Mmm!"

—Ragdolly

PISTACHIO CRANBERRY BARK

"This recipe was in my first TOH (Taste of Home) magazine, but I haven't tried it until this past Christmas. I sure have been missing out. It was SO delicious! I made it with white chocolate chips, instead of candy coating, and it still turned out great. I loved the combination of pistachios and cranberries together. My husband and I loved it so much, I made it twice during the Christmas season. It's really hard for me to limit myself to a couple pieces at a time. I plan on making this every Christmas season. So good!"

—*kristinscott*

[2006]

PISTACHIO CRANBERRY BARK

yield: about 1 pound ∾ prep: 20 min. + chilling

This bark makes a lovely holiday gift from the kitchen. Fill a plate or cup with candy, then gather up clear cellophane around it and tie with red and green ribbons.

—*Susan Wacek, Pleasanton, California*

- 2 cups (12 ounces) semisweet chocolate chips
- 5 ounces white candy coating, chopped
- 1 cup chopped pistachios, toasted, *divided*
- 3/4 cup dried cranberries, *divided*

1. In a microwave-safe bowl, melt semisweet chips; stir until smooth. Repeat with white candy coating.

2. Stir 3/4 cup pistachios and half of the cranberries into semisweet chocolate. Thinly spread onto a waxed paper-lined baking sheet. Drizzle with the candy coating.

3. Cut through candy with a knife to swirl. Sprinkle with the remaining pistachios and cranberries. Chill until firm. Break into pieces. Store in an airtight container in the refrigerator.

[1994]

COW PIES CANDY

yield: 2 dozen ∾ prep/total time: 20 min.

A barnyard birthday party just wouldn't be complete without cow pies! The kids loved 'em once they got a taste of these yummy treats packed with raisins and almonds and covered in rich milk chocolate.

—*Karen Kenney, Harvard, Illinois*

- 2 cups (12 ounces) milk chocolate chips
- 1 tablespoon shortening
- 1/2 cup raisins
- 1/2 cup chopped slivered almonds

1. In a heavy saucepan or microwave, melt the chocolate chips and shortening over low heat, stirring until smooth. Remove from the heat; stir in the raisins and almonds. Drop by tablespoonfuls onto waxed paper. Chill until ready to serve.

[2005]

CHERRY CHOCOLATE CUPS

yield: 2 dozen ∾ prep: 30 min. + chilling

These outstanding treats taste like you spent hours working on them.

—*Michelle Smith, Sykesville, Maryland*

- 2-1/2 ounces semisweet chocolate
- 2 teaspoons shortening, *divided*
- 2-1/2 ounces white baking chocolate
- 1/2 cup dried cherries, chopped
- 1/2 cup boiling water
- 1/4 teaspoon almond extract
- 1 package (8 ounces) cream cheese, softened
- 3 tablespoons confectioners' sugar
- 1 drop red food coloring
- 1/4 teaspoon grated lemon peel

1. In a microwave, melt the semisweet chocolate and 1 teaspoon shortening; stir until smooth. Brush evenly on the inside of 12 paper or foil miniature muffin cup liners. Repeat with white baking chocolate and the remaining shortening. Chill until firm, about 25 minutes.

2. Meanwhile, in a small bowl, combine the cherries, water and extract; let stand for 5 minutes. Drain, reserving liquid.

3. In a small bowl, combine the cream cheese, confectioners' sugar, food coloring, lemon peel and 2 tablespoons reserved cherry liquid; beat on medium-low speed for 2 minutes or until smooth. Fold in the cherries.

4. Cut a small hole in the corner of a pastry or plastic bag; insert a tip. Fill with cherry mixture. Pipe into chocolate cups. Refrigerate for 1 hour or until firm. Carefully remove from liners.

[1998]

CHOCOLATE CARAMEL CANDY

yield: about 8 dozen ∞ **prep: 45 min. + chilling**

(Pictured on page 234)

This dazzling candy tastes like a Snickers bar but has homemade flavor beyond compare. When I entered it in a recipe contest at our harvest festival, it won five ribbons, including grand prize and the judges' special award.

—*Jane Meek, Pahrump, Nevada*

2 teaspoons butter
1 cup milk chocolate chips
1/4 cup butterscotch chips
1/4 cup creamy peanut butter
FILLING:
1/4 cup butter
1 cup sugar
1/4 cup evaporated milk
1-1/2 cups marshmallow creme
1/4 cup creamy peanut butter
1 teaspoon vanilla extract
1-1/2 cups chopped salted peanuts
CARAMEL LAYER:
1 package (14 ounces) caramels
1/4 cup heavy whipping cream
ICING:
1 cup (6 ounces) milk chocolate chips
1/4 cup butterscotch chips
1/4 cup creamy peanut butter

1. Line a 13-in. x 9-in. pan with foil; butter the foil with 2 teaspoons butter and set aside. In a small saucepan, combine the milk chocolate chips, butterscotch chips and peanut butter; stir over low heat until melted and smooth. Spread into prepared pan. Refrigerate until set.

2. For filling, in a small heavy saucepan, melt butter over medium heat. Add sugar and milk; bring to a gentle boil. Reduce heat to medium-low; boil and stir for 5 minutes. Remove from the heat; stir in marshmallow creme, peanut butter and vanilla. Add peanuts. Spread over first layer. Refrigerate until set.

3. For caramel layer, in a small heavy saucepan, combine caramels and cream; stir over low heat until melted and smooth. Cook and stir 4 minutes longer. Spread over the filling. Refrigerate until set.

4. For icing, in another saucepan, combine the chips and peanut butter; stir over low heat until melted and smooth. Pour over the caramel layer. Refrigerate for at least 4 hours or overnight.

5. Remove from the refrigerator 20 minutes before cutting. Using foil, lift fudge from pan. Gently peel off foil and cut into 1-in. squares. Store in an airtight container.

[2008]

HOMEMADE PEANUT BUTTER CUPS

yield: 3 dozen ∞ **prep: 20 min. + chilling**

Make a lasting impression on Valentine's Day or any occasion with this luscious candy featuring a dark chocolate shell and a gooey peanut butter center. Your sweetie will appreciate the colorful sprinkles on top, too.

—*Lavonne Hegland*
Saint Michael, Minnesota, Field Editor

1 cup creamy peanut butter, *divided*
4-1/2 teaspoons butter, softened
1/2 cup confectioners' sugar
1/2 teaspoon salt
2 cups (12 ounces) semisweet chocolate chips
4 milk chocolate candy bars (1.55 ounces *each*), coarsely chopped
Colored sprinkles, optional

1. In a small bowl, combine 1/2 cup peanut butter, butter, confectioners' sugar and salt until smooth; set aside.

2. In a microwave, melt the chocolate chips, candy bars and remaining peanut butter; stir until smooth.

3. Drop teaspoonfuls of chocolate mixture into paper-lined miniature muffin cups. Top each with a scant teaspoonful of peanut butter mixture; top with another teaspoonful of chocolate mixture. Decorate with sprinkles if desired. Refrigerate until set. Store in an airtight container.

FOUR-CHIP FUDGE

"Definitely the best and smoothest fudge around!!! Making it for years! Don't remember where I got the recipe, so if someone could help with a year/date they started, I'd be appreciative!"
—fishwoman

[2002]

FOUR-CHIP FUDGE

yield: about 4-1/2 pounds
prep: 25 min. + chilling

I stir up this wonderful creamy fudge every Christmas. My friend Marlene gave me the recipe years ago, and I've passed it on to everyone who tries it. Flavored with four different kinds of chips, this is the best fudge I've ever tasted!

—Delores Wigginston, Prudenville, Michigan

1-1/2 teaspoons plus 3/4 cup butter, *divided*
  1 can (14 ounces) sweetened condensed milk
  3 tablespoons 2% milk
  1 package (12 ounces) semisweet chocolate chips
  1 package (11-1/2 ounces) milk chocolate chips
  1 package (10 ounces) peanut butter chips
  1 cup butterscotch chips
  1 jar (7 ounces) marshmallow creme
1/2 teaspoon almond extract
1/2 teaspoon vanilla extract
  1 cup chopped walnuts

1. Line a 13-in. x 9-in. pan with foil and grease the foil with 1-1/2 teaspoons of butter; set aside. In a large heavy saucepan, melt the remaining butter over low heat. Add the next six ingredients. Cook and stir constantly until smooth. (Mixture will first appear separated; continue stirring until fully blended). Remove from the heat; stir in marshmallow creme and extracts until well blended. Stir in the nuts.

2. Spread the fudge into prepared pan. Refrigerate until set. Lift out of the pan and remove foil; cut into squares. Store in the refrigerator.

[2000]

CHOCOLATE TRUFFLES

yield: about 4 dozen   prep: 20 min. + chilling

You may be tempted to save this recipe for a special occasion since these smooth, creamy chocolates are divine. But with just a few ingredients, they're easy to make anytime.

—Darlene Wiese-Appleby, Creston, Ohio

  3 cups (18 ounces) semisweet chocolate chips
  1 can (14 ounces) sweetened condensed milk
  1 tablespoon vanilla extract
Chopped flaked coconut, chocolate sprinkles, colored spinkles, baking cocoa *and/or* finely chopped nuts, optional

1. In a microwave-safe bowl, melt chocolate chips and milk; stir until smooth. Stir in vanilla. Chill for 2 hours or until mixture is easy to handle.

2. Shape into 1-in. balls. Roll in the coconut, sprinkles, cocoa or nuts if desired.

[1999]

SUGARED PEANUT CLUSTERS

yield: 6 cups   prep: 15 min. + cooling

I made these nuts for my aunt's birthday, and everybody loved them. I've also given them as Christmas gifts.

—Gail McClantoc, Sweet Water, Alabama

  2 teaspoons butter, softened
1-1/2 cups sugar
1/2 cup brewed coffee
  1 tablespoon light corn syrup
  1 teaspoon ground cinnamon
  1 teaspoon vanilla extract
  1 jar (16 ounces) dry roasted peanuts

1. Butter two baking sheets with the 2 teaspoons butter; set aside. In a heavy saucepan, combine the sugar, coffee,

corn syrup and cinnamon. Bring to a boil over medium heat, stirring occasionally. Cook until a candy thermometer reads 234°-240° (soft-ball stage). Remove from the heat; stir in vanilla. Add the peanuts; stir quickly.

2. Pour onto prepared baking sheets. Quickly separate into small clumps with two forks. Cool completely. Store in an airtight container.

Editor's Note: We recommend that you test your candy thermometer before each use by bringing water to a boil; the thermometer should read 212°. Adjust your recipe temperature up or down based on your test.

[2007]

PEANUT BUTTER PRETZEL BITES
yield: 8-1/2 dozen
prep: 1-1/2 hours + standing

Bite into these special sweets to discover delicious peanut flavor and a salty pretzel crunch.

—*Lois Farmer, Logan, West Virginia*

- 1 package (14 ounces) caramels
- 1/4 cup butter, cubed
- 2 tablespoons water
- 5 cups miniature pretzels
- 1 jar (18 ounces) chunky peanut butter
- 26 ounces milk chocolate candy coating, melted

1. In a microwave, melt caramels with butter and water; stir until smooth. Spread one side of each pretzel with 1 teaspoon peanut butter; top with 1/2 teaspoon caramel mixture. Place on waxed paper-lined baking sheets. Refrigerate until set.

2. Using a small fork, dip each pretzel into melted chocolate coating until completely covered; allow excess to drip off. Place on waxed paper. Let stand until set. Store in an airtight container in a cool dry place.

Editor's Note: This recipe was tested in a 1,100-watt microwave.

[2003]

ENGLISH TOFFEE
yield: about 2 pounds
prep: 20 min. + standing

Each Christmas I make several pounds of candy and cookies for friends, neighbors and business associates. This tasty toffee is covered in chocolate and sprinkled with nuts, and it won't stick to your teeth!

—*Don McVay, Wilsonville, Oregon*

- 1 tablespoon plus 2 cups butter, softened, *divided*
- 2 cups sugar
- 1 tablespoon light corn syrup
- 1/4 teaspoon salt
- 1 cup milk chocolate chips
- 1 cup chopped pecans

1. Grease a 15-in. x 10-in. x 1-in. pan with 1 tablespoon butter; set aside. In a large heavy saucepan, melt remaining butter. Add the sugar, corn syrup and salt; cook and stir over medium heat until a candy thermometer reads 295° (hard-crack stage). Quickly pour into prepared pan. Let stand at room temperature until cool, about 1 hour.

2. In a microwave, melt the chocolate chips; stir until smooth. Spread over the toffee. Sprinkle with pecans. Let stand for 1 hour. Break into bite-size pieces. Store in an airtight container at room temperature.

Editor's Note: We recommend that you test your candy thermometer before each use by bringing water to a boil; the thermometer should read 212°. Adjust your recipe temperature up or down based on your test.

PEANUT BUTTER PRETZEL BITES

❝These are fabulous! Instead of purchasing gifts for teachers, we bake for them. These pretzel bites are a hit with everyone who has received them, and I get requests for these each holiday season! The kids all get involved in making these with alot of "taste testing" going on while we're making them! Enjoy!❞
—*aambrozich*

[2006]

CARAMEL PECAN CANDY

yield: about 6-1/2 dozen
prep: 35 min. + chilling

Sweet and chewy, these delectable layered squares are a great treat. I have also made this recipe in a 9-inch pie pan and cut it into small pieces. You can't eat very much at one time.

—*Dick Deacon, Lawrenceville, Georgia*

1/3 cup plus 1/2 cup butter, *divided*
20 cream-filled chocolate sandwich cookies, crushed
1 package (14 ounces) caramels
3 cups chopped pecans, toasted

TOPPING:

3/4 cup semisweet chocolate chips
3 tablespoons butter
3 tablespoons heavy whipping cream
3 tablespoons light corn syrup
3/4 teaspoon vanilla extract

---

1. In a large saucepan, melt 1/3 cup butter over medium heat; stir in the cookie crumbs. Press into an ungreased 9-in. square baking dish. Bake at 325° for 10-12 minutes or until set. Cool on a wire rack. Meanwhile, in a small saucepan, melt the caramels and the remaining butter over low heat. Stir in the pecans. Pour over crust. Cool.

2. For topping, in a small saucepan, combine the chocolate chips, butter, cream and corn syrup. Cook and stir over low heat until smooth. Remove from the heat; stir in vanilla. Pour over caramel layer. Cool on a wire rack. Refrigerate until chocolate hardens. Let candy stand at room temperature for 5-10 minutes before cutting into 1-in. squares. Store in the refrigerator.

[2010]

HOMEMADE MARSHMALLOWS

yield: about 9-1/2 dozen ∞ **prep: 55 min. + standing**

My grandpa considered this his favorite treat. At Christmas, he would be busy making marshmallows for his family and friends.

—*Diana Byron, New London, Ohio*

---

2 teaspoons butter
3 envelopes unflavored gelatin
1 cup cold water, *divided*
2 cups sugar
1 cup light corn syrup
1/8 teaspoon salt
1 teaspoon clear vanilla extract

Optional toppings: melted chocolate, hot fudge *and/or* caramel ice cream topping
Optional garnishes: baking cocoa, confectioners' sugar, crushed assorted candies, chopped nuts, colored sugars *and/or* sprinkles

---

1. Line a 13-in. x 9-in. pan with foil and grease the foil with butter; set aside. In a large metal bowl, sprinkle gelatin over 1/2 cup cold water; set aside. In a large heavy saucepan, combine the sugar, corn syrup, salt and remaining water. Bring to a boil, stirring occasionally. Cook, without stirring, until a candy thermometer reads 240° (soft-ball stage).

2. Remove from the heat and gradually add to gelatin. Beat on high speed until mixture is thick and the volume is doubled, about 15 minutes. Beat in vanilla. Spread into prepared pan. Cover and let stand at room temperature for 6 hours or overnight.

3. Using foil, lift marshmallows out of pan; gently peel off foil. With a knife or pizza cutter coated with cooking spray, cut into 1-in. squares. Dip or drizzle half of the marshmallows with toppings if desired; coat with garnishes as desired. Roll remaining marshmallows in the garnishes of your choice. Store in an airtight container in a cool dry place.

Editor's Note: We recommend that you test your candy thermometer before each use by bringing water to a boil; the thermometer should read 212°. Adjust your recipe temperature up or down based on your test.

[1993]

SALTED PEANUT CHEWS

yield: 2 dozen   **prep: 25 min.**   **bake: 15 min.**

I took these great treats to an evening reunion. They disappeared fast, and soon people were asking for the recipe.

—Irene Yoder, Millersburg, Ohio

- 1-1/2 **cups all-purpose flour**
- 1/2 **cup packed brown sugar**
- 3/4 **cup butter, softened,** *divided*
- 3 **cups miniature marshmallows**
- 2 **cups peanut butter chips**
- 2/3 **cup corn syrup**
- 2 **teaspoons vanilla extract**
- 2 **cups crisp rice cereal**
- 2 **cups salted peanuts**

---

1. In a large bowl, combine the flour, brown sugar and 1/2 cup butter. Press into an ungreased 13-in. x 9-in. baking pan. Bake at 350° for 12-15 minutes or until lightly browned.

2. Sprinkle with marshmallows; return to the oven for 3-5 minutes or until marshmallows begin to melt. Set aside.

3. In a large saucepan, cook and stir the peanut butter chips, corn syrup, vanilla and remaining butter until smooth. Remove from the heat; stir in cereal and peanuts. Pour over prepared crust, spreading to cover. Cool on a wire rack before cutting into bars.

[2011]

CRUNCHY CHOCOLATE MINT BALLS

yield: 4-1/2 dozen   **prep: 45 min. + chilling cook: 5 min. + freezing**

My mom made these every year when I was growing up. We'd have an ice cream container full of them in the freezer that never lasted until Christmas. I now make them every year for my family.

—Amanda Triff, Dartmouth, Nova Scotia

- 1 **package (10 ounces) mint chocolate chips**
- 1/4 **cup butter, softened**
- 1 **can (14 ounces) sweetened condensed milk**
- 1-1/4 **cups chocolate wafer crumbs (about 22 wafers)**

White jimmies

---

1. In a double boiler or metal bowl over hot water, melt chips and butter; stir until smooth. Stir in milk. Add wafer crumbs; mix to coat. Refrigerate for 1 hour or until easy to handle.

2. Roll into 1-in. balls; roll in jimmies. Place on a waxed paper-lined 15-in. x 10-in. x 1-in. baking pan; freeze until firm. Transfer to a resealable plastic freezer bag. May be frozen for up to 3 months.

3. To use frozen balls: Thaw at room temperature.

[2009]

WONDERFUL CANDIES TWO WAYS

yield: 9 dozen   **prep: 2-1/2 hours**

(Pictured on page 239)

This recipe makes a big batch of two different kinds of delectable candies. They're great not only for Valentine's Day, but also for the holidays or any special gathering.

—Jeanne Trudell, Del Norte, Colorado

- 1 **cup butter, melted**
- 1 **can (14 ounces) sweetened condensed milk**
- 3 **pounds confectioners' sugar**

COOKIES & CREME BONBONS:
- 1/2 **cup cream-filled chocolate sandwich cookie crumbs**
- 1 **pound white candy coating, melted**

CHOCOLATE-COVERED CHERRIES:
- 54 **maraschino cherries (about two 10-ounce jars), patted dry**
- 1 **pound milk chocolate candy coating, melted**

---

1. In a large bowl, combine butter and milk. Gradually beat in confectioners' sugar until a smooth dough is formed. Divide in half; cover with plastic wrap.

2. For bonbons, stir cookie crumbs into one portion of dough. Shape into 1-in. balls. Dip into white candy coating; allow excess to drip off. Place on waxed paper-lined baking sheets. Chill until firm.

3. For chocolate-covered cherries, shape remaining portion of dough into 1-in. balls; flatten to 2-in. circles. Wrap each circle around a cherry and gently reshape into a ball. Dip into milk chocolate coating; allow excess to drip off. Place on waxed paper-lined baking sheets. Chill until firm. Store in an airtight container.

MOTHER LODE PRETZELS

"Really good and fairly easy to make. I bought the mini-pretzel rods so that I didn't have to cut full size rods and it worked out really well. The caramel is hard to keep melted, but that was really the only thing that was even remotely difficult. Will definitely make again."

—*gretcheepoo*

[2012]

AMARETTO CREAM TRUFFLES

yield: 30 servings   ∽   prep: 30 min. + chilling

The velvety texture of the almond filling with the sensational chocolate coating make these truffles truly heavenly. I like to give them as gifts during the holidays.

—*Sherry Day, Pinckney, Michigan*

> 5 ounces semisweet chocolate, chopped
> 4 ounces milk chocolate, chopped
> 1/3 cup heavy whipping cream
> 2 tablespoons Amaretto
> 1 teaspoon vanilla extract
> 2 tablespoons sugar
> 2 tablespoons baking cocoa

1. Place chocolates in a small bowl. In a small saucepan, bring cream just to a boil. Pour over chocolates; whisk until smooth. Stir in Amaretto and vanilla. Cool to room temperature, stirring occasionally. Cover and refrigerate for 1-1/2 hours or until easy to handle.

2. In a small bowl, combine the sugar and cocoa. Shape the chocolate mixture into 1-in. balls; roll in cocoa mixture. Store candy in an airtight container in the refrigerator.

[2008]

MOTHER LODE PRETZELS

yield: 4-1/2 dozen
prep: 35 min. + standing

I brought these savory-sweet pretzels to a family gathering, and they disappeared from the dessert tray before dessert was even served! My family raves about how good they are.

—*Carrie Bennett, Madison, Wisconsin*

> 1 package (10 ounces) pretzel rods
> 1 package (14 ounces) caramels
> 1 tablespoon evaporated milk
> 1-1/4 cups miniature semisweet chocolate chips

> 1 cup plus 2 tablespoons butterscotch chips
> 2/3 cup milk chocolate toffee bits
> 1/4 cup chopped walnuts, toasted

1. With a sharp knife, cut pretzel rods in half; set aside. In a large saucepan over low heat, melt caramels with milk. In a large shallow bowl, combine the chips, toffee bits and walnuts.

2. Pour caramel mixture into a 2-cup glass measuring cup. Dip the cut end of each pretzel piece two-thirds of the way into caramel mixture (reheat in microwave if mixture becomes too thick for dipping). Allow the excess caramel to drip off, then roll pretzels in the chip mixture. Place pretzels on waxed paper until set. Store in an airtight container.

[1997]

TIGER BUTTER CANDY

yield: about 1-1/2 pounds
prep/total time: 20 min.

This candy is big on peanut butter flavor and fun to make.

—*Pamela Pogue, Mineola, Texas*

> 1 pound white candy coating, coarsely chopped
> 1/2 cup chunky peanut butter
> 1/2 cup semisweet chocolate chips
> 4 teaspoons half-and-half cream

1. In a microwave, melt coating and peanut butter; stir until smooth. Pour onto a foil-lined baking sheet coated with cooking spray; spread into a thin layer.

2. Repeat with chips and cream. Pour and swirl over peanut butter layer. Freeze for 5 minutes or until set. Break into small pieces.

Editor's Note: This recipe was tested in a 1,100-watt microwave.

[1998]

CASHEW CRICKLE

yield: about 2 pounds ∞ **prep: 10 min.**
cook: 30 min. + cooling

Cashews add excellent flavor to this golden
brickle. You can always substitute your favorite
type of nut.

—Kathy Kittell
Lenexa, Kansas, Field Editor

---

2 cups sugar
1 cup light corn syrup
1/2 cup water
3 tablespoons butter
1 teaspoon vanilla extract
1/2 teaspoon baking soda
2 cups salted cashews

---

1. In a large saucepan, combine the
sugar, corn syrup and water. Bring to
a boil, stirring constantly, until the
sugar is dissolved. Cook, without
stirring, over medium heat until a
candy thermometer reads 300°
(hard-crack stage).

2. Remove from the heat; stir in butter,
vanilla and baking soda. Add cashews.
Pour into a buttered 15-in. x 10-in. x
1-in. pan. Cool; break into pieces.

Editor's Note: We recommend that you
test your candy thermometer before each use
by bringing water to a boil; the thermometer
should read 212°. Adjust your recipe
temperature up or down based on your test.

[2004]

SOFT CHEWY CARAMELS

yield: about 2-1/2 pounds
prep: 5 min. ∞ **cook: 20 min. + cooling**

One of my first experiences with cooking was
helping my mother make these caramels for
Christmas. We'd make up to 12 batches each year.
Today, I do at least 95 percent of the cooking at
home, but my wife does much of the baking.

—Robert Sprenkle, Hurst, Texas

---

1 tablespoon plus 1 cup butter, *divided*
2-1/4 cups packed brown sugar
1 can (14 ounces) sweetened
   condensed milk
1 cup dark corn syrup

---

1. Line a 15-in. x 10-in. x 1-in. pan
with foil; grease the foil with 1
tablespoon butter. In a heavy
saucepan over medium heat, melt
remaining butter. Add the brown
sugar, milk and corn syrup. Cook
and stir until candy thermometer
reads 250° (hard-ball stage).

2. Pour into prepared pan (do not
scrape saucepan). Cool caramels
completely. Using foil, lift caramels
out of pan; gently peel off foil. Cut
into 1-in. squares.

Editor's Note: We recommend that you
test your candy thermometer before each use
by bringing water to a boil; the thermometer
should read 212°. Adjust your recipe
temperature up or down based on your test.

SOFT CHEWY CARAMELS

❝I made this recipe for gifts
last holiday season and
people wanted to know
what candy shop in town I
got them from. They said
that they had never tasted
caramels as good as
these.❞
—chamb1km

USING CANDY THERMOMETERS

For accurate temperature readings, it's important
that you have the candy thermometer attached
to the side of the saucepan.

new year's eve

[2012]
CHEDDAR GOUGERES
yield: 3 dozen
prep: 30 min. ❧ bake: 15 min.

For a simple but delicious finger food, try these flavorful puffs for your next party. They're easy to make yet always impress guests. I like to use the sharpest cheddar I can find, but the recipe works well with milder cheese, too.

—*Bridget Klusman, Otsego, Michigan*

1	cup water
1/4	cup butter, cubed
2-1/2	teaspoons kosher salt, *divided*
1	cup all-purpose flour
4	eggs
1-1/2	cups shredded sharp cheddar cheese
1/2	cup minced fresh chives
2	garlic cloves, minced

1. In a large saucepan, bring the water, butter and 1/2 teaspoon salt to a boil. Add flour all at once and stir until a smooth ball forms. Remove from the heat; let stand for 5 minutes. Add the eggs, one at a time, beating well after each addition. Continue beating until mixture is smooth and shiny. Stir in the cheese, chives and garlic.

2. Drop by tablespoonfuls 1 in. apart onto greased baking sheets. Sprinkle with the remaining salt. Bake at 375° for 14-16 minutes or until golden brown. Serve warm.

[1994]
CAJUN PARTY MIX SNACK
yield: 8 cups
prep: 10 min. ❧ bake: 40 min.

This is a crisp snack with punch. Once you get started eating it, it's hard to stop.

—*Miriam Hershberger*
Holmesville, Ohio, Former Field Editor

2-1/2	cups Corn Chex
2	cups Rice Chex
2	cups Crispix
1	cup miniature pretzels
1	cup mixed nuts
1/2	cup butter, melted
1	tablespoon dried parsley flakes
1	teaspoon celery salt
1	teaspoon garlic powder
1/4	to 1/2 teaspoon cayenne pepper
1/4	teaspoon hot pepper sauce

1. In a large bowl, combine the cereals, pretzels and nuts. Pour into an ungreased 15-in. x 10 - in. x 1-in. baking pan. Combine the remaining ingredients; pour over cereal mixture and stir to coat.

2. Bake the mix at 250° for 40-60 minutes, stirring every 15 minutes. Store in an airtight containers.

CAJUN PARTY MIX SNACK

❝It was a welcome difference from what is commonly made. Could be a bit spicy for some but we truly liked it.❞

—*Church chef*

[2011]

BLUE CHEESE-ONION STEAK BITES

yield: 4 dozen ✎ **prep: 15 min.** ✎ **cook: 35 min.**

(Pictured on page 237)

I love the flavor pairing of blue cheese and steak. Adding garlic and onion make it even better. This is a hearty appetizer for parties or a great light lunch.

—*Jo-Ellen Neil, Arroyo Grande, California*

---

    3 large onions, thinly sliced into rings
    3 tablespoons butter
   12 garlic cloves, minced
    4 beef tenderloin steaks (6 ounces each)
  1/4 teaspoon salt
  1/4 teaspoon pepper
    1 loaf (10-1/2 ounces) French bread baguette, cut into 1/4-inch slices
SPREAD:
    4 ounces cream cheese, softened
    1 cup (4 ounces) crumbled blue cheese
  1/8 teaspoon salt
  1/8 teaspoon pepper

---

1. In a large skillet, saute onions in butter until onions are softened. Reduce heat to medium-low; cook, stirring occasionally, for 30 minutes or until onions are golden brown. Add garlic; cook 1 minute longer.

2. Meanwhile, sprinkle beef with salt and pepper. Using long-handled tongs, moisten a paper towel with cooking oil and lightly coat the grill rack.

3. Grill steaks, covered, over medium heat or broil 4 in. from the heat for 5-7 minutes on each side or until meat reaches desired doneness (for medium-rare, a thermometer should read 145°; medium, 160°; well-done, 170°). Cut into thin slices.

4. Place the bread on ungreased baking sheets. Bake at 400° for 4-6 minutes or until lightly browned.

5. Meanwhile, place the cream cheese, blue cheese, salt and pepper in a food processor; cover and process until blended. Spread each bread slice with 1 teaspoon cheese mixture; top with steak and onions.

BLUE CHEESE-ONION STEAK BITES

"I made this one night for my husband, and since then whenever I ask what he's in the mood for for dinner...he always says this!!! So I'm off to the store to make it again tonight."
—*AimeeB*

PASS THE HORS D'OEURVES

When you are hosting a party and serving just appetizers, it can be hard to judge how many appetizers you will need. In general, plan on serving 6 to 8 different items and calculate that each guest will have a total of 10 to 14 pieces.

—*Taste of Home Cooking Experts*

LAYERED SHRIMP DIP

"This was so good, I could have eaten it with a spoon! I used light cream cheese, and next time will use 2% fat cheese to lighten it up even more. I will definitely make this one a permanent card in my recipe box!"

—Summy

[2000]

CRANBERRY QUENCHER
yield: 6 quarts ∽ prep/total time: 5 min.
(Pictured on page 235)

You need just three items to stir up this delicious, rosy fruit punch. Float a few fresh cranberries on top or garnish each glass with a pineapple wedge.

—Dorothy Smith
El Dorado, Arkansas, Former Field Editor

---

1 bottle (64 ounces) cranberry-apple juice
1 can (46 ounces) pineapple juice, chilled
3/4 cup thawed lemonade *or* orange juice concentrate

---

1. In a large container or punch bowl, combine the juices. Stir in lemonade concentrate. Serve in chilled glassed over ice.

[1997]

LAYERED SHRIMP DIP
yield: 12-16 servings
prep: 15 min. + chilling

Eyes light up when I set this special snack on the buffet table. It has a terrific combination of flavors and is a colorful addition to any spread.

—Sue Broyles, Cherokee, Texas, Field Editor

---

1 package (3 ounces) cream cheese, softened
6 tablespoons salsa, *divided*
1/2 cup cocktail sauce
3 cans (6 ounces *each*) small shrimp, rinsed and drained
1 can (2-1/4 ounces) sliced ripe olives, drained
1 cup (4 ounces) shredded cheddar cheese
1 cup (4 ounces) shredded Monterey Jack cheese
Sliced green onions
Tortilla chips

1. In a small bowl, combine cream cheese and 3 tablespoons salsa; spread into an ungreased 9-in. pie plate. Combine the cocktail sauce and the remaining salsa; spread over cream cheese.

2. Arrange the shrimp evenly over top. Sprinkle with olives. Combine cheeses; sprinkle over top. Add the onions. Chill. Serve with tortilla chips.

[2008]

THREE-CHEESE PESTO PIZZA
yield: 16 slices ∽ prep/total time: 30 min.

With a ready-made crust, this pizza can be on a serving tray in half an hour. The triple cheese blend will make these slices go fast.

—Pat Stevens
Granbury, Texas, Field Editor

1/2 cup finely chopped red onion
1/2 cup finely chopped sweet red pepper
1 tablespoon olive oil
1 prebaked 12-inch pizza crust
1/2 cup prepared pesto
1 cup (4 ounces) crumbled feta cheese
1 cup (4 ounces) shredded part-skim mozzarella cheese
1 cup (4 ounces) shredded Parmesan cheese
1 can (4-1/4 ounces) chopped ripe olives
1 medium tomato, thinly sliced

---

1. In a small skillet, saute the onion and red pepper in oil until tender. Remove from the heat; set aside.

2. Place the crust on an ungreased 14-in. pizza pan. Spread the pesto to within 1/2 in. of edges. Layer with cheeses, onion mixture, olives and tomato.

3. Bake at 400° for 15-18 minutes or until cheese is melted.

[2010]

CHERRY-BRANDY BAKED BRIE

yield: 8 servings ∽ prep/total time: 20 min.

(Pictured on page 240)

No one will believe this impressive appetizer is so easy to make. You can substitute dried cranberries or apricots for the cherries and apple juice for the brandy.

—*Kevin Phebus, Katy, Texas*

---

  1 round (8 ounces) Brie cheese
1/2 cup dried cherries
1/2 cup chopped walnuts
1/4 cup packed brown sugar
1/4 cup brandy *or* unsweetened apple juice
French bread baguette, sliced and toasted *or* assorted crackers

---

1. Place cheese in a 9-in. pie plate. Combine cherries, walnuts, brown sugar and brandy; spoon over cheese.

2. Bake the Brie at 350° for 15-20 minutes or until cheese is softened. Serve with the baguette.

[2011]

PARTY PITAS

yield: 2 dozen ∽ prep/total time: 25 min.

These dainty mini sandwiches are easy to make with store-bought deli turkey. Greek vinaigrette and olives give them a Mediterranean flair.

—*Awynne Thurstenson*
Siloam Springs, Arkansas, Field Editor

---

  4 whole wheat pita pocket halves
1/3 cup Greek vinaigrette
1/2 pound thinly sliced deli turkey
  1 jar (7-1/2 ounces) roasted sweet red peppers, drained and patted dry
  2 cups fresh baby spinach
 24 pitted Greek olives
 24 frilled toothpicks

---

1. Brush insides of pita pockets with vinaigrette; fill with turkey, peppers and spinach. Cut each pita pocket into six wedges.

2. Thread olives onto toothpicks; use to secure wedges.

[2006]

BASIL CREAM CHEESE BRUSCHETTA

yield: 1 dozen ∽ prep/total time: 20 min.

This appealing appetizer takes classic bruschetta to new heights. Instead of olive oil, these savory treats are spread with reduced-fat cream cheese, then topped with tomato, green onion and ripe olives.

Michelle Wentz, Fort Polk, Louisiana

---

 12 slices French bread (12 inch thick)
1/2 cup chopped seeded tomato
  2 tablespoons chopped green onion
  1 tablespoon chopped ripe olives
  4 ounces reduced-fat ice cream cheese
  1 tablespoon minced fresh basil

---

1. Place bread on an ungreased baking sheet. Broil 6-8 in. from the heat for 3-4 minutes or until golden brown. Meanwhile, in a small bowl, combine the tomato, onion and olives; set aside.

2. Combine cream the cheese and basil; spread over the untoasted side of bread. Broil 3 minutes longer or until the cheese is melted and edges are golden brown. Top with the tomato mixture. Serve warm.

CHERRY-BRANDY BAKED BRIE

"Great recipe! I made this for a holiday party and everyone loved it. I used the brandy and served it with cinnamon sugar pita chips. I'm still getting requests for the recipe."
—*luvingLI*

[2010]

GREEK DELI KABOBS
yield: 2 dozen
prep/total time: 30 min. + marinating

These pretty skewers combine marinated cheese, veggies, and meat in a fun and fresh appetizer that's a snap to make.

—Vikki Spengler, Ocala, Florida

2 jars (7-1/2 ounces each) roasted sweet red peppers, drained
1 pound part-skim mozzarella cheese, cut into 1/2-inch cubes
24 fresh broccoli florets
24 slices hard salami
1/2 cup Greek vinaigrette

1. Cut the red peppers into 24 strips; place strips in a large resealable plastic bag. Add remaining ingredients. Seal the bag and turn to coat; refrigerate for 4 hours or overnight.

2. Drain and discard marinade. Thread cheese, vegetables and meat onto frilled toothpicks or short skewers.

[2012]

SOUTHERN BLACK-EYED PEAS
yield: 6 servings
prep/total time: 20 min. + standing ∾ cook: 45 min.

I find pork the secret to a good black-eyed pea recipe. A double dose of ham for flavor and slow and gentle cooking creates this perfect side dish.

—Emory Doty, Jasper, Georgia

1 pound dried black-eyed peas, sorted and rinsed
1 large onion, chopped
2 tablespoons olive oil
2 ounces sliced salt pork belly, chopped
6 garlic cloves, minced
2 bay leaves
1 tablespoon minced fresh thyme *or* 1 teaspoon dried thyme

1/4 teaspoon crushed red pepper flakes
1/4 teaspoon pepper
1 carton (32 ounces) reduced-sodium chicken broth
2 smoked ham hocks

1. Place peas in a Dutch oven; add water to cover by 2 in. Bring to a boil; boil for 2 minutes. Remove from the heat; cover the peas and let stand for 1 hour. Drain and rinse peas, discarding liquid; set aside.

2. In the same pan, saute the onion in oil until tender. Add the pork belly, garlic, bay leaves, thyme, pepper flakes and pepper; cook 1 minute longer.

3. Add the broth, ham hocks and peas; bring to a boil. Reduce heat; simmer, uncovered, for 35-40 minutes or until peas are tender, stirring occasionally and adding additional water if desired.

4. Discard the bay leaves. Remove the ham hocks; cool slightly. Remove meat from the bones if desired; finely chop and return to pan. Discard bones.

[2010]

SAVORY STUFFED FIGS
yield: 2 dozen ∾ prep/total time: 30 min.
grill: 5 min.

I use this three-ingredient recipe when I want a sweet and savory appetizer that's simple to make. It can be made ahead and is nice for elegant or casual parties.

—Maggie Zabinko, Anchorage, Alaska

12 bacon strips
24 dried figs
24 pecan halves

1. Cut the bacon strips in half widthwise. In a large skillet, cook bacon over medium heat until partially cooked but not crisp. Remove to paper towels to drain; keep warm.

2. Cut a lengthwise slit down the center of each fig; fill with a pecan half. Wrap each with a piece of bacon.

3. Grill, covered, over medium heat or broil 4 in. from the heat for 5-8 minutes or until bacon is crisp; turn once.

valentine's day

[2001]

CHOCOLATE HAZELNUT TRUFFLES

yield: 2 dozen ❧ **prep: 25 min. + chilling**

I've given these delectable candies with a nutty surprise inside to teachers and friends.

—*Debra Pedrazzi, Ayer, Massachusetts*

- 3/4 cup confectioners' sugar
- 2 tablespoons baking cocoa
- 4 milk chocolate candy bars (1.55 ounces each)
- 6 tablespoons butter
- 1/4 cup heavy whipping cream
- 24 whole hazelnuts
- 1 cup ground hazelnuts, toasted

1. In a large bowl, sift together the confectioners' sugar and cocoa; set aside. In a small saucepan, melt candy bars and butter. Add the cream and reserved cocoa mixture. Cook and stir over medium-low heat until mixture is thickened and smooth. Pour into an 8-in. square dish. Cover and refrigerate overnight.

2. Using a melon baller or spoon, shape candy into 1-in. balls; press a hazelnut into each. Reshape balls and roll in ground hazelnuts. Store in an airtight container in the refrigerator.

[2000]

AVOCADO ORANGE SALAD

yield: 2 servings ❧ **prep/total time: 10 min.**

My mom passed this recipe on to me. It's a longtime family favorite. The tangy oranges, crisp lettuce and mellow avocado are terrific together.

—*Catherine Shelton, Las Vegas, Nevada*

- 2 cups torn mixed salad greens
- 1 medium navel orange, peeled and sectioned
- 1 large ripe avocado, peeled and sliced
- 1 small onion, chopped

CITRUS DRESSING:
- 1/4 cup canola oil
- 2 tablespoons orange juice
- 1 tablespoon lemon juice
- 1 tablespoon sugar
- 1/2 teaspoon grated orange peel
- 1/8 teaspoon salt
- 1/8 teaspoon celery seed

1. On two salad plates, arrange the greens, orange, avocado and onion. In a small bowl, whisk the dressing ingredients. Drizzle over salads.

[2009]

GRILLED SHRIMP WITH APRICOT SAUCE

yield: 2 skewers (2/3 cup sauce)
prep/total time: 20 min.

Succulent, bacon-wrapped shrimp get a flavor boost from the sweet-hot sauce. Served on skewers, they make a fabulous addition to a romantic meal.

—*Carole Resnick, Cleveland, Ohio*

- 1/4 cup apricot preserves
- 1 tablespoon apricot nectar
- 1/8 teaspoon ground chipotle powder
- 6 uncooked large shrimp, peeled and deveined
- 3 slices Canadian bacon, halved

1. In a small bowl, combine the preserves, apricot nectar and chipotle powder. Chill until serving.

2. Thread shrimp and bacon onto two metal or soaked wooden skewers. Grill, covered, over medium heat for 3-4 minutes on each side or until shrimp turn pink. Serve with sauce.

TUSCAN PORK MEDALLIONS

"My mother-in-law made this for Memorial Day weekend and I had to have the recipe. It is absolutely delicious, one of the most memorable meals I have had in a long time. Whether for an intimate dinner, a family weekday dinner or a large dinner party this cannot fail to impress. Leftovers taste even better if that's possible, too. I would have given this even more stars if I could have done. Thank you for a truly amazing recipe."

—LeLimey

[2007]

CHOCOLATE-PECAN PUDDING CAKES

yield: 6 servings ∾ **prep: 15 min.**
bake: 25 min. + cooling

Sinful chocolate mounds are topped with a dollop of cream. I've been cooking since I was 7. My parents and grandparents provided my early experience. My grandfather was a professional baker. Enjoy this treat!

—Cory Tower, Columbus, Nebraska

1	cup all-purpose flour
2/3	cup sugar
6	tablespoons baking cocoa, *divided*
2	teaspoons baking powder
1/4	teaspoon salt
1/2	cup 2% milk
1/4	cup butter, melted
1	teaspoon vanilla extract
1/2	cup coarsely chopped pecans
2/3	cup packed brown sugar
3/4	cup hot water

Whipped cream, optional

1. In a large bowl, combine the flour, sugar, 3 tablespoons cocoa, baking powder and salt. Combine the milk, butter and vanilla; stir into dry ingredients just until combined. Stir in the pecans. Spoon into six greased 6-oz. custard cups.

2. Combine brown sugar and remaining cocoa; sprinkle over the batter. Pour 2 tablespoons hot water over each cup. Place cups on a baking sheet.

3. Bake at 350° for 25-30 minutes or until toothpick inserted in cake portion comes out clean. Cool on wire racks for 15 minutes. Run a knife around the edge of each cup; invert onto dessert plates. Serve warm with whipped cream if desired.

[2010]

TUSCAN PORK MEDALLIONS

yield: 2 servings ∾ **prep/total time: 30 min.**

(Pictured on page 235)

Pork tenderloin gets delightful Italian flavor from prosciutto, tomatoes and garden herbs. The beautifully browned slices are quick enough for weeknights, yet special enough for holidays.

—Lorraine Caland, Thunder Bay, Ontario

3/4	pound pork tenderloin, cut into 1-inch slices
1/4	teaspoon salt
1/8	teaspoon pepper
1	tablespoon butter
2	thin slices prosciutto *or* deli ham, chopped
2	garlic cloves, minced
1-1/2	teaspoons minced fresh sage *or* 1/2 teaspoon dried sage leaves
2	tablespoons balsamic vinegar
1/2	cup heavy whipping cream
3/4	cup chopped plum tomatoes
4	fresh basil leaves, thinly sliced
1	teaspoon grated Parmesan cheese

1. Sprinkle pork with salt and pepper. In a large skillet over medium heat, cook pork in butter until a thermometer reads 145°. Remove; let meat stand for 5 minutes.

2. Meanwhile, in the same skillet, saute prosciutto in the drippings until browned. Add garlic and sage; cook 1 minute longer. Add vinegar, stirring to loosen browned bits from pan.

3. Stir in cream; bring to a boil. Reduce heat; cook and stir for 1-2 minutes or until slightly thickened. Add tomatoes and pork; heat through. Sprinkle each serving with basil and cheese.

[2006]

RIBEYES WITH MUSHROOMS

yield: 2 servings
prep/total time: 5 min. + marinating
cook: 10 min.

This easy entree takes just minutes to make and is ideal to serve on Valentine's Day to a meat-and-potatoes guy. The hearty steak is well-seasoned with a robust marinade and served with a fresh mushroom sauce.

—Lissa Hutson, Phelan, California

8	green onions, sliced
2	garlic cloves, minced
1	cup beef broth
2	tablespoons balsamic vinegar
1/2	teaspoon dried thyme
1/2	teaspoon pepper
2	beef ribeye steaks (8 ounces each)
1	cup sliced fresh mushrooms

1. In a small bowl, combine the first six ingredients. Place the steaks in a large resealable plastic bag; add half of the marinade. Seal bag and turn to coat; refrigerate for 1-2 hours. Cover and refrigerate remaining marinade.

2. Drain and discard marinade from steaks. Broil steaks 4-6 in. from the heat for 5-6 minutes on each side or until meat reaches desired doneness (for medium-rare, a thermometer should read 145°; medium, 160°; well-done, 170°).

3. Meanwhile, place remaining marinade in a small saucepan. Bring to a boil over medium heat; cook and stir for 1 minute. Stir in the mushrooms. Serve with steaks.

[2003]

GREEN BEAN STIR-FRY

yield: 2 servings
prep/total time: 10 min.

Soy sauce and peanut butter flavor these crisp-tender beans. They're a nice change from the usual green bean salads and casseroles. With a sesame seed crunch, this dish always wows guests and brings plenty of recipe requests.

—Robin Joss, Ashburn, Virginia

1	tablespoon reduced-sodium soy sauce
2	garlic cloves, minced
1	teaspoon sesame seeds, toasted
1	teaspoon brown sugar
1	teaspoon peanut butter
3/4	pound fresh green beans, trimmed
4-1/2	teaspoons vegetable oil

1. In a small bowl, combine the soy sauce, garlic, sesame seeds, brown sugar and peanut butter; set aside.

2. In a large skillet, stir-fry green beans in oil until crisp-tender. Remove from the heat. Add the soy sauce mixture; stir to coat.

BALSAMIC VINEGAR

Over the years balsamic vinegar has gone from an exotic ingredient to a pantry staple. This Italian vinegar is a dark, thick liquid with a sweet-smelling aroma. It adds a rich, dark color to dishes. When a dark color is undesirable, use white balsamic vinegar.

—Taste of Home Cooking Experts.

GREEN BEAN STIR-FRY

"One of my favorite recipes. I've made it several times and my 10-year-old son loves it. I also gave the recipe to my mother and she loved it."

—jlc1978blue

---

easter

SPRINGTIME
ASPARAGUS
MEDLEY

*"*This is awesome. I made
it after finding asparagus on
sale at the grocer's. What a
treat! I will make it over and
over, and have already passed
it on to others!*"*
—JessCostello

[2007]

SPRINGTIME ASPARAGUS MEDLEY

yield: 8-10 servings.
prep/total time: 25 min.

Seasonal and tasty, this colorful side dish is delicious served warm or cold. I get lots of compliments on the zesty sauce.

—Millie Vickery, Lena, Illinois, Field Editor

1	cup water
1-1/2	pounds fresh asparagus, trimmed and cut into 2-inch pieces
2	small tomatoes, cut into wedges
3	tablespoons cider vinegar
3/4	teaspoon Worcestershire sauce
1/3	cup sugar
1	tablespoon grated onion
1/2	teaspoon salt
1/2	teaspoon paprika
1/3	cup canola oil
1/3	cup sliced almonds, toasted
1/3	cup crumbled blue cheese, optional

1. In a large saucepan, bring water to a boil. Add asparagus; cover and cook for 3-5 minutes or until crisp-tender. Drain. Add the tomatoes; cover and keep warm.

2. In a blender, combine the vinegar, Worcestershire sauce, sugar, onion, salt and paprika; cover and process until smooth. While processing, gradually add oil in a steady stream. Pour over asparagus mixture and toss to coat.

3. Transfer to a serving bowl; sprinkle with almonds and blue cheese if desired. Serve warm.

[1993]

PLUM-GLAZED LAMB

yield: 10-12 servings.   **prep: 5 min.**
bake: 2-1/2 hours

Fruity and flavorful, this wonderful glaze is simple to prepare, and its hint of garlic really complements the lamb. The recipe makes enough glaze to baste the lamb during roasting and leaves plenty to pass when serving.

—Ann Eastman, Santa Monica, California

1	leg of lamb (4 to 5 pounds)
	Salt and pepper to taste
2	cans (15 ounces *each*) plums, pitted
2	garlic cloves
1/4	cup lemon juice
2	tablespoons reduced-sodium soy sauce
2	teaspoons Worcestershire sauce
1	teaspoon dried basil

1. Place lamb, fat side up, on a rack in a shallow baking pan. Season with salt and pepper. Bake at 325° for 2-1/2 to 3 hours or until meat reaches desired doneness (for medium-rare, a thermometer should read 145°; medium, 160°; well-done, 170°).

2. Meanwhile, drain plums, reserving 1/2 cup syrup. In a food processor, process plums, reserved syrup, garlic, lemon juice, soy sauce, Worcestershire sauce and basil until smooth; set aside half of plum sauce.

3. Baste lamb every 15 minutes during the last hour of roasting. In a small saucepan, simmer reserved sauce for 5 minutes; serve with meat.

[2005]

ORANGE-GLAZED BUNNY ROLLS

**yield: 1 dozen ∞ prep: 45 min. + rising
bake: 15 min. + cooling**

(Pictured on page 233)

I make these tender yeast rolls for special occasions. Orange marmalade gives the frosting a pleasant citrus flavor. Shape the rolls any way you like.

—*Gerri Brown, Canfield, Ohio*

- 2 packages (1/4 ounce each) active dry yeast
- 1/4 cup warm water (110° to 115°)
- 1 cup warm 2% milk (110° to 115°)
- 1/2 cup shortening
- 2 eggs
- 1/3 cup sugar
- 1/4 cup orange juice
- 2 tablespoons grated orange peel
- 1 teaspoon salt
- 5 to 5-1/2 cups all-purpose flour

GLAZE:
- 2 cups confectioners' sugar
- 1/4 cup water
- 1 tablespoon orange marmalade
- 1/2 teaspoon butter, softened

1. In a large bowl, dissolve yeast in warm water. Add the milk, shortening, eggs, sugar, orange juice, orange peel, salt and 3 cups flour; beat until smooth. Stir in enough remaining flour to form a soft dough.

2. Turn onto a floured surface; knead until smooth and elastic, about 6-8 minutes. Place in a greased bowl, turning once to grease top. Cover; let rise in a warm place until doubled; about 1 hour.

3. Punch dough down; turn on a lightly floured surface. Divide into 13 pieces. Shape 12 pieces into 12-in. ropes. Fold each in half; twist top half of the open end twice to form ears. Place 2 in. apart on greased baking sheets. Shape remaining dough into 12 balls. Place one on the loop end of each roll to form a tail; press into dough. Cover and let rise until doubled, about 30 minutes.

4. Bake at 375° for 12-15 minutes or until golden brown. Cool on wire racks. In a small bowl, combine glaze ingredients; beat until blended. Spread over rolls.

[2003]

JIM'S HONEY-GLAZED HAM

**yield: 10 servings ∞ prep: 10 min.
bake: 1 hour**

The aroma of this ham cooking in the oven is absolutely wonderful. It comes out moist, juicy and lightly browned.

—*Jim Whelan, Sebastian, Florida*

- 1 boneless fully cooked ham (3 to 4 pounds)
- 1/2 cup water
- 1 cup honey
- 1/2 cup packed brown sugar
- 1 teaspoon ground cloves
- 1/2 teaspoon ground mustard

1. Score the ham, making diamond shapes 1/2 in. deep. Place on a rack in a well-greased foil-lined roasting pan. Add water to pan. In a small bowl, combine the honey, brown sugar, cloves and mustard; pour over ham.

2. Bake, uncovered, at 325° for 1 to 1-1/2 hours or until a thermometer reads 140°, basting with pan juices often. Add additional water to the pan if necessary.

ORANGE-GLAZED BUNNY ROLLS

"Love these rolls. I roll them into spirals to enjoy them all year round!"
—colllege_kid

[2011]

MARMALADE CANDIED CARROTS

yield: 8 servings ∾ prep/total time: 30 min.

These crisp-tender carrots have a citrusy sweet flavor that really dresses up this veggie. It's my favorite carrot recipe.

—*Heather Clemmons, Supply, North Carolina*

    2   pounds fresh baby carrots
    2/3 cup orange marmalade
    3   tablespoons packed brown sugar
    2   tablespoons butter
    1/2 chopped pecans, toasted
    1   teaspoon rum extract

1. Place carrots in a steamer basket; place in a large saucepan over 1 in. of water. Bring to a boil; cover and steam for 12-15 minutes or until crisp-tender.

2. Meanwhile, in a small saucepan, combine marmalade, brown sugar and butter; cook and stir over medium heat until mixture is thickened and reduced to about 1/2 cup. Stir in pecans and extract.

3. Place carrots in a large bowl; drizzle with glaze and stir gently to coat.

[2007]

LOADED RED POTATO CASSEROLE

yield: 9 servings ∾ prep: 25 min. ∾ bake: 20 min.

This potato casserole has the same flavor of the potato skins you can order as a restaurant appetizer. It's an ideal dish for parties, tailgating and potlucks.

—*Charlane Gathy, Lexington, Kentucky*

    16   small red potatoes
    1/2   cup 2% milk
    1/4   cup butter, cubed
    1/2   teaspoon pepper
    1/8   teaspoon salt
    1-1/2 cups (6 ounces) shredded cheddar cheese, *divided*
    1/2   cup crumbled cooked bacon
    1   cup (8 ounces) sour cream
    2   tablespoons minced chives

1. Place potatoes in a Dutch oven and cover with water. Bring to a boil. Reduce heat; cover and cook for 15-20 minutes or until tender. Drain.

2. Mash potatoes with the milk, butter, pepper and salt. Transfer to a greased 13-in. x 9-in. baking dish. Sprinkle with 1 cup cheese and bacon.

3. Dollop with sour cream; sprinkle with chives and the remaining cheese. Bake, uncovered, at 350° for 20-25 minutes or until cheese is melted.

[2009]

SPRING GREENS WITH BEETS AND GOAT CHEESE

yield: 8 servings ∾ prep/total time: 20 min.

I love to put small variations on this salad, depending on what I have on hand, but this version is my absolute favorite. I just fell in love with the flavor combinations.

—*Kristin Kossak, Bozeman, Montana*

    2/3 cup pecan halves
    3   tablespoons balsamic vinegar, *divided*
    1   tablespoon water
    1   tablespoon sugar
    1/4 cup olive oil
    2   tablespoons maple syrup
    1   teaspoon stone-ground mustard
    1/8 teaspoon salt
    1   package (5 ounces) spring mix salad greens
    1   can (14-1/2 ounces) sliced beets, drained
    1   cup crumbled goat cheese

1. In a large heavy skillet, cook the pecans, 1 tablespoon vinegar and water over medium heat until nuts are toasted, about 4 minutes. Sprinkle with sugar. Cook and stir for 2-4 minutes or until sugar is melted. Spread on foil to cool.

2. In a small bowl, whisk the oil, syrup, mustard, salt and remaining vinegar. Refrigerate until serving.

3. In a large bowl, combine salad greens and dressing; toss to coat. Divide among eight salad plates. Top with beets, goat cheese and glazed pecans.

[2008]

LEMONY WHITE CHOCOLATE CHEESECAKE

yield: 12 servings ～ prep: 30 min. ～ bake: 65 min. + chilling

(*Pictured on page 235*)

Although it takes some time to prepare this eye-catching cheesecake, the combination of tangy lemon and rich white chocolate is hard to beat. It's always a hit!

—*Marlene Schollenberger, Bloomington, Indiana*

1-1/4 cups all-purpose flour
   2 tablespoons confectioners' sugar
   1 teaspoon grated lemon peel
 1/2 cup cold butter, cubed
FILLING:
   4 packages (8 ounces *each*) cream cheese, softened
1-1/4 cups sugar
 10 ounces white baking chocolate, melted and cooled
   2 tablespoons all-purpose flour
   2 tablespoons heavy whipping cream
   2 tablespoons lemon juice
   2 teaspoons grated lemon peel
   2 teaspoons vanilla extract
   4 eggs, lightly beaten

1. Place a 9-in. springform pan on a double thickness of heavy-duty foil (about 18 in. square). Securely wrap foil around pan; set aside.

2. In a small bowl, combine the flour, confectioners' sugar and peel; cut in butter until crumbly. Press onto the bottom and 1 in. up the sides of prepared pan. Place on a baking sheet. Bake at 325° for 25-30 minutes or until golden brown. Cool on a wire rack.

3. In a large bowl, beat cream cheese and sugar until smooth. Beat in the white chocolate, flour, cream, lemon juice, lemon peel and vanilla. Add eggs; beat on low speed just until combined. Pour into crust.

4. Place pan in a large baking pan; add 1 in. of hot water to larger pan. Bake at 325° for 65-85 minutes or until center is just set and top appears dull.

5. Remove the pan from water bath. Cool on a wire rack for 10 minutes. Carefully run a knife around edge of pan to loosen; cool 1 hour longer. Refrigerate overnight. Remove sides of pan.

LEMONY WHITE CHOCOLATE CHEESECAKE

"This is amazing! It has replaced my holiday cheescake that I have been making for years. I do add white chocolate ganache on the top, sometimes with berries. You will love it. The crust makes it stand above the rest! I am so tired of graham cracker crusts. We will be having this for Easter. It is so delicious!"
— *flyglo*

[1997]

APRICOT GELATIN SALAD

yield: 12-16 servings
prep/total time: 20 min. + chilling

I serve this smooth, fluffy salad all year for special meals, but it's especially fitting around Easter with its pretty color and fruity flavor. The apricot pieces in the salad are an unexpected treat.

—*Ellen Benninger, Greenville, Pennsylvania*

- 1 package (6 ounces) apricot *or* orange gelatin
- 2 cups boiling water
- 1 can (20 ounces) crushed pineapple
- 1 package (8 ounces) cream cheese, softened
- 1 can (15 ounces) apricot halves, drained and chopped
- 1/2 cup chopped walnuts
- 1 carton (8 ounces) frozen whipped topping, thawed

Additional chopped walnuts, optional

1. In a bowl, dissolve gelatin in water. Drain pineapple, reserving juice. Add pineapple to gelatin and set aside.

2. In a bowl, beat the cream cheese and pineapple juice until smooth. Stir in the gelatin mixture; chill until partially set, stirring occasionally.

3. Stir in the apricots and walnuts. Fold in whipped topping. Pour into a 13-in. x 9-in. dish. Sprinkle with the walnuts if desired. Chill until firm.

[2007]

FESTIVE RICE SALAD

yield: 8 servings
prep/total time: 30 min. + cooling

I once had a similar salad at a friend's house and I was determined to re-create it at home. After several tries, I came up with this concoction of flavors in which opposites attract. It's easy to prepare and colorful, too.

—*Terri Simpson, Palm Harbor, Florida*

- 3/4 cup uncooked long grain rice
- 1 package (10 ounces) frozen peas, thawed
- 1 small sweet red pepper, chopped
- 3/4 cup chopped green onions
- 1/2 cup dried cranberries

DRESSING:
- 1/2 cup canola oil
- 1/3 cup white vinegar
- 3 tablespoons sugar
- 1/2 teaspoon dill weed
- 1/4 teaspoon ground mustard
- 1/8 teaspoon pepper

1. Cook rice according to package directions; cool. In a large bowl, combine the rice, peas, red pepper, onions and cranberries. In a small bowl, whisk the dressing ingredients. Drizzle over salad and toss to coat. Refrigerate until serving.

[2003]

AU GRATIN PARTY POTATOES

yield: 60 (3/4-cup) servings
prep: 45 min.   bake: 45 min.

When putting on a party for their American Legion Post, my father and uncle prepared this yummy potato dish. I've used the recipe for smaller groups by making a half or quarter of it. It's simple to divide.

-*Crystal Kolady, Henrietta, New York*

- 20 pounds potatoes, peeled, cubed, and cooked
- 4 cans (12 ounces each) evaporated milk
- 3 packages (16 ounces each) process cheese (Velveeta), cubed
- 1 cup butter, cubed
- 2 tablespons salt
- 2 teaspoons pepper

Paprika, optional

1. In several large bowls, combine potatoes, milk, cheese, butter, salt and pepper. Transfer to four greased 13-in. x 9-in. baking dishes.

2. Bake, uncovered, at 350° for 45-50 minutes or until bubbly. Sprinkle with paprika if desired.

[2010]

STRAWBERRY-RHUBARB MERINGUE PIE

yield: 8 servings ⟳ **prep: 55 min.** ⟳ **bake: 40 min. + chilling**

This pie is a rite of spring at our house, and many people have enjoyed sharing it with us. We love that it's both sweet and tart with a mild almond accent.

—Jessie Grearson, Falmouth, Maine

1/2	cup all-purpose flour
1/4	cup whole wheat pastry flour
1/4	cup ground almonds
1/2	teaspoon salt
1/4	cup ground almonds
1/2	teaspoon salt
1/4	cup cold butter, cubed
2	tablespoons cold water

FILLING:

1	egg, lightly beaten
3/4	cup sugar
2	tablespoons all-purpose flour
1/4	teaspoon ground cinnamon
2	cups chopped fresh *or* frozen rhubarb, thawed
1-1/2	cups sliced fresh stawberries

MERINGUE:

3	egg whites
1/4	teaspoon almond extract
6	tablespoons sugar

1. In a food processor, combine the all-purpose flour, pastry flour, almonds and salt; cover and pulse until blended. Add butter; cover and pulse until mixture resembles coarse crumbs. While processing, gradually add water until dough forms a ball.

2. Roll out pastry to fit a 9-in. pie plate. Transfer pastry to pie plate. Trim pastry to 1/2 in. beyond edge of plate; flute edges.

3. In a large bowl, combine the egg, sugar, flour and cinnamon; stir in rhubarb and strawberries. Transfer to prepared crust. Bake at 375° for 35-40 minutes or until the filling is bubbly. Place pie on a wire rack; keep warm. Reduce heat to 350°.

4. In a large bowl, beat egg whites and extract on medium speed until soft peaks form. Gradually beat in sugar, 1 tablespoon at a time, on high until stiff peaks form. Spread over hot filling, sealing edges to crust.

5. Bake for 15 minutes or until golden brown. Cool on a wire rack for 1 hour; refrigerate for 1-2 hours before serving.

[2001]

PINEAPPLE ICED TEA

yield: 5 servings ⟳ **prep/total time: 10 min. + chilling**

With five teenagers, we go through lots of beverages. This thirst-quenching tea is easy to mix up and has a sparkling citrus flavor we all enjoy.

—Kathy Kittell, Lenexa, Kansas, Field Editor

4	cups water
7	individual tea bags
1	cup unsweetened pineapple juice
1/3	cup lemon juice
2	tablespoons sugar

1. In a large saucepan, bring water to a boil. Remove from the heat.

2. Add the tea bags; cover and steep for 3-5 minutes. Discard tea bags. Stir in the pineapple juice, lemon juice and sugar until sugar is dissolved. Refrigerate overnight for the flavors to blend. Serve over ice.

AVOID WATERED-DOWN DRINKS

Ice cubes add a refreshing chill to beverages, but as they melt, the flavor of the drink will be diluted. To keep that beverage chill and delicious flavor, make ice cubes using the ingredients of the drink. For example, in the Pineapple Iced Tea above, make ice cubes from either prepared tea or pineapple juice.

—Taste of Home Cooking Experts

graduation

[1995]

MEXICAN PIZZA

yield: 12-16 servings
prep: 20 min. + chilling
bake: 10 min. + cooling

(*Pictured on page 237*)

My husband and I came up with the recipe for these loaded snack squares. Our whole family likes the Southwestern flavor.

—Sandy McKenzie
Braham, Minnesota, Field Editor

2	tubes (8 ounces each) refrigerated crescent rolls
1	package (8 ounces) cream cheese, softened
1	cup (8 ounces) sour cream
1	pound ground beef
1	envelope taco seasoning
1	can (2-1/4 ounces) sliced ripe olives, drained
1	medium tomato, chopped
3/4	cup shredded cheddar cheese
3/4	cup shredded part-skim mozzarella cheese
1	cup shredded lettuce

---

1. Unroll crescent roll dough and place in an ungreased 15-in. x 10-in. x 1-in. baking pan. Flatten dough to fit the pan, sealing seams and perforations. Bake at 375° for 8-10 minutes or until light golden brown; cool on a wire rack.

2. In a small bowl, combine cream cheese and sour cream until blended; spread over crust. Chill 30 minutes.

3. Meanwhile, in a large skillet, cook beef over medium heat until no longer pink; drain. Stir in taco seasoning. Add water according to package directions and simmer for 5 minutes, stirring occasionally. Spread over cream cheese layer. Top with the olives, tomato, cheeses and lettuce. Cut into serving-size pieces. Serve immediately or refrigerate.

[2008]

SUMMER VEGETABLE SALAD

yield: 6 servings      **prep: 15 min. + chilling**

We're always looking for ways to use our garden produce in the summer, and this salad is great because you can use whatever vegetables you have on hand. You'll love the dill dressing.

—Mari Roseberry, *Dunning, Nebraska*

1	cup fresh cauliflowerets
1	cup fresh baby carrots
1	cup sliced red onion
1	cup halved grape tomatoes
1	cup chopped zucchini
3	tablespoons cider vinegar
2	tablespoons olive oil
1	teaspoon dill weed
1/2	teaspoon salt
1/2	teaspoon ground mustard
1/4 to 1/2	teaspoon garlic powder
1/4	teaspoon pepper

---

1. In a large bowl, combine cauliflower, carrots, onion, tomatoes and zucchini. In a small bowl, whisk the remaining ingredients. Pour over vegetables and toss to coat.

2. Cover and refrigerate for at least 2 hours, stirring occasionally. Serve with a slotted spoon.

MEXICAN PIZZA

"I prepared this as a quick and "lighter" dinner. We had a super busy weekend and I wanted something quick and not so heavy on the tummy. Everyone loved it...just perfect for a quick dinner. I'm taking it to my next ladies' gathering. Yum."

—*dkbaes*

[2000]

OAT SNACK MIX

yield: about 6 cups ∞ **prep: 10 min.**
bake: 45 min. + cooling

Kids of all ages seem to enjoy the creative combination of ingredients in this not-so-sweet mix. My three children would rather munch on this snack than on candy.

—*Patti Brandt, Reedsburg, Wisconsin*

1/2 **cup butter, cubed**
1/3 **cup honey**
1/4 **cup packed brown sugar**
  1 **teaspoon ground cinnamon**
1/2 **teaspoon salt**
  3 **cups square oat cereal**
1-1/2 **cups old-fashioned oats**
  1 **cup chopped walnuts**
1/2 **cup dried cranberries**
1/2 **cup chocolate-covered raisins**

1. In a saucepan, combine first five ingredients. Cook until butter is melted and sugar is dissolved; stir until smooth.

2. In a large bowl, combine the cereal, oats and nuts. Drizzle with butter mixture; toss to coat.

3. Transfer to a greased 15-in. x 10-in. x 1-in. baking pan. Bake, uncovered, at 275° for 45 minutes, stirring every 15 minutes. Cool for 15 minutes, stirring occasionally. Stir in cranberries and chocolate-covered raisins. Store in an airtight container.

[2007]

ORANGE GELATIN PRETZEL SALAD

yield: 15 servings ∞ **prep: 30 min. + chilling**

Salty pretzels pair nicely with the candy-like fruit in this layered gelatin salad. It provides a pretty potluck dish.

—*Peggy Boyd, Northport, Alabama*

  2 **cups crushed pretzels**
  3 **teaspoons plus 3/4 cup sugar,** *divided*
3/4 **cup butter, melted**
  2 **packages (3 ounces** *each***) orange gelatin**
  2 **cups boiling water**
  2 **cans (8 ounces** *each***) crushed pineapple, drained**
  1 **can (11 ounces) mandarin oranges, drained**

  1 **package (8 ounces) cream cheese, softened**
  2 **cups whipped topping**
Additional whipped topping, optional

1. In a small bowl, combine pretzels and 3 teaspoons sugar; stir in butter. Press into an ungreased 13-in. x 9-in. baking dish. Bake at 350° for 10 minutes. Cool on a wire rack.

2. In a large bowl, dissolve gelatin in boiling water. Add pineapple and oranges. Chill until partially set, about 30 minutes.

3. In a bowl, beat cream cheese and remaining sugar until smooth. Fold in whipped topping. Spread over crust. Gently spoon gelatin mixture over cream cheese layer. Cover and refrigerate for 2-4 hours or until firm.

4. Cut into squares. Garnish with additional whipped topping if desired.

[2008]

GRADUATION PUNCH

yield: 3-3/4 gallons ∞ **prep: 15 min. + cooling**

Enjoyed for over 30 years in our family, this was the punch my mom served when I graduated from high school. And I made it when my own kids graduated!

—*Deb Waggoner, Grand Island, Nebraska, Field Editor*

1-1/2 **cups sugar**
  8 **quarts water,** *divided*
  4 **envelopes unsweetened strawberry Kool-Aid mix**
  3 **cans (6 ounces** *each***) frozen orange juice concentrate, thawed**
2-1/4 **cups thawed lemonade concentrate**
  2 **cans (46 ounces** *each***) unsweetened pineapple juice**
  2 **liters ginger ale, chilled**

1. In a large saucepan, combine the sugar and 2 qts. water. Cook and stir over medium heat until sugar is dissolved. Remove from the heat; stir in Kool-Aid mix. Cool completely.

2. Just before serving, divide the syrup between two large containers or punch bowls; add the concentrates, pineapple juice and remaining water to each. Stir in ginger ale.

[2009]

TOFFEE POKE CAKE

yield: 15 servings ∾ prep: 25 min.
bake: 25 min. + chilling

This recipe is my family's and friends' very favorite dessert. I love making it, because it is so simple.

—*Jeanette Hoffman, Oshkosh, Wisconsin*

- 1 package (18-1/4 ounces) chocolate cake mix
- 1 jar (17 ounces) butterscotch-caramel ice cream topping
- 1 carton (12 ounces) frozen whipped topping, thawed
- 3 Heath candy bars (1.4 ounces each), chopped

1. Prepare and bake the cake according to package directions, using a greased 13-in. x 9-in. baking pan. Cool on a wire rack.

2. Using the handle of a wooden spoon, poke holes in cake. Pour 3/4 cup caramel topping into holes. Spoon remaining caramel over cake. Top with whipped topping. Sprinkle with candy. Refrigerate for at least 2 hours before serving.

[2008]

SICILIAN SALAD

yield: 8 servings ∾ prep/total time: 25 min.

Cheese cubes give substance to this beautiful, mild and fresh-tasting pasta salad. It makes a great side in any season.

—*Ben Haen, Baldwin, Wisconsin*

- 1 package (7 ounces) small pasta shells
- 1 can (14-1/2 ounces) Italian diced tomatoes, drained
- 1 large tomato, diced
- 1 cup cubed part-skim mozzarella cheese
- 1/2 cup chopped red onion
- 1/3 cup sliced ripe olives, drained
- 1/4 cup minced fresh parsley
- 1/4 cup olive oil
- 1 to 1-1/4 teaspoons salt
- 1/4 teaspoon pepper

1. Cook pasta according to package directions; drain and rinse in cold water.

2. In a large salad bowl, combine the pasta, tomatoes, cheese, onion, olives and parsley. Drizzle with oil; sprinkle with salt and pepper. Toss to coat. Cover and refrigerate until serving.

[1997]

TANGY BARBECUE SANDWICHES

yield: 14-18 servings ∾ prep: 10 min. ∾ cook: 8 hours

Since I prepare the beef for these hearty sandwiches in the slow cooker, it's easy to fix a meal for a hungry bunch. The savory homemade sauce ensures I come home with no leftovers.

—*Debbi Smith, Crossett, Arkansas, Former Field Editor*

- 3 cups chopped celery
- 1 cup chopped onion
- 1 cup ketchup
- 1 cup barbecue sauce
- 1 cup water
- 2 tablespoons white vinegar
- 2 tablespoons Worcestershire sauce
- 2 tablespoons brown sugar
- 1 teaspoon chili powder
- 1 teaspoon salt
- 1/2 teaspoon pepper
- 1/2 teaspoon garlic powder
- 1 boneless beef chuck roast (3 to 4 pounds), trimmed and cut in half
- 14 to 18 hamburger buns, split

1. In a 5-qt. slow cooker, combine first 12 ingredients. Add roast. Cover and cook on high for 1 hour. Reduce heat to low and cook 6-8 hours longer or until the meat is tender.

2. Remove roast; cool. Shred meat and return to sauce; heat through. Using a slotted spoon, fill each bun with about 1/2 cup of meat mixture.

ORANGE-GLAZED BUNNY ROLLS, page 225

MUSHROOM PUFFS, page 244

CHOCOLATE CARAMEL CANDY, page 209

CRANBERRY QUENCHER, page 218

MAKE-AHEAD MASHED POTATOES, page 258

LEMONY WHITE CHOCOLATE CHEESECAKE, page 227

TUSCAN PORK MEDALLIONS, page 222

SPOOKY SPIDER CAKE, page 251

ROASTED HARVEST VEGETABLES, page 256

PILGRIM HAT COOKIES, page 260

MEXICAN PIZZA, page 230

BLUE CHEESE-ONION STEAK BITES, page 217

GRANDMA'S POTATO SALAD, page 241

SPECIAL-OCCASION CHOCOLATE CAKE, page 250

CARAMEL MARSHMALLOW DELIGHTS, page 207

WONDERFUL CANDIES TWO WAYS, page 213

BEEF RIB ROAST, page 264

YUMMY MUMMY CHEESE SPREAD, page 254

CHERRY-BRANDY BAKED BRIE, page 219

SWEET ONION BBQ BURGERS, page 242

4th of july

[1994]

GRANDMA'S POTATO SALAD

yield: 18 servings   prep: 20 min. + chilling

(Pictured on page 238)

Our Fourth of July feast wouldn't be complete without this cool, old-fashioned potato salad. It's my grandma's treasured recipe.

—*Sue Gronholz*
Beaver Dam, Wisconsin, Field Editor

- 1 **cup water**
- 1/2 **cup butter, cubed**
- 1/4 **cup white vinegar**
- 2 **eggs**
- 1/2 **cup sugar**
- 4-1/2 **teaspoons cornstarch**
- 3/4 **cup Miracle Whip**
- 3/4 **cup heavy whipping cream, whipped**
- 6 **pounds red salad potatoes, cooked, peeled and sliced**
- 1/2 **cup chopped onion**
- 1/4 **cup sliced green onions**
- 1 **teaspoon salt**
- 1/2 **teaspoon pepper**
- 3 **hard-cooked eggs, sliced**

Paprika

1. In a double boiler or metal bowl over hot water, heat the water, butter and vinegar. In a small bowl, beat eggs; add sugar and cornstarch. Add to butter mixture; cook and stir constantly until thick, about 5-7 minutes. Remove from the heat and allow to cool.

2. Stir in Miracle Whip; fold in whipped cream. In a bowl, toss potatoes, onion, green onions, salt and pepper. Pour dressing over potato mixture and toss gently. Chill. Garnish with hard-cooked eggs and sprinkle with paprika.

[1995]

MINTED MELON SALAD

yield: 12-14 servings
prep: 20 min. + chilling

People can't resist digging into a salad made with colorful summer fruits. The unique dressing is what makes this salad a hit. I get compliments whenever I serve it, especially when I put it on the table in a melon boat. It's a warm-weather treat.

—*Terry Saylor, Vermillion, South Dakota*

- 1 **cup water**
- 3/4 **cup sugar**
- 3 **tablespoons lime juice**
- 1-1/2 **teaspoons chopped fresh mint**
- 3/4 **teaspoon aniseed**

Dash salt

- 5 **cups cubed watermelon (about 1/2 melon)**
- 3 **cups cubed cantaloupe (about 1 medium melon)**
- 3 **cups cubed honeydew (about 1 medium melon)**
- 2 **cups peach slices (about 2 peaches)**
- 1 **cup fresh blueberries**

1. In a small saucepan, bring the first six ingredients to a boil. Boil for 2 minutes; remove from the heat. Cover and cool syrup completely.

2. Combine fruit in a very large bowl; add syrup and stir to coat. Cover and chill for at least 2 hours, stirring occasionally.

3. Drain before serving. Spoon into watermelon bowl or 8-qt. serving bowl.

MINTED MELON SALAD

❝Very fresh and light; perfect for a summer afternoon! ❞
—*melodious88*

[2008]

RANCH COLESLAW

yield: 6 servings ∞ prep/total time: 15 min.

Lime and cilantro add refreshing accents to this tangy, yummy slaw. It's perfect for a summer get-together.

—*Laurel Leslie, Sonora, California*

- 3 cups coleslaw mix
- 1/2 cup shredded cheddar cheese
- 1/4 cup canned Mexicorn
- 1 jalapeno pepper, seeded and chopped
- 2 tablespoons chopped red onion
- 1 tablespoon minced fresh cilantro
- 1/2 cup ranch salad dressing
- 1-1/2 teaspoons lime juice
- 1/2 teaspoon ground cumin

1. In a large bowl, combine the first six ingredients. In a small bowl, whisk the salad dressing, lime juice and cumin. Pour over coleslaw; toss to coat. Refrigerate until serving.

Editor's Note: Wear disposable gloves when cutting hot peppers; the oils can burn skin. Avoid touching your face.

[2005]

SWEET ONION BBQ BURGERS

yield: 4 servings
prep: 30 min. + marinating ∞ grill: 15 min.
(*Pictured on page 240*)

Sometimes we don't even bother with a bun for these moist, flavorful burgers. Smoked cheese, grilled onions and a special sauce make them out of the ordinary.

—*Christie Gardiner, Pleasant Grove, Utah*

- 1/2 cup dry bread crumbs
- 2 teaspoons onion salt
- 2 teaspoons brown sugar
- 1 egg, lightly beaten
- 1 pound ground beef
- 1-1/4 cups barbecue sauce

SAUCE:
- 1/2 cup mayonnaise
- 1/2 cup barbecue sauce
- 1 teaspoon brown sugar

ONION TOPPING:
- 2 tablespoons butter
- 1/4 cup honey
- 2 large sweet onions, thinly sliced
- 4 slices smoked cheddar cheese
- 4 hamburger buns, split

1. In a large bowl, combine bread crumbs, onion salt and brown sugar. Add egg. Crumble beef over mixture and mix well. Shape into four patties. Place in a shallow dish; pour barbecue sauce over patties. Cover and refrigerate for 2-4 hours.

2. In a small bowl, combine sauce ingredients; cover and refrigerate until serving. For topping, melt butter in a small skillet. Stir in honey until blended. Add onions; saute for 15-20 minutes or until tender and lightly browned. Remove from the heat and keep warm.

3. Drain and discard barbecue sauce from patties. Grill patties, uncovered, over medium-hot heat for 5-7 minutes on each side or until the juices run clear. Top each with a cheese slice; grill 1 minute longer or until the cheese is melted. Serve on buns with sauce and onion topping.

[2009]

RASPBERRY LEMONADE PIE

yield: 8 servings ∞ prep: 10 min. + freezing

You can't beat this refreshing freezer dessert as the finale for an outdoor summer meal. The tangy fruit flavors combined with the chocolate crust and vanilla ice cream are to-die-for.

—*Sue Stewart, Hales Corners, Wisconsin*

- 1/3 cup sweetened raspberry lemonade drink mix
- 1/2 cup water
- 2 cups vanilla ice cream, softened
- 1 carton (8 ounces) frozen whipped topping, thawed
- 1 chocolate crumb crust (9 inches)

Chocolate syrup, optional

1. In a large bowl, combine drink mix and water. Add ice cream; beat on low speed for 2 minutes or until blended. Fold in whipped topping. Spoon into crust.

2. Freeze for 4 hours or until firm. Remove from the freezer 10 minutes before serving. Serve with the chocolate syrup if desired.

[2010]

NEW ENGLAND BAKED BEANS

yield: 12 servings (2/3 cup each)
prep: 1-1/2 hours + soaking
bake: 2-1/2 hours

For a potluck or picnic, you can't beat this classic side that starts with a pound of dried beans. Molasses and maple syrup give it a slight sweetness.

—Pat Medeiros
Tiverton, Rhode Island, Field Editor

1	pound dried great northern beans
1/2	pound thick-sliced bacon strips, chopped
2	large onions, chopped
3	garlic cloves, minced
2	cups ketchup
1-1/2	cups packed dark brown sugar
1/3	cup molasses
1/3	cup maple syrup
1/4	cup Worcestershire sauce
1/2	teaspoon salt
1/4	teaspoon coarsely ground pepper

1. Sort beans and rinse with cold water. Place beans in a Dutch oven; add enough water to cover by 2 in. Bring to a boil; boil for 2 minutes. Remove from the heat; cover and let stand for 1-4 hour or until beans are softened.

2. Drain and rinse beans, discarding liquid. Return beans to Dutch oven; add 6 cups water. Bring to a boil. Reduce heat; cover and simmer for 1 hour or until beans are almost tender.

3. In a large skillet, cook the bacon over medium heat until crisp. Using a slotted spoon, remove to paper towels; drain, reserving 2 tablespoons of the drippings. Saute onions in drippings until tender. Add garlic; cook 1 minute longer. Stir in the ketchup, brown sugar, molasses, syrup, Worcestershire sauce, salt and pepper.

4. Drain beans, reserving cooking liquid; place in an ungreased 3-qt. baking dish. Stir in onion mixture and bacon. Cover and bake at 300° for 2-1/2 hours or until beans are tender and reach desired consistency, stirring every 30 minutes. Add reserved cooking liquid as needed.

[2007]

GRILLED CORN ON THE COB

yield: 8 servings ∽ prep: 20 min. + soaking
grill: 25 min.

I'd never grilled corn until last summer when my sister-in-law served it for us. What a treat! So simple, yet delicious, grilled corn is now a must for my favorite summer menu.

—Angela Leinenbach
Mechanicsvlle, Virginia, Field Editor

8	medium ears sweet corn
1/2	cup butter, softened
2	tablespoons minced fresh basil
2	tablespoons minced fresh parsley
1/2	teaspoon salt

1. Soak the corn in cold water for 20 minutes. Meanwhile, in a small bowl, combine butter, basil, parsley and salt. Carefully peel back corn husks to within 1 in. of bottoms; remove silk. Spread butter mixture over the corn.

2. Rewrap corn in husks and secure with kitchen string. Grill corn, covered, over medium heat for 25-30 minutes or until tender, turning occasionally. Cut strings and peel back husks.

NEW ENGLAND BAKED BEANS

"This recipe is time-consuming but well worth the effort. I have been looking for a great baked bean recipe and this is it. Do not change a thing. Sweet and rich baked beans. Great."
—*tubber1*

shower

[2008]

CHERRY-CHICKEN SALAD CROISSANTS

yield: 7 servings ∞ **prep/total time: 15 min.**

I love cherries and happened to come across this recipe one day. It's a real hit with my family, and a friend's husband even took it to work to share with the office staff.

—**Martha Goodrich, Wilmington, Delaware**

2-1/2 cups cubed cooked chicken breast
2/3 cup dried cherries
1/3 cup chopped celery
1/3 cup chopped tart apple
1/3 cup chopped pecans, toasted
1/2 cup mayonnaise
4 teaspoons buttermilk
1/2 teaspoon salt
1/8 teaspoon pepper
7 croissants, split

---

1. In a large bowl, combine the chicken, cherries, celery, apple and pecans. In another bowl, combine the mayonnaise, buttermilk, salt and pepper; add to chicken mixture and mix well. Spoon 1/2 cup chicken salad onto each croissant.

[2012]

CITRUS CHAMPAGNE SPARKLER

yield: 11 servings ∞ **prep/total time: 10 min.**

Here's a festive beverage to use when toasting the bride at her shower.

—**Sharon Tipton, Winter Garden, Florida**

1-1/4 cups orange juice
1/3 cup orange liqueur
1/3 cup brandy
1/4 cup sugar

1/4 cup lemon juice
1/4 cup unsweetened pineapple juice
6 cups chilled Champagne

---

1. In a pitcher, combine the first six ingredients, stirring until the sugar is dissolved. Pour 1/4 cup into each Champagne flute or wine glass. Top with Champagne.

[2004]

MUSHROOM PUFFS

yield: 20 appetizers ∞ **prep/total time: 20 min.**

(Pictured on page 234)

You can make these attractive appetizers in a jiffy with refrigerated crescent roll dough. The tasty little spirals disappear fast at parties!

—**Marilin Rosborough, Altoona, Pennsylvania**

---

4 ounces cream cheese, cubed
1 can (4 ounces) mushroom stems and pieces, drained
1 tablespoon chopped onion
1/8 teaspoon hot pepper sauce
1 tube (8 ounces) crescent roll dough

---

1. In a blender, combine the cream cheese, mushrooms, onion and hot pepper sauce; cover and process until blended. Unroll crescent dough; separate into four rectangles. Press perforations to seal. Spread mushroom mixture over dough.

2. Roll up jelly-roll style, starting with a long side. Cut each roll into five slices; place on an ungreased baking sheet. Bake at 425° for 8-10 minutes or until puffed and golden brown.

[2011]

LACY BRANDY SNAPS

**yield: about 4 servings ∾ prep: 30 min.
bake: 10 min./batch + cooling**

This crisp, delicate cookie is simply scrumptious.

—*Natalie Bremson, Plantation, Florida*

---

    6 tablespoons unsalted butter, cubed
  1/3 cup sugar
    3 tablespoons light corn syrup
  2/3 cup all-purpose flour
    2 teaspoons brandy
    1 teaspoon ground ginger
FILLING:
    4 cups heavy whipping cream
1-3/4 cups confectioners' sugar
  1/2 cup brandy
Grated chocolate, optional

---

1. In a small saucepan, combine the butter, sugar and corn syrup. Cook and stir over medium heat until butter is melted. Remove from the heat. Stir in the flour, brandy and ginger.

2. Drop by teaspoonfuls, three at a time, 3 in. apart onto a parchment paper-lined baking sheet. Bake at 350° for 7-8 minutes or until golden brown.

3. Cool for 30-45 seconds. Working quickly, loosen each cookie and curl around a thick wooden spoon handle. (If cookies become to cool to shape, return to the oven for 1 minute to soften.) Remove from spoon handle to wire rack to cool completely.

4. For filling, in a large bowl, beat cream until it begins to thicken. Add the confectioners' sugar and brandy; beat until stiff peaks form. Just before serving, pipe cream mixture into the cookies. Sprinkle ends with chocolate if desired. Refrigerate leftovers.

[1999]

SEVEN-FRUIT SALAD

**yield: 8-10 servings
prep: 20 min. + chilling**

A tongue-tingling lime dressing complements the colorful variety of fruit in this delightful salad. It's always a hit at summer get-togethers. It looks lovely on a buffet and is very refreshing on a hot day.

—*Judi Cottrell, Grand Blanc, Michigan*

  1/2 cup lime juice
  1/2 cup water
  1/2 cup sugar
    2 medium nectarines, thinly sliced
    1 large firm banana, thinly sliced
    1 pint blueberries
    1 pint fresh strawberries, sliced
1-1/2 cups watermelon balls
    1 cup green grapes
    1 kiwifruit, peeled and chopped

---

1. In a large bowl, combine the lime juice, water and sugar; stir until sugar is dissolved. Add nectarines and banana; toss to coat.

2. In a 2-1/2-qt. glass bowl, combine the remaining fruits. Add the nectarine mixture; stir gently. Cover and refrigerate for 1 hour. Serve with a slotted spoon.

KEEPING SALADS COLD

To keep salads or dips cold, place food in a plastic bowl and set in a larger bowl filled with ice cubes or crushed ice. Replenish ice for chilling as it melts.

—*Taste of Home Cooking Experts*

SEVEN-FRUIT SALAD

❝I've been making this for several years now. It is a very good, easy and simple, refreshing salad. I make it the night before—except for the bananas, adding them just before serving for a great breakfast.❞
—*cwbuff*

DULCE DE LECHE CHEESECAKE

DULCE DE LECHE CHEESECAKE

"If I could give this 10 stars, I would! So delicious. I was hesitant about adding the chili powder to the chocolate, but since I was making this for a Mexican dinner, I decided to go for it. I am so glad I did—I love the flavor. Don't be afraid to try it!"
— Peache_77

[2011]

DULCE DE LECHE CHEESECAKE

**yield: 16 servings   prep: 40 min.
bake: 1 hour + chilling**

I'm originally from Paraguay, and dulce de leche reminds me of where I came from. If you can't find it at your grocery store, try caramel ice cream topping instead. It tastes different, but this decadent dessert will still be amazing.

—Sonia Lipham, Ranburne, Alabama

1-3/4	cups crushed gingersnap cookies (about 35 cookies)
1/4	cup finely chopped walnuts
1	tablespoon sugar
1/2	teaspoon ground cinnamon
6	tablespoons butter, melted

FILLING:

3	packages (8 ounces *each*) cream cheese, softened
1	cup plus 2 tablespoons sugar
1/4	cup 2% milk
2	tablespoons all-purpose flour
1	teaspoon vanilla extract
3	eggs, lightly beaten
1	can (13.4 ounces) dulce de leche
1	cup (6 ounces) semisweet chocolate chips
1-1/2	teaspoons chili powder

---

1. Place a greased 9-in. springform pan on a double thickness of heavy-duty foil (about 18 in. square). Securely wrap foil around pan. In a large bowl, combine the cookie crumbs, walnuts, sugar, cinnamon and butter. Press onto the bottom and 2 in. up the sides of prepared pan.

2. In a large bowl, beat cream cheese and sugar until smooth. Beat in the milk, flour and vanilla. Add eggs; beat on low speed just until combined. Pour into crust.

3. Pour dulce de leche into a microwave-safe bowl; microwave at 50% power until softened. Drop dulce de leche by tablespoonfuls over batter; cut through batter with a knife to swirl.

4. Place springform pan in a large baking pan; add 1 in. of hot water to larger pan. Bake at 350° for 60-70 minutes or until center is just set and top appears dull.

5. Remove the springform pan from water bath. Cool on a wire rack for 10 minutes. Carefully run a knife around edge of pan to loosen; cool 1 hour longer.

6. In a microwave-safe bowl, melt chips; stir until smooth. Stir in chili powder. Spread over cheesecake. Refrigerate overnight. Remove sides of pan.

[2001]

RASPBERRY ICED TEA

**yield: about 2 quarts
prep: 10 min. + chilling**

One sip and you'll likely agree this is the best flavored tea you've ever tasted.

—Christine Wilson
Sellersville, Pennsylvania

8-1/4	cups water, *divided*
2/3	cup sugar
5	individual tea bags
3	to 4 cups unsweetened raspberries

---

1. In a large saucepan, bring 4 cups water to a boil. Stir in sugar until dissolved. Remove from the heat; add tea bags. Steep for 5-8 minutes. Discard tea bags. Add 4 cups water.

2. In another saucepan, bring raspberries and remaining water to a boil. Reduce heat; simmer, uncovered, for 3 minutes. Strain and discard pulp. Add the raspberry juice to the tea mixture. Serve in chilled glasses over ice.

[2011]

BERRY DELIGHTFUL SPINACH SALAD
yield: 8 servings ∾ prep: 35 min.

A homemade dressing and sugared pecans dress up this fabulous fruit-filled green salad. When fresh berries are out of season, try substituting dried fruits.

—*Bonnie Jost, Manitowoc, Wisconsin*

- 1/2 **cup sugar**
- 1 **cup chopped pecans**
- 1 **package (6 ounces) fresh baby spinach**
- 2 **cups sliced fresh stawberries**
- 1 **cup fresh blueberries**

DRESSING:
- 1/4 **cup balsamic vinegar**
- 2/3 **cup fresh strawberries**
- 1 **teaspoon sugar**
- 3/4 **teaspoon onion powder**
- 1/2 **teaspoon salt**
- 1/4 **teaspoon pepper**
- 2/3 **cup olive oil**

1. In a small heavy skillet over medium-low heat, cook sugar until it begins to melt. Gently drag melted sugar to the center of pan so sugar melts evenly. Cook, without stirring, until sugar is dark reddish brown, about 15 minutes.

2. Remove from the heat; stir in the pecans. Pour onto a foil-lined baking sheet; cool completely. Break pecans apart if necessary.

3. In a salad bowl, combine the spinach, strawberries and blueberries. Place first six dressing ingredients in a blender; cover and process until pureed. While processing, gradually add the oil in a steady stream.

4. Just before serving, drizzle the salad with dressing; toss to coat. Top with sugared pecans.

[2001]

FOUR-TOMATO SALSA
yield: 14 cups ∾ prep/total time: 20 min.

A variety of tomatoes, onions and peppers makes this chunky salsa so good. Whenever I try to take a batch to a get-together, it's hard to keep my family from finishing it off first! It's a super snack with tortilla chips or as a relish with meat.

—*Connie Siese, Wayne, Michigan*

- 7 **plum tomatoes, chopped**
- 7 **medium red tomatoes, chopped**
- 3 **medium yellow tomatoes, chopped**
- 3 **medium orange tomatoes, chopped**
- 1 **teaspoon salt**
- 2 **tablespoons lime juice**
- 2 **tablespoons olive oil**
- 1 **medium white onion, chopped**
- 1 **medium red onion, chopped**
- 2 **green onions, chopped**
- 1/2 **cup *each* chopped green, sweet red, orange and yellow pepper**
- 3 **pepperoncinis, chopped**
- 1/3 **cup mild pickled pepper rings, chopped**
- 1/2 **cup minced fresh parsley**
- 2 **tablespoons minced fresh cilantro**
- 1 **tablespoon dried chervil**

Tortilla chips

1. In a colander, combine the tomatoes and salt. Let drain for 10 minutes.

2. Transfer to a large bowl. Stir in the lime juice, oil, onions, peppers, parsley, cilantro and chervil. Serve with tortilla chips. Refrigerate leftovers for up to 1 week.

Editor's Note: Look for pepperoncinis (pickled peppers) and pickled banana peppers in the pickle and olive aisle of your grocery store.

BERRY DELIGHTFUL SPINACH SALAD

"I made it for a party and my father-in-law and several guests told me several times that they really liked the salad. I did not have the blueberries, and it was still excellent! For Easter I brought my father-in-law a jar full of the salad dressing made with farm-fresh strawberries."

— *mmpense*

[2011]

ARTICHOKE MUSHROOM LASAGNA

yield: 12 servings ∽ **prep: 30 min.**
bake: 1 hour + standing

White wine adds delightful flavor to this hearty vegetarian entree. No one will miss the meat!

—*Bonnie Jost, Manitowoc, Wisconsin*

- 1 pound sliced baby portobello mushrooms
- 2 tablespoons butter
- 3 garlic cloves, minced
- 2 cans (14 ounces *each*) water-packed artichoke hearts, rinsed, drained and chopped
- 1 cup chardonnay *or* other white wine
- 1/4 teaspoon salt
- 1/4 teaspoon pepper

SAUCE:
- 1/4 cup butter, cubed
- 1/4 cup all-purpose flour
- 3-1/2 cups 2% milk
- 2-1/2 shredded Parmesan cheese
- 1 cup chardonnay *or* other white wine

ASSEMBLY:
- 9 no-cook lasagna noodles
- 4 cups (16 ounces) shredded part-skim mozzarella cheese, *divided*

1. In a large skillet, saute mushrooms in butter until tender. Add garlic; cook 1 minute longer. Add the artichokes, wine, salt and pepper; cook over medium heat until liquid is evaporated.

2. For the sauce, in a large saucepan over medium heat, melt butter. Stir in flour until smooth; gradually add milk. Bring to a boil; cook and stir for 1 minute or until thickened. Stir in Parmesan cheese and wine.

3. Spread 1 cup sauce into a greased 13-in. x 9-in. baking dish. Layer with three noodles, 1-2/3 cups sauce, 1 cup mozzarella and 1-1/3 cups artichoke mixture. Repeat layers twice.

4. Cover and bake at 350° for 45 minutes. Sprinkle with remaining mozzarella cheese. Bake, uncovered, 15-20 minutes longer or until cheese is melted. Let stand for 15 minutes before cutting.

[2006]

PARTY ANTIPASTO SALAD

yield: 50 (3/4-cup) servings ∽ **prep: 1 hour + marinating**

This colorful salad is a tasty crowd-pleaser. Guests love the homemade, from-scratch dressing, which is a nice change from bottled Italian.

—*Linda Harrington, Hudson, New Hampshire, Field Editor*

- 2 packages (1 pound *each*) spiral pasta
- 4 cups chopped green peppers
- 4 cups chopped seeded tomatoes
- 3 cups chopped onions
- 2 cans (15 ounces *each*) garbanzo beans *or* chickpeas, rinsed and drained
- 1 pound thinly sliced Genoa salami, julienned
- 1 pound sliced pepperoni, julienned
- 1/2 pound provolone cheese, cubed
- 1 cup pitted ripe olives, halved
- 1-1/2 cups olive oil
- 1 cup red wine vinegar
- 1/2 cup sugar
- 2 tablespoons dried oregano
- 2 teaspoons salt
- 1 teaspoon pepper

1. Cook pasta according to package directions. Drain and rinse in cold water. In several large bowls, combine the pasta, green peppers, tomatoes, onions, beans, salami, pepperoni, cheese and olives.

2. In a large bowl, whisk oil, vinegar, sugar, oregano, salt and pepper. Pour over pasta salad; toss to coat. Cover and refrigerate for 4 hours or overnight.

birthday

[2001]

TROPICAL ISLAND CHICKEN
yield: 8 servings
prep: 10 min. + marinating ∾ grill: 45 min.

The marinade makes a savory statement in this all-time-favorite chicken recipe that I served at our son's pirate-theme birthday party. It smelled so good on the grill that guests could hardly wait to try a piece!

—*Sharon Hanson, Franklin, Tennessee*

1/2 cup reduced-sodium soy sauce
1/3 cup canola oil
1/4 cup water
2 tablespoons dried minced onion
2 tablespoons sesame seeds
1 tablespoon sugar
4 garlic cloves, minced
1 teaspoon ground ginger
3/4 teaspoon salt
1/8 teaspoon cayenne pepper
2 broiler/fryer chickens (3 to 4 pounds *each*), quartered

1. In a small bowl, combine the first 10 ingredients. Set aside 1/3 cup for basting; cover and refrigerate. Pour the remaining marinade into a large resealable plastic bag. Add chicken; seal and turn to coat. Refrigerate for 8 hours or overnight.

2. Prepare grill for indirect heat, using a drip pan. Place chicken over drip pan and grill, covered, over indirect medium heat for 45-60 minutes or until a thermometer reads 180°, turning and basting often with reserved marinade.

[2005]

VEGETABLE TRIO
yield: 4 servings ∾ prep/total time: 25 min.

This side is a pretty mix of garden-fresh green beans and carrots. It's a nice accompaniment with any meal.

—*Mary Lou Wayman, Salt Lake City, Utah*

4 large carrots, julienned
1/2 pound fresh green beans, cut into 2-inch pieces
1-1/2 cups sliced fresh mushrooms
1 teaspoon salt
1/2 teaspoon dried thyme
2 tablespoons butter

1. In a large skillet, cook and stir the carrots, green beans, mushrooms, salt and thyme in butter over medium-heat for 15 minutes or until beans are crisp-tender.

[2006]

FRUITY PUNCH
yield: about 2 quarts ∾ prep/total time: 10 min.

I mix three refreshing juices with ginger ale for this pretty party-perfect punch. It's the freshest way to quench your thirst at a summer gathering.

—*Anna Minegar*
Zolfo Springs, Florida, Former Field Editor

2 cups orange juice, chilled
2 cups unsweetened pineapple juice, chilled
2 cups sweetened pink grapefruit juice drink, chilled
3 cans (12 ounces *each*) ginger ale, chilled

1. In a punch bowl or pitcher, combine the juices. Refrigerate until serving. Just before serving, stir in ginger ale. Serve over ice.

[2008]

SPECIAL-OCCASION CHOCOLATE CAKE

yield: 12 servings ∞ **prep: 40 min.**
bake: 25 min. + cooling

(Pictured on page 239)

This cake won Grand Champion at the 2000 Alaska State Fair and you will see why once you taste it. This decadent chocolate cake boasts a ganache filling and fudge frosting.

—*Cindi Paulson, Anchorage, Alaska, Field Editor*

1	cup baking cocoa
2	cups boiling water
1	cup butter, softened
2-1/4	cups sugar
4	eggs
1-1/2	teaspoons vanilla extract
2-3/4	cups all-purpose flour
2	teaspoons baking soda
1/2	teaspoon baking powder
1/2	teaspoon salt

GANACHE:

10	ounces semisweet chocolate, chopped
1	cup heavy whipping cream
2	tablespoons sugar

FROSTING:

1	cup butter, softened
4	cups confectioners' sugar
1/2	cup baking cocoa
1/4	cup 2% milk
2	teaspoons vanilla extract

GARNISH:

3/4	cup sliced almonds, toasted

1. In a small bowl, combine the cocoa and water; set aside. In a large bowl, cream butter and sugar until light and fluffy. Add eggs, one at a time, beating well after each addition. Beat in the vanilla. Combine the flour, baking soda, baking powder and salt; add to creamed mixture alternately with cocoa mixture, beating well after each addition.

2. Pour into three greased and floured 9-in. round baking pans. Bake at 350° for 25-30 minutes or until a toothpick inserted near the center comes out clean. Cool for 10 minutes before removing from pans to wire racks to cool completely.

3. For ganache, place chocolate in a small bowl. In a small heavy saucepan over low heat, bring cream and sugar to a boil. Pour over chocolate; whisk gently until smooth. Refrigerate for 35-45 minutes or until ganache begins to thicken, stirring occasionally.

4. For frosting, in a large bowl, beat the butter until fluffy. Add confectioners' sugar, cocoa, milk and vanilla; beat until smooth.

5. Place one cake layer on a serving plate; spread with 1 cup frosting. Top with the second layer and 1 cup ganache; sprinkle with 1/2 cup almonds. Top with the third layer; frost top and sides of cake. Warm the ganache until pourable; pour over cake, allowing some ganache to drape down the sides. Sprinkle with the remaining almonds. Refrigerate until serving.

[1997]

HERBED WILD RICE

yield: 8 servings ∞ **prep: 15 min.**
bake: 70 min.

Like many cooking enthusiasts, I've discovered good food pleases the palate and soothes the soul! This rice has a nice nutty flavor and the wonderful aroma of sage.

—*David Collin, Martinez, California*

1	cup sliced green onions
2	tablespoons butter
1	cup uncooked wild rice
3	cups chicken broth
1	teaspoon rubbed sage
3/4	teaspoon dried thyme
1/2	teaspoon salt, optional

1. In a large saucepan over medium heat, saute the onions in butter until tender, about 5 minutes. Add the rice; cook for 8-10 minutes. Add broth, sage, thyme and salt if desired.

2. Pour into an ungreased 1-1/2-qt. baking dish. Cover and bake at 350° for 70-80 minutes or until rice is tender and liquid is absorbed.

halloween

[2008]

SPOOKY SPIDER CAKE

yield: 18-20 servings   **prep: 2 hours**
bake: 40 min. + cooling

(Pictured on page 236)

Get ready to wow the crowd with this appetizing arachnid. By using different frosting techniques and traditional Halloween candy, you too can create this fun creepy crawler!

—*Gina Feger, Louisville, Kentucky*

CHOCOLATE CAKE:

- 1 **package (18-1/4 ounces) chocolate cake mix**
- 1-1/2 **cups water**
- 2 **eggs**

WHITE CAKE:

- 1 **package (18-1/4 ounces) white cake mix**
- 1-1/3 **cups water**
- 2 **eggs**

FROSTING:

- 2 **cups shortening**
- 1/4 **cup plus 2 tablespoons water,** *divided*
- 2 **teaspoons clear vanilla extract**
- 2 **pounds confectioners' sugar**
- 2 **tablespoons meringue powder**

Purple and black paste food coloring

- 3/4 **cup baking cocoa**
- 1/4 **teaspoon light corn syrup**

ASSEMBLY:

- 2 **wooden dowels (2 inches x 1/4 inch)**
- 1 **cardboard cake circle (6 inches)**
- 16 **wooden toothpicks**
- 8 **black twist licorice ropes**
- 20 **pieces candy corn**

1. In a large bowl, beat the chocolate cake mix, water and eggs on low speed for 30 seconds. Beat on medium for 2 minutes. Pour into the two halves of a greased and floured sports ball baking pan. Bake at 350° for 40-50 minutes or until a toothpick inserted near the center comes out clean.

2. Meanwhile, in another bowl, beat the white cake mix, water and eggs on low speed for 30 seconds. Beat on medium for 2 minutes. Pour into two greased and floured 9-in. round baking pans. Bake for 30-35 minutes or until a toothpick comes out clean.

3. Cool all cakes for 10 minutes before removing from pans to wire racks to cool completely.

4. For frosting, using a heavy-duty stand mixer, combine the shortening, 1/4 cup water and vanilla. Combine confectioners' sugar and meringue powder; beat into shortening mixture.

5. For base cake: Tint 2-1/4 cups frosting purple. Using a serrated knife, level tops of white cakes if necessary. Place one cake layer on a serving plate; spread with 1 cup frosting. Top with remaining cake layer. Spread remaining tinted frosting over top and sides of cake.

6. Combine 3 cups frosting, cocoa and remaining water until smooth; tint black. Combine 1/4 cup black frosting and corn syrup. Using round tip #2 and black frosting with corn syrup, pipe webs and spiders around sides of cake.

7. With 3/4 cup white frosting and shell tip #18, pipe border along bottom edge of cake. Insert dowels into center of cake. Cut cardboard circle to measure 3-1/4 in.; place over cake.

8. For spider cake: Using a serrated knife, level the rounded side of one chocolate cake; attach to cake circle with a small amount of black frosting. Spread top with 1/3 cup black frosting; top with remaining chocolate cake.

9. Using grass tip #233 and black frosting, pipe hair over cake. With white frosting and round tip # 12, pipe eyes and teeth. Pipe pupils with round tip #2 and black frosting. For legs, insert a toothpick into the ends of each licorice rope. Insert one end into side of spider; insert other end into top of purple cake. Garnish with candy corn.

[2006]

TOMBSTONE TREATS

yield: about 16 servings ∞ **prep: 45 min.**
bake: 10 min. + cooling

My brother loves Rice Krispies squares, and my mom loves sugar cookies. So I came up with a cute treat they'd both like.

—*Jill Wright, Dixon, Illinois*

3	tablespoons butter
4	cups miniature marshmallows
7-1/2	cups crisp rice cereal
1	tube (18 ounces) refrigerated sugar cookie dough
2/3	cup all-purpose flour
32	wooden toothpicks
1	teaspoon water
4	drops green food coloring
1-1/2	cups flaked coconut
	Black decorating gel
	Vanilla frosting
1	cup (6 ounces) semisweet chocolate chips, melted
	Candy pumpkins

1. In a large saucepan over low heat, melt butter. Stir in marshmallows until completely melted. Remove from the heat. Stir in cereal until well coated. Press into a greased 13-in. x 9-in. pan with a buttered spatula. Cool.

2. In a large bowl, beat cookie dough and flour until combined. On a lightly floured surface, roll out dough to 1/4-in. thickness. Trace tombstone pattern onto waxed paper; cut out 16 tombstones from dough. Place 2 in. apart on ungreased baking sheets.

3. Along the bottom edge of each cookie, insert two toothpicks halfway into the dough. Bake at 350° for 8-10 minutes or until edges are golden brown. Remove to wire racks to cool.

4. In a large resealable plastic bag, combine the water and green food coloring. Add coconut; seal bag and shake to coat. Toast coconut; set aside. Using black gel, tint frosting gray. Frost sugar cookies; decorate with black gel.

5. Cut cereal bars into 3-in. x 2-in. rectangles; spread with melted chocolate. Using toothpicks, insert cookies into cereal bars. Decorate with coconut and candies as desired.

[1995]

SPICE COOKIES WITH PUMPKIN DIP

yield: about 20 dozen (3 cups dip) ∞ **prep: 20 min.**
bake: 10 min./batch

My husband and two kids are sure to eat the first dozen of these cookies warm from the oven—before the next tray is even done. A co-worker gave me the recipe for the pumpkin dip, which everyone loves with the delectable spice cookies.

—*Kelly McNeal, Derby, Kansas*

1-1/2	cups butter, softened
2	cup sugar
2	eggs
1/2	cup molasses
4	cups all-purpose flour
4	teaspoons baking soda
2	teaspoons ground cinnamon
1	teaspoon *each* ground ginger and cloves
1	teaspoon salt

Additional sugar
PUMPKIN DIP:

1	package (8 ounces) cream cheese, softened
2	cups pumpkin pie filling
2	cups confectioners' sugar
1/2	to 1 teaspoon ground cinnamon
1/4	to 1/2 teaspoon ground ginger

1. In a large bowl, cream butter and sugar until light and fluffy. Beat in eggs and molasses. Combine the flour, baking soda, cinnamon, ginger, cloves and salt; add to creamed mixture and mix well. Chill overnight.

2. Shape into 1/2-in. balls; roll in additional sugar. Place 2 in. apart on ungreased baking sheets. Bake at 375° for 6 minutes or until the edges begin to brown. Cool for 2 minutes before removing to a wire rack.

3. For dip, beat cream cheese in a large bowl until smooth. Beat in pumpkin pie filling. Add the sugar, cinnamon and ginger and mix well. Serve with cookies. Store leftover dip in the refrigerator.

[2009]

SWAMP JUICE A LA SLIME

yield: 10 servings (2 quarts) ∽ **prep: 25 min. + freezing**

The green goo oozing down the sides of the eerie wine glasses make this fruity beverage perfect for any Halloween party.

—*Melissa Ann Beier, Howell, Michigan*

1/2 cup light corn syrup
Green paste food coloring
   5 cups unsweetened pineapple juice
   2 cups white grape juice
   2 drops yellow food coloring, optional
   1 cup club soda, chilled
Fresh pineapple slices, optional

---

1. Refrigerate 10 champagne flutes or cocktail glasses until chilled. In a small bowl, combine the corn syrup and green food coloring; dip rims of chilled glasses into mixture. Turn glasses upright, allowing mixture to slightly run down sides of glasses. Freeze until firm.

2. In a pitcher, combine juices and yellow food coloring if desired. Refrigerate until chilled.

3. Just before serving, stir club soda into juice mixture. Pour the juice into prepared glasses; garnish with pineapple if desired.

[2007]

TRICK-OR-TREAT TURNOVERS

yield: 8 servings ∽ **prep: 30 min.
bake: 10 min.**

I carved these clever pumpkin pastries to feed my hungry bunch at Halloween. The ground beef filling has a hint of onion and mustard.

—*Marge Free, Brandon, Mississippi*

1/2 pound ground beef
   1 tablespoon finely chopped onion
   4 ounces cubed part-skim mozzarella cheese
1/4 cup prepared mustard
   2 tubes (16.3 ounces *each*) large refrigerated flaky biscuits
   1 egg, lightly beaten

---

1. In a large skillet, cook beef and onion over medium heat until meat is no longer pink; drain. Add cheese and mustard; cook and stir until cheese is melted. Cool slightly.

2. Flatten each biscuit into a 4-in. circle; place four biscuits in each of two greased 15-in. x 10-in. x 1-in. baking pans. Spoon 2 heaping tablespoons of meat mixture onto each.

3. Using a sharp knife or cookie cutters, cut out jack-o'-lantern faces from remaining biscuit circles; place over meat mixture and pinch edges to seal tightly. Reroll the scraps if desired and cut out stems for pumpkins.

4. Brush with the egg. Bake at 350° for 10-15 minutes or until golden brown.

[1996]

QUICK GHOST COOKIES

yield: about 3 dozen ∽ **prep/total time: 30 min.**

For a fun treat, I spruce up store-bought cookies for the Halloween. These are a real hit with goblins of all ages.

—*Denise Smith, Lusk, Wyoming, Field Editor*

---

   1 pound white candy coating, coarsely chopped
   1 package (1 pound) Nutter Butter peanut butter cookies
Miniature semisweet chocolate chips

---

1. In a microwave, melt candy coating; stir until smooth. Dip cookies into coating, covering completely; allow excess to drip off. Place on waxed paper.

2. Brush the ends with a pastry brush dipped in coating where fingers touched cookies. While coating is still warm, place two chips on each cookie for eyes. Let stand until set. Store in an airtight container.

[2007]

APPLE SNACK MIX

yield: 4 quarts ∞ prep/total time: 15 min.

The alphabet cereal and apple chips along with a handful of other popular treats, makes this fun mix a cute gift for a teacher or party favor.

—*Rosemary Pacha, Brighton, Iowa*

2	packages (3 ounces *each*) dried apple chips
3	cups French Toast Crunch cereal
2	cups miniature pretzels
2	cups dry roasted peanuts
1-1/2	cups Frosted Cheerios
1-1/2	cups Apple Cinnamon Cheerios
1-1/2	cups yogurt-covered raisins
1-1/2	cups small apple-flavored red and green jelly beans
2/3	cup sunflower kernels

1. In a bowl, combine all the ingredients. Store in an airtight container.

[2002]

CHOCOLATE CARAMEL APPLES

yield: 8 servings ∞ prep: 15 min. + cooling

Caramel apples get dressed up for this harvest time holiday with chocolate, crunchy nuts and bitty toffee bits.

—*Linda Smith, Frederick, Maryland*

1	package (14 ounces) caramels
2	tablespoons water
4	wooden sticks
4	large tart apples
2	cups chopped pecans *or* peanuts
1	cup (6 ounces) semisweet chocolate chips
1	teaspoon shortening
1	cup English toffee bits *or* almond brickle chips

1. In a large microwave-safe bowl, microwave the caramels and water,

uncovered, on high for 45 seconds; stir. Microwave for 20-40 seconds or until caramels are melted; stir until smooth.

2. Insert wooden sticks into apples; dip apples into caramel mixture, turning to coat. Coat with nuts; set on waxed paper to cool.

3. Meanwhile, melt chocolate chips and shortening; stir until smooth. Drizzle over apples. Sprinkle with toffee bits. Place on waxed paper to cool. Cut into wedges to serve.

Editor's Note: This recipe was tested in a 1,100-watt microwave.

[2006]

YUMMY MUMMY CHEESE SPREAD

yield: 1 cheese log ∞ prep/total time: 30 min.

(Pictured on page 240)

My annual Halloween bash wouldn't be the same without the now famous Mummy Man. When kids first see Mummy Man, they wonder if he's edible. I assure them, and we hack off a foot or an arm with some crackers.

—*Rebecca Eremich, Barberton, Ohio*

2	port wine cheese logs (12 ounces *each*)
1	package (8 ounces) cream cheese, softened
1	tablespoon 2% milk
2	whole peppercorns
1	pimiento strip

1. Cut the cheese logs into pieces for mummy's head, body, arms and legs; arrange on a serving plate.

2. In small bowl, beat cream cheese and milk. Cut a small hole in the corner of a pastry or plastic bag; insert basket weave tip #47. Pipe rows across the mummy, creating bandages. Add peppercorns for eyes and pimiento strip for mouth. Chill until serving.

APPLE SNACK MIX

❝I didn't make these—my friend did, using Granny Smith apples. I'm not a caramel gal but these were incredible! The tartness of the apple was the perfect foil for all that sweetness.❞
—*adnissi*

---

thanksgiving

[2000]

FESTIVE TOSSED SALAD

yield: 8-10 servings
prep/total time: 15 min.

With its unique medley of fruits and appealing look, this salad is a holiday tradition at our house. Our three grown daughters have come to expect it. One forkful reminds us of all the things we can be thankful for.

—*Jauneen Hosking, Waterford, Wisconsin*

1/2 cup sugar
1/3 cup red wine vinegar
2 tablespoons lemon juice
2 tablespoons finely chopped onion
1/2 teaspoon salt
2/3 cup canola oil
2 to 3 teaspoons poppy seeds
10 cups torn romaine
1 cup (4 ounces) shredded Swiss cheese
1 medium apple, chopped
1 medium pear, chopped
1/4 cup dried cranberries
1/2 to 1 cup chopped cashews

1. In a blender, combine sugar, vinegar, lemon juice, onion and salt. Cover and process until blended. With blender running, gradually add oil. Add poppy seeds and blend.

2. In a salad bowl, combine the romaine, cheese, apple, pear and cranberries. Drizzle with desired amount of dressing. Add cashews; toss to coat.

[2002]

MALLOW-TOPPED SWEET POTATOES

yield: 10-12 servings ✂ **prep: 10 min.**
bake: 45 min.

My grandmother always served this sweet potato casserole at Thanksgiving. The puffy marshmallow topping gives the dish a festive look, and spices enhance the sweet potato flavor.

—*Edna Hoffman*
Hebron, Indiana, Field Editor

6 cups hot mashed sweet potatoes (prepared without milk and butter)
1 cup 2% milk
6 tablespoons butter, softened
1/2 cup packed brown sugar
1 egg
1-1/2 teaspoons ground cinnamon
1-1/2 teaspoons vanilla extract
3/4 teaspoon ground allspice
1/2 teaspoon salt
1/4 teaspoon ground nutmeg
18 large marshmallows

1. In a large bowl, beat the sweet potatoes, milk, butter, brown sugar, egg, cinnamon, vanilla, allspice, salt and nutmeg until smooth.

2. Transfer to a greased shallow 2-1/2-qt. baking dish. Bake, uncovered, at 325° for 40-45 minutes or until heated through. Top with the marshmallows. Bake 5-10 minutes longer or until the marshmallows just begin to puff and brown.

MALLOW-TOPPED SWEET POTATOES

"I've prepared this recipe since it came out in the 2002 magazine (*Taste of Home*). Everyone loves it and tries to guess what spices are in it!"
—*tuscalooso*

[2001]

NUTTY FUDGE TORTE

yield: 12-14 servings ∾ **prep: 25 min.**
bake: 45 min. + cooling

This dessert is so yummy and beautiful, you'd never guess it's easy to make (it starts with a convenient packaged cake mix). Rich, moist and fudgy, it never fails to draw compliments... as well as requests for the recipe.

—*Kay Berg, Lopez Island, Washington*

1/2	cup semisweet chocolate chips
1/3	cup sweetened condensed milk
1	package (18-1/4 ounces) devil's food cake mix
1/3	cup canola oil
1	teaspoon ground cinnamon
1	can (15 ounces) sliced pears, drained
2	eggs
1/3	cup chopped pecans, toasted
2	teaspoons water
1/4	cup caramel ice cream topping, warmed
1/2	teaspoon 2% milk

Whipped cream *or* vanilla ice cream and additional toasted pecans, optional

1. In a microwave, melt chocolate chips and condensed milk; stir until smooth. Set aside. In a large bowl, combine cake mix, oil and cinnamon until crumbly. Set aside 1/2 cup for topping.

2. In a blender, cover and process pears until smooth. Add to remaining cake mixture with eggs; beat on low speed for 30 seconds. Beat on medium for 2 minutes.

3. Pour into a greased 9-in. springform pan. Drop melted chocolate by tablespoonfuls over batter. Combine the pecans, water and reserved cake mixture; crumble over chocolate.

4. Bake at 350° for 45-50 minutes or until a toothpick inserted near the center comes out clean. Cool on a wire rack

for 10 minutes. Carefully run a knife around the edge of pan to loosen.

5. Remove sides of pan. Combine the caramel topping and milk until smooth; drizzle on serving plates. Top with a slice of torte. Serve with whipped cream or ice cream and sprinkle with pecans if desired.

[2010]

ROASTED HARVEST VEGETABLES

yield: 9 servings ∾ **prep: 20 min.**
bake: 30 min.

(Pictured on page 236)

This is a favorite side dish to serve any time we're having company. I like to pair it with just about any roasted meat.

—*Amy Logan, Mill Creek, Pennsylvania*

8	small red potatoes, quartered
2	small onions, quartered
1	medium zucchini, halved and sliced
1	medium yellow summer squash, halved and sliced
1/2	pound fresh baby carrots
1	cup fresh cauliflowerets
1	cup fresh broccoli florets
1/4	cup olive oil
1	tablespoon garlic powder
1-1/2	teaspoons dried rosemary, crushed
1/2	teaspoon dried thyme
1/4	teaspoon salt
1/4	teaspoon pepper

1. Place vegetables in a large bowl. In a small bowl, whisk the remaining ingredients; drizzle over vegetables and toss to coat.

2. Transfer to two greased 15-in. x 10-in. x 1-in. baking pans. Bake, uncovered, at 400° for 30-35 minutes or until tender, stirring occasionally.

ROASTED HARVEST VEGETABLES

"I am not a big vegetable fan. However, this dish won me over! It is delicious and so easy to prepare. I like that I'm getting so many vegetables at once! I'm thinking the next time I make it I will add some red, green, and yellow peppers, garlic...maybe even some tomato. It smelled so good while it was cooking that when I took it out of the oven, I was eating it straight from the pan!"

—*Ninee1*

[1998]

TRADITIONAL PUMPKIN PIE

yield: 2 pies (6-8 servings each) ∽ **prep: 20 min.** ∽ **bake: 40 min.**

Most families would agree that Thanksgiving dinner isn't complete until slices of pumpkin pie are passed. Here, brown sugar, cinnamon, cloves, nutmeg and ginger add spark to canned pumpkin.

—*Gloria Warczak, Cedarburg, Wisconsin, Field Editor*

---

    2 cups all-purpose flour
  3/4 teaspoon salt
  2/3 cup shortening
    4 to 6 tablespoons cold water
FILLING:
    6 eggs
    1 can (29 ounces) solid-pack pumpkin
    2 cups packed brown sugar
    2 teaspoons ground cinnamon
    1 teaspoon salt
  1/2 teaspoon *each* ground cloves, nutmeg and ginger
    2 cups evaporated milk

1. In a large bowl, combine flour and salt; cut in shortening until crumbly. Gradually add water, tossing with a fork until dough forms a ball. Divide pastry in half. On a floured surface, roll out each portion to fit a 9-in. pie plate. Place pastry in plates; trim pastry to 1/2 in. beyond edge of plate. Flute edges. If desired, reroll scraps and make pastry cutouts; place cutouts on pies when they are completely cooled.

2. For filling, beat eggs in a large bowl. Add the pumpkin, brown sugar, cinnamon, salt, cloves, nutmeg and ginger; beat just until combined. Gradually stir in milk. Pour into pastry shells.

3. Bake at 450° for 10 minutes. Reduce heat to 350°; bake 40-45 minutes longer or until a knife inserted near the center comes out clean. Cool pies on wire racks for 1 hour. Refrigerate for at least 3 hours before serving. Refrigerate leftovers.

TRADITIONAL PUMPKIN PIE

"Pumpkin pie is one of my faves. I've never made a homemade one until I used this recipe. Far exceeds store-bought pumpkin pie!! Very simple recipe and I used the frozen deep dish pie shells rather than making the shell. Absolutely delicious!!"
—akoehler79

MAKING PASTRY CUTOUTS FOR A SINGLE-CRUST PIE

1. Roll out dough to 1/8-in. thickness. Cut out with 1-in. to 1-1/2-in. cookie cutters.

2. Score designs on cutout with a sharp knife if desired.

3. Bake at 400° on ungreased baking sheets for 6-8 minutes.

4. Remove to a wire rack to cool. Arrange over cooled filling on baked pie.

—*Taste of Home Cooking Experts*

[2011]

MAKE-AHEAD MASHED POTATOES

yield: 10 servings ∞ prep: 25 min.
bake: 40 min.

(Pictured on page 235)

Creamy mashed potatoes get even better when topped with a savory trio of cheese, onions and bacon. Plus, these potatoes offer make-ahead appeal.

—*Amanda Sauer, University City, Missouri*

3	pounds potatoes (about 9 medium), peeled and cubed
1	package (8 ounces) cream cheese, softened
1/2	cup sour cream
1/2	cup butter, cubed
1/4	cup 2% milk
1-1/2	teaspoons onion powder
1	teaspoon salt
1	teaspoon garlic powder
1/2	teaspoon pepper
6	bacon strips, chopped
1	cup (4 ounces) shredded cheddar cheese
3	green onions, chopped

1. Place potatoes in a Dutch oven and cover with water. Bring to a boil. Reduce heat; cover and cook for 10-15 minutes or until tender. Drain; mash potatoes with cream cheese, sour cream and butter. Stir in milk and seasonings.

2. In a small skillet, cook bacon over medium heat until crisp. Using a slotted spoon, remove to paper towels to drain.

3. Transfer potato mixture to a greased 13-in. x 9-in. baking dish; sprinkle with cheese, onions and bacon. Cover and refrigerate until ready to use.

4. Remove potatoes from the refrigerator 30 minutes before baking. Bake, uncovered, at 350° for 40-50 minutes or until heated through.

[2002]

GINGERED CRANBERRY CHUTNEY

yield: 3 cups ∞ prep: 25 min.
cook: 15 min.

This colorful chutney is a super side dish or condiment served with pork, ham or poultry. It also makes a nice holiday gift.

—*Marion Lowery*
Medford, Oregon, Former Field Editor

1	cup packed brown sugar
1/3	cup red wine vinegar
1/2	teaspoon ground ginger
1/8	teaspoon cayenne pepper
1/8	teaspoon salt
2	pounds fresh pears, peeled and diced
1	package (12 ounces) fresh *or* frozen cranberries, thawed
1/2	teaspoon ground cinnamon

1. In a large saucepan, combine the brown sugar, vinegar, ginger, cayenne and salt. Bring to a boil. Add pears. Reduce heat; cover and simmer for 10 minutes or until pears are tender.

2. Strain, reserving the liquid. Return the liquid to pan; set the pears aside. Stir cranberries into pan. Cook over medium heat until the berries pop, about 3 minutes, stirring occasionally.

3. Strain the berries, reserving the liquid. Return liquid to pan; set the berries aside. Bring liquid to a boil; cook, uncovered, until liquid is reduced to 1/2 cup. Stir in pears, cranberries and cinnamon. Serve warm or cold. Store in the refrigerator.

MAKE-AHEAD MASHED POTATOES

"This was wonderful!! I made it for my parents on Monday and we loved it so much when my husband came home Saturday, I made it again!"
—BNavarro0331

[2011]

STUFFED PORK LOIN WITH CURRANT SAUCE

yield: 12 servings (1-1/4 cups sauce) ∞ **prep: 30 min.**
bake: 1 hour + standing

This is a great entree to serve any time of year, but especially around the holidays. It looks so pretty with the red currant sauce, garnished with fresh parsley.

—*Gloria Bradley, Naperville, Illinois*

3/4 cup chopped walnuts, toasted
3/4 pound bulk pork sausage
1 medium apple, peeled and finely chopped
1 garlic clove, minced
1 egg, beaten
1 tablespoon minced fresh parsley
1/4 teaspoon salt
1/4 teaspoon pepper
1 boneless whole pork loin roast (3 to 4 pounds)
1/3 cup apple butter
SAUCE:
1 cup red currant jelly
2 tablespoons honey
1 tablespoon dried currants
2 teaspoons cider vinegar
1/4 teaspoon hot pepper sauce

---

1. Place walnuts in a food processor; cover and process until ground. Set aside.

2. In a large skillet, cook the sausage, apple and garlic over medium heat until meat is no longer pink. Drain; cool slightly. Stir in the ground walnuts, egg, parsley, salt and pepper.

3. Cut a lengthwise slit down the center of the roast to within 1/2 in. of bottom. Open roast so it lies flat. Starting at the center, split each half of roast horizontally to within 1/2 in. of edge. Open halves so roast lies flat. Cover with plastic wrap. Flatten to 1/2-in. thickness. Remove plastic.

4. Brush roast with apple butter; spoon sausage mixture over the top. Roll up jelly-roll style, starting with a long side. Tie with kitchen string at 2-in. intervals. Place on a rack in a shallow baking pan.

5. Bake, uncovered, at 350° for 1 to 1-1/2 hours or until a thermometer reads 160°. Let stand for 10-15 minutes before slicing. In a small saucepan, heat the sauce ingredients until smooth. Serve with roast.

[2006]

CRANBERRY PUMPKIN BREAD

yield: 2 loaves (16 slices each) ∞ **prep: 20 min.**
bake: 70 min. + cooling

Put leftover cranberries and pumpkin to great use in this moist quick bread. It's very good with my Secondhand Turkey casserole for an after-Thanksgiving meal.

—*Dixie Terry, Goreville, Illinois, Field Editor*

3-3/4 cups all-purpose flour
3 cups sugar
4 teaspoons pumpkin pie spice
2 teaspoons baking soda
1 teaspoon salt
4 eggs
1 can (15-ounces) solid-pack pumpkin
1/2 cup canola oil
2 cups fresh or frozen cranberries, thawed
1 cup chopped walnuts

---

1. In a large bowl, combine the flour, sugar, pumpkin pie spice, baking soda and salt. In another bowl, whisk the eggs, pumpkin and oil; stir into dry ingredients just until moistened. Fold in cranberries and walnuts.

2. Spoon into two greased 9-in. x 5-in. loaf pans. Bake at 350° for 70-80 minutes or until a toothpick inserted near the center comes out clean. Cool for 10 minutes before removing from the pans to wire racks to cool completely.

USING CRANBERRIES YEAR-ROUND

Cranberries add a tart, refreshing flavor to breads, relishes, desserts and entrees. Stock up in the fall when they are readily available, and freeze them for year-round use. Simply lay the bag flat in the freezer. They will stay fresh for about 9 months.

—*Taste of Home Cooking Experts*

TURKEY WITH APPLE STUFFING

"Apple stuffing tastes so much better than normal stuffing that my family wants it as often as they can have it. Since my son is an awesome cook, he tends to take over and cook Christmas dinner, and this stuffing is one he makes every year. "
—*tkarinas*

[2006]

TURKEY WITH APPLE STUFFING

yield: 10-12 servings ∞ **prep: 20 min.**
bake: 3-3/4 hours + standing

Complementing your golden bird, the well-seasoned bread stuffing is sparked by a festive sweetness from apples and raisins. It's a staple on our holiday menu.

—*Nancy Zimmerman*
Cape May Court House, New Jersey
Field Editor

1-1/2	cups chopped celery
3/4	cup chopped onion
3/4	cup butter, cubed
9	cups day-old cubed whole wheat bread
3	cups finely chopped apples
3/4	cup raisins
1-1/2	teaspoons salt
1-1/2	teaspoons dried thyme
1/2	teaspoon rubbed sage
1/4	teaspoon pepper
1	turkey (14 to 16 pounds)
Additional butter, melted	

---

1. In a Dutch oven, saute the celery and onion in butter until tender. Remove from heat; stir in bread cubes, apples, raisins, salt, thyme, sage and pepper.

2. Just before baking, loosely stuff the turkey with 4 cups stuffing. Place the remaining stuffing in a greased 2-qt. baking dish; refrigerate until ready to bake. Skewer the turkey openings; tie drumsticks together. Place breast side up on a rack in a roasting pan. Brush with melted butter.

3. Bake, uncovered, at 325° for 3-3/4 to 4 hours or until a thermometer reads 180° for the turkey and 165° for the stuffing, basting occasionally with pan drippings. (Cover loosely with foil if turkey browns too quickly.)

4. Bake the additional stuffing, covered, for 20-30 minutes. Uncover; bake 10 minutes longer or until lightly browned. Cover turkey and let stand for 20 minutes before removing the stuffing and carving. If desired, thicken pan drippings for gravy.

Editor's Note: Stuffing may be prepared as directed and baked separately in a greased 3-qt. baking dish. Cover and bake at 325° for 30 minutes. Uncover and bake 10 minutes longer or until lightly browned.

[2008]

PILGRIM HAT COOKIES

yield: 32 cookies ∞ **prep: 1 hour**

(Pictured on page 236)

We dreamed up this combination for a yummy treat to take to school before our Thanksgiving break. Everyone loved them!

—*Megan and Mitchell Vogel*
Jefferson, Wisconsin

1	cup vanilla frosting
7	drops yellow food coloring
32	miniature peanut butter cups
1	package (11-1/2 ounces) fudge-striped cookies
32	pieces orange mini Chiclets gum

---

1. In a small shallow bowl, combine the frosting and food coloring. Remove paper liners from peanut butter cups.

2. Holding the bottom of a peanut butter cup, dip top of cup in yellow frosting. Position over center hole on the bottom of cookie, forming the hatband and crown. Add a buckle of Chiclets gum. Repeat with remaining cups and cookies.

christmas

[1997]

HOMEMADE EGGNOG
yield: 3-1/2 quarts ∞ **prep: 50 min. + chilling**

After just one taste, folks will know this holiday treat is homemade, not a store-bought variety.

—*Pat Waymire*
Yellow Springs, Ohio, Field Editor

12	eggs
1-1/2	cups sugar
1/2	teaspoon salt
2	quarts whole milk, *divided*
2	tablespoons vanilla extract
1	teaspoon ground nutmeg
2	cups heavy whipping cream

Additional nutmeg, optional

---

1. In a heavy 4-qt. saucepan, whisk together eggs, sugar and salt. Gradually add 1 qt. of milk. Cook and stir over low heat until a thermometer reads 160°-170°, about 30-35 minutes.

2. Pour into a large heatproof bowl; stir in the vanilla, nutmeg and remaining milk. Place bowl in an ice-water bath, stirring frequently until mixture is cool. If mixture separates, process in a blender until smooth. Cover and refrigerate for at least 3 hours.

3. When ready to serve, beat cream in a large bowl on high until soft peaks form; whisk gently into cooled milk mixture. Pour into a chilled 5-qt. punch bowl. Sprinkle with nutmeg if desired.

Editor's Note: Eggnog may be stored, covered, in the refrigerator for several days. Whisk before serving.

[2009]

PEAS A LA FRANCAISE
yield: 12 servings (1/2 cup each)
prep/total time: 30 min.

I love peas, and this recipe is a favorite. It features tiny pearl onions touched with thyme and chervil, and its presentation is lovely.

—*Christine Frazier, Auburndale, Florida*

1-1/2	cups pearl onions, trimmed
1/4	cup butter, cubed
1/4	cup water
1	tablespoon sugar
1	teaspoon salt
1/4	teaspoon dried thyme
1/4	teaspoon dried chervil
1/4	teaspoon pepper
2	packages (16 ounces *each*) frozen peas, thawed
2	cups shredded lettuce

---

1. In a large saucepan, bring 6 cups water to a boil. Add the onions; boil for 5 minutes. Drain and rinse in cold water; peel.

2. In the same saucepan, melt butter over medium heat. Stir in the onions, water, sugar and seasonings. Add peas and lettuce; stir until blended. Cover and cook for 6-8 minutes or until tender.

3. Serve with a slotted spoon.

HOMEMADE EGGNOG

"Never liked eggnog until I made this. I do not buy eggnog in the store because nothing tastes like this recipe! Yummy!!"
—*Dshiggy5@aol.com*

[2006]

FROZEN PEPPERMINT DELIGHT
yield: 12-15 servings ∽ prep: 25 min. + freezing

If you're looking for a dessert that's festive, delicious and easy to make, this is the one for you. Drizzled in hot fudge sauce and loaded with pretty peppermint pieces, this tempting treat will have guests asking for seconds.

—Pam Lancaster, Willis, Virginia

- 1 **package (16.6 ounces) cream-filled chocolate sandwich cookies, crushed**
- 1/2 **cup butter, melted**
- 1 **gallon peppermint ice cream, slightly softened**
- 1 **carton (12 ounces) frozen whipped topping, thawed**
- 1 **jar (11-3/4 ounces) hot fudge ice cream topping, warmed**

Crushed peppermint candy

1. In a large bowl, combine the cookie crumbs and butter. Press into an ungreased 13-in. x 9-in. dish. Spread the ice cream over crust; top with whipped topping. Cover and freeze until solid. May be frozen for up to 2 months.

2. Just before serving, drizzle with hot fudge topping and sprinkle with peppermint candy.

[1998]

CHRISTMAS CAULIFLOWER
**yield: 8-10 servings ∽ prep: 25 min.
bake: 25 min.**

A Swiss cheese sauce gives this vegetable casserole an extra-special taste. I have served it every Christmas for many years.

—Betty Claycomb, Alverton, Pennsylvania, Field Editor

- 1 **large head cauliflower, broken into florets**
- 1/4 **cup chopped green pepper**
- 1 **jar (7.3 ounces) sliced mushrooms, drained**
- 1/4 **cup butter, cubed**
- 1/3 **cup all-purpose flour**
- 2 **cups 2% milk**
- 1 **cup (4 ounces) shredded Swiss cheese**
- 2 **tablespoons diced pimientos**

- 1 **teaspoon salt**

Paprika, optional

1. In a large saucepan, bring 1 in. of water and the cauliflower to a boil. Reduce heat; cover and cook for 5-15 minutes or until crisp-tender; drain and pat dry.

2. Meanwhile in a large saucepan, saute green pepper and mushrooms in butter for 2 minutes or until crisp-tender. Add flour; gradually stir in milk. Bring to a boil; cook and stir for 2 minutes or until thickened. Remove from the heat; stir in cheese until melted. Add pimientos and salt.

3. Place half of the cauliflower in a greased 2-qt. baking dish; top with half of the sauce. Repeat layers. Bake, uncovered, at 325° for 25 minutes or until bubbly. Sprinkle with paprika if desired.

[1997]

LEMON PARSLEY POTATOES
yield: 10-12 servings ∽ prep/total time: 20 min.

For a simply delicious side dish, I often prepare these potatoes. I like the fact that there are few ingredients and they take such little time to prepare.

—Dorothy Pritchett, Wills Point, Texas, Field Editor

- 3 **pounds small red new potatoes, quartered**
- 1/2 **cup butter, melted**
- 3 **tablespoons lemon juice**
- 3 **tablespoons minced fresh parsley**

1. Cook potatoes in boiling salted water until tender, about 15 minutes; drain. Combine butter, lemon juice and parsley; pour over the potatoes and stir gently to coat.

[2003]

CHOCOLATE YULE LOG

yield: 12 servings ∽ **prep: 65 min. + chilling** ∽ **bake: 15 min. + cooling**

This eye-catching dessert is guaranteed to delight holiday dinner guests. Chocolate lovers will lick their lips over the yummy cocoa cake, mocha filling and frosting. For a festive touch, I garnish the log with marzipan holly leaves and berries.

—*Jenny Hughson, Mitchell, Nebraska, Former Field Editor*

5	eggs, *separated*
1	cup sugar, *divided*
1/2	cup cake flour
1/4	cup baking cocoa
1/4	teaspoon salt
1/2	teaspoon cream of tartar

MOCHA CREAM FILLING:

1	cup heavy whipping cream
1/2	cup confectioners' sugar
1-1/2	teaspoons instant coffee granules

MOCHA BUTTERCREAM FROSTING:

1/3	cup butter, softened
1/3	cup baking cocoa
2	cups confectioners' sugar
1-1/2	teaspoons vanilla extract
1	tablespoon brewed coffee
2	to 3 tablespoons 2% milk

1. Line a 15-in. x 10-in. x 1-in. baking pan with parchment paper; grease the paper. Place egg whites in a small bowl; let stand at room temperature for 30 minutes.

2. In a large bowl, beat egg yolks on high until light and fluffy. Gradually add 1/2 cup sugar, beating until thick and lemon-colored. Combine the flour, cocoa and salt; gradually add to egg yolk mixture until blended.

3. Beat egg whites on medium until foamy. Add cream of tartar; beat until soft peaks form. Gradually add remaining sugar, 1 tablespoon at a time, beating on high until stiff peaks form. Stir a fourth into chocolate mixture. Fold in remaining egg whites until no streaks remain.

4. Spread batter evenly in prepared pan. Bake at 350° for 12-15 minutes or until the cake springs back (do not overbake). Cool for 5 minutes; invert onto a linen towel dusted with confectioners' sugar. Peel off parchment paper. Roll up in the towel, starting with a short side. Cool on a wire rack.

5. In a large bowl, beat cream until it begins to thicken. Add confectioners' sugar and coffee granules. Beat until stiff peaks form; chill. Unroll cooled cake; spread filling to within 1/2 in. of edges. Roll up again. Place on serving platter; chill.

6. In a large bowl, beat frosting ingredients until smooth. Frost cake. Using a fork, make lines resembling tree bark.

CHOCOLATE YULE LOG

" I make this every year for our traditional family Christmas Eve. It gets devoured as soon as it gets put out."
—*GSHughes*

[2007]

BEEF RIB ROAST

**yield: 10-12 servings   prep: 15 min.
bake: 2 hours + standing**

(Pictured on page 239)

My mom topped beef roast with bacon and onion. Whenever I prepare it, I can't help but reminisce about the wonderful life she gave me and my brothers.

—Betty Abel Jellencich, Utica, New York

- 1 bone-in beef rib roast (4 to 5 pounds)
- 1 garlic clove, minced
- 1 teaspoon salt
- 1/2 teaspoon pepper
- 1 small onion, sliced
- 6 to 8 bacon strips

1. Place the roast, fat side up, on a rack in a shallow roasting pan. Rub with the garlic, salt and pepper; top with onion and bacon.

2. Bake, uncovered, at 325° for 2-3 hours or until meat reaches desired doneness (for medium-rare, a thermometer should read 145°; medium, 160°; well-done, 170°).

3. Transfer to warm serving platter. Let stand for 10-15 minutes before slicing.

[1997]

CRUNCHY TOSSED SALAD

yield: 12 servings   prep: 20 min. + chilling

Count on compliments, not leftovers, when you share this fun, crunchy salad at your next gathering. It's so easy to toss together, and someone always asks for the recipe.

—Deb Weisberger, Mullett Lake, Michigan

- 1/2 cup canola oil
- 1/4 cup sugar
- 2 tablespoons vinegar
- 1 teaspoon salt
- 1/4 teaspoon pepper
- 1 large head iceberg lettuce, sliced
- 6 bacon strips, cooked and crumbled
- 1/3 cup sliced almonds, toasted
- 1/4 cup sesame seeds, toasted
- 4 green onions, sliced
- 3/4 cup chow mein noodles

1. In a small bowl, whisk the oil, sugar, vinegar, salt and pepper; shake well. Chill for 1 hour.

2. Just before serving, in a salad bowl, combine the lettuce, bacon, almonds, sesame seeds and onions in a large bowl. Whisk dressing and pour over salad; toss to coat. Top with chow mein noodles.

[1996]

WASSAIL PUNCH

**yield: about 3-1/2 quarts
prep/total time: 25 min.**

Cloves and cinnamon dress up a blend of fruit juices for special occasions. The spicy warm drink is sure to help you forget about any nip in the air.

—Dorothy Anderson, Ottawa, Kansas

- 2 quarts apple cider
- 2 cups orange juice
- 2 cups pineapple juice
- 1/2 cup sugar
- 1/2 cup lemon juice
- 12 whole cloves
- 4 cinnamon sticks (3 to 4 inches)

Orange slices and cranberries, optional

1. In a Dutch oven, bring the first seven ingredients to a boil. Reduce heat; simmer, uncovered, for 10-15 minutes.

2. Discard the cinnamon and cloves. Garnish with orange slices and cranberries if desired. Serve warm.

CRUNCHY TOSSED SALAD

"Our extended family loves this salad. A niece fixed it for a holiday meal and it's on every table when we have a get-together. There's never so much as a noodle left."

—4Appys

[1998]

STUFFED CROWN ROAST OF PORK

yield: 8 servings ∞ prep: 15 min.
bake: 1-1/2 hours

It looks so elegant that everyone thinks I really fussed when I serve this roast. But it's actually so easy! The biggest challenge is to remember to order the crown roast from the meat department ahead of time. My family loves the succulent pork and savory bread stuffing.

—Betty Claycomb
Alverton, Pennsylvania, Field Editor

1 pork loin crown roast (5 to 6 pounds, about 10 ribs)
1/2 teaspoon seasoned salt
MUSHROOM STUFFING:
1 cup sliced fresh mushrooms
1/2 cup diced celery
1/4 cup butter, cubed
3 cups day-old cubed bread
1/4 teaspoon salt
1/4 teaspoon pepper
1/3 cup apricot preserves
1 cup whole fresh cranberries, optional

1. Place roast, rib ends up, in a shallow roasting pan; sprinkle with seasoned salt. Cover rib ends with foil. Bake, uncovered, at 350° for 1 hour.

2. Meanwhile, saute mushrooms and celery in butter until tender. Stir in the bread cubes, salt and pepper. Spoon into the center of the roast. Brush sides of roast with preserves. Bake 30-45 minutes longer or until a thermometer inserted into stuffing and meat between ribs both read 145°; remove foil. Let meat stand for 10 minutes before slicing.

3. If desired, thread cranberries on a 20-in. piece of thin string or thread. Transfer roast to a serving platter. Loop the cranberry string in and out of the rib ends.

[2006]

NINE-LAYER SALAD

yield: 6-8 servings ∞ prep: 30 min. + chilling

Creamy and crunchy, this delightful dish is loaded with popular salad ingredients such as green pepper, green onions, frozen peas and bacon. It's a colorful accompaniment to Mom's spaghetti.

—Anne Halfhill, Worthington, Ohio

4 cups torn iceberg lettuce
4 cups fresh baby spinach
1 cup *each* chopped green pepper, celery and green onions
1 package (10 ounces) frozen peas, thawed and patted dry
1-1/2 cups mayonnaise
1/2 cup shredded Parmesan cheese
1/2 cup shredded Romano cheese
1 cup crumbled cooked bacon

1. In a large salad bowl, layer the lettuce, spinach, green pepper, celery, onions and peas. Spread with mayonnaise. Combine the cheeses; sprinkle cheeses and bacon over mayonnaise. Cover and refrigerate overnight.

CARVING A CROWN ROAST

Remove the stuffing and place in a serving bowl. With a long, sharp knife, cut between each rib bone, creating individual rib chops.

—Taste of Home Cooking Experts

STUFFED CROWN ROAST OF PORK

"I always thought pork crown roasts were a lot of fuss, until I finally got up my courage and tried this recipe. It was easy and looked and tasted terrific! It looks like you're a gourmet cook, which I definitely am not. However, I admit I didn't do the cranberry garnish. Terrific recipe for the holidays, especially New Year's."
—cwbuff

[1998]

CHOCOLATE TRUFFLE COOKIES

yield: 4 dozen ∾ **prep: 25 min.**
bake: 10 min./batch

Here's a snack for serious chocolate lovers.
These enticing cookies are crisp on the outside
and soft on the inside, somewhat bittersweet
and very chocolaty. I usually make them to
share at get-togethers...otherwise, I'd eat them
all myself! I'm always asked for the recipe.

—*Delaine Fortenberry*
 McComb, Mississippi

4	ounces unsweetened chocolate
2	cups (12 ounces) semisweet chocolate chips, divided
1/3	cup butter
1	cup sugar
3	eggs
1-1/2	teaspoons vanilla extract
1/2	cup all-purpose flour
2	tablespoons baking cocoa
1/4	teaspoon baking powder
1/4	teaspoon salt
	Confectioners' sugar

1. In a microwave or double boiler, melt unsweetened chocolate, 1 cup of chocolate chips and butter; cool for 10 minutes.

2. In a bowl, beat sugar and eggs for 2 minutes. Beat in vanilla and the chocolate mixture.

3. Combine flour, cocoa, baking powder and salt; beat into chocolate mixture. Stir in remaining chocolate chips. Cover and chill for at least 3 hours.

4. Remove about 1 cup of dough. With lightly floured hands, roll into 1-in. balls. Place on ungreased baking sheets.

5. Bake at 350° for 10-12 minutes or until lightly puffed and set. Cool on pan 3-4 minutes before removing to a wire rack to cool completely.

6. Repeat with remaining dough. Dust with confectioners' sugar.

[2002]

SURPRISE PACKAGE COOKIES

yield: 3-1/2 dozen ∾ **prep: 25 min.**
bake: 10 min./batch

Each of these buttery cookies has a chocolate
mint candy inside. They're my very favorite
cookie and are always part of our Christmas
cookie trays.

—*Lorraine Meyer, Bend, Oregon*

1	cup butter, softened
1	cup sugar
1/2	cup packed brown sugar
2	eggs
1	teaspoon vanilla extract
3	cups all-purpose flour
1	teaspoon baking powder
1/2	teaspoon salt
65	mint Andes candies

1. In a bowl, cream butter and sugars. Add eggs, one at a time, beating well after each addition. Beat in vanilla. Combine the flour, baking powder and salt; gradually add to creamed mixture. Cover and refrigerate for 2 hours or until easy to handle.

2. With floured hands, shape a tablespoonful of dough around 42 candies, forming rectangular cookies. Place 2 in. apart on greased baking sheets.

3. Bake at 375° for 10-12 minutes or until edges are golden brown. Remove to wire racks to cool. In a microwave or saucepan, melt the remaining candies; drizzle over cookies.

SURPRISE PACKAGE COOKIES

"If you are looking to have a chocolate exclamation point in your Christmas cookie selection, this recipe is it! Kind of like molten chocolate lava cake in a cookie form. I omitted the powdered sugar dusting and think they taste better and less messy to eat (who needs evidence anyway?). This recipe ROCKS!"
—*Amy A. Davidson*

[2005]

ALMOND VENETIAN DESSERT

yield: 2 dozen ∾ **prep: 35 min.** ∾ **bake: 15 min. + chilling**

These beautiful bars feature three colorful cake-like layers, an apricot filling and a chocolate topping.

—*Reva Becker, Farmington Hills, Michigan*

1/2 **cup almond paste**
3/4 **cup butter, softened**
1/2 **cup sugar**
  2 **eggs,** *separated*
1/4 **teaspoon almond extract**
  1 **cup all-purpose flour**
1/8 **teaspoon salt**
  5 **drops green food coloring**
  4 **drops red food coloring**
2/3 **cup apricot preserves**
  3 **ounces semisweet chocolate, chopped**

1. Grease the bottoms of three 8-in. square baking dishes. Line with waxed paper and grease the paper; set aside.

2. Place almond paste in a large bowl; break up with a fork. Add the butter, sugar, egg yolks and extract; beat until smooth and fluffy. Stir in flour and salt. In another bowl, beat egg whites until soft peaks form. Stir a fourth of the whites into the dough, then fold in the remaining whites (dough will be stiff).

3. Divide the dough evenly into three portions, about 2/3 cup each. Tint one portion green, one portion red and leave the remaining portion white. Spread each portion into a prepared pan. Bake at 350° for 13-15 minutes or until edges are golden brown Immediately invert onto wire racks; remove waxed paper. Place another wire rack on top and turn over. Cool completely.

4. Place the green layer on a large piece of plastic wrap. Spread evenly with 1/3 cup apricot preserves. Top with white layer and spread with remaining preserves. Top with red layer. Bring the plastic over layers. Slide onto a baking sheet and set a cutting board on top to compress the layers. Refrigerate overnight.

5. In a microwave-safe bowl, melt chocolate. Remove cutting board and unwrap dessert. Spread melted chocolate over top; let stand until set. With a sharp knife, trim edges. Cut into 2-in. x 5/8-in. bars. Store in an airtight container.

[2009]

PAPA'S SUGAR COOKIES

yield: 8 dozen ∾ **prep: 20 min.** ∾ **bake: 10 min./batch**

My grandchildren love these sugar cookies. These crisp cookies will melt in your mouth. Their subtle macadamia nut, cinnamon and orange peel flavors go perfectly together.

—*Lee Doverspike, North Ridgeville, Ohio*

   1 **cup butter, softened**
   1 **cup canola oil**
   1 **cup sugar**
   1 **cup confectioners' sugar**
   2 **eggs**
   2 **teaspoons butter flavoring**
   1 **tablespoon grated orange peel**
   1 **tablespoons vanilla extract**
5-1/2 **cups all-purpose flour**
  1/4 **cup ground macadamia nuts**
1-1/2 **teaspoons baking soda**
   1 **teaspoon salt**
   1 **teaspoon cream of tartar**
   1 **teaspoon ground cinnamon**
Additional granulated sugar

1. In a large bowl, beat the butter, oil and sugars until well blended. Add eggs, one at a time, beating well after each addition. Beat in the butter flavoring, orange peel and vanilla.

2. Combine the flour, nuts, baking soda, salt, cream of tartar and cinnamon; gradually add to butter mixture and mix well. Cover and refrigerate for 1 hour or until easy to handle.

3. Roll into 1-in. balls, then roll in additional sugar. Place 2 in. apart on ungreased baking sheets. Flatten with a glass dipped in additional sugar.

4. Bake at 350° for 10-12 minutes or until edges begin to brown. Remove to wire racks.

[2002]

BREAD AND BUTTER PICKLES

yield: 7 pints ❧ prep: 30 min.
process: 15 min.

My mom always made these crisp pickles when we were kids, and she gave me the recipe. They are pleasantly tart and so good.

—Karen Owen
Rising Sun, Indiana, Field Editor

4	pounds cucumbers, sliced
8	small onions, sliced
1/2	cup canning salt
5	cups sugar
4	cups white vinegar
2	tablespoons mustard seed
2	teaspoons celery seed
1-1/2	teaspoons ground turmeric
1/2	teaspoon ground cloves

---

1. In a large container, combine the cucumbers, onions and salt. Cover with crushed ice and mix well. Let stand for 3 hours. Drain; rinse and drain again.

2. In a Dutch oven, combine the sugar, vinegar and seasonings; bring to a boil. Add cucumber mixture; return to a boil. Remove from the heat.

3. Carefully ladle hot mixture into hot pint jars, leaving 1/2-in. headspace. Remove air bubbles, wipe rims and adjust lids. Process for 15 minutes in a boiling-water canner.

Editor's Note: The processing time listed is for altitudes of 1,000 feet or less. For altitudes up to 3,000 feet, add 5 minutes; 6,000 feet, add 10 minutes; 8,000 feet, add 15 minutes; 10,000 feet, add 20 minutes.

[2004]

SPICED APPLESAUCE

yield: 9 cups ❧ prep: 20 min.
cook: 30 min.

(Pictured on page 290)

Cardamom and mace add a bit of unusual spicy flavor to this homemade applesauce. This is a great way to use autumn's apple bounty.

—Janet Thomas
McKees Rocks, Pennsylvania
Field Editor

6	pounds tart apples (about 18 medium), peeled and quartered
1	cup apple cider *or* juice
3/4	cup sugar
2	tablespoons lemon juice
1	cinnamon stick (3 inches)
1	teaspoon ground ginger
1	teaspoon vanilla extract
1/2	teaspoon ground nutmeg
1/2	teaspoon ground mace
1/4	to 1/2 teaspoon ground cardamom

---

1. Place all ingredients in a Dutch oven. Cover and cook over medium-low heat for 30-40 minutes or until apples are tender; stir occasionally. Remove from the heat; discard the cinnamon stick. Mash the apples to desired consistency. Serve warm or cold. Store in the refrigerator.

[2009]

GARDEN TOMATO RELISH

yield: 10 pints
prep: 1-1/2 hours + simmering
process: 20 min.

What a super way to make the most of your garden harvest and have a tasty topping on hand for hot dogs, hamburgers and more. The relish is also a wonderful homemade gift.

—*Kelly Martel, Tillsonburg, Ontario*

10	pounds tomatoes
3	large sweet onions, finely chopped
2	medium sweet red peppers, finely chopped
2	medium green peppers, finely chopped
2	teaspoons mustard seed
1	teaspoon celery seed
4-1/2	cups white vinegar
2-1/2	cups packed brown sugar
3	tablespoons canning salt
2	teaspoons ground ginger
2	teaspoons ground cinnamon
1	teaspoon ground allspice
1	teaspoon ground cloves
1	teaspoon ground nutmeg

1. In a large saucepan, bring 8 cups water to a boil. Add tomatoes, a few at a time; boil for 30 seconds. Drain and immediately place tomatoes in ice water. Drain and pat dry; peel and finely chop. Place in a stockpot. Add onions and peppers.

2. Place mustard and celery seed on a double thickness of cheesecloth; bring up corners of cloth and tie with string to form a bag. Add spice bag and the remaining ingredients to the pot. Bring to a boil. Reduce heat; cover and simmer for 60-70 minutes or until slightly thickened. Discard spice bag.

3. Carefully ladle relish into hot 1-pint jars, leaving 1/2-in. headspace. Remove air bubbles; wipe the rims and adjust lids. Process in boiling-water canner for 20 minutes.

Editor's Note: The processing time listed is for altitudes of 1,000 feet or less. For altitudes up to 3,000 feet, add 5 minutes; 6,000 feet, add 10 minutes; 8,000 feet, add 15 minutes; 10,000, add 20 minutes.

[1998]

CREOLE SEASONING MIX

yield: 1 batch (about 1/2 cup)
prep/total time: 5 min.

Rather than buying another jar of seasoning, I make up this zippy blend to use in recipes that call for Creole or Cajun seasoning.

—*Marian Platt*
Sequim, Washington, Field Editor

2	tablespoons plus 1-1/2 teaspoons paprika
2	tablespoons garlic powder
1	tablespoon salt
1	tablespoon onion powder
1	tablespoon dried oregano
1	tablespoon dried thyme
1	tablespoon cayenne pepper
1	tablespoon pepper

1. Combine all the ingredients. Store in an airtight container. Use to season chicken, seafood, steaks or vegetables.

GARDEN TOMATO RELISH

"This is a wonderful recipe. We canned about 20 jars of it this summer using tomatoes we grew in our garden. It's delicious on chicken and pork chops as well as a dip for chips."
—sstewart29

FRUITY CRANBERRY CHUTNEY

"I was looking for an alternative to cranberry sauce and found this recipe in the *Taste of Home* Thanksgiving magazine. It was such a hit that I now keep a container of it in the fridge all year long. I added a half cup of white sugar because I like things on the sweet side, but if you you like dishes with a slight tartness to them, the recipe is perfect as is. It makes a large amount but keeps well in the fridge for a long time. We eat it with all sorts of meals— poultry, ham, roast pork, even fish. Buy some extra bags of cranberries during the holidays and put them in the freezer—you'll want to make this in all seasons!"

—*Rhonda Rose*

[2011]

HAPPY HOT DOG RELISH

yield: 1-1/2 cups   **prep/total time: 25 min.**

This sweet-tart relish, combining cranberry sauce and sauerkraut, is so good! It's also a nice complement to hamburgers, baked ham and roast pork.

—*Elizabeth Carlson, Corvallis, Oregon*

1	medium onion, chopped
1	tablespoon olive oil
1	cup whole-berry cranberry sauce
1	tablespoon Dijon mustard
1	teaspoon sugar
1/2	teaspoon garlic powder
1/4	teaspoon hot pepper sauce
1/2	cup sauerkraut, rinsed and drained

1. In a small saucepan, saute onion in oil until tender. Add the cranberry sauce, mustard, sugar, garlic powder and pepper sauce. Cook and stir for 5-10 minutes or until cranberry sauce is melted. Add sauerkraut; heat through.

[2007]

FRUITY CRANBERRY CHUTNEY

yield: about 5 cups   **prep: 15 min.** **cook: 55 min. + chilling**

An enticing blend of fruits and spices comes alive in this versatile chutney. It goes nicely with turkey and ham. We also enjoy it as an appetizer, spooned over cream cheese and served with crackers.

—*Pat Stevens,*
Granbury, Texas, Field Editor

2-1/4	cups packed brown sugar
1-1/2	cups cranberry juice
1/2	cup cider vinegar
1/2	teaspoon ground ginger
1/4	teaspoon ground allspice
2	packages (12 ounces each) fresh or frozen cranberries
2	medium oranges, peeled and sectioned
1	medium tart apple, peeled and coarsely chopped
1/2	cup dried currants or golden raisins
1/2	cup dried apricots, coarsely chopped
2	tablespoons finely grated orange peel

1. In a large saucepan, combine the brown sugar, cranberry juice, vinegar, ginger and allspice. Bring to a boil. Reduce heat; simmer, uncovered, for 2 minutes or until sugar is dissolved.

2. Stir in the cranberries, oranges, apple, currants, apricots and orange peel. Return to a boil. Reduce heat; simmer, uncovered, for 45 minutes or until thickened, stirring occasionally. Cool to room temperature. Transfer to a serving bowl; cover and refrigerate until chilled.

[1993]

NO-SALT SEASONING

yield: 1/3 cup   **prep/total time: 5 min.**

When you first start on a low-salt diet, everything tastes bland until your taste buds have time to adjust. This seasoning will help overcome that blandness. Some people still reach for the salt shaker out of habit. Put this seasoning on the table instead of salt.

—*Roma Lea, Short Baldwyn, Mississippi*

5	teaspoons onion powder
1	tablespoon garlic powder
1	tablespoon paprika
1	tablespoon ground mustard
1	teaspoon dried thyme
1/2	teaspoon pepper
1/2	teaspoon celery seed

1. Combine all ingredients in a small jar with a shaker top. Use for seasoning broiled fish, poultry, soups, stews and cooked vegetables or place it on the table to be used individually.

3. Drain and rinse the cucumber mixture; add sugar mixture and stir well. Pack into 1-pt. freezer containers, leaving 1-in. headspace. Cover and freeze for up to 6 weeks. Thaw before serving.

[2006]

HONEY ALMOND BUTTER
yield: 1-1/2 cups ∞ prep: 10 min. + chilling

To me, nothing tastes better than a warm homemade muffin right from the oven, topped with this yummy flavored butter. It's also wonderfully delicious on toast, quick breads and biscuits.

—Pat Hockett, Ocala, Florida, Field Editor

1	cup butter, softened
1/4	cup honey
1	tablespoon brown sugar
1/2	teaspoon almond extract

1. In a small bowl, beat the butter, honey, brown sugar and extract until light and fluffy. Transfer to a sheet of plastic wrap; roll into a log. Refrigerate until chilled. Unwrap and slice or place on a butter dish.

[1997]

EASY FREEZER PICKLES
yield: 6 pints ∞ prep: 15 min. + freezing

These crisp, no-cook pickle slices are so simple to fix.

—Lucile Johnson, Red Oak, Iowa

8	pounds cucumbers, thinly sliced
1	cup thinly sliced onion
3	tablespoons salt
4	cups sugar
2	cups white vinegar
1	teaspoon celery seed
1	teaspoon ground turmeric
1	teaspoon mustard seed

1. In a large container, combine cucumbers, onion and salt. Let stand for 3 hours, stirring occasionally.

2. In a bowl, combine the remaining ingredients; let stand for 2-3 hours, stirring often.

[2010]

ZUCCHINI RELISH
yield: 4 cups ∞ prep: 20 min. + standing
cook: 15 min. + chilling
(Pictured on page 296)

Mom likes to make this crisp and colorful relish when zucchini is in season and Dad's little patch has produced to excess.

—Nancy Kreiser, Lebanon, Pennsylvania

4	cups diced zucchini
1	large onion, thinly sliced
2	celery ribs, sliced
2	medium carrots, sliced
1	medium sweet red pepper, sliced
2	tablespoons salt
3/4	cup sugar
1/2	cup water
1/2	cup cider vinegar
1/2	teaspoon celery seed

Dash onion salt
Dash ground turmeric

1. In a large bowl, combine all the vegetables; sprinkle with salt and cover with cold water. Let stand for 3 hours; rinse and drain.

2. In a large saucepan, bring the remaining ingredients to a boil. Stir in zucchini mixture and return to a boil. Reduce heat; simmer, uncovered, for 5 minutes. Transfer to a large bowl; cool to room temperature. Cover and refrigerate for at least 2 days.

HONEY ALMOND BUTTER

"This is so delicious. I made it to go with some corn bread. I can't wait to make some homemade rolls to slather this on!"
—Cooper78

MANGO CRANBERRY SALSA

[2008]

MANGO CRANBERRY SALSA

yield: 4-1/2 cups ∞ prep/total time: 25 min.

I got this recipe from a friend. It's definitely worth the effort if you want to wow your gang at Thanksgiving. The leftovers are great with chicken or ham.

—Rebecca Littlejohn
Meadow Vista, California

- 1-1/2 cups whole-berry cranberry sauce
- 3 tangerines, peeled, seeded and chopped
- 1 medium mango, peeled and diced
- 1 cup diced fresh pineapple
- 1/4 cup finely chopped red onion
- 1/4 cup minced fresh cilantro
- 1 jalapeno pepper, seeded and finely chopped

1. In a bowl, combine all the ingredients. Cover and refrigerate until serving.

Editor's Note: Wear disposable gloves when cutting hot peppers; the oils can burn skin. Avoid touching your face.

[2003]

CHEESE SAUCE FOR VEGGIES

yield: 1-1/2 cups ∞ prep/total time: 10 min.

This tasty cheese sauce, flavored with ground mustard, curry and marjoram, is especially good over broccoli and cauliflower. I like to add a sprinkling of crumbled bacon on top.

—Ruth Bogdanski, Grants Pass, Oregon

- 2 cups (8 ounces) shredded cheddar cheese
- 3/4 cup plus 2 tablespoons evaporated milk
- 3/4 teaspoon ground mustard
- 1/2 teaspoon dried marjoram
- Dash to 1/8 teaspoon curry powder

1. In a small saucepan, combine all the ingredients. Cook and stir over medium-low heat until the cheese is melted. Serve warm over broccoli or other cooked vegetables.

[2007]

VERSATILE CHILI-CHEESE SAUCE

yield: 4 cups ∞ prep/total time: 30 min.

It's so good, there's no limit to how this sauce can be enjoyed. We use it as a fondue—a dip for tortilla chips or vegetables—or poured over grilled chicken, baked potatoes, etc.

—Darlene Brenden
Salem, Oregon, Field Editor

- 1/4 cup butter, cubed
- 1/4 cup all-purpose flour
- 2 cups heavy whipping cream
- 1 cup (8 ounces) sour cream
- 1 can (4 ounces) chopped green chilies, undrained
- 3 teaspoons chicken bouillon granules
- 1 cup (4 ounces) shredded cheddar cheese
- 1/2 cup shredded Monterey Jack cheese
- 1/4 teaspoon pepper

1. In a large saucepan, melt butter. Stir in the flour until smooth; gradually add cream. Bring to a boil; cook and stir for 2 minutes or until thickened.

2. Stir in the sour cream, chilies and bouillon. Reduce heat to medium; cook and stir for 3-4 minutes or until heated through. Add cheeses and pepper. Cook until bubbly and cheese is melted, stirring occasionally.

[2002]

BRUCE'S HOT BARBECUE SAUCE

yield: 4 quarts   prep: 20 min.
cook: 1 hour

The heat is on when you brush on this tongue-tingling sauce! You'll also detect a hint of fruity sweetness, thanks to the apricots. This recipe makes a lot; you can make smaller batches or share it with friends.

—Bruce Fisher, East Bloomfield, New York

2 cans (15 ounces each) apricot halves, drained
4 cups packed brown sugar
4 cups cider vinegar
1 can (29 ounces) tomato sauce
2 cups ketchup
1 cup maple syrup
1 cup prepared mustard
1/2 cup orange juice
1/2 cup honey
3 tablespoons salt
1/2 cup molasses
3 tablespoons chicken bouillon granules
2 to 4 tablespoons crushed red pepper flakes
2 tablespoons garlic powder
2 tablespoons onion powder
2 tablespoons Worcestershire sauce
2 tablespoons reduced-sodium soy sauce
1 tablespoon pepper
2 tablespoons Liquid Smoke, optional

1. In a blender, puree the apricots until smooth. Pour into a large Dutch oven; add the next 17 ingredients. Bring to a boil. Reduce heat; simmer, uncovered, for 1 hour or until flavors are blended, stirring occasionally.

2. Stir in Liquid Smoke if desired. Cool. Store in the refrigerator.

[1995]

CREAMY HORSERADISH SAUCE

yield: 3-1/2 cups   prep/total time: 15 min.

My favorite way to use this sauce is on cold roast beef sandwiches. But it really complements a variety of foods.

—Florence Palmer, Marshall, Illinois

1 cup heavy whipping cream
1 cup mayonnaise
1/8 teaspoon salt
1/4 cup prepared horseradish

1. In a bowl, whip the cream until soft peaks form. Add the mayonnaise and salt; blend thoroughly. Fold in the horseradish. Chill until serving. Use as a condiment with roast beef, corned beef, pork or sandwiches.

[2009]

SASSY BLUE CHEESE POTATO TOPPER

yield: 2-1/2 cups   prep/total time: 5 min.

This topper works great on a spud or even as a dip with your favorite corn chips. I think it's best made a day ahead of time.

*—Ronald James Bishop
Ridgefield, Washington*

2 cups mayonnaise
1 jar (5 ounces) blue cheese spread
1/4 cup finely chopped onion
1/4 cup minced fresh parsley
2 garlic cloves, minced
1/4 teaspoon Worcestershire sauce
Baked potatoes

1. In a small bowl, beat the mayonnaise and blue cheese spread until smooth. Stir in the onion, parsley, garlic and Worcestershire sauce. Serve the cheese sauce over potatoes.

BRUCE'S HOT BARBECUE SAUCE

"This is my family's favorite on pork ribs on the grill. It is SPICY, so be sure how spicy your gang likes their sauce, and if not sure go light—you can always add more pepper. I love this recipe especially since it makes enough to last me almost the whole summer."
—suwest

FOOLPROOF GRAVY

[1999]

SPICY MUSTARD SPREAD

yield: about 1/3 cup
prep/total time: 10 min.

This zippy spread makes taste buds sit up and take notice. It's super on vegetables, hot dogs and hamburgers, in potato salad and more.

—*Audrey Thibodeau, Gilbert, Arizona*

- 1/4 cup butter, softened
- 2 tablespoons ground mustard
- 2 tablespoons white vinegar
- 1/4 teaspoon garlic salt
- 4 drops hot pepper sauce

1. In a bowl, combine the ingredients until smooth. Serve with hot dogs, vegetables or meat. Refrigerate.

[2010]

FOOLPROOF GRAVY

yield: 2-1/3 cups ∽ **prep/total time: 20 min.**

Make Thanksgiving or other special-occasion dinners easy with this can't-miss recipe. Use the drippings from your roasted turkey, and the gravy is done in just 20 minutes.

—*Edie DeSpain*
Logan, Utah, Field Editor

Drippings from 1 roasted turkey
- 1/2 to 1 cup turkey *or* chicken broth
- 1/4 cup plus 1 tablespoon all-purpose flour
- 1/2 cup fat-free milk
- 1 teaspoon chicken bouillon granules
- 1/4 teaspoon poultry seasoning
- 1/8 teaspoon white pepper

1. Pour drippings into a 2-cup measuring cup. Skim and discard fat. Add enough broth to drippings to measure 2 cups. Transfer to a saucepan; bring to a boil.

2. In a bowl, combine flour and milk until smooth. Gradually stir into the drippings mixture. Stir in bouillon,

poultry seasoning and white pepper. Bring to a boil; cook and stir for 2 minutes or until thickened.

[2012]

GINGERBREAD SPICE JELLY

yield: 5 half-pints
prep: 15 min. + standing ∽ **process: 10 min.**
(Pictured on page 291)

For two years in a row, my jelly has won purple champion ribbons at our county fair. I have made this simple jelly as gifts for many years and people are thrilled to receive it. In fact, they return my jelly jars for a refill every year.

—*Robin Nagel, Whitehall, Montana*

- 2-1/2 cups water
- 18 gingerbread spice tea bags
- 4-1/2 cups sugar
- 1/2 cup unsweetened apple juice
- 2 teaspoons butter
- 2 pouches (3 ounces *each*) liquid fruit pectin

1. In a large saucepan, bring water to a boil. Remove from the heat; add tea bags. Cover and steep for 30 minutes.

2. Discard tea bags. Stir in the sugar, apple juice and butter. Bring to a full rolling boil over high heat, stirring constantly. Stir in the pectin. Boil for 1 minute, stirring constantly.

3. Remove from the heat; skim off foam. Carefully ladle hot mixture into hot half-pint jars, leaving 1/4-in. headspace. Remove air bubbles; wipe rims and adjust lids. Process for 10 minutes in a boiling-water canner. (Jelly may take up to 2 weeks to fully set.)

Editor's Note: The processing time listed is for altitudes of 1,000 feet or less. Add 1 minute to the processing time for each 1,000 feet of additional altitude.

[1994]

WILD PLUM JELLY

yield: about 8 half-pints ∞ **prep: 55 min.**
process: 5 min.

(Pictured on page 293)

I've had this recipe for ages. Each year when the wild plums are ripe, I'll fill my pail and make this jelly. It's so good served with toast, pancakes or waffles!

—*Ludell Heuser, Mt. Horeb, Wisconsin*

---

5   pounds wild plums, halved and pitted
4   cups water
1   package (1-3/4 ounces) powdered fruit pectin
7-1/2   cups sugar

1. In a stockpot, simmer plums and water until tender, about 30 minutes. Line a strainer with four layers of cheesecloth; place over a bowl. Place plum mixture in strainer; cover with edges of cheesecloth. Let stand for 30 minutes or until the liquid measures 5-1/2 cups.

2. Return liquid to the pan. Add pectin; stir and bring to a boil. Add sugar; bring to a full rolling boil. Boil for 1 minute, stirring constantly.

3. Remove from the heat; skim off any foam. Carefully ladle hot mixture into hot sterilized half-pint jars, leaving 1/4-in. headspace. Remove air bubbles; wipe rims and adjust lids. Process for 5 minutes in a boiling-water canner.

Editor's Note: The processing time listed is for altitudes of 1,000 feet or less. Add 1 minute to the processing time for each 1,000 feet of additional altitude.

HOW TO PROCESS JELLIES & JAMS

1. Wash jars and two-piece caps in hot, soapy water; rinse throughly. Dry bands on a towel. Put jars in a large kettle with enough water to cover; simmer to 180°. Remove from heat. Place lids in a small saucepan and cover with water; simmer to 180°. Remove from heat.

2. Place the rack in canner. Add several inches of water; bring to a simmer. Meanwhile, prepare the recipe. Ladle or pour hot mixture into hot jars, leaving the recommended amount of headspace for expansion during processing.

3. Wipe threads and rim of jar with clean damp cloth. Place warm lids on jars with sealing compound on the glass. Screw band onto the jars just until resistance is met.

4. Immediately after filling each jar, use a jar lifter to place the jar onto the rack in the canner, making sure the jars are not touching. Lower rack when filled. If necessary, add enough boiling water to canner to cover jar lids by 1 to 2 in. Cover canner with its lid. Adjust heat to hold a steady rolling boil. Start counting the processing time when the water returns to a boil. If the water level decreases while processing, add additional boiling water.

5. When the processing time has ended, remove jar lifter. Stand upright on a towel, out of drafts, leaving 1 to 2 in. of space around each jar. After 12 to 24 hours, test each of the lids to determine if they have sealed by pressing the center of the lid. If it is concave (indented), remove the band and try to lift the lid. If lid is secure, the jar is vacuum-sealed. Wipe jars to remove any food. Label and date jars.

HOT PEPPER JELLY

[2001]

yield: 5 half-pints ✺ **prep: 15 min.**
process: 5 min.

We enjoy this fiery pepper spread on crackers with cream cheese. It also makes a terrific holiday gift. For a milder flavor and different color, substitute a green bell pepper for the red one, jalapeno peppers for the habaneros and green food coloring instead of red.

—Richard Harris, Kingston, Tennessee

1-1/2   cups white vinegar
    1   medium sweet red pepper, cut into wedges
 2/3   cup chopped habanero peppers
    6   cups sugar, *divided*
    2   pouches (3 ounces ea*ch*) liquid fruit pectin
    1   teaspoon red food coloring, optional
Cream cheese and crackers

1. Place vinegar and peppers in a blender; cover and puree. Add 2 cups sugar; blend well. Pour into a saucepan. Stir in the remaining sugar; bring to a boil. Strain mixture and return to pan. Stir in pectin and food coloring if desired. Return to a rolling boil over high heat. Boil for 2 minutes, stirring constantly.

2. Remove from the heat; skim off foam. Carefully ladle hot mixture into hot sterilized half-pint jars, leaving 1/4-in. headspace. Remove air bubbles, wipe rims and adjust lids. Process for 5 minutes in a boiling-water canner.

3. Serve with cream cheese on crackers.

Editor's Note: Wear disposable gloves when cutting hot peppers; the oils can burn skin. Avoid touching your face. The processing time listed is for altitudes of 1,000 feet or less. Add 1 minute to the processing time for each 1,000 feet of additional altitude.

HOT PEPPER JELLY

❝I have made this two times now and both times I have had requests for more! YUMMY! Wear gloves and a mask though when making. Fumes can be a little overwhelming.❞
—JMartin1265

ORANGE RHUBARB SPREAD

[2006]

yield: 5 half-pints ✺ **prep: 5 min.**
cook: 20 min. + standing

This tangy spread is easy to make and tastes especially good on hot, buttered cinnamon toast. The recipe makes enough to have on hand well beyond the growing season.

—Betty Nyenhuis, Oostburg, Wisconsin

  4   cups diced fresh *or* frozen rhubarb
  2   cups water
  1   can (6 ounces) frozen orange juice concentrate, thawed
  1   package (1-3/4 ounces) powdered fruit pectin
  4   cups sugar

1. In a large saucepan, bring rhubarb and water to a boil. Reduce heat; simmer, uncovered, for 7-8 minutes or until rhubarb is tender. Drain and reserve cooking liquid. Cool rhubarb and liquid to room temperature.

2. Place the rhubarb in a blender; cover and process until pureed. Transfer to a 4-cup measuring cup; add enough reserved cooking liquid to measure 2-1/3 cups. Return to the saucepan.

3. Add orange juice concentrate and pectin; bring to a full rolling boil, stirring constantly. Stir in sugar. Return to a full rolling boil; boil and stir for 1 minute. Remove from the heat; skim off foam.

4. Pour into jars or freezer containers; cool to room temperature, about 1 hour. Cover and let stand overnight or until set, but not longer than 24 hours. Refrigerate for up to 3 weeks or freeze for up to 12 months.

[2005]

HABANERO APRICOT JAM

yield: 11 half-pints ∽ **prep: 15 min.**
process: 5 min.

This zippy and versatile jam was a blue-ribbon winner at our county fair. I mix it with applesauce as a condiment for pork, with cranberry sauce for poultry and with cream cheese as a spread on celery sticks. It's a beautiful color...and in "hot" demand as a gift item!

—*Janet Eckhoff, Woodland, California*

- 3-1/2 pounds fresh apricots
- 6 tablespoons bottled lemon juice
- 2 to 4 habanero peppers, seeded
- 1 package (1-3/4 ounces) powdered fruit pectin
- 7 cups sugar

1. Pit and chop apricots; place in a Dutch oven. Stir in the lemon juice. Place habaneros in a blender; add a small amount of apricot mixture. Cover and process until smooth. Return to the pan.

2. Stir in pectin. Bring to a full rolling boil, stirring constantly. Stir in sugar; return to a full rolling boil. Boil for 1 minute, stirring constantly.

3. Remove from the heat; skim off foam. Carefully ladle hot mixture into hot sterilized half-pint jars, leaving 1/4-in. headspace. Wipe rims and adjust lids. Process for 5 minutes in a boiling-water canner.

4. For best results, let processed jam stand at room temperature for 2 weeks to set up.

Editor's Note: Wear disposable gloves when cutting hot peppers; the oils can burn skin. Avoid touching your face. The processing time listed is for altitudes of 1,000 feet or less. Add 1 minute to the processing time for each 1,000 feet of additional altitude.

[1996]

FOUR-BERRY SPREAD

yield: about 7 half-pints ∽ **prep: 20 min.**
process: 10 min.

For a big berry taste, you can't beat this tasty spread. With a flavorful foursome of blackberries, blueberries, raspberries and strawberries, this lovely jam brightens any breakfast.

—*Marie St. Thomas*
Sterling, Massachusetts

- 1 cup fresh *or* frozen blackberries
- 1 cup fresh *or* frozen blueberries
- 1-1/2 cups fresh *or* frozen strawberries
- 1-1/2 cups fresh *or* frozen raspberries
- 1 package (1-3/4 ounces) powdered fruit pectin
- 7 cups sugar

1. Crush berries in a Dutch oven. Stir in pectin; bring to a full rolling boil over high heat, stirring constantly. Stir in sugar; return to a full rolling boil. Boil for 1 minute, stirring constantly.

2. Remove from the heat; skim off any foam. Carefully ladle hot mixture into hot half-pint jars, leaving 1/4-in. headspace. Remove air bubbles, wipe rims and adjust lids. Process for 10 minutes in a boiling-water canner.

Editor's Note: The processing time listed is for altitudes of 1,000 feet or less. Add 1 minute to the processing time for each 1,000 feet of additional altitude.

HABANERO APRICOT JAM

"I couldn't decide whether to use two peppers (I was afraid it would be mild) or four (because it would be too hot), so I settled for three...and it was just perfect! This jam rocks. I've been canning for over twenty years now and was looking for something a little different...Prep was pretty easy, using the food processor on pulse to give me a nice texture and the blender to combine the habaneros with the apricot mixture. The flavor is incredible and it makes eleven half-pints, so it's nice for gift giving."
—*linsvin*

~ COOKIES & BARS ~

JEWELED COOKIE SLICES

"These are my husband's favorite cookies. He will buy the candied fruit as a hint that he would like me to make some for him.**"**

—SueLaurito

[1999]

JEWELED COOKIE SLICES

yield: about 2-1/2 dozen
prep: 20 min. + chilling
bake: 10 min. + cooling

I often mark recipes with "G" for good, "VG" for very good; this seasonal favorite is marked "VVG"! I usually double the recipe.

—Rosella Peters
Gull Lake, Saskatchewan
Former Field Editor

1/3	cup butter, melted
1/3	cup sugar
1/4	cup packed brown sugar
1	egg
1/2	teaspoon vanilla extract
1-1/2	cups all-purpose flour
1	teaspoon baking powder
1/8	teaspoon baking soda
1/8	teaspoon ground nutmeg
1/2	cup chopped candied pineapple *or* red and green candied cherries
2	tablespoons chopped blanched almonds

---

1. In a large bowl, cream butter and sugars until light and fluffy. Beat in egg and vanilla. Combine dry ingredients; gradually add to the butter mixture and mix well. Stir in the pineapple and almonds. Spread evenly into a foil-lined 8-in. x 4-in. loaf pan. Cover and refrigerate for at least 2 hours.

2. Invert dough onto a cutting board; remove foil. Cut into 1/4-in. slices; place on greased baking sheets. Bake at 350° for 10-12 minutes or until lightly browned. Remove to wire racks.

[1998]

SOFT MOLASSES JUMBLES

yield: 4 dozen ∽ prep: 15 min.
bake: 10 min./batch

These old-fashioned cookies are given a new twist with raisins and chocolate chips.

—Margaret Adamson
Gaithersburg, Maryland

2/3	cup butter, softened
1/2	cup sugar
1	egg
1/2	cup molasses
1/2	cup buttermilk
2-1/2	cups all-purpose flour
1	teaspoon baking soda
1/2	teaspoon ground cinnamon
1/4	teaspoon salt
1/8	teaspoon ground ginger
1/2	cup raisins
1/2	cup semisweet chocolate chips

---

1. In a large bowl, cream butter and sugar until light and fluffy. Beat in egg. Combine molasses and buttermilk. Combine the dry ingredients; gradually add to creamed mixture alternately with molasses mixture, beating well after each addition. Stir in raisins and chocolate chips.

2. Drop by tablespoonfuls 2 in. apart onto greased baking sheets. Bake at 350° for 10-12 minutes or until set. Cool for 2 minutes before removing from pans to wire racks.

[2000]

TRIPLE-CHOCOLATE KISSES

yield: 3-1/2 dozen ∽ prep: 30 min.
bake: 15 min./batch

These crisp meringue cookies with a chocolate center are easy to make but look like you spent a lot of time. When our son and daughter-in-law moved into their first home on Valentine's Day, I prepared them a nice dinner and gave them a batch of these treats.

—*Evelyn Lindburg, Shenandoah, Iowa*

 2 egg whites
 1/4 teaspoon cream of tartar
 1/4 teaspoon almond extract
 1/2 cup sugar
 1 ounce semisweet chocolate, grated
 42 milk chocolate kisses
Baking cocoa

1. Place egg whites in a bowl; let stand at room temperature for 30 minutes.

2. Add the cream of tartar and extract; beat on medium speed until soft peaks form. Gradually add the sugar, 1 tablespoon at a time, beating on high until stiff glossy peaks form and sugar is dissolved. Fold in grated chocolate.

3. Insert a medium open-star tip in a pastry or plastic bag. Fill bag with the meringue. On lightly greased baking sheets, pipe forty-two 1-in. circles.

4. Press a chocolate kiss into the center of each. Pipe meringue around each kiss in continuous circles from the base to the top until kiss is completely covered. Dust with cocoa.

5. Bake cookies at 325° for 15-18 minutes or until the edges are lightly browned. Remove to wire racks.

[1998]

WHOLE WHEAT TOFFEE SANDIES

yield: about 12 dozen ∽ prep: 35 min.
bake: 15 min./batch

Crisp and loaded with goodies, these are my husband's favorite cookies. I used to bake them in large batches when our sons still lived at home. Now I whip them up for our grandchildren.

—*Alice Kahnk, Kennard, Nebraska*

 1 cup butter, softened
 1 cup sugar
 1 cup confectioners' sugar
 1 cup canola oil
 2 eggs
 1 teaspoon almond extract
 3-1/2 cups all-purpose flour
 1 cup whole wheat flour
 1 teaspoon baking soda
 1 teaspoon cream of tartar
 1 teaspoon salt
 2 cups chopped almonds
 1 package (8 ounces) milk chocolate English toffee bits
Additional sugar

1. In a large bowl, cream the butter and sugars until light and fluffy. Beat in the oil, eggs and extract. Combine flours, baking soda, cream of tartar and salt; gradually add to the creamed mixture and mix well. Stir in the almonds and toffee bits.

2. Shape into 1-in. balls; roll in the sugar. Place 2 in. apart on ungreased baking sheets and flatten with a fork. Bake cookies at 350° for 12-14 minutes or until lightly browned. Remove to wire racks.

WHOLE WHEAT TOFFEE SANDIES

"Oh, my word! These are the best cookies of all time! They are light and crispy and buttery...everything good sandies are supposed to be. They are delicious, and after making them once, they became the family-favorite cookie. Thank you Alice for sharing your wonderful recipe with the rest of us. You rock! :)"

—*Missionary*

[2003]

WATERMELON SLICE COOKIES

yield: about 3 dozen
prep: 25 min. + chilling
bake: 10 min./batch

(*Pictured on page 296*)

When I made these rich butter cookies for a neighborhood event, one neighbor thought they were so attractive that she kept one in her freezer for the longest time so she could show it to friends and relatives.

—*Sue Ann Benham, Valparaiso, Indiana*

3/4	cup butter, softened
3/4	cup sugar
1	egg
1/2	teaspoon almond extract
2	cups all-purpose flour
1/4	teaspoon baking powder
1/8	teaspoon salt

Red and green gel food coloring

1/3	cup raisins
1	teaspoon sesame seeds

---

1. In a large bowl, cream butter and sugar until light and fluffy. Beat in the egg and extract. Combine the flour, baking powder and salt; gradually add to the creamed mixture and mix well. Set aside 1 cup of dough.

2. Tint remaining dough red; shape into a 3-1/2-in.-long log. Wrap in plastic wrap. Tint 1/3 cup of the reserved dough green; wrap in plastic wrap. Wrap the remaining plain dough. Refrigerate for 2 hours or until firm.

3. On a lightly floured surface, roll the plain dough into a 8-1/2-in. x 3-1/2-in. rectangle. Place red dough log on the end of a short side of the rectangle; roll up.

4. Roll the green dough into a 10-in. x 3-1/2-in. rectangle. Place red and white log on the end of a short side on green dough; roll up. Wrap in plastic wrap; refrigerate overnight.

5. Unwrap and cut into 3/16-in. slices (just less than 1/4 in.). Place 2 in. apart on ungreased baking sheets. Cut raisins into small pieces. Lightly press raisin bits and sesame seeds into red dough to resemble watermelon seeds.

6. Bake at 350° for 9-11 minutes or until firm. Immediately cut cookies in half. Remove to wire racks.

[1993]

CRISP SUGAR COOKIES

yield: 8 dozen   **prep: 15 min. + chilling**
bake: 10 min.

My grandmother always had sugar cookies in her pantry, and we grandchildren would empty that big jar quickly because those cookies were the best! I now regularly bake these wonderful cookies to share with friends.

—*Evelyn Poteet, Hancock, Maryland*

1	cup butter, softened
2	cups sugar
2	eggs
1	teaspoon vanilla extract
5	cups all-purpose flour
1-1/2	teaspoons baking powder
1	teaspoon baking soda
1/2	teaspoon salt
1/4	cup 2% milk

---

1. In a large bowl, cream butter and sugar until light and fluffy. Add the eggs and vanilla. Combine flour, baking powder, baking soda and salt; add to creamed mixture alternately with milk. Cover and refrigerate for 15-30 minutes or until easy to handle.

2. On a floured surface, roll out dough to 1/8-in. thickness. Cut out cookies into desired shapes. Place 2 in. apart on greased baking sheets.

3. Bake cookies at 350° for 10 minutes or until the edges are lightly browned. Remove to wire racks.

[2009]

ICE CREAM KOLACHKES

yield: 10 dozen ∞ **prep: 1 hour + chilling**
bake: 15 min./batch

(Pictured on page 291)

These sweet pastries have Polish and Czech roots and can also be spelled "kolaches." They are usually filled with poppy seeds, nuts, jam or a mashed fruit mixture. The ice cream is a unique twist on traditional kolachkes, and it's simplest to use a square cookie cutter to cut the dough.

—Diane Turner
Brunswick, Ohio, Field Editor

- 2 cups butter, softened
- 1 pint vanilla ice cream, softened
- 4 cups all-purpose flour
- 2 tablespoons sugar
- 2 cans (12 ounces each) apricot *and/or* raspberry cake and pastry filling
- 1 to 2 tablespoons confectioners' sugar, optional

1. In the bowl of a heavy-duty stand mixer, beat butter and ice cream until blended (mixture will appear curdled). Add flour and sugar; mix well. Divide dough into four portions; cover and chill for 2 hours or until easy to handle.

2. On a lightly floured surface, roll one portion of dough into a 12-in. x 10-in. rectangle; cut into 2-in. squares. Place a teaspoonful of filling in the center of each square. Overlap two opposite corners of dough over filling; pinch tightly to seal. Place 2 in. apart on ungreased baking sheets. Repeat with remaining dough and filling.

3. Bake at 350° for 11-14 minutes or until bottoms are lightly browned. Cool for 1 minute before removing from pan to wire racks. Sprinkle with confectioners' sugar if desired.

Editor's Note: This recipe was tested with Solo brand cake and pastry filling. Look for it in the baking aisle.

[1998]

CHOCOLATE MERINGUE STARS

yield: about 4 dozen ∞ **prep: 25 min.**
bake: 30 min./batch + cooling

Looking for light, delicate yet chewy cookies perfect for holiday munching? Try these! Their big chocolate flavor makes it difficult to keep the kids away from them long enough to get any on the cookie tray.

—Edna Lee, Greeley, Colorado

- 3 egg whites
- 3/4 teaspoon vanilla extract
- 3/4 cup sugar
- 1/4 cup baking cocoa

GLAZE:
- 3 ounces semisweet chocolate, chopped
- 1 tablespoon shortening

1. Place egg whites in a large bowl; let stand at room temperature for 30 minutes. Add the vanilla; beat on medium speed until soft peaks form. Gradually add the sugar, about 2 tablespoons at a time, beating until stiff peaks form and sugar is dissolved. Gently fold in cocoa.

2. Insert a #8b large open star tip into a pastry or plastic bag; fill half full with meringue. Pipe stars, about 1-1/4 in. in diameter, or drop meringue by rounded teaspoonfuls onto parchment paper-lined baking sheets.

3. Bake at 300° for 30-35 minutes or until lightly browned. Remove from paper to wire racks.

4. In a microwave, melt the chocolate and shortening; stir until smooth. Dip the cookies halfway into glaze; allow the excess to drip off. Place on waxed paper; let stand until set.

ICE CREAM KOLACHKES

" This recipe is so simple to make, my family makes it very often. We love it and will be keeping this recipe for a long time to come. **"**
—tkarinas

OLD-FASHIONED WHOOPIE PIES

"These were incredible. I was looking for a scratch recipe and not a cake mix, and this was so perfect. It seems like it would take a long time, but it doesn't really. I used Crisco for the cookie and half butter-half Crisco for the filling. I was imagining a icing filling, but it was more like a stiff pudding taste..like vanilla. They are so good. I tinted the filling green for St. Paddy's Day. Will definitely make again!!"

—silly girl

[1998]

OLD-FASHIONED WHOOPIE PIES

yield: 2 dozen ∞ **prep: 35 min. + chilling**
bake: 10 min./batch + cooling

Who can resist soft chocolate sandwich cookies filled with a layer of fluffy white frosting? Mom has made these for years...they're a treat that never lasted very long with me and my two brothers around.

—Maria Costello, Monroe, North Carolina

1/2	cup baking cocoa
1/2	cup hot water
1/2	cup shortening
1-1/2	cups sugar
2	eggs
1	teaspoon vanilla extract
2-2/3	cups all-purpose flour
1	teaspoon baking powder
1	teaspoon baking soda
1/4	teaspoon salt
1/2	cup buttermilk

FILLING:

3	tablespoons all-purpose flour

Dash salt

1	cup 2% milk
3/4	cup shortening
1-1/2	cups confectioners' sugar
2	teaspoons vanilla extract

---

1. In a small bowl, combine cocoa and water. Cool for 5 minutes. In a large bowl, cream shortening and sugar until light and fluffy. Beat in the eggs, vanilla and cocoa mixture. Combine dry ingredients; gradually add to creamed mixture alternately with buttermilk, beating well after each addition.

2. Drop by rounded tablespoonfuls 2 in. apart onto greased baking sheets. Flatten slightly with a spoon. Bake at 350° for 10-12 minutes or until firm to the touch. Remove to wire racks to cool completely.

3. In a small saucepan, combine flour and salt. Gradually whisk in milk until smooth; cook and stir over medium-high heat until thick, 5-7 minutes. Remove from the heat. Cover and refrigerate until completely cool.

4. In a small bowl, cream the shortening, sugar and vanilla until light and fluffy. Add milk mixture; beat for 7 minutes or until fluffy. Spread filling on half of the cookies; top with the remaining cookies. Store in the refrigerator.

[1995]

PECAN MELTAWAYS

yield: 4 dozen ∞ **prep: 15 min. + chilling**
bake: 10 min./batch

(Pictured on page 295)

These sugared nut-filled balls are a tradition in our house at Christmastime.

—Alberta McKay
Bartlesville, Oklahoma, Field Editor

1	cup butter, softened
1/2	cup confectioners' sugar
1	teaspoon vanilla extract
2-1/4	cups all-purpose flour
1/4	teaspoon salt
3/4	cup chopped pecans

Additional confectioners' sugar

---

1. In a large bowl, cream butter and confectioners' sugar until light and fluffy. Beat in vanilla. Combine flour and salt; gradually add to creamed mixture and mix well. Stir in pecans. Refrigerate until chilled.

2. Roll dough into 1-in. balls and place on ungreased baking sheets. Bake at 350° for 10-12 minutes or until cookies are set. Roll warm cookies in additional confectioners' sugar; cool completely on wire racks. Roll cooled cookies again in confectioners' sugar.

[1995]

PEANUT BUTTER SANDWICH COOKIES

yield: 44 sandwich cookies ∞ **prep: 20 min.**
bake: 10 min./batch + cooling

I'm a busy mother. I work in our school office and help my husband on our hog and cattle farm. When I find time to bake a treat, I like it to be a special one like this. The creamy filling gives traditional peanut butter cookies a new twist.

—Debbie Kokes, Tabor, South Dakota

- 1 cup butter-flavored shortening
- 1 cup creamy peanut butter
- 1 cup sugar
- 1 cup packed brown sugar
- 3 eggs
- 1 teaspoon vanilla extract
- 3 cups all-purpose flour
- 2 teaspoons baking soda
- 1/4 teaspoon salt

FILLING:
- 1/2 cup creamy peanut butter
- 3 cups confectioners' sugar
- 1 teaspoon vanilla extract
- 5 to 6 tablespoons milk

1. In a large bowl, cream the shortening, peanut butter and sugars until light and fluffy, about 4 minutes. Beat in eggs and vanilla. Combine the flour, baking soda and salt; add to creamed mixture and mix well.

2. Shape into 1-in. balls and place 2 in. apart on ungreased baking sheets. Flatten to 3/8-in. thickness with fork. Bake at 375° for 7-8 minutes or until golden. Remove from pans to wire racks to cool completely.

3. For filling, in a large bowl, beat the peanut butter, confectioners' sugar, vanilla and enough milk to achieve spreading consistency. Spread filling on half of the cookies and top each with another cookie.

[1997]

CHOCOLATE NUT COOKIES

yield: about 5 dozen ∞ **prep: 25 min.**
bake: 10 min.

Folks are quick to grab one of these cookies when they see they're chocolate. Once they discover the nuts and white chips, they grab a second and sometimes a third. This recipe moved with me from Kentucky to Arizona and now to Ohio!

—Farralee Baldwin, Centerville, Ohio

- 1 cup butter, softened
- 3/4 cup packed brown sugar
- 1/2 cup sugar
- 1 egg
- 1 teaspoon almond extract
- 2 cups all-purpose flour
- 1/4 cup baking cocoa
- 1 teaspoon baking soda
- 1/2 teaspoon salt
- 1 cup white baking chips
- 1 cup chopped almonds

1. In a large bowl, cream the butter and sugars until light and fluffy. Beat in egg and extract. Combine the flour, cocoa, baking soda and salt; gradually add to creamed mixture and mix well. Stir in the chips and nuts.

2. Drop dough by teaspoonfuls onto ungreased baking sheets. Bake at 375° for 7-9 minutes. Cool the cookies on pans for 1 minute before removing from pans to wire racks.

PEANUT BUTTER SANDWICH COOKIES

"Very good! Everybody loved them. I added a thin layer of grape jam (you could use your favorite) along with the peanut butter filling, and that was excellent, too."
—*mamacubed*

[2010]

MOLASSES COOKIES WITH A KICK

yield: 8 dozen ∞ prep: 40 min. + chilling
bake: 10 min./batch

*This is a combination of spices that I have used
for a long time. It's also one of my mother's
favorite cookies. I get requests from her to make
them year-round!*

—*Tamara Rau, Medina, North Dakota*

3/4	cup butter, softened
1/2	cup sugar
1/2	cup packed brown sugar
1/4	cup molasses
1	egg
1-1/2	teaspoons minced fresh gingerroot
2-1/4	cups all-purpose flour
1	teaspoon ground cinnamon
3/4	teaspoon baking soda
1/2	teaspoon ground cloves
1/4	to 1/2 teaspoon cayenne pepper
1/4	teaspoon salt
1/4	teaspoon ground nutmeg
1/8	teaspoon each ground white pepper, cardamom and coriander
3/4	cup turbinado (washed raw) sugar

1. In a large bowl, cream the butter and
sugars until light and fluffy. Beat in the
molasses, egg and ginger. Combine the
flour, cinnamon, baking soda, cloves,
cayenne, salt, nutmeg, white pepper,
cardamom and coriander; gradually
add to creamed mixture and mix well.
Cover and refrigerate for 1-1/2 hours
or until easy to handle.

2. Roll into 1/2-in. balls; roll in turbinado
sugar. Place 3 in. apart on lightly
greased baking sheets.

3. Bake at 350° for 8-10 minutes or until
set. Cool cookies for 2 minutes before
removing from the pans to wire racks.

[2007]

ICED PUMPKIN COOKIES

yield: 3 dozen ∞ prep: 45 min.
bake: 15 min./batch + cooling

*My son, Joshua, especially likes testing—or
should I say consuming—these chunky cookies.*

—*Johna Nilson, Vista, California*

1	cup butter, softened
1/2	cup sugar
1/2	cup packed brown sugar
1	egg
1	cup canned pumpkin
1	cup all-purpose flour
1	cup whole wheat flour
1-1/2	teaspoons ground cinnamon
1	teaspoon baking powder
1	teaspoon ground ginger
1/2	teaspoon salt
1/2	teaspoon baking soda
1/2	teaspoon ground nutmeg
1/4	teaspoon ground cloves
1	cup granola without raisins
1	cup chopped walnuts
1	cup white baking chips
1	cup dried cranberries
ICING:	
1/4	cup butter, softened
2	cups confectioners' sugar
3	tablespoons 2% milk

1. In a large bowl, cream the butter and
sugars until light and fluffy. Beat in the
egg and pumpkin. Combine the flours,
cinnamon, baking powder, ginger, salt,
baking soda, nutmeg and cloves;
gradually add to creamed mixture and
mix well. Stir in the granola, walnuts,
chips and cranberries.

2. Drop by tablespoonfuls 2 in. apart onto
greased baking sheets. Bake at 350° for
15-18 minutes or until lightly browned.
Remove to wire racks to cool completely.

3. In a small bowl, combine the icing
ingredients until smooth. Spread over
cooled cookies. Store in the refrigerator.

[2008]

LARA'S TENDER GINGERSNAPS

yield: 3 dozen ∽ **prep: 15 min. + chilling
bake: 10 min./batch**

(Pictured on page 292)

Soft gingersnaps embody the tastes and smells of the Christmas season but are perfect for any fall gathering. I enjoy the flavors of cloves, cinnamon and ginger blended into one delicious cookie.

—*Lara Pennell, Mauldin, South Carolina*

> 1 cup packed brown sugar
> 3/4 cup butter, melted
> 1 egg
> 1/4 cup molasses
> 2-1/4 cups all-purpose flour
> 1-1/2 teaspoons ground ginger
> 1 teaspoon baking soda
> 1 teaspoon ground cinnamon
> 1/2 teaspoon ground cloves
> 1/4 cup sugar

1. In a large bowl, beat brown sugar and butter until blended. Beat in egg and molasses. Combine the flour, ginger, baking soda, cinnamon and cloves; gradually add to brown sugar mixture and mix well (dough will be stiff). Cover and refrigerate for at least 2 hours.

2. Shape dough into 1 in. balls. Roll in sugar. Place 2 in. apart on baking sheets coated with cooking spray.

3. Bake at 350° for 9-11 minutes or until set. Cool for 1 minute before removing from pans to wire racks.

[2002]

CHEWY MACAROONS

yield: 4-1/2 dozen ∽ **prep: 5 min.
bake: 10 min./batch**

My family loves these scrumptious cookies on special occasions.

—*Marcia Hostetter
Canton, New York, Former Field Editor*

> 5-1/3 cups flaked coconut
> 1 can (14 ounces) sweetened condensed milk
> 2 teaspoons vanilla extract

1. In a bowl, combine all the ingredients. Drop 2 in. apart onto greased baking sheets. Bake at 350° for 10-12 minutes or until lightly browned. With a spatula dipped in water, immediately remove to wire racks.

[1998]

LEMON CRISP COOKIES

**yield: about 4 dozen
prep/total time: 30 min.**

These quick-to-fix treats are a snap to make using a boxed cake mix. The sunny yellow color, big lemon flavor and delightful crunch are sure to bring smiles.

—*Julia Livingston
Frostproof, Florida, Field Editor*

> 1 package (18-1/4 ounces) lemon cake mix
> 1 cup crisp rice cereal
> 1/2 cup butter, melted
> 1 egg, lightly beaten
> 1 teaspoon grated lemon peel

1. In a large bowl, combine all ingredients (dough will be crumbly). Shape into 1-in. balls. Place 2 in. apart on ungreased baking sheets. Bake at 350° for 10-12 minutes or until set. Cool the cookies for 1 minute, before removing from pans to wire rack.

CHEWY MACAROONS

❝I loved these cookies, and if you cook them just right, they have a crispy coconut shell and a chewy center, which is perfect. (They stick to the pan if you don't cook them long enough.) I used fat-free sweetened condensed milk to make them more diet-friendly, so I wouldn't feel guilty downing five or six in one sitting!❞
—*epatters*

OATMEAL SANDWICH COOKIES

[2009]

MACAROON KISSES

yield: 4 dozen ∞ prep: 45 min. + chilling
bake: 10 min./batch + cooling

(Pictured on page 294)

These cookies are sure to delight the coconut and chocolate lover. That flavor combination is absolutely irresistible!

—Lee Roberts, Racine, Wisconsin

1/3 cup butter, softened
1 package (3 ounces) cream cheese, softened
3/4 cup sugar
1 egg yolk
2 teaspoons almond extract
1-1/2 cups all-purpose flour
2 teaspoons baking powder
1/2 teaspoon salt
5 cups flaked coconut, *divided*
48 milk chocolate kisses
Coarse sugar

1. In a large bowl, cream the butter, cream cheese and sugar until light and fluffy. Beat in the egg yolk and extract. Combine the flour, baking powder and salt; gradually add to creamed mixture and mix well. Stir in 3 cups coconut. Cover and refrigerate for 1 hour or until dough is easy to handle.

2. Roll dough into 1-in. balls, then roll in the remaining coconut. Place 2 in. apart on ungreased baking sheets.

3. Bake at 350° for 10-12 minutes or until lightly browned. Immediately press a chocolate kiss into the center of each cookie; sprinkle with coarse sugar. Cool on pan for 2-3 minutes or until chocolate is softened. Remove from pans to wire racks.

[2001]

OATMEAL SANDWICH COOKIES

yield: about 4-1/2 dozen ∞ prep: 25 min.
bake: 10 min. + cooling

These fun treats put a sweet fluffy filling between two chewy oatmeal cookies. They're perfect for snacking and to carry in lunch boxes. At bake sales, they sell instantly.

—Jan Woodall, Indianapolis, Indiana
Former Field Editor

1-1/2 cups shortening
2-2/3 cups packed brown sugar
4 eggs
2 teaspoons vanilla extract
2-1/4 cups all-purpose flour
2 teaspoons ground cinnamon
1-1/2 teaspoons baking soda
1 teaspoon salt
1/2 teaspoon ground nutmeg
4 cups old-fashioned oats
FILLING:
3/4 cup shortening
3 cups confectioners' sugar
1 jar (7 ounces) marshmallow creme
1 to 3 tablespoons 2% milk

1. In a large bowl, cream shortening and brown sugar until light and fluffy. Beat in eggs and vanilla. Combine the flour, cinnamon, baking soda, salt and nutmeg; gradually add to the creamed mixture and mix well. Stir in the oats.

2. Drop by rounded teaspoonfuls 2 in. apart onto lightly greased baking sheets. Bake at 350° for 10-12 minutes or until golden brown. Remove to wire racks to cool completely.

3. For filling, in a small bowl, cream the shortening, sugar and marshmallow creme. Add enough milk to achieve spreading consistency. Spread filling on the bottom of half of the cookies; top with remaining cookies.

[2004]

PEANUT BUTTER CHRISTMAS MICE

yield: about 5 dozen ∞ prep: 30 min.
bake: 10 min./batch + cooling

With their red licorice tails, candy noses and peanut ears, these chewy "mice" were always a hit at classroom parties. Even in their teens, my children still asked me to make these cookies for the holidays.

—*Nancy Rowse, Bella Vista, Arkansas*

- 1 cup creamy peanut butter
- 1/2 cup butter, softened
- 1/2 cup sugar
- 1/2 cup packed brown sugar
- 1 egg
- 1 teaspoon vanilla extract
- 1-1/2 cups all-purpose flour
- 1/2 teaspoon baking soda
- 1/2 cup peanut halves
- 2 tablespoons green and red M&M's miniature baking bits
- 4 teaspoons miniature semisweet chocolate chips
- Cake decorator holly leaf and berry candies
- 60 to 66 pieces red shoestring licorice (2 inches each)

1. In a large bowl, cream peanut butter, butter, and sugars until light and fluffy. Beat in egg and vanilla. Combine flour and baking soda; gradually add to the creamed mixture and mix well. (Dough will be soft). Refrigerate for 1 hour or until easy to handle.

2. Roll into 1-in. balls. Place 2 in. apart on ungreased baking sheets. Pinch each ball at one end to taper. Insert two peanut halves in center of each ball for ears. Add one M&M baking bit for nose and two chocolate chips for eyes. Arrange holly and berry candies in front of one ear.

3. Bake at 350° for 8-10 minutes or until set. Gently insert one licorice piece into each warm cookie for tail. Remove to wire racks.

Editor's Note: Reduced-fat peanut butter is not recommended for this recipe.

[1997]

GRANDPA'S COOKIES

yield: about 10 dozen
prep: 20 min. + chilling ∞ bake: 10 min.

My grandpa, a widower, raised his three sons on his own and did all the cooking and lots of baking. I can still picture him making these tasty old-fashioned cookies.

—*Karen Baker, Dover, Ohio*

- 2 cups butter, softened
- 4 cups packed brown sugar
- 4 eggs
- 1/2 cup water
- 1 teaspoon vanilla extract
- 7 cups all-purpose flour
- 1 tablespoon cream of tartar
- 1 tablespoon baking soda

1. In several large bowls, cream butter and brown sugar until light and fluffy. Beat in the eggs, water and vanilla. Combine the remaining ingredients; gradually add to creamed mixture and mix well.

2. Shape into three rolls; wrap with plastic wrap. Chill 4 hours or overnight.

3. Cut the rolls into 1/4-in. slices; place 2 in. apart on greased baking sheets. Bake at 375° for 8-10 minutes or until lightly browned. Remove to wire racks to cool.

PEANUT BUTTER CHRISTMAS MICE

❝We have been making these mice cookies for years (since they appeared in my *Taste of Home* magazine). My kids love making them and eating them. The kids insist on taking photos of the group—of them in their hands and of them half in their mouth with the tail hanging out. What can be more fun for a kid than pretending! They turn out just like the photo. We do without the holly and berry, but they still look as cute as can be.❞

—*mieoliphant*

[2004]

COCONUT PECAN COOKIES

yield: 6-1/2 dozen ∞ prep: 30 min.
bake: 10 min./batch + cooling

With chocolate chips and coconut in the cookie and a yummy pecan-coconut frosting these will remind you of German chocolate cake. A drizzle of chocolate tops them off in a festive way.

—*Diane Selich, Vassar, Michigan*

1 egg, lightly beaten
1 can (5 ounces) evaporated milk
2/3 cup sugar
1/4 cup butter, cubed
1-1/4 cups flaked coconut
1/2 cup chopped pecans
COOKIE DOUGH:
1 cup butter, softened
3/4 cup sugar
3/4 cup packed brown sugar
2 eggs
1 teaspoon vanilla extract
2-1/4 cups all-purpose flour
1 teaspoon baking soda
1 teaspoon salt
4 cups (24 ounces) semisweet chocolate chips, *divided*
1/4 cup flaked coconut

1. For frosting, in a large saucepan, combine the egg, milk, sugar and butter. Cook and stir over medium-low heat for 10-12 minutes or until slightly thickened and mixture reaches 160° or is thick enough to coat the back of a metal spoon. Stir in coconut and pecans. Set aside.

2. In a large bowl, cream the butter and sugars until light and fluffy. Beat in the eggs and vanilla. Combine the flour, baking soda and salt; gradually add to creamed mixture and mix well. Stir in 2 cups chips and coconut.

3. Drop by tablespoonfuls 2 in. apart onto ungreased baking sheets. Bake

cookies at 350° for 8-10 minutes or until lightly browned. Cool cookies for 10 minutes before removing from pans to wire racks to cool completely.

4. In a microwave, melt the remaining chocolate chips; stir until smooth. Spread frosting over cooled cookies; drizzle with melted chocolate.

[2004]

CANDY CANE SNOWBALLS

yield: 5 dozen ∞ prep: 25 + chilling
bake: 20 min./batch

I bake dozens of different kinds of Christmas cookies to give to family and friends. I came up with this recipe when I had leftover candy canes that I wanted to use up. The snowballs are dipped in a white candy coating, then into crushed peppermint candy.

—*Debby Anderson, Stockbridge, Georgia*

2 cups butter, softened
1 cup confectioners' sugar
1 teaspoon vanilla extract
3-1/2 cups all-purpose flour
1 cup chopped pecans
8 ounces white candy coating, coarsely chopped
1/3 to 1/2 cup crushed peppermint candy

1. In a large bowl, cream the butter and confectioners' sugar until light and fluffy. Beat in vanilla. Gradually add flour and mix well. Stir in the pecans. Refrigerate for 3-4 hours or until easy to handle.

2. Roll into 1-in. balls. Place 2 in. apart on ungreased baking sheets. Bake cookies at 350° for 18-20 minutes or until lightly browned. Remove to wire racks to cool completely.

3. In a microwave, melt candy coating; stir until smooth. Dip the top of each cookie into the candy coating; allow excess to drip off. Dip into peppermint candy. Place on waxed paper; let stand until set.

COCONUT PECAN COOKIES

"Excellent! Love the topping with a bit of crunch in the cookie. Made these for a cookie exchange and they were a hit."
—*dgmenm6*

SWEDISH RASPBERRY ALMOND BARS, page 323

CHEWY BROWNIE COOKIES, page 312

SCOTCH SHORTBREAD COOKIES, page 305

SPICED APPLESAUCE, page 268

ICE CREAM KOLACHKES, page 281

GINGERBREAD SPICE JELLY, page 274

LARA'S TENDER GINGERSNAPS, page 285

FROSTED COOKIE BROWNIES, page 325

WILD PLUM JELLY, page 275

RANGER COOKIES, page 302

PECAN GOODY CUPS, page 313

MACAROON KISSES, page 286

SHORTBREAD LEMON BARS, page 322

CHOCOLATE-DIPPED BROWNIES, page 318

CARAMEL HEAVENLIES, page 318

PECAN MELTAWAYS, page 282

WATERMELON SLICE COOKIES, page 280

LEMON CHEESECAKE SQUARES, page 315

ZUCCHINI RELISH, page 271

HOLIDAY SPRITZ, page 300

[2004]
CHOCOLATE CARAMEL THUMBPRINTS

yield: about 2-1/2 dozen
prep: 25 min. + chilling
bake: 10 min./batch

Covered in chopped nuts and drizzled with chocolate, these cookies are delicious and pretty, too. Everybody looks forward to munching on them during the holidays.

—Elizabeth Marino
San Juan Capistrano, California

- 1/2 cup butter, softened
- 2/3 cup sugar
-   1 egg, separated
-   2 tablespoons 2% milk
-   1 teaspoon vanilla extract
-   1 cup all-purpose flour
- 1/3 cup baking cocoa
- 1/4 teaspoon salt
-   1 cup finely chopped pecans

FILLING:
- 12 to 14 caramels
-   3 tablespoons heavy whipping cream
- 1/2 cup semisweet chocolate chips
-   1 teaspoon shortening

1. In a large bowl, cream butter and sugar until light and fluffy. Beat in the egg yolk, milk and vanilla. Combine the flour, cocoa and salt; gradually add to creamed mixture and mix well. Cover and refrigerate for 1 hour or until easy to handle.

2. Roll into 1-in. balls. Beat egg white. Place egg white in a shallow bowl. Place nuts in another shallow bowl. Dip balls into egg white and coat with nuts.

3. Place 2 in. apart on greased baking sheets. Using the end of a wooden spoon handle, make a 3/8-to 1/2-in. indentation in the center of each ball. Bake at 350° for 10-12 minutes or until set. Remove to wire racks.

4. In a large heavy saucepan, melt caramels with cream over low heat; stir until smooth. Using about 1/2 teaspoon caramel mixture, fill each cookie. In a microwave, melt chocolate chips and shortening; stir until smooth. Drizzle over cookies.

[2001]
BERRY SHORTBREAD DREAMS

yield: about 3-1/2 dozen
prep: 20 min. + chilling
bake: 15 min./batch

Raspberry jam adds fruity sweetness to these rich-tasting cookies.

—Mildred Sherrer
Fort Worth, Texas, Former Field Editor

-   1 cup butter, softened
- 2/3 cup sugar
- 1/2 teaspoon almond extract
-   2 cups all-purpose flour
- 1/3 to 1/2 cup seedless raspberry jam

GLAZE:
-   1 cup confectioners' sugar
- 1/2 teaspoon almond extract
-   2 to 3 teaspoons water

1. In a large bowl, cream butter and sugar until light and fluffy. Beat in extract; gradually add flour until dough forms a ball. Cover and refrigerate for 1 hour or until dough is easy to handle.

2. Roll into 1-in. balls; place 1 in. apart on ungreased baking sheets. Using the end of a wooden spoon handle, make an indentation in centers. Fill with jam. Bake at 350° for 14-18 minutes or until edges are lightly browned. Remove to wire racks.

3. Spoon additional jam into cookies if desired. Mix confectioners' sugar, extract and enough water to achieve drizzling consistency; drizzle over cookies.

CHOCOLATE CARAMEL THUMBPRINTS

"I have frozen these delicious cookies many times with no problems. I love these cookies. They look so pretty sitting on a plate. I have sold them at charity food sales and have people coming back year after year to purchase them."
— *netsie*

[2005]

FRUIT PIZZA SUPREME

yield: 20 servings ∾ **prep: 30 min.**
bake: 10 min. + chilling

*I like to prepare this easy, colorful treat first
thing in the morning when we're expecting
guests that evening.*

—Nina Vilhauer
Mina, South Dakota, Field Editor

- 1 tube (16-1/2 ounces) refrigerated
  sugar cookie dough
- 2 packages (8 ounces *each*) cream
  cheese, softened
- 1 cup confectioners' sugar
- 1 teaspoon vanilla extract
- 1 carton (8 ounces) frozen whipped
  topping, thawed
- 1 cup fresh strawberries, halved
- 1 cup seedless red grapes
- 1 cup fresh blueberries
- 2 kiwifruit, peeled and sliced
- 1 can (11 ounces) mandarin oranges,
  drained
- 1 cup sugar
- 3 tablespoons cornstarch
- 1 cup orange juice
- 1/4 cup unsweetened pineapple juice

---

1. Pat cookie dough onto the bottom of
an ungreased 15-in. x 10-in. x 1-in.
baking pan. Bake at 350° for 10-12
minutes or until deep golden brown.
Cool completely on a wire rack.

2. In a large bowl, beat the cream cheese,
confectioners' sugar and vanilla until
smooth. Fold in whipped topping.
Spread over the crust. Arrange fruit
on top.

3. In a small saucepan, combine the
sugar, cornstarch, orange juice and
pineapple juice until smooth. Bring to
a boil; cook and stir for 2 minutes or
until thickened. Cool; drizzle over
fruit. Refrigerate until chilled.

[2007]

CHOCOLATE CHIP
OATMEAL COOKIES

yield: about 7 dozen ∾ **prep: 20 min.**
bake: 10 min./batch

*Crazy about chocolate chips? This chewy cookie
has plenty, not to mention lots of heart-healthy
oatmeal. The gang will come back repeatedly for
another taste...so this big batch is perfect.*

—Diane Neth, Menno, South Dakota

- 1 cup butter, softened
- 3/4 cup sugar
- 3/4 cup packed brown sugar
- 2 eggs
- 1 teaspoon vanilla extract
- 3 cups quick-cooking oats
- 1-1/2 cups all-purpose flour
- 1 package (3.4 ounces) instant vanilla
  pudding mix
- 1 teaspoon baking soda
- 1 teaspoon salt
- 2 cups (12 ounces) semisweet
  chocolate chips
- 1 cup chopped nuts

---

1. In a large bowl, cream butter and
sugars until light and fluffy. Beat in
eggs and vanilla. Combine the oats,
flour, dry pudding mix, baking soda
and salt; gradually add to creamed
mixture and mix well. Stir in chocolate
chips and nuts.

2. Drop by rounded teaspoonfuls 2 in.
apart onto ungreased baking sheets.
Bake at 375° for 10-12 minutes or until
lightly browned. Remove to wire racks.

[1997]

MOUNTAIN COOKIES
yield: 4 dozen ∞ prep: 30 min.
bake: 10 min./batch + cooling

*I've been making these deliciously different
cookies for over 10 years. My kids especially
like the creamy coconut filling. Wherever I
take these treats to share, people ask for the
recipe. You'll be hard-pressed to eat just one!*

—Jeanne Adams, Richmond, Vermont

- 1 cup butter, softened
- 1 cup confectioners' sugar
- 2 teaspoons vanilla extract
- 2 cups all-purpose flour
- 1/2 teaspoon salt

FILLING:
- 1 package (3 ounces) cream cheese, softened
- 1 cup confectioners' sugar
- 2 tablespoons all-purpose flour
- 1 teaspoon vanilla extract
- 1/2 cup finely chopped pecans
- 1/2 cup flaked coconut

TOPPING:
- 1/2 cup semisweet chocolate chips
- 2 tablespoons butter
- 2 tablespoons water
- 1/2 cup confectioners' sugar

1. In a large bowl, cream butter and sugar until light and fluffy. Beat in vanilla. Combine flour and salt; gradually add to the creamed mixture and mix well.

2. Shape into 1-in. balls; place 2 in. apart on ungreased baking sheets. Make a deep indentation in the center of each cookie. Bake at 350° for 10-12 minutes or until the edges just start to brown. Remove to wire racks to cool completely.

3. For the filling, in a large bowl, beat the cream cheese, sugar, flour and vanilla until smooth. Add pecans and coconut. Spoon 1/2 teaspoon into each cookie.

4. For topping, in a microwave, melt chocolate chips and butter with water; stir until smooth. Stir in sugar. Drizzle over cookies.

[2004]

FROSTED RHUBARB COOKIES
yield: about 5 dozen ∞ prep: 20 min.
bake: 15 min./batch + cooling

*Since these cookies freeze well, I make a lot of
them during rhubarb season. They are best
when you use young tender stalks.*

—Ann Marie Moch
Kintyre, North Dakota, Field Editor

- 1 cup shortening
- 1-1/2 cups packed brown sugar
- 2 eggs
- 3 cups all-purpose flour
- 1 teaspoon baking soda
- 1/2 teaspoon salt
- 1-1/2 cups diced fresh rhubarb
- 3/4 cup flaked coconut

CREAM CHEESE FROSTING:
- 1 package (3 ounces) cream cheese, softened
- 1 tablespoon butter, softened
- 3 teaspoons vanilla extract
- 1-1/2 cups confectioners' sugar

1. In a bowl, cream shortening and brown sugar until light and fluffy. Beat in eggs. Combine the flour, baking soda and salt; gradually add to the creamed mixture.

2. Stir in rhubarb and coconut. Drop by tablespoonfuls 2 in. apart onto greased baking sheets. Bake cookies at 350° for 12-15 minutes or until lightly browned. Remove to wire racks to cool completely.

3. In a large bowl, beat the cream cheese, butter and vanilla. Gradually beat in the confectioners' sugar until smooth. Spread over cooled cookies. Store in the refrigerator.

FROSTED RHUBARB COOKIES

❝I make this every spring/summer and there are never any left!❞
—abbysue

[1998]

DIPPED VANILLAS

yield: about 2-1/2 dozen ∞ prep: 30 min. + chilling
bake: 10 min./batch + chilling

A touch of chocolate makes these classics stand out on the holiday cookie tray. They're a tradition at our home for Christmas.

—*Karen Bourne, Magrath, Alberta, Field Editor*

 1/2 cup butter, softened
 1/2 cup ground almonds
 1/4 cup sugar
   1 teaspoon vanilla extract
   1 cup all-purpose flour
   2 tablespoons cornstarch
   2 ounces semisweet chocolate
 1/2 teaspoon shortening

---

1. In a small bowl, beat the butter, almonds, sugar and vanilla until blended. Gradually add the flour and cornstarch and mix well. Roll into 1-in. balls; shape into crescents and place on greased baking sheets.

2. Bake at 375° for 8-10 minutes or until lightly browned. Remove to wire racks to cool completely.

3. In a microwave, melt chocolate and shortening; stir until smooth. Dip one end of each crescent into chocolate; allow excess to drip off. Place on waxed paper-lined baking sheets. Decorate as desired. Refrigerate for 30 minutes or until set.

[2008]

HOLIDAY SPRITZ

yield: 7 dozen ∞ prep: 30 min. ∞ bake: 10 min./batch

(Pictured on page 296)

I substituted rum extract for vanilla in a classic spritz recipe, and the end result was a cookie that tasted a lot like eggnog.

—*Lisa Varner, Charleston, South Carolina, Field Editor*

---

   1 cup butter, softened
   1 cup confectioners' sugar
   1 egg
 1-1/2 teaspoons rum extract
 2-1/2 cups all-purpose flour
 1/4 teaspoon salt
Colored sugar

---

1. In a large bowl, cream butter and confectioners' sugar until light and fluffy. Beat in egg and extract. Combine flour and salt; gradually add to the creamed mixture and mix well.

2. Using a cookie press fitted with the disk of your choice, press cookies 1 in. apart onto ungreased baking sheets. Sprinkle with colored sugar.

3. Bake at 375° for 6-9 minutes or until lightly browned. Cool cookies for 2 minutes before removing from pans to wire racks.

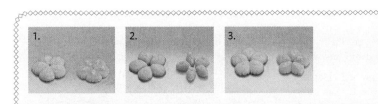

MAKING PERFECTLY SHAPED SPRITZ

If you are making spritz cookies for the first time, it may take some practice with the cookie press to make perfectly shaped cookies.

1. Too Big: The design will lose its form.

2. Too Small: The design will not meet at all the indentations. The cookie will be too small and break easily.

3. Just Right: The baked cookie will have a uniform design and crisp indentations.

[1997]

WHITE VELVET CUTOUTS

yield: about 7 dozen
prep: 25 min. + chilling
bake: 10 min./batch + cooling

We make these cutouts every Christmas and give lots of them as gifts. Last year, we baked a batch a week all through December to be sure we'd have plenty for ourselves, too. These rich cookies melt in your mouth!

—Kim Hinkle, Wauseon, Ohio

---

    2 cups butter, softened
    1 package (8 ounces) cream cheese,
       softened
    2 cups sugar
    2 egg yolks
    1 teaspoon vanilla extract
4-1/2 cups all-purpose flour
BUTTER CREAM FROSTING:
3-1/2 cups confectioners' sugar, *divided*
    3 tablespoons butter, softened
    1 tablespoon shortening
  1/2 teaspoon vanilla extract
    3 to 4 tablespoons 2% milk, *divided*
Red and/or green food coloring, optional

---

1. In a large bowl, cream the butter and cream cheese and sugar until light and fluffy. Beat in egg yolks and vanilla. Gradually add the flour and mix well. Cover and chill 2 hours or until firm.

2. Roll out on a floured surface to 1/4-in. thickness. Cut into 3-in. shapes; place 1 in. apart on greased baking sheets. Bake cookies at 350° for 10-12 minutes or until set (not browned). Cool for 5 minutes before removing from pans to wire racks to cool completely.

3. For frosting, in a large bowl, combine 1-1/2 cups confectioners' sugar, butter, shortening, vanilla and 3 tablespoons milk; beat until smooth. Gradually add remaining sugar; beat until light and fluffy, about 3 minutes. Add enough remaining milk and food coloring until frosting reaches desired consistency. Frost cookies.

[2006]

CHEWY APPLE OATMEAL COOKIES

yield: 4 dozen   prep: 20 min.
bake: 10 min./batch

My family has always loved oatmeal raisin cookies, but I wanted to try something new with the classic recipe. We enjoy apples, and I thought the dried fruit would make a good addition to an oatmeal cookie.

—Jan Marshall, Fenton, Missouri

---

    1 cup butter, softened
    1 cup packed brown sugar
  1/2 cup sugar
    2 eggs
    1 teaspoon vanilla extract
1-1/2 cups all-purpose flour
    2 teaspoons ground cinnamon
    1 teaspoon baking soda
  1/4 teaspoon salt
    3 cups old-fashioned oats
  1/2 cup chopped dried apples

---

1. In a large bowl, cream butter and sugars until light and fluffy. Beat in eggs and vanilla. Combine the flour, cinnamon, baking soda and salt; gradually add to creamed mixture and mix well. Stir in oats and apples.

2. Drop by rounded tablespoonfuls 2 in. apart onto ungreased baking sheets. Bake at 350° for 10-12 minutes or until golden brown. Cool the cookies for 1 minute before removing from pans to wire racks.

WHITE VELVET CUTOUTS

"This is a delicious cookie. Last time I made them, I didn't have time to roll out and cut the cookies, so I rolled the dough into a log, wrapped it in plastic and refrigerated it as the recipe states. I then sliced the cookies into 1/4-inch rounds and baked as directed. They came out perfect!"

—Kristin White

[2012]

TRIPLE-GINGER GINGERSNAPS

yield: 4 dozen ∾ **prep: 35 min. + chilling**
bake: 10 min./batch

I made batch after batch of these soft, chewy gingersnaps to get me through my queasy first trimester of pregnancy. These snaps pack a punch with both crystallized and minced fresh ginger. They keep for weeks in the freezer or up to one week in an airtight container.

—*Jess Follen, Waunakee, Wisconsin*

2/3	cup butter, softened
1	cup packed brown sugar
1/4	cup molasses
1	egg
2	teaspoons minced fresh gingerroot
1	cup all-purpose flour
3/4	cup whole wheat flour
3	teaspoons ground ginger
1-1/2	teaspoons baking soda
1/2	teaspoon fine sea salt *or* kosher salt
1/2	teaspoon ground nutmeg
1/4	teaspoon ground cloves
3	tablespoons crystallized ginger, finely chopped
1/4	cup sugar
1-1/2	teaspoons ground cinnamon

---

1. In a large bowl, cream the butter and brown sugar until light and fluffy. Beat in molasses, egg and fresh ginger. Combine the flours, ground ginger, baking soda, salt, nutmeg and cloves; gradually add to creamed mixture and mix well. Stir in crystallized ginger. Cover and refrigerate for 1 hour or until easy to handle.

2. In a small bowl, combine sugar and cinnamon. Shape dough into 1-in. balls; roll in sugar mixture. Place 3 in. apart on parchment-lined baking sheets. Bake at 350° for 10-12 minutes or until set. Cool for 2 minutes before removing from pans to wire racks.

[2008]

RANGER COOKIES

yield: 7-1/2 dozen ∾ **prep: 25 min.**
bake: 10 min./batch

(Pictured on page 294)

These golden brown cookies are crispy on the outside and cake-like on the inside. Their tasty blend of oats, rice cereal, coconut and brown sugar have made them a favorite with our family. You won't be able to eat just one.

—*Mary Lou Boyce, Wilmington, Delaware*

1	cup shortening
1	cup sugar
1	cup packed brown sugar
2	eggs
1	teaspoon vanilla extract
2	cups all-purpose flour
1	teaspoon baking soda
1/2	teaspoon baking powder
1/2	teaspoon salt
2	cups quick-cooking oats
2	cups crisp rice cereal
1	cup flaked coconut

---

1. In a large bowl, cream the shortening and sugars until light and fluffy. Beat in the eggs and vanilla. Combine the flour, baking soda, baking powder and salt; gradually add to creamed mixture and mix well. Stir in the oats, cereal and coconut.

2. Drop by rounded tablespoonfuls 2 in. apart onto ungreased baking sheets. Bake at 350° for 7-9 minutes or until golden brown. Remove to wire racks.

RANGER COOKIES

"These cookies are great and low-calorie, too (as long as you don't eat eight of them like me)!"

— *rharkless*

[2009]

MOCHA NUT BALLS

yield: 4-1/2 dozen ∞ **prep: 20 min.**
bake: 15 min./batch

*These tender, flavorful cookies are so addictive;
I always know I have to make a double batch.
The family demands it!*

—*Janet Sullivan, Buffalo, New York*

- 1 cup butter, softened
- 1/2 cup sugar
- 2 teaspoons vanilla extract
- 1-3/4 cups all-purpose flour
- 1/3 cup baking cocoa
- 1 tablespoon instant coffee granules
- 1 cup finely chopped pecans *or* walnuts

Confectioners' sugar

1. In a large bowl, cream butter and sugar until light and fluffy. Beat in vanilla. Combine the flour, cocoa and coffee granules; gradually add to creamed mixture and mix well. Stir in pecans. Roll into 1-in. balls. Place 2 in. apart on ungreased baking sheets.

2. Bake at 325° for 14-16 minutes or until firm. Cool for 1-2 minutes before removing from pans to wire racks. Roll warm cookies in confectioners' sugar.

[2005]

PECAN SWIRLS

yield: 7 dozen ∞ **prep: 25 min. + chilling**
bake: 10 min. + cooling

*Cream cheese makes the cookies rich and
tender, and the sweet filling showcases pecans.*

—*Wanda Rascoe, Shreveport, Louisiana*

- 2 cups butter, softened
- 2 packages (8 ounces ea*ch*) cream cheese, softened
- 2 teaspoons vanilla extract
- 4 cups all-purpose flour
- 1/2 teaspoon salt
- 2-1/4 cups finely chopped pecans
- 1-1/3 cups sugar

1. In a large bowl, cream the butter and cream cheese until light and fluffy. Beat in vanilla. Combine flour and salt; gradually add to creamed mixture and mix well. Divide into three portions. Wrap each in plastic wrap; refrigerate for 2 hours or until easy to handle.

2. On a lightly floured surface, roll each portion into a 16-in. x 9-in. rectangle. Combine pecans and sugar; sprinkle over dough to within 1/2 in. of edges. Roll up each rectangle tightly jelly-roll style, starting with a long side. Wrap in plastic wrap; refrigerate for 2 hours.

3. Unwrap and cut into 3/8-in. slices. Place 2-in. apart on lightly greased baking sheets. Bake at 400° for 12-14 minutes or until lightly browned. Remove to wire racks.

[1999]

EASY PEANUT BUTTER COOKIES

yield: about 2 dozen
prep/total time: 30 min.

*With only four ingredients, these cookies
couldn't be easier for our son, Jacob, to help
whip up. He thinks it's fun helping prepare
meals and snacks.*

—*Valerie Ellsworth, Belvidere, Illinois*

- 1 cup peanut butter
- 1 cup sugar
- 1 egg
- 1 teaspoon vanilla extract

1. In a large bowl, cream peanut butter and sugar until light and fluffy, about 4 minutes. Beat in the egg and vanilla.

2. Shape level tablespoonfuls into balls. Place 2 in. apart on ungreased baking sheets; flatten with a fork. Bake at 350° for 16-18 minutes or until set. Cool for 5 minutes before removing from pans to wire racks.

EASY PEANUT BUTTER COOKIES

"I've made these, and it really is just four ingredients...amazed me, too, but they are really, really good. I'm going to add chopped peanuts to my next batch."
—*sharonbolden*

[1998]

PISTACHIO THUMBPRINTS

yield: about 7 dozen   prep: 45 min.
bake: 10 min./batch

These mild pistachio-flavored cookies disappear in a wink.

—*Elizabeth Probelski*
Port Washington, Wisconsin

---

  1 **cup butter, softened**
1/3 **cup confectioners' sugar**
  1 **egg**
  1 **teaspoon vanilla extract**
3/4 **teaspoon almond extract**
  2 **cups all-purpose flour**
  1 **package (3.4 ounces) instant pistachio pudding mix**
1/2 **cup miniature chocolate chips**
  2 **cups finely chopped pecans**
FILLING:
  2 **tablespoons butter, softened**
  2 **cups confectioners' sugar**
  1 **teaspoon vanilla extract**
  2 **to 3 tablespoons 2% milk**
GLAZE:
1/2 **cup semisweet chocolate chips**
  2 **teaspoons shortening**

---

1. In a large bowl, cream butter and sugar until smooth and fluffy. Beat in the egg and extracts. Combine the flour and dry pudding mix; gradually add to the creamed mixture and mix well. Stir in the chocolate chips.

2. Shape into 1-in. balls; roll in nuts. Place 2 in. apart on greased baking sheets; make a thumbprint in center of each cookie. Bake at 350° for 10-12 minutes. Remove to wire racks to cool completely.

3. For filling, in a bowl, beat the butter, confectioners' sugar, vanilla and enough of the milk to achieve desired consistency. Spoon into the center of cooled cookies.

4. For glaze, if desired, melt the chocolate chips and shortening in a microwave and stir until smooth. Drizzle over the cookies. Let stand until set.

[2006]

FUDGY MINT COOKIES

yield: about 3 dozen   prep: 10 min.
bake: 10 min./batch + cooling

Chocolate lovers will get a double dose with this tender cake-like cookie and its chocolate mint middle. They're especially popular served with a big scoop of mint chocolate chip ice cream!

—*Renee Schwebach*
Dumont, Minnesota, Field Editor

---

  1 **package (18-1/4 ounces) devil's food cake mix**
1/2 **cup butter, softened**
  1 **tablespoon water**
  2 **eggs**
  2 **tablespoons confectioners' sugar**
  2 **packages (5 ounces *each*) chocolate-covered thin mints**

---

1. In a large bowl, beat the cake mix, butter and water until well combined. Beat in eggs. Shape into 1-in. balls; roll in confectioners' sugar. Place 2 in. apart on ungreased baking sheets.

2. Bake at 375° for 8-10 minutes or until set. Immediately press a mint into the center of each cookie. Cool for 2 minutes before removing from pans to wire racks.

[2003]

RASPBERRY RIBBONS

yield: about 5 dozen ∞ **prep: 20 min.**
bake: 20 min. + cooling

*I make these attractive, buttery cookies to serve
at our remote guest lodge, and all the girls in
the kitchen are addicted to them!*

—*Patsy Wolfenden*
Golden, British Columbia

---

1 **cup butter, softened**
1/2 **cup sugar**
1 **egg**
1 **teaspoon vanilla extract**
2-1/4 **cups all-purpose flour**
1/2 **teaspoon baking powder**
1/4 **teaspoon salt**
1/2 **cup raspberry jam**
GLAZE:
1 **cup confectioners' sugar**
2 **tablespoons evaporated milk**
1/2 **teaspoon vanilla extract**

---

1. In a large bowl, cream butter and sugar until light and fluffy. Beat in egg and vanilla. Combine flour, baking powder and salt; gradually add to the creamed mixture and mix well.

2. Divide the dough into four portions; shape each into a 10-in. x 2-1/2-in. log. Place 4 in. apart on greased or foil-lined baking sheets. Make a 1/2-in. depression down the center of each log. Bake at 350° for 10 minutes.

3. Fill the depressions with jam. Bake 10-15 minutes longer or until lightly browned. Cool for 2 minutes. Remove to a cutting board; cut the logs into 3/4-in. slices. Place on wire racks.

4. In a small bowl, combine the glaze ingredients. Drizzle over the warm cookies. Cool completely.

[1993]

SCOTCH SHORTBREAD COOKIES

yield: 4 dozen ∞ **prep: 15 min.**
bake: 25 min.

(Pictured on page 289)

*This simple three-ingredient recipe makes
wonderfully rich, tender cookies. Serve them
with fresh berries of the season for a nice, light
dessert. You'll get smiles when you provide
these for afternoon tea or a bridal shower.*

—*Marlene Hellickson*
Big Bear City, California

---

4 **cups all-purpose flour**
1 **cup sugar**
1 **pound cold butter, cubed**

---

1. In a large bowl, combine the flour and sugar. Cut in the butter until mixture resembles fine crumbs. Knead dough until smooth, about 6-10 times. Pat dough into an ungreased 15-in. x 10-in. x 1-in. baking pan. Pierce with a fork.

2. Bake at 325° for 25-30 minutes or until lightly browned. Cut into squares while warm. Remove to wire racks.

Editor's Note: This recipe makes a dense, crisp bar, so it does not call for baking powder or baking soda.

SHORTBREAD COOKIES

Shortbread relies on butter to impart its wonderful, rich flavor and the buttery, melt-in-your-mouth quality. It is not time to economize when making these cookies. Use real good-quality stick butter; otherwise, you may be disappointed with the results.

—*Taste of Home Cooking Experts*

SCOTCH SHORTBREAD COOKIES

"These could not be any easier to make or more delicious to eat. This was my first time making shortbreads and they could not have been any better. Best ones I've ever had!"
—*MelissaV81*

COLOSSAL BATCH OF OATMEAL COOKIES

"These were wonderful! I did make a couple dozen plain, and they were great! I did not put in the nuts, just chips. I used a medium Pampered Chef scoop for mine, and it made eight dozen. Will be my oatmeal cookie recipe from now on!"

—wefarm2live

[2001]

CHRISTMAS SUGAR COOKIES

yield: about 8 dozen
prep: 20 min. + chilling
bake: 10 min./batch + cooling

Sour cream keeps my favorite sugar cookies extra moist. Dress them up with a drizzle of tinted white chocolate, or dip them in white chocolate, then sprinkle with crushed candy canes.

—Lisa MacLean, Winslow, Arizona

1	cup butter, softened
2	cups confectioners' sugar
1	egg
1/4	cup sour cream
1/4	cup honey
2	teaspoons vanilla extract
3-1/2	cups all-purpose flour
1	teaspoon baking soda
1	teaspoon cream of tartar
1/2	teaspoon ground mace
1/8	teaspoon salt

White candy coating
Green paste food coloring

1. In a large bowl, cream butter and sugar until light and fluffy. Beat in egg. Beat in the sour cream, honey and vanilla. Combine dry ingredients; gradually add to creamed mixture and mix well. Cover and chill for 2 hours or until easy to handle.

2. On a lightly floured surface, roll out dough to 1/8-in. thickness. Cut with a floured 3-in. cookie cutter. Place 1 in. apart on ungreased baking sheets.

3. Bake at 325° for 8-10 minutes or until lightly browned. Remove to wire racks to cool completely.

4. In a microwave, melt white coating; stir until smooth. Stir in food coloring; drizzle over cookies.

[2009]

COLOSSAL BATCH OF OATMEAL COOKIES

yield: about 13-1/2 dozen ⌇ prep: 20 min.
bake: 10 min./batch

I divide this dough into thirds and make three different types of cookies—one with chocolate chips and nuts, one with raisins and one with butterscotch chips.

—Lisa Cooper, Paris, Texas

2	cups butter, softened
3/4	cup butter-flavored shortening
3-1/4	cups packed brown sugar
1-1/4	cups sugar
5	eggs
2/3	cup buttermilk
4	teaspoons vanilla extract
6	cups quick-cooking oats
5-3/4	cups all-purpose flour
1	tablespoon baking soda
2-1/2	teaspoons salt
1	package (10 to 11 ounces) butterscotch chips
1	cup chopped pecans

1. In a very large bowl, cream the butter, shortening and sugars until light and fluffy. Beat in the eggs, buttermilk and vanilla. Combine the oats, flour, baking soda and salt; gradually add to the creamed mixture and mix well. Stir in chips and pecans.

2. Drop by rounded tablespoonfuls 3 in. apart onto ungreased baking sheets. Bake at 375° for 10-12 minutes or until golden brown. Remove to wire racks.

[2007]
PISTACHIO CRANBERRY BISCOTTI

yield: 16 cookies ∞ **prep: 15 min. + chilling**
bake: 35 min. + cooling

My friends were delighted to receive batches of this fruit and nut biscotti mix as gifts. Layer the dry ingredients in a clear jar, add a bow and attach the instructions for preparation and baking.

—**Dawn Fagerstrom**
Warren, Minnesota, Field Editor

- 2 **cups all-purpose flour**
- 2 **teaspoons baking powder**
- 1/2 **teaspoon ground cinnamon**
- 2/3 **cup sugar, *divided***
- 3/4 **cup pistachios**
- 3/4 **cup dried cranberries *or* cherries**

ADDITIONAL INGREDIENTS:
- 1/3 **cup butter, softened**
- 2 **eggs**

1. Combine flour and baking powder; pour into a wide-mouth 1-qt. glass container with a tight-fitting lid. Sprinkle cinnamon around edge of container. Layer with 1/3 cup sugar, pistachios and cranberries, packing each layer tightly (do not mix). Pour remaining sugar down the center. Cover and store in a cool dry place for up to 6 months.

2. To prepare biscotti: In a large bowl, beat butter and eggs. Gradually stir in biscotti mix (dough will be sticky). Chill for 30 minutes.

3. Divide dough in half. On an ungreased baking sheet, shape each half into a 10-in. x 2-in. rectangle. Bake at 350° for 25-30 minutes or until firm. Cool for 5 minutes.

4. Transfer to a cutting board; cut diagonally with a serrated knife into 3/4-in.-thick slices. Place cut side

down on an ungreased baking sheet. Bake for 5 minutes. Turn and bake 5-6 minutes longer or until golden brown. Remove to wire racks to cool. Store in an airtight container.

[2008]
COCONUT CRUNCH COOKIES

yield: about 4-1/2 dozen ∞ **prep: 30 min.**
bake: 10 min./batch

These sweet drop cookies are loaded with coconut and chocolate chips. Their crisp edges and soft centers add up to a perfect cookie.

—**Maria Regakis**
Somerville, Massachusetts, Field Editor

- 1 **cup butter, softened**
- 3/4 **cup sugar**
- 3/4 **cup packed brown sugar**
- 2 **eggs**
- 2 **teaspoons vanilla extract**
- 1 **teaspoon almond extract**
- 2 **cups all-purpose flour**
- 1 **teaspoon baking soda**
- 3/4 **teaspoon salt**
- 2 **cups flaked coconut**
- 1 **package (11-1/2 ounces) milk chocolate chips**
- 1-1/2 **cups finely chopped almonds**

1. In a large bowl, cream the butter and sugars until light and fluffy. Beat in eggs and extracts. Combine the flour, baking soda and salt; gradually add to the creamed mixture and mix well. Stir in the coconut, chocolate chips and almonds.

2. Drop by rounded teaspoonfuls 2 in. apart onto ungreased baking sheets. Bake at 375° for 9-11 minutes or until lightly browned. Cool the cookies for 1 minute before removing from pans to wire racks.

COCONUT CRUNCH COOKIES

"These cookies are more than good—they are so flavorful. Chocolate, coconut and almonds—like an Almond Joy in a cookie. Crisp on the bottom and soft in the middle. After making them at home, I made them for an office party, and they were a big hit. Did not modify the recipe; did not see the need to. I have to control myself from eating too many."
—*soulfulcook*

[2002]

GINGERBREAD SNOWFLAKES

yield: about 5 dozen
prep: 30 min. + chilling
bake: 10 min./batch

Cutting my favorite gingerbread cookie dough into snowflake shapes and decorating them with white icing was ideal for a winter-themed get-together I hosted. I like to share these crunchy treats on the way home from cutting our fresh Christmas tree.

—Shelly Rynearson
Oconomowoc, Wisconsin

- 1 cup butter, softened
- 1 cup sugar
- 1 cup molasses
- 1/4 cup water
- 5 cups all-purpose flour
- 2-1/2 teaspoons ground ginger
- 1-1/2 teaspoons baking soda
- 1-1/2 teaspoons ground cinnamon
- 1/2 teaspoon ground allspice
- 1/4 teaspoon salt

FROSTING:
- 3-3/4 cups confectioners' sugar
- 1/4 cup water
- 1-1/2 teaspoons light corn syrup
- 1/2 teaspoon vanilla extract

1. In a large bowl, cream butter and sugar until light and fluffy. Beat in molasses and water. Combine the flour, ginger, baking soda, cinnamon, allspice and salt; gradually add to creamed mixture and mix well. Cover and refrigerate for 1 hour or until easy to handle.

2. On a lightly floured surface, roll out to 1/4-in. thickness. Cut with 2-1/2-in. cookie cutters dipped in flour. Place 2 in. apart on ungreased baking sheets.

3. Bake at 350° for 10-12 minutes or until edges are firm. Remove to wire racks.

4. In a small bowl, combine the frosting ingredients; beat until smooth. Transfer to a plastic bag. Cut a small hole in a corner of the bag; pipe the frosting onto the cookies.

[2006]

ALMOND COOKIES

yield: 3 dozen   **prep: 10 min.**
bake: 10 min./batch + cooling

I began making these delightful cookies after enjoying similar ones at my favorite Chinese restaurant. They're crisp and have a wonderful almond flavor.

—Beverly Preston, Fond du Lac, Wisconsin

- 1 cup shortening
- 1/2 cup plus 3 tablespoons sugar, *divided*
- 1/4 cup packed brown sugar
- 1 egg
- 1 teaspoon almond extract
- 2 cups all-purpose flour
- 1-1/2 teaspoons baking powder
- 1/8 teaspoon salt
- 3 tablespoons sliced almonds

1. In a small bowl, cream the shortening, 1/2 cup sugar and brown sugar until light and fluffy. Beat in egg and extract. Combine the flour, baking powder and salt; gradually add to creamed mixture and mix well.

2. Shape into 1-in. balls. Roll in remaining sugar. Place 2 in. apart on ungreased baking sheets. Flatten with the bottom of a glass. Press three almond slices into the center of each.

3. Bake at 350° for 9-11 minutes or until edges are lightly browned. Cool the cookies for 2 minutes before removing from pans to wire racks.

[1993]

MOM'S SOFT RAISIN COOKIES

yield: 6 dozen ✑ **prep: 25 min.**
bake: 15 min.

With four sons in the service during World War II, my mother sent these favorite cookies as a taste from home to "her boys" in different parts of the world. These days, my grandchildren are enjoying them as we did, along with my stories of long ago.

—**Pearl Cochenour, Williamsport, Ohio**

- 2 **cups raisins**
- 1 **cup water**
- 1 **cup shortening**
- 1-3/4 **cups sugar**
- 2 **eggs, lightly beaten**
- 1 **teaspoon vanilla extract**
- 3-1/2 **cups all-purpose flour**
- 1 **teaspoon baking powder**
- 1 **teaspoon baking soda**
- 1 **teaspoon salt**
- 1/2 **teaspoon ground cinnamon**
- 1/2 **teaspoon ground nutmeg**
- 1/2 **cup chopped walnuts**

1. Combine raisins and water in a small saucepan; bring to a boil. Cook for 3 minutes; remove from the heat and let cool (do not drain).

2. In a large bowl, cream shortening and sugar until light and fluffy. Beat in eggs and vanilla. Combine dry ingredients; gradually add to creamed mixture and mix well. Stir in nuts and raisins.

3. Drop by teaspoonfuls 2 in. apart on greased baking sheets. Bake at 350° for 12-14 minutes. Remove to wire racks.

[1999]

DAD'S CHOCOLATE CHIP COOKIES

yield: 5 dozen ✑ **prep: 15 min.**
bake: 10 min./batch

These hearty classic chocolate chip cookies were always a favorite at our house.

—**Art Winter, Trumbull, Connecticut**

- 1/3 **cup butter, softened**
- 2/3 **cup shortening**
- 1 **cup sugar**
- 1 **cup packed brown sugar**
- 2 **eggs**
- 2 **teaspoons vanilla extract**
- 3-1/2 **cups all-purpose flour**
- 1 **teaspoon salt**
- 1 **teaspoon baking soda**
- 2 **cups (12 ounces) semisweet chocolate chips**
- 1 **cup chopped walnuts**

1. In a large bowl, cream the butter, shortening and sugars until light and fluffy. Beat in the eggs and vanilla. Combine flour, salt and baking soda; gradually add to creamed mixture and mix well. Stir in the chocolate chips and nuts.

2. Drop by rounded tablespoonfuls onto ungreased baking sheets. Bake at 350° for 10-11 minutes or until golden brown. Remove to wire racks.

SCOOP THE COOKIE DOUGH

For uniform-sized drop cookies use an ice cream scoop. A 1-tablespoon size scoop is perfect to make 2-inch cookies. Scrape the excess dough from the top of the scoop, or the cookies will not be identical.

—*Taste of Home Cooking Experts*

DAD'S CHOCOLATE CHIP COOKIES

"This is an excellent recipe. My daughter and I made them and they turned out delicious. We used half white chocolate chips and half mini chocolate chips. We also sprayed the pans, even though it says 'ungreased.' A++++++ "
—*winnafrog3*

BUTTER COOKIES

"Consistently requested and appropriate for every occasion. Sooo rich but uber delicious and quite simply, in my opinion, the best iced cookies ever."

—*Hayleigh*

[1999]

CINNAMON CRACKLE COOKIES

yield: about 6 dozen ∾ prep: 15 min.
bake: 10 min./batch

A blend of cinnamon, nutmeg and orange plus lemon peel gives these sugar cookies excellent flavor. Keep a batch in the freezer for a special and speedy snack.

—*Vicki Lair, Albert Lea, Minnesota*

1/2	cup butter, softened
1/2	cup shortening
1	cup sugar
1/2	cup packed brown sugar
1	egg
1	teaspoon vanilla extract
1/2	teaspoon almond extract
2-1/2	cups all-purpose flour
1	tablespoon ground cinnamon
2	teaspoons baking soda
2	teaspoons cream of tartar
2	teaspoons ground nutmeg
2	teaspoons grated orange peel
1	teaspoon grated lemon peel
1/2	teaspoon salt

Additional sugar

1. In a large bowl, cream the butter, shortening and sugars until light and fluffy. Beat in the egg and extracts. Combine the flour, cinnamon, baking soda, cream of tartar, nutmeg, orange and lemon peel and salt; gradually add to the creamed mixture.

2. Shape into 1-in. balls; roll in additional sugar. Place 2 in. apart on ungreased baking sheets. Bake at 350° for 10-15 minutes or until lightly browned. Remove to wire racks to cool.

[1997]

BUTTER COOKIES

yield: about 6-1/2 dozen ∾ prep: 25 min.
bake: 10 min.

These cookies are favorites of my nephews, who love the creamy frosting.

—*Ruth Griggs, South Hill, Virginia*

1	cup butter, softened
3/4	cup sugar
1	egg
1/2	teaspoon vanilla extract
2-1/2	cups all-purpose flour
1	teaspoon baking powder
1/4	teaspoon salt

FROSTING:

1/2	cup butter, softened
4	cups confectioners' sugar
1	teaspoon vanilla extract
3	to 4 tablespoons 2% milk

Red food coloring, optional

1. In a large bowl, cream butter and sugar until light and fluffy. Beat in egg and vanilla. Combine the flour, baking powder and salt; add to creamed mixture and mix well.

2. Place the dough in a cookie press fitted with a heart plate; form cookies on ungreased baking sheets. Bake at 375° for 6-8 minutes or until set but not brown. Remove to wire racks to cool completely.

3. Beat butter, sugar and vanilla until smooth. Blend in enough milk to reach desired spreading consistency. Add food coloring to a portion or all of the frosting if desired. Frost cookies.

[2009]

ITALIAN COOKIES

yield: 7 dozen ∞ prep: 20 min.
bake: 10 min./ batch + cooling

My 100% Italian husband will tell you these are his favorite cookies. I make them often and definitely every Christmas (if not, people get upset). They're good with or without the icing and sprinkles.

—Marie Forte
Raritan, New Jersey, Field Editor

1/2	pound butter, softened
1/2	cup sugar
6	eggs
2	teaspoons vanilla *or* anise extract
4	cups all-purpose flour
4	teaspoons baking powder

ICING:

3-3/4	cups confectioners' sugar
2	teaspoons vanilla extract
5	to 6 tablespoons 2% milk

DECORATIONS:

Flaked coconut *or* assorted sprinkles

1. In a large bowl, cream butter and sugar until light and fluffy. Beat in eggs and extract. Combine the flour and baking powder; gradually add to the creamed mixture and mix well.

2. Drop by rounded teaspoonfuls onto ungreased baking sheets. Bake at 350° for 9-11 minutes or until bottoms are lightly browned. Remove to wire racks to cool completely.

3. For icing, in a small bowl, combine the confectioners' sugar, vanilla and enough of the milk to achieve desired consistency. Dip cookies in icing; allow excess to drip off. Place on waxed paper; decorate as desired. Let stand until set.

[2006]

CHIPPY PEANUT BUTTER COOKIES

yield: about 4 dozen ∞ prep: 25 min.
bake: 15 min./batch

"Hey, these are good!" is the happy remark I often hear when I cook or bake for my family. As simple as it may seem, all I do is follow directions. This works exceptionally well when it comes to making cookies. I've learned to modify recipes, too, which is what I did to create these chewy treats.

—Ian Badeer, Hickman, Nebraska

1	cup butter, softened
1	cup creamy peanut butter
1	cup sugar
1	cup packed brown sugar
2	eggs
1	teaspoon vanilla extract
2-1/4	cups all-purpose flour
2	teaspoons baking soda
1/4	teaspoon salt
1	package (10 ounces) swirled milk chocolate and peanut butter chips

1. In a large bowl, cream the butter, peanut butter and sugars until light and fluffy. Beat in eggs and vanilla. Combine the flour, baking soda and salt; gradually add to creamed mixture and mix well. Stir in chips.

2. Drop by rounded tablespoonfuls onto ungreased baking sheets. Bake at 350° for 12-15 minutes or until golden brown. Cool for 2 minutes before removing from pans to wire racks.

Editor's Note: This recipe was tested with Nestle swirled milk chocolate and peanut butter chips.

CHIPPY PEANUT BUTTER COOKIES

"I have made other peanut butter cookies before, and my husband and I agree that these have the best dough. I did not have the swirled chips, so I used half chocolate chips and half peanut butter chips. These are so good we have a hard time not sneaking a few every time we walk in the kitchen. I will be making these again soon because chocolate and peanut butter go great together."
—lvmyhbby

CHEWY BROWNIE COOKIES

"I made 18 dozen of these cookies to give away at Christmas, and they are easy and delicious. Highly recommend these. The texture is great and they are plump, not flat, cookies. Super recipe and a definite keeper."
—jthibeau

[2004]

LEMON MELTAWAYS
yield: about 5 dozen
prep: 15 min. + chilling
bake: 10 min.

Both the cookie and the frosting are sparked with fabulous lemon in these melt-in-your-mouth goodies.

—*Mary Houchin*
Lebanon, Illinois, Field Editor

3/4 cup butter, softened
1/3 cup confectioners' sugar
1 teaspoon lemon juice
1-1/4 cups all-purpose flour
1/2 cup cornstarch
FROSTING:
1/4 cup butter, softened
3/4 cup confectioners' sugar
1 teaspoon lemon juice
1 teaspoon grated lemon peel
1 to 3 drops yellow food coloring, optional

---

1. In a large bowl, cream the butter and confectioners' sugar until light and fluffy; beat in lemon juice. Combine flour and cornstarch; gradually add to the creamed mixture and mix well. Shape into two 8-in. rolls; wrap each roll in plastic wrap. Refrigerate for 2 hours or until firm.

2. Unwrap dough and cut into 1/4-in. slices. Place 2 in. apart on ungreased baking sheets. Bake at 350° for 8-12 minutes or until the cookies are firm to the touch. Remove to wire racks to cool completely.

3. For frosting, in a small bowl, beat the butter and confectioners' sugar until smooth. Stir in the lemon juice, lemon peel and food coloring if desired. Frost cooled cookies.

[1994]

CHEWY BROWNIE COOKIES
yield: 3 dozen ∞ prep: 10 min.
bake: 10 min./batch

(*Pictured on page 289*)

Biting into these chocolaty cookies reveals they're like chewy brownies inside.

—*Jonie Adams, Albion, Michigan*

2/3 cup shortening
1-1/2 cups packed brown sugar
2 eggs
1 tablespoon water
3 teaspoons vanilla extract
1-1/2 cups all-purpose flour
1/3 cup baking cocoa
1/2 teaspoon salt
1/4 teaspoon baking soda
2 cups (12 ounces) semisweet chocolate chips
1/2 cup chopped walnuts *or* pecans, optional

---

1. In a large bowl, cream shortening and sugar until light and fluffy. Beat in the eggs, water and vanilla. Combine the flour, cocoa, salt and baking soda; gradually add to creamed mixture and beat just until blended. Stir in the chocolate chips and nuts if desired.

2. Drop by rounded teaspoonfuls 2 in. apart on ungreased baking sheets. Bake at 375° for 7-9 minutes; do not overbake. Cool for 2 minutes before removing from pans to wire racks.

[2005]

ROSETTES

yield: about 2-1/2 dozen ∽ **prep: 10 min.**
cook: 1 hour

Shaped like delicate snowflakes, these crisp rosettes make a lovely winter dessert. We make these Norwegian treats for Christmas and special occasions.

—Rita Christianson
   Glenburn, North Dakota, Field Editor

---

   2 **eggs**
   1 **cup 2% milk**
   1 **teaspoon sugar**
 1/4 **teaspoon salt**
   1 **cup all-purpose flour**
Oil for deep-fat frying
Confectioners' sugar

---

1. In a small bowl, beat the eggs, milk, sugar and salt. Gradually add flour; beat until smooth.

2. In a deep-fat fryer or electric skillet, heat 2-1/2 in. of oil to 375°. Place the rosette iron in hot oil for 30 seconds. Blot iron on paper towels, then dip the iron in batter to three-fourths the way up the sides (do not let batter run over top of iron). Immediately place in hot oil; loosen the rosette with fork and remove iron.

3. Fry for 1-2 minutes on each side or until golden brown. Remove to a wire rack covered with paper towels. Repeat with remaining batter. Sprinkle with confectioners' sugar before serving.

[2006]

PECAN GOODY CUPS

yield: 4 dozen ∽ **prep: 35 min. + chilling**
bake: 20 min./batch

(Pictured on page 294)

These miniature tarts feature whole pecans, a caramel-like filling and a buttery cream cheese crust. They're sure to disappear fast at Christmas or anytime.

—Janice Hose, Hagerstown, Maryland

 3/4 **cup butter, softened**
   2 **packages (3 ounces each) cream cheese, softened**
   2 **cups all-purpose flour**
FILLING:
1-1/2 **cups packed brown sugar**
   2 **eggs**
   1 **tablespoon butter, melted**
  48 **pecan halves**

---

1. In a large bowl, beat the butter and cream cheese until light and fluffy. Gradually add the flour, beating until the mixture forms a ball. Cover and refrigerate for 15 minutes.

2. For filling, in a small bowl, combine the brown sugar, eggs and butter.

3. Roll dough into 1-in. balls. Press onto the bottoms and up the sides of greased miniature muffin cups. Spoon filling into the cups; top each with a pecan half.

4. Bake at 350° for 20-25 minutes or until golden brown. Cool the cookie for 2-3 minutes before removing from pans to wire racks.

ROSETTES

❝Just like my Italian grandma and aunts used to make :)❞
—JMartinelli13

CHUNKY BLOND BROWNIES

"My boyfriend says this recipe actually deserves six stars."
—casserroll

[2007]

SUNFLOWER-CHERRY GRANOLA BARS

yield: 2-1/2 dozen ∞ prep: 30 min. + cooling

These chewy granola bars have plenty of fiber; the cherries add just the right amount of tang.

—*Laura McDowell, Lake Villa, Illinois*

4	cups old-fashioned oats
1	cup sliced almonds
1	cup flaked coconut
1	cup sugar
1	cup light corn syrup
1	cup creamy peanut butter
1/2	cup raisins
1/2	cup dried cherries
1/2	cup sunflower kernels

---

1. Spread oats into an ungreased 15-in. x 10-in. x 1-in. baking pan. Bake at 400° for 15-20 minutes or until lightly browned. Meanwhile, spread almonds and coconut into another ungreased 15-in. x 10-in. x 1-in. baking pan. Bake for 8-10 minutes or until lightly toasted.

2. In a Dutch oven over medium heat, bring sugar and corn syrup to a boil. Cook and stir for 2-3 minutes or until sugar is dissolved. Remove from the heat; stir in the peanut butter until combined. Add the raisins, cherries, sunflower kernels, and toasted oats, almonds and coconut.

3. Using a metal spatula, press mixture into an ungreased 15-in. x 10-in. x 1-in. baking pan. Cool in pan on a wire rack to room temperature. Cut into bars.

[1998]

CHUNKY BLOND BROWNIES

yield: 2 dozen ∞ prep: 15 min.
bake: 25 min. + cooling

Every bite of these blondies is packed with chunks of white and semisweet chocolate and macadamia nuts. It's a treat that stands out.

—*Rosemary Dreiske*
Lemmon, South Dakota

1/2	cup butter, softened
3/4	cup sugar
3/4	cup packed brown sugar
2	eggs
2	teaspoons vanilla extract
1-1/2	cups all-purpose flour
1	teaspoon baking powder
1/2	teaspoon salt
1	cup white baking chips
1	cup semisweet chocolate chunks
1	jar (3 ounces) macadamia nuts *or* 3/4 cup blanched almonds, chopped, *divided*

---

1. In a large bowl, cream the butter and sugars until light and fluffy. Beat in the eggs and vanilla. Combine the flour, baking powder and salt; gradually add to creamed mixture and mix well. Stir in white chips, chocolate chunks and 1/2 cup nuts.

2. Spoon into a greased 13-in. x 9-in. baking pan; spread over the bottom of pan. Sprinkle with the remaining nuts. Bake at 350° for 25-30 minutes or until top begins to crack and is golden brown. Cool in pan on a wire rack; cut into bars.

SOFTENED BUTTER

When a recipe calls for softened butter, it should be soft enough that a knife easily glides through it. If it was heated in the microwave and there are small pools of melted butter, let it solidify before using.

—*Taste of Home Cooking Experts*

[2001]

LEMON CHEESECAKE SQUARES

yield: 20 servings   **prep: 15 min.**
bake: 30 min.

(Pictured on page 296)

Whether I'm hosting friends or sending a plate to work with my husband, these creamy, elegant cheesecake squares are always a hit. It's a wonderful make-ahead dessert that easily serves a large group.

—*Peggy Reddick, Cumming, Georgia*

- 3/4 cup shortening
- 1/3 cup packed brown sugar
- 1-1/4 cups all-purpose flour
- 1 cup rolled oats
- 1/4 teaspoon salt
- 1/2 cup seedless raspberry jam

FILLING:

- 4 packages (8 ounces each) cream cheese, softened
- 1-1/2 cups sugar
- 1/4 cup all-purpose flour
- 1/3 cup lemon juice
- 4 teaspoons grated lemon peel
- 4 eggs, lightly beaten

1. In a large bowl, cream shortening and brown sugar until light and fluffy. Combine the flour, oats and salt; gradually add to the creamed mixture and mix well.

2. Press dough into a greased 13-in. x 9-in. baking dish. Bake at 350° for 15-18 minutes or until golden brown. Spread with jam.

3. Meanwhile, in a large bowl, beat the cream cheese, sugar and flour until smooth. Beat in lemon juice and peel. Add eggs; beat on low speed just until combined. Carefully spoon over jam.

4. Bake at 350° for 30-35 minutes or until center is almost set. Cool in pan on a wire rack. Store in the refrigerator.

[2007]

GLAZED PEANUT BUTTER BARS

yield: 4 dozen   **prep: 15 min.**
bake: 20 min. + cooling

Memories of lunchtime at school and my Aunt Shelly's kitchen come to mind when I bite into these sweet, chewy bars. My husband is the biggest fan of these PB and chocolate treats.

—*Janis Luedtke, Westminster, Colorado*

- 3/4 cup butter, softened
- 3/4 cup creamy peanut butter
- 3/4 cup sugar
- 3/4 cup packed brown sugar
- 2 eggs
- 2 teaspoons water
- 1-1/2 teaspoons vanilla extract
- 1-1/2 cups all-purpose flour
- 1-1/2 cups quick-cooking oats
- 3/4 teaspoon baking soda
- 1/2 teaspoon salt

GLAZE:

- 1-1/4 cups milk chocolate chips
- 1/2 cup butterscotch chips
- 1/2 cup creamy peanut butter

1. In a large bowl, cream the butter, peanut butter and sugars until light and fluffy, about 4 minutes. Beat in the eggs, water and vanilla. Combine flour, oats, baking soda and salt; gradually add to creamed mixture and mix well.

2. Spread into a greased 15-in. x 10-in. x 1-in. baking pan. Bake at 325° for 18-22 minutes or until lightly browned.

3. For glaze, in a microwave, melt chips and peanut butter; stir until smooth. Pour over warm bars; spread evenly. Cool completely in pan on a wire rack before cutting.

LEMON CHEESECAKE SQUARES

"I was thrilled the first time I made these bars when my husband said that they were pretty good! I love lemon, but he usually doesn't care for it. These bars are the exception. Besides the wonderful, not-too-strong lemon flavor, these also have a wonderful creamy consistency. The layer of jam is a nice touch, which you can increase to 2/3 cup if desired."

—*HeatherHH*

CHEWY PEANUT
BUTTER BARS

"My family has enjoyed this recipe since it first came out years ago. Sometimes I melt butterscotch chips with semisweet and spread on top and chill a bit. Or I cut in triangles and dip half in the same mixture or just chocolate alone, although mainly we just enjoy this chewy treat as is."
—ekladar

[2007]

HAZELNUT MOCHA BROWNIES

yield: 16 servings ⁓ **prep: 35 min.**
bake: 25 min. + chilling

Flavored instant coffee adds great taste to this brownie recipe I made up while cooking with my young daughter. Emma's not interested in eating sweets (odd, eh?), but she does love helping.

—Anna Ginsberg, Austin, Texas

1-1/2　cups semisweet chocolate chips, divided
　3/4　cup butter, cubed
　　1　tablespoon hazelnut-flavored instant coffee granules
　　2　eggs
　2/3　cup packed brown sugar
　　1　teaspoon vanilla extract
　3/4　cup all-purpose flour
　1/2　teaspoon baking powder
　1/4　teaspoon salt
　1/4　cup chopped hazelnuts, toasted
FROSTING:
　1/2　cup semisweet chocolate chips
　　1　tablespoon butter
　1/4　cup heavy whipping cream
1-1/2　teaspoons instant hazelnut-flavored coffee granules
　1/2　cup confectioners' sugar
　　1　teaspoon vanilla extract

1. In a microwave, melt 1 cup chocolate chips and butter with coffee granules; stir until smooth. Cool slightly.

2. In a large bowl, beat eggs and brown sugar; stir in chocolate mixture and vanilla. Combine flour, baking powder and salt; gradually add to chocolate mixture. Stir in hazelnuts and the remaining chips.

3. Pour into a greased 9-in. square baking pan. Bake at 325° for 22-26 minutes or until a toothpick inserted near the

center comes out clean. Cool in the pan on a wire rack.

4. For frosting, in a microwave, melt the chocolate chips and butter with cream and coffee granules; stir until smooth. Cool to room temperature.

5. Transfer to a small bowl; beat on high speed for 2 minutes. Beat in the confectioners' sugar and vanilla until fluffy. Frost brownies; refrigerate for at least 30 minutes before cutting.

[1998]

CHEWY PEANUT BUTTER BARS

yield: 2 dozen ⁓ **prep: 10 min.**
bake: 30 min.

My peanut butter bars have been a favorite treat at my house for years. These simple-to-prepare bars are so good they never last long.

—Deb DeChant, Milan, Ohio

　1/2　cup butter, cubed
　1/2　cup creamy peanut butter
1-1/2　cups sugar
　　1　cup all-purpose flour
　　2　eggs, lightly beaten
　　1　teaspoon vanilla extract

1. In a microwave, melt the butter and peanut butter; stir until smooth. Combine sugar and flour; gradually add to butter mixture and mix well. Beat in eggs and vanilla.

2. Spread into a greased 13-in. x 9-in. baking pan. Bake at 350° for 28-32 minutes or until lightly browned and edges start to pull away from sides of pan. Cool in pan on a wire rack.

Editor's Note: Reduced-fat peanut butter is not recommended for this recipe.

[1999]

M&M OAT BARS
**yield: 6 dozen · prep: 20 min.
bake: 10 min. + cooling**

These irresistible bars make for an easy way to sweeten any occasion.

—Renee Schwebach
  Dumont, Minnesota, Field Editor

1/2 **cup butter, softened**
  1 **cup packed brown sugar**
  1 **egg**
  1 **teaspoon vanilla extract**
1-1/4 **cups all-purpose flour**
1/2 **teaspoon baking soda**
1/2 **teaspoon salt**
  2 **cups quick-cooking oats**
  1 **package (14 ounces) caramels**
  3 **tablespoons water**
  1 **cup (6 ounces) miniature semisweet chocolate chips**
  1 **cup chopped walnuts**
  1 **cup plain M&M's**
  3 **ounces white candy coating**

---

1. In a large bowl, cream the butter and brown sugar until light and fluffy. Beat in egg and vanilla. Combine the flour, baking soda and salt; add to creamed mixture and mix well. Stir in oats.

2. Press into a greased 15-in. x 10-in. x 1-in. baking pan. Bake at 350° for 10-15 minutes or until golden brown. Cool in pan on a wire rack.

3. In a microwave, melt caramels with water; stir until smooth. Spread over crust. Sprinkle with the chips, nuts and M&M's. Gently press into the caramel mixture. Melt candy coating; drizzle over the top. Let stand for 5 minutes or until set. Cut into bars.

Editor's Note: Confectionery coating (also called almond bark or candy coating) is found in the baking section of most grocery stores.

[2004]

CHOCOLATE RIBBON BARS
yield: 2 dozen · prep: 20 min. + chilling

No one will be able to eat just one of these bars, full of butterscotch, peanut butter and chocolate flavor. Unlike similar crispy cereal treats, these aren't sticky! Over the years I've accumulated quite a few recipes from my co-workers, and this one is easy to prepare.

—Gail Wiese, Athens, Wisconsin

---

  1 **package (10 to 11 ounces) butterscotch chips**
  1 **cup peanut butter**
  8 **cups crisp rice cereal**
  2 **cups (12 ounces) semisweet chocolate chips**
1/4 **cup butter, cubed**
  2 **tablespoons water**
3/4 **cup confectioners' sugar**

---

1. In a microwave, melt the butterscotch chips and peanut butter; stir until smooth. Gradually stir in cereal until well coated. Press half of the mixture into a greased 13-in. x 9-in. pan; set remaining mixture aside.

2. In a microwave, melt semisweet chips and butter. Stir in water until blended. Gradually add the confectioners' sugar, stirring until smooth.

3. Spread over cereal layer. Cover and refrigerate for 10 minutes or until the chocolate layer is set. Spread the remaining cereal mixture over the top. Chill before cutting.

Editor's Note: Reduced-fat peanut butter is not recommended for this recipe.

CHOCOLATE RIBBON BARS

"These are good! My 10-year old and her friends gobbled them up."
—Aquarelle

CARAMEL HEAVENLIES

[1998]

CHOCOLATE-DIPPED BROWNIES

yield: 3 dozen ∽ prep: 30 min. + freezing
bake: 35 min. + cooling

(Pictured on page 295)

My family calls these bars "the world's chocolatiest brownies" and is more than happy to gobble up a batch whenever I make them. They're a delicious part of our holiday cookie collection.

—*Jackie Archer, Clinton, Iowa*

3/4	**cup sugar**
1/3	**cup butter, cubed**
2	**tablespoons water**
4	**cups (24 ounces) semisweet chocolate chips,** *divided*
1	**teaspoon vanilla extract**
2	**eggs**
3/4	**cup all-purpose flour**
1/2	**teaspoon salt**
1/4	**teaspoon baking soda**
2	**tablespoons shortening**

GARNISHES: Chopped pecans, jimmies and/ or nonpareils, optional

1. In a large saucepan, bring the sugar, butter and water to a boil over medium heat. Remove from the heat; stir in 1 cup chocolate chips and vanilla until smooth. Cool for 5 minutes. Beat in eggs. Combine the flour, salt and baking soda; add to chocolate mixture. Stir in 1 cup chocolate chips.

2. Pour into a greased 9-in. square baking pan. Bake at 325° for 35 minutes or until set. Cool completely in pan on a wire rack.

3. Place in the freezer for 30-40 minutes or until firm (do not freeze completely). Cut into bars.

4. In a microwave-safe bowl, melt the remaining chips and shortening; stir until smooth. Using a small fork, dip brownies to completely coat; allow excess to drip off. Place on waxed paper-lined baking sheets. Sprinkle with garnishes if desired. Let stand until set.

[1997]

CARAMEL HEAVENLIES

yield: about 6 dozen ∽ prep: 20 min.
bake: 15 min.

(Pictured on page 295)

My mom made these dressy, sweet cookies for cookie exchanges when I was a little girl, letting me sprinkle on the almonds and coconut. They're so easy to fix that sometimes I can't wait 'til Christmas to make a batch.

—*Dawn Burns, Lake St. Louis, Missouri*

12	**whole graham crackers**
2	**cups miniature marshmallows**
3/4	**cup butter**
3/4	**cup packed brown sugar**
1	**teaspoon ground cinnamon**

TOP 100 RECIPE

COATING BARS AND BROWNIES WITH CHOCOLATE

Melt the chocolate chips, baking chocolate or candy coating according to recipe directions. If necessary, transfer chocolate to a narrow container. To cover an entire bar in chocolate, use two forks to dip the bar into the chocolate and lift up. Gently shake the bar to remove excess chocolate. Place on a waxed paper-lined baking sheet to set at room temperature. If the chocolate cools too much to coat the bars properly, rewarm and continue dipping.

1 teaspoon vanilla extract
1 cup sliced almonds
1 cup flaked coconut

1. Line a 15-in. x 10-in. x 1-in. baking pan with foil. Place graham crackers in pan; cover with marshmallows. In a saucepan over medium heat, cook and stir butter, brown sugar and cinnamon until the butter is melted and sugar is dissolved. Remove from the heat; stir in vanilla.

2. Spoon over marshmallows. Sprinkle with nuts and coconut. Bake at 350° for 14-16 minutes or until browned. Cool completely in pan on a wire rack. Cut into 2-in. squares, then cut each square in half to form triangles.

[2012]

SWEET & SALTY POPCORN BARS

yield: 2-1/2 dozen ∽ prep: 20 min. + cooling

The name says it all. You have the sweet from the M&Ms and marshmallows, and the salty from the popcorn and peanuts. Kids of all ages will enjoy snacking on these bars.

—Nina Vilhauer
Mina, South Dakota, Field Editor

4 quarts popped popcorn
1 package (14 ounces) milk chocolate M&M's
3 cups salted peanuts
1 package (16 ounces) large marshmallows
1 cup butter, cubed

1. In a large bowl, combine the popcorn, M&M's and peanuts. In a large saucepan, combine the marshmallows and butter. Cook and stir over medium-low heat until mixture is melted. Stir into the popcorn mixture.

2. Press into two greased 13-in. x 9-in. pans. Cool; cut into bars.

[2005]

MERINGUE COCONUT BROWNIES

yield: 3 to 3-1/2 dozen ∽ prep: 30 min.
bake: 30 min. + cooling

Looking for an ooey-gooey brownie that's delicious and different? This luscious recipe combines a shortbread-like crust and a brown sugar meringue with chocolate, coconut and nuts.

—Diane Bridge, Clymer, Pennsylvania

3/4 cup butter, softened
1-1/2 cups packed brown sugar, *divided*
1/2 cup sugar
3 eggs, *separated*
1 teaspoon vanilla extract
2 cups all-purpose flour
1 teaspoon baking powder
1/4 teaspoon baking soda
1/4 teaspoon salt
2 cups (12 ounces) semisweet chocolate chips
1 cup flaked coconut
3/4 cup chopped walnuts

1. In a large bowl, cream butter, 1/2 cup brown sugar and sugar until light and fluffy. Beat in the egg yolks and vanilla. Combine flour, baking powder, baking soda and salt; gradually add to creamed mixture just until blended (batter will be thick). Spread into a greased 13-in. x 9-in. baking pan. Sprinkle with the chocolate chips, coconut and walnuts.

2. In another large bowl and with clean beaters, beat egg whites until soft peaks form. Gradually beat in the remaining brown sugar, 1 tablespoon at a time. Beat until stiff peaks form. Spread over the top.

3. Bake at 350° for 30-35 minutes or until a toothpick inserted near the center comes out clean (do not overbake). Cool in pan on a wire rack. Cut into bars. Store in the refrigerator.

MERINGUE COCONUT BROWNIES

"I made this recipe for a co-worker's birthday, and the whole office flipped for them! The name doesn't quite capture this delicious little treasure. My co-workers renamed them 'little gooey magic bites.' They are divine!"
— arinrose

[2008]

CHOCOLATE-GLAZED ALMOND BARS

yield: 40 bars ∞ prep: 25 min.
bake: 20 min. + cooling

With a moist almond filling and a flaky golden crust, these bars are sure to be the perfect dessert for any get-together.

—*Robin Hart*
North Brunswick, New Jersey

- 2 cups all-purpose flour
- 1/2 cup packed brown sugar
- 1/2 teaspoon salt
- 3/4 cup cold butter, cubed
- 3 egg whites
- 1 cup sugar
- 1 can (12-1/2 ounces) almond cake and pastry filling
- 2 cups sliced almonds
- 4 ounces bittersweet chocolate, chopped

1. In a large bowl, combine the flour, brown sugar and salt. Cut in the butter until mixture resembles coarse crumbs. Pat into a 13-in. x 9-in. baking pan coated with cooking spray. Bake at 350° for 18-22 minutes or until edges are lightly browned.

2. Meanwhile, in a large bowl, whisk egg whites, sugar and almond filling until blended. Stir in almonds. Pour over crust. Bake for 20-25 minutes or until set. Cool completely in pan on a wire rack.

3. In a microwave, melt chocolate; stir until smooth. Drizzle over top. Let stand until set. Cut into bars. Store in an airtight container in the refrigerator.

Editor's Note: This recipe was tested with Solo brand cake and pastry filling. Look for it in the baking aisle.

CHOCOLATE-GLAZED ALMOND BARS

"They are a lot easier to make than they look, and they taste like you spent hours on them. Sooo yummy!"
—*bethandal*

[1995]

CHOCOLATE RASPBERRY BARS

yield: 3 dozen ∞ prep: 20 min. + chilling
bake: 15 min. + cooling

Chocolate and raspberry jam go together so well in these rich, sweet bars. Their make-ahead convenience is perfect for hectic days.

—*Kathy Smedstad, Silverton, Oregon*

- 1 cup all-purpose flour
- 1/4 cup confectioners' sugar
- 1/4 cup butter, cubed
FILLING:
- 1/2 cup seedless raspberry jam
- 4 ounces cream cheese, softened
- 2 tablespoons 2% milk
- 1 cup white baking chips, melted
GLAZE:
- 3/4 cup semisweet chocolate chips
- 2 tablespoons shortening

1. In a small bowl, combine flour and confectioners' sugar; cut in butter until crumbly. Press into an ungreased 9-in. square baking pan. Bake at 375° for 15-18 minutes or until browned. Spread jam over the warm crust.

2. In a small bowl, beat cream cheese and milk until smooth. Add white chips; beat until smooth. Spread carefully over jam layer. Cool completely. Refrigerate for 1 hour or until set.

3. For glaze, melt chocolate chips and shortening in a microwave; stir until smooth. Spread over filling. Refrigerate for 10 minutes. Cut into bars; chill 1 hour longer or until set. Store in the refrigerator.

[2002]

FUDGY MINT SQUARES

yield: about 4 dozen
prep: 25 min. + chilling
bake: 30 min. + cooling

We've had this recipe since I was in junior high school. No one can resist the fudgy brownie base, cool minty cheesecake filling and luscious chocolate glaze in these mouthwatering bars.

—Heather Campbell
  Lawrence, Kansas, Field Editor

10	tablespoons butter, *divided*
3	ounces unsweetened chocolate, chopped
3	eggs
1-1/2	cups sugar
2	teaspoons vanilla extract
1	cup all-purpose flour
1	package (8 ounces) cream cheese, softened
1	tablespoon cornstarch
1	can (14 ounces) sweetened condensed milk
1	teaspoon peppermint extract
4	drops green food coloring, optional
1	cup (6 ounces) semisweet chocolate chips
1/2	cup heavy whipping cream

1. In a microwave, melt 8 tablespoons butter and unsweetened chocolate; stir until smooth. Cool slightly. In a small bowl, beat 2 eggs, sugar and vanilla. Beat in the chocolate mixture until blended. Gradually stir in the flour.

2. Spread into a greased 13-in. x 9-in. baking pan. Bake at 350° for 15-20 minutes or until top is set.

3. In a large bowl, beat the cream cheese and remaining butter until fluffy. Add the cornstarch; beat until smooth. Gradually beat in milk and remaining egg. Beat in extract and food coloring if desired.

4. Pour over the crust. Bake for 15-20 minutes or until center is almost set. Cool in pan on a wire rack.

5. In a small heavy saucepan, combine chocolate chips and cream. Cook and stir over medium heat until chips are melted. Cool for 30 minutes or until lukewarm, stirring occasionally. Pour over cream cheese layer. Chill for 2 hours or until set before cutting.

[1997]

TRIPLE-FUDGE BROWNIES

yield: 4 dozen ✎ **prep: 10 min.**
bake: 30 min.

When you're in a hurry to make dessert, here's a "mix of mixes" that's so convenient and quick. The result is a big pan of very rich, fudgy brownies. Friends who ask me for the recipe are amazed that it's so easy.

—Denise Nebel
  Wayland, Iowa, Former Field Editor

1	package (3.9 ounces) instant chocolate pudding mix
1	package (18-1/4 ounces) chocolate cake mix
2	cups (12 ounces) semisweet chocolate chips

Confectioners' sugar
Vanilla ice cream, optional

1. Prepare pudding according to package directions. Whisk in the dry cake mix. Stir in chocolate chips.

2. Pour into a greased 15-in. x 10-in. x 1-in. baking pan. Bake at 350° for 30-35 minutes or until the top springs back when lightly touched. Cool in pan on a wire rack.

3. Dust with confectioners' sugar. Serve with ice cream if desired.

FUDGY MINT SQUARES

❝Of the 10 Christmas sweets I made, this is the one that got the most oohs and aahs. Fabulous!❞
—glitterchatter

SHORTBREAD LEMON BARS

[2000]

SHORTBREAD LEMON BARS

yield: 3 dozen ∞ prep: 25 min.
bake: 15 min. + chilling

(Pictured on page 295)

I've put together two family cookbooks over the years, and this recipe ranks among my favorites. The special lemon bars have a yummy shortbread crust and refreshing flavor. I'm never afraid to make this dessert for guests because I know it will be a hit with everyone.

—Margaret Peterson, Forest City, Iowa

1-1/2	cups all-purpose flour
1/2	cup confectioners' sugar
1	teaspoon grated lemon peel
1	teaspoon grated orange peel
3/4	cup cold butter, cubed

FILLING:

4	eggs
2	cups sugar
1/3	cup lemon juice
1/4	cup all-purpose flour
2	teaspoons grated lemon peel
2	teaspoons grated orange peel
1	teaspoon baking powder

TOPPING:

2	cups (16 ounces) sour cream
1/3	cup sugar
1/2	teaspoon vanilla extract

1. In a food processor, combine the flour, confectioners' sugar, and lemon and orange peel. Add butter; cover and process until mixture forms a ball.

2. Pat into a greased 13-in. x 9-in. baking pan. Bake at 350° for 12-14 minutes or until set and edges are lightly browned.

3. In a large bowl, combine all the filling ingredients. Pour over hot crust. Bake for 14-16 minutes or until set and lightly browned.

4. In a small bowl, combine topping ingredients. Spread over filling.

5. Bake the bars 7-9 minutes longer or until topping is set. Cool in pan on a wire rack. Refrigerate overnight. Cut into bars just before serving. Store in the refrigerator.

[2005]

CHUNKY PECAN BARS

yield: about 6 dozen ∞ prep: 15 min.
bake: 20 min. + cooling

Most folks can't eat just one of these rich, gooey bars. They taste just like chocolate pecan pie.

—Hazel Baldner, Austin, Minnesota

1-1/2	cups all-purpose flour
1/2	cup packed brown sugar
1/2	cup cold butter, cubed

FILLING:

3	eggs
3/4	cup sugar
3/4	cup dark corn syrup
2	tablespoons butter, melted
1	teaspoon vanilla extract
1-3/4	cups semisweet chocolate chunks
1-1/2	cups coarsely chopped pecans

1. In a small bowl, combine the flour and brown sugar; cut in the butter until crumbly. Press into a greased 13-in. x 9-in. baking pan. Bake at 350° for 10-15 minutes or until golden brown.

2. Meanwhile, in a large bowl, whisk the eggs, sugar, corn syrup, butter and vanilla until blended. Stir in chocolate chunks and pecans. Pour over crust.

3. Bake for 20-25 minutes or until set. Cool completely in pan on a wire rack. Cut into bars. Store in the refrigerator.

[2006]

RHUBARB OAT BARS
yield: 16 bars   prep: 20 min.
bake: 25 min. + cooling

These soft bars provide just the right amount of tartness and sweetness. They are unbeatable!

—Renette Cressey
Fort Mill, South Carolina

1-1/2   **cups chopped fresh *or* frozen rhubarb**
   1   **cup packed brown sugar,** *divided*
   4   **tablespoons water,** *divided*
   1   **teaspoon lemon juice**
   4   **teaspoons cornstarch**
   1   **cup old-fashioned oats**
3/4   **cup all-purpose flour**
1/2   **cup flaked coconut**
1/2   **teaspoon salt**
1/3   **cup butter, melted**

---

1. In a large saucepan, combine rhubarb, 1/2 cup brown sugar, 3 tablespoons water and lemon juice. Bring to a boil. Reduce the heat to medium; cook and stir for 4-5 minutes or until rhubarb is tender.

2. Combine cornstarch and remaining water until smooth; gradually stir into rhubarb mixture. Bring to a boil; cook and stir for 2 minutes or until thickened. Remove from the heat; set aside.

3. In a bowl, combine oats, flour, coconut, salt and remaining brown sugar. Stir in butter until mixture is crumbly.

4. Press half of the mixture into a greased 8-in. square baking dish. Spread with the rhubarb mixture. Sprinkle with the remaining oat mixture and press down lightly.

5. Bake at 350° for 25-30 minutes or until golden brown. Cool in pan on a wire rack. Cut into squares.

Editor's Note: If using frozen rhubarb, measure rhubarb while still frozen, then thaw completely. Drain in a colander, but do not press liquid out.

[2011]

SWEDISH RASPBERRY ALMOND BARS
yield: 2 dozen   prep: 35 min.
bake: 20 min. + cooling
(Pictured on page 289)

When I was a single mom with a young child and little money, my Swedish neighbor brought me a batch of these cookies at Christmas. My daughter's an adult now, and I still make these wonderful cookies.

—Marina Castle
La Crescenta, California, Field Editor

3/4   **cup butter, softened**
3/4   **cup confectioners' sugar**
1-1/2   **cups all-purpose flour**
3/4   **cup seedless raspberry jam**
   3   **egg whites**
   6   **tablespoons sugar**
1/2   **cup flaked coconut**
   1   **cup sliced almonds,** *divided*
Additional confectioners' sugar

---

1. In a large bowl, cream the butter and confectioners' sugar until light and fluffy. Gradually add the flour and mix well. Press onto the bottom of a greased 13-in. x 9-in. baking pan. Bake at 350° for 18-20 minutes or until lightly browned.

2. Spread jam over crust. In a large bowl and with clean beaters, beat egg whites until soft peaks form. Gradually beat in sugar, 1 tablespoon at a time, on high until stiff peaks form. Fold in coconut and 1/2 cup almonds. Spread over jam. Sprinkle with remaining almonds. Bake at 350° for 18-22 minutes or until golden brown. Cool in pan on a wire rack.

RHUBARB OAT BARS

"I'm always looking for ways to get my husband and daughter to share my love of rhubarb, and this recipe is it! I'm always asked for the recipe whenever I bring them places. I think another fruit would be good in the filling, too."
—nott818

FROSTED BANANA BARS

[2000]

FROSTED BANANA BARS

yield: 3-4 dozen ∾ **prep: 15 min.**
bake: 20 min. + cooling

I make these moist bars whenever I have ripe bananas on hand, then store them in the freezer to share later at a potluck. With creamy frosting and big banana flavor, this treat is a real crowd-pleaser.

—Debbie Knight, Marion, Iowa

- 1/2 cup butter, softened
- 1-1/2 cups sugar
- 2 eggs
- 1 cup (8 ounces) sour cream
- 1 teaspoon vanilla extract
- 2 cups all-purpose flour
- 1 teaspoon baking soda
- 1/4 teaspoon salt
- 2 medium ripe bananas, mashed (about 1 cup)

FROSTING:
- 1 package (8 ounces) cream cheese, softened
- 1/2 cup butter, softened
- 2 teaspoons vanilla extract
- 3-3/4 to 4 cups confectioners' sugar

1. In a large bowl, cream butter and sugar until light and fluffy. Add the eggs, sour cream and vanilla. Combine the flour, baking soda and salt; gradually add to the creamed mixture. Stir in bananas.

2. Spread into a greased 15-in. x 10-in. x 1-in. baking pan. Bake at 350° for 20-25 minutes or until a toothpick inserted near the center comes out clean (do not overbake). Cool completely in pan on a wire rack.

3. For frosting, in a large bowl, beat the cream cheese, butter and vanilla until fluffy. Gradually beat in enough of the confectioners' sugar to achieve desired consistency. Frost the bars. Store in the refrigerator.

[1997]

SCANDINAVIAN ALMOND BARS

yield: about 4 dozen ∾ **prep: 20 min.**
bake: 20 min.

Delicate and crisp with a rich butter and almond flavor, these cookies are irresistible.

—Melva Baumer, Millmont, Pennsylvania

- 1 cup sugar
- 1/2 cup butter, softened
- 1 egg
- 1/2 teaspoon almond extract
- 1-3/4 cups all-purpose flour
- 2 teaspoons baking powder
- 1/4 teaspoon salt
- 1 tablespoon 2% milk
- 1/2 cup sliced almonds, chopped

ICING:
- 1 cup confectioners' sugar
- 1/4 teaspoon almond extract
- 1 to 2 tablespoons 2% milk

1. In a large bowl, cream sugar and butter until light and fluffy. Beat in egg and extract. Combine dry ingredients; add to creamed mixture and mix well.

2. Divide dough into fourths; form into 12-in. x 3-in. rectangles. Place 5 in. apart on greased baking sheets. Brush with milk; sprinkle with almonds.

3. Bake at 325° for 18-20 minutes or until firm to the touch and edges are lightly browned. Cool on pans for 5 minutes, then cut diagonally into 1-in. slices. Remove to wire racks to cool completely.

4. In a small bowl, combine the confectioners' sugar, extract and enough milk to achieve desired consistency; drizzle over bars.

[2005]

FROSTED COOKIE BROWNIES

yield: 15 servings ∾ **prep: 30 min.**
bake: 40 min. + cooling

(Pictured on page 293)

Years ago, my children and I came up with these bars by combining two of their favorite treats. With a crisp cookie crust and a fluffy frosting, these brownies are the most-requested treats at our house.

—*Alicia French, Colton, California*

- 1 tube (18 ounces) refrigerated chocolate chip cookie dough
- 3 cups miniature marshmallows
- 2 cups (12 ounces) semisweet chocolate chips
- 1 cup butter, cubed
- 4 eggs
- 2 teaspoons vanilla extract
- 1 cup all-purpose flour
- 1/2 teaspoon baking powder
- 1/4 teaspoon salt
- 1 cup chopped walnuts

FROSTING:
- 2 cups miniature marshmallows
- 6 tablespoons milk
- 1/4 cup butter, softened
- 2 ounces unsweetened chocolate
- 3 cups confectioners' sugar

1. Press cookie dough into a greased 13-in. x 9-in. baking pan. Bake at 350° for 10 minutes.

2. Meanwhile, in a large saucepan, combine the marshmallows, chips and butter; cook and stir over low heat until melted and smooth. Transfer to a large bowl; cool. Beat in eggs and vanilla. Combine the flour, baking powder and salt; gradually stir into marshmallow mixture. Stir in nuts.

3. Spread over cookie crust. Bake for 30-35 minutes or until a toothpick inserted near the center comes out clean. Cool completely in pan on a wire rack.

4. For frosting, in a small saucepan, combine the marshmallows, milk, butter and chocolate. Cook and stir over low heat until smooth. Remove from the heat; beat in confectioners' sugar until smooth. Frost brownies. Cut into bars.

[2004]

PEANUT BUTTER BROWNIES

yield: 4 dozen ∾ **prep: 30 min.** ∾ **bake: 20 min. + chilling**

I modified a recipe for layered brownies by adding chunky peanut butter. It's a real crowd-pleaser!

—*Judy Sims, Weatherford, Texas*

- 1-1/2 cups butter, *divided*
- 3/4 cup baking cocoa, *divided*
- 4 eggs
- 2 cups sugar
- 1 teaspoon vanilla extract
- 1-1/2 cups all-purpose flour
- 1/2 teaspoon salt
- 1 jar (18 ounces) chunky peanut butter
- 1/3 cup 2% milk
- 10 large marshmallows
- 2 cups confectioners' sugar

1. In a small saucepan, melt 1 cup butter; stir in 1/2 cup cocoa until smooth. Remove from the heat. In a large bowl, beat the eggs, sugar and vanilla until blended. Combine flour and salt; gradually add to egg mixture. Beat in cocoa mixture.

2. Transfer to a greased 15-in. x 10-in. x 1-in. baking pan. Bake at 350° for 18-22 minutes or until toothpick inserted near the center comes out clean. Cool for 3-4 minutes on a wire rack.

3. Meanwhile, in a microwave, melt peanut butter, uncovered, at 50% power for 2 minutes, stirring once. Stir until peanut butter is blended. Spread peanut butter over warm brownies. Refrigerate for 45 minutes or until peanut butter is set.

4. In a heavy saucepan, combine the milk, remaining cocoa, marshmallows and remaining butter. Cook and stir over medium heat until butter and marshmallows are melted and mixture is smooth. Remove from the heat. Gradually stir in confectioners' sugar until smooth. Spread over peanut butter layer. Refrigerate for at least 30 minutes. Cut into squares.

Editor's Note: This recipe was tested in a 1,100-watt microwave.

[2009]

CHOCOLATE NUT BARS

yield: 3 dozen ✆ prep: 30 min.
bake: 15 min. + cooling

When I ask my husband what he would like me to bake, he often asks for these fudgy, nutty bars. They are his first choice!

—*Lisa Darling, Scottsville, New York*

- 1 cup butter, softened
- 2 cups all-purpose flour
- 1/2 cup sugar
- 1/4 teaspoon salt
- 1 can (14 ounces) sweetened condensed milk
- 2 cups (12 ounces) semisweet chocolate chips, *divided*
- 1 teaspoon vanilla extract
- 1/2 cup chopped macadamia nuts
- 1/2 cup chopped walnuts
- 1/2 cup chopped pecans
- 1/2 cup milk chocolate chips

1. In a large bowl, beat butter until fluffy. Add flour, sugar and salt; beat just until crumbly. Set aside 1 cup for topping. Press remaining crumb mixture into a greased 13-in. x 9-in. baking pan. Bake at 350° for 10-12 minutes or until set and edges begin to brown.

2. Meanwhile, in a small saucepan, combine the milk and 1-1/2 cups semisweet chocolate chips. Cook and stir until the chips are melted. Remove from the heat; stir in vanilla. Spread mixture over crust.

3. Combine the nuts and milk chocolate chips with the remaining semisweet chocolate chips and crumb mixture. Sprinkle over filling. Bake for 15-20 minutes or until center is set. Cool in pan on a wire rack. Cut into bars.

[2002]

APRICOT
MERINGUE BARS

yield: 32 bars ✆ prep: 15 min.
bake: 25 min. + cooling

Their sweet apricot filling and delicate meringue topping make these bars everyone's favorite. I wouldn't dream of hosting a get-together without serving them.

—*Kristine Fossmeyer, Huntley, Illinois*

- 3 cups all-purpose flour
- 1 cup sugar, *divided*
- 1 cup cold butter, cubed
- 4 eggs, *separated*
- 1 teaspoon vanilla extract
- 2 cans (12 ounces *each*) apricot filling
- 1/2 cup chopped pecans

1. In a large bowl, combine the flour and 1/2 cup sugar; cut in the butter until crumbly. Add the egg yolks and vanilla. Press into a greased 15-in. x 10-in. x 1-in. baking pan.

2. Bake at 350° for 12-15 minutes or until lightly browned. Spread apricot filling over crust.

3. In a small bowl, beat egg whites on medium speed until soft peaks form. Gradually beat in the remaining sugar, 1 tablespoon at a time, on high until stiff glossy peaks form and sugar is dissolved. Spread the meringue evenly over filling; sprinkle with pecans.

4. Bake at 350° for 25-30 minutes or until the meringue is lightly browned. Cool in pan on a wire rack (the meringue will crack). Cut into bars. Store in the refrigerator.

[1998]

COOKIES 'N' CREAM BROWNIES

yield: 2 dozen ∞ **prep: 15 min.**
bake: 25 min. + cooling

You won't want to frost these brownies, since the marbled top is too pretty to cover up. Besides, the yummy cream cheese layer makes them taste like they're already frosted. The crushed cookies add extra chocolate flavor and a fun crunch.

—Darlene Brenden
    Salem, Oregon, Field Editor

1	package (8 ounces) cream cheese, softened
1/4	cup sugar
1	egg
1/2	teaspoon vanilla extract

BROWNIE LAYER:

1/2	cup butter, melted
1/2	cup sugar
1/2	cup packed brown sugar
1/2	cup baking cocoa
2	eggs
1	teaspoon vanilla extract
1/2	cup all-purpose flour
1	teaspoon baking powder
12	cream-filled chocolate sandwich cookies, crushed

1. In a small bowl, beat the cream cheese, sugar, egg and vanilla until smooth; set aside. For brownie layer, combine the butter, sugars and cocoa in a large bowl. Beat in eggs. Combine flour and baking powder; gradually add to cocoa mixture. Stir in cookie crumbs.

2. Pour brownie batter into a greased 11-in. x 7-in. baking pan. Spoon cream cheese mixture over batter; cut through batter with a knife to swirl. Bake at 350° for 25-30 minutes or until a toothpick inserted near the center comes out with moist crumbs. Cool completely in pan on a wire rack. Cut into bars. Store in the refrigerator.

[2001]

BUTTERSCOTCH CASHEW BARS

yield: 3-1/2 dozen ∞ **prep: 20 min.**
bake: 15 min. + cooling

I knew these nutty bars were a success when I took them on our annual family vacation. My husband couldn't stop eating them...and my sister-in-law, who is a great cook, asked for the recipe. It makes a big batch, which is good because they go quickly!

—Lori Berg, Wentzville, Missouri

1	cup plus 2 tablespoons butter, softened
3/4	cup plus 2 tablespoons packed brown sugar
2-1/2	cups all-purpose flour
1-3/4	teaspoons salt

TOPPING:

1	package (10 to 11 ounces) butterscotch chips
1/2	cup plus 2 tablespoons light corn syrup
3	tablespoons butter
2	teaspoons water
2-1/2	cups salted cashew halves

1. In a large bowl, cream the butter and brown sugar until light and fluffy. Combine the flour and salt; add to creamed mixture just until combined.

2. Press into a greased 15-in. x 10-in. x 1-in. baking pan. Bake at 350° for 10-12 minutes or until lightly browned.

3. Meanwhile, in a small saucepan, combine the butterscotch chips, corn syrup, butter and water. Cook and stir over medium heat until the chips and butter are melted.

4. Spread over the crust. Sprinkle with cashews; press down lightly. Bake for 11-13 minutes or until the topping is bubbly and lightly browned. Cool in pan on a wire rack. Cut into bars.

BUTTERSCOTCH CASHEW BARS

"My husband and two teenage sons love, love, love this recipe. If you're a fan of cashews, and who isn't, you will love these sweet and salty bars!"
—imvideomom

TURKEY SALTIMBOCCA

*"I tried this dish last night from the *2011* (*Taste of Home*) *Annual Recipes* book and it was delicious. I had leftover new potatoes, which I fried up in the same skillet with the turkey, and I also had leftover green and red peppers and green onions. Probably not your typical fare with this dish, but my husband loved it."*

—*grosslynn*

[2010]

TURKEY SALTIMBOCCA

yield: 2 servings ∞ **prep/total time: 30 min.**

This Italian twist on the holiday staple combines sage and prosciutto for a tempting turkey tenderloin that's so good you won't believe it's made in a skillet.

—*Deirdre Dee Cox, Milwaukee, Wisconsin*

1	turkey breast tenderloin (8 ounces)
1/8	teaspoon pepper
1/4	cup all-purpose flour
2	tablespoons butter, *divided*
1-1/2	teaspoons olive oil
1	thin slice prosciutto *or* deli ham, cut into thin strips
2	tablespoons minced fresh sage
1/4	cup white wine *or* chicken broth

1. Cut tenderloin in half lengthwise; flatten each half to 1/2-in. thickness. Sprinkle with pepper. Place flour in a large shallow bowl; add turkey, one piece at a time, and turn to coat.

2. In a large skillet, cook the turkey in 1 tablespoon butter and oil over medium heat for 3-4 minutes on each side or until no longer pink. Remove and keep warm.

3. In the same skillet, saute prosciutto and sage in 1-1/2 teaspoons butter until slightly crisp. Add wine, stirring to loosen browned bits from the pan. Bring to a boil; cook until liquid is slightly reduced. Remove from the heat; stir in remaining butter. Serve with turkey.

[2002]

BATTER-FRIED FISH

yield: 2 servings ∞ **prep/total time: 15 min.**

Whether I'm fixing cod fillets or my husband's catch of the day, this batter makes the fish fry up golden and crispy. Club soda gives it a different twist, and the sweet and zippy sauce complements the fish nicely.

—*Nancy Johnson*
Connersville, Indiana, Field Editor

1/2	pound cod
2	tablespoons all-purpose flour
2 to 3	tablespoons cornstarch
1/4	teaspoon *each* garlic powder, onion powder, salt, cayenne pepper and paprika
1/8	teaspoon dried oregano
1/8	teaspoon dried thyme
1/3	cup club soda
Oil for frying	
1/4	cup orange marmalade
1 to 2	tablespoons prepared horseradish

1. Rinse fillets in cold water; pat dry. Place flour in a large resealable plastic bag; add fish one piece at a time. Seal bag; toss to coat. In a shallow bowl, combine the cornstarch, seasonings and soda.

2. In a heavy skillet, heat 1 in. of oil. Dip floured fillets into batter; fry over medium heat for 2-3 minutes on each side or until the fish flakes easily with a fork. Combine the marmalade and horseradish; serve with fish.

[2009]

OMELET CROISSANTS

yield: 2 servings ✎ **prep/total time: 30 min.**

(Pictured on page 351)

Bacon and eggs never tasted so good, stacked with cheese, greens, tomato and more in this grilled meal-in-one.

—Edna Coburn
  Tucson, Arizona, Field Editor

3	eggs
1	tablespoon water
1	teaspoon chicken bouillon granules
1	green onion, finely chopped
2	tablespoons finely chopped sweet red pepper
1/4	teaspoon lemon-pepper seasoning
1/2	teaspoon butter
2	croissants, split
4-1/2	teaspoons ranch salad dressing
4	slices Canadian bacon
4	slices Muenster cheese
1/2	cup fresh arugula
4	thin slices tomato

---

1. In a small bowl, whisk the eggs, water and bouillon; set aside.

2. In a small nonstick skillet over medium heat, cook the onion, red pepper and lemon-pepper in butter until tender.

3. Add the egg mixture. As eggs set, push cooked edges toward the center, letting uncooked portion flow underneath. When the eggs are completely set, fold omelet in half and cut into two wedges.

4. Spread croissants with salad dressing. On the croissant bottoms, layer with the bacon, omelet, cheese, arugula and tomato. Replace croissant tops.

5. Cook sandwich on a panini maker or indoor grill for 2-4 minutes or until cheese is melted.

[2008]

SIRLOIN WITH BLUE CHEESE BUTTER

yield: 2 servings ✎ **prep: 25 min. + chilling**
grill: 10 min.

Few meats are as mouthwatering as a juicy, grilled steak. And when you top a tender sirloin with a savory blue cheese and walnut butter, it's mouthwatering and memorable.

—Sharon Johnson, Minneapolis, Minnesota

1/2	cup crumbled blue cheese
1/4	cup butter, softened
1/4	cup chopped walnuts, toasted
2	tablespoons minced fresh parsley
1-3/4	teaspoons minced fresh rosemary, *divided*
6	large garlic cloves, peeled
1/4	teaspoon salt
1/4	teaspoon pepper
2	beef top sirloin steak (6 ounces *each*)

---

1. In a small bowl, combine the blue cheese, butter, walnuts, parsley and 3/4 teaspoon rosemary. Shape into a 5-in. log; wrap in plastic wrap. Chill for 30 minutes or until firm.

2. In a small food processor, combine the garlic, salt, pepper and remaining rosemary. Cover and process until blended. Rub over both sides of steaks.

3. Grill steaks, covered, over medium heat or broil 4-6 in. from the heat for 5-6 minutes on each side or until the meat reaches desired doneness (for medium-rare, a thermometer should read 145°; medium, 160°; well-done, 170°).

4. Unwrap blue cheese butter; cut two 1/2-in.-slices from log. Place one slice on each steak. Rewrap remaining butter; refrigerate for 1 week or freeze for up to 3 months.

SIRLOIN WITH BLUE CHEESE BUTTER

"I have made this several times and it is delicious! I don't care for steak, but the blue cheese butter makes it delish!"
—sulynn051467

[1995]

STUFFED CORNISH HENS

yield: 2 servings ∞ prep: 45 min. + cooling
bake: 1 hour

(Pictured on page 348)

With a golden and flavorful stuffing, these tender hens are a special-occasion entree for just the two of us.

—*Wanda Jean Sain*
Hickory, North Carolina

2 tablespoons finely chopped onion
1/3 cup uncooked long grain rice
4 tablespoons butter, *divided*
3/4 cup water
1/2 cup condensed cream of celery soup, undiluted
1 tablespoon lemon juice
1 teaspoon minced chives
1 teaspoon dried parsley flakes
1 teaspoon chicken bouillon granules
2 Cornish game hens (20 to 24 ounces each)
Salt and pepper to taste
1/2 teaspoon dried tarragon

1. In a small skillet, saute onion and rice in 2 tablespoons butter until rice is browned. Add the water, soup, lemon juice, chives, parsley and bouillon. Bring to a boil. Reduce heat; cover and simmer for 25 minutes or until rice is tender and liquid is absorbed. Remove from the heat and cool slightly.

2. Sprinkle hen cavities with salt and pepper; stuff with rice mixture. Place with breast side up on a rack in an ungreased 13-in. x 9-in. baking pan. Melt remaining butter and add the tarragon; brush some over the hens.

3. Cover loosely and bake at 375° for 30 minutes. Uncover; bake 30-45 minutes longer or until a thermometer reads 180° for the hens and 165° for the stuffing, basting frequently with tarragon butter.

[2003]

SAUSAGE MACARONI BAKE

yield: 2 servings ∞ prep: 20 min.
bake: 20 min.

You're both bound to enjoy this satisfying Italian-style bake. Oregano seasons the pork sausage, macaroni and tomato sauce mixture that's topped with a sprinkling of Parmesan cheese. It really hits the spot when you want a quick not-so-big meal.

—*Kelli Bucy, Red Oak, Iowa*

1/2 cup uncooked elbow macaroni
1/2 pound bulk pork sausage
1/4 cup chopped green pepper
2 tablespoons chopped onion
1/4 teaspoon dried oregano
1/8 teaspoon pepper
1 can (8 ounces) tomato sauce
1/2 cup water
4 tablespoons grated Parmesan cheese, *divided*

1. Cook macaroni according to package directions; drain and set aside.

2. In a large skillet, cook the sausage over medium heat until no longer pink; drain. Add the green pepper, onion, oregano and pepper. Stir in the tomato sauce and water. Bring to a boil. Reduce heat; simmer, uncovered, for 5 minutes.

3. Stir in the macaroni and 2 tablespoons cheese. Transfer to an ungreased 1-qt. baking dish. Sprinkle with remaining cheese. Bake, uncovered, at 350° for 20-25 minutes or until bubbly.

[1994]

MIDGET POT ROAST

yield: 2 servings ∞ prep: 10 min.
bake: 2 hours

(Pictured on page 346)

Do you want a pot roast with big, old-fashioned flavor that does not serve eight? Try this one that I enjoy making for my husband and me.

—*Marian Platt*
Sequim, Washington, Field Editor

---

2   beef shanks (about 1-1/2 pounds)
3   tablespoons all-purpose flour, *divided*
1-1/2   cups cold water, *divided*
1/2   cup beef broth
1   tablespoon onion soup mix
1   garlic clove, minced
1   teaspoon Worcestershire sauce
1/4   teaspoon dried thyme
1   large potato, peeled and cut into eighths
2   medium carrots, cut into 2-inch pieces
6   pearl onions
Salt and pepper to taste

---

1. Sprinkle the meat with 1 tablespoon flour; place in a shallow 2-qt. baking dish. Mix 1 cup water, broth, soup mix, garlic, Worcestershire sauce and thyme; pour over meat. Cover and bake at 325° for 1-1/2 hours.

2. Turn meat; add the potato, carrots and onions. Cover; return to oven for 30-45 minutes or until meat and vegetables are tender. Remove meat and vegetables and keep warm.

3. To prepare gravy, skim fat from pan juices. Measure 1 cup of the juices and place in a small saucepan. Combine remaining flour and cold water until smooth; stir into juices. Bring to a boil; cook and stir for 2 minutes or until thickened. Season with salt and pepper. Serve with meat and vegetables.

[1997]

LAZY LASAGNA

yield: 2 servings ∞ prep/total time: 30 min.

Lasagna may seem like more work than it's worth to some people. But one day when I had a craving for it, I devised this simple recipe.

—*Carol Mead*
Los Alamos, New Mexico, Field Editor

---

1   cup spaghetti sauce
3/4   cup shredded part-skim mozzarella cheese
1/2   cup 4% cottage cheese
1-1/2   cups cooked wide noodles
2   tablespoons grated Parmesan cheese

---

1. Warm the spaghetti sauce; stir in mozzarella and cottage cheeses. Fold in noodles. Pour into two 2-cup baking dishes coated with cooking spray. Sprinkle with the Parmesan cheese.

2. Bake casseroles, uncovered, at 375° for 20 minutes or until bubbly.

LAZY LASAGNA

"Very yummy and easy! Has been a hit with everyone I've made it for. Hamburger meat would be a good idea if you wanted a truer lasagna feel, but I like this one as it is."
—*kategaffney*

POT ROAST DONENESS TEST

Pot roasts are done when a long-handled fork can be inserted into the thickest part of the roast easily. If the pot roast is cooked until it falls apart, the meat is actually overcooked and will be stringy, tough and dry.

[2006]

HONEY-MUSTARD CHICKEN

yield: 2 servings ∞ **prep/total time: 30 min.**

This entree combines my husband's love for mustard with my love for anything sweet, like honey. The yummy curry taste really sends this dish over the top! We like it with rice pilaf.

—Lisa Varner, Charleston, South Carolina, Field Editor

- 1/4 cup honey
- 2 tablespoons butter, melted
- 2 tablespoons Dijon mustard
- 1 tablespoon orange juice
- 1/8 teaspoon curry powder
- 2 boneless skinless chicken breast halves
- 1 tablespoon vegetable oil
- 1/8 teaspoon salt
- 1/8 teaspoon pepper

---

1. In a small bowl, combine the honey, butter, mustard, orange juice and curry powder. Spoon half into a greased 8-in. square baking dish.

2. In a skillet, brown chicken in oil. Sprinkle with salt and pepper. Place over sauce; turn to coat.

3. Bake, uncovered, at 350° for 15 minutes. Drizzle with remaining sauce. Bake 5-10 minutes longer or until a thermometer reads 170°.

[2011]

PRESTO BEEF STEW

yield: 2 servings ∞ **prep/total time: 30 min.**

This quick, flavorful dinner for two couldn't be easier. Just combine sauteed mushrooms with shredded beef, then serve with golden-brown biscuits. Sometimes I add sliced green onions to the stew.

—Karla Johnson, East Helena, Montana

- 2 individually frozen biscuits
- 2 tablespoons butter
- 2 cups sliced fresh mushrooms
- 1 package (17 ounces) refrigerated beef roast au jus
- 1/4 teaspoon pepper
- 2 tablespoons cornstarch
- 1 cup cold water

---

1. Bake biscuits according to package directions.

2. Meanwhile, in a large saucepan over medium heat, melt butter. Add mushrooms; cook and stir until tender. Shred the beef with two forks; add to the pan. Add the pepper. Combine cornstarch and water until smooth; stir into stew. Bring to a boil; cook and stir for 1-2 minutes or until thickened.

3. Divide the stew between two bowls; top each with a biscuit.

[2004]

SHRIMP PASTA PRIMAVERA

yield: 2 servings ∞ **prep/total time: 15 min.**

They say the way to a man's heart is through his stomach. So when I invite that special guy to dinner, I like to prepare something equally special. This well-seasoned pasta dish has lots of flavor, and it won't hurt your budget!

—Shari Neff, Takoma Park, Maryland

- 4 ounces uncooked angel hair pasta
- 8 jumbo shrimp, peeled and deveined
- 6 fresh asparagus spears, trimmed and cut into 2-inch pieces
- 1/4 cup olive oil
- 2 garlic cloves, minced
- 1/2 cup sliced fresh mushrooms
- 1/2 cup chicken broth
- 1 small plum tomato, peeled, seeded and diced
- 1/4 teaspoon salt
- 1/8 teaspoon crushed red pepper flakes
- 1 tablespoon *each* minced fresh basil, oregano, thyme and parsley
- 1/4 cup grated Parmesan cheese

---

1. Cook pasta according to package directions. Meanwhile, in a large skillet, saute shrimp and asparagus in oil for 3-4 minutes or until shrimp turn pink. Add garlic; cook 1 minute longer. Add the mushrooms, broth, tomato, salt and pepper flakes; simmer, uncovered, for 2 minutes.

2. Drain the pasta. Add the pasta and seasoning to skillet; toss to coat. Sprinkle with the cheese.

[2010]

HAMBURGER NOODLE BAKE

yield: 2 servings ∞ prep: 35 min.
bake: 20 min.

(Pictured on page 351)

Cream cheese and cottage cheese nicely balance the saucy ground beef and noodles in this hearty casserole. It's been a favorite for years.

—*Charissa Dunn, Bartlesville, Oklahoma*

- 2 cups uncooked egg noodles
- 1/2 pound lean ground beef (90% lean)
- 2 tablespoons finely chopped onion
- 1 can (8 ounces) tomato sauce
- 1/4 teaspoon sugar
- 1/8 teaspoon salt
- 1/8 teaspoon garlic salt
- Dash pepper
- 1/4 cup cream-style cottage cheese
- 2 ounces cream cheese, softened
- 1 tablespoon thinly sliced green onion
- 1 tablespoon chopped green pepper
- 1 tablespoon sour cream
- 2 tablespoons grated Parmesan cheese

1. Cook noodles according to package directions. Meanwhile, in a large skillet, cook beef and onion until meat is no longer pink; drain. Remove from the heat; stir in the tomato sauce, sugar, salt, garlic salt and pepper.

2. In a small bowl, combine the cottage cheese, cream cheese, green onion, green pepper and sour cream.

3. Drain noodles; place half of noodles in a greased 1-qt. baking dish. Spoon half of beef mixture over the top. Layer with cottage cheese mixture and the remaining noodles. Top with the remaining beef mixture; sprinkle with Parmesan cheese.

4. Cover and bake at 350° for 20-25 minutes or until heated through.

[2009]

RUBBED GRILLED T-BONES

yield: 2 servings ∞ prep: 10 min. + standing
grill: 10 min.

This recipe is perfect for empty-nesters. The rub is so flavorful, you don't need to add sauce!

—*Alaina Showalter*
Clover, South Carolina, Field Editor

- 2 beef T-bone steaks (1 inch thick and 12 ounces each)
- 2 tablespoons olive oil
- 1/2 cup packed brown sugar
- 1/2 teaspoon seasoned salt
- 1/2 teaspoon lemon-pepper seasoning
- 1/2 teaspoon lime-pepper seasoning *or* additional lemon-pepper seasoning
- 1/4 teaspoon garlic powder

1. Rub the steaks with oil. Combine the remaining ingredients; rub over steaks. Let stand for 10 minutes before grilling.

2. Grill, covered, over medium heat for 5-7 minutes on each side or until the meat reaches desired doneness (for medium-rare, a thermometer should read 145°; medium, 160°; well-done, 170°).

DONENESS TEST FOR STEAK

To test for doneness, insert an instant-read thermometer horizontally from the side, making sure to get the reading in the center of the steak.

—*Taste of Home Cooking Experts*

RUBBED GRILLED T-BONES

"Wonderful flavor! We don't use anything but this recipe. We use it on all steaks and usually forget to oil the steaks first, but it turns out great anyway! Once you try this recipe, you'll never want a steak any other way. Made our cookouts famous! :)"
—*lorrielu*

[2006]

PORK FRIED RICE

yield: 2 servings ∞ prep/total time: 30 min.

(Pictured on page 347)

We love pork roast, but we know there will be leftovers. I like to use them up in this fast-to-fix stir-fry dish.

—*Joyce Kramer*
Donalsonville, Georgia, Field Editor

- 1 tablespoon canola oil
- 1 egg, lightly beaten
- 3/4 cup cubed cooked pork
- 1/4 cup finely chopped onion
- 1/4 cup canned bean sprouts, rinsed and drained
- 2 cups cold cooked long grain rice
- 1/4 cup chicken broth
- 1 tablespoon reduced-sodium soy sauce
- 1 green onion, sliced
- 1/4 teaspoon sugar

Dash pepper

1. In a large skillet or wok, heat oil over medium-high heat; add the egg. As the egg sets, lift edges, letting uncooked portion flow underneath. When egg is completely cooked, remove to a plate and keep warm.

2. In the same pan, stir-fry pork, onion and bean sprouts for 2-3 minutes or until pork and onion are tender. Add rice and broth; cover and simmer for 1-2 minutes or until heated through.

3. Chop egg into small pieces; add to the rice mixture. Stir in soy sauce, green onion, sugar and pepper.

PORK FRIED RICE

❝We like this, but I like to stir-fry strips of the leftover pork in a bit of BBQ sauce first, then I add about 1 cup of cooked rice for however many servings I need.❞
—*FluffyinCD*

[2004]

CHICKEN WITH LEMON SAUCE

yield: 2 servings ∞ prep/total time: 20 min.

This delicious Italian dish is easy to prepare, yet it looks like you fussed.

—*Brenda Hoffman, Stanton, Michigan*

- 2 boneless skinless chicken breast halves (5 ounces each)
- 5 tablespoons all-purpose flour, *divided*
- 1/4 cup grated Parmesan cheese
- 3/4 teaspoon salt, *divided*
- 1/2 teaspoon pepper, *divided*
- 2 eggs
- 2 tablespoons butter, *divided*
- 1 tablespoon olive oil
- 3/4 cup chicken broth
- 1/2 cup apple juice
- 1 tablespoon lemon juice
- 1 tablespoon minced fresh parsley

1. Flatten chicken to 1/4-in. thickness. In a shallow bowl, combine 4 tablespoons flour, cheese, 1/2 teaspoon salt and 1/4 teaspoon pepper. In another shallow bowl, beat the eggs. Coat the chicken with flour, then dip into the egg mixture.

2. In a large skillet, cook the chicken in 1 tablespoon butter and oil over medium heat for 3-5 minutes on each side or until no longer pink. Remove and keep warm.

3. In a small bowl, combine remaining salt and pepper; stir in broth until smooth. Add apple juice to the skillet, stirring to loosen any browned bits. Stir broth mixture and add to the pan. Bring to a boil; cook and stir for 1-2 minutes or until thickened.

4. Stir in lemon juice; cook for 1 minute. Add parsley and remaining butter; cook and stir until butter is melted. Serve with chicken.

[1999]

CHICKEN CAESAR SALAD

yield: 2 servings ∽ **prep/total time: 25 min.**

This restaurant-style, main-dish salad may sound fancy, but in reality it couldn't be easier to make.

—Kay Andersen, Bear, Delaware

- 2 boneless skinless chicken breast halves (1/2 pound)
- 2 teaspoons olive oil
- 1/8 teaspoon dried basil
- 1/8 teaspoon dried oregano
- 1/4 teaspoon garlic salt, optional
- 1/4 teaspoon pepper
- 1/4 teaspoon paprika
- 4 cups torn romaine
- 1 small tomato, thinly sliced

Creamy Caesar salad dressing

Caesar salad croutons, optional

1. Brush chicken with oil. Combine the basil, oregano, garlic salt if desired, pepper and paprika; sprinkle over chicken. Grill, uncovered, over medium-low heat for 12-15 minutes or until a thermometer reads 170°, turning several times.

2. Arrange romaine and tomato on plates. Cut chicken into strips; arrange over salads. Drizzle with dressing. Sprinkle with croutons if desired.

[2010]

BERRY-PORT GAME HENS

yield: 2 servings ∽ **prep: 20 min.**
bake: 50 min.

This recipe uses only five ingredients to create a simple but elegant entree. It's one of my favorite dishes to serve.

—Josephine Piro, Easton, Pennsylvania

- 1 large orange
- 2 Cornish game hens (20 to 24 ounces *each*)
- 1/2 teaspoon salt
- 1/2 teaspoon pepper
- 1 cup ruby port wine *or* grape juice
- 1/4 cup seedless strawberry jam
- 5 teaspoons stone-ground mustard

1. Finely grate peel from orange to measure 1 teaspoon. Cut orange in half widthwise; cut a thin slice from each half. Quarter slices and set aside. Juice the orange to measure 1/4 cup.

2. Loosen skin around hen breasts and thighs; place orange slices under the skin.

3. Place hens in a greased 13-in. x 9-in. baking dish. Sprinkle with salt and pepper. Bake, uncovered, at 350° for 40 minutes. Meanwhile, in a small saucepan, combine the wine, jam and orange juice. Bring to a boil. Reduce heat; simmer, uncovered, for 6-8 minutes or until slightly thickened. Stir in the mustard and orange peel.

4. Set aside 1/2 cup sauce for serving; brush remaining sauce over hens. Bake the hens 10-20 minutes longer or until a thermometer reads 180°, basting occasionally with pan juices. Warm reserved sauce; serve with hens.

[1999]

ITALIAN TURKEY BREAST

yield: 2 servings ∽ **prep/total time: 20 min.**

My husband and I enjoy this Italian-style turkey dish when we want a delightful change of pace. The dressed-up turkey slices are never dry, and they cook in just minutes.

—Helen Vail, Glenside, Pennsylvania

- 1 tablespoon all-purpose flour
- 1/8 teaspoon pepper
- 2 turkey breast slices (3 ounces *each*)
- 2 teaspoons olive oil
- 1 teaspoon butter
- 1 can (8 ounces) no-salt-added tomato sauce
- 1 teaspoon *each* dried oregano, basil and thyme
- 2 teaspoons shredded part-skim mozzarella cheese
- 1 teaspoon nonfat Parmesan cheese topping

1. In a large resealable plastic bag, combine flour and pepper; add turkey slices. Seal bag and turn to coat.

2. In a large skillet over medium heat, brown turkey in oil and butter. Combine the tomato sauce, oregano, basil and thyme; pour over turkey. Bring to a boil; reduce heat. Cover and simmer for 3-4 minutes or until no turkey is longer pink. Sprinkle with cheeses.

[2004]

TOMATO 'N' CHEESE PASTA

yield: 2 servings ∞ prep: 25 min.
bake: 10 min.

Garlic, basil and oregano add pizzazz to this savory side dish. The pasta is tender and moist, and there's plenty of cheese flavor. I like to serve it alongside steaks or chicken.

—*Dawn Dhooghe, Concord, North Carolina*

1	cup uncooked small tube pasta
1	small onion, chopped
1	tablespoon olive oil
2	garlic cloves, minced
1	can (14-1/2 ounces) Italian diced tomatoes
1/2	teaspoon dried basil
1/2	teaspoon dried oregano
1/4	teaspoon sugar
1/4	teaspoon pepper
1/4	cup shredded part-skim mozzarella cheese
1/4	cup grated Parmesan cheese

1. Cook the pasta according to package directions. In a small saucepan, saute onion in oil until tender. Add garlic; cook 1 minute longer. Stir in the tomatoes, basil, oregano, sugar and pepper. Bring to a boil. Reduce heat; simmer, uncovered, for 15 minutes. Drain pasta; stir into saucepan.

2. Transfer to a greased 1-qt. baking dish. Top with cheeses. Bake, uncovered, at 375° for 10-15 minutes or until cheese is melted.

TOMATO 'N' CHEESE PASTA

"This makes a great meatless main dish, too, and is easily doubled. I bake it in individual gratin dishes and serve with garlic bread and a green salad."
—*Aquarelle*

[2005]

MINIATURE HAM LOAF

yield: 2 servings ∞ prep: 15 min.
bake: 30 min.

(Pictured on page 349)

Shredded carrots add color and flavor to this downsized ham loaf. A buttery glaze and slices of pineapple put the finishing touches on this satisfying entree.

—*Carol Dunne, Middle Village, New York*

1	egg
1	small carrot, shredded
1/4	cup chopped onion
1/3	cup seasoned bread crumbs
1	tablespoon dried parsley flakes
1	teaspoon prepared mustard
1/2	pound ground fully cooked ham
1	can (8 ounces) unsweetened sliced pineapple
1	tablespoon brown sugar
1	teaspoon cornstarch
1	tablespoon butter
1	tablespoon lemon juice

1. In a small bowl, combine the first six ingredients. Crumble the ham over mixture and mix well. Shape into a loaf and place in a greased baking dish. Bake at 350° for 20 minutes.

2. Meanwhile, drain pineapple, reserving juice; set pineapple aside. In a small saucepan, combine the brown sugar, cornstarch and reserved juice until smooth. Bring to a boil; cook and stir for 1 minute or until thickened. Stir in butter and lemon juice.

3. Brush the sauce over ham loaf; top with three pineapple slices. (Save remaining pineapple for another use.) Bake 10-15 minutes longer or until a thermometer reads 160°. Let stand for 5 minutes before slicing.

[2005]

CHICKEN BISCUIT BAKE

yield: 2 servings ✐ **prep: 20 min.**
bake: 30 min.

(Pictured on page 346)

This recipe looks fussy but doesn't take long to assemble...plus it gives me time to put my feet up and read the paper while it bakes. It's nice with just a salad and some fruit.

—*Gail Cory-Betz, Newport, Washington*

1/2	cup plus 1 tablespoon all-purpose flour
1/2	teaspoon baking powder
Dash salt	
3	tablespoons cold butter
2	tablespoons beaten egg
1/4	cup buttermilk

FILLING:

2	tablespoons butter
2	tablespoons all-purpose flour
1	cup 2% milk
1	tablespoon chicken bouillon granules
Dash poultry seasoning	
Dash onion powder	
1/2	cup cubed cooked chicken
1/2	cup frozen mixed vegetables
1/2	cup 4% cottage cheese

---

1. In a small bowl, combine the flour, baking powder and salt; cut in the butter until mixture resembles coarse crumbs. Set aside 1 teaspoon beaten egg; stir the remaining egg into buttermilk. Add to crumb mixture; stir until dough forms a ball.

2. Turn onto a floured surface; knead 10 times or until smooth. Divide dough in half. On a lightly floured surface, roll out one portion to fit the bottom of a greased 1-qt. baking dish. Place in dish.

3. For filling, in a small saucepan, melt the butter over medium heat. Stir in flour until smooth. Gradually add the milk, bouillon, poultry seasoning and onion powder. Bring to a boil; cook and stir for 1-2 minutes or until thickened. Remove from the heat. Stir in the chicken, vegetables and cottage cheese. Pour into baking dish.

4. Roll out remaining dough to fit top of dish; place over filling. Brush with reserved egg. Bake at 350° for 30-35 minutes or until golden brown.

[1998]

BEEF TENDERLOIN IN MUSHROOM SAUCE

yield: 2 servings ✐ **prep/total time: 30 min.**

It doesn't take much fuss to fix a special meal for two. Here's the delicious proof.

—*Denise McNab, Warminster, Pennsylvania*

1	teaspoon canola oil
4	tablespoons butter, *divided*
2	beef tenderloin steaks (8 ounces *each*)
1/2	cup chopped fresh mushrooms
1	tablespoon chopped green onion
1	tablespoon all-purpose flour
1/8	teaspoon salt
Dash pepper	
2/3	cup chicken *or* beef broth
1/8	teaspoon browning sauce, optional

---

1. In a large skillet, heat oil and 2 tablespoons of butter over medium-high heat. Cook steaks for 6-7 minutes on each side or until meat reaches desired doneness (for medium-rare, a thermometer should read 145°; medium, 160°; well-done, 170°). Remove to a serving platter; keep warm.

2. To pan juices, add the mushrooms, onions and remaining butter; saute until vegetables are tender. Stir in the flour, salt and pepper; gradually stir in broth until smooth. Add browning sauce if desired. Bring to a boil; cook and stir for 2 minutes or until thickened. Serve with the steaks.

[2004]

BUTTERFLIED PORK CHOP DINNER

**yield: 2 servings   prep: 10 min.
cook: 35 min.**

The sliced apple and sweet potatoes that complement these tender pork chops remind me of a crisp fall day, but I enjoy this hearty main dish any time of year, served with salad and dinner rolls.

—Angela Leinenbach
Mechanicsville, Virginia, Field Editor

2	butterflied pork chops (3/4 inch thick and 3 ounces each)
1	tablespoon butter
1	cup apple juice or cider, *divided*
1	teaspoon rubbed sage
3/4	teaspoon salt
1/2	teaspoon pepper
2	medium sweet potatoes, peeled and cut into 1/2-inch slices
1	green onion, thinly sliced
1	medium tart apple, peeled, cored and cut into 1/4-inch rings
2	teaspoons cornstarch

1. In a large skillet, brown pork chops in butter; drain. Remove from skillet and keep warm. In same skillet, combine 3/4 cup apple juice, sage, salt and pepper. Add sweet potatoes and green onion. Bring to a boil. Reduce heat.

2. Cover and simmer for 10 minutes; add apple rings and pork chops. Cover and simmer for 13-15 minutes or until apple rings and sweet potatoes are tender and meat is no longer pink.

3. With a slotted spoon, remove the pork chops, sweet potatoes and apple to serving plates; keep warm.

4. Combine cornstarch and remaining apple juice until smooth. Gradually stir into pan juices. Bring to a boil; cook and stir for 1-2 minutes or until thickened. Serve with pork chops, sweet potatoes and apple.

[1993]

LIME BROILED CATFISH

yield: 2 servings   prep/total time: 15 min.

(Pictured on page 347)

To serve a reduced-calorie dish that is ready in about 15 minutes, I came up with this fast recipe. I think the lime juice adds a fresh flavor to the mild taste of the fish.

—Nick Nicholson, Clarksdale, Mississippi

1	tablespoon butter
2	tablespoons lime juice
1/2	teaspoon salt, optional
1/4	teaspoon pepper
1/4	teaspoon garlic powder
2	catfish fillets (6 ounces each)

Lime slices *or* wedges, optional
Fresh parsley, optional

1. Melt butter in a small saucepan. Stir in the lime juice, salt if desired, pepper and garlic powder. Remove from the heat and set aside.

2. Place fillets in a shallow baking pan. Brush each fillet generously with lime-butter sauce. Broil for 5-8 minutes or until the fish flakes easily with a fork.

3. Remove to a warm serving dish; spoon pan juices over each fillet. Garnish with lime slices and parsley if desired.

BUTTERFLIED PORK CHOP DINNER

"I made this the other night using apple cider instead of the apple juice. It was so strong and potent that no one could eat it. I made the sauce with apple juice though, and it was so delicous and sweet. I might try this recipe again but just use the juice instead."
—littleann1

[2002]

BEEF PAPRIKA

yield: 2 servings   **prep: 25 min.**
cook: 1-1/2 hours

My husband, Don, and I loved this savory dish when we first sampled it at a party. Of course, I had to have the recipe, which I have downsized to serve just the two of us.

—*Nancy Nielsen, Orange, Connecticut*

- 3/4 **pound beef stew meat, cut into 3/4-inch cubes**
- 2 **teaspoons canola oil**
- 1 **small onion, thinly sliced**
- 1 **garlic clove, minced**
- 3/4 **cup water,** *divided*
- 1/4 **cup ketchup**
- 1 **teaspoon brown sugar**
- 3/4 **teaspoon paprika**
- 3/4 **teaspoon Worcestershire sauce**
- 1/2 **teaspoon salt**
- 1/4 **teaspoon Dijon mustard**

Dash cayenne pepper

- 1 **tablespoon all-purpose flour**

Hot cooked noodles

1. In a large saucepan, brown the beef in oil on all sides. Add the onion; cook until onion is tender. Add the garlic; cook 1 minute longer. Add 1/2 cup of water, ketchup, brown sugar, paprika, Worcestershire sauce, salt, mustard and cayenne; mix well. Bring to a boil. Reduce heat; cover and simmer for 1-1/2 to 1-3/4 hours or until the beef is tender.

2. Combine flour and remaining water until smooth; gradually stir into the stew. Bring to a boil; cook and stir for 2 minutes or until thickened. Serve with the noodles.

[2007]

HERB-CRUSTED RED SNAPPER

yield: 2 servings   **prep: 25 min.**

An appetizing blend of herbs complements the mild flavor of these flaky fillets. Red pepper flakes give the entree its zip.

—*Nella Parker, Hersey, Michigan*

- 1 **tablespoon dry bread crumbs**
- 1 **teaspoon dried basil**
- 1 **teaspoon paprika**
- 1/2 **teaspoon salt**
- 1/2 **teaspoon fennel seeds**
- 1/2 **teaspoon dried thyme**
- 1/2 **teaspoon dried oregano**
- 1/4 **teaspoon pepper**
- 1/4 **teaspoon crushed red pepper flakes**
- 2 **red snapper fillets (5 ounces each), skin removed**
- 2 **teaspoons canola oil**

1. In a food processor, combine the first nine ingredients; cover and process until fennel is finely ground. Transfer to a shallow bowl; dip fillets in herb mixture, coating both sides.

2. In a heavy skillet over medium-high heat, cook fillets in oil for 3-4 minutes on each side or until fish flakes easily with a fork.

RED SNAPPER SUBSTITUTION

Most supermarkets carry a limited selection of fish and may not have red snapper when you want it. Select another fish with similar qualities. Red snapper is a mild, lean fish. Cod, grouper, mahi mahi, sole, tilapia and whiting would be good substitutes.

—*Taste of Home Cooking Experts*

HERB-CRUSTED RED SNAPPER

"My husband is a sworn fish hater, but he and my toddler both love this! I usually use it for salmon instead of snapper."
—*ghttogrl*

[2009]

SAILOR SANDWICHES WITH CAESAR MAYO

yield: 2 servings ∞ **prep: 25 min.**
broil: 10 min.

(Pictured on page 350)

This recipe was inspired by Patricia Cornwall's detective novels, since the characters ate Sailor Sandwiches. I thought I could put a New England spin on them by combining these great ingredients.

—*Lesley Pew, Lynn, Massachusetts*

- 1/4 cup 2% milk
- 1/4 cup cornmeal
- 2 tablespoons all-purpose flour
- 1 tablespoon grated Parmesan cheese
- 1/2 teaspoon dried oregano
- 1/4 teaspoon garlic powder
- 1/4 teaspoon salt
- 1/4 teaspoon pepper
- 2 cod *or* haddock fillets (6 ounces *each*)
- 1 tablespoon butter, melted

CAESAR MAYO:

- 4 teaspoons grated Parmesan cheese
- 4 teaspoons mayonnaise
- 4 teaspoons olive oil
- 1 tablespoon lemon juice
- 1 tablespoon Worcestershire sauce
- 3/4 teaspoon garlic powder
- 1/2 teaspoon ground mustard
- 1/4 teaspoon hot pepper sauce

SANDWICHES:

- 2 kaiser rolls, split and toasted
- 2 lettuce leaves
- 1 small tomato, thinly sliced
- 2 slices sweet onion

---

1. Place the milk in a shallow bowl. In another shallow bowl, combine the cornmeal, flour, cheese and seasonings. Dip the fish in the milk, then in the cornmeal mixture.

2. Place on a greased broiler pan; drizzle with butter. Broil 4 in. from the heat for 8-10 minutes or until the fish flakes easily with a fork.

3. Combine the mayonnaise ingredients; spread over rolls. On roll bottoms, layer with fish, lettuce, tomato and onion. Replace tops.

[2010]

CURRIED APRICOT PORK CHOPS

yield: 2 servings ∞ **prep/total time: 30 min.**

A fresh fruit glaze that's both sweet and savory drapes these tender chops. They're pretty enough to serve for a special night in.

—*Trisha Kruse, Eagle, Idaho, Field Editor*

- 2 tablespoons apricot nectar
- 1 tablespoon plus 1-1/2 teaspoons apricot preserves
- 1 tablespoon Dijon mustard
- 1 tablespoon reduced-sodium soy sauce
- 1 teaspoon curry powder
- 2 boneless pork loin chops (5 ounces *each*)
- 1/8 teaspoon salt
- 1/8 teaspoon pepper
- 1-1/2 teaspoons canola oil
- 1/2 cup sliced fresh apricots
- 2 green onions, sliced

---

1. In a small bowl, combine the first five ingredients; set aside. Sprinkle pork chops with salt and pepper. In a small nonstick skillet, cook chops in oil for 4-5 minutes on each side or until a thermometer reads 145°. Remove and set aside.

2. Add apricots and onions to the pan; cook and stir for 2 minutes. Stir in nectar mixture. Return pork chops to the pan and heat through, spooning the sauce over the top. Cook until slightly thickened.

SAILOR SANDWICHES WITH CAESAR MAYO

"So far I have made these sandwiches three times. The first time I made them with cod, the second time with tilapia, the third with chicken breast (our lunch guest had a severe fish allergy). Very delicious sandwich that my husband actually requests, so it must be good! All three times the sandwiches turned out tasty. The Caesar Mayo makes the difference."
—*skyeyes*

[2000]

TANGY GLAZED CHICKEN

yield: 2 servings   prep: 15 min.
cook: 30 min.

This finger-licking citrus sauce offers a hint of sweet apple jelly, making it perfect over bone-in chicken breasts. Serve them with potatoes or rice and a salad if you wish.

—*Barbara Haney, St Louis, Missouri*

  2   bone-in chicken breast halves
         (8 ounces *each*)
1/4   teaspoon salt, optional
4-1/2 teaspoons butter
  1   small onion, thinly sliced
  1   celery rib, thinly sliced
1/2   cup chicken broth
1/2   cup apple jelly
  3   tablespoons orange juice
  1   tablespoon minced fresh parsley
1/4   to 1/2 teaspoon dried thyme

1. Sprinkle chicken with salt if desired. In a large skillet, melt butter over medium heat; brown chicken on all sides. Remove and keep warm.

2. In the pan drippings, saute the onion and celery until tender. Add the remaining ingredients; cook and stir until jelly is melted. Return the chicken to pan. Cook, uncovered, for 30-35 minutes or a thermometer reads 170°. Remove skin if desired. Top chicken with onion mixture.

[2002]

GINGERED GARLIC SHRIMP

yield: 2 servings   prep/total time: 20 min.

(Pictured on page 349)

Ginger and garlic nicely complement the tender shrimp in this delicious pasta dish.

—*Rebecca Baird*
Salt Lake City, Utah, Field Editor

  1   tablespoon minced fresh gingerroot
  2   garlic cloves, minced
  2   tablespoons butter
  2   tablespoons olive oil
  2   plum tomatoes, diced
3/4   cup chicken broth
  3   teaspoons minced fresh parsley,
         divided
  3   teaspoons minced fresh basil, *divided*
1-1/2 teaspoon cornstarch
  1   tablespoon cold water
1/2   pound uncooked medium *or* large
         shrimp, peeled and deveined
  2   cups cooked angel hair pasta

1. In a large skillet, saute ginger and garlic in butter and oil for 1 minute or until tender. Stir in the tomatoes, broth, 1-1/2 teaspoons parsley and 1-1/2 teaspoons basil. Combine the cornstarch and cold water until smooth; add to skillet. Bring to a boil; cook and stir for 2 minutes or until thickened.

2. Reduce heat; add the shrimp. Simmer, uncovered, for 2-3 minutes or until the shrimp turn pink. Add the pasta and remaining parsley and basil; toss to coat.

TANGY GLAZED CHICKEN

"This is probably my husband's favorite chicken recipe. I thicken the sauce with 1/2 teaspoon or more of cornstarch so it is not so runny. I also add a bit more apple jelly as needed for that wonderful flavor. I like to serve this with spinach noodles, a veggie and corn muffins. "
—*Buddy's girl*

[2011]

ASIAN MANGO CHICKEN

yield: 2 servings ∞ prep: 25 min.
cook: 15 min.

This unique entree will brighten any table. Its vibrant colors draw you in while the lively blend of flavors will keep you coming back to this recipe time and again.

—Jessica Feist, Brookfield, Wisconsin

   2   boneless skinless chicken breast
       halves (6 ounces each)
   1   tablespoon sesame or canola oil
   1   tablespoon rice vinegar
   1   garlic clove, minced
   1   teaspoon honey
 1/2   teaspoon green curry paste
   1   medium mango, peeled and diced
   1   green onion, finely chopped
   2   tablespoons diced peeled cucumber
   2   tablespoons finely chopped sweet red
       pepper
 1/8   teaspoon cayenne pepper
Chopped dry roasted peanuts

1. In a large skillet over medium heat, cook chicken in oil for 4-5 minutes on each side or until a thermometer reads 170°. Remove and keep warm.

2. Add the vinegar, garlic, honey and curry paste to the pan; cook and stir for 1-2 minutes to allow flavors to blend. Return chicken to the pan.

3. Combine the mango, onion, cucumber, red pepper and cayenne. Serve with chicken. Sprinkle with peanuts.

ASIAN MANGO CHICKEN

"Wonderful combination of flavors! Absolutely the only thing I'd change is that I'd like a little more sauce next time, so I'd double (or more!) those ingredients. Served it over jasmine rice, and it was not only pretty but really good! Thanks for sharing this one!"
—btaylor123

[2007]

CORNED BEEF SUPPER

yield: 2 servings
prep: 25 min. ∞ cook: 4 hours

What better way to celebrate St. Patrick's Day than with this hearty one-pot meal. I often fix it for the holiday, but it's good any time of the year.

—Dawn Fagerstrom
Warren, Minnesota, Field Editor

   1   small onion, sliced
   4   small carrots, cut into chunks
   2   medium potatoes, cut into chunks
   1   corned beef brisket with spice packet
       (1 pound)
 1/3   cup unsweetened apple juice
   2   whole cloves
   1   tablespoon brown sugar
 1/2   teaspoon grated orange peel
 1/2   teaspoon prepared mustard
   2   cabbage wedges

1. Place onion in a 3-qt. slow cooker. Top with the carrots, potatoes and brisket. Combine apple juice, cloves, brown sugar, orange peel, mustard and contents of spice packet; pour over brisket. Cover and cook on high for 3-4 hours.

2. Add the cabbage; cover and cook 30 minutes longer or until meat and vegetables are tender. Strain and discard cloves; serve pan juices with corned beef and vegetables.

[2002]
CHILI FOR TWO
yield: 2 servings ✎ **prep/total time: 25 min.**
(Pictured on page 352)

This flavorful chili is still thick and hearty even though it makes a small batch. I serve it with a salad of grapefruit and avocado slices.

—*Norma Grogg, St. Louis, Missouri*

1/4 **pound ground beef**
1/4 **cup chopped onion**
 1 **garlic clove, minced**
 1 **can (16 ounces) chili beans, undrained**
 1 **can (14-1/2 ounces) diced tomatoes, undrained**
1-1/2 **teaspoons chili powder**
1/2 **teaspoon ground cumin**

1. In a large saucepan, cook the beef and onion over medium heat until meat no longer pink. Add the garlic; cook 1 minute longer. Drain. Stir in remaining ingredients; bring to a boil.

2. Reduce heat; cover and simmer for 10-15 minutes or until heated through.

[2006]
SKILLET LAMB CHOPS
yield: 2 servings ✎ **prep: 5 min.**
cook: 40 min.

These mildly seasoned chops are so satisfying. They make a great entree—particularly if you enjoy lamb—for holiday dinners.

—*Alpha Wilson*
Roswell, New Mexico, Field Editor

 2 **lamb shoulder blade chops (8 ounces each)**
 2 **tablespoons canola oil**
1/2 **cup warm water**
 1 **teaspoon lemon juice**
 1 **teaspoon dried minced onion**
1/2 **teaspoon dried oregano**

1/4 **teaspoon salt**
1/8 **teaspoon pepper**

1. In a large skillet, brown lamb chops in oil. Add the remaining ingredients; bring to a boil. Reduce heat; cover and simmer for 30-35 minutes or until meat reaches desired doneness (for medium-rare, a thermometer should read 145°; medium, 160°; well-done, 170°).

[1997]
ELEGANT PORK CHOPS
yield: 2 servings ✎ **prep/total time: 30 min.**
(Pictured on page 345)

My recipe for these pork chops is so easy. It has wonderful old-fashioned flavor without the fuss or mess. Plus, the chops stay very moist.

—*Nila Towler*
Baird, Texas, Former Field Editor

 2 **pork loin chops (1 inch thick)**
 1 **tablespoon canola oil**
 1 **can (10-3/4 ounces) condensed cream of mushroom soup, undiluted**
3/4 **cup 2% milk**
3/4 **cup uncooked instant rice**
1/8 **teaspoon onion powder**
1/8 **teaspoon garlic powder**
Dash pepper

1. In a small skillet, brown pork chops in oil on both sides over medium heat; set aside. In an ungreased 8-in. square baking dish, combine soup, milk, rice and seasonings. Top with pork chops.

2. Cover the dish and bake at 350° for 15-20 minutes. Uncover and bake 5 minutes longer or until a thermometer reads 145°. Let stand for 5 minutes before serving.

CHILI FOR TWO

“ This is the best recipe for chili I have ever found. My grandkids love it. It's easy too! I do use 1/2 pound meat in mine to make it thicker. When the kids aren't eating with me, I add 1/8 teaspoon cayenne to give it some heat. ”
—*nanabuela*

[1996]

SALMON SALAD SANDWICHES

yield: 2 servings ∾ prep/total time: 10 min.

These are perfect to pack in your kids' lunch boxes when they can't face another boring sandwich. We love the salmon, cream cheese and dill tucked inside a crusty roll. The carrots and celery add a nice crunch.

—Yvonne Shust, Shoal Lake, Manitoba

1   package (3 ounces) cream cheese, softened
1   tablespoon mayonnaise
1   tablespoon lemon juice
1   teaspoon dill weed
1/4 to 1/2 teaspoon salt
1/8 teaspoon pepper
1   can (6 ounces) pink salmon, drained, bones and skin removed
1/2 cup shredded carrot
1/2 cup chopped celery
Lettuce leaves
2   whole wheat buns, split

1. In a large bowl, beat cream cheese, mayonnaise, lemon juice, dill, salt and pepper until smooth. Add salmon, carrot and celery and mix well. Place a lettuce leaf and about 1/2 cup salmon salad on each bun.

[2001]

APPLE PUFF PANCAKE

yield: 2 servings ∾ prep/total time: 30 min.

For a light breakfast, lunch or brunch entree, this fluffy baked pancake is very little fuss. It's economical, too.

—Sharon Emery, New Burnside, Illinois

1/2 cup all-purpose flour
1/8 teaspoon salt
2   eggs
1/2 cup 2% milk
1   tablespoon butter, melted
1   medium tart apple, peeled and chopped
1/2 cup apple jelly
1/8 teaspoon ground cinnamon

1. In a small bowl, combine flour and salt. Add the eggs, milk and butter. Pour into a greased 8-in. square baking pan. Bake at 400° for 20-25 minutes or until lightly browned.

2. Meanwhile, combine the chopped apple, jelly and cinnamon in a saucepan. Cook and stir until jelly is melted. Cut pancake into fourths; place two pieces on each plate. Top with apple mixture.

[2012]

SEARED SCALLOPS WITH CITRUS HERB SAUCE

yield: 2 servings ∾ prep/total time: 20 min.

Tender, sweet scallops are topped with a herb-garlic sauce that makes this dish very special. I serve it with angel hair pasta.

—April Lane, Greeneville, Tennessee

3/4 pound sea scallops
1/4 teaspoon salt
1/4 teaspoon pepper
1/8 teaspoon paprika
3   tablespoons butter, *divided*
1   garlic clove, minced
2   tablespoons dry sherry *or* chicken broth
1   tablespoon lemon juice
1/8 teaspoon minced fresh oregano
1/8 teaspoon minced fresh tarragon

1. Pat the scallops dry with paper towels; sprinkle with the salt, pepper and paprika. In a large skillet, heat 2 tablespoons butter over medium-high heat. Add the scallops; sear for 1-2 minutes on each side or until golden brown and firm. Remove from the skillet and keep warm.

2. Wipe skillet clean if necessary. Saute the garlic in remaining butter until tender; stir in the sherry. Cook until liquid is almost evaporated; stir in the remaining ingredients. Serve with scallops.

ELEGANT PORK CHOPS, page 343

MIDGET POT ROAST, page 331

CHICKEN BISCUIT BAKE, page 337

SENSATIONAL TIRAMISU, page 373

HOMEMADE BUTTERSCOTCH PUDDING, page 374

LIME BROILED CATFISH, page 338

PORK FRIED RICE, page 334

STUFFED CORNISH HENS, page 330

MINIATURE HAM LOAF, page 336

CHOCOLATE CAYENNE SOUFFLES, page 366

GINGERED GARLIC SHRIMP, page 341

CARAMEL APPLE BREAD PUDDING, page 371

SAILOR SANDWICHES WITH CAESAR MAYO, page 340

APPLE-CHERRY PORK CHOPS, page 355

HAMBURGER NOODLE BAKE, page 333

OMELET CROISSANTS, page 329

CINNAMON BISCUIT PEACH COBBLER, page 371

PEAR PERFECTION, page 364

CHILI FOR TWO, page 343

CHOCOLATE RASPBERRY CHEESECAKE, page 376

[2004]

CREAMED CHICKEN OVER BISCUITS

yield: 2 servings — prep/total time: 20 min.

A friend of mine prepared this homey dish for my husband and me after our first son was born. I've made just a few minor modifications over the years. We love all of the heartwarming comfort it offers in every bite.

—Pam Kelley, Uniontown, Ohio

- 1 cup cubed peeled potato
- 1/2 cup diced carrot
- 2 tablespoons butter
- 2 tablespoons all-purpose flour
- 1 cup 2% milk
- 2-1/2 teaspoons chicken bouillon granules
- 1/8 teaspoon pepper
- 1/2 pound boneless skinless chicken breasts, cooked and cubed
- 1/2 cup frozen peas, thawed
- 4 warm buttermilk biscuits

1. Place potato and carrot in a small saucepan. Cover with water. Bring to a boil. Reduce heat; cover and simmer for 8-10 minutes or until vegetables are tender. Drain and set aside.

2. In a large skillet, melt butter. Stir in the flour until smooth. Gradually whisk in milk. Add bouillon and pepper. Bring to a boil; cook and stir for 2 minutes or until thickened. Stir in the chicken, peas and potato mixture; heat through. Serve with biscuits.

[2009]

CAROLINA CRAB CAKES

yield: 2 servings — prep: 10 min. + chilling cook: 10 min.

I think these little rounds are spiced just right, and the mustard sauce is the ideal accent. If you're a fan of crab cakes, these are a must-try!

—Katie Sloan
  Charlotte, North Carolina, Field Editor

- 1 egg, lightly beaten
- 1/2 cup soft bread crumbs
- 1/4 cup mayonnaise
- 1 teaspoon grated onion
- 1/2 teaspoon minced fresh parsley
- 1/2 teaspoon Worcestershire sauce
- 1/8 teaspoon seafood seasoning
- 1/8 teaspoon ground mustard
- Dash pepper
- Dash hot pepper sauce
- 1 can (6 ounces) crabmeat, drained, flaked and cartilage removed
- 1 tablespoon canola oil
- **MUSTARD SAUCE:**
- 2 tablespoons mayonnaise
- 2 tablespoons sour cream
- 1 tablespoon Dijon mustard
- 1/2 teaspoon lemon juice
- 1/2 teaspoon Worcestershire sauce

1. In a small bowl, combine the first 10 ingredients. Fold in crab. Refrigerate for 30 minutes. Meanwhile, combine sauce ingredients.

2. In a large skillet, heat oil over medium heat. Drop crab mixture by 1/4 cupfuls into the pan; cook for 3-5 minutes on each side or until golden brown. Serve with sauce.

CAROLINA CRAB CAKES

❝I had never made crab cakes, but knowing *Taste of Home's* reputation, I knew they had to be good. They were better than good; they were scrumptious and a new favorite!❞
—RealtorSherry

[2003]

OMELET QUESADILLA

yield: 2 servings   prep/total time: 15 min.

I came up with these crispy quesadillas because we found breakfast burritos too messy. They're fast to fix, fun to eat, filling and healthy—and you can add or subtract ingredients to fit individual tastes.

—*Terri Capps, Wichita, Kansas*

- 1 cup sliced fresh mushrooms
- 2 tablespoons chopped onion
- 1/2 cup egg substitute
- 2 tablespoons chopped fresh tomato
- 2 flour tortillas (10 inches)
- 4 thin slices lean ham (1/2 ounce *each*)
- 1/4 cup shredded part-skim mozzarella cheese
- 1/4 cup shredded reduced-fat cheddar cheese
- 3 tablespoons salsa

1. In a small nonstick skillet coated with cooking spray, cook mushrooms and onion over medium heat until tender. Add egg substitute and tomato; cook and stir until set.

2. Place one tortilla in a large nonstick skillet; top with the ham, egg mixture, cheeses and remaining tortilla. Cook over medium heat, carefully turning once, until lightly browned on both sides and cheese is melted. Cut into four wedges. Serve with salsa.

QUESO FRESCO

Also known as queso blanco, queso fresco is a soft, moist, fresh Mexican cheese that melts easily. Use this cheese to give any dish authentic Mexican flair.

—*Taste of Home Cooking Experts*

OMELET QUESADILLA

"Thank you for making a healthy recipe for two. It is wonderful. Add some green chilis to pep it up a bit."
—*dmsaari*

[2007]

BROCCOLI CHICKEN FETTUCCINE

yield: 2 servings
prep/total time: 25 min.

I served this with Chive Garlic Bread (page 479), and my finicky, young grandson absolutely loved it!

—*Elaine Mizzles, Ben Wheeler, Texas*

- 4 ounces uncooked fettuccine
- 1/2 pound boneless skinless chicken breasts, cut into 1-inch pieces
- 1 small onion, halved and sliced
- 2 tablespoons butter
- 4 garlic cloves, minced
- 1 can (10-3/4 ounces) condensed cream of chicken soup, undiluted
- 1 cup chicken broth
- 1-1/2 cups frozen broccoli florets, thawed
- 1 can (4 ounces) mushroom stems and pieces, drained
- 1 teaspoon onion powder
- 1/2 teaspoon pepper
- 1/4 cup shredded Parmesan cheese

1. Cook fettuccine according to package directions. Meanwhile, in a large skillet, saute chicken and onion in butter until no longer pink. Add the garlic; cook 1 minute longer. Stir in the soup, broth, broccoli, mushrooms, onion powder and pepper. Bring to a boil.

2. Drain fettuccine; add to chicken mixture. Reduce heat; cover and simmer for 5 minutes or until heated through. Sprinkle with cheese.

[2005]
MINI SALMON LOAF

yield: 2 servings ∽ **prep: 15 min.**
bake: 40 min.

This nicely textured salmon loaf accompanied by a pleasing dill sauce is perfect for two. I've made it many, many times.

—*Patricia Gould, Canaan, New Hampshire*

- 3/4 cup chopped celery
- 1/2 cup chopped onion
- 2 tablespoons canola oil
- 1 cup soft bread crumbs
- 1 egg, lightly beaten
- 2 tablespoons 2% milk
- 1/4 teaspoon salt
- 1/4 teaspoon pepper
- 1 can (7-1/2 ounces) salmon, drained, bones and skin removed

DILL SAUCE:

- 1/2 cup mayonnaise
- 1/4 cup sour cream
- 1 tablespoon lemon juice
- 1 tablespoon 2% milk
- 2 teaspoons snipped fresh dill
- 1/2 teaspoon sugar
- 1/8 teaspoon pepper

1. In a small skillet, saute the celery and onion in oil until tender. In a large bowl, combine the bread crumbs, egg, milk, salt, pepper and celery mixture. Crumble salmon over mixture and mix well. Transfer to a greased 5-3/4-in. x 3-in. x 2-in. loaf pan.

2. Bake at 350° for 40-45 minutes or until a thermometer reads 160°. In a small bowl, combine the sauce ingredients. Serve with salmon loaf.

[2007]
APPLE-CHERRY PORK CHOPS

yield: 2 servings ∽ **prep/total time: 30 min.**

(Pictured on page 350)

You'll never want pork chops any other way once you try this recipe! I season the juicy chops with a fragrant herb rub and serve them with a scrumptious apple and cherry sauce.

—*Doris Heath*
 Franklin, North Carolina
 Former Field Editor

- 2 boneless pork loin chops (1/2 inch thick and 5 ounces *each*)
- 1/4 teaspoon dried thyme
- 1/8 teaspoon salt
- 1 tablespoon olive oil
- 2/3 cup apple juice
- 1 small red apple, sliced
- 2 tablespoons dried cherries *or* cranberries
- 2 tablespoons chopped onion
- 1 teaspoon cornstarch
- 1 tablespoon cold water

1. Sprinkle pork chops with thyme and salt. In a large skillet, cook pork in oil for 3-4 minutes on each side or until a thermometer reads 145°. Remove and let meat stand for 5 minutes.

2. Meanwhile, in the same skillet, combine the apple juice, apple, cherries and onion. Bring to a boil. In a small bowl, combine cornstarch and water until smooth; stir into skillet. Cook and stir for 1-2 minutes or until thickened. Spoon over pork chops.

APPLE-CHERRY PORK CHOPS

❝This went together really quickly and tasted fantastic. I used the cranberries as dried cherries are hard to come by here in Australia. Served it with mashed potato and steamed veggies for a weekend supper. Two thumbs up!❞
—*Louise.Hooper*

CHICKEN PARMIGIANA

"This is really good! I've made it many times. The sauce is great, and we serve it over angel hair pasta. Wonderful!"
—LauraManning

[2004]

CHICKEN PARMIGIANA
yield: 2 servings ∽ **prep: 20 min.**
cook: 30 min.

These tender crumb-coated chicken breasts are topped with a savory homemade spaghetti sauce and served over pasta. You can adjust the seasonings in this dish to your taste. My husband and I like lots of garlic, onion and herbs in everything.

—*Heather Sauter, Silver Spring, Maryland*

1	small onion, chopped
1	tablespoon olive oil
4	garlic cloves, minced
1	can (15 ounces) tomato sauce
1	can (14-1/2 ounces) stewed tomatoes
1	teaspoon each dried basil, thyme and oregano
1/4	teaspoon pepper
1/4	cup 2% milk
1/2	cup all-purpose flour
1	egg, lightly beaten
1/4	cup seasoned bread crumbs
1/4	cup grated Parmesan cheese
1	teaspoon salt-free garlic and herb seasoning
2	boneless skinless chicken breast halves (4 ounces each)
2	tablespoons butter
1/2	cup shredded mozzarella cheese

Hot cooked spaghetti

1. In a small saucepan, saute onion in oil until tender. Add garlic; cook 1 minute longer. Add tomato sauce, tomatoes, herbs and pepper. Bring to a boil. Reduce heat; cover and simmer for 20 minutes or until heated through.

2. Meanwhile, place the milk, flour and egg in separate shallow bowls. In another bowl, combine the bread crumbs, Parmesan cheese and herb seasoning. Dip chicken in milk; roll in flour. Dip in egg, then coat with crumb mixture.

3. In a small skillet, brown chicken in butter over medium heat until golden brown and a thermometer reads 170°. Sprinkle with mozzarella cheese. Cover and cook 3-4 minutes longer or until cheese is melted. Serve with the spaghetti and tomato sauce.

[2000]

BARLEY BURGER STEW
yield: 2 servings ∽ **prep: 15 min.**
cook: 50 min.

I found this hearty stew recipe in an old cookbook purchased at a flea market. The blend of beef and barley really hits the spot on days when there's a chill in the air.

—*Judy McCarthy, Derby, Kansas*

1/2	pound ground beef
1	small onion, chopped
1/4	cup chopped celery
2-1/4	cups tomato juice
1/2	cup water
1/4	cup medium pearl barley
1	to 1-1/2 teaspoons chili powder
1/2	teaspoon salt
1/4	teaspoon pepper

1. In a large saucepan over medium heat, cook the beef, onion and celery until meat is no longer pink; drain. Stir in the tomato juice, water, barley, chili powder, salt and pepper. Bring to a boil. Reduce heat; cover and simmer for 50-60 minutes or until barley is tender.

[2008]

MIXED GREENS WITH GARLIC-BASIL VINAIGRETTE

yield: 2 servings ∾ **prep/total time: 20 min.**

Toasted almonds add flavor, texture, crunch and extra nutrition to this tart, cranberry-studded green salad. The recipe includes a tongue-tingling homemade dressing that's a breeze to make.

—Dawn Bryant, Thedford, Nebraska

> 3 tablespoons olive oil
> 1 tablespoon raspberry vinegar
> 1 tablespoon chopped fresh basil
> 2 teaspoons brown sugar
> 1/2 teaspoon Dijon mustard
> 1 garlic clove, minced
> Dash pepper
> 3 cups torn mixed salad greens
> 2 tablespoons chopped dried cranberries
> 2 tablespoons sliced almonds, toasted

1. In a small bowl, whisk the oil, vinegar, basil, brown sugar, mustard, garlic and pepper. Divide salad greens between two plates; drizzle with the dressing. Sprinkle with cranberries and almonds.

[2006]

SESAME-SOY BROCCOLI FLORETS

yield: 2 servings ∾ **prep/total time: 15 min.**

We love to eat healthy, and this recipe has an Asian flare with a touch of sweetness that's sure to satisfy even those who turn up their noses at broccoli.

—Marianne Bauman, Modesto, California

> 2 cups fresh *or* frozen broccoli florets
> 1 tablespoon sugar
> 1 tablespoon olive oil
> 1 tablespoon reduced-sodium soy sauce
> 2 teaspoons rice vinegar
> 2 teaspoons sesame seeds, toasted

1. Place the broccoli in a steamer basket; place in a saucepan over 1 in. of water. Bring to a boil; cover and steam for 5-7 minutes or until crisp-tender.

2. Meanwhile, in a small saucepan, combine the sugar, oil, soy sauce and vinegar. Cook and stir over medium heat until the sugar is dissolved. Transfer the broccoli to a serving bowl. Drizzle with soy sauce mixture; sprinkle with sesame seeds.

[1994]

BASIL BUTTERED BEANS

yield: 2 servings ∾ **prep/total time: 10 min.**

I find that these beans make a versatile side. The small-portioned, fresh-tasting dish goes great with any meat entree.

—Laura Porter, Sheridan, Oregon

> 2 cups fresh green beans, cut into 2-inch pieces
> 2 tablespoons chopped onion
> 2 tablespoons chopped celery
> 1/4 cup water
> 2 tablespoons butter, melted
> 1-1/2 teaspoons minced fresh basil *or* 1/2 teaspoon dried basil
> 1/4 teaspoon salt
> 1/8 teaspoon pepper

1. In a large saucepan, combine the beans, onion, celery and water; bring to a boil. Boil, uncovered, for 10-15 minutes or until beans are tender. Drain. Add the butter, basil, salt and pepper; stir to coat.

MIXED GREENS WITH GARLIC-BASIL VINAIGRETTE

"This dressing is fabulous as a marinade or condiment for grilled fish or chicken too. It's really great!"
—*imclever5150*

[2004]

STUFFED SQUASH
FOR TWO

yield: 2 servings ∽ **prep: 20 min.**
bake: 65 min.

*My husband and I loved this recipe as
newlyweds, and now that our children are
grown, we are enjoying it again. As soon as the
weather turns cool, we get hungry for this
squash dish, filled with savory ground beef and
topped with a sprinkling of cheese.*

—*Barbara Rohlck, Sioux Falls, South Dakota*

1	medium acorn squash
1	tablespoon butter, melted
2	tablespoons brown sugar
3/4	teaspoon salt, *divided*
1/8	teaspoon pepper
1/2	pound ground beef
3	tablespoons chopped celery
3	tablespoons chopped onion
2	tablespoons all-purpose flour
1/2	teaspoon rubbed sage
3/4	cup 2% milk
1	cup salad croutons
1/4	cup shredded cheddar cheese

1. Cut the squash in half; discard seeds.
   Place the squash cut side down in an
   11-in. x 7-in. baking pan; add 1/2 in. of
   hot water.

2. Bake squash, uncovered, at 350° for
   30 minutes. Drain water from the pan;
   turn squash cut side up. Brush with
   butter; sprinkle with the brown sugar,
   1/4 teaspoon salt and pepper. Bake
   30-40 minutes or longer or until the
   squash is tender.

3. Meanwhile, in small skillet, cook the
   beef, celery and onion over medium
   heat until the meat is no longer pink;
   drain. Stir in flour, sage and remaining
   salt. Gradually stir in milk. Bring to a
   boil; cook and stir for 2 minutes or
   until thickened.

4. Remove from the heat; stir in croutons.
   Spoon into the squash halves. Sprinkle
   with cheese. Bake 5 minutes longer or
   until cheese is melted.

[2011]

HERB GARDEN
VEGETABLES

yield: 2 servings ∽ **prep/total time: 30 min.**

*I wanted to use all the wonderful vegetables
and herbs growing in our garden, so I came up
with this easy and tasty medley.*

—*Julie Stella, Champlin, Minnesota*

1/4	pound fresh green beans, trimmed
3/4	cup fresh sugar snap peas
1	tablespoon olive oil
3/4	cup julienned zucchini
3/4	cup julienned yellow summer squash
3/4	teaspoon *each* minced fresh rosemary, sage, basil and thyme
1/4	teaspoon crushed red pepper flakes
2	tablespoons crumbled blue cheese

1. In a small skillet over medium heat,
   cook the beans and peas in oil for
   3 minutes. Add the zucchini, squash,
   herbs and pepper flakes; cook and stir
   3-5 minutes longer or until vegetables
   are crisp-tender. Sprinkle with cheese
   just before serving.

FREEZE EXTRA HERBS

You can freeze chopped herbs in
freezer containers or bags and just
use the amount you need directly
from the freezer.

—*Taste of Home Cooking Experts*

STUFFED SQUASH
FOR TWO

❝I made this dish for the first
time and guarantee I will be
making it again and again. It
was delicious.❞
—*gypsymal*

[1995]

BROCCOLI CHEDDAR SOUP

yield: 2 servings ∽ prep/total time: 20 min.

This cheesy soup doesn't need to be made in big batches to be good.

—*Cheryl McRae, West Valley, Utah*

1/4	cup chopped onion
1/4	cup butter, cubed
1/4	cup all-purpose flour
1/4	teaspoon salt
1/4	teaspoon pepper
1-1/2	cups 2% milk
3/4	cup chicken broth
1	cup cooked chopped fresh *or* frozen broccoli
1/2	cup shredded cheddar cheese

---

1. In a small saucepan, saute the onion in butter until tender. Stir in flour, salt and pepper until blended; gradually add the milk and broth. Bring sauce to a boil; cook and stir for 2 minutes or until thickened.

2. Add the broccoli. Cook and stir until heated through. Remove from the heat; add the cheese, stirring until melted.

[2003]

CHEESY TEXAS TOAST

yield: 2 servings ∽ prep/total time: 15 min.

My husband and I love garlic bread, but to make a whole loaf is a waste for just the two of us, so I came up with this cheesy recipe. You can prepare it in a snap, and it's tasty, too!

—*LaDonna Reed*
Ponca City, Oklahoma, Field Editor

2	tablespoons butter, softened
4	slices French bread (1 inch thick)
1/4	to 1/2 teaspoon garlic powder
1	cup (4 ounces) shredded part-skim mozzarella cheese

Chopped green onions *or* parsley, optional

---

1. Spread butter over bread. Sprinkle with garlic powder and cheese. Place on an ungreased baking sheet.

2. Bake at 400° for 5-7 minutes or until cheese is melted. Sprinkle with onions or parsley if desired. Serve warm.

[2009]

CREAMY BOW TIE PASTA

yield: 2 servings ∽ prep/total time: 25 min.

Bring a little zip to your dinnertime routine with this saucy, seasoned pasta. It's a great accompaniment to almost any main course.

—*Kathy Kittell*
Lenexa, Kansas, Field Editor

1	cup uncooked bow tie pasta
1-1/2	teaspoons butter
2-1/4	teaspoons olive oil
1-1/2	teaspoons all-purpose flour
1/2	teaspoon minced garlic

Dash salt

Dash dried basil

Dash crushed red pepper flakes

3	tablespoons 2% milk
2	tablespoons chicken broth
1	tablespoon water
2	tablespoons shredded Parmesan cheese
1	tablespoon sour cream

---

1. Cook the pasta according to package directions. Meanwhile, in a small saucepan, melt the butter. Stir in the oil, flour, garlic and seasonings until blended. Gradually add milk, broth and water. Bring to a boil; cook and stir for 2 minutes or until slightly thickened.

2. Remove from the heat; stir in cheese and sour cream. Drain the pasta; toss with sauce.

CREAMY BOW TIE PASTA

"OMG, we started out cooking this as a side dish for two, just like the recipe says. Changed my mind while cooking, and wound up tripling the recipe to serve as a main dish for two, with bread and a salad on the side. Very, very yummy. It's a keeper."
—*kegs1*

[1997]

BAKED BEANS FOR TWO

yield: 2 servings ∽ prep: 5 min.
bake: 30 min.

A few additional ingredients dress up canned beans. This recipe can be easily doubled.

—Eldora Yoder, Versailles, Missouri

- 1 can (16 ounces) pork and beans
- 3 tablespoons ketchup
- 2 tablespoons chopped onion
- 2 to 3 teaspoons brown sugar
- 2 to 3 teaspoons honey
- 1 teaspoon prepared mustard
- 1/2 teaspoon Worcestershire sauce
- 1/8 teaspoon prepared horseradish

1. In an ungreased 1-qt. baking dish, combine all the ingredients. Bake, uncovered, at 350° for 30-40 minutes or until heated through.

[2004]

SUMMER SQUASH CASSEROLE

yield: 2 servings ∽ prep: 10 min.
bake: 25 min.

Onion and cheddar cheese perk up the rich flavor of summer squash in this comforting casserole. A crispy cornflake-crumb topping adds a little crunch.

—Katherine Metz, Jacksonville, Florida

- 2 small yellow summer squash, sliced
- 1/4 cup chopped onion
- 1/2 teaspoon salt, *divided*
- 1 egg
- 1/4 cup mayonnaise
- 2 teaspoons sugar

Pepper to taste

- 1/4 cup shredded cheddar cheese
- 2 tablespoons crushed cornflakes
- 1-1/2 teaspoons butter, melted

1. In a small saucepan, combine squash, onion and 1/4 teaspoon salt. Cover with water. Bring to a boil. Reduce the heat; simmer, uncovered, for 2 minutes or until squash is crisp-tender. Drain.

2. In a small bowl, whisk egg, mayonnaise, sugar, pepper and remaining salt until blended. Stir in cheese and squash mixture. Transfer to a greased 2-cup baking dish. Toss the cornflakes and butter; sprinkle over top.

3. Bake the squash, uncovered, at 350° for 25-30 minutes or until golden brown and bubbly.

[2001]

CHICKEN VEGETABLE SOUP

yield: 2 servings ∽ prep: 10 min.
cook: 35 min.

I love eating a big bowl of this colorful fresh-tasting soup on a winter's day. What a great way to warm up!

—Ruth Wimmer, Bland, Virginia

- 2 cups chicken broth
- 1 cup fresh *or* frozen corn
- 1 small celery rib, chopped
- 1 small carrot, chopped
- 1 small onion, chopped
- 1 cup cubed cooked chicken
- 1/2 cup canned diced tomatoes

Salt and pepper to taste

1. In a large saucepan, combine the first five ingredients. Bring to a boil. Reduce heat; cover and simmer for 25-30 minutes or until vegetables are tender. Stir in the chicken, tomatoes, salt and pepper; heat through.

BAKED BEANS FOR TWO

"I love baked beans, but the canned versions always need a little help. This recipe is the help they need. I followed the recipe and added four broiled Eckrich smoky links, maple flavor, mixed the sauce in the sausage drippings, then added to the beans and baked for 30 minutes. Mmm, very good."
—*goodcook321*

[1998]

HONEY-LIME FRUIT SALAD

yield: 2 servings   prep/total time: 10 min.

When my husband and I yearn for something a little different at mealtime, I fix this unique fruit salad. It's really light and refreshing.

—*Emma Magielda, Amsterdam, New York*

1-1/2   cups torn salad greens
    1   can (11 ounces) mandarin oranges, drained
    1   small red apple, sliced
    3   tablespoons thawed limeade *or* lemonade concentrate
    3   tablespoons honey
    3   tablespoons canola oil
  1/2   teaspoon poppy seeds

1. On two salad plates, arrange the greens, oranges and apple. In a small bowl, whisk the remaining ingredients. Drizzle over salads.

[1999]

PECAN GREEN BEANS

yield: 2 servings   prep/total time: 20 min.

Being a teenager, my great-grandson Derek has developed his own tastes and doesn't always care for the same things I do. But this recipe is a tasty vegetable dish we both enjoy.

—*Ruby Williams*
Bogalusa, Louisiana, Former Field Editor

1-1/2   cups cut fresh green beans
    2   tablespoons chopped pecans
    1   tablespoon butter
  1/4   teaspoon salt
  1/8   teaspoon pepper

1. Place beans in a saucepan and cover with water; bring to a boil. Cook, uncovered, for 8-10 minutes or until crisp-tender.

2. Meanwhile, in a skillet, saute pecans in butter for 3 minutes or until golden brown. Drain the beans; add to skillet. Sprinkle with the salt and pepper; toss to coat.

[2002]

CHICKEN BEAN PASTA SOUP

yield: 2 servings   prep/total time: 30 min.

This comforting and colorful soup is loaded with old-fashioned goodness. The flavorful broth is chock-full of veggies, chicken and macaroni. By changing the vegetables, you can make it different every time.

—*Margery Bryan*
Moses Lake, Washington
Former Field Editor

  1/2   cup chopped onion
  1/2   cup chopped carrot
    1   tablespoon butter
    1   can (14-1/2 ounces) chicken broth
  2/3   cup cubed cooked chicken
  1/2   cup cauliflowerets
  1/2   cup canned kidney beans, rinsed and drained
  1/4   cup uncooked elbow macaroni
    1   cup torn fresh spinach
  1/8   teaspoon pepper
Seasoned salad croutons, optional

1. In a large saucepan, saute onion and carrot in butter for 4 minutes or until crisp-tender. Stir in the broth, chicken, cauliflower, beans and macaroni. Bring to a boil.

2. Reduce the heat; cover and simmer for 15-20 minutes or until the macaroni and vegetables are tender. Add spinach and pepper; cook and stir until spinach is wilted. Garnish with the croutons if desired.

CHICKEN BEAN PASTA SOUP

"Very good soup, would also taste good with leftover beef instead of chicken."
—*katlaydee3*

[1995]

BISCUITS FOR TWO

yield: 4 biscuits ∞ prep/total time: 20 min.

A friend shared this recipe with me. I think the biscuits taste wonderful warm from the oven.

—*Sylvia Mccoy, Lees Summit, Missouri*

1	cup all-purpose flour
2-1/2	teaspoons baking powder
1	teaspoon sugar
1/2	teaspoon salt
1/8	teaspoon cream of tartar
1/4	cup shortening
1/2	cup 2% milk

1. In a small bowl, combine the first five ingredients. Cut in shortening until mixture resembles coarse crumbs. Stir in the milk just until moistened. Turn onto a lightly floured surface; knead 8-10 times.

2. Pat or roll out to 1/2-in. thickness; cut with a floured 2-1/2-in. biscuit cutter.

3. Place on a greased baking sheet. Bake at 450° for 10-12 minutes or until golden brown. Serve warm.

BISCUITS FOR TWO

"I've been making these biscuits for a couple of years now and wouldn't think of going back to canned! They are delicious, and turn out light and fluffy every time. Last night I made them with butter-flavored shortening and let them sit a few minutes before baking, and they rose even higher. My husband has only one 'word' for these, Mmmmmmmmmm."

—*walkingfit*

[2010]

CREAMY BUTTERNUT SQUASH SOUP

yield: 2 servings ∞ prep: 15 min.
cook: 20 min.

I used to live in Australia, where this soup is served often. Once I tried it, I knew I had to have the recipe so I could make it at home. It's now one of my favorites.

—*Tiffany Pope, Draper, Utah*

1/4	cup chopped onion
1	tablespoon butter
3	cups cubed peeled butternut squash
1	medium potato, peeled and cubed
1-1/2	cups water
1-1/2	teaspoons chicken bouillon granules
1/4	teaspoon salt
Dash pepper	
1/4	cup evaporated milk

1. In a small saucepan, saute onion in butter until tender. Add squash and potato; cook and stir for 2 minutes. Add water, bouillon, salt and pepper; bring to a boil. Reduce heat; cover and simmer for 15-20 minutes or until the vegetables are tender.

2. Cool slightly. In a blender, cover and process soup until smooth. Return to the pan; stir in milk and heat through.

[2006]

TOMATO RICE PILAF

yield: 2 servings ∞ prep/total time: 25 min.

Parsley, green onions and tomatoes add festive color to this mild rice dish. I serve this pilaf quite often as a change from potatoes because it complements any type of meat.

—*Carole Fraser, North York, Ontario*

2	teaspoons butter
1/2	cup uncooked long grain rice
1	small onion, sliced
1-1/4	cups chicken broth
2	tablespoons chopped green onion
2	tablespoons chopped tomato
2	tablespoons minced fresh parsley

1. In a 3-cup microwave-safe dish, melt the butter. Stir in the rice and onion. Microwave, uncovered, on high for 2-3 minutes or until rice is lightly browned and onion is tender, stirring once. Add the broth.

2. Cover and cook on high for 13-15 minutes or until liquid is absorbed. Stir in the green onion, tomato and parsley.

Editor's Note: This recipe was tested in a 1,100-watt microwave.

[2010]

TWICE-BAKED
SWEET POTATOES

yield: 2 servings ∾ **prep: 20 min.**
bake: 15 min.

*Everyone loves twice-baked potatoes, but
they're even better made with sweet potatoes!
The microwave helps turn ordinary potatoes
into a dish fit for a holiday.*

—*Darlene Brenden*
Salem, Oregon, Field Editor

2 medium sweet potatoes
2 ounces cream cheese, softened
2 tablespoons sour cream
1 tablespoon butter
1/4 teaspoon salt
2 tablespoons brown sugar
1/2 teaspoon ground cinnamon

1. Scrub and pierce potatoes; place on a
microwave-safe plate. Microwave,
uncovered, on high for 12-14 minutes
or until tender, turning once.

2. When cool enough to handle, cut a
thin slice off the top of each potato
and discard. Scoop out pulp, leaving a
thin shell. In a large bowl, mash the
pulp. Add cream cheese, sour cream,
butter and salt; mix well. Spoon into
potato shells.

3. Place on a baking sheet. Sprinkle with
brown sugar and cinnamon. Bake,
uncovered, at 425° for 12-15 minutes
or until heated through and topping is
golden brown.

Editor's Note: This recipe was tested in a
1,100-watt microwave.

[1998]

VEGETABLE RAMEKINS

yield: 2 servings ∾ **prep/total time: 30 min.**

*Our children and grandchildren live far away,
so my husband, Jim, and I frequently plan a
quiet dinner by candlelight. We have these
ramekins often since we can pull fresh things
from our garden all year. It is a colorful and
delicious side dish.*

—*Dona Alsover, Upland, California*

1 small zucchini *or* yellow summer
squash, halved and cut into 1/2-inch
slices
1/4 cup chopped green pepper
1/3 cup broccoli florets
1 medium carrot, julienned
1 medium potato, peeled, cooked and
cubed
2 tablespoons butter
2 tablespoons all-purpose flour
3/4 cup 2% milk
1/4 teaspoon garlic salt
1/8 teaspoon coarsely ground pepper
1/4 cup shredded cheddar cheese
1 tablespoon minced fresh parsley
1 tablespoon chopped walnuts

1. In a large saucepan over medium heat,
cook squash, green pepper, broccoli
and carrot in boiling water until
crisp-tender; drain. Stir in the potato.

2. Spoon into two greased ovenproof
10-oz. custard cups or baking dishes.
In a small saucepan, melt butter; stir in
the flour, milk, garlic salt and pepper
until smooth. Cook for 2-3 minutes,
gradually adding the cheese in small
amounts; cook and stir until the
cheese is melted.

3. Pour over vegetables. Sprinkle with
parsley and walnuts. Bake, uncovered,
at 350° for 20-25 minutes or until
sauce is bubbly.

TWICE-BAKED
SWEET POTATOES

"This recipe is fabulous
and easy. I have made it
a couple of times. I add
2 tablespoons of sugar to
one potato or 4
tablespoons to two
potatoes. Other than
that, no changes. Love
this recipe!"
—*SheKendra*

[1993]

CHOCOLATE BREAD PUDDING

yield: 2 servings ∽ **prep: 15 min. + standing**
bake: 30 min.

This is a fun recipe because the chocolate makes it different from traditional bread pudding. It's a rich, comforting dessert.

—Mildred Sherrer
Fort Worth, Texas, Former Field Editor

---

    2 ounces semisweet chocolate
  1/2 cup half-and-half cream
  2/3 cup sugar
  1/2 cup 2% milk
    1 egg
    1 teaspoon vanilla extract
  1/4 teaspoon salt
    4 slices day-old bread, crusts removed
       and cut into cubes (about 3 cups)
Confectioners' sugar *or* whipped cream,
  optional

---

1. In a small microwave-wave bowl, melt the chocolate; stir until smooth. Stir in cream; set aside.

2. In a large bowl, whisk the sugar, milk, egg, vanilla and salt. Stir in chocolate mixture. Add bread cubes and toss to coat. Let stand for 15 minutes.

3. Spoon into two greased 2-cup souffle dishes. Bake at 350° for 30 to 35 minutes or until a knife inserted near the center comes out clean.

4. If desired, sprinkle the bread pudding with confectioners' sugar or top with a dollop of whipped cream.

[2011]

PEAR PERFECTION

yield: 2 servings ∽ **prep: 20 min.**
cook: 30 min. + chilling

(Pictured on page 352)

What makes this dessert especially great is that it can be made in advance and year-round. I use lime sherbet for St. Patrick's Day and pineapple sherbet for Easter. For a yuletide touch, add a sprinkle of pomegranate seeds.

—Pat Neaves, *Lees Summit, Missouri*

  1/2 cup pomegranate juice
  1/4 cup orange juice
1-1/2 teaspoons lemon juice
  1/4 cup sugar
    1 teaspoon grated lemon peel
    1 large pear, peeled, halved and cored
    1 tablespoon semisweet chocolate chips
    1 tablespoon white baking chips
  2/3 cup raspberry sherbet
    2 tablespoons sliced almonds

---

1. In a small saucepan, bring the juices, sugar and lemon peel to a boil. Reduce heat; carefully add pear halves. Cover and simmer for 8-10 minutes or until tender. Remove pears with a slotted spoon; refrigerate for 1 hour.

2. Bring the poaching liquid to a boil; cook until liquid is reduced to about 2 tablespoons. Cool.

3. In a microwave, melt chocolate and baking chips in separate bowls; stir until smooth. Drizzle chocolate on a plate. Place the pear halves on plate; top with sherbet. Drizzle with the poaching liquid and the melted white chips. Sprinkle with the almonds. Serve immediately.

[2000]

PEACH CRISP CUPS

yield: 2 servings ∾ prep: 10 min. ∾ bake: 30 min.

There may be only two servings in this comforting, old-fashioned dessert, but they're bursting with peach flavor.

—*Aida Von Babbel, Coquitlam, British Columbia*

- 2 medium peaches, peeled and sliced
- 2 teaspoons sugar
- 2 tablespoons quick-cooking oats
- 2 tablespoons all-purpose flour
- 1 tablespoon brown sugar
- 2 teaspoons chopped almonds
- 5 teaspoons cold butter
- 1/4 teaspoon almond extract

---

1. In a small bowl, combine peaches and sugar. Transfer to two greased 6-oz. baking dishes. In a small bowl, combine the oats, flour, brown sugar and almonds. Cut in the butter until mixture resembles coarse crumbs. Sprinkle with almond extract; toss. Sprinkle over the peaches.

2. Bake, uncovered, at 375° for 30 minutes or until bubbly and golden brown.

[2008]

LEMON PUDDING SOUFFLES

yield: 2 servings ∾ prep: 20 min.
bake: 25 min.

With their tangy lemon flavor, these creamy souffles make the perfect finale for a special meal. It's fun to dress up each dessert with an edible flower.

—*Lily Julow, Gainesville, Florida, Field Editor*

- 1 egg, *separated*
- 1/3 cup sugar
- 1/3 cup 2% milk
- 1 tablespoon butter, melted
- 1 tablespoon all-purpose flour

Dash salt

- 2 tablespoons lemon juice
- 1/2 teaspoon grated lemon peel

Coarse sugar, edible pansies and fresh mint leaves, optional

---

1. In a small bowl, beat egg yolk until slightly thickened. Gradually add sugar, beating until thick and lemon-colored. Beat in the milk, butter, flour and salt. Stir in lemon juice and peel.

2. In a small bowl, beat egg white until stiff peaks form. With a spatula, stir a fourth of the egg white into lemon mixture until no white streaks remain. Fold in remaining egg white until combined.

3. Divide between two ungreased 6-oz. ramekins or custard cups. Place in an 8-in. square baking dish; add 1 in. of hot water to dish.

4. Bake at 350° for 25-30 minutes or until the tops are golden brown. If desired, sprinkle with coarse sugar, and garnish with pansies and mint. Serve immediately.

Editor's Note: Verify that flowers are edible and have not been treated with chemicals.

[2003]

CHILLED
STRAWBERRY CREAM

yield: 2 servings ∾ prep: 10 min. + chilling

Made with only three ingredients, this cool, refreshing dessert goes together in a jiffy, yet it's pretty enough for a special occasion.

—*Ann Main, Moorefield, Ontario*

- 2 cups frozen unsweetened whole strawberries
- 1/4 cup confectioners' sugar
- 1/2 cup heavy whipping cream

---

1. Place the strawberries and sugar in a food processor; cover and process until finely chopped.

2. In a small bowl, beat cream until stiff peaks form. Fold into berries. Pour into serving dishes. Refrigerate or freeze for 25 minutes.

[2012]

CHOCOLATE CAYENNE SOUFFLES

(Pictured on page 349)

yield: 2 servings ∽ **prep: 25 min.** ∽ **bake: 15 min.**

This rich, chocolately souffle has a surprise ending...a little kick of heat from the cayenne pepper. It's very yummy.

—*Diane Halferty, Corpus Christi, Texas*

1	egg
1	teaspoon plus 1 tablespoon butter, *divided*
2	teaspoons plus 4 tablespoons sugar, *divided*
2	tablespoons all-purpose flour
1/2	cup 2% milk
2	ounces semisweet chocolate, chopped
1/8	teaspoon cayenne pepper

Dash salt

---

1. Separate egg; let stand at room temperature for 30 minutes. Coat two 6-oz. ramekins with 1 teaspoon butter and sprinkle with 2 teaspoons sugar. Place ramekins on a baking sheet; set aside.

2. In a small saucepan over medium heat, melt remaining butter. Stir in 2 tablespoons sugar and the flour until smooth. Gradually whisk in milk. Bring to a boil, stirring constantly. Cook and stir 1-2 minutes longer or until thickened. Whisk in the chocolate, cayenne and salt until the chocolate is melted. Transfer to a small bowl.

3. Stir a small amount of hot mixture into the egg yolk; return all to the bowl, stirring constantly. Cool slightly.

4. In another bowl and with clean beaters, beat egg white on medium speed until soft peaks form. Gradually beat in remaining sugar on high until stiff peaks form. With a spatula, stir a fourth of the egg white into chocolate mixture until no white streaks remain. Fold in remaining egg white until combined. Transfer to prepared ramekins.

5. Bake at 400° for 12-15 minutes or until the tops are puffed and centers appear set. Serve immediately.

[1999]

BLUEBERRY CAKE CUPS

yield: 2 servings ∽ **prep: 10 min.**
bake: 25 min.

For a tasty serving of cake just for two, serve these yummy desserts. It is a great treat utilizing summer blueberries.

—*Suzanne McKinley, Lyons, Georgia, Former Field Editor*

1/4	cup all-purpose flour
1/4	cup sugar
1/2	teaspoon baking powder

Dash salt

1/4	cup 2% milk
1	tablespoon butter, melted
1	cup blueberries, *divided*

---

1. In a small bowl, combine the flour, sugar, baking powder and salt. Stir in milk and butter just until moistened.

2. Divide half of the berries between two greased 10-oz. custard cups. Top with batter and remaining berries. Bake at 375° for 25-30 minutes or until golden brown. Serve warm.

[1995]

QUICK CHERRY TURNOVERS

yield: 4 turnovers ∽ **prep/total time: 20 min.**

Refrigerated crescent rolls let you make these fruit-filled pastries in a hurry. Feel free to experiment with other pie fillings.

—*Elleen Oberrueter, Danbury, Iowa*

1	tube (8 ounces) refrigerated crescent rolls
1	cup cherry pie filling
1/2	cup confectioners' sugar
1	to 2 tablespoons milk

---

1. Unroll crescent roll dough and separate into four squares; place on an ungreased baking sheet. Press seams and perforations together. Spoon 1/4 pie filling in one corner of each square. Fold to make triangles; pinch to seal.

2. Bake at 375° for 10-12 minutes or until golden. Combine sugar and milk to achieve drizzling consistency. Drizzle over turnovers; serve warm.

[2004]

CHOCOLATE LAYER CAKE

yield: 4 servings ∞ prep: 30 min. ∞ bake: 30 min. + cooling

You can "halve" your cake and eat it, too, with this chocolaty classic. My mother came up with the delicious dessert after we kids left the nest. Today, I split this tempting two-layer treat with my husband.

—*Verna Mae Floyd, Highlands, Texas*

1/4	cup shortening
1	cup sugar
1	egg
1/2	teaspoon vanilla extract
1	cup all-purpose flour
1/4	cup baking cocoa
1	teaspoon baking powder
1/4	teaspoon baking soda
1/4	teaspoon salt
3/4	cup 2% milk

FROSTING:

1/2	cup butter, softened
2-1/2	cups confectioners' sugar
1/2	cup baking cocoa
1	teaspoon vanilla extract
2	to 3 tablespoons hot water

1. In a large bowl, cream shortening and sugar until light and fluffy. Beat in egg and vanilla. Combine the flour, cocoa, baking powder, baking soda and salt; add to creamed mixture alternately with milk, beating well after each addition.

2. Pour into a greased and floured 9-in. round baking pan. Bake at 350° for 30-35 minutes or until a toothpick inserted near the center comes out clean. Cool in pan for 10 minutes before removing to a wire rack to cool completely.

3. For frosting, in a small bowl, cream butter until light and fluffy. Gradually beat in the confectioners' sugar, cocoa, vanilla and enough water to achieve spreading consistency.

4. Cut cake horizontally into two layers. Place bottom layer on a serving plate; spread with 1/2 cup frosting. Top with remaining layer. Spread remaining frosting over top and sides of cake.

CHOCOLATE LAYER CAKE

"This is a great recipe when a full-size cake isn't needed. I baked mine in an 8-in. square pan, then cut in half and stacked to frost. The frosting recipe is a keeper. I used a bit of warmed milk instead of water though. Thanks for sharing this one with us!"

—*carrolcofer*

PREPARING A CAKE PAN

1. Grease the sides and bottom of the pan by spreading shortening with a paper towel over the interior of the pan.

2. Sprinkle 1 to 2 tablespoons of flour into the greased pan; tilt the pan to coat bottom and sides. Turn pan over and tap to remove any excess flour.

[2004]

RUSTIC FRUIT TART

yield: 2 servings ∞ **prep: 20 min. + standing bake: 25 min.**

My husband Don and I love pie, but we can't eat a whole 9-inch pie by ourselves. So I make these easy tarts using rhubarb and fruit from our red raspberry bushes. Sometimes I substitute apples, peaches or our homegrown blueberries for the rhubarb.

—*Naomi Olson, Hamilton, Michigan*

- 1 cup all-purpose flour
- 1/2 teaspoon salt
- 1/4 cup canola oil
- 2 tablespoons milk
- 1 cup diced fresh *or* frozen rhubarb, thawed
- 1 cup fresh *or* frozen raspberries, thawed
- 1/2 cup sugar
- 2 tablespoons quick-cooking tapioca

GLAZE:

- 6 tablespoons confectioners' sugar
- 1 teaspoon water
- 1/8 teaspoon almond extract

1. In a large bowl, combine flour and salt. Add oil and milk, tossing with a fork until mixture forms a ball. Shape the dough into a disk; wrap in plastic wrap. Refrigerate for at least 1 hour.

2. In another bowl, combine the rhubarb, raspberries, sugar and tapioca; let stand for 15 minutes. Unwrap the dough and place on a parchment-lined baking sheet. Cover with waxed paper and roll the dough into an 11-in. circle. Discard waxed paper.

3. Spoon fruit mixture into the center of dough to within 2 in. of the edges. Fold edges of dough over fruit, leaving center uncovered. Bake at 400° for 25-30 minutes or until crust is golden brown and filling is bubbly. Remove to a wire rack. Combine glaze ingredients until smooth. Drizzle over warm tart.

Editor's Note: If using frozen rhubarb, measure rhubarb while still frozen, then thaw completely. Drain in a colander, but do not press liquid out.

[2007]

CINNAMON-RAISIN BREAD PUDDING

yield: 2 servings ∞ **prep: 5 min. bake: 35 min.**

This rich bread pudding recipe goes together in minutes. There's plenty of old-fashioned cinnamon flavor.

—*Edna Hoffman*
Hebron, Indiana, Field Editor

- 1 cup cubed cinnamon-raisin bread
- 1 egg
- 2/3 cup 2% milk
- 3 tablespoons brown sugar
- 1 tablespoon butter, melted
- 1/2 teaspoon ground cinnamon
- 1/4 teaspoon ground nutmeg
- Dash salt
- 1/3 cup raisins

1. Place bread cubes in a greased 2-cup baking dish. In a small bowl, whisk egg, milk, brown sugar, butter, cinnamon, nutmeg and salt until blended. Stir in raisins. Pour over bread; let stand for 15 minutes or until bread is softened.

2. Bake at 350° for 35-40 minutes or until a knife inserted near the center comes out clean. Serve warm.

CINNAMON-RAISIN BREAD PUDDING

"The first time I made this recipe, it was part of a dinner that I was taking to a sick friend. I doubled it as I wanted enough for my husband and me, too. It was so good that I made it again the very next day. I am now copying the recipe as that same friend raved about it and wanted the recipe."
—*Katmom51*

[2001]

LI'L PECAN PIES

yield: 2 servings ✎ **prep: 15 min. + chilling**
bake: 35 min.

These tempting little tarts have all the rich traditional taste of a full-size pecan pie in a much smaller package.

—*Christine Boitos, Livonia, Michigan*

- 1/2 cup all-purpose flour
- 1/8 teaspoon salt
- 3 tablespoons shortening
- 4 teaspoons cold water

FILLING:

- 1/3 cup pecan halves
- 1 egg
- 1/3 cup corn syrup
- 1/3 cup packed brown sugar
- 1/2 teaspoon vanilla extract

Whipped cream, optional

---

1. In a bowl, combine flour and salt; cut in shortening until crumbly. Gradually add the water, tossing with fork until the dough forms a ball. Cover and refrigerate for at least 30 minutes.

2. Divide dough in half. Roll each half into a 6-in. circle. Transfer to two 4-1/2-in. tart pans; fit pastry into pans, trimming if necessary. Arrange pecans in shells.

3. In a bowl, combine egg, corn syrup, brown sugar and vanilla; mix well. Pour over the pecans. Place shells on a baking sheet. Bake at 375° for 35-40 minutes or until a knife inserted near the center comes out clean. Cool the pies on a wire rack. Top with whipped cream if desired.

[2008]

PEACHES 'N' CREAM CUPS

yield: 2 servings ✎ **prep: 10 min. + chilling**

For a no-fuss dessert that's as cool and refreshing as a summer breeze, try these tasty treats with a gingersnap crust and creamy yogurt filling.

—*Suzanne McKinley*
Lyons, Georgia, Former Field Editor

- 1 gingersnap cookie, crumbled
- 1/4 teaspoon ground ginger
- 3/4 cup (6 ounces) peach yogurt
- 1/4 cup cream cheese, softened
- 1/4 teaspoon vanilla extract
- 1/3 cup sliced peaches, drained and chopped

---

1. In a small bowl, combine crumbs and ginger; set aside. In a small bowl, beat the yogurt, cream cheese and vanilla until smooth. Fold in peaches.

2. Spoon into two 6-oz. custard cups; cover and refrigerate for 1 hour. Just before serving, sprinkle with reserved crumb mixture.

LI'L NUT PIES

If pecans are not your favorite type of nut, you can use an equal amount of a different variety, such as walnut halves, macadamia nuts, whole blanched almonds, whole cashews or even peanuts.

—*Taste of Home Cooking Experts*

LI'L PECAN PIES

"My husband and I loved these, and I will definitely be making them again. I baked them in my small Pyrex glass bowls and it worked out perfectly."
—*cmm_bama*

∾ DESSERTS ∾

[2007]

BLACK FOREST DREAM DESSERT

yield: 12 servings ∾ **prep: 45 min. + chilling**

This rich, chilled dessert seems to hit the spot on a hot summer's day. The recipe makes a large dessert, but my family never complains if there happen to be leftovers!

—Angela Leinenbach
Mechanicsvlle, Virginia, Field Editor

1	cup all-purpose flour
2	tablespoons sugar
1/2	cup cold butter, cubed
1/2	cup flaked coconut
1/2	cup chopped walnuts, toasted
1	package (8 ounces) cream cheese, softened
1	cup confectioners' sugar
1	carton (8 ounces) frozen whipped topping, thawed, *divided*
1	can (21 ounces) cherry pie filling
1-1/2	cups semisweet chocolate chips
2-1/2	cups cold milk
2	packages (3.4 ounces *each*) instant vanilla pudding mix

Chocolate curls, optional

1. In a large bowl, combine the flour and sugar; cut in butter until crumbly. Stir in coconut and walnuts. Press into an ungreased 13-in. x 9-in. baking dish. Bake at 350° for 15-18 minutes or until lightly browned. Cool on a wire rack.

2. In a small bowl, beat the cream cheese and confectioners' sugar until smooth. Fold in 1 cup whipped topping. Spread over crust. Top with pie filling; cover and chill.

3. In a microwave, melt chocolate chips; stir until smooth. In a large bowl, whisk the milk and pudding mixes for 2 minutes. Let stand for 2 minutes or until soft-set. Whisk a small amount of pudding into melted chocolate. Return all to the pudding, whisking constantly. Pour over the cherry filling. Refrigerate for 2 hours or until set.

4. Just before serving, spread remaining whipped topping over dessert. Garnish with chocolate curls if desired.

CREATING CHOCOLATE CURLS

Adding a pretty chocolate garnish to any dessert is a cinch. Use a vegetable peeler to "peel" curls from a solid block of chocolate. To keep the strips intact, allow them to fall gently onto a plate or a single layer of waxed paper. If you get only shavings, your chocolate may be too hard, so warm it slightly.

[2009]

CINNAMON BISCUIT PEACH COBBLER

**yield: 12 servings ∽ prep: 30 min.
bake: 20 min.**

(Pictured on page 351)

As a high school English teacher, I don't always have time to make the gourmet meals I would like. This recipe is a quick, simple treat that I made once and now have to bring to every gathering! If short on time, substitute refrigerated biscuits and sprinkle with the walnut and cinnamon mixture.

—*Fawna Eastman, Lewiston, Montana*

- 1-1/2 cups all-purpose flour
- 1 tablespoon plus 1/3 cup packed brown sugar, *divided*
- 2 teaspoons baking powder
- 1/4 teaspoon salt
- 1/4 teaspoon baking soda
- 6 tablespoons cold butter, cubed
- 1/2 cup 2% milk
- 2 tablespoons butter, melted
- 3/4 cup chopped walnuts
- 3/4 teaspoon ground cinnamon

FILLING:
- 1 cup packed brown sugar
- 2 tablespoons cornstarch
- 3/4 teaspoon grated lemon peel
- 1 cup water
- 9 cups sliced peeled peaches

1. In a small bowl, combine the flour, 1 tablespoon brown sugar, baking powder, salt and baking soda; cut in cold butter until mixture resembles coarse crumbs. Stir in milk just until blended.

2. Transfer to a floured surface; knead 10-12 times. Pat into a 12-in. square. Brush with melted butter.

3. Combine the walnuts, cinnamon and remaining brown sugar; sprinkle over dough to within 1/2 in. of edge. Roll up jelly-roll style. Seal dough; set aside.

4. For filling, in a large saucepan, combine the brown sugar, cornstarch and lemon peel. Gradually stir in

water until blended. Add peaches. Bring to a boil. Cook and stir for 2 minutes or until thickened and bubbly. Transfer to a greased 13-in. x 9-in. baking dish.

5. Cut biscuit dough into twelve 1-in. slices; arrange the biscuits over filling. Bake, uncovered, at 400° for 20-25 minutes or until golden brown.

[2008]

CARAMEL APPLE BREAD PUDDING

**yield: 8 servings ∽ prep: 15 min.
bake: 35 min.**

(Pictured on page 349)

Tender, sweet pudding with delicious apple pieces, spices and a luscious low-fat caramel topping make a rich-tasting comfort dish without all the fat. Yum!

—*Michelle Borland, Peoria, Illinois*

- 1 cup unsweetened applesauce
- 1 cup fat-free milk
- 1/2 cup packed brown sugar
- 1/2 cup egg substitute
- 1 teaspoon vanilla extract
- 1/2 teaspoon ground cinnamon
- 5 cups cubed day-old bread
- 1/2 cup chopped peeled apple
- 1/2 cup fat-free whipped topping
- 1/2 cup fat-free caramel ice cream topping

1. In a large bowl, combine the applesauce, milk, brown sugar, egg substitute, vanilla and cinnamon. Fold in bread cubes and apple; let stand for 15 minutes or until bread is softened.

2. Pour into an 8-in. square baking dish coated with cooking spray. Bake, uncovered, at 325° for 35-40 minutes or until a knife inserted near the center comes out clean. Serve warm with whipped topping and caramel topping. Refrigerate leftovers.

[2009]

PUMPKIN WALNUT CHEESECAKE

yield: 12 servings ∽ prep: 40 min.
bake: 1-1/2 hours + chilling

One of my Bunco friends gave me this recipe, and it has quickly become a family favorite. It's a great dessert for Thanksgiving, and you can't eat just one slice!

—*Susan Garoutte, Georgetown, Texas, Field Editor*

- 2 cups graham cracker crumbs
- 1/4 cup sugar
- 6 tablespoons butter, melted

FILLING:
- 3 packages (8 ounces each) cream cheese, softened
- 3/4 cup sugar
- 3/4 cup packed dark brown sugar
- 1 can (15 ounces) solid-pack pumpkin
- 1/4 cup heavy whipping cream
- 1 teaspoon ground cinnamon
- 1 teaspoon ground cloves
- 5 eggs, lightly beaten

TOPPING:
- 6 tablespoons butter, softened
- 1 cup packed dark brown sugar
- 1 cup chopped walnuts

1. Place a greased 9-in. springform pan on a double thickness of heavy-duty foil (about 18 in. square). Securely wrap foil around pan. In a small bowl, combine cracker crumbs and sugar; stir in butter. Press onto the bottom and 1 in. up the sides of prepared pan.

2. In a large bowl, beat cream cheese and sugars until smooth. Beat in the pumpkin, cream, cinnamon and cloves until blended. Add eggs; beat on low speed just until combined. Pour over crust. Place the springform pan in a large baking pan; add 1 in. of hot water to larger pan.

3. Bake at 325° for 1 hour. For topping, in a small bowl, combine butter and brown sugar. Stir in walnuts. Carefully sprinkle over hot cheesecake.

4. Bake 30 minutes longer or until center is just set. Remove springform pan from water bath. Cool on a wire rack for 10 minutes. Carefully run a knife around edge of pan to loosen; cool 1 hour longer. Refrigerate overnight. Remove sides of pan.

[2008]

FROZEN STRAWBERRY DESSERT

yield: 9 servings ∽ prep: 25 min. + freezing

The strawberry flavor comes through in every bite. People always comment on the nice and chewy shortbread crust and delectable crumbled topping.

—*Gayleen Grote, Battleview, North Dakota*

- 1 cup all-purpose flour
- 1/4 cup packed brown sugar
- 1/2 cup cold butter, cubed
- 1/2 cup chopped pecans
- 2 cups frozen unsweetened strawberries, thawed
- 1 cup sugar
- 1 teaspoon lemon juice
- 1 cup heavy whipping cream, whipped

1. In a small bowl, combine flour and brown sugar; cut in butter until crumbly. Stir in pecans. Press into an ungreased 9-in. square baking pan. Bake at 350° for 14-16 minutes or until lightly browned. Cool on a wire rack.

2. Crumble the baked pecan mixture; set aside 1/2 cup for topping. Sprinkle the remaining mixture into an 8-in. square dish.

3. In a large bowl, beat the strawberries, sugar and lemon juice until blended. Fold in whipped cream. Spread evenly into dish. Sprinkle with reserved pecan mixture. Cover and freeze for 8 hours or overnight.

[2010]

SENSATIONAL TIRAMISU

yield: 12 servings   ⚭   **prep: 25 min.**
cook: 10 min. + chilling

(Pictured on page 347)

This light version of the popular Italian dessert is moist and creamy, and it cuts so well into pretty layered squares. You'll love the blend of coffee, Kahlua and cream cheese flavors.

—**Mary Walters, Westerville, Ohio**

- 1 **package (8 ounces) reduced-fat cream cheese**
- 2/3 **cup confectioners' sugar**
- 1-1/2 **cups reduced-fat whipped topping,** *divided*
- 1/2 **cup plus 1 tablespoon sugar**
- 3 **egg whites**
- 1/4 **cup water**
- 2 **packages (3 ounces** *each***) ladyfingers, split**
- 1/2 **cup boiling water**
- 2 **tablespoons coffee liqueur**
- 1 **tablespoon instant coffee granules**
- 1/2 **teaspoon baking cocoa**

1. In a small bowl, beat the cream cheese and confectioners' sugar until smooth. Fold in 1 cup whipped topping and set aside.

2. Combine 1/2 cup sugar, egg whites and water in a small heavy saucepan over low heat. With a hand mixer, beat on low speed for 1 minute. Continue beating on low over low heat until mixture reaches 160°, about 8-10 minutes. Pour into a large bowl. Beat on high until stiff peaks form, about 7 minutes. Fold into the cream cheese mixture.

3. Arrange half of ladyfingers in an ungreased 11-in. x 7-in. dish. Combine the boiling water, coffee liqueur, coffee granules and remaining sugar; brush half of mixture over ladyfingers. Top with half of cream cheese mixture. Repeat layers. Spread the remaining whipped topping over the top; sprinkle with cocoa. Refrigerate for 2 hours before serving.

[2006]

CARAMEL APPLE CRISP

yield: 12-14 servings   ⚭   **prep: 20 min.**
bake: 45 min.

When my children and I make this scrumptious layered dessert at home, we use a variety of apples to give it a nice combination of flavors.

—**Michelle Brooks, Clarkston, Michigan**

- 3 **cups old-fashioned oats**
- 2 **cups all-purpose flour**
- 1-1/2 **cups packed brown sugar**
- 1 **teaspoon ground cinnamon**
- 1 **cup cold butter, cubed**
- 8 **cups thinly sliced peeled tart apples**
- 1 **package (14 ounces) caramels, halved**
- 1 **cup apple cider,** *divided*

1. In a large bowl, combine the oats, flour, brown sugar and cinnamon; cut in butter until crumbly. Press half of the mixture into a greased 13-in. x 9-in. baking dish. Layer with half of the apples, caramels and 1 cup oat mixture. Repeat layers. Pour 1/2 cup cider over top.

2. Bake the crisp, uncovered, at 350° for 30 minutes. Drizzle with the remaining cider; bake 15-20 minutes longer or until apples are tender.

SENSATIONAL TIRAMISU

❝This recipe truly is sensational! My whole family thought it was the best tiramisu recipe that I've made. I'm making a double batch for the Italian themed party we're having at work. I'm sure it will be the hit of the party.❞
—*bake master*

NUTTY APPLE STREUSEL DESSERT

I make this for Thanksgiving instead of an apple pie. My family LOVES it.
—*mamalou1962*

[2012]

HOMEMADE BUTTERSCOTCH PUDDING
yield: 6 servings ⚬ **prep: 5 min.**
cook: 25 min. + chilling

(Pictured on page 347)

When I was a child, my grandmother would make this silky pudding as a special treat. The rich butterscotch flavor made this one of my favorite desserts.

—*Teresa Wilkes, Pembroke, Georgia*

- 1/2 cup sugar
- 1/2 cup packed dark brown sugar
- 3 tablespoons cornstarch
- 1/4 teaspoon salt
- 1/4 teaspoon ground nutmeg
- 3 cups 2% milk
- 3 egg yolks
- 2 tablespoons butter, cubed
- 2 teaspoons vanilla extract

Whipped cream, optional

1. In a large heavy saucepan, combine the first five ingredients. Stir in milk until smooth. Cook and stir over medium-high heat until thickened and bubbly. Reduce the heat to low; cook and stir 2 minutes longer. Remove from heat.

2. Stir a small amount of hot mixture into egg yolks; return all to the pan. Bring to a gentle boil, stirring constantly; cook 2 minutes or until the mixture is thickened and coats the back of a spoon. Remove from the heat.

3. Stir in the butter and vanilla. Cool for 15 minutes, stirring occasionally. Transfer to six dessert dishes. Cover and refrigerate until chilled. Garnish with whipped cream.

[1998]

NUTTY APPLE STREUSEL DESSERT
yield: 6-8 servings ⚬ **prep: 20 min.**
bake: 6 hours

Many people don't think of using a slow cooker to make dessert, but I like finishing up our dinner and having this hot, scrumptious apple treat waiting to be served up. I can start it in the afternoon and not give it another thought.

—*Jacki Every, Rotterdam, New York*

- 6 cups sliced peeled tart apples
- 1-1/4 teaspoons ground cinnamon
- 1/4 teaspoon ground allspice
- 1/4 teaspoon ground nutmeg
- 3/4 cup 2% milk
- 2 tablespoons butter, softened
- 3/4 cup sugar
- 2 eggs
- 1 teaspoon vanilla extract
- 1/2 cup biscuit/baking mix

TOPPING:
- 1 cup biscuit/baking mix
- 1/3 cup packed brown sugar
- 3 tablespoons cold butter
- 1/2 cup sliced almonds

Ice cream *or* whipped cream, optional

1. In a large bowl, toss apples with the cinnamon, allspice and nutmeg. Place in a greased 3-qt. slow cooker. In a small bowl, combine the milk, butter, sugar, eggs, vanilla and baking mix. Spoon over apples.

2. For topping, combine biscuit mix and brown sugar in a large bowl; cut in butter until crumbly. Add almonds; sprinkle over apples.

3. Cover and cook on low for 6-8 hours or until the apples are tender. Serve with ice cream or whipped cream if desired.

[2011]

LEMON DREAM CHEESECAKE

yield: 16 servings ∽ **prep: 30 min.**
bake: 55 min. + chilling

Light and lemony, this creamy cheesecake is a perfect dessert.

—*Bonnie Jost, Manitowoc, Wisconsin*

2 cups graham cracker crumbs
6 tablespoons butter, melted
1/4 cup sugar
FILLING:
4 packages (8 ounces *each*) cream cheese, softened
1 cup sugar
1/2 cup heavy whipping cream
1/4 cup lemon juice
2 tablespoons all-purpose flour
1 tablespoon grated lemon peel
2-1/2 teaspoons vanilla extract
1 teaspoon lemon extract
10 drops yellow food coloring, optional
5 eggs, lightly beaten

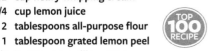

1. In a small bowl, combine cracker crumbs, butter and sugar. Press onto the bottom and 2 in. up the sides of a greased 10-in. springform pan. Place pan on a baking sheet. Bake at 325° for 10 minutes. Cool on a wire rack.

2. In a large bowl, beat cream cheese and sugar until smooth. Beat in the cream, lemon juice, flour, lemon peel, extracts and food coloring if desired. Add eggs; beat on low speed just until combined. Pour into crust. Return pan to baking sheet.

3. Bake for 55-65 minutes or until center is almost set. Cool on a wire rack for 10 minutes. Carefully run a knife around edge of pan to loosen; cool 1 hour longer. Refrigerate overnight. Remove sides of pan.

[1996]

COCONUT CRUNCH DELIGHT

yield: 12-16 servings
prep: 15 min. + chilling

I tasted this light dessert years ago at a potluck and got the recipe from my mom's dear friend. I've made it dozens of times since for my family and friends, who go wild over it. This is a terrific way to end a heavy meal.

—*Debby Chiorino, Pt. Hueneme, California*

1/2 cup butter, melted
1 cup all-purpose flour
1-1/4 cups flaked coconut
1/4 cup packed brown sugar
1 cup slivered almonds
2-2/3 cups cold milk
1/2 teaspoon coconut extract
2 packages (3.4 ounces *each*) instant vanilla pudding mix
2 cups whipped topping
Fresh strawberries, optional

1. In a large bowl, combine butter, flour, coconut, brown sugar and almonds; press lightly into a greased 13-in. x 9-in. baking dish. Bake at 350° for 25-30 minutes or until golden brown, stirring every 10 minutes to form coarse crumbs. Cool.

2. Divide crumb mixture in half; press half into the same baking pan. In a large bowl, whisk the milk, extract and pudding mixes for 2 minutes. Let stand for 2 minutes or until soft-set.

3. Fold in whipped topping; spoon over the crust. Top with remaining crumb mixture. Cover and refrigerate overnight. Garnish with fresh strawberries if desired.

MAKING A CHEESECAKE CRUMB CRUST

1. Place cookies or crackers in a heavy-duty resealable plastic bag. Seal bag, pushing out as much air as possible. Press a rolling pin over the bag, crushing the cookies or crackers into fine crumbs. Or process cookies and crackers in a food processor.

2. Use a flat-bottomed measuring cup or glass to firmly press the prepared crumb mixture onto the bottom (and up the sides if recipe directs) of a springform pan.

[2010]

CHOCOLATE RASPBERRY CHEESECAKE

yield: 16 servings prep: 40 min.
bake: 65 min. + chilling

(Pictured on page 352)

My husband loves cheesecake, and this favorite is from a cookbook I bought long ago for $1 at a yard sale. We love raspberries and chocolate—they make a fabulous combination.

—*Mickey Turner, Grants Pass, Oregon, Field Editor*

1-1/2 cups cream-filled chocolate sandwich cookie crumbs
  2 tablespoons butter, melted
  4 packages (8 ounces *each*) cream cheese, softened
1-1/4 cups sugar
  1 cup (8 ounces) sour cream
  1 teaspoon vanilla extract
  3 eggs, lightly beaten
  9 ounces semisweet chocolate, chopped
1/2 cup seedless raspberry preserves
TOPPING:
  6 ounces semisweet chocolate, chopped
1/3 cup heavy whipping cream
Fresh raspberries and whipped cream, optional

1. Place a greased 9-in. springform pan on a double thickness of heavy-duty foil (about 18 in. square). Securely wrap foil around pan. Combine cookie crumbs and butter; press onto the bottom of the prepared pan.

2. In a large bowl, beat cream cheese and sugar until smooth. Beat in sour cream and vanilla. Add eggs; beat on low speed just until combined. Set aside 1-1/2 cups; pour remaining batter over crust.

3. In a microwave-safe bowl, melt chocolate; stir in preserves until blended. Stir in reserved batter just until blended. Drop by tablespoonfuls over the plain batter (do not swirl). Place springform pan in a large baking pan; add 1 in. of hot water to larger pan.

4. Bake at 325° for 65-75 minutes or until center is just set and top appears dull. Remove springform pan from water bath. Cool on a wire rack for 10 minutes. Carefully run a knife around edge of pan to loosen; cool 1 hour longer.

5. For topping, place chocolate in a small bowl. In a small saucepan, bring cream just to a boil. Pour over the chocolate; whisk until smooth. Cool slightly. Spread over top of cheesecake. Refrigerate overnight. Garnish with the raspberries and whipped cream if desired. Remove sides of pan.

[2001]

PRETZEL DESSERT

yield: 16 servings prep: 20 min. + chilling

The recipe makes a big batch of this sweet and salty, creamy and crunchy treat. That's fine with us because any dessert that's left over is super the next day, too.

—*Rita Winterberger, Huson, Montana*

  2 cups crushed pretzels
3/4 cup sugar
3/4 cup butter, cubed
  2 envelopes whipped topping mix (Dream Whip)
  1 cup cold 2% milk
  1 teaspoon vanilla extract
  1 package (8 ounces) cream cheese, softened
  1 cup confectioners' sugar
  1 can (21 ounces) cherry pie filling

1. In a large bowl, combine pretzels, sugar and butter; set aside 1/2 cup for topping. Press the remaining mixture into an ungreased 13-in. x 9-in. dish.

2. In a large bowl, beat the whipped topping mix, milk and vanilla on high speed for 4 minutes or until soft peaks form. Add cream cheese and confectioners' sugar; beat until smooth.

3. Spread half over crust. Top with pie filling and remaining cream cheese mixture. Sprinkle with reserved pretzel mixture. Refrigerate overnight.

[2009]

CHOCOLATE COOKIE CHEESECAKE

yield: 12 servings ∽ **prep: 30 min.**
bake: 50 min. + chilling

This is great for parties because it is popular with all ages and can be made in advance. People really go wild when this is served as part of a dessert buffet. It's usually the first to go!

—Lisa Varner
Charleston, South Carolina, Field Editor

1-1/2 **cups cream-filled chocolate sandwich cookie crumbs (about 16 cookies)**
3 **tablespoons butter, melted**
4 **packages (8 ounces each) cream cheese, softened**
1 **cup sugar**
1-1/2 **cups semisweet chocolate chips, melted and cooled**
3 **teaspoons vanilla extract**
4 **eggs, lightly beaten**
20 **chocolate cream-filled chocolate sandwich cookies, coarsely chopped**

1. In a small bowl, combine the cookie crumbs and butter. Press onto the bottom of greased 9-in. springform pan. Refrigerate while preparing filling.

2. In a large bowl, beat cream cheese and sugar until smooth. Beat in chocolate and vanilla. Add the eggs; beat on low speed just until combined. Fold in half of chopped cookies. Pour over crust. Sprinkle with remaining cookies. Place pan on a baking sheet.

3. Bake at 325° for 50-60 minutes or until the center is almost set and top appears dull. Cool on a wire rack for 10 minutes. Carefully run a knife around edge of pan to loosen; cool 1 hour longer. Refrigerate overnight. Remove side of pan.

[1999]

HONEY BAKED APPLES

yield: 6 servings ∽ **prep: 10 min.**
bake: 1 hour

These tender apples smell so good while they're in the oven, and they taste even better. We enjoy the golden raisins inside and the soothing taste of honey, which is a yummy change from the traditional cinnamon and sugar seasoning.

—Chere Bell, Colorado Springs, Colorado

2-1/4 **cups water**
3/4 **cup packed brown sugar**
3 **tablespoons honey**
6 **large tart apples**
1 **cup golden raisins**
Vanilla ice cream, optional

1. In a small saucepan, bring water, brown sugar and honey to a boil. Remove from the heat.

2. Core apples and peel the top third of each. Place in an ungreased 9-in. pie plate. Fill apples with raisins; sprinkle any remaining raisins into pan. Pour sugar syrup over apples.

3. Bake, uncovered, at 350° for 1 hour or until tender, basting occasionally. Serve with ice cream if desired.

CHOCOLATE COOKIE CHEESECAKE

❝I made this for a gourmet Valentine's dinner I did at my house. It was a big hit! They all loved it! Sort of like a chocolate mousse cake but not overly sweet.❞
—Samo21

CORING AN APPLE

1. Use an apple corer to core a whole apple. Push apple corer down into center of a washed apple. Twist and remove the center seeds and membranes.

2. Core an apple quarter by cutting out the core with a sharp knife.

MINI CHERRY CHEESECAKES

[1995]

MINI CHERRY CHEESECAKES

yield: 12 servings ∽ prep: 20 min. + chilling
bake: 15 min. + cooling

These individual cheesecakes make a festive dessert that's just right for cooks who don't have a lot of time for fussy recipes.

—Kay Keller, Morenci, Michigan

- 1 cup vanilla wafer crumbs
- 3 tablespoons butter, melted
- 1 package (8 ounces) cream cheese, softened
- 1/3 cup sugar
- 2 teaspoons lemon juice
- 1-1/2 teaspoons vanilla extract
- 1 egg, lightly beaten

TOPPING:

- 1 pound pitted canned *or* frozen tart red cherries
- 1/2 cup sugar
- 2 tablespoons cornstarch

Red food coloring, optional

1. In a small bowl, combine crumbs and butter. Press gently onto the bottom of 12 paper-lined muffin cups. In a large bowl, combine cream cheese, sugar, lemon juice and vanilla. Add the egg; beat on low speed just until combined. Spoon into crusts.

2. Bake at 375° for 12-15 minutes or until centers are almost set. Cool completely.

3. Drain cherries, reserving 1/2 cup juice in a saucepan; discard remaining juice. To the reserved juice, add the cherries, sugar, cornstarch and food coloring if desired. Bring to a boil; cook for 1 minute or until thickened. Cool; spoon over cheesecakes. Chill for at least 2 hours.

[2009]

APPLE-RAISIN BREAD PUDDING

yield: 12 servings (1-1/4 cups sauce)
prep: 20 min. ∽ bake: 40 min.

Our six children love to have this bread pudding for breakfast on a chilly morning instead of dessert. It makes the kitchen smell warm and cozy.

—Janelle Fahnestock, Lititz, Pennsylvania

- 3 tablespoons butter, melted
- 1 loaf (1 pound) day-old cinnamon-raisin bread, cubed
- 3 cups chopped peeled tart apples
- 7 eggs, lightly beaten
- 2-1/2 cups 2% milk
- 3/4 cup sugar
- 3 teaspoons vanilla extract

VANILLA SAUCE:

- 2/3 cup sugar
- 1 tablespoon cornstarch
- 1/8 teaspoon salt
- 1 cup cold water
- 1 tablespoon butter
- 1 teaspoon vanilla extract

1. Pour butter into a 13-in. x 9-in. baking dish. Combine bread cubes and apples; sprinkle over butter. In a large bowl, whisk the eggs, milk, sugar and vanilla. Pour over the bread; let stand for 15 minutes or until bread is softened.

2. Bake, uncovered, at 325° for 40-45 minutes or until a knife inserted near the center comes out clean.

3. In a small saucepan, combine the sugar, cornstarch, salt and water until smooth. Bring to a boil over low heat, stirring constantly. Cook and stir sauce for 1-2 minutes or until thickened. Remove from the heat; stir in butter and vanilla. Serve with the warm bread pudding.

[2009]

LAYERED TURTLE CHEESECAKE

yield: 12 servings ∞ prep: 40 min.
bake: 1-1/4 hours + chilling

After receiving a request for a special turtle cheesecake and not finding a good recipe, I created my own. Everyone is thrilled with the results and this cheesecake remains a favorite at the coffee shop where I work.

—Sue Gronholz
Beaver Dam, Wisconsin, Field Editor

- 1 cup all-purpose flour
- 1/3 cup packed brown sugar
- 1/4 cup finely chopped pecans
- 6 tablespoons cold butter, chopped

FILLING:

- 4 packages (8 ounces *each*) cream cheese, softened
- 1 cup sugar
- 1/3 cup packed brown sugar
- 1/4 cup plus 1 teaspoon all-purpose flour, *divided*
- 2 tablespoons heavy whipping cream
- 1-1/2 teaspoons vanilla extract
- 4 eggs, lightly beaten
- 1/2 cup milk chocolate chips, melted and cooled
- 1/4 cup caramel ice cream topping
- 1/3 cup chopped pecans

GANACHE:

- 1/2 cup milk chocolate chips
- 1/4 cup heavy whipping cream
- 2 tablespoons chopped pecans

Optional garnish: pecan halves and additional caramel ice cream topping

1. Place a greased 9-in. springform pan on a double thickness of heavy-duty foil (about 18 in. square). Securely wrap foil around pan.

2. In a small bowl, combine the flour, brown sugar and pecans; cut in butter until crumbly. Press onto the bottom of prepared pan. Place pan on a baking sheet. Bake at 325° for 12-15 minutes or until set. Cool on a wire rack.

3. In a large bowl, beat cream cheese and sugars until smooth. Beat in 1/4 cup flour, cream and vanilla. Add the eggs; beat on low speed just until combined. Remove 1 cup batter to a small bowl; stir in melted chocolate until blended. Spread over crust.

4. Combine the caramel topping and remaining flour; stir in the pecans. Drop by tablespoonfuls over the chocolate batter. Top with remaining batter. Place springform pan in a large baking pan; add 1 in. of hot water to larger pan.

5. Bake at 325° for 1-1/4 to 1-1/2 hours or until center is just set and top appears dull. Remove springform pan from water bath. Cool on a wire rack for 10 minutes. Carefully run a knife around edge of pan to loosen; cool 1 hour longer. Refrigerate overnight.

6. Place chips in a small bowl. In a small saucepan, bring cream just to a boil. Pour over chips; whisk until smooth. Cool slightly, stirring occasionally.

7. Spread over cheesecake. Sprinkle with chopped pecans. Refrigerate until set. Remove sides of pan. Garnish with pecan halves and additional caramel topping if desired.

LAYERED TURTLE CHEESECAKE

"I made this for a surprise birthday party, and the birthday girl loved it! She still raves about it, and her birthday was 6 months ago! But once piece is all you need because, be warned, this is VERY SWEET!"
—pepperpepperj

[2008]

MASCARPONE CHEESECAKE

yield: 12 servings
prep: 30 min. ∞ **bake: 50 min. + chilling**

This rich dessert is sure to delight with its creamy filling, whipped topping and sweet caramel drizzle. It makes an ideal ending to a special meal.

—Deanna Polito-Laughinghouse
Raleigh, North Carolina

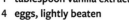

3/4 cup graham cracker crumbs
3 tablespoons sugar
3 tablespoons butter, melted
FILLING:
2 packages (8 ounces *each*) cream cheese, softened
2 cartons (8 ounces *each*) Mascarpone cheese
1 cup sugar
1 tablespoon lemon juice
1 tablespoon vanilla extract
4 eggs, lightly beaten
TOPPING:
1 envelope whipped topping mix (Dream Whip)
1 tablespoon caramel ice cream topping

1. Place a greased 9-in. springform pan on a double thickness of heavy-duty foil (about 18 in. square). Securely wrap foil around pan.

2. In a small bowl, combine cracker crumbs and sugar; stir in butter. Press onto the bottom of prepared pan. Place the pan on a baking sheet. Bake at 325° for 10 minutes. Cool on a wire rack.

3. For filling, in a large bowl, beat cheeses, sugar, lemon juice and vanilla until smooth. Add eggs; beat on low speed just until combined. Pour over crust. Place the springform pan in a large baking pan; add 1 in. of hot water to larger pan.

4. Bake at 325° for 50-60 minutes or until center is just set and top appears dull. Remove springform pan from water bath. Cool on a wire rack for 10 minutes.

Carefully run a knife around the edge of pan to loosen; cool 1 hour longer.

5. Refrigerate overnight. Remove sides of pan. Before serving, prepare topping mix according to package directions. Garnish cheesecake with whipped topping; drizzle with caramel. Refrigerate leftovers.

[2008]

PUMPKIN GINGERBREAD TRIFLE

yield: 25 servings (1 cup each)
prep: 40 min. + chilling

Soft layers of pumpkin, spicy gingerbread and creamy whipped topping make this decadent trifle a feast for your eyes and your stomach.

—Amy Geiser, Fairlawn, Ohio

2 packages (14-1/2 ounces *each*) gingerbread cake mix
1 package (4.6 ounces) cook-and-serve vanilla pudding mix
3 cups 2% milk
1 can (29 ounces) solid-pack pumpkin
1/2 cup packed brown sugar
1 carton (12 ounces) frozen whipped topping, thawed, *divided*

1. Prepare and bake gingerbread according to package directions, using two greased 9-in. round baking pans. Cool completely on wire racks.

2. Meanwhile, for pudding, in a large saucepan, combine pudding mix and milk; stir until smooth. Cook and stir over medium heat until mixture comes to a boil. Cook and stir 1-2 minutes longer or until thickened. Remove from the heat; cool to room temperature. Combine pumpkin and brown sugar; stir into pudding.

3. In a 4-qt. glass serving bowl, crumble one gingerbread cake; gently press down. Top with half of pudding mixture and whipped topping. Repeat layers. Cover and refrigerate overnight.

MEASURING BROWN SUGAR

The moisture in brown sugar tends to trap air between the crystals, so it should be firmly packed when measuring. *Taste of Home* recipes specify packed brown sugar in the ingredients.

[2008]

LAYERED MOCHA CHEESECAKE

yield: 16 servings ∞ prep: 30 min.
bake: 55 min. + chilling

In my search for the perfect mocha cheesecake, I ended up combining a few of my favorite recipes to create this delicious version. It's as much a feast for the eyes as for the palate!

—*Sue Gronholz, Beaver Dam, Wisconsin, Field Editor*

1-1/2 cups cream-filled chocolate sandwich cookie crumbs
1/4 cup butter, melted
FILLING:
2 tablespoons plus 1-1/2 teaspoons instant coffee granules
1 tablespoon boiling water
1/4 teaspoon ground cinnamon
4 packages (8 ounces *each*) cream cheese, softened
1-1/2 cups sugar
1/4 cup all-purpose flour
2 teaspoons vanilla extract
4 eggs, lightly beaten
2 cups (12 ounces) semisweet chocolate chips, melted and cooled
GLAZE:
1/2 cup semisweet chocolate chips
3 tablespoons butter
Chocolate-covered coffee beans, optional

1. Place greased 9-in. springform pan on a double thickness of heavy-duty foil (about 18 in. square). Securely wrap foil around pan.

2. Combine cookie crumbs and butter; press onto the bottom of prepared pan. In a small bowl, combine the coffee granules, water and cinnamon; set aside.

3. In a large bowl, beat the cream cheese, sugar, flour and vanilla until smooth. Add eggs; beat on low speed just until combined.

4. Divide batter in half. Stir melted chocolate into one portion; pour over crust. Stir coffee mixture into the remaining batter; spoon over chocolate layer. Place springform pan in a large baking pan; add 1 in. of hot water to larger pan.

5. Bake at 325° for 60-65 minutes or until center is just set and top appears dull. Remove springform pan from water bath. Cool on a wire rack for 10 minutes.

Carefully run a knife around edge of pan to loosen; cool 1 hour longer. Refrigerate overnight.

6. In a microwave, melt chocolate chips and butter; stir until smooth. Spread over cheesecake. Garnish with coffee beans if desired. Refrigerate leftovers.

[2012]

WARM CHEESECAKE CREPES

yield: 8 servings ∞ prep: 15 min. ∞ bake: 20 min.

I usually make the crepes, filling and sauce for this recipe the day before. The next day, I assemble them for baking and warm the sauce. It might seem complicated, but it's not difficult, and the results are so worth it!

—*Pattie Prescott, Manchester, New Hampshire*

1 package (8 ounces) cream cheese, softened
1 cup 4% cottage cheese
1/4 cup sugar
2 eggs, beaten
1 teaspoon vanilla extract
16 prepared crepes (9 inches)
SAUCE:
1 can (20 ounces) pineapple tidbits
1/4 cup sugar
2 tablespoons cornstarch
1/2 cup orange juice
1/2 cup canned mandarin oranges
1-1/2 cups fresh strawberries, quartered

1. In a small bowl, beat the cream cheese, cottage cheese and sugar until well blended. Beat in eggs and vanilla. Spread about 2 tablespoons filling down the center of each crepe; roll up. Place in two ungreased 11-in. x 7-in. baking dishes. Bake at 350° for 18-22 minutes or until a thermometer reads 160°.

2. Drain pineapple, reserving juice. In a small saucepan, combine sugar, cornstarch, orange juice and reserved pineapple juice. Bring to a boil; cook and stir for 2 minutes or until thickened. Remove from the heat; stir in fruit. Serve with crepes.

[2007]

PRALINE CHOCOLATE DESSERT
**yield: 14-16 servings ∞ prep: 25 min. + chilling
bake: 10 min. + cooling**

A cookie crumb crust, luscious layers of praline and cream cheese and a chocolate glaze make this rich dessert a show-stopper. It's worth the extra effort, and it freezes well, too.

—Korrie Bastian, Clearfield, Utah

---

  2 **cups cream-filled chocolate sandwich cookie crumbs**
1/2 **cup butter, melted**
  1 **cup chopped pecans**
PRALINE:
1-1/2 **cups butter, cubed**
  1 **cup packed brown sugar**
  1 **teaspoon vanilla extract**
FILLING:
  2 **packages (8 ounces *each*) cream cheese, softened**
1/2 **cup confectioners' sugar**
1/3 **cup packed brown sugar**
GANACHE:
  1 **cup (6 ounces) semisweet chocolate chips**
1/2 **cup heavy whipping cream**
Pecan halves

---

1. In a small bowl, combine cookie crumbs and butter. Press onto the bottom of a greased 9-in. springform pan. Place on a baking sheet. Bake at 350° for 10 minutes. Cool on a wire rack. Sprinkle with pecans.

2. In a large saucepan over medium heat, bring butter and brown sugar to a boil, stirring constantly. Reduce heat; simmer, uncovered, for 10 minutes. Remove from the heat; stir in the vanilla. Pour over the pecans. Refrigerate for 1-2 hours or until set.

3. In a large bowl, beat filling ingredients until smooth. Spread over praline layer. Refrigerate for 1-2 hours or until set.

4. For ganache, place chocolate chips in a small bowl. In a small saucepan, bring cream just to a boil. Pour over the chocolate; whisk until smooth. Spread over filling. Refrigerate for 1-2 hours or until set.

5. Carefully run a knife around edge of pan to loosen; remove sides of pan. Garnish with the pecan halves. Refrigerate leftovers.

[2004]

PEARS WITH RASPBERRY SAUCE
yield: 4 servings ∞ prep/total time: 20 min.

This dish came about when I was expecting company and wanted to make a light, pretty dessert with items that I already had on hand. My guests really enjoyed it. I now make it as often as I can.

—Constance Rak, Westlake, Ohio

---

  1 **package (10 ounces) frozen sweetened raspberries, thawed**
  4 **medium firm pears**
  2 **cups white grape juice**
  1 **cup sugar**
  2 **tablespoons lemon juice**
Whipped cream

---

1. Place raspberries in a blender; cover and process until pureed. Strain, reserving juice; set aside. Discard the seeds. Core pears from bottom, leaving stems intact. Peel pears; set aside.

2. In a large saucepan, bring the grape juice, sugar and lemon juice to a boil; add pears. Reduce heat; cover and simmer for 5-7 minutes or until tender; drain.

3. For each serving, spoon raspberry sauce on plate, then top with a pear. Garnish with whipped cream.

CORING A PEAR

To core a fresh pear, insert an apple corer into the bottom of the pear to within 1 in. of its top. Twist the corer to cut around the core, then slowly pull the corer out of the pear to remove the core. If you don't have an apple corer, use a sharp knife or vegetable peeler to cut the core from the bottom of the pear.

[2010]

MAGNOLIA DREAM CHEESECAKE

yield: 16 servings ∽ **prep: 50 min.**
bake: 1-1/2 hours + chilling

Your guests will be amazed when they learn that this gorgeous cheesecake was made by you. This Italian-style dessert is flavored with a delightful combination of hazelnut and peach.

—**Charlene Chambers**
Ormond Beach, Florida

- 1 cup hazelnuts, toasted, *divided*
- 12 whole graham crackers
- 1/4 cup sugar
- 6 tablespoons unsalted butter, melted

FILLING:
- 1-1/2 pounds ricotta cheese
- 2 packages (8 ounces *each*) cream cheese, softened
- 2 cups (16 ounces) sour cream
- 1-1/2 cups sugar
- 6 tablespoons all-purpose flour
- 4 tablespoons hazelnut liqueur, *divided*
- 6 eggs, lightly beaten
- 3 medium peaches, sliced

1. Place a greased 10-in. springform pan on a double thickness of heavy-duty foil (about 18 in. square). Securely wrap foil around pan.

2. Place hazelnuts in a food processor; cover and pulse until coarsely chopped. Set aside 1/4 cup for garnish. Add the graham crackers and sugar to food processor; cover and process until finely chopped. Add butter; process until blended. Press onto the bottom and 1 in. up the sides of prepared pan. Place pan on a baking sheet. Bake at 325° for 10 minutes. Cool on a wire rack.

3. In a large bowl, beat the ricotta, cream cheese, sour cream and sugar until well blended. Beat in flour and 2 tablespoons liqueur. Add eggs; beat on low speed just until combined. Pour into the crust. Place springform pan in a large baking pan; add 1 in. of hot water to larger pan.

4. Bake at 325° for 1-1/2 hours or until center is just set and top appears dull. Remove springform pan from the water bath. Cool on a wire rack for 10 minutes. Carefully run a knife around edge of the pan to loosen; cool 1 hour longer. Refrigerate overnight.

5. Toss peaches with remaining liqueur; arrange over top of the cheesecake. Sprinkle the reserved hazelnuts in the center. Remove sides of pan.

[2008]

CRANBERRY FLUFF

yield: 10 servings ∽ **prep: 20 min. + chilling**

This tangy pink fluff gets crunch from chopped apples and nuts. It's delightful as a salad or dessert, and it keeps well in the refrigerator. I serve any leftovers with sandwiches the next day.

—*Tena Huckleby, Greeneville, Tennessee*

- 4 cups fresh *or* frozen cranberries
- 3 cups miniature marshmallows
- 3/4 cup sugar
- 2 cups finely chopped apples
- 1/2 cup green grapes, quartered
- 1/2 cup chopped walnuts
- 1/4 teaspoon salt
- 1 cup heavy whipping cream, whipped

1. Place cranberries in a food processor; cover and process until finely chopped. Transfer to a large bowl; stir in the marshmallows and sugar. Cover and refrigerate overnight.

2. Just before serving, stir in the apples, grapes, walnuts and salt. Fold in the whipped cream.

CRANBERRY FLUFF

❝We make this recipe every Thanksgiving, and it makes a bunch, but there are never any leftovers! Everyone loves this.❞
—dwilliams

ALMOND CHICKEN SALAD

"At first I wasn't sure that the flavors would work well together. But after trying it, I was wrong. This salad has something for all your taste buds. The combination of flavors and textures is excellent. Sometimes I add chopped apple for even more flavor."
—Angelique177

[1995]

ALMOND CHICKEN SALAD
yield: 6-8 servings
prep/total time: 15 min.

My mother used to prepare this salad for an evening meal during the hot summer months. It also serves well as a delicious but quick luncheon or potluck dish. You can't beat the tasty combination of chicken, grapes and almonds.

—*Kathy Kittell*
Lenexa, Kansas, Field Editor

- 4 cups cubed cooked chicken
- 1-1/2 cups seedless green grapes, halved
- 1 cup chopped celery
- 3/4 cup sliced green onions
- 3 hard-cooked eggs, chopped
- 1/2 cup Miracle Whip
- 1/4 cup sour cream
- 1 tablespoon prepared mustard
- 1 teaspoon salt
- 1/2 teaspoon pepper
- 1/4 teaspoon onion powder
- 1/4 teaspoon celery salt
- 1/8 teaspoon ground mustard
- 1/8 teaspoon paprika
- 1/2 cup slivered almonds, toasted
- 1 kiwifruit, peeled and sliced, optional

1. In a large bowl, combine the chicken, grapes, celery, onions and eggs. In another bowl, combine the next nine ingredients; stir until smooth.

2. Pour over the chicken mixture and toss gently. Stir in almonds and serve immediately, or refrigerate and add the almonds just before serving. Garnish with kiwi if desired.

[2007]

COLORFUL CHICKEN 'N' SQUASH SOUP
yield: 14 servings (5-1/2 quarts)
prep: 25 min.   cook: 1-1/2 hours

When I turned 40, I decided to live a healthier lifestyle, which included cooking healthier for my family. I make this soup every week, and everyone loves it.

—*Trina Bigham, Fairhaven, Massachusetts*

- 1 broiler/fryer chicken (4 pounds), cut up
- 13 cups water
- 5 pounds butternut squash, peeled and cubed (about 10 cups)
- 1 bunch kale, trimmed and chopped
- 6 medium carrots, chopped
- 2 large onions, chopped
- 3 teaspoons salt

1. Place chicken and water in a stockpot. Slowly bring to a boil. Reduce heat; cover and simmer for 1 hour or until chicken is tender.

2. Remove the chicken from broth. Strain broth and skim fat. Return broth to the pan; add the squash, kale, carrots and onions. Bring to a boil. Reduce heat; cover and simmer for 25-30 minutes or until vegetables are tender.

3. When the chicken is cool enough to handle, remove meat from bones and cut into bite-size pieces. Discard bones and skin. Add chicken and salt to soup; heat through.

[2000]

FRUIT-PECAN PORK ROAST

yield: 10-12 servings ∞ **prep: 20 min.**
bake: 65 min. + standing

(Pictured on page 407)

This spectacular roast was a huge hit with members of the cooking club I belong to. The sweet, tangy fruit glaze looks lovely and is a wonderful complement to the juicy pork. It's a family favorite for special occasions and holidays.

—*Gay Flynn, Bellevue, Nebraska*

- 1 **boneless rolled pork loin roast (3-1/2 pounds)**
- 1/2 **cup chopped green onions**
- 4 **tablespoons butter,** *divided*
- 1/4 **cup orange juice**
- 1 **bay leaf**
- 1 **can (14 ounces) whole-berry cranberry sauce**
- 1/2 **cup chicken broth**
- 1/2 **cup chopped pecans**
- 1 **tablespoon red wine vinegar**
- 1/4 **teaspoon salt**
- 1/8 **teaspoon pepper**
- 1/8 **teaspoon sugar**
- 1/4 **cup apricot preserves**

1. Place the roast on a rack in a shallow roasting pan. Bake, uncovered, at 350° for 45 minutes.

2. Meanwhile, in a large skillet, saute the onions in 1 tablespoon of butter for 1 minute. Add the orange juice and bay leaf; cook and stir over medium-high heat until thickened, about 4 minutes. Add the cranberry sauce, broth, pecans and vinegar; cook and stir until slightly thickened, about 5 minutes. Reduce heat; stir in the salt, pepper, sugar and remaining butter until butter is melted. Discard bay leaf.

3. Remove 1/4 cup sauce and stir in the preserves; spoon over roast. Set the remaining sauce aside. Bake 20-30 minutes longer or until a thermometer reads 145°. Let meat stand for 10 minutes before slicing. Serve with reserved sauce.

[1993]

NUTTY OVEN-FRIED CHICKEN

yield: 6-8 servings ∞ **prep: 10 min.**
bake: 1 hour

(Pictured on page 401)

The pecans that give this dish its unique nutty flavor are plentiful in the South, and so is chicken. I love to make and serve this easy dish because the chicken comes out moist, tasty and crispy.

—*Diane Hixon*
Niceville, Florida, Field Editor

- 1/2 **cup evaporated milk**
- 1 **cup biscuit/baking mix**
- 1/3 **cup finely chopped pecans**
- 2 **teaspoons paprika**
- 1/2 **teaspoon salt**
- 1/2 **teaspoon poultry seasoning**
- 1/2 **teaspoon rubbed sage**
- 1 **broiler/fryer chicken (3 to 4 pounds), cut up**
- 1/3 **cup butter, melted**

1. Place the milk in a shallow bowl. In another shallow bowl, combine the baking mix, pecans and seasonings. Dip chicken pieces in milk, then coat generously with pecan mixture.

2. Place in a lightly greased 13-in. x 9-in. baking dish. Drizzle with butter. Bake, uncovered, at 350° for 1 hour or until chicken is golden brown and crispy and juices run clear.

FRUIT-PECAN PORK ROAST

"This roast was very moist and tender. I added lemon zest and a dash of nutmeg to the sauce, it was perfection. I will make this again."
—*alleytt*

[2010]

SLOW COOKER TAMALE PIE

yield: 8 servings ∞ prep: 25 min.
cook: 7 hours

Canned beans and corn bread/muffin mix speed up the prep on this crowd-pleasing main dish that's perfect for busy evenings and carry-in dinners.

—*Jill Pokrivka, York, Pennsylvania*

- 1 **pound ground beef**
- 1 **teaspoon ground cumin**
- 1/2 **teaspoon salt**
- 1/2 **teaspoon chili powder**
- 1/4 **teaspoon pepper**
- 1 **can (15 ounces) black beans, rinsed and drained**
- 1 **can (14-1/2 ounces) diced tomatoes with mild green chilies, undrained**
- 1 **can (11 ounces) whole kernel corn, drained**
- 1 **can (10 ounces) enchilada sauce**
- 2 **green onions, chopped**
- 1/4 **cup minced fresh cilantro**
- 1 **package (8-1/2 ounces) corn bread/ muffin mix**
- 2 **eggs**
- 1 **cup (4 ounces) shredded Mexican cheese blend**

Sour cream and additional minced fresh cilantro, optional

1. In a large skillet, cook the beef over medium heat until no longer pink; drain. Stir in cumin, salt, chili powder and pepper.

2. Transfer to a 4-qt. slow cooker; stir in the beans, tomatoes, corn, enchilada sauce, onions and cilantro. Cover and cook on low for 6-8 hours or until heated through.

3. In a small bowl, combine muffin mix and eggs; spoon over meat mixture. Cover and cook 1 hour longer or until a toothpick inserted near the center comes out clean.

4. Sprinkle with the cheese; cover and let stand for 5 minutes. Serve with sour cream and additional cilantro if desired.

[2001]

PEPPERONI PIZZA CHILI

yield: 8 servings ∞ prep: 5 min.
cook: 40 min.

I came up with this recipe one day when I was really craving pizza but didn't want to fuss with making a crust. I just put the pizza in a bowl instead!

—*Marilouise Wyatt, Cowen, West Virginia*

- 1 **pound ground beef**
- 1 **can (16 ounces) kidney beans, rinsed and drained**
- 1 **can (15 ounces) pizza sauce**
- 1 **can (14-1/2 ounces) Italian stewed tomatoes**
- 1 **can (8 ounces) tomato sauce**
- 1-1/2 **cups water**
- 1 **package (3-1/2 ounces) sliced pepperoni**
- 1/2 **cup chopped green pepper**
- 1 **teaspoon pizza seasoning *or* Italian seasoning**
- 1 **teaspoon salt**

Shredded part-skim mozzarella cheese, optional

1. In a large saucepan, cook beef over medium heat until no longer pink; drain. Stir in the beans, pizza sauce, tomatoes, tomato sauce, water, pepperoni, green pepper, pizza seasoning and salt. Bring to a boil. Reduce heat; simmer, uncovered, for 30 minutes or until the chili reaches desired thickness. Sprinkle with cheese if desired.

SLOW COOKER TAMALE PIE

" Excellent!! My husband and I are on low-fat, low-salt cardiac diets, so I substituted ground turkey for the ground beef, and left out the salt...and it was STILL delicious. I froze the leftovers, and it was great reheated, too. I'm getting ready for my monthly cooking day, and my husband made a special request for more Slow Cooker Tamale Pie. Thank you! "

—*Ozark-ian*

[2009]

FLATBREAD TACOS WITH RANCH SOUR CREAM

yield: 8 servings ∽ **prep/total time: 30 min.**

(Pictured on page 408)

These tasty flatbread tacos are made with convenient refrigerated biscuits and are ideal for serving buffet-style. Set out the toppings and let everyone make their own!

—*Jennifer Eggebraaten*
Bothell, Washington

1 cup (8 ounces) sour cream
2 teaspoons ranch salad dressing mix
1 teaspoon lemon juice
1-1/2 pounds ground beef
1 can (15 ounces) pinto beans, rinsed and drained
1 can (14-1/2 ounces) diced tomatoes, undrained
1 envelope taco seasoning
1 tablespoon hot pepper sauce
1 tube (16.3 ounces) large refrigerated buttermilk biscuits
Optional toppings: sliced ripe olives and shredded lettuce and cheddar cheese

1. In a small bowl, combine sour cream, dressing mix and lemon juice; chill until serving.

2. In a large skillet, cook the beef over medium heat until meat is no longer pink; drain. Add the beans, tomatoes, taco seasoning and pepper sauce; heat through.

3. Meanwhile, roll out each biscuit into a 6-in. circle. In a small nonstick skillet over medium heat, cook each biscuit for 30-60 seconds on each side or until golden brown; keep warm.

4. To serve, spread each flatbread with 2 tablespoons ranch sour cream; top each with 2/3 cup meat mixture. Sprinkle with toppings if desired.

[2011]

CHAMPION LAMB BURGERS

yield: 6 servings ∽ **prep/total time: 25 min.**

This recipe is a wonderful alternative to beef burgers. The rosemary onions make it especially delicious. It's so good, I serve it all year long.

—*Charlene Chambers*
Ormond Beach, Florida

2 large red onions, thinly sliced
2 teaspoons olive oil
1 tablespoon red wine vinegar
2 teaspoons minced fresh rosemary
1-1/2 teaspoons sugar
1 teaspoon stone-ground mustard
1/4 teaspoon salt
1/4 teaspoon pepper
BURGERS:
2 pounds ground lamb
2 garlic cloves, minced
1 teaspoon salt
1/4 teaspoon pepper
6 pita pocket halves
2 tablespoons olive oil
1-1/2 cups spring mix salad greens

1. In a large skillet, saute onions in oil until tender. Add the vinegar, rosemary, sugar, mustard, salt and pepper; cook 5 minutes longer. Keep warm.

2. Crumble lamb into a large bowl; sprinkle with garlic, salt and pepper and mix well. Shape into six patties. Grill burgers, covered, over medium heat or broil 4 in. from the heat for 4-6 minutes on each side or until a thermometer reads 160° and juices run clear.

3. Brush pita pockets with oil; lightly grill on both sides. Serve burgers in pita pockets with lettuce and onions.

FLATBREAD TACOS WITH RANCH SOUR CREAM

"This was a good and simple dinner to make. I substituted plain Greek yogurt for the sour cream and my son loved it. He states it is fantastic as a dip for artichokes."
—*piquilting*

CHICKEN IN POTATO BASKETS

"My sister has made this several times, including last night when we were over. She uses store-bought rotisserie chicken, which adds even more flavor, and she found a frozen peas and mini-pearl onion mix that was great in there! (She did use the sauteed onion in the beginning, too.) So easy, and perfect with a simple salad and a dinner roll."

—drtrish

[1994]

CHICKEN AND DUMPLING CASSEROLE

yield: 6-8 servings   prep: 30 min.
bake: 40 min.

This savory casserole is one of my husband's favorites. He loves the fluffy dumplings with plenty of gravy poured over them. The basil adds just the right touch of flavor.

—Sue Mackey
Jackson, Wisconsin, Field Editor

1/2	cup chopped onion
1/2	cup chopped celery
1/4	cup butter, cubed
2	garlic cloves, minced
1/2	cup all-purpose flour
2	teaspoons sugar
1	teaspoon salt
1	teaspoon dried basil
1/2	teaspoon pepper
4	cups chicken broth
1	package (10 ounces) frozen green peas
4	cups cubed cooked chicken

DUMPLINGS:

2	cups biscuit/baking mix
2	teaspoons dried basil
2/3	cup 2% milk

1. In a large saucepan, saute the onion and celery in butter until tender. Add garlic; cook 1 minute longer. Stir in the flour, sugar, salt, basil and pepper until blended. Gradually add broth; bring to a boil. Cook and stir for 1 minute or until thickened; reduce heat. Add peas and cook for 5 minutes, stirring constantly. Stir in chicken. Pour into a greased 13-in. x 9-in. baking dish.

2. For the dumplings, in a small bowl, combine baking mix and basil. Stir in milk with a fork until moistened. Drop by tablespoonfuls into 12 mounds over chicken mixture.

3. Bake casserole, uncovered, at 350° for 30 minutes. Cover and bake 10 minutes longer or until a toothpick inserted in a dumpling comes out clean.

[2001]

CHICKEN IN POTATO BASKETS

yield: 6 servings   prep: 20 min.
bake: 30 min.

These petite pies with their hash brown crusts are so pretty that I like to serve them for special luncheons. Chock-full of meat and vegetables in a creamy sauce, they're a meal in one and a great way to use up leftover chicken or turkey.

—Helen Lamison, Carnegie, Pennsylvania

4-1/2	cups frozen shredded hash brown potatoes, thawed
6	tablespoons butter, melted
1-1/2	teaspoons salt
1/4	teaspoon pepper

FILLING:

1/2	cup chopped onion
1/4	cup butter, cubed
1/4	cup all-purpose flour
2	teaspoons chicken bouillon granules
1	teaspoon Worcestershire sauce
1/2	teaspoon dried basil
2	cups 2% milk
3	cups cubed cooked chicken
1	cup frozen peas, thawed

1. In a large bowl, combine the potatoes, butter, salt and pepper. Press into six greased 10-oz. custard cups; set aside.

2. In a large saucepan, saute the onion in butter. Add the flour, bouillon, Worcestershire sauce and basil. Stir in the milk. Bring to a boil; cook and stir for 2 minutes or until thickened. Add the chicken and peas. Spoon into prepared crusts.

3. Bake, uncovered, at 375° for 30-35 minutes or until crust is golden brown.

[2006]

CHICKEN AND ASPARAGUS KABOBS

yield: 6 servings
prep: 25 min. + marinating ∞ **grill: 10 min.**

(*Pictured on page 406*)

These Asian-flavored kabobs, served with a tasty dipping sauce, are special enough to make for guests at your next backyard get-together. Sometimes I substitute salmon for the chicken.

—*Kelly Townsend, Syracuse, Nebraska*

DIPPING SAUCE:
- 2 cups mayonnaise
- 1/4 cup sugar
- 1/4 cup reduced-sodium soy sauce
- 2 tablespoons sesame seeds, toasted
- 1 tablespoon sesame oil
- 1/2 teaspoon white pepper

KABOBS:
- 1/4 cup soy sauce
- 2 tablespoons brown sugar
- 2 tablespoons water
- 1 tablespoon sesame oil
- 1 teaspoon crushed red pepper flakes
- 1 teaspoon minced fresh gingerroot
- 1-1/2 pounds boneless skinless chicken breasts, cut into 1-1/2-inch pieces
- 1 pound fresh asparagus, trimmed and cut into 2-inch pieces
- 2 tablespoons olive oil
- 1/2 teaspoon salt

1. In a small bowl, combine the sauce ingredients. Cover and refrigerate for 2-4 hours.

2. In a large resealable plastic bag, combine the soy sauce, brown sugar, water, sesame oil, pepper flakes and ginger. Add the chicken; seal bag and turn to coat. Refrigerate for 2 hours, turning occasionally.

3. Drain and discard marinade. In a large bowl, toss the asparagus with olive oil and salt. On six metal or soaked wooden skewers, alternately thread one chicken piece and two asparagus pieces.

4. Grill, covered, over medium heat for 4-5 minutes on each side or until the chicken is no longer pink and the asparagus is crisp-tender. Serve with dipping sauce.

[2009]

"SECRET'S IN THE SAUCE" BBQ RIBS

yield: 5 servings ∞ **prep: 10 min.**
cook: 6 hours

(*Pictured on page 404*)

A sweet, rich sauce makes these ribs so tender that the meat literally falls off the bones. And the aroma is wonderful. Yum!

—*Tanya Reid*
Winston-Salem, North Carolina

- 2 racks pork baby back ribs (about 4-1/2 pounds)
- 1-1/2 teaspoons pepper
- 2-1/2 cups barbecue sauce
- 3/4 cup cherry preserves
- 1 tablespoon Dijon mustard
- 1 garlic clove, minced

1. Cut ribs into serving-size pieces; sprinkle with the pepper. Place in a 5- or 6-qt. slow cooker. Combine the remaining ingredients; pour over the ribs. Cover and cook on low for 6-8 hours or until the meat is tender. Serve with sauce.

"SECRET'S IN THE SAUCE" BBQ RIBS

"Turned out great for me. I didn't have cherry preserves so substituted red currant jelly instead. Super easy and tasty for a busy weeknight dinner or weekend when you want to take it easy."
—*cwbuff*

FARMHOUSE PORK AND APPLE PIE

"This is a great way to use up leftover pork roast, too! I doubled the amount of mashed potatoes to get it to look like the picture, and added cut green beans to make it a one-pot meal. Great down-home flavor!"

—cwbuff

[2004]

PINEAPPLE-STUFFED CORNISH HENS

yield: 2 servings ～ **prep: 20 min.**
bake: 55 min.

My mother brought this recipe back with her from Hawaii about 25 years ago. The tender meat, pineapple-coconut stuffing and sweet-sour sauce made it a favorite of my family and friends. I keep copies of the recipe on hand to share.

—*Vicki Corners, Rock Island, Illinois*

2	Cornish game hens (20 to 24 ounces each)
1/2	teaspoon salt, *divided*
1	can (8 ounces) crushed pineapple
3	cups cubed day-old bread (1/2-inch cubes), crusts removed
1	celery rib, chopped
1/2	cup flaked coconut
2/3	cup butter melted, *divided*
1/4	teaspoon poultry seasoning
2	tablespoons steak sauce
2	tablespoons cornstarch
2	tablespoons brown sugar
1	cup water
1	tablespoon lemon juice

1. Sprinkle the inside of hens with 1/4 teaspoon salt; set aside. Drain pineapple, reserving juice. In a large bowl, combine the pineapple, bread cubes, celery and coconut. Add 6 tablespoons butter; toss to coat.

2. Loosely stuff hens; tie legs together with kitchen string. Place on a rack in a greased shallow roasting pan. Place remaining stuffing in a greased 1-1/2-cup baking dish; cover and set aside. Add poultry seasoning and remaining salt to remaining butter.

3. Spoon some butter mixture over the hens. Bake, uncovered, at 350° for 40 minutes, basting twice with the butter mixture.

4. Stir the steak sauce and reserved pineapple juice into remaining butter mixture; baste hens. Bake reserved stuffing with hens for 30 minutes; baste hens twice.

5. Uncover stuffing and baste hens with the remaining butter mixture. Bake 15-20 minutes longer or until a thermometer reads 185° for hens and 165° for stuffing in hens. Remove hens from pan; keep warm.

6. Pour drippings into a saucepan, skim fat. Combine the cornstarch, brown sugar, water and lemon juice until smooth; add to the drippings. Bring to a boil; cook and stir for 1-2 minutes or until thickened. Serve with the hens and stuffing.

[1995]

FARMHOUSE PORK AND APPLE PIE

yield: 10 servings ～ **prep: 70 min.**
bake: 2 hours

I've always loved pork and apples together, and this recipe combines them nicely to create a comforting main dish. It calls for a bit of preparation, but my family and I agree that its wonderful flavor makes it well worth the extra effort.

—*Suzanne Strocsher, Bothell, Washington*

1	pound sliced bacon, cut into 2-inch pieces
3	medium onions, chopped
3	pounds boneless pork, cut into 1-inch cubes
3/4	cup all-purpose flour
Canola oil, optional	
3	medium tart apples, peeled and chopped
1	teaspoon rubbed sage
1/2	teaspoon ground nutmeg
1	teaspoon salt
1/4	teaspoon pepper
1	cup apple cider

1/2   cup water
4   medium potatoes, peeled and cubed
1/2   cup milk
5   tablespoons butter, *divided*
Additional salt and pepper
Minced fresh parsley, optional

1. Cook bacon in an ovenproof 12-in. skillet until crisp. Using a slotted spoon, remove to paper towels to drain. In drippings, saute onions until tender; remove with slotted spoon and set aside. Dust pork lightly with flour. Brown a third at a time in drippings, adding oil if needed. Remove from the heat and drain.

2. To the pork, add the bacon, onions, apples, sage, nutmeg, salt and pepper. Stir in cider and water. Cover and bake at 325° for 2 hours or until pork is tender.

3. Place potatoes in a large saucepan and cover with water. Bring to a boil. Reduce heat; cover and cook for 10-15 minutes or until tender.

4. Drain and mash potatoes with milk and 3 tablespoons butter. Add salt and pepper to taste. Remove skillet from oven and spread potatoes over pork mixture.

5. Melt the remaining butter; brush over potatoes. Broil 6 in. from the heat for 5 minutes or until topping is browned. Sprinkle with parsley if desired.

[2002]

SEAFOOD LASAGNA
yield: 12 servings   ∞   prep: 35 min.
bake: 35 min. + standing
(*Pictured on page 405*)

This rich, satisfying dish, adapted from a recipe given to me by a friend, is my husband's favorite. I usually serve it on his birthday. It's loaded with scallops, shrimp and crab in a creamy sauce. I consider this the "crown jewel" in my repertoire of recipes.

—Elena Hansen, Ruidoso, New Mexico

1   green onion, finely chopped
2   tablespoons canola oil
2   tablespoons plus 1/2 cup butter, *divided*
1/2   cup chicken broth
1   bottle (8 ounces) clam juice
1   pound bay scallops
1   pound uncooked small shrimp, peeled and deveined

1   package (8 ounces) imitation crabmeat, chopped
1/4   teaspoon white pepper, *divided*
1/2   cup all-purpose flour
1-1/2   cups 2% milk
1/2   teaspoon salt
1   cup heavy whipping cream
1/2   cup shredded Parmesan cheese, *divided*
9   lasagna noodles, cooked and drained

1. In a large skillet, saute onion in oil and 2 tablespoons butter until tender. Stir in broth and clam juice; bring to a boil. Add scallops, shrimp, crab and 1/8 teaspoon pepper; return to a boil. Reduce the heat; simmer, uncovered, for 4-5 minutes or until the shrimp turn pink and scallops are firm and opaque, stirring gently. Drain, reserving cooking liquid; set the seafood mixture aside.

2. In a large saucepan, melt the remaining butter; stir in flour until smooth. Combine the milk and reserved cooking liquid; gradually add to the saucepan. Add salt and remaining pepper. Bring to a boil; cook and stir for 2 minutes or until thickened.

3. Remove from the heat; stir in the cream and 1/4 cup cheese. Stir 3/4 cup white sauce into seafood mixture.

4. Spread 1/2 cup white sauce in a greased 13-in. x 9-in. baking dish. Top with three noodles; spread with half of the seafood mixture and 1-1/4 cups sauce. Repeat layers. Top with remaining noodles, sauce and cheese.

5. Bake, uncovered, at 350° for 35-40 minutes or until golden brown. Let stand for 15 minutes before cutting.

WHY USE CLAM JUICE?

Clam juice, which is the strained liquid from shucked clams, adds a briny flavor to dishes and is a popular addition to seafood dishes. Look for bottled clam juice in the canned seafood aisle of your supermarket.

—*Taste of Home Cooking Experts*

[1997]

SPICY BEAN AND BEEF PIE

yield: 8 servings ∾ prep: 20 min.
bake: 30 min.

(Pictured on page 408)

*My daughter helped me create this recipe one
day when we wanted a one-dish meal that was
something other than a casserole. It slices nicely
and is a fun and filling dish.*

—Debra Dohy
Newcomerstown, Ohio, Field Editor

- 1 **pound ground beef**
- 2 **to 3 garlic cloves, minced**
- 1 **can (11-1/2 ounces) condensed bean
  with bacon soup, undiluted**
- 1 **jar (16 ounces) thick and chunky
  picante sauce,** *divided*
- 1/4 **cup cornstarch**
- 1 **tablespoon chopped fresh parsley**
- 1 **teaspoon paprika**
- 1 **teaspoon salt**
- 1/4 **teaspoon pepper**
- 1 **can (16 ounces) kidney beans, rinsed
  and drained**
- 1 **can (15 ounces) black beans, rinsed
  and drained**
- 2 **cups (8 ounces) shredded cheddar
  cheese,** *divided*
- 3/4 **cup sliced green onions,** *divided*

Pastry for double-crust pie (10 inches)
- 1 **cup (8 ounces) sour cream**
- 1 **can (2-1/4 ounces) sliced ripe olives,
  drained**

1. In a large skillet, cook beef over medium
   heat until beef is no longer pink. Add
   garlic; cook 1 minute longer. Drain.

2. In a large bowl, combine soup, 1 cup
   picante sauce, cornstarch, parsley,
   paprika, salt and pepper. Fold in beans,
   1-1/2 cups cheese, 1/2 cup onions and
   the beef mixture.

3. Line pie plate with bottom pastry; fill
   with bean mixture. Top with remaining
   pastry; seal and flute edges. Cut slits in
   top crust.

4. Bake at 425° for 30-35 minutes or until
   crust is lightly browned. Let stand for
   5 minutes before cutting. Garnish with
   the sour cream, olives and remaining
   picante sauce, cheese and onions.

[2012]

GARDEN VEGGIE LASAGNA

yield: 12 servings ∾ prep: 50 min.
bake: 35 min. + standing

*My husband and I really enjoy traditional
lasagna, and I'm always looking for new ways
to jazz up this dish. I had just loaded up on
veggies from the farmer's market and decided
to try a veggie lasagna. It's now our go-to meal
when we are craving our Italian favorite!*

—Samantha Neal
Morgantown, West Virginia

- 2 **medium zucchini, sliced diagonally
  1/4 inch thick**
- 2 **cups fresh broccoli florets**
- 2 **large carrots, julienned**
- 2 **medium sweet red peppers, julienned**
- 1/4 **cup olive oil**
- 2 **garlic cloves, minced**
- 3/4 **teaspoon dried thyme**
- 1/2 **teaspoon** *each* **salt and pepper**

SAUCE:
- 2 **cups finely chopped baby portobello
  mushrooms**
- 1 **large onion, finely chopped**
- 2 **garlic cloves, minced**
- 2 **tablespoons olive oil**
- 2 **cans (28 ounces** *each***) crushed
  tomatoes**
- 3 **teaspoons Italian seasoning**
- 3/4 **teaspoon** *each* **salt and pepper**

FILLING:
- 1-1/4 **cups ricotta cheese**
- 1 **package (8 ounces) cream cheese,
  softened**
- 3/4 **cup grated Parmesan cheese**
- 1 **egg, lightly beaten**
- 2 **teaspoons dried basil**

ASSEMBLY:

- 12 no-cook lasagna noodles
- 3 cups (12 ounces) shredded mozzarella and provolone cheese blend

1. Place the first nine ingredients in a large bowl; toss to coat. Arrange the vegetables on two greased 15-in. x 10-in. x 1-in baking pans. Bake at 425° for 10-15 minutes or until tender, stirring occasionally.

2. Meanwhile, in a Dutch oven, saute mushrooms, onion and garlic in oil until tender. Stir in remaining sauce ingredients; bring to a boil. Reduce heat; simmer, uncovered, for 10-12 minutes, stirring occasionally.

3. In a large bowl, combine the filling ingredients. Spread 1 cup sauce into a greased 13-in. x 9-in. baking dish. Layer a third of the noodles, a third of the ricotta cheese mixture, half of the vegetables, a third of the remaining sauce and a third of the cheese blend; repeat layers. Top with the remaining noodles, ricotta mixture, sauce and cheese blend.

4. Cover and bake at 350° for 35-40 minutes or until bubbly. Let stand for 15 minutes before cutting.

[2005]

SPINACH CRAB CHICKEN
yield: 4 servings ∾ prep: 45 min.
cook: 40 min.

I altered a friend's recipe for crab-stuffed chicken to include one of my favorite vegetables.
—*Vicki Melies, Elkhorn, Nebraska*

- 1/2 cup finely chopped onion
- 1/4 cup chopped fresh mushrooms
- 1/4 cup finely chopped celery
- 3 tablespoons butter
- 3 tablespoons all-purpose flour
- 1/2 teaspoon salt, *divided*
- 1 cup chicken broth
- 1/2 cup 2% milk
- 4 boneless skinless chicken breast halves (6 ounces *each*)
- 1/8 teaspoon white pepper
- 1/2 cup dry bread crumbs
- 1 can (6 ounces) crabmeat, drained, flaked and cartilage removed
- 12 fresh spinach leaves, chopped
- 1 tablespoon minced fresh parsley
- 1 cup (4 ounces) shredded Swiss cheese

Hot cooked rice

1. For sauce, in a large skillet, saute onion, mushrooms and celery in butter until tender. Stir in flour and 1/4 teaspoon salt until blended. Gradually add broth and milk. Bring to a boil; cook and stir for 1-2 minutes or until thickened. Remove from the heat.

2. Flatten chicken to 1/4-in. thickness; sprinkle with pepper and remaining salt. In a large bowl, combine the bread crumbs, crab, spinach and parsley; stir in 1/2 cup sauce. Spoon 1/4 cup down the center of each chicken breast half. Roll up; secure with toothpicks. Place seam side down in a greased 13-in. x 9-in. baking dish. Top with the remaining sauce.

3. Cover dish and bake at 375° for 35-45 minutes or until chicken is no longer pink. Sprinkle with cheese. Broil 4-6 in. from the heat for 5 minutes or until lightly browned. Discard toothpicks. Serve with rice.

SPINACH CRAB CHICKEN

"My husband, who doesn't generally like me to make new recipes and is a fussy eater, liked this as did I. I try new stuff anyway!"
—*mar4bill*

[2000]

TRADITIONAL LASAGNA

yield: 12 servings ∽ **prep: 30 min. plus simmering**
bake: 70 min. + standing

(Pictured on page 401)

*My family first tasted this rich, classic lasagna at a friend's home
on Christmas Eve. We were so impressed that it became our own
holiday tradition as well. I also prepare it other times of the year.
It's requested often by my sister's Italian in-laws—I consider
that the highest compliment!*

—*Lorri Foockle, Granville, Illinois*

1	pound ground beef
3/4	pound bulk pork sausage
3	cans (8 ounces *each*) tomato sauce
2	cans (6 ounces *each*) tomato paste
2	garlic cloves, minced
2	teaspoons sugar
1	teaspoon Italian seasoning
1	teaspoon salt
1/2	teaspoon pepper
3	eggs
3	tablespoons minced fresh parsley
3	cups (24 ounces) 4% small-curd cottage cheese
1	carton (8 ounces) ricotta cheese
1/2	cup grated Parmesan cheese
9	lasagna noodles, cooked and drained
6	slices provolone cheese
3	cups (12 ounces) shredded part-skim mozzarella cheese, *divided*

1. In a large skillet, cook beef and sausage over medium
heat until no longer pink; drain. Add the tomato sauce,
tomato paste, garlic, sugar, seasoning, salt and pepper.
Bring to a boil. Reduce heat; simmer, uncovered, for
1 hour, stirring occasionally.

2. In a large bowl, combine eggs and parsley. Stir in the
cottage cheese, ricotta and Parmesan cheese.

3. Spread 1 cup meat sauce in an ungreased 13-in. x 9-in.
baking dish. Layer with three noodles, provolone
cheese, 2 cups cottage cheese mixture, 1 cup
mozzarella, three noodles, 2 cups meat sauce,
remaining cottage cheese mixture and 1 cup
mozzarella. Top with the remaining noodles, meat
sauce and mozzarella (dish will be full).

4. Cover and bake at 375° for 50 minutes. Uncover; bake
20 minutes longer or until heated through. Let stand
for 15 minutes before cutting.

[2006]

STUFFED HAM WITH RAISIN SAUCE

yield: 12-14 servings ∽ **prep: 30 min.** ∽ **bake: 1-3/4 hours**

*This impressive ham is a great centerpiece for a holiday
dinner, but I've made it most often for brunch. I always hear
compliments when I serve it.*

—*Jeanne Miller, Big Sky, Montana*

1	boneless fully cooked ham (6 to 7 pounds)
1	large onion, chopped
1/4	cup butter, cubed
2	cups corn bread stuffing mix
1-1/2	cups chopped pecans, toasted
1/2	cup minced fresh parsley
1/4	cup egg substitute
2	tablespoons prepared mustard
1/2	cup honey
2	tablespoons orange juice concentrate

RAISIN SAUCE:

1/2	cup packed brown sugar
2	tablespoons all-purpose flour
1/2	teaspoon ground mustard
1/2	cup raisins
1-1/2	cups water
1/4	cup cider vinegar

1. Using a sharp thin-bladed knife and beginning at one
end of the ham, carefully cut a 2-1/2-in. circle about
6 in. deep; remove cutout. Cut a 1-1/2-in. slice from
the end of removed piece; set aside.

2. Continue cutting a 2-1/2-in. tunnel halfway through
ham, using a spoon to remove pieces of ham (save
for another use). Repeat from opposite end of ham,
cutting and removing ham until a tunnel has been
cut through entire length of ham.

3. In a small skillet, saute onion in butter until tender. In
a large bowl, combine the stuffing mix, pecans, parsley,
egg substitute and mustard. Stir in onion. Stuff ham;
cover end openings with reserved ham slices. Place in
a shallow roasting pan.

4. Bake, uncovered, at 325° for 1-1/4 hours. In a small saucepan, combine the honey and orange juice concentrate; cook and stir for 1-2 minutes or until blended. Brush over ham. Bake 30 minutes longer or until a thermometer reads 140°.

5. For sauce, combine brown sugar, flour, mustard and raisins in a saucepan. Gradually add water and vinegar. Bring to a boil; cook and stir for 1-2 minutes or until thickened. Serve with ham.

Editor's Note: Two fully cooked boneless ham halves can be substituted for the whole ham. Simply hollow out each ham; loosely spoon stuffing into each half, then bake as directed.

[1998]

SURPRISE SAUSAGE BUNDLES

yield: 16 servings ∞ prep: 45 min. + rising ∞ bake: 20 min.

(Pictured on page 406)

Kielbasa and sauerkraut star in a tasty filling for these scrumptious stuffed rolls, which make a great dinner with soup or salad. My family also loves leftover bundles right out of the refrigerator for a quick lunch.

—*Barb Ruis*
Grandville, Michigan, Field Editor

- 6 **bacon strips, diced**
- 1 **cup chopped onion**
- 1 **can (16 ounces) sauerkraut, rinsed and well drained**
- 1/2 **pound smoked kielbasa *or* Polish sausage, coarsely chopped**
- 2 **tablespoons brown sugar**
- 1/2 **teaspoon garlic salt**
- 1/4 **teaspoon caraway seeds**
- 1/8 **teaspoon pepper**
- 1 **package (16 ounces) hot roll mix**
- 2 **eggs**
- 1 **cup warm water (120° to 130°)**
- 2 **tablespoons butter, softened**

Poppy seeds

1. In a large skillet, cook the bacon over medium heat until crisp. Using a slotted spoon, remove to paper towels. Reserve 2 tablespoons drippings. Saute onion in drippings until tender. Stir in the sauerkraut, sausage, brown sugar, garlic salt, caraway and pepper. Cook and stir for 5 minutes. Remove from the heat; add bacon. Set aside to cool.

2. In a large bowl, combine contents of the roll mix and yeast packets. Stir in one egg, water and butter to form a soft dough. Turn dough onto a floured surface; knead until smooth and elastic, about 5 minutes. Cover dough with a large bowl; let stand for 5 minutes.

3. Divide dough into 16 pieces. On a floured surface, roll out each piece into a 4-in. circle. Top each with 1/4 cup filling. Fold dough around filling, forming a ball; pinch edges to seal. Place seam side down on greased baking sheets. Cover loosely with plastic wrap that has been coated with cooking spray. Let rise in a warm place for 15 minutes.

4. Beat the remaining egg; brush over bundles. Sprinkle with poppy seeds. Bake at 350° for 16-17 minutes or until golden brown. Serve warm.

SURPRISE SAUSAGE BUNDLES

"These little bundles are great on a cold day with a bowl of soup. They are also easy to pack in a school/work lunch to be eaten cold or heated in a microwave."
—*lisakostelecky*

[1994]

TERIYAKI SHISH KABOBS
yield: 6-8 servings
prep: 20 min. + marinating ∽ **grill: 15 min.**

My father worked for an airline in the 1960s, when I was a teenager, and my family lived on the island of Guam in the South Pacific. A friend of Mother's there gave her this wonderful recipe. We ate this delicious warm-weather dish often, and now I prepare it for my family.

—*Suzanne Pelegrin, Ocala, Florida*

- 1 cup ketchup
- 1 cup sugar
- 1 cup reduced-sodium soy sauce
- 2 teaspoons garlic powder
- 2 teaspoons ground ginger
- 1 beef top sirloin steak (1-1/2 inches thick and 2 pounds), cut into 1-1/2-inch cubes
- 1/2 fresh pineapple, trimmed and cut into 1-inch chunks
- 2 to 3 small zucchini, cut into 1-inch chunks
- 1/2 pound medium fresh mushrooms
- 1/2 pound pearl onions
- 1 large green or sweet red pepper, cut into 1-inch pieces

1. Combine first five ingredients in a large resealable plastic bag; reserving half the marinade. Add beef. Seal bag and turn to coat; refrigerate overnight. Cover and refrigerate reserved marinade.

2. Drain and discard marinade from the beef. Thread meat, pineapple and vegetables alternately on metal or soaked wooden skewers.

3. Grill over hot heat for 15-20 minutes, turning often, or until meat reaches desired doneness and the vegetables are tender.

4. In a small saucepan, bring reserved marinade to a boil; boil for 1 minute. Remove the meat and vegetables from skewers; serve with marinade.

[2008]

PEPPERONI
SPINACH QUICHE
yield: 8 servings ∽ prep: 25 min.
bake: 25 min.

(*Pictured on page 403*)

Several years ago, I had to come up with a dish to serve at a pool party, and this colorful quiche was a hit. It's also great on an antipasto tray, cut into wedges.

—*Elynor (Elly) Townsend*
Summerfield, Florida

- 1 tube (8 ounces) refrigerated crescent rolls
- 1 large sweet red pepper, chopped
- 1 tablespoon olive oil
- 1 garlic clove, minced
- 5 eggs, lightly beaten

SEEDING AND SLICING
SWEET PEPPERS

Holding the pepper by the stem, slice from the top of the pepper down, using a chef's knife. Use this technique to slice around the seeds when a recipe calls for julienned or chopped.

1/2 cup shredded part-skim mozzarella cheese
1/2 cup frozen chopped spinach, thawed and squeezed dry
1/4 cup sliced pepperoni, cut into strips
1/4 cup half-and-half cream
2 tablespoons grated Parmesan cheese
1 tablespoon minced fresh parsley
1 tablespoon minced fresh basil *or* 1 teaspoon dried basil
Dash pepper

1. Separate crescent dough into eight triangles; place in an ungreased 9-in. fluted tart pan with removable bottom with points toward the center. Press onto the bottom and up the sides to form a crust; seal seams. Set aside.

2. In a small skillet, saute the red pepper in oil until tender. Add the garlic; cook 1 minute longer. Remove from the heat. In another small bowl, combine the remaining ingredients; stir in the red pepper mixture. Pour into crust.

3. Bake at 375° for 25-30 minutes or until a knife inserted near the center comes out clean. Let stand for 5 minutes before cutting.

[1996]

HERBED TURKEY AND DRESSING

yield: 14-16 servings (18 cups dressing)
prep: 55 min. + chilling   **bake:** 5 hours
(*Pictured on page 403*)

Whenever I serve this succulent golden turkey and delectable dressing, guests fill their plates and I'm buried in compliments. This recipe always makes a holiday dinner one to remember. It's well worth the time.

—Marilyn Clay, Palatine, Illinois

BASTING SAUCE:
2-1/4 cups chicken broth
1/2 cup butter, cubed
1/2 teaspoon salt
1 teaspoon dried thyme
1/4 teaspoon *each* dried marjoram, rubbed sage and dried rosemary, crushed
1/4 cup minced fresh parsley
2 tablespoons minced chives

DRESSING:
1 loaf (1 pound) sliced bread
1 pound bulk pork sausage
1/2 cup butter, cubed
4 cups thinly sliced celery
3 cups thinly sliced carrots
1/2 pound fresh mushrooms, chopped
1/2 pound cubed fully cooked ham
2 cups green onions
2 cups chopped pecans
1 large tart apple, chopped
1 cup chopped dried apricots
1 tablespoon rubbed sage
2 teaspoons dried marjoram
1 teaspoon dried rosemary, crushed
1 teaspoon salt
1/8 teaspoon ground nutmeg
1 cup egg substitute
1 turkey (16 to 18 pounds)
1 cup chicken broth

1. In a small saucepan, combine the broth, butter and salt; bring to a boil. Add herbs; set aside.

2. Toast bread; cut into 1/2-in. cubes. Place in a bowl. In a skillet, cook the sausage over medium heat until no longer pink; remove with slotted spoon and add to the bread. Add the butter to drippings; saute the celery, carrots, mushrooms, ham and onions for 15 minutes.

3. Add to the bread mixture; stir in the nuts, fruit and seasonings. Add the egg substitute and 3/4 cup basting sauce; mix lightly.

4. Stuff the turkey with about 8 cups dressing. Skewer openings; tie the drumsticks together. Place on rack in roasting pan. Baste with some of the remaining basting sauce.

5. Bake, uncovered, at 325° for 5 to 5-1/2 hours or until a thermometer reads 180° for the turkey and 165° for the stuffing, basting every 30 minutes. When turkey begins to brown, cover lightly with foil.

6. Add the broth to remaining dressing; toss to coat. Place in a greased 2-1/2-qt. baking dish; refrigerate. Remove from the refrigerator 30 minutes before baking. Cover and bake at 325° for 1 hour; uncover and bake 10 minutes.

[2010]

CHICKEN FLORENTINE MEATBALLS

yield: 6 servings ∽ **prep: 40 min.** ∽ **cook: 20 min.**

Served over squash and a chunky, mushroom-tomato sauce, these tender meatballs are tops when it comes to great flavor.

—*Diane Nemitz, Ludington, Michigan*

---

  2 eggs, lightly beaten
  1 package (10 ounces) frozen chopped spinach, thawed and squeezed dry
1/2 cup dry bread crumbs
1/4 cup grated Parmesan cheese
  1 tablespoon dried minced onion
  1 garlic clove, minced
1/4 teaspoon salt
1/8 teaspoon pepper
  1 pound ground chicken
  1 medium spaghetti squash

SAUCE:
1/2 pound sliced fresh mushrooms
  2 teaspoons olive oil
  1 can (14-1/2 ounces) diced tomatoes, undrained
  1 can (8 ounces) tomato sauce
  2 tablespoons minced fresh parsley
  1 garlic clove, minced
  1 teaspoon dried oregano
  1 teaspoon dried basil

---

1. In a large bowl, combine the first eight ingredients. Crumble chicken over mixture and mix well. Shape into 1-1/2-in. balls.

2. Place meatballs on a rack in a shallow baking pan. Bake, uncovered, at 400° for 20-25 minutes or until no longer pink. Meanwhile, cut squash in half lengthwise; discard seeds. Place squash cut side down on a microwave-safe plate. Microwave, uncovered, on high for 15-18 minutes or until tender.

3. For sauce, in a large nonstick skillet, saute mushrooms in oil until tender. Stir in the remaining ingredients. Bring to a boil. Reduce heat; simmer, uncovered, for 8-10 minutes or until slightly thickened. Add meatballs and heat through.

4. When squash is cool enough to handle, use a fork to separate strands. Serve with meatballs and sauce.

Editor's Note: Recipe was tested in a 1,100-watt microwave.

[2003]

TEMPURA CHICKEN WINGS

yield: 2-1/2 dozen ∽ **prep: 40 min.**
bake: 25 min.

When I moved to Kansas City from Texas, I brought many of my mom's best-loved recipes with me, including these saucy sweet-and-sour wings. This recipe turned a friend of mine, who's not a fan of chicken, into a real wing lover.

—*Susan Wuckowitsch, Lenexa, Kansas*

---

15 whole chicken wings (about 3 pounds)
  1 cup cornstarch
  3 eggs, lightly beaten
Oil for deep-fat frying
1/2 cup sugar
1/2 cup white vinegar
1/2 cup currant jelly
1/4 cup reduced-sodium soy sauce
  3 tablespoons ketchup
  2 tablespoons lemon juice

---

1. Cut chicken wings into three sections; discard wing tip section. Place cornstarch in a large resealable plastic bag; add chicken wings, a few at a time, and shake to coat evenly. Place eggs in a shallow bowl; dip wings in eggs.

2. In an electric skillet or deep-fat fryer, heat oil to 375°. Fry the wings for 8 minutes or until golden brown and juices run clear, turning occasionally. Drain the wings on paper towels.

3. In a small saucepan, combine the sugar, vinegar, jelly, soy sauce, ketchup and lemon juice. Bring to a boil. Reduce heat; simmer, uncovered, for 10 minutes.

4. Place chicken wings in a greased 15-in. x 10-in. x 1-in. baking pan. Pour half of the sauce over wings. Bake, uncovered, at 350° for 15 minutes. Turn wings; top with remaining sauce. Bake 10-15 minutes longer or until coating is set.

Editor's Note: Uncooked chicken wing sections (wingettes) may be substituted for whole chicken wings.

[2003]

ONION BEEF AU JUS

yield: 12 servings ∾ **prep: 20 min.**
bake: 2-1/2 hours + standing

(Pictured on page 403)

Garlic, onions, soy sauce and onion soup mix flavor the tender beef in these hot, savory sandwiches that are served with a tasty, rich broth for dipping. The seasoned beef makes delicious cold sandwiches, too.

—*Marilyn Brown, West Union, Iowa*

  1 beef rump roast *or* bottom round roast (4 pounds)
  2 tablespoons canola oil
  2 large sweet onions, cut into 1/4-inch slices
  6 tablespoons butter, softened, *divided*
  5 cups water
1/2 cup reduced-sodium soy sauce
  1 envelope onion soup mix
  1 garlic clove, minced
  1 teaspoon browning sauce, optional
  1 loaf (1 pound) French bread
  1 cup (4 ounces) shredded Swiss cheese

1. In a Dutch oven over medium-high heat, brown roast on all sides in oil; drain. In a large skillet, saute onions in 2 tablespoons butter until tender. Add the water, soy sauce, soup mix, garlic and browning sauce if desired. Pour over roast. Cover and bake at 325° for 2-1/2 hours or until meat is tender.

2. Let stand for 10 minutes before slicing. Return meat to pan juices. Slice bread in half lengthwise; cut into 3-in. sections. Spread remaining butter over bread.

3. Place on a baking sheet. Broil 4-6 in. from the heat for 2-3 minutes or until golden brown. Top with beef and onions; sprinkle with cheese. Broil 4-6 in. from the heat for 1-2 minutes or until cheese is melted. Serve with pan juices.

[1996]

BLUEBERRY FRENCH TOAST

yield: 6-8 servings (1-3/4 cups sauce)
prep: 30 min. + chilling ∾ **bake: 55 min.**

This is the best breakfast dish I have ever tasted. Luscious blueberries are tucked into the French toast and in the sauce that goes over the top. With the cream cheese and berry combination, this dish reminds me of dessert. The recipe was shared with me by a local blueberry grower.

—*Patricia Axelsen, Aurora, Minnesota, Field Editor*

 12 slices day-old white bread, crusts removed
  2 packages (8 ounces *each*) cream cheese
  1 cup fresh *or* frozen blueberries
 12 eggs, lightly beaten
  2 cups 2% milk
1/3 cup maple syrup *or* honey
SAUCE:
  1 cup sugar
  2 tablespoons cornstarch
  1 cup water
  1 cup fresh *or* frozen blueberries
  1 tablespoon butter

1. Cut the bread into 1-in. cubes; place half in a greased 13-in. x 9-in. baking dish. Cut the cream cheese into 1-in. cubes; place over bread. Top with the blueberries and remaining bread cubes.

2. In a large bowl, whisk the eggs, milk and syrup. Pour over bread mixture. Cover and refrigerate for 8 hours or overnight.

3. Remove from the refrigerator 30 minutes before baking. Cover and bake at 350° for 30 minutes. Uncover; bake 25-30 minutes longer or until a knife inserted near the center comes out clean.

4. In a small saucepan, combine the sugar, cornstarch and water until smooth. Bring to a boil over medium heat; cook and stir for 3 minutes or until thickened. Stir in blueberries; reduce heat. Simmer for 8-10 minutes or until berries have burst. Stir in the butter until melted. Serve with French toast.

Editor's Note: If using frozen blueberries, do not thaw.

[1997]

RYE PARTY PUFFS
yield: 4-1/2 dozen ∽ prep: 30 min.
bake: 20 min. + cooling

I can't go anywhere without taking along my puffs. They're pretty enough for a wedding reception yet also hearty enough to snack on while watching football on television. A platterful of these will disappear even with a small group.

—Kelly Williams, Morganville, New Jersey, Field Editor

- 1 cup water
- 1/2 cup butter, cubed
- 1/2 cup all-purpose flour
- 1/2 cup rye flour
- 2 teaspoons dried parsley flakes
- 1/2 teaspoon garlic powder
- 1/4 teaspoon salt
- 4 eggs
- Caraway seeds

CORNED BEEF FILLING:
- 2 packages (8 ounces each) cream cheese, softened
- 2 packages (2 ounces each) thinly sliced deli corned beef, chopped
- 1/2 cup mayonnaise
- 1/4 cup sour cream
- 2 tablespoons minced chives
- 2 tablespoons diced onion
- 1 teaspoon spicy brown or horseradish mustard
- 1/8 teaspoon garlic powder
- 10 small pimiento-stuffed olives, chopped

1. In a large saucepan over medium heat, bring water and butter to a boil. Add the flours, parsley, garlic powder and salt all at once; stir until a smooth balls forms. Remove from the heat; let stand for 5 minutes. Beat in eggs, one at a time. Beat until smooth.

2. Drop batter by rounded teaspoonfuls 2 in. apart onto greased baking sheets. Sprinkle with caraway. Bake at 400° for 18-20 minutes or until golden. Remove to wire racks. Immediately cut a slit in each puff to allow steam to escape; cool.

3. In a large bowl, combine first eight filling ingredients. Stir in olives. Split puffs; add the filling. Refrigerate.

[1999]

CAPPUCCINO MUFFINS
yield: about 14 muffins (3/4 cup spread)
prep: 15 min. ∽ bake: 20 min.

(Pictured on page 404)

These are my favorite muffins to serve with a cup of coffee or a tall glass of cold milk. Not only are they great for breakfast, they make a tasty dessert or midnight snack. I get lots of recipe requests whenever I serve them. The espresso spread is also super on a bagel.

—Janice Schulz, Racine, Wisconsin

ESPRESSO SPREAD:
- 4 ounces cream cheese, cubed
- 1 tablespoon sugar
- 1/2 teaspoon instant coffee granules
- 1/2 teaspoon vanilla extract
- 1/4 cup miniature semisweet chocolate chips

MUFFINS:
- 2 cups all-purpose flour
- 3/4 cup sugar
- 2-1/2 teaspoons baking powder
- 1 teaspoon ground cinnamon
- 1/2 teaspoon salt
- 1 cup 2% milk
- 2 tablespoons instant coffee granules
- 1/2 cup butter, melted
- 1 egg
- 1 teaspoon vanilla extract
- 3/4 cup miniature semisweet chocolate chips

1. In a food processor, combine all the spread ingredients; cover and process until well blended. Transfer to a small bowl; cover and refrigerate until serving.

2. In a large bowl, combine flour, sugar, baking powder, cinnamon and salt. In another bowl, combine milk and coffee granules until coffee is dissolved. Add the butter, egg and vanilla. Stir into dry ingredients just until moistened. Fold in chocolate chips.

3. Fill greased or paper-lined muffin cups two-thirds full. Bake at 375° for 17-20 minutes or until a toothpick inserted near the center comes out clean. Cool for 5 minutes before removing from pans to wire racks. Serve warm with espresso spread.

ZUCCHINI CUPCAKES, page 416

TRADITIONAL LASAGNA, page 394

NUTTY OVEN-FRIED CHICKEN, page 385

MARVELOUS MEDITERRANEAN VEGETABLES, page 410

HERBED TURKEY AND DRESSING, page 397

ONION BEEF AU JUS, page 399

PEPPERONI SPINACH QUICHE, page 396

SOUTH-OF-THE-BORDER CAPRESE SALAD, page 411

"SECRET'S IN THE SAUCE" BBQ RIBS, page 389

CAPPUCCINO MUFFINS, page 400

TOMATO CORN SALAD, page 410

APPLE PIE BARS, page 418

SEAFOOD LASAGNA, page 391

BLOND BROWNIES A LA MODE, page 419

CHICKEN AND ASPARAGUS KABOBS, page 389

RASPBERRY STREUSEL COFFEE CAKE, page 416

SURPRISE SAUSAGE BUNDLES, page 395

FRUIT-PECAN PORK ROAST, page 385

STRAWBERRY CHEESECAKE ICE CREAM, page 414

SPICY BEAN AND BEEF PIE, page 392

FLATBREAD TACOS WITH RANCH SOUR CREAM, page 387

[1993]

LEMON CHEESE BRAID BREAD

yield: 12-14 servings ∽ **prep: 30 min. + rising**
bake: 25 min.

This recipe came from my mom, who is an excellent cook. She always gets raves when she serves it. Although it's fairly simple to make, when you finish you'll feel a sense of accomplishment because it tastes delicious and looks so impressive.

—*Grace Dickey, Hillsboro, Oregon, Fied Editor*

1	package (1/4 ounce) active dry yeast
3	tablespoons warm water (110° to 115°)
1/3	cup 2% milk
1/4	cup sugar
1/4	cup butter, melted
2	eggs
1/2	teaspoon salt
3	to 3-1/2 cups all-purpose flour

FILLING:

2	packages (one 8 ounces, one 3 ounces) cream cheese, softened
1/2	cup sugar
1	egg
1	teaspoon grated lemon peel

ICING:

1/2	cup confectioners' sugar
1/4	teaspoon vanilla extract
2	to 3 teaspoons 2% milk

1. In a large bowl, dissolve yeast in warm water. Add the milk, sugar, butter, eggs, salt and 2 cups flour; beat on low speed for 3 minutes. Stir in enough of remaining flour to form a soft dough.

2. Turn onto a floured surface; knead until smooth and elastic, about 6-8 minutes. Place in a greased bowl, turning once to grease top. Cover and let rise in a warm place until doubled, about 1 hour.

3. Meanwhile, in a small bowl, beat the filling ingredients until fluffy; set aside.

4. Punch the dough down. Turn onto a lightly floured surface; roll into a 14-in. x 12-in. rectangle. Place on a greased baking sheet. Spread filling down center third of rectangle. On each long side, cut 1-in.-wide strips, 3 in. into center. Starting at one end, fold alternating strips at an angle across filling. Seal end. Cover and let rise for 30 minutes.

5. Bake at 375° for 25-30 minutes or until golden brown. Cool on a wire rack. Combine the confectioners' sugar, vanilla and enough milk to achieve drizzling consistency; drizzle over warm bread.

[1996]

MEXICAN CHICKEN CORN CHOWDER

yield: 6-8 servings (2 quarts)
prep/total time: 30 min.

I like to make this smooth, creamy soup when company comes to visit. Its zippy flavor is full of Southwestern flair. My family enjoys dipping slices of homemade bread in this chowder to soak up every bite!

—*Susan Garoutte, Georgetown, Texas, Field Editor*

1-1/2	pounds boneless skinless chicken breasts, cut into 1-inch pieces
1/2	cup chopped onion
3	tablespoons butter
1	to 2 garlic cloves, minced
1	cup hot water
2	teaspoons chicken bouillon granules
1/2	to 1 teaspoon ground cumin
2	cups half-and-half cream
2	cups (8 ounces) shredded Monterey Jack cheese
1	can (14-3/4 ounces) cream-style corn
1	can (4 ounces) chopped green chilies, undrained
1/4	to 1 teaspoon hot pepper sauce
1	medium tomato, chopped

Minced fresh cilantro, optional

1. In a Dutch oven, brown chicken and onion in butter until chicken is no longer pink. Add the garlic; cook 1 minute longer. Add water, bouillon and cumin; bring to a boil. Reduce heat; cover and simmer for 5 minutes.

2. Stir in the cream, cheese, corn, chilies and hot pepper sauce. Cook and stir over low heat until cheese is melted; add tomato. Sprinkle with cilantro if desired.

[2011]

MARVELOUS MEDITERRANEAN VEGETABLES

yield: 9 servings
prep: 25 min. + marinating ∽ **grill: 10 min.**

(*Pictured on page 402*)

With so many outdoor barbecues in the summer, I came up with this simple and tasty dish to complement any entree. I like to prepare it earlier in the day and let it marinate for the afternoon. The veggies are also great wrapped in a tortilla for a sandwich.

—Cathy Godberson, Oakville, Ontario

- 3 large portobello mushrooms, sliced
- 1 *each* medium sweet red, orange and yellow pepper, sliced
- 1 medium zucchini, sliced
- 10 fresh asparagus spears, cut into 2-inch lengths
- 1 small onion, sliced and separated into rings
- 3/4 cup grape tomatoes
- 1/2 cup fresh sugar snap peas
- 1/2 cup fresh broccoli florets
- 1/2 cup pitted Greek olives
- 1 bottle (14 ounces) Greek vinaigrette
- 1/2 cup crumbled feta cheese

1. In a large resealable plastic bag, combine mushrooms, peppers and zucchini. Add the asparagus, onion, tomatoes, peas, broccoli and olives. Pour vinaigrette into bag; seal bag and turn to coat. Refrigerate for at least 30 minutes.

2. Discard marinade. Transfer vegetables to a grill wok or basket. Grill, uncovered, over medium heat for 8-12 minutes or until tender, stirring frequently. Place on a serving plate; sprinkle with cheese.

Editor's Note: If you do not have a grill wok or basket, use a disposable foil pan. Poke holes in the bottom of the pan with a meat fork to allow liquid to drain.

[2008]

TOMATO CORN SALAD

yield: 7 servings ∽ **prep/total time: 30 min.**

(*Pictured on page 404*)

Warm and colorful, this tantalizing side dish bursts with refreshing vegetable flavor. Fresh herbs and Dijon mustard add extra pizzazz.

—Carrie Componile, Roselle Park, New Jersey

- 3 large tomatoes, chopped
- 1 small red onion, halved and thinly sliced
- 1/3 cup chopped green onions
- 1/4 cup balsamic vinegar
- 3 tablespoons minced fresh basil
- 1 tablespoon minced fresh cilantro
- 1 teaspoon salt
- 1/2 teaspoon pepper
- 4 cups fresh corn (about 9 ears of corn)
- 2 tablespoons olive oil
- 3 garlic cloves, peeled and thinly sliced
- 1 tablespoon Dijon mustard

1. In a large bowl, combine the first eight ingredients. In a large skillet, saute corn in oil until tender. Add the garlic; cook 1 minute longer. Stir in mustard. Add to vegetable mixture; toss to coat. Serve with a slotted spoon.

[1999]

COLORFUL CORN SALAD

yield: 16-18 servings ∽ **prep/total time: 15 min.**

This colorful, tasty corn salad is an excellent way to perk up a summer picnic. The seasonings add a bold, refreshing Southwestern flavor that brings people back for seconds.

—Helen Koedel, Hamilton, Ohio

- 2 packages (10 ounces *each*) frozen corn, thawed
- 2 cups diced green pepper
- 2 cups diced sweet red pepper
- 2 cups diced celery
- 1 cup minced fresh parsley
- 1 cup chopped green onions
- 1/2 cup shredded Parmesan cheese
- 2 teaspoons ground cumin

1-1/2 teaspoons salt
3/4 teaspoon pepper
1/2 teaspoon hot pepper sauce
1/8 teaspoon cayenne pepper
3 tablespoons olive oil
2 garlic cloves, minced
6 tablespoons lime juice

1. In a large bowl, combine the first 12 ingredients. In a microwave-safe dish, combine oil and garlic. Microwave, uncovered, on high for 30 seconds. Cool. Whisk in lime juice. Pour over corn mixture and toss to coat. Cover and refrigerate until serving.

Editor's Note: Recipe was tested in a 1,100-watt microwave.

[2009]

SOUTH-OF-THE-BORDER CAPRESE SALAD

yield: 6 servings (1 cup dressing) ∽ prep/total time: 30 min.
(Pictured on page 404)

Plump heirloom tomatoes are the stars of this garden-fresh medley, topped with a sweet-tart dressing and crumbled cheese.
—*Kathleen Merkley, Layton, Utah*

CILANTRO VINAIGRETTE:
1/3 cup white wine vinegar
1/2 cup fresh cilantro leaves
3 tablespoons sugar
1 jalapeno pepper, seeded and chopped
1 garlic clove, peeled and quartered
3/4 teaspoon salt
2/3 cup olive oil
SALAD:
4 cups torn mixed salad greens
3 large heirloom *or* other tomatoes, sliced
1/2 cup crumbled queso fresco *or* diced part-skim mozzarella cheese
1/4 teaspoon salt
1/8 teaspoon pepper
1-1/2 teaspoons fresh cilantro leaves

1. In a blender, combine the first six ingredients. While processing, gradually add oil in a steady stream.

2. Arrange greens on a serving platter; top with tomatoes. Sprinkle with cheese, salt and pepper.

3. Just before serving, drizzle the salad with 1/2 cup dressing; garnish with cilantro leaves. Refrigerate leftover dressing.

Editor's Note: Wear disposable gloves when cutting hot peppers; the oils can burn skin. Avoid touching your face.

[1994]

DELUXE GERMAN POTATO SALAD

yield: 14-16 servings ∽ prep/total time: 30 min.

I make this salad for all occasions because it goes well with any kind of meat. I often take the warm salad to bring-a-dish events, and there's never any left over. The celery, carrots and mustard are a special touch not usually found in traditional German potato salad.

—*Betty Perkins, Hot Springs, Arkansas, Former Field Editor*

1/2 pound sliced bacon, diced
1 cup thinly sliced celery
1 cup chopped onion
1 cup sugar
2 tablespoons all-purpose flour
1 teaspoon salt
3/4 teaspoon ground mustard
1 cup cider vinegar
1/2 cup water
5 pounds unpeeled small red potatoes, cooked and sliced
2 medium carrots, shredded
2 tablespoons minced fresh parsley
Additional salt, optional

1. In a large skillet, cook bacon over medium heat until crisp. Using a slotted spoon, remove to paper towels; drain, reserving 1/4 cup drippings. Saute celery and onion in drippings until tender.

2. In a large bowl, combine sugar, flour, salt, mustard, vinegar and water until smooth. Add to skillet. Bring to a boil. Cook and stir for 1-2 minutes until thickened.

3. In a large serving bowl, combine potatoes, carrots and parsley; drizzle with sauce; stir gently to coat. Season with additional salt; garnish with the reserved bacon. Serve warm. Refrigerate leftovers.

[1993]

SPINACH-TOPPED TOMATOES

yield: 6 servings ∞ prep: 20 min.
bake: 15 min.

The perfect taste of summer, this colorful side dish is sure to please. The spinach and tomato, combined with the Parmesan cheese, give it a fabulous fresh flavor. My daughter especially loves this dish, which I make often.

—*Ila Mae Alderman, Galax, Virginia, Former Field Editor*

- 1 package (10 ounces) frozen chopped spinach
- 2 chicken bouillon cubes
Salt
- 3 large tomatoes, halved
- 1 cup soft bread crumbs
- 1/2 cup grated Parmesan cheese
- 1/2 cup chopped onion
- 1/2 cup butter, melted
- 1 egg, lightly beaten
- 1 garlic clove, minced
- 1/4 teaspoon pepper
- 1/8 teaspoon cayenne pepper
Shredded Parmesan cheese, optional

1. In a large saucepan, cook the spinach according to package directions with bouillon; drain well. Cool slightly; press out excess liquid.

2. Lightly salt the tomato halves; place with cut side down on a paper towel for 15 minutes to absorb excess moisture.

3. Meanwhile, in a small bowl, combine the spinach, bread crumbs, cheese, onion, butter, egg, garlic, pepper and cayenne pepper.

4. Place tomato halves, cut side up, in a shallow baking dish. Divide the spinach mixture over tomatoes.

Sprinkle with shredded cheese if desired. Bake at 350° for about 15 minutes or until heated through.

[2011]

GREEN BEAN MUSHROOM PIE

yield: 8-10 servings ∞ prep: 45 min. ∞ bake: 25 min.

Fresh green bean flavor stands out in this pretty lattice-topped pie. A flaky golden crust holds the savory bean, mushroom and cream cheese filling. It tastes wonderfully different every time I make it depending on the variety of mushroom I use.

—*Tara Walworth, Maple Park, Illinois*

- 3 cups sliced fresh mushrooms
- 4 tablespoons butter, *divided*
- 2-1/2 cups chopped onions
- 6 cups cut fresh green beans (1-inch pieces)
- 2 teaspoons minced fresh thyme *or* 3/4 teaspoon dried thyme
- 1/2 teaspoon salt
- 1/4 teaspoon pepper
- 1 package (8 ounces) cream cheese, cubed
- 1/2 cup 2% milk
CRUST:
- 2-1/2 cups all-purpose flour
- 2 teaspoons baking powder
- 1 teaspoon dill weed
- 1/4 teaspoon salt
- 1 cup cold butter, cubed
- 1 cup (8 ounces) sour cream
- 1 egg
- 1 tablespoon heavy whipping cream

1. In a large skillet, saute mushrooms in 1 tablespoon butter until tender; drain and set aside. In the same skillet, saute onions and beans in remaining butter

MAKING SOFT BREAD CRUMBS

Tear several slices of fresh white, French or whole wheat bread into 1-in. pieces. Place in a food processor or blender; cover and push pulse button several times to make coarse crumbs. One slice of bread yields about 1/2 cup crumbs.

for 18-20 minutes or until beans are crisp-tender. Add the thyme, salt, pepper, cream cheese, milk and mushrooms. Cook and stir until the cheese is melted. Remove from the heat; set aside.

2. In a large bowl, combine the flour, baking powder, dill and salt. Cut in butter until mixture resembles coarse crumbs. Stir in sour cream to form a soft dough.

3. Divide dough in half. On a well-floured surface, roll out one portion to fit a deep-dish 9-in. pie plate; trim pastry even with edge.

4. Pour the green bean mixture into crust. Roll out remaining pastry; make a lattice crust. Trim, seal and flute edge.

5. In a small bowl, beat the egg and cream; brush over lattice top. Bake at 400° for 25-35 minutes or until golden brown.

[1998]

CHEDDAR PEAR PIE

yield: 6-8 servings ∽ prep: 10 min.
bake: 25 min. + cooling

I take this pie to lots of different gatherings, and I make sure to have copies of the recipe with me since people always ask for it. It's amusing to see some folks puzzling over what's in the filling.

—*Cynthia LaBree, Elmer, New Jersey*

  4 large ripe pears, peeled and thinly sliced
1/3 cup sugar
  1 tablespoon cornstarch
1/8 teaspoon salt
  1 frozen pie shell (9 inches)
TOPPING:
1/2 cup shredded cheddar cheese
1/2 cup all-purpose flour
1/4 cup sugar
1/4 teaspoon salt
1/4 cup butter, melted

1. In a large bowl, combine the pears, sugar, cornstarch and salt; toss gently to coat. Pour into pie shell.

2. For topping, combine the cheese, flour, sugar and salt; stir in butter until crumbly. Sprinkle over filling.

3. Bake at 425° for 25-35 minutes or until crust is golden brown and cheese is melted. Cool on a wire rack for 15-20 minutes. Serve warm. Store in the refrigerator.

[2006]

CHUNKY APPLE CAKE

yield: 12-14 servings ∽ prep: 20 min.
bake: 40 min. + cooling

This tender, moist cake is full of old-fashioned comfort, and the yummy brown sugar sauce makes it special. For a festive occasion, top with a dollop of whipped cream.

—*Debi Benson, Bakersfield, California*

1/2 cup butter, softened
  2 cups sugar
1/2 teaspoon vanilla extract
  2 eggs
  2 cups all-purpose flour
1-1/2 teaspoons ground cinnamon
  1 teaspoon ground nutmeg
1/2 teaspoon salt
1/2 teaspoon baking soda
  6 cups chopped peeled tart apples
BUTTERSCOTCH SAUCE:
1/2 cup packed brown sugar
1/4 cup butter, cubed
1/2 cup heavy whipping cream

1. In a large bowl, cream the butter, sugar and vanilla. Add eggs, one at a time, beating well after each addition. Combine the flour, cinnamon, nutmeg, salt and baking soda; gradually add to creamed mixture and mix well (batter will be stiff). Stir in apples until well combined.

2. Spread into a greased 13-in. x 9-in. baking dish. Bake at 350° for 40-45 minutes or until top is lightly browned and springs back when lightly touched. Cool for 30 minutes before serving.

3. Meanwhile, in a small saucepan, combine brown sugar and butter. Cook over medium heat until butter is melted. Gradually add the cream. Bring to a slow boil over medium heat, stirring constantly. Remove from the heat. Serve with cake.

[2007]

ELEGANT CHOCOLATE TORTE

yield: 16 servings ∞ **prep: 50 min.**
bake: 30 min. + cooling

When I want to serve a really special dessert, I turn to this recipe. The four-layer cake has a yummy pudding-like filling.

—*Lois Gallup Edwards, Woodland, California*

1/3	cup all-purpose flour
3	tablespoons sugar
1/4	teaspoon salt
1-3/4	cups 2% milk
1	cup chocolate syrup
1	egg, lightly beaten
1	tablespoon butter
1	teaspoon vanilla extract

BATTER:

1/2	cup butter, softened
1-1/4	cups sugar
4	eggs
1	teaspoon vanilla extract
1-1/4	cups all-purpose flour
1/3	cup baking cocoa
3/4	teaspoon baking soda
1/4	teaspoon salt
1-1/2	cups chocolate syrup
1/2	cup water

FROSTING:

2	cups heavy whipping cream
1/4	cup chocolate syrup
1/4	teaspoon vanilla extract

1. For filling, in a small saucepan, combine the flour, sugar and salt. Stir in milk and syrup until smooth. Bring to a boil over medium heat, stirring constantly; cook and stir for 1-2 minutes or until thickened.

2. Remove from the heat. Stir a small amount of hot mixture into egg; return all to the pan, stirring constantly. Bring to a gentle boil; cook and stir for 2 minutes. Remove from heat; stir in butter and vanilla. Cool to room temperature, stirring often.

3. In a large bowl, cream butter and sugar until light and fluffy. Add eggs, one at a time, beating well after each. Stir in vanilla. Combine dry ingredients; add to creamed mixture alternately with syrup and water. Beat just until combined.

4. Pour into two greased and floured 9-in. round baking pans. Bake at 350° for 30-35 minutes or until a toothpick inserted near the center comes out clean. Cool for 10 minutes; remove from the pans to wire racks to cool.

5. Cut each cake in half horizontally. Place one bottom layer on a serving plate; spread with a third of the filling. Repeat layers twice. Top with remaining cake. In a large bowl, beat the frosting ingredients until stiff peaks form; spread or pipe over top and sides of cake.

[2004]

STRAWBERRY CHEESECAKE ICE CREAM

yield: 1 gallon ∞ **prep: 15 min. + cooling**
process: 20 min./batch + freezing

(*Pictured on page 408*)

The custard-like ice cream is so rich and creamy that it tastes like you fussed for hours. But it's easy to make and pretty, too.

—*Irene Yoder, Fillmore, New York*

3	cups sugar
3	tablespoons all-purpose flour
Dash salt	
8	cups milk
4	eggs, lightly beaten
1	package (8 ounces) cream cheese, cubed
1	teaspoon vanilla extract
3	cups fresh *or* frozen unsweetened strawberries, thawed
2	cups heavy whipping cream

1. In a heavy saucepan, combine the sugar, flour and salt. Gradually add milk until smooth. Bring to a boil over medium heat; cook and stir for 2 minutes or until thickened. Remove from the heat; cool slightly.

2. Whisk a small amount of hot milk mixture into the eggs; return all to the pan, whisking constantly. Cook and stir over low heat until mixture reaches at least 160° and coats the back of a metal spoon. Stir in the cream cheese until melted.

3. Remove from the heat. Cool quickly by placing pan in a bowl of ice water; stir for 2 minutes. Stir in vanilla. Press plastic wrap onto surface of custard. Refrigerate for several hours or overnight.

4. Stir strawberries and cream into custard. Fill cylinder of ice cream freezer two-thirds full; freeze according to the manufacturer's directions. Refrigerate remaining mixture until ready to freeze. When ice cream is frozen, transfer to a freezer container; freeze for 2-4 hours before serving.

[2012]

CHOCOLATE & PEANUT BUTTER MOUSSE CHEESECAKE

yield: 16 servings ∞ prep: 50 min. + freezing

This no-bake cheesecake with distinctive layers of chocolate, peanut butter mousse and a silky ganache on top takes time to assemble, but it's worth the effort to create a dessert with grand-champion appeal.

—*JaNon Furrer, Prescott, Arizona*

1-1/2 cups chocolate wafer crumbs
1/4 cup butter, melted
MOUSSE LAYERS:
5 ounces cream cheese, softened
3/4 cup creamy peanut butter
2 tablespoons butter, softened
1-1/4 cups confectioners' sugar
1-1/4 cups heavy whipping cream
5 ounces bittersweet chocolate, chopped
1 milk chocolate candy bar (3-1/2 ounces), chopped
1/3 cup sugar
1/4 cup 2% milk
1 teaspoon vanilla extract
GANACHE:
6 ounces bittersweet chocolate, chopped
2/3 cup heavy whipping cream
1 teaspoon vanilla extract

1. In a small bowl, combine wafer crumbs and butter. Press onto the bottom of a greased 9-in. springform pan; set aside.

2. For peanut butter mousse, in a small bowl, beat the cream cheese, peanut butter and butter until smooth. Add the confectioners' sugar; beat until smooth. In another bowl, beat cream until soft peaks form. With a spatula, fold half of the whipped cream into peanut butter mixture. Spread over crust.

3. For chocolate mousse, place bittersweet and milk chocolates in a small bowl. In a small saucepan, combine the sugar and milk; bring just to a boil. Pour over the chocolate; whisk until smooth. Stir in vanilla. Cool to room temperature, stirring occasionally, about 5 minutes. Gently fold in remaining whipped cream. Spread over peanut butter layer; cover and freeze for 2 hours or until firm.

4. For ganache, place chocolate in a small bowl. In a small saucepan, bring cream just to a boil. Pour over chocolate; whisk until smooth. Stir in vanilla. Cool slightly, stirring occasionally. Pour over chocolate mousse. Cover and refrigerate for 1 hour or until ganache is set.

5. Carefully run a knife around edge of springform pan to loosen; remove sides of pan.

[2005]

COOKIE DOUGH TRUFFLES

yield: 5-1/2 dozen ∞ prep: 1 hour + chilling

The flavorful filling at the center of these yummy candies tastes like genuine chocolate chip cookie dough, without the worry of raw eggs. That's what makes them so appealing.

—*Lanita Dedon, Slaughter, Louisiana*

1/2 cup butter, softened
3/4 cup packed brown sugar
1 teaspoon vanilla extract
2 cups all-purpose flour
1 can (14 ounces) sweetened condensed milk
1/2 cup miniature semisweet chocolate chips
1/2 cup chopped walnuts
1-1/2 pounds dark chocolate candy coating, coarsely chopped

1. In a large bowl, cream the butter and brown sugar until light and fluffy. Beat in vanilla. Gradually add flour, alternately with milk, beating well after each addition. Stir in chocolate chips and walnuts.

2. Shape into 1-in. balls; place on waxed paper-lined baking sheets. Loosely cover and refrigerate for 1-2 hours or until firm.

3. In a microwave, melt candy coating; stir until smooth. Dip balls in coating; allow excess to drip off. Place on waxed paper-lined baking sheets. Refrigerate until firm, about 15 minutes. If desired, remelt remaining candy coating and drizzle over candies. Store in the refrigerator.

[1997]

ZUCCHINI CUPCAKES

yield: 1-1/2 to 2 dozen ✒ prep: 20 min.
bake: 20 min. + cooling

(Pictured on page 401)

I asked my grandmother for this recipe after trying these irresistible spice cupcakes at her home. I love their creamy caramel frosting. They make a delectable dessert.

—*Virginia LaPierre*
Greensboro Bend, Vermont, Field Editor

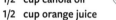

3	eggs
1-1/3	cups sugar
1/2	cup canola oil
1/2	cup orange juice
1	teaspoon almond extract
2-1/2	cups all-purpose flour
2	teaspoons ground cinnamon
2	teaspoons baking powder
1	teaspoon baking soda
1	teaspoon salt
1/2	teaspoon ground cloves
1-1/2	cups shredded zucchini

CARAMEL FROSTING:

1	cup packed brown sugar
1/2	cup butter, cubed
1/4	cup 2% milk
1	teaspoon vanilla extract
1-1/2	to 2 cups confectioners' sugar

1. In a large bowl, beat the eggs, sugar, oil, orange juice and extract. Combine dry ingredients; gradually add to egg mixture and mix well. Stir in zucchini.

2. Fill paper-lined muffin cups two-thirds full. Bake at 350° for 20-25 minutes or until toothpick inserted near the center comes out clean. Cool for 10 minutes before removing to a wire rack.

3. For frosting, combine brown sugar, butter and milk in a saucepan. Bring to a boil over medium heat; cook and stir for 2 minutes or until thickened. Remove from the heat; stir in the vanilla. Cool to lukewarm.

4. Gradually beat in confectioners' sugar until frosting reaches spreading consistency. Frost cupcakes.

[2003]

RASPBERRY STREUSEL COFFEE CAKE

yield: 12-16 servings ✒ prep: 25 min. + cooling
bake: 40 min.

(Pictured on page 406)

One of my mother's friends used to bring this over at the holidays, and it never lasted long. With the tangy raspberry filling, tender cake and crunchy topping, it has become a favorite at our house.

—*Amy Mitchell, Sabetha, Kansas*

3-1/2	cups unsweetened raspberries
1	cup water
2	tablespoons lemon juice
1-1/4	cups sugar
1/3	cup cornstarch

BATTER:

3	cups all-purpose flour
1	cup sugar
1	teaspoon baking powder
1	teaspoon baking soda
1	cup cold butter, cubed
2	eggs, lightly beaten
1	cup (8 ounces) sour cream
1	teaspoon vanilla extract

TOPPING:

1/2	cup all-purpose flour
1/2	cup sugar
1/4	cup butter, softened
1/2	cup chopped pecans

GLAZE:

1/2	cup confectioners' sugar
2	teaspoons 2% milk
1/2	teaspoon vanilla extract

1. In a large saucepan, cook the raspberries and water over medium heat for 5 minutes. Add the lemon juice. Combine sugar and cornstarch; stir into the fruit mixture. Bring to a boil; cook and stir for 2 minutes or until thickened. Cool.

2. In a large bowl, combine flour, sugar, baking powder and baking soda. Cut in butter until mixture resembles coarse crumbs. Stir in the eggs, sour cream and vanilla (batter will be stiff).

3. Spread half into a greased 13-in. x 9-in. baking dish. Spread raspberry filling over batter; spoon remaining batter over filling. Combine the topping ingredients; sprinkle over top.

4. Bake at 350° for 40-45 minutes or until golden brown. Combine the glaze ingredients; drizzle over warm cake.

[1998]

VERY CHOCOLATE BROWNIES
yield: 3 dozen ∽ prep: 20 min. + chilling
bake: 25 min. + cooling

I've spent years trying different recipes in search of the perfect brownie...and this divine version might be it. The fluffy melt-in-your-mouth top layer is absolutely heavenly. It's impossible to eat just one!

—Arlene Butler, Ogden, Utah, Field Editor

3/4 cup butter, cubed
4 ounces unsweetened chocolate, chopped
3 eggs
2 cups sugar
1 teaspoon vanilla extract
1 cup all-purpose flour
1 cup coarsely chopped walnuts
TOPPING:
1 cup (6 ounces) semisweet chocolate chips
2 tablespoons butter
1/4 cup water
1 cup heavy whipping cream, whipped

1. In a microwave, melt butter and chocolate; stir until smooth. Cool slightly. In a large bowl, beat eggs and sugar. Stir in vanilla and chocolate mixture. Gradually add flour to chocolate mixture. Stir in walnuts.

2. Line a 13-in. x 9-in. baking pan with foil and grease the foil. Pour batter into pan. Bake at 350° for 25-30 minutes or until a toothpick inserted near the center comes out with moist crumbs (do not overbake). Cool completely.

3. For topping, melt the chocolate chips and butter with water in a microwave; stir until smooth. Cool to room temperature. Fold in the whipped cream. Spread over brownies. Chill before cutting. Refrigerate leftovers.

[2012]

MACADAMIA & COCONUT CARAMELS
yield: 1-1/2 pounds ∽ prep: 25 min.
cook: 25 min. + chilling

I collect recipes and cookbooks from all over the world. I actually cook from them and serve my family and guests new and different dishes. These smooth caramels have a scrumptious macadamia-coconut flavor. It was a winner in my book.

—Sharon Delaney-Chronis
South Milwaukee, Wisconsin

1 teaspoon plus 1/2 cup butter, *divided*
1 cup packed light brown sugar
1/2 cup light corn syrup
1/4 teaspoon cream of tartar
3/4 cup sweetened condensed milk
1/2 cup flaked coconut
1/2 cup chopped macadamia nuts
1/2 teaspoon vanilla extract

1. Line an 8-in. square baking dish with foil and grease the foil with 1 teaspoon butter; set aside.

2. In a large heavy saucepan, combine the brown sugar, corn syrup, cream of tartar and remaining butter; bring to a boil over medium heat, stirring constantly. Remove from the heat; gradually stir in milk. Cook and stir over medium-low heat until a candy thermometer reads 244° (firm-ball stage).

3. Remove from the heat; stir in remaining ingredients. Pour into prepared dish. Refrigerate until set, at least 2 hours.

4. Using foil, lift candy out of dish. Gently peel off foil; cut caramel into 1-in. squares. Wrap individually in waxed paper; twist ends. Store in an airtight container.

Editor's Note: We recommend that you test your candy thermometer before each use by bringing water to a boil; the thermometer should read 212°. Adjust your recipe temperature up or down based on your test.

[2002]

APPLE PIE BARS

yield: about 2 dozen ∞ prep: 30 min.
bake: 45 min. + cooling

(Pictured on page 405)

This is the only one of the many wonderful recipes that my mother handed down to me. These delicious bars, with their flaky crust and scrumptious fruit filling, are the perfect way to serve apple pie to a crowd.

—**Janet English, Pittsburgh, Pennsylvania**

- 4 cups all-purpose flour
- 1 teaspoon salt
- 1 teaspoon baking powder
- 1 cup shortening
- 4 egg yolks
- 2 tablespoons lemon juice
- 8 to 10 tablespoons cold water

FILLING:
- 7 cups finely chopped peeled apples
- 2 cups sugar
- 1/4 cup all-purpose flour
- 2 teaspoons ground cinnamon

Dash ground nutmeg

GLAZE:
- 1 cup confectioners' sugar
- 1 tablespoon 2% milk
- 1 tablespoon lemon juice

1. In a large bowl, combine the flour, salt and baking powder. Cut in shortening until mixture resembles coarse crumbs. In a small bowl, whisk the egg yolks, lemon juice and water; gradually add to flour mixture, tossing with a fork until dough forms a ball. Divide in half. Chill for 30 minutes.

2. Roll out one portion of dough between two large sheets of waxed paper into a 17-in. x 12-in. rectangle. Transfer to an ungreased 15-in. x 10-in. x 1-in. baking pan. Press pastry onto the bottom and up the sides of pan; trim pastry even with top edge.

3. In a large bowl, toss the apples, sugar, flour, cinnamon and nutmeg; spread over crust. Roll out the remaining pastry to fit top of pan; place over filling. Trim edges; brush edges between pastry with water or milk; pinch to seal. Cut slits in top.

4. Bake at 375° for 45-50 minutes or until golden brown. Cool on a wire rack. Combine glaze ingredients until smooth; drizzle over bars before cutting.

[2007]

SPECIAL MOCHA CUPCAKES

yield: 1 dozen ∞ prep: 25 min. ∞ bake: 20 min. + cooling

Topped with a fluffy frosting and chocolate sprinkles, these extra-rich, extra-delicious cupcakes smell wonderful while baking and taste even better!

—**Mary Bilyeu, Ann Arbor, Michigan**

- 1 cup sugar
- 1/2 cup cold brewed coffee
- 1/2 cup canola oil
- 2 eggs
- 3 teaspoons cider vinegar
- 3 teaspoons vanilla extract
- 1-1/2 cups all-purpose flour
- 1/3 cup baking cocoa
- 1 teaspoon baking soda
- 1/2 teaspoon salt

MOCHA FROSTING:
- 3 tablespoons milk chocolate chips
- 3 tablespoons semisweet chocolate chips
- 1/3 cup butter, softened
- 2 cups confectioners' sugar
- 1 to 2 tablespoons brewed coffee
- 1/2 cup chocolate sprinkles

1. In a large bowl, beat the sugar, coffee, oil, eggs, vinegar and vanilla until well blended. In a small bowl, combine the flour, cocoa, baking soda and salt; gradually beat into coffee mixture until blended.

2. Fill paper-lined muffin cups three-fourths full. Bake at 350° for 20-25 minutes or until a toothpick inserted near the center comes out clean. Cool for 10 minutes before removing from pan to a wire rack to cool.

3. For frosting, in a microwave, melt chips and butter; stir until smooth. Transfer to a large bowl. Gradually beat in confectioners' sugar and enough coffee to achieve desired consistency. Pipe frosting onto cupcakes. Top with sprinkles; gently press down.

[2004]

ALMOND SUGAR COOKIES

yield: about 4-1/2 dozen
prep/total time: 30 min.

It's a tradition in our house to start baking Christmas cookies early in the season and try some new recipes every year. This nutty, glazed melt-in-your-mouth cookie is one of my favorites.

—Lisa Hummell, Phillipsburg, New Jersey

> 1 cup butter, softened
> 3/4 cup sugar
> 1 teaspoon almond extract
> 2 cups all-purpose flour
> 1/2 teaspoon baking powder
> 1/4 teaspoon salt
>
> Additional sugar
> GLAZE:
> 1 cup confectioners' sugar
> 1-1/2 teaspoons almond extract
> 2 to 3 teaspoons water
> Green food coloring, optional
> Sliced almonds, toasted

1. In a large bowl, cream butter and sugar until light and fluffy. Beat in almond extract. Combine the flour, baking powder and salt; gradually add to creamed mixture and mix well. Roll into 1-in. balls.

2. Place 2 in. apart on ungreased baking sheets. Coat bottom of a glass with cooking spray; dip in sugar. Flatten cookies with prepared glass, dipping glass in sugar again as needed.

3. Bake at 400° for 7-9 minutes or until edges are lightly browned. Cool for 1 minute before removing to wire racks.

4. In a small bowl, whisk together the confectioners' sugar, almond extract and enough water to achieve glaze consistency. Tint with food coloring if desired; drizzle over cookies. Sprinkle with almonds.

[2005]

BLOND BROWNIES A LA MODE

yield: 20 servings ✆ prep: 25 min.
bake: 25 min. + cooling

(Pictured on page 405)

We have a lot of church socials and I'm always looking for something new and different to prepare. These brownies, drizzled with a sweet maple sauce, are a sure hit...with or without the ice cream.

—Pat Parker, Chester, South Carolina

> 3/4 cup butter, softened
> 2 cups packed brown sugar
> 4 eggs
> 2 teaspoons vanilla extract
> 2 cups all-purpose flour
> 2 teaspoons baking powder
> 1 teaspoon salt
> 1-1/2 cups chopped pecans
> MAPLE CREAM SAUCE:
> 1 cup maple syrup
> 2 tablespoons butter
> 1/4 cup evaporated milk
> Vanilla ice cream and chopped pecans

1. In a large bowl, cream butter and brown sugar until light and fluffy. Beat in eggs and vanilla. Combine the flour, baking powder and salt; gradually add to creamed mixture. Stir in pecans.

2. Spread into a greased 13-in. x 9-in. baking pan. Bake at 350° for 25-30 minutes or until a toothpick inserted near the center comes out clean. Cool on a wire rack.

3. For the sauce, combine syrup and butter in a saucepan. Bring to a boil; cook and stir for 3 minutes. Remove from the heat; stir in milk. Cut brownies into squares; cut in half if desired.

4. Place on dessert plates with a scoop of ice cream. Top with sauce; sprinkle with pecans.

ALMOND SUGAR COOKIES

"These have become a Christmas tradition since my daughter first made them several years ago. They are wonderful and everyone loves the flavor. Make them just once, you'll be convinced—and hooked."
—dln57

[2008]

LEMON CHIFFON CAKE

yield: 12-16 servings ∞ prep: 25 min.
bake: 50 min. + cooling

This light, airy cake was my dad's top choice. My mom revamped the original recipe to include lemons. I'm not much of a baker, so I don't make it very often. But it is well worth the effort.

—Trisha Kammers, Clarkston, Washington

7	eggs, *separated*
2	cups all-purpose flour
1-1/2	cups sugar
3	teaspoons baking powder
1	teaspoon salt
3/4	cup water
1/2	cup canola oil
4	teaspoons grated lemon peel
2	teaspoons vanilla extract
1/2	teaspoon cream of tartar

LEMON FROSTING:

1/3	cup butter, softened
3	cups confectioners' sugar
1/4	cup lemon juice
4-1/2	teaspoons grated lemon peel
Dash salt	

1. Place egg whites in a large bowl; let stand at room temperature for 30 minutes.

2. In a large bowl, combine the flour, sugar, baking powder and salt. In another bowl, whisk the egg yolks, water, oil, lemon peel and vanilla; add to dry ingredients and beat until well blended. Add cream of tartar to egg whites; beat on medium speed until soft peaks form. Fold into batter.

3. Gently spoon into an ungreased 10-in. tube pan. Cut through batter with a knife to remove air pockets. Bake on the lowest oven rack at 325° for 50-55 minutes or until cake springs back when lightly touched. Immediately invert pan; cool completely, about 1 hour.

4. Run a knife around sides and center tube of pan. Remove cake to a serving plate. In a small bowl, combine frosting ingredients; beat until smooth. Frost top of cake.

[1999]

CHOCOLATE CHIP COOKIE DOUGH CHEESECAKE

yield: 12-14 servings ∞ prep: 25 min.
bake: 45 min. + chilling

I created this recipe to combine two of my all-time favorites: cheesecake for the grown-up in me and chocolate chip cookie dough for the little girl in me. Sour cream offsets the sweetness and adds a nice tang. Everyone who tries this scrumptious treat loves it.

—Julie Craig, Kewaskum, Wisconsin

1-3/4	cups crushed chocolate chips cookies *or* chocolate wafer crumbs
1/4	cup sugar
1/3	cup butter, melted

FILLING:

3	packages (8 ounces *each*) cream cheese, softened
1	cup sugar
1	cup (8 ounces) sour cream
1/2	teaspoon vanilla extract
3	eggs, lightly beaten

COOKIE DOUGH:

1/4	cup butter, softened
1/4	cup sugar
1/4	cup packed brown sugar
1	tablespoon water
1	teaspoon vanilla extract
1/2	cup all-purpose flour
1-1/2	cups miniature semisweet chocolate chips, *divided*

1. In a small bowl, combine cookie crumbs and sugar; stir in butter. Press onto the bottom and 1 in. up the sides of a greased 9-in. pan. Place pan on a baking sheet; set aside.

2. In a large bowl, beat cream cheese and sugar until smooth. Beat in sour cream and vanilla. Add eggs; beat on low speed just until combined. Pour over crust; set aside.

3. In another bowl, cream butter and sugars until light and fluffy. Add water and vanilla. Gradually add flour and mix well. Stir in 1 cup chocolate chips.

4. Drop dough by teaspoonfuls over filling, gently pushing dough below surface (dough should be completely covered by filling). Place pan on a baking sheet.

5. Bake at 350° for 45-55 minutes or until center is almost set. Cool on a wire rack for 10 minutes. Carefully run a knife around edge of pan to loosen; cool 1 hour longer. Refrigerate overnight.

6. Remove sides of pan. Sprinkle with remaining chips. Refrigerate leftovers.

[1995]

MOCHA TRUFFLES

yield: about 5-1/2 dozen ∾ prep: 25 min. + chilling

Nothing compares to the melt-in-your-mouth flavor of these truffles or to the simplicity of the recipe. Whenever I make them for my family or friends, they're quickly devoured. No one has to know how easy they are to prepare!

—*Stacy Abell, Olathe, Kansas*

2 packages (12 ounces each) semisweet chocolate chips
1 package (8 ounces) cream cheese, softened
3 tablespoons instant coffee granules
2 teaspoons water
1 pound dark chocolate candy coating, coarsely chopped
White candy coating, optional

1. In a microwave-safe bowl, melt chocolate chips; stir until smooth. Beat in cream cheese. Dissolve coffee in water; add to cream cheese and beat until smooth.

2. Chill until firm enough to shape. Shape into 1-in. balls and place on waxed paper-lined baking sheet. Chill for 1-2 hours or until firm.

3. In a microwave, melt chocolate coating; stir until smooth. Dip balls in chocolate; allow excess to drip off. Place on waxed paper; let stand until set. Melt white coating and drizzle over truffles if desired.

Editor's Note: Dark, white or milk chocolate confectionery coating is found in the baking section of most grocery stores. It is sometime labeled "almond bark" or "candy coating" and is often sold in bulk packages (1 to 1-1/2 pounds). It is the product used for dipping chocolate. A substitute for 6 ounces chocolate coating would be 1 cup semisweet, dark or white chocolate chips and 1 tablespoon shortening melted together. Truffles can be frozen for several months before dipping in chocolate. Thaw in the refrigerator before dipping.

[2000]

PEAR CUSTARD BARS

yield: 16 bars ∾ prep: 30 min. + chilling
bake: 30 min. + cooling

When I take this crowd-pleasing treat to a potluck, I always come home with an empty pan. Cooking and baking come naturally for me.

—*Jeannette Nord, San Juan Capistrano, California*

1/2 cup butter, softened
1/3 cup sugar
1/4 teaspoon vanilla extract
3/4 cup all-purpose flour
2/3 cup chopped macadamia nuts
FILLING/TOPPING:
1 package (8 ounces) cream cheese, softened
1/2 cup sugar
1 egg
1/2 teaspoon vanilla extract
1 can (15-1/4 ounces) pear halves, drained
1/2 teaspoon sugar
1/2 teaspoon ground cinnamon

1. In a large bowl, cream butter and sugar until light and fluffy. Beat in vanilla. Gradually add flour to creamed mixture. Stir in nuts.

2. Press into a greased 8-in. square baking pan. Bake at 350° for 20 minutes or until lightly browned. Cool on a wire rack.

3. In a small bowl, beat cream cheese until smooth. Beat in the sugar, egg and vanilla. Pour over crust.

4. Cut pears into 1/8-in. slices; arrange in a single layer over filling. Combine sugar and cinnamon; sprinkle over pears.

5. Bake at 375° for 28-30 minutes (center will be soft-set and will become firmer upon cooling). Cool on a wire rack for 45 minutes.

6. Cover and refrigerate for at least 2 hours before cutting. Store in the refrigerator.

[2011]

BEST MAPLE-CRANBERRY CHEESECAKE

yield: 16 servings (2 cups compote) ∞ **prep: 30 min.**
bake: 1-1/4 hours + chilling

This maple cheesecake recipe may look intimidating, but it's not. If you make one holiday dessert, this is the five-star dessert to showcase.

—*Tonya Burkhard-Jones, Davis, Illinois*

2 cups graham cracker crumbs
1/3 cup butter, melted
3 tablespoons sugar
1/2 teaspoon ground cinnamon
FILLING:
1-1/2 cups maple syrup
3 packages (8 ounces *each*) cream cheese, softened
1/2 cup packed brown sugar
2/3 cup sour cream
3 tablespoons all-purpose flour
2 teaspoons vanilla extract
1/4 teaspoon salt
4 eggs, lightly beaten
COMPOTE:
2 cups fresh *or* frozen cranberries, thawed
2/3 cup dried cranberries
1 cup maple syrup
1/2 cup packed brown sugar

1. Place a greased 9-in. springform pan on a double thickness of heavy-duty foil (about 18 in. square). Securely wrap foil around pan.

2. Combine the cracker crumbs, butter, sugar and cinnamon; press onto the bottom and 1-1/2 in. up the sides of prepared pan. Place pan on a baking sheet.

Bake at 375° for 8-10 minutes or until set. Cool on a wire rack. Reduce heat to 325°.

3. Meanwhile, place maple syrup in a small saucepan. Bring to a boil; cook until syrup is reduced to about 1 cup. Cool to room temperature; set aside.

4. In a large bowl, beat cream cheese and brown sugar until smooth. Beat in the sour cream, flour, vanilla, salt and cooled syrup. Add eggs; beat on low speed just until combined. Pour into crust. Place springform pan in a large baking pan; add 1 in. of hot water to larger pan.

5. Bake at 325° for 1-1/4 to 1-1/2 hours or until center is just set and top appears dull. Remove springform pan from water bath. Cool on a wire rack for 10 minutes. Carefully run a knife around edge of pan to loosen; cool 1 hour longer. Refrigerate overnight. Remove sides of pan.

6. In a large saucepan, combine the cranberries, syrup and brown sugar. Cook over medium heat until the berries pop, about 10 minutes. Serve warm with cheesecake.

[2001]

THREE-CHIP ENGLISH TOFFEE

yield: about 2-1/2 pounds
prep: 15 min. + chilling ∞ **cook: 30 min.**

With its devilishly decadent texture and scrumptiously rich flavor, this is the ultimate toffee! Drizzled on top are three different kinds of melted chips, plus a sprinkling of walnuts. Packaged in colorful tins, these pretty pieces make great gifts.

—*Lana Petfield, Richmond, Virginia*

1/2 teaspoon plus 2 cups butter, *divided*
2 cups sugar
1 cup slivered almonds

BAKING A CHEESECAKE IN A WATER BATH

1. Using a double thickness of heavy-duty foil, make an 18-in. square. Center springform pan on foil, then tightly mold foil around pan.

2. Place springform pan in a larger pan, such as a larger shallow baking dish or roasting pan. Set dish on rack in oven. Using a large kettle or large measuring cup, carefully pour hot water into larger pan to a depth of 1 in.

1 cup milk chocolate chips

1 cup chopped walnuts

1/2 cup semisweet chocolate chips

1/2 cup white baking chips

1-1/2 teaspoons shortening

1. Butter a 15-in. x 10-in. x 1-in. pan with 1/2 teaspoon butter. In a heavy saucepan over medium-low heat, bring sugar and remaining butter to a boil, stirring constantly. Cover and cook for 2-3 minutes.

2. Uncover; add almonds. Cook and stir with a clean spoon until a candy thermometer reads 300° (hard-crack stage) and mixture is golden brown.

3. Pour into prepared pan (do not scrape sides of saucepan). Surface will be buttery. Cool for 1-2 minutes. Sprinkle with milk chocolate chips. Let stand for 1-2 minutes; spread chocolate over the top. Sprinkle with walnuts; press down gently with the back of a spoon. Chill for 10 minutes.

4. In a microwave, melt semisweet chips; stir until smooth. Drizzle over the walnuts. Refrigerate for 10 minutes. Melt vanilla chips and shortening; stir until smooth. Drizzle over the walnuts. Cover and refrigerate for 1-2 hours. Break into pieces.

Editor's Note: We recommend that you test your candy thermometer before each use by bringing water to a boil; the thermometer should read 212°. Adjust your recipe temperature up or down based on your test. If toffee separates during cooking, add 1/2 cup hot water and stir vigorously. Bring back up to 300° and proceed as recipe directs.

[2010]

CHOCOLATE TRUFFLE CAKE

yield: 16 servings ∞ prep: 35 min. + chilling
bake: 25 min. + cooling

Love chocolate? Then this tender, luxurious layer cake is for you. With a ganache glaze and a fabulous bittersweet filling, the indulgence is so worth it.

—Jo Ann Koerkenmeier, Damiansville, Illinois

2-1/2 cups 2% milk

1 cup butter, cubed

8 ounces semisweet chocolate, chopped

3 eggs

2 teaspoons vanilla extract

2-2/3 cups all-purpose flour

2 cups sugar

1 teaspoon baking soda

1/2 teaspoon salt

FILLING:

6 tablespoons butter, cubed

4 ounces bittersweet chocolate, chopped

2-1/2 cups confectioners' sugar

1/2 cup heavy whipping cream

GANACHE:

10 ounces semisweet chocolate, chopped

2/3 cup heavy whipping cream

1. In a large saucepan, cook the milk, butter and chocolate over low heat until melted. Remove from the heat; let stand for 10 minutes.

2. In a large bowl, beat eggs and vanilla; stir in chocolate mixture until smooth. Combine flour, sugar, baking soda and salt; gradually add to chocolate mixture and mix well (batter will be thin).

3. Transfer to three greased and floured 9-in. round baking pans. Bake at 325° for 25-30 minutes or until a toothpick inserted near the center comes out clean. Cool for 10 minutes before removing from pans to wire racks to cool completely.

4. For filling, in a small saucepan, melt the butter and chocolate. Stir in the confectioners' sugar and cream until smooth.

5. For the ganache, place the chocolate in a small bowl. In a small saucepan, bring the cream just to a boil. Pour over the chocolate; whisk until smooth. Cool, stirring occasionally, until the ganache reaches a spreading consistency.

6. Set aside 1/2 cup filling for garnish. Place one cake layer on a serving plate; spread with half of remaining filling. Repeat layers. Top with remaining cake layer. Spread ganache over top and sides of cake. Decorate with reserved filling. Store in the refrigerator.

SPANISH RICE *supper*

[1993]

"You can count on combining this casserole with the flavorful salad, simple biscuits and lovely pudding dessert to satisfy your hungry family. It's tasty, filling and quick."

HAMBURGER SPANISH RICE

yield: 4-6 servings ∞ **prep: 5 min.** ∞ **cook: 30 min.**

When I need to make dinner in a hurry, this is one of my go-to dishes. Even though we're retired, I often work on crafts or paint right up until mealtime.

—*Bernice Morris, Marshfield, Missouri, Field Editor*

- 1 **pound lean ground beef (90% lean)**
- 1 **medium onion, chopped**
- 1/2 **green pepper, chopped**
- 1 **cup uncooked instant rice**
- 1 **can (15 ounces) tomato sauce**
- 3/4 **cup hot water**
- 1 **teaspoon prepared mustard**
- 1 **teaspoon Worcestershire sauce**
- 1 **teaspoon salt**
- 1 **teaspoon sugar**

1. In a large skillet, brown the beef, onion, green pepper and rice over medium heat until meat is no longer pink and vegetables are tender. Stir in the remaining ingredients. Bring to a boil. Reduce heat; cover and simmer 20-25 minutes or until the rice is tender.

INSTANT BROWN RICE

To beef up the nutrients and fiber in Hamburger Spanish Rice use 1 cup instant brown rice for the white rice.

—*Taste of Home Cooking Experts*

AMBROSIA PUDDING

yield: 4-6 servings ∞ **prep/total time: 20 min.**

For a special way to round out a quick dinner, try this dessert. Serving this in a parfait glass showcases the layers.

—*Debbie Jones, California, Maryland*

2	cups cold 2% milk
1	package (3.4 ounces) instant vanilla pudding mix
1/4	cup honey
2	teaspoons grated orange peel
1/4	teaspoon vanilla extract
1	cup heavy whipping cream, whipped
1	banana, sliced
1	can (11 ounces) mandarin oranges, drained
1/4	cup flaked coconut
1/4	cup sliced almonds

---

1. In a large bowl, whisk the milk and pudding mix for 2 minutes. Let stand for 2 minutes or until soft-set. Add the honey, orange peel and vanilla. Fold in the whipped cream.

2. In individual dessert dishes, layer half of the pudding, banana slices, orange sections, coconut and almonds. Repeat layers. Chill.

QUICK BISCUITS

yield: 9 biscuits ∞ **prep/total time: 25 min.**

Choose these biscuits for a satisfying accompaniment to any meal. I never made biscuits until I tried this two-ingredient recipe. Now my husband wants biscuits all the time.

—*Diane Hixon, Niceville, Florida, Field Editor*

2	cups self-rising flour
1	cup heavy whipping cream

---

1. In a large bowl, combine the flour and cream. Turn out onto a floured surface; knead for 5 minutes or until no longer sticky.

2. Roll dough to a 1/2-in. thickness. Cut into 3-in. biscuits.

3. Place on a greased baking sheet. Bake at 450° for 8 to 10 minutes.

Editor's Note: As a substitute for 2 cups self-rising flour, place 1 tablespoon baking powder and 1 teaspoon salt in a measuring cup. Add all-purpose flour to measure 1 cup. Combine with an additional 1 cup all-purpose flour.

WILTED LETTUCE SALAD

yield: 6 servings ∞ **prep/total time: 15 min.**

The bacon drippings become part of the dressing and give the salad a fabulous flavor!

—*Alberta McKay*
  Bartlesville, Oklahoma, Former Field Editor

8	cups torn leaf lettuce *or* spinach
1/4	cup sliced green onions
Pepper to taste	
3	bacon strips, diced
1	tablespoon white wine vinegar
2	teaspoons lemon juice
1/2	teaspoon sugar
1/4	teaspoon salt
1	hard-cooked egg, chopped

---

1. In a large bowl, combine the lettuce and onions in a large salad bowl. Sprinkle with pepper; set aside.

2. In a large skillet, cook the bacon over medium heat until crisp. Stir the vinegar, lemon juice, sugar and salt into the drippings. Pour over the lettuce and toss gently until well coated. Top with the hard-cooked egg. Serve immediately.

MAKING HARD-COOKED EGGS

To hard-cook large eggs, place a single layer of eggs in a saucepan and add enough water to cover by 1 inch. Put a lid on the pan and bring to a boil. Remove from the heat and let stand for 15 minutes. Immediately rinse with cold water and cover with ice water until completely cool. This will prevent a dark ring from forming on the surface of the yolks. After cooking, crackle the shells all over before peeling by gently tapping on the kitchen counter.

—*Taste of Home Cooking Experts*

SUPER SKILLET *entree*

[1994]

"Fantastic entrees can be made in a skillet in minutes—including the chicken dish that follows. Round your meal out with savory rolls, a no-bake pie and your favorite salad or veggies and dinner is ready."

QUICK CHICKEN CACCIATORE

yield: 4 servings ∞ prep: 10 min. ∞ cook: 30 min.

(Pictured on page 447)

My family enjoys this zesty chicken dish. I like it, too, since it is so simple to make.

—Marcia Hostetter, Canton, New York, Field Editor

- 1 medium green pepper, cut into strips
- 1 medium onion, sliced into rings
- 8 ounces fresh mushrooms, sliced
- 1 tablespoon olive oil
- 4 boneless skinless chicken breast halves (4 ounces *each*)
- 1 can (15 ounces) tomato sauce
- 1 can (4 ounces) chopped green chilies
- 1/4 to 1/2 teaspoon dried basil
- 1/4 to 1/2 teaspoon dried oregano
- 1/8 to 1/4 teaspoon garlic powder
- Dash cayenne pepper
- Cooked spaghetti *or* rice, optional

1. In a large skillet, saute green pepper, onion and mushrooms in olive oil for 4-5 minutes or until crisp-tender. Place the chicken breasts over the vegetables.

2. In a small bowl, combine tomato sauce, chilies and seasonings. Pour over the chicken; cover and simmer for 20 minutes or until a thermometer inserted into the chicken breast reads 170°. Before serving, cut chicken breasts into slices if desired. Serve with spaghetti or rice if desired.

NO-COOK COCONUT PIE

yield: 6-8 servings ∞ prep/total time: 15 min.

A quick meal does not have to go without dessert. If you don't think so, just try my creamy No-Cook Coconut Pie.

—*Jeanette Fuehring, Concordia, Missouri, Former Field Editor*

    2 packages (3.4 ounces *each*) instant vanilla pudding mix
2-3/4 cups cold 2% milk
    1 teaspoon coconut extract
    1 carton (8 ounces) frozen whipped topping, thawed
  1/2 cup flaked coconut
    1 graham cracker crust (9 inches)
Toasted coconut

1. In a large bowl, beat the dry pudding mixes, milk and coconut extract on low speed until combined. Beat on high for 2 minutes. Fold in whipped topping and coconut.

2. Pour into the crust. Sprinkle with toasted coconut. Chill until ready to serve. Refrigerate leftovers.

MINI BLUE CHEESE ROLLS

yield: 4-6 servings ∞ prep/total time: 25 min.

Here's a fun, quick way to dress up refrigerated breadsticks.

—*Myrtle Albrecht*
Shingle Springs, California, Former Field Editor

1/4 cup butter, cubed
1/2 cup crumbled blue cheese
  1 tube (11 ounces) refrigerated breadsticks

1. In a large saucepan, melt butter and blue cheese over low heat. Unroll dough. Separate into six sections. Cut each double breadstick into six pieces; place in a foil-lined 11-in. x 7-in. baking pan. Pour cheese mixture over dough.

2. Bake at 400° for 20 minutes or until butter is absorbed and rolls are lightly browned. Carefully lift foil out of pan; transfer rolls to a serving plate. Serve warm.

CLASSIC *salisbury steak*

[1995]

"Warm yourself up with this old-fashioned entree, which is ideal for hectic days and nights."

SALISBURY STEAK

yield: 4 servings ∞ prep/total time: 25 min.

(Pictured on page 444)

I often double the recipe and freeze one batch of cooked steaks and gravy for an even faster meal on an especially busy night.

—*Carol Callahan, Rome, Georgia*

  1/3 cup chopped onion
  1/4 cup crushed saltines
    1 egg white, lightly beaten
    2 tablespoons 2% milk
    1 tablespoon prepared horseradish
  1/4 teaspoon salt, optional
  1/8 teaspoon pepper
    1 pound lean ground beef (90% lean)
    1 jar (12 ounces) beef gravy
1-1/4 to 1-1/2 cups sliced fresh mushrooms
    2 tablespoons water
Hot cooked noodles, optional

1. In a large bowl, combine the onion, saltines, egg white, milk, horseradish, salt if desired, and pepper. Crumble beef over mixture. Shape into four oval patties.

2. In a large skillet over medium heat, cook patties for 5-6 minutes on each side or until no pink remains and a thermometer reads 160°.

3. Remove patties and keep warm. Add gravy, mushrooms and water to skillet; cook for 3-5 minutes or until heated through. Serve with patties and noodles if desired.

QUICK CARROTS

yield: 4 servings ∞ prep/total time: 15 min.

This recipe is a versatile, colorful side dish. The carrots and green onions are a combination your family is sure to enjoy.

—Florence Jacoby, Granite Falls, Minnesota

        2   cups fresh *or* frozen sliced carrots
        1   tablespoon butter
        2   tablespoons sliced green onions
        1   tablespoon water
     1/4   teaspoon salt
    Chopped fresh parsley

1. In a large saucepan, combine first five ingredients. Cover and simmer for 8-10 minutes or until the carrots are crisp tender. Sprinkle with parsley.

SAUSAGE SKILLET SUPPER

❝I substituted turkey bulk sausage for the pork sausage to lower the fat content, but kept all the other ingredients the same. It is not only fast but delicious!**❞**
—*tinkaandme*

BANANA PUDDING DESSERT

**yield: 6-8 servings
prep/total time: 15 min.**

This creamy dessert with mild banana taste is comfort food that tastes like you fussed.

—Hazel Merrill, Greenville, South Carolina

        1   package (3.4 ounces) instant vanilla
             pudding mix
    1-1/4   cups cold water
        1   can (14 ounces) sweetened
             condensed milk
        2   cups whipped topping
       24   to 32 vanilla wafers
        3   large firm bananas, sliced

1. In a large bowl, combine the pudding mix, water and milk; beat on low speed for 2 minutes. Chill for 5 minutes. Fold in the whipped topping.

2. In individual dessert dishes, layer with the wafers, pudding, bananas and more pudding. Top each with a wafer. Chill until serving.

SAVORY SAUSAGE *meal*

[1996]

❝These family-style dishes are great to serve, especially during the busy school year.**❞**

SAUSAGE SKILLET SUPPER

**yield: 6-8 servings
prep/total time: 30 min.**

This simple and satisfying entree is a favorite of my family's. It is prepared in no time!

*—Mildred Sherrer
Fort Worth, Texas, Former Field Editor*

        1   pound bulk pork sausage
        1   can (16 ounces) kidney beans, rinsed
             and drained
        1   can (14-1/2 ounces) stewed tomatoes,
             undrained
        1   cup uncooked long grain rice
        1   cup water
      2/3   cup picante sauce *or* salsa

1. In a large skillet, crumble the sausage. Cook oven medium heat until no longer pink; drain. Add the remaining ingredients; bring to a boil. Reduce heat; cover and simmer for 20-25 minutes or until rice is tender.

SPEEDY RICE PUDDING
yield: 8-10 servings
prep/total time: 30 min.

This delicious pudding has a rich, old-fashioned flavor, but it's quick to make especially for my great-grandchildren.

—*Ann Vershowske, West Allis, Wisconsin*

- 4 cups 2% milk
- 1 egg, lightly beaten
- 1 package (3 ounces) cook-and-serve vanilla pudding mix
- 1 cup uncooked instant rice
- 1/4 cup raisins
- 1/4 teaspoon ground cinnamon
- 1/8 teaspoon ground nutmeg

1. In a large saucepan, combine the milk, egg and pudding mix. Add rice and raisins. Bring to a boil over medium heat, stirring constantly. Cook and stir for 2 minutes or until mixture reaches 160°. Remove from the heat; cool for 5 minutes, stirring twice.

2. Spoon into individual desserts dishes or a serving bowl. Serve immediately or cover with plastic wrap and refrigerate. Sprinkle with cinnamon and nutmeg just before serving.

LEMON GARLIC BREAD
yield: 8-10 servings
prep/total time: 25 min.

These bread slices are deliciously different with a hint of lemon.

—*Adeline Piscitelli, Sayreville, New Jersey*

- 1 loaf (1 pound) French bread
- 1/2 cup butter, melted
- 2 tablespoons grated Parmesan cheese
- 4 teaspoons lemon juice
- 1 tablespoon grated lemon peel
- 1 garlic clove, minced
- 1/4 teaspoon pepper

1. Cut bread diagonally into 1-in. slices. Combine the remaining ingredients; brush over cut sides of bread. Wrap loaf in foil. Bake at 400° for 15-20 minutes or until heated through.

HONEY POPPY SEED DRESSING
yield: about 2/3 cup
prep/total time: 10 min.
(Pictured on page 443)

This simple, fast dressing is a light and refreshing way to dress up a plain lettuce salad.

—*Michelle Bentley, Waukesha, Wisconsin*

- 1/3 cup canola oil
- 1/4 cup honey
- 2 tablespoons cider vinegar
- 2 teaspoons poppy seeds
- 1/2 teaspoon salt

1. In a small bowl, whisk the ingredients. Serve over a green salad or fresh fruit. Store in the refrigerator.

HOW TO MELT CRYSTALLIZED HONEY

Liquid honey will naturally crystallize over time. You can still use the honey, but it will need to be melted. Place the jar in warm water and stir until the crystals dissolve. Or place honey in a microwave-safe container and microwave on high, stirring every 30 seconds, until the crystals dissolve.

—*Taste of Home Cooking Experts*

SPEEDY RICE PUDDING

"My husband and daughter just love this recipe. I make it an easier way by just putting everything in the pan at once and letting it cook."

—*CathyGribler*

HAM & RICE *pair up for dinner*

[1997]

"Two mealtime basics—ham and rice—create a savory, out-of-the-ordinary dinner spread. Get ready for lots of satisfied smiles and very few leftovers."

APRICOT HAM ROLLS

yield: 4 servings ∽ **prep/total time: 30 min.**

This is the kind of hearty dish we 10 kids would devour after doing chores on our parents' farm. Mom always had lots of hungry mouths to appreciate her good food. When I'm short on cooking time, I rely on this tasty recipe.

—**Carolyn Hannay, Antioch, Tennessee**

1-2/3	cups apricot nectar, *divided*
1	tablespoon Dijon mustard
1/2	teaspoon salt
1	cup uncooked instant rice
2	tablespoons minced fresh parsley
8	thin slices fully cooked ham
2	tablespoons maple syrup

1. In a large saucepan over medium heat, combine 1-1/3 cups apricot nectar, mustard and salt; bring to a boil. Stir in rice. Remove from heat; cover and let stand for 6-8 minutes or until the liquid is absorbed. Add parsley and fluff with a fork.

2. Place about 1/4 cup of rice mixture on each slice of ham. Overlap two opposite corners of ham over rice mixture; secure with a toothpick.

3. In a large skillet over medium-high heat, combine syrup and remaining nectar; bring to a boil. Add ham rolls; reduce heat. Cover and simmer for about 5 minutes or until heated through, basting occasionally with the sauce. Remove toothpicks.

MICROWAVE CHERRY CRISP

yield: 4-6 servings ∽ **prep/total time: 20 min.**

(Pictured on page 442)

Microwaving this crisp is a time-saving method that produces a treat with old-fashioned flavor. It tastes just like the old-time crisp with half the fuss and mess.

—*Debra Morello, Edwards, California*

  1 **can (21 ounces) cherry pie filling**
3/4 **cup packed brown sugar**
2/3 **cup quick-cooking oats**
1/3 **cup all-purpose flour**
1/4 **cup butter, cubed**
Vanilla ice cream, optional

1. Spoon filling into a greased 9-in. pie plate. In a small bowl, combine brown sugar, oats and flour; cut in butter until crumbly. Sprinkle over filling. Microwave on high for 7-9 minutes. Serve warm with ice cream if desired.

Editor's Note: This recipe was tested in a 1,100-watt microwave.

BROCCOLI STIR-FRY

yield: 4 servings ∽ **prep/total time: 10 min.**

Broccoli stir-fried with lemon pepper makes an easy but delicious side dish.

—*Susan Davis, Vernon Hills, Illinois*

  3 **cups fresh broccoli florets**
1/4 **cup butter, cubed**
1-1/2 **teaspoons lemon-pepper seasoning**

1. In a large skillet over medium-high heat, stir-fry the broccoli in butter and lemon-pepper until crisp-tender, about 2 minutes.

FUN KABOB *meal*

[1998]

❝When summertime comes around it's hard to pull yourself from outdoor activities to make dinner. Here's a quick-to-the-table meal that will have you back outdoors in no time.❞

BROILED BEEF KABOBS

yield: 4 servings ∽ **prep/total time: 25 min.**

This recipe is a fun summer main dish, and is seasoned in a snap with a tangy homemade marinade. They are so easy to prepare!

—*Margery Bryan, Moses Lake, Washington, Former Field Editor*

  1 **tablespoon olive oil**
  1 **tablespoon lemon juice**
  1 **tablespoon water**
  2 **teaspoon Dijon mustard**
  1 **teaspoon honey**
1/2 **teaspoon dried oregano**
1/4 **teaspoon pepper**
  1 **pound beef top sirloin steak (1 inch thick), cut into 1-inch cubes**
  2 **small green *and/or* sweet red peppers, cut into 1-inch pieces**
 12 **large fresh mushrooms**
Hot cooked rice

1. In a large bowl, combine the first seven ingredients. Add the beef, peppers and mushrooms; toss to coat. Thread meat and vegetables alternately on metal or soaked wooden skewers.

2. Broil 3 in. from the heat, turning often, until meat reaches desired doneness and vegetables are tender, about 12-16 minutes. Serve with rice.

APPLE-NUT TOSSED SALAD

yield: 4 servings ∞ **prep/total time: 10 min.**

When you want an alternative to a plain salad, give this one a try. A light dressing tops crunchy apples, walnuts and greens sprinkled with blue cheese.

—*Maureen Reubelt, Gales Ferry, Connecticut*

- 3 cups torn Bibb lettuce
- 1/2 cup chopped apple
- 1 tablespoon chopped green onion
- 1 to 2 tablespoons chopped walnuts
- 1 to 2 tablespoons crumbled blue cheese
- 3 tablespoons olive oil
- 1 teaspoon Dijon mustard
- 3/4 teaspoon sugar

Salt and pepper to taste

1. In a large bowl, combine the lettuce, apple, onion, walnuts and blue cheese. In a large bowl, whisk the oil, mustard, sugar, salt and pepper. Pour over salad and toss to coat.

STRAWBERRY LEMON PARFAITS

yield: 4 servings ∞ **prep/total time: 10 min.**

This parfait makes a cool, elegant dessert that's such a cinch to fix.

—*Joy Beck, Cincinnati, Ohio*

- 1 pint fresh strawberries
- 3 tablespoons sugar
- 3 cups (24 ounces) lemon yogurt

1. In a food processor, combine the strawberries and sugar. Process for 20-30 seconds or until the berries are coarsely chopped. Divide half of the mixture into four parfait glasses. Top with yogurt and remaining berries.

SAY OLÉ *to supper*

[1999]

❝Spice up suppertime with this Southwestern-style meal.❞

CHICKEN QUESADILLAS

yield: 6 servings ∞ **prep/total time: 30 min.**

(Pictured on page 445)

This recipe has an impressive look and taste with little preparation. The leftover chicken gets Mexican flair from cumin in this fun main dish.

—*Linda Wetzel, Woodland Park, Colorado*

- 2-1/2 cups shredded cooked chicken
- 2/3 cup salsa
- 1/3 cup sliced green onions
- 3/4 to 1 teaspoon ground cumin
- 1/2 teaspoon salt
- 1/2 teaspoon dried oregano
- 6 flour tortillas (8 inches)
- 1/4 cup butter, melted
- 2 cups (8 ounces) shredded Monterey Jack cheese

Sour cream and guacamole

1. In a large skillet, combine the first six ingredients. Cook, uncovered, over medium heat for 10 minutes or until heated through, stirring occasionally.

2. Brush one side of tortillas with butter; place buttered side down on a lightly greased baking sheet. Spoon 1/3 cup chicken mixture over half of each tortilla; sprinkle with 1/3 cup cheese.

3. Fold plain side of tortilla over the cheese. Bake at 375° for 9-11 minutes or until crisp and golden brown. Cut into wedges; serve with the sour cream and guacamole.

BERRY PINEAPPLE PARFAITS

yield: 6 servings   prep/total time: 20 min.

(Pictured on page 443)

Here's a surefire winner that's bound to satisfy all of the tastes that sit at your table.

—Ruth Andrewson
Leavenworth, Washington
Former Field Editor

---

3   cups whole fresh strawberries
3   to 4 tablespoons sugar
12   scoops vanilla ice cream
1   can (8 ounces) crushed pineapple, drained
Whipped topping

---

1. Set aside six strawberries for garnish. Slice the remaining strawberries and toss with the sugar; let the strawberries stand for 10 minutes.

2. Spoon half of the sliced berries into six parfait glasses. Top with half of the ice cream and half of the pineapple. Repeat layers. Top with the whipped topping and reserved strawberries.

ZIPPY BEANS AND RICE

yield: 6 servings   prep/total time: 20 min.

This is a super side dish, and we also enjoy it as a light entree with corn bread and salad.

—Darlene Owen, Reedsport, Oregon

---

1   can (15 ounces) black beans, rinsed and drained
1   can (10 ounces) diced tomatoes and green chilies, undrained
1   cup frozen corn
3/4   cup water
1   medium jalapeno pepper, seeded and chopped
1   teaspoon salt, optional
1   cup uncooked instant white *or* brown rice
1   green onion, sliced

---

1. In a large skillet, combine the beans, tomatoes, corn, water, jalapeno and salt if desired. Bring to a boil; stir the in rice.

2. Cover and remove from the heat. Let stand for 5 minutes or until liquid is absorbed. Fluff with a fork. Sprinkle with onion.

Editor's Note: Wear disposable gloves when cutting hot peppers; the oils can burn skin. Avoid touching your face.

ZIPPY BEANS AND RICE

"This is an EXCELLENT side to any Spanish dish! The whole family loves it, plus it is sooo easy to make!"
—toddandfawn

SEEDING JALAPENO PEPPERS

Chili peppers, such as jalapenos, contain a skin irritant that's called capsaicin. When handling chili peppers, wear rubber or plastic gloves and avoid touching your face, eyes or mouth. Wash hands and the cutting surface thoroughly with hot, soapy water when finished.

SUPER EASY *stroganoff*

[2000]

"This classic, satisfying meal will please your family without taking much time from your to-do list."

MUSHROOM BEEF STROGANOFF
yield: 6 servings ∽ **prep/total time: 30 min.**

I've had this recipe for more years than I care to count and have used it countless times. You can serve it over noodles or rice.
—*Robin De La Gardelle, Concord, California*

2	tablespoons butter
1	tablespoon canola oil
1-1/2	pounds beef top sirloin steak, thinly sliced
1	pound fresh mushrooms, sliced
1	can (10-3/4 ounces) condensed cream of mushroom soup, undiluted
2	cups (16 ounces) sour cream
1	cup chopped green onions
1/2	teaspoon dried thyme
1/2	teaspoon dried marjoram

Hot cooked noodles *or* rice

---

1. In a large skillet, heat butter and oil over medium-high heat. Brown steak; remove with a slotted spoon and keep warm. Add mushrooms; saute until tender. Return steak to pan. Add the soup, sour cream, onions, thyme and marjoram; heat gently (do not boil). Serve with noodles or rice.

HERBED TOSSED SALAD

yield: about 1-1/3 cups dressing ∽ prep/total time: 10 min.

Ten minutes are all you need to toss together this green salad. The homemade dressing features garlic, oregano and basil.

—*Margery Bryan*
Moses Lake, Washington, Former Field Editor

1 cup canola oil
1/3 cup tarragon vinegar
1 garlic clove, minced
2 teaspoons minced fresh oregano *or* 1/2 teaspoon dried oregano
1 teaspoon salt
3/4 to 1 teaspoon minced fresh basil *or* 1/4 teaspoon dried basil
1/2 teaspoon minced fresh parsley
Mixed salad greens
Sliced cucumber and sweet red pepper

1. In a small bowl, whisk the first seven ingredients. In a large salad bowl, combine greens, cucumber and red pepper. Drizzle with dressing; toss to coat.

CANDY BAR CROISSANTS

yield: 8 servings ∽ prep: 15 min. ∽ bake: 15 min. + cooling
(Pictured on page 446)

These croissants taste as good as they look. This rich, buttery treat combines convenient refrigerated crescent rolls and chocolate bars.

—*Beverly Sterling, Gasport, New York*

1 tube (8 ounces) refrigerated crescent rolls
1 tablespoon butter, softened
2 plain milk chocolate candy bars (1.55 ounces each), broken into small pieces
1 egg, lightly beaten
2 tablespoons sliced almonds

1. Unroll crescent roll dough; separate into triangles. Brush with butter. Arrange candy bar pieces evenly over triangles; roll up from the wide end.

2. Place point side down on a greased baking sheet; curve ends slightly. Brush with egg and sprinkle with almonds. Bake at 375° for 11-13 minutes or until golden brown. Cool on a wire rack.

NO-FUSS *yuletide supper*

[2001]

"When the hustle and bustle of the holiday season comes along, here's a delightful meal that gives a taste of Christmastime."

CRANBERRY PORK MEDALLIONS

yield: 3 servings ∽ prep/total time: 20 min.

This juicy pork with its festive cranberry glaze is simple to make. It tastes so special and looks so good, people will think you fussed. Serve with refrigerated mashed potatoes and frozen green beans for a super meal.

—*Maria Brennan, Waterbury, Connecticut*

1 pork tenderloin (about 1 pound), cut into 1/2-inch slices
3 tablespoons olive oil
1 medium onion, finely chopped
1 garlic clove, minced
3 tablespoons sugar
3/4 cup apple juice
1/2 cup cranberry juice
1/2 cup fresh *or* frozen cranberries, thawed
2 teaspoons Dijon mustard
1/2 teaspoon minced fresh rosemary *or* 1/8 teaspoon dried rosemary, crushed
Additional cranberries and fresh rosemary, optional

1. In a large nonstick skillet, brown pork in oil for 3-4 minutes on each side. Remove and set aside.

2. In the same skillet, saute the onion, garlic and sugar until onion is caramelized and tender. Stir in the apple juice, cranberry juice, cranberries, mustard and rosemary. Bring mixture to a boil. Reduce heat; simmer, uncovered, for 5-6 minutes or until sauce is reduced by half.

3. Return the pork to pan; heat through. Sprinkle with additional cranberries and rosemary if desired.

CHOCOLATE RAISIN TRUFFLES

yield: 2-1/2 dozen ∞ prep/total time: 20 min.

These sweet morsels have wonderful flavor and are inexpensive to make.

—*Diane Hixon, Niceville, Florida, Field Editor*

1 cup milk chocolate chips
1/4 cup light corn syrup
2 tablespoons confectioners' sugar
1-1/2 teaspoons vanilla extract
1-1/2 cups raisins
Nonpareils, sprinkles and/or ground nuts

1. In a microwave-safe bowl, melt chips. Stir in the corn syrup, confectioners' sugar and vanilla until smooth. Stir in raisins until evenly coated.

2. Drop by teaspoonfuls onto waxed paper-lined baking sheet. Roll truffles in nonpareils, sprinkles or nuts.

Editor's Note: This recipe was tested in a 1,100-watt microwave.

HONEY-MUSTARD SALAD DRESSING

yield: 8 servings, 1 cup ∞ prep/total time: 10 min.

This delicious dressing has only four ingredients, but it's big on flavor. My family loves this thick, tangy golden topping over a mixture of fresh greens and mushrooms.

—*Joanne Hof, Los Alamos, New Mexico*

3 tablespoons honey
2 tablespoons Dijon mustard
1/4 cup cider vinegar
1/2 cup canola oil
Salad greens and sliced fresh mushrooms

1. In a small bowl, combine the honey and mustard until smooth. Add the vinegar; whisk until blended. Slowly add the oil while beating with a whisk. Serve over salad greens and mushrooms.

SIMPLE STEAK *dinner*

[2002]

"Here's a quick meal that is sure to satisfy the steak lovers in your family."

PEPPERED RIB EYE STEAKS

yield: 4 servings ∞ prep/total time: 20 min.

These steaks are an easy yet elegant-looking entree that grill up nice and juicy with a pleasant peppery zip.

—*Julee Wallberg, Salt Lake City, Utah*

2 tablespoons canola oil
1/2 teaspoon paprika
1/2 teaspoon pepper
1/4 teaspoon *each* salt, garlic powder and lemon-pepper seasoning
1/8 teaspoon *each* dried oregano, crushed red pepper flakes, ground cumin and cayenne pepper
4 beef ribeye steaks (1 inch thick and about 10 ounces each)

1. In a large bowl, combine the oil and seasonings; rub over steaks. Grill steaks, covered, over medium heat or broil 3-4 in. from the heat for 7-10 minutes on each side or until meat reaches desired doneness (for medium-rare, a thermometer should read 145°; medium, 160°; well-done, 170°). Baste occasionally with the seasoning mixture. Let stand for 3-5 minutes before serving.

NO-BAKE FUDGY OAT COOKIES
yield: about 3 dozen ∾ prep/total time: 15 min.

I got this recipe from my mother-in-law, and my grown daughter asked me to share it with her so she could make them for Christmas.

—Elizabeth Hunter, Prosperity, South Carolina, Field Editor

2-1/4	cups quick-cooking oats
1	cup flaked coconut
1/2	cup 2% milk
1/4	cup butter, cubed
2	cups sugar
1/2	cup baking cocoa
1	teaspoon vanilla extract

1. In a large bowl, combine oats and coconut; set aside. In a large saucepan, combine milk and butter. Stir in sugar and cocoa. Bring to a boil. Add oat mixture; cook for 1 minute, stirring constantly. Remove from the heat; stir in vanilla.

2. Drop by rounded tablespoonfuls 1 in. apart onto waxed paper. Let stand until set.

COLORFUL RICE MEDLEY
yield: 4 servings ∾ prep/total time: 15 min.
(Pictured on page 443)

With only a gram of fat and less than 200 calories per serving, this delightful side dish is sure to brighten up any meal. Shredded carrot, red onion and fresh parsley give it a festive look.

—Terri Griffin, Salisbury, Maryland

2	cups water
2	cups uncooked instant rice
1/3	cup shredded carrot
1/4	cup finely chopped red onion
1-1/2	teaspoons steak sauce
1	teaspoon butter
1/2	to 1-1/2 teaspoons salt
1/2	teaspoon pepper
1	teaspoon minced fresh parsley

1. In a large saucepan, bring water to a boil. Stir in rice. Remove from the heat; cover and let stand for 3 minutes. Stir in the remaining ingredients. Cover and let stand 5 minutes longer.

SPEEDY SUMMERTIME *meal*

[2003]

❝If you can't beat the heat, at least you can be out of the kitchen in a flash with this quick-to-make dinner.❞

CHICKEN ENCHILADAS
yield: 4 servings ∾ prep/total time: 30 min.

This recipe puts a little zip into any menu. The rolled tortillas are filled with a hearty mixture of cheese, chicken and green chilies and then topped with a creamy sauce and more cheese. I sometimes use leftover turkey instead of chicken.

—Karen Bourne, Magrath, Alberta, Field Editor

2	tablespoons butter
1/4	cup all-purpose flour
2-1/2	cups chicken broth
1	teaspoon dried coriander
1	can (4 ounces) chopped green chilies, *divided*
2	cups cubed cooked chicken
1	cup (4 ounces) shredded Monterey Jack cheese
8	flour tortillas (8 inches), warmed
1	cup (4 ounces) shredded cheddar cheese

1. Melt butter in a large saucepan. Stir in flour until smooth. Gradually add broth. Bring to a boil; cook and stir for 2 minutes or until thickened. Stir in coriander and half of the chilies. In a large bowl, combine the chicken, Monterey Jack cheese and remaining chilies.

2. Spoon 1/3 cup chicken mixture onto each tortilla; roll up. Place seam side down in an ungreased 13-in. x 9-in. baking dish. Pour sauce over enchiladas. Sprinkle with cheddar cheese. Bake, uncovered, at 375° for 15-18 minutes or until heated through and cheese is melted.

GUACAMOLE TOSSED SALAD

yield: 4 servings   prep/total time: 15 min.

The fresh-tasting blend of avocados, tomatoes, red onion and greens in my salad get added pizzazz from crumbled cooked bacon and a slightly spicy vinaigrette.

—Lori Fischer, Chino Hills, California

2	medium tomatoes, seeded and chopped
1/2	small red onion, sliced and separated into rings
6	bacon strips, cooked and crumbled
1/3	cup canola oil
2	tablespoons cider vinegar
1	teaspoon salt
1/4	teaspoon pepper
1/4	teaspoon hot pepper sauce
2	large ripe avocados, peeled and cubed
4	cups torn salad greens

1. In a large bowl, combine the tomatoes, onion and bacon; set aside.

2. In a small bowl, whisk the oil, vinegar, salt, pepper and hot pepper sauce. Pour over tomato mixture; toss gently. Add avocados.

3. Place greens in a large salad bowl; add avocado mixture and toss to coat.

PEANUT BUTTER CASHEW SUNDAES

yield: 4 servings   prep/total time: 5 min.

These tasty sundaes make a cool finale to any summer meal...and they go together in a snap.

—Betty Claycomb, Alverton, Pennsylvania, Field Editor

1/3	cup light corn syrup
1/4	cup peanut butter
4	scoops ice cream
1/2	cup salted cashews

1. In a small bowl, combine the corn syrup and peanut butter until blended. Serve over the ice cream and sprinkle with cashews.

COLORFUL *cuisine*

[2004]

"These burgers really get you out of the house since they are grilled in the outdoors. "

FRENCH ONION BURGERS

yield: 4 servings   prep/total time: 20 min.

(Pictured on page 446)

I created French Onion Burgers one day when I needed to stretch a pound of hamburger. When we have high school boys help with baling hay, this is one of their favorite foods to enjoy after the work is done.

—Beth Johnson, Dalton, Ohio

1	can (4 ounces) mushroom stems and pieces, drained and diced
1	can (2.8 ounces) french-fried onions
1	tablespoon Worcestershire sauce
1/2	teaspoon salt
1	pound ground beef
4	hamburger buns, split

Lettuce leaves and tomato slices

1. In a large bowl, combine the mushrooms, onions, Worcestershire sauce and salt. Crumble the beef over mixture and mix well. Shape into four patties.

2. Grill, uncovered, over medium heat or broil 4 in. from the heat for 6-9 minutes on each side or a until a thermometer reads 160° and juices run clear. Serve on buns with lettuce and tomato.

OLD GLORY ANGEL FOOD

yield: 8 servings ∞ **prep/total time: 20 min.**

Old Glory Angel Food makes a glorious dessert for your Fourth of July celebration. It's easy to assemble, but the triple layers and stars-and-stripes topping look like you fussed. One July, we invited a couple over for a backyard barbecue. The woman had recently become a United States citizen, so I created this cake for her. It was a big hit.

—Anne Nabbefeld, Hortonville, Wisconsin

- 1 loaf-shaped angel food cake (10-1/2 ounces)
- 1 carton (8 ounces) frozen whipped topping, thawed
- 1 cup quartered fresh strawberries
- 1 cup fresh blueberries

Additional blueberries and strawberries

1. Split cake horizontally into thirds. Place bottom layer on a serving platter. Combine 1 cup whipped topping and strawberries; spread over bottom layer. Top with second cake layer.

2. Combine 1 cup whipped topping and blueberries; spread over the second layer. Top with remaining cake layer. Spread with the remaining whipped topping. Arrange additional berries over top of cake to form a flag.

CRANBERRY LEMONADE

yield: 4 servings ∞ **prep: 5 min. cook: 15 min. + chilling**

With its pretty pink blush and tart refreshing flavor, Cranberry Lemonade is sure to satisfy, glass after glass after glass.

—Darlene Brenden
Salem, Oregon, Field Editor

- 3/4 cup sugar
- 2/3 cup lemon juice
- 3 cups cold water
- 1 cup cranberry juice

1. In a small saucepan, combine the sugar and lemon juice. Cook and stir over medium heat until the sugar is dissolved. Stir in the water and cranberry juice.

2. Cool; pour the lemonade into a pitcher. Refrigerate until chilled. Serve over ice.

CRANBERRY LEMONADE

"This tasted a little too tart for me so I added a little more sugar. My family loved it!"
—mcgee64

BUYING GROUND BEEF

When selecting a package of ground beef, look for the following:

1. Meat that is a bright, cherry-red color. There should be no gray or brown patches.

2. A package with no holes, tears or excessive liquid, which could indicate improper handling and storage.

3. The sell-by date on the package. It should be before the day of your purchase. If it is the same date, then use it that day or freeze it for later.

—Taste of Home Cooking Experts

SOPHISTICATED
but easy scampi

[2005]

It will feel like you're dining luxuriously at a white tablecloth restaurant when you savor this meal.

SHRIMP SCAMPI
yield: 4 servings ∞ prep/total time: 20 min.
(*Pictured on page 448*)

It looks like you spent hours at the stove when you serve this scampi, but it's a snap to prepare. Lemon and herbs enhance the shrimp, and bread crumbs add a pleasing crunch. Served over pasta, this main dish is pretty enough for company.
—*Lori Packer, Omaha, Nebraska*

- 3 to 4 garlic cloves, minced
- 1/4 cup butter, cubed
- 1/4 cup olive oil
- 1 pound uncooked medium shrimp, peeled and deveined
- 1/4 cup lemon juice
- 1/2 teaspoon pepper
- 1/4 teaspoon dried oregano
- 1/2 cup grated Parmesan cheese
- 1/4 cup dry bread crumbs
- 1/4 cup minced fresh parsley

Hot cooked angel hair pasta

---

1. In a 10-in. ovenproof skillet, saute garlic in butter and oil for 1 minute or until tender. Stir in the shrimp, lemon juice, pepper and oregano; cook and stir for 2-3 minutes or until shrimp turn pink. Sprinkle with the cheese, bread crumbs and parsley.

2. Broil 6 in. from the heat for 2-3 minutes or until topping is golden brown. Serve with pasta.

OLIVE 'N' FIG CHICKEN, page 458 with STOVETOP ORZO MEDLEY, page 459

MICROWAVE CHERRY CRISP, page 431

SALSA VERDE, page 457

FRESH MOZZARELLA SANDWICHES, page 454

BERRY PINEAPPLE PARFAITS, page 433

COLORFUL RICE MEDLEY, page 437

GINGER PEAR SIPPER, page 460

HONEY POPPY SEED DRESSING, page 429

SALISBURY STEAK, page 427

MEXICAN PORK CHOPS , page 452 with BROCCOLI WITH LEMON SAUCE, page 453

CHICKEN FLORENTINE PANINI, page 450 with RAMEN CORN CHOWDER, page 451

CHICKEN QUESADILLAS, page 432

TACO SALAD, page 456

CHICKEN TORTILLA CHOWDER, page 457

FRENCH ONION BURGERS, page 438

CANDY BAR CROISSANTS, page 435

BANANA COLADA SUNDAES, page 455

QUICK CHICKEN CACCIATORE, page 426

SHRIMP SCAMPI, page 440 with GARLIC-ALMOND GREEN BEANS, page 449

PEPPER-RUBBED RED SNAPPER, page 453 with PROSCIUTTO TORTELLINI, page 454

GARLIC-ALMOND GREEN BEANS

yield: 4 servings ∞ prep/total time: 20 min.

(Pictured on page 448)

The beans in this recipe stay so bright and crisp and add a pop of color to any entree. To speed things up even more, you could use frozen green beans instead of fresh.

—Genny Monchamp, Redding, California

- 1 pound fresh green beans
- 2 garlic cloves, minced
- 1 tablespoon olive oil
- 1/4 cup slivered almonds, toasted

Pepper to taste

1. Place the beans in a large saucepan and cover with water. Bring to a boil; cook, uncovered, for 8-10 minutes or until crisp-tender.

2. Meanwhile, in a large skillet, cook garlic in oil for 1 minute. Drain beans. Add the beans, almonds and pepper to skillet; toss to coat.

GRANOLA FUDGE CLUSTERS

yield: about 2-1/2 dozen
prep/total time: 25 min.

This recipe is short and sweet, calling for only four ingredients. I always make a double batch because no one can eat just one.

—Loraine Meyer, Bend, Oregon

- 1 cup (6 ounces) semisweet chocolate chips
- 1 cup butterscotch chips
- 1-1/4 cups granola cereal without raisins
- 1 cup chopped walnuts

1. In a microwave-safe bowl, melt the chocolate and butterscotch chips; stir until smooth. Stir in the granola and walnuts.

2. Drop by tablespoonfuls onto waxed paper-lined baking sheets. Refrigerate for 15 minutes or until firm.

GRANOLA FUDGE CLUSTERS

" Our family loves this quick and easy recipe. Our 10-year-old daughter usually makes this. It tastes like a chocolate bar, but only better. We substitute peanut butter chips in place of the butterscotch chips. YUM! "
—gaylene1126

TOASTING NUTS

Toasting nuts enhances their flavor and makes them more crunchy. To toast nuts, spread in a 15-in. x 10-in. x 1-in. baking pan. Bake at 350° for 5-10 minutes or until lightly browned, stirring occasionally. Or spread in a dry, nonstick skillet and heat over low heat until lightly browned, stirring occasionally.

—Taste of Home Cooking Experts

QUICK, FUN *lunch*

[2006]

"Soup, salad and a yummy toasted sandwich make a great comforting lunch."

CHICKEN FLORENTINE PANINI
yield: 4 servings ∞ **prep/total time: 25 min.**
(*Pictured on page 445*)

This grilled sandwich combines chicken with provolone cheese, spinach and red onion.
—*Lee Bremson, Kansas City, Missouri*

CHICKEN
FLORENTINE
PANINI

" Used focaccia bread instead
of sourdough...wonderful!**"**
—*angelasandoval*

1	**package (6 ounces) fresh baby spinach**
2	**teaspoons olive oil**
8	**slices sourdough bread**
1/4	**cup creamy Italian salad dressing**
8	**slices provolone cheese**
1/2	**pound shaved deli chicken**
2	**slices red onion, separated into rings**
1/4	**cup butter, softened**

1. In a large skillet, saute spinach in oil for 2 minutes or until wilted; drain.

2. Spread four bread slices with salad dressing. Layer with a cheese slice, chicken, spinach, onion and another cheese slice. Top with remaining bread. Butter outsides of sandwiches.

3. Cook on a panini maker or indoor grill until bread is browned and cheese is melted.

RAMEN CORN CHOWDER

yield: 4 servings ✑ **prep/total time: 15 min.**

(*Pictured on page 445*)

This chowder tastes as good as if it simmered for hours, but it's ready in 15 minutes. I thought the original recipe was lacking in flavor, so I jazzed it up with extra corn and bacon bits.

—*Darlene Brenden*
Salem, Oregon, Field Editor

2 cups water
1 package (3 ounces) chicken ramen noodles
1 can (15-1/4 ounces) whole kernel corn, drained
1 can (14-3/4 ounces) cream-style corn
1 cup 2% milk
1 teaspoon dried minced onion
1/4 teaspoon curry powder
3/4 cup shredded cheddar cheese
1 tablespoon crumbled cooked bacon
1 tablespoon minced fresh parsley

1. In a small saucepan, bring water to a boil. Break noodles into large pieces. Add the noodles and contents of seasoning packet to water. Reduce heat to medium. Cook, uncovered, for 2-3 minutes or until the noodles are tender.

2. Stir in the corn, cream-style corn, milk, onion and curry; heat through. Stir in the cheese, bacon and parsley until blended.

OLIVE THOUSAND ISLAND SALAD DRESSING

yield: 2 cups ✑ **prep/total time: 15 min.**

Why buy bottled salad dressing when you can make fresh, delicious, homemade Thousand Island Dressing in a jiffy? This tangy version is fabulous.

—*Elizabeth Montgomery*
Allston, Massachusetts

1-1/2 cups mayonnaise
1/2 cup chili sauce
1 hard-cooked egg, chopped
2 tablespoons finely chopped celery
2 tablespoons finely chopped green pepper
2 tablespoons chopped pimiento-stuffed olives
1 tablespoon grated onion

1. In a small bowl, combine all the ingredients. Cover and refrigerate until serving.

PLAN AHEAD & KEEP COOKED BACON IN THE FREEZER

When recipes call for a tablespoon of crumbled cooked bacon, cook up several slices at a time. Use the amount you need for your recipes, then crumble and freeze the rest. The next time you need some crumbled bacon it will be ready to use.

—*Taste of Home Cooking Experts*

RAMEN CORN CHOWDER

❝SO EASY!!! I love this recipe!!! It's definitely going to be an old standby in my house. The ingredients are easy to keep on hand, it's relatively inexpensive, and (most importantly) it takes no time to make. One pot, no mixing, no simmering, etc. I really, really love it. I replaced the chicken ramen with mushroom ramen, since my boyfriend and I are vegetarians. I also replaced the crumbled bacon with Morningstar Farms vegetarian bacon. And I added some hickory smoked salt. Delicious!❞
— *slug9000*

SOUTH-OF-THE-BORDER
supper

[2007]

"Here are some simple solutions to get a meal on the table in no time and add a festive flair to dinner."

MEXICAN PORK CHOPS
yield: 4 servings ∞ **prep/total time: 25 min.**

(Pictured on page 444)

We enjoy Mexican Pork Chops and serve them over rice to catch the spicy sauce. You can use mild, medium or hot salsa. If the pork chops are too spicy hot, you can eliminate the cumin-chili powder rub.

—*Nancy Negvesky, Somerville, New Jersey, Field Editor*

- 1 teaspoon ground cumin
- 1 teaspoon chili powder
- 4 boneless pork loin chops (1/2 inch thick and 4 ounces each)
- 1 tablespoon canola oil
- 1-1/4 cups salsa
- 1 teaspoon baking cocoa
- 1/8 teaspoon ground cinnamon
- 2 tablespoons minced fresh cilantro
- 1 green onion, chopped

1. Combine cumin and chili powder; rub over both sides of pork. In a large skillet, brown pork chops in oil on both sides over medium heat.

2. In a small bowl, combine the salsa, cocoa and cinnamon; pour over pork. Bring sauce to a boil. Reduce heat; simmer, uncovered, for 3-4 minutes on each side or until a thermometer reads 145°, stirring sauce occasionally. Let stand for 5 minutes before serving. Sprinkle with cilantro and green onion.

BROCCOLI WITH LEMON SAUCE

yield: 4 servings ∞ **prep/total time: 20 min.**

(Pictured on page 444)

I enjoyed a delicious broccoli dish in Mexico a few years ago and tried making it in my own kitchen. I think my version tastes very much like what I had at the restaurant.

—*Nancy Larkin, Maitland, Florida, Field Editor*

1   bunch broccoli, cut into spears
1/2   cup sour cream
3   to 4 tablespoons 2% milk
1   teaspoon lemon juice
1/2   teaspoon grated lemon peel

1. Place broccoli in a steamer basket; place in a large saucepan over 1 in. of water. Bring to a boil; cover and steam for 5-7 minutes or until crisp-tender.

2. Meanwhile, in a small microwave-safe bowl, combine the sour cream, milk, lemon juice and peel. Microwave, uncovered, at 50% power for 1-1/2 minutes or until heated through, stirring every 30 seconds. Serve with broccoli.

Editor's Note: This recipe was tested in a 1,100-watt microwave.

INDIVIDUAL STRAWBERRY TRIFLES

yield: 4 servings ∞ **prep/total time: 20 min.**

These delicious little trifles are loaded with berries and pound cake cubes, then drizzled with a decadent homemade chocolate sauce. I like to sprinkle each one with a little powdered sugar.

—*Karen Scaglione, Nanuet, New York*

1/2   cup semisweet chocolate chips
1/2   cup heavy whipping cream
2   tablespoons orange juice
2   cups sliced fresh strawberries
4   slices pound cake, cubed

1. In a small saucepan, melt chocolate chips with cream over low heat; stir until blended. Remove from the heat; stir in orange juice. Cool to room temperature.

2. In four dessert glasses or bowls, layer strawberries, cake cubes and chocolate mixture.

SKILLET SEAFOOD *menu*

[2008]

"You can run errands, attend after-school events and even work late if you must, and still have time to make this fabulous fish dinner."

PEPPER-RUBBED RED SNAPPER

yield: 4 servings ∞ **prep/total time: 15 min.**

(Pictured on page 448)

I found the recipe for this red snapper several years ago while living in Corpus Christi. It's often requested when guests visit, and it sure comes in handy when the boys come home with a great catch.

—*Windy Byrd, Sweeny, Texas*

1/2   teaspoon onion powder
1/2   teaspoon garlic powder
1/2   teaspoon dried thyme
1/2   teaspoon white pepper
1/2   teaspoon cayenne pepper
1/2   teaspoon pepper
1/8   teaspoon salt
4   red snapper fillets (8 ounces *each*)
3   tablespoons butter, melted

1. In a small bowl, combine the first seven ingredients. Dip fillets in butter, then rub with spice mixture.

2. In a large nonstick skillet, cook fillets over medium-high heat for 2-4 minutes on each side or until fish flakes easily with a fork.

PROSCIUTTO TORTELLINI

yield: 4 servings ❧ **prep/total time: 20 min.**

(*Pictured on page 448*)

I spruce up store-bought frozen cheese tortellini with peas, prosciutto and a smooth, cheesy sauce. You can't beat this side dish for speed and satisfying taste.

—*Scott Jones, Tulsa, Oklahoma*

- 1 package (19 ounces) frozen cheese tortellini
- 1 tablespoon all-purpose flour
- 1 cup half-and-half cream
- 1/2 cup shredded part-skim mozzarella cheese
- 1/2 cup shredded Parmesan cheese
- 10 thin slices prosciutto, chopped
- 1 package (10 ounces) frozen peas
- 1/4 teaspoon white pepper

1. Cook tortellini according to package directions. Meanwhile, in a large skillet, combine flour and cream until smooth; stir in the cheeses. Bring to a boil; cook and stir for 2 minutes or until thickened. Reduce heat.

2. Drain tortellini; add to the cheese sauce. Stir in the prosciutto, peas and pepper. Cook for 5 minutes or until heated through.

FROSTY ALMOND DESSERT

yield: 4 servings ❧ **prep/total time: 10 min.**

You can treat your family to a homemade dessert without a lot of labor when you whip up this confection. Everyone will love its yummy flavor.

—*Phyllis Schmalz, Kansas City, Kansas*

- 4 cups low-fat vanilla frozen yogurt
- 1 cup ice cubes
- 1/2 cup hot fudge ice cream topping
- 1/4 teaspoon almond extract
- Whipped topping and baking cocoa, optional

1. In a blender, place half of the yogurt, ice cubes, fudge topping and extract; cover and process for 1-2 minutes or until smooth. Stir if necessary. Pour into chilled dessert glasses.

2. Repeat with the remaining yogurt, ice, fudge topping and extract. Garnish with whipped topping and baking cocoa if desired.

FRESH TASTING *fare*

[2009]

❝When you're looking for a lighter-style meal that won't weigh you down during the dog days of summer, try this refreshing dinner. You can add avocados to the sandwiches and use fresh Walla Walla onions when they're in season.❞

FRESH MOZZARELLA SANDWICHES

yield: 4 servings ❧ **prep/total time: 15 min.**

(*Pictured on page 442*)

We love this fast, fresh sandwich, especially when it's too warm to turn on the oven. I like to pair it with a fruity white wine and pasta salad or fancy potato chips.

—*Stacey Johnson, Tacoma, Washington*

- 8 slices sourdough bread, toasted
- 1/4 cup wasabi mayonnaise
- 1/2 pound fresh mozzarella cheese, sliced
- 2 medium tomatoes, sliced
- 4 thin slices sweet onion
- 8 fresh basil leaves

1. Spread the toast with mayonnaise. On four slices, layer the cheese, tomatoes, onion and basil; top with the remaining toast.

BANANA COLADA SUNDAES

yield: 8 servings ∞ prep/total time: 20 min.

(Pictured on page 446)

This is my number one standby when I don't have much time to prepare a dessert but still want to wow my guests. Smiling, satisfied faces are guaranteed!

—Kristin Kossak, Bozeman, Montana

- 6 tablespoons butter, cubed
- 1/3 cup packed brown sugar
- 1/3 cup orange juice
- 2 teaspoons ground cinnamon
- 4 medium bananas, sliced
- 1/2 teaspoon rum extract
- 3 pints vanilla ice cream
- 1/2 cup flaked coconut, toasted

1. In a small saucepan, combine the butter, brown sugar, orange juice and cinnamon. Cook and stir over medium heat for 4-5 minutes or until sauce is smooth. Stir in bananas; heat through. Remove from the heat; stir in extract.

2. Serve warm over ice cream. Sprinkle with coconut.

SWEET ONION, TOMATO & CUKE SALAD

yield: 10 servings ∞ prep/total time: 15 min.

Crisp, fresh veggies combine with feta and zesty dressing in this fast fix. You'll want to make it again and again.

—Mickey Turner
Grants Pass, Oregon, Field Editor

- 3 large tomatoes, chopped
- 3 large cucumbers, peeled, halved, seeded and sliced
- 1 large sweet onion, halved and thinly sliced
- 1/2 cup olive oil
- 3 tablespoons mayonnaise
- 2 tablespoons rice vinegar
- 1 tablespoon Dijon mustard
- 1 garlic clove, minced
- 1/2 teaspoon salt
- 1/4 teaspoon pepper
- 1/4 cup crumbled feta cheese

1. In a large bowl, combine the tomatoes, cucumbers and onion. In a small bowl, whisk the oil, mayonnaise, vinegar, mustard, garlic, salt and pepper. Pour over tomato mixture and toss to coat. Sprinkle with cheese.

SWEET ONION, TOMATO & CUKE SALAD

❝ My husband and I love this salad! The dressing is great and the feta adds an interesting and savory twist.❞
—jenniferpero

SEEDING CUCUMBERS

Peel or score cucumber if desired. Cut lengthwise in half. Using a teaspoon, run the tip under the seeds to loosen and remove.

MEXICAN *fiesta*

[2010]

"Take a quick trip south to Mexico with this 30-minute meal. Your family will say olé!"

TACO SALAD

yield: 6 servings ∾ **prep/total time: 30 min.**

(*Pictured on page 445*)

Even with my family's busy schedule, I enjoy cooking from scratch. We love this easy taco salad made with ground pork. If I don't fix it often enough, they ask for it.

—*Sherry Duval, Baltimore, Maryland*

- 1 **pound ground pork** *or* **beef**
- 1 **envelope taco seasoning**
- 1 **can (16 ounces) kidney beans, rinsed and drained**
- 3/4 **cup water**
- 10 **cups torn romaine**
- 2 **medium tomatoes, chopped**
- 1/3 **cup chopped onion**
- 2 **cups (8 ounces) shredded cheddar cheese**
- 1/2 **to 3/4 cup Western salad dressing**

Tortilla chips, crushed

Sour cream and guacamole, optional

1. In a large skillet, cook pork over medium heat until no longer pink; drain. Stir in the taco seasoning, beans and water. Bring to a boil. Reduce heat; simmer, uncovered, for 5 minutes, stirring occasionally. Remove from the heat; cool for 10 minutes.

2. In a large bowl, combine the romaine, tomatoes, onion and cheese. Stir in pork mixture. Drizzle with salad dressing and toss to coat. Sprinkle with chips. Serve immediately with sour cream and guacamole if desired.

CHICKEN TORTILLA CHOWDER

yield: 10 servings (2-1/2 quarts)
prep/total time: 30 min.

(*Pictured on page 446*)

A restaurant-style soup starting with a can?
It's possible with this creamy, comforting soup.

—*Dana Rood, Oreana, Illinois*

---

2 cans (10-3/4 ounces *each*) condensed
   cream of potato soup, undiluted
2 cans (10-3/4 ounces *each*) condensed
   cream of chicken soup, undiluted
2 cups 2% milk
1 can (14-1/2 ounces) reduced-sodium
   chicken broth
1 can (11 ounces) Mexicorn, drained
1 package (9 ounces) ready-to-serve
   roasted chicken breast strips,
   chopped
1 can (4 ounces) chopped green chilies
3 flour tortillas (8 inches), cut into
   2-inch x 1/2-inch strips
1 cup (4 ounces) shredded cheddar
   cheese
Additional shredded cheddar cheese,
   optional

---

1. In a large saucepan, combine soups,
   milk and broth. Heat through, stirring
   frequently. Add the corn, chicken and
   chilies; bring to a boil. Stir in tortilla
   strips. Reduce heat; simmer, uncovered,
   for 5 minutes. Stir in cheese until
   melted. Sprinkle each serving with
   additional cheese if desired.

SALSA VERDE

yield: 2-1/2 cups ∽ **prep: 15 min. + chilling**

(*Pictured on page 442*)

This salsa is fresh and creamy! It's great as
a chip dip or as a topper for tacos and other
Mexican dishes. You can adjust the spiciness
as you want.

—*Paul and Nanette Hilton*
   Las Vegas, Nevada

---

8 tomatillos, husks removed
1 medium ripe avocado, peeled and
   pitted
1 small onion, halved
1 jalapeno pepper, peeled and pitted
1/3 cup fresh cilantro leaves
1/2 teaspoon salt
Tortilla chips

---

1. In a large saucepan, bring 4 cups
   water to a boil. Add the tomatillos.
   Reduce heat; simmer, uncovered, for
   5 minutes. Drain.

2. Place the avocado, onion, jalapeno,
   cilantro, salt and tomatillos in a food
   processor. Cover and process until
   blended. Refrigerate until chilled.
   Serve with chips.

Editor's Note: Wear disposable gloves
when cutting hot peppers; the oils can burn
skin. Avoid touching your face.

CHICKEN TORTILLA CHOWDER

❝This was delicious and
very easy. We substituted
ground, cooked chorizo
for the chicken strips, and
it was just fantastic. I will
definitely make this again.
I think I will add an
additional can of
Mexicorn next time.❞
—*leesquinn*

ABOUT TOMATILLOS

Tomatillos are green, tomato-like fruit with a papery outer husk and a lemon-herb flavor. To
remove the husk, pull back one of the tips of the husk from the bottom to the top. Rinse
husked tomatillos under cold running water and pat dry before using.

—*Taste of Home Cooking Experts*

NO-FUSS *company dishes*

[2011]

❝Who says quick meals are only for weeknights? Weekends can be packed with activities, too. This menu makes a fabulous company meal without sacrificing a free day in the kitchen.**❞**

OLIVE 'N' FIG CHICKEN

yield: 4 servings ∾ **prep/total time: 25 min.**

(Pictured on page 441)

I love green olives and figs, so I put this together with the chicken to have a salty-sweet combination. I found the green olive tapenade at my grocery store and the fig preserves at a specialty store.

—Carol Hull, Hermiston, Oregon

- 4 boneless skinless chicken breast halves (5 ounces each)
- 1/4 teaspoon garlic salt
- 1/4 teaspoon lemon-pepper seasoning
- 2 tablespoons olive oil
- 1 jar (6.35 ounces) green olive tapenade
- 2 tablespoons fig preserves

Sliced pimiento-stuffed olives, optional

1. Flatten chicken to 1/2-inch thickness; sprinkle with garlic salt and lemon pepper. In a large skillet, cook chicken in oil over medium heat for 4-5 minutes on each side or until a thermometer reads 170°. Remove and keep warm.

2. In the same skillet, cook tapenade and fig preserves over medium heat until heated through, stirring to loosen browned bits from pan. Return chicken to the pan; cook on low heat for 2-3 minutes or until chicken is heated through. Garnish with olives if desired.

TIPSY ROASTED PEACHES

yield: 4 servings ∽ **prep/total time: 20 min.**

Roasting frozen peaches in a simple brandy sauce turns them into a decadent topping for toasted pound cake. Whipped cream and crunchy almonds are fast finishing touches.

—*Susan Martin, Oshkosh, Wisconsin*

1/3 cup brandy
1/3 cup honey
  3 tablespoons butter
  2 cups frozen unsweetened sliced peaches
  4 slices pound cake, toasted
1/2 cup heavy whipping cream, whipped
  3 tablespoons sliced almonds, toasted

1. In a small saucepan, combine brandy, honey and butter; heat through. Keep sauce warm.

2. Combine peaches and 3 tablespoons brandy mixture; transfer to a greased 15-in. x 10-in. x 1-in. baking pan. Bake at 400° for 10-15 minutes or until tender.

3. To assemble, place the toasted pound cake on four dessert plates. Top with the peaches and the remaining brandy mixture. Garnish with the whipped cream and almonds.

STOVETOP ORZO MEDLEY

yield: 8 servings ∽ **prep/total time: 30 min.**

(Pictured on page 441)

A burst of butter and a colorful array of vegetables make this pretty pasta side good enough for company. Use a blend of exotic mushrooms to make it extra special.

—*Marie Rizzio, Interlochen, Michigan*

1-1/4 cups uncooked orzo pasta
    2 shallots, finely chopped
    1 tablespoon olive oil
  3/4 pound fresh snow peas
  1/2 pound assorted fresh mushrooms (such as portobello, button and/or shiitake), thinly sliced
  1/4 cup pine nuts
    2 tablespoons butter
    1 teaspoon salt
  1/2 teaspoon coarsely ground pepper
  1/4 cup finely chopped sweet red pepper

1. Cook the orzo according to package directions. Meanwhile, in a large skillet, saute shallots in oil for 2 minutes. Add peas and mushrooms; cook 3 minutes longer. Add pine nuts; cook and stir until vegetables are tender.

2. Drain orzo; stir in the shallot mixture, butter, salt and pepper until blended. Sprinkle with red pepper.

STOVETOP ORZO MEDLEY

❝This is such a flavorful & EASY dish to make! Added some chicken so it would fill my husband up a little better and it was PERFECT!! It's a staple in my home.❞
—*floskall*

ORZO: A VERSATILE PASTA

Orzo is a rice-shaped pasta. It's used for soups, pilafs, casseroles and can be used as a substitute for rice. Nutritionally speaking, rice and orzo are similar. Ounce for ounce, they contain similar amounts of fat, sugar, carbohydrates and even sodium.

—*Taste of Home Cooking Experts*

SOUP & SANDWICH *spread*

[2012]

"A warm sandwich along with a steaming bowl of soup is just the right combo to make you feel all cozy on a chilly autumn evening."

GINGER PEAR SIPPER

yield: 1 serving ∾ **prep/total time: 5 min.**

(Pictured on page 443)

Dress up any meal with this simple-to-make drink. It's pretty and refreshing.

—*Susan Westerfield, Albuquerque, New Mexico*

- 3 ounces ginger ale, chilled
- 3 ounces pear nectar, chilled
- 1 slice fresh pear

1. In a tall glass, combine ginger ale and pear nectar; garnish with pear slice.

ITALIAN SAUSAGE & BEAN SOUP

yield: 6 servings (2 quarts)
prep: 15 min. ∾ **cook: 20 min.**

This recipe is complete comfort food. There's nothing better than soup when there's a bite in the air. As an added bonus, the spices in the soup are awesome when you have a winter cold.

—*Stacey Bennett, Locust Grove, Virginia*

- 1 pound bulk hot Italian sausage
- 2 cans (15-1/2 ounces *each*) great northern beans, rinsed and drained
- 1 package (16 ounces) coleslaw mix
- 1 jar (24 ounces) garlic and herb spaghetti sauce
- 3 cups water

1. In a Dutch oven, cook the sausage over medium heat until no longer pink; drain.

2. Stir in all the remaining ingredients. Bring to a boil. Reduce heat; simmer, uncovered, for 20 minutes or until flavors are blended.

MEDITERRANEAN TURKEY PANINI

yield: 4 servings ∾ **prep/total time: 25 min.**

I love making this panini for my friends. For potlucks, I make several and cut them in fourths for a terrific appetizer.

—*Martha Muellenberg, Vermillion, South Dakota*

- 4 ciabatta rolls, split
- 1 jar (24 ounces) marinara sauce, *divided*
- 1 container (4 ounces) crumbled feta cheese
- 1 jar (7-1/2 ounces) marinated quartered artichoke hearts, drained and chopped
- 2 plum tomatoes, sliced
- 1 pound sliced deli turkey

1. Spread each ciabatta bottom with 2 tablespoons marinara sauce. Top with feta cheese, artichokes, tomato and turkey. Spread each ciabatta top with 2 tablespoons marinara sauce; place over turkey.

2. Cook on a panini maker or indoor grill for 4-5 minutes or until the cheese is melted. In a small microwaveable bowl, microwave remaining marinara sauce until warmed; serve with sandwiches.

GET RIGHT TO COOKING WITH A WELL-STOCKED KITCHEN

In a perfect world, you would plan out weekly or even monthly menus and have all the ingredients on hand to make each night's dinner. The reality, however, is you likely haven't thought about dinner until you've walked through the door.

With a reasonably stocked pantry, refrigerator and freezer, you'll still be able to serve a satisfying meal in short order. Consider these tips.

- **QUICK-COOKING MEATS** like boneless chicken breasts, chicken thighs, pork tenderloin, pork chops, ground meats, Italian sausage, sirloin and flank steaks, fish fillets and shrimp should be stocked in the freezer. Wrap the individually (except shrimp) so you can remove only the amount you need. For the quickest defrosting, wrap meat for freezing in small, thin packages.

- **FROZEN VEGETABLES** prepackaged in plastic bags are a real time-saver. Simply pour out the amount needed. No preparation required!

- **PASTAS, RICE, RICE MIXES AND COUSCOUS** are great staples to have in the pantry —and they generally have a long shelf life. Remember, thinner pastas, such as angel hair, cook faster than thicker pastas. Fresh (refrigerated) pasta cooks faster than dried.

- **DAIRY PRODUCTS** like milk, sour cream, cheeses (shredded, cubed or crumbled), eggs, yogurt and butter or margarine are more perishable, so check the use-by date on packages and replace as needed.

- **CONDIMENTS,** such as ketchup, mustard, mayonnaise, salad dressings, salsa, taco sauce, soy sauce, stir-fry sauce, lemon juice, etc., add flavor to many dishes. Personalize this list to suit your family's tastes.

- **FRESH FRUIT AND VEGETABLES** can make a satisfying predinner snack. Oranges and apples are not as perishable as bananas. Ready-to-use salad greens are handy for an instant salad.

- **DRIED HERBS, SPICES, VINEGARS** and seasoning mixes add flavor and keep for months.

- **PASTA SAUCES, OLIVES, BEANS,** broths, canned tomatoes, canned vegetables, and canned or dried soups are vital to have on hand for a quick meal—and many of these items are common recipe ingredients.

- **A POSTED GROCERY LIST** is an irreplaceable reference for your family. When an item is used up or almost gone, just tell your loved ones to add that to the list for the next shopping trip. This way, you won't completely run out of an item, and you'll save time when writing your grocery list.

HOME-STYLE *pot roast dinner*

[1993]

"My mother simply loved to cook. She was well-known for her delicious everyday dinners. Plus, it seemed she was always cooking for a wedding reception or some other party. My sister and I liked to help her whenever we could, and I certainly learned my way around the kitchen thanks to Mom."

—*Adeline Piscitelli, Sayreville, New Jersey*

OLD-FASHIONED POT ROAST

yield: 6-8 servings ∞ **prep: 15 min.** ∞ **cook: 2 hours**

I got this recipe from my mom, a great cook. My sister, dad and I loved it when she made her pot roast. Later, I served this dish in our restaurant for many years. It's a recipe that just says "home cooking."

- 1 boneless beef chuck roast (about 3 pounds)
- 6 tablespoons all-purpose flour, *divided*
- 6 tablespoons butter, *divided*
- 3 cups hot water
- 2 teaspoons beef bouillon granules
- 1 medium onion, quartered
- 1 celery rib, cut into pieces
- 1 teaspoon salt
- 1/2 teaspoon pepper
- 4 carrots, cut into 2-inch pieces

1. Sprinkle the roast with 1 tablespoon flour. In a Dutch oven, brown the roast on all sides in half of the butter. Add the water, bouillon, onion, celery, salt and pepper; bring to a boil. Reduce heat, cover and simmer for 1 hour.

2. Add carrots; cover and simmer 45-60 minutes longer or until meat is tender. Remove meat and carrots to a serving platter and keep warm. Strain cooking juices; set aside.

3. In the same Dutch oven, melt the remaining butter. Stir in the remaining flour; cook and stir until bubbly. Add 2 cups of the cooking juices and blend until smooth. Cook and stir until thickened; add additional cooking juices until gravy has desired consistency.

GARLIC-BUTTERED GREEN BEANS

yield: 6 servings ∞ prep/total time: 15 min.

These dressed-up beans are simple to make but look and taste special. They're a perfect side dish for nearly any meal.

- 1 **pound fresh *or* frozen green beans**
- 1/2 **cup sliced fresh mushrooms**
- 6 **tablespoons butter, cubed**
- 2 **to 3 teaspoons onion powder**
- 1 **to 1-1/2 teaspoons garlic powder**

Salt and pepper to taste

1. Place the green beans in a large saucepan, cover with water. Bring to a boil. Reduce heat; cover and cook for 8-10 minutes or until crisp-tender.

2. Meanwhile, in a large skillet, saute mushrooms in butter until tender. Add the onion powder and garlic powder. Drain the beans; add to skillet and toss. Season with salt and pepper.

PARSLEY POTATOES

yield: 6-8 servings
prep/total time: 30 min.

The fresh flavor of parsley is perfect with hot buttered potatoes. I used this recipe when I did all the cooking at our restaurant, and the customers loved it.

- 2 **pounds potatoes, peeled and cut into 2-inch pieces**
- 1/2 **cup butter, melted**
- 1/4 **cup minced fresh parsley**

Salt and pepper to taste

1. Place the potatoes in a large saucepan and cover with water. Bring to a boil. Reduce heat; cover and cook for 10-15 minutes or until tender. Drain.

2. Combine butter and parsley; pour over the potatoes and toss to coat. Season with salt and pepper.

PEACH BAVARIAN

yield: 8-10 servings
prep: 15 min. + chilling

(*Pictured on page 481*)

Fruit molds are my specialty, and I enjoy making and serving them. This one, with its refreshing peach taste, makes a colorful salad or dessert. It goes great with my mom's pot roast.

- 1 **can (15-1/4 ounces) sliced peaches**
- 2 **packages (3 ounces *each*) peach *or* apricot gelatin**
- 1/2 **cup sugar**
- 2 **cups boiling water**
- 1 **teaspoon almond extract**
- 1 **carton (8 ounces) frozen whipped topping, thawed**

Additional sliced peaches, optional

1. Drain peaches, reserving 2/3 cup juice. Chop the peaches into small pieces; set aside.

2. In a large bowl, dissolve the gelatin and sugar in boiling water. Stir in reserved syrup. Chill until slightly thickened. Stir the extract into whipped topping; gently fold in gelatin mixture. Fold in the peaches.

3. Pour into a 6-cup mold coated with cooking spray. Refrigerate overnight. Unmold onto a serving platter; garnish with additional peaches if desired.

OLD-FASHIONED POT ROAST

"Our supermarket has a sale on chuck roast, so I decided I'd make pot roast for dinner since it's been so cold. It had been so long since I made this dish that I came onto this (Taste of Home) website and found this recipe. It was outstanding and took almost no time to cook. I'm sure the leftovers will be even better. Thanks for sharing."
— bowrain99

OLD-TIME
beef & potato dinner

[1994]

"My mom has a reputation among family and friends for making the very best roast beef. She was born to be a good cook and rarely measures anything. On chilly days our home was filled with the heavenly aroma of her pot roast. Her secret ingredient for its rich flavor is brewed coffee."

—*Linda Gaido, New Brighton, Pennsylvania*

MOM'S ROAST BEEF
yield: 8 servings ∾ **prep: 20 min.** ∾ **cook: 2-1/2 hours**

(Pictured on page 484)

Everyone loves slices of this fork-tender roast beef and its savory gravy. This well-seasoned roast is Mom's specialty!

- 1 beef eye round roast (about 2-1/2 pounds)
- 1 tablespoon canola oil
- 1 medium onion, chopped
- 1 cup brewed coffee
- 1 cup cold water, *divided*
- 1 teaspoon beef bouillon granules
- 2 teaspoons dried basil
- 1 teaspoon dried rosemary, crushed
- 1 garlic clove, minced
- 1 teaspoon salt
- 1/2 teaspoon pepper
- 1/4 cup all-purpose flour

1. In a Dutch oven, brown roast in oil on all sides. Add onion; cook and stir until tender. Add the coffee, 3/4 cup water and bouillon to the pan. Combine the basil, rosemary, garlic, salt and pepper; sprinkle over the roast.

2. Bring to a boil. Reduce heat; cover and simmer for 2-1/2 hours or until meat is tender. Remove roast; let stand for 10 minutes before slicing.

3. Combine the flour and remaining water until smooth; stir into pan juices. Bring to a boil. Cook and stir for 1-2 minutes or until thickened. Serve gravy with roast.

OVEN-ROASTED POTATOES

yield: 4 servings ∞ prep: 10 min.
bake: 45 min.

(Pictured on page 488)

These golden, melt-in-your-mouth potatoes go perfectly with roast beef. They make a homey side dish that's also convenient because they can share the oven with the baked apple slices Mom serves for dessert.

4	large baking potatoes (about 2 pounds)
2	tablespoons butter, melted
2	teaspoons paprika
1	teaspoon salt
1/2	teaspoon pepper

1. Peel the potatoes and cut into large chunks; place in a shallow 2-qt. baking dish. Drizzle with the butter; toss to coat. Sprinkle with the paprika, salt and pepper.

2. Bake, uncovered, at 350° for 45-60 minutes or until potatoes are tender.

COUNTRY GREEN BEANS

yield: 4 servings ∞ prep/total time: 25 min.

This deliciously different way to dress up green beans is sure to become a hit at your house, too. The garlic, chopped ham and onion blend so well with the beans. It's a beautiful and tasty side dish that has real appeal.

1	pound fresh green beans, trimmed
1/4	cup chopped onion
1/4	cup cubed fully cooked ham
1/4	cup butter, cubed
1/4	cup water
1	garlic clove, minced
1/2	teaspoon salt
1/4	teaspoon pepper

1. In a large saucepan, combine all the ingredients. Bring to a boil. Reduce heat; cover and simmer for 8-10 minutes or until beans are crisp-tender. Drain if necessary.

BAKED APPLE SLICES

yield: 4 servings ∞ prep: 10 min.
bake: 45 min. + cooling

Nothing beats these tender apple slices over ice cream for satisfying harvest flavor. This old-fashioned treat gives a new twist to traditional baked apples. They are also excellent served over waffles or with ham.

3	large tart apples, peeled and sliced
3/4	cup sugar
1/4	cup apple cider *or* juice
3	teaspoons ground cinnamon
1/4	teaspoon ground nutmeg
1/4	teaspoon ground ginger
1/2	cup butter, cubed
1/2	cup walnuts *or* raisins

Vanilla ice cream

1. Place apples in a greased 1-qt. baking dish. In a small bowl, combine the sugar, cider, cinnamon, nutmeg and ginger; pour over apples. Dot with butter. Sprinkle with the nuts.

2. Bake, uncovered, at 350° for 45-60 minutes or until apples are tender. Serve warm with ice cream.

COUNTRY GREEN BEANS

"I don't cook with fresh vegetables but I wanted to start. I began with this green bean recipe and it was delicious. I'm doing it again this weekend."
— *Punskee*

SAUCY *spareribs & more*

[1995]

"A cherished childhood memory is stepping into the house after Sunday services and having the enchanting aroma of my mom's spareribs just envelop me. My mom, Thelma Arnold, taught me that cooking is an adventure, not a chore. To her, a high compliment from family or guests was a look of delight at a first mouthful. She liked to serve her finger-licking-good ribs with baked potatoes, garden peas and rolls."

—*Judy Clark, Elkhart, Indiana*

TANGY SPARERIBS

yield: 6-8 servings ∾ **prep: 30 min.** ∾ **bake: 1-1/2 hours**

I'll never forget the wonderful aroma of these spareribs cooking when I was growing up. They have a real old-fashioned flavor. Who can resist when that mouthwatering homemade barbecue sauce clings to every morsel?

4	to 5 pounds pork spareribs
1	medium onion, finely chopped
1/2	cup finely chopped celery
2	tablespoons butter
1	cup water
1	cup ketchup
1/3	cup lemon juice
2	tablespoons brown sugar
2	tablespoons white vinegar
1	tablespoon Worcestershire sauce
1/2	teaspoon ground mustard
1/8	teaspoon pepper
1/8	teaspoon chili powder

1. Cut ribs into serving-size pieces; place on a rack in a shallow roasting pan. Bake, uncovered, at 350° for 45 minutes.

2. Meanwhile in a large saucepan, saute onion and celery in butter for 4-5 minutes or until tender. Stir in the remaining ingredients. Bring to a boil. Reduce heat; cook and stir until slightly thickened, about 10 minutes. Remove from the heat.

3. Drain fat from roasting pan. Pour sauce over ribs. Bake 45-60 minutes longer or until tender.

ICEBOX BUTTERHORNS

yield: 2 dozen ∞ **prep: 15 min. + chilling**
bake: 15 min. + rising

These beautiful golden rolls just melt in your mouth! People will be impressed when these butterhorns appear on your table.

- 2 packages (1/4 ounce *each*) active dry yeast
- 1/4 cup warm water (110° to 115°)
- 2 cups warm milk (110° to 115°)
- 1/2 cup sugar
- 1 egg, lightly beaten
- 1 teaspoon salt
- 6-1/2 cups all-purpose flour
- 3/4 cup butter, melted
- Additional melted butter

1. In a large bowl, dissolve yeast in warm water. Add the milk, sugar, egg, salt and 3 cups flour; beat until smooth. Beat in butter and remaining flour (dough will be slightly sticky). DO NOT KNEAD. Place in a greased bowl. Cover and refrigerate overnight.

2. Punch down dough and divide in half. On a floured surface, roll each half into a 12-in. circle. Cut each circle into pie-shaped wedges. Beginning at the wide end, roll up each wedge. Place rolls, point side down, 2 in. apart on greased baking sheets. Cover and let rise in a warm place until doubled, about 1 hour.

3. Bake at 350° for 15-20 minutes or until golden brown. Immediately brush tops with melted butter. Remove from pans to wire racks to cool.

CHEERY CHERRY COOKIES

yield: 4 dozen ∞ **prep: 10 min.** ∞ **bake: 10 min./batch**

With a tall glass of ice-cold milk, a couple of cherry cookies really hit the spot for dessert or as a snack.

- 3/4 cup butter, softened
- 1 cup packed brown sugar
- 1 egg
- 2 tablespoons 2% milk
- 1 teaspoon vanilla extract
- 2 cups all-purpose flour
- 1/2 teaspoon salt
- 1/2 teaspoon baking soda
- 1/2 cup maraschino cherries, well drained and chopped
- 1/2 cup chopped pecans
- 1/2 cup flaked coconut

1. In a large bowl, cream butter and brown sugar until light and fluffy. Beat in egg, milk and vanilla. Combine flour, salt and baking soda; gradually add to creamed mixture and mix well. Fold in cherries, pecans and coconut.

2. Drop by teaspoonfuls onto ungreased baking sheets. Bake at 375° for 10-12 minutes or until golden brown. Remove to wire racks to cool.

HOMEMADE FROZEN CUSTARD

yield: 1-1/2 quarts ∞ **prep: 20 min. + freezing**

My siblings and I had a hard time finding room for dessert after Mom's meals, but when we were ready, we could count on some creamy frozen custard.

- 4 cups milk
- 1-1/4 cups sugar
- 1/3 cup cornstarch
- 1/8 teaspoon salt
- 4 eggs
- 1 can (14 ounces) sweetened condensed milk
- 2 tablespoons vanilla extract

1. In a large saucepan, heat milk to 175°; stir in sugar, cornstarch and salt until dissolved. Whisk a small amount of the hot mixture into the eggs. Return all to the pan, whisking constantly. Cook and stir over low heat until mixture reaches at least 160° and coats the back of a metal spoon.

2. Remove from the heat. Cool quickly by placing pan in a bowl of ice water; stir for 2 minutes. Stir in condensed milk and vanilla. Press waxed paper onto surface of custard. Refrigerate for several hours or overnight.

3. Fill cylinder of ice cream freezer two-thirds full; freeze according to the manufacturer's directions. Refrigerate remaining mixture until ready to freeze. When ice cream is frozen, transfer to a freezer container; freeze for 2-4 hours before serving.

TRADITIONAL
german meal

[1996]

❝I was just 18 when I married and came to America from Germany. Since it was my first time away from my family, I was very homesick. One thing I found that helped to ease my longing for home and my mother, Annelies Hupfeld, was to cook some of her Sunday dinners, such as the rouladen dinner that follows.❞

—*Karen Cousineau, Burlington, North Carolina*

BEEF ROULADEN

yield: 8 servings ∾ prep: 35 min. ∾ cook: 1-3/4 hours

(*Pictured on page 484*)

Our family was poor when I was growing up in Germany, so we ate garden vegetables for many weekday meals. When Mother made meat for a Sunday dinner, it was a terrific treat. My favorite is this tender beef dish, which gets great flavor from Dijon mustard.

1/4 cup Dijon mustard
   8 slices beef top round steak (1/4 inch thick and about 2 pounds)
Salt and pepper to taste
   8 bacon strips
   1 large onion, cut into thin wedges
   3 tablespoons canola oil
   3 cups beef broth
1/3 cup all-purpose flour
1/2 cup water
Chopped fresh parsley, optional

---

1. Lightly spread mustard on each slice of steak; sprinkle with salt and pepper. Place 1 bacon strip and a few onion wedges on each slice; roll up; secure with toothpicks.

2. In a large skillet, brown beef in oil until no longer pink; drain. Add broth; bring to a boil. Reduce heat; cover and simmer for 1-1/2 hours or until meat is tender.

3. Remove meat and keep warm. Combine flour and water until smooth; gradually stir into broth. Bring to a boil, stirring constantly until thickened and bubbly. Remove toothpicks from rolls and return to gravy; heat through. Sprinkle with parsley if desired.

SPICED RED CABBAGE

yield: 6 servings ∞ **prep: 10 min.** ∞ **cook: 1-1/4 hours**

When it comes to vegetable dishes, this traditional one is at the top of my list. The wonderful sweet-sour aroma and taste remind me of home. Plus, it looks so pretty on the table.

- 1/2 medium head red cabbage, diced
- 1 tablespoon canola oil
- 1/2 cup chopped onion
- 1 medium tart apple, quartered
- 3 tablespoons tarragon vinegar
- 1 tablespoon sugar
- 1 bay leaf
- 1 teaspoon salt, optional
- 1/4 teaspoon pepper
- 1/8 teaspoon ground cloves

1. In a large saucepan, bring 1 in. of water and cabbage to a boil. Reduce heat; cover and simmer for 3-5 minutes or until crisp-tender; drain. Return to pan; stir in remaining ingredients. Cover and simmer for 1 hour or until cabbage is tender. Discard bay leaf.

SPECIAL POTATO DUMPLINGS

yield: 6-8 servings ∞ **prep: 45 min. + chilling** ∞ **cook: 15 min.**

(Pictured on page 484)

These moist dumplings are an extra-special way to serve potatoes. The bread centers add a comforting touch, and the potato flavor really comes through. They go so well with my mother's Beef Rouladen and gravy.

- 5 to 6 medium potatoes
- 5 tablespoons all-purpose flour
- 1 egg, lightly beaten
- 1-1/2 teaspoons salt
- 1/4 teaspoon ground nutmeg
- 2 slices white bread, toasted
- 1/3 cup mashed potato flakes, optional

Melted butter and toasted bread crumbs, optional

1. Place the potatoes in a large saucepan and cover with water. Bring to a boil. Reduce heat; cover and simmer for 15-20 minutes or until tender. Drain. Refrigerate for 2 hours or overnight.

2. Peel and grate potatoes. In a large bowl, combine the flour, egg, salt and nutmeg. Add potatoes and mix until a stiff batter is formed, adding additional flour if necessary.

3. Slice toasted bread into 24 squares, 1/2-in. each; shape 2 tablespoons of the potato mixture around two bread squares, forming a 2-in. ball.

4. In a large stock pot, bring salted water to a boil; add the test dumpling. Reduce the heat; cover and simmer for 15-20 minutes or until dumpling is no longer sticky in the center.

5. If test dumpling falls apart during cooking, add mashed potato flakes to the batter. Let batter sit for 5 minutes; form remaining dumplings. Add to boiling water; return to a boil and follow the same cooking procedure.

6. Remove the dumplings with a slotted spoon to a serving bowl. If desired, drizzle with butter and sprinkle with bread crumbs.

APPLE DATE CRISP

yield: 6-8 servings ∞ **prep: 20 min.** ∞ **bake: 35 min.**

My mother loves to make this old-fashioned dessert, and my father, brother and I love to eat it. Each serving is chock-full of apple slices, crunchy nuts and chewy dates. It's a satisfying way to end a delicious meal.

- 8 cups sliced peeled tart apples
- 2 cups chopped dates
- 2/3 cup packed brown sugar
- 1/2 cup all-purpose flour
- 1 teaspoon ground cinnamon
- 1/3 cup cold butter, cubed
- 1 cup chopped nuts

Additional apple slices, optional

1. In an ungreased 13-in. x 9-in. baking dish, combine apples and dates. In a small bowl, combine the sugar, flour and cinnamon; cut in butter until crumbly. Add nuts; sprinkle over apples.

2. Bake at 375° for 35-40 minutes or until the apples are tender. Serve warm. Garnish with apple slices if desired.

SOUTHWESTERN
inspired dinner

[1997]

❝My mother, Lupe Mirabal, had the daily challenge of preparing economical foods that could feed a family of 10 and would appeal to all of us. She used her skills as a nutritionist to fix foods that would fit into my father's diet and still be tasty and keep us well-fed. I'm grateful for the cooking skills I learned from her, and I make her delicious recipes for my own family.❞

—*Jerri Moror, Rio Rancho, New Mexico*

CHICKEN TORTILLA BAKE
yield: 6-8 servings ⌘ **prep: 20 min.** ⌘ **bake: 30 min.**

Mother frequently made this heartwarming casserole when I was growing up. Our family would scrape the pan clean. Chicken, cheese and zippy green chilies are a classic, comforting mix.

- 3 cups shredded cooked chicken
- 2 cans (4 ounces each) chopped green chilies
- 1 cup chicken broth
- 1 can (10-3/4 ounces) condensed cream of mushroom soup, undiluted
- 1 can (10-3/4 ounces) condensed cream of chicken soup, undiluted
- 1 small onion, finely chopped
- 12 corn tortillas, warmed
- 2 cups (8 ounces) shredded cheddar cheese, *divided*

1. In a large bowl, combine the chicken, chilies, broth, soups and onion; set aside. Layer half of the tortillas in a greased 13-in. x 9-in. baking dish, cutting to fit pan if desired. Top with half of the chicken mixture and half of the cheese. Repeat layers.

2. Bake, uncovered, at 350° for 30 minutes or until heated through.

SOUTHWESTERN CORN CHIP SALAD

yield: 8 servings ∞ prep/total time: 15 min.

You get an explosion of Southwestern flavor in every bite of this deliciously different salad. It's a favorite for kids of all ages since it mixes beans and cheese, tasty vegetables and crisp corn chips.

2-1/2 cups corn chips
1/2 head iceberg lettuce, torn
1 cup (4 ounces) shredded Mexican cheese blend *or* cheddar cheese
1 can (15 ounces) pinto beans, rinsed and drained
1 small tomato, seeded and diced
1/4 to 1/2 cup salad dressing of your choice
2 tablespoons sliced green onions
1 to 2 tablespoons chopped green chilies
1 small avocado, peeled and sliced

1. In a serving bowl or platter, toss together the chips, lettuce, cheese, beans, tomato, salad dressing, onions and chilies. Top with avocado. Serve immediately.

QUICK SPANISH RICE

yield: 6 servings ∞ prep/total time: 30 min.

We were always glad to see a big bowl of this festive rice on the table. My mom developed this mild version using ingredients she had on hand. It pairs perfectly with chicken or any other meat.

1 cup uncooked long grain rice
2 tablespoons canola oil
1 small onion, chopped
1 garlic clove, minced
1/2 teaspoon salt, optional
1 cup water
1 cup chicken *or* vegetable broth
2 large tomatoes, peeled and chopped
1/3 cup frozen peas, thawed
1/3 cup diced cooked carrots

1. In a large skillet over medium heat, saute rice in oil until lightly browned. Add the onion, garlic and salt if desired; cook over low heat until onion is tender.

2. Add water and broth. Bring to a boil. Reduce heat; cover and simmer until water is almost absorbed. Stir in the tomatoes, peas and carrots; cover and cook until liquid is absorbed and vegetables are heated through.

ANISE CUTOUT COOKIES

yield: 5 dozen ∞ prep: 20 min. ∞ bake: 15 min./batch

Mother prepared these soft cookies for holidays and special-occasion meals. My seven siblings and I gobbled them up as fast as she made them. I still can't resist the cinnamon-sugar coating.

2 cups shortening
1 cup sugar
2 eggs
2 teaspoons aniseed
6 cups all-purpose flour
1 tablespoon baking powder
1 teaspoon salt
1/4 cup apple juice
1/2 cup sugar
1 teaspoon ground cinnamon

1. In a bowl, cream the shortening and sugar until fluffy; add the eggs and aniseed. Combine the flour, baking powder and salt; add to the creamed mixture. Add apple juice and mix well.

2. On a floured surface, knead until well blended, about 4-5 minutes. Roll dough to 1/2-in. thickness; cut into 2-in. shapes. Place 2 in. apart on greased baking sheets.

3. Bake at 375° for 12-16 minutes or until lightly browned. Combine sugar and cinnamon; roll cookies in the mixture while still warm. Cool on wire racks.

COMFORTING *family supper*

[1998]

"Just as my mom, Ruth Toth, did for years, I love cooking for others. I've collected lot of recipes, but the best ones are those Mom passed on to me, and now I am sharing them with my daughter-in-law and granddaughter. This is one of my mom's best meals.
—*Barbara Hyatt, Folsom, California*

CITY KABOBS

yield: 4-6 servings ∽ prep: 20 min. ∽ cook: 20 min.

(*Pictured on page 488*)

This old-fashioned mock chicken dish, actually made of tender perfectly seasoned pork, is one that my mom relied on often during 55 years of marriage. The delicious gravy is really good over mashed potatoes.

- 2 pounds boneless pork, cut into 1-inch cubes
- 1/2 cup all-purpose flour
- 1/2 teaspoon garlic salt
- 1/4 teaspoon pepper
- 1/4 cup butter, cubed
- 3 tablespoons canola oil
- 1 envelope onion soup mix
- 1 can (14-1/2 ounces) chicken broth
- 1 cup water

Hot mashed potatoes

1. Thread pork on small wooden skewers. Combine the flour, garlic salt and pepper on a plate; roll kabobs in flour mixture until coated.

2. In a large skillet over medium heat, brown kabobs in butter and oil, turning frequently; drain. Sprinkle with soup mix. Add broth and water. Bring to a boil. Reduce heat; cover and simmer for 8-10 minutes or until tender.

3. Remove kabobs and keep warm. If desired, thicken pan juices and serve with mashed potatoes and kabobs.

OIL AND VINEGAR DRESSING

yield: 2 cups ∾ prep/total time: 10 min.

The goodness of crisp salad ingredients comes through when topped with this simple homemade dressing. It tastes so fresh.

- 1 cup sugar
- 1 tablespoon ground mustard
- 1 teaspoon salt
- 1/2 teaspoon pepper
- 1/2 teaspoon paprika
- 1/2 cup hot water
- 1/4 cup cider vinegar
- 2 garlic cloves, halved
- 1/4 cup canola oil

Mixed salad greens and shredded red cabbage

1. In a 1-qt. jar with a tight-fitting lid, combine the first five ingredients. Add water, vinegar and garlic; shake until sugar is dissolved. Add oil; shake well. Refrigerate. Just before serving, remove garlic from dressing. Drizzle over salad greens and red cabbage.

CHUNKY CINNAMON APPLESAUCE

yield: 6 cups ∾ prep: 20 min.
cook: 20 min.

As a girl, I was amazed when Mom turned fresh apples into this delightful mixture. I'm not sure if I liked it so much because it was made with candies or because it tasted wonderful.

- 8 medium tart apples, peeled and quartered
- 1 cup water
- 1 cup sugar
- 1/4 cup red-hot candies

1. Place apples and water in a 5-qt. saucepan. Cover and cook over medium-low heat for 15-20 minutes or until tender.

2. Mash until sauce is desired consistency. Add sugar and candies. Cook, uncovered, until sugar and candies are dissolved; stirring frequently. Remove from the heat; cool. Refrigerate until serving.

MOM'S CUSTARD PIE

yield: 8 servings ∾ prep: 25 min.
bake: 40 min. + cooling

Just a single bite of this traditional treat takes me back to the days when Mom would fix this pie for Dad, Grandfather and me. Mom also regularly prepared pies for large gatherings.

- 1 unbaked pastry shell (9 inches)
- 4 eggs
- 1/2 cup sugar
- 1/4 teaspoon salt
- 1 teaspoon vanilla extract
- 2-1/2 cups 2% milk
- 1/4 teaspoon ground nutmeg

1. Line unpricked pastry shell with a double thickness of heavy-duty foil. Bake at 450° for 8 minutes. Remove foil; bake 5 minutes longer. Remove from the oven and set aside.

2. Separate one egg; set the white aside. In a small bowl, beat the yolk and remaining eggs just until combined. Blend in the sugar, salt and vanilla. Stir in milk. Beat reserved egg white until stiff peaks form; fold into egg mixture.

3. Carefully pour into crust. Cover the edges of the pie with foil. Bake at 350° for 25 minutes. Remove foil; bake 15-20 minutes longer or until a knife inserted near the center comes out clean. Cool on a wire rack. Sprinkle with nutmeg. Store in the refrigerator.

MOM'S CUSTARD PIE

"I saw this recipe in *Taste of Home* online a year or so ago. I tried it and my family loves it. I made this Custard Pie as a baked custard. I didn't change the recipe at all—just baked in small dishes covered 3/4 with water in a turkey pan. Yes, I use a turkey pan. My family likes this recipe so much I have to double it. This custard doesn't have a water on top after the custard has been cooled. I don't know, but maybe it's the egg that has been beaten and added. Thank you, Taste of Home, for all the great recipes that you have supplied."
—carolynstower

FAMILY-PLEASING *supper*

[1999]

"For my mom, Edythe Wagy, preparing an evening meal for our family was not a chore but a labor of love. In those days, she was a real homemaker. She not only loved to sew, cook and bake, she also strived to make our home a warm and inviting place. Mom hosted many large gatherings when my two brothers and I were growing up. Everyone looked forward to a satisfying meal like the one that follows."
—Linda McGinty, Parma, Ohio

SO-TENDER SWISS STEAK

yield: 8 servings ∞ **prep: 30 min.** ∞ **bake: 2 hours**

Swiss steak with wonderful gravy was an often-requested main dish around our house when I was growing up. Mom took pride in preparing scrumptious, hearty meals like this for our family and guests.

- 1/4 **cup all-purpose flour**
- 1/2 **teaspoon salt**
- 1/4 **teaspoon pepper**
- 2 **pounds beef top round steak, cut into serving-size pieces**
- 2 **tablespoons canola oil**
- 1 **medium onion, thinly sliced**
- 2 **cups water**
- 2 **tablespoons Worcestershire sauce**

GRAVY:
- 1/4 **cup all-purpose flour**
- 1/4 **teaspoon salt**
- 1/8 **teaspoon pepper**
- 1-1/4 **cups beef broth or water**

Hot cooked noodles or mashed potatoes, optional

1. In a large resealable plastic bag, combine the flour, salt and pepper. Add the steak, a few pieces at a time and shake to coat. Remove meat from bag and pound with a mallet to tenderize.

2. In a Dutch oven over medium-high heat , brown the steak in oil on both sides. Arrange the onion slices between layers of the meat. Add the water and Worcestershire sauce.

3. Cover and bake at 325° for 2 to 2-1/2 hours or until meat is very tender. Remove to a serving platter and keep warm.

4. In a small bowl, combine the flour, salt, pepper and broth until smooth; stir into pan juices. Bring to a boil over medium heat; cook and stir for 2 minutes or until thickened. Serve steak and gravy with noodles or mashed potatoes if desired.

CAULIFLOWER CASSEROLE

(Pictured on page 488)

yield: 6-8 servings ∞ **prep: 15 min.** ∞ **bake: 30 min.**

To dress up cauliflower, my mom used a delightful mixture of a cheesy sauce, colorful pepper pieces and crushed cornflakes. We enjoyed this casserole so much that leftovers were rare.

- 1 **medium head cauliflower, broken into florets**
- 1 **cup (8 ounces) sour cream**
- 1 **cup (4 ounces) shredded cheddar cheese**
- 1/2 **cup crushed cornflakes**
- 1/4 **cup chopped green pepper**
- 1/4 **cup chopped sweet red pepper**
- 1 **teaspoon salt**
- 1/4 **cup grated Parmesan cheese**

Paprika

1. Place 1 in. of water in a saucepan; add cauliflower. Bring to a boil. Reduce heat; cover and simmer for 5-10 minutes or until crisp-tender. Drain.

2. In a large bowl, combine the cauliflower, sour cream, cheddar cheese, cornflakes, peppers and salt; transfer to a greased 2-qt. baking dish. Sprinkle with Parmesan cheese and paprika.

3. Bake, uncovered, at 325° for 30-35 minutes or until heated through.

STRAWBERRY PEAR GELATIN

yield: 12-16 servings ⤳ **prep: 15 min. + chilling**

Mother always had a way of making every dish she served just a little more special. A good example is this fluffy salad. It's both fruity and refreshing.

1 can (29 ounces) pears
1 package (6 ounces) strawberry gelatin
1 package (8 ounces) cream cheese, cubed
1 carton (8 ounces) frozen whipped topping, thawed
Mandarin oranges, optional

1. Drain pears, reserving juice. Chop pears and set aside. Add water to the juice to measure 3 cups. Place in a saucepan; bring to a boil. Add gelatin and stir until dissolved. Whisk in cream cheese until smooth. Refrigerate until slightly thickened. Whisk in whipped topping until smooth. Add chopped pears.

2. Transfer to a 13-in. x 9-in. dish. Cover and refrigerate until firm. Cut into squares. Garnish with mandarin oranges if desired.

SMOOTH & CREAMY GELATIN

If the gelatin is not completely dissolved when it is heated, the salad may have little gritty pieces in it. Cut the cream cheese into cubes then let soften at room temperature for 20 minutes. Whisk the cream cheese into the gelatin mixture until no lumps remain.

—*Taste Of Home Cooking Experts*

MOM'S CHOCOLATE CAKE

yield: 12-15 servings ⤳ **prep: 20 min. + cooling**
bake: 35 min. + cooling

Over the years, Mother has become known for wonderful from-scratch desserts like this old-fashioned chocolate cake topped with a yummy, rich frosting. It was difficult, but my brothers and I always managed to save room for dessert.

2 ounces unsweetened chocolate, broken into pieces
1/2 cup boiling water
1/2 cup shortening
2 cups packed brown sugar
2 eggs, *separated*
2 cups sifted cake flour
2 teaspoons baking powder
1/2 teaspoon baking soda
1/2 teaspoon salt
1/2 cup buttermilk
1/2 cup water
1/2 cup chopped walnuts
1 teaspoon vanilla extract
COCOA FROSTING:
6 tablespoons butter, softened
3-1/2 cups confectioners' sugar
1/2 cup baking cocoa
1-1/2 teaspoons vanilla extract
Pinch salt
4 to 6 tablespoons milk

1. In a small bowl, stir chocolate in boiling water until melted; cool for 10 minutes.

2. In a bowl, cream shortening and brown sugar. Beat in egg yolks and chocolate mixture. Combine flour, baking powder, baking soda and salt; add to creamed mixture alternately with buttermilk. Gradually beat in water, nuts and vanilla.

3. In a small bowl, beat egg whites until soft peaks form; fold into batter. Pour into a greased 13-in. x 9-in. baking pan. Bake at 350° for 35-40 minutes or until toothpick inserted near center comes out clean. Cool on wire rack.

4. In a bowl, cream butter. Combine sugar and cocoa; gradually add to butter with vanilla, salt and enough milk to achieve desired spreading consistency. Frost cake.

SOUTHERN *sunday supper*

[2000]

"When my brother and I were growing up, Mom, Maxine Haynes, and Dad both loved to cook. Even though there were only four of us, they cooked like they were feeding an army. Over the years, Mom and Dad owned and operated three restaurants. Mom's favorite meal—the one featured here—was on every menu."

—*Sandra Pichon, Memphis, Tennessee, Field Editor*

SUNDAY PORK ROAST

yield: 10-12 servings ∞ prep: 20 min. ∞ bake: 1 hour 20 minutes + standing
(*Pictured on page 486*)

Mom has prepared this delectable main dish numerous times over the years for our family, friends and customers at the restaurants she and Dad owned. It has a remarkable flavor.

 4 tablespoons all-purpose flour, *divided*
 1 teaspoon salt
 1 teaspoon pepper
 1 bay leaf, very finely crushed *or* ground
1/2 teaspoon dried thyme
 1 bone-in pork loin roast (4 to 5 pounds)
 2 medium onions, chopped
 2 medium carrots, chopped
 1 celery rib, chopped
2-1/3 cups cold water, *divided*
1/3 cup packed brown sugar

1. Combine 2 tablespoons flour, salt, pepper, bay leaf and thyme; rub over entire roast. Place roast with fat side up on a rack in a large shallow roasting pan. Arrange vegetables around the roast. Pour 2 cups cold water into pan.

2. Bake, uncovered, at 350° for 50 minutes, basting with pan juices every 30 minutes.

3. Sprinkle with brown sugar. Bake 30-40 minutes longer or until a thermometer reads 145°. Let meat stand for 10 minutes before slicing.

4. Meanwhile, strain pan drippings into a 2-cup measuring cup. Add water to measure 1-2/3 cups; skim fat. Discard vegetables. Return drippings to pan. Combine the remaining flour and cold water until smooth. Gradually stir into drippings. Bring to a boil; cook and stir for 2 minutes or until thickened. Serve with roast.

MOM'S SWEET POTATO BAKE
yield: 8-10 servings ∽ **prep: 10 min.** ∽ **bake: 45 min.**

Mom loves sweet potatoes and fixed them often in this creamy, comforting casserole. With its nutty topping, this side dish could almost serve as a dessert. It's a yummy treat!

- 3 cups cold mashed sweet potatoes (prepared without milk *or* butter)
- 1 cup sugar
- 3 eggs
- 1/2 cup 2% milk
- 1/4 cup butter, softened
- 1 teaspoon salt
- 1 teaspoon vanilla extract

TOPPING:
- 1/2 cup packed brown sugar
- 1/2 cup chopped pecans
- 1/4 cup all-purpose flour
- 2 tablespoons cold butter

1. In a large bowl, beat the sweet potatoes, sugar, eggs, milk, butter, salt and vanilla until smooth. Transfer to a greased 2-qt. baking dish.

2. In a small bowl, combine the brown sugar, pecans and flour; cut in butter until crumbly. Sprinkle over potato mixture. Bake, uncovered, at 325° for 45-50 minutes or until a thermometer reads 160°.

COUNTRY TURNIP GREENS
yield: 8-10 servings ∽ **prep: 10 min.** ∽ **cook: 50 min.**

This easy recipe results in a delicious dish of cooked greens sure to please any palate. The key is the rich flavor of pork and onion simmered with the fresh greens.

- 3/4 pound lean salt pork *or* bacon, diced
- 4-1/2 pounds fresh turnip greens, trimmed
- 1-1/2 cups water
- 1 large onion, chopped
- 1 teaspoon sugar
- 1/4 to 1/2 teaspoon pepper

1. In a Dutch oven, cook salt pork until lightly browned. Drain, reserving 2 tablespoons of drippings.

2. Stir the remaining ingredients into the reserved drippings. Bring to a boil. Reduce heat; cover and simmer for 45 minutes or until greens are tender.

DIXIE PIE
yield: 2 pies (6-8 servings each)
prep: 20 min. + cooling ∽ **bake: 30 min. + cooling**

When Mom baked this old-fashioned sugar pie, family members would clamor for second servings. We love the combination of cinnamon, coconut, nuts and raisins. She'd sometimes toss in a few chocolate chips for variety. Thanksgiving and Christmas dinner were not complete without this dessert.

Pastry for two single-crust pies (9 inches)
- 1-1/2 cups raisins
- 1 cup butter, softened
- 1 cup sugar
- 1 cup packed brown sugar
- 6 eggs
- 2 teaspoons vanilla extract
- 2 to 4 teaspoons ground cinnamon
- 1 cup chopped nuts
- 1 cup flaked coconut

Whipped topping and additional chopped nuts, optional.

1. Line two 9-in. pie plates with pastry. Trim pastry to 1/2 in. beyond edge of plate; flute edges. Line crusts with a double thickness of heavy-duty foil. Bake at 450° for 10 minutes. Discard foil. Cool on wire racks.

2. Place raisins in a saucepan and cover with water; bring to a boil. Remove from the heat; set aside. In a large bowl, cream butter and sugars until light and fluffy. Beat in eggs, vanilla and cinnamon until blended.

3. Drain raisins. Stir the raisins, nuts and coconut into creamed mixture (mixture will appear curdled). Pour into the crusts.

4. Bake at 350° for 30-35 minutes or until set. Cool on wire racks. Garnish with whipped topping and nuts if desired.

LASAGNA *and the fixings*

[2001]

*"*I remember my mom, Cindy Robbins, always making sure we had a home-cooked meal when we were growing up, no matter how busy the day. Mom is a self-taught cook who enjoys preparing food. When my sister and I were younger, she would make us our favorite dinners on our birthdays. I always chose this lasagna.*"*

—*Kim Orr, West Grove, Pennsylvania*

MOM'S LASAGNA

yield: 12 servings ∞ **prep: 40 min.**
bake: 45 min. + standing

(Pictured on page 487)

One of my mom's special recipes, this Italian classic is requested time and again. The made-from-scratch sauce gives each cheesy slice home-style flavor and a softer texture than many other versions of lasagna.

- 1   pound ground beef
- 2   garlic cloves, minced
- 1-1/2 cups water
- 1   can (15 ounces) tomato sauce
- 1   can (6 ounces) tomato paste
- 1/2 to 1 envelope onion soup mix
- 1   teaspoon dried oregano
- 1/2 teaspoon sugar
- 1/4 teaspoon pepper
- 9   lasagna noodles, cooked and drained
- 2   cups (16 ounces) 4% cottage cheese
- 4   cups (16 ounces) shredded part-skim mozzarella cheese
- 2   cups grated Parmesan cheese

1. In a large saucepan, cook beef over medium heat until meat is no longer pink. Add garlic; cook 1 minute longer. Drain. Stir in the water, tomato sauce and paste, soup mix, oregano, sugar and pepper. Bring to a boil. Reduce heat; cover and simmer for 30 minutes.

2. Spoon 1/2 cup meat sauce into a greased 13-in. x 9-in. baking dish. Layer with three noodles and a third of the cottage cheese, mozzarella, meat sauce and Parmesan cheese. Repeat layers twice.

3. Cover and bake at 350° for 40 minutes or until bubbly and heated through. Uncover; bake 5-10 minutes longer. Let stand for 10 minutes before cutting.

THOUSAND ISLAND SALAD DRESSING

yield: 1-1/2 cups ∞ **prep/total time: 10 min.**

This comforting homemade dressing is chock-full of tasty ingredients, including chopped onion, celery and hard-cooked eggs. It's a delightful topping for any crisp green salad.

- 1   cup mayonnaise
- 1/4 cup chili sauce
- 2   hard-cooked eggs, chopped
- 2   tablespoons chopped green onion
- 2   tablespoons chopped celery
- 4-1/2 teaspoons finely chopped onion
- 1   teaspoon paprika
- 1/2 teaspoon salt
- Salad greens

1. In a small bowl, combine all the ingredients. Cover and refrigerate until serving. Serve with salad greens.

CHIVE GARLIC BREAD

yield: 12 servings ∞ **prep/total time: 30 min.**

(Pictured on page 483)

A purchased loaf of French bread gets a real boost with a few simple ingredients. Garlic and chives make the savory slices irresistible. Along with lasagna or another Italian main dish, we munch them until the last crumbs have vanished!

- 1/4 **cup butter, softened**
- 1/4 **cup grated Parmesan cheese**
- 2 **tablespoons minced chives**
- 1 **garlic clove, minced**
- 1 **loaf (1 pound) French bread, cut into 1-inch slices**

1. In a small bowl, combine the butter, cheese, chives and garlic. Spread on one side of each slice of bread; wrap in a large piece of heavy-duty foil. Seal the edges.

2. Place on a baking sheet. Bake at 350° for 25-30 minutes or until heated through.

OLD-FASHIONED CARROT CAKE

yield: 12 servings ∞ **prep: 30 min. bake: 35 min. + cooling**

(Pictured on page 487)

A pleasingly moist cake, this treat is the one I requested that my mom make each year for my birthday. It's dotted with sweet carrots and a hint of cinnamon. The fluffy buttery frosting is scrumptious with chopped walnuts stirred in. One piece of this cake is never enough!

- 4 **eggs**
- 2 **cups sugar**
- 1 **cup canola oil**
- 2 **cups all-purpose flour**
- 2 **to 3 teaspoons ground cinnamon**
- 3/4 **teaspoon baking soda**
- 1/2 **teaspoon baking powder**
- 1/4 **teaspoon salt**
- 1/4 **teaspoon ground nutmeg**
- 2 **cups grated carrots**

FROSTING:
- 1/2 **cup butter, softened**
- 1 **package (3 ounces) cream cheese, softened**
- 1 **teaspoon vanilla extract**
- 3-3/4 **cups confectioners' sugar**
- 2 **to 3 tablespoons 2% milk**
- 1 **cup chopped walnuts**

Orange and green food coloring, optional

1. In a large bowl, combine the eggs, sugar and oil. Combine the flour, cinnamon, baking soda, baking powder, salt and nutmeg; beat into egg mixture. Stir in carrots.

2. Pour into two greased and floured 9-in. round baking pans. Bake at 350° for 35-40 minutes or until a toothpick inserted near the center comes out clean. Cool for 10 minutes before removing from pans to wire racks to cool completely.

3. For frosting, in another large bowl, cream butter and cream cheese until light and fluffy. Beat in the vanilla. Gradually beat in confectioners' sugar. Add enough milk to achieve desired spreading consistency. Reserve 1/2 cup frosting for decorating if desired. Stir walnuts into remaining frosting.

4. Spread frosting between layers and over top and sides of cake. If decorating the cake, tint 1/4 cup reserved frosting orange and 1/4 cup green. Cut a small hole in the corner of pastry or plastic bag; insert #7 round pastry tip. Fill the bag with orange frosting. Pipe twelve carrots on top of cake, so that each slice will have a carrot. Using #67 leaf pastry tip and the green frosting, pipe a leaf at the top of each carrot.

5. Store cake in the refrigerator.

CHIVE GARLIC BREAD

"Delicious, homemade garlic bread. This is a no-fail recipe!"
—*lurky, 27*

CLASSIC *easter feast*

[2002]

"Easter was a memorable time when I was growing up on our family farm. After coming home from church in the morning, Mom, June Mullin, would serve the most terrific Easter dinner later in the afternoon. Preparing delicious recipes like the ones that follow was one of the many ways she showed her love for us."

—*Lorrie Bailey, Pulaski, Iowa*

PINEAPPLE MUSTARD HAM

yield: 16-20 servings ∞ prep: 5 min.
bake: 2-1/4 hours

Sweet and spicy ingredients combine in a fruity glaze to top my mom's delightful ham, which was one of her many specialities. Our family enjoyed it many times for Easter. The horseradish and mustard in the glaze add delicious zip to the ham.

- 1 fully cooked bone-in spiral-sliced ham (8 to 10 pounds)
- 1 jar (12 ounces) apple jelly
- 1 jar (12 ounces) pineapple ice cream topping
- 1 container (1-3/4 ounces) ground mustard
- 2 tablespoons prepared horseradish
- 1 tablespoon pepper

1. Place ham on a rack in a shallow roasting pan. Cover and bake at 325° for 1-3/4 hours.

2. In a small bowl, combine remaining ingredients until blended. Pour over the ham. Bake, uncovered, 30-45 minutes longer or until a thermometer reads 140°.

BROCCOLI VEGETABLE SALAD

yield: 16-20 servings ∞ prep/total time: 15 min.

Carrot, celery and tomatoes go so well with broccoli and cauliflower in this crisp, refreshing salad with a light vinaigrette dressing. My mom used this popular salad to round out a variety of different meals. Even when made ahead, it didn't get soggy.

- 1 medium head cauliflower, broken into florets (about 8 cups)
- 1 medium bunch broccoli, cut into florets (about 5 cups)
- 3 large tomatoes, chopped
- 1 medium onion, chopped
- 2 celery ribs, chopped
- 1 medium carrot, shredded

DRESSING:
- 3/4 cup canola oil
- 3 tablespoons lemon juice
- 1 teaspoon salt
- 1/2 teaspoon sugar
- 1/2 teaspoon pepper

1. In a large salad bowl, combine the cauliflower, broccoli, tomatoes, onion, celery and carrot. In a small bowl, whisk the dressing ingredients. Pour over vegetables and toss to coat.

CINNAMON-PECAN COFFEE CAKES, page 501

PEACH BAVARIAN, page 463

TENDER FLANK STEAK, page 498

CHIVE GARLIC BREAD, page 479

NENA'S PAPAS RELLENAS, page 506

BROILED GRAPEFRUIT, page 500

BEEF ROULADEN, page 468 with SPECIAL POTATO DUMPLINGS, page 469

MOM'S ROAST BEEF, page 464

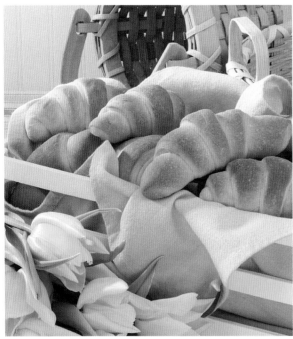

BUTTERY CRESCENTS, page 493

ORANGE 'N' RED ONION SALAD, page 497

CARROT SALAD, page 505

CHEDDAR TWICE-BAKED POTATOES, page 499

SUNDAY PORK ROAST, page 476

MOM'S LASAGNA, page 478

OLD-FASHIONED CARROT CAKE, page 479

RASPBERRY TOSSED SALAD, page 491

CITY KABOBS, page 472

OVEN-ROASTED POTATOES, page 465

LEMON BAKED ALASKA, page 493

CAULIFLOWER CASSEROLE, page 474

HOT CROSS BUNS

**yield: 2 dozen   prep: 40 min. + rising
bake: 15 min. + cooling**

These golden buns, with a light seasoning from cinnamon and allspice, were a family Easter tradition. My mom made them only once a year using her mother's recipe. Icing crosses make a tasty topping and reflect the meaning of the holiday.

- 2 packages (1/4 ounce *each*) active dry yeast
- 1/4 cup warm water (110° to 115°)
- 1 cup warm 2% milk (110° to 115°)
- 1/2 cup sugar
- 1/4 cup shortening
- 2 eggs
- 2 teaspoons salt
- 1 teaspoon ground cinnamon
- 1/4 teaspoon ground allspice
- 4-1/2 to 5 cups all-purpose flour
- 1 cup dried currants
- 1 egg white, lightly beaten

ICING:
- 1-3/4 cups confectioners' sugar
- 1/2 teaspoon vanilla extract
- 4 to 6 teaspoons 2% milk

1. In a large bowl, dissolve yeast in warm water. Add the milk, sugar, shortening, eggs, salt, cinnamon, allspice and 3 cups flour. Beat until smooth. Stir in currants and enough remaining flour to form a soft dough.

2. Turn onto a floured surface; knead until smooth and elastic, about 6-8 minutes. Place in a greased bowl, turning once to grease top. Cover and let rise in a warm place until doubled, about 1 hour.

3. Punch dough down. Cover and let rest for 10 minutes. On a lightly floured surface, roll out to 1/2-in. thickness. Cut with a floured 2-1/2-in. biscuit cutter. Place 2 in. apart on lightly greased baking sheets. Cover and let rise until doubled, about 30 minutes.

4. Brush with egg white. Bake at 350° for 12-15 minutes or until golden brown. Remove from the pans to wire racks to cool.

5. For icing, in a small bowl, combine the sugar, vanilla and enough milk to achieve piping consistency. Pipe a cross on top of each bun.

STRAWBERRY SATIN PIE

yield: 6-8 servings   prep: 1-1/2 hours + chilling

My mom loved to spoil us with tempting desserts like this pretty springtime treat. Toasted sliced almonds sprinkled over the bottom crust, a smooth-as-satin filling and a lovely strawberry glaze make this a memorable pie.

- 1 pastry shell (9 inches), baked
- 1/2 cup sliced almonds, toasted
- 1/2 cup sugar
- 3 tablespoons all-purpose flour
- 3 tablespoons cornstarch
- 1/2 teaspoon salt
- 2 cups 2% milk
- 1 egg, lightly beaten
- 1 teaspoon vanilla extract
- 1/2 cup heavy whipping cream, whipped

GLAZE:
- 3 cups fresh strawberries
- 1 cup water
- 1/3 cup sugar
- 2 tablespoons cornstarch
- 12 drops red food coloring, optional

1. Cover bottom of pie shell with almonds; set aside. In a small saucepan, combine the sugar, flour, cornstarch and salt. Gradually stir in milk until smooth. Bring to a boil; cook and stir for 2 minutes or until thickened.

2. Remove from the heat. Stir a small amount of hot filling into egg. Return all to the pan, stirring constantly. Bring to a gentle boil; cook and stir 2 minutes longer. Remove from the heat. Stir in vanilla. Cool to room temperature. Fold in whipped cream. Pour into pie shell. Cover and refrigerate for at least 2 hours.

3. Mash 1 cup strawberries; set remaining berries aside. In a small saucepan, bring crushed berries and water to a boil; cook, uncovered, for 2 minutes. Strain through cheesecloth; discard fruit and set liquid aside to cool.

4. In another saucepan, combine sugar and cornstarch; gradually stir in berry liquid until blended. Bring to a boil; cook and stir for 2 minutes or until thickened. Stir in food coloring if desired. Cool for 20 minutes.

5. Slice the reserved strawberries; arrange over chilled filling. Pour glaze evenly over berries. Refrigerate for at least 1 hour before serving.

FRENCH *christmas menu*

[2003]

"My mom, Nancy Larkin, is a true artist—both on canvas and in the kitchen. So it was no surprise when she returned from an art workshop in Provence, France, that she was all enthused about the meals she had there. That year for Christmas, Mom wanted us to experience the cuisine of France. So she fashioned a wonderful feast with a French accent."

—*Kerry Sullivan, Longwood, Florida*

HERBED ROAST BEEF

yield: 10-12 servings ∞ prep: 10 min. ∞ bake: 2-1/2 hours + standing

A savory herb rub flavors this juicy roast that makes an impression every time my mom serves it for dinner. The creamy horseradish sauce adds a little kick to the crispy coated slices of beef.

- 2 **teaspoons fennel seed, crushed**
- 2 **teaspoons dried rosemary, crushed**
- 2 **teaspoons *each* dried basil, marjoram, savory and thyme**
- 2 **teaspoons rubbed sage**
- 2 **bone-in beef rib roasts (4 to 6 pounds *each*)**
- 2 **medium onions, sliced**
- 6 **fresh rosemary sprigs**

HORSERADISH SAUCE:
- 1-1/2 **cups (12 ounces) sour cream**
- 1/4 **cup prepared horseradish**
- 2 **tablespoons minced chives**
- 3 **tablespoons lemon juice**

1. In a small bowl, combine the fennel seed, crushed rosemary, basil, marjoram, savory, thyme and sage; rub over roasts. Place with fat side up on a rack in a roasting pan. Top with onions and rosemary sprigs.

2. Bake, uncovered, at 350° for 2-1/2 to 3-1/2 hours or until meat reaches desired doneness (for medium-rare, a thermometer should read 145°; medium, 160°; well-done, 170°).

3. Discard onions and rosemary. Let roasts stand for 10-15 minutes before slicing. Meanwhile, in a small bowl, combine the sauce ingredients. Serve with beef.

ROASTED ROOT VEGETABLES

yield: 10-12 servings   prep: 15 min.
bake: 45 min.

Pleasantly seasoned with rosemary and garlic, this appealing side dish showcases good-for-you turnips, carrots and potatoes. It's a nice homey addition to our family's holiday meal.

- 5 medium red potatoes, cubed
- 4 medium carrots, cut into 1/2-inch slices
- 2 small turnips, peeled and cubed
- 1 garlic clove, minced
- 2 to 4 tablespoons olive oil
- 1 tablespoon minced fresh rosemary *or* 1 teaspoon dried rosemary, crushed
- 1/2 teaspoon salt
- 1/4 teaspoon pepper

1. Place the potatoes, carrots, turnips and garlic in a greased 13-in. x 9-in. baking dish. Drizzle with oil; sprinkle with rosemary, salt and pepper. Stir to coat.

2. Bake vegetables , uncovered, at 350° for 35 minutes. Increase temperature to 450°; bake 10-15 minutes longer or until vegetables are tender.

RASPBERRY TOSSED SALAD

yield: 12 servings   prep/total time: 15 min.

(Pictured on page 487)

Red raspberries brighten this tossed green salad, making it the perfect ingredient for a festive yuletide menu. Raspberry juice adds a special touch to the oil and vinegar dressing.

- 9 cups torn mixed salad greens
- 3 cups fresh *or* frozen unsweetened raspberries
- 2 tablespoons olive oil
- 2 tablespoons cider vinegar
- 4 teaspoons sugar
- 1/8 teaspoon salt

Dash pepper

1. In a large salad bowl, gently combine the salad greens and 2-3/4 cups raspberries. Mash the remaining berries; strain, reserving juice and discarding seeds.

2. In a small bowl, whisk the raspberry juice, oil, vinegar, sugar, salt and pepper. Drizzle over salad; gently toss to coat.

ORANGE CHANTILLY CREAM

yield: 12 servings
prep/total time: 30 min.

Mom first tried this recipe from a French cookbook many years ago. She decorated the top of each light fluffy dessert cup with a slice of fresh orange from our trees! Everyone loved it.

- 12 medium navel oranges
- 4-1/2 cups heavy whipping cream
- 1 cup confectioners' sugar
- 2-1/4 teaspoons orange extract
- 1/3 cup orange juice

1. Cut a thin slice off the top of each orange. With a grapefruit spoon, scoop out pulp. Invert oranges onto paper towels to drain. Remove and discard membrane from orange pulp.

2. In a large bowl, beat cream until it begins to thicken. Add confectioners' sugar and extract; beat until stiff peaks form. Beat in orange juice. Fold in reserved orange pulp. Spoon into orange shells. Cover and refrigerate until serving.

ORANGE CHANTILLY CREAM

"I made these for dessert on Mother's Day. They took no time at all, but I let my mother think I worked all day on them."
—lori827

SOUP *salad & roll*

[2004]

❝My mom, Marie Weeks, has a recipe for every occasion, whether she's competing in a cooking contest, organizing a meal at church or feeding family and friends. Of course, everyone has their favorite "Marie recipe," but everyone agrees that her famous Buttery Crescents are the best you've ever tasted. The crescents go great with her seafood bisque.❞ —*Kevin Weeks, North Palm Beach, Florida*

SPICY SEAFOOD BISQUE
yield: 10-12 servings (about 3 quarts)
prep: 10 min.   ∞   cook: 40 min.

This spicy soup, featuring shrimp, crabmeat and tomatoes, gets its zip from hot pepper sauce and cayenne pepper. It's easy to prepare and dresses up any meal. Of all the recipes I've borrowed from my mom, this soup is the one that I've made most often.

- 1/2 cup chopped onion
- 1/2 cup chopped celery
- 2 tablespoons butter
- 4 cups chicken broth
- 3 cups tomato juice
- 1 can (14-1/2 ounces) diced tomatoes, undrained
- 1 tablespoon Worcestershire sauce
- 1 teaspoon seafood seasoning
- 1 teaspoon dried oregano
- 1/2 teaspoon garlic powder
- 1/2 teaspoon hot pepper sauce
- 1/4 teaspoon cayenne pepper
- 1 bay leaf
- 1/2 cup uncooked small shell pasta *or* elbow macaroni
- 1 pound uncooked medium shrimp, peeled and deveined
- 1 can (6 ounces) crabmeat, drained, flaked and cartilage removed

1. In a large saucepan, saute onion and celery in butter until tender. Add the broth, tomato juice, tomatoes, Worcestershire sauce and seasonings; bring to a boil. Reduce heat; cover and simmer for 20 minutes.

2. Discard bay leaf. Add pasta to the soup; cook, uncovered, until pasta is tender. Add shrimp and crab; simmer 5 minutes longer or until shrimp turn pink.

CHICKEN ROMAINE SALAD
yield: 12 servings (3/4 cup each)   ∞   prep/total time: 25 min.

Mom invented this colorful salad by combining romaine lettuce with toasted pecans, chicken strips, grapes, dried cranberries and cheddar cheese. I think she's particularly proud of this recipe.

- 3 tablespoons butter, melted
- 1 cup chopped pecans
- 1/2 teaspoon salt
- 1/4 cup all-purpose flour
- 1/2 pound boneless skinless chicken breasts, cut into 1-inch pieces
- 1/2 cup canola oil
- 7 cups torn romaine
- 1 cup seedless red grapes
- 1/2 cup dried cranberries
- 1/2 cup shredded sharp cheddar cheese
- 1 cup Vidalia onion *or* honey mustard salad dressing

1. Pour butter into a 15-in. x 10-in. x 1-in. baking pan; stir in pecans and salt. Bake at 350° for 10 minutes, stirring twice. Set aside.

2. Place flour in a large resealable plastic bag; add the chicken, a few pieces at a time, and shake to coat. In an electric skillet, heat oil to 375°. Fry chicken in batches for 2-3 minutes or until no longer pink, turning occasionally. Drain on paper towels.

3. In a large salad bowl, combine the romaine, grapes, cranberries and cheese. Add chicken and reserved nuts; toss to combine. Serve with dressing.

BUTTERY CRESCENTS

yield: 2 dozen (24 servings, 1 per serving)
prep: 20 min. + rising ∾ bake: 15 min.
(Pictured on page 485)

These golden brown rolls are my mother's bread of choice for holiday meals. No one in our extended family can imagine a celebratory meal without them. They have such a rich taste that you might not need to butter them!

- 1 package (1/4 ounce) active dry yeast
- 1/2 cup warm water (110° to 115°)
- 1/2 cup warm 2% milk (110° to 115°)
- 1/2 cup butter, softened
- 1/3 cup sugar
- 1 egg
- 3/4 teaspoon salt
- 4 to 4-1/2 cups all-purpose flour
- Additional butter, melted

1. In a large bowl, dissolve yeast in warm water. Add the milk, butter, sugar, egg, salt and 2 cups flour. Beat on medium speed for 2 minutes. Stir in enough remaining flour to form a soft dough.

2. Turn onto a floured surface; knead until smooth and elastic, about 6-8 minutes. Place in a greased bowl, turning once to grease top. Cover and let rise in a warm place until doubled, about 1 hour.

3. Punch the dough down. Turn onto a floured surface; divide in half. Roll each portion into a 12-in. circle; cut each circle into 12 wedges. Roll up wedges from the wide end and place pointed end down 2 in. apart on greased baking sheets. Curve ends to form crescents. Cover and let rise in a warm place until doubled, about 30 minutes.

4. Bake at 375° for 12-14 minutes or until golden brown. Brush with melted butter. Remove from pans to wire racks to cool.

LEMON BAKED ALASKA

yield: 8-10 servings
prep: 25 min. + freezing ∾ bake: 5 min.
(Pictured on page 488)

This impressive dessert, piled high with vanilla ice cream, lemon sauce and meringue, won my mother the grand prize in a local cooking contest as a first-time entrant. It's the perfect finale to a special meal.

- 1 cup sugar
- 2 eggs
- 2 egg yolks, lightly beaten
- 1/3 cup lemon juice
- 1/8 teaspoon salt
- 6 tablespoons butter
- 1 teaspoon grated lemon peel
- 1-1/2 quarts vanilla ice cream, softened
- 1 pastry shell (9 inches), baked
- **MERINGUE:**
- 5 egg whites
- 1/2 cup plus 2 tablespoons sugar
- 1/2 teaspoon cream of tartar
- 1 teaspoon vanilla extract

1. In a large saucepan, combine the sugar, eggs, lemon juice and salt. Cook and stir over medium heat until mixture reaches 160° or is thick enough to coat the back of a metal spoon. Stir in butter and lemon peel until blended. Cool completely. Refrigerate until chilled.

2. Spread half of the ice cream into pastry shell. Top with lemon mixture and remaining ice cream. Cover and freeze overnight.

3. In a small heavy saucepan, combine the egg whites, sugar and cream of tartar. With a hand mixer, beat on low speed for 1 minute. Continue beating over low heat until egg mixture reaches 160°, about 12 minutes.

4. Remove from the heat. Add the vanilla; beat and until stiff peaks form. Immediately spread over frozen pie. Bake at 450° for 3-5 minutes or until lightly browned. Serve immediately.

MEMORABLE *sunday meal*

[2005]

"My fondest food-related memories center on my mother's kitchen. My mom, Sarah Catterson, taught school for a short time before I was born. From then on, she devoted her time to taking care of her family. There weren't a lot of convenience foods back then, so Mom made everything from scratch. I liked to help her, and learned how to cook in the process. On Sundays, our big meal was served at noon, and she often served a roast, such as this stuffed pork roast."

—*Lois Frazee, Fernley, Nevada*

PORK TENDERLOIN WITH STUFFING

yield: 6 servings ∽ **prep: 20 min.** ∽ **bake: 20 min.**

For an impressive entree that goes together with ease, you must try my mom's tenderloin. Sauteed veggies keep the bread stuffing moist, and the pork is so flavorful.

- 4 celery ribs, chopped
- 1 small onion, chopped
- 2 tablespoons butter
- 6 cups cubed day-old bread (1/2-inch cubes)
- 1/2 teaspoon salt
- 1/4 teaspoon pepper
- 2 pork tenderloins (1 pound *each*)
- 2 tablespoons canola oil

1. In a small skillet, saute celery and onion in butter until tender. In a large bowl, combine the bread cubes, celery mixture, salt and pepper; set aside.

2. Cut a lengthwise slit down the center of each tenderloin to within 1/2 in. of bottom. Open tenderloins so they lie flat; cover with plastic wrap. Flatten to 1/2-in. thickness. In a large skillet, brown pork in oil on all sides over medium-high heat.

3. Spoon stuffing onto one tenderloin. Top with the second tenderloin; tie with kitchen string. Place on a rack in a shallow roasting pan.

4. Bake, uncovered, at 425° for 20-30 minutes or until a thermometer inserted into meat reads 145°. Let meat stand for 5 minutes before slicing.

PARSNIP PANCAKES

yield: 6 servings ∞ **prep/total time: 30 min.**

Instead of rice or potatoes with her meal, my mom chose these delicate pancakes that are crispy on the outside and tender inside. The parsnips have a pleasant sweetness, while the chives add a hint of onion flavor.

- 2 pounds parsnips, peeled
- 1 teaspoon salt
- 1/2 cup chopped onion
- 1/4 cup all-purpose flour
- 1 egg, lightly beaten
- 1 tablespoon minced chives
- 2 to 4 tablespoons canola oil

1. Place parsnips in a large saucepan and cover with water; add salt. Bring to a boil over medium-high heat. Reduce heat; cover and cook for 15-20 minutes or until tender.

2. Drain. Place parsnips in a large bowl; mash. Stir in onion, flour, egg and chives.

3. Heat 2 tablespoons oil in a large nonstick skillet over medium heat. Drop batter by 1/4 cupfuls into oil. Fry in batches until golden brown on both sides, using remaining oil as needed. Drain on paper towels.

RASPBERRY SQUARES

yield: 12-16 servings ∞ **prep: 20 min. + chilling bake: 10 min. + cooling**

This refreshing dessert has a rich shortbread-like crust with a creamy center and pretty red gelatin top layer. It's easy enough for everyday, but cheery enough to dish up for guests, too.

- 1 cup all-purpose flour
- 1/2 cup finely chopped pecans
- 1/4 cup packed brown sugar
- 1/2 cup butter, melted
- 2 packages (8 ounces *each*) cream cheese, softened
- 3/4 cup sugar
- 1 carton (8 ounces) frozen whipped topping, thawed
- 2 packages (3 ounces *each*) raspberry gelatin
- 2 cups boiling water
- 2 cups cold water

1. In a large bowl, combine the flour, pecans and brown sugar; stir in butter until crumbly. Press into an ungreased 13-in. x 9-in. baking dish. Bake at 350° for 10-13 minutes or until lightly browned. Cool on a wire rack.

2. In a large bowl, beat cream cheese and sugar until smooth; fold in whipped topping. Spread over crust. Cover and refrigerate for 1 hour.

3. In a small bowl, dissolve gelatin in boiling water; stir in cold water. Spoon over cream cheese layer. Chill until firm. Cut into squares.

ZUCCHINI APPLE SALAD

yield: 6 servings ∞ **prep/total time: 15 min.**

You'll want to serve this salad in a glass bowl because it's so colorful. Everyone will enjoy its fresh-tasting crunch, and you'll like how quickly it goes together!

- 2 medium red apples, chopped
- 2 small zucchini, chopped
- 1/2 cup coarsely chopped walnuts
- 2/3 cup Italian salad dressing

1. In a serving bowl, combine the apples, zucchini and walnuts. Drizzle with salad dressing; toss to coat.

PARSNIP PANCAKES

❝These are the absolute best! I have made them again and again. I have a friend whose favorite veggie is parsnips and this is a great change instead of just boiled with a slathering of butter. I would really recommend you try them!❞
—cornysas

ELEGANT *stuffed cornish hens*

[2006]

"Cooking for a crowd came naturally for my mom, Antoinette DeGear, since she grew up with five siblings and raised eight of her own kids. When I was a child, she always seem to be cooking. With such a large family, huge gatherings were the norm and we often had dinner parties for 30 or more people. In my opinion, her best meal is the one that follows."

—*Jodi Grable, Springfield, Missouri*

HENS WITH APRICOT RICE STUFFING
yield: 4 servings ∽ prep: 25 min. ∽ bake: 2 hours

When you want to impress guests, you can't beat these lovely Cornish game hens. Apricots and apricot preserves give the tender meat and moist wild rice stuffing a fruity flavor that everyone in our family loves.

- 1 **cup sliced fresh mushrooms**
- 3/4 **cup chopped pecans**
- 1/2 **cup chopped onion**
- 6 **tablespoons butter,** *divided*
- 1 **cup cooked wild rice**
- 1/2 **cup chopped dried apricots**
- 1 **tablespoon minced fresh parsley**
- 1/2 **teaspoon salt**
- 1/4 **teaspoon pepper**
- 1/8 **teaspoon cayenne pepper**
- 4 **Cornish game hens (20 to 24 ounces each)**
- 1/2 **cup apricot preserves**
- 1 **tablespoon white vinegar**

1. In a large skillet, saute the mushrooms, pecans and onion in 4 tablespoons butter until tender. Stir in the rice, apricots, parsley, salt, pepper and cayenne.

2. Spoon about 3/4 cup rice mixture into each hen; tie legs together. Place hens, breast side up, on a rack in a shallow roasting pan. Melt remaining butter; drizzle over hens.

3. Bake, uncovered, at 350° for 1-3/4 to 2 hours or until a thermometer reads 180° for hens and 165° for stuffing. In a small saucepan, warm preserves and vinegar; spoon over hens. Bake 15 minutes longer.

BACON SQUASH SAUTE

yield: 4 servings prep/total time: 20 min.

This delicious medley is my favorite way to serve zucchini and squash. The bacon and onion add just the right amount of flavor and crunch.

- 6 bacon strips, diced
- 2 small zucchini, cut into 1/4-inch slices
- 2 small yellow summer squash, cut into 1/4-inch slices
- 1 medium onion, thinly sliced

1. In a large skillet, cook the bacon over medium heat until crisp; remove bacon to paper towels. Drain, reserving 2 tablespoons drippings.

2. In the drippings, saute the zucchini, yellow squash and onion for 6-8 minutes or until crisp-tender. Sprinkle with the bacon.

ORANGE 'N' RED ONION SALAD

yield: 4 servings prep/total time: 15 min.

(Pictured on page 485)

Drizzled with a tangy dressing, this appealing salad makes a colorful and tasty alternative to the usual tossed salad. Plus, you can assemble it in minutes.

- 4 cups torn romaine
- 2 medium navel oranges, peeled and sectioned
- 1 small red onion, sliced and separated into rings
- 1/4 cup olive oil
- 3 tablespoons red wine vinegar
- 1 teaspoon sugar
- 1/4 teaspoon salt
- 1/8 teaspoon pepper

1. On a serving platter, arrange the romaine, oranges and onion. In a small bowl, whisk the remaining ingredients; drizzle over salad.

BANANA CREAM PIE

yield: 6-8 servings prep: 10 min. cook: 15 min. + chilling

Cream pies are my mom's specialty, and this dreamy dessert has a wonderful banana flavor. It looks so pretty topped with almonds, and it cuts easily, too.

- 1 cup sugar
- 1/4 cup cornstarch
- 1/2 teaspoon salt
- 3 cups 2% milk
- 2 eggs, lightly beaten
- 3 tablespoons butter
- 1-1/2 teaspoons vanilla extract
- 2 large firm bananas
- 1 pastry shell (9 inches), baked
- 1 cup heavy whipping cream, whipped
- 1 tablespoon sliced almonds, toasted

1. In a large saucepan, combine the sugar, cornstarch, salt and milk until smooth. Cook and stir over medium-high heat until thickened and bubbly. Reduce heat; cook and stir 2 minutes longer. Remove from the heat. Stir a small amount of hot filling into eggs; return all to the pan. Bring to a gentle boil; cook and stir 2 minutes longer.

2. Remove from the heat. Gently stir in butter and vanilla. Press plastic wrap onto surface of custard; cover and refrigerate for 30 minutes.

3. Slice the bananas into pastry shell; pour custard over top. Spread with whipped cream; sprinkle with almonds. Chill for 6-8 hours or overnight. Refrigerate leftovers.

BACON SQUASH SAUTE

"Add fresh tomatoes...a few red pepper flakes and soy sauce, and serve over rice as a main dish...One of our summer favorites!"
—grammadi323

HEARTY *steak & potatoes*

[2007]

"My mother, Tammy Ahrens, was the oldest of seven children and learned how to cook and can at an early age. She put those skills to good use cooking for a family of 13. For each of our birthdays, she made our favorite meal. My favorite is here."

—*Heather Ahrens, Columbus, Ohio*

TENDER FLANK STEAK

yield: 6 servings ∞ prep: 10 min. + marinating
cook: 20 min.

(*Pictured on page 482*)

This marinated steak is so moist that it will become one of your favorite ways to serve beef. It is also delicious prepared on the grill. It can easily be cut into thin slices, and leftovers are perfect for sandwiches!

- 1 cup reduced-sodium soy sauce
- 1/4 cup lemon juice
- 1/4 cup honey
- 6 garlic cloves, minced
- 1 beef flank steak (1-1/2 pounds)

1. In a large resealable plastic bag, combine the soy sauce, lemon juice, honey and garlic; add steak. Seal bag and turn to coat; refrigerate for 6-8 hours.

2. Drain and discard marinade. Broil 4-6 in. from the heat or grill over medium heat for 8-10 minutes on each side or until meat reaches desired doneness (for medium-rare, a thermometer should read 145°; medium, 160°; well-done, 170°). Thinly slice steak across the grain.

ROMAINE WITH ORANGES

yield: 6 servings ∞ prep: 20 min. + chilling

Mandarin oranges give this crisp, cool salad a refreshing tang that will perk up any meal. There's even orange juice in the light vinaigrette that glistens as it coats the greens.

- 6 cups torn romaine
- 2 medium navel oranges, peeled and sectioned
- 6 slices red onion, separated into rings

DRESSING:
- 1/4 cup olive oil
- 2 tablespoons orange juice
- 2 teaspoons cider vinegar
- 1/4 teaspoon salt

Dash ground mustard

1. In a large salad bowl, toss the romaine, oranges and onion. In a small bowl, whisk the dressing ingredients. Drizzle over salad and toss to coat. Cover and refrigerate until chilled; toss before serving.

CHEDDAR TWICE-BAKED POTATOES

yield: 6 servings   prep: 20 min.
bake: 1 hour 20 min.

(Pictured on page 485)

Our family rarely has Mom's steak without these easy-to-fix potatoes. They're creamy and full of bacon, cheese and onion flavor.

- 6 large baking potatoes
- 8 tablespoons butter, *divided*
- 1/4 pound sliced bacon, diced
- 1 medium onion, finely chopped
- 1/2 cup 2% milk
- 1 egg
- 1/2 teaspoon salt
- 1/8 teaspoon white pepper
- 1 cup (4 ounces) shredded cheddar cheese

1. Scrub and pierce potatoes; rub each with 1 teaspoon butter. Place on a baking sheet. Bake at 375° for 1 hour or until tender.

2. Meanwhile, in a small skillet, cook bacon over medium heat until crisp. Remove to paper towels; drain, reserving 1 tablespoon drippings. In the drippings, saute onion until tender; set aside.

3. When potatoes are cool enough to handle, cut a thin slice off the top of each and discard. Scoop out pulp, leaving a thin shell. In a small bowl, mash pulp with remaining butter. Stir in the milk, egg, salt and pepper. Stir in the cheese, bacon and onion.

4. Spoon into the potato shells. Place on a baking sheet. Bake at 375° for 20-25 minutes or until heated through.

PISTACHIO ICE CREAM DESSERT

yield: 9 servings   prep: 20 min. + freezing

Both creamy and crunchy, this fabulous frozen dessert is a favorite at our house. You'll love the pistachio flavor and toffee candy topping.

- 1 cup crushed butter-flavored crackers
- 1/4 cup butter, melted
- 3/4 cup cold 2% milk
- 1 package (3.4 ounces) instant pistachio pudding mix
- 1 quart vanilla ice cream, softened
- 1 carton (8 ounces) frozen whipped topping, thawed
- 2 packages (1.4 ounces each) Heath candy bars, crushed

1. In a small bowl, combine cracker crumbs and butter. Press into an ungreased 9-in. square baking pan. Bake at 325° for 7-10 minutes or until lightly browned. Cool on a wire rack.

2. Meanwhile, in a large bowl, whisk the milk and pudding mix for 2 minutes. Let stand for 2 minutes or until soft-set. Stir in ice cream; pour over crust. Cover and freeze for 2 hours or until firm.

3. Spread with whipped topping; sprinkle with crushed candy bars. Cover and freeze for 1 hour or until firm.

PISTACHIO ICE CREAM DESSERT

"This is delicious! I have made this a few times, substituting with different ice creams and different flavored puddings and even using different candy bars. All have turned out well. It is easy to make so have fun with it!!"
—sd20

HEARTWARMING *morning menu*

[2008]

“When my sisters and I were growing up, the heartbeat of our home was the kitchen, and our mother, Marie Caldwell LaBrozzi, was the heart. We spent hours in the kitchen—gathered for meals, a game or a serious talk. We choose the following breakfast menu as our mom's best meal, because it was one of the times we'd have Mom to ourselves. Of course, the food was fantastic, too.”

—Vicki Holloway, Joelton, Tennessee

EGG SCRAMBLE

yield: 10 servings   prep: 15 min.   cook: 20 min.

Perfect for a special-occasion breakfast or holiday brunch, this easy egg scramble is warm and hearty, with potatoes, ham, cheese and sweet red and green peppers.

- 1-1/2 cups diced peeled potatoes
- 1/2 cup chopped sweet red pepper
- 1/2 cup chopped green pepper
- 1/2 cup chopped onion
- 2 teaspoons canola oil, *divided*
- 2 cups cubed fully cooked ham
- 16 eggs
- 2/3 cup sour cream
- 1/2 cup 2% milk
- 1 teaspoon onion salt
- 1/2 teaspoon garlic salt
- 1/4 teaspoon pepper
- 2 cups (8 ounces) shredded cheddar cheese, *divided*

1. Place potatoes in a small saucepan and cover with water. Bring to a boil. Reduce heat; cover and simmer for 10-15 minutes or until tender. Drain.

2. In a large skillet, saute half of the peppers and onion in 1 teaspoon oil until tender. Add half of the ham and potatoes; saute 2-3 minutes longer.

3. Meanwhile, in a blender, combine the eggs, sour cream, milk, onion salt, garlic salt and pepper. Cover and process until smooth. Pour half over vegetable mixture; cook and stir over medium heat until eggs are completely set. Sprinkle with 1 cup cheese. Repeat with remaining ingredients.

BROILED GRAPEFRUIT

yield: 10 servings   prep/total time: 25 min.

(Pictured on page 483)

This easy-to-prepare dish lends eye-catching appeal to a winter morning meal. Brown sugar sweetens the tart fruit, and the sugared grapes add a lovely accent.

- 5 medium pink grapefruit
- 1/4 cup packed brown sugar
- 2 tablespoons plus 1/4 cup sugar, *divided*
- 2 tablespoons butter, melted
- Seedless red and green grape clusters

1. Cut each grapefruit in half horizontally. With a sharp knife, cut around each section to loosen fruit. Place grapefruit halves, cut side up, in a 15-in. x 10-in. x 1-in. baking pan.

2. Combine brown sugar and 2 tablespoons sugar; sprinkle over grapefruit. Drizzle with butter. Broil 4 in. from the heat until sugar is bubbly.

3. For garnish, rinse grape clusters and dip in remaining sugar. Place on grapefruit; serve warm.

HOT COCOA

yield: 10 servings (2-1/2 quarts)
prep/total time: 15 min.

Treat your family to this comforting, homemade cocoa as you decorate the tree or open holiday gifts. Vanilla and almond extracts make it taste even more special.

- 1 cup sugar
- 2/3 cup baking cocoa
- 1/4 teaspoon salt
- 8 cups 2% milk
- 2/3 cup water
- 2 teaspoons vanilla extract
- 1/2 teaspoon almond extract
- **Miniature marshmallows, optional**

1. In a large saucepan, combine the sugar, cocoa and salt. Stir in milk and water. Cook and stir over medium heat until heated through. Remove from the heat; stir in extracts. Serve in mugs with marshmallows if desired.

CINNAMON-PECAN COFFEE CAKES

yield: 2 loaves (12 slices each)
prep: 30 min. + rising
bake: 25 min. + cooling

(Pictured on page 481)

With their decorative cinnamon swirls, these lovely braids taste as good as they look! And their aroma while baking will make your mouth water. You could decorate the drizzle of icing with pecans and candied cherries.

- 6 to 6-1/2 cups all-purpose flour
- 2 packages (1/4 ounce each) active dry yeast
- 1-1/2 teaspoons salt
- 1/2 teaspoon sugar
- 1-1/2 cups water
- 1/2 cup plus 2 tablespoons butter, softened, *divided*
- 2 eggs
- 1 cup chopped pecans
- 1/2 cup packed brown sugar
- 1 teaspoon ground cinnamon

GLAZE:
- 2 cups confectioners' sugar
- 1/4 teaspoon almond extract
- 2 to 3 tablespoons water

1. In a large bowl, combine 3 cups flour, yeast, salt and sugar. In a small saucepan, heat water and 1/2 cup butter to 120°-130°. Add to dry ingredients; beat just until moistened. Add eggs; beat until smooth. Stir in enough remaining flour to form a soft dough (dough will be sticky).

2. Turn onto a floured surface; knead until smooth and elastic, about 6-8 minutes. Place in a greased bowl, turning once to grease top. Cover and let rise in a warm place until doubled, about 1 hour.

3. Punch dough down. Divide into six portions. Roll out each portion into a 12-in. x 6-in. rectangle. Melt remaining butter; brush over dough. Combine pecans, brown sugar and cinnamon; sprinkle over dough to within 1/2 in. of edges. Roll up jelly-roll style, starting with a long side; pinch seams to seal.

4. Place three ropes seam side down on a greased baking sheet and braid; pinch ends to seal and tuck under. Repeat with remaining ropes. Cover and let rise until doubled, about 45 minutes.

5. Bake ropes at 325° for 25-30 minutes or until golden brown. Cool for 10 minutes before removing from pans to wire racks.

6. In a small bowl, combine the confectioners' sugar, extract and enough water to achieve desired consistency; drizzle over warm loaves. Serve warm.

HOT COCOA

"This is the only hot cocoa recipe I use. The ladies in my Bible study are addicted to it!"
—*ArkRatLady51*

DOWN-HOME *chicken supper*

[2009]

"For most of her life, my mom, Enoth Bratten, made do with whatever was on hand. Yet she could transform the simplest ingredients into a delicious meal for our family of nine. She rarely used recipes, and many dishes came from the huge garden she had. On Sundays, she often served this down-home meal."

—*Ginny Werkmeister, Tilden, Nebraska*

FRIED CHICKEN WITH PAN GRAVY

yield: 6 servings (1-1/2 cups gravy)
prep: 15 min.   cook: 45 min.

Mom's traditional fried chicken always cooked up golden brown and crispy. Drizzled with the pan gravy, this dish is real comfort food.

- 1 cup all-purpose flour
- 3/4 teaspoon salt
- 1/4 teaspoon dried thyme
- 1/4 teaspoon rubbed sage
- 1/4 teaspoon pepper
- 1 broiler/fryer chicken (3-1/2 to 4 pounds), cut up
- Oil for frying
- GRAVY:
- 2 tablespoons all-purpose flour
- 1/8 teaspoon salt
- 1-1/3 cups 2% milk

1. In a large resealable plastic bag, combine the first five ingredients. Add chicken, a few pieces at a time, and shake to coat.

2. In a large skillet over medium-high heat, heat 1/4 in. of oil; fry chicken until browned on all sides. Reduce heat; cover and cook for 30-35 minutes or until juices run clear, turning occasionally. Uncover and cook 5 minutes longer. Remove chicken to paper towels and keep warm.

3. For gravy, pour the drippings and loosened brown bits into a measuring cup. Skim the fat, reserving 3 tablespoons. In a small bowl, combine flour, salt and drippings until blended; pour into a small saucepan. Gradually stir in milk. Bring to a boil; cook and stir for 2 minutes or until thickened. Serve with chicken.

GARDEN COLESLAW

yield: 4 servings   prep/total time: 10 min.

As soon as the first head of cabbage was barely big enough to harvest, Mom made this refreshing slaw. We kids shredded the cabbage while Mom whipped up the sweet cream dressing.

- 3 cups shredded cabbage
- 1/4 cup chopped green pepper
- 1 green onion, thinly sliced
- 1/4 cup mayonnaise
- 1/4 cup heavy whipping cream
- 1 tablespoon sugar
- 1 tablespoon cider vinegar
- 1/4 teaspoon salt

1. In a large bowl, combine cabbage, pepper and onion. In a small bowl, combine the remaining ingredients; pour over cabbage mixture and toss to coat.

CREAMED POTATOES & PEAS

yield: 6 servings
prep: 10 min. ∞ cook: 25 min.

Early in June, we helped Mom pick the first green sweet peas of the season. She combined them with potatoes and green onion to create this creamy dish, which we all loved.

- 1 **pound small red potatoes**
- 2-1/2 **cups frozen peas**
- 1/4 **cup butter, cubed**
- 1 **green onion, sliced**
- 1/4 **cup all-purpose flour**
- 1/2 **teaspoon salt**

Dash pepper

- 2 **cups 2% milk**

1. Scrub and quarter potatoes; place in a large saucepan and cover with water. Bring to a boil. Reduce heat; cover and simmer for 10 minutes. Add peas; cook 5 minutes longer or until vegetables are tender.

2. Meanwhile, in another large saucepan, melt butter. Add onion; saute until tender. Stir in flour, salt and pepper until blended; gradually add the milk. Bring to a boil. Reduce heat; cook and stir for 1-2 minutes or until thickened. Drain the potatoes and peas; toss with the sauce.

COCONUT CREAM ANGEL PIE

yield: 8 servings ∞ prep: 30 min.
bake: 20 min. + chilling

Mom whipped up this wonderful pie on impulse, using an ancient whisk and an old skillet. I am still amazed that it turned out perfect every time.

- 1/2 **cup sugar**
- 1/4 **cup cornstarch**
- 1/4 **teaspoon salt**

- 2 **cups whole milk**
- 3 **egg yolks, lightly beaten**
- 1/2 **cup flaked coconut**
- 1 **tablespoon butter**
- 1-1/2 **teaspoons vanilla extract**
- 1 **pastry shell (9 inches), baked**

MERINGUE:

- 3 **egg whites**
- 1/4 **teaspoon cream of tartar**
- 1/4 **teaspoon vanilla extract**
- 6 **tablespoons sugar**
- 1/4 **cup flaked coconut**

1. In a small heavy saucepan, combine the sugar, cornstarch and salt. Add milk; stir until smooth. Cook and stir over medium-high heat until thickened and bubbly. Reduce heat to low; cook and stir for 2 minutes longer.

2. Remove from the heat. Stir a small amount of hot filling into the egg yolks; return all to the pan, stirring constantly. Bring to a gentle boil; cook and stir 2 minutes longer. Remove from the heat; stir in coconut, butter and vanilla. Pour into prepared shell.

3. In a small bowl, beat the egg whites, cream of tartar and vanilla on medium speed until soft peaks form. Gradually beat in sugar, 1 tablespoon at a time, on high until stiff peaks form. Spread meringue over hot filling, sealing edges to crust. Sprinkle with coconut.

4. Bake at 350° for 17-20 minutes or until golden brown. Cool the pie on a wire rack for 1 hour. Refrigerate for at least 3 hours before serving. Store leftovers in the refrigerator.

CREAMED POTATOES & PEAS

"Oh my goodness!! This is a great side. My grandma used to prepare cream peas, never with potatoes. It was one of my favorite dishes. My daughter made this for a family get-together, and we ate it all. Great recipe!"
—*likemama*

MEMORIES *of india*

[2010]

"If there's one thing I never forget to say to my mother, Jemima Madhavan, after dinner it's, 'Good food, Mom!' I can't remember my mother ever making a bad meal. It's the best Indian food I've ever tasted. Here's a sampling of my favorite dishes that she makes."

—*Anand Madhavan, Lincoln, Nebraska*

CHICKEN KORMA

yield: 4 servings ∞ **prep: 20 min.**
cook: 25 min.

There were days, like after basketball practice, when all I wanted to do was refuel with my mother's korma. It's filling, spicy and delicious.

- 1 large potato, peeled and cut into 1/2-inch cubes
- 1 large onlon, chopped
- 1 cinnamon stick (3 inches)
- 1 bay leaf
- 3 whole cloves
- 1 tablespoon canola oil
- 1 pound boneless skinless chicken breasts, cut into 1/2-inch cubes
- 1 garlic clove, minced
- 1 teaspoon curry powder
- 1/2 teaspoon minced fresh gingerroot
- 2 medium tomatoes, seeded and chopped
- 1 teaspoon salt
- 1/2 cup sour cream
Hot cooked rice

1. Place potato in a small saucepan and cover with water. Bring to a boil. Reduce heat; cover and cook for 10-15 minutes or until tender. Drain.

2. In a large skillet, saute the onion, cinnamon, bay leaf and cloves in oil until onion is tender. Add the chicken, garlic, curry and ginger; cook and stir for 1 minute. Stir in the tomatoes, salt and potato.

3. Cover and cook for 10-15 minutes or until chicken is no longer pink. Remove from the heat; discard cinnamon, bay leaf and cloves. Stir in sour cream. Serve with rice.

CURRY POWDER

yield: 2 tablespoons ∞ **prep/total time: 10 min.**

A little curry powder goes a long way. Use my mom's personal blend instead of store-bought to flavor her delicious recipes.

- 3 cardamom pods
- 2 teaspoons ground coriander
- 2 teaspoons ground cumin
- 1 teaspoon ground turmeric
- 1/2 teaspoon chili powder
- 1/2 teaspoon pepper
- 1/8 teaspoon fennel seed

1. Remove seeds from cardamom pods. In a spice grinder or with a mortar and pestle, combine cardamom seeds with remaining ingredients; grind until mixture becomes a powder. Store in an airtight container for up to 1 year.

MINTED RICE WITH GARBANZO CURRY

yield: 3 servings ∾ **prep: 20 min.** ∾ **cook: 20 min.**

Fluffy flavored rice and tender beans in a well-seasoned, aromatic sauce make this easy, meatless main dish a fitting introduction to Indian cooking.

- 1 cinnamon stick (3 inches)
- 2 whole cloves
- 1/8 teaspoon cumin seeds
- 2 teaspoons canola oil
- 1 cup uncooked long grain rice
- 2 cups water
- 1/2 cup minced fresh mint

GARBANZO CURRY:

- 1 medium onion, chopped
- 1 cinnamon stick (3 inches)
- 1 tablespoon canola oil
- 1 teaspoon curry powder
- 1 garlic clove, minced
- 1/4 teaspoon minced fresh gingerroot
- 1 can (15 ounces) garbanzo beans *or* chickpeas, rinsed and drained
- 1 cup water
- 1 can (8 ounces) tomato sauce
- 2 tablespoons lemon juice
- 1/2 teaspoon salt
- 1/2 cup minced fresh cilantro

1. In a large saucepan over medium heat, saute cinnamon, cloves and cumin seeds in oil until aromatic, about 1-2 minutes. Add rice; cook and stir until lightly browned. Add water and mint. Bring to a boil. Reduce heat; cover and simmer for 15-20 minutes or until rice is tender.

2. Meanwhile, in a large skillet, saute onion and cinnamon in oil until onion is tender. Add the curry, garlic and ginger; cook 1 minute longer. Add the garbanzo beans, water, tomato sauce, lemon juice and salt; bring to a boil. Reduce heat; simmer, uncovered, for 4-6 minutes or until slightly thickened. Discard cinnamon; stir in cilantro.

3. Fluff rice with a fork. Discard cinnamon and cloves. Serve with garbanzo curry.

CUCUMBER SALAD

yield: 6 servings ∾ **prep/total time: 15 min.**

A staple of Indian meals, this cooling cucumber dish is often served alongside a spicy Indian entree.

- 1/2 cup plain yogurt
- 1/2 cup sour cream
- 1/4 teaspoon salt
- 1-1/2 cups chopped cucumbers
- 1 medium onion, chopped
- 1 medium tomato, seeded and chopped
- 1 tablespoon chopped seeded jalapeno pepper

Fresh cilantro leaves, optional

1. In a large bowl, combine the yogurt, sour cream and salt. Add the cucumbers, onion, tomato and jalapeno; stir until blended. Garnish with cilantro if desired.

CARROT SALAD

yield: 4 servings ∾ **prep: 15 min. + chilling**

(Pictured on page 485)

Creamy and crunchy, this refreshing salad can be served alone, on the side or with rice. Raisins add a nice touch of sweetness.

- 2 medium carrots, grated
- 1 medium tomato, seeded and chopped
- 1/2 cup plain yogurt
- 1/2 cup sour cream
- 1/4 cup raisins
- 1/4 cup finely chopped red onion
- 1/2 teaspoon salt

Fresh cilantro leaves and coarsely ground pepper, optional

1. In a small bowl, combine the first seven ingredients. Cover and refrigerate until chilled. Garnish with cilantro and pepper if desired.

COOKING *to a cuban beat*

[2011]

"The food my mother, Nena Linares, put on the table was a mouthwatering blend of cultures. Mom, who lives in Los Angeles, was born in Cuba; her parents were transplants from Spain. Early on, she learned the basics of French and Spanish cooking from her grandmother. Her mother-in-law showed her how to make authentic Cuban food, and our Sicilian stepdad, Fred, taught her the Italian classics. When my brother, Rick, and I were growing up, there was always something ready in the fridge or on the stove for us to eat. And everything was from scratch. Here are a few of her best dishes."

—*Marina Castle, La Crescenta, California, Field Editor*

NENA'S PAPAS RELLENAS
yield: 2-1/2 dozen ∞ prep: 45 min.
cook: 5 min./batch

(Pictured on page 483)

A Cuban classic, these satisfying, crispy-coated potato balls are filled with a savory ground beef mixture known as picadillo.

2-1/2   **pounds potatoes (about 8 medium), peeled and cut into wedges**
1   **pound lean ground beef (90% lean)**
1   **small green pepper, finely chopped**
1   **small onion, finely chopped**
1/2   **cup tomato sauce**
1/2   **cup sliced green olives with pimientos**
1/2   **cup raisins**
1-1/4   **teaspoons salt,** *divided*
1-1/4   **teaspoons pepper,** *divided*
1/2   **teaspoon paprika**
1   **teaspoon garlic powder**
2   **eggs, lightly beaten**
1   **cup seasoned bread crumbs**
Oil for deep-fat frying

---

1. Place potatoes in a large saucepan and cover with water. Bring to a boil. Reduce heat; cover and cook for 15-20 minutes or until tender.

2. Meanwhile, in a large skillet, cook the beef, green pepper and onion over medium heat until meat is no longer pink; drain. Stir in the tomato sauce, olives, raisins, 1/4 teaspoon salt, 1/4 teaspoon pepper and paprika; heat through.

3. Drain potatoes; mash with garlic powder and remaining salt and pepper. Shape 2 tablespoons potatoes into a patty; place a heaping tablespoonful of filling in the center. Shape potatoes around filling, forming a ball. Repeat.

4. Place eggs and bread crumbs in separate shallow bowls. Dip potato balls in the eggs, then roll in bread crumbs. In an electric skillet or deep fryer, heat oil to 375°. Fry potato balls, a few at a time, for 1-2 minutes or until golden brown. Drain on paper towels.

Editor's Note: Instead of frying the papas rellenas, you may place them on baking sheets and bake at 450° for 20 minutes or until heated through.

NO-FUSS AVOCADO ONION SALAD

yield: 12 servings
prep/total time: 20 min.

My mother could take a simple salad and make it incredibly delicious, like this one, which is a favorite of mine.

- 3 medium ripe avocados, peeled and thinly sliced
- 1 large sweet onion, halved and thinly sliced
- 1/3 cup olive oil
- 1/4 cup stone-ground mustard
- 2 tablespoons lemon juice
- 1 tablespoon honey

1. Arrange the avocados and onion on a large platter. In a small bowl, whisk the oil, mustard, lemon juice and honey; drizzle over the vegetables.

CUBAN BLACK BEANS

yield: 9 servings
prep: 20 min. + soaking   cook: 1-3/4 hours

This hearty side dish starts with a sofrito, a combination of finely minced onions and green peppers. The tomato puree and sherry give the beans a distinctive flavor.

- 2 cups dried black beans, rinsed
- 1 bay leaf
- 3 medium green peppers, chopped
- 2 medium onions, chopped
- 1/2 cup olive oil
- 6 garlic cloves, minced
- 1 can (15 ounces) tomato puree
- 1/2 cup sherry *or* chicken broth
- 2 tablespoons sugar
- 3/4 teaspoon salt

1. Soak beans according to package directions. Drain and rinse beans, discarding liquid. Place beans in a large saucepan; add 6 cups water and bay leaf. Bring to a boil. Reduce heat; cover and simmer for 1-1/2 to 2 hours or until tender.

2. Meanwhile, in a large skillet, saute peppers and onions in oil until tender. Add garlic; cook 1 minute longer. Stir in tomato puree, sherry, sugar and salt. Bring to a boil. Reduce heat; simmer, uncovered, for 8-10 minutes or until thickened. Drain beans; discard bay leaf. Stir beans into tomato mixture.

ARROZ CON LECHE (RICE PUDDING)

yield: 4 servings   prep: 5 min.
cook: 30 min.

Sweet and simple, this creamy dessert is real comfort food in any language. You'll love the warm raisin and cinnamon flavors. It's great served cold, too.

- 1-1/2 cups water
- 1/2 cup uncooked long grain rice
- 1 cinnamon stick (3 inches)
- 1 cup sweetened condensed milk
- 3 tablespoons raisins

1. In a small saucepan, combine the water, rice and cinnamon. Bring to a boil. Reduce heat; simmer, uncovered, for 15-20 minutes or until the water is absorbed.

2. Stir in milk and raisins. Bring to a boil. Reduce heat; simmer, uncovered, for 10-15 minutes or until thick and creamy, stirring frequently. Discard cinnamon. Serve warm or cold.

CUBAN BLACK BEANS

"Delicious! I had some canned black beans in my pantry and decided to make this to pair with pork chops and yellow rice, and what a wonderful flavor! Even my husband, who doesn't care for black beans, loved it."
—aug2295

A TRIP *to armenia*

LAHMAJOON (ARMENIAN PIZZA)
yield: 6 servings ∞ prep: 25 min. ∞ bake: 10 min.

When I was little, we would roll homemade yeast dough tissue-paper thin and bake it right on the oven rack until it was crisp before adding meat, onion and parsley. These days I rely on flour tortillas instead.

- 3/4 **cup drained petite diced tomatoes**
- 1/2 **cup finely chopped onion**
- 1/3 **cup minced fresh parsley**
- 1/4 **cup finely chopped green pepper**
- 2 **tablespoons tomato paste**
- 1 **teaspoon dried mint**
- 1 **garlic clove, minced**
- 1/4 **teaspoon salt**
- 1/4 **teaspoon paprika**
- 1/8 **teaspoon cayenne pepper**
- 1/8 **teaspoon pepper**
- 3/4 **pound extra-lean ground beef (95% lean)**
- 12 **flour tortillas (8 inches)**

1. In a large bowl, combine the tomatoes, onion, parsley, green pepper, tomato paste, mint, garlic, salt, paprika, cayenne and pepper. Crumble the beef over mixture and mix well.

2. Place the tortillas on greased baking sheets. Spread 1/4 cup of meat mixture onto each tortilla to within 1/2 in. of edges (tortillas will not be completely covered). Bake at 425° for 9-12 minutes or until meat is no longer pink and edges of tortillas begin to brown.

VERMICELLI RICE PILAF

yield: 8 servings ∞ prep/total time: 30 min.

At the holidays, I use butter and white rice in this recipe, just like my mom and generations of Armenian women did. But most days I saute the vermicelli in olive oil and substitute brown rice for white.

- 1/2 cup broken uncooked vermicelli (1-inch lengths)
- 3 tablespoons butter
- 3 cups reduced-sodium chicken broth
- 2 cups uncooked basmati rice
- 1 cup water
- 1 teaspoon salt
- 1/2 teaspoon pepper

1. In a large saucepan, saute vermicelli in butter for 4-5 minutes or until golden brown. Add the broth, rice, water, salt and pepper. Bring to a boil. Reduce heat; cover and simmer for 15-20 minutes or until rice is tender. Fluff with a fork.

ARMENIAN OKRA

yield: 8 servings ∞ prep/total time: 30 min.

We always use fresh okra in from our garden for this recipe when I was a kid, but I've found that frozen, thawed okra works fine, too. To get the full effect, you must spoon this over the rice pilaf so it soaks up the sauce.

- 2 medium onions, halved and sliced
- 1 tablespoon olive oil
- 1-1/2 cups vegetable *or* chicken broth
- 1/4 cup tomato paste
- 1/2 teaspoon salt
- 1/2 teaspoon pepper
- 1-1/2 pounds fresh or frozen okra, thawed
- 1 cup dried apricots
- 1 tablespoon lemon juice

1. In a large skillet, saute onions in oil until tender. Add the broth, tomato paste, salt and pepper. Bring to a boil.

2. Stir in the okra, apricots and lemon juice. Return to a boil. Reduce heat; cover and simmer for 10-12 minutes or until okra is tender.

ARMENIAN GARDEN SALAD

yield: 16 servings (3/4 cup each)
prep/total time: 20 min.

Armenians are really big on salads, with everything chopped very fine. We even heap them on Armenian pizza and fold everything over like a salad sandwich.

- 1 bunch romaine, torn
- 2 medium tomatoes, chopped
- 1 medium cucumber, seeded and chopped
- 1 medium sweet red pepper, chopped
- 1 small red onion, thinly sliced
- 1 tablespoon minced fresh parsley
- 1 teaspoon minced fresh basil
- 1 teaspoon minced fresh mint

DRESSING:
- 1/4 cup white wine vinegar
- 1/4 cup olive oil
- 1 garlic clove, minced
- 1 teaspoon lemon juice
- 1/2 teaspoon dried tarragon
- 1/2 teaspoon pepper
- 1/4 teaspoon salt

1. In a salad bowl, combine the first eight ingredients. In a small bowl, whisk the dressing ingredients. Drizzle over salad; toss to coat. Serve immediately.

THE SECRET OF MULTITASKING

My mom is adept at multitasking. She learned that from her mother, who everyone said flowed through the kitchen with ease and elegance. Their secret: a cheat sheet. When entertaining, they kept a list of everything that needed to be done, including which dishes were to be used for each course. The dessert plates and coffee machine were set up in one corner; the platters for the main course waited in another corner. Now that's how I entertain!

—Jean Ecos, Hartland, Wisconsin

SUNDAY'S *barbecued chicken*

[1993]

"My husband, Rawley, and I raised our family on a dairy farm for over 20 years. So, for many years, I've cooked big meals for family and farmhands. I created my own cookbook and it features two of my favorite types of recipes—make-aheads and oven dishes—which allow me to attend to other matters while the food cooks."

—*Esther Shank, Harrisonburg, Virginia, Field Editor*

OVEN BARBECUED CHICKEN

yield: 6-8 servings ∽ prep: 25 min. ∽ bake: 45 min.

Chicken and Sunday dinner go together in my mind, and this oven dish is perfect for me. I brown the chicken and mix up the sauce, then pop the chicken in the oven when we leave for church. We have a wonderful meal waiting for us when we come home.

1	broiler/fryer chicken, cut up (3 to 4 pounds)
2	tablespoons canola oil
1/3	cup chopped onion
3	tablespoons butter
3/4	cup ketchup
1/2	cup hot water
1/3	cup cider vinegar
3	tablespoons brown sugar
1	tablespoon Worcestershire sauce
2	teaspoons prepared mustard
1/4	teaspoon salt
1/8	teaspoon pepper

1. In a large skillet, brown chicken in oil in batches. Drain chicken on paper towels.

2. Meanwhile, in a small saucepan, saute onion in butter until tender; stir in the remaining ingredients. Simmer, uncovered, for 15 minutes.

3. Place the chicken in an ungreased 13-in. x 9-in. baking dish. Pour the barbecue sauce over the chicken. Bake, uncovered, at 350° for 45-60 minutes or until chicken juices run clear, basting occasionally.

FAVORITE BROCCOLI SALAD

yield: 6-8 servings ∽ prep/total time: 20 min.

"Fresh tasting, so colorful and delicious dressing" are some of the compliments I get whenever I serve this broccoli salad with a meal or take it to a church dinner. Although I use many other good salad recipes, I'm especially fond of this one.

1	bunch broccoli, separated into florets
1	head cauliflower, separated into florets
8	bacon strips, cooked and crumbled
1	cup chopped seeded tomatoes
1/3	cup chopped onion
2	hard-cooked eggs, sliced
1	cup mayonnaise
1/3	cup sugar
2	tablespoons cider vinegar

1. In a large salad bowl, combine the broccoli, cauliflower, bacon, tomatoes, onion and eggs; set aside.

2. In another bowl, combine the mayonnaise, sugar and vinegar. Just before serving, pour dressing over salad and toss to coat.

DELUXE CHOCOLATE MARSHMALLOW BARS

yield: about 3 dozen ∽ prep: 25 min.
bake: 20 min. + chilling

(*Pictured on page 542*)

I'd have to say that I've been asked to share this chocolaty layered recipe more than any other in my collection. They're a longtime favorite of our three daughters. I can't even begin to count how many times I've made them.

3/4 cup butter, softened
1-1/2 cups sugar
3 eggs
1 teaspoon vanilla extract
1-1/3 cups all-purpose flour
3 tablespoons baking cocoa
1/2 teaspoon baking powder
1/2 teaspoon salt
1/2 cup chopped nuts, optional
4 cups miniature marshmallows

TOPPING:
1-1/3 cups semisweet chocolate chips
1 cup peanut butter
3 tablespoons butter
2 cups crisp rice cereal

1. In a small bowl, cream the butter and sugar until light and fluffy. Add eggs, one at a time, beating well after each addition. Beat in vanilla.

2. Combine flour, cocoa, baking powder and salt; gradually add to the creamed mixture. Stir in nuts if desired. Spread in a greased 15-in. x 10-in. x 1-in. baking pan.

3. Bake at 350° for 15-18 minutes. Sprinkle with marshmallows; bake 2-3 minutes longer. Remove to a wire rack. Using a knife dipped in water, spread melted marshmallows evenly over top. Cool brownies completely.

4. For topping, combine the chocolate chips, peanut butter and butter in a small saucepan. Cook and stir over low heat until blended. Remove from the heat; stir in cereal. Spread over bars immediately. Chill.

MEXICAN CORN BREAD

yield: 8-10 servings ∽ prep: 15 min.
bake: 30 min.

This tasty corn bread is easy to mix up. I serve it often with a meal or hearty bowl of soup as an alternative to rolls. Cheddar cheese makes it especially flavorful, and the diced peppers add nice color.

1 cup yellow cornmeal
1/3 cup all-purpose flour
2 tablespoons sugar
2 teaspoons baking powder
1 teaspoon salt
1/2 teaspoon baking soda
2 eggs
1 cup buttermilk
1 can (8-1/4 ounces) cream-style corn
1/3 cup canola oil
1/3 cup chopped onion
2 tablespoons chopped green pepper
1/2 cup shredded cheddar cheese

1. In a large bowl, combine the first six ingredients. Whisk together the eggs, buttermilk, corn, oil, onion and green pepper. Stir into dry ingredients just until moistened. Fold in cheese.

2. Pour into a greased 10-in. ovenproof skillet or 9-in. square baking pan. Bake at 350° for 30-35 minutes or until a toothpick inserted near the center comes out clean.

DELUXE CHOCOLATE MARSHMALLOW BARS

"I made these the other day and they were excellent. I had to give them away because I kept eating them. I changed the recipe by using 2 cups of Chex cereal, then crushed it instead of using Rice Krispies. I also used crunchy peanut butter because that was what I had in the house."
—Pamkevin

BERRY *special luncheon*

[1994]

❝I'm an avid cook and since "berry" is part of my last name, it's no wonder that strawberries and raspberries top my list of favorite spring and summertime ingredients! I created this meal many years ago for a cooking class I taught at a gourmet cooking shop. The class loved it, and I've served this meal countless times since. ❞

—*Janet Mooberry, Peoria, Illinois, Field Editor*

SPINACH CHICKEN SALAD
yield: 8-10 servings ∞ prep: 20 min. + chilling
(Pictured on page 539)

Dazzle your hungry visitors with this crunchy salad. It showcases an interesting mixture of chicken, pasta, spinach and other vegetables. The delectable dressing complements the bright ingredients. A hearty plateful makes a satisfying entree.

- 5 cups cubed cooked chicken (about 3 whole breasts)
- 2 cups green grape halves
- 1 cup snow peas
- 2 cups packed torn spinach
- 2-1/2 cups sliced celery
- 7 ounces spiral pasta *or* elbow macaroni, cooked and drained
- 1 jar (6 ounces) marinated artichoke hearts, drained and quartered
- 1/2 large cucumber, sliced
- 3 green onions with tops, sliced

DRESSING:
- 1/2 cup canola oil
- 1/4 cup sugar
- 2 tablespoons white wine vinegar
- 1 teaspoon salt
- 1/2 teaspoon dried minced onion
- 1 teaspoon lemon juice
- 2 tablespoons minced fresh parsley

Large spinach leaves, optional
Oranges slices, optional

1. In a large bowl, combine the chicken, grapes, peas, spinach, celery, pasta, artichoke hearts, cucumber and green onions. Cover and refrigerate. In a small bowl, whisk the remaining ingredients. Cover and refrigerate.

2. Just before serving, whisk the dressing and pour over salad; toss to coat. If desired, serve on a spinach leaf and garnish with oranges.

SPRINGTIME PUNCH
yield: 16-20 servings (3 quarts)
prep: 15 min. + chilling

I use this punch to start off a party. Its blend of lemon, orange and pineapple juices creates the sunny color and fruity flavor, while ginger ale adds zesty fizz. Floating fresh strawberries in the punch bowl will add flair to this beverage.

- 2 cups sugar
- 2-1/2 cups water
- 1 cup lemon juice (3 to 4 lemons)
- 1 cup orange juice (2 to 3 oranges)
- 3/4 cup thawed pineapple juice concentrate
- 2 quarts ginger ale, chilled

1. In a large saucepan, bring the sugar and water to a boil. Boil for 10 minutes; remove from the heat. Stir in the lemon, orange and pineapple juices. Refrigerate. Just before serving; transfer to a punch bowl; stir in the ginger ale.

COOL RASPBERRY SOUP

yield: 4-6 servings ∞ **prep: 10 min. + chilling**

An exquisite combination of spices and a rich berry flavor make this beautiful soup so refreshing.

- 1 package (20 ounces) frozen unsweetened raspberries, thawed
- 1-1/4 cups water
- 1/4 cup white wine, optional
- 1 cup cran-raspberry juice
- 1/2 cup sugar
- 1-1/2 teaspoons ground cinnamon
- 3 whole cloves
- 1 tablespoon lemon juice
- 1 cup (8 ounces) raspberry yogurt
- 1/2 cup sour cream

1. In a blender, puree raspberries, water and wine if desired. Transfer to a saucepan; add cran-raspberry juice, sugar, cinnamon and cloves. Bring just to a boil over medium heat. Remove from the heat; strain and allow to cool.

2. Whisk in lemon juice and yogurt. Refrigerate. To serve, pour into bowls and top with a dollop of sour cream.

SKY-HIGH STRAWBERRY PIE

yield: 8-10 servings ∞ **prep: 20 min.** ∞ **cook: 5 min. + chilling**

This pie is my specialty. It's fairly simple to make but so dramatic to serve. The ultimate taste of spring, this luscious dessert has such big, fresh berry taste, I've had many requests to bring it to gatherings.

- 3 quarts fresh strawberries, *divided*
- 1-1/2 cups sugar
- 6 tablespoons cornstarch
- 2/3 cup water
- Red food coloring, optional
- 1 deep-dish pastry shell (10 inches), baked
- 1 cup heavy whipping cream
- 4-1/2 teaspoons instant vanilla pudding mix

1. In a large bowl, mash enough berries to equal 3 cups. In a large saucepan, combine sugar and cornstarch. Stir in mashed berries and water. Bring to a boil over medium heat, stirring constantly. Cook and stir for 2 minutes or until thickened.

2. Remove from the heat; add food coloring if desired. Pour into a large bowl. Chill for 20 minutes, stirring occasionally, until mixture is just slightly warm. Fold in the remaining berries. Pile into pastry shell. Chill for 2-3 hours.

3. In a small bowl, whip the cream until soft peaks form. Sprinkle dry pudding mix over cream and whip until stiff. Pipe around edge of pie or dollop on individual slices.

CINNAMON TWISTS

yield: 4 dozen ∞ **prep: 25 min. + rising**
bake: 15 min.

These delightful golden twists are perfect as part of a holiday meal. The brown sugar and cinnamon give them a delicate, spicy flavor.

- 1 package (1/4 ounce) active dry yeast
- 3/4 cup warm water (110° to 115°), *divided*
- 4 to 4-1/2 cups all-purpose flour
- 1/4 cup sugar
- 1-1/2 teaspoons salt
- 1/2 cup warm 2% milk (110° to 115°)
- 1/4 cup butter, softened
- 1 egg

FILLING:
- 1/4 cup butter, melted
- 1/2 cup packed brown sugar
- 4 teaspoons ground cinnamon

1. In a large bowl, dissolve yeast in 1/4 cup warm water. Add 2 cups flour, sugar, salt, milk, butter, egg and remaining water; beat on medium speed for minutes. Stir in enough remaining flour to form a soft dough.

2. Turn onto a floured surface; knead until smooth and elastic, about 6-8 minutes. Place dough in a greased bowl, turning once to grease top. Cover and let rise in a warm place until doubled, about 1 hour.

3. Punch down dough. Roll into a 16-in. x 12-in. rectangle. Brush with butter. Combine brown sugar and cinnamon; sprinkle over butter. Let dough rest for 6 minutes. Cut lengthwise into three 16-in. x 4-in. strips. Cut each strip into sixteen 4-in. x 1-in. pieces. Twist and place on greased baking sheets. Cover and let rise until doubled, about 30 minutes.

4. Bake at 350° for 15 minutes or until golden brown.

CAN'T-*miss cookout*

TERIYAKI FINGER STEAKS

yield: 6 servings ∽ **prep: 15 min. + marinating**
grill: 10 min.

(Pictured on page 541)

When these flavorful skewered steaks are sizzling on the grill, the aroma makes everyone around stop what they're doing and come to see what's cooking. The tasty marinade is easy to make, and these little steaks are quick to cook and fun to eat.

1/2	cup reduced-sodium soy sauce
1/4	cup cider vinegar
2	tablespoons brown sugar
2	tablespoons finely chopped onion
1	tablespoon canola oil
1	garlic clove, minced
1/2	teaspoon ground ginger
1/8	teaspoon pepper
2	pounds beef top sirloin steak

1. In a large resealable plastic bag, combine the first eight ingredients. Trim fat from steak and slice across the grain into 1/2-in. strips. Add the beef to bag; seal bag and turn to coat. Refrigerate for 2-3 hours.

2. Drain and discard marinade. Loosely thread the meat strips onto six metal or soaked wooden skewers. Grill, uncovered, over medium-hot heat for 7-10 minutes or until meat reaches desired doneness, turning often.

STRAWBERRY-GLAZED FRUIT SALAD

yield: 6-8 servings ∽ **prep: 10 min. + chilling**

I first tasted this delightful salad at a friend's house when she served it with dinner. It tastes so good made with fresh strawberries. After sampling it, no one would ever believe how incredibly easy it is to prepare.

1	quart fresh strawberries, halved
1	can (20 ounces) pineapple chunks, drained
4	firm bananas, sliced
1	jar *or* pouch (16 ounces) strawberry glaze

1. In a large bowl, gently toss the strawberries, pineapple and bananas; fold in glaze. Chill for 1 hour.

Editor's Note: Strawberry glaze can often be found in the produce section of your grocery store.

SELECTING A FIRM BANANA

Firm bananas have a yellow skin and green tips. If the skin is green, you can hasten ripening by placing them in a paper bag with or without an apple.

—*Taste of Home Cooking Experts*

CHOCOLATE ALMOND CHEESECAKE

**yield: 12 servings ∞ prep: 20 min. + chilling
bake: 45 min. + cooling**

*My family enjoys a good meal, but we all save room for dessert
when this cheesecake is part of the menu. Its rich chocolate flavor
is so satisfying when we're craving something sweet and creamy.*

1-1/4 cups graham cracker crumbs
1-1/2 cups sugar, *divided*
  1/2 cup plus 2 tablespoons baking cocoa, *divided*
  1/4 cup butter, melted
    2 packages (8 ounces *each*) cream cheese, softened
    1 cup (8 ounces) sour cream
1-1/2 teaspoons almond extract, *divided*
    3 eggs, lightly beaten
    1 cup heavy whipping cream
  1/4 cup confectioners' sugar
  1/4 cup sliced almonds, toasted

1. In a small bowl, combine the cracker crumbs, 1/4 cup sugar, 2 tablespoons cocoa and butter. Press onto bottom of a 9-in. springform pan; chill.

2. In a large bowl, beat the cream cheese, sour cream and remaining sugar until smooth. Beat in 1 teaspoon extract and remaining cocoa. Add the eggs; beat on low speed just until combined.

3. Pour into crust. Bake at 350° for 45-50 minutes or until the center is almost set. Cool on a wire rack for 10 minutes. Carefully run a knife around edge of pan to loosen; cool for 1 hour longer. Refrigerate overnight. Remove the sides of pan.

4. In a large bowl, beat the cream until it begins to thicken. Add confectioners' sugar and remaining extract; beat until stiff peaks form. Spread evenly over cheesecake. Sprinkle with almonds. Store in refrigerator.

SKILLET HERBED RICE PILAF

**yield: 6 servings ∞ prep: 15 min.
cook: 15 min. + standing**

*I have been serving this dish for so many years that when my
daughter, Jennifer, was 12, she was already an expert at making
it. What a great help for a busy working mom like me!*

    1 cup uncooked long grain rice
    1 cup chopped celery
  3/4 cup chopped onion
  1/4 cup butter, cubed
2-1/2 cups water
    1 package (2 to 2-1/2 ounces) chicken noodle soup mix
    2 tablespoons fresh minced parsley
    1 teaspoon dried thyme
  1/4 teaspoon rubbed sage
  1/4 teaspoon pepper
    1 tablespoon chopped pimientos, optional

1. In a large skillet, cook the rice, celery and onion in butter, stirring constantly, until rice is browned. Stir in the water, soup mix, parsley, thyme, sage and pepper; bring to a boil. Reduce heat; cover and simmer for 15 minutes. Stir in the pimientos if desired.

2. Remove from the heat and let stand, covered, for 10 minutes. Fluff with a fork.

SOFTENING CREAM CHEESE

It will take about 30 minutes at room temperature to soften cream cheese. It is soft when you can easily make an indentation in it with your finger.

—*Taste of Home Cooking Experts*

FARM-*style fare*

[1996]

"I was raised on a farm and am now married to a farmer. I draw on a heritage of good country cooking! We grow grain and raise hogs on a farm owned by my husband, Dennis, and his two brothers' family. Over the years, I've created quite a library of fabulous pork recipes."

—*Patricia Staudt, Marble Rock, Iowa, Field Editor*

ITALIAN MEAT LOAVES

yield: 10 servings ∽ **prep: 15 min.** ∽ **bake: 45 min.**

We raise hogs, so pork is something I often use in my cooking. These miniature meat loaves made with ground pork and Italian herbs are very tasty. Our children especially like the topping of ketchup and Parmesan cheese.

- 2 **eggs, lightly beaten**
- 3/4 **cup cracker** *or* **bread crumbs**
- 1/2 **cup 2% mllk**
- 1/2 **cup plus 2 tablespoons grated Parmesan cheese,** *divided*
- 1/4 **cup finely chopped onion**
- 1 **teaspoon Worcestershire sauce**
- 1 **teaspoon garlic salt**
- 1 **teaspoon Italian seasoning,** *divided*
- 2 **pounds ground pork**
- 1/4 **cup ketchup**

1. In a large bowl, combine the eggs, bread crumbs, milk, 1/2 cup cheese, onion, Worcestershire sauce, garlic salt and 1/2 teaspoon Italian seasoning. Crumble pork over mixture and mix well. Shape into 10 individual loaves.

2. Place on a rack in a greased large shallow baking pan. Spread ketchup over loaves; sprinkle with remaining cheese and Italian seasoning.

3. Bake, uncovered, at 350° for 45-55 minutes until a thermometer reads 160°.

OATMEAL DINNER ROLLS

yield: 1-1/2 dozen ∾ prep: 40 min. + rising ∾ bake: 20 min.

(Pictured on page 542)

These fluffy rolls go perfectly with any meal. They have a delicious homemade flavor that's irresistible. They're not hard to make, and they bake up nice and high.

- 2 cups water
- 1 cup quick-cooking oats
- 3 tablespoons butter
- 1 package (1/4 ounce) active dry yeast
- 1/3 cup warm water (110° to 115°)
- 1/3 cup packed brown sugar
- 1 tablespoon sugar
- 1-1/2 teaspoons salt
- 4-3/4 to 5-1/4 cups all-purpose flour

1. In a large saucepan, bring water to a boil; add oats and butter. Cook and stir for 1 minute. Remove from the heat; cool to lukewarm.

2. In a large bowl, dissolve yeast in warm water. Add the oat mixture, sugars, salt and 4 cups of flour; beat until smooth. Add enough remaining flour to form a soft dough.

3. Turn onto a floured surface; knead until smooth and elastic, about 6-8 minutes. Place in a greased bowl, turning once to grease top. Cover and let rise in a warm place until doubled, about 1 hour.

4. Punch dough down; allow to rest for 10 minutes. Shape into 18 balls. Place in two greased 9-in. round baking pans. Cover and let rise until doubled, about 45 minutes.

5. Bake at 350° for 20-25 minutes or until golden brown. Remove from pan to wire racks.

TANGY COLESLAW

yield: 10 servings ∾ prep: 10 min. + chilling

If you've been searching for the perfect coleslaw, give this one a try! It has a terrific crunch, and the simple dressing is sweet and tangy all in one. This is a great way to get your family to eat cabbage. We love it.

- 1/2 large head cabbage, shredded
- 2 large carrots, shredded
- 1/2 cup finely chopped green pepper
- 2 tablespoons finely chopped onion

DRESSING:

- 1/4 cup sugar
- 3 tablespoons cider vinegar
- 2 tablespoons canola oil
- 1 teaspoon celery seed
- 1/2 teaspoon salt

1. In a large bowl, combine the cabbage, carrots, green pepper and onion. In a small bowl, whisk the dressing ingredients. Pour over cabbage mixture and toss to coat. Cover and chill for 4 hours before serving.

PEANUT BUTTER BARS

yield: 3-4 dozen ∾ prep: 15 min.
bake: 20 min. + cooling

These bars can be dressed up for festive occasions by substituting colored icing for the peanut butter frosting.

- 1/2 cup butter, softened
- 1/2 cup sugar
- 1/2 cup packed brown sugar
- 1/2 cup creamy peanut butter
- 1 egg
- 1 teaspoon vanilla extract
- 1 cup all-purpose flour
- 1/2 cup quick-cooking oats
- 1 teaspoon baking soda
- 1/4 teaspoon salt
- 1 cup (6 ounces) semisweet chocolate chips

ICING:

- 1/2 cup confectioners' sugar
- 2 tablespoons creamy peanut butter
- 2 tablespoons milk

1. In a large bowl, cream the butter, sugars and peanut butter until light and fluffy. Beat in egg and vanilla. Combine the flour, oats, baking soda and salt; gradually add into the creamed mixture and mix well. Spread into a greased 13-in. x 9-in. baking pan. Sprinkle with the chocolate chips.

2. Bake at 350° for 20-25 minutes or until lightly browned. Cool on a wire rack for 10 minutes.

3. Combine icing ingredients; drizzle over the top. Cool completely. Cut into bars.

STICK-TO-YOUR RIBS *dinner*

[1997]

"My husband, Lee, and I enjoy entertaining and sharing the bounty from our garden in casual meals. We're Montana transplants who used to barbecue often for dinners at our ranch. The plum-sauced ribs that are the center of this meal were a hit on our ranch and at our new home in Kentucky. "

—*Marie Hoyer, Hodgenville, Kentucky, Former Field Editor*

RIBS WITH PLUM SAUCE

yield: 6 servings ❧ **prep: 10 min.** ❧ **bake: 1-1/2 hours**

(Pictured on page 537)

I found the recipe for this tangy-sweet basting sauce when a surplus of plums sent me searching for new ideas to use all the fruit. In summer, I like to finish the ribs on the grill, brushing on the sauce after first baking them in the oven. Depending on how many people you are serving, consider making a double batch

- 5 to 6 pounds pork spareribs
- 3/4 cup reduced-sodium soy sauce
- 3/4 cup plum jam *or* apricot preserves
- 3/4 cup honey
- 2 to 3 garlic cloves, minced

1. Cut ribs into serving-size pieces; place with bone side down on a rack in a shallow roasting pan. Cover and bake at 350° for 1 hour or until ribs are tender; drain.

2. In a small bowl, combine the remaining ingredients; baste with some of the marinade. Bake at 350° or grill over medium heat, uncovered, for 30 minutes longer, turning and basting occasionally with remaining marinade.

ZUCCHINI CAKE

yield: 20-24 servings ❧ **prep: 20 min.**
bake: 35 min. + cooling

What gardener doesn't have extra zucchini? When it's abundant, I shred and freeze plenty so I have it on hand to bake this moist sheet cake all year long. The cream cheese frosting is yummy, and the big panful always goes fast at a picnic or potluck.

- 2 cups shredded zucchini
- 2 cups sugar
- 1 cup canola oil
- 4 eggs
- 2-1/2 cups all-purpose flour
- 1-1/2 teaspoons ground cinnamon
- 1 teaspoon salt
- 1/2 teaspoon baking powder
- 1/2 teaspoon baking soda
- 1/2 cup chopped walnuts, optional

FROSTING:
- 1 package (3 ounces) cream cheese, softened
- 1/4 cup butter, softened
- 1 tablespoon 2% milk
- 1 teaspoon vanilla extract
- 2 cups confectioners' sugar

Additional chopped walnuts, optional

1. In a large bowl, beat the zucchini, sugar, oil and eggs until well blended. Combine the flour, cinnamon, salt, baking powder and baking soda; gradually beat into zucchini mixture until blended. Fold in walnuts if desired.

2. Pour into a greased 13-in. x 9-in. baking pan. Bake at 350° for 35-40 minutes or until a toothpick inserted near the center comes out clean. Cool.

3. For frosting, in a small bowl, beat the cream cheese, butter, milk and vanilla until smooth. Add confectioners' sugar and mix well. Frost cake. Sprinkle with nuts if desired. Store in the refrigerator.

CREAMY POTATO STICKS

yield: 6 servings ∞ prep: 15 min.
bake: 55 min.

This homey potato side dish harks back to my ranch kitchen in Montana, where my husband and I raised four sons and a daughter. Hearty eaters, they always spooned up big servings of this casserole. Cutting the potatoes into sticks is a nice change.

1/4 cup all-purpose flour
1/2 teaspoon salt
1-1/2 cups 2% milk
1 can (10-3/4 ounces) condensed cream of celery soup, undiluted
1/2 pound process cheese (Velveeta), cubed
5 to 6 large baking potatoes, peeled
1 cup chopped onion
Paprika

1. In a small saucepan, combine the flour and salt; gradually whisk in milk until smooth. Bring to a boil; cook and stir for 2 minutes. Remove from the heat; whisk in soup and cheese until smooth. Set aside.

2. Cut potatoes into 4-in. x 1/2-in. x 1/2-in. sticks; place in a greased 13-in. x 9-in. baking dish. Sprinkle with the onion. Top with cheese sauce. Bake, uncovered, at 350° for 55-60 minutes or until potatoes are tender. Sprinkle with paprika.

BROCCOLI TOMATO SALAD

yield: 6-8 servings ∞ prep: 20 min. + chilling

Garden-fresh tomatoes and broccoli florets brighten this summertime salad with distinctive flavor and eye-catching color. My homemade dressing mixes up in a jiffy and complements the vegetables.

1 large bunch broccoli, separated into florets
2 large tomatoes, cut into wedges
3/4 cup sliced fresh mushrooms
2 green onions, sliced
DRESSING:
3/4 cup olive oil
1/3 cup tarragon vinegar
2 tablespoons water
1 teaspoon lemon juice
1 teaspoon sugar
1 teaspoon salt, optional
3/4 teaspoon dried thyme
1 garlic clove, minced
1/2 teaspoon celery seed
1/4 teaspoon Italian seasoning
1/4 teaspoon lemon-pepper seasoning
1/4 teaspoon paprika
1/4 teaspoon ground mustard

1. Place broccoli in a large saucepan with 1 inch of water. Bring to a boil. Reduce heat; cover and simmer for 3-5 minutes or until crisp-tender. Rinse with cold water and drain. Place in a large bowl; add tomatoes, mushrooms and onions.

2. In a small bowl, whisk dressing ingredients. Pour over salad; toss gently. Cover and chill for 1 hour. Serve with a slotted spoon.

CREAMY POTATO STICKS

"Really good flavor. I was in a hurry, so I substituted frozen unseasoned steak fries. It worked great. A definite keeper. "
—ferretmama

DELIGHTFUL *midday brunch*

[1998]

"Brunch is a great meal to mark special occasions. At our house, we've celebrated birthdays, confirmations and graduations with this midmorning menu. "

—*Patricia Throlson, Clear Lake, Minnesota, Former Field Editor*

SUNDAY BRUNCH CASSEROLE

yield: 8 servings ∾ **prep: 20 min.** ∾ **bake: 35 min.**

"Isn't it about time for you to make your 'egg pie'?" my husband and sons inquire, using the nickname they've given this hearty casserole. It's nice enough for a brunch or a family supper.

- 1/2 **pound sliced bacon**
- 1/2 **cup chopped onion**
- 1/2 **cup chopped green pepper**
- 12 **eggs, lightly beaten**
- 1 **cup 2% milk**
- 1 **package (16 ounces) frozen shredded hash brown potatoes, thawed**
- 1 **cup (4 ounces) shredded cheddar cheese**
- 1 **teaspoon salt**
- 1/2 **teaspoon pepper**
- 1/4 **teaspoon dill weed**

1. In a large skillet, cook the bacon over medium heat until crisp. Remove to paper towels; drain, reserving 2 tablespoons drippings. Crumble bacon and set aside. In same skillet, saute onion and green pepper in drippings until tender; remove with a slotted spoon.

2. In a large bowl, whisk eggs and milk. Stir in the hash browns, cheese, salt, pepper, dill, onion mixture and reserved bacon.

3. Transfer to a greased 13-in. x 9-in. baking dish. Bake, uncovered, at 350° for 35-45 minutes or until a knife inserted near the center comes out clean.

PINEAPPLE HAM BAKE

yield: 8 servings ∾ **prep: 10 min.**
bake: 30 min.

This side dish is simple to fix, and the tangy pineapple flavor goes well with the casserole.

- 2 **cans (8 ounces *each*) unsweetened crushed pineapple**
- 2/3 **cup packed brown sugar**
- 1 **tablespoon white vinegar**
- 2 **teaspoons ground mustard**
- 1 **pound fully cooked ham, cut into 1/4-ince pieces**

1. Combine the first four ingredients in an ungreased 2-qt. baking dish. Stir in ham.

2. Bake, uncovered, at 350° for 30-40 minutes or until heated through. Serve with a slotted spoon.

PAT'S BLUEBERRY MUFFINS

yield: 1 dozen ∽ **prep/total time: 30 min.**

Yummy and golden, these muffins are packed with plenty of berries and are a great addition to a brunch menu. But at our house, muffins aren't just relegated to mornings!

- 2 cups all-purpose flour
- 1/3 cup plus 2 tablespoons sugar
- 1 tablespoon baking powder
- 1 teaspoon salt
- 1 cup fresh *or* frozen blueberries, thawed
- 1 egg
- 1 cup 2% milk
- 1/4 cup butter, melted

1. In a large bowl, combine the flour, sugar, baking powder and salt. Add blueberries. In another bowl, beat the egg and milk; stir in butter. Stir into the dry ingredients just until moistened.

2. Fill greased or paper-lined muffin cups two-thirds full. Bake at 400° for 20-25 minutes or until a toothpick inserted near the center comes out clean. Serve warm.

FROZEN FRUIT CUPS

yield: 10 servings ∽ **prep: 10 min. + freezing**

Individual servings of this rosy-orange fruit blend are refreshing and attractive parts of brunch. Freeze the salad in clear, disposable plastic glasses, or set foil cupcake liners inside sauce dishes or sherbet glasses.

- 2 cans (20 ounces *each*) crushed pineapple, undrained
- 2 packages (10 ounces *each*) frozen sweetened sliced strawberries, thawed
- 1 can (20 ounces) fruit cocktail, undrained
- 1 can (12 ounces) frozen orange juice concentrate, thawed
- 3/4 cup thawed lemonade concentrate
- 6 medium firm bananas, cubed

1. In a large bowl, combine all ingredients. Pour into foil-lined muffin cups or individual plastic beverage glasses. Freeze until solid. When ready to serve, thaw for 30-45 minutes before serving.

OVERNIGHT COFFEE CAKE

yield: 6-8 servings ∽ **prep: 15 min. + chilling** ∽ **bake: 40 min.**

It's so convenient to mix up this old-fashioned breakfast treat the night before and bake it fresh the morning you serve it. We like the cake's light texture and nutty brown sugar topping spiced with cinnamon and nutmeg.

- 1/3 cup butter, softened
- 1/2 cup sugar
- 1/4 cup packed brown sugar
- 1 egg, lightly beaten
- 1 cup all-purpose flour
- 1/2 teaspoon baking powder
- 1/4 teaspoon baking soda
- 1/2 teaspoon ground cinnamon
- 1/2 cup buttermilk

TOPPING:
- 1/4 cup packed brown sugar
- 1/4 cup finely chopped pecans
- 1/4 teaspoon ground cinnamon
- 1/8 teaspoon ground nutmeg, optional

1. In a large bowl, cream butter and sugars until light and fluffy. Beat in egg. Combine the flour, baking powder, baking soda and cinnamon; gradually add to creamed mixture alternately with buttermilk, beating well after each addition.

2. Spread into a greased 8-in. square baking pan. Combine topping ingredients; sprinkle over batter. Cover and refrigerate overnight.

3. Bake, uncovered, at 350° for 40-45 minutes or until a toothpick inserted near the center comes out clean. Cool on a wire rack.

FESTIVE *make-ahead menu*

[1999]

"My husband, Roger, and I often celebrate Christmas at home with a few of our children and grandchildren. With so many people in the house, I'd rather spend time with them than cooking in the kitchen. My menu consists mainly of make-ahead foods, so I can relax, too."

—*Audrey Thibodeau, Gilbert, Arizona, Former Field Editor*

ROSEMARY PORK ROAST

yield: 8 servings ∞ **prep: 10 min. + marinating**
bake: 1 hour + standing

Tender and full of flavor, this lovely roast is an impressive main dish for a Christmas dinner or any special occasion. The aroma of roasting pork is enhanced by rosemary and garlic. This entree is just mouthwatering.

- 1 cup thinly sliced/chopped green onions
- 4-1/2 cups chicken broth, divided
- 1/2 cup red wine vinegar
- 1/4 cup olive oil
- 8 garlic cloves, minced
- 2 tablespoons minced fresh rosemary *or* 2 teaspoons dried rosemary, crushed
- 1/2 teaspoon pepper
- 1 boneless pork loin roast (3 to 3-1/2 pounds)
- 1 teaspoon salt, optional
- 2 tablespoons cornstarch
- 1/4 cup cold water

1. In a large bowl, combine the onions, 1/2 cup broth, vinegar, oil, garlic, rosemary and pepper. Pour half of the marinade into a large resealable plastic bag. Add the pork; seal bag and turn to coat. Refrigerate for 4-8 hours, turning occasionally. Cover and refrigerate remaining marinade.

2. Drain and discard marinade from pork. Place with fat side up in an ungreased shallow roasting pan.

3. In a large bowl, combine reserved marinade with remaining broth; pour over roast. Sprinkle with salt if desired. Bake, uncovered, at 350° for 1 to 1-1/4 hours or until a thermometer reads 145°. Let meat stand for 10 minutes before slicing.

4. Meanwhile, skim fat from the pan juices. Combine cornstarch and water until smooth; stir into juices. Bring to a boil over medium heat; cook and stir for 2 minutes or until thickened. Serve with roast.

APPLE SWEET POTATO BAKE

yield: 8 servings ∞ **prep: 15 min.** ∞ **bake: 30 min.**

I like to serve this side with roast pork. The nutmeg and allspice complement both the apples and the sweet potatoes.

- 3 cups sliced peeled cooked sweet potatoes
- 3 cups sliced peeled tart apples (about 2 large)
- 3/4 cup packed brown sugar
- 3/4 teaspoon ground nutmeg
- 1/4 teaspoon ground allspice
- 1/4 teaspoon salt
- Dash pepper
- 1 tablespoon butter

1. In a greased 1-1/2-qt. baking dish, layer half of the sweet potatoes and apples. In a small bowl, combine the brown sugar, nutmeg, allspice, salt and pepper; sprinkle half over apples. Dot with half of the butter. Repeat layers.

2. Cover and bake at 350° for 15 minutes. Baste with pan juices. Bake, uncovered, 15 minutes longer or until apples are tender.

CRANBERRY SHIVER

yield: 10 servings ∽ prep: 15 min. + freezing

Cool and refreshing, this pretty dessert is delightfully sweet-tart and makes the perfect ending to a bountiful holiday meal.

- 1 package (12 ounces) fresh *or* frozen cranberries
- 3 cups water, *divided*
- 1-3/4 cups sugar
- 1/4 cup lemon juice
- 1 teaspoon grated orange peel

Fresh mint, optional

1. In a large saucepan, bring cranberries and 2 cups water to a boil. Reduce heat; simmer for 5 minutes. Press through a strainer to remove skins; discard skins.

2. Transfer to a large bowl. Stir in the sugar, lemon juice, orange peel and remaining water. Pour into an 8-in. square pan. Cover and freeze until ice begins to form around the edges of the pan, about 1-1/2 hours; stir. Freeze until mushy, about 30 minutes.

3. Spoon into a freezer container; cover and freeze. Remove from the freezer 20 minutes before serving. Scoop into small dishes; garnish with mint if desired.

FANCY BAKED POTATOES

yield: 8 servings ∽ prep: 1-1/4 hours + cooling
bake: 35 min.

I can't count the times I've turned to this recipe when company is coming. The potato filling is creamy and rich-tasting. But the best part is not having the hassle of mashing potatoes at the last minute.

- 4 large baking potatoes
- 2 teaspoons canola oil, optional
- 2 tablespoons butter
- 1/4 cup 2% milk
- 1/2 cup sour cream
- 1/2 teaspoon salt
- 1/4 teaspoon pepper
- 1 jar (2 ounces) diced pimientos, drained, *divided*
- 2 tablespoons minced chives, *divided*

1. Scrub and pierce potatoes; rub with oil if desired. Bake at 375° for 1 hour or until tender. Cool.

2. Cut each potato in half lengthwise. Scoop out the pulp, leaving thin shells. In a large bowl, mash pulp with butter. Stir in milk, sour cream, salt, pepper and half of pimientos and chives. Spoon into potato shells. Place on a baking sheet. Bake, uncovered, at 375° for 20-30 minutes or until heated. Sprinkle with remaining pimientos and chives.

HOLLY BERRY COOKIES

yield: 2 dozen ∽ prep: 30 min. + chilling
bake: 10 min. + cooling

What would Christmas be without overflowing tins of cookies? These festive, filled cookies are ones my family looks forward to each year. Plus, you can freeze them for up to 2 months.

- 2 cups all-purpose flour
- 1 cup sugar
- 1 teaspoon ground cinnamon
- 3/4 teaspoon baking powder
- 1/4 teaspoon salt
- 1/2 cup cold butter, cubed
- 1 egg
- 1/4 cup 2% milk
- 2/3 cup seedless raspberry jam

GLAZE:
- 2 cups confectioners' sugar
- 2 tablespoons 2% milk
- 1/2 teaspoon vanilla extract

Red hot candies
Green food coloring

1. In a large bowl, combine the first five ingredients. Cut in butter until mixture resembles coarse crumbs. In a small bowl, beat egg and milk. Add to crumb mixture just until moistened. Cover and refrigerate for 1 hour or until dough is easy to handle.

2. On a lightly floured surface, roll out dough to 1/8-in. thickness. Cut with a 2-in. round cookie cutter. Place on ungreased baking sheets. Bake at 375° for 8-10 minutes or until edges are lightly browned. Cool on wire racks. Spread jam on half of the cookies; top each with another cookie.

3. In a small bowl, combine the sugar, milk and vanilla until smooth; spread over cookies. Decorate with red-hots before glaze is set. Let dry. Using a small, new paintbrush and green food coloring, paint holly leaves on cookies.

A PICNIC *spread*

[2000]

"A picnic is such fun for everyone, especially when you take along delicious foods that are easy to prepare. I've devised a portable menu that family and friends say is perfect for summertime outings. However, it is also my traditional Fourth of July meal. We just have the picnic on our patio."

—*Marion Lowery, Medford, Oregon, Former Field Editor*

GRILLED ORANGE CHICKEN STRIPS

yield: 4 servings ∾ **prep: 15 min. + marinating** ∾ **grill: 10 min.**

These savory marinated chicken strips are great for a picnic or backyard barbecue. I grill them right along with sausages and hot dogs. Skewering the chicken makes it easy to handle, but you can put the strips directly on the grill or broil them in the oven if you prefer.

- 2 tablespoons chopped fresh orange segments
- 1/4 cup orange juice
- 1/4 cup olive oil
- 2 teaspoons lime juice
- 3 garlic cloves, minced
- 1 teaspoon dried thyme
- 1 teaspoon dried oregano
- 1 teaspoon ground cumin
- 1/2 teaspoon salt, optional
- 1 pound boneless skinless chicken breasts, cut into 1/4-inch strips

1. Combine the first nine ingredients in a resealable plastic bag; add chicken and turn to coat. Seal and refrigerate for 1 hour.

2. Drain and discard marinade. Thread meat on metal or soaked wooden skewers. Grill, uncovered, over medium-hot heat for 6-8 minutes or until juices run clear, turning often.

PICNIC FRUIT PUNCH

yield: 5 quarts prep/total time: 10 min.

This pink cooler is deliciously thirst-quenching on a warm day. Seeing its color, folks guess it might be pink lemonade. They're pleasantly surprised to discover the bubbly blend includes cranberry, pineapple, orange and lemon juices.

8 cups cranberry juice
3 cups pineapple juice
3 cups orange juice
1/4 cup lemon juice
1 liter ginger ale, chilled
1 medium navel orange, sliced

1. In a large container, combine juices; refrigerate. Just before serving, transfer to a punch bowl; stir in ginger ale and orange slices.

GOLDEN RAISIN OATMEAL COOKIES

**yield: 4 dozen prep: 15 min.
bake: 15 min./batch**

Here's a slightly different twist on a traditional cookie jar treat. These crisp, chewy oatmeal cookies feature golden raisins and have a mild orange tang.

3/4 cup butter, softened
1 cup packed brown sugar
1/2 cup sugar
1 egg
2 tablespoons water
1 teaspoon vanilla extract
3 cups quick-cooking oats
2/3 cup all-purpose flour
2 tablespoons grated orange peel
1 teaspoon ground cinnamon
1/2 teaspoon baking soda
2/3 cup golden raisins

1. In a large bowl, cream butter and sugars until light and fluffy. Beat in the egg, water and vanilla. Combine the oats, flour, orange peel, cinnamon and baking soda; gradually add to creamed mixture and mix well. Stir in raisins (dough will be stiff).

2. Drop by level tablespoonfuls 2 in. apart onto ungreased baking sheets. Bake at 350° for 12-15 minutes or until the edges are lightly browned. Remove to wire racks to cool.

SALAMI PASTA SALAD

**yield: 8 servings
prep: 15 min. + marinating**

Popular any time of the year, this crowd-pleasing pasta salad is perfect for summer picnics. Made the day before, it has a pleasant vinaigrette dressing sparked with herbs. I set aside the Parmesan cheese and add it just before the salad is served.

3 cups uncooked penne pasta
8 ounces hard salami, cubed
1/2 cup minced fresh parsley
4 green onions, sliced
1/2 cup olive oil
1/4 cup cider vinegar
4 teaspoons minced fresh oregano *or* 1 teaspoon dried oregano
4 teaspoons minced fresh basil *or* 1 teaspoon dried basil
2 garlic cloves, minced
1 teaspoon salt
1/4 teaspoon pepper
1/2 cup shredded Parmesan cheese

1. In a large saucepan, cook the pasta according to package directions; rinse in cold water and drain. Transfer to a large bowl; add salami, parsley and onions.

2. In a small bowl, whisk the oil, vinegar and seasonings. Drizzle over the pasta mixture and toss to coat. Cover and refrigerate overnight. Just before serving, stir in the cheese.

SALAMI PASTA SALAD

"This is delicious! Everyone compliments me on this dish when I make it, and I make it often for family and friend get-togethers."
—*Chickadee, 4242*

SAVORY *salmon fare*

[2001]

"Since I didn't start cooking as a child, I suppose you could call me a 'late bloomer' in the kitchen. But after I started working in a restaurant years ago, I realized I wanted to spend as much time as I could with foods and started a catering business with my best friend. Like most of my menus, this one came together as I mixed and matched recipes. This one's been a winner for me."

—*Kathy Schrecengost, Oswego, New York, Former Field Editor*

MAPLE TERIYAKI SALMON FILLETS

**yield: 4 servings   prep: 10 min. + marinating
broil: 15 min.**

Maple syrup and apple juice provide the mildly sweet marinade for these salmon fillets. Whether they are broiled or grilled, the fillets glaze nicely when basted.

- 1/3 **cup apple juice**
- 1/3 **cup maple syrup**
- 3 **tablespoons reduced-sodium soy sauce**
- 2 **tablespoons finely chopped onion**
- 2 **garlic cloves, minced**
- 4 **salmon fillets (6 ounces each)**

1. In a small bowl, combine the apple juice, maple syrup, soy sauce, onion and cloves. Remove 1/2 cup marinade for basting; cover and refrigerate. Pour the remaining marinade into a large resealable plastic bag. Add the salmon; seal bag and turn to coat. Refrigerate for 1-3 hours.

2. Drain and discard marinade. Broil salmon 4 in. from the heat for 5 minutes. Baste with reserved marinade. Broil 8-10 minutes longer or until fish flakes easily with fork, basting frequently.

SPINACH SALAD WITH ORANGES

**yield: 4-6 servings (about 3/4 cup dressing)
prep/total time: 15 min.**

The tangy dressing for this refreshing salad has the right sweet-tart balance to suit my taste

- 1 **package (10 ounces) fresh spinach, torn**
- 1 **can (11 ounces) mandarin oranges, drained**
- 1 **cup sliced fresh mushrooms**
- 3 **bacon strips, cooked and crumbled**

DRESSING:
- 3 **tablespoons ketchup**
- 2 **tablespoons cider vinegar**
- 1-1/2 **teaspoons Worcestershire sauce**
- 1/4 **cup sugar**
- 2 **tablespoons chopped onion**
- 1/8 **teaspoon salt**

Dash pepper
- 1/2 **cup canola oil**

1. In a large salad bowl, toss the spinach, oranges, mushrooms and bacon; set aside.

2. In a blender, combine ketchup, vinegar, Worcestershire sauce, sugar, onion, salt and pepper; cover and process until smooth. While processing, gradually add oil in a steady stream. Serve with salad.

GARLIC SOUP

yield: 4-6 servings
prep/total time: 25 min.

This recipe can be prepared a day ahead and can easily be doubled or tripled. I garnish each serving with a dab of sour cream. By adding chicken and rice, you can turn it into a main course.

- 2 small onions, chopped
- 1/2 cup butter, cubed
- 3 garlic cloves, minced
- 6 tablespoons all-purpose flour
- 6 cups chicken broth
- 1/4 to 1/2 teaspoon cayenne pepper

1. In a large saucepan, saute onions in butter until tender, about 2-3 minutes. Add the garlic; cook 1 minute longer. Stir in flour until blended. Gradually add broth. Bring to a boil; cook and stir for 2 minutes or until thickened. Reduce heat; simmer, uncovered, for 15 minutes. Stir in cayenne.

POPPY SEED BUNDT CAKE

yield: 12 servings ∞ **prep: 15 min.**
bake: 50 min. + cooling

This cake tastes so old-fashioned, you might be tempted not to tell anyone it starts with a mix! A hint of coconut and the tender texture make it simply scrumptious. All you need to dress it up is a dusting of confectioners' sugar.

- 1 package (18-1/4 ounces) yellow cake mix
- 1 package (3.4 ounces) instant vanilla pudding mix
- 1 cup water
- 1/2 cup canola oil
- 3 eggs
- 1/2 teaspoon coconut extract

- 1/2 cup flaked coconut
- 2 tablespoons poppy seeds
- **Confectioners' sugar**

1. In a large bowl, combine cake mix, dry pudding mix, water, oil, eggs and extract; beat on low speed for 30 seconds. Beat on medium for 2 minutes. Stir in the coconut and poppy seeds.

2. Pour into a greased and floured 10-in. fluted tube pan. Bake at 350° for 48-52 minutes or until a toothpick inserted near the center comes out clean. Cool for 10 minutes before removing from pan to a wire rack to cool completely. Dust with confectioners' sugar.

NOODLE RICE PILAF

yield: 4 servings ∞ **prep: 5 min.**
cook: 30 min.

By adding a few fine egg noodles to a rice pilaf, you can have a deliciously different side dish. Terrific with fish, this also goes well with meat or poultry.

- 1 cup uncooked long grain rice
- 1/2 cup uncooked fine egg noodles *or* vermicelli
- 1/4 cup butter, cubed
- 2-3/4 cups chicken broth
- 2 tablespoons minced fresh parsley

1. In a large saucepan, cook and stir the rice and noodles in butter for 3-4 minutes or until lightly browned. Stir in broth; bring to a boil. Reduce heat; cover and simmer for 20-25 minutes or until broth is absorbed and rice is tender. Stir in parsley.

GARLIC SOUP

"Everyone loves this soup when I make it. I leave the chicken in and add barley to make a main-course meal. I serve it with delicious, moist tea biscuits."
—deannacollin

SPECIAL *company meal*

[2002]

"Growing up with a working mom and as the eldest of five boys, I was assigned cooking duty. I didn't mind, since I had a keen interest in cooking. In college I started a small catering business and continued with it while we raised our children."

—*Mark Trinklein, Racine, Wisconsin, Field Editor*

STUFFED BEEF TENDERLOIN

yield: 12 servings ∞ **prep: 25 min. + marinating**
bake: 1-1/2 hours + standing
(*Pictured on page 539*)

Slices of this elegant but easy special-occasion roast look so attractive, and you'll be delighted with the flavor.

- 1 cup olive oil
- 2 tablespoons Worcestershire sauce
- 1 teaspoon *each* dried oregano, basil and thyme
- 1 teaspoon garlic salt
- 1 teaspoon salt
- 1/2 teaspoon pepper
- 1 beef tenderloin roast (3 to 4 pounds)

STUFFING:
- 2 cups sliced fresh mushrooms
- 1/2 cup sliced green onions
- 1 can (8 ounces) water chestnuts, drained and chopped
- 1/2 cup butter, cubed
- 2 cups seasoned bread crumbs
- 3/4 cup egg substitute
- 1/4 cup grated Parmesan cheese
- 1/2 teaspoon dried oregano
- 1/2 teaspoon dried rosemary, crushed
- 1 teaspoon fennel seed
- 1/2 teaspoon pepper

1. In a resealable bag, combine first eight ingredients. Make a lengthwise slit about three-fourths of the way through the tenderloin. Place in bag; seal and turn to coat. Refrigerate for 4 hours or overnight.

2. In a large skillet, saute mushrooms, onions and water chestnuts in butter until onion is tender. Remove from the heat. Stir in remaining stuffing ingredients. Drain and discard marinade. Open tenderloin; spoon stuffing on one side. Close and tie with kitchen string. Place in a greased shallow roasting pan.

3. Bake, uncovered, at 350° for about 1-1/2 hours or until meat reaches desired doneness (for medium-rare, a thermometer should read 145°; medium, 160°; well-done, 170°). Let stand for 10-15 minutes before removing string and slicing.

MOCHA BUNDT CAKE

yield: 12-16 servings ∞ **prep: 15 min.**
bake: 55 min. + cooling

Bittersweet chocolate and strong coffee pair up to deliver distinctive taste in this moist cake.

- 12 ounces bittersweet chocolate
- 1-1/2 cups butter
- 2-1/4 cups sugar
- 3 eggs
- 2 cups strong brewed coffee
- 2 teaspoons rum extract
- 1-1/2 teaspoons vanilla extract
- 3 cups all-purpose flour
- 1-1/2 teaspoons baking soda
- 3/4 teaspoon salt
- Confectioners' sugar
- Whipped cream, optional

1. Melt chocolate and butter; stir until smooth; pour into a large bowl. Beat in sugar until smooth. Add eggs, one at a time, beating well after each addition. Beat in coffee and extracts. Combine flour, baking soda and salt; gradually add to the chocolate mixture and mix well.

2. Pour into a greased and floured 10-in. fluted tube pan. Bake at 325° for 55-65 minutes or until a toothpick inserted near the center comes out clean. Cool for 10 minutes before inverting onto a wire rack to cool completely. Dust with confectioners' sugar. Serve with whipped cream if desired.

FRUIT SALAD WITH RASPBERRY VINAIGRETTE
yield: 1-1/4 cups ∽ **prep/total time: 10 min.**

A bright, homemade berry dressing is the finishing touch to this lovely fresh fruit salad. It adds a burst of color to any table.

- 1 package (10 ounces) frozen sweetened raspberries, thawed and drained
- 1/3 cup seedless raspberry jam
- 2 tablespoons cider vinegar
- 2 tablespoons lemon juice
- 1/2 cup olive oil
- 1/8 teaspoon salt
- Dash pepper
- Dash ground nutmeg
- Assorted fresh fruit

1. In a blender, puree raspberries. Strain; discard seeds. Return puree to blender. Add jam, vinegar and lemon juice; cover and process until smooth. Add oil, salt, pepper and nutmeg; cover and process until blended. Serve with fruit.

ALMOND WILD RICE
yield: 10 servings ∽ **prep: 25 min.**
cook: 55 min.

Made with both brown rice and wild rice, this popular pilaf has a hint of fruity sweetness thanks to golden raisins.

- 5-1/2 cups chicken broth, *divided*
- 1 cup golden raisins
- 6 tablespoons butter, *divided*
- 1 cup uncooked wild rice
- 1 cup uncooked brown rice

- 1 cup sliced *or* slivered almonds
- 1/2 cup minced fresh parsley
- 1/4 teaspoon salt
- 1/4 teaspoon pepper

1. In a saucepan, bring 1/2 cup broth to a boil. Remove from heat; add raisins and set aside (do not drain). In a large saucepan, bring 3 cups broth and 2 tablespoons butter to a boil. Add wild rice; cover and simmer for 55-60 minutes or until the rice is tender; drain if necessary.

2. In large saucepan, combine the brown rice, 2 tablespoons butter and remaining broth. Bring to a boil. Reduce heat; cover and simmer for 35-40 minutes or until rice is tender; drain if necessary.

3. In a small skillet, saute the almonds in remaining butter until lightly browned. In a serving bowl, combine the wild rice, brown rice, raisin mixture, almonds, parsley, salt and pepper.

CHEDDAR POTATO SOUP
yield: 8 servings ∽ **prep/total time: 30 min.**

My home state is famous for cheese, which I use in many recipes. Cheddar gives this creamy soup a sunny color and tantalizing taste.

- 1/3 cup chopped onion
- 1/3 cup chopped celery
- 2 tablespoons butter
- 4 cups diced peeled potatoes
- 3 cups chicken *or* vegetable broth
- 2 cups (8 ounces) shredded cheddar cheese
- 2 cups 2% milk
- 1/4 teaspoon pepper
- Dash paprika
- Seasoned croutons and minced fresh parsley

1. In a saucepan, saute onion and celery in butter. Add potatoes and broth; bring to a boil. Reduce heat; cover and simmer for 10-15 minutes or until potatoes are tender. Cool slightly.

2. Puree in small batches in a blender until smooth; return to pan. Stir in cheese, milk, pepper and paprika. Cook and stir over low heat until the cheese is melted. Garnish with croutons and parsley.

CROWD-PLEASING *cuisine*

BEEF BRISKET IN GRAVY

yield: 6-8 servings ∞ prep: 20 min.
bake: 2 hours + standing

This tender roast has remained our very favorite family main dish over many years. Often, I make it ahead and reheat the beef in the gravy. It's delicious served with hot cooked noodles or mashed potatoes.

    1 fresh beef brisket (about 2 pounds)
    2 tablespoons canola oil
    1 cup hot water
    1 envelope beefy onion soup mix
    2 tablespoons cornstarch
  1/2 cup cold water

1. In a Dutch oven, brown brisket in oil on both sides over medium-high heat; drain. Combine hot water and soup mix; pour over brisket. Cover and bake at 325° for 2 to 2-1/2 hours or until meat is tender.

2. Remove brisket to a serving platter. Let stand for 10-15 minutes. Meanwhile, combine cornstarch and cold water until smooth; gradually stir into pan juices. Bring to a boil; cook and stir for 2 minutes or until thickened. Thinly slice meat across the grain; serve with the gravy.

Editor's Note: This is a fresh beef brisket, not corned beef.

PILLOW-SOFT ROLLS

yield: 2 dozen ∞ prep: 45 min. + chilling
bake: 15 min.

If you set these freshly baked rolls on the counter to cool and leave the room, they may not be there when you return! They are always a treat, my children and grandchildren tell me. Sour cream adds richness to the dough.

3-3/4 to 4-1/2 cups all-purpose flour
  1/2 cup sugar
    2 packages (1/4 ounce each) active dry yeast
1-1/4 teaspoons salt
    1 cup (8 ounces) sour cream
  1/2 cup water
    2 eggs
    1 tablespoon butter, melted

1. In a large bowl, combine 1-1/4 cups flour, sugar, yeast and salt. In a small saucepan, heat sour cream and water to 120°-130°. Add to dry ingredients; beat until blended. Beat in eggs until smooth. Stir in enough remaining flour to form a soft dough.

2. Turn dough onto a lightly floured surface; knead until smooth and elastic, about 6-8 minutes. Place in a greased bowl, turning once to grease top. Cover and refrigerate overnight.

3. Punch the dough down. Turn onto a lightly floured surface; roll out to 1/2-in. thickness. Cut with a floured 2-1/2-in. biscuit cutter. Using dull edge of a table knife, make an off-center crease in each roll. Fold along crease so the small half is on the top; press along folded edge.

4. Place in a greased 15-in. x 10-in. x 1-in. baking pan, allowing edges to touch. Cover and let rise in a warm place until doubled, about 25 minutes. Brush the tops with butter. Bake at 375° for 12-15 minutes or until golden brown.

LEMON TART

yield: 6-8 servings ✎ **prep: 10 min. + chilling**
bake: 10 min. + cooling

Here's a luscious way to end a meal! Smooth and creamy, with a refreshing lemon taste, this tart gets rave reviews. Every time I serve it to someone new, it results in a request for the recipe.

- 1 cup sugar
- 1/4 cup cornstarch
- 1 cup 2% milk
- 3 egg yolks, lightly beaten
- 1/4 cup butter, cubed
- 1 tablespoon grated lemon peel
- 1/3 cup lemon juice
- 1 cup (8 ounces) sour cream

Pastry for single-crust pie (9 inches), baked
Whipped topping

1. In a large saucepan, combine sugar and cornstarch. Gradually add milk until smooth. Cook and stir over medium-high heat until thickened. Reduce heat; cook and stir 2 minutes longer. Remove from the heat. Stir a small amount of hot liquid into egg yolks; return all to the pan. Bring to a gentle boil, stirring constantly. Cook 2 minutes longer (mixture will be very thick).

2. Remove from the heat; stir in butter and lemon peel. Gently stir in lemon juice. Cover and cool completely.

3. Fold in sour cream. Pour into pastry shell. Refrigerate pie for at least 2 hours before cutting. Garnish with the whipped topping.

GOLDEN CARROT COINS

yield: 6-8 servings
prep/total time: 25 min.

Once you try this simple yet scrumptious side dish, you'll never serve plain carrots again!

- 1/4 cup butter, cubed
- 3/4 cup chicken broth
- 2 teaspoons sugar
- 2 teaspoons salt
- 1/8 teaspoon pepper
- 14 medium carrots, cut into 1/4-inch slices
- 3 tablespoons minced fresh parsley
- 2 teaspoons lemon juice

1. In a large saucepan, melt butter. Stir in the broth, sugar, salt and pepper; bring to a boil. Add carrots. Return to a boil. Reduce heat; cover and simmer for 8-10 minutes or until carrots are crisp-tender. Stir in parsley and lemon juice. Serve with a slotted spoon.

BLUE CHEESE VINAIGRETTE

yield: 2-1/2 cups ✎ **prep/total time: 10 min.**

Even people who aren't big blue cheese fans have told me how much they enjoy this tangy dressing. It's refreshing and the flavors blend well, whether you serve it over lettuce or fresh spinach.

- 1 cup cider vinegar
- 1/4 to 1/2 cup sugar
- 1/2 to 1 cup crumbled blue cheese, *divided*
- 1 small onion, chopped
- 1 tablespoon Dijon mustard
- 2 garlic cloves, minced
- 1/2 teaspoon salt
- 1 cup canola oil

Torn salad greens and vegetables of your choice

1. In a blender, combine the vinegar, sugar, 1/2 cup blue cheese, onion, mustard, garlic and salt. Cover and process until smooth. While processing, gradually add oil in a steady stream until dressing is thickened. Stir in the remaining blue cheese if desired. Serve over salad. Cover and refrigerate leftover dressing.

ENTERTAIN *italian-style*

[2004]

"As unbelievable as it may sound, I started cooking when I was 5. My maternal grandfather owned three Italian restaurants and kept me perched at his side in the kitchens of his businesses. My first job was to tear salad greens."

—*Barbara McCalley, Allison Park, Pennsylvania, Former Field Editor*

BAKED MUSHROOM CHICKEN

yield: 4 servings ∾ prep: 20 min. ∾ bake: 20 min.

I love to entertain in any fashion—from casual gatherings to multicourse dinners. Our home is the favorite "eating place" for many of our friends and family. That's a wonderful compliment! So I always have enthusiastic tasters for new recipes or tried-and-true ones like those that make up my favorite meal featured here.

- 4 boneless skinless chicken breast halves (1 pound)
- 1/4 cup all-purpose flour
- 3 tablespoons butter, *divided*
- 1 cup sliced fresh mushrooms
- 1/2 cup chicken broth
- 1/4 teaspoon salt
- 1/8 teaspoon pepper
- 1/3 cup shredded part-skim mozzarella cheese
- 1/3 cup grated Parmesan cheese
- 1/4 cup sliced green onions

1. Flatten each chicken breast half to 1/4-in. thickness. Place flour in a resealable plastic bag; add chicken, a few pieces at a time. Seal and shake to coat.

2. In a large skillet, brown chicken in 2 tablespoons butter on both sides. Transfer to a greased 11-in. x 7-in. baking dish. In the same skillet, saute mushrooms in the remaining butter until tender. Add the broth, salt and pepper. Bring to a boil; cook for 5 minutes or until liquid is reduced to 1/2 cup. Spoon over chicken.

3. Bake, uncovered, at 375° for 15 minutes or until the chicken is no longer pink. Sprinkle with cheeses and green onions. Bake 5 minutes longer or until cheese is melted.

BERRY VINAIGRETTE

yield: 3/4 cup ∾ prep/total time: 5 min.

(Pictured on page 544)

This dressing is wonderful on tossed, fresh salad greens and your favorite salad ingredients. Because the raspberry flavor comes from jam, this versatile vinaigrette is convenient to make year-round.

- 3 tablespoons seedless raspberry jam
- 2/3 cup canola oil
- 1/3 cup red wine vinegar
- 1/4 teaspoon salt
- 1/4 teaspoon pepper

1. Place jam in a small microwave-safe bowl. Microwave, uncovered, on high for 10-15 seconds or until jam is melted. Whisk in the oil, vinegar, salt and pepper. Store in the refrigerator.

CHEESECAKE PRALINE SQUARES

yield: 15 servings ✎ prep: 20 min.
bake: 1 hour + chilling

A smooth cheesecake layer, a nutty crust, and a praline-like topping make this dessert extra special. I fix these squares often for friends or when my big Italian family gets together.

2-1/2 cups all-purpose flour
   1 cup butter, melted
 2/3 cup finely chopped pecans
   2 tablespoons confectioners' sugar
FILLING:
   3 packages (8 ounces *each*) cream cheese, softened
 2/3 cup sugar
   1 can (14 ounces) sweetened condensed milk
   2 teaspoons vanilla extract
 1/2 teaspoon grated lemon peel
   4 eggs, lightly beaten
TOPPING:
   1 cup packed brown sugar
   1 cup heavy whipping cream
   1 cup chopped pecans
1-1/2 teaspoons vanilla extract

1. In a large bowl, combine flour, butter, pecans and confectioners' sugar. Press into an ungreased 13-in. x 9-in. baking dish. Bake at 350° for 20-24 minutes or until lightly browned. Cool pan on a wire rack.

2. In a large bowl, beat the cream cheese and sugar until smooth. Add the milk, vanilla and lemon peel. Add eggs; beat on low speed just until combined. Pour over crust.

3. Bake at 350° for 35-40 minutes or until edges are lightly browned. Cool on a wire rack.

4. In a small saucepan, combine brown sugar and cream. Cook and stir over medium heat until mixture comes to a boil. Reduce heat; simmer, uncovered,

for 10 minutes. Remove from the heat; stir in pecans and vanilla. Pour over cheesecake. Refrigerate for 4 hours or overnight. Cut into squares.

TOMATO BASIL BRUSCHETTA

yield: 20 appetizers
prep/total time: 30 min.

This is one of the appetizers my friends request most. There is rarely a single piece left over when I serve it. The red pepper flakes and basil add a nice little kick to the taste.

   3 tablespoons olive oil, *divided*
   1 loaf (1 pound) Italian bread, cut into 1/2-inch slices
1-1/2 cups chopped seeded plum tomatoes
   1 jar (4 ounces) diced pimientos, rinsed and drained
   2 tablespoons chopped fresh basil
   1 teaspoon red wine vinegar
   1 teaspoon minced fresh parsley
   1 garlic clove, minced
 1/4 teaspoon salt
 1/4 teaspoon crushed red pepper flakes
 1/8 teaspoon pepper
   1 tablespoon grated Romano cheese
Fresh basil leaves

1. Using 2 tablespoons oil, lightly brush one side of bread slices. Place bread oil side up on an ungreased baking sheet. Bake at 350° for 15 minutes or until lightly browned.

2. In a large bowl, combine the tomatoes, pimientos, chopped basil, vinegar, parsley, garlic, salt, pepper flakes and pepper; stir in cheese.

3. Place a whole basil leaf on each slice of toasted bread. Top with the tomato mixture. Drizzle with remaining olive oil. Serve immediately.

TOMATO BASIL BRUSCHETTA

❝This has got to be the best thing I have ever put into my mouth! The flavor is so fresh and clean. I love to pick the tomato and basil right out of the garden to add to the freshness. So good!❞
—*irishprincess874*

SPRING DINNER *for company*

[2005]

❝Easter has always been a special time for my husband, Jeff, and me to gather with our relatives for a very wonderful meal. Our family likes to linger for hours around the table, talking and laughing together. The following menu has my top picks for our Easter meals. ❞

—Lavonn Bormuth, Westerville, Ohio, Field Editor

HAM WITH CHERRY SAUCE

yield: 8-10 servings ∾ **prep: 10 min.** ∾ **bake: 1-3/4 hours**

There's nothing I'd rather serve for Easter dinner or another springtime occasion than succulent baked ham. My recipe features a rub that adds flavor to the meat plus my mother-in-law's delicious cherry sauce with a hint of almond.

- 1 fully cooked bone-in ham (6 to 8 pounds)
- 1 cup packed brown sugar
- 3 tablespoons maple syrup
- 1 teaspoon ground mustard
- 1/2 cup sugar
- 3 tablespoons cornstarch
- 1 cup cold water
- 1 can (16 ounces) pitted dark sweet cherries, undrained
- 2 tablespoons lemon juice
- 1 teaspoon almond extract

1. Place ham in a roasting pan. Score surface of ham with shallow diagonal cuts, making diamond shapes. Combine the brown sugar, syrup and mustard; rub over ham and press into cuts.

2. Cover and bake at 325° for 1-3/4 to 2 hours or until a thermometer reads 140° and ham is heated through.

3. For cherry sauce, in a small saucepan, combine the sugar, cornstarch and water until smooth. Add cherries. Bring to a boil; cook and stir for 2 minutes or until thickened. Remove from the heat; stir in lemon juice and extract. Serve with ham.

GOLDEN SCALLOPED POTATOES

yield: 8 servings ✦ **prep: 20 min.**
bake: 1 hour

Homemade scalloped potatoes are a must with ham. We all enjoy the great taste of the rich cream sauce in this dish. My mother-in-law shared the often-used recipe with me.

1/4 **cup butter**
3 **tablespoons all-purpose flour**
1 **teaspoon salt**
Dash pepper
3 **cups 2% milk**
5 **large Yukon Gold potatoes, peeled and thinly sliced**

1. In a large saucepan over medium heat, melt the butter. Stir in the flour, salt and pepper until smooth. Gradually add the milk. Bring to a boil; cook and stir for 2 minutes or until thickened.

2. Place potatoes in a greased 9-in. square baking dish. Add sauce and stir gently to coat. Cover and bake at 325° for 30 minutes. Uncover; bake 30-40 minutes longer or until potatoes are tender.

ALMOND-ORANGE TOSSED SALAD

yield: 8 servings ✦ **prep: 20 min.**
cook: 15 min. + cooling

Another highlight of my Easter menu is this pretty salad, with its slightly sweet homemade dressing and crispy sugar-toasted almonds. I've often taken the salad to potlucks because everyone enjoys it so much.

2 **tablespoons sugar**
1/2 **cup sliced almonds**
4 **cups torn iceberg lettuce**
4 **cups torn romaine**
1 **can (11 ounces) mandarin oranges, drained**
1 **large ripe avocado, peeled and cubed**
1/2 **cup diced celery**
2 **green onions, sliced**
DRESSING:
1/4 **cup canola oil**
2 **tablespoons sugar**
2 **tablespoons cider vinegar**
2 **teaspoons minced fresh parsley**

1/4 **teaspoon salt**
1/4 **teaspoon pepper**

1. In a small skillet over medium-low heat, cook sugar without stirring for 12-14 minutes or until melted. Add almonds; stir quickly to coat. Remove from the heat; pour onto waxed paper to cool.

2. In a large serving bowl, combine the lettuce, romaine, oranges, avocado, celery, onions and almonds. In a small bowl, whisk the dressing ingredients. Pour over salad; toss gently to coat.

DOUBLE-CRUST RHUBARB PIE

yield: 8 servings ✦ **prep: 20 min.** ✦ **bake: 45 min. + cooling**

Old-fashioned and delicious, rhubarb pie is truly springtime comfort food. I buy rhubarb in season, cut it up and freeze it so I can enjoy this pie any time of year.

1 **cup sugar**
3 **tablespoons all-purpose flour**
1/2 **teaspoon ground cinnamon**
2 **eggs, lightly beaten**
4 **cups chopped fresh rhubarb *or* frozen rhubarb**
Pastry for double-crust pie (9 inches)
1 **tablespoon butter**

1. In a large bowl, combine the sugar, flour and cinnamon. Add eggs; whisk until smooth. Gently stir in rhubarb. Line a 9-in. pie plate with bottom pastry; add filling. Dot with butter.

2. Roll out remaining pastry to fit top of pie; place over filling. Trim, seal and flute edges. Cut slits in top.

3. Bake at 400° for 45-50 minutes or until crust is golden brown and filling is bubbly. Cool on a wire rack. Store in the refrigerator.

Editor's Note: If using frozen rhubarb, measure rhubarb while still frozen, then thaw completely. Drain in a colander, but do not press liquid out.

SAVORY *seafood supper*

[2006]

*"*My personal cooking pleasures didn't begin until I was an adult. I have come a long way and now am even asked to prepare foods for weddings and showers on occasion. I must admit, however, that I much prefer the simple pleasures of cooking for my husband, Ron, family, friends and coworkers. The simple, delicious meal that follows is one that Ron and I enjoy.*"*

—*Sundra Hauck, Bogalusa, Louisiana, Field Editor*

SUNDAY SHRIMP PASTA BAKE

yield: 8 servings ∞ **prep: 30 min.** ∞ **bake: 25 min.**

(Pictured on page 542)

Pasta is popular in our home, so my best meal would almost have to have it in the main course. In this delicious casserole, pasta complements the shrimp our local fishermen bring in.

- 12 ounces uncooked vermicelli
- 1 medium green pepper, chopped
- 5 green onions, chopped
- 6 tablespoons butter, cubed
- 6 garlic cloves, minced
- 2 tablespoons all-purpose flour
- 2 pounds cooked medium shrimp, peeled and deveined
- 1 teaspoon celery salt
- 1/8 teaspoon pepper
- 1 pound process cheese (Velveeta), cubed
- 1 can (10 ounces) diced tomatoes and green chilies, drained
- 1 can (4 ounces) mushroom stems and pieces, drained
- 1 tablespoon grated Parmesan cheese

1. Cook vermicelli according to the package directions. Meanwhile, in a large skillet, saute green pepper and onions in butter until tender. Add garlic; cook 1 minute longer. Gradually stir in flour until blended. Stir in the shrimp, celery salt and pepper; cook, uncovered, over medium heat for 5-6 minutes or until heated through.

2. In a microwave-safe bowl, combine the process cheese, tomatoes and mushrooms. Microwave, uncovered, on high for 3-4 minutes or until cheese is melted, stirring occasionally. Add to shrimp mixture. Drain vermicelli; stir into skillet.

3. Pour spaghetti mixture into a greased 13-in. x 9-in. baking dish. Sprinkle with the Parmesan cheese. Bake, uncovered, at 350° for 25-30 minutes or until heated through.

Editor's Note: Recipe was tested in a 1,100-watt microwave.

CITRUS QUENCHER

yield: 8 servings (2-1/2 quarts)
prep/total time: 5 min.

Sparkling and refreshing, my quencher complements a meal with just the right tartness. It's so easy to mix up that I serve this sunny beverage year-round.

- 2 liters lemon-lime soda, chilled
- 3/4 cup limeade concentrate
- 1/2 cup orange juice

1. In a large pitcher, combine all the ingredients. Serve over ice.

RIBS WITH PLUM SAUCE, page 518

FLORIDA CITRUS MERINGUE PIE, page 553

SPINACH CHICKEN SALAD, page 512

CHUNKY CRAWFISH SPREAD, page 545

STUFFED BEEF TENDERLOIN, page 528

LOW COUNTRY GRILL, page 550

SIMPLE SAUSAGE LASAGNA, page 546

TERIYAKI FINGER STEAKS, page 514

FROTHY MEXI-MOCHA COFFEE, page 552

BISCUIT-Y BELL PEPPER MUFFINS, page 551

DELUXE CHOCOLATE MARSHMALLOW BARS, page 511

OATMEAL DINNER ROLLS, page 517

SUNDAY SHRIMP PASTA BAKE, page 536

HEARTY RED BEANS AND RICE, page 571

CARIBBEAN CHICKEN CAESAR SALAD, page 552

RANCH MAC & CHEESE, page 558

CREAMY PASTA PRIMAVERA, page 564

SAUERBRATEN, page 548

CHEESE-STUFFED SHELLS, page 560

BERRY VINAIGRETTE, page 532

OLIVE-CUCUMBER TOSSED SALAD

yield: 8 servings
prep: 15 min. + marinating

You get lots of flavor from this easy-to-fix salad. It's refreshing but bold with zip from the Creole seasoning and saltiness from the olives.

- 1 cup Italian salad dressing
- 2 medium cucumbers, peeled, halved, seeded and sliced
- 1 cup pimiento-stuffed olives, halved
- 1 teaspoon Creole seasoning
- 2 packages (10 ounces each) ready-to-serve salad greens

1. In a large bowl, combine the salad dressing, cucumbers, olives and Creole seasoning. Cover and refrigerate for at least 30 minutes.

2. Just before serving, place the salad greens in a large bowl; add cucumber mixture and toss to coat.

Editor's Note: The following spices may be substituted for 1 teaspoon Creole seasoning: 1/4 teaspoon each salt, garlic powder and paprika; and a pinch each of dried thyme, ground cumin and cayenne pepper.

CHUNKY CRAWFISH SPREAD

yield: 3 cups ∞ **prep: 20 min. + chilling**
(*Pictured on page 539*)

Seafood is plentiful here, and crawfish is my favorite. I like to serve this tasty appetizer while the main course is finishing up in the oven.

- 1 package (16 ounces) frozen cooked crawfish tails, thawed
- 1 package (8 ounces) cream cheese, softened
- 1 medium green pepper, finely chopped
- 1 medium sweet red pepper, finely chopped
- 1 small onion, finely chopped
- 6 garlic cloves, minced
- 1/2 to 1 teaspoon Creole seasoning
- 1/2 teaspoon salt
- 6 to 12 drops hot pepper sauce
Assorted crackers

1. Chop crawfish; pat dry. In a small bowl, beat cream cheese until smooth. Add the peppers, onion, garlic, Creole seasoning, salt and hot pepper sauce; stir in the crawfish. Cover and refrigerate for at least 2 hours. Serve with crackers.

Editor's Note: The following spices may be substituted for 1 teaspoon Creole seasoning: 1/4 teaspoon each salt, garlic powder and paprika; and a pinch each of dried thyme, ground cumin and cayenne pepper.

NO-BAKE CHOCOLATE PIE

yield: 8 servings ∞ **prep: 15 min. + chilling**

This chocolaty pie is simple and light enough to accent even the heaviest meal. It's an Amish recipe that has been in my file for several years.

- 7 milk chocolate candy bars (1.55 ounces each), chopped
- 20 large marshmallows
- 1/2 cup 2% milk
- 2 cups whipped topping
- 1 graham cracker crust (9 inches)
Additional whipped topping, optional

1. In a large heavy saucepan, combine the candy bars, marshmallows and milk. Cook and stir over low heat until smooth. Remove from the heat; cool. Fold in the whipped topping; pour into the crust.

2. Cover and refrigerate for 4 hours or overnight. Garnish with additional whipped topping if desired.

OLIVE-CUCUMBER TOSSED SALAD

"Absolutely delicious! I have made this 3 times already and have friends asking for the recipe! I didn't have the Creole seasoning so I used the suggested substitutions and it was outstanding. To make it slightly healthier, however, I use the "free zesty Italian" dressing. Deliciously healthy!"
—*amandastarr*

EASY, *cheesy supper*

SIMPLE SAUSAGE LASAGNA

**yield: 12 servings ∞ prep: 20 min.
bake: 55 min. + standing**

(Pictured on page 540)

When I saw a lasagna recipe that did not call for precooking the noodles, I was anxious to try this time-saving shortcut. Making some changes and additions to suit my taste, I developed this popular dish that I now call my own.

- 1 **pound bulk pork sausage**
- 1 **jar (26 ounces) spaghetti sauce**
- 1/2 **cup water**
- 2 **eggs, lightly beaten**
- 3 **cups (24 ounces) 4% cottage cheese**
- 1/3 **cup grated Parmesan cheese**
- 1 **to 2 tablespoons dried parsley flakes**
- 1/2 **teaspoon *each* garlic powder, pepper, dried basil and oregano**
- 9 **uncooked lasagna noodles**
- 3 **cups (12 ounces) shredded part-skim mozzarella cheese**

1. In a large skillet, cook sausage over medium heat until no longer pink; drain. Stir in spaghetti sauce and water. Simmer, uncovered, for 10 minutes. Meanwhile, in a large bowl, combine eggs, cottage cheese, Parmesan cheese, parsley and seasonings.

2. Spread 1/2 cup meat sauce into a greased 13-in. x 9-in. baking dish. Layer with three noodles and a third of the cheese mixture, meat sauce and mozzarella cheese. Repeat layers twice.

3. Cover and bake at 375° for 45 minutes. Uncover; bake 10 minutes longer or until a thermometer reads 160°. Let stand for 15 minutes before serving.

HOT CHEDDAR-MUSHROOM SPREAD

yield: 3 cups ∞ prep/total time: 25 min.

One of my high school friends brought this fuss-free appetizer to a get-together and the rest of us couldn't get enough of it. I've since made it for family parties and potlucks, where it is always a hit.

- 2 **cups mayonnaise**
- 2 **cups (8 ounces) shredded cheddar cheese**
- 2/3 **cup grated Parmesan cheese**
- 4 **cans (4-1/2 ounces *each*) sliced mushrooms, drained**
- 1 **envelope ranch salad dressing mix**

Minced fresh parsley
Assorted crackers

1. In a large bowl, combine the mayonnaise, cheeses, mushrooms and dressing mix. Spread into a greased 9-in. pie plate.

2. Bake, uncovered, at 350° for 20-25 minutes or until the cheese is melted. Sprinkle with parsley. Serve with the crackers.

CHEDDAR SQUASH SOUP

yield: 6 servings ∽ prep/total time: 30 min.

This delectable soup feels like fall! Its golden color and rich, satisfying flavor have made it a favorite of mine, which is really amazing, because I was convinced I didn't like squash until I tried this recipe.

- 5 medium leeks (white portion only), sliced
- 2 tablespoons butter
- 1-1/2 pounds butternut squash, peeled, seeded and cubed (about 4 cups)
- 4 cups chicken broth
- 1/4 teaspoon dried thyme
- 1/4 teaspoon pepper
- 1-3/4 cups shredded cheddar cheese
- 1/4 cup sour cream
- 2 tablespoons thinly sliced green onion

1. In a large saucepan, saute leeks in butter until tender. Stir in the squash, broth, thyme and pepper. Bring to a boil. Reduce heat; cover and simmer for 10-15 minutes or until squash is tender. Cool slightly.

2. In a blender, cover and process squash mixture in small batches until smooth; return all to the pan. Bring to a boil. Reduce heat to low. Add cheese; stir until soup is heated through and cheese is melted. Garnish with sour cream and onion.

CARAMEL-PECAN CHEESECAKE PIE

yield: 6-8 servings ∽ prep: 15 min.
bake: 35 min. + chilling

In fall or any time of year, this nutty, rich and delicious pie is one I am proud to serve. While it seems very special, it's a snap to make.

- 1 sheet refrigerated pie pastry
- 1 package (8 ounces) cream cheese, softened
- 1/2 cup sugar
- 4 eggs
- 1 teaspoon vanilla extract
- 1-1/4 cups chopped pecans
- 1 jar (12-1/4 ounces) fat-free caramel ice cream topping

TOP 100 RECIPE

1. Line a 9-in. pie plate with pastry. Trim and flute edges. In a small bowl, beat the cream cheese, sugar, 1 egg and vanilla until smooth. Spread into pastry shell; sprinkle with pecans.

2. In a small bowl, whisk remaining eggs; gradually whisk in caramel topping until blended. Pour slowly over pecans.

3. Bake at 375° for 35-40 minutes or until lightly browned (loosely cover edges with foil after 20 minutes if pie browns too quickly). Cool on a wire rack for 1 hour. Refrigerate for 4 hours or overnight before slicing.

Editor's Note: This recipe was tested with Smucker's ice cream topping.

BROCCOLI WITH MUSTARD SAUCE

yield: 4 servings ∽ prep/total time: 25 min.

Stir up this smooth, delicious sauce in a jiffy in the microwave, and you'll be delighted with how it complements steamed vegetables. Start with fresh veggies or make things even easier by using a frozen blend.

- 2 pounds fresh broccoli florets, cauliflowerets *or* sliced carrots
- 1/2 cup mayonnaise
- 1/3 cup 2% milk
- 1/4 cup grated Parmesan cheese
- 1/4 cup shredded Swiss cheese
- 2 teaspoons lemon juice
- 2 teaspoons prepared mustard

Salt and pepper to taste

1. Place broccoli in a steamer basket; place in a large saucepan over 1 in. of water. Bring to a boil; cover and steam for 5-8 minutes or until crisp-tender.

2. Meanwhile, in a small microwave-safe bowl, combine the remaining ingredients. Cover and microwave at 50% power for 2 minutes or until heated through, stirring every 30 seconds. Drain broccoli. Serve with sauce.

Editor's Note: This recipe was tested in a 1,100-watt microwave.

A TASTE *of germany*

[2008]

"While I am of German descent, my mother did not cook traditional German food. I learned about the cuisine through our county extension office. When it was my turn to give a lesson to the extension group, I got classic German dishes from four area ladies who were originally from Germany. I enjoyed the recipes so much that I make this meal for my family."

—*Patricia Rutherford, Winchester, Illinois, Field Editor*

SAUERBRATEN

yield: 6 servings   prep: 25 min. + marinating   bake: 3 hours

(*Pictured on page 544*)

This is a tasty example of traditional German fare. Its definitive pickled tang is pleasing and sure to delight German food lovers.

    4 cups water
    2 cups red wine vinegar
   12 whole cloves
    2 bay leaves
    3 teaspoons salt
    3 teaspoons brown sugar
    1 boneless beef chuck roast, *or* beef rump roast *or* bottom round roast (4 pounds)
  1/4 cup all-purpose flour
    2 tablespoons canola oil
    1 large onion, cut into wedges
    5 medium carrots, cut into 1-1/2-inch pieces
    2 celery ribs, cut into 1-1/2-inch pieces

1. In a large bowl, combine the water, vinegar, cloves, bay leaves, salt and brown sugar. Remove 2 cups to a small bowl; cover and refrigerate. Pour remaining marinade into a 2-gal. resealable plastic bag. Add roast; seal bag and turn to coat. Refrigerate for 1-2 days, turning twice each day.

2. Discard marinade and spices. Pat roast dry; dredge in flour. In a large skillet over medium-high heat, brown roast in oil on all sides. Transfer to a small roasting pan. Add the onion, carrots, celery and reserved marinade.

3. Cover and bake at 325° for 3 to 3-1/2 hours or until meat is tender. With a slotted spoon, remove meat and vegetables to a serving platter. Strain cooking juices; thicken if desired.

RED CABBAGE WITH APPLE

yield: 6 servings   **prep: 15 min.**
cook: 40 min.

This delicious combination has a sweet and tart flavor with a hint of bacon and apple that goes perfectly with sauerbraten.

- 3 bacon strips, diced
- 1 medium onion, chopped
- 1 medium apple, peeled and chopped
- 1 small head red cabbage, chopped
- 1 cup water
- 1/4 cup white wine vinegar
- 1 tablespoon sugar
- 1/2 teaspoon salt

1. In a large saucepan, cook the bacon over medium heat until crisp. Using a slotted spoon, remove to paper towels to drain.

2. In the drippings, saute onion and apple until tender. Stir in the remaining ingredients. Bring to a boil. Reduce heat; cover and simmer for 30 minutes or until tender. Stir in reserved bacon.

BLACK FOREST CAKE

yield: 6-8 servings   **prep: 10 min.**
bake: 25 min. + chilling

Cake is a favorite German dessert. When my daughter went to Germany on a backpacking trip, she said the streets were lined with pastry shops.

- 1 package (9 ounces) chocolate cake mix
- 1/2 cup water
- 1 egg
- 1 package (3 ounces) cream cheese, softened
- 2 tablespoons sugar
- 1 carton (8 ounces) frozen whipped topping, thawed
- 1 can (21 ounces) cherry pie filling

1. In a small bowl, beat the cake mix, water and egg on medium speed for 3-4 minutes. Pour into a greased 9-in. springform pan; place pan on a baking sheet.

2. Bake at 350° for 23-25 minutes or until cake springs back when lightly touched. Cool on a wire rack.

3. In a small bowl, beat cream cheese and sugar until fluffy; fold in whipped topping. Spread the pie filling over cake; top with cream cheese mixture. Cover and refrigerate for 4 hours. Remove sides of pan.

CRUMB-COATED SPAETZLE

yield: 6 servings   **prep/total time: 20 min.**

Spaetzle is a cross between a curly noodle and a small dumpling. It's a traditional German accompaniment to all types of roasts, especially sauerbraten.

- 2 cups all-purpose flour
- 1 teaspoon salt
- 2 eggs, lightly beaten
- 3/4 cup 2% milk
- 1/2 cup dry bread crumbs
- 1/2 cup butter, melted

1. In a small bowl, combine flour and salt. Whisk in eggs and milk until smooth.

2. Fill a large stockpot three-fourths full with water; bring to a boil. With a rubber spatula, press dough through a colander into boiling water. Cook and stir gently for 4-5 minutes or until spaetzle float and are tender.

3. Combine bread crumbs and butter. With a slotted spoon, transfer spaetzle to a large bowl; add crumb mixture and toss to coat.

FORMING SPAETZLE

Place colander over boiling water; press dough through holes of colander. Cook until tender, about 5 minutes.

SEAFOOD GRILL *with the extras*

[2009]

"For our 2009, 2010 and 2011 meals, our contributors sent in their favorite recipes—but for these years each recipe comes from a different individual. We brought together these star combinations to create three complementary, cohesive menus. For 2012 we went back to one complete meal from one contributor. We hope your family will be delighted with this Southern-inspired seafood meal from 2009."

LOW COUNTRY GRILL

yield: 6 servings ∞ prep: 20 min. ∞ grill: 50 min.

(Pictured on page 540)

Grilling is one of my family's favorite ways of cooking. This recipe comes together quickly.

—Alaina Showalter, Clover, South Carolina, Field Editor

---

  2 tablespoons olive oil
  1 teaspoon salt, *divided*
  1 teaspoon garlic powder, *divided*
  1 teaspoon seafood seasoning, *divided*
 12 small red potatoes, quartered
1/3 cup butter, melted
  1 pound smoked kielbasa *or* Polish sausage
  3 medium ears sweet corn, cut in half
1-1/2 pounds uncooked medium shrimp, peeled and deveined

1. In a large bowl, combine the oil with 1/4 teaspoon each salt, garlic powder and seafood seasoning. Add the potatoes; toss to coat. Spoon onto a greased double thickness of heavy-duty foil (about 18 in. square).

2. Fold foil around potatoes and seal tightly. Grill, covered, over medium heat for 30-35 minutes or until tender, turning once. Set aside and keep warm.

3. In a small bowl, combine the butter with remaining salt, garlic powder and seafood seasoning. Grill the kielbasa and corn, covered, over medium heat for 10-12 minutes or until kielbasa is heated through and corn is tender, turning occasionally and basting corn with half of the butter mixture. Keep warm.

4. Thread shrimp onto four metal or soaked wooden skewers; grill, covered, over medium heat for 3-4 minutes on each side or until shrimp turn pink, basting with remaining butter mixture. Slice kielbasa into six pieces before serving. Carefully open foil from the potatoes to allow steam to escape.

MEXICAN LAYERED SALAD

yield: 10 servings ∞ prep/total time: 20 min.

Here's a popular dish I like to prepare in advance, adding the cheese and chips just before serving. It's a slightly different version of the layered salad.

—Joan Hallford, North Richland Hills, Texas Field Editor

---

  4 cups torn romaine
  1 large cucumber, peeled, halved and sliced
  3 medium tomatoes, chopped
  2 medium ripe avocados, peeled and sliced
  2 large green peppers, chopped
1-1/2 cups mayonnaise
1/4 cup canned chopped green chilies
  2 teaspoons chili powder
1/2 teaspoon onion powder
1/4 teaspoon salt
1/4 teaspoon garlic powder
  1 cup crushed tortilla chips
1/2 cup shredded cheddar cheese

1. In a 2-qt. trifle bowl or glass serving bowl, layer first five ingredients. Combine mayonnaise, chilies and seasonings; spread over the top. Sprinkle with chips and cheese.

GLAZED APPLE PIE SQUARES

yield: 2 dozen ∽ **prep: 1 hour** ∽ **bake: 45 min. + cooling**

For a change from apple pie, try these glazed bars. They're glazed and a little bit sweeter. The dough is firm enough that you can eat them with your hands. They're best when apples are in season.

—*Diane Turner, Brunswick, Ohio, Field Editor*

2-1/2 cups all-purpose flour
   1 teaspoon salt
   1 cup cold butter, cubed
   1 egg, *separated*
   3 to 4 tablespoons 2% milk
   1 cup crushed cornflakes
   9 cups thinly sliced peeled tart apples (about 10 medium)
   1 cup plus 2 tablespoons sugar, *divided*
   2 teaspoons ground cinnamon, *divided*
1/2 teaspoon ground nutmeg
GLAZE:
   1 cup confectioners' sugar
1/2 teaspoon vanilla extract
   1 to 2 tablespoons 2% milk

1. In a large bowl, combine flour and salt; cut in butter until mixture resembles coarse crumbs. In a measuring cup, combine egg yolk and enough milk to measure 1/3 cup. Gradually add to the flour mixture, tossing with a fork until dough forms a ball.

2. Divide dough in half. Roll one portion into a thin 15-in. x 10-in. rectangle. Transfer to the bottom of an ungreased 15-in. x 10-in. x 1-in. baking pan. Sprinkle with cornflakes.

3. In a large bowl, combine the apples, 1 cup sugar, 1-1/2 teaspoons cinnamon and nutmeg; toss to coat. Spoon over the crust.

4. Roll remaining dough into a thin 15-in. x 10-in. rectangle; place over apple filling. Beat the egg white; brush over the pastry. Combine the remaining sugar and cinnamon; sprinkle over the top. Bake at 350° for 45-50 minutes or until golden brown.

5. For glaze, combine the confectioners' sugar, vanilla and enough milk to achieve a drizzling consistency. Drizzle over warm pastry. Cool completely on a wire rack. Cut into squares.

BISCUIT-Y BELL PEPPER MUFFINS

yield: 10 muffins ∽ **prep: 15 min.**
bake: 20 min.

(Pictured on page 541)

I like to use three or four different colors of pepper for these easy muffins. When you cut one open, it looks like a rainbow!

—*Rachel Garcia, Arlington, Virginia, Field Editor*

1/2 cup butter, cubed
1/3 cup finely chopped green onions
1/3 cup finely chopped sweet red pepper
1/4 cup finely chopped sweet yellow pepper
   2 eggs
2/3 cup sour cream
1-1/2 cups all-purpose flour
   2 tablespoons sugar
1-1/2 teaspoons baking powder
3/4 teaspoon salt
1/2 teaspoon dried basil
1/4 teaspoon baking soda
1/4 teaspoon dried tarragon

1. In a small skillet, melt the butter. Add the onions and peppers; saute until tender. Remove from the heat; cool for 5 minutes.

2. In a small bowl, whisk eggs and sour cream. Stir in the onion mixture until blended. In a large bowl, combine the remaining ingredients. Stir in sour cream mixture just until moistened.

3. Fill greased or paper-lined muffin cups two-thirds full. Bake at 350° for 20-25 minutes or until a toothpick inserted near the center comes out clean. Serve warm.

THE FLAVORS *of summer*

[2010]

"The refreshing blend of ingredients for this meal combination will make you feel like you're taking a mini vacation to a warm-weather destination. Imagine the ocean breezes as you dig into this scrumptious fare!"

CARIBBEAN CHICKEN CAESAR SALAD

yield: 4 servings ∞ **prep/total time: 30 min.**

(*Pictured on page 543*)

A friend of mine loved the food served at her wedding reception. Afterward, we re-created the menu, including this salad with its refreshing citrus accent.

—*Barbara Carlucci, Orange Park, Florida, Field Editor*

- 1 pound boneless skinless chicken breasts, cut into 1-inch pieces
- 1/2 cup thawed nonalcoholic pina colada mix, *divided*
- 1 cup tangerine *or* mandarin orange segments
- 1 celery rib, chopped
- 2 tablespoons crushed pineapple
- 1 green onion, chopped
- 4 pitted ripe olives, sliced
- 2 tablespoons plus 2 teaspoons lemon juice
- 4 teaspoons mayonnaise
- 2 teaspoons grated Parmesan cheese
- 1 to 2 garlic cloves, minced
- 1/8 teaspoon salt
- 1/8 teaspoon pepper
- 4 cups torn romaine *or* iceberg lettuce

1. Combine chicken and 1/4 cup pina colada mix. In a large skillet coated with cooking spray, cook and stir chicken mixture over medium heat until chicken is no longer pink. Remove from the heat; set aside.

2. Combine the tangerines, celery, pineapple, onion and olives in a large bowl. In a small bowl, combine the lemon juice, mayonnaise, cheese, garlic, salt, pepper and the remaining pina colada mix. Add chicken and romaine to the tangerine mixture; drizzle with dressing and toss to coat.

FROTHY MEXI-MOCHA COFFEE

yield: 4 servings ∞ **prep/total time: 15 min.**

(*Pictured on page 541*)

Knowing that this cup of coffee is waiting for me on the other side of the alarm clock makes for a great start to my morning!

—*Maria Regakis, Somerville, Massachusetts, Field Editor*

- 1 cup packed brown sugar
- 4 ounces semisweet chocolate, chopped
- 2 orange peel strips (1 to 3 inches)
- 1/2 teaspoon ground cinnamon
- 1/4 teaspoon ground allspice
- 3 cups hot strong brewed coffee
- 1/2 cup half-and-half cream, warmed

Optional garnishes: cinnamon sticks, orange peel and whipped cream

1. Place the first five ingredients in a blender; cover and process until chocolate is finely chopped. Add coffee; cover and process for 1-2 minutes or until chocolate is melted. Transfer to a small saucepan; heat through.

2. Return mixture to blender; add cream. Cover and process until frothy. Strain, discarding solids; serve in mugs. Garnish with cinnamon sticks, orange peel and whipped cream if desired.

FLORIDA CITRUS MERINGUE PIE

yield: 8 servings ∞ prep: 30 min.
bake: 15 min. + chilling

(*Pictured on page 538*)

*Why limit a great dessert to just one kind of citrus fruit? Thanks to
orange and lemon, this lovely pie packs a bold, sweet-tart flavor!*
—*Barbara Carlucci, Orange Park, Florida, Field Editor*

Pastry for single-crust pie (9 inches)
  1 cup sugar
  5 tablespoons cornstarch
1/2 teaspoon salt
  1 cup water
  1 cup orange juice
  4 egg yolks, lightly beaten
1/2 cup lemon juice
  2 tablespoons butter
  1 teaspoon grated lemon peel
  1 teaspoon grated orange peel
MERINGUE:
  3 egg whites
  1 teaspoon vanilla extract
  6 tablespoons sugar

1. Roll out pastry to fit a 9-in. pie plate. Transfer pastry to
   pie plate. Trim pastry to 1/2 in. beyond edge of plate; flute
   edges. Line unpricked pastry with a double thickness of
   heavy-duty foil.

2. Bake at 450° for 8 minutes. Remove foil; bake 5-7 minutes
   longer or until lightly browned. Cool on a wire rack.
   Reduce heat to 350°.

3. Meanwhile, in a large saucepan, combine the sugar,
   cornstarch and salt. Gradually stir in water and orange
   juice until smooth. Cook and stir over medium-high heat
   until thickened and bubbly. Reduce heat; cook and stir
   2 minutes longer (mixture will be thick).

4. Remove from the heat. Stir a small amount of the hot
   mixture into egg yolks; return all to the pan, stirring
   constantly. Bring to a gentle boil; cook and stir 2 minutes
   longer. Remove from the heat. Gently stir in the lemon
   juice, butter, and lemon and orange peel. Pour into
   prepared crust.

5. In a large bowl, beat egg whites and vanilla on medium
   speed until soft peaks form. Gradually beat in the sugar,
   1 tablespoon at a time, on high until stiff glossy peaks form
   and the sugar is dissolved. Spread over the hot filling, sealing
   edges to crust.

6. Bake at 350° for 12-15 minutes or until meringue is golden
   brown. Cool on a wire rack for 1 hour. Refrigerate for at
   least 3 hours before serving. Store in the refrigerator.

BASIL, FETA & ROASTED PEPPER MUFFINS

yield: 9 muffins ∞ prep: 20 min.
bake: 20 min.

*Anything with basil is always a winner. It pairs especially well with
the salty feta and sweet peppers in these savory, biscuit-like muffins.*
—*Maria Regakis, Somerville, Massachusetts, Field Editor*

  2 cups all-purpose flour
  2 teaspoons baking powder
1/2 teaspoon salt
1/2 teaspoon baking soda
  1 egg
  1 cup buttermilk
1/4 cup olive oil
3/4 cup crumbled feta cheese
1/2 cup chopped roasted sweet red peppers
  3 tablespoons minced fresh basil *or* 1 tablespoon dried basil

1. In a large bowl, combine the flour, baking powder, salt
   and baking soda. In another bowl, combine the egg,
   buttermilk and oil. Stir into dry ingredients just until
   moistened. Fold in the cheese, peppers and basil.

2. Fill greased muffin cups three-fourths full. Bake at 375°
   for 16-20 minutes or until a toothpick inserted near the
   center comes out clean. Cool for 5 minutes before
   removing from pan to a wire rack. Serve warm.

BACKYARD *dining*

[2011]

❝Treat your family to some grilled chicken with slaw, fresh bean salad and a cool and creamy dessert. They'll love the blend of flavors and textures after a day in the great outdoors.❞

SMOKY GARLIC AND SPICE CHICKEN

yield: 4 servings ∾ **prep: 20 min. + marinating grill: 1 hr. + standing**

A soy sauce-based marinade gives this moist, crispy chicken a rich flavor. To make chicken satay, I vary the ingredients a bit and marinate the meat longer.

—Tina Repak Mirilovich
Johnstown, Pennsylvania, Field Editor

- 1/3 cup reduced-sodium soy sauce
- 3 tablespoons lime juice
- 6 garlic cloves, minced
- 1 tablespoon olive oil
- 1 tablespoon ground cumin
- 1 teaspoon paprika
- 1/2 teaspoon dried oregano
- 1/2 teaspoon pepper
- 1 broiler/fryer chicken (3 to 4 pounds), split in half lengthwise

1. In a large resealable plastic bag, combine the first eight ingredients. Add the chicken; seal bag and turn to coat. Refrigerate for 8 hours or overnight.

2. Drain and discard marinade. Moisten a paper towel with cooking oil; using long-handled tongs, lightly coat the grill rack. Prepare grill for indirect heat, using a drip pan.

3. Place chicken cut side down over drip pan and grill, covered, over indirect medium heat for 1 to 1-1/4 hours or until a thermometer reads 180°, turning occasionally. Let stand for 10 minutes before carving.

BLUE CHEESE SLAW

yield: 10 servings ∾ **prep: 40 min. + chilling**

I'm apt to add blue cheese to anything I can think of, including this tangy slaw. I make it ahead of time because the longer it sits, the better it tastes.

—Nicole Clayton, Prescott, Arizona, Field Editor

- 4 cups shredded green cabbage
- 4 cups shredded red cabbage
- 4 large carrots, shredded

DRESSING:
- 1 cup mayonnaise
- 2 tablespoons Dijon mustard
- 1 tablespoon stone-ground mustard
- 1 tablespoon cider vinegar
- 1/2 teaspoon celery salt
- 1/4 teaspoon salt
- 1/4 teaspoon coarsely ground pepper
- 1-1/2 cups (6 ounces) crumbled blue cheese
- 1/4 cup minced fresh parsley

1. In a large bowl, combine cabbages and carrots. In a small bowl, combine mayonnaise, mustards, vinegar, celery salt, salt and pepper. Pour over the cabbage mixture; toss to coat. Stir in the cheese and parsley. Refrigerate for at least 2 hours.

LEMONADE CHEESECAKE PARFAITS

yield: 6 parfaits ∾ **prep: 40 min. + chilling**

My friends like the tartness of the pink lemonade layer against the sweetness of the cheesecake layer. For a pretty look, I top the parfaits with crushed pomegranate seeds and lemon zest.

—*Teena Petrus*
  Johnstown, Pennsylvania, Field Editor

   2 whole graham crackers, crushed
   1 cup half-and-half cream
1-3/4 cups sugar, *divided*
   2 tablespoons lemon juice, *divided*
   2 envelopes unflavored gelatin
   1 package (8 ounces) cream cheese, softened
   3 teaspoons grated lemon peel, *divided*
   1 teaspoon vanilla extract
1-1/4 cups cold water
   1 tablespoon grenadine syrup
Dash salt

1. Divide the graham crackers among six dessert dishes. In a small saucepan, combine the cream, 1 cup sugar and 1 tablespoon lemon juice. Sprinkle 1 envelope of gelatin over the cream mixture; let stand for 1 minute or until softened. Heat over low heat, stirring until gelatin and sugar are both completely dissolved.

2. In a large bowl, beat the cream cheese until smooth. Beat in gelatin mixture. Stir in 1 teaspoon lemon peel and vanilla. Pour into glasses over graham crackers, about 1/2 cup in each. Cover and refrigerate until firm.

3. In a small saucepan, combine the water, grenadine, salt and remaining sugar and lemon juice. Sprinkle the remaining gelatin over the water mixture; let stand for 1 minute. Heat over low heat, stirring until gelatin and sugar are completely dissolved. Pour 2 tablespoons mixture into each parfait glass. Cover and refrigerate until firm.

4. Refrigerate the remaining grenadine mixture until it is syrupy, about 30 minutes. With a hand mixer, beat until frothy. Divide among glasses. Cover and refrigerate until firm. Garnish with remaining lemon peel.

COOL BEANS SALAD

yield: 6 servings ∾ **prep/total time: 20 min.**

Beans and rice together make a complete protein. So, depending on the serving size, this colorful dish could be a side or a meatless entree. The basmati rice adds a unique flavor and the dressing gives it a bit of a tang.

—*Janelle Lee*
  Appleton, Wisconsin, Field Editor

   3 cups cooked basmati rice
   1 can (16 ounces) kidney beans, rinsed and drained
   1 can (15 ounces) black beans, rinsed and drained
1-1/2 cups frozen corn, thawed
   4 green onions, sliced
   1 small sweet red pepper, chopped
 1/4 cup minced fresh cilantro
DRESSING:
 1/2 cup olive oil
 1/4 cup red wine vinegar
   1 tablespoon sugar
   1 garlic clove, minced
   1 teaspoon salt
   1 teaspoon ground cumin
   1 teaspoon chili powder
 1/4 teaspoon pepper

1. In a large bowl, combine the first seven ingredients. In a small bowl, whisk the dressing ingredients; pour over salad and toss to coat. Chill until serving.

COOL BEANS SALAD

"This stuff rocks! My husband could not stay out of it. When you make it, double the recipe because it will be gone in a flash!"
—*mullinta*

THE FINEST *italian*

[2012]

"Impress your guests with a sumptuous Italian menu. The flavor combinations within each dish are divine, and I think the items in one of my favorite meals complement each other wonderfully. The recipes may sound exotic, but they are simple to prepare."
—*Trisha Kruse, Eagle, Idaho, Field Editor*

SAGE & PROSCIUTTO CHICKEN SALTIMBOCCA

yield: 4 servings ∞ **prep/total time: 25 min.**

The Italian word "saltimbocca" means to "jump into one's mouth." This wonderful dish fulfills the promise with prosciutto and fresh sage leaves.

- 1/2 **cup plus 2 teaspoons all-purpose flour,** *divided*
- 4 **boneless skinless chicken breast halves (6 ounces** *each***)**
- 1/2 **teaspoon salt**
- 1/4 **teaspoon pepper**
- 8 **fresh sage leaves**
- 8 **thin slices prosciutto** *or* **deli ham**
- 2 **tablespoons olive oil**
- 1 **tablespoon butter**
- 1/2 **cup chicken broth**
- 2 **tablespoons lemon juice**
- 2 **tablespoons white wine** *or* **additional chicken broth**

1. Place 1/2 cup flour in a shallow bowl; set aside. Flatten chicken breasts to 1/4-in. thickness. Sprinkle both sides with salt and pepper; top each breast half with 2 sage leaves and 2 slices prosciutto, pressing to adhere. Dip chicken sides only in flour to coat.

2. In a large skillet, heat oil and butter over medium heat; cook chicken for 3-4 minutes on each side or until lightly browned and thermometer reads 170°. Remove and keep warm.

3. Place the remaining flour in a small bowl. Whisk in the chicken broth, lemon juice and wine; add to skillet, stirring to loosen browned bits from pan. Bring to a boil; cook and stir for 1 minute or until thickened. Serve with chicken.

ROSEMARY ROASTED POTATOES AND ASPARAGUS

yield: 4 servings ∞ **prep: 10 min.**
bake: 35 min.

Showcase asparagus when you dress it in fresh rosemary and red potatoes for an earthy counterpoint to the fresh, green spears. Add minced garlic and you get a gorgeous, flavorful side dish.

- 1/2 pound fingerling potatoes, cut into 1-inch pieces
- 1/4 cup olive oil, *divided*
-   2 tablespoons minced fresh rosemary *or* 2 teaspoons dried rosemary, crushed
-   2 garlic cloves, minced
-   1 pound fresh asparagus, trimmed
- 1/4 teaspoon salt
- 1/4 teaspoon freshly ground pepper

1. In a small bowl, combine the potatoes, 2 tablespoons oil, rosemary and garlic; toss to coat. Transfer to a greased 15-in. x 10-in. x 1-in. baking pan. Bake, uncovered, at 400° for 20 minutes, stirring once.

2. Drizzle asparagus with remaining oil; add to the pan. Bake 15-20 minutes longer or until vegetables are tender, stirring occasionally. Sprinkle with salt and pepper.

ORANGE CHOCOLATE RICOTTA PIE

yield: 8 servings ∞ **prep: 20 min.**
bake: 40 min. + cooling

A traditional Italian dessert served during the holidays and for special occasions, the orange and chocolate flavors make a classic Italian pairing. The result is rich and tangy—a perfect finale to a Mediterranean-style dinner.

-   2 cartons (15 ounces *each*) ricotta cheese
-   2 eggs, lightly beaten
- 1/2 cup dark chocolate chips
- 1/3 cup sugar
-   1 tablespoon grated orange peel
-   2 tablespoons orange liqueur, optional

Pastry for double-crust pie (9 inches)

1. In a large bowl, combine ricotta cheese, eggs, chocolate chips, sugar, orange peel and orange liqueur if desired.

2. Roll out half of the pastry to fit a 9-in. pie plate; transfer pastry to pie plate. Fill with ricotta mixture. Roll out remaining pastry; make a lattice crust. Trim, seal and flute edges. Bake at 425° for 40-45 minutes or until crust is golden brown.

MEDITERRANEAN ROMAINE SALAD

yield: 6 servings ∞ **prep/total time: 30 min.**

My mother taught me how to make a salad of artichoke hearts, roasted red peppers, red onion and olives. It's a traditional Genovese accompaniment to a family dinner or a main dish for a light supper when you add chicken or shrimp.

- 2-1/2 cups cubed French bread
-   1 tablespoon olive oil
-   1 garlic clove, minced
-   1 jar (7-1/2 ounces) marinated quartered artichoke hearts, drained
-   1 cup roasted sweet red peppers, thinly sliced
-   1 medium cucumber, peeled and thinly sliced
-   1 celery rib, sliced
-   1 can (2-1/4 ounces) sliced ripe olives, drained
- 1/3 cup thinly sliced red onion
- 1/2 cup balsamic vinaigrette
-   1 bunch romaine, torn

Freshly ground pepper
Shaved Parmesan cheese

1. Place cubed bread on an ungreased 15-in. x 10-in. x 1-in. baking pan. Combine oil and garlic; drizzle over bread and toss to coat. Bake at 400° for 6-8 minutes or until golden brown, stirring once. Set aside.

2. In a small bowl, combine the artichokes, red peppers, cucumber, celery, olives, red onion and vinaigrette. Just before serving, place romaine in a large bowl. Add artichoke mixture and croutons; toss to coat. Sprinkle with the pepper; top with cheese.

RANCH MAC & CHEESE

"This recipe is a favorite in my house! I was on the search for a great mac & cheese, and I found it with this one! The best part is that it is different than your everyday mac & cheese. I chose to add crumbled crackers mixed with butter to the top and bake it for 20 mins. Awsome recipe... Thanks Michelle!!"

—abbie23

[1995]

RANCH MAC & CHEESE

yield: 8 servings ⮾ prep/total time: 30 min.

(Pictured on page 543)

I came up with the recipe for this creamy and satisfying macaroni and cheese, which has a special twist. My husband requests it often.

—Michelle Rotunno
Independence, Missouri

- 1 package (16 ounces) elbow macaroni
- 1 cup 2% milk
- 1/4 cup butter, cubed
- 1 envelope ranch salad dressing mix
- 1 teaspoon garlic salt
- 1 teaspoon garlic pepper blend
- 1 teaspoon lemon-pepper seasoning
- 1 cup (4 ounces) shredded Monterey Jack cheese
- 1 cup (4 ounces) shredded Colby cheese
- 1 cup (8 ounces) sour cream
- 1/2 cup crushed saltines
- 1/3 cup grated Parmesan cheese

TOP 100 RECIPE

1. Cook macaroni according to package directions. Meanwhile, in a Dutch oven, combine the milk, butter, dressing mix and seasonings; heat through. Stir in Monterey Jack and Colby cheeses until melted. Stir in sour cream.

2. Drain macaroni; stir into the cheese sauce with the saltines. Sprinkle with Parmesan cheese.

[1995]

HOMEMADE PASTA SAUCE

**yield: 2 quarts ⮾ prep: 20 min.
cook: 3-1/4 hours**

When my tomatoes ripen, the first things I make are BLTs and this fanatastic homemade spaghetti sauce.

—Sondra Bergy
Lowell, Michigan, Former Field Editor

- 4 medium onions, chopped
- 1/2 cup canola oil
- 12 cups chopped peeled fresh tomatoes
- 4 garlic cloves, minced
- 3 bay leaves
- 4 teaspoons salt
- 2 teaspoons dried oregano
- 1-1/4 teaspoons pepper
- 1/2 teaspoon dried basil
- 2 cans (6 ounces *each*) tomato paste
- 1/3 cup packed brown sugar
- Hot cooked spaghetti

1. In a Dutch oven, saute onions in oil until tender. Add tomatoes, garlic, bay leaves, salt, oregano, pepper and basil. Bring to a boil. Reduce heat; cover and simmer for 2 hours, stirring occasionally.

2. Add tomato paste and brown sugar; simmer, uncovered, for 1 hour. Discard the bay leaves. Serve with spaghetti.

Editor's Note: Browned ground beef or Italian sausage can be added to the cooked sauce if desired. The sauce also freezes well.

[2007]

CHEESE RAVIOLI WITH ZUCCHINI

yield: 4 servings ∞ prep: 15 min.
cook: 20 min.

Whipping cream lends rich flavor to the lovely sauce for this colorful medley.

—*Maria Regakis*
Somerville, Massachusetts, Field Editor

- 1 cup heavy whipping cream
- 1/2 cup chicken broth
- 1 package (9 ounces) refrigerated cheese ravioli
- 1 small onion, finely chopped
- 1 tablespoon butter
- 1 medium sweet red pepper, julienned
- 3 cups julienned zucchini
- 1/2 teaspoon salt
- 1/4 teaspoon garlic powder
- 3/4 cup grated Parmesan cheese, *divided*
- 1 to 2 tablespoons minced fresh basil
- 1 tablespoon minced fresh parsley

1. In a large saucepan, bring cream and broth to a boil. Reduce heat; simmer, uncovered, for 10-15 minutes or until reduced to 1 cup. Meanwhile, cook ravioli according to package directions.

2. In a large skillet, saute onion in butter for 2 minutes. Add the red pepper; cook 2 minutes longer. Stir in the zucchini, salt and garlic powder; cook for 1-2 minutes or until vegetables are crisp-tender. Keep warm.

3. Stir 1/2 cup cheese, basil and parsley into cream sauce; cook for 1 minute. Drain ravioli; add to skillet with cream sauce. Toss to coat. Sprinkle with the remaining cheese.

[2009]

CABERNET MARINARA PASTA

yield: 4 servings ∞ prep: 20 min.
cook: 20 min.

Red wine and fresh herbs accent the sweet sauce that highlights this fancy but fuss-free pasta dish. It makes an excellent meatless entree but can also be served on the side with meat or poultry.

—*Sarah Vasques, Milford, New Hampshire*

- 1 cup chopped sweet onion
- 2 tablespoons olive oil
- 3 garlic cloves, crushed
- 1/2 cup Cabernet Sauvignon *or other dry red wine*
- 1 can (28 ounces) crushed tomatoes
- 3 plum tomatoes, chopped
- 1 tablespoon sugar
- 1 fresh basil sprig
- 1 fresh thyme sprig
- 2 cups uncooked penne pasta

Parmesan and Romano cheeses

1. In a large saucepan, cook onion in oil over medium heat until tender. Add garlic; cook 1 minute longer. Stir in the wine and bring to a boil. Reduce heat; cook for 6-8 minutes or until liquid is reduced by half.

2. Add crushed tomatoes, plum tomatoes, sugar, basil and thyme; bring to a boil. Reduce heat; cover and simmer for 15 minutes. Meanwhile, cook pasta according to package directions.

3. Discard basil and thyme. Drain pasta; toss with sauce. Top with cheeses.

CHEESE RAVIOLI WITH ZUCCHINI

❝I make this all the time; it is my favorite. It tastes like you're eating at a five-star restuarant.❞
—*drangel*

[1995]

CHEESE-STUFFED SHELLS

**yield: 12 servings prep: 35 min.
bake: 50 min.**

(Pictured on page 544)

When I was living in California, I tasted this rich, cheesy pasta dish at a neighborhood Italian restaurant. I got the recipe and made a few changes to it in my own kitchen.

—Lori Mecca, Grants Pass, Oregon

- 1 pound bulk Italian sausage
- 1 large onion, chopped
- 1 package (10 ounces) frozen chopped spinach, thawed and squeezed dry
- 1 package (8 ounces) cream cheese, cubed
- 1 egg, lightly beaten
- 2 cups (8 ounces) shredded part-skim mozzarella cheese, *divided*
- 2 cups (8 ounces) shredded cheddar cheese
- 1 cup 4% cottage cheese
- 1 cup grated Parmesan cheese
- 1/4 teaspoon salt
- 1/4 teaspoon pepper
- 1/8 teaspoon ground cinnamon, optional
- 24 jumbo pasta shells, cooked and drained

SAUCE:
- 1 can (29 ounces) tomato sauce
- 1 tablespoon dried minced onion
- 1-1/2 teaspoons dried basil
- 1-1/2 teaspoons dried parsley flakes
- 2 garlic cloves, minced
- 1 teaspoon sugar
- 1 teaspoon dried oregano
- 1/2 teaspoon salt
- 1/4 teaspoon pepper

1. In a large skillet, cook sausage and onion over medium heat until meat is no longer pink; drain. Transfer to a large bowl. Stir in the spinach, cream cheese and egg. Add 1 cup mozzarella cheese, cheddar cheese, cottage cheese, Parmesan cheese, salt, pepper and cinnamon if desired.

2. Stuff pasta shells with sausage mixture. Arrange in two 11-in. x 7-in. baking dishes coated with cooking spray. Combine the sauce ingredients; spoon over shells.

3. Cover and bake at 350° for 45 minutes. Uncover; sprinkle with remaining mozzarella. Bake 5-10 minutes longer or until bubbly and cheese is melted. Let stand for 5 minutes before serving.

[2011]

PRESTO PASTA

yield: 9 servings prep/total time: 20 min.

When the temperature and humidity rise, this easy, breezy pasta is just the ticket to help you play it cool.

—Debbie Verdini, Yardley, Pennsylvania

- 8 ounces linguine
- 4 cups fresh baby spinach
- 1-1/2 cups julienned roasted sweet red peppers
- 4 garlic cloves, minced
- 3 tablespoons olive oil
- 1 can (6 ounces) pitted ripe olives, drained
- 1/4 teaspoon salt
- 1/8 teaspoon pepper

1. Cook linguine according to package directions. Meanwhile, in a large skillet over medium heat, cook the spinach, peppers and garlic in oil until spinach is wilted.

2. Drain linguine; toss with spinach mixture, olives, salt and pepper. Serve warm or at room temperature.

CHEESE-STUFFED SHELLS

"My family LOVES these! They're super simple to make, and the cinnamon makes them out of this world! Do NOT skip it! This really is just such a great recipe with very little prep work and such a beautiful finish."

—Jayshree

[2009]

DOUBLE-CHEESE MACARONI

yield: 12 servings (1 cup each)
prep: 25 min. ∞ **bake: 20 min.**

A friend passed this recipe on to me and I made some changes, which created this definite crowd-pleaser. I make it for every family get-together, and I haven't found anyone, child or adult, who doesn't want some of this ooey-gooey macaroni and cheese.

—Sabrina DeWitt, Cumberland, Maryland

- 1 package (16 ounces) elbow macaroni
- 3 cups (24 ounces) 4% cottage cheese
- 1/2 cup butter, cubed
- 1/2 cup all-purpose flour
- 1 teaspoon salt
- 1/2 teaspoon white pepper
- 1/4 teaspoon garlic salt
- 3 cups half-and-half cream
- 1 cup 2% milk
- 4 cups (16 ounces) shredded cheddar cheese

TOPPING:
- 1 cup dry bread crumbs
- 1/4 cup butter, melted

1. Cook macaroni according to package directions. Meanwhile, place cottage cheese in a food processor; cover and process until smooth. Set aside.

2. In a large saucepan, melt butter. Stir in the flour, salt, pepper and garlic salt until smooth. Gradually add cream and milk. Bring to a boil; cook and stir for 2 minutes or until thickened.

3. Drain macaroni; transfer to a bowl. Add cheddar cheese, cottage cheese and white sauce; toss to coat. Transfer to a greased 13-in. x 9-in. baking dish. (Dish will be full.) Combine bread crumbs and butter; sprinkle over top.

4. Bake, uncovered, at 400° for 20-25 minutes or until bubbly.

[2000]

VERY VEGGIE LASAGNA

yield: 12 servings ∞ **prep: 40 min.**
bake: 1 hour + standing

I concocted this quick and easy recipe to use up some of the abundant fresh produce from my garden. When I made a batch to share at a church potluck, I received lots of compliments.

—Berniece Baldwin, Glennie, Michigan

- 2 medium carrots, julienned
- 1 medium zucchini, cut into 1/4-inch slices
- 1 yellow summer squash, cut into 1/4-inch slices
- 1 medium onion, sliced
- 1 cup fresh broccoli florets
- 1/2 cup sliced celery
- 1/2 cup julienned sweet red pepper
- 1/2 cup julienned green pepper
- 1/2 to 1 teaspoon salt
- 2 tablespoons canola oil
- 2 garlic cloves, minced
- 3-1/2 cups spaghetti sauce
- 14 lasagna noodles, cooked and drained
- 4 cups (16 ounces) shredded part-skim mozzarella cheese

1. In a large skillet, stir-fry vegetables and salt in oil until crisp-tender. Add garlic; cook 1 minute longer.

2. Spread 3/4 cup spaghetti sauce in the greased 13-in. x 9-in. baking dish. Arrange seven noodles over sauce, overlapping as needed. Layer with half of the vegetables, spaghetti sauce and cheese. Repeat layers.

3. Cover and bake at 350° for 60-65 minutes or until bubbly. Let stand for 15 minutes before cutting.

VERY VEGGIE LASAGNA

"This is a wonderful recipe that is even loved by a guy who typically wants meaty meals!"
—delidella

[2008]

PASTA WITH CREAM SAUCE

yield: 8 servings ⚭ **prep: 15 min.** ⚭ **cook: 25 min.**

This beautiful pasta is well coated with a delicious garlic-cream sauce. It's a versatile dish that can be served as a side dish or a main dish.

—Amy Sauser, Omaha, Nebraska, Field Editor

----

  1 package (16 ounces) bow tie pasta
  1 small red onion, chopped
  3 tablespoons olive oil
  4 large garlic cloves, minced
3/4 cup chicken broth
1-1/2 teaspoons minced fresh basil
1-1/2 teaspoons minced fresh oregano
1/4 teaspoon salt
1/4 teaspoon pepper
  1 cup heavy whipping cream

----

1. Cook the pasta according to package directions. Meanwhile, in a large skillet, saute onion in oil until tender. Add garlic; cook 1 minute longer. Stir in the broth, basil, oregano, salt and pepper. Bring to a boil; cook for 8 minutes or until reduced by about half. Stir in cream.

2. Cook, uncovered, 8-10 minutes longer or until sauce is reduced to 1-1/4 cups. Drain pasta; toss with sauce.

[2006]

POTATO GNOCCHI

yield: 6-8 servings ⚭ **prep: 30 min.
cook: 10 min./batch**

My Italian mother remembers her mother making these dumplings for special occasions. She still has the bowl Grandma mixed the dough in, which will be passed down to me some day.

**—Tina Repak Mirilovich
Johnstown, Pennsylvania, Field Editor**

----

  4 medium potatoes, peeled and quartered
  1 egg, lightly beaten
1-1/2 teaspoons salt, *divided*
1-3/4 to 2 cups all-purpose flour

  3 quarts water
Spaghetti sauce, warmed

----

1. Place potatoes in a saucepan and cover with water. Bring to a boil. Reduce heat; cover and cook for 15-20 minutes or until tender. Drain and mash.

2. Place 2 cups mashed potatoes in a large bowl (save any remaining mashed potatoes for another use). Stir in egg and 1 teaspoon salt. Gradually beat in flour until blended (dough will be firm and elastic).

3. Turn onto a lightly floured surface; knead 15 times. Roll into 1/2-in.-wide ropes. Cut ropes into 1-in. pieces. Press down with a lightly floured fork.

4. In a Dutch oven, bring water and remaining salt to a boil. Add gnocchi in small batches; cook for 8-10 minutes or until gnocchi float to the top and are cooked through. Remove with a slotted spoon. Serve immediately with spaghetti sauce.

MAKING GNOCCHI

1. Mash or rice the potatoes and sprinkle with flour. Make a well and pour in egg, salt and seasonings.

2. Roll the dough into four ropes and cut each rope into 1-in. dumplings.

3. Press each piece between your thumb and a floured fork to make grooves for catching butter or sauce.

[2007]

SPAETZLE DUMPLINGS

yield: 6 servings ∞ prep/total time: 15 min.

These tender homemade noodles take only minutes to make. You can enjoy them topped with gravy or simply buttered and sprinkled with parsley.

—*Pamela Eaton, Monclova, Ohio*

---

2   cups all-purpose flour
4   eggs, lightly beaten
1/3 cup 2% milk
2   teaspoons salt
8   cups water
1   tablespoon butter

---

1. In a large bowl, stir flour, eggs, milk and salt until smooth (dough will be sticky). In a large saucepan, bring the water to a boil. Pour dough into a colander or spaetzle maker coated with cooking spray; place over the boiling water.

2. With a wooden spoon, press dough until small pieces drop into boiling water. Cook for 2 minutes or until dumplings are tender and float. Remove with a slotted spoon; toss with butter.

[1995]

VEGETABLE NOODLE CASSEROLE

yield: 12-14 servings ∞ prep: 15 min.
bake: 45 min.

If you're looking for a filling side dish, this recipe fits the bill. It combines vegetables and hearty noodles in a delectable cream sauce. Whenever I serve this the pan is scraped clean.

—*Jeanette Hios, Brooklyn, New York*

---

1   can (10-3/4 ounces) condensed cream of chicken soup, undiluted
1   can (10-3/4 ounces) condensed cream of broccoli soup, undiluted

1-1/2 cups 2% milk
1   cup grated Parmesan cheese, *divided*
3   garlic cloves, minced
2   tablespoons dried parsley flakes
1/2 teaspoon pepper
1/4 teaspoon salt
1   package (16 ounces) wide egg noodles, cooked and drained
1   package (16 ounces) frozen California-blend vegetables, thawed
2   cups frozen corn, thawed

---

1. In a large bowl, combine the soups, milk, 3/4 cup cheese, garlic, parsley, pepper and salt. Stir in the noodles and vegetables.

2. Pour into a greased 13-in. x 9-in. baking dish. Sprinkle with remaining cheese. Cover and bake at 350° for 45-50 minutes or until heated through.

[2008]

NUTTY CHEESE TORTELLINI

yield: 3 servings ∞ prep/total time: 20 min.

I like to plant Italian flat-leaf parsley in a long terra-cotta planter, so I have it on hand. The Italian parsley really lends itself to this dish.

—*Barbara Penatzer, Vestal, New York*

---

1   package (9 ounces) refrigerated cheese tortellini
1/2 cup butter, cubed
1/2 cup minced fresh parsley
1/3 cup chopped walnuts, toasted
1/4 cup shredded Parmesan cheese
Coarsely ground pepper to taste

---

1. Cook tortellini according to package directions; drain and keep warm.

2. In the same pan, melt butter. Stir in the tortellini, parsley and walnuts; toss to coat. Sprinkle pasta mixture with the cheese and pepper.

SPAETZLE DUMPLINGS

❝I make this recipe all of the time, and depending what I am making it for, I sometimes do a half or third of whole wheat. The flavor changes a bit, but it isn't a bad change, just different. One of my favorite ways to use this recipe is to have chopped tomatoes, chives, garlic powder and Parmesan with about a quarter cup butter in a bowl. When the spatzle is done, I drain and pour into the bowl. Toss and add some of cream and pepper. My family really likes it. I love this recipe--thanks.❞
—*jeanemed*

[1997]

CLASSIC LASAGNA

yield: 12 servings ∞ prep: 45 min.
bake: 55 min. + standing

My parents were Hungarian, but I've always had a weakness for Italian food. This traditional lasagna is thick, meaty and cheesy—just the way I like it.

—*Suzanne Barker, Bellingham, Washington*

1/2 pound bulk Italian sausage
1/2 pound ground beef
1-1/2 cups chopped onion
1 cup chopped carrot
1/4 teaspoon crushed red pepper flakes
3 garlic cloves, minced
2 cans (28 ounces each) diced tomatoes, undrained
2 tablespoons tomato paste
1 teaspoon *each* sugar, dried oregano and basil
1 teaspoon salt
1 teaspoon pepper, *divided*
2 cartons (15 ounces each) ricotta cheese
3/4 cup grated Parmesan cheese, *divided*
1 egg
1/3 cup minced fresh parsley
1 package (12 ounces) lasagna noodles, cooked, rinsed and drained
2 cups (8 ounces) shredded part-skim mozzarella cheese

1. In a large saucepan, cook the sausage, beef, onion, carrot and pepper flakes over medium heat until meat is no longer pink. Add garlic; cook 1 minute longer. Drain.

2. Add the tomatoes, tomato paste, sugar, oregano, basil, salt and 1/2 teaspoon pepper; bring to a boil. Reduce heat; simmer, uncovered, for 45 minutes or until thick, stirring occasionally.

3. In a small bowl, combine the ricotta, 1/2 cup Parmesan cheese, egg, parsley and remaining pepper.

4. In a greased 13-in. x 9-in. baking dish, layer a fourth of the noodles, a third of the ricotta mixture, a fourth of the meat sauce and 1/2 cup mozzarella cheese. Repeat layers twice. Top with the remaining noodles, sauce and Parmesan cheese.

5. Cover and bake at 400° for 45 minutes. Sprinkle with remaining mozzarella; bake, uncovered, 10 minutes longer or until a thermometer reads 160°. Let stand for 15 minutes before serving.

[2010]

CREAMY PASTA PRIMAVERA

yield: 6 servings ∞ prep/total time: 30 min.

(*Pictured on page 544*)

This pasta dish is a wonderful blend of tender, crisp, colorful vegetables and a creamy Parmesan cheese sauce.

—*Darlene Brenden
Salem, Oregon, Field Editor*

2 cups uncooked gemelli *or* spiral pasta
1 pound fresh asparagus, trimmed and cut into 2-inch pieces
3 medium carrots, cut into strips
2 teaspoons canola oil
2 cups cherry tomatoes, halved
1 garlic clove, minced
1/2 cup grated Parmesan cheese
1/2 cup heavy whipping cream
1/4 teaspoon pepper

1. Cook pasta according to package directions. In a large skillet, saute asparagus and carrots in oil until crisp-tender. Add the tomatoes and garlic; cook 1 minute longer.

2. Stir in the cheese, cream and pepper. Drain the pasta; toss with the asparagus mixture.

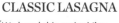

CLASSIC LASAGNA

"We loved this recipe! I've made it three times now for family gatherings, and it's always much appreciated. I used all ground beef (no sausage) and substituted 2 teaspoons dried parsley flakes for the fresh parsley. Delicious!"

—*ronayne*

[2008]

SAVORY PUMPKIN RAVIOLI

yield: 6 servings ∞ **prep: 2 hours
cook: 10 min.**

*This recipe may sound complicated, but if you
follow the simple steps, it really isn't. The result
will be pure pumpkin heaven. I like to sprinkle
the ravioli with Parmesan as well. You can also
add salt and pepper to the rich sage sauce.*

—*Christopher Presutti
Jacksonville, Florida*

2-1/2 to 3 cups all-purpose flour
  5 eggs
  1 tablespoon olive oil
FILLING:
  1 small pie pumpkin (about 2-1/4
    pounds), peeled and cut into
    1-inch cubes
  4 teaspoons chopped shallot
1/3 cup butter, cubed
  2 teaspoons minced fresh sage
3/4 teaspoon minced fresh thyme
1/4 teaspoon salt
1/4 teaspoon pepper
2/3 cup heavy whipping cream
  1 small bay leaf
  1 egg, lightly beaten
SAUCE:
  1 cup heavy whipping cream
  3 tablespoons butter
  2 teaspoons minced fresh sage

1. Place 2-1/2 cups flour in a large bowl;
make a well in the center. Beat eggs
and oil; pour into well. Stir together,
forming a ball. Turn onto a floured
surface; knead until smooth and
elastic, about 8-10 minutes, adding
remaining flour if necessary to keep
dough from sticking. Cover and let rest
for 30 minutes.

2. Meanwhile, in a large skillet, saute
pumpkin and shallot in butter until
tender. Add the sage, thyme, salt and
pepper. Transfer to a food processor;
cover and process until blended.
Return to the pan; stir in the cream
and bay leaf. Bring to a boil, stirring
constantly. Reduce the heat; simmer,
uncovered, for 15-20 minutes or until
thickened. Discard bay leaf.

3. Divide pasta dough into fourths; roll
one portion to 1/16-in. thickness.
(Keep remaining dough covered until
ready to use.) Working quickly, place
rounded teaspoonfuls of filling 1 in.
apart over half of pasta sheet. Brush
around filling with egg. Fold sheet
over; press down to seal. Cut into
squares with a pastry wheel. Repeat
with remaining dough and filling.

4. Bring a stockpot of salted water to a
boil. Add ravioli. Reduce the heat to a
gentle simmer; cook for 1-2 minutes or
until the ravioli float to the top and are
tender. Drain and keep warm.

5. In a small saucepan, bring cream to a
boil; cook, uncovered, until reduced by
half. Stir in butter and sage. Serve with
the ravioli.

Editor's Note: If pumpkin is not available,
use butternut squash.

COOKING PASTA

Cooking times vary with the size and
variety of pasta. Dried pasta can take
from 5 to 15 minutes to cook; fresh
pasta can cook in as little as 2 to 3
minutes. Follow the recommended
cooking directions on packaged pasta.

—*Taste of Home Cooking Experts*

SAVORY PUMPKIN RAVIOLI

"These were very tasty! I
don't shy away from a
complex recipe, and
these were worth the
time in making. :)"
—*williamsegraves*

[2012]

OVER-THE-TOP BAKED ZITI

yield: 8 servings
prep: 20 min. + simmering ∽ **bake: 20 min.**

*I adapted a ziti recipe to remove ingredients my kids did not like,
such as ground beef, garlic and onions. The revised recipe was
not only a success with my family but at potlucks, too. It is also
very versatile. You can use jarred sauce and double or triple the
recipe. It freezes well, too.*

—*Kimberley Pitman*
Smyrna, Delaware, Former Field Editor

- 2 cans (29 ounces *each*) tomato puree
- 1 can (12 ounces) tomato paste
- 1 medium onion, chopped
- 1/4 cup minced fresh parsley
- 2 tablespoons dried oregano
- 4 teaspoons sugar
- 3 garlic cloves, minced
- 1 tablespoon dried basil
- 1 teaspoon salt
- 1/2 teaspoon pepper

ZITI:
- 1 package (16 ounces) ziti
- 1 egg, beaten
- 1 carton (15 ounces) reduced-fat ricotta cheese
- 2 cups (8 ounces) shredded part-skim mozzarella cheese, *divided*
- 3/4 cup grated Parmesan cheese
- 1/4 cup minced fresh parsley
- 1/2 teaspoon salt
- 1/4 teaspoon pepper

1. In a 3- or 4-qt. slow cooker, combine the first 10 ingredients. Cover and cook on low for 4 hours.

2. Cook the ziti according to package directions. In a large bowl, combine egg, ricotta cheese, 1 cup mozzarella, Parmesan, parsley, salt, pepper and 5 cups sauce. Drain ziti; stir into the cheese mixture.

3. Transfer to a 13-in. x 9-in. baking dish coated with cooking spray. Pour the remaining sauce over the top; sprinkle with the remaining mozzarella cheese. Bake ziti at 350° for 20-25 minutes or until bubbly.

[2007]

MEDITERRANEAN COUSCOUS

yield: 4 servings ∽ **prep/total time: 15 min.**

*With garlic, tomatoes and Parmesan cheese, this is a great side
dish for just about any entree. It relies on a boxed item to get
started; then it's just a matter of adding a few ingredients.*

—*Beth Tomlinson, Morgantown, West Virginia*

- 2 tablespoons chopped onion
- 2 tablespoons olive oil, *divided*
- 3 teaspoons minced garlic
- 1-1/4 cups water
- 1 package (5.6 ounces) couscous with toasted pine nuts
- 1-1/2 teaspoons chicken bouillon granules
- 1/2 cup cherry tomatoes, halved
- 2 tablespoons grated Parmesan cheese

1. In a small skillet, saute onion in 1 tablespoon oil for 3-4 minutes or until tender. Add the garlic; cook 1 minute longer.

2. In a saucepan, combine water, contents of seasoning packet from couscous mix, bouillon and remaining oil. Bring to a boil. Stir in onion mixture and couscous. Cover and remove from the heat; let stand for 5 minutes. Fluff with a fork. Stir in tomatoes and cheese.

[2008]

BASIL NOODLES

yield: 8 servings ∽ **prep: 30 min. + standing**
cook: 5 min.

*Here's a simple way to make noodles from scratch, and it's our
favorite way to use up our summer crop of basil. We even grow a
monster leaf variety just to create this homemade pasta!*

—*Janine Colasurdo, Chesapeake, Virginia*

- 1-1/4 cups fresh basil leaves
- 3 cups all-purpose flour
- 3 eggs
- 1/4 cup plus 1 tablespoon water
- 2 teaspoons olive oil

1. Place basil in a food processor; cover and process until finely chopped. Add flour; process until blended. Add the eggs, water and oil. Process for 15-20 seconds or until dough forms a ball.

2. Turn onto a floured surface; knead until smooth and elastic, about 8-10 minutes. Cover and let rest for 30 minutes. Divide into fourths.

3. On a floured surface, roll each portion of dough to 1/16-in. thickness. Roll up jelly-roll style and cut into 1/4-in. slices. Separate and unroll the slices. Hang to dry or let stand on a clean towel for 1 hour. Cook the noodles in boiling salted water for 4-5 minutes or until tender; drain.

[1994]

PASTA WITH ASPARAGUS

yield: 4-6 servings
prep/total time: 20 min.

Many terrific recipes change hands at the monthly get-togethers of my ladies' bridge group. That's where I discovered this zippy, tempting dish. The garlic, asparagus, Parmesan cheese and red pepper flakes create an irresistible taste combination.

—*Jean Fisher, Redlands, California*

 5 garlic cloves, minced
 1 teaspoon crushed red pepper flakes
 2 to 3 dashes hot pepper sauce
 1/4 cup olive oil
 1 tablespoon butter
 1 pound fresh asparagus, cut into 1-1/2-inch pieces
Salt to taste
 1/4 teaspoon pepper
 1/4 cup shredded Parmesan cheese
 1/2 pound mostaccioli *or* elbow macaroni, cooked and drained

1. In a large skillet, cook the garlic, red pepper flakes and hot pepper sauce in oil and butter for 1 minute. Add the asparagus, salt and pepper; saute until asparagus is crisp-tender, about 8-10 minutes. Stir in cheese. Pour over hot pasta and toss to coat. Serve immediately.

[2001]

SPINACH CHEESE MANICOTTI

yield: 4 servings   ∞   **prep: 20 min.**
bake: 30 min.

The creamy cheese filling in these yummy stuffed shells has pretty flecks of spinach.

—*Margaret Truxton*
Pinehurst, North Carolina

 1 medium onion, finely chopped
 1 tablespoon canola oil
 3 garlic cloves, minced
1-1/2 cups ricotta cheese
 1 cup (4 ounces) shredded part-skim mozzarella cheese, *divided*
 4 ounces cream cheese, softened
 6 tablespoons grated Parmesan cheese, *divided*
 1 teaspoon Italian seasoning
 1/2 teaspoon pepper
 1 package (10 ounces) frozen chopped spinach, thawed and squeezed dry
 8 manicotti shells, cooked and drained
 1 jar (26 ounces) spaghetti sauce

1. In a small skillet, saute onion in oil for 3 minutes. Add garlic; cook 1 minute longer. Set aside.

2. In a large bowl, combine the ricotta, 1/2 cup mozzarella cheese, cream cheese, 4 tablespoons Parmesan cheese, Italian seasoning and pepper; beat until smooth. Stir in the onion mixture and spinach. Stuff into the manicotti shells.

3. Pour half of the spaghetti sauce into a greased 13-in. x 9-in. baking dish. Arrange shells over sauce; top with the remaining sauce.

4. Cover and bake at 350° for 25 minutes. Uncover; sprinkle with the remaining mozzarella and Parmesan cheeses. Bake 5-10 minutes longer or until the cheese is melted.

PASTA WITH ASPARAGUS

❝Delicious!! I doubled the recipe, with the exception of the red pepper flakes, and we thought it was seasoned perfectly.❞
— *tjreese*

[1994]

LASAGNA WITH WHITE SAUCE

yield: 10-12 servings ∞ prep: 40 min.
bake: 40 min.

I'm an old-fashioned country cook and love preparing recipes like this one that uses staples I normally keep on hand. Unlike most lasagnas, this one doesn't call for precooking the noodles. It's so simple that my children sometimes make it after school and have it ready when I get home from work.

—*Angie Price, Bradford, Tennessee*

- 1 pound ground beef
- 1 large onion, chopped
- 1 can (14-1/2 ounces) diced tomatoes, undrained
- 2 tablespoons tomato paste
- 1 teaspoon beef bouillon granules
- 1-1/2 teaspoons Italian seasoning
- 1 teaspoon salt
- 1/2 teaspoon pepper
- 1/4 teaspoon cayenne pepper

WHITE SAUCE:
- 2 tablespoons butter
- 3 tablespoons all-purpose flour
- 1 teaspoon salt
- 1/4 teaspoon pepper
- 2 cups 2% milk
- 1-1/4 cups shredded mozzarella cheese, *divided*
- 10 to 12 uncooked lasagna noodles

1. In a Dutch oven, cook the beef and onion over medium heat until meat is no longer pink; drain. Add tomatoes, tomato paste, bouillon and seasonings. Cover and cook over medium-low heat for 20 minutes, stirring occasionally.

2. Meanwhile, melt butter in a large saucepan; stir in the flour, salt and pepper until blended. Gradually add milk. Bring to a boil; cook and stir for

2 minutes or until thickened. Remove from the heat and stir in half of the cheese; set aside.

3. Pour half of the meat sauce into an ungreased 13-in. x 9-in. baking dish. Layer with half the lasagna noodles and remaining meat sauce. Top with the remaining noodles. Pour the white sauce over noodles. Sprinkle with the remaining cheese.

4. Cover and bake at 400° for 40 minutes or until bubbly and noodles are tender.

[1997]

GREEN RICE

yield: 10-12 servings ∞ prep: 15 min.
bake: 55 min.

Don't turn away from this recipe because of its name. It's a creamy, comforting dish I know your family will come to love as much as mine does.

—*Ruth Glabe, Oronoco, Minnesota*

- 2 cups uncooked long grain rice
- 1-1/2 cups 2% milk
- 1 pound shredded process American cheese
- 1 cup chopped green pepper
- 1 cup minced fresh parsley
- 1/4 cup canola oil
- 1 to 2 garlic cloves, minced

Salt and pepper to taste

1. Cook the rice according to package directions. Add remaining ingredients. Transfer to a greased 2-1/2-qt. baking dish. Bake, uncovered, at 350° for 55-60 minutes or until the green pepper is tender.

LASAGNA WITH WHITE SAUCE

"My family loves lasagna, but I never have ricotta cheese on hand. This recipe uses staples that I always have on hand, and it is delicious."
—*jeankr*

[2000]

MUSHROOM WILD RICE

yield: 12 servings ∞ **prep: 1 hour 20 min.
bake: 30 min.**

*This colorful casserole is a standout from my
mother's collection of family recipes. Excellent
texture and taste guarantee it won't play
second fiddle to either the turkey or the
pumpkin pie at holiday meals.*

—*Charlene Baert, Winnipeg, Manitoba*

4	cups water
1	cup uncooked wild rice
1	teaspoon butter
1-1/2	teaspoons salt, *divided*
1/2	cup uncooked brown rice
8	bacon strips, diced
2	cups sliced fresh mushrooms
1	large onion, chopped
1	medium green pepper, chopped
1	medium sweet red pepper, chopped
1	celery rib, thinly sliced
1	can (14-1/2 ounces) beef broth
2	tablespoons cornstarch
1/4	cup cold water
1/2	cup slivered almonds

1. In a large saucepan, combine water,
wild rice, butter and 1/2 teaspoon salt;
bring to a boil. Reduce heat; cover and
simmer for 40 minutes. Stir in the
brown rice. Cover and simmer for
25-30 minutes longer or until the rice
is tender.

2. Meanwhile, in a large skillet, cook the
bacon until crisp. Using a slotted
spoon, remove bacon to paper towels.
Drain; reserve 2 tablespoons drippings.
In drippings, saute mushrooms, onion,
peppers and celery until vegetables are
tender. Stir in the broth and remaining
salt. Bring to a boil.

3. Combine the cornstarch and cold
water until smooth; stir into mushroom
mixture. Cook and stir for 2 minutes
or until thickened; stir in the almonds
and bacon. Drain the rice; add the
mushroom mixture.

4. Transfer to a greased 13-in. x 9-in.
baking dish. Cover and bake at 350°
for 25 minutes. Uncover and bake 5-10
minutes longer or until heated through.

[1998]

BAKED RICE PILAF

yield: 4 servings ∞ **prep: 10 min.
bake: 40 min.**

*I'm always in search of inexpensive yet
delicious dishes like this one to serve at
potlucks. This fluffy rice tastes as good as
it looks.*

—*Sheree Feero, Golden, Colorado*

1-3/4	cups water
1	cup shredded carrot
1	cup chopped celery
3/4	cup uncooked long grain rice
3	tablespoons minced fresh parsley
2	tablespoons finely chopped onion
2	tablespoons butter, melted
1	tablespoon chicken bouillon granules

1. In an ungreased 8-in. square baking
dish, combine all the ingredients.
Cover and bake at 375° for 40-45
minutes or until rice is tender, stirring
after 25 minutes.

BAKED RICE PILAF

❝Very good pilaf. I
particularly like that you
just mix everything in one
dish and pop it in the oven
—time is a premium for
me during the week. No-
fuss recipes like this make
the difference between a
real meal for my family and
everyone scrounging
for themselves.**❞**
—*cwbuff*

RICE CROQUETTES

"I saw this recipe from Lucia in the *Taste of Home* magazine many years ago. Anyway, I tried it and my family absolutely loved it. I have been making it ever since, and if you ask all 3 of my kids, 'What is your favorite thing your Mom makes for you,' I guarantee the unanimous answer would be rice croquettes. I have tons of recipes and honestly, if I had to choose my favorite staple, this would be it. I am surprised that nobody has rated it yet...please try it because it is an awesome recipe. Thanks, Lucia, for many years of these yummy croquettes...my kids thank you too!!"

—3dogday

[2012]

LENTIL WHITE BEAN PILAF

yield: 10 servings ∽ prep: 35 min.
cook: 15 min.

I make this when I have leftover cooked grains on hand. Rosemary brings out the earthy flavors of the grains.

—Juli Meyers, Hinesville, Georgia

- 1 cup dried lentils, rinsed
- 1/2 cup quick-cooking barley
- 1/2 cup quinoa, rinsed
- 1/3 cup uncooked long grain rice
- 1/2 pound sliced baby portobello mushrooms
- 3 medium carrots, finely chopped
- 3 celery ribs, finely chopped
- 1 large onion, finely chopped
- 1/4 cup butter, cubed
- 3 garlic cloves, minced
- 2 teaspoons minced fresh rosemary *or* 1/2 teaspoon dried rosemary, crushed
- 1/2 cup vegetable broth
- 1/2 teaspoon salt
- 1/2 teaspoon pepper
- 2 cups canned white kidney *or* cannellini beans, rinsed and drained

1. Cook the lentils, barley, quinoa and rice according to package directions; set aside.

2. In a Dutch oven, saute the mushrooms, carrots, celery and onion in butter until tender. Add garlic and rosemary; cook 1 minute longer. Add broth, salt and pepper, stirring to loosen browned bits from pan. Stir in beans and the cooked lentils, barley, quinoa and rice; heat through.

Editor's Note: Look for quinoa in the cereal, rice or organic food aisle.

[1996]

RICE CROQUETTES

yield: 16 croquettes
prep: 45 min. + cooling ∽ cook: 15 min.

As a newlywed, I used to agonize over meal preparation. Now I enjoy trying new recipes, and some—like this tasty dish—turn out to be very popular with my family. These croquettes are crisp and golden. They also add some fun to a simple dinner like roasted chicken and salad.

—Lucia Edwards, Cotati, California

- 1/2 cup chopped onion
- 2 tablespoons butter
- 1 cup uncooked long grain rice
- 2-1/4 cups chicken broth
- 2 tablespoons chopped fresh parsley
- 1 egg, lightly beaten
- 1/2 cup grated Parmesan cheese
- 1 teaspoon dried basil
- 1/4 teaspoon pepper
- 1/2 cup dry bread crumbs
- Canola oil
- Additional fresh parsley, optional

1. In a large saucepan, saute the onion in butter until tender. Add the rice; saute 3 minutes. Stir in the broth and parsley; bring to a boil. Reduce heat; cover and simmer for 20 minutes. Cool for 30 minutes.

2. Stir in egg, cheese, basil and pepper. Moisten hands with water and shape 1/4 cupfuls into logs. Roll in crumbs.

3. In an electric skillet, heat 1/4 in. of oil to 365°. Fry croquettes, a few at a time, for 3-4 minutes or until crisp and golden, turning often. Drain on paper towels. Sprinkle with parsley if desired.

[1997]

HEARTY RED
BEANS AND RICE

yield: 8-10 servings

prep: 15 min. + soaking ∽ **cook: 2 hours**

(Pictured on page 542)

I take this dish to many potlucks and never fail to bring home an empty pot. I learned about the mouthwatering combination of meats, beans and seasonings while working for the Navy in New Orleans. If you want to get a head start, cover the beans with the water and let soak overnight. Drain them the next day and continue with the recipe as directed.

—*Kathy Jacques, Chesterfield, Michigan*

- 1 pound dried kidney beans
- 2 teaspoons garlic salt
- 1 teaspoon Worcestershire sauce
- 1/4 teaspoon hot pepper sauce
- 1 quart water
- 1/2 pound fully cooked ham, diced
- 1/2 pound fully cooked smoked sausage, diced
- 1 cup chopped onion
- 1/2 cup chopped celery
- 3 garlic cloves, minced
- 1 can (8 ounces) tomato sauce
- 2 bay leaves
- 1/4 cup minced fresh parsley
- 1/2 teaspoon salt
- 1/2 teaspoon pepper
- Hot cooked rice

1. Place the dried beans in a Dutch oven; add water to cover by 2 in. Bring to a boil; boil for 2 minutes. Remove from the heat; cover and let stand for 1 to 4 hours or until softened.

2. Drain beans and discard liquid. Add the garlic salt, Worcestershire sauce, hot pepper sauce and water; bring to a boil. Reduce heat; cover and simmer for 1-1/2 hours.

3. Meanwhile, in a large skillet, saute ham and sausage until lightly browned. Remove with a slotted spoon to bean mixture. Saute the onion and celery in drippings until tender. Add garlic; cook 1 minute longer. Add to bean mixture. Stir in tomato sauce and bay leaves. Cover and simmer for 30 minutes or until beans are tender.

4. Discard bay leaves. Measure 2 cups of beans; mash and return to the bean mixture. Stir in the parsley, salt and pepper. Serve over rice.

[2010]

NUTTY WILD RICE

yield: 5 servings ∽ **prep: 15 min.**

cook: 50 min.

You'll go nuts for this wild rice side dish and its hearty crunch. Served warm, this rice packs a zesty bite.

—*Heather Webb, Channelview, Texas*

- 2-1/2 cups water
- 1/2 cup uncooked wild rice
- 1 tablespoon reduced-sodium soy sauce
- 6 green onions, sliced
- 1 tablespoon butter
- 2/3 cup sliced almonds, toasted
- 1/4 cup sunflower kernels
- 3 tablespoons sesame seeds, toasted
- 1/4 teaspoon salt

1. In a large saucepan, bring the water, rice and soy sauce to a boil. Reduce heat; cover and simmer for 45-60 minutes or until rice is tender.

2. Meanwhile, in a small skillet, saute onions in butter until tender. Stir in the remaining ingredients; heat through. Remove from the heat.

3. Drain the rice if necessary. Stir in the onion mixture.

NUTTY WILD RICE

"Delicious and easy.**"**
—*stubbzmom*

[1999]

NUTTY BARLEY BAKE

**yield: 6 servings ∾ prep: 15 min.
bake: 1-1/4 hours**

When I started bringing this distinctive dish to holiday dinners, a lot of people had never seen barley in anything but soup. They have since dubbed me "the barley lady," and now I wouldn't dare bring anything but this dish. Even if I double the recipe, I come home with an empty pan.

—Renate Crump, Los Angeles, California

- 1 medium onion, chopped
- 1 cup medium pearl barley
- 1/2 cup slivered almonds *or* pine nuts
- 1/4 cup butter, cubed
- 1/2 cup minced fresh parsley
- 1/4 cup thinly sliced green onions
- 1/4 teaspoon salt
- 1/8 teaspoon pepper
- 2 cans (14-1/2 ounces *each*) beef broth

Additional parsley, optional

1. In a large skillet, saute onion, barley and nuts in butter until barley is lightly browned. Stir in parsley, green onions, salt and pepper.

2. Transfer to a greased 2-qt. baking dish. Stir in the broth. Bake, uncovered, at 350° for 1-1/4 hours or until the barley is tender and the liquid is absorbed. Sprinkle with parsley if desired.

[1999]

FRIED RICE

yield: 9 servings ∾ prep/total time: 15 min.

Turn leftover rice into a tasty new side dish. It's a snap to put together.

—Suzanne McKinley
Lyons, Georgia, Former Field Editor

- 1/2 cup chopped green pepper
- 1/2 cup egg substitute

- 4 cups cooked rice
- 2 tablespoons reduced-sodium soy sauce

1. In a skillet coated with cooking spray, saute green pepper until crisp-tender. Add egg substitute; cook and stir until egg is completely set. Chop egg into small pieces. Add rice and soy sauce; heat through.

[1993]

HERBED RICE PILAF

**yield: 8 servings ∾ prep: 15 min.
bake: 50 min.**

The zesty flavor of onion is great with the crunch of celery in this recipe. It's a tasty side dish for any meal. I sometimes add chopped shrimp, chicken or beef to make it into a one-dish meal.

—Norma Poole
Auburndale, Florida, Former Field Editor

- 2 cups uncooked long grain rice
- 1 cup chopped celery
- 1/2 cup chopped onion
- 1/4 cup butter, cubed
- 4 cups chicken broth
- 1 teaspoon Worcestershire sauce
- 1 teaspoon reduced-sodium soy sauce
- 1 teaspoon dried oregano
- 1 teaspoon dried thyme

1. In a large skillet, saute the rice, celery and onion in butter until the rice is lightly browned and the vegetables are tender.

2. Spoon into a greased 2-qt. baking dish. Combine all the remaining ingredients; pour over rice mixture. Cover and bake at 325° for 50 minutes or until rice is tender.

NUTTY BARLEY BAKE

❝This recipe is so good that I've served it with everything from roast beef to roast chicken to ham. It started as a holiday instead-of-stuffing dish for my family, but now I make it any time of the year.❞
—*FriedaG*

[2008]

TOMATO 'N' CORN RISOTTO

yield: 5 servings ∾ **prep: 15 min.**
cook: 35 min.

This is one of my favorite recipes because it uses items from the garden. Milk and Parmesan cheese give this side dish a creaminess everyone's sure to enjoy.

—*Angela Lively, Baxter, Tennessee*

2-1/2 cups water
2 cups whole milk
3 tablespoons chicken broth
1 large onion, finely chopped
2 tablespoons butter
1 garlic clove, minced
3/4 cup uncooked arborio rice
1-1/3 cups fresh corn (about 5 ears of corn)
1 medium tomato, peeled, seeded and chopped
1/2 cup grated Parmesan cheese
1/2 cup fresh basil leaves, thinly sliced
1/2 teaspoon salt
Pepper to taste

1. In a large saucepan, heat the water, milk and broth; keep warm.

2. In a large skillet, saute onion in butter until tender. Add garlic; cook 1 minute longer. Add rice; cook and stir for 2-3 minutes. Stir in 1 cup of the hot water mixture. Cook and stir until all liquid is absorbed.

3. Add remaining water mixture, 1/2 cup at a time, stirring constantly. Allow the liquid to absorb between additions. Cook until risotto is creamy and rice is almost tender.(Cooking time is about 20 minutes.) Stir in the remaining ingredients; heat through.

[2008]

MEXICORN GRITS

yield: 10 servings ∾ **prep: 20 min.**
bake: 35 min.

I grew up on grits and have fixed them in various ways. I decided to put a new twist on them with this recipe, and my husband says it's a keeper. Even the leftovers are good.

—*Barbara Moorhead*
Gaffney, South Carolina

4 cups 2% milk
1/2 cup plus 1/3 cup butter, *divided*
1 cup quick-cooking grits
2 eggs
1 can (11 ounces) Mexicorn, drained
1 can (4 ounces) chopped green chilies
1 cup (4 ounces) shredded Mexican cheese blend
1 teaspoon salt
1/4 teaspoon white pepper
1 cup shredded Parmesan cheese

1. In a large saucepan, bring the milk and 1/2 cup butter to a boil. Slowly stir in the grits. Reduce heat; cook and stir for 5-7 minutes.

2. In a small bowl, whisk eggs. Stir a small amount of hot grits into eggs; return all to the pan, stirring constantly. Melt the remaining butter; stir into grits. Add corn, chilies, cheese, salt and pepper.

3. Transfer to a greased 2-qt. baking dish. Sprinkle with the Parmesan cheese. Bake, uncovered, at 350° for 35-40 minutes or until a knife inserted near the center comes out clean.

TOMATO 'N' CORN RISOTTO

"Amazing flavors! Delicious and creamy!"
—*missnatlynn*

PIES & TARTS

[1997]

PERFECT RHUBARB PIE

yield: 8 servings ∞ **prep: 20 min. + standing**
bake: 55 min. + cooling

Nothing hides the tangy rhubarb in this lovely pie, which has just the right balance of sweet and tart. Serving this dessert is a nice way to celebrate the end of winter!

—*Ellen Benninger, Greenville, Pennsylvania*

　4　**cups sliced fresh *or* frozen rhubarb**
　4　**cups boiling water**
1-1/2　**cups sugar**
　3　**tablespoons all-purpose flour**
　1　**teaspoon quick-cooking tapioca**
　1　**egg**
　2　**teaspoons cold water**
Pastry for double-crust pie (9 inches)
　1　**tablespoon butter**

---

1. Place the rhubarb in a colander; pour water over rhubarb and set aside. In a large bowl, combine the sugar, flour and tapioca. Add drained rhubarb; toss to coat. Let stand for 15 minutes. Beat egg and cold water; add to the rhubarb mixture until well blended.

2. Line a 9-in. pie plate with bottom pastry. Add filling. Dot with butter. Cover with remaining pastry; flute edges. Cut slits in top crust.

3. Bake at 400° for 15 minutes. Reduce heat to 350°; bake 40-50 minutes longer or until crust is golden brown and the filling is bubbly. Cool on a wire rack.

PERFECT RHUBARB PIE

❝I have been making this pie since I first saw it in *Taste of Home* years ago. I have made it for church groups, and every time I do I hear, 'I haven't had rhubarb pie this good since Grandma passed away.' Now that is a compliment. Thanks again!❞
—*karter*

Editor's Note: If using frozen rhubarb, measure rhubarb while still frozen, then thaw completely. Drain in a colander, but do not press liquid out.

[2005]

PARADISE PINEAPPLE PIE

yield: 2 pies (6 servings each)
prep: 20 min. + chilling

This quick-to-fix recipe makes two yummy pies that will be a hit at any carry-in dinner. Lemon juice and crushed pineapple flavor the fluffy filling that's topped with a sprinkling of coconut. I like to garnish with a sprig of mint.

—*Bonnie Baumgardner*
　Sylva, North Carolina

　1　**can (14 ounces) sweetened condensed milk**
　1　**carton (12 ounces) frozen whipped topping, thawed**
　1　**can (20 ounces) crushed pineapple, drained**
1/3　**cup lemon juice**
　2　**graham cracker crusts (8 inches)**
　1　**cup flaked coconut, toasted**

---

1. Place the milk in a large bowl; fold in whipped topping. Add pineapple and lemon juice; stir for 2 minutes or until slightly thickened.

2. Pour into crusts. Sprinkle with the coconut. Cover and refrigerate for at least 2 hours.

[2007]

RASPBERRY PATCH CREAM PIE

yield: 6-8 servings ∾ **prep: 35 min. + chilling**

Our family loves raspberries, and this pie keeps the flavor and firmness of the berries intact. The combination of the berry gelatin and cream cheese layers keeps everyone coming back for seconds.

—*Allison Anderson, Raymond, Washington*

- 1 cup graham cracker crumbs
- 1/2 cup sugar
- 5 tablespoons butter, melted

FILLING:
- 1 package (8 ounces) cream cheese, softened
- 1/4 cup confectioners' sugar
- 2 teaspoons 2% milk
- 1 teaspoon vanilla extract

TOPPING:
- 3/4 cup sugar
- 3 tablespoons cornstarch
- 1-1/3 cups cold water
- 1/4 cup raspberry gelatin powder
- 3 cups fresh raspberries

1. In a small bowl, combine the cracker crumbs, sugar and butter. Press onto the bottom and up the sides of an ungreased 9-in. pie plate. Bake at 350° for 9-11 minutes or until set. Cool on a wire rack.

2. For filling, in a small bowl, combine the cream cheese, confectioners' sugar, milk and vanilla. Carefully spread the filling over the crust.

3. For topping, in a small saucepan, combine the sugar, cornstarch and water until smooth. Bring to a boil; cook and stir for 2 minutes or until thickened. Remove from the heat; stir in the gelatin until dissolved. Cool to room temperature. Refrigerate until slightly thickened.

4. Arrange raspberries over filling. Spoon gelatin mixture over berries. Refrigerate until set.

[2005]

STRAWBERRY TARTLETS

yield: 1 dozen ∾ **prep: 25 min.**
bake: 10 min. + cooling

(Pictured on page 597)

This elegant-looking dessert is easy to make, and the cute wonton "cups" can be made in advance. They're a different way to present fresh strawberries when entertaining. The recipe is easy to double, too.

—*Joy Van Meter, Thornton, Colorado*

- 12 wonton wrappers
- 3 tablespoons butter, melted
- 1/3 cup packed brown sugar
- 3/4 cup Mascarpone cheese
- 2 tablespoons honey
- 2 teaspoons orange juice
- 3 cups fresh strawberries, sliced

Whipped cream and fresh mint, optional

1. Brush one side of each wonton wrapper with butter. Place brown sugar in a shallow bowl; press buttered side of wontons into sugar to coat. Press wontons sugared side up into greased muffin cups.

2. Bake at 325° for 7-9 minutes or until edges are lightly browned. Cool on a wire rack.

3. In a small bowl, combine the cheese, honey and orange juice until smooth. Spoon about 1 tablespoon into each wonton cup. Top with strawberries. Garnish with whipped cream and mint if desired.

STRAWBERRY TARTLETS

❝This was my favorite recipe of the year!! The brown sugar melts in the wonton giving it a caramelized base, and then the honey with the cheese pulls it all together. This is my new favorite dessert and they look so elegant—you can bring them to any dinner party. The only negative: They do not refrigerate well. If there are any left over, the wontons become soft and droopy. The good news: There probably won't be any left over!!❞

—*pallen0703*

[2008]

FRESH RASPBERRY PIE

yield: 6-8 servings ∞ prep: 35 min. + chilling
bake: 50 min. + cooling

(Pictured on page 599)

This pretty raspberry pie was practically a staple at our house during the late summer. Our family had raspberry bushes, so the pie was always made with fresh-picked berries.

—*Emily Dennis, Hancock, Michigan*

- 2 cups all-purpose flour
- 1 tablespoon sugar
- 1/2 teaspoon salt
- 3/4 cup shortening
- 1 egg, lightly beaten
- 3 tablespoons cold water
- 1 tablespoon white vinegar

FILLING:

- 1-1/3 cups sugar
- 2 tablespoons quick-cooking tapioca
- 2 tablespoons cornstarch
- 5 cups fresh *or* frozen unsweetened raspberries, thawed
- 1 tablespoon butter

TOPPING:

- 1 tablespoon 2% milk
- 1 tablespoon sugar

1. In a large bowl, combine the flour, sugar and salt; cut in shortening until mixture resembles coarse crumbs. Combine the egg, water and vinegar; stir into the flour mixture just until moistened. Divide dough in half so that one ball is slightly larger than the other; wrap each in plastic wrap. Refrigerate for 30 minutes or until easy to handle.

2. In another large bowl, combine sugar, tapioca, cornstarch and raspberries; let stand for 15 minutes.

3. On a lightly floured surface, roll out larger ball of dough to fit a 9-in. pie plate. Transfer dough to pie plate; trim even with edge. Add raspberry filling; dot with butter.

4. Roll out remaining dough to fit top of pie; place over filling. Trim, seal and flute edges. Cut slits in top. Brush with milk; sprinkle with sugar.

5. Bake at 350° for 50-55 minutes or until crust is golden brown and filling is bubbly. Cool on a wire rack.

Editor's Note: If using frozen raspberries, do not thaw before adding to filling.

[2006]

CRUMBLEBERRY PIE

yield: 6-8 servings ∞ prep: 15 min. ∞ bake: 50 min.

Blueberries peek through the golden crumb topping of this tantalizing pear-and-berry pie. It's best served warm.

—*Maria Regakis, Somerville, Massachusetts, Field Editor*

Pastry for single-crust pie (9 inches)

- 6 tablespoons butter, softened
- 1/2 cup sugar
- 2 eggs
- 1 cup finely ground almonds
- 1/4 cup all-purpose flour
- 1 large pear, peeled and thinly sliced

TOPPING:

- 3/4 cup all-purpose flour
- 1/3 cup packed brown sugar
- 1/4 teaspoon almond extract
- 1/3 cup cold butter, cubed
- 1 cup fresh *or* frozen blueberries

1. Line a 9-in. pie plate with pastry; set aside. In a small bowl, cream butter and sugar until light and fluffy. Add eggs, one at a time, beating well after each addition. Stir in almonds and flour.

2. Spread into pastry shell. Arrange pear slices over filling. Bake at 350° for 25-30 minutes or until light golden brown.

3. For topping, in a large bowl, combine the flour, brown sugar and extract; cut in butter until crumbly. Sprinkle blueberries over pears; sprinkle with crumb topping.

4. Bake 25-30 minutes longer or until golden brown. Serve warm. Refrigerate leftovers.

Editor's Note: If using frozen blueberries, do not thaw before adding to filling.

[2000]
CARAMEL PEAR PIE
yield: 6-8 servings
prep: 15 min. + standing
bake: 55 min. + cooling

A dear friend shared the recipe for this attractive pie. The caramel drizzle and streusel topping make it almost too pretty to eat. Knowing this dessert is waiting is great motivation for our children to eat all their vegetables.

—Mary Kaehler, Lodi, California

- 6 cups sliced peeled ripe pears (about 6 medium)
- 1 tablespoon lemon juice
- 1/2 cup plus 3 tablespoons sugar, *divided*
- 2 tablespoons quick-cooking tapioca
- 3/4 teaspoon ground cinnamon
- 1/4 teaspoon salt
- 1/4 teaspoon ground nutmeg
- Pastry for single-crust pie (9 inches)
- 3/4 cup old-fashioned oats
- 1 tablespoon all-purpose flour
- 1/4 cup cold butter, cubed
- 18 caramels
- 5 tablespoons 2% milk
- 1/4 cup chopped pecans

1. In a large bowl, combine pears and lemon juice. In another bowl, combine 1/2 cup sugar, tapioca, cinnamon, salt and nutmeg. Add to pears; stir gently. Let stand for 15 minutes.

2. Pour into pastry shell. In a small bowl, combine the oats, flour and remaining sugar. Cut in butter until crumbly. Sprinkle over pears. Bake at 400° for 45 minutes.

3. Meanwhile, in a saucepan over low heat, melt caramels with milk. Stir until smooth; add pecans. Drizzle over pie. Bake 8-10 minutes longer or until crust is golden brown and filling is bubbly. Cool on a wire rack.

[1998]
DUTCH APPLE PIE
yield: 6-8 servings ∞ **prep: 20 min.**
bake: 40 min. + cooling

(Pictured on page 593)

Everything about this dessert makes it the top request for family gatherings. The delightful crust cuts beautifully to reveal a filling with pieces of diced apple. At harvesttime or any time, you cannot beat this delectable apple pie.

—Brenda DuFresne, Midland, Michigan

- 2 cups all-purpose flour
- 1 cup packed brown sugar
- 1/2 cup quick-cooking oats
- 3/4 cup butter, melted

FILLING:
- 2/3 cup sugar
- 3 tablespoons cornstarch
- 1-1/4 cups cold water
- 3 cups diced peeled tart apples
- 1 teaspoon vanilla extract

TOP 100 RECIPE

1. In a large bowl, combine the flour, brown sugar, oats and butter; set aside 1 cup for topping. Press remaining crumb mixture into an ungreased 9-in. pie plate; set aside.

2. For filling, combine the sugar, cornstarch and water in a large saucepan until smooth; bring to a boil. Cook and stir for 2 minutes or until thickened. Remove from the heat; stir in apples and vanilla.

3. Pour into crust; top with reserved crumb mixture. Bake at 350° for 40-45 minutes or until crust is golden brown. Cool on a wire rack.

CARAMEL PEAR PIE

"I made this pie for a pie baking contest put on by my college last year—and I won it! I got raves and raves. Even after the judges finished testing, I went to get the remains of my pie to take home, but there were none! Thanks for sharing such a great recipe!"

—Nelson Needs

WASHINGTON STATE APPLE PIE

"I made this for a bbq cookout last fall and it was a hit! I cheated and used a store-bought refrigerator pie crust (I am scared to make one from scratch after my first diaster!). The filling is sweet and warm...just like apple pie ought to be!"

—peach08

[2008]

RUSTIC AUTUMN FRUIT TART

yield: 6 servings ∽ prep: 25 min. + chilling
bake: 40 min. + cooling

(Pictured on page 597)

This impressive dessert was a hit at my house. It's fast, easy and delicious! An apricot jam glaze lends a pretty sheen to the buttery pastry that envelops tender apple and pear slices.

—Jennifer Wickes, Pine Beach, New Jersey

1/2	cup butter, softened
4	ounces cream cheese, softened
1-1/2	cups all-purpose flour
2	large apples, peeled and thinly sliced
1	medium pear, peeled and thinly sliced
4-1/2	teaspoons cornstarch
1/2	teaspoon ground cinnamon
1/4	teaspoon ground cardamom
1/4	teaspoon ground nutmeg
1/4	cup orange juice
1/3	cup packed brown sugar
1/2	cup apricot jam, warmed

1. In a small bowl, beat butter and cream cheese until smooth. Gradually add flour, beating just until mixture forms a ball. Cover and refrigerate for 1 hour.

2. In a large bowl, combine the apples and pear. In a small bowl, combine the cornstarch and spices; stir in orange juice until smooth. Stir in brown sugar until blended. Add to apple mixture and stir gently to coat.

3. On a lightly floured surface, roll out dough into a 14-in. circle. Transfer to a parchment paper-lined baking sheet. Spoon filling over the pastry to within 2 in. of edges. Fold up edges of pastry over filling, leaving center uncovered.

4. Bake at 375° for 40-45 minutes or until the crust is golden and filling is bubbly. Spread with the apricot jam. Using parchment paper, slide tart onto a wire rack to cool.

[1993]

WASHINGTON STATE APPLE PIE

yield: 6-8 servings ∽ prep: 25 min.
bake: 45 min. + cooling

(Pictured on page 595)

This pie won Grand Champion in the Apple Pie category at the 1992 Okanogan County Fair. The pie looks traditional, but making your own filling gives it a different flair and great taste.

—Dolores Scholz, Tonasket, Washington
Former Field Editor

6	cups sliced peeled tart apples (about 5 to 6 medium)
2	tablespoons water
1	tablespoon lemon juice
1/2	cup sugar
1/2	cup packed brown sugar
3	tablespoons all-purpose flour
1	teaspoon ground cinnamon
1/4	teaspoon ground nutmeg
1/8	teaspoon ground ginger
1/8	teaspoon salt

Pastry for double-crust pie (9 inches)

1. In a saucepan, combine the apples, water and lemon juice; cook over medium-low heat just until the apples are tender. Remove from the heat and cool (do not drain).

2. In a large bowl, combine the sugars, flour, cinnamon, nutmeg, ginger and salt; add apples and toss to coat. Place bottom pastry in pie plate; add apple mixture. Cover with top pastry; seal and flute edges. Cut slits in top crust.

3. Bake at 450° for 10 minutes. Reduce the heat to 350°; bake 35-45 minutes longer or until golden brown. Cool on a wire rack.

[1994]

CHERRY PIE

yield: 6-8 servings ∽ prep: 20 min. + standing ∽ bake: 55 min. + cooling

(*Pictured on page 600*)

A real all-American pie is a tart cherry pie. In my family, it is always a delicious treat when I serve a slice of this pretty dessert.

—Frances Poste, Wall, South Dakota, Field Editor

PASTRY:
1-1/2 cups all-purpose flour
1/2 teaspoon salt
1/2 cup shortening
1/4 cup ice water

FILLING:
2 cans (14-1/2 ounces *each*) pitted tart cherries
1 cup sugar
3 tablespoons quick-cooking tapioca
1/4 teaspoon almond extract
1/4 teaspoon salt
Red food coloring, optional
1 tablespoon butter

1. In a large bowl, combine flour and salt; cut in shortening until crumbly. Gradually add water, tossing with a fork until dough forms a ball. Divide dough in half. Roll out one portion. Line a 9-in. pie plate with bottom crust; trim pastry even with edge.

2. Drain cherries, reserving 1/4 cup juice. In a large bowl, combine the sugar, tapioca, extract, salt, food coloring if desired and reserved juice. Gently stir in the cherries; let stand for 15 minutes.

3. Pour into the crust. Dot with butter. Roll out remaining pastry; make a lattice crust. Seal and flute edges. Bake at 375° for 55-60 minutes. Cool on a wire rack.

CHERRY PIE

"This is great. My dad can be picky about his pies, and he adored it. I had frozen cherries on hand so I thawed and used those. The pie came out terrific, and gosh it was pretty while it lasted. :)"
—*lightedway*

MAKING A LATTICE TOP

1. Line bottom of a 9-in. pie plate with half the pastry for a double-crust pie, and add filling. Roll remaining dough into an 11-in. circle. Cut 1-in.-wide strips using a knife or pizza cutter. Lay half the strips across the pie, about 1 in. apart.

2. Fold back every other strip about halfway. Lay a strip of dough across center of pie at a right angle to the other strips. Unfold strips over the center strip. Fold back the alternate strips; place second cross strip in place. Continue to add strips until pie is covered with lattice.

CRUMB-TOPPED CHERRY PIE

[2006]

CRUMB-TOPPED CHERRY PIE

yield: 6-8 servings ∞ **prep: 25 min.**
bake: 35 min. + cooling

(Pictured on page 597)

*This pie was my dad's favorite and one my
mom made frequently for Sunday dinner. We
had a farm, so mom made her own butter and
ice cream, and she used our fresh dairy
products for this pie's great topping.*

—*Sandy Jenkins, Elkhorn, Wisconsin*

1-1/4 cups all-purpose flour
1/2 teaspoon salt
1/2 cup canola oil
2 tablespoons 2% milk
FILLING:
1-1/3 cups sugar
1/3 cup all-purpose flour
2 cans (14-1/2 ounces each) pitted tart
    cherries, drained
1/4 teaspoon almond extract
TOPPING:
1/2 cup all-purpose flour
1/2 cup sugar
1/4 cup cold butter, cubed
1 cup heavy whipping cream
1 tablespoon confectioners' sugar
1/8 teaspoon vanilla extract

---

1. In a small bowl, combine flour and salt.
Combine oil and milk; stir into flour
mixture with a fork just until blended.
Pat evenly onto the bottom and up the
sides of a 9-in. pie plate; set aside.

2. In a large bowl, combine the filling
ingredients; pour into the crust. For
topping, combine the flour and sugar;
cut in butter until crumbly. Sprinkle
over the filling.

3. Bake at 425° for 35-45 minutes or until
crust is golden brown and filling is
bubbly. Cool on a wire rack.

4. Just before serving, in a small bowl,
beat cream until it begins to thicken.
Add confectioners' sugar and vanilla;
beat until soft peaks form. Serve with
the pie.

[1997]

PURPLE PLUM PIE

yield: 8 servings ∞ **prep: 20 min.**
bake: 50 min. + cooling

*I can never resist a tart, tempting slice of this
beautiful pie. It's a down-home dessert that
makes any meal special. This pie is a terrific
way to put bountiful summer plums to use.*

—*Michelle Beran, Claflin, Kansas*

---

4 cups sliced fresh plums (about 1-1/2
    pounds)
1 tablespoon lemon juice
1/2 cup sugar
1/4 cup all-purpose flour
1/4 teaspoon salt
1/4 teaspoon ground cinnamon
Frozen deep-dish pie shell
TOPPING:
1/2 cup sugar
1/2 cup all-purpose flour
1/4 teaspoon ground cinnamon
1/4 teaspoon ground nutmeg
3 tablespoons cold butter

---

1. In a large bowl, sprinkle plums with
lemon juice. Combine the sugar, flour,
salt and cinnamon. Add to plums; toss
gently to coat. Pour into pie shell.

2. For topping, in a small bowl, combine
the sugar, flour, cinnamon and nutmeg;
cut in butter until crumbly. Sprinkle
over filling.

3. Bake at 375° for 50-60 minutes or until
filling is bubbly. Cover edges of crust
during the last 20 minutes to prevent
overbrowning. Cool on a wire rack.

[2011]

BLUEBARB PIE

yield: 8 servings ∽ **prep: 50 min. + chilling** ∽ **bake: 40 min. + cooling**

The jewel tones of rhubarb and blueberries are nestled in a flaky, homemade crust. This pie makes a fabulous summertime treat.

—*Steve Gyuro, Franklin, Wisconsin*

2	**cups all-purpose flour**
1	**teaspoon salt**
2/3	**cup shortening**
6	**to 8 tablespoons ice water**

FILLING:

1-1/2	**cups sugar**
3	**tablespoons quick-cooking tapioca**
1/4	**teaspoon salt**
4	**cups sliced fresh *or* frozen rhubarb, thawed**
2	**cups fresh *or* frozen blueberries, thawed**
1	**tablespoon butter**
1	**teaspoon 2% milk**

Coarse sugar *or* additional granulated sugar, optional

---

1. In a small bowl, combine flour and salt; cut in the shortening until crumbly. Gradually add water, tossing with a fork until dough forms a ball. Divide dough in half so that one portion is slightly larger than the other; wrap each in plastic wrap. Refrigerate dough for 4 hours or until easy to handle.

2. On a lightly floured surface, roll out larger portion of dough to fit a 9-in. deep-dish pie plate. Transfer pastry to pie plate. Trim pastry even with edge.

3. For filling, in a large bowl, combine the sugar, tapioca and salt. Add the rhubarb and blueberries; toss to coat. Let stand for 15 minutes. Transfer to crust. Dot with butter.

4. Roll out remaining pastry to fit top of pie. Place over filling. Trim, seal and flute edges. Cut slits in pastry. Brush with milk; sprinkle with coarse sugar if desired.

5. Bake at 400° for 40-45 minutes or until crust is golden brown and filling is bubbly. Cover edges with foil during the last 15 minutes to prevent overbrowning if necessary. Cool on a wire rack.

Editor's Note: If using frozen rhubarb, measure rhubarb while still frozen, then thaw completely. Drain in a colander, but do not press liquid out.

BLUEBARB PIE

"Delicious! With whipped topping on top or a scoop of vanilla ice cream, this makes a nice, patriotic (red, white, blue) dessert for 4th of July or Memorial Day."
—*mbandboys*

[2004]

CRANBERRY PECAN PIE

yield: 6-8 servings   **prep: 25 min. + chilling**
bake: 45 min. + chilling

I first prepared this pie at Thanksgiving to share with my coworkers. It was such a success! Now I freeze cranberries while they are in season so that I can make it year-round.

—*Dawn Liet Hartman, Mifflinburg, Pennsylvania*

6	tablespoons shortening
1-1/2	teaspoons buttermilk
2	tablespoons hot water
1	cup all-purpose flour
1/2	teaspoon salt

FILLING:

3	eggs
1	cup corn syrup
2/3	cup sugar
1/4	cup butter, melted
1	teaspoon vanilla extract
2	cups fresh cranberries
1	cup chopped pecans

1. In a small bowl, cream shortening and buttermilk until smooth. Gradually add water, beating until light and fluffy. Beat in the flour and salt. Wrap pastry in plastic wrap; refrigerate for 4 hours or overnight.

2. Roll out pastry to fit a 9-in. pie plate. Trim pastry to 1/2 in. beyond edge of plate; flute edges. In a large bowl, combine the eggs, corn syrup, sugar, butter and vanilla until blended. Stir in cranberries and pecans. Pour into crust.

3. Bake at 425° for 10 minutes. Reduce heat to 350°; bake 35-40 minutes longer or until filling is almost set. Cool completely on a wire rack. Cover pie and refrigerate overnight before slicing.

[2005]

CREAM CHEESE BLUEBERRY PIE

yield: 6-8 servings   **prep: 20 min. + chilling**

(Pictured on page 600)

This pie will have everyone's approval—you'll probably get requests for the recipe, too!

—*Lisieux Bauman, Cheektowaga, New York*

4	ounces cream cheese, softened
1/2	cup confectioners' sugar
1/2	cup heavy whipping cream, whipped

Pastry for single-crust pie (9 inches), baked

2/3	cup sugar
1/4	cup cornstarch
1/2	cup water
1/4	cup lemon juice
3	cups fresh *or* frozen blueberries

1. In a small bowl, beat cream cheese and confectioners' sugar until smooth. Fold in whipped cream. Spread into pie shell.

2. In a large saucepan, combine sugar, cornstarch, water and lemon juice until smooth; stir in blueberries. Bring to a boil over medium heat; cook and stir for 2 minutes or until thickened. Cool. Spread over cream cheese layer. Refrigerate until serving.

MEASURING SHORTENING

Press shortening into a dry measuring cup with a spatula to make sure it is solidly packed without air pockets. With a metal spatula or flat side of a knife, level with the rim. Some shortenings come in sticks and may be measured like butter.

[2007]

PEACHES 'N' CREAM TART

yield: 10 servings ∽ prep: 30 min.
bake: 15 min. + chill

Fresh peach slices and big, juicy raspberries crown this beautiful tart. An almond-flavored cream filling and macaroon crust complement the fruits. It's the perfect dessert for company during peach season.

—*Brenda Harmon, Hastings, Minnesota*

- 2 cups crumbled soft macaroon cookies
- 1 cup ground pecans
- 3 tablespoons butter, melted
- 1/2 cup heavy whipping cream
- 1 package (8 ounces) cream cheese, softened
- 1/3 cup sugar
- 2 teaspoons orange juice
- 1 teaspoon vanilla extract
- 1/4 teaspoon almond extract
- 4 medium peaches, peeled and sliced *or* 3 cups frozen unsweetened sliced peaches, thawed
- 2 tablespoons lemon juice
- 1/2 cup fresh raspberries
- 1/4 cup apricot preserves
- 2 teaspoons honey

1. In a food processor, combine the crumbled cookies, pecans and butter; cover and process until blended. Press cookie mixture onto the bottom and up the sides of an ungreased 11-in. fluted tart pan with a removable bottom.

2. Place pan on a baking sheet. Bake at 350° for 12-14 minutes or until golden brown. Cool completely on a wire rack.

3. In a small bowl, beat cream until soft peaks form; set aside. In another small bowl, beat cream cheese and sugar until smooth. Beat in orange juice and extracts. Fold in whipped cream. Spread over crust.

4. In a small bowl, combine peaches and lemon juice. Arrange peaches and raspberries over filling.

5. In a small saucepan, combine preserves and honey. Cook and stir over low heat until melted; strain. Brush over fruit. Store in the refrigerator.

[2010]

FIVE-FRUIT PIE

yield: 8 servings ∽ prep: 40 min.
bake: 45 min. + cooling

(*Pictured on page 596*)

This recipe gets compliments galore! I've given it to new neighbors or anyone who needed a pick-me-up. They all love it!

—*Jean Ross, Oil City, Pennsylvania*

- 1-1/2 cups sugar
- 3 tablespoons cornstarch
- 2 tablespoons quick-cooking tapioca
- 1 cup chopped peeled tart apples
- 1 cup chopped fresh *or* frozen rhubarb
- 1 cup *each* fresh *or* frozen raspberries, blueberries and sliced strawberries

CRUST:
- 2 cups all-purpose flour
- 1/2 teaspoon salt
- 1/2 cup shortening
- 1 egg
- 1/4 cup cold water
- 2 teaspoons white vinegar
- 2 tablespoons half-and-half cream
- 2 tablespoons coarse sugar

1. In a large bowl, combine the sugar, cornstarch, tapioca and fruit; let stand for 15 minutes. In another bowl, combine flour and salt; cut in shortening until mixture resembles coarse crumbs. Combine the egg, water and vinegar; stir into flour mixture just until moistened.

2. Divide dough in half so that one portion is slightly larger than the other. On a lightly floured surface, roll out larger portion to fit a 9-in. pie plate. Transfer pastry to pie plate; trim pastry even with edge. Spoon fruit mixture into crust.

3. Roll out remaining pastry to fit top of pie; make a lattice crust. Trim, seal and flute edges. Brush with cream; sprinkle with coarse sugar.

4. Bake at 375° for 45-55 minutes or until crust is golden brown and filling is bubbly. Cool on a wire rack.

Editor's Note: If using frozen fruit, measure fruit while still frozen, then thaw completely. Drain in a colander, but do not press liquid out.

[1998]

WHITE CHOCOLATE FRUIT TART

yield: 16 servings ∞ prep: 30 min.
bake: 25 min. + chilling

It takes a little time to make, but this tart is absolutely marvelous, especially in summer when fresh fruit is in abundance.

—*Claire Darby, New Castle, Delaware*

3/4	cup butter, softened
1/2	cup confectioners' sugar
1-1/2	cups all-purpose flour

FILLING:

1	package (10 to 12 ounces) white baking chips, melted and cooled
1/4	cup heavy whipping cream
1	package (8 ounces) cream cheese, softened
1	can (20 ounces) pineapple chunks
1	pint fresh strawberries, sliced
1	can (11 ounces) mandarin oranges, drained
2	kiwifruit, peeled and sliced

GLAZE:

3	tablespoons sugar
2	teaspoons cornstarch
1/2	teaspoon lemon juice

WHITE CHOCOLATE FRUIT TART

"I've made this beautiful dessert dozens of times over the past 10 years. It is always delicious, and there are never any leftovers! It's a must, whether it be for a fancy family gathering or a backyard picnic with friends."
—*msbeth2u*

1. In a small bowl, cream butter and confectioners' sugar until light and fluffy. Gradually add the flour and mix well.

2. Press into an ungreased 11-in. fluted tart pan with removable bottom or 12-in. pizza pan with sides. Bake at 300° for 25-30 minutes or until lightly browned. Cool on a wire rack.

3. For filling, in a small bowl, beat melted chips and cream. Add cream cheese; beat until smooth. Spread over crust. Refrigerate for 30 minutes.

4. Drain the pineapple, reserving 1/2 cup juice. Arrange pineapple, strawberries, oranges and kiwi over filling.

5. For glaze, in a small saucepan, combine the sugar and cornstarch. Stir in lemon juice and reserved pineapple juice until smooth. Bring to a boil over medium heat; cook and stir for 2 minutes or until thickened. Cool.

Brush glaze over the fruit. Refrigerate for 1 hour before serving. Store tart in the refrigerator.

PEELING KIWI TWO WAYS

1. Cut both ends from fruit. Using a spoon, scoop out the flesh.

2. Cut both ends from fruit. Using a vegetable peeler, peel off fuzzy, brown skin. Cut into slices, wedges or chunks with a sharp knife or egg slicer.

[1995]

PEACH CREAM PIE

yield: 6-8 servings ∞ **prep: 15 min.**
bake: 50 min. + cooling

The sour cream filling and cinnamon crumb topping complement the fruit flavor in this yummy pie.

—Denise Goedeken
Platte Center, Nebraska, Former Field Editor

1-1/2   cups all-purpose flour
1/2   teaspoon salt
1/2   cup cold butter, cubed
FILLING:
  4   cups unsweetened sliced peaches (about 6 medium)
  1   cup sugar, *divided*
  2   tablespoons all-purpose flour
  1   egg
1/2   teaspoon vanilla extract
1/4   teaspoon salt
  1   cup (8 ounces) sour cream
TOPPING:
1/3   cup sugar
1/3   cup all-purpose flour
  1   teaspoon ground cinnamon
1/4   cup cold butter, cubed

---

1. In a small bowl, combine the flour and salt; cut in the butter until crumbly. Press into a 9-in. pie plate.

2. For filling, place peaches in a large bowl; sprinkle with 1/4 cup sugar and toss gently to coat. In another small bowl, combine flour, egg, vanilla, salt and remaining sugar; fold in sour cream. Stir into peaches.

3. Pour filling into the crust. Bake at 400° for 15 minutes. Reduce heat to 350°; bake for 20 minutes.

4. Meanwhile prepare topping. In a small bowl, combine sugar, flour and cinnamon. Cut in butter until crumbly. Sprinkle over top of pie. Bake at 450° 15 minutes or until topping is browned. Cool on a wire rack. Store in the refrigerator.

[2010]

BERRY DELICIOUS TART

yield: 12 servings ∞ **prep: 25 min.**
bake: 30 min. + cooling

(Pictured on page 596)

After trying a little of this and a little of that, this is my result. I love berries and am always trying to find something new to do with them. Everyone loved this tart and asked for the recipe.

—Angela Moorhead, Cambridge, Ontario

---

  1   cup all-purpose flour
1/3   cup plus 1/4 cup sugar, *divided*
1/2   cup cold butter, cubed
1/2   cup seedless strawberry jam
  1   package (8 ounces) cream cheese, softened
  1   egg, lightly beaten
  1   teaspoon vanilla extract
  2   cups fresh *or* frozen unsweetened mixed berries, thawed and drained
TOPPING:
3/4   cup packed brown sugar
1/3   cup old-fashioned oats
1/2   cup all-purpose flour
1/4   cup cold butter, cubed

---

1. In a small bowl, combine flour and 1/3 cup sugar; cut in the butter until crumbly. Press onto the bottom and 1 in. up the sides of a greased 9-in. springform pan.

2. Place pan on a baking sheet. Bake at 375° for 8-10 minutes or until crust is lightly browned. Cool on a wire rack.

3. Spread jam over crust. In a small bowl, beat cream cheese and remaining sugar until smooth. Add egg and vanilla; beat on low speed just until combined. Pour over jam; sprinkle with berries.

4. In a small bowl, combine the brown sugar, oats and flour; cut in butter until crumbly. Sprinkle over filling.

5. Bake for 30-35 minutes or until bubbly and golden brown. Cool on a wire rack for 10 minutes. Carefully run a knife around edge of pan to loosen; cool 30 minutes longer. Serve warm or cold.

[2009]

CHOCOLATE GANACHE TARTS

yield: 2 dozen ∞ prep: 30 min. + chilling
bake: 20 min. + cooling

(Pictured on page 593)

Decadent, chocolate mousse-like filling and a flaky, tender crust make this very special. Be sure to coat hands well with flour when pressing the dough into pastry cups.

—Lorraine Caland, Thunder Bay, Ontario

1/2	cup butter, softened
1	package (3 ounces) cream cheese, softened
1	cup all-purpose flour
1/2	cup semisweet chocolate chips
1/2	cup milk chocolate chips
2/3	cup heavy whipping cream

Whipped cream, fresh raspberries and confectioners' sugar, optional

1. In a small bowl, beat butter and cream cheese until smooth; beat in flour. Drop dough by scant tablespoonfuls into greased miniature muffin cups; with well-floured hands, press dough onto bottoms and up sides of cups.

2. Bake at 325° for 20-25 minutes or until golden brown. Cool tarts for 5 minutes before removing from the pans to wire racks to cool completely.

3. Place chocolate chips in a small bowl. In a small saucepan, bring cream just to a boil. Pour over chocolate; whisk until smooth. Transfer to a small bowl; cover and refrigerate until firm.

4. Beat the chocolate mixture until soft peaks form. Pipe or spoon into the tart shells. Garnish with whipped cream, raspberries and confectioners' sugar if desired.

[2002]

CHOCOLATE MALLOW PIE

yield: 8 servings ∞ prep: 15 min. + chilling
bake: 10 min. + chilling

(Pictured on page 599)

This rich and fudgy cream cheese pie should serve eight, but it never does because so many folks request a second slice! I've been cooking more than 60 years and this is the best chocolate pie recipe I've found.

—Louise Genn, Cosmopolis, Washington

1-1/4	cups cream-filled chocolate sandwich cookie crumbs (about 14 cookies)
1/4	cup butter, melted
2	tablespoons sugar
2	packages (one 8 ounces, one 3 ounces) cream cheese, softened
1/2	cup chocolate syrup
1-1/3	cups semisweet chocolate chips, melted
1	carton (8 ounces) frozen whipped topping, thawed
2	cups miniature marshmallows

Chocolate curls, optional

1. In a large bowl, combine the cookie crumbs, butter and sugar. Press onto the bottom and up the sides of a 9-in. pie plate. Bake at 375° for 8-10 minutes or until crust is set; cool completely on a wire rack.

2. In a large bowl, beat cream cheese and chocolate syrup until blended. Beat in the melted chips. Set aside 1/4 cup of whipped topping. Fold marshmallows and remaining whipped topping into chocolate mixture.

3. Spoon into crust. Refrigerate for at least 8 hours or overnight. Garnish with reserved whipped topping and chocolate curls if desired.

[2010]

STRAWBERRIES & CREAM PIE

yield: 8 servings ✎ **prep: 20 min. + chilling**

(*Pictured on page 593*)

Every time I take this pie to a family dinner, church event or anything else, it disappears quickly. I've even started taking the recipe with me because I'm always asked for it.

—*Angela Moore, Tollesboro, Kentucky*

- 1 cup (6 ounces) semisweet chocolate chips, *divided*
- 3 teaspoons shortening, *divided*
- 1 graham cracker crust (10 inches)
- 1 package (8 ounces) cream cheese, softened
- 1/2 cup sugar
- 1/2 cup sour cream
- 1 teaspoon vanilla extract
- 1 carton (8 ounces) frozen whipped topping, thawed
- 2 cups fresh strawberries, halved
- 1/2 cup seedless strawberry jam

---

1. In a microwave, melt 3/4 cup chocolate chips and 2 teaspoons shortening; stir until smooth. Brush over the crust. Refrigerate until firm.

2. In a small bowl, beat the cream cheese, sugar, sour cream and vanilla until smooth. Fold in whipped topping. Spoon into crust. Refrigerate for 1 hour.

3. Arrange strawberries over pie. In a microwave, heat jam until melted; brush over the top. Melt remaining chocolate chips and shortening; stir until smooth. Drizzle over pie. Refrigerate until chilled.

[2008]

FROSTY TOFFEE BITS PIE

yield: 6-8 servings
prep: 10 min. + freezing

(*Pictured on page 598*)

On a hot summer day, or to finish off a wonderful meal any time, this dessert tastes oh-so-good!

—*LaDonna Reed*
Ponca City, Oklahoma, Field Editor

- 1 package (3 ounces) cream cheese, softened
- 2 tablespoons sugar
- 1/2 cup half-and-half cream
- 1 carton (8 ounces) frozen whipped topping, thawed
- 1 package (8 ounces) milk chocolate English toffee bits, *divided*
- 1 graham cracker crust (9 inches)

---

1. In a large bowl, beat cream cheese and sugar until smooth. Beat in cream until blended. Fold in whipped topping and 1 cup toffee bits.

2. Spoon into crust; sprinkle with the remaining toffee bits. Cover and freeze overnight. Remove from the freezer 10 minutes before serving.

FROSTY TOFFEE BITS PIE

"This pie is so delicious. I drizzled each piece with Hershey's chocolate syrup before serving. I made it for Father's Day and I'm making it for the Fourth of July with Butterfingers crushed up instead of the toffee to change it up a bit. You could use lots of different crushed up candy bars in this, like the Dairy Queen Blizzard!"
—*badkitty*

MELTING CHOCOLATE

It's best to melt chocolate chips at reduced power in the microwave. Stir at 30-second to 1-minute intervals.

—*Taste of Home Cooking Experts*

[2008]

LEMON MERINGUE PIE

yield: 8 servings ∞ prep: 35 min.
bake: 15 min. + chilling

This is my grandmother's recipe. It's a lovely, special dessert that feels like home.

—*Merle Dyck, Elkford, British Columbia, Field Editor*

 1/2 cup sugar
 1/4 cup cornstarch
Pinch salt
   2 cups cold water
   2 egg yolks, lightly beaten
   3 tablespoons lemon juice
   1 teaspoon grated lemon peel
   1 teaspoon butter
MERINGUE:
   3 egg whites
 1/8 teaspoon cream of tartar
   6 tablespoons sugar
Pastry for single-crust pie (9 inches), baked

---

1. In a large saucepan, combine sugar, cornstarch and salt. Stir in water until smooth. Cook and stir over medium heat until thickened and bubbly, about 2 minutes. Reduce heat; cook and stir 2 minutes longer.

2. Remove from the heat. Gradually stir 1 cup hot filling into egg yolks; return all to the pan. Bring to a gentle boil; cook and stir for 2 minutes. Remove from the heat. Gently stir in lemon juice, peel and butter until butter is melted. Set aside and keep warm.

3. For meringue, in a small bowl, beat the egg whites and cream of tartar on medium speed until soft peaks form. Gradually beat in sugar, 1 tablespoon at a time, on high until stiff glossy peaks form and sugar is dissolved.

4. Pour filling into crust. Spread the meringue over hot filling, sealing the edges to the crust. Bake at 350° for 15 minutes or until meringue is golden brown. Cool the pie on a wire rack for 1 hour; refrigerate for at least 3 hours before serving.

[2009]

MINTY ICE CREAM PIE

yield: 6-8 servings ∞ prep: 25 min. + freezing

I love ice cream desserts like this one because they can be fixed in advance and kept on hand for unexpected company. And they never fail to please! This minty pie is always a refreshing treat.

—*Lorraine Darocha, Mountain City, Tennessee*

---

   1 package (3 ounces) cream cheese, softened
   2 tablespoons sugar
   2 cups heavy whipping cream, *divided*
 1/4 cup chopped walnuts
   1 chocolate crumb crust (9 inches)
   2 packages (4-3/4 ounces *each*) chocolate-covered peppermint candies, *divided*
   1 pint chocolate ice cream *or* fudge ripple ice cream
 1/4 cup hot fudge ice cream topping, warmed
   2 tablespoons confectioners' sugar
   1 teaspoon peppermint extract
   2 to 3 drops green food coloring, optional

---

1. In a small bowl, beat cream cheese and sugar until smooth. Beat in 1 cup cream until soft peaks form. Fold in the walnuts. Spread into crust. Coarsely chop 1 package peppermint candies; fold into the ice cream. Spread over cream cheese mixture. Drizzle with fudge topping. Freeze for 1 hour.

2. In a small bowl, beat remaining cream until it begins to thicken. Add the confectioners' sugar, extract and food coloring if desired; beat until stiff peaks form. Garnish the pie with whipped cream mixture and remaining candies. Freeze. Remove from the freezer 15 minutes before serving.

MERINGUE PEAKS

Make easy work of this fancy decorating technique by using an offset spatula to create the peaks. Gently touch the spatula to the meringue and then quickly pull it back. The meringue will come to a point.

[1998]
CHOCOLATE RASPBERRY PIE

yield: 6-8 servings ∞ **prep: 30 min. + chilling
bake: 15 min. + chilling**

(*Pictured on page 596*)

*After tasting this pie at my sister-in-law's
house, I had to have the recipe. I love the
chocolate and raspberry layers separated by a
dreamy cream layer. It's a joy to serve this
standout treat!*

—Ruth Bartel, Morris, Manitoba

Pastry for single-crust pie (9 inches)
- 3 tablespoons sugar
- 1 tablespoon cornstarch
- 2 cups fresh *or* frozen unsweetened raspberries, thawed

FILLING:
- 1 package (8 ounces) cream cheese, softened
- 1/3 cup sugar
- 1/2 teaspoon vanilla extract
- 1/2 cup heavy whipping cream, whipped

TOPPING:
- 2 ounces semisweet chocolate
- 3 tablespoons butter

1. Line unpricked pie shell with a double thickness of heavy-duty foil. Bake at 450° for 8 minutes. Remove foil; bake 5 minutes longer. Cool on a wire rack.

2. In a large saucepan, combine sugar and cornstarch. Stir in raspberries; bring to a boil over medium heat. Boil and stir for 2 minutes. Remove from the heat; cool for 15 minutes. Spread into the shell; refrigerate.

3. In a large bowl, beat the cream cheese, sugar and vanilla until fluffy. Fold in whipped cream. Carefully spread over raspberry layer. Cover and refrigerate for at least 1 hour.

4. In a microwave, melt chocolate and butter; stir until smooth. Cool for 4-5 minutes. Pour over the filling. Cover and chill for at least 2 hours. Store in the refrigerator.

[2008]
STRAWBERRY CUSTARD PIES

**yield: 6 pies (8 servings each)
prep: 35 min. + chilling**

*These pies were a spring special at a restaurant
where I used to work. Whoever was cook that
day had to bake them first thing in the morning
and again in the afternoon, as soon as
strawberries were ready.*

—Caroline Park
Pritchard, British Columbia

- 4-1/2 cups sugar
- 3/4 cup cornstarch
- 4-1/2 cups cold water
- 3 packages (3 ounces each) strawberry gelatin
- 1 tablespoon lemon juice
- 6 packages (3 ounces each) cook-and-serve vanilla pudding mix
- 6 pastry shells (9 inches), baked
- 3 pounds fresh strawberries, halved

Whipped cream, optional

1. In a large saucepan, combine sugar and cornstarch; gradually stir in water until smooth. Bring to a boil; cook and stir for 2 minutes or until thickened. Remove from the heat. Stir in gelatin and lemon juice until gelatin is dissolved. Cool to room temperature.

2. Prepare pudding mixes according to package directions. Pour into pastry shells. Top with strawberries. Carefully spoon gelatin mixture over berries. Refrigerate until set. Garnish with whipped cream if desired.

STRAWBERRY CUSTARD PIES

❝WOW! This is now my favorite pie. My family couldn't get enough of them. I'm glad the recipe made a big batch. I can't wait to make them again.❞
—*katejudy311*

[2009]

TURTLE PRALINE TART

yield: 16 servings ～ prep: 35 min. + chilling

(Pictured on page 593)

This rich dessert is my own creation, and I'm very proud of it. It's easy enough to make for every day but special enough to serve guests or take to a potluck.

—*Kathleen Specht, Clinton, Montana*

- 1 sheet refrigerated pie pastry
- 36 caramels
- 1 cup heavy whipping cream, *divided*
- 3-1/2 cups pecan halves
- 1/2 cup semisweet chocolate chips, melted

1. Unroll the pastry on a lightly floured surface. Transfer pastry to an 11-in. fluted tart pan with removable bottom; trim edges.

2. Line unpricked pastry shell with a double thickness of heavy-duty foil. Bake at 450° for 8 minutes. Remove foil; bake 5-6 minutes longer or until light golden brown. Cool the crust on a wire rack.

3. In a large saucepan, combine caramels and 1/2 cup cream. Cook and stir over medium-low heat until the caramels are melted. Stir in pecans. Spread filling evenly into the crust. Drizzle with melted chocolate.

4. Cover and refrigerate for 30 minutes or until set. Whip remaining cream; serve with tart.

TURTLE PRALINE TART

❝Out of this world! Soooo good!❞
—*shirleypozi*

[2005]

BAVARIAN STRAWBERRY PIE

yield: 6-8 servings
prep: 15 min.
bake: 30 min. + chilling

A coconut crust and pretty, fluffy filling make this dessert special. When the strawberries ripen here in our Hudson Valley, many churches feature them at festivals.

—*Kathy Anderson*
Wallkill, New York, Field Editor

- 2-1/2 cups flaked coconut
- 1/3 cup butter, melted
- 1 quart fresh strawberries, sliced
- 3/4 cup sugar
- 1 envelope unflavored gelatin
- 1/2 cup cold water
- 2 teaspoons lemon juice
- 1 cup heavy whipping cream, whipped

1. In a small bowl, combine coconut and butter. Press onto the bottom and up the sides of a greased 9-in. pie plate. Bake at 300° for 30-35 minutes or until lightly browned (cover edges loosely with foil to prevent overbrowning if necessary). Cool on a wire rack.

2. In a large bowl, combine strawberries and sugar; let stand for 15 minutes. In a small saucepan, sprinkle gelatin over cold water; let stand for 1 minute. Cook and stir over medium heat until gelatin is dissolved; stir in lemon juice. Stir into strawberry mixture. Cool to room temperature. Fold in whipped cream. Pour into crust. Refrigerate for at least 4 hours before slicing.

[1997]

CHERRY ALMOND MOUSSE PIE

yield: 8-10 servings
prep: 25 min. + chilling

Christmas is the perfect time to treat your family and guests to a luscious pie with chocolate, cherries and nuts in a creamy vanilla mousse. It's a sweet yet light dessert.

—Dorothy Pritchett
Wills Point, Texas, Former Field Editor

- 1 can (14 ounces) sweetened condensed milk, *divided*
- 1 ounce unsweetened chocolate
- 1/2 teaspoon almond extract, *divided*
- 1 frozen pie shell (9 inches), baked
- 1 jar (10 ounces) maraschino cherries, drained
- 1 package (8 ounces) cream cheese, softened
- 1 cup cold water
- 1 package (3.4 ounces) instant vanilla pudding mix
- 1 cup heavy whipping cream, whipped
- 1/2 cup chopped toasted almonds

Chocolate curls, optional

1. In a saucepan over low heat, cook and stir 1/2 cup milk and chocolate until the chocolate is melted and mixture is thickened, about 4 minutes. Stir in 1/4 teaspoon extract. Pour into the pie shell; set aside.

2. Set aside eight whole cherries for garnish. Chop the remaining cherries; set aside. In a large bowl, beat cream cheese until fluffy. Gradually beat in water and remaining milk. Beat in

pudding mix and remaining extract. Fold in the whipped cream. Stir in the chopped cherries and almonds.

3. Pour over pie. Chill 4 hours or until set. Garnish with whole cherries and chocolate curls if desired.

[2006]

EGGNOG PUMPKIN PIE

yield: 6-8 servings ✎ **prep: 10 min.**
bake: 1 hour + cooling

This pie of my mom's is the absolute best pumpkin pie I have ever tasted. Eggnog is the special ingredient in the creamy custard filling.

—Terri Gonzalez, Roswell, New Mexico

- 1 can (15 ounces) solid-pack pumpkin
- 1-1/4 cups eggnog
- 2/3 cup sugar
- 3 eggs
- 1-1/2 teaspoons pumpkin pie spice
- 1/4 teaspoon salt

Pastry for single-crust pie (9 inches)

1. In a large bowl, combine the pumpkin, eggnog, sugar, eggs, pumpkin pie spice and salt. Pour into pastry shell.

2. Bake at 375° for 60-65 minutes or until a knife inserted near the center comes out clean. Cool the pie on a wire rack. Refrigerate until serving.

Editor's Note: This recipe was tested with commercially prepared eggnog.

CHERRY ALMOND MOUSSE PIE

"When I saw this recipe, I was thrilled. I love almond and chocolate and cherries! It was creamy and sweet but not too sweet. Like my husband says to me, 'They had you at heavy cream!' It was so tasty. I don't like pie crust, so I used an Oreo cookie crust instead. Amazing taste and beautiful enough for company!"
—Wilberst

[2008]

GINGER-STREUSEL
PUMPKIN PIE

yield: 8 servings ∽ **prep: 25 min.**
bake: 55 min. + cooling

*I love to bake and have spent a lot of time
making goodies for my family and friends. The
streusel topping gives this pie a special touch
your family will love.*

—*Sonia Parvu, Sherrill, New York*

1	sheet refrigerated pie pastry
3	eggs, lightly beaten
1	can (15 ounces) solid-pack pumpkin
1-1/2	cups heavy whipping cream
1/2	cup sugar
1/4	cup packed brown sugar
1-1/2	teaspoons ground cinnamon
1/2	teaspoon salt
1/4	teaspoon ground allspice
1/4	teaspoon ground nutmeg
1/4	teaspoon ground cloves

STREUSEL:

1	cup all-purpose flour
1/2	cup packed brown sugar
1/2	cup cold butter, cubed
1/2	cup chopped walnuts
1/3	cup finely chopped crystallized ginger

1. On a lightly floured surface, unroll
pastry. Transfer pastry to a 9-in. pie
plate. Trim pastry to 1/2 in. beyond
edge of plate; flute edges.

2. In a large bowl, whisk eggs, pumpkin,
cream, sugars, cinnamon, salt, allspice,
nutmeg and cloves. Pour into pastry
shell. Bake at 350° for 40 minutes.

3. In a small bowl, combine flour and
brown sugar; cut in the butter until
crumbly. Stir in walnuts and ginger.
Gently sprinkle over filling.

4. Bake 15-25 minutes longer or until a
knife inserted near the center comes
out clean. Cool the pie on a wire rack.
Refrigerate leftovers.

[2008]

BERRY SMOOTHIE PIE

yield: 6 servings ∽ **prep: 10 min. + chilling**

(Pictured on page 594)

*This refreshing dessert is so beautiful and
tastes sensational. Your family will love it,
just like mine!*

—*Jill Bonanno, Prineville, Oregon*

1	package (.3 ounce) sugar-free strawberry gelatin
1/3	cup reduced-calorie reduced-sugar cranberry juice
3/4	cup (6 ounces) raspberry yogurt
3	cups chopped fresh strawberries
1	reduced-fat graham cracker crust (8 inches)

Fat-free whipped topping, optional

1. In a small microwave-safe bowl,
sprinkle gelatin over cranberry juice;
let stand for 1 minute. Microwave on
high for 40 seconds; stir. Let stand for
1 minute or until the gelatin is
completely dissolved.

2. In a blender, combine gelatin mixture,
yogurt and strawberries; cover and
process until blended. Pour into crust.
Refrigerate for 4 hours or until set.
Serve with whipped topping if desired.

BERRY
SMOOTHIE PIE

"This tastes just like a
smoothie! My entire
family loved it! I will
definitely make it again!"
—*tinaoocumma*

TURTLE PRALINE TART, page 590

CHOCOLATE GANACHE TARTS, page 586

DUTCH APPLE PIE, page 577

STRAWBERRIES & CREAM PIE, page 587

BERRY SMOOTHIE PIE, page 592

BAKLAVA TARTLETS, page 604

WASHINGTON STATE APPLE PIE, page 578

CHOCOLATE RASPBERRY PIE, page 589

BERRY DELICIOUS TART, page 585

FIVE-FRUIT PIE, page 583

STRAWBERRY TARTLETS, page 575

RUSTIC AUTUMN FRUIT TART, page 578

CRUMB-TOPPED CHERRY PIE, page 580

FROSTY KEY LIME PIE, page 603

FROSTY TOFFEE BITS PIE, page 587

FRESH RASPBERRY PIE, page 576

CHOCOLATE MALLOW PIE, page 586

QUICK BANANA CREAM PIE, page 605

CREAM CHEESE BLUEBERRY PIE, page 582

CHERRY PIE, page 579

[1998]

LEMON SUPREME PIE

yield: 6-8 servings ∽ **prep: 25 min. + chilling**
∽ **bake: 15 min. + chilling**

The combination of the cream cheese topping and tart lemon filling is wonderful.

—*Jana Beckman, Wamego, Kansas*

Frozen deep-dish pie shell
LEMON FILLING:
- 1-1/4 cups sugar, *divided*
- 6 tablespoons cornstarch
- 1/2 teaspoon salt
- 1-1/4 cups water
- 2 tablespoons butter
- 2 teaspoons grated lemon peel
- 4 to 5 drops yellow food coloring, optional
- 1/2 cup lemon juice

CREAM CHEESE FILLING:
- 2 packages (one 8 ounces, one 3 ounces) cream cheese, softened
- 3/4 cup confectioners' sugar
- 1-1/2 cups whipped topping
- 1 tablespoon lemon juice

---

1. Line unpricked pie shell with a double thickness of heavy-duty foil. Bake at 450° for 8 minutes. Remove foil; bake 5 minutes longer. Cool on a wire rack.

2. For lemon filling, combine 3/4 cup sugar, cornstarch and salt. Stir in water until smooth. Bring to a boil over medium-high heat. Reduce heat; add the remaining sugar. Cook and stir for 2 minutes or until thickened and bubbly. Remove from the heat; stir in butter, lemon peel and food coloring if desired. Gently stir in lemon juice. Cool to room temperature, about 1 hour.

3. For cream cheese filling, beat the cream cheese and sugar in a large bowl until smooth. Fold in whipped topping

and lemon juice. Refrigerate 1/2 cup for garnish. Spread remaining cream cheese mixture into pie shell; top with lemon filling. Refrigerate overnight.

4. Place reserved cream cheese mixture in a pastry bag with a #21 star tip; pipe stars onto pie. Store in the refrigerator.

[2002]

HOMEMADE EGGNOG PIE

yield: 8 servings ∽ **prep: 40 min. + chilling**

This dessert is a festive finale. It is delightfully rich and scrumptious.

—*Katherine Kuhlemeier*
 Pearl City, Illinois, Former Field Editor

- 1-1/8 teaspoons unflavored gelatin
- 1/4 cup cold water
- 3/4 cup sugar
- 2 tablespoons cornstarch
- 2/3 cup 2% milk
- 3 egg yolks, lightly beaten
- 1 teaspoon vanilla extract
- 1-1/2 cups heavy whipping cream, whipped
Pastry for single-crust pie (9 inches)
- 1/8 teaspoon ground nutmeg

---

1. In a small bowl, soften gelatin in cold water; set aside.

2. In a large saucepan, combine sugar and cornstarch. Gradually stir in milk until smooth. Bring to a boil; cook and stir for 2 minutes or until thickened. Remove from the heat. Stir a small amount of hot mixture into egg yolks. Return all to the pan; bring to a gentle boil, stirring constantly. Remove from the heat; stir in gelatin and vanilla.

3. Cool to room temperature, stirring occasionally. Fold in whipped cream. Pour into pie shell. Sprinkle with the nutmeg. Refrigerate until set, about 2 hours.

LEMON SUPREME PIE

"Soooooo good. Tastes just like the pie we get at Bakers Square, but not anymore, because now I can make it! Thanks for such a great recipe."
—*pixie9999*

[2008]

BERRY CHEESECAKE PIE

yield: 6-8 servings ✎ **prep: 20 min.**
bake: 35 min. + chilling

Since I don't care for traditional pie crust, I usually eat only the filling of pie. That changed when I discovered this recipe. Boasting a luscious cheesecake flavor, this unique pie gets creative with phyllo dough.

—Deanne Causey, Midland, Texas

- 8 sheets phyllo dough (14 inches x 9 inches)
- 6 tablespoons butter, melted
- 2 packages (8 ounces *each*) cream cheese, softened
- 1/2 cup sugar
- 1 teaspoon vanilla extract
- 2 eggs, lightly beaten
- 2 cups fresh *or* frozen blueberries
- 1/2 cup strawberry jelly
- 1 cup whipped topping

Sliced fresh strawberries and additional blueberries, optional

1. Place one phyllo sheet in a greased 9-in. pie plate; brush with butter. Repeat seven times; trim edges. (Keep remaining phyllo covered with plastic wrap and a damp towel to prevent it from drying out.)

2. Bake at 425° for 6-8 minutes or until edges are lightly browned (center will puff up). Cool on a wire rack.

3. For filling, in a large bowl, beat the cream cheese, sugar and vanilla until smooth. Add the eggs; beat on low speed just until combined. Fold in the blueberries. Spoon into crust.

4. Bake at 350° for 10 minutes; cover edges with foil to prevent overbrowning. Bake 23-27 minutes longer or until center is almost set. Cool the pie on a wire rack for 1 hour. Refrigerate until chilled.

5. In a small bowl, beat the jelly until smooth; spread over the filling. Spread with whipped topping. Garnish with strawberries and additional blueberries if desired.

Editor's Note: If using frozen blueberries, use without thawing to avoid discoloring the batter.

[1994]

PEANUT BUTTER PIE

yield: 8-10 servings
prep: 20 min. + cooling

Who can resist a tempting chocolate crumb crust and a creamy filling with big peanut butter taste? Be prepared to take an empty plate home when you serve this pie at your next potluck.

—Doris Doherty, Albany, Oregon

- 1-1/4 cups chocolate cookie crumbs (20 cookies)
- 1/4 cup sugar
- 1/4 cup butter, melted

FILLING:
- 1 package (8 ounces) cream cheese, softened
- 1 cup creamy peanut butter
- 1 cup sugar
- 1 tablespoon butter, softened
- 1 teaspoon vanilla extract
- 1 cup heavy whipping cream, whipped

Grated chocolate *or* chocolate cookie crumbs, optional

1. In a small bowl, combine the cookie crumbs and sugar; stir in the butter. Press the crumbs onto the bottom and up the sides of a 9-in. pie plate. Bake at 375° for 10 minutes. Cool on a wire rack.

2. For filling, beat cream cheese, peanut butter, sugar, butter and vanilla in a large bowl until smooth. Fold in the whipped cream. Gently spoon into the crust. Garnish the pie with chocolate or cookie crumbs if desired. Store in the refrigerator.

MAKING COOKIE CRUMBS

Place cookies in a heavy-duty resealable plastic bag. Seal bag, pushing out as much air as possible. Press a rolling pin over the bag, crushing the cookies into fine crumbs. Or, process cookies in a food processor.

—*Taste of Home Cooking Experts*

[1998]

PISTACHIO PUDDING TARTS
yield: 4 dozen ∞ prep: 30 min.
bake: 15 min./batch + cooling

For St. Patrick's Day or anytime you want a treat that's green, refreshing and delightful, try these tempting tarts.

—Bettye Linster, Atlanta, Georgia

- 1 cup butter, softened
- 1 package (8 ounces) cream cheese, softened
- 2 cups all-purpose flour
- 1-3/4 cups cold 2% milk
- 1 package (3.4 ounces) instant pistachio pudding mix

1. In a large bowl, combine butter and cream cheese until smooth. Gradually add flour until blended.

2. Shape into 48 balls (1 in. each); press onto the bottom and up the sides of ungreased miniature muffin cups. Bake at 400° for 12-15 minutes or until lightly browned. Cool for 5 minutes; carefully remove from pans to a wire rack to cool completely.

3. For filling, in a large bowl, whisk milk and pudding for 2 minutes. Let stand for 2 minutes or until set. Cover and refrigerate for 5 minutes. Spoon into tart shells.

[1998]

COCONUT PIE
yield: 6 servings ∞ prep: 10 min.
bake: 50 min.

This old-fashioned dessert is easy to assemble, so it's one I rely on when dinnertime's fast approaching. I sometimes sprinkle slices with cinnamon or nutmeg.

—Virginia Krites, Cridersville, Ohio

- 2 cups 2% milk
- 1 cup sugar

- 4 eggs
- 1/2 cup all-purpose flour
- 6 tablespoons butter
- 1 teaspoon vanilla extract
- 1/2 teaspoon salt
- 1 cup flaked coconut

1. In a blender, combine the first seven ingredients. Cover and process for 10 seconds; scrape the sides. Process for another 10 seconds. Add the coconut; process for 2 seconds or until blended. Pour into a greased 10-in. pie plate.

2. Bake at 350° for 50-55 minutes or until a knife inserted near the center comes out clean. Serve warm.

[2007]

FROSTY KEY LIME PIE
yield: 6-8 servings
prep: 20 min. + freezing

(Pictured on page 597)

Credit whipped cream for the fluffy-smooth texture and key lime juice for luscious flavor of this frozen refresher.

—Lisa Feld
Grafton, Wisconsin, Field Editor

- 1 can (14 ounces) sweetened condensed milk
- 6 tablespoons key lime juice
- 2 cups heavy whipping cream, whipped, *divided*
- 1 graham cracker crust (9 inches)

1. In a large bowl, combine milk and lime juice. Refrigerate 1/4 cup whipped cream for garnish. Fold a fourth of the remaining whipped cream into lime mixture; fold in the remaining whipped cream. Spoon into the crust. Cover and freeze overnight.

2. Remove the pie from the freezer 10-15 minutes before serving. Garnish with reserved whipped cream.

FROSTY KEY LIME PIE

"I made this pie a few days ago, and my husband and I both LOVED it! Tangy with a hint of sweetness, it was perfectly balanced and absolutely delicious! I used regular lime juice in place of the key lime juice and it worked just fine. I was amazed at how high the pie was after I piled it into the crust! The next time I make it, I'm going to try spreading Cool Whip over the top—my husband's suggestion—and split the pie into two instead of one singular. All in all, a wonderful and refreshing pie for spring! This recipe is definitely one I'm going to keep!"
—Edyne Jurai

COCONUT CHOCOLATE PIE

For fun, I substituted the milk with coconut milk. It cooked up beautifully, and for coconut fans, it was extra fantastic! (It was a rich, full-bodied coconut milk.)

—Marcia Phillips

[2006]

COCONUT CHOCOLATE PIE

yield: 6-8 servings ∞ prep: 20 min. + chilling

Everyone loves my fudgy Almond Joy pie. It's pretty, cuts easily and is absolutely delicious.

—Cheryl Wilt
Eglon, West Virginia, Field Editor

1/2 cup sugar
1/3 cup cornstarch
1/4 cup baking cocoa
1/4 teaspoon salt
1-1/2 cups 2% milk
16 fun-size Almond Joy candy bars, chopped
1 teaspoon vanilla extract
Pastry for single-crust pie (9 inches), baked
Whipped cream

1. In a large saucepan, combine the sugar, cornstarch, cocoa and salt. Stir in the milk until smooth. Bring to a boil over medium heat, cook and stir for 2 minutes or until thickened (mixture will thicken quickly). Remove from heat.

2. Add chopped candy bars and vanilla; stir until chocolate is melted. Pour into pie shell. Press plastic wrap onto the filling. Refrigerate until set, about 4 hours. Remove plastic wrap. Slice and serve with whipped cream.

[2006]

CARAMEL PECAN PIE

yield: 6-8 servings
prep: 25 min. ∞ bake: 35 min. + cooling

This is hands-down the best pecan pie —it's so good, it's scary! I make it for Thanksgiving because there will be others around to share it with me.

—Dorothy Reinhold, Malibu, California

36 caramels
1/4 cup water
1/4 cup butter, cubed
3 eggs
3/4 cup sugar
1 teaspoon vanilla extract
1/8 teaspoon salt
1-1/3 cups chopped pecans, toasted
Frozen deep-dish pie shell
Pecan halves, optional

1. In a small heavy saucepan, combine caramels, water and butter. Cook and stir over low heat until caramels are melted. Remove from the heat; set aside.

2. In a small bowl, beat eggs, sugar, vanilla and salt until smooth. Gradually add caramel mixture. Stir in chopped pecans. Pour into pie shell. If desired, arrange pecan halves over filling.

3. Bake the pie at 350° for 35-40 minutes or until set. Cool the pie on a wire rack. Refrigerate leftovers.

[2007]

BAKLAVA TARTLETS

yield: 45 tartlets ∞ prep/total time: 25 min.

(Pictured on page 594)

Want a quick treat that's delicious and easy to make? These tartlets will do the trick. You can serve them right away, but they're better after chilling for about an hour in the refrigerator.

—Ashley Eagon, Kettering, Ohio

2 cups finely chopped walnuts
3/4 cup honey
1/2 cup butter, melted
1 teaspoon ground cinnamon
1 teaspoon lemon juice
1/4 teaspoon ground cloves
3 packages (1.9 ounces each) frozen miniature phyllo tart shells

1. In a small bowl, combine the first six ingredients; spoon 2 teaspoonfuls into each tart shell. Cover and refrigerate until serving.

[2003]

SWEET POTATO CUSTARD PIE

yield: 8 servings ∞ prep: 25 min.
bake: 45 min. + cooling

I love to bake and experiment with ingredients. I came up with a hit when I developed this deliciously different pie.

—**Kathy Roberts, New Hebron, Mississippi**

2	small sweet potatoes, peeled and chopped
3/4	cup marshmallow creme
1/2	cup butter, cubed
1	can (5 ounces) evaporated milk
3	eggs
1	teaspoon vanilla extract
1/4	teaspoon almond extract
3/4	cup sugar
1/4	cup packed brown sugar
1	tablespoon all-purpose flour
1/8	teaspoon ground cinnamon
1/8	teaspoon ground nutmeg

Pastry for single-crust pie (9 inches)
1/2 cup whipping topping

1. Place the sweet potatoes in a large saucepan and cover with water. Bring to a boil. Reduce the heat; cover and simmer for 10 minutes or until tender. Drain potatoes and place in large bowl; mash. Add the marshmallow creme and butter; beat until smooth. Beat in the milk, eggs and extracts.

2. Combine the sugars, flour, cinnamon and nutmeg; gradually beat into potato mixture and mix well. Pour into the pie shell.

3. Bake at 350° for 45-50 minutes or until a knife inserted near the center comes out clean. Cool the pie on a wire rack. Serve with the whipped topping. Refrigerate leftovers.

[2002]

QUICK BANANA CREAM PIE

yield: 8 servings ∞ prep/total time: 10 min.

(Pictured on page 599)

This fluffy, no-bake pie is full of old-fashioned flavor, with only a fraction of the work. It uses instant vanilla pudding and it's whipped up in minutes.

—**Perlene Hoekema**
Lynden, Washington, Field Editor

1	cup cold 2% milk
1	package (3.4 ounces) instant vanilla pudding mix
1/2	teaspoon vanilla extract
1	carton (12 ounces) frozen whipped topping, thawed, *divided*
1	graham cracker crust (9 inches)
2	medium firm bananas, sliced

Additional banana slices, optional

1. In a large bowl, whisk the milk and pudding mix for 2 minutes. Let stand for 2 minutes or until soft-set; beat in the vanilla. Fold in 3 cups of the whipped topping.

2. Pour 1-1/3 cups of the pudding mixture into pie crust. Layer with banana slices and remaining pudding mixture. Top with the remaining whipped topping. Garnish with additional banana slices if desired. Refrigerate until serving.

STORING BANANAS

Once bananas are ripe, they can be stored in the refrigerator or freezer. The skin will turn black in the refrigerator, but the flesh will keep for several days. Frozen bananas are great for smoothies.

—*Taste of Home Cooking Experts*

QUICK BANANA CREAM PIE

Awesome! My guest LOVED it!
—*conwaycom2*

✑ PORK & LAMB ✑

GRILLED PORK ROAST

❝I've made this many times, and it's consistently good every time. To cut the grilling time in half, I cut the roast in half lengthwise before marinating. Overcooking will result in a dry roast, so I suggest using a leave-in thermometer while grilling.❞

—LauraManning

[1999]

GRILLED PORK ROAST

yield: 8 servings
prep: 10 min. + marinating
grill: 1-1/2 hours + standing

(Pictured on page 633)

We enjoy the mild mustard flavor of this juicy, tender pork roast. With a little advance preparation, this roast is simple since it creates no dirty dishes, and I get the rest of the meal ready while it cooks.

—*Myra Innes, Auburn, Kansas, Field Editor*

2/3 cup canola oil
1/3 cup reduced-sodium soy sauce
1/4 cup red wine vinegar
2 tablespoons lemon juice
2 tablespoons Worcestershire sauce
2 garlic cloves, minced
1 to 2 tablespoons ground mustard
1 to 2 teaspoons pepper
1 teaspoon salt
1 boneless pork loin roast (2-1/2 to 3 pounds)

---

1. In a large resealable plastic bag, combine the first nine ingredients; add the pork. Seal the bag and turn to coat. Refrigerate overnight.

2. Prepare grill for indirect heat. Drain and discard marinade. Grill the roast, covered, over indirect heat for 50-60 minutes or until a thermometer reads 145°. Let meat stand for 10 minutes before slicing.

[2002]

SESAME PORK TENDERLOIN

yield: 8 servings
prep: 15 min. + marinating ✑ bake: 20 min.

Pork tenderloin gets dressed up for company in this easy-to-fix yet special main dish. The meat is tender and flavorful. Sesame seeds and ginger go together so well.

—*Sue Mackey*
Jackson, Wisconsin, Field Editor

1/2 cup reduced-sodium soy sauce
3 tablespoons olive oil
2 teaspoons minced fresh gingerroot
1 to 3 garlic cloves, minced
2 pork tenderloins (1 pound each)
1/2 cup honey
1/4 cup packed brown sugar
1/3 cup sesame seeds, toasted

---

1. In a large resealable plastic bag, combine the soy sauce, oil, ginger and garlic. Add pork; seal and turn to coat. Refrigerate for 4 hours or overnight, turning occasionally.

2. Drain and discard marinade. Place pork on a greased rack in a foil-lined shallow roasting pan. Combine the honey and brown sugar; spoon over pork. Sprinkle with sesame seeds.

3. Bake, uncovered, at 425° for 20-25 minutes or until a thermometer reads 145°. Let meat stand for 5 minutes before slicing.

[2009]

PORK TENDERLOIN WITH FIG-ORANGE GLAZE

yield: 6 servings ∞ **prep: 40 min. + chilling** ∞ **bake: 20 min.**

Here's an entree that's low in fat and calories but doesn't make you feel deprived! The sauce is bursting with fig flavor, seasonings and citrus flair.

—*Kathy Pettit, Los Angeles, California*

1-1/2 teaspoons garlic powder

3/4 teaspoon pepper

1/2 teaspoon salt

1/2 teaspoon fennel seed, crushed

1/2 teaspoon rubbed sage

1/2 teaspoon dried thyme

1/8 teaspoon cayenne pepper

2 pork tenderloins (3/4 pound *each*)

GLAZE:

2/3 cup reduced-sodium chicken broth

2 tablespoons brown sugar

1 tablespoon molasses

1/2 teaspoon balsamic vinegar

1/4 teaspoon ground cumin

1/8 teaspoon kosher salt

Dash white pepper

Dash ground cinnamon

10 dried figs

1/2 cup chopped orange segments

1/4 cup water

1 tablespoon olive oil

---

1. In a small bowl, combine the first seven ingredients; rub over the pork. Cover and refrigerate for at least 2 hours.

2. For glaze, in a large saucepan, combine the broth, brown sugar, molasses, vinegar and seasonings. Stir in figs and orange. Cook and stir over medium heat until mixture comes to a boil. Reduce heat; simmer, uncovered, for 15-18 minutes or until figs are tender. Stir in water; cool slightly. Transfer to a blender; cover and process until smooth.

3. In a large nonstick skillet, brown pork in oil on all sides. Spread with half of fig-orange glaze. Place pork on a rack in a shallow roasting pan lined with foil.

4. Bake at 350° for 20-25 minutes or until a thermometer reads 145°, basting occasionally with remaining glaze. Let meat stand for 5 minutes before slicing.

PORK TENDERLOIN WITH FIG-ORANGE GLAZE

"Excellent! Very easy to prepare. My family loves it. I am always asked for the recipe. I put the rub on the night before. It is delicious."
— *lyndireed*

[2009]

BRAIDED PORK TENDERLOINS

yield: 8 servings (3/4 cup sauce)
prep: 30 min. + marinating ∽ grill: 10 min.

(Pictured on page 640)

For a summertime family dinner, I served a jerk-spiced marinated pork tenderloin. Braiding the meat, which is easy to do, makes for an attractive presentation.

—*Jim Rude, Janesville, Wisconsin*

2	pork tenderloins (1 pound *each*)
1/2	cup mango nectar
1/4	cup plus 1 tablespoon spiced rum *or* additional mango nectar, *divided*
2	tablespoons olive oil
2	tablespoons Caribbean jerk seasoning, *divided*
2	garlic cloves, minced
1	tablespoon heavy whipping cream
1	cup chopped peeled mango

1. Cut tenderloins in half lengthwise; cut each half into three strips to within 1-in. of one end. In a large resealable plastic bag, combine the mango nectar, 1/4 cup rum, oil, 1 tablespoon jerk seasoning and garlic; add pork. Seal bag and turn to coat; refrigerate for up to 4 hours.

2. Drain and discard marinade. Place the tenderloin halves on a clean cutting board and braid; secure the loose ends with toothpicks. Sprinkle with remaining jerk seasoning.

3. Grill braids, covered, over medium heat for 4-5 minutes on each side or until a thermometer reads 145°. Discard toothpicks. Let stand for 5 minutes before slicing.

4. Meanwhile, place the cream, remaining rum and mango in a food processor. Cover and process until smooth. Transfer to a small saucepan; heat through. Serve with pork.

[2003]

CHERRY-STUFFED PORK LOIN

yield: 10-12 servings ∽ prep: 55 min.
bake: 1 hour + standing

(Pictured on page 634)

This easy pork roast is moist and has a wonderful stuffing. It looks and tastes impressive, and the gravy is a great complement.

—*James Korzenowski, Fennville, Michigan*

1	cup dried cherries
1/2	cup water
2/3	cup chopped onion
1/2	cup chopped celery
1/2	cup minced fresh parsley
1/4	cup shredded carrot
1	tablespoon rubbed sage
1	teaspoon minced fresh rosemary
3	tablespoons butter
1/2	teaspoon minced garlic
2-1/2	cups salad croutons
1	cup chicken broth
1/2	teaspoon pepper, *divided*
1/4	teaspoon ground nutmeg
1/4	teaspoon almond extract
1	boneless whole pork loin roast (about 3 pounds)

GRAVY:

1-3/4	cups chicken broth
1/2	cup water
1/2	cup heavy whipping cream
1/2	teaspoon minced fresh rosemary

1. In a small saucepan, bring cherries and water to a boil. Remove from the heat; set aside (do not drain).

2. In a large skillet, saute the onion, celery, parsley, carrot, sage and rosemary in butter until tender. Add garlic; cook 1 minute longer. Remove from the heat. Stir in the croutons, broth, 1/4 teaspoon pepper, nutmeg, extract and cherries. Let stand until the liquid is absorbed.

3. Cut a lengthwise slit down the center of the roast to within 1/2 in. of bottom. Open roast so it lies flat; cover with plastic wrap. Flatten to 3/4-in. thickness. Remove plastic; spread stuffing over meat to within 1 in. of edges. Close the roast; tie several times with

kitchen string and secure the ends with toothpicks. Place roast fat side up on a rack in a shallow roasting pan. Sprinkle with the remaining pepper.

4. Bake, uncovered, at 350° for 1 to 1-1/4 hours or until a thermometer reads 145°. Let meat stand for 10 minutes before slicing.

5. Meanwhile, add broth and water to roasting pan; stir to loosen browned bits. Pour into a small saucepan. Bring to a boil over medium-high heat; cook until reduced by half. Stir in cream and rosemary. Bring to a boil. Reduce heat; simmer, uncovered, until thickened. Serve with roast.

[2007]

SLOW-COOKED PORK AND BEANS
yield: 12 servings ∞ prep: 15 min.
cook: 6 hours

This is a hearty slow cooker meal that is also good for a potluck. A generous helping of tender pork and beans is perfect alongside a slice of warm corn bread.

—*Patricia Hager, Nicholasville, Kentucky*

1   boneless whole pork loin roast (3 pounds)
1   medium onion, sliced
3   cans (15 ounces each) pork and beans
1-1/2   cups barbecue sauce
1/4   cup packed brown sugar
1   teaspoon garlic powder

1. Cut the roast in half; place in a 5-qt. slow cooker. Top with the onion. In a large bowl, combine beans, barbecue sauce, brown sugar and garlic powder; pour over meat. Cover and cook on low for 6-8 hours or until the meat is tender.

2. Remove the roast; shred with two forks. Return meat to the slow cooker; heat through.

[2010]

ROAST PORK WITH APPLES & ONIONS
yield: 8 servings ∞ prep: 25 min.
bake: 45 min. + standing

The sweetness of the apples and onions really complements the roast pork. With its crisp skin and melt-in-your-mouth flavor, this is my family's favorite weekend dinner.

—*Lily Julow*
Gainesville, Florida, Field Editor

1   boneless whole pork loin roast (2 pounds)
1/4   teaspoon salt
1/4   teaspoon pepper
1   tablespoon olive oil
3   large Golden Delicious apples, cut into wedges
2   large onions, cut into wedges
5   garlic cloves, peeled
1   tablespoon minced fresh rosemary *or* 1 teaspoon dried rosemary, crushed

1. Sprinkle roast with salt and pepper. In a large nonstick skillet, brown roast in oil on all sides. Place in a shallow roasting pan coated with cooking spray. Arrange the apples, onions and garlic around roast; sprinkle with rosemary.

2. Bake, uncovered, at 350° for 45-60 minutes or until a thermometer reads 145°, turning the apples, onions and garlic once. Let meat stand for 10 minutes before slicing.

ROAST PORK WITH APPLES & ONIONS

"This was so good. My husband normally does not like cooked onions, but the apples flavored them so well. I had Fuji apples and used them in this dish. Delicious!"
—*Oregongrandma*

[2011]

SLOW-COOKED CARNITAS

yield: 12 servings ∞ prep: 20 min.
cook: 6 hours

(Pictured on page 639)

This hearty entree is delicious and easy to simmer in a slow cooker all day long. Instead of using tortillas, I sometimes place the pork on top of shredded lettuce for a tasty salad.

—*Lisa Glogow, Aliso VIejo, California*

---

  1 boneless pork shoulder butt roast (3 to 4 pounds)
  3 garlic cloves, thinly sliced
  2 teaspoons olive oil
  1/2 teaspoon salt
  1/2 teaspoon pepper
  1 bunch green onions, chopped
1-1/2 cups minced fresh cilantro
  1 cup salsa
  1/2 cup chicken broth
  1/2 cup tequila *or* additional chicken broth
  2 cans (4 ounces *each*) chopped green chilies
  12 flour tortillas (8 inches), warmed
Fresh cilantro leaves, sliced red onion and chopped tomatoes, optional

---

1. Cut roast in half; place in a 5-qt. slow cooker. Sprinkle with garlic, oil, salt and pepper. Add the onions, cilantro, salsa, broth, tequila and chilies. Cover and cook on low for 6-8 hours or until meat is tender.

2. Remove meat; cool slightly. Shred with two forks and return to slow cooker; heat through. Spoon about 2/3 cup meat mixture onto each tortilla; serve with toppings of your choice.

[1995]

TUSCAN PORK ROAST

yield: 10 servings
prep: 10 min. + standing
bake: 1 hour + standing

Everyone's eager to eat after the wonderful aroma of this roast tempts us all afternoon. This is a great Sunday dinner with little fuss.

—*Elinor Stabile, Canmore, Alberta*

---

  5 to 8 garlic cloves, peeled
  1 tablespoon dried rosemary, crushed
  1 tablespoon olive oil
  1/2 teaspoon salt
  1 boneless pork loin roast (3 to 4 pounds)

---

1. In a food processor, combine garlic, rosemary, oil and salt; cover and process until mixture becomes a paste. Rub over the roast; cover and let stand for 30 minutes.

2. Place roast fat side up on a greased baking rack in a shallow roasting pan. Bake, uncovered, at 350° for 1 to 1-1/4 hours or until a thermometer reads 145°. Let meat stand for 10 minutes before slicing.

SLOW-COOKED CARNITAS

"Fantastic! Just the right amount of liquid to keep the pork from getting dry, but not dripping out of the tortilla. We love Mexican restaurant-made carnitas but had never made one at home that I cared to repeat until now—wonderful!"
—*susitravl*

PEELING GARLIC

Using the blade of a chef's knife, crush garlic clove. Peel away skin. Chop or mince as directed in the recipe.

—*Taste of Home Cooking Experts*

[1994]

PORK CHOPS WITH SCALLOPED POTATOES

yield: 6 servings ∞ prep: 25 min.
bake: 1-1/2 hours

Mom always managed to put a delicious, hearty meal on the table for us and our farmhands. This all-in-one main dish is not only hearty but has a comforting flavor, too.

—Bernice Morris
Marshfield, Missouri, Field Editor

---

    3 tablespoons butter
    3 tablespoons all-purpose flour
1-1/2 teaspoons salt
  1/4 teaspoon pepper
    1 can (14-1/2 ounces) chicken broth
    6 pork rib *or* loin chops (3/4 inch thick)
    2 tablespoons canola oil
Additional salt and pepper, optional
    6 cups thinly sliced peeled potatoes
       (about 4 pounds)
    1 medium onion, sliced
Paprika and minced fresh parsley, optional

---

1. In a small saucepan, melt butter; stir in the flour, salt and pepper until smooth. Add broth. Bring to a boil; cook and stir for 1 minute or until thickened. Remove from the heat and set aside. In a large skillet, brown the pork chops in oil; sprinkle with additional salt and pepper if desired.

2. In a greased 13-in. x 9-in. baking dish, layer with potatoes and onion. Pour broth mixture over layers. Place pork chops on top.

3. Cover and bake at 350° for 1 hour; uncover and bake 30 minutes longer or until the meat and potatoes are tender. If desired, sprinkle with the paprika and parsley.

[1995]

PORK CHOPS OLE

yield: 4-6 servings ∞ prep: 15 min.
bake: 1 hour

(Pictured on page 637)

This recipe is a fun and simple way to give pork chops south-of-the-border flair. The flavorful seasoning, rice and melted cheddar cheese make this dish a crowd-pleaser.

—Laura Turner, Channelview, Texas

---

    6 pork loin chops (1/2 inch thick)
    2 tablespoons canola oil
Seasoned salt and pepper to taste
1-1/2 cups water
    1 can (8 ounces) tomato sauce
  3/4 cup uncooked long grain rice
    2 tablespoons taco seasoning
    1 medium green pepper, chopped
  1/2 cup shredded cheddar cheese

---

1. In a large skillet, brown the pork chops in oil; sprinkle with the seasoned salt and pepper.

2. Meanwhile, in a greased 13-in. x 9-in. baking dish, combine the water, tomato sauce, rice and taco seasoning.

3. Arrange chops over rice; top with green pepper. Cover and bake at 350° for 1 hour or until rice and meat are tender. Uncover and sprinkle with cheese.

SLICING POTATOES

For thin, even slices of potatoes, use the slicing slot on a standard grater or a mandoline.

—*Taste of Home Cooking Experts*

PORK CHOPS OLE

"This is one of my family's favorite ways to enjoy pork chops. I've substituted brown rice and it is still very good. This recipe is also very easy to make."
—*shecooksalot*

BREADED PORK CHOPS

"We always had pork chops breaded with saltines while growing up. Got away from doing breading this way and used store-bought breadings. Went back to this breading a year ago, and it's the BEST; no more store-bought for me."
—*GavinsNana*

[1996]

SPICED PORK CHOPS

**yield: 4 servings ∞ prep: 20 min.
bake: 30 min.**

Being a widow who likes to cook big meals, I frequently invite family and friends for dinner. On busy days, I rely on this easy recipe, which I got from a dear friend. It's hearty and satisfying, and people really enjoy it.

—Joan MacKinnon, Brooklyn, Nova Scotia

1/2	cup all-purpose flour
1-1/2	teaspoons garlic powder
1-1/2	teaspoons ground mustard
1-1/2	teaspoons paprika
1/2	teaspoon celery salt
1/4	teaspoon ground ginger
1/8	teaspoon dried oregano
1/8	teaspoon dried basil
1/8	teaspoon salt

Pinch pepper

4	pork loin chops (about 3/4 inch thick and 8 ounces each)
1	to 2 tablespoons canola oil
1	cup ketchup
1	cup water
1/4	cup packed brown sugar

---

1. In a large resealable plastic bag, combine the first 10 ingredients. Add pork chops, a few at a time; seal bag and toss to coat.

2. In a large skillet, brown chops in oil on both sides. Place in a greased 13-in. x 9-in. baking dish. In a small bowl, combine the ketchup, water and brown sugar; pour over chops.

3. Bake chops, uncovered, at 350° for 30 minutes or until a thermometer reads 145°. Let stand for 5 minutes before serving.

[1993]

BREADED PORK CHOPS

yield: 6 servings ∞ prep/total time: 20 min.

(Pictured on page 634)

These traditional pork chops have a wonderful home-cooked flavor like the ones Mom used to make. The breading makes them crispy outside and tender and juicy inside. Why not treat your family to them tonight?

**—Deborah Amrine
Fort Myers, Florida, Field Editor**

1	egg, lightly beaten
1/2	cup 2% milk
1-1/2	cups crushed saltines
6	boneless pork loin chops (4 ounces each)
1/4	cup canola oil

---

1. In a shallow bowl, combine egg and milk. Place cracker crumbs in another shallow bowl. Dip each pork chop in the egg mixture, then coat with the cracker crumbs, patting to make a thick coating.

2. In a large skillet, cook chops in oil for 4-5 minutes on each side or until a thermometer reads 145°. Let meat stand for 5 minutes before serving.

BONELESS PORK LOIN CHOPS

Boneless loin chops are great for your diet and menu. These lean, versatile chops cook quickly and can be use for many recipes, not just for pork chops. They can be cut into strips for stir-fries, and cubed for kabobs, stews or chili. Thick chops can be stuffed and thinner ones flattened for cutlets.

—*Taste of Home Cooking Experts*

[1996]

PORK CHOP CASSEROLE

yield: 6 servings ∞ prep: 25 min.
bake: 55 min.

One bite of these tender pork chops smothered in a creamy sauce and we could taste the care Mother put into her cooking. She was happy to share the recipe with guests who requested it after trying this delicious dish at our house.

—*Nancy Duty, Jacksonville, Florida*

- 3/4 cup all-purpose flour
- 1 teaspoon salt
- 1/2 teaspoon pepper
- 6 bone-in pork loin chops (3/4 inch thick and 8 ounces *each*)
- 2 tablespoons canola oil
- 1 can (10-3/4 ounces) condensed cream of mushroom soup, undiluted
- 1 cup (8 ounces) sour cream, *divided*
- 2/3 cup chicken broth
- 1/2 teaspoon ground ginger
- 1/4 teaspoon dried rosemary, crushed
- 1 can (2.8 ounces) french-fried onions, *divided*

1. In a large plastic resealable bag, combine the flour, salt and pepper. Add pork chops, one at a time, and shake to coat.

2. In a large skillet, brown pork chops in oil on both sides. Arrange in a single layer in an ungreased 13-in. x 9-in. baking dish. In a large bowl, combine the soup, 1/2 cup sour cream, broth, ginger and rosemary; pour over chops. Sprinkle with half of onions.

3. Cover and bake the chops at 350° for 45-50 minutes or until tender. Stir the remaining sour cream into the sauce. Sprinkle with remaining onions. Bake, uncovered, for 10 minutes or until onions are browned.

[1995]

BARBECUED SPARERIBS

yield: 4 servings
prep: 10 min + simmering ∞ bake: 10 min.

My husband is a meat cutter at a supermarket and likes to find new ways to barbecue or smoke meat. Several years ago, he discovered this recipe for pork ribs covered in a rich tangy sauce. It was an instant success with our family and friends.

—*Bette Brotzel, Billings, Montana*

- 4 pounds pork spareribs, cut into serving-size pieces
- 1 medium onion, quartered
- 2 teaspoons salt
- 1/4 teaspoon pepper

SAUCE:
- 1/2 cup packed brown sugar
- 1/2 cup cider vinegar
- 1/2 cup ketchup
- 1/4 cup Worcestershire sauce
- 1/4 cup chili sauce
- 2 tablespoons chopped onion
- 1 tablespoon lemon juice
- 1/2 teaspoon ground mustard
- 1 garlic clove, minced

Dash cayenne pepper

1. In a Dutch oven, place ribs and onion; sprinkle with salt and pepper. Add enough water to cover ribs; bring to a boil. Reduce heat; cover and simmer for 1-1/2 hours or until the meat is tender; drain.

2. Meanwhile, in a small saucepan, combine sauce ingredients. Simmer, uncovered, for 1 hour or until slightly thickened, stirring occasionally.

3. Arrange ribs on a rack in a broiler pan. Brush with sauce. Broil 5 in. from the heat for 5 minutes on each side, brushing frequently with sauce.

BARBECUED SPARERIBS

"Just made these tonight; they were DELICIOUS! Cooked exactly like the recipe said. Only wished I had doubled the recipe— no leftovers!"
—*lahall64*

[1996]

SPICY CABBAGE ROLLS

yield: 8-10 servings ∽ prep: 20 min.
bake: 1 hour 20 min.

(Pictured on page 638)

This delightfully delicious recipe came from my Aunt Helen. I serve it alongside ham or turkey for the holidays or on its own with rolls and a crunchy, green salad.

—*Darlene King, Estevan, Saskatchewan*

1	large head cabbage
2	cups cooked barley
2	garlic cloves, minced
1-1/2	cups chopped onion
2	tablespoons reduced-sodium soy sauce
2	tablespoons ketchup
1	tablespoon brown sugar
2	to 3 teaspoons ground ginger
1/2	teaspoon salt
1/4	teaspoon pepper
2	pounds ground pork

SAUCE:

1	can (15 ounces) tomato sauce
1/2	cup chili sauce
1	teaspoon reduced-sodium soy sauce
1/8	teaspoon cayenne pepper

1. Cook the cabbage in boiling water just until outer leaves pull away easily from head. Set aside 10 large leaves for rolls. (Refrigerate remaining cabbage for another use.) Meanwhile, in a large bowl, combine the barley, garlic, onion, soy sauce, ketchup, brown sugar, ginger, salt and pepper. Crumble pork over mixture and mix well.

2. Cut out the thick vein from bottom of each leaf, making a V-shaped cut. Place about 1/2 cup of the pork mixture on a cabbage leaf; overlap cut ends of leaf. Fold in sides. Beginning from the cut end, roll up. Repeat. Place rolls, seam side down in a greased 13-in. x 9-in. baking dish.

3. In a small saucepan over medium heat, combine the sauce ingredients; cook and stir until smooth. Pour over rolls. Cover and bake at 350° for 80-90 minutes or a thermometer reads 160°.

[2000]

PORK AND ONION KABOBS

yield: 6 servings
prep: 15 min. + marinating ∽ grill: 15 min.

A sweet and savory marinade brings out the best in pork, as these grilled kabobs prove. They're a super supper, easy to prepare and fun to serve to company. The pork is so tasty grilled with onion wedges.

—*Mary Lou Wayman, Salt Lake City, Utah*

1/2	cup reduced-sodium soy sauce
1/4	cup chili sauce
1/4	cup honey
2	tablespoons olive oil
2	tablespoons finely chopped onion
2	teaspoons curry powder
2	pounds boneless pork, cut into 1-inch cubes
3	medium onions, cut into 1-inch wedges

1. In a small bowl, combine the first six ingredients. Remove half for basting; cover and refrigerate. Pour remaining marinade into a large resealable plastic bag. Add the pork; seal bag and turn to coat. Cover and refrigerate for 3 hours or overnight.

2. Drain and discard marinade. On six metal or soaked wooden skewers, alternately thread pork and onions.

3. Grill, uncovered, over medium heat for 5 minutes; turn. Baste with reserved marinade. Continue turning and basting for 10-15 minutes or until meat is tender.

[1997]

GINGERED PORK AND ASPARAGUS

yield: 4 servings ∽ **prep: 10 min. + marinating
cook: 15 min.**

*My husband and I really enjoy fresh asparagus. So we were
thrilled when I found this recipe for asparagus and juicy pork
slices smothered in a snappy ginger sauce.*

—Kathleen Purvis, Franklin, Tennessee

---

6 tablespoons apple juice
6 tablespoons reduced-sodium soy sauce
4 garlic cloves, minced
1 tablespoon ground ginger
1 pound pork tenderloin, thinly sliced
2 tablespoons canola oil, *divided*
1 pound fresh asparagus, cut into 1-inch pieces
1-1/2 teaspoons cornstarch
Hot cooked rice, optional

---

1. In a bowl, combine the first four ingredients; set aside
   1/3 cup. Pour the remaining marinade into a large
   resealable plastic bag; add pork. Seal bag and turn to
   coat; refrigerate for 1 hour. Cover and refrigerate the
   reserved marinade.

2. Drain and discard marinade. In a large skillet or wok,
   stir-fry half of the pork in 1 tablespoon oil for 2-3
   minutes or until tender. Remove the pork with a
   slotted spoon; set aside. Repeat with remaining pork
   and oil.

3. In the same skillet, stir-fry asparagus for 2-3 minutes
   or until crisp-tender. Combine the cornstarch and
   reserved marinade until smooth; stir into skillet. Bring
   mixture to a boil; cook and stir for 2 minutes or until
   thickened. Return the pork to skillet and heat through.
   Serve with rice if desired.

[1994]

PORK AND GREEN CHILI CASSEROLE

yield: 6 servings ∽ **prep: 20 min.
bake: 30 min.**

*I work at a local hospital and also part-time for some area
doctors, so I'm always on the lookout for good, quick recipes to fix
for my family. Some of my co-workers and I exchange recipes.
This zippy casserole is one that was brought to a picnic at my
house. People raved over it.*

—Dianne Esposite, New Middletown, Ohio

1-1/2 pounds boneless pork, cut into 1/2-inch cubes
1 tablespoon canola oil
1 can (15 ounces) black beans, rinsed and drained
1 can (10-3/4 ounces) condensed cream of chicken soup,
  undiluted
1 can (14-1/2 ounces) diced tomatoes, undrained
2 cans (4 ounces *each*) chopped green chilies
1 cup quick-cooking brown rice
1/4 cup water
2 to 3 tablespoons salsa
1 teaspoon ground cumin
1/2 cup shredded cheddar cheese

---

1. In a large skillet, brown pork in oil; drain. Add the
   beans, soup, tomatoes, chilies, rice, water, salsa and
   cumin; cook and stir until bubbly.

2. Pour into an ungreased 2-qt. baking dish. Bake,
   uncovered, at 350° for 30 minutes or until casserole is
   bubbly. Sprinkle with cheese; let stand for 5 minutes
   before serving.

PORK AND GREEN CHILI CASSEROLE INGREDIENT SUBSTITUTIONS

This dish is so versatile that if you don't have the exact
ingredient, it's easy to make substitutions. For the pork,
try chicken or crumbled sausage. For the soup, use
cream of mushroom or celery. For the beans, kidney or
pinto would be great, too. For the cheese, use taco or
Mexican cheese blends.

—Taste of Home Cooking Experts

FAMILY FAVORITE KABOBS

"I halved this and made it for just myself and my husband, and then a couple weeks later, made it when my parents came to visit. It was a hit both times! I love the versatility of the recipe—you can use other meat, and you don't have to use all the ingredients for the skewers if you don't want to. This makes a lot, but the leftovers are great as well!"

—caree929

[2008]

FAMILY FAVORITE KABOBS

yield: 6 servings

prep: 30 min. + marinating ∽ **grill: 10 min.**

These hearty, meat-and-potato skewers have a little something to please everyone, from pineapple to pork. I cook these kabobs even in winter; I just shovel a path to the grill.

—**Dione Steffens, Dimmitt, Texas**

6	small red potatoes, halved
1-1/2	cups canola oil
1/3	cup lemon juice
1/3	cup Worcestershire sauce
1/4	cup white wine vinegar
1/4	cup reduced-sodium soy sauce
3	tablespoons prepared mustard
2	tablespoons minced fresh parsley
3	teaspoons pepper
2	garlic cloves, minced
2	pork tenderloins (1 pound *each*), cut into 1-inch cubes
3	medium ears sweet corn, cut into 1-inch wheels
1	large onion, cut into wedges
1	large green pepper, cut into 1-inch pieces
1	package (11-1/2 ounces) cherry tomatoes
1/2	pound medium fresh mushrooms
1-1/2	cups cubed fresh pineapple

1. Place potatoes in a large saucepan and cover with water. Bring to a boil. Reduce heat; cover and simmer for 15-20 minutes or until tender. Drain and cool slightly; set aside.

2. In a small bowl, combine the oil, lemon juice, Worcestershire sauce, vinegar, soy sauce, mustard, parsley, pepper and garlic. Pour half into a large resealable plastic bag; add the pork. Pour remaining marinade into another large resealable plastic bag, add the vegetables and pineapple. Seal both bags and turn to coat; refrigerate for 2 hours. Drain and discard both marinades.

3. On 12 metal or soaked wooden skewers, alternately thread pork with vegetables and pineapple. Grill, covered, over medium heat for 10-15 minutes or until pork is tender, turning often.

[1998]

MAPLE COUNTRY RIBS

yield: 4 servings ∽ **prep: 25 min.**

bake: 1-1/2 hours

I brought this recipe with me from Quebec after my husband and I were married. The rich maple flavor impressed my in-laws the first time I made dinner for them.

—**Anne-Marie Fortin, Swanton, Vermont**

3	pounds bone-in country-style pork ribs
1	cup maple syrup
1/2	cup applesauce
1/4	cup ketchup
3	tablespoons lemon juice
1/4	teaspoon *each* salt, pepper, paprika, garlic powder and ground cinnamon

1. Place ribs in a Dutch oven. Cover with water; bring to a boil. Reduce heat and simmer for 10 minutes. Drain.

2. Place ribs in a greased 13-in. x 9-in. baking dish. In a small bowl, combine the remaining ingredients; pour half over ribs.

3. Bake, uncovered, at 325° for 1-1/2 hours or until tender, basting often with remaining sauce.

[2010]

BALSAMIC PORK SCALLOPINE

yield: 12 servings ∞ **prep: 25 min.**
cook: 30 min.

I developed this delightful dish by tweaking my veal scallopine recipe. Thinly sliced pork is an economical alternative and a tasty success!

—*Mary Cokenour, Monticello, Utah*

- 3 pounds pork sirloin cutlets
- 1-1/2 cups all-purpose flour
- 1/2 cup olive oil
- 2 tablespoons butter
- 1 medium onion, chopped
- 1/2 cup chopped roasted sweet red peppers
- 6 garlic cloves, minced
- 1 can (14-1/2 ounces) reduced-sodium chicken broth
- 1/2 cup minced fresh basil *or* 2 tablespoons dried basil
- 1/2 cup balsamic vinegar
- 1/2 teaspoon pepper

NOODLES:
- 1 package (16 ounces) egg noodles
- 1/2 cup half-and-half cream
- 1/4 cup grated Romano cheese
- 1/4 cup butter, cubed
- 1/2 teaspoon pepper
- 1/4 teaspoon garlic powder

1. Dredge pork cutlets in flour. Heat oil and butter in a large skillet over medium-high heat; add the pork and brown in batches. Set aside.

2. Add onion and red peppers to the pan; saute until onion is tender. Add garlic; cook 1 minute longer. Add the broth, basil, vinegar and pepper. Return pork to the pan, layering if necessary.

3. Cover and cook over low heat for 15-20 minutes or until meat is tender.

4. Meanwhile, in a Dutch oven, cook noodles according to the package directions. Drain; stir in the cream, cheese, butter, pepper and garlic powder. Serve with pork.

[2006]

CREAMY CABBAGE-PORK STEW

yield: 6 servings ∞ **prep: 20 min.**
cook: 5 hours

Savory flavors blend beautifully in this hearty dish. In a pinch, I use a ring of garlic bologna cut into chunks in place of the pork shoulder and make it on the stovetop until the vegetables are tender.

—*Ruth Ann Stelfox*
Raymond, Alberta, Field Editor

- 1 boneless pork shoulder butt roast (1 pound), cut into 3/4-inch cubes
- 1 tablespoon canola oil
- 2 cans (10-3/4 ounces *each*) condensed cream of celery soup, undiluted
- 1-1/2 cups apple juice
- 2 medium red potatoes, cut into 1-inch chunks
- 3 medium carrots, sliced
- 1/4 teaspoon caraway seeds
- 1/4 teaspoon pepper
- 3 cups coarsely chopped cabbage
- 1/2 cup 2% milk

1. In a large skillet over medium-high heat, brown the pork cubes in oil on all sides; drain.

2. Transfer to a 3-qt. slow cooker; stir in the soup, apple juice, potatoes, carrots, caraway and pepper. Cover and cook on high for 3-4 hours.

3. Add the cabbage and milk. Cover and cook 2 hours longer or until meat and vegetables are tender.

BALSAMIC PORK SCALLOPINE

"I have two recipes with pork and balsamic glaze. I made this one first because I had all the ingredients in my pantry. After making this, I threw the other recipe away. This is amazing!! I used penne pasta instead of noodles due to personal preference; other than that, I made it exactly to the recipe. It was a huge hit and will definitely become part of our menu!! Can't wait to serve it to my married children!"
— *punkinlips*

[2010]

ITALIAN PORK STEW

yield: 8 servings (2 quarts) ∞ **prep: 30 min.**
cook: 1-1/2 hours

(Pictured on page 636)

Don't skip the anchovy paste! It gives a good, salty flavor but doesn't taste fishy at all. Add a salad and crusty bread for an incredible meal.

—*Lynne German*
Cumming, Georgia, Field Editor

2/3 cup all-purpose flour
2 pounds boneless pork loin, cut into 1-inch pieces
4 tablespoons olive oil, *divided*
1 large onion, chopped
5 garlic cloves, crushed
1 can (28 ounces) diced tomatoes, undrained
1 cup dry red wine *or* beef broth
3 bay leaves
1 cinnamon stick (3 inches)
1 tablespoon tomato paste
1 tablespoon red wine vinegar
1 teaspoon anchovy paste
1 teaspoon *each* dried oregano, basil and sage leaves
1/2 teaspoon salt
1/2 teaspoon crushed red pepper flakes
1/4 teaspoon pepper
1/4 cup minced fresh parsley
Hot cooked bow tie pasta
Grated Parmesan cheese

---

1. Place flour in a large resealable plastic bag. Add the pork, a few pieces at a time, and shake to coat. In a Dutch oven, brown the pork in 3 tablespoons oil in batches. Remove and keep warm.

2. In the same pan, saute the onion in remaining oil until crisp-tender. Add garlic; cook 1 minute longer. Stir in the tomatoes, wine, bay leaves, cinnamon, tomato paste, vinegar, anchovy paste, herbs, salt, pepper flakes, pepper and pork; bring to a boil.

3. Reduce heat; cover and simmer for 1-1/2 hours, stirring occasionally. Stir in parsley. Cover and cook 30-60 minutes longer or until meat is tender. Skim fat; discard bay leaves and cinnamon.

4. Serve with pasta; sprinkle with cheese.

[2003]

BEST BABY-BACK RIBS

yield: 4 servings ∞ **prep: 10 min.**
bake: 1-1/2 hours

(Pictured on page 635)

My dad encouraged me when I was young to pursue my interest in cooking. As I got older, I experimented more, and there were many successes, including these ribs.

—*Rick Consoli, Orion, Michigan*

---

4 pounds pork baby back ribs
1 teaspoon garlic powder
1 teaspoon seasoned salt
1 teaspoon pepper
1 medium onion, sliced
1 cup ketchup
1 cup chili sauce
1/4 cup packed brown sugar
1 tablespoon dried minced onion
1 tablespoon Liquid Smoke, optional
1 tablespoon molasses

---

1. Place ribs bone side down in a large roasting pan. Combine garlic powder, seasoned salt and pepper; sprinkle over ribs. Top with sliced onion. Cover tightly and bake at 350° for 1 hour.

2. In a large bowl, combine the remaining ingredients. Drain fat from the pan; discard sliced onion. Brush ribs with half of barbecue sauce.

3. Cover and bake 30-60 minutes longer or until ribs are tender. Serve with remaining sauce.

ITALIAN PORK STEW

"I have made it several times as written with pork and love it. It is equally good with venison."
—*avidcookGA*

[1995]

SWEET-AND-SOUR PORK

yield: 4 servings ❧ **prep/total time: 25 min.**

After my sister moved away to the university, I used to visit her on weekends. She often made this wonderful and tangy pork dish. Now, every time I make it for my family, it reminds me of those special visits.

—*Cherry Williams, St. Albert, Alberta*

1   can (14 ounces) pineapple tidbits
2   tablespoons cornstarch
2   tablespoons brown sugar
3/4   teaspoon salt
1/4   teaspoon ground ginger
1/4   teaspoon pepper
1/3   cup water
1/3   cup ketchup
2   tablespoons white vinegar
2   tablespoons reduced-sodium soy sauce
1   pound pork tenderloin, cut into 1-1/2-inch x 1/4-inch strips
1   medium onion, chopped
2   tablespoons canola oil
1   green pepper, cut into thin strips
Hot cooked rice

1. Drain pineapple, reserving juice; set aside. In a small bowl, combine the cornstarch, brown sugar, salt, ginger and pepper. Stir in the water, ketchup, vinegar, soy sauce and reserved juice until smooth.

2. In a large skillet or wok, stir-fry pork and onion in oil for 4-8 minutes or until tender. Stir the pineapple juice mixture; add to the skillet. Bring to a boil; cook and stir for 1-2 minutes or until thickened.

3. Add green pepper and reserved pineapple. Reduce heat; cover and cook for 5 minutes. Serve with rice.

[2008]

SCALLOPED POTATOES 'N' HAM

yield: 6 servings ❧ **prep: 25 min.**
bake: 1 hour

(Pictured on page 636)

I'm a home health nurse and got this recipe from one of my elderly clients, who had used it for years. Now, it's one of my family's favorites. It will never curdle, thanks to the secret ingredient of powdered nondairy creamer.

—*Kathy Johnson, Lake City, South Dakota*

3/4   cup powdered nondairy creamer
1-3/4   cups water
3   tablespoons butter
3   tablespoons all-purpose flour
2   tablespoons dried minced onion
1   teaspoon salt
3/4   teaspoon paprika
6   large potatoes, peeled and thinly sliced
2   cups diced fully cooked ham
1   cup (4 ounces) shredded cheddar cheese

1. In a small bowl, combine the creamer and water until smooth. In a small saucepan, melt butter. Stir in the flour, onion, salt and paprika until smooth; gradually add creamer mixture. Bring to a boil; cook and stir for 1-2 minutes or until thickened.

2. In a greased shallow 2-1/2-qt. baking dish, combine potatoes and ham. Pour sauce over the top.

3. Cover and bake at 350° for 15 minutes. Uncover; bake 40-50 minutes longer or until potatoes are tender. Sprinkle with cheese; bake for 5-10 minutes or until edges are bubbly and the cheese is melted.

SCALLOPED POTATOES 'N' HAM

❝This is the BEST scalloped potato recipe I have found. My family loves it. I now make for the holidays. Fast and easy!❞
—*debdeb1*

[1994]

HAM-STUFFED MANICOTTI

yield: 8 servings ✎ prep: 20 min.
bake: 30 min.

Here's a fun and different use for ham. Combined with the manicotti, it's unexpected yet delicious. The creamy cheese sauce makes this casserole perfect for chilly days. I'm always asked for the recipe whenever I serve it.

—*Dorothy Anderson, Ottawa, Kansas*

8	manicotti shells
1/2	cup chopped onion
1	tablespoon canola oil
3	cups (1 pound) ground fully cooked ham
1	can (4 ounces) sliced mushrooms, drained
1	cup (4 ounces) shredded Swiss cheese, *divided*
3	tablespoons grated Parmesan cheese
1/4	to 1/2 cup chopped green pepper
3	tablespoons butter
3	tablespoons all-purpose flour
2	cups 2% milk

Paprika
Chopped fresh parsley

---

1. Cook manicotti according to package directions; set aside. In a large skillet, saute onion in oil until tender. Remove from the heat. Add ham, mushrooms, half of Swiss and Parmesan cheeses; set aside.

2. In a small saucepan, saute the green pepper in butter until tender. Stir in the flour until combined. Add milk; cook and stir for 2 minutes or until thickened. Stir a quarter of the sauce into ham mixture.

3. Stuff each shell with about 1/3 cup of filling. Place in a greased 11-in. x 7-in. baking dish. Top with remaining sauce; sprinkle with paprika.

4. Cover and bake at 350° for 30 minutes or until heated through. Sprinkle with the parsley and remaining Swiss cheese before serving.

Editor's Note: Recipe can easily be doubled for a larger group.

[2006]

CREAMY HAM 'N' MACARONI

yield: 6 servings ✎ prep: 20 min.
bake: 20 min.

The original comfort food, macaroni and cheese gets a makeover with the addition of cubed ham and grated Parmesan. Kids will love it!

—*Christy Looper*
Colorado Springs, Colorado

2	cups uncooked elbow macaroni
1/4	cup butter, cubed
1/4	cup all-purpose flour
2	cups 2% milk
4	teaspoons chicken bouillon granules
1/4	teaspoon pepper
2	cups (8 ounces) shredded cheddar cheese, *divided*
1-1/2	cups cubed fully cooked ham
1/4	cup grated Parmesan cheese

---

1. Cook macaroni according to package directions; drain and set aside. In a large saucepan, melt butter over low heat; whisk in the flour until smooth. Whisk in the milk, bouillon and pepper. Bring to a boil; cook and stir for 2 minutes or until thickened. Remove from the heat. Stir in 1 cup cheddar cheese, ham, Parmesan cheese and macaroni.

2. Transfer to a greased 2-qt. baking dish. Sprinkle with remaining cheddar cheese. Bake, uncovered, at 350° for 20-25 minutes or until bubbly. Let stand for 5 minutes before serving.

HAM-STUFFED MANICOTTI

❝Wonderful change from the heavy cheese or spinach recipes out there. I used more fresh mushrooms than the recipe called for. I also used fontina cheese instead of the Swiss; it was what I had on hand. Will definitely make this again and try it with the Swiss cheese.❞

—*mom23kids*

[1997]

HAM AND VEGETABLE LINGUINE

yield: 4 servings ∞ **prep/total time: 20 min.**

I've been pleasing dinner guests with this delectable pasta dish, which was based on one in a favorite Italian cookbook. The delicate cream sauce blends well with the colorful and hearty mix of vegetables. I chop the vegetables ahead and later prepare this dish in a snap.

—*Kerry Kerr McAvoy, Rockford, Michigan*

- 1 package (8 ounces) linguine
- 1/2 pound fresh asparagus, trimmed and cut into 1-inch pieces
- 1/2 pound fresh mushrooms, sliced
- 1 medium carrot, thinly sliced
- 1 medium zucchini, diced
- 2 cups julienned fully cooked ham
- 1/4 cup butter
- 1 cup heavy whipping cream
- 1/2 cup frozen peas
- 3 green onions, sliced
- 1/4 cup grated Parmesan cheese
- 1 teaspoon dried basil
- 3/4 teaspoon salt
- Dash ground nutmeg
- Dash pepper
- Additional Parmesan cheese, optional

1. Cook linguine according to package directions. Meanwhile, in a large skillet, saute the asparagus, mushrooms, carrot, zucchini and ham in butter until the vegetables are tender.

2. Add the cream, peas, onions, Parmesan cheese, basil, salt, nutmeg and pepper; bring to a boil. Reduce heat; simmer for 3 minutes or until heated through, stirring frequently.

3. Rinse and drain the linguine; add to the vegetable mixture and toss to coat. Sprinkle with Parmesan if desired.

[2009]

HAM & SWEET POTATO KABOBS

yield: 8 kabobs

prep: 25 min. + marinating ∞ **grill: 15 min.**

I serve these kabobs with a green salad for an easy, thrifty meal. The buttery, brown sugar marinade highlights everything on the skewer.

—*Sandra Hill, Wilson, New York*

- 1 large sweet potato, peeled and cubed
- 1 can (20 ounces) unsweetened pineapple chunks
- 1/4 cup butter, melted
- 4 teaspoons brown sugar
- 1 pound fully cooked boneless ham, cut into 1-inch cubes
- 2 yellow summer squash, cut into 3/4-inch slices
- 2 large apples, cubed

1. Place sweet potato in a small saucepan; cover with water. Bring to a boil. Reduce heat; cover and cook for 10-15 minutes or until almost tender. Drain; set aside.

2. Drain pineapple, reserving juice; set the pineapple aside. In a small bowl, combine the butter, brown sugar and reserved juice. Place the ham, squash, apples, sweet potato and pineapple in a large resealable plastic bag; add the juice mixture. Seal the bag and turn to coat; refrigerate for 1 hour.

3. Drain and discard marinade. On eight metal or soaked wooden skewers, alternately thread ham, sweet potato, squash, apples and pineapple. Grill, covered, over medium heat for 15-20 minutes or until the apples are tender, turning occasionally.

HAM AND VEGETABLE LINGUINE

"I bake hams often, so I'm always on the lookout for recipes in which I can use the leftovers. This recipe is excellent! Thanks, Kerry!"
—*cwbuff*

[2007]

HAM-POTATO PHYLLO BAKE

yield: 12-15 servings   prep: 30 min.
bake: 20 min.

(Pictured on page 640)

I'm often asked to bring this savory dish to potlucks. The phyllo is crisp and golden brown, and the dill tastes so good with the rich filling.

—Tracy Hartsuff, Charlotte, Michigan

- 3 pounds red potatoes, peeled and thinly sliced
- 1 medium onion, chopped
- 8 tablespoons butter, *divided*
- 20 sheets phyllo dough (14 inches x 9 inches)
- 2 cups (16 ounces) sour cream
- 2 cups cubed fully cooked ham
- 2 cups (8 ounces) shredded cheddar cheese
- 7 teaspoons dill weed, *divided*
- 2 teaspoons garlic powder
- 1 teaspoon salt
- 1/2 teaspoon pepper
- 1 egg, lightly beaten
- 2 tablespoons half-and-half cream

---

1. Place the potatoes in a Dutch oven and cover with water. Bring to a boil; reduce heat. Cover and cook for 10-15 minutes or until tender; drain. In a small skillet, saute the onion in 1 tablespoon butter until tender; set aside.

2. Melt remaining butter. Brush a 13-in. x 9-in. baking dish with some of the butter. Unroll phyllo sheets; trim to fit into dish. (Keep dough covered with plastic wrap and a damp cloth while assembling.) Place one phyllo sheet in the prepared dish; brush with butter. Repeat twice.

3. Top with half of sour cream, potatoes, onion, ham and cheese. Combine 6 teaspoons dill, garlic powder, salt and pepper; sprinkle half over the cheese. Layer with three more phyllo sheets,

brushing each with butter. Top with remaining sour cream, potatoes, onion, ham, cheese and seasoning mixture.

4. Layer with remaining phyllo dough, brushing each sheet with the butter. Combine egg and cream; brush over top. Sprinkle with remaining dill.

5. Bake, uncovered, at 350° for 20-25 minutes or until heated through. Let stand for 5 minutes. Cut into squares.

[1999]

HURRY-UP HAM 'N' NOODLES

yield: 4 servings   prep/total time: 25 min.

I created this rich-tasting entree. It is ready to serve in almost the time it takes to cook the noodles. I've made it for luncheons and potlucks, but mostly I make it on days when I'm in a hurry to get something on the table.

—Lucille Howell, Portland, Oregon

- 5 to 6 cups uncooked wide egg noodles
- 1/4 cup butter, cubed
- 1 cup heavy whipping cream
- 1-1/2 cups julienned fully cooked ham
- 1/2 cup grated Parmesan cheese
- 1/4 cup thinly sliced green onions
- 1/4 teaspoon salt
- 1/8 teaspoon pepper

---

1. Cook the noodles according to the package directions. Meanwhile, in a large skillet, melt butter over medium heat. Gradually whisk in the cream. Bring to a boil, stirring constantly; cook and stir for 2 minutes longer or until thickened.

2. Add the ham, cheese, onions, salt and pepper; cook, uncovered, until heated through. Drain noodles; add to ham mixture. Toss to coat; heat through.

HURRY-UP HAM 'N' NOODLES

"I have made this dish several times, and it always is wonderful. It's very easy and quick to prepare, and the green onion gives it great flavor. Try adding a small can of mushrooms. This is a family favorite."
—bherek

[1993]

SUGAR-GLAZED HAM

yield: 10-14 servings   prep: 5 min.
bake: 1-3/4 hours

This old-fashioned sugar glaze gives your ham a pretty, golden-brown coating just like Grandma used to make. The mustard and vinegar complement the brown sugar and add tangy flavor. Be prepared to serve seconds!

—*Carol Strong Battle*
Heathsville, Virginia, Field Editor

- 1 **fully cooked bone-in ham (5 to 7 pounds)**
- 1 **cup packed brown sugar**
- 2 **teaspoons prepared mustard**
- 1 **to 2 tablespoons cider vinegar**

1. Score ham about 1/2-in. deep with a sharp knife. Place ham on a rack in a shallow baking pan. Bake at 325° for 1-3/4 to 2-1/4 hours or until a thermometer reads 140°.

2. In a small bowl, combine the brown sugar, mustard and enough vinegar to make a thick paste. During the last hour of baking, brush glaze on ham every 15 minutes.

[1995]

APRICOT BAKED HAM

yield: 10-14 servings   prep: 10 min.
bake: 1-3/4 hours

Ham is a wonderful choice for a holiday meal. Once it's in the oven, it practically takes care of itself until dinnertime. I serve it because everyone in my family loves it! The sugary crust makes the ham beautiful to serve.

—*Marge Clark, West Lebanon, Indiana*

- 1 **fully cooked bone-in ham (5 to 7 pounds)**
- 20 **whole cloves**
- 1/2 **cup apricot preserves**
- 3 **tablespoons ground mustard**
- 1/2 **cup packed light brown sugar**

1. Place the ham on a rack in a shallow roasting pan. Score the surface of the ham, making diamond shapes 1/2 in. deep; insert a clove in each diamond. Combine the preserves and mustard; spread over ham. Pat brown sugar into apricot mixture.

2. Bake at 325° for 1-3/4 to 2-1/4 hours or until a thermometer reads 140°.

SUGAR-GLAZED HAM

"I took this to a church Easter Sunday dinner and everyone was coming back for more. It was tender and sooooooo good! Definitely a keeper."
—*mamamartha*

BONE-IN HAM

1. Place ham fat side up on a carving board. Using a meat fork to anchor the ham, make a horizontal cut with a carving knife from the one side of the ham to the bone. Position the cut in about the middle of the ham along the natural break between the muscles. Make a second cut from the top of the ham to the first cut. Remove the large meaty area of the ham from the bone. Remove the two remaining large meaty sections in the same manner. The meat left on the ham bone may be used for soup or picked off and used in salads or casseroles.

2. Place the meaty piece of meat cut side down on a cutting board. Cut into slices.

[2011]

FONTINA HAM STROMBOLI

**yield: 2 loaves (8 servings each)
prep: 40 min.   bake: 30 min.**

Pesto seasons these savory meat- and cheese-stuffed slices that my gang loves. The loaves can be frozen baked or unbaked.

—*Nancy Piano*
Nevada City, California
Former Field Editor

---

1 large onion, chopped
1 tablespoon olive oil
1 garlic clove, minced
2 loaves (1 pound *each*) frozen bread dough, thawed
1/2 cup prepared pesto, *divided*
2 teaspoons dried basil
1/2 pound sliced deli ham
1/2 pound thinly sliced prosciutto *or* additional deli ham
1/2 pound sliced fontina cheese
1/4 cup grated Parmesan cheese

---

1. In a large skillet, saute the onion in oil until tender. Add garlic; cook 1 minute longer. Cool completely.

2. On two greased baking sheets, roll each loaf into a 16-in. x 10-in rectangle. Spread each with 2 tablespoons pesto; sprinkle with onion mixture and basil. Arrange ham, prosciutto and fontina cheese over each rectangle to within 1/2 in. of edges.

3. Roll up jelly-roll style, starting with a long side; pinch seams to seal and tuck ends under.

4. Brush with the remaining pesto and sprinkle with Parmesan cheese. Bake at 350° for 30-35 minutes or until the loaves are golden brown. Cool for 5 minutes before slicing.

FONTINA HAM STROMBOLI

"This recipe was awesome! Perfect cold day lunch, with a nice bowl of soup. And it is so easily adapted to your preference. I made it once with all the ingredients suggested, once with salami and American cheese and then with meatballs and Parmesan cheese. All were top-notch!"
—*aug2295*

[1995]

HAM LOAVES

**yield: 12 servings   prep: 10 min.
bake: 1-1/4 hours**

If your family enjoys meat loaf, they will like this, too. The brown sugar mixture makes it so tasty.

—*Carol Van Sickle, Versailles, Kentucky*

---

4 cups dry bread crumbs
4 eggs, lightly beaten
1 cup 2% milk
2 pounds ground pork
2 pounds ground fully cooked ham
1-1/2 cups packed brown sugar
3/4 cup water
1/2 cup white vinegar
1 teaspoon ground mustard

---

1. In a large bowl, combine the bread crumbs, eggs and milk. Crumble pork and ham over mixture and mix well. Shape into 12 ovals, using 1 cup of mixture for each.

2. Place in an ungreased 15-in. x 10-in. x 1-in. baking pan. Combine the brown sugar, water, vinegar and mustard; pour over loaves.

3. Bake, uncovered, at 350° for 1 hour 15 minutes or until a thermometer reads 160°, basting every 15-20 minutes. Place the loaves on a serving platter; drizzle with pan juices.

LEFTOVER HAM

Leftover ham can be easily made into ham salad for sandwiches. Mix ham with mayonnaise, mustard and add-ins such as pickle relish, chopped olives, celery, onion, shredded cheese or peppers.

—*Taste of Home Cooking Experts*

GRILLED HAM STEAK

[1993]

yield: 6 servings ∞ prep/total time: 30 min.

Here's a quick and impressive ham dish to prepare. It tastes great with the smoky grill flavor and tangy sauce.

—*Sharon Mensing*
Greenfield, Iowa, Field Editor

- 1/4 cup apricot *or* plum preserves
- 1 tablespoon prepared mustard
- 1 teaspoon lemon juice
- 1/8 teaspoon ground cinnamon
- 1 ham steak (about 2 pound and 1-inch thick)

1. In a small saucepan, combine the preserves, mustard, lemon juice and cinnamon. Cook and stir over low heat for 2-3 minutes. Set glaze aside. Score edges of ham.

2. Grill, uncovered, over medium heat for 8-10 minutes on each side, brushing with glaze during the last few minutes of grilling.

HAM WITH PINEAPPLE SALSA

[2006]

yield: 4 servings ∞ prep/total time: 25 min.

(*Pictured on page 640*)

A dear friend shared this recipe when she moved from Hawaii to Colorado. Now it's one of my favorite ways to serve ham.

—*Dawn Wilson, Buena Vista, Colorado*

- 1 can (8 ounces) crushed pineapple, drained
- 2 tablespoons orange marmalade
- 1 tablespoon minced fresh cilantro
- 2 teaspoons lime juice
- 2 teaspoons chopped jalapeno pepper
- 1/4 teaspoon salt
- 1 bone-in fully cooked ham steak (1-1/2 pounds)

1. For salsa, in a small bowl, combine the first six ingredients; set aside.

2. Place the ham steak on an ungreased rack in a broiler pan. Broil 4-6 in. from the heat for 4-5 minutes on each side or until a thermometer reads 140°. Cut into serving-size pieces; serve with salsa.

Editor's Note: Wear disposable gloves when cutting hot peppers; the oils can burn skin. Avoid touching your face.

ITALIAN SAUSAGE AND PEPPERS

[2003]

yield: 12 servings ∞ prep: 15 min.
cook: 30 min.

My sister was hosting a birthday party and asked me to bring sausage and peppers. I'd never made them before, so I altered a braised pepper recipe. Now family members request this dish often.

—*Jeanne Corsi, Arnold, Pennsylvania*

- 3 pounds Italian sausage links, cut into 3/4-inch slices
- 4 medium green peppers, cut into thin strips
- 1 medium onion, thinly sliced and quartered
- 1 tablespoon butter
- 1 tablespoon olive oil
- 3 tablespoons chicken broth
- 6 plum tomatoes, coarsely chopped
- 1 tablespoon minced fresh parsley
- 1/2 teaspoon salt
- 1/4 teaspoon pepper
- 1/2 teaspoon lemon juice

1. In a Dutch oven, cook the sausage over medium heat until no longer pink; drain. Add the remaining ingredients.

2. Cover and cook for 30 minutes or until vegetables are tender; stir occasionally. Serve with a slotted spoon.

GRILLED HAM STEAK

"EXCELLENT!!! Our new favorite way to make ham. It's also excellent with pineapple preserves and grilled pineapple slices on the side."
—*ashulman*

[2009]

PENNE & SAUSAGE CASSEROLES

yield: 2 casseroles (8 servings each) ∞ **prep: 50 min.** ∞ **bake: 30 min.**

This hearty casserole has been a consistent hit with my family and friends. It feeds a lot of people and comes together relatively quickly, making it ideal for bring-a-dish events.

—*John Venturino, Concord, California*

1-1/2 pounds uncooked penne pasta
   1 pound bulk Italian sausage
   1 pound sliced fresh mushrooms
   1 large onion, chopped
   3 tablespoons olive oil
   6 garlic cloves, minced
   1 tablespoon dried oregano
1-1/2 cups dry red wine *or* beef broth, *divided*
   2 cans (14-1/2 ounces *each*) stewed tomatoes, cut up
   1 can (15 ounces) tomato sauce
   1 cup beef broth
   4 cups (16 ounces) shredded part-skim mozzarella cheese
   4 cups (16 ounces) shredded fontina cheese
Minced fresh parsley, optional

---

1. Cook pasta according to package directions. Meanwhile, in a Dutch oven, cook sausage over medium heat until no longer pink; drain and set aside.

2. In the same Dutch oven, saute mushrooms and onion in oil until tender. Add garlic and oregano; cook 1 minute longer. Stir in 1 cup wine. Bring to a boil; cook until liquid is reduced by half. Stir in the tomatoes, tomato sauce, broth, sausage and remaining wine. Bring to a boil. Reduce heat; cover and simmer for 15 minutes.

3. Drain pasta. Spread 1/2 cup sauce in each of two greased 13-in. x 9-in. baking dishes. Divide half of the pasta between the dishes; layer each with 2-1/2 cups sauce and 1 cup each of the cheeses. Repeat layers.

4. Cover and bake at 350° for 25 minutes. Uncover; bake 5-10 minutes longer or until bubbly and cheese is melted. Sprinkle with parsley if desired.

PENNE & SAUSAGE CASSEROLES

"This is an excellent casserole. I did increase the meat in it as my family is big on meat. The kitchen smells like a top-of-the-line Italian restaurant while it's cooking, and the taste delivers that promise."
—dglong

SAUSAGE LINK SUBSTITUTION

Italian sausage links can be used in place of the bulk sausage. One link is about 4 ounces. So, use 4 to 5 for a pound of sausage. Using a sharp knife, slit the casing lengthwise and remove it from the link. Crumble the sausage into the skillet to cook. You can also place the sausage in the skillet and mash with a potato masher or wooden spoon to break up.

—*Taste of Home Cooking Experts*

[2006]

APPLE SAUSAGE-STUFFED SQUASH

yield: 2 servings ⮚ **prep: 30 min.**
bake: 20 min.

Acorn squash serves as a fitting bowl for the flavorful apple, pork and cheese stuffing. It makes a great autumn dish.

—Carol Mays, Oregon, Wisconsin

1	medium acorn squash
6	ounces bulk pork sausage
1/2	cup chopped celery, optional
2	tablespoons chopped onion
1/2	cup chopped peeled tart apple
1	teaspoon all-purpose flour
1	egg, lightly beaten
1/4	cup sour cream
1/8	teaspoon salt
1/3	cup diced process cheese (Velveeta)

---

1. Cut squash in half; remove seeds. Place cut side down in a greased 13-in. x 9-in. baking dish. Cover and bake at 350° for 25-30 minutes or until tender.

2. Meanwhile, in a small skillet, cook the sausage, celery if desired and onion over medium heat, until meat is no longer pink. Add apple; cook and stir for 3 minutes. Drain.

3. In a small bowl, combine the flour, egg and sour cream until smooth; stir into sausage mixture.

4. Turn squash over; sprinkle cut sides with salt. Stuff with sausage mixture. Bake, uncovered, for 15-20 minutes or until a thermometer inserted in the stuffing reads 160°. Sprinkle with the cheese; bake 5 minutes longer or until cheese is melted.

[1998]

CORN DOG CASSEROLE

yield: 12 servings ⮚ **prep: 25 min.**
bake: 30 min.

(Pictured on page 636)

Reminiscent of traditional corn dogs, this fun main dish really hits the spot on fall days. It's perfect for the football parties my husband and I often host. It tastes especially good right from the oven.

—Marcy Suzanne Olipane
Belleville, Illinois

2	cups thinly sliced celery
2	tablespoons butter
1-1/2	cups sliced green onions
1-1/2	pounds hot dogs
2	eggs
1-1/2	cups 2% milk
2	teaspoons rubbed sage
1/4	teaspoon pepper
2	packages (8-1/2 ounces *each*) corn bread/muffin mix
2	cups (8 ounces) shredded sharp cheddar cheese, *divided*

---

1. In a small skillet, saute celery in butter for 5 minutes. Add onions; saute for 5 minutes longer or until vegetables are tender. Place in a large bowl and set aside.

2. Cut hot dogs lengthwise into quarters, then cut into thirds. In same skillet, saute hot dogs for 5 minutes or until lightly browned; add to vegetables. Set aside 1 cup.

3. In a large bowl, whisk the eggs, milk, sage and pepper. Add remaining hot dog mixture. Stir in the corn bread mixes. Add 1-1/2 cups of cheese. Spread into a shallow 3-qt. baking dish. Top with the reserved hot dog mixture and remaining cheese.

4. Bake, uncovered, at 400° for 30 minutes or until golden brown.

CORN DOG CASSEROLE

"This is seriously yummy. My kids could eat either this or meat loaf for dinner every night."
—Red Molly

KIELBASA CABBAGE SKILLET

I have made this a couple of times and we love it. I use diced tomatoes instead of the tomato sauce, and my husband likes caraway seeds added to it.

—kmacquard

[2007]

CREAMY PEPPERONI ZITI

yield: 9 servings ∞ prep: 15 min.
bake: 25 min.

You can easily feed a crowd with this simple dish that's ready in about 40 minutes. Its comforting sauce will become a fast favorite at your next potluck or weeknight dinner.

—*Charlane Gathy, Lexington, Kentucky*

- 1 package (16 ounces) ziti *or* small tube pasta
- 1 can (10-3/4 ounces) condensed cream of mushroom soup, undiluted
- 3/4 cup shredded part-skim mozzarella cheese
- 3/4 cup chopped pepperoni
- 1/2 cup *each* chopped onion, mushrooms, green pepper and tomato
- 1/2 cup half-and-half cream
- 1/4 cup chicken broth
- 1/4 teaspoon salt
- 1/4 teaspoon garlic powder
- 1/4 teaspoon pepper
- 1/2 cup grated Parmesan cheese

1. Cook the pasta according to package directions; drain. In a large bowl, combine the pasta, soup, mozzarella cheese, pepperoni, onion, mushrooms, green pepper, tomato, cream, broth and seasonings.

2. Transfer to a greased 13-in. x 9-in. baking dish. Sprinkle with Parmesan cheese. Cover and bake at 350° for 20 minutes. Uncover; bake 5-10 minutes longer or until bubbly.

[2005]

KIELBASA CABBAGE SKILLET

yield: 8-10 servings ∞ prep: 10 min.
cook: 1-1/4 hours

(Pictured on page 636)

Spicy kielbasa sausage and plentiful cabbage and potatoes give this dish a pleasing Old-World flair. My husband never liked cabbage before I made this, but now he does!

—*Romaine Wetzel*
Ronks, Pennsylvania, Field Editor

- 1 pound smoked kielbasa *or* Polish sausage, cut into 1/2-inch slices
- 4 tablespoons butter, *divided*
- 1 large head cabbage (4 pounds), coarsely chopped
- 2 medium onions, chopped
- 3 cans (8 ounces *each*) tomato sauce
- 1/2 cup sugar
- 1 tablespoon paprika
- 3 to 4 large potatoes, peeled and cubed

1. In a Dutch oven, brown the sausage in 2 tablespoons butter; remove and set aside. In the same pan, saute cabbage and onions in remaining butter until onions are tender.

2. In a small bowl, combine the tomato sauce, sugar and paprika; pour over cabbage mixture. Bring to a boil. Reduce heat; cover and simmer for 20 minutes. Add the potatoes and reserved sausage. Cover and simmer for 30 minutes or until the potatoes are tender.

ABOUT POLISH SAUSAGE

Smoked Polish sausage is available in most supermarkets. Fresh Polish sausage can be found in some specialty markets and must be fully cooked before eating. Polish sausage can be made with pork or beef, and for those watching their weight, with turkey.

—*Taste of Home Cooking Experts*

[2001]

FARMERS MARKET SAUSAGE PIE

yield: 8 servings ❧ **prep: 15 min. + cooling
bake: 35 min. + standing**

*Our son named this savory pie for the
Saturday morning farmers market that's held
near our state capitol building. Most of the
fresh ingredients called for in the recipe can be
found there and baked into this deliciously
different entree.*

—Teri Schuman, Oregon, Wisconsin

4	Italian sausage links, casings removed, halved and cut into 1/2-inch pieces
1	medium tomato, cut into chunks
1	small yellow tomato, cut into chunks
1	cup thinly sliced zucchini
1	cup thinly sliced yellow summer squash
1/2	cup julienned green pepper
1/2	cup julienned sweet red pepper
1	tablespoon Italian salad dressing mix
1/2	teaspoon garlic powder
1/4	to 1/2 teaspoon fennel seed, crushed

Pastry for double-crust pie (9 inches)

1	cup (4 ounces) shredded cheddar cheese
1	cup (4 ounces) shredded mozzarella cheese

1. In a large skillet, cook sausage over medium heat until no longer pink; drain. Stir in the tomatoes, zucchini, yellow squash, peppers, salad dressing mix, garlic powder and fennel seed. Cook and stir for 10 minutes; drain. Cool for 10 minutes.

2. Line a 9-in. pie plate with the bottom pastry; trim pastry even with edge. Fill with sausage mixture. Sprinkle with cheeses. Roll out remaining pastry to fit top of pie; place over filling. Trim, seal and flute edges. Cut slits in top.

3. Bake at 375° for 35-40 minutes or until the filling is bubbly and crust is golden brown. Let pie stand for 10 minutes before cutting.

[2009]

SPEEDY JAMBALAYA

yield: 8 servings ❧ **prep/total time: 30 min.**

(Pictured on page 634)

*Spicy sausage and colorful sweet peppers make
this classic Cajun dish look as appetizing as it
tastes. It's impossible to say no to seconds!*

—Nicole Filizetti, Jacksonville, Florida

1-1/3	cups uncooked long grain rice
1	large onion, halved and sliced
1	medium green pepper, sliced
1	medium sweet red pepper, sliced
2	teaspoons olive oil
3	garlic cloves, minced
1	can (28 ounces) diced tomatoes, undrained
3	bay leaves
1	teaspoon salt
1	teaspoon paprika
1/2	teaspoon dried thyme
1/2	teaspoon pepper
1/4	teaspoon hot pepper sauce
2	cans (15-1/2 ounces *each*) black-eyed peas, rinsed and drained
3/4	pound fully cooked andouille *or* Italian sausage links, sliced
1/4	cup minced fresh parsley

1. Cook the rice according to package directions. Meanwhile, in a large skillet, saute the onion and peppers in oil for 4 minutes. Add garlic; cook 1 minute longer. Stir in the tomatoes, bay leaves, salt, paprika, thyme, pepper and pepper sauce. Bring to a boil.

2. Reduce heat; simmer, uncovered, for 5 minutes. Stir in the peas and sausage; heat through. Discard bay leaves. Serve with rice. Sprinkle with parsley.

SPEEDY JAMBALAYA

❝I made this today and am going to be sure to make it many more times. I did half the recipe as there are only three of us. I used one can of black-eyed peas and a 15-oz. can of tomatoes along with half the other amounts, and it was very tasty.❞
— *cafritz*

[2007]

THREE-CHEESE SAUSAGE LASAGNA

yield: 12 servings ∞ prep: 30 min.
bake: 30 min. + standing

(Pictured on page 638)

Here's a nice alternative to traditional lasagna, and it's so easy to prepare! It has a simple white sauce and lots of savory Italian sausage.

—*Lesley Cormier, Pepperell, Massachusetts*

1-1/2	pounds bulk Italian sausage
6	tablespoons butter
6	tablespoons all-purpose flour
1	teaspoon salt
1	teaspoon pepper
3	cups 2% milk
9	lasagna noodles, cooked and drained
6	slices part-skim mozzarella cheese, cut in half
6	slices provolone cheese, cut in half
1/3	cup grated Romano cheese

1. In a large skillet, cook sausage over medium heat until no longer pink; drain and set aside.

2. In a small saucepan, melt butter. Stir in the flour, salt and pepper until smooth; gradually stir in milk. Bring to a boil over medium heat; cook and stir for 2 minutes or until thickened. Remove from the heat.

3. In a greased 13-in. x 9-in. baking dish, layer a fourth of the white sauce, three noodles, half of the sausage and four pieces each of mozzarella and provolone cheeses. Repeat layers once. Spoon half of the remaining sauce over the top. Layer with remaining noodles, sauce, mozzarella and provolone cheeses; sprinkle with Romano cheese.

4. Bake, uncovered, at 350° for 30-35 minutes or until heated through. Let stand for 15 minutes before cutting.

[2006]

MEATY MANICOTTI

yield: 7 servings ∞ prep: 20 min.
bake: 45 min.

This simple dish has been very popular at family gatherings and potlucks. You can assemble it ahead of time.

—*Lori Thompson, New London, Texas*

14	uncooked manicotti shells
1	pound bulk Italian sausage
3/4	pound ground beef
2	garlic cloves, minced
2	cups (8 ounces) shredded part-skim mozzarella cheese
1	package (3 ounces) cream cheese, cubed
1/4	teaspoon salt
4	cups meatless spaghetti sauce, *divided*
1/4	cup grated Parmesan cheese

1. Cook manicotti shells according to package directions. Meanwhile, in a large skillet, cook sausage and beef over medium heat until meat is no longer pink. Add garlic; cook 1 minute longer. Drain. Remove from the heat. Cool for 10 minutes.

2. Drain shells and rinse in cold water. Stir the mozzarella cheese, cream cheese and salt into meat mixture. Spread 2 cups spaghetti sauce in a greased 13-in. x 9-in. baking dish.

3. Stuff each shell with about 1/4 cupful meat mixture; arrange over sauce. Pour remaining sauce over top. Sprinkle with Parmesan cheese.

4. Cover and bake at 350° for 40 minutes. Uncover; bake 5-10 minutes longer or until bubbly and heated through.

[2009]

STAMP-OF-APPROVAL SPAGHETTI SAUCE

yield: 12 servings (3 quarts)
prep: 30 min. ∞ **cook: 8 hours**

My father is very opinionated —especially about food, and this recipe received his almost unreachable stamp of approval. I have yet to hear a disagreement from anyone who has tried it!

—Melissa Taylor, Higley, Arizona

2	pounds ground beef
3/4	pound bulk Italian sausage
4	medium onions, finely chopped
8	garlic cloves, minced
4	cans (14-1/2 ounces *each*) diced tomatoes, undrained
4	cans (6 ounces *each*) tomato paste
1/2	cup water
1/4	cup sugar
1/4	cup Worcestershire sauce
1	tablespoon canola oil
1/4	cup minced fresh parsley
2	tablespoons minced fresh basil *or* 2 teaspoons dried basil
1	tablespoon minced fresh oregano *or* 1 teaspoon dried oregano
4	bay leaves
1	teaspoon rubbed sage
1/2	teaspoon salt
1/2	teaspoon dried marjoram
1/2	teaspoon pepper

Hot cooked spaghetti

1. In a Dutch oven, cook the beef, sausage and onions over medium heat until the meat is no longer pink. Add garlic; cook 1 minute longer. Drain.

2. Transfer to a 5-qt. slow cooker. Stir in the tomatoes, tomato paste, water, sugar, Worcestershire sauce, oil and seasonings. Cover and cook on low for 8-10 hours. Discard bay leaves. Serve with spaghetti.

[2010]

FIRE ISLAND ZITI

yield: 5 servings ∞ **prep: 30 min.**
cook: 20 min.

(Pictured on page 634)

I've always been fascinated by Fire Island and thought the name was fitting for this slightly spicy pasta dish.

—Candace Reed, DeSoto, Texas

2	pounds plum tomatoes, halved lengthwise
3	tablespoons olive oil, *divided*
2	garlic cloves, minced
1	teaspoon salt
8	ounces ziti *or* small tube pasta
2	cups fresh broccoli florets
1	pound Italian sausage links, cut into 1/2-inch slices
1/2	teaspoon crushed red pepper flakes
1/3	cup grated Romano cheese

1. Toss the tomatoes with 2 tablespoons oil, garlic and salt. Place cut side down in a 15-in. x 10-in. x 1-in. baking pan. Bake at 450° for 20-25 minutes or until tender. Chop the tomatoes when cool enough to handle.

2. Cook the ziti according to package directions, adding broccoli during the last 4 minutes. Meanwhile, in a large skillet over medium heat, cook sausage in remaining oil until no longer pink. Add pepper flakes; cook 1 minute longer. Stir in tomatoes; heat through.

3. Drain ziti mixture; toss with sausage mixture. Sprinkle with cheese.

STAMP-OF-APPROVAL SPAGHETTI SAUCE

"I always try to make my own sauce as opposed to the jarred variety because it cuts the sodium in half. This recipe was easy to put together once the meat was browned, and it smelled and tasted amazing. I will never buy jarred sauces again! I added zucchini to mine, too."
—cricketbean

ITALIAN SPIRAL MEAT LOAF

[2011]

ITALIAN SPIRAL MEAT LOAF

yield: 12 servings ∞ prep: 40 min ∞ bake: 1-1/4 hours

(*Pictured on page 633*)

Take a classic comfort food to delicious new heights with this impressive recipe. Sausage, pizza sauce and mozzarella give this entree its Italian accent.

—*Megan Krumm, Schererville, Indiana*

2	eggs, lightly beaten
1	cup pizza sauce, *divided*
1	cup seasoned bread crumbs
1	medium onion, chopped
1	medium green pepper, chopped
1	teaspoon dried oregano
1	garlic clove, minced
1/2	teaspoon salt
1/4	teaspoon pepper
2	pounds lean ground beef (90% lean)
1	pound bulk Italian sausage
1/2	pound sliced deli ham
2	cups (8 ounces) shredded part-skim mozzarella cheese, *divided*
1	jar (6 ounces) sliced mushrooms, drained

---

1. In a large bowl, combine the eggs, 3/4 cup pizza sauce, bread crumbs, onion, green pepper, oregano, garlic, salt and pepper. Crumble beef and sausage over mixture and mix well.

2. On a piece of parchment paper, pat beef mixture into a 12-in. x 10-in. rectangle. Layer with ham, 1-1/2 cups cheese and mushrooms over beef mixture to within 1 in. of edges. Roll up jelly-roll style, starting with a short side and peeling parchment paper away as you roll. Seal seam and ends. Place seam side down in a greased 13-in. x 9-in. baking dish; brush with remaining pizza sauce.

3. Bake, uncovered, at 375° for 1 hour. Sprinkle with cheese. Bake 15-20 minutes longer or until no pink remains and a thermometer reads 160°. Using two large spatulas, carefully transfer meat loaf to a serving platter.

ITALIAN SPIRAL MEAT LOAF

"I made this meat loaf tonight. It was the best meat loaf that I have ever tasted. Yes, all of my other meat loaf recipes are history. No, I did not make any changes to this recipe; I think it is perfect.

It makes a lot, but I am looking forward to the good sandwiches it is going to make. When I make it again, and I know I will, I will probably turn it into two—one to cook and one to freeze. You have got to try this one. It is wonderful! My family gave it a 10, and they are not even fond of meat loaf."

—*GFEZ6*

ITALIAN SPIRAL MEAT LOAF, page 632

GRILLED PORK ROAST, page 606

HERBED LAMB KABOBS, page 641

FIRE ISLAND ZITI, page 631

BREADED PORK CHOPS, page 612

SPEEDY JAMBALAYA, page 629

CHERRY-STUFFED PORK LOIN, page 608

BEST BABY-BACK RIBS, page 618

ITALIAN PORK STEW, page 618

CORN DOG CASSEROLE, page 627

SCALLOPED POTATOES 'N' HAM, page 619

KIELBASA CABBAGE SKILLET, page 628

PORK CHOPS OLE, page 611

WYOMING LAMB STEW, page 642

THREE-CHEESE SAUSAGE LASAGNA, page 630

SPICY CABBAGE ROLLS, page 614

SLOW-COOKED CARNITAS, page 610

BRAIDED PORK TENDERLOINS, page 608

HAM WITH PINEAPPLE SALSA, page 625

HAM-POTATO PHYLLO BAKE, page 622

[2007]

HERBED LAMB KABOBS

yield: 8 servings
prep: 15 min. + marinating ∽ **grill: 20 min.**
(*Pictured on page 633*)

*This colorful kabob wouldn't be the same
without its delicious herb marinade and
tender-crisp vegetables. Together, they add
delicious flavor and texture to the lamb pieces.*

—*Janet Dingler, Cedartown, Georgia*

1	cup canola oil
1	medium onion, chopped
1/2	cup lemon juice
1/2	cup minced fresh parsley
3	to 4 garlic cloves, minced
2	teaspoons salt
2	teaspoons dried marjoram
2	teaspoons dried thyme
1/2	teaspoon pepper
2	pounds boneless lamb
1	medium red onion, cut into wedges
1	large green pepper, cut into 1-inch pieces
1	large sweet red pepper, cut into 1-inch pieces

1. In a small bowl, combine the first nine
ingredients. Pour 1 cup into a large
resealable plastic bag; add lamb. Seal
bag and turn to coat; refrigerate for 6-8
hours. Cover and refrigerate remaining
marinade for basting.

2. Drain and discard marinade. On eight
metal or soaked wooden skewers,
alternately thread lamb and vegetables.
Grill, uncovered, over medium-hot
heat for 8-10 minutes on each side or
until meat reaches desired doneness
(for medium-rare, a thermometer
should read 145°; medium, 160°;
well-done, 170°), basting frequently
with reserved marinade.

[2004]

TRADITIONAL LAMB STEW

yield: 4 servings ∽ **prep: 10 min.**
cook: 1 hour

*This is a delicious, nourishing and economical
dish. The flavor improves if you make the stew
the day before you serve it.*

—*Margery Richmond, Fort Collins, Colorado*

1-1/2	pounds lamb stew meat
2	tablespoons olive oil, *divided*
3	large onions, quartered
3	medium carrots, cut into 1-inch pieces
4	small potatoes, peeled and cubed
1	can (14-1/2 ounces) beef broth
1	teaspoon salt
1/4	teaspoon pepper
1	tablespoon butter
1	tablespoon all-purpose flour
1-1/2	teaspoons minced fresh parsley
1-1/2	teaspoons minced chives
1/2	teaspoon minced fresh thyme

1. In a Dutch oven, brown the meat in
1 tablespoon oil until meat is no longer
pink. Remove with a slotted spoon; set
aside. Add onions, carrots and remaining
oil to pan. Cook for 5 minutes or until
onions are tender stirring occasionally.
Add the potatoes, broth, salt, pepper
and lamb; bring to a boil.

2. Remove from the heat. Cover and bake
at 350° for 50-60 minutes or until
meat and vegetables are tender.

3. With a slotted spoon, remove meat
and vegetables to a large bowl; set
aside and keep warm. Pour pan juices
into another bowl; set aside.

4. In Dutch oven, melt butter. Stir in the
flour until smooth. Gradually whisk in
pan juices. Bring to a boil; cook and
stir for 2 minutes or until thickened.
Stir in the parsley, chives, thyme, meat
and vegetables; heat through.

TRADITIONAL LAMB STEW

❝Best lamb stew I ever
made. Easy, flavorful.
Husband loved it.❞
—*budlight*

RACK OF LAMB

❝These racks of lamb are so tasty. The oven roasting makes them tender, and the bread-crumb topping is my favorite part! When my husband and I want to impress guests, this does the trick. It even converts those who say they don't like lamb.❞

—*Trilby Yost*

[1998]

WYOMING LAMB STEW

yield: 6 servings ∽ prep: 30 min.
bake: 2 hours

(Pictured on page 637)

This satisfying stew was recommended to me by Jackie Palm, whose area ranch ships out several thousand head of lambs. Even though my husband, Randy, and I are empty nesters, I always make a big batch of this flavorful stew with its rich gravy. Since we have a busy cattle ranch and I also substitute teach, leftovers always come in handy.

—*Sandra Ramsey, Elk Mountain, Wyoming*

> 5 bacon strips, diced
> 1/4 cup all-purpose flour
> 1 teaspoon salt
> 1/2 teaspoon pepper
> 6 lamb shanks (about 6 pounds)
> 1 can (28 ounces) diced tomatoes, undrained
> 1 can (14-1/2 ounces) beef broth
> 1 can (8 ounces) tomato sauce
> 2 cans (4 ounces each) mushroom stems and pieces, drained
> 2 medium onions, chopped
> 1 cup chopped celery
> 1/2 cup minced fresh parsley
> 2 tablespoons prepared horseradish
> 1 tablespoon cider vinegar
> 2 teaspoons Worcestershire sauce
> 1 garlic clove, minced

1. In a Dutch oven, cook the bacon over medium heat until crisp. Using a slotted spoon, remove to paper towels to drain, reserving drippings. Reserve bacon for garnish; refrigerate.

2. In a large resealable plastic bag, combine flour, salt and pepper; add lamb shanks, one at a time and shake to coat. In bacon drippings, brown shanks on all sides; drain. Add the remaining ingredients. Bring to a boil.

3. Cover and bake at 325° for 2 to 2-1/2 hours or until the meat is very tender; skim fat. Garnish with bacon.

Editor's Note: If you like, make the stew a day ahead. Cool, then refrigerate. Before reheating, lift off fat from top of stew. Bring to a boil over medium-high heat. Reduce heat; cover and simmer until heated through.

[2003]

RACK OF LAMB

yield: 8 servings ∽ prep: 10 min.
bake: 30 min.

I first started cooking in college and have continued to do so ever since. Grilling is what I like best, but I think this rack of lamb is better baked than grilled.

—*Bob Paffenroth, Brookfield, Wisconsin*

> 4 racks of lamb (1 to 1-1/2 pounds *each*), trimmed
> 2 tablespoons Dijon mustard
> 1 cup soft bread crumbs
> 1/4 cup minced fresh parsley
> 1/4 teaspoon salt
> 1/4 teaspoon pepper
> 1/4 cup butter, melted
> 1 garlic clove, minced

1. Place lamb on a rack in a greased large roasting pan; brush with mustard. In a small bowl, combine the bread crumbs, parsley, salt and pepper. Press onto the meat. Combine the butter and garlic; drizzle over meat.

2. Bake, uncovered, at 375° for 30-35 minutes or until meat reaches desired doneness (for medium-rare, a thermometer should read 145°; medium, 160°; well-done, 170°). Remove from the oven and cover loosely with foil. Let stand for 5-10 minutes before slicing.

[2004]

ROSEMARY LEG OF LAMB
yield: 10-12 servings ∾ prep: 10 min.
bake: 1-1/2 hours

Roast lamb is a treat for our family at Easter and on other special occasions. Before roasting the meat, I rub on a mixture of garlic, rosemary, salt and pepper, which enhances the flavor.

—*Marie Hattrup, Sparks, Nevada, Field Editor*

  4 garlic cloves, minced
  1 to 2 tablespoons minced fresh rosemary *or* 1 teaspoon dried rosemary, crushed
  1 teaspoon salt
1/2 teaspoon pepper
  1 bone-in leg of lamb (7 to 9 pounds), trimmed
  1 teaspoon cornstarch
1/4 cup beef broth

1. In a small bowl, combine the seasonings; rub over meat. Place on a rack in a large roasting pan.

2. Bake, uncovered, at 350° for 1-1/2 to 2-1/2 hours or until the meat reaches desired doneness (for medium-rare, a thermometer should read 145°; medium, 160°; well-done, 170°;). Let stand for 10 minutes before slicing.

3. Meanwhile, pour pan drippings and loosened brown bits into a small saucepan. Skim the fat. Combine cornstarch and broth until smooth. Whisk into the drippings. Bring to a boil; cook and stir for 1-2 minutes or until thickened. Serve with lamb.

[2011]

CHERRY-GLAZED LAMB CHOPS
yield: 2 servings ∾ prep/total time: 25 min.

An elegant, deep brown reduction sauce studded with bits of cherry makes this entree ideal for a special dinner.

—*Kerry Dingwall, Ponte Vedra, Florida, Field Editor*

  1 teaspoon dried rosemary, crushed
1/4 teaspoon salt
1/4 teaspoon pepper, *divided*
  4 lamb loin chops (4 ounces *each*)
  1 garlic clove, minced
1/4 cup beef broth

1/4 cup cherry preserves
1/4 cup balsamic vinegar

1. Combine the rosemary, salt and 1/8 teaspoon pepper; rub over lamb chops. In a large skillet coated with cooking spray, cook chops over medium heat for 4-6 minutes on each side or until meat reaches desired doneness (for medium-rare, a thermometer should read 145°; medium, 160°; well-done, 170°). Remove and keep warm.

2. Add garlic to the pan; cook for 1 minute. Stir in the broth, preserves, vinegar and remaining pepper; cook for 2-4 minutes or until thickened. Return chops to the pan; turn to coat. Sprinkle with additional dried rosemary if desired.

[2012]

GREEK MEAT LOAF WITH TZATZIKI SAUCE
yield: 8 servings ∾ prep: 20 min.
bake: 55 min. + standing

This is a great spin on classic meat loaf. I love it because I can sneak spinach in on my meat-and-potatoes family. Plus, I get to make a whole other meal the next night with the leftovers.

—*Mandy Rivers, Lexington, South Carolina*

   2 eggs
   1 package (10 ounces) frozen chopped spinach, thawed and squeezed dry
   1 cup dry bread crumbs
   1 small onion, finely chopped
 1/4 cup grated Romano cheese
   2 teaspoons dried oregano
1-1/2 teaspoons garlic powder
 1/2 teaspoon salt
   2 pounds ground lamb *or* ground beef
   1 cup refrigerated tzatziki sauce

1. In a large bowl, combine eggs, spinach, bread crumbs, onion, cheese, oregano, garlic powder and salt. Crumble lamb over mixture and mix well. Shape into a loaf and place in a greased 11-in. x 7-in. baking dish.

2. Bake, uncovered, at 350° for 55-60 minutes or until no pink remains and a thermometer reads 160°. Let stand 15 minutes before slicing. Serve with the sauce.

CORN TORTILLA CHICKEN LASAGNA

"LOVED this inexpensive, easy recipe. I used pinto beans (although I would probably use black beans next time), a Mexican shredded cheese blend, and medium salsa. It was delicious. It tasted great left over, too, although the bottom layer of tortillas got a bit soggy. I will definitely be making it again, at the request of my fiance! He even bragged about it to his mom... score!"
—*JustLikeMoms*

[2007]

CORN TORTILLA CHICKEN LASAGNA

yield: 2 casseroles (12 servings each)
prep: 40 min. ∞ bake: 35 min. + standing

(*Pictured on page 675*)

This Southwest-style lasagna will satisfy a hungry crowd. It can be stretched with extra beans, and it's super-easy to put together. People love it!

—*Susan Seymar, Valatie, New York*

36	corn tortillas (6 inches)
6	cups shredded *or* cubed cooked chicken breast
2	cans (one 28 ounces, one 16 ounces) kidney beans, rinsed and drained
3	jars (16 ounces *each*) salsa
3	cups (24 ounces) sour cream
3	large green peppers, chopped
3	cans (3.8 ounces *each*) sliced ripe olives, drained
3	cups (12 ounces) shredded Monterey Jack cheese
3	cups (12 ounces) shredded cheddar cheese

1. In each of two greased 13-in. x 9-in. baking dishes, arrange six tortillas. Layer each with 1 cup chicken, 2/3 cup kidney beans, 1 cup salsa, 1/2 cup sour cream, 1/2 cup green pepper, about 1/3 cup olives, 1/2 cup Monterey Jack cheese and 1/2 cup cheddar cheese. Repeat layers twice.

2. Cover and bake at 350° for 25 minutes. Uncover; bake 10-15 minutes longer or until cheese is melted. Let stand for 10 minutes before serving.

[2002]

FOUR-PASTA BEEF BAKE

yield: 2 casseroles (8-10 servings each)
prep: 15 min. ∞ bake: 25 min.

(*Pictured on page 674*)

This hearty casserole looks and tastes a lot like lasagna, but it's quicker to prepare since you don't have to layer it. It disappears fast when I share it at a gathering. Served with rolls and a salad, it makes an easy and satisfying supper.

—*Harriet Stichter*
Milford, Indiana, Field Editor

8	cups uncooked pasta (four assorted pasta shapes of your choice)
2	pounds ground beef
2	medium green peppers, chopped
2	medium onions, chopped
2	cups sliced fresh mushrooms
4	jars (26 ounces *each*) meatless spaghetti sauce
2	eggs, lightly beaten
4	cups (16 ounces) shredded part-skim mozzarella cheese

1. Cook the pasta according to package directions. Meanwhile, in a large skillet, cook the beef, peppers, onions and mushrooms over medium heat until meat is no longer pink; drain.

2. Drain pasta and place in a large bowl; stir in the beef mixture, two jars of spaghetti sauce and eggs.

3. Transfer to two greased 3-qt. baking dishes. Top with remaining sauce; sprinkle with cheese. Bake, uncovered, at 350° for 25-30 minutes or until a thermometer reads 160°.

[2010]

GINGERBREAD PANCAKES WITH BANANA CREAM

yield: 42 pancakes (4-2/3 cups topping)
prep: 25 min.   **cook:** 5 min./batch

(Pictured on page 679)

If you like gingerbread, you'll be thrilled with these pancakes. They're good any time of year, but make a yuletide brunch or Breakfast with Santa fundraiser especially festive.

—Barbara Brittain
  Santee, California, Former Field Editor

2	cups heavy whipping cream
1/3	cup confectioners' sugar
2	medium bananas, chopped
3/4	cup butter, softened
1-1/2	cups packed brown sugar
6	eggs
1-1/2	cups molasses
6	cups all-purpose flour
4-1/2	teaspoons baking powder
1	tablespoon ground ginger
1	tablespoon ground cinnamon
2-1/4	teaspoons salt
3/4	teaspoon ground allspice
4	cups 2% milk

---

1. In a large bowl, beat the cream until it begins to thicken. Add confectioners' sugar; beat until soft peaks form. Fold in bananas. Cover and chill until serving.

2. In a very large bowl, cream butter and brown sugar until light and fluffy. Add eggs, one at a time, beating well after each addition. Beat in the molasses. Combine flour, baking powder, ginger, cinnamon, salt and allspice; add to the creamed mixture alternately with milk, beating well after each addition.

3. Pour the batter by 1/4 cupfuls onto a greased hot griddle; turn when bubbles form on top. Cook until the second side is golden brown. Serve with the banana cream.

[2006]

MEAT 'N' CHEESE STROMBOLI

yield: 2 loaves (8 servings each)
prep: 25 min.   **bake:** 15 min.

(Pictured on page 674)

This tasty Italian-style sandwich can be served warm or at room temperature, and it heats up nicely in the microwave. Friends request it when I'm asked to bring something for a party.

—Sue Shea, Defiance, Ohio

1	medium onion, sliced and separated into rings
1	medium green pepper, sliced into rings
1	tablespoon butter
2	loaves (16 ounces *each*) frozen bread dough, thawed
1/2	pound thinly sliced hard salami
1/2	pound thinly sliced deli ham
8	ounces sliced part-skim mozzarella cheese
1/2	pound sliced mild cheddar cheese
1/2	teaspoon Italian seasoning
1/4	teaspoon garlic powder
1/8	teaspoon pepper
1	egg, lightly beaten
1	teaspoon poppy seeds

---

1. In a large skillet, saute onion and green pepper in butter until crisp-tender and set aside.

2. On two greased baking sheets, roll each loaf of dough into a 15-in. x 12-in. rectangle. Arrange salami, ham and cheeses lengthwise over half of each rectangle to within 1/2 in. of edges. Top with onion mixture; sprinkle with Italian seasoning, garlic powder and pepper. Fold dough over filling; pinch edges to seal.

3. Brush with egg and sprinkle with poppy seeds. Bake at 400° for 15-20 minutes or until golden brown. Cool for 5 minutes before slicing.

MEAT 'N' CHEESE STROMBOLI

"I have made this many times. It is so good and makes great leftovers also. I always get rave reviews when I make it for our football parties."
—cricket59

ITALIAN SAUSAGE EGG BAKE

"I have been making this every year for the past three years at Christmas and Easter. I have a crowd of 20 for breakfast on those holidays, and they look forward to it every time. It is so easy to whip up and clean up on those busy mornings is limited to one pan. The taste is yummy and it's very filling. We also serve it with French toast."
—jenn1972

[2007]

ITALIAN SAUSAGE EGG BAKE

yield: 12 servings ∞ prep: 20 min. + chilling
bake: 50 min.

This hearty entree warms up any breakfast or brunch menu with its herb-seasoned flavor.

—*Darlene Markham*
Rochester, New York, Field Editor

8	slices white bread, cubed
1	pound Italian sausage links, casings removed and sliced
2	cups (8 ounces) shredded sharp cheddar cheese
2	cups (8 ounces) shredded part-skim mozzarella cheese
9	eggs, lightly beaten
3	cups 2% milk
1	teaspoon dried basil
1	teaspoon dried oregano
1	teaspoon fennel seed, crushed

1. Place bread cubes in a greased 13-in. x 9-in. baking dish; set aside. In a large skillet, cook the sausage over medium heat until no longer pink; drain. Spoon the sausage over bread; sprinkle with the cheeses.

2. In a large bowl, whisk the eggs, milk and seasonings; pour over casserole. Cover and refrigerate overnight.

3. Remove the dish from the refrigerator 30 minutes before baking. Bake, uncovered, at 350° for 50-55 minutes or until a knife inserted near center comes out clean. Let casserole stand for 5 minutes before cutting.

[1996]

BARBECUED PORK SANDWICHES

yield: 25 servings ∞ prep: 15 min.
cook: 4 hours

When our office held a bridal shower, we presented the future bride with a collection of our favorite recipes. I included this one. I like serving this savory pork as an alternative to a typical ground beef barbecue.

—*Karla Labby, Otsego, Michigan*

2	boneless pork loin roasts (3 pounds each)
1	cup water
2	teaspoons salt
2	cups ketchup
2	cups diced celery
1/3	cup steak sauce
1/4	cup packed brown sugar
1/4	cup white vinegar
2	teaspoons lemon juice
25	hamburger buns, split

1. Place roasts in an 8-qt. Dutch oven; add water and salt. Cover and cook on medium-low heat for 2-1/2 hours or until a thermometer reads 145°.

2. Remove the roasts; let stand for 10 minutes. Shred the meat with a fork; set aside. Skim fat from cooking liquid and discard. Drain, reserving 1 cup cooking liquid. Add the meat, ketchup, celery, steak sauce, brown sugar, vinegar and lemon juice. Cover and cook over medium-low heat for 1-1/2 hours. Serve on buns.

[1994]

CHICKEN SUPREME WITH GRAVY

yield: 70-80 servings ∽ **prep: 1 hour**
bake: 1 hour 20 min.

A group of friends and I have met often throughout the years to swap our favorite recipes. This tried-and-true dish has always been well received.

—Bernice Hartje, Cavalier, North Dakota

1-1/2 bunches celery, diced (about 6 cups)
  6 medium onions, diced (about 4 cups)
  2 cups butter, cubed
  3 loaves day-old white bread (1-1/2 pounds *each*), cut into 1-inch cubes
  3 tablespoons salt
  3 tablespoons rubbed sage
  1 tablespoon baking powder
  2 teaspoons pepper
 12 eggs
  9 cups 2% milk
 24 cups diced cooked chicken (about 6 chickens)
  3 cans (14-1/2 ounces *each*) chicken broth
GRAVY:
  8 cans (10-3/4 ounces *each*) condensed cream of chicken and mushroom soup, undiluted
  9 to 10 cups water

1. In several Dutch ovens, saute celery and onions in butter. In several large bowls, combine the bread, salt, sage, baking powder and pepper; toss to coat. Stir in celery mixture. Beat eggs and milk; add to bread mixture.

2. Divide half of chicken among four 13-in. x 9-in. greased baking dishes. Cover with half of the bread mixture. Repeat layers. Pour about 1/3 cups broth into each dish.

3. Cover and bake at 325° for 70 minutes or until hot and bubbly; uncover and bake 10-15 minutes longer.

4. For gravy, in a stockpot, combine soup and water. Bring to a boil. Reduce heat; simmer, uncovered, for 10 minutes. Serve with chicken.

[2006]

PEPPERY ROAST BEEF

yield: 10-12 servings ∽ **prep: 5 min.**
bake: 2-1/2 hours + standing

With its spicy coating and creamy horseradish sauce, this tender roast is sure to be the star of any meal, whether it's a sit-down dinner or serve-yourself potluck.

—Maureen Brand, Somers, Iowa

  1 tablespoon olive oil
  1 tablespoon seasoned pepper
  2 garlic cloves, minced
1/2 teaspoon dried thyme
1/4 teaspoon salt
  1 boneless beef eye round roast (4 to 5 pounds)
HORSERADISH SAUCE:
  1 cup (8 ounces) sour cream
  2 tablespoons lemon juice
  2 tablespoons 2% milk
  2 tablespoons prepared horseradish
  1 tablespoon Dijon mustard
1/4 teaspoon salt
1/8 teaspoon pepper

1. In a small bowl, combine the oil, seasoned pepper, garlic, thyme and salt; rub over roast. Place fat side up on a rack in a shallow roasting pan.

Bake, uncovered, at 325° for 2-1/2 to 3 hours or until the meat reaches desired doneness (for medium-rare, a thermometer should read 145°; medium, 160°; well-done, 170°). Let stand for 10 minutes before slicing.

2. In a small bowl, combine the sauce ingredients. Serve with roast.

CHICKEN SUPREME WITH GRAVY

"I make this for our church suppers and it's one of the favorites! I would recommend adding less milk until you see if you need it all or it could get soupy. I serve this with mashed potatoes, gravy, a vegetable and cranberry sauce. It's a real crowd-pleaser!"
—hatti

MEATY SPINACH MANICOTTI

❝This recipe is delicious! It does take some time; stuffing manicotti shells is always putzie, but definitely worth it. A great dish for guests, it looks fancy and tastes like it, too. Halve the recipe for a smaller group or freeze the leftovers. It's also a good do-ahead dish. You can prep it, throw it in the fridge and bake it just before you're ready to serve.❞

—*RD2Cook*

[2001]

MEATY SPINACH MANICOTTI

yield: 14-16 servings ∾ prep: 30 min.
bake: 45 min.

(*Pictured on page 680*)

This hearty stuffed pasta dish will feed a crowd. Tangy tomato sauce tops manicotti that's filled with a wonderful blend of Italian sausage, chicken, spinach and mozzarella cheese. Be prepared to share the recipe!

—*Pat Schroeder, Elkhorn, Wisconsin*

---

 2 **packages (8 ounces each) manicotti shells**
 1/4 **cup butter, cubed**
 1/4 **cup all-purpose flour**
 2-1/2 **cups 2% milk**
 3/4 **cup grated Parmesan cheese**
 1 **pound bulk Italian sausage**
 4 **cups cubed cooked chicken or turkey**
 2 **packages (10 ounces each) frozen chopped spinach, thawed and squeezed dry**
 2 **eggs, lightly beaten**
 1 **cup (4 ounces) shredded part-skim mozzarella cheese**
 2 **jars (24 ounces each) spaghetti sauce**
 1/4 **cup minced fresh parsley**

---

1. Cook manicotti according to package directions. Meanwhile, melt butter in a saucepan. Stir in the flour until smooth; gradually add milk. Bring to a boil; cook and stir for 2 minutes or until thickened. Stir in Parmesan cheese until melted; set aside. Drain manicotti; set aside.

2. In a large skillet, cook sausage over medium heat until no longer pink; drain. Add the chicken, spinach, eggs, mozzarella cheese and 3/4 cup white sauce. Stuff into manicotti shells.

3. Spread 1/2 cup spaghetti sauce in each of two ungreased 13-in. x 9-in. baking dishes. Top with manicotti. Pour the remaining spaghetti sauce over top.

4. Reheat the remaining white sauce, stirring constantly. Pour over spaghetti sauce. Bake, uncovered, at 350° for 45-50 minutes or until a thermometer inserted in the filling reads 160°. Sprinkle with parsley.

[2002]

SAUSAGE EGG BAKE

yield: 12 servings ∾ prep: 10 min.
bake: 40 min.

This hefty egg dish is wonderful for any meal of the day. I fix it frequently for special occasions, too, because it's easy to prepare and really versatile. For a change, use spicier sausage or substitute a flavored cheese blend.

—*Molly Swallow, Pocatello, Idaho*

---

 1 **pound bulk Italian sausage**
 2 **cans (10-3/4 ounces each) condensed cream of potato soup, undiluted**
 9 **eggs, lightly beaten**
 3/4 **cup 2% milk**
 1/4 **teaspoon pepper**
 1 **cup (4 ounces) shredded cheddar cheese**

---

1. In a large skillet, cook sausage over medium heat until no longer pink; drain. Stir in soup. In a large bowl, whisk eggs, milk and pepper; stir in sausage mixture.

2. Transfer to a lightly greased 11-in. x 7-in. baking dish. Sprinkle with cheese. Bake, uncovered, at 375° for 40-45 minutes or until a knife inserted near the center comes out clean.

[2007]

CLASSIC TURKEY TETRAZZINI

yield: 12 servings ∞ **prep: 30 min.**
bake: 30 min.

This classic casserole is so easy to make and works well with either leftover turkey or fresh turkey cutlets. You can also substitute flavored bread crumbs for the plain ones and jarred, roasted red pepper for the fresh variety.

—*Shannon Weddle, Berryville, Virginia*

1	package (16 ounces) spaghetti
2	medium onions, chopped
9	tablespoons butter, *divided*
1	pound sliced fresh mushrooms
1	large sweet red pepper, chopped
1/2	cup all-purpose flour
1	teaspoon salt
6	cups 2% milk
1	tablespoon chicken bouillon granules
6	cups cubed cooked turkey breast
1	cup grated Parmesan cheese
1-1/2	cups dry bread crumbs
4	teaspoons minced fresh parsley

1. Cook spaghetti according to package directions. Meanwhile, in a Dutch oven, saute onions in 6 tablespoons butter until tender. Add mushrooms and red pepper; saute 4-5 minutes longer or until vegetables are tender.

2. Stir in flour and salt until blended. Gradually whisk in milk and bouillon. Bring to a boil; cook and stir for 2 minutes or until thickened. Stir in turkey and cheese; heat through. Remove from the heat.

3. Drain spaghetti; add to turkey mixture and mix well. Transfer to one greased 13-in. x 9-in. baking dish and one greased 11-in. x 7-in. baking dish.

4. Melt the remaining butter; toss with bread crumbs. Sprinkle over the casseroles. Bake, uncovered, at 350° for 30-35 minutes or until heated through. Sprinkle with the parsley.

[2009]

MAKE ONCE, EAT TWICE LASAGNA

yield: 2 lasagnas (12 servings each)
prep: 35 min. ∞ **bake: 50 min. + standing**

Our family loves this recipe accompanied with a green salad and garlic bread. It's so handy on lazy days or when guests arrive to have an extra, ready-made pan in the freezer.

—*Geri Davis, Prescott, Arizona*

1	package (16 ounces) lasagna noodles
3	pounds ground beef
3	jars (26 ounces *each*) spaghetti sauce
2	eggs, lightly beaten
1-1/2	pounds ricotta cheese
6	cups (24 ounces) shredded part-skim mozzarella cheese, *divided*
1	tablespoon dried parsley flakes
1	teaspoon salt
1/2	teaspoon pepper
1	cup grated Parmesan cheese

1. Cook noodles according to package directions. Meanwhile, in a Dutch oven, cook beef over medium heat until no longer pink; drain. Remove from the heat; stir in spaghetti sauce. In a large bowl, combine the eggs, ricotta cheese, 4-1/2 cups mozzarella cheese, parsley, salt and pepper.

2. Drain noodles. Spread 1 cup meat sauce in each of two greased 13-in. x 9-in. baking dishes. Layer each with three noodles, 1 cup ricotta mixture and 1-1/2 cups meat sauce. Repeat layers twice. Top with Parmesan cheese and remaining mozzarella cheese.

3. Cover and freeze one lasagna for up to 3 months. Cover and bake remaining lasagna at 375° for 45 minutes. Uncover; bake 10 minutes longer or until bubbly. Let stand for 10 minutes before cutting.

4. To use frozen lasagna: Thaw in the refrigerator overnight. Remove from refrigerator 30 minutes before baking. Cover and bake at 375° for 60-70 minutes or until heated through. Uncover; bake 10 minutes longer. Let stand for 10 minutes before cutting.

[2000]

GREEK PASTA AND BEEF

yield: 12 servings ∞ prep: 30 min. ∞ bake: 45 min.

This casserole gives everyday macaroni and cheese an international flavor. A coworker who's a pro at Greek cooking shared the recipe.

—Dorothy Bateman, Carver, Massachusetts, Former Field Editor

1	package (16 ounces) elbow macaroni
1	pound ground beef
1	large onion, chopped
1	garlic clove, minced
1	can (8 ounces) tomato sauce
1/2	cup water
1	teaspoon salt
1/2	teaspoon ground cinnamon
1/4	teaspoon ground nutmeg
1/4	teaspoon pepper
1	egg, lightly beaten
1/2	cup grated Parmesan cheese

SAUCE:

1/4	cup butter
1/4	cup all-purpose flour
1/4	teaspoon ground cinnamon
3	cups 2% milk
2	eggs, lightly beaten
1/3	cup grated Parmesan cheese

GREEK PASTA AND BEEF

❝I have made this recipe numerous times since seeing it in the magazine in October 2000. My husband is of Greek descent and loves when I make this.**❞**
— *churmusidn*

---

1. Cook macaroni according to package directions. In a large skillet, cook beef and onion over medium heat until meat is no longer pink. Add garlic; cook 1 minute longer. Drain. Stir in the tomato sauce, water and seasonings. Cover and simmer for 10 minutes, stirring occasionally. Drain macaroni.

2. In a large bowl, combine the macaroni, egg and cheese; set aside. For sauce, in a large saucepan, melt butter; stir in flour and cinnamon until smooth. Gradually add milk. Bring to a boil over medium heat; cook and stir for 2 minutes or until slightly thickened. Remove from the heat. Stir a small amount of hot mixture into eggs; return all to pan, stirring constantly. Stir in cheese.

3. In a greased 3-qt. baking dish, spread half of the macaroni mixture. Top with beef mixture and remaining macaroni mixture. Pour sauce over the top. Bake, uncovered, at 350° for 45-50 minutes or until a thermometer reads 160°. Let stand for 5 minutes before serving.

[1993]

REUNION CASSEROLE

yield: 8-10 servings ∞ prep: 15 min.
bake: 45 min.

(Pictured on page 676)

Here's a noodle casserole just like Mom used to make! Its down-home taste has great appeal at a family gathering or as a dish to pass. It's also easy to prepare and can be assembled ahead of time. No leftovers!

—Bernice Morris
Marshfield, Missouri, Field Editor

- 1 pound ground beef
- 1/2 pound bulk spicy pork sausage
- 1 cup chopped onion
- 2 cups (8 ounces) shredded cheddar cheese, *divided*
- 1 medium green pepper, chopped
- 1 can (11 ounces) whole kernel corn, drained
- 1 can (10-3/4 ounces) condensed tomato soup, undiluted
- 1 can (8 ounces) tomato sauce
- 1/3 cup sliced pimiento-stuffed olives
- 1 garlic clove, minced
- 1/2 teaspoon salt
- 8 ounces wide noodles, cooked and drained

---

1. In a large Dutch oven, cook the beef, sausage and onion over medium heat until meat is no longer pink; drain. Stir in 1 cup of the cheese, the green pepper, corn, soup, tomato sauce, olives, garlic, salt and noodles.

2. Transfer to a greased 13-in. x 9-in. baking dish. Sprinkle with remaining cheese. Cover and bake at 350° for 35 minutes or until bubbly. Uncover; bake 10 minutes longer or until cheese is melted.

[2007]

PICNIC CHICKEN

yield: 24 servings (4 cups dip)
prep: 20 min. ∞ bake: 1 hour + chilling

I made this well-seasoned chicken one evening for dinner and served it hot from the oven. While raiding the fridge the next day, I discovered how delicious it was cold and created the creamy yogurt dip to go with it.

—Ami Okasinski, Memphis, Tennessee

- 3 eggs
- 3 tablespoons water
- 1-1/2 cups dry bread crumbs
- 2 teaspoons paprika
- 1 teaspoon salt
- 1/2 teaspoon *each* dried marjoram, thyme and rosemary, crushed
- 1/2 teaspoon pepper
- 1 cup butter, melted
- 12 chicken drumsticks
- 12 bone-in chicken thighs

CREAMY LEEK DIP:
- 1 cup heavy whipping cream
- 1-1/2 cups plain yogurt
- 1 envelope leek soup mix
- 1 cup (4 ounces) shredded Colby cheese

---

1. In a shallow bowl, whisk eggs and water. In another shallow bowl, combine bread crumbs and seasonings. Divide butter between two 13-in. x 9-in. baking dishes.

2. Dip chicken pieces in egg mixture, then coat with crumb mixture. Place in prepared pans. Bake, uncovered, at 375° for 1 hour or until a thermometer reads 180°, turning once. Cool for 30 minutes; refrigerate until chilled.

3. For dip, in a small bowl, beat cream until stiff peaks form. In another bowl, combine the yogurt, soup mix and cheese; fold in whipped cream. Cover and refrigerate until serving. Serve with cold chicken.

PICNIC CHICKEN

"Great recipe. Everyone who tasted it loved it— and that's a lot of people since the recipe makes so much. I did skin the chicken and used Herbs de Provence instead of the three separate herbs called for. A definite keeper and a great make-ahead recipe. Reheats perfectly! Will make again and again. Thanks."
—2008reneeq

CREAMY CHICKEN NOODLE BAKE

[2009]

CREAMY CHICKEN NOODLE BAKE

yield: 12 servings (1 cup each)
prep: 25 min. ∞ **bake: 40 min. + standing**

Talk about a potluck pleaser! This comforting, creamy casserole is bursting with tender chunks of chicken. Even the pickiest eater will gobble up this tasty bake.

—*Shirley Unger, Bluffton, Ohio*

4	cups uncooked egg noodles
1/2	cup butter, *divided*
1/4	cup all-purpose flour
1/2	teaspoon salt
1/8	teaspoon white pepper
3-1/2	cups 2% milk
4	cups cubed cooked chicken
2	jars (12 ounces *each*) chicken gravy
1	jar (2 ounces) diced pimientos, drained
1/2	cup cubed process cheese (Velveeta)
1/2	cup dry bread crumbs
4	teaspoons butter, melted

---

1. Cook noodles according to package directions. Meanwhile, in a Dutch oven, melt 6 tablespoons butter. Stir in the flour, salt and pepper until smooth. Gradually add milk. Bring to a boil; cook and stir for 1-2 minutes or until thickened. Remove from the heat. Stir in the chicken, gravy and pimientos.

2. Drain noodles; toss with remaining butter. Stir into chicken mixture. Transfer to a greased 13-in. x 9-in. baking dish.

3. Cover and bake at 350° for 30-35 minutes or until bubbly. Combine the cheese, bread crumbs and melted butter. Sprinkle around edges of the casserole. Bake, uncovered, for 10 minutes longer or until golden brown. Let stand for 10 minutes before serving.

[2003]

ZESTY SLOPPY JOES

yield: 16 servings ∞ **prep: 15 min.**
cook: 1 hour

My mother-in-law created this recipe in the early 1950s. Our family likes these classic sloppy joes served with pickles and potato chips.

—*Sharon McKee, Denton, Texas*

2	pounds lean ground beef (90% lean)
1	large green pepper, chopped
2	cans (14-1/2 ounces *each*) diced tomatoes, undrained
2	cans (8 ounces *each*) tomato sauce
1	can (6 ounces) tomato paste
2	tablespoons Worcestershire sauce
1	tablespoon sugar
2	teaspoons celery salt *or* celery seed
2	teaspoons onion salt *or* onion powder
1	teaspoon paprika
1/4	to 1/2 teaspoon cayenne pepper
3	bay leaves
16	hamburger buns, split

---

1. In a Dutch oven, cook beef and green pepper over medium heat until meat is no longer pink; drain. Stir in the tomatoes, tomato sauce, tomato paste and seasonings. Bring to a boil. Reduce heat; cover and cook over low heat for 30 minutes.

2. Cook, uncovered, 30-40 minutes longer or until thickened. Discard bay leaves. Serve 1/2 cup of meat mixture on each bun.

HOW MUCH CHICKEN?

Generally, 3/4 pound of boneless skinless chicken breasts will yield 2 cups of cubed cooked chicken and 3-1/2-pound whole chicken will yield about 3 cups.

—*Taste of Home Cooking Experts*

[2010]

TEX-MEX CHILI

yield: 12 servings (1-1/3 cups each)
prep: 20 min. ∞ cook: 6 hours

Hearty and spicy, this is a man's chili for sure. You can also simmer it on the stove, if you prefer.

—Eric Hayes, Antioch, California

3	pounds beef stew meat
1	tablespoon canola oil
3	garlic cloves, minced
3	cans (16 ounces each) kidney beans, rinsed and drained
3	cans (15 ounces each) tomato sauce
1	can (14-1/2 ounces) diced tomatoes, undrained
1	cup water
1	can (6 ounces) tomato paste
3/4	cup salsa verde
1	envelope chili seasoning
2	teaspoons dried minced onion
1	teaspoon chili powder
1/2	teaspoon crushed red pepper flakes
1/2	teaspoon ground cumin
1/2	teaspoon cayenne pepper

Shredded cheddar cheese and minced fresh cilantro

1. In a large skillet, brown beef in oil in batches. Add the garlic; cook 1 minute longer. Transfer to a 6-qt. slow cooker.

2. Stir in the remaining ingredients. Cover and cook on low for 6-8 hours or until meat is tender. Garnish each serving with cheese and cilantro.

[1998]

SANDWICH FOR A CROWD

yield: 12-14 servings ∞ prep: 10 min. + chilling

My husband and I live on a 21-acre horse ranch and are pleased to invite friends to enjoy it with us. When entertaining, I rely on no-fuss, make-ahead entrees like this satisfying sandwich.

—Helen Hougland, Spring Hill, Kansas

2	loaves (1 pound each) unsliced Italian bread
1	package (8 ounces) cream cheese, softened
1	cup (4 ounces) shredded cheddar cheese
3/4	cup sliced green onions
1/4	cup mayonnaise
1	tablespoon Worcestershire sauce
1	pound thinly sliced fully cooked ham
1	pound thinly sliced roast beef
12	to 14 thin slices dill pickle

1. Cut the bread in half lengthwise. Hollow out top and bottom of loaves, leaving a 1/2-in. shell (discard removed bread or save for another use).

2. In a large bowl, combine cheeses, onions, mayonnaise and Worcestershire sauce; spread over cut sides of bread. Layer with ham and roast beef on bottom and top halves; place pickles on bottom halves. Gently press halves together.

3. Wrap sandwiches in plastic wrap and refrigerate for at least 2 hours. Cut into 1-1/2-in. slices.

[2006]

BOW TIE SEAFOOD SALAD

yield: 32 servings (1 cup each) ∞ prep: 25 min. + chilling

I served this satisfying pasta salad to a group of hospital volunteers who were quick with compliments. It's brimming with shrimp and imitation crab and accented with dill.

—Lily Julow, Gainesville, Florida, Field Editor

3	pounds uncooked bow tie pasta
1-1/2	pounds imitation crabmeat, chopped
1	pound frozen cooked salad shrimp, thawed
4	celery ribs, chopped
1	cup finely chopped green onions
1	medium green pepper, diced
4	cups mayonnaise
1/4	cup dill pickle relish
1/4	cup Dijon mustard
1	tablespoon salt
1	tablespoon dill weed
3/4	teaspoon pepper

1. Cook pasta according to package directions; drain and rinse in cold water. Place in a large bowl; add the crab, shrimp, celery, onions and green pepper.

2. In another bowl, whisk the mayonnaise, pickle relish, mustard, salt, dill and pepper. Pour over pasta mixture and toss to coat. Cover salad and refrigerate for at least 2 hours before serving.

HOME-STYLE MEAT LOAF

"I looked through 120 meat loaf recipes on TOH.com (tasteofhome.com) and all my magazines to find this one. I cook dinners every week at church, and we made this last year. I had so many people ask for the recipe. I froze the leftovers, reheated slowly in some stock and made them into hot meat loaf sandwiches. Yum."
—jamie667

[2004]

ITALIAN SPAGHETTI BAKE
yield: 2 casseroles (8 servings each)
prep: 20 min.   ∽   bake: 20 min.
(Pictured on page 678)

This satisfying recipe makes two large baking dishes. The tasty layers of meat sauce, spaghetti and gooey cheese are sure to appeal to pizza-loving kids...and adults. You'll bring home empty pans when you take this to a potluck.

—*Janice Fredrickson, Elgin, Texas*

2	packages (one 16 ounces, one 8 ounces) spaghetti
1-1/2	pounds ground beef
1	large green pepper, chopped
1	medium onion, chopped
2	cans (15 ounces each) tomato sauce
1	package (8 ounces) sliced pepperoni
1	can (8 ounces) mushroom stems and pieces, drained
1	can (3.8 ounces) sliced ripe olives, drained
1/2	teaspoon dried basil
1/2	teaspoon dried oregano
1/4	teaspoon garlic salt
1/4	teaspoon pepper
4	cups (16 ounces) shredded part-skim mozzarella cheese
1/2	cup grated Parmesan cheese

1. Cook spaghetti according to package directions. Meanwhile, in a Dutch oven, cook the beef, green pepper and onion over medium heat until meat is no longer pink; drain. Stir in tomato sauce, pepperoni, mushrooms, olives and seasonings. Drain spaghetti.

2. Spoon 1 cup meat mixture into each of two greased 13-in. x 9-in. baking dishes. Layer with spaghetti and the remaining meat mixture. Sprinkle with cheeses.

3. Cover and freeze one casserole for up to 3 months. Bake the remaining casserole, uncovered, at 350° for 20-25 minutes or until heated through.

4. To use frozen casserole: Thaw in the refrigerator overnight. Remove from the refrigerator 30 minutes before baking. Cover and bake at 350° for 40 minutes. Uncover; bake 5-10 minutes longer or until cheese is melted.

[2002]

HOME-STYLE MEAT LOAF
yield: 5 meat loaves (12 servings each)
prep: 45 min.
bake: 1-1/4 hours + standing

Down-home meat loaf is hard to resist, and with this recipe I can make sure that lots of friends and family get a chance to enjoy such a specialty. Guests seem to like the fact that this version uses both ground beef and ground pork.

—*Allison Craig, Ormstown, Quebec*

6	eggs, lightly beaten
4	cups 2% milk
4	cups dry bread crumbs
2-1/2	cups shredded carrots
1-1/4	cups chopped onions
5	teaspoons salt
4	teaspoons pepper
10	pounds ground beef
5	pounds ground pork

1. In two very large bowls, combine the first seven ingredients. Crumble meat over the top and mix well.

2. Shape into five loaves; place each in an ungreased 13-in. x 9-in. baking pan. Bake, uncovered, at 350° for 75-85 minutes or until a thermometer reads 160°. Drain; let stand for 10 minutes before slicing.

[1999]

SAUSAGE SANDWICH SQUARES

yield: 12-15 servings
prep: 35 min. + rising ∞ **bake: 20 min.**

(Pictured on page 677)

As Sunday-school teachers, my husband and I often host youth groups, so I dreamed up this handy recipe to feed some hungry teenagers. They loved the pizza-like sandwich and still request it when they visit.

—*Mary Merrill, Bloomingdale, Ohio*

1 **package (1/4 ounce) active dry yeast**
1-1/3 **cups warm water (110° to 115°), *divided***
1/2 **teaspoon salt**
3 **to 3-1/2 cups all-purpose flour**
1 **pound bulk Italian sausage**
1 **medium sweet red pepper, diced**
1 **medium green pepper, diced**
1 **large onion, diced**
4 **cups (16 ounces) shredded part-skim mozzarella cheese**
1 **egg**
1 **tablespoon water**
2 **tablespoons grated Parmesan cheese**
2 **tablespoons minced fresh parsley**
1/2 **teaspoon dried oregano**
1/8 **teaspoon garlic powder**

1. In a large bowl, dissolve yeast in 1/2 cup warm water. Add the salt, remaining water and 2 cups flour. Beat until smooth. Add enough remaining flour to form a firm dough.

2. Turn onto a floured surface; knead until smooth and elastic, about 6 minutes. Place in a greased bowl, turning once to grease top. Cover and let rise in a warm place until doubled, about 50 minutes.

3. In a large skillet, cook sausage over medium heat until no longer pink; remove with a slotted spoon and set aside. In the drippings, saute peppers and onion until tender; drain.

4. Press half of the dough onto the bottom and 1/2 in. up the sides of a greased 15-in. x 10-in. x 1-in. baking pan. Spread sausage evenly over the crust. Top with the peppers and onion. Sprinkle with mozzarella cheese. Roll out remaining dough to fit pan; place over cheese and seal the edges.

5. In a small bowl, beat the egg and water. Stir in the remaining ingredients. Brush over dough. Cut slits in top. Bake at 400° for 20-25 minutes or until golden brown. Cut into squares.

[2006]

SLOW-COOKED TURKEY SANDWICHES

yield: 22 servings ∞ **prep: 15 min.**
cook: 3 hours

These sandwiches have been such a hit at office potlucks that I keep copies of the recipe in my desk to hand out.

—*Diane Twait Nelsen, Ringsted, Iowa*

6 **cups cubed cooked turkey**
2 **cups cubed process cheese (Velveeta)**
1 **can (10-3/4 ounces) condensed cream of chicken soup, undiluted**
1 **can (10-3/4 ounces) condensed cream of mushroom soup, undiluted**
1/2 **cup finely chopped onion**
1/2 **cup chopped celery**
22 **wheat sandwich buns, split**

1. In a 3-qt. slow cooker, combine the first six ingredients. Cover and cook on low for 3-4 hours or until onion and celery are tender and cheese is melted. Stir mixture before spooning 1/2 cup onto each bun.

MINCING PARSLEY

Here's a simple trimming tip. Don't clean up a cutting board! Simply place parsley in a small glass container and snip sprigs with kitchen shears until minced.

[2009]

TEXAS-STYLE BEEF BRISKET

yield: 12 servings
prep: 25 min. + marinating
cook: 6-1/2 hours

(Pictured on page 676)

A friend tried this recipe and liked it, so I thought I would try it, too. When my husband told me how much he liked it, I knew I'd be making it often.

—**Vivian Warner, Elkhart, Kansas**

3	tablespoons Worcestershire sauce
1	tablespoon chili powder
2	bay leaves
2	garlic cloves, minced
1	teaspoon celery salt
1	teaspoon pepper
1	teaspoon Liquid Smoke, optional
1	fresh beef brisket (6 pounds)
1/2	cup beef broth

BARBECUE SAUCE:

1	medium onion, chopped
2	tablespoons canola oil
2	garlic cloves, minced
1	cup ketchup
1/2	cup molasses
1/4	cup cider vinegar
2	teaspoons chili powder
1/2	teaspoon ground mustard

1. In a large resealable plastic bag, combine the Worcestershire sauce, chili powder, bay leaves, garlic, celery salt, pepper and Liquid Smoke if desired. Cut brisket in half; add to bag. Seal bag and turn to coat. Refrigerate overnight.

2. Transfer beef to a 5- or 6-qt. slow cooker; add broth. Cover and cook on low for 6-8 hours or until tender.

3. For sauce, in a small saucepan, saute onion in oil until tender. Add garlic; cook 1 minute longer. Stir in the remaining ingredients; heat through.

4. Remove brisket from the slow cooker; discard bay leaves. Place 1 cup cooking juices in a measuring cup; skim fat. Add to the barbecue sauce. Discard remaining juices.

5. Return brisket to the slow cooker; top with sauce mixture. Cover and cook on high for 30 minutes. Thinly slice across the grain; serve with sauce.

Editor's Note: This recipe uses a fresh beef brisket, not corned beef.

[2004]

BACON-COLBY LASAGNA

yield: 2 casseroles (12 servings each)
prep: 20 min. bake: 45 min. + standing

With both bacon and ground beef, this filling dish is a real crowd-pleaser. The recipe came from my grandmother. I've learned so much from helping her in the kitchen.

—**Cathy McCartney, Davenport, Iowa**

2	pounds ground beef
2	medium onions, chopped
2	pounds sliced bacon, cooked and crumbled
2	cans (15 ounces *each*) tomato sauce
2	cans (14-1/2 ounces *each*) diced tomatoes, undrained
2	tablespoons sugar
1	teaspoon salt
24	lasagna noodles, cooked and drained
8	cups (32 ounces) shredded Colby cheese

1. In a Dutch oven, cook beef and onions over medium heat until meat is no longer pink; drain. Stir in the bacon, tomato sauce, tomatoes, sugar and salt; cook until heated through.

2. Spread 1 cup meat sauce in each of two greased 13-in. x 9-in. baking dishes. Layer four noodles, 1-2/3 cups meat sauce, and 1-1/3 cups cheese in each dish. Repeat layers twice.

BACON-COLBY LASAGNA

"This recipe was delicious. A coworker ate three plates. I made it with ground turkey instead of ground beef. Really delicious."
—lab7137

---

3. Cover and bake at 350° for 40 minutes. Uncover; bake 5-10 minutes longer or until bubbly. Let stand for 15 minutes before cutting.

[2007]

CHICKEN SALAD WITH A TWIST

yield: 12 servings ∞ prep: 30 min. + chilling

(Pictured on page 678)

This colorful salad will disappear fast at your next potluck. I got the recipe from my cousin, who always has great dishes at her parties—and this one's no exception!

—*Valerie Holt, Cartersville, Georgia*

8	ounces uncooked spiral pasta
2-1/2	cups cubed cooked chicken
1	medium onion, chopped
2	celery ribs, chopped
1	medium cucumber, seeded and chopped
1/2	cup sliced ripe olives
1/3	cup zesty Italian salad dressing
1/3	cup mayonnaise
2	teaspoons spicy brown *or* horseradish mustard
1	teaspoon lemon juice
1/2	teaspoon salt
1/4	teaspoon pepper
3	plum tomatoes, chopped

1. Cook the pasta according to package directions; drain and rinse in cold water. In a large bowl, combine the pasta, chicken, onion, celery, cucumber and olives.

2. In a small bowl, whisk Italian dressing, mayonnaise, mustard, lemon juice, salt and pepper. Pour over salad and toss to coat. Cover the salad and refrigerate for 2 hours or until chilled. Just before serving, fold in tomatoes.

[1997]

DINNER IN A DISH

yield: 12 servings ∞ prep: 15 min.
bake: 35 min.

I haven't found anyone yet who can resist this saucy casserole topped with mashed potatoes. The frozen peas and canned tomatoes add color and make a helping or two a complete meal.

—*Betty Kay Sitzman*
Wray, Colorado, Field Editor

2	pounds ground beef
1	medium onion, chopped
2	cans (14-1/2 ounces each) diced tomatoes, undrained
3	cups frozen peas
2/3	cup ketchup
1/4	cup minced fresh parsley
2	tablespoons all-purpose flour
2	teaspoons beef bouillon granules
2	teaspoons dried marjoram
1	teaspoon salt
1/2	teaspoon pepper
6	cups hot mashed potatoes (prepared with milk and butter)
2	eggs

1. In a large skillet, cook the beef and onion over medium heat until the beef is no longer pink; drain. Stir in the next nine ingredients. Bring to a boil; cook and stir for 2 minutes.

2. Pour into an ungreased shallow 3-qt. baking dish. Combine the potatoes and eggs. Drop by 1/2 cupfuls onto the beef mixture.

3. Bake, uncovered, at 350° for 35-40 minutes or until bubbly and potatoes are lightly browned.

DINNER IN A DISH

❝This is delicious. I like to make 'dirty mashed potatoes' for on top (using cooked, but not peeled red-skinned potatoes and preparing them with milk and butter).❞
—*mrs_h*

[1994]

BAKED SPAGHETTI

yield: 12 servings ∾ prep: 20 min.
bake: 30 min.

(Pictured on page 673)

Every time I make this cheesy dish, I get requests for the recipe. It puts a different spin on spaghetti and is great for any meal. The leftovers, if there are any, also freeze well for a quick meal later on in the week.

—*Ruth Koberna, Brecksville, Ohio*

---

1   cup chopped onion
1   cup chopped green pepper
1   tablespoon butter
1   can (28 ounces) diced tomatoes, undrained
1   can (4 ounces) mushroom stems and pieces, drained
1   can (2-1/4 ounces) sliced ripe olives, drained
2   teaspoons dried oregano
1   pound ground beef, browned and drained, optional
12 ounces spaghetti, cooked and drained
2   cups (8 ounces) shredded cheddar cheese
1   can (10-3/4 ounces) condensed cream of mushroom soup, undiluted
1/4 cup water
1/4 cup grated Parmesan cheese

---

1. In a large skillet, saute onion and green pepper in butter until tender. Add the tomatoes, mushrooms, olives, oregano. Add ground beef if desired. Simmer, uncovered, for 10 minutes.

2. Place half of the spaghetti in a greased 13-in. x 9-in. baking dish. Layer with half of the vegetable mixture and 1 cup of cheddar cheese. Repeat layers.

3. In a small bowl, combine the soup and water until smooth; pour over the casserole. Sprinkle with the Parmesan cheese. Bake, uncovered, at 350° for 30-35 minutes or until heated through.

BAKED SPAGHETTI

❝Tried this at home for a different twist on the normal spaghetti and my family loved it. I did add garlic powder and salt; other than that, it was perfect. I also cook for my church weekly, so since it was a hit at home, I made it for 125+ church members and received great reviews.❞

—CyndyRH

[2008]

CHILI FOR A CROWD

yield: 24 servings (1 cup each)
prep: 20 min. ∾ cook: 1-1/4 hours

(Pictured on page 675)

A coworker made this hearty, well-seasoned chili for a potluck at work, and I just had to have the recipe. It freezes nicely, too.

—*Linda Boehme, Fairmont, Minnesota*

---

5   pounds ground beef
3   large onions, chopped
5   celery ribs, chopped
2   cans (28 ounces *each*) diced tomatoes, undrained
2   cans (16 ounces *each*) kidney beans, rinsed and drained
1   can (28 ounces) pork and beans
2   cans (10-3/4 ounces *each*) condensed tomato soup, undiluted
2-2/3 cups water
1/4 cup chili powder
3   teaspoons salt
2   teaspoons garlic powder
2   teaspoons seasoned salt
2   teaspoons pepper
1   teaspoon ground cumin
1   teaspoon *each* dried thyme, oregano and rosemary, crushed
1/2 teaspoon cayenne pepper

---

1. In a stockpot, cook beef, onions and celery over medium heat until meat is no longer pink; drain. Stir in remaining ingredients. Bring to a boil. Reduce heat; simmer, uncovered, for 1 hour or until desired thickness is achieved.

CHILI TOPPINGS

Part of the fun of eating chili is in the toppings. Here are a few to try: jalapeno pepper, crushed tortilla chips, ripe olives, green onions, cheese, sour cream or tomatoes.

—*Taste of Home Cooking Experts*

[2000]

PINEAPPLE PEPPER CHICKEN

yield: 12 servings   prep: 30 min.
bake: 1 hour

(Pictured on page 680)

I came up with this recipe years ago by combining a couple of family favorites. Easy and versatile, it's great for potlucks. I can make the sauce ahead and use all wings or leg quarters —whatever is on sale. This is a welcome entree at senior citizen fellowship dinners.

—*Phyllis Minter, Wakefield, Kansas*

4	cups unsweetened pineapple juice
2-1/2	cups sugar
2	cups white vinegar
1-1/2	cups water
1	cup packed brown sugar
2/3	cup cornstarch
1/2	cup ketchup
6	tablespoons reduced-sodium soy sauce
2	teaspoons chicken bouillon granules
3/4	teaspoon ground ginger
2	broiler/fryer chickens (3 to 3-1/2 pounds each), cut up
3	tablespoons canola oil
1	can (8 ounces) pineapple chunks, drained
1	medium green pepper, julienned

1. In a large saucepan, combine the first 10 ingredients; stir until smooth. Bring to a boil; cook and stir for 2 minutes or until thickened. Set aside. In a large skillet over medium-high heat, brown the chicken in oil on all sides.

2. Place chicken in two greased 13-in. x 9-in. baking dishes. Pour reserved sauce over chicken. Bake, uncovered, at 350° for 45 minutes or until chicken juices run clear. Add pineapple and green pepper. Bake 15 minutes longer or until heated through.

[2008]

CHUNKY TURKEY SOUP

yield: 12 servings (1-1/3 cups each)
prep: 20 min. + simmering   cook: 40 min.

This hefty, chunky soup is the perfect answer to your Turkey Day leftovers. Combining the earthy flavors of curry and cumin, no one will mistake it for canned soup!

—*Jane Scanlon, Marco Island, Florida*

1	leftover turkey carcass (from a 12– to 14-pound turkey)
4-1/2	quarts water
1	medium onion, quartered
1	medium carrot, cut into 2-inch pieces
1	celery rib, cut into 2-inch pieces

SOUP:

2	cups shredded cooked turkey
4	celery ribs, chopped
2	cups frozen corn
2	medium carrots, sliced
1	large onion, chopped
1	cup uncooked orzo pasta
2	tablespoons minced fresh parsley
4	teaspoons chicken bouillon granules
1	teaspoon salt
1	teaspoon curry powder
1/2	teaspoon ground cumin
1/2	teaspoon pepper

1. Place the turkey carcass in a stockpot; add the water, onion, carrot and celery. Slowly bring to a boil over low heat; cover and simmer for 1-1/2 hours.

2. Discard the carcass. Strain the broth through a cheesecloth-lined colander. If using immediately, skim fat. Or cool, then refrigerate for 8 hours or overnight; remove fat from surface before using. (The broth may be refrigerated for up to 3 days or frozen for 4-6 months.)

3. Place soup ingredients in a stockpot; add broth. Bring to a boil. Reduce heat; cover and simmer for 30 minutes or until pasta and vegetables are tender.

CHUNKY TURKEY SOUP

"Used bouillon cubes, more carrots and homemade noodles. Will throw out all other turkey and chicken soup recipes and use only this one from now on. Fantastic!"
—*dusty222*

[2007]

HAM BUNDLES

yield: 2 dozen ∽ **prep: 55 min. + rising**
bake: 20 min.

Whenever I serve ham, I can't wait for the leftovers so I can make these ham buns. My husband often warms them up for breakfast.

—*Chris Sendelbach, Henry, Illinois*

1	package (1/4 ounce) active dry yeast
1/4	cup warm water (110° to 115°)
3/4	cup warm 2% milk (110° to 115°)
1/2	cup shortening
3	eggs, lightly beaten
1/2	cup sugar
1-1/2	teaspoons salt
4-1/2	to 4-3/4 cups all-purpose flour

FILLING:

1	large onion, finely chopped
5	tablespoons butter, *divided*
4	cups cubed fully cooked ham, coarsely ground
4	bacon strips, cooked and crumbled, optional
1/4	to 1/3 cup sliced pimiento-stuffed olives, optional
1/2	to 3/4 cup shredded cheddar cheese, optional

1. In a large bowl, dissolve yeast in warm water. Add the milk, shortening, eggs, sugar, salt and 2 cups flour; beat until smooth. Add enough remaining flour to form a soft dough.

2. Turn onto a lightly floured surface; knead until smooth and elastic, about 8 minutes. Place in a greased bowl, turning once to grease top. Cover and let rise in a warm place until doubled, about 1 hour.

3. Meanwhile, in a large skillet, saute the onion in 2 tablespoons butter until tender. Add the ham and mix well; set aside.

4. Punch dough down. Turn onto a lightly floured surface; divide into thirds. Roll each portion into a 16-in. x 8-in. rectangle. Cut each rectangle into eight squares. Place a tablespoonful of the ham mixture in the center of each square. Add bacon, olives and/or cheese if desired. Fold up corners to center of dough; seal edges.

5. Place 2 in. apart on greased baking sheets. Cover and let rise in a warm place until doubled, about 45 minutes.

6. Melt remaining butter; brush over dough. Bake at 350° for 16-20 minutes or until golden brown and filling is heated through. Refrigerate leftovers.

[2005]

MINI SAUSAGE QUICHES

yield: 4 dozen ∽ **prep: 25 min.**
bake: 20 min.

These bite-size quiches are loaded with sausage and cheese, and their crescent-roll base makes preparation a snap. Serve these adorable little muffinettes at any brunch or potluck gathering.

—*Jan Mead*
Milford, Connecticut, Former Field Editor

1/2	pound bulk hot Italian sausage
2	tablespoons dried minced onion
2	tablespoons minced chives
1	tube (8 ounces) refrigerated crescent rolls
4	eggs, lightly beaten
2	cups (8 ounces) shredded Swiss cheese
1	cup (8 ounces) 4% cottage cheese
1/3	cup grated Parmesan cheese

Paprika

---

1. In a large skillet, brown sausage and onion over medium heat for 4-5 minutes or until meat is no longer pink; drain. Stir in chives.

2. On a lightly floured surface, unroll crescent dough into one long rectangle; seal seams and perforations.

HAM BUNDLES

❝I really liked this recipe. The one thing I changed was to use frozen bread loaves instead of making homemade bread. I let them thaw, then rolled, cut, stuffed, and let them rise.❞

—*snoope*

Cut into 48 pieces. Press onto the bottom and up the sides of greased miniature muffin cups.

3. Fill each with about 2 teaspoons of the sausage mixture. In a large bowl, combine the eggs and cheeses. Spoon 2 teaspoonfuls over sausage mixture. Sprinkle with paprika.

4. Bake at 375° for 20-25 minutes or until a knife inserted in the center comes out clean. Cool for 5 minutes before removing from pans to wire racks. Serve warm. Refrigerate leftovers.

[2010]

HOT WING DIP

yield: 4-1/2 cups ∽ prep: 10 min.
cook: 1 hour

(Pictured on page 674)

Since I usually have all the ingredients on hand, this is a great go-to recipe when unexpected guests show up.

—*Coleen Corner, Grove City, Pennsylvania*

- 2 **cups shredded cooked chicken**
- 1 **package (8 ounces) cream cheese, cubed**
- 2 **cups (8 ounces) shredded cheddar cheese**
- 1 **cup ranch salad dressing**
- 1/2 **cup Louisiana-style hot sauce**
Tortilla chips *and/or* **celery sticks**
Minced fresh parsley, optional

1. In a 3-qt. slow cooker, combine the chicken, cream cheese, cheddar cheese, salad dressing and hot sauce. Cover and cook on low for 1-2 hours or until cheese is melted. Serve with chips and/or celery. Sprinkle with parsley if desired.

[2008]

SUN-DRIED TOMATO SPREAD

yield: 28 servings (1/4 cup each)
prep: 15 min. ∽ bake: 20 min.

This creamy, bubbly spread is sure to please. Baked to a golden brown, the cream cheese and mayonnaise give this appetizer a mild flavor.

—*Valerie Elkinton, Gardner, Kansas*

- 2 **packages (8 ounces** *each***) cream cheese, softened**
- 2 **cups mayonnaise**
- 1/4 **cup finely chopped onion**
- 4 **garlic cloves, minced**
- 1 **jar (7 ounces) oil-packed sun-dried tomatoes, drained and chopped**
- 2/3 **cup chopped roasted sweet red peppers**
- 2 **cups (8 ounces) shredded part-skim mozzarella cheese**
- 2 **cups (8 ounces) shredded Italian cheese blend**
- 1 **cup shredded Parmesan cheese,** *divided*
Assorted crackers

1. In a large bowl, combine the cream cheese, mayonnaise, onion and garlic until blended. Stir in tomatoes and red peppers. Stir in the mozzarella cheese, Italian cheese blend and 3/4 cup Parmesan cheese.

2. Transfer to a greased 13-in. x 9-in. baking dish. Sprinkle with remaining Parmesan cheese. Bake, uncovered, at 350° for 18-22 minutes or until edges are bubbly and lightly browned. Serve with crackers.

SUN-DRIED TOMATO SPREAD

"After making this for a family gathering, I'm now being asked all the time to bring this dish! I don't use the roasted sweet red peppers and also, I sometimes add crab. Mmmmmm."

—*gmandatory2*

[2007]

BARBECUE BEEF TACO PLATE

yield: 40-50 servings ∞ **prep: 20 min.**
cook: 20 min.

I prepared this filling appetizer for 200 people at a cookout, and it was gone before I knew it! Everyone loved the barbecued ground beef, veggie and cheese combination.

—Iola Egle
Bella Vista, Arkansas, Field Editor

---

    4   pounds ground beef
    2   envelopes taco seasoning
    1   cup water
    4   packages (8 ounces *each*) cream
        cheese, softened
    1   cup 2% milk
    2   envelopes ranch salad dressing mix
    4   cans (4 ounces *each*) chopped green
        chilies, drained
    1   cup chopped green onions
    3   to 4 cups shredded romaine
    2   cups (8 ounces) shredded cheddar
        cheese
    4   medium tomatoes, seeded and
        chopped
    2   to 3 cups honey barbecue sauce
    2   to 3 packages (13-1/2 ounces *each*)
        tortilla chips

---

1. In a Dutch oven, cook the beef over medium heat until no longer pink; drain. Stir in taco seasoning and water. Bring to a boil. Reduce heat; simmer, uncovered, for 15 minutes.

2. In a large bowl, beat the cream cheese, milk and dressing mix until blended. Spread over two 14-in. plates. Layer with the beef mixture, chilies, onions, romaine, cheese and tomatoes. Drizzle with barbecue sauce.

3. Arrange some tortilla chips around the edge; serve with remaining chips.

BARBECUE BEEF TACO PLATE

❝I was hesitant at first to try this recipe because the barbecue and taco flavors clashed in my mind, but now, this has to be one of my favorite recipes. Thanks.❞
—*kathypercy*

[2008]

SOUTHWESTERN NACHOS

yield: 30 servings ∞ **prep: 40 min.**
cook: 7-1/4 hours

(Pictured on page 675)

Guests will go crazy when you serve two heaping pans of this cheesy nacho casserole featuring tender chunks of pork. And don't worry about filling the chip bowl...the tortilla chips are conveniently baked right in the dish!

—Kelly Byler, Goshen, Indiana

---

    2   boneless whole pork loin roasts
        (3-1/2 pounds *each*)
    1   cup unsweetened apple juice
    6   garlic cloves, minced
    1   teaspoon salt
    1   teaspoon Liquid Smoke, optional
2-1/2   cups barbecue sauce, *divided*
  1/3   cup packed brown sugar
    2   tablespoons honey
    1   package (10 ounces) tortilla chip
        scoops
1-1/2   cups frozen corn
    1   can (15 ounces) black beans, rinsed
        and drained
    1   medium tomato, seeded and chopped
    1   medium red onion, chopped
  1/3   cup minced fresh cilantro
    1   jalapeno pepper, seeded and chopped
    2   teaspoons lime juice
    1   package (16 ounces) process cheese
        (Velveeta), cubed
    2   tablespoons 2% milk

---

1. Cut each roast in half; place in two 5-qt. slow cookers. Combine the apple juice, garlic, salt and Liquid Smoke if desired; pour over the meat. Cover and cook on low for 7-8 hours or until the meat is tender.

2. Shred pork with two forks; place in a very large bowl. Stir in 2 cups barbecue sauce, brown sugar and honey. Divide tortilla chips between

two greased 13-in. x 9-in. baking dishes; top with pork mixture. Combine corn, beans, tomato, onion, cilantro, jalapeno and lime juice; spoon over pork mixture.

3. Bake, uncovered, at 375° for 15-20 minutes or until heated through. Meanwhile, in a small saucepan, melt cheese with milk. Drizzle cheese sauce and remaining barbecue sauce over nachos.

Editor's Note: Wear disposable gloves when cutting hot peppers; the oils can burn skin. Avoid touching your face.

[2006]

SPICY RANCH CHICKEN WINGS
yield: about 4 dozen ∽ prep: 20 min. + marinating
bake: 40 min.

My mother gave me this recipe more than 10 years ago. Since then, I've made these lip-smacking wings for countless parties and get-togethers.

—*Tracy Peters, Corinth, Mississippi*

---

    4 pounds whole chicken wings
  3/4 cup hot pepper sauce
  1/4 cup butter, melted
    3 tablespoons cider vinegar
    1 envelope ranch salad dressing mix
  1/2 teaspoon paprika

---

1. Cut the chicken wings into three sections; discard wing tip sections. In a gallon-size resealable plastic bag, combine hot pepper sauce, butter and vinegar. Add chicken wings; seal bag and toss to coat evenly. Refrigerate for 4-8 hours.

2. Place chicken on racks in two greased 15-in. x 10-in. x 1-in. baking pans. Sprinkle with the dressing mix and paprika. Bake, uncovered, at 350° for 40-50 minutes or until juices run clear.

Editor's Note: Uncooked chicken wing sections (wingettes) may be substituted for whole chicken wings.

[2004]

THREE-MEAT STROMBOLI
yield: 4 loaves (8 slices each) ∽ prep: 20 min. + rising
bake: 25 min.

Here's a spicy appetizer that will have your group clamoring for more. No one believes me when I tell them it's a simple recipe. And I never have any leftovers.

—*Jude Mulvey, East Schodack, New York*

---

    4 loaves (1 pound *each*) frozen bread dough, thawed
  1/2 pound thinly sliced deli salami
  1/2 pound thinly sliced deli ham
  1/2 pound thinly sliced pepperoni
  1/2 pound thinly sliced provolone cheese
    2 cups (8 ounces) shredded part-skim mozzarella cheese
  1/2 cup grated Romano *or* Parmesan cheese
    1 tablespoon garlic powder
    1 tablespoon dried oregano
    1 teaspoon dried parsley flakes
    1 teaspoon pepper
    1 egg yolk, lightly beaten

---

1. Let the dough rise until doubled, according to the package directions.

2. Punch down. Roll each loaf into a 15-in. x 12-in. rectangle. Arrange a fourth of salami, ham, pepperoni and provolone cheese over each rectangle. Sprinkle each with a fourth of the mozzarella cheese, Romano cheese, garlic powder, oregano, parsley and pepper.

3. Roll up each rectangle jelly-roll style, beginning with a long side. Seal seams and ends. Place seam side down on two greased baking sheets. Brush with egg yolk.

4. Bake at 375° for 25-30 minutes or until golden brown. Let stand for 5 minutes before slicing. Serve warm. Refrigerate leftovers.

[2007]

CHOCOLATE CHIP CINNAMON ROLLS

yield: 4 dozen ∽ prep: 45 min. + rising ∽ bake: 25 min./batch

(Pictured on page 677)

I started adding chocolate chips to my cinnamon rolls because several children didn't like the raisins in them. The chocolate and cinnamon are a fun flavor combination. My family loves them, and so does my Sunday school class.

—Patty Wynn, Pardeeville, Wisconsin

4 packages (1/4 ounce *each*) active dry yeast
2-1/2 cups warm water (110° to 115°)
3 cups warm 2% milk (110° to 115°)
1/2 cup butter, softened
2 eggs
3/4 cup honey
4 teaspoons salt
14 cups all-purpose flour
FILLING:
6 tablespoons butter, softened
2-1/4 cups packed brown sugar
1 package (12 ounces) miniature semisweet chocolate chips
3 teaspoons ground cinnamon
GLAZE:
3 cups confectioners' sugar
6 tablespoons butter, softened
1 teaspoon vanilla extract
6 to 8 tablespoons milk

1. In a large bowl, dissolve yeast in warm water; let stand for 5 minutes. Add the milk, butter, eggs, honey, salt and 3 cups flour; beat on low for 3 minutes. Stir in enough remaining flour to form a soft dough.

2. Turn onto a floured surface; knead until smooth and elastic, 6-8 minutes. Place in a large greased bowl; turning once. Cover and let rise in a warm place until doubled, about 1 hour.

3. Punch dough down. Turn onto a floured surface; divide into four pieces. Roll each into a 14-in. x 8-in. rectangle; spread with butter. Combine the brown sugar, chips and cinnamon; sprinkle over dough to within 1/2 in. of edges and press into dough.

4. Roll up jelly-roll style, starting with a long side; pinch seam to seal. Cut each roll into 12 slices. Place cut side down in four greased 13-in. x 9-in. baking dishes. Cover and let rise until doubled, about 30 minutes.

5. Bake at 350° for 25-30 minutes or until golden brown. Cool for 5 minutes; remove from pans to wire racks.

6. For glaze, in a large bowl, combine the confectioners' sugar, butter, vanilla and enough milk to achieve desired consistency; drizzle over warm rolls.

Editor's Note: This recipe can be halved to fit into a mixing bowl.

CHOCOLATE CHIP CINNAMON ROLLS

❝I made these today, and I must say, they turned out awesome! In fact I had to take a picture of them. I only made one change: I halved the recipe as I didn't want 4 dozen. I also sprinkled cinnamon sugar on the dough before putting the chocolate chip mixture on because we like a lot of cinnamon flavor in our rolls. YUMMY!❞
— *ladyhuskerfan*

[2008]

DELIGHTFUL FRUIT SALAD

yield: 24 servings (3/4 cup each)
prep: 35 min. + chilling

I use this recipe as a salad, but my friends say it's good enough to be a dessert! Add more—or less—whipped topping to taste.

—Elaine Bailey, Bloomfield, Indiana

- 1 cup sugar
- 2 tablespoons all-purpose flour
- 1/2 teaspoon salt
- 1-3/4 cups unsweetened pineapple juice
- 2 eggs, lightly beaten
- 1 tablespoon lemon juice
- 1 package (16 ounces) acini di pepe pasta
- 3 cans (11 ounces *each*) mandarin oranges, drained
- 2 cans (20 ounces *each*) pineapple chunks, drained
- 1 can (20 ounces) crushed pineapple, drained
- 1 cup miniature marshmallows
- 1 cup flaked coconut
- 1 carton (12 ounces) frozen whipped topping, thawed

1. In a small saucepan, combine the sugar, flour and salt. Gradually stir in pineapple juice. Bring to a boil, stirring constantly. Stir a small amount of hot mixture into eggs; return all to the pan, stirring constantly. Bring to a gentle boil; cook and stir 2 minutes longer. Remove from the heat. Gently stir in lemon juice.

2. Transfer to a large bowl. Cool to room temperature without stirring. Cover surface of dressing with waxed paper; refrigerate until cooled.

3. Cook the pasta according to package directions; drain and rinse in cold water. Place in a very large bowl; stir in the oranges, pineapple, marshmallows, coconut and dressing. Fold in whipped topping. Cover and chill.

Editor's Note: Acini di pepe are tiny pellets of pasta. This recipe was tested with DaVinci brand pasta. You may substitute 1 pound of macaroni or other pasta if desired.

[1997]

HASH BROWN CASSEROLE

yield: 12-16 servings **prep: 10 min.**
bake: 55 min.

People always go back for seconds whenever I serve these rich, creamy potatoes. This dish is a snap to fix using quick convenient packaged ingredients. It travels well, too.

—Susan Auten
 Dallas, Georgia, Field Editor

- 2 cans (10-3/4 ounces *each*) condensed cream of potato soup, undiluted
- 1 cup (8 ounces) sour cream
- 1/2 teaspoon garlic salt
- 1 package (2 pounds) frozen hash brown potatoes
- 2 cups (8 ounces) shredded cheddar cheese
- 1/2 cup grated Parmesan cheese

1. In a large bowl, combine the soup, sour cream and garlic salt. Stir in potatoes and cheddar cheese.

2. Pour into a greased 13-in. x 9-in. baking dish. Top with the Parmesan. Bake, uncovered, at 350° for 55-60 minutes or until the potatoes are tender.

SWITCH OUT

Don't have cream of potato soup for Hash Brown Casserole? Use cream of mushroom or celery.

—*Taste of Home Cooking Experts*

HASH BROWN CASSEROLE

"I took this to a neighborhood potluck and everyone loved it so much they insisted on getting the recipe. I cut the recipe in half for my own family and sometimes add chopped ham.**"**
—*cafritz*

GRILLED GREEK POTATO SALAD

GRILLED GREEK POTATO SALAD

"My sister made this for graduation. She added the potatoes when they were still warm and the cheese melted a little bit. It was the best potato salad I have ever had. It has become a family favorite."
—*kindyklein*

[2009]

GRILLED GREEK POTATO SALAD

yield: 16 servings (3/4 cup each)
prep: 30 min. ∽ grill: 20 min.

(Pictured on page 674)

My most requested summer recipe, this salad is wonderful warm, cold or at room temperature. Because it's dressed with a vinaigrette, not mayonnaise, it's ideal for outdoor occasions.

—*Robin Jungers, Campbellsport, Wisconsin*

- 3 pounds small red potatoes, halved
- 2 tablespoons olive oil
- 1/2 teaspoon salt
- 1/4 teaspoon pepper
- 1 large sweet yellow pepper, chopped
- 1 large sweet red pepper, chopped
- 1 medium red onion, halved and sliced
- 1 medium cucumber, chopped
- 1-1/4 cups grape tomatoes, halved
- 1/2 pound fresh mozzarella cheese, cubed
- 3/4 cup Greek vinaigrette
- 1/2 cup halved Greek olives
- 1 can (2-1/4 ounces) sliced ripe olives, drained
- 2 tablespoons minced fresh oregano *or* 1 teaspoon dried oregano

1. Drizzle potatoes with oil and sprinkle with salt and pepper; toss to coat. Grill potatoes, covered, over medium heat or broil 4 in. from the heat for 20-25 minutes or until tender.

2. Place in a large bowl. Add remaining ingredients; toss to coat. Serve salad warm or cold.

[2008]

PUMPKIN PECAN LOAVES

yield: 3 loaves (12 slices each)
prep: 20 min. ∽ bake: 45 min. + cooling

This recipe is too good not to share! Three loaves easily feed a crowd, or you can use them as gifts. Either way, these spice-swirled loaves get gobbled up fast.

—*Robin Guthrie, Victorville, California*

- 3/4 cup packed brown sugar
- 1/2 cup all-purpose flour
- 1/3 cup cold butter, cubed
- 1 cup chopped pecans, *divided*
- 2 packages (16 ounces *each*) pound cake mix
- 1 can (15 ounces) solid-pack pumpkin
- 4 eggs
- 3/4 cup water
- 2 teaspoons baking soda
- 2 teaspoons pumpkin pie spice

1. For streusel, combine the brown sugar and flour in a bowl; cut in butter until mixture resembles coarse crumbs. Stir in 1/2 cup pecans; set aside.

2. In a large bowl, combine the pound cake mix, pumpkin, eggs, water, baking soda and pumpkin pie spice; beat on low speed for 30 seconds. Beat on medium for 2 minutes. Fold in the remaining pecans.

3. Divide half of the batter among three greased and floured 8-in. x 4-in. loaf pans. Sprinkle with half of the streusel. Top with remaining batter and streusel.

4. Bake at 350° for 45-50 minutes or until a toothpick inserted near the center comes out clean. Cool for 10 minutes before removing from pans to wire racks to cool completely.

[2005]

CARROT CABBAGE SLAW

yield: 12 servings   prep/total time: 20 min.

(Pictured on page 677)

With a light, homemade honey mayonnaise dressing, this crunchy salad complements almost any main dish.

—*Geordyth Sullivan, Miami, Florida*

- 4 cups shredded cabbage
- 2 cups shredded carrots
- 2 medium Golden Delicious apples, chopped
- 1 cup raisins
- 1/2 cup chopped walnuts
- 1/2 cup honey
- 1 tablespoon lemon juice
- 1 cup (8 ounces) sour cream
- 1/4 teaspoon salt
- 1/8 teaspoon pepper
- 1/8 to 1/4 teaspoon ground nutmeg, optional

1. In a large serving bowl, combine the cabbage, carrots, apples, raisins and walnuts.

2. In a small bowl, combine the honey and lemon juice until smooth. Stir in the sour cream, salt, pepper and nutmeg if desired. Stir into cabbage mixture. Chill until serving.

[2007]

HEARTY BEEF SOUP

yield: 32 servings (8 quarts)
prep: 1 hour   cook: 40 min.

This quick-to-fix soup feeds a lot of hungry people. The tender sirloin pieces and diced veggies make a satisfying meal.

—*Marcia Severson, Hallock, Minnesota, Former Field Editor*

- 4 pounds beef top sirloin steak, cut into 1/2-inch cubes
- 4 cups chopped onions
- 1/4 cup butter
- 4 quarts hot water
- 4 cups sliced carrots
- 4 cups cubed peeled potatoes
- 2 cups chopped cabbage
- 1 cup chopped celery
- 1 large green pepper, chopped
- 8 teaspoons beef bouillon granules
- 1 tablespoon seasoned salt
- 1 teaspoon dried basil
- 1 teaspoon pepper
- 4 bay leaves
- 6 cups tomato juice

1. In two Dutch ovens, brown the beef and onions in butter in batches; drain. Add water, vegetables and seasonings; bring to a boil. Reduce heat; cover and simmer for 20 minutes.

2. Add tomato juice; cover and simmer 10 minutes longer or until the beef and vegetables are tender. Discard bay leaves.

[2002]

BIG-BATCH MEXICAN CORN BREAD

yield: 18-24 servings   prep: 10 min.
bake: 50 min.

I work at an elementary school, and a couple of times a year we have a gathering where everyone brings a favorite dish to pass. A friend shared this delicious corn bread and it was a big hit.

—*Sandy Gaulitz, Spring, Texas*

- 2 packages (8-1/2 ounces *each*) corn bread/muffin mix
- 1 medium onion, chopped
- 2 cups (8 ounces) shredded cheddar cheese
- 1 can (14-3/4 ounces) cream-style corn
- 1-1/2 cups (12 ounces) sour cream
- 4 eggs, lightly beaten
- 1 can (4 ounces) chopped green chilies
- 1/3 cup canola oil
- 1 tablespoon finely chopped jalapeno pepper

1. In a large bowl, combine corn bread mix and onion. Combine the remaining ingredients; add to the corn bread mixture just until moistened. Pour into a greased 13-in. x 9-in. baking dish.

2. Bake at 350° for 50-55 minutes or until lightly browned and the edges pull away from sides of pan and a toothpick inserted near the center comes out clean. Serve warm. Refrigerate leftovers.

Editor's Note: Wear disposable gloves when cutting hot peppers; the oils can burn skin. Avoid touching your face.

[2008]

NUT-TOPPED STRAWBERRY RHUBARB MUFFINS

yield: 1-1/2 dozen
prep: 25 min. ∾ **bake: 20 min. + cooling**

A sweet, crispy topping highlights these tender muffins that are filled with two favorite spring fruits. They're perfect for a brunch or a grab-and-go breakfast.

—Audrey Stallsmith, Hadley, Pennsylvania

2-3/4 cups all-purpose flour
1-1/3 cups packed brown sugar
2-1/2 teaspoons baking powder
1/2 teaspoon baking soda
1/2 teaspoon ground cinnamon
1/4 teaspoon salt
1 egg
1 cup buttermilk
1/2 cup canola oil
2 teaspoons vanilla extract
1 cup chopped fresh strawberries
3/4 cup diced fresh *or* frozen rhubarb
TOPPING:
1/2 cup chopped pecans
1/3 cup packed brown sugar
1/2 teaspoon ground cinnamon
1 tablespoon cold butter

1. In a large bowl, combine the first six ingredients. In another bowl, whisk the egg, buttermilk, oil and vanilla. Stir into the dry ingredients just until moistened. Fold in strawberries and rhubarb. Fill greased or paper-lined muffin cups two-thirds full.

2. In a small bowl, combine the pecans, brown sugar and cinnamon. Cut in the butter until mixture resembles coarse crumbs. Sprinkle over batter.

3. Bake at 400° for 20-25 minutes or until a toothpick inserted near center comes out clean. Cool for 5 minutes; remove from pans to wire racks. Serve warm.

NUT-TOPPED STRAWBERRY RHUBARB MUFFINS

"Great muffins! Even my husband, who doesn't like rhubarb, gobbled them up!"
—JEVINK

Editor's Note: If using frozen rhubarb, measure rhubarb while still frozen, then thaw completely. Drain in a colander, but do not press liquid out.

[1995]

FESTIVE FRUIT SALAD

yield: 16-20 servings
prep/total time: 30 min.

This refreshing, colorful salad has become a favorite of everyone who's tried it. My bowl always comes home empty when I take this salad to a party or cookout.

—Gail Sellers, Savannah, Georgia

1 medium fresh pineapple
3 medium apples (red, yellow and green), cubed
1 small cantaloupe, cubed
1 large firm banana, sliced
1 pint strawberries, halved
1 pint blueberries
4 cups seedless red and green grapes
3 kiwifruit, peeled and sliced
DRESSING:
1 package (3 ounces) cream cheese, softened
1/2 cup confectioners' sugar
2 teaspoons lemon juice
1 carton (8 ounces) frozen whipped topping, thawed
Additional berries for garnish, optional

1. Peel and core pineapple; cut into cubes. Place in a 3- or 4-qt. glass serving bowl. Stir in remaining fruit.

2. In a large bowl, beat the cream cheese until fluffy. Gradually add sugar and lemon juice and mix well. Fold in the whipped topping.

3. Spread over fruit. Garnish with the additional berries if desired. Store leftovers in the refrigerator.

[2008]

FROSTED PINEAPPLE LEMON GELATIN

yield: 12 servings ❧ **prep: 30 min. + chilling**

(Pictured on page 678)

A fruity, summery treat, this dessert uses ginger ale to add a sparkling touch.

—Penny Burpeau
Londonderry, New Hampshire

- 1 can (20 ounces) crushed pineapple
- 2 packages (3 ounces each) lemon gelatin
- 2 cups boiling water
- 2 cups ginger ale, chilled
- 2 large firm bananas, sliced
- 1/2 cup sugar
- 2 tablespoons all-purpose flour
- 1 egg, lightly beaten
- 2 tablespoons butter
- 1 cup heavy whipping cream

1. Drain pineapple, reserving juice; set the pineapple aside. In a large bowl, dissolve gelatin in boiling water. Stir in the ginger ale, bananas and reserved pineapple. Transfer to a 13-in. x 9-in. dish. Refrigerate until firm.

2. For topping, combine sugar and flour in a small saucepan. Gradually whisk in the reserved pineapple juice. Bring to a boil over medium heat; cook and stir for 2 minutes or until thickened.

3. Remove from the heat. Stir a small amount into egg; return all to the pan, stirring constantly. Cook and stir until a thermometer reads 160° and mixture is thickened. Remove from the heat; stir in butter. Cool to room temperature.

4. In a small bowl, beat the cream on high speed until stiff peaks form. Gently fold into custard. Spread over gelatin. Refrigerate for 1 hour or until chilled.

[2004]

APPLE-FETA TOSSED SALAD

yield: 12 servings ❧ **prep/total time: 30 min.**

A friend of mine shared this recipe with me after I raved about her delightful salad at dinner. I have served it for years now, and no matter where I take it, I have to bring along copies of the recipe to hand out.

—Marlene Clark, Apple Valley, California

- 2 tablespoons butter
- 1 cup walnut halves
- 1 tablespoon sugar
- 1/8 teaspoon pepper
- 5 cups torn romaine
- 5 cups torn red leaf lettuce
- 1 medium red apple, chopped
- 1 medium green apple, chopped
- 1/2 to 1 cup crumbled feta cheese

DRESSING:
- 6 tablespoons white wine vinegar
- 2 tablespoons finely chopped onion
- 1-1/2 teaspoons Dijon mustard
- 2 garlic cloves, minced
- 1/2 teaspoon sugar
- 1/4 teaspoon dried oregano
- 1/8 teaspoon salt
- 1/8 teaspoon dried parsley flakes
- 1/8 teaspoon pepper

1. In a skillet, melt butter over medium heat. Add walnuts; sprinkle with sugar and pepper. Stir until well coated.

2. Spread onto a baking sheet. Bake at 350° for 15 minutes or until lightly browned, stirring every 5 minutes. Cool on a wire rack.

3. Meanwhile, in a large bowl, combine the romaine, red lettuce, apples and feta cheese; set aside. In a blender, combine dressing ingredients; cover and process until blended. Drizzle over the salad; toss to coat. Sprinkle with sugared walnuts.

APPLE-FETA TOSSED SALAD

❝I really like the flavors! I used store-bought candied walnuts to save a few minutes. The dressing is delicious, although I added about a tablespoon of olive oil to cut the vinegar a little. Perfect for colder months when it's hard to find veggies for your salad!❞
—Laves_girl

MUSHROOM GREEN
BEAN CASSEROLE

❝I have made this recipe every
Thanksgiving for 10 years! My
husband loves the hint of hot
pepper, sauteed mushrooms
& water chestnuts. Definitely
better than the 'other' green
bean bake!❞
—smfrueh

[1999]

MUSHROOM GREEN
BEAN CASSEROLE

yield: 14 servings ∽ **prep: 15 min.**
bake: 25 min.

*Most traditional green bean casseroles center
around mushroom soup and french-fried
onions. This from-scratch variation features
fresh mushrooms, sliced water chestnuts and
slivered almonds.*

—*Pat Richter, Lake Placid, Florida*

1	pound fresh mushrooms, sliced
1	large onion, chopped
1/2	cup butter
1/4	cup all-purpose flour
1	cup half-and-half cream
1	jar (16 ounces) process cheese spread
2	teaspoons reduced-sodium soy sauce
1/2	teaspoon pepper
1/8	teaspoon hot pepper sauce
1	can (8 ounces) sliced water chestnuts, drained
2	packages (16 ounces each) frozen French-style green beans, thawed and well drained
2	to 3 tablespoons slivered almonds

---

1. In a large skillet, saute mushrooms and
   onion in butter. Stir in the flour until
   blended. Gradually stir in cream. Bring
   to a boil; cook and stir for 2 minutes or
   until thickened. Reduce heat; add the
   cheese spread, soy sauce, pepper and
   hot pepper sauce, stirring until cheese
   is melted. Remove from the heat; stir
   in water chestnuts.

2. Place the beans in an ungreased 3-qt.
   baking dish. Pour the cheese mixture
   over top. Sprinkle with almonds. Bake,
   uncovered, at 375° for 25-30 minutes
   or until bubbly.

[2005]

GIANT GREEN SALAD

yield: 85 servings ∽ **prep/total time: 30 min.**

*I tried this delightful salad at a friend's house
and couldn't wait to have the recipe. It makes a
beautiful presentation for winter holidays, too.*

—*Rebecca Cook Jones*
  Henderson, Nevada, Field Editor

3	tablespoons butter
4	cups walnut halves
1/4	cup sugar
4	bunches romaine, torn
16	cups torn leaf lettuce
6	cups dried cranberries
4	medium sweet yellow peppers, diced
4	cups (16 ounces) crumbled feta cheese

Coarsely ground pepper, optional
DRESSING:

4	envelopes Italian salad dressing mix
2	cups canola oil
1	cup balsamic vinegar
3/4	cup water

---

1. In a large heavy skillet, melt the butter.
   Add the walnuts; cook over medium
   heat until toasted, about 4 minutes.
   Sprinkle with sugar; cook and stir for
   2-4 minutes or until sugar is melted.
   Spread on foil to cool.

2. Meanwhile, in several large salad
   bowls, combine the romaine, lettuce,
   cranberries, yellow peppers, cheese
   and pepper if desired. In a large bowl,
   whisk the dressing ingredients. Pour
   over salad and toss to coat. Sprinkle
   with sugared walnuts.

[2008]

REFRIGERATOR PICKLES

yield: 6 cups ⌘ prep: 25 min. + chilling

These pickles are so good and easy to prepare, you'll want to keep them on hand all the time. My in-laws provide me with produce just so I'll make more!

—Loy Jones, Anniston, Alabama

- 3 cups sliced peeled cucumbers
- 3 cups sliced peeled yellow summer squash
- 2 cups chopped sweet onions
- 1-1/2 cups white vinegar
- 1 cup sugar
- 1/2 teaspoon salt
- 1/2 teaspoon celery seed
- 1/2 teaspoon mustard seed

1. Place the cucumbers, squash and onions in a large bowl; set aside. In a small saucepan, combine the remaining ingredients; bring to a boil. Cook and stir just until the sugar is dissolved. Pour over cucumber mixture; cool.

2. Cover tightly and refrigerate for at least 24 hours. Serve with a slotted spoon.

[2012]

GRILLED POTATO ANTIPASTO SALAD

yield: 20 servings (3/4 cup each)
prep: 20 min. ⌘ grill: 20 min.

Grilling the potatoes gives them a fresh and interesting flavor. With the sweet peppers, cheeses and meat, this salad is not only colorful, but hearty, too. I've served it warm, cold and at room temperature. It's fabulous at any temp.

—Marianna Falce
Osceola Mills, Pennsylvania

- 3 pounds small red potatoes
- 1/4 cup olive oil
- 1/2 teaspoon salt
- 1/4 teaspoon pepper
- 1 package (8 ounces) sliced pepperoni
- 1/2 pound cubed fully cooked ham

- 1 large sweet red pepper, chopped
- 1 large sweet yellow pepper, chopped
- 1 large onion, halved and thinly sliced
- 1 cup chopped cucumber
- 1 cup cubed part-skim mozzarella cheese
- 1 cup cubed cheddar cheese
- 1 cup Italian salad dressing
- 1 can (2-1/4 ounces) sliced ripe olives, drained

1. Scrub potatoes and cut into wedges. Place in a large bowl. Add the oil, salt and pepper; toss to coat.

2. Transfer potatoes to a grill wok or basket. Grill, covered, over medium heat for for 20-25 minutes or until tender, turning occasionally. Transfer to a large bowl. Add the remaining ingredients; toss to coat. Serve warm or cold.

Editor's Note: If you don't want to grill the potatoes, they can be roasted at 425° for 20 minutes or until tender.

[1995]

SUMMER SQUASH SALAD

yield: 12-16 servings ⌘ prep: 15 min. + chilling

Here's a colorful and tasty alternative to coleslaw. Like most gardeners, we usually have an abundance of squash and zucchini in summer, so this dish is inexpensive to prepare and a great way to put this fresh produce to use.

—Diane Hixon, Niceville, Florida, Field Editor

- 4 cups julienned zucchini
- 4 cups julienned yellow squash
- 2 cups sliced radishes
- 1 cup canola oil
- 1/3 cup cider vinegar
- 2 tablespoons Dijon mustard
- 2 tablespoons snipped fresh parsley
- 1-1/2 teaspoons salt
- 1 teaspoon dill weed
- 1/2 teaspoon pepper

1. In a large bowl, toss zucchini, squash and radishes. In a bowl, whisk the remaining ingredients. Pour over vegetables. Cover and refrigerate for at least 2 hours.

[2008]

FIVE-TOPPING BREAD

yield: 2 loaves (10 wedges each)
prep: 30 min. + rising ∞ bake: 20 min.

I love making bread, and you can't go wrong with this recipe. These tender, golden brown loaves have a great combination of seasonings and go perfectly with any meal or sandwiches!

—*Traci Wynne*
Denver, Pennsylvania, Field Editor

---

1 package (1/4 ounce) active dry yeast
3/4 cup warm water (110° to 115°)
1 cup warm 2% milk (110° to 115°)
1/4 cup sugar
1/4 cup butter, softened
1 egg, *separated*
2 teaspoons salt, *divided*
4 to 4-1/2 cups all-purpose flour
1 tablespoon water
1 teaspoon *each* poppy seeds, sesame seeds and caraway seeds
1 teaspoon dried minced onion

---

1. In a large bowl, dissolve yeast in warm water. Add the milk, sugar, butter, egg yolk, 1-1/2 teaspoons salt and 2 cups flour. Beat dough on medium speed for 3 minutes. Stir in enough remaining flour to form a soft dough (dough will be sticky).

2. Turn onto a floured surface; knead until smooth and elastic, about 6-8 minutes. Place in a bowl coated with cooking spray, turning once to coat top. Cover and let rise in a warm place until doubled, about 1 hour.

3. Punch dough down. Turn onto a lightly floured surface; divide in half. Shape into two round loaves. Place each on a baking sheet coated with cooking spray. Beat egg white and water; brush over loaves.

4. Combine the poppy seeds, sesame seeds, caraway seeds, onion and remaining salt; sprinkle over loaves. Cover and let rise in a warm place until doubled, about 30 minutes.

5. Bake at 375° for 20-25 minutes or until golden brown. Cut bread into wedges; serve warm.

[2006]

ROMAINE SALAD WITH AVOCADO DRESSING

yield: 12 servings ∞ prep/total time: 25 min.

This colorful salad looks great on a buffet table and tastes even better. The crunchy corn chips are a nice change from croutons.

—*Sandra Forsyth, Edmonton, Alberta*

---

1 medium ripe avocado, peeled and cubed
1/2 cup mayonnaise
1/4 cup canola oil
3 tablespoons lemon juice
2 garlic cloves, peeled
1/2 teaspoon salt
1/4 teaspoon hot pepper sauce
1 bunch romaine, torn
3 medium tomatoes, cut into wedges
1 cup (4 ounces) shredded cheddar cheese
1 can (2-1/4 ounces) sliced ripe olives, drained
2 green onions, chopped
Corn chips

---

1. For dressing, place the first seven ingredients in a blender; cover and process until blended.

2. In a large bowl, combine the romaine, tomatoes, cheese, olives and onions. Pour dressing over salad; toss to coat. Sprinkle with corn chips.

FIVE-TOPPING BREAD

❝I made this bread for a bake sale at church. A lady called and asked me if I made the bread or bought it because it was so good and looked so professionally done. Great recipe for bread.**❞**
—*clowmom*

BAKED SPAGHETTI, page 658

MEAT 'N' CHEESE STROMBOLI, page 645

GRILLED GREEK POTATO SALAD, page 666

HOT WING DIP, page 661

FOUR-PASTA BEEF BAKE, page 644

CORN TORTILLA CHICKEN LASAGNA, page 644

SOUTHWESTERN NACHOS, page 662

CHILI FOR A CROWD, page 658

REUNION CASSEROLE, page 651

TEXAS-STYLE BEEF BRISKET, page 656

CHOCOLATE CHIP CINNAMON ROLLS, page 664

CARROT CABBAGE SLAW, page 667

SAUSAGE SANDWICH SQUARES, page 655

VANILLA FRUIT SALAD, page 688

FROSTED PINEAPPLE LEMON GELATIN, page 669

ITALIAN SPAGHETTI BAKE, page 654

CHICKEN SALAD WITH A TWIST, page 657

GINGERBREAD PANCAKES WITH BANANA CREAM, page 645

PINEAPPLE PEPPER CHICKEN, page 659

MEATY SPINACH MANICOTTI, page 648

[2009]

ROASTED VEGGIE PASTA

yield: 16 servings (3/4 cup each)
prep: 40 min. ∽ **bake: 25 min.**

My sister gave me this recipe years ago and it has become a favorite make-ahead and company meal. For a heartier dish, pair it with ham and dinner rolls.

—*Robyn Baney, Lexington Park, Maryland*

- 4 small zucchini, halved lengthwise and cut into 1-inch slices
- 2 large onions, cut into wedges
- 2 medium yellow summer squash, halved lengthwise and cut into 1-inch slices
- 2 large sweet yellow peppers, cut into 1-inch pieces
- 1 cup fresh baby carrots, halved lengthwise
- 2 tablespoons olive oil
- 3-1/2 cups uncooked fusilli pasta
- 2 cups (8 ounces) shredded fontina cheese
- 1-1/2 cups heavy whipping cream
- 1/2 cup canned diced tomatoes in sauce
- 1/2 cup grated Parmesan cheese, *divided*
- 2 garlic cloves, minced
- 1/2 teaspoon salt
- 1/4 teaspoon pepper

1. In a large bowl, combine the first six ingredients. Transfer to two greased 15-in. x 10-in. x 1-in. baking pans. Bake at 450° for 20-25 minutes or until crisp-tender; set aside. Reduce the heat to 350°.

2. Cook the pasta according to package directions; drain. Add the fontina cheese, cream, tomatoes, 1/4 cup Parmesan cheese, garlic, salt and pepper to the pasta. Stir in vegetable mixture.

3. Transfer to a greased 13-in. x 9-in. baking dish (dish will be full). Sprinkle with the remaining Parmesan cheese. Bake, uncovered, for 25-30 minutes or until bubbly.

[2003]

THREE-POTATO SALAD

yield: 15 servings ∽ **prep: 20 min. + chilling**
cook: 20 min.

This pretty salad made with white, red and sweet potatoes is as delicious as it looks. The mild dill dressing enhances the tender spuds and onion, especially if you refrigerate it overnight. Even those who don't like sweet potatoes like this salad.

—*Nan Cairo, Greenwood, Delaware*

- 3 medium russet potatoes, peeled and cubed
- 3 medium unpeeled red potatoes, cubed
- 1 large sweet potato, peeled and cubed
- 1 medium onion, chopped
- 1 cup mayonnaise
- 2 tablespoons sugar
- 1 tablespoon white vinegar
- 1 teaspoon salt
- 3/4 teaspoon dill weed
- 1/2 teaspoon pepper

1. Place all of the potatoes in a Dutch oven; cover with water. Cover and bring to a boil. Reduce heat; cook for 20-30 minutes or until tender. Drain and cool.

2. Place potatoes in a large bowl; add onion. In a small bowl, combine the remaining ingredients. Pour over the potato mixture and toss gently to coat. Cover and refrigerate overnight.

THREE-POTATO SALAD

"I brought this salad to a two-day open house at work...customers came back the second day just to eat the potato salad! Awesome recipe!"
—*Marcia Kenimer*

3. Cut corn from cobs; place in a large bowl. Stir in the bread, tomatoes, cheese, basil, asparagus and roasted vegetable mixture. Combine oil and vinegar; drizzle over mixture and toss to coat.

[2010]

ROASTED VEGETABLE SALAD

yield: 12 servings (2/3 cup each)
prep: 30 min. ∞ bake: 20 min.

For even more flavor, mix field greens and crisp, crumbled bacon into this appealing veggie salad. Or whisk a tablespoon of honey into the dressing. Guests will love it!

—*Laura McAllister*
Morganton, North Carolina

- 1 **pound small red potatoes, quartered**
- 2 **medium ears sweet corn, halved**
- 1/2 **pound baby portobello mushrooms, halved**
- 1 **medium sweet red pepper, cut into strips**
- 2 **medium leeks (white portion only), cut into 2-inch lengths**
- 1/4 **cup plus 2 tablespoons olive oil, divided**
- 1/2 **teaspoon salt**
- 1/4 **teaspoon pepper**
- 1/2 **pound fresh asparagus, cut into 2-Inch lengths**
- 2 **garlic cloves, minced**
- 1/2 **teaspoon crushed red pepper flakes**
- 2 **cups cubed French bread**
- 10 **cherry tomatoes, halved**
- 1 **cup (4 ounces) crumbled feta cheese**
- 1 **cup thinly sliced fresh basil leaves**

DRESSING:
- 1/3 **cup olive oil**
- 1/4 **cup red wine vinegar**

---

1. In a large bowl, combine the first five ingredients. Drizzle with 1/4 cup oil; sprinkle with salt and pepper and toss to coat. Place in two greased 15-in. x 10-in. x 1-in. baking pans. Bake at 425° for 20-25 minutes or until the potatoes are tender.

2. Meanwhile, in a large skillet, saute the asparagus in remaining oil until tender. Add garlic and pepper flakes; cook 1 minute longer.

ROASTED VEGETABLE SALAD

❝This dish was sooo yummy! Just the thing for our family dinners—satisfying side dish as well as a vegetarian main dish for the vegetarian in the family.❞
—*donnasc*

[2001]

BAKED POTATO CASSEROLE

yield: 20-24 servings ∞ prep: 15 min.
bake: 50 min.

I created this baked potato casserole with input from friends and neighbors. It makes a great all-around side dish for special meals.

—*Karen Berlekamp, Maineville, Ohio*

- 5 **pounds red potatoes, cooked and cubed**
- 1 **pound sliced bacon, cooked and crumbled**
- 1 **pound cheddar cheese, cubed**
- 4 **cups (16 ounces) shredded cheddar cheese**
- 1 **large onion, finely chopped**
- 1 **cup mayonnaise**
- 1 **cup (8 ounces) sour cream**
- 1 **tablespoon minced chives**
- 1 **teaspoon salt**
- 1/2 **teaspoon pepper**

---

1. In a very large bowl, combine potatoes and bacon. In another large bowl, combine the remaining ingredients; add to the potato mixture and gently toss to coat.

2. Transfer to a greased 4-1/2-qt. baking dish. Bake, uncovered, at 325° for 50-60 minutes or until bubbly and lightly browned.

[2008]

FANCY BEAN SALAD
yield: 12 servings (3/4 cup each)
prep: 20 min. + chilling

Bursting with a colorful crunch, this bean salad is a snap to make—thanks to canned goods and store-bought salad dressing.

—Iola Egle, Bella Vista, Arkansas, Field Editor

- 1 package (16 ounces) frozen gold and white corn, thawed
- 1 can (16 ounces) kidney beans, rinsed and drained
- 1 can (15 ounces) garbanzo beans *or* chickpeas, rinsed and drained
- 1 can (15 ounces) black beans, rinsed and drained
- 1 medium cucumber, finely chopped
- 1 cup finely chopped sweet onion
- 1 medium sweet red pepper, finely chopped
- 1 cup fat-free honey Dijon salad dressing

1. In a large bowl, combine the first seven ingredients. Pour salad dressing over mixture and toss to coat. Cover and refrigerate until serving.

[2007]

CHEDDAR LOAVES
yield: 2 loaves (12 slices each)
prep: 25 min. + rising   bake: 35 min. + cooling

Swirls of cheddar cheese give these loaves an exquisite flavor. Try a slice or two for sandwiches, toasted for breakfast or served on the side with a Caesar salad.

—Agnes Ward, Stratford, Ontario

- 3 teaspoons active dry yeast
- 1/2 cup warm water (110° to 115°)
- 2 cups warm 2% milk (110° to 115°)
- 2 tablespoons butter, melted
- 2 eggs
- 3 teaspoons sugar
- 2 teaspoons salt
- 6 to 6-1/2 cups all-purpose flour
- 2 cups (8 ounces) shredded sharp cheddar cheese

1. In a large bowl, dissolve yeast in warm water. Add the milk, butter, eggs, sugar, salt and 6 cups flour. Beat on medium speed for 3 minutes. Stir in enough remaining flour to form a soft dough.

2. Turn onto a lightly floured surface; knead until smooth and elastic, about 6-8 minutes. Place in a greased bowl, turning once to grease top. Cover and let rise in a warm place until doubled, about 1 hour.

3. Punch the dough down. Turn onto a lightly floured surface; knead cheese into the dough. Divide in half; shape each portion into a 6-in. round loaf. Place on greased baking sheets. Cover and let rise until doubled, about 45 minutes.

4. Bake at 350° for 35-40 minutes or until golden brown. Remove the bread from pans to wire racks to cool. Refrigerate leftovers.

[2009]

MEDITERRANEAN SALAD
yield: 28 servings (3/4 cup each)
prep/total time: 20 min.

Got a crowd coming over for a backyard barbecue? This crisp, big-batch salad makes a great accompaniment to any main dish you fix on the grill.

—Pat Stevens, Granbury, Texas, Field Editor

- 18 cups torn romaine (about 2 large bunches)
- 1 medium cucumber, sliced
- 1 cup crumbled feta cheese
- 1 cup cherry tomatoes, quartered
- 1 small red onion, thinly sliced
- 1/2 cup julienned roasted sweet red peppers
- 1/2 cup pitted Greek olives, halved

DRESSING:
- 2/3 cup olive oil
- 1/4 cup red wine vinegar
- 1 garlic clove, minced
- 1 teaspoon Italian seasoning
- 1/4 teaspoon salt
- 1/4 teaspoon pepper

1. In a very large salad bowl, combine the first seven ingredients. In a small bowl, whisk the dressing ingredients. Drizzle over salad and toss to coat.

[2001]

MOCHA WALNUT BROWNIES

yield: about 2 dozen ∽ **prep: 20 min.**
bake: 30 min.

*These rich, cake-like brownies are generously
topped with a scrumptious mocha frosting.
They're a great dessert to serve company...or to
share when you need a dish to pass. Be sure to
hold back a few if you want leftovers!*

—*Jill Bonanno, Prineville, Oregon*

4	ounces unsweetened chocolate, chopped
1	cup butter, cubed
4	eggs
2	cups sugar
1	teaspoon vanilla extract
1-1/4	cups all-purpose flour
1/2	teaspoon baking powder
1/2	teaspoon salt
1	cup chopped walnuts

MOCHA FROSTING:

4	cups confectioners' sugar
1/2	cup butter, melted
1/3	cup baking cocoa
1/4	cup strong brewed coffee
2	teaspoons vanilla extract

---

1. In a microwave, melt the chocolate
and butter; stir until smooth. Cool
slightly. In a large bowl, beat eggs and
sugar. Stir in the vanilla and chocolate
mixture. Combine the flour, baking
powder and salt; gradually add to the
chocolate mixture. Stir in walnuts.

2. Pour batter into a greased 13-in. x 9-in.
baking pan. Bake at 375° for 30-35
minutes or until a toothpick inserted
near the center comes out clean. Cool
on a wire rack.

3. In a large bowl, beat all the frosting
ingredients until smooth. Spread over
the cooled brownies.

MOCHA WALNUT BROWNIES

"Great brownies! Nice and
chewy—and the frosting is
the best."
—*katlaydee3*

[2010]

LEMON DELIGHT TRIFLE

yield: 12 servings (1 cup each)
prep: 30 min. + chilling

*I like to serve this lemony treat in a trifle bowl.
If you don't have one, a glass 13-in. x 9-in. dish
will also work well.*

—*Kim Wallace*
Dennison, Ohio, Field Editor

3-1/2	cups cold 2% milk
2	packages (3.4 ounces *each*) instant lemon pudding mix
1	package (8 ounces) cream cheese, softened
1/2	cup butter, softened
1/2	cup confectioners' sugar
1	carton (12 ounces) frozen whipped topping, thawed, *divided*
1	package (12 to 14 ounces) lemon cream-filled sandwich cookies, crushed

---

1. In a large bowl, whisk the milk and
pudding mix for 2 minutes. Let stand
for 2 minutes or until soft-set.

2. In another bowl, beat cream cheese,
butter and confectioners' sugar until
smooth. Gradually stir in the pudding
until blended.

3. Set aside 1/4 cup each of whipped
topping and crushed cookies for
garnish. Fold the remaining whipped
topping into the pudding mixture.

4. Place half of the remaining cookies in
a 3-qt. glass bowl; top with half of the
pudding mixture. Repeat layers once.
Garnish with the reserved whipped
topping and crushed cookies. Refrigerate
until serving.

[1994]

CARAMEL APPLE CAKE

yield: 12-16 servings ⚬ **prep: 30 min.**
bake: 1-1/2 hours + cooling

When I go to potlucks, family gatherings or on hunting and fishing trips with my husband and son, this cake is one of my favorite desserts to bring. It's so flavorful and stays moist as long as it lasts, which isn't long!

—Marilyn Paradis
  Woodburn, Oregon, Field Editor

1-1/2 cups canola oil
1-1/2 cups sugar
  1/2 cup packed brown sugar
    3 eggs
    3 cups all-purpose flour
    2 teaspoons ground cinnamon
    1 teaspoon baking soda
  1/2 teaspoon salt
  1/2 teaspoon ground nutmeg
3-1/2 cups diced peeled apples
    1 cup chopped walnuts
    2 teaspoons vanilla extract
CARAMEL ICING:
  1/2 cup packed brown sugar
  1/3 cup half-and-half cream
  1/4 cup butter, cubed
Dash salt
    1 cup confectioners' sugar
Chopped walnuts, optional

1. In a large bowl, combine the oil, sugars and eggs until well blended. Combine the flour, cinnamon, baking soda, salt and nutmeg; gradually add to the sugar mixture until blended. Fold in apples, walnuts and vanilla.

2. Pour into a greased and floured 10-in. tube pan. Bake at 325° for 1-1/2 hours or until a toothpick inserted near the center comes out clean. Cool in pan for 10 minutes before removing to a wire rack to cool completely.

3. In a small heavy saucepan over medium-low heat, cook and stir the brown sugar, cream, butter and salt until sugar is dissolved. Transfer to a small bowl; cool to room temperature. Beat in the confectioners' sugar until smooth; drizzle over the cake. Sprinkle with nuts if desired.

[2004]

PECAN PIE BARS

yield: 6-8 dozen ⚬ **prep: 20 min.**
bake: 45 min.

I love to cook large quantities and do most of the cooking for our church functions. People seem to enjoy these luscious bars even more than pecan pie.

—Clara Honeyager
  North Prairie, Wisconsin

    6 cups all-purpose flour
1-1/2 cups sugar
    1 teaspoon salt
    2 cups cold butter, cubed
FILLING:
    8 eggs
    3 cups sugar
    3 cups corn syrup
  1/2 cup butter, melted
    3 teaspoons vanilla extract
    5 cups chopped pecans

1. In a large bowl, combine the flour, sugar and salt. Cut in the butter until crumbly. Press onto the bottom and up the sides of two greased 15-in. x 10-in. x 1-in. baking pans. Bake at 350° for 18-22 minutes or until crust edges are beginning to brown and bottom is set.

2. For filling, combine the eggs, sugar, corn syrup, butter and vanilla in a large bowl. Stir in pecans. Pour over crust.

3. Bake 25-30 minutes longer or until edges are firm and center is almost set. Cool in pans on wire racks. Cut into bars. Refrigerate until serving.

CARAMEL APPLE CAKE

"This cake has become an absolute favorite with family and friends. A coworker once said: It makes music in my mouth! The best apple cake recipe I have ever made. Thank you, Marilyn!"
—PennyPoppins

[2001]

PEANUT BUTTER SHEET CAKE

yield: 20-24 servings ∽ **prep: 15 min.**
bake: 20 min. + cooling

I received the recipe for Peanut Butter Sheet Cake from a minister's wife, and my family loves it.

—*Brenda Jackson, Garden City, Kansas*

2	cups all-purpose flour
2	cups sugar
1	teaspoon baking soda
1/2	teaspoon salt
1	cup water
3/4	cup butter, cubed
1/2	cup chunky peanut butter
1/4	cup canola oil
2	eggs
1/2	cup buttermilk
1	teaspoon vanilla extract

GLAZE:

2/3	cup sugar
1/3	cup evaporated milk
1	tablespoon butter
1/3	cup chunky peanut butter
1/3	cup miniature marshmallows
1/2	teaspoon vanilla extract

1. In a large bowl, combine the flour, sugar, baking soda and salt; set aside. In a small saucepan, bring water and butter just to a boil; stir in peanut butter and oil until blended. Add to dry ingredients. Combine the eggs, buttermilk and vanilla; add to peanut butter mixture and mix well.

2. Pour into a greased 15-in. x 10-in. x 1-in. baking pan. Bake at 350° for 20-25 minutes or until a toothpick inserted near the center comes out clean.

3. Meanwhile, combine the sugar, milk and butter in a large saucepan. Bring to a boil, stirring constantly; cook and stir for 2 minutes. Remove from the

heat; stir in peanut butter, marshmallows and vanilla until the marshmallows are melted. Spoon over the warm cake and carefully spread the glaze over the top. Cool completely.

Editor's Note: Reduced-fat peanut butter is not recommended for this recipe.

[1998]

BUTTERSCOTCH PECAN DESSERT

yield: 16-20 servings
prep: 15 min. + chilling
bake: 20 min. + cooling

Light and creamy, this terrific treat never lasts long when I serve it. The fluffy cream cheese layer topped with cool butterscotch pudding is a lip-smacking combination.

—*Becky Harrison, Albion, Illinois*

1/2	cup cold butter, cubed
1	cup all-purpose flour
3/4	cup chopped pecans, *divided*
1	package (8 ounces) cream cheese, softened
1	cup confectioners' sugar
1	carton (8 ounces) frozen whipped topping, thawed, *divided*
3-1/2	cups cold 2% milk
2	packages (3.4 *or* 3.5 ounces *each*) instant butterscotch *or* vanilla pudding mix

1. In a small bowl, cut the butter into the flour until crumbly; stir in 1/2 cup pecans. Press into an ungreased 13-in. x 9-in. baking dish. Bake at 350° for 20 minutes or until lightly browned. Cool.

2. In a small bowl, beat the cream cheese and sugar until fluffy. Fold in 1 cup whipped topping; spread over crust.

3. In a large bowl, whisk the milk and pudding mix for 2 minutes. Let stand for 2 minutes or until soft-set; pour over cream cheese layer. Refrigerate

---

PEANUT BUTTER SHEET CAKE

❝This cake is VERY GOOD! I added my own touch....1/2 to 3/4 cup of chocolate chips in the frosting (at the same time you add the marshmallows and peanut butter). And wow! You have chocolate to go along with your peanut butter! This cake got rave reviews at the office for the Boss Day celebration!❞

—*bartim718*

---

for 15-20 minutes or until set. Top with remaining whipped topping and pecans. Refrigerate for 1-2 hours.

[2002]

TOFFEE CHIP COOKIES
yield: 12 dozen ∽ **prep: 15 min.**
bake: 10 min./batch

These cookies combine several mouthwatering flavors. The generous size of the batch gives me plenty of scrumptious cookies to have on hand and extras to send to our sons at college.

—*Kay Frances Ronnenkamp*
Albion, Nebraska

- 1 cup butter, softened
- 1/2 cup canola oil
- 1 cup sugar
- 1 cup packed brown sugar
- 2 eggs
- 1 teaspoon vanilla extract
- 3-1/2 cups all-purpose flour
- 1 teaspoon cream of tartar
- 1 teaspoon baking soda
- 1 teaspoon salt
- 3 cups crisp rice cereal
- 1 cup quick-cooking oats
- 1 cup flaked coconut
- 1 cup chopped pecans
- 1 cup milk chocolate English toffee bits *or* brickle toffee bits

1. In a large bowl, beat the butter, oil and sugars until blended. Beat in eggs, then vanilla. Combine the flour, cream of tartar, baking soda and salt; add to sugar mixture and mix well. Stir in remaining ingredients.

2. Drop by tablespoonfuls 2 in. apart onto ungreased baking sheets. Bake at 350° for 10-12 minutes or until lightly browned. Remove to wire racks to cool.

[2011]

RAZZY JAZZY BERRY TARTS
yield: 3 dozen ∽ **prep: 1 hour**
bake: 25 min.

I serve these fresh-fruit tarts at summer parties. I often add slivered almonds to the filling.

—*Nicole Chatron, Tulsa, Oklahoma*

- 1 cup butter, softened
- 2 packages (3 ounces *each*) cream cheese, softened
- 2 cups all-purpose flour
- 1/2 teaspoon salt
- 1-1/2 cups fresh blueberries
- 2/3 cup blueberry preserves
- 1-1/2 cups fresh raspberries
- 2/3 cup seedless raspberry jam

1. In a large bowl, beat butter and cream cheese until smooth. Combine flour and salt; gradually add to creamed mixture. Drop by scant tablespoonfuls into 36 greased miniature muffin cups. With well-floured hands, press dough onto bottoms and up sides of cups; flute edges if desired.

2. Bake tarts at 325° for 20-25 minutes or until golden brown. Cool for 5 minutes before removing from pans to wire racks to cool completely.

3. On a lightly floured surface, roll remaining dough to 1/8-in. thickness. Cut stars with a floured 1-1/2-in. star-shaped cookie cutter; cut 1/4-in. stripes with a small knife. Place the stars and stripes on ungreased baking sheets. Bake at 325° for 4-6 minutes or until lightly browned.

4. In a small bowl, combine blueberries and blueberry preserves; spoon into half of the tarts. In another bowl, combine raspberries and raspberry jam; spoon into remaining tarts. Top with cut-outs.

TOFFEE CHIP COOKIES

"I have been making these since they first appeared in the magazine to great reviews. Everyone wants the recipe. My son is now allergic to tree nuts, so I left out the nuts and they still were yummy! They've even been requested as a repeat at a cookie party."
—*Kathleen C.*

LAYERED LEMON PIES

[2010]

LAYERED LEMON PIES

yield: 2 pies (10 servings each)
prep: 55 min. + chilling

*My sister shared this recipe with me and it is
simply fabulous. The secret to the great flavor
is using fresh lemon juice.*

—*Nanette Sorensen, Taylorsville, Utah*

Pastry for two single-crust pies (9 inches)
- 1-1/2   cups sugar
- 6   tablespoons cornstarch
- 1/4   teaspoon salt
- 2   cups cold water
- 3   egg yolks, lightly beaten
- 1/3   cup lemon juice
- 1/4   cup butter, cubed
- 1   teaspoon grated lemon peel
- 1   teaspoon lemon extract
- 3   drops yellow food coloring, optional

SECOND LAYER:
- 1   package (8 ounces) cream cheese, softened
- 1   cup confectioners' sugar
- 1-1/2   cups cold 2% milk
- 2   packages (3.4 ounces each) instant lemon pudding mix

TOPPING:
- 1   package (8 ounces) cream cheese, softened
- 1   cup confectioners' sugar
- 1   carton (16 ounces) frozen whipped topping, thawed

1. Line two 9-in. pie plates with pastry; trim and flute edges. Line unpricked pastry with a double thickness of heavy-duty foil. Bake at 450° for 8 minutes. Remove foil; bake 5-7 minutes longer or until golden brown. Cool on wire racks.

2. In a large saucepan, combine the sugar, cornstarch and salt. Stir in water until smooth. Cook and stir over medium-high heat until thickened and bubbly. Reduce heat; cook and stir 2 minutes longer. Remove from the heat.

3. Stir a small amount of hot filling into egg yolks; return all to the pan, stirring constantly. Bring to a gentle boil; cook and stir 2 minutes longer. Remove from the heat. Gently stir in the lemon juice, butter, lemon peel, extract and food coloring if desired. Cool to room temperature without stirring. Spread lemon mixture into crusts. Refrigerate for 30 minutes or until firm.

4. In a large bowl, beat the cream cheese and confectioners' sugar until smooth. Gradually beat in milk. Add pudding mix; beat 2 minutes longer. Let stand for 2 minutes or until soft-set. Gently spread over lemon layer. Refrigerate for 30 minutes or until set.

5. For topping, in a large bowl, beat the cream cheese and confectioners' sugar until smooth. Fold in whipped topping. Spread over tops of pies. Refrigerate until set.

[1997]

VANILLA FRUIT SALAD

yield: 64 servings (1/2 cup each)
prep: 30 min. + chilling

(*Pictured on page 678*)

*I often serve this fruit salad as a side dish with
a variety of main courses. It has a nice sweet
taste, which also makes it perfect for dessert.*

—*Geraldine Grisdale*
Mt. Pleasant, Michigan, Field Editor

- 5   cans (20 ounces each) plus 1 can (8 ounces) pineapple chunks
- 4   packages (5.1 ounces each) instant vanilla pudding mix
- 8   cans (15 ounces each) mandarin oranges, drained
- 10   medium red apples, chopped

1. Drain pineapple, reserving juice; set the pineapple aside. Add enough cold water to juice to make 6 cups.

2. In a very large bowl, whisk the juice mixture and pudding mix for 2 minutes. Let stand for 2 minutes or until soft-set. Stir in oranges, apples and reserved pineapple. Refrigerate until chilled.

3. Fold in marshmallows and whipped cream. Spoon over the cherry layer; sprinkle with the pecans. Cover and refrigerate for 2 hours or until set.

[2007]

CHERRY GELATIN SUPREME

yield: 12 servings ∞ **prep: 20 min. + chilling**

When I was growing up, this yummy, easy-to-make dessert was always on the menu at holiday functions. Years ago, my aunt gave me the recipe, and now when I make it for my family, I think of her.

—Janice Rathgeb, Brighton, Illinois

  2 cups water, *divided*
  1 package (3 ounces) cherry gelatin
  1 can (21 ounces) cherry pie filling
  1 package (3 ounces) lemon gelatin
  1 package (3 ounces) cream cheese, softened
1/3 cup mayonnaise
  1 can (8 ounces) crushed pineapple, undrained
  1 cup miniature marshmallows
1/2 cup heavy whipping cream, whipped
  2 tablespoons chopped pecans

1. In a large saucepan, bring 1 cup water to a boil. Stir in cherry gelatin until dissolved. Stir in pie filling. Pour into an 11-in. x 7-in. dish. Cover and refrigerate for 2 hours or until set.

2. In a small saucepan, bring remaining water to a boil. Stir in lemon gelatin until dissolved. In a small bowl, beat the cream cheese and mayonnaise until smooth. Beat in lemon gelatin and pineapple. Cover and refrigerate for 45 minutes.

[2005]

PUMPKIN PIES FOR A GANG

yield: 8 pies (6-8 servings each)
prep: 50 min. ∞ **bake: 1 hour + cooling**

When I think of cooking for a crowd during fall, pumpkin pie always comes to mind. Guests love this traditional treat, and the recipe is perfect for a large gathering...it fills eight pie shells.

—Edna Hoffman
Hebron, Indiana, Field Editor

    4 packages (15 ounces *each*) refrigerated pie pastry
  16 eggs, lightly beaten
    4 cans (29 ounces *each*) solid-pack pumpkin
1/2 cup dark corn syrup
    9 cups sugar
1-1/4 cups all-purpose flour
    1 cup nonfat dry milk powder
    4 teaspoons salt
    4 teaspoons *each* ground ginger, cinnamon and nutmeg
    1 teaspoon ground cloves
    8 cups 2% milk

1. Unroll pastry; line eight 9-in. pie plates with one sheet of pastry. Flute edges; set aside. In very large bowl, combine the eggs, pumpkin and corn syrup. In another large bowl, combine the dry ingredients; place half in each of two large bowls. Stir half of the pumpkin mixture into each bowl. Gradually stir in milk until smooth.

2. Pour into pie shells. Bake at 350° for 60-70 minutes or until a knife inserted near the center comes out clean. Cool on wire racks. Store in the refrigerator.

PUMPKIN PIES FOR A GANG

"My husband is in the Army and we hang out with a lot of the single soldiers. This recipe is loved by them all! It has become tradition that, for all the dinner parties we have, we make these. But we never seem to have enough—even though the recipe makes eight pies!"
—chocoholic chicka

HONEY-GLAZED HENS WITH FRUIT STUFFING

"My wife and I found this recipe and wanted to try something different and light. We had never tried hens before, so although both nervous at first, we decided to go for it. And OH MY GOD, we were quite pleased. My family (4 kids included) all LOVED it!!! The taste was impeccable, with the honey and the fruit stuffing combined, awesome... we ate the entire hen and are trying it again for family and friends on Thanksgiving."
—*smashe2003*

[2010]

HONEY-GLAZED HENS WITH FRUIT STUFFING

**yield: 4 servings ❧ prep: 30 min.
bake: 1 hour + standing**

(Pictured on page 713)

My husband really likes Cornish hens, so I searched for a recipe I could use during the holidays. My family loves this fruit stuffing.

—Denise Albers
Freeburg, Illinois, Field Editor

1/2	cup butter, cubed
1/4	cup chopped onion
1/4	cup chopped celery
4	cups cubed day-old bread
1/2	cup dried fruit bits
1/2	cup water
1/8	teaspoon ground allspice

CORNISH HENS:

4	Cornish game hens (20 to 24 ounces each)
1/4	teaspoon salt
1/8	teaspoon pepper
2	tablespoons butter, melted
1	tablespoon honey

---

1. In a large skillet over medium heat, melt butter. Add onion and celery; cook and stir until tender. Stir in the bread, fruit bits, water and allspice; cover and cook for 2-3 minutes or until heated through.

2. Loosely stuff hens with stuffing. Tuck wings under hens; tie drumsticks together. Sprinkle with the salt and pepper. Place breast side up on a rack in a shallow roasting pan. Combine butter and honey; drizzle over hens.

3. Bake, uncovered, at 350° for 1 to 1-1/2 hours or until a thermometer reads 180° for the hens and 165° for stuffing, basting occasionally with pan drippings. Cover loosely with foil if hens brown too quickly. Cover and let stand for 10 minutes before serving.

[1998]

SWEET 'N' SPICY CHICKEN

yield: 4 servings ❧ prep/total time: 20 min.

My family loves this tender chicken that has a spicy sauce. Peach preserves add just a touch of sweetness, while taco seasoning and salsa give this dish some kick. This entree can be made even zippier yet by adding more taco seasoning and using spicier salsa.

—Sheri White, Higley, Arizona

3	tablespoons taco seasoning
1	pound boneless skinless chicken breasts, cut into 1/2-inch cubes
1	to 2 tablespoons canola oil
1	jar (11 ounces) chunky salsa
1/2	cup peach preserves

Hot cooked rice

---

1. Place the taco seasoning in a large resealable plastic bag; add chicken and toss to coat.

2. In a large skillet, brown the chicken in oil until no longer pink. Combine the salsa and preserves; stir into skillet. Bring to a boil. Reduce heat; cover and simmer for 2-3 minutes or until heated through. Serve with rice.

[2008]

CHICKEN & TOMATO RISOTTO

yield: 4 servings ⸺ prep: 25 min.
cook: 25 min.

(Pictured on page 715)

If you're looking for Italian comfort food, this is it! By using store-bought spaghetti sauce, you save time when preparing this creamy dish. You'll enjoy every bite!

—*Lorraine Caland, Thunder Bay, Ontario*

3 cups chicken broth
1 pound boneless skinless chicken breasts, cut into 1-inch cubes
1 tablespoon olive oil
1-1/2 cups sliced fresh mushrooms
1 medium onion, chopped
2 tablespoons butter
1 garlic clove, minced
1 cup uncooked arborio rice
1 cup meatless spaghetti sauce
1/4 cup grated Parmesan cheese

1. In a small saucepan, heat broth and keep warm. In a large skillet, saute chicken in oil until no longer pink. Remove and keep warm.

2. In the same skillet, saute the mushrooms and onion in butter until crisp-tender. Add garlic; cook 1 minute longer. Add rice; cook and stir for 3 minutes. Carefully stir in 1 cup warm broth. Cook and stir until all of the liquid is absorbed.

3. Add the remaining broth, 1/2 cup at a time, stirring constantly. Allow the liquid to absorb between additions. Cook until risotto is creamy and rice is almost tender. (Cooking time is about 20 minutes.)

4. Stir in the spaghetti sauce, cheese and reserved chicken; cook and stir until mixture is thickened.

[2012]

SKILLET-ROASTED LEMON CHICKEN WITH POTATOES

yield: 4 servings ⸺ prep: 20 min.
bake: 25 min.

This is a meal I have my students make in our nutrition unit. It has a delicious lemon-herb flavor and is simple to make.

—*Mindy Rottmund*
Lancaster, Pennsylvania

1 tablespoon olive oil, *divided*
1 medium lemon, thinly sliced
4 garlic cloves, minced and *divided*
1/4 teaspoon grated lemon peel
1/2 teaspoon salt, *divided*
1/4 teaspoon pepper, *divided*
8 boneless skinless chicken thighs (4 ounces *each*)
1/4 teaspoon dried rosemary, crushed
1 pound fingerling potatoes, halved lengthwise
8 cherry tomatoes

1. Grease a 10-inch cast-iron skillet with 1 teaspoon oil. Arrange lemon slices in a single layer in skillet.

2. Combine 1 teaspoon oil, 2 minced garlic cloves, lemon peel, 1/4 teaspoon salt and 1/8 teaspoon pepper; rub over chicken. Place over lemon.

3. In a large bowl, combine rosemary and the remaining oil, garlic, salt and pepper. Add potatoes and tomatoes; toss to coat. Arrange over chicken. Bake, uncovered, at 450° for 25-30 minutes or until chicken is no longer pink and potatoes are tender.

CHICKEN & TOMATO RISOTTO

"So easy and so delicious! I added asparagus, which really added a nice fresh texture. I also replaced the onion with leek. This is definitely one of my favorite risottos to make!"
—*ChrissyLukken*

[2011]

NUTTY CHICKEN STIR-FRY

yield: 5 servings ∾ prep: 20 min.
cook: 15 min.

(Pictured on page 713)

*My daughter makes this yummy stir-fry often
for our family. It goes together so quickly. The
peanuts and chunky peanut butter give it a nice
crunch. Leftovers, if there are any, are great!*

—*Shirley Conrad
High Amana, Iowa, Field Editor*

1 pound boneless skinless chicken
breasts, chopped
1 tablespoon canola oil
1 package (16 ounces) frozen stir-fry
vegetable blend
6 garlic cloves, minced
2 tablespoons brown sugar
4 teaspoons cornstarch
3/4 teaspoon ground ginger
1/2 cup chicken broth
1/3 cup reduced-sodium soy sauce
1/4 cup chunky peanut butter
5 to 6 drops hot pepper sauce
3 cups shredded cabbage
3/4 cup salted peanuts, chopped
Hot cooked rice

1. In a large skillet or wok, stir-fry the
chicken in oil for 2 minutes. Add the
vegetables; cook 4 minutes longer. Add
garlic; stir-fry until the chicken is no
longer pink and the vegetables are
crisp-tender.

2. In a small bowl, combine the brown
sugar, cornstarch and ginger; stir in the
broth, soy sauce, peanut butter and
pepper sauce until blended. Pour over
chicken mixture.

3. Bring to a boil; cook and stir for 2
minutes or until thickened. Add the
cabbage; cook 2 minutes longer or
until crisp-tender. Sprinkle with the
peanuts. Serve with rice.

[1999]

CHICKEN STROGANOFF

yield: 4 servings ∾ prep/total time: 30 min.

*I came up with this recipe, a variation on beef
Stroganoff, as a way to use up roasted chicken.
It was a hit. I'm usually the only one in my
family who enjoys noodles, but even our son
will have more when they're topped with the
creamy poultry dish.*

—*Laura Schimanski, Coaldale, Alberta*

4 bacon strips, diced
1 pound boneless skinless chicken
breasts, cut into 1/4-inch strips
1 medium onion, chopped
2 jars (4-1/2 ounces *each*) sliced
mushrooms, drained
2 garlic cloves, minced
1-1/2 cups chicken broth
1/2 teaspoon salt
1/8 teaspoon paprika
Pepper to taste
2 tablespoons all-purpose flour
1 cup (8 ounces) sour cream
Hot cooked noodles
Additional paprika, optional

1. In a large skillet, cook the bacon until
crisp. Using a slotted spoon, remove
bacon to paper towels to drain;
reserving 2 tablespoons drippings; set
bacon aside.

2. In the drippings, cook the chicken,
onion and mushrooms until the
chicken is no longer pink. Add garlic;
cook 1 minute longer. Add the broth,
salt, paprika, pepper and bacon. Cover
and simmer for 10 minutes.

3. Combine flour and sour cream until
smooth; add to the skillet. Bring to a
boil; cook and stir for 2 minutes or
until thickened. Serve with noodles.
Sprinkle with paprika if desired.

CHICKEN STROGANOFF

❝This recipe is really good
and it was hard not to have
a second helping!❞
—*4Huskers*

[1997]

GRILLED GAME HENS

yield: 4 servings ∞ **prep: 5 min. + marinating grill: 35 min.**

I love to cook and bake just about everything, but grilling is my specialty. These game hens pick up wonderful flavor from a sweet and refreshing marinade.

—Kriss Erickson, Kalauea, Hawaii

2	Cornish game hens (20 to 24 ounces each), split lengthwise
1/2	cup olive oil
2/3	cup white wine vinegar
8	garlic cloves, minced
1/3	cup minced fresh cilantro
1/3	cup honey
1/3	cup reduced-sodium soy sauce
2	to 3 tablespoons ground ginger
1/2	teaspoon crushed red pepper flakes

Dash pepper

---

1. Place the hens in a large resealable plastic bag. In a small bowl, combine the remaining ingredients. Pour half of the marinade into the bag; add the hens. Seal the bag and turn to coat. Refrigerate for at least 1 hour. Cover and refrigerate remaining marinade.

2. Drain and discard marinade from hens. Place hens in a 13-in. x 9-in. disposable foil pan. Pour the reserved marinade over hens; cover pan.

3. Grill, covered, over medium-hot heat for 35-40 minutes or until a thermometer reads 180° in the thigh and meat juices run clear, basting frequently. Place the hens directly over heat for the last 3-4 minutes of cooking time, turning once.

[2008]

FORGOTTEN JAMBALAYA

yield: 11 servings ∞ **prep: 35 min. cook: 4-1/4 hours**

(Pictured on page 715)

During chilly months, I fix this jambalaya at least once a month. It's so easy...just chop the vegetables, dump everything in the slow cooker and forget it! Even my sons, who are picky about spicy things, like this dish.

—Cindi Coss, Coppell, Texas

1	can (14-1/2 ounces) diced tomatoes, undrained
1	can (14-1/2 ounces) beef *or* chicken broth
1	can (6 ounces) tomato paste
2	medium green peppers, chopped
1	medium onion, chopped
3	celery ribs, chopped
5	garlic cloves, minced
3	teaspoons dried parsley flakes
2	teaspoons dried basil
1-1/2	teaspoons dried oregano
1-1/4	teaspoons salt
1/2	teaspoon cayenne pepper
1/2	teaspoon hot pepper sauce
1	pound boneless skinless chicken breasts, cut into 1-inch cubes
1	pound smoked sausage, halved and cut into 1/4-inch slices
1/2	pound uncooked medium shrimp, peeled and deveined

Hot cooked rice

---

1. In a 5-qt. slow cooker, combine the tomatoes, broth and tomato paste. Stir in the green peppers, onion, celery, garlic, seasonings and pepper sauce. Stir in chicken and sausage.

2. Cover and cook on low for 4-6 hours or until chicken is no longer pink. Stir in the shrimp. Cover and cook 15-30 minutes longer or until shrimp turn pink. Serve with rice.

FORGOTTEN JAMBALAYA

"This was soooo unbelievably good! I only made a half recipe to try the first time, and I didn't have shrimp, but it was so good anyways. The flavor was perfect, not too spicy. And of course being able to throw it all in the slow cooker is such a bonus! I use mine as often as I can to make life easier."
—bdstickles

[2004]

GRILLED THIGHS AND DRUMSTICKS

yield: 12-14 servings
prep: 10 min. + marinating
grill: 30 min.

This chicken is juicy, has great barbecue flavor and makes a big batch, so it's perfect for summer picnics and family reunions.

—*Brenda Beachy, Belvidere, Tennessee*

2-1/2 **cups packed brown sugar**
2 **cups water**
2 **cups cider vinegar**
2 **cups ketchup**
1 **cup canola oil**
4 **tablespoons salt**
3 **tablespoons prepared mustard**
4-1/2 **teaspoons Worcestershire sauce**
1 **tablespoon reduced-sodium soy sauce**
1 **teaspoon pepper**
1 **teaspoon Liquid Smoke, optional**
10 **pounds bone-in chicken thighs and chicken drumsticks**
1/2 **teaspoon seasoned salt**

1. In a large bowl, combine the first 11 ingredients. Pour the marinade into two large resealable plastic bags; add equal amounts of the chicken to each bag. Seal the bags and turn to coat; refrigerate overnight.

2. Drain and discard marinade. Prepare grill for indirect heat. Using long-handled tongs, moisten a paper towel with cooking oil and lightly coat the grill rack.

3. Sprinkle chicken with seasoned salt. Grill chicken skin side down, covered, over indirect medium heat for 15-20 minutes on each side or until a thermometer reads 180°.

GRILLED THIGHS AND DRUMSTICKS

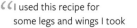

"I used this recipe for some legs and wings I took camping with me. It kept in the cooler very well and was very tasty!!"
—*Planetcaravan19f*

[2000]

ORANGE WALNUT CHICKEN

yield: 4 servings
prep: 10 min. + marinating
cook: 30 min.

(*Pictured on page 714*)

For an impressive main dish that's not tricky to prepare, try this mouthwatering chicken. With orange juice concentrate, orange juice, lemon juice and marmalade, the pretty sauce has a zesty taste.

—*TerryAnn Moore, Vineland, New Jersey*

1/3 **cup thawed orange juice concentrate**
5 **tablespoons canola oil,** *divided*
2 **tablespoons reduced-sodium soy sauce**
2 **garlic cloves, minced**
4 **boneless skinless chicken breast halves (4 ounces** *each***)**
1/2 **cup coarsely chopped walnuts**
1 **tablespoon butter**
4 **green onions, thinly sliced,** *divided*
1/2 **cup orange marmalade**
1/2 **cup orange juice**
1/4 **cup lemon juice**
2 **tablespoons honey**
1 **to 2 tablespoons grated orange peel**
2 **to 3 teaspoons grated lemon peel**
1/2 **teaspoon salt**
1/8 **teaspoon pepper**
Hot cooked rice

1. In a small bowl, combine the orange juice concentrate, 4 tablespoons oil, soy sauce and garlic. Pour half of the marinade into a large resealable plastic bag; add the chicken. Seal bag and turn to coat; chill for 2-3 hours. Cover and refrigerate the remaining marinade.

2. Discard the marinade from the chicken. In a large skillet, cook the chicken in remaining oil until a thermometer reads 170°.

3. Meanwhile, in a small saucepan, saute the walnuts in butter until lightly browned; remove and set aside. Set aside 1/4 cup green onions for garnish.

4. Add remaining onions to saucepan; saute until tender. Add the next eight ingredients and reserved marinade. Bring to a boil. Reduce heat; simmer, uncovered, for 5-10 minutes or until sauce reaches desired consistency. Serve chicken with rice and sauce. Garnish with reserved walnuts and onions.

[1995]

PARMESAN CHICKEN

yield: 6-8 servings ∽ prep: 10 min.
bake: 40 min.

The savory coating on this chicken has the satisfying flavor of Parmesan cheese. It's easy enough to be a family weekday meal yet impressive enough to serve to guests. When I serve this chicken, there are never any leftovers.

—*Schelby Thompson*
Camden Wyoming, Delaware

1/2 **cup butter, melted**
2 **teaspoons Dijon mustard**
1 **teaspoon Worcestershire sauce**
1/2 **teaspoon salt**
1 **cup dry bread crumbs**
1/2 **cup grated Parmesan cheese**
6 **to 8 boneless skinless chicken breast halves**

1. In a pie plate or shallow bowl, combine butter, mustard, Worcestershire sauce and salt. In a plastic bag, combine the crumbs and cheese. Dip the chicken in butter mixture, then shake in crumb mixture, a few pieces at a time.

2. Place chicken in an ungreased 13-in. x 9-in. baking pan. Drizzle with any remaining butter mixture. Bake at 350° for 40-45 minutes or until a thermometer reads 170°.

[1998]

STUFFED CHICKEN ROLLS

yield: 6 servings ∽ prep: 25 min. + chilling
cook: 4 hours

The wonderful aroma that comes from this moist, delicious chicken as it cooks sparks our appetites. The ham and cheese rolled inside is a tasty surprise. They're especially nice served over rice or pasta.

—*Jean Sherwood, Kenneth City, Florida*

6 **boneless skinless chicken breast halves (8 ounces each)**
6 **slices fully cooked ham**
6 **slices Swiss cheese**
1/4 **cup all-purpose flour**
1/4 **cup grated Parmesan cheese**
1/2 **teaspoon rubbed sage**
1/4 **teaspoon paprika**
1/4 **teaspoon pepper**
1/4 **cup canola oil**
1 **can (10-3/4 ounces) condensed cream of chicken soup, undiluted**
1/2 **cup chicken broth**
Chopped fresh parsley, optional

1. Flatten chicken to 1/8-in. thickness. Place ham and cheese on each breast. Roll up and tuck in ends; secure with a toothpick.

2. In a large resealable plastic bag, combine flour, cheese, sage, paprika and pepper; add the chicken. Seal bag; toss to coat. Cover and refrigerate for 1 hour.

3. In a large skillet, brown chicken in oil over medium-high heat. Transfer to a 5-qt. slow cooker. Combine soup and broth; pour over chicken. Cover and cook on low for 4-5 hours or until chicken is tender. Remove toothpicks. Garnish with parsley if desired.

STUFFED CHICKEN ROLLS

"This is really good. I didn't have rubbed sage, so I used rubbed thyme instead. I thickened the juice with a cornstarch/water mixture at the end of the cooking time. It was really good over rice. This was a little more work than most slow cooker recipes but worth the effort. I'll definitely be making this again."
—*LauraManning*

[2011]

SAUCY GARLIC CHICKEN

yield: 6 servings ∞ prep: 40 min. + cooling
bake: 35 min.

Roasted garlic lends a rich flavor to this appetizing entree, and it complements the spinach nicely. Ideal for entertaining, the recipe can be assembled in advance and baked when guests arrive.

—*Joanna Johnson, Flower Mound, Texas*

  4 whole garlic bulbs
  2 tablespoons olive oil, *divided*
  1 package (9 ounces) fresh baby spinach
3/4 teaspoon salt, *divided*
1/2 teaspoon coarsely ground pepper, *divided*
  6 boneless skinless chicken breast halves
     (6 ounces *each*)
  6 tablespoons butter, cubed
  6 tablespoons all-purpose flour
  3 cups 2% milk
2-1/2 cups grated Parmesan cheese, *divided*
1/8 teaspoon nutmeg
Hot cooked pasta
Chopped tomato and minced fresh parsley, optional

1. Remove papery outer skin from garlic (do not peel or separate cloves). Cut tops off of garlic bulbs; brush bulbs with 1 tablespoon oil. Wrap each bulb in heavy-duty foil. Bake at 425° for 30-35 minutes or until softened. Cool for 10-15 minutes.

2. Meanwhile, place spinach in a greased 13-in. x 9-in. baking dish; sprinkle with 1/4 teaspoon each of salt and pepper. In a large skillet, brown chicken in remaining oil on both sides; place over spinach.

3. In a large saucepan, melt butter. Stir in flour until smooth; gradually add the milk. Bring to a boil; cook and stir for 1-2 minutes or until thickened. Stir in 2 cups cheese, nutmeg and remaining salt and pepper.

4. Transfer to a blender; squeeze softened garlic into the blender. Cover and process until smooth. Pour the mixture over chicken.

5. Cover and bake at 425° for 30-35 minutes or until a thermometer reads 170° and sauce is bubbly. Uncover; sprinkle with the remaining cheese. Bake 5 minutes longer. Serve with pasta. Sprinkle with the tomato and parsley if desired.

[2006]

COLORFUL CHICKEN FETTUCCINE

yield: 6 servings ∞ prep/total time: 30 min.

This surefire entree is a delicious option if you find yourself in a time crunch. I like to prepare and freeze fresh veggies ahead of time for use in recipes like this one. The rest is as easy as 1-2-3!

—*Ginger Kelly, Cranberry Township, Pennsylvania*

 10 ounces uncooked fettuccine
  1 pound boneless skinless chicken breasts, cut into strips
  1 tablespoon canola oil
  1 cup julienned carrots
  1 medium sweet red pepper, julienned
  1 medium green pepper, julienned
  2 cups fresh broccoli florets
  4 teaspoons cornstarch
  1 can (14-1/2 ounces) chicken broth
  1 tablespoon lemon juice
1/2 teaspoon salt
1/2 teaspoon dried thyme
  2 tablespoons sour cream
1/2 cup shredded Parmesan cheese

1. Cook the fettuccine according to package directions. Meanwhile, in a large skillet, saute chicken in oil until no longer pink. Remove and keep warm. In the same pan, saute carrots for 1 minute. Add peppers and broccoli; saute 3-4 minutes longer or until vegetables are crisp-tender.

2. In a small bowl, combine the cornstarch, broth, lemon juice, salt and thyme until blended; stir into vegetables. Bring to a boil; cook and stir for 2 minutes. Remove from the heat. Stir in sour cream.

3. Drain fettuccine; place in a large bowl. Add the chicken, vegetable mixture and cheese; toss to coat.

[2003]

PINEAPPLE CHICKEN STIR-FRY

yield: 6 servings ∽ **prep/total time: 25 min.**

The brown sugar called for in this recipe gives the chicken a superior taste.

—Mel Miller, Perkins, Oklahoma

---

 1 can (20 ounces) unsweetened pineapple tidbits
 2 tablespoons cornstarch
 1/4 cup cider vinegar
 1/4 cup ketchup
 2 tablespoons brown sugar
 2 tablespoons reduced-sodium soy sauce
 1/4 teaspoon ground ginger
 1-1/2 pounds boneless skinless chicken breasts, cubed
 3 tablespoons canola oil, *divided*
 1/2 teaspoon garlic salt
 2 medium carrots, sliced
 1 medium green pepper, julienned
 1 medium tomato, cut into wedges
Hot cooked rice

---

1. Drain pineapple, reserving the juice; set pineapple aside. In a small bowl, combine the cornstarch and reserved juice until smooth. Stir in the vinegar, ketchup, brown sugar, soy sauce and ginger; set aside.

2. In a wok or large skillet, stir-fry chicken in 2 tablespoons oil for 5-6 minutes or until no longer pink; sprinkle with the garlic salt. Remove and keep warm.

3. Stir-fry the carrots in remaining oil for 4 minutes. Add the green pepper; cook and stir until vegetables are crisp-tender. Add chicken and pineapple.

4. Stir pineapple juice mixture; pour into pan. Bring to a boil; cook and stir for 1-2 minutes or until thickened. Add the tomato wedges. Serve with rice.

[2007]

HUNGARIAN CHICKEN PAPRIKASH

yield: 6 servings ∽ **prep: 20 min. bake: 1-1/2 hours**

My mom learned to make this tender chicken dish when she volunteered to help prepare the dinners served at her church. It's my favorite main dish, and the gravy, seasoned with paprika, sour cream and onions, is the best.

—Pamela Eaton, Monclova, Ohio

---

 1 large onion, chopped
 1/4 cup butter, cubed
 4 to 5 pounds broiler/fryer chicken pieces
 2 tablespoons paprika
 1 teaspoon salt
 1/2 teaspoon pepper
 1-1/2 cups hot water
 2 tablespoons cornstarch
 2 tablespoons cold water
 1 cup (8 ounces) sour cream

---

1. In a large skillet, saute onion in butter until tender. Sprinkle the chicken with paprika, salt and pepper; place in an ungreased roasting pan. Spoon onion mixture over chicken. Add hot water. Cover and bake at 350° for 1/2 hours or until chicken juices run clear.

2. Remove chicken and keep warm. In a small bowl, combine the cornstarch and cold water until smooth. Gradually add to the pan juices with onion. Bring to a boil over medium heat; cook and stir for 2 minutes or until thickened. Remove from the heat. Stir in the sour cream. Serve with chicken.

HUNGARIAN CHICKEN PAPRIKASH

"This recipe tastes just like what my mom used to make when I was younger. I cut the chicken into pieces for faster cooking time and made egg noodles with it. Delicious!"
—*PucciBaby*

[2011]

LEMON-SAGE CHICKEN

**yield: 4 servings ∞ prep: 30 min.
bake: 15 min.**

I had completely forgotten about this recipe my mom made and just recently found a copy of the fantastic dish. Wonderful battered chicken is served with a rich sauce that makes this an exquisite entree for company.

—*Denise Kleffman, Gardena, California*

4	boneless skinless chicken breast halves (6 ounces ea*ch*)
3	eggs, lightly beaten
1/4	cup grated Parmesan and Romano cheese blend
1	tablespoon minced fresh parsley
1	teaspoon dried basil
1/2	teaspoon salt
1/8	teaspoon pepper
1/2	cup all-purpose flour
2	tablespoons olive oil

SAUCE:

2	tablespoons chopped shallot
3	garlic cloves, minced
1/4	cup white wine
4-1/2	teaspoons lemon juice
1	tablespoon minced fresh parsley
1	teaspoon dried sage leaves
1	teaspoon grated lemon peel
1/2	cup heavy whipping cream
3	tablespoons cold butter

1. Flatten chicken to 1/2-in. thickness. In a shallow bowl, combine the eggs, cheese and seasonings. Place flour in another shallow bowl. Coat chicken with flour, then dip in egg mixture.

2. In a large skillet, brown the chicken in oil in batches. Transfer to a greased 15-in. x 10-in. x 1-in. baking pan. Bake, uncovered, at 375° for 15-20 minutes or until a thermometer reads 170°.

3. In the drippings, saute shallot until tender. Add garlic; cook 1 minute longer. Add wine, lemon juice, herbs and lemon peel; cook over medium heat until liquid is reduced by half. Add cream; cook until thickened, stirring occasionally. Stir in the butter until melted. Serve sauce with chicken.

[2000]

HERBED CHICKEN QUARTERS

**yield: 4 servings
prep: 15 min. + marinating ∞ grill: 1 hour**

I often grill chicken in the summer, and this herbed version is a big hit with our daughters. A salad and seasoned potatoes make great complements to the plump, juicy chicken.

—*Erika Aylward, Clinton, Michigan*

4	medium lemons, cut into wedges
1/2	cup canola oil
8	garlic cloves, minced
4	teaspoons minced fresh basil
2	teaspoons minced fresh thyme
2	teaspoons salt
1/2	teaspoon cayenne pepper
1	broiler/fryer chicken (about 3 pounds), quartered

1. Gently squeeze juice from lemons into a large resealable plastic bag; leave lemon wedges in the bag. Add the oil, garlic, basil, thyme, salt and cayenne; add the chicken. Seal the bag and turn to coat. Refrigerate the chicken for 24 hours, turning frequently.

2. Drain and discard marinade. Grill the chicken, covered, over medium heat, turning every 15 minutes, for 1 hour or until juices run clear and a thermometer reads 180° in the thigh.

LEMON-SAGE CHICKEN

❝This is the best chicken dish I have ever made. And that was without the wine (subbed chicken broth). The only thing I would do differently is to whisk the sauce in a blender until it's smooth.❞

—*ayodaly*

[1997]

CRISPY FRIED CHICKEN

yield: 8 servings ∞ **prep: 10 min.** ∞ **cook: 10 min./batch**

Always a picnic favorite, this chicken is delicious hot or cold.

—*Jeanne Schnitzler, Lima, Montana*

---

    4 cups all-purpose flour, *divided*
    2 tablespoons garlic salt
    1 tablespoon paprika
    3 teaspoons pepper, *divided*
2-1/2 teaspoons poultry seasoning
    2 eggs
1-1/2 cups water
    1 teaspoon salt
    2 broiler/fryer chickens (3-1/2 to 4 pounds ea*c*h), cut up
Oil for deep-fat frying

1. In a large resealable plastic bag, combine 2-2/3 cups flour, garlic salt, paprika, 2-1/2 teaspoons pepper and poultry seasoning. In a shallow bowl, beat eggs and water; add salt, pepper and remaining flour. Dip chicken in egg mixture, then place in the bag, a few pieces at a time. Seal bag and shake to coat.

2. In a deep-fat fryer, heat oil to 375°. Fry chicken, several pieces at a time, for 5-6 minutes on each side or until golden brown and juices run clear. Drain on paper towels.

CRISPY FRIED CHICKEN

❝Undoubtedly the best homemade crispy fried chicken I have ever had. Wish I had thought of it.❞
—*Karen1027*

CUTTING UP A WHOLE CHICKEN

1. Pull the leg and thigh away from the body. With a small sharp knife, cut through the skin to expose the joint.

2. Cut through joint, then cut the skin around the thigh to free the leg. Repeat with other leg.

3. Separate drumstick from thigh by cutting skin at the joint. Bend drumstick to expose joint; cut through joint and skin.

4. Pull wing away from the body. Cut through skin to expose joint. Cut through joint and skin to separate wing from body. Repeat.

5. Snip along each side of the backbone between rib joints with kitchen or poultry shears.

6. Hold chicken breast in both hands (skin side down) and bend it back to snap breastbone. Turn over. With a knife, cut in half along breastbone. Breastbone will remain attached to one of the halves.

OLD-FASHIONED CHICKEN POTPIE

[2006]

OLD-FASHIONED CHICKEN POTPIE

yield: 8 servings ∽ **prep: 1-1/2 hours bake: 40 min. + standing**

This buttery, 2-crust pie is stuffed with tender chicken pieces, vegetables, seasonings and a creamy sauce.

—*Sue Davis, Wausau, Wisconsin*

3	to 4 pounds bone-in chicken breast halves
1-1/2	quarts water
1	small onion, peeled
1	celery rib
1	large carrot
1-1/2	teaspoons salt, *divided*
Pastry for double-crust pie (9 inches)	
1/2	cup all-purpose flour
1/2	teaspoon onion salt
1/2	teaspoon celery salt
1/4	teaspoon pepper

---

1. In a stockpot, bring the chicken, water, onion, celery, carrot and 1/2 teaspoon salt to a boil. Reduce heat; cover and simmer for 50-60 minutes or until chicken is tender.

2. Remove the chicken and vegetables from the broth. Set aside until cool enough to handle. Meanwhile, line a 9-in. deep-dish pie plate with bottom pastry; trim even with edge of plate. Set aside.

3. Remove chicken from bones; discard skin and bones and cut chicken into cubes. Set aside. Chop the onion, celery and carrot. Strain broth and skim fat; set broth aside.

4. In a small bowl, combine the flour, onion salt, celery salt, pepper and remaining salt. Add 1/2 cup broth; whisk until smooth. In a large saucepan, bring 3 cups of broth to a boil; whisk in flour mixture. Cook and

stir for 2 minutes or until thickened. Remove from the heat; add chicken and vegetables. Pour into crust.

5. Roll out remaining pastry to fit top of pie; place over filling. Trim, seal and flute edges. Cut slits in top.

6. Cover edges loosely with foil. Bake at 400° for 40-45 minutes or until golden brown and filling is bubbly. Let stand for 15 minutes before cutting.

[2009]

CHICKEN WITH ROSEMARY BUTTER SAUCE

yield: 4 servings ∽ **prep/total time: 25 min.**

This simply elegant entree requires almost no effort but will win you many compliments. You'll love the mellow sauce!

—*Connie McDowell, Greenwood, Delaware*

4	boneless skinless chicken breast halves (4 ounces *each*)
4	tablespoons butter, *divided*
1/2	cup white wine *or* chicken broth
1/2	cup heavy whipping cream
1	tablespoon minced fresh rosemary

TOP 100 RECIPE

---

1. In a large skillet over medium heat, cook chicken in 1 tablespoon butter for 4-5 minutes on each side or until a thermometer reads 170°. Remove and keep warm.

2. Add the wine to the pan; cook over medium-low heat, stirring to loosen browned bits from pan. Add the cream and bring to a boil. Reduce heat; cook and stir until slightly thickened. Stir in rosemary and remaining butter until blended. Serve sauce with chicken.

[2003]

CRESCENT-WRAPPED DRUMSTICKS

yield: 4 servings (2 drumsticks each)
prep: 50 min.   bake: 15 min.

Looking for a different way to do drumsticks? A friend shared this recipe with me. The drums are simmered in barbecue sauce and then wrapped in crescent roll dough that's sprinkled with Parmesan cheese and Italian seasoning.

—**Paula Plating**
Colorado Springs, Colorado

---

8 chicken drumsticks
1/4 cup butter, cubed
1/2 cup barbecue sauce
1 tube (8 ounces) refrigerated crescent rolls
1 egg, lightly beaten
2 teaspoons grated Parmesan cheese
2 teaspoons Italian seasoning
2 teaspoons sesame seeds, toasted

---

1. Remove and discard skin from the drumsticks. In a large skillet, melt the butter over medium heat; stir in the barbecue sauce. Add drumsticks. Bring to a boil. Reduce the heat; cover and simmer for 30 minutes or until a thermometer reads 180°, turning occasionally. Remove the chicken from pan; cool slightly.

2. Separate the crescent dough into eight triangles; place on a lightly greased 15-in. x 10-in. x 1-in. baking pan. Brush the dough with some of the beaten egg; sprinkle with the cheese and Italian seasoning.

3. Place meaty portion of each drumstick at the tip of each triangle, with bony portion extended beyond one long side of triangle. Wrap drumstick in dough; place seam side down. Brush with remaining egg; sprinkle with sesame seeds.

4. Bake chicken at 375° for 13-15 minutes or until crust is golden brown and a thermometer reads 180°.

[2012]

MOROCCAN CHICKEN STEW

yield: 6 servings   prep: 20 min.
bake: 45 min.

The fragrant aroma of this dish will have your family gathering in the kitchen before it's done. And it's so easy to do. Place the ingredients in a Dutch oven and bake!

—**Veronica Gantley, Norfolk, Virginia**

---

2 pounds boneless skinless chicken thighs, cut into 2-inch pieces
2 medium sweet potatoes, peeled and cut into 2-inch pieces
1 cup chicken broth
1 small onion, coarsely chopped
2 tablespoons honey
1 tablespoon olive oil
1 teaspoon pepper
1 teaspoon ground allspice
1/4 teaspoon salt
Dash ground cinnamon
Dash ground nutmeg
1 cup dried cranberries
1/4 cup chopped pistachios, toasted
Hot cooked couscous, optional

---

1. In a Dutch oven, combine the first 11 ingredients. Cover and bake at 400° for 30 minutes.

2. Uncover; sprinkle with the cranberries. Bake 15-20 minutes longer or until the chicken is no longer pink. Sprinkle with pistachios. Serve with couscous if desired.

CRESCENT-WRAPPED DRUMSTICKS

"This is awesome! Very easy to prepare and tastes great. My mom called it "Poor Man's Chicken Wellington!" Don't worry what the crescent roll seam side looks like (as I was)—when it bakes, they come out perfectly. I can see myself making this for a crowd in the future!"
—*HeidiSB*

CHICKEN CORDON BLEU CALZONES

"This was a big hit with the family and was easy to make. Can't wait to tell the other Army wives about it!"
—katinahall

[2001]

CHICKEN CORDON BLEU CALZONES

yield: 4 servings ∞ prep: 40 min.
bake: 15 min.

This recipe combines the delicate flavor of chicken Cordon Bleu with the look of beef Wellington.

—*Kathy Gounaud, Warwick, Rhode Island*

4   boneless skinless chicken breasts (4 ounces each)
1   cup sliced fresh mushrooms
1/2 medium onion, chopped
2   tablespoons butter
3   tablespoons cornstarch
1-1/4 cups 2% milk
1   tablespoon minced fresh basil *or* 1 teaspoon dried basil
1   teaspoon salt
1/4 teaspoon pepper
1   package (17.3 ounces) frozen puff pastry, thawed
8   thin slices deli ham
4   slices provolone cheese
Additional milk, optional

1. Place chicken in a greased 2-qt. baking dish; cover with water. Cover and bake at 350° for 30 minutes or until a thermometer reads 170°.

2. Meanwhile, in a small skillet, saute the mushrooms and onion in butter until tender. Combine cornstarch and milk until smooth; stir into skillet. Add the seasonings. Bring to a boil; cook and stir for 2 minutes or until thickened.

3. Drain chicken. Cut pastry sheets in half widthwise. On one side of each half, place a chicken breast, 1/4 cup mushroom mixture, two ham slices and one cheese slice. Fold pastry over filling and seal edges.

4. Place on a greased baking sheet. Brush the tops with milk if desired. Bake at 400° for 15-20 minutes or until puffed and golden.

[2010]

BBQ CHICKEN BAKED POTATOES

yield: 10 servings ∞ prep: 15 min.
cook: 6-1/4 hours

(Pictured on page 715)

These baked potatoes are meals in themselves, with a smoky barbecue flavor that will make your mouth water. You can top them with your favorite cheese and garnish.

—*Amber Massey, Fort Worth, Texas*

4-1/2 pounds bone-in chicken breast halves, skin removed
2   tablespoons garlic powder
1   large red onion, sliced into thick rings
1   bottle (18 ounces) honey barbecue sauce
1   cup Italian salad dressing
1/2 cup packed brown sugar
1/2 cup cider vinegar
1/4 cup Worcestershire sauce
2   tablespoons Liquid Smoke, optional
10 medium potatoes, baked
Crumbled blue cheese and chopped green onions, optional

1. Place chicken in a greased 5- or 6-qt. slow cooker; sprinkle with the garlic powder and top with onion. Combine barbecue sauce, salad dressing, brown sugar, vinegar, Worcestershire sauce and Liquid Smoke if desired; pour over the chicken.

2. Cover and cook on low for 6-8 hours or until chicken is tender. When cool enough to handle, remove the chicken from bones; discard bones and onion. Skim fat from cooking juices.

3. Shred meat with two forks and return to slow cooker; heat through. Serve with potatoes, blue cheese and green onions if desired.

[2002]

SWISS MUSHROOM CHICKEN

yield: 4 servings ∞ **prep/total time: 30 min.**

Everyone enjoys the golden chicken breasts topped with ham, melted Swiss cheese and fresh mushrooms. It's easy to prepare but looks and tastes special enough for company.

—*Jan Baxter, Humarock, Massachusetts*

- 4 boneless skinless chicken breast halves (4 ounces each)
- 1 egg
- 1 cup crushed butter-flavored crackers (about 25 crackers)
- 3/4 teaspoon salt
- 1/2 pound fresh mushrooms, sliced
- 2 tablespoons butter, *divided*
- 4 slices deli ham *or* thinly sliced hard salami
- 4 slices Swiss cheese

1. Flatten chicken to 1/4-in. thickness. In a shallow bowl, lightly beat the egg. Combine cracker crumbs and salt in another shallow bowl. Dip chicken in egg, then roll in crumbs; set aside.

2. In a large ovenproof skillet, saute the mushrooms in 1 tablespoon butter until tender; remove and set aside. In the same skillet, cook chicken over medium heat in remaining butter for 3-4 minutes on each side or until no longer pink.

3. Top each chicken breast half with a ham slice, mushrooms and a cheese slice. Broil 4-6 in. from the heat for 1-2 minutes or until cheese is melted.

[1996]

CRISPY BAKED CHICKEN

yield: 4-6 servings ∞ **prep: 15 min. bake: 50 min.**

My siblings and I couldn't wait to sit down to supper when Mom was making this delicious chicken. The cornmeal in the coating gives each juicy, golden piece a wonderful crunch.

—*Karen Wingate, Coldwater, Kansas*

- 1/2 cup cornmeal
- 1/2 cup all-purpose flour
- 1-1/2 teaspoons salt
- 1-1/2 teaspoons chili powder
- 1/2 teaspoon dried oregano
- 1/4 teaspoon pepper
- 1/2 cup 2% milk
- 1 broiler/fryer chicken (3 to 3-1/2 pounds), cut up
- 1/3 cup butter, melted

1. In a shallow bowl combine the first six ingredients. Pour the milk in another shallow bowl. Dip the chicken in milk, then roll in the cornmeal mixture.

2. Place chicken in a greased 13-in. x 9-in. baking pan. Drizzle with butter. Bake, uncovered, at 375° for 50-55 minutes or until juices run clear.

SWISS MUSHROOM CHICKEN

"This is one of my family's favorite recipes, and I would make it every couple of months, but my husband likes to save it for more special occasions. The flavors are wonderful together. I make it with good quality deli ham, exotic blend mushrooms (cremini, shiitake, oyster), Townhouse crackers, and add a little black pepper to the crumb mixture. I don't bother with broiling. I just leave a little heat on and cover the pan with a lid until the cheese melts. Heavenly!"
—*laswd*

FLATTENING A CHICKEN BREAST

Place boneless chicken breasts between two pieces of waxed paper or plastic wrap or in a resealable plastic bag. Starting in the center and working out to edges, pound lightly with the flat side of a meat mallet until the chicken is even in thickness.

[2000]

CHICKEN FAJITAS
yield: 6 servings
prep: 20 min. + marinating
cook: 5 min.

This recipe goes together in a snap and is very popular at my house. If you don't like your food spicy, just leave out the red pepper flakes.

—Julie Sterchi
Jackson, Missouri, Field Editor

- 4 tablespoons canola oil, *divided*
- 2 tablespoons lemon juice
- 1-1/2 teaspoons seasoned salt
- 1-1/2 teaspoons dried oregano
- 1-1/2 teaspoons ground cumin
- 1 teaspoon garlic powder
- 1/2 teaspoon chili powder
- 1/2 teaspoon paprika
- 1/2 teaspoon crushed red pepper flakes, optional
- 1-1/2 pounds boneless skinless chicken breast, cut into thin strips
- 1/2 medium sweet red pepper, julienned
- 1/2 medium green pepper, julienned
- 4 green onions, thinly sliced
- 1/2 cup chopped onion
- 6 flour tortillas (8 inches), warmed
- Shredded cheddar cheese, taco sauce, salsa, guacamole and sour cream

1. In a large resealable plastic bag, combine 2 tablespoons oil, lemon juice and seasonings; add chicken. Seal and turn to coat; refrigerate for 1-4 hours.

2. In a large skillet, saute peppers and onions in remaining oil until crisp-tender. Remove and keep warm.

3. Discard marinade. In same skillet, cook chicken over medium-high heat for 5-6 minutes or until no longer pink. Return pepper mixture to pan; heat through.

4. Spoon the filling down the center of tortillas; fold in half. Serve with the cheese, taco sauce, salsa, guacamole and sour cream.

[2008]

ALMOND CHICKEN WITH APRICOT SAUCE
yield: 6 servings   prep: 15 min.
bake: 30 min.

With its fruity, slightly sweet sauce, this tender chicken entree is full of flavor, not fat. When my children were all still living at home, they would rate a new recipe on a scale of 1 to 10. This one earned a 10 every time!

—Erma Yoder, Millersburg, Indiana

- 1 cup apricot spreadable fruit
- 3 tablespoons reduced-sodium soy sauce
- 2 tablespoons finely chopped onion
- 4 teaspoons cider vinegar
- 1 teaspoon ground mustard
- 6 boneless skinless chicken breast halves (6 ounces *each*)
- 1/2 cup sliced almonds
- 1 tablespoon butter, melted

1. In a shallow bowl, combine the first five ingredients; transfer 1/2 cup to a serving bowl and set aside. Dip the chicken in remaining apricot mixture. Place in a 13-in. x 9-in. baking dish coated with cooking spray.

2. Sprinkle the almonds over chicken; drizzle with butter. Bake, uncovered, at 350° for 30-35 minutes or until a thermometer reads 170°. Serve with reserved apricot sauce.

BUYING CHICKEN

When purchasing chicken or other meats, check to make sure it is before the "sell-by" date listed on the label. Use within a few days of the sell-by date, or freeze for longer storage.

—*Taste of Home Cooking Experts*

CHICKEN FAJITAS

"Awesome recipe! Better than Mexican restaurant chicken fajitas."
—*malugen_06*

[2001]

LEMON CREAM CHICKEN
yield: 6 servings ✄ **prep: 5 min.**
cook: 45 min.

If you want an entree that's quick, easy and elegant, you can't beat this one. The lemon cream sauce is what makes it irresistible. It goes so nicely with the chicken and mushrooms.

—Mary Anne McWhirter
Pearland, Texas, Former Field Editor

- 1/2 cup plus 1 tablespoon all-purpose flour, *divided*
- 1/2 teaspoon salt
- 1/2 teaspoon pepper
- 6 boneless skinless chicken breast halves (4 ounces *each*)
- 1/4 cup butter, cubed
- 1 cup chicken broth
- 1 cup heavy whipping cream, *divided*
- 3 tablespoons lemon juice
- 1/2 pound fresh mushrooms, sliced

---

1. In a large resealable plastic bag, combine 1/2 cup flour, salt and pepper; add the chicken, a few pieces at a time. Seal bag and shake to coat.

2. In a large skillet, cook the chicken in butter for 8-9 minutes on each side or until a thermometer reads 170°. Remove the chicken; cover and keep warm.

3. Add broth to the drippings. Bring to a boil over medium heat; stir to loosen browned bits from pan. Simmer, uncovered, for 10 minutes or until broth is reduced to 1/3 cup. Stir in 3/4 cup cream, lemon juice and mushrooms. Cook over medium-low heat for 5 minutes.

4. Combine remaining flour and cream until smooth; stir into skillet. Bring to a boil; cook and stir for 2 minutes or until thickened. Return chicken to skillet and heat through.

[1995]

CAJUN CHICKEN PASTA
yield: 2 servings ✄ **prep/total time: 25 min.**

Our pasta began as a special, but due to its overwhelming popularity, we made it a permanent part of our menu. In the 9 years we've been open, we have become a favorite restaurant with locals and travelers alike because our food is not typical hotel fare.

—Monroe Street Grille
Tallahassee, Florida

- 2 teaspoons Cajun seasoning
- 2 boneless skinless chicken breast halves (4 ounces *each*), cut into thin strips
- 2 tablespoons butter
- 8 slices *each* green and sweet red pepper
- 4 large fresh mushrooms, sliced
- 1 green onion, sliced
- 1 to 2 cups heavy whipping cream
- 1/4 teaspoon dried basil
- 1/4 teaspoon lemon-pepper seasoning
- 1/4 teaspoon salt
- 1/8 teaspoon garlic powder
- 1/8 teaspoon pepper
- 4 ounces linguine, cooked and drained

Grated Parmesan cheese, optional

---

1. Place Cajun seasoning in a large resealable plastic bag; add the chicken. Seal bag and shake to coat.

2. In a large skillet over medium heat, saute the chicken in butter until no longer pink, about 5-7 minutes. Add the peppers, mushrooms and onion; cook and stir for 2-3 minutes or until the vegetables are tender. Reduce heat. Add the cream and seasonings; heat through. Add linguine and toss to coat; heat through. Sprinkle with the cheese if desired.

LEMON CREAM CHICKEN

"Delicious! My family loves it when I make this for dinner! We like a lot of sauce, as we serve it over rice, so I do not reduce the broth to 1/3 cup. Instead, I add a couple more tablespoons of lemon juice—always from fresh lemons—and mix cornstarch instead of flour with the cream for a nice, smooth sauce. Fabulous!"
—SandyC79

MASCARPONE-PESTO CHICKEN ROLLS

[2010]

MASCARPONE-PESTO CHICKEN ROLLS

yield: 4 servings ∽ prep: 20 min.
bake: 35 min.

(Pictured on page 718)

Who could resist the savory flavor of these golden-brown roll-ups spiraled with delectable mascarpone cheese and prepared pesto? What's more, they're easy to make.

—*Sheryl Little, Sherwood, Arkansas*

4 boneless skinless chicken breast
  halves (6 ounces *each*)
3/4 teaspoon garlic salt
1/2 cup Mascarpone cheese
1/4 cup prepared pesto
1 egg
2 teaspoons water
1 cup seasoned bread crumbs
8 teaspoons butter, melted, *divided*
8 ounces uncooked fettuccine
Fresh basil leaves, optional

1. Flatten chicken to 1/4-in. thickness; sprinkle with garlic salt. Combine the cheese and pesto; spread over chicken. Roll up each from a short side and secure with toothpicks.

2. In a shallow bowl, whisk the egg and water. Place the bread crumbs in a separate shallow bowl. Dip chicken in egg mixture, then coat with crumbs. Place seam side down in a greased 11-in. x 7-in. baking dish. Drizzle with 4 teaspoons butter. Bake the chicken, uncovered, at 350° for 35-40 minutes or until a thermometer reads 170°. Discard the toothpicks.

3. Meanwhile, cook fettuccine according to package directions. Drain fettuccine; toss with remaining butter. Serve with chicken. Garnish with basil if desired.

"Very good! Flavor is bursting. Before this recipe, I had never heard of mascarpone cheese. Next time I'm going to try adding some mozzarella cheese to make it cheesier. This recipe is very quick and easy and comes out like a difficult, fancy meal. I love it."
—*Daddycooks*

[2005]

ASIAN CHICKEN THIGHS

yield: 5 servings ∽ prep: 15 min.
cook: 50 min.

A thick, tangy sauce coats the golden chicken pieces in this savory skillet recipe. I like to serve them over long grain rice or with a helping of ramen noodle slaw.

—*Dave Farrington*
Midwest City, Oklahoma

5 bone-in chicken thighs (about
  1-3/4 pounds), skin removed
5 teaspoons olive oil
1/3 cup warm water
1/4 cup packed brown sugar
2 tablespoons orange juice
2 tablespoons reduced-sodium soy
  sauce
2 tablespoons ketchup
1 tablespoon white vinegar
4 garlic cloves, minced
1/2 teaspoon crushed red pepper flakes
1/4 teaspoon Chinese five-spice powder
2 teaspoons cornstarch
2 tablespoons cold water
Hot cooked rice
Sliced green onions

1. In a large skillet over medium heat, cook chicken in oil for 8-10 minutes on each side or until no longer pink. In a small bowl, whisk the warm water, brown sugar, orange juice, soy sauce, ketchup, vinegar, garlic, pepper flakes and five-spice powder.

2. Pour over the chicken. Bring to a boil. Reduce heat; simmer, uncovered, for 30-35 minutes or until the chicken is tender, turning occasionally.

3. Combine the cornstarch and cold water until smooth; gradually stir into the pan. Bring to a boil; cook and stir for 2 minutes or until thickened. Serve with rice. Garnish with green onions.

[2007]

CHICKEN SPARERIBS

yield: 4 servings ∞ **prep: 5 min.**
cook: 30 min.

(Pictured on page 717)

Inexpensive chicken thighs get all gussied up in a zippy sparerib-style sauce that's irresistible.

—Janice Porterfield, Atlanta, Texas

8 bone-in chicken thighs (about 3 pounds)
2 tablespoons canola oil
1 cup water
2/3 cup packed brown sugar
2/3 cup reduced-sodium soy sauce
1/2 cup apple juice
1/4 cup ketchup
2 tablespoons cider vinegar
2 garlic cloves, minced
1 teaspoon crushed red pepper flakes
1/2 teaspoon ground ginger
2 tablespoons cornstarch
2 tablespoons cold water

1. In a Dutch oven, brown chicken over medium heat in oil in batches on both sides; drain. Return all of the chicken to the pan.

2. In a large bowl, combine the water, brown sugar, soy sauce, apple juice, ketchup, vinegar, garlic, pepper flakes and ginger; pour over chicken. Bring to a boil. Reduce heat; cover and simmer for 20-25 minutes or until a thermometer reads 180°.

3. Remove chicken to a platter and keep warm. Combine cornstarch and water until smooth; stir into the cooking juices. Bring to a boil; cook and stir for 2 minutes or until thickened. Serve with the chicken.

[2001]

BRUSCHETTA CHICKEN

yield: 4 servings ∞ **prep: 10 min.**
bake: 30 min.

(Pictured on page 717)

My husband and I enjoy serving this tasty chicken to company as well as family. It looks like we fussed, but it's really fast and easy to fix. I found the recipe years ago and it's become a trusted dish. It usually prompts recipe requests.

—Carolin Cattoi-Demkiw
Lethbridge, Alberta

1/2 cup all-purpose flour
1/2 cup egg substitute
4 boneless skinless chicken breast halves (4 ounces each)
1/4 cup grated Parmesan cheese
1/4 cup dry bread crumbs
1 tablespoon butter, melted
2 large tomatoes, seeded and chopped
3 tablespoons minced fresh basil
2 garlic cloves, minced
1 tablespoon olive oil
1/2 teaspoon salt
1/4 teaspoon pepper

TOP 100 RECIPE

1. Place the flour and egg substitute in separate shallow bowls. Dip chicken in flour, then in eggs; place in a greased 13-in. x 9-in. baking dish. Combine the cheese, bread crumbs and butter; sprinkle over chicken.

2. Loosely cover baking dish with foil. Bake at 375° for 20 minutes. Uncover; bake 5-10 minutes longer or until a thermometer reads 170°.

3. Meanwhile, in a small bowl, combine the remaining ingredients. Spoon over the chicken. Return to the oven for 3-5 minutes or until tomato mixture is heated through.

CHICKEN SPARERIBS

"This recipe is amazing. I made this on a whim because I had all the ingredients and I was looking for something different. My entire family went nuts for it. The sauce is amazing. My boyfriend saved the leftover sauce and put it on pretty much everything he ate for the next couple of days. He thinks the sauce is better than any store-bought barbecue sauce he has ever had. Definitely will be making this for many, many, many years to come."
—foodeater

[2010]

GINGER CHICKEN

yield: 4 servings ∞ **prep: 20 min. + chilling cook: 15 min.**

Ginger and soy sauce lend an Asian flair to this hearty and healthy main dish.

—*Ben Haen, Baldwin, Wisconsin*

- 1 egg white, lightly beaten
- 1 tablespoon reduced-sodium soy sauce
- 1 teaspoon cornstarch
- 1/8 teaspoon white pepper
- 1 pound boneless skinless chicken breasts, cut into 1-inch pieces

SAUCE:
- 1/2 teaspoon cornstarch
- 2 tablespoons rice vinegar
- 2 tablespoons reduced-sodium soy sauce
- 1 teaspoon sugar

STIR-FRY:
- 1 tablespoon plus 2 teaspoons peanut oil, *divided*
- 1 medium green pepper, julienned
- 3 green onions, cut into 1-inch lengths
- 1/2 cup canned bamboo shoots, finely chopped
- 2 to 3 teaspoons minced fresh gingerroot
- 1/4 cup slivered almonds, toasted

Hot cooked rice, optional

1. In a large resealable plastic bag, combine the egg white, soy sauce, cornstarch and pepper. Add chicken; seal bag and turn to coat. Refrigerate for 30 minutes. For sauce, combine the cornstarch, vinegar, soy sauce and sugar until smooth; set aside.

2. Drain chicken and discard marinade. In a large skillet or wok, stir-fry the chicken in 1 tablespoon oil until no longer pink. Remove and keep warm.

3. Stir-fry green pepper and onions in remaining oil for 2 minutes. Add bamboo shoots and ginger; stir-fry 3-4 minutes longer or until vegetables are crisp-tender.

4. Stir the sauce mixture and add to the pan. Bring to a boil; cook and stir for 2 minutes or until thickened. Add the chicken and heat through. Sprinkle with the almonds. Serve with the rice if desired.

[2005]

BARBECUED CHICKEN

yield: 4-6 servings ∞ **prep: 20 min. bake: 55 min.**

I still have the card for this recipe that a friend gave me 25 years ago.

—*Norma Harder*
Saskatoon, Saskatchewan, Field Editor

- 1 broiler/fryer chicken (4 to 5 pounds), cut up
- 1 tablespoon canola oil
- 1/2 cup chicken broth
- 1/2 cup ketchup
- 1/4 cup cider vinegar
- 1 tablespoon brown sugar
- 1/2 teaspoon curry powder
- 1/2 teaspoon paprika
- 1/4 teaspoon salt
- 1/4 teaspoon ground mustard
- 1/8 teaspoon chili powder

Pinch pepper
- 2 tablespoons onion soup mix

1. In a large skillet, brown the chicken on all sides in oil in batches; drain. Place chicken in a greased 13-in. x 9-in baking dish and an 8-in. square baking dish.

2. Combine the broth, ketchup, vinegar, brown sugar, curry powder, paprika, salt, mustard, chili powder and pepper; pour over chicken. Sprinkle with the soup mix. Cover and bake at 350° for 55-65 minutes or until the chicken juices run clear.

GINGER CHICKEN

"This dish has an excellent flavor and I think just about any vegetables could be substituted in place of the ones in the recipe and it would still be delicious."
—*anselr*

[2003]

CRISPY ONION CHICKEN

yield: 4 servings ∞ prep: 10 min.
bake: 30 min.

My family loves chicken, and I'm always trying new ways to prepare it. This golden-brown chicken, with its crunchy french-fried onion coating, is great with rice, baked potatoes, macaroni salad or potato salad.

—*Charlotte Smith*
 McDonald, Pennsylvania

1/2 cup butter, melted
 1 tablespoon Worcestershire sauce
 1 teaspoon ground mustard
1/2 teaspoon garlic salt
1/4 teaspoon pepper
 1 can (6 ounces) cheddar *or* original french-fried onions, crushed
 4 boneless skinless chicken breast halves (4 ounces each)

1. In a shallow bowl, combine the butter, Worcestershire sauce, mustard, garlic salt and pepper. In another shallow bowl, add 1/2 cup french-fried onions. Dip chicken in the butter mixture, then coat with onions.

2. Place in a greased 9-in. square baking pan. Top with the remaining onions; drizzle with any of the remaining butter mixture. Bake, uncovered, at 350° for 30-35 minutes or until a thermometer reads 170°.

STUFFING A BONE-IN CHICKEN BREAST

To form a pocket for stuffing, carefully loosen skin on chicken breast with your fingers. Place stuffing between meat and skin.

—*Taste of Home Cooking Experts*

[1997]

STUFFED CHICKEN BREASTS

yield: 6 servings ∞ prep: 20 min.
bake: 1-1/2 hours

Mushroom-and-rice stuffing turns plain chicken breasts into a terrific main dish that your family will remember.

—*Pat Neu, Gainesville, Texas*

1-1/2 cups sliced fresh mushrooms
1-1/3 cups uncooked instant rice
 1/4 cup chopped onion
 1/4 cup chopped celery leaves
 1/4 cup butter
1-1/2 cups water
1-1/2 teaspoons salt
 1/2 teaspoon dried oregano
 1/2 teaspoon rubbed sage
 1/2 teaspoon dried thyme
 1/4 teaspoon pepper
 1/3 cup chopped pecans, toasted
 6 bone-in chicken breast halves (8 ounces each)

1. In a large saucepan, saute mushrooms, rice, onion and celery leaves in butter until onion is tender. Add water and seasonings; bring to a boil. Reduce heat; cover and simmer for 5-7 minutes or until the rice is tender and liquid is absorbed. Stir in the pecans.

2. Stuff 1/2 cup of rice mixture under the skin of each chicken breast half. Place in a greased 13-in. x 9-in. baking dish. Bake, uncovered, at 350° for 1-1/2 hours or until a thermometer reads 170°.

STUFFED CHICKEN BREASTS

"I like stuffed recipes, and this one not only is very tasty but the stuffing goes easily under the skin of the chicken breasts. A really nice entree for company or when you feel like treating your family. I spooned the extra stuffing around the breasts and baked it, covered, for 30-35 min., then uncovered for the last half hour."
—*cwbuff*

[2002]

PUFF PASTRY CHICKEN BUNDLES

yield: 8 servings ∞ prep: 30 min. ∞ bake: 25 min.

Inside these golden puff pastry "packages", chicken breasts rolled with spinach, herbed cream cheese and walnuts are a savory surprise. I like to serve this elegant entree when we have guests or are celebrating a holiday or special occasion.

—Brad Moritz, Limerick, Pennsylvania, Field Editor

8	boneless skinless chicken breast halves (about 6 ounces *each*)
1	teaspoon salt
1/2	teaspoon pepper
40	large spinach leaves
2	cartons (8 ounces *each*) spreadable chive and onion cream cheese
1/2	cup chopped walnuts, toasted
2	sheets frozen puff pastry, thawed
1	egg
1/2	teaspoon cold water

1. Cut a lengthwise slit in each chicken breast to within 1/2 in. of the other side; open meat so it lies flat. Cover with plastic wrap; pound to flatten to 1/8-in. thickness. Remove the plastic wrap. Sprinkle salt and pepper over chicken.

2. In a small saucepan, bring 1 in. of water to a boil; add spinach. Cover and cook for 1-2 minutes or until wilted; drain. Place five spinach leaves on each chicken breast. Spoon 2 tablespoons of cream cheese down the center of each chicken breast; sprinkle with walnuts. Roll up chicken and tuck in ends.

3. Unroll puff pastry; cut into eight portions. Roll each into an 8-in. x 7-in. rectangle. Combine egg and cold water; brush over edges of pastry. Place chicken at one short end; roll up tightly, tucking in ends.

4. Place on a greased 15-in. x 10-in. x 1-in. baking sheet. Bake at 350° for 25-30 minutes or until meat is no longer pink.

PUFF PASTRY CHICKEN BUNDLES

"Very good and easy to make! Flavor and texture was great. Hardest part of this recipe is finding spinach in my town!"
—Bruha1

FLATTENING A CHICKEN BREAST

1. Hold sharp knife parallel to cutting board and along one long side of breast; cut almost in half, leaving breast attached at one side.

2. Open breast so it lies flat; cover with plastic wrap. Using flat side of a meat mallet, lightly pound to 1/4-in. thickness. Remove plastic wrap and proceed as recipe directs.

[2010]

SUMMERTIME ORZO & CHICKEN

yield: 4 servings ∞ prep/total time: 30 min.

This easy-as-can-be main dish is likely to become a summer staple at your house. It's that good! If you prefer, grill the chicken breasts instead of cooking in a skillet.

—Fran MacMillan
West Melbourne, Florida

3/4 cup uncooked orzo pasta
1 pound boneless skinless chicken breasts, cut into 1-inch pieces
1 medium cucumber, chopped
1 small red onion, chopped
1/4 cup minced fresh parsley
2 tablespoons lemon juice
1 tablespoon olive oil
1 teaspoon salt
1/4 teaspoon pepper
1/4 cup crumbled reduced-fat feta cheese

1. Cook the pasta according to package directions. Meanwhile, in a large skillet coated with cooking spray, cook the chicken over medium heat for 6-8 minutes or until no longer pink.

2. In a large bowl, combine cucumber, onion, parsley and chicken. Drain pasta; stir into chicken mixture. In a small bowl, whisk the lemon juice, oil, salt and pepper. Pour over chicken mixture; toss to coat. Serve warm or cold. Just before serving, sprinkle with cheese.

[2009]

CORNMEAL OVEN-FRIED CHICKEN

**yield: 6 servings ∞ prep: 20 min.
bake: 40 min.**

This dish perks up the dinner table. Its flavorful cornmeal coating is a crisp and tasty variation from the usual.

—Deb Williams, Peoria, Arizona

1/2 cup dry bread crumbs
1/2 cup cornmeal
1/3 cup grated Parmesan cheese
1/4 cup minced fresh parsley *or* 4 teaspoons dried parsley flakes
3/4 teaspoon garlic powder
1/2 teaspoon salt
1/2 teaspoon onion powder
1/2 teaspoon dried thyme
1/2 teaspoon pepper
1/2 cup buttermilk
1 broiler/fryer chicken (3 to 4 pounds), cut up and skin removed
1 tablespoon butter, melted

1. In a large resealable plastic bag, combine the first nine ingredients. Place the buttermilk in a shallow bowl. Dip chicken in buttermilk, then add to bag, a few pieces at a time, and shake to coat.

2. Place in a 13-in. x 9-in. baking pan coated with cooking spray. Bake at 375° for 10 minutes; drizzle with butter. Bake 30-40 minutes longer or until juices run clear.

SUMMERTIME ORZO & CHICKEN

"This was so yummy! I had it warm for dinner, then had it cold for lunch the next day. Both ways were good. The flavors go together perfectly, and it is a perfect summer meal, nice and light. I used a rotisserie chicken for convenience, and dried parsley. This is a very easy and quick recipe, and I am excited to keep making it over and over."
—*meganshakes*

FETA FACTS

Feta is a white, salty, semi-firm cheese. Traditionally it was made from sheep or goat's milk but is now also made with cow's milk. After feta is formed in a special mold, it's sliced into large pieces, salted and soaked in brine. Although feta cheese is mostly associated with Greek cooking, "feta" comes from the Italian word "fette," meaning slice of food.

—*Taste of Home Cooking Experts*

[2005]

BACON-CHEESE TOPPED CHICKEN

yield: 4 servings
prep: 40 min. + marinating
bake: 20 min.

(Pictured on page 715)

Mushrooms, bacon and Monterey Jack cheese top these tender marinated chicken breasts that provide a flavorful dining experience with just a little fuss. I get compliments whenever I serve them. They're one of my family's favorites.

—*Melanie Kennedy*
Battle Ground, Washington

1/2 cup Dijon mustard
1/2 cup honey
4-1/2 teaspoons canola oil, *divided*
1/2 teaspoon lemon juice
4 boneless skinless chicken breast halves
1/4 teaspoon salt
1/8 teaspoon pepper
Dash paprika
2 cups sliced fresh mushrooms
2 tablespoons butter
1 cup (4 ounces) shredded Monterey Jack cheese
1 cup (4 ounces) shredded cheddar cheese
8 bacon strips, partially cooked
2 teaspoons minced fresh parsley

1. In a small bowl, combine the mustard, honey, 1-1/2 teaspoons oil and lemon juice. Pour 1/2 cup marinade into a large resealable plastic bag; add the chicken. Seal the bag and turn to coat; refrigerate for 2 hours. Cover and refrigerate the remaining marinade.

2. Drain and discard marinade from chicken. In a large skillet over medium heat, brown chicken in remaining oil on all sides. Sprinkle with salt, pepper and paprika. Transfer to a greased 11-in. x 7-in. baking dish.

3. In the same skillet, saute mushrooms in butter until tender. Spoon reserved marinade over chicken. Top with the cheeses and mushrooms. Place the bacon strips in a crisscross pattern over chicken.

4. Bake, uncovered, at 375° for 20-25 minutes or until a thermometer reads 170°. Sprinkle with parsley.

[2010]

CAPRESE CHICKEN WITH BACON

yield: 4 servings ∞ **prep: 20 min.**
bake: 20 min.

Smoky bacon, fresh basil, ripe tomatoes and gooey mozzarella top these appealing chicken breasts. The aroma as they bake is irresistible!

—*Tammy Hayden, Quincy, Michigan*

8 bacon strips
4 boneless skinless chicken breast halves (6 ounces *each*)
1 tablespoon olive oil
1/2 teaspoon salt
1/4 teaspoon pepper
2 plum tomatoes, sliced
6 fresh basil leaves, thinly sliced
4 slices part-skim mozzarella cheese

1. Place bacon in an ungreased 15-in. x 10-in. x 1-in. baking pan. Bake at 400° for 8-10 minutes or until partially cooked but not crisp. Remove to paper towels to drain.

2. Place chicken in an ungreased 13-in. x 9-in. baking pan; brush with oil and sprinkle with salt and pepper. Top with tomatoes and basil. Wrap each in two bacon strips arranging bacon in a crisscross pattern.

3. Bake, uncovered, at 400° for 20-25 minutes or until a thermometer reads 170°. Top with the cheese; bake 1 minute longer or until melted.

BACON-CHEESE TOPPED CHICKEN

"I love the flavors in this recipe. I have made it three or four times. When I make it for just my husband & me, I cut the ingredients in half and substitute precooked bacon pieces for the strips."
—*grammiegreat*

TURKEY HASH, page 735

NUTTY CHICKEN STIR-FRY, page 692

HONEY-GLAZED HENS WITH
FRUIT STUFFING, page 690

ORANGE WALNUT CHICKEN, page 694

FORGOTTEN JAMBALAYA, page 693

BACON-CHEESE TOPPED CHICKEN, page 712

CHICKEN & TOMATO RISOTTO, page 691

BBQ CHICKEN BAKED POTATOES, page 702

ROAST CHRISTMAS GOOSE, page 728

CHICKEN CHEESE LASAGNA, page 722

CHICKEN 'N' HASH BROWN BAKE, page 726

BRUSCHETTA CHICKEN, page 707

CHICKEN SPARERIBS, page 707

TURKEY WITH CURRIED CREAM SAUCE, page 739

MASCARPONE-PESTO CHICKEN ROLLS, page 706

TURKEY STEW WITH DUMPLINGS, page 736

TURKEY ENCHILADAS, page 738

TURKEY BREAST WITH VEGETABLES, page 732

TURKEY DRUMSTICK DINNER, page 733

PHEASANT AND WILD RICE, page 729

[2009]

LEMON BASIL CHICKEN

yield: 6 servings ∞ **prep: 15 min.**
bake: 1-1/4 hours + standing

For Sunday dinner or any time, this tender, fragrant chicken makes a special meal.

—*Marguerite Marshall, Carencro, Louisiana*

- 1 medium lemon
- 2 garlic cloves, peeled, *divided*
- 1/4 cup minced fresh basil, *divided*
- 1 broiler/fryer chicken (3 to 4 pounds)
- 2 tablespoons butter, melted
- 1/2 teaspoon salt
- 1/4 teaspoon pepper

1. Finely grate enough peel from the lemon to measure 2 teaspoons. Cut lemon in half; squeeze juice from one half. Set aside. Slice one garlic clove; place sliced garlic, 2 tablespoons basil and the remaining lemon half in the chicken cavity.

2. Place chicken, breast side up, in a shallow roasting pan; rub with reserved lemon juice. Mince remaining garlic; combine with butter and reserved lemon peel. Rub mixture over chicken. Sprinkle with salt, pepper and remaining basil.

3. Bake, uncovered, at 375° for 1-1/4 to 1-1/2 hours or until meat juices run clear.

[2005]

PEACHY CHICKEN

yield: 4 servings ∞ **prep/total time: 30 min.**

This sweet and refreshing chicken dish is great for weeknights, but attractive enough for guests. I like to serve this over rice.

—*Bill Brown, Haddonfield, New Jersey*

- 4 boneless skinless chicken breast halves (4 ounces each)
- 1 tablespoon canola oil
- 1 tablespoon butter
- 1 can (15-1/4 ounces) sliced peaches, undrained
- 1/2 cup packed brown sugar

- 1/2 cup orange juice
- 1 envelope onion soup mix
Hot cooked rice, optional

1. In a large skillet over medium heat, brown chicken in oil and butter; remove and keep warm. Stir in the peaches with juice, brown sugar, orange juice and soup mix to the skillet. Bring to a boil; cook and stir for 2 minutes. Reduce heat; return chicken to the pan.

2. Simmer, uncovered, for 15-20 minutes or until a thermometer reads 170°. Serve with rice if desired.

[2004]

CHICKEN WITH PAPRIKA CREAM

yield: 6 servings ∞ **prep/total time: 25 min.**

Chicken with Paprika Cream is quick to make when you buy boned and skinned chicken breasts. Serving it over rice lets you get every last bit of the tasty paprika cream.

—*Marilou Robinson, Portland, Oregon*

- 6 boneless skinless chicken breast halves (4 ounces each)
- 6 tablespoons butter, *divided*
- 1 tablespoon canola oil
- 6 green onions, chopped
- 1 to 2 tablespoons paprika
- 2 cups heavy whipping cream
- 1 teaspoon salt
- 1/4 teaspoon pepper
Hot cooked rice
Additional chopped green onions, optional

1. In a large skillet, brown chicken in 1 tablespoon butter and oil over medium heat. Cover and cook for 5-7 minutes or until a thermometer reads 170°. Remove chicken; keep warm.

2. In same skillet, saute the onions until tender. Reduce heat to medium. Add paprika and remaining butter; heat until butter is melted. Stir in the cream, salt and pepper; cook and stir until sauce is thickened, about 4 minutes. Serve with chicken and rice. Garnish with onions if desired.

HUBBY'S FAVORITE CREPES

[2011]

HUBBY'S FAVORITE CREPES

yield: 5 servings ∞ prep: 30 min.
cook: 15 min.

This is a great way to use up leftover chicken. It always brings a smile to my husband's face when he comes in for supper and sees it on the table.

—Joanne Sieg, River Hills, Manitoba

1/4	cup butter, cubed
1/2	pound sliced fresh mushrooms
1/4	cup finely chopped onion
1/4	cup all-purpose flour
2	cups 2% milk
2	teaspoons chicken bouillon granules
1/2	teaspoon Italian seasoning
1/4	teaspoon pepper
1/2	cup sour cream
3	tablespoons sherry *or* chicken broth
2	cups finely chopped cooked chicken
2	tablespoons minced fresh parsley, *divided*
15	prepared crepes (9 inches)

Additional sour cream, optional

---

1. In a large skillet over medium-high heat, melt butter. Add mushrooms and onion; saute until tender. Sprinkle with flour; stir until blended. Gradually add milk. Stir in bouillon, Italian seasoning and pepper.

2. Bring mixture to a boil; cook and stir for 2 minutes or until thickened. Stir in the sour cream and sherry. Remove 1 cup sauce; set aside. Stir chicken and 1 tablespoon parsley into remaining mixture; heat through.

3. Spread 3 tablespoons filling down the center of each crepe; roll up. Drizzle reserved sauce over the top. Sprinkle with remaining parsley. Serve with additional sour cream if desired.

[1993]

CHICKEN CHEESE LASAGNA

yield: 12 servings ∞ prep: 25 min.
bake: 35 min. + standing

(Pictured on page 716)

I like to make a double batch of this lasagna and freeze one for another day. The filling can also be stuffed in manicotti shells.

—Mary Ann Kosmas
Minneapolis, Minnesota
Former Field Editor

1	medium onion, chopped
1/2	cup butter, cubed
1	garlic clove, minced
1/2	cup all-purpose flour
1	teaspoon salt
2	cups chicken broth
1-1/2	cups 2% milk
4	cups (16 ounces) shredded part-skim mozzarella cheese, *divided*
1	cup grated Parmesan cheese, *divided*
1	teaspoon dried basil
1	teaspoon dried oregano
1/2	teaspoon white pepper
2	cups (15 to 16 ounces) ricotta cheese
1	tablespoon minced fresh parsley
9	lasagna noodles, cooked and drained
2	packages (10 ounces *each*) frozen spinach, thawed and well drained
2	cups cubed cooked chicken

---

1. In a large saucepan, saute the onion in butter until tender. Add garlic; cook 1 minute longer. Stir in flour and salt until blended; cook until bubbly. Gradually stir in broth and milk. Bring to a boil; cook and stir for 1 minute or until thickened. Stir in 2 cups mozzarella, 1/2 cup Parmesan cheese, basil, oregano and pepper; set aside.

2. In a large bowl, combine ricotta cheese, parsley and remaining mozzarella; set aside. Spread one-quarter of the cheese sauce into a greased 13-in. x 9-in.

baking dish; cover with one-third of the noodles. Layer with half of the ricotta mixture, half of the spinach and half of the chicken.

3. Cover with one-quarter of the cheese sauce and one-third of the noodles. Repeat the layers of ricotta mixture, spinach, chicken and one-quarter cheese sauce. Cover with remaining noodles and cheese sauce.

4. Sprinkle with remaining Parmesan cheese. Bake at 350°, uncovered, for 35-40 minutes. Let stand 15 minutes.

[2009]

CHICKEN ENCHILADA BAKE

yield: 10 servings ∞ prep: 20 min.
bake: 50 min. + standing

Your family is going to gobble up this cheesy, Southwestern chicken bake, and they will ask for it again and again. It's real comfort food!

—*Melanie Burns, Pueblo West, Colorado*

4-1/2 cups cubed rotisserie chicken
1 can (28 ounces) green enchilada sauce
1-1/4 cups (10 ounces) sour cream
9 corn tortillas (6 inches), cut into 1-1/2-inch pieces
4 cups (16 ounces) shredded Monterey Jack cheese

1. In a greased 13-in. x 9-in. baking dish, layer half of the chicken, enchilada sauce, sour cream, tortillas and cheese. Repeat layers.

2. Cover and bake at 375° for 40 minutes. Uncover; bake 10 minutes longer or until bubbly. Let stand for 15 minutes before serving.

[2010]

GREEK CHICKEN PASTA

yield: 5 servings ∞ prep/total time: 25 min.

This hearty main dish has great Mediterranean flavor. I left out the olives, and my family still loved it.

—*Susan Stetzel*
Gainesville, New York, Field Editor

2 cups uncooked penne pasta
1/4 cup butter, cubed
1 large onion, chopped
1/4 cup all-purpose flour
1 can (14-1/2 ounces) reduced-sodium chicken broth
3 cups cubed rotisserie chicken
1 jar (7-1/2 ounces) marinated quartered artichoke hearts, drained
1 cup (4 ounces) crumbled feta cheese
1/2 cup chopped oil-packed sun-dried tomatoes
1/3 cup sliced pitted Greek olives
2 tablespoons minced fresh parsley

1. Cook the pasta according to the package directions.

2. Meanwhile, in a large ovenproof skillet, melt butter. Add the onion; saute until tender. Stir in the flour until blended; gradually add the broth. Bring to a boil; cook and stir for 2 minutes or until thickened. Stir in the chicken, artichoke hearts, cheese, tomatoes and olives.

3. Drain pasta; stir into the pan. Broil 3-4 in. from the heat for 5-7 minutes or until bubbly and golden brown. Sprinkle with parsley.

GREEK CHICKEN PASTA

"This recipe is FABULOUS! It tastes like something I ordered at a high-end restaurant! I did not include the Greek olives, and I baked boneless skinless chicken breasts in Italian dressing and then cubed them for the recipe. I even cut the butter down a bit and it was still amazing!"
—*jennifergooding*

[2008]

CREAMY CHICKEN ENCHILADAS

yield: 10 servings ∽ prep: 30 min.
bake: 35 min.

My daughter brought 10 pans of these yummy enchiladas to my wedding reception and it was the biggest hit of all the food. So many people wanted the recipe we sent it out with our Christmas cards.

—*Pat Coffee, Kingston, Washington*

1	package (8 ounces) cream cheese, softened
2	tablespoons water
2	teaspoons onion powder
2	teaspoons ground cumin
1/2	teaspoon salt
1/4	teaspoon pepper
5	cups diced cooked chicken
20	flour tortillas (6 inches), room temperature
2	cans (10-3/4 ounces *each*) condensed cream of chicken soup, undiluted
2	cups (16 ounces) sour cream
1	cup 2% milk
2	cans (4 ounces *each*) chopped green chilies
2	cups (8 ounces) shredded cheddar cheese

1. In a large bowl, beat the cream cheese, water, onion powder, cumin, salt and pepper until smooth. Stir in chicken.

2. Place 1/4 cup chicken mixture down the center of each tortilla. Roll up and place seam side down in two greased 13-in. x 9-in. baking dishes. In a large bowl, combine the soup, sour cream, milk and chilies; pour over enchiladas.

3. Bake, uncovered, at 350° for 30-40 minutes or until heated through. Sprinkle with cheese; bake 5 minutes longer or until cheese is melted.

CREAMY CHICKEN ENCHILADAS

"These are so good, every time I make them, I can't believe that I made them. Have shared this recipe with family and friends, someone always asks. Thank you, we LOVE it."

—*VStarVickie*

[1993]

THREE-CHEESE CHICKEN BAKE

yield: 12-15 servings ∽ prep: 15 min.
bake: 55 min.

This is a hearty, comforting casserole that's always a crowd-pleaser. The combination of flavors and interesting colors ensures I come home with an empty dish!

—*Vicki Raatz*
Waterloo, Wisconsin, Former Field Editor

1/2	cup chopped onion
1/2	cup chopped green pepper
3	tablespoons butter
1	can (10-3/4 ounces) condensed cream of chicken soup, undiluted
1	jar (8 ounces) sliced mushrooms, drained
1	jar (2 ounces) diced pimientos, drained
1/2	teaspoon dried basil
1	package (8 ounces) noodles, cooked and drained
3	cups diced cooked chicken
2	cups ricotta cheese
2	cups (8 ounces) shredded cheddar cheese
1/2	cup grated Parmesan cheese
1/4	cup buttered bread crumbs

1. In a large skillet, saute onion and green pepper in butter until tender. Remove from the heat. Stir in soup, mushrooms, pimientos and basil; set aside.

2. In a large bowl, combine the noodles, chicken and cheeses; add mushroom sauce and mix well. Transfer to a greased 13-in. x 9-in. baking dish.

3. Bake, uncovered, at 350° for 40-45 minutes or until bubbly. Sprinkle with crumbs. Bake 15 minutes longer or until browned.

[2007]

CHICKEN MANICOTTI

yield: 7 servings ∞ **prep: 30 min.**
bake: 35 min.

I like making this dish for special occasions.
You can also use low-fat ingredients, and it
turns out just as good.

—**Liz Lorch, Spirit Lake, Iowa**

 2 packages (3 ounces *each*) cream
   cheese, softened
 1 cup (8 ounces) sour cream
1/4 cup minced fresh parsley
1/2 teaspoon salt
1/4 teaspoon pepper
 4 cups cubed cooked chicken
 1 medium onion, finely chopped
 1 can (8 ounces) mushroom stems and
   pieces, drained
 1 tablespoon butter
14 manicotti shells, cooked and drained
SAUCE:
 6 tablespoons butter
 6 tablespoons all-purpose flour
1/4 teaspoon salt
3-1/2 cups 2% milk
 3 cups (12 ounces) shredded Monterey
   Jack *or* cheddar cheese
 4 tablespoons shredded Parmesan
   cheese, *divided*

1. In a large bowl, beat the cream cheese
until fluffy. Beat in the sour cream,
parsley, salt and pepper until blended.
Stir in chicken. In a small skillet, cook
onion and mushrooms in butter until
tender; add to chicken mixture. Stuff
into manicotti shells.

2. In a large saucepan, melt butter. Stir in
flour and salt until smooth. Gradually
whisk in milk. Bring to a boil; cook and
stir for 2 minutes or until thickened. Stir
in 2-1/2 cups Monterey Jack cheese and
2 tablespoons Parmesan cheese just
until melted.

3. Spread about 1/2 cup cheese sauce in
each of two greased 11-in. x 7-in.
dishes. Top with stuffed shells and
remaining sauce.

4. Cover and bake at 350° for 25 minutes.
Uncover; sprinkle with remaining
cheeses. Bake 10-15 minutes longer or
until bubbly and cheese is melted.

[2009]

QUICK CHICKEN AND DUMPLINGS

yield: 6 servings ∞ **prep/total time: 30 min.**

Using precooked chicken and ready-made
biscuits, this hearty dish is comfort food made
super simple. It's the perfect way to warm up
on chilly nights.

—**Lakeya Astwood, Schenectady, New York**

 6 individually frozen biscuits
1/4 cup chopped onion
1/4 cup chopped green pepper
 1 tablespoon olive oil
 4 cups shredded rotisserie chicken
 2 cans (14-1/2 ounces *each*) reduced-
   sodium chicken broth
 1 can (4 ounces) mushroom stems and
   pieces, drained
 1 teaspoon chicken bouillon granules
 1 teaspoon minced fresh parsley
1/2 teaspoon dried sage leaves
1/4 teaspoon dried rosemary, crushed
1/4 teaspoon pepper

1. Cut each biscuit into fourths; set aside.
In a large saucepan, saute onion and
green pepper in oil until tender. Stir in
chicken, broth, mushrooms, bouillon,
parsley, sage, rosemary and pepper.

2. Bring to a boil. Reduce the heat; add
the biscuits for dumplings. Cover and
simmer for 10 minutes or until a
toothpick inserted near the center of a
dumpling comes out clean (do not lift
cover while simmering).

CHICKEN MANICOTTI

"I love this recipe. It's great
to freeze as well."
—*samantha_phill*

CHICKEN 'N' HASH BROWN BAKE

[1994]

CHICKEN 'N' HASH BROWN BAKE

yield: 8-10 servings ∽ **prep:** 10 min.
bake: 50 min.

(Pictured on page 717)

The first time I served this dish for company was to a family with five children. The kids and the adults love it! This is one recipe I often make for potlucks.

—*Ruth Andrewson*
Leavenworth, Washington
Former Field Editor

---

1 **package (32 ounces) frozen cubed hash brown potatoes, thawed**
1 **teaspoon salt**
1/4 **teaspoon pepper**
4 **cups diced cooked chicken**
1 **can (4 ounces) mushroom stems and pieces, drained**
1 **cup (8 ounces) sour cream**
2 **cups chicken broth *or* stock**
1 **can (10-3/4 ounces) condensed cream of chicken soup, undiluted**
2 **teaspoons chicken bouillon granules**
2 **tablespoons finely chopped onion**
2 **tablespoons finely chopped sweet red pepper**
1 **garlic clove, minced**
Paprika
1/4 **cup sliced almonds**

---

1. Spread potatoes in an ungreased 13-in. x 9-in. baking dish. Sprinkle with salt and pepper. Sprinkle the chicken and mushrooms over the top. Combine the sour cream, broth, soup, bouillon, onion, red pepper and garlic; pour over the mushrooms.

2. Sprinkle with paprika and almonds. Bake, uncovered, at 350° for 50-60 minutes or until heated through.

[2007]

BISCUIT-TOPPED LEMON CHICKEN

yield: 15 servings (30 biscuits)
prep: 40 min. ∽ **bake:** 35 min.

This homey recipe combines two of my favorite things —hot, crusty biscuits and a flavorful lemon-pepper sauce. I've taken it to potlucks and given it as gifts with potatoes and carrots baked in.

—*Pattie Ishee, Stringer, Mississippi*

---

2 **large onions, finely chopped**
4 **celery ribs, finely chopped**
1 **cup butter, cubed**
2 **garlic cloves, minced**
8 **green onions, thinly sliced**
2/3 **cup all-purpose flour**
8 **cups 2% milk**
12 **cups cubed cooked chicken**
2 **cans (10-3/4 ounces *each*) condensed cream of chicken soup, undiluted**
1/2 **cup lemon juice**
2 **tablespoons grated lemon peel**
2 **teaspoons pepper**
1 **teaspoon salt**
CHEDDAR BISCUITS:
5 **cups self-rising flour**
2 **cups 2% milk**
2 **cups (8 ounces) shredded cheddar cheese**
1/4 **cup butter, melted**

---

1. In a Dutch oven, saute onions and celery in butter. Add the garlic; cook 1 minute longer. Add green onions. Stir in flour until blended; gradually add the milk. Bring to a boil; cook and stir for 2 minutes or until thickened.

2. Stir in chicken, soup, lemon juice and peel, pepper and salt; heat through. Pour into two greased 13-in. x 9-in. baking dishes; set aside.

3. In a large bowl, combine the biscuit ingredients just until moistened. Turn onto a lightly floured surface; knead

8-10 times. Pat or roll out to 3/4-in. thickness. With a floured 2-1/2-in. biscuit cutter, cut out 30 biscuits.

4. Place over chicken mixture. Bake, uncovered, at 350° for 35-40 minutes or until golden brown.

Editor's Note: As a substitute for each cup of self-rising flour, place 1-1/2 teaspoons baking powder and 1/2 teaspoon salt in a measuring cup. Add all-purpose flour to measure 1 cup.

[1994]

POTLUCK CORDON BLEU CASSEROLE
yield: 8-10 servings ✎ prep: 25 min. bake: 30 min.

Whenever I'm invited to attend a potluck, people usually ask me to bring this tempting casserole. The chicken, ham and cheese are delectable combined with the crunchy topping. Whenever I bake a turkey, I'll prepare the leftovers for this dish, since it is great with either chicken or turkey.

—Joyce Paul, Moose Jaw, Saskatchewan

```
  4  cups cubed cooked chicken or turkey
  3  cups cubed fully cooked ham
  1  cup (4 ounces) shredded cheddar cheese
  1  cup chopped onion
1/4  cup butter, cubed
1/3  cup all-purpose flour
  2  cups half-and-half cream
  1  teaspoon dill weed
1/8  teaspoon ground mustard
1/8  teaspoon ground nutmeg
TOPPING:
  1  cup dry bread crumbs
  2  tablespoons butter, melted
1/4  teaspoon dill weed
1/4  cup shredded cheddar cheese
1/4  cup chopped walnuts
```

1. In a large bowl, combine the chicken, ham and cheese; set aside. In a large saucepan, saute onion in butter until tender. Add flour; stir until blended. Gradually add cream, stirring constantly. Bring to a boil; cook and stir for 1-2 minutes or until thickened. Stir in the dill, mustard and nutmeg. Remove from the heat and pour over meat mixture.

2. Spoon into a greased 13-in. x 9-in. baking dish. In a small bowl, combine the bread crumbs, butter and dill. Stir in cheese and walnuts. Sprinkle over casserole.

3. Bake casserole, uncovered at 350° for 30 minutes or until heated through.

[1999]

CHICKEN CRESCENT WREATH
yield: 6-8 servings ✎ prep: 15 min. bake: 20 min.

Chicken Crescent Wreath is an impressive-looking main dish that's a snap to prepare. Even when my cooking time is limited, I can still serve this delicious wreath. The red pepper and green broccoli add a festive touch.

—Marlene Denissen, St. Croix Falls, Wisconsin

```
  2  tubes (8 ounces each) refrigerated crescent rolls
  1  cup (4 ounces) shredded Colby-Monterey Jack cheese
2/3  cup condensed cream of chicken soup, undiluted
1/2  cup chopped fresh broccoli
1/2  cup chopped sweet red pepper
1/4  cup chopped water chestnuts
  1  can (5 ounces) white chicken, drained or 3/4 cup
     cubed cooked chicken
  2  tablespoons chopped onion
```

1. Arrange crescent rolls on a 12-in. pizza pan, forming a ring with pointed ends facing the outer edge of pan and wide ends overlapping.

2. Combine the remaining ingredients; spoon over wide ends of rolls. Fold points over filling and tuck under wide ends (filling will be visible).

3. Bake at 375° for 20-25 minutes or until golden brown.

TOTING FOOD TO A POTLUCK

Use an insulated food carrier to keep your food hot while transporting. If you don't have one, wrap the dish in a large towel to keep in the heat.

—Taste of Home Cooking Experts

CHILI CHICKEN ENCHILADAS

"Great enchiladas! Good for us, as they only make four which is plenty for just two of us. I boiled one large bone-in chicken breast half, and it yielded just enought meat for the recipe, so they're economical too. Easy to put together....delicious....love this recipe! "
— vewebber58

[2007]

CHILI CHICKEN ENCHILADAS

yield: 4 enchiladas ∽ prep: 20 min.
bake: 25 min.

Rich and saucy, this south-of-the-border entree makes a hearty meal. Whenever I take dinner to friends who are ill, these enchiladas seem to make them feel better.

—Alicia Johnson, Hillsboro, Oregon

- 1/4 **cup chopped onion**
- 1 **tablespoon butter**
- 2 **garlic cloves, minced**
- 2 **tablespoons all-purpose flour**
- 1 **cup chicken broth**
- 1 **can (4 ounces) chopped green chilies**
- 1/4 **teaspoon ground coriander**
- 1/8 **teaspoon pepper**
- 1 **cup (4 ounces) shredded Monterey Jack cheese, *divided***
- 1/2 **cup sour cream**
- 2 **cups chopped cooked chicken**
- 4 **flour tortillas (8 inches)**

Sliced ripe olives, chopped tomatoes and green onions, optional

---

1. In a small saucepan, saute onion in butter until tender. Add garlic; cook 1 minute longer. Combine flour and broth until smooth; gradually add to the pan.

2. Stir in chilies, coriander and pepper. Bring to a boil; cook and stir for 2 minutes or until thickened. Remove from the heat; add 1/2 cup cheese and sour cream, stirring until the cheese is melted.

3. Combine chicken and 3/4 cup sauce. Place about 1/2 cup chicken mixture down the center of each tortilla. Roll up and place seam side down in a greased 11-in. x 7-in. baking dish. Pour remaining sauce over enchiladas.

4. Bake enchiladas , uncovered, at 350° for 20 minutes. Sprinkle with the remaining cheese. Bake 5-10 minutes longer or until the cheese is melted. Garnish with olives, tomatoes and green onions if desired.

[2004]

ROAST CHRISTMAS GOOSE

yield: 8 servings ∽ prep: 10 min.
bake: 2-1/4 hours + standing

(Pictured on page 716)

I have such fond childhood memories of my mother serving this golden-brown Christmas goose. To flavor the meat, Mom stuffed the bird with peeled and quartered fruit that's discarded after baking.

—Rosemarie Forcum
Heathsville, Virginia, Former Field Editor

- 1 **domestic goose (10 to 12 pounds)**

Salt and pepper
- 1 **medium apple, peeled and quartered**
- 1 **medium navel orange, peeled and quartered**
- 1 **medium lemon, peeled and quartered**
- 1 **cup hot water**

---

1. Sprinkle the goose cavity with salt and pepper. Place the apple, orange and lemon in the cavity. Place goose breast side up on a rack in a large shallow roasting pan. Prick skin well with a fork. Pour water into pan.

2. Bake, uncovered, at 350° for 2-1/4 to 3 hours or until a thermometer reads 180°. If necessary, drain fat from pan as it accumulates. Cover goose with foil and let stand for 20 minutes before carving. Discard fruit.

[2002]

TURKEY BREAST FLORENTINE

**yield: 6-8 servings ∽ prep: 30 min.
bake: 1-1/2 hours + standing**

A lovely dish for guests, this spinach-stuffed turkey breast looks beautiful when you slice it for serving. I've also spooned the filling into a pocket slit in a boneless center-cut pork roast with delicious results.

—Shirley Goehring, Lodi, California, Field Editor

- 1 boneless skinless turkey breast half (3 to 4 pounds)
- 5 bacon strips
- 3/4 cup chopped onion
- 3 tablespoons all-purpose flour
- 3/4 teaspoon dried tarragon
- 1/2 teaspoon salt
- 1/4 teaspoon pepper
- 1-1/2 cups milk
- 1 package (10 ounces) frozen chopped spinach, thawed and squeezed dry
- 1 jar (4-1/2 ounces) sliced mushrooms, drained
- 1 tablespoon butter, melted
- 1/3 cup shredded Swiss cheese

1. Make a lengthwise slit down the center of the turkey breast to within 1/2 in. of bottom. Open meat so it lies flat; cover with plastic wrap. Flatten to 1/2-in. thickness. Remove plastic; set aside.

2. In a large skillet, cook two bacon strips until crisp. Drain, reserving drippings. Crumble bacon; set aside. In the drippings, saute onion until tender. Stir in flour, tarragon, salt and pepper until blended. Gradually stir in milk. Bring to a boil; cook and stir for 2 minutes or until thickened. Remove from the heat.

3. Refrigerate 1/2 cup sauce. Add spinach, mushrooms and crumbled bacon to the remaining sauce; spread over turkey breast. Starting at a short end, roll up and tuck in ends; tie with kitchen string. Place on a rack in a greased shallow roasting pan. Brush with butter. Cover loosely with foil.

4. Bake at 350° for 1 hour. Remove foil. Cut remaining bacon strips in half; place over the turkey. Bake 25-35 minutes longer or until turkey is no longer pink.

5. Discard string. Let turkey stand for 10 minutes before slicing. Meanwhile, heat the reserved sauce; stir in cheese until melted. Serve with turkey.

[1993]

PHEASANT AND WILD RICE

**yield: 6-8 servings ∽ prep: 20 min.
bake: 1 hour + standing**

(Pictured on page 720)

Everyone in my family hunts, so we have an abundance of game. This recipe also works well with wild turkey or grouse and even with chicken if you prefer. I love to make this dish on special occasions and for guests.

—Deb Arndt, Hillsboro, Wisconsin

- 1 can (10-3/4 ounces) condensed cream of mushroom soup, undiluted
- 2-2/3 cups water
- 3/4 cup chopped onion
- 2-1/2 teaspoons dried parsley flakes
- 2 teaspoons salt
- 2 teaspoons garlic powder
- 2 teaspoons dried oregano
- 1-1/2 teaspoons paprika
- 1 teaspoon pepper
- 1 tablespoon all-purpose flour
- 1 large oven roasting bag
- 6 bacon strips, cut up
- 2 cups uncooked wild rice
- 1/2 pound sliced fresh mushrooms
- 1 large pheasant, halved *or* two small pheasants (about 4 pounds)

1. In a large saucepan, combine first nine ingredients; bring to a boil.

2. Meanwhile, place flour in oven bag; shake to coat. Place oven bag in a 13-in. x 9-in. baking pan; add the bacon. Sprinkle rice and mushrooms over bacon. Add pheasant. Pour soup mixture into bag.

3. Cut six 1/2-in. slits in top of bag; close bag with tie provided. Bake at 350° for 1 to 1-1/2 hours or until a thermometer reads 180°. Let stand for 10 minutes before carving.

[2010]

CHAMPAGNE-BASTED TURKEY

yield: 14 servings (1-2/3 cups gravy) ∽ **prep: 20 min.**
bake: 3-1/2 hours + standing

I've prepared this recipe every Thanksgiving for years, and we all love it. The secret is to use lots of fresh parsley and to keep basting. The result is a tender, delightful turkey.

—*Sharon Hawk, Edwardsville, Illinois*

- 1 turkey (14 to 16 pounds)
- 1/4 cup butter, softened
- 1 teaspoon salt
- 1 teaspoon celery salt
- 3/4 teaspoon pepper
- Fresh sage and parsley sprigs, optional
- 2 cups Champagne *or* other sparkling wine
- 2 medium onions, chopped
- 1-1/2 cups minced fresh parsley
- 1 cup condensed beef consomme, undiluted
- 1/2 teaspoon dried thyme
- 1/2 teaspoon dried marjoram

GRAVY:
- 1 tablespoon butter
- 1 tablespoon all-purpose flour

1. Pat turkey dry. Combine the butter, salt, celery salt and pepper; rub over the outside and inside of turkey. Place sage and parsley sprigs in cavity if desired. Tuck wings under turkey; tie drumsticks together. Place breast side up on a rack in a roasting pan.

2. Bake, uncovered, at 325° for 30 minutes. In a large bowl, combine Champagne, onions, parsley, consomme, thyme and marjoram; pour into pan. Bake turkey for 3 to 3-1/2 hours longer or until a thermometer reads 180° in the thigh, basting occasionally with Champagne mixture. Cover loosely with foil if turkey browns too quickly. Cover and let stand for 20 minutes before slicing.

3. For gravy, strain drippings into a small bowl. In a small saucepan, melt butter. Stir in the flour until smooth; gradually add drippings. Bring to a boil; cook and stir for 2 minutes or until thickened. Serve with turkey.

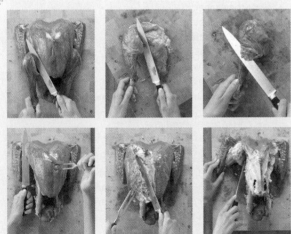

CARVING A TURKEY

1. Place bird on a carving board and remove any stuffing. Holding the end of the drumstick, pull the leg away from the body and cut between the thigh joint and body to remove the entire leg. Repeat with other leg.

2. To separate the drumstick and thigh, cut through the connecting joint.

3. Holding the drumstick by the end, slice meat into 1/4-in. slices. Cut thigh meat parallel to the bone into 1/4-in. slices.

4. Hold the bird with a meat fork and make a deep cut into the breast meat just above the wing area.

5. Slice down from the top of the breast into the cut made in Step 4. Slice meat 1/4 in. thick. Repeat Steps 4 and 5 on other side of bird.

6. To remove wings, cut through the connecting joints by the wing bones and backbone.

[1995]

MARINATED THANKSGIVING TURKEY

yield: 8 servings
prep: 10 min. + marinating
grill: 2-1/2 hours + standing

My family enjoys this turkey because it cooks up tender, tasty and golden brown. The marinade flavors the meat well. I like grilling it since it adds that tempting barbecued flavor.

—**Ken Churches**
Kailua-Kona, Hawaii, Field Editor

1-1/2 **cups chicken broth**
   2 **cups water**
   1 **cup reduced-sodium soy sauce**
 2/3 **cup lemon juice**
   2 **garlic cloves, minced**
1-1/2 **teaspoons ground ginger**
   1 **teaspoon pepper**
   1 **turkey (12 to 13 pounds)**

---

1. Combine the first seven ingredients; set aside 1 cup for basting. Pour the remaining marinade into a 2-gallon resealable plastic bag. Add the turkey and seal bag; turn to coat. Refrigerate overnight, turning several times. Cover and refrigerated reserved marinade.

2. Drain and discard marinade.

3. Grill Method: Prepare grill for indirect medium heat. Tuck wings under turkey and place with breast side down on grill rack. Grill, covered, for 1 hour.

4. If using a charcoal grill, add 10 briquettes to coals; turn the turkey. Baste with reserved marinade. Cover and cook for 1-1/2 to 2 hours, adding 10 briquettes to maintain heat and brushing with marinade every 30 minutes until thermometer reads 180° in the thigh. Cover and let stand 20 minutes before carving.

5. Conventional Roasting Method: Place turkey on a rack in a large roaster. Bake, uncovered, at 325° for 3 to 3-1/2 hours or until thermometer reads 180° in the thigh. Baste frequently with reserved marinade. When turkey begins to brown, cover lightly with foil.

[2000]

HERBED TURKEY BREAST

yield: 10-12 servings ∾ **prep: 10 min.**
bake: 1-1/2 hours

I always serve turkey for our Thanksgiving meal. But instead of roasting a whole bird, I opt for a turkey breast since most of us prefer white meat. The herb butter basting sauce keeps it so moist, and it's easy to carve.

—**Ruby Williams**
Bogalusa, Louisiana, Former Field Editor

1/2 **cup butter, cubed**
1/4 **cup lemon juice**
  2 **tablespoons reduced-sodium soy sauce**
  2 **tablespoons finely chopped green onions**
  1 **tablespoon rubbed sage**
  1 **teaspoon dried thyme**
  1 **teaspoon dried marjoram**
1/4 **teaspoon pepper**
  1 **bone-in turkey breast (5-1/2 to 6 pounds)**

---

1. In a small saucepan, combine the first eight ingredients; bring to a boil. Remove from the heat. Place turkey in a shallow roasting pan; drizzle with the butter mixture.

2. Bake, uncovered, at 325° for 1-1/2 to 2 hours or until a thermometer reads 170°, basting every 30 minutes.

MARINATED THANKSGIVING TURKEY

❝I made this recipe for our first Thanksgiving at home. Wow. My husband couldn't stop stuffing his face—and he doesn't generally like turkey!❞
—*mrsb1218*

TURKEY BREAST WITH VEGETABLES

"This recipe is fantastic!"
—*mykamartin*

[2007]

TURKEY BREAST WITH VEGETABLES

yield: 6 servings ∞ prep: 20 min.
bake: 2-1/4 hours + standing

(Pictured on page 719)

This recipe offers the convenient option of baking just the turkey breast. Prepared with herbs and crisp-tender vegetables, no one will miss the rest of the bird. It's a breeze to prepare. Plus, it allows you to spend more precious time with your family.

—*Doris Russell, Fallston, Maryland*

1/4 cup plus 1 tablespoon olive oil, *divided*
1 tablespoon minced fresh rosemary
2 teaspoons fennel seed, crushed
3 garlic cloves, minced
1 pound fresh baby carrots
3 large onions, cut into eighths
8 small red potatoes, cut in half
1 bone-in turkey breast (6 pounds)
1/2 teaspoon salt
1/4 teaspoon pepper
1/8 teaspoon garlic powder
1/2 cup chicken broth

---

1. In a large resealable plastic bag, combine 1/4 cup oil, rosemary, fennel seed and garlic. Add the carrots, onions and potatoes; shake to coat.

2. Place turkey breast in a shallow roasting pan. Rub turkey skin with remaining oil; sprinkle with the salt, pepper and garlic powder. Arrange vegetables around turkey.

3. Bake turkey, uncovered, at 325° for 2-1/4 to 2-3/4 hours or until a thermometer reads 170°, basting occasionally with broth. Cover and let stand for 10 minutes before carving.

[2000]

NUTTY TURKEY SLICES

yield: 3-6 servings
prep/total time: 20 min.

Here's a flavorful way to dress up turkey breast slices. You can really taste the walnuts in the crunchy golden coating.

—*Nancy Schmidt*
Center, Colorado, Field Editor

3/4 cup ground walnuts
1/4 cup grated Parmesan cheese
1/2 teaspoon Italian seasoning
1/2 teaspoon paprika
1 package (17.6 ounces) turkey breast cutlets
3 tablespoons butter
1 teaspoon cornstarch
1/2 cup chicken broth
2 teaspoons lemon juice

---

1. In a large resealable plastic bag, combine the walnuts, cheese, Italian seasoning and paprika. Add turkey, a few pieces at a time, and shake to coat.

2. In a large skillet over medium heat, brown turkey in batches in butter for 3-4 minutes on each side or until no longer pink; remove and keep warm.

3. Combine the cornstarch, broth and lemon juice until smooth; gradually add to the skillet. Stir to loosen browned bits and bring to a boil; cook and stir for 1 minute or until thickened. Serve with turkey.

GRINDING NUTS

When using a food processor to grind nuts, they can easily go from finely ground into nut butter. Keep an eye on them as you are grinding and use the pulse feature.

—*Taste of Home Cooking Experts*

[1996]

TURKEY DRUMSTICK DINNER

yield: 4 servings ✑ **prep: 25 min.**
bake: 2-1/2 hours

(Pictured on page 719)

I discovered this recipe a long time ago and love it since it uses tasty turkey drumsticks. Our family and friends enjoy this savory meat-and-potatoes meal.

—Alice Balliet, Kane, Pennsylvania

4 turkey drumsticks (12 ounces each)
2 tablespoons canola oil
1 tablespoon butter
1 medium onion, sliced
1 can (14-1/2 ounces) stewed tomatoes
3 chicken bouillon granules
1 teaspoon garlic salt
1/2 teaspoon dried oregano
1/2 teaspoon dried basil
4 large potatoes, peeled, cooked and quartered
2 medium zucchini, cut into 3/4-inch slices
2 tablespoons cornstarch
2 tablespoons water
Chopped fresh parsley

1. In a large skillet, brown drumsticks in oil and butter. Place in a 3-qt. Dutch oven. Top with onion slices. In the same skillet, combine the tomatoes, bouillon and seasonings.

2. Pour over the drumsticks. Cover and bake at 325° for 2 hours or until a thermometer reads 180° basting once or twice. Add potatoes and zucchini. Cover and bake 20 minutes longer or until vegetables are tender. Remove drumsticks and vegetables to a serving dish and keep warm.

3. Combine the cornstarch and water until smooth; stir into tomato mixture. Bring to a boil; reduce heat. Cook and

stir for 1-2 minutes or until thickened. Serve with drumsticks and vegetables. Sprinkle with parsley.

[1994]

TURKEY STIR-FRY

yield: 6 servings ✑ **prep/total time: 30 min.**

Here's a tasty way to prepare turkey any time of year. My family loves the tender turkey strips, colorful vegetables and crunchy cashews. You don't always have to fix the whole bird to enjoy the wonderful taste of turkey.

—Julianne Johnson, Grove City, Minnesota

1-1/2 pounds boneless turkey breast halves, cut into strips
1 tablespoon canola oil
1 small onion, chopped
1 carrot, julienned
1/2 medium green pepper, sliced
2 cups fresh mushrooms, sliced
3 tablespoons cornstarch
1 cup chicken broth
3 tablespoons reduced-sodium soy sauce
1/2 teaspoon ground ginger
2 cups pea pods, trimmed
Cooked rice, optional
1/3 cup cashews, optional

1. In a large skillet or wok, stir-fry turkey in oil over medium-high heat until no longer pink, about 5-6 minutes. Remove the turkey and keep warm. Stir-fry the onion, carrot, green pepper and mushrooms until crisp-tender, about 5 minutes.

2. In a bowl, combine cornstarch, broth, soy sauce and ginger until smooth. Stir into skillet. Bring to boil; cook and stir for 2 minutes or until thickened.

3. Add turkey and pea pods; cook and stir until heated through. Serve with rice if desired. Top with cashews.

TURKEY DRUMSTICK DINNER

❝This is delicious! My kids and I all loved it. It was easy to fix and the drumsticks (I used chicken instead of turkey) came out very tender and flavorful.❞
—kelbuz

BRINED GRILLED TURKEY BREAST

"I have made this recipe many times. It is absolutely the best recipe that I have ever made with turkey. Sometimes I have made it in the oven, and I leave about an inch of the brine in the Dutch oven, then baste as usual. I cover it if it seems to get too brown. I cooked it for the time recommended on the package for a breast or whole turkey."
—gardeninggirl1951

[2009]

BRINED GRILLED TURKEY BREAST

yield: 6 servings ∽ prep: 20 min. + chilling
grill: 1-1/4 hours + standing

You'll want to give thanks for this awesome turkey! Moist, slightly sweet and with a hint of spice, this was one of our best turkeys ever.

—*Tina Repak Mirilovich*
Johnstown, Pennsylvania, Field Editor

2 quarts cold water, *divided*
1/2 cup kosher salt
1/2 cup packed brown sugar
1 tablespoon whole peppercorns
1 boneless skinless turkey breast half
(2 to 3 pounds)
BASTING SAUCE:
1/4 cup canola oil
1/4 cup sesame oil
1/4 cup reduced-sodium soy sauce
3 tablespoons lemon juice
2 tablespoons honey
3 garlic cloves, minced
1/4 teaspoon dried thyme
1/4 teaspoon crushed red pepper flakes

1. In a large saucepan, combine 1 quart water, salt, brown sugar and the peppercorns. Bring to a boil. Cook and stir until salt and sugar are dissolved. Remove from the heat. Add remaining cold water to cool the brine to room temperature.

2. Place a large resealable plastic bag inside a second plastic bag; add turkey breast. Carefully pour cooled brine into bag. Squeeze out as much air as possible; seal bags and turn to coat. Place in a pan. Refrigerate for 4-6 hours.

3. Prepare grill for indirect heat, using a drip pan. Meanwhile, combine basting sauce ingredients. Place the turkey over drip pan and grill, covered, over indirect medium heat for 1-1/4 to 1-1/2

hours or until a thermometer reads 170°, basting occasionally with sauce. Cover turkey and let stand for 10 minutes before slicing.

Editor's Note: This recipe was tested with Morton brand kosher salt. It is best not to use a prebasted turkey breast for this recipe. However, if you do, omit the salt in the recipe.

[1997]

MARINATED TURKEY TENDERLOINS

yield: 4 servings ∽ prep: 5 min. + marinating
grill: 20 min.

When they taste my grilled specialty, guests say this turkey melts in their mouths.

—*Denise Nebel*
Wayland, Iowa, Former Field Editor

1/4 cup apple juice
1/4 cup reduced-sodium soy sauce
1/4 cup canola oil
2 tablespoons lemon juice
2 tablespoons dried minced onion
1 teaspoon vanilla extract
1/4 teaspoon ground ginger
Dash *each* garlic powder and pepper
2 turkey breast tenderloins
(1/2 pound *each*)

1. In a large resealable plastic bag, combine the apple juice, soy sauce, oil, lemon juice, onion, vanilla, ginger, garlic powder and pepper; add the turkey. Seal bag and turn to coat. Refrigerate for at least 2 hours.

2. Drain and discard marinade. Grill turkey, covered, over medium heat for 8-10 minutes on each side or until a thermometer reads 170°.

4. In another large bowl, combine turkey, soup, garlic powder and 1/4 cup sour cream; spoon over stuffing mixture. Drain potatoes; mash in a large bowl. Beat in the cream cheese, pepper, salt and remaining sour cream; spread over turkey mixture. Sprinkle with cheese.

5. Bake, uncovered, at 350° for 30-35 minutes or until heated through.

[2008]

TASTES LIKE THANKSGIVING CASSEROLE

yield: 8 servings ∽ prep: 30 min.
bake: 30 min.

This hearty, rich-tasting main dish is sure to be a hit with your family. It's a wonderful way to use up Thanksgiving turkey, and you can substitute 5-1/2 cups leftover mashed potatoes for the 6 potatoes.

—*Mary Lou Timpson*
Colorado City, Arizona

6	medium potatoes, peeled and cut into chunks
1-1/4	cups chopped celery
3/4	cup chopped onion
1/2	cup butter, cubed
6	cups unseasoned stuffing cubes
1	teaspoon poultry seasoning
1/4	teaspoon rubbed sage
1	cup chicken broth
4	cups cubed cooked turkey
2	cans (10-3/4 ounces *each*) condensed cream of chicken soup, undiluted
1	teaspoon garlic powder
3/4	cup sour cream, *divided*
4	ounces cream cheese, softened
1/2	teaspoon pepper
1/4	teaspoon salt
1-1/2	cups (6 ounces) shredded cheddar cheese

1. Place the potatoes in a Dutch oven and cover with water. Bring to a boil. Reduce heat; cover and cook for 10-15 minutes or until tender.

2. Meanwhile, in a large skillet, saute the celery and onion in butter until tender. Remove from the heat.

3. In a large bowl, combine the stuffing cubes, poultry seasoning and sage. Stir in broth and celery mixture. Transfer to a greased 13-in. x 9-in. baking dish.

[1998]

TURKEY HASH

yield: 8 servings ∽ prep/total time: 30 min.

(Pictured on page 713)

This mild-tasting dish comes recommended by my family, and it's a good use for leftover turkey, too.

—*Edna Hoffman*
Hebron, Indiana, Field Editor

1	medium onion, chopped
1/2	cup chopped green pepper
1/2	cup chopped sweet red pepper
2	tablespoons butter
6	cups diced cooked potatoes
2	cups cubed cooked turkey
1/2	teaspoon salt, optional
1/8	teaspoon cayenne pepper
1/8	teaspoon ground nutmeg

1. In a large skillet, saute the onion and peppers in butter until tender. Add the potatoes, turkey, salt if desired, cayenne and nutmeg. Cook and stir over low heat for 20 minutes or until lightly browned and heated through.

TASTES LIKE THANKSGIVING CASSEROLE

"The most delicious casserole! They are not kidding when they say "tastes like Thanksgiving"... it does. I used chicken when I didn't have turkey and it tasted almost as good. Great recipe. I tried to cut down to only one can of chicken soup but I ended up using both."
—*chasmar*

TURKEY PASTA SUPREME

"The name is apt—this recipe is supreme! The sauce is simple but delicious. I altered nothing and it came out great. I served it when my brother-in-law and his wife visited, and they loved it. Terrific and a light way to use up turkey leftovers at holiday time."
—cwbuff

[1999]

TURKEY STEW WITH DUMPLINGS

yield: 10-12 servings ∞ **prep: 30 min.**
cook: 45 min.

(Pictured on page 718)

My husband and I love dumplings, and this mild-tasting, homey dish has flavorful ones floating on a tasty turkey and vegetable stew. It really hits the spot on chilly fall and winter days.

—*Rita Taylor, St. Cloud, Minnesota*

---

    8 medium carrots, cut into 1-inch
       chunks
    4 celery ribs, cut into 1-inch chunks
    1 cup chopped onion
  1/2 cup butter, cubed
    2 cans (10-1/2 ounces *each*) condensed
       beef consomme, undiluted
4-2/3 cups water, *divided*
    2 teaspoons salt
  1/4 teaspoon pepper
    3 cups cubed cooked turkey
    2 cups frozen cut green beans
  1/2 cup all-purpose flour
    2 teaspoons Worcestershire sauce
DUMPLINGS:
1-1/2 cups all-purpose flour
    2 teaspoons baking powder
    1 teaspoon salt
    2 tablespoons minced parsley
  1/8 teaspoon poultry seasoning
  3/4 cup 2% milk
    1 egg

---

1. In a Dutch oven, saute carrots, celery and onion in butter for 10 minutes. Add the consomme, 4 cups water, salt and pepper. Bring to a boil. Reduce the heat; cover and cook over low heat for 15 minutes or until the vegetables are tender.

2. Add the turkey and beans; cook for 5 minutes. Combine the flour, Worcestershire sauce and remaining water until smooth; stir into turkey

mixture. Bring to a boil. Reduce heat; cover and simmer for 5 minutes or until thickened.

3. For dumplings, in a large bowl, combine flour, baking powder and salt. Stir in the parsley and poultry seasoning. Combine milk and egg; stir into flour mixture just until moistened. Drop by tablespoonfuls onto simmering stew. Cover and simmer for 20 minutes or until a toothpick inserted in a dumpling comes out clean (do not lift the cover while simmering).

[1995]

TURKEY PASTA SUPREME

yield: 4 servings ∞ **prep/total time: 20 min.**

Since this dish combines turkey and pasta, even our children love it. It's fun to make turkey a different way, and you can't beat the creamy, cheesy sauce. This recipe also helps stretch my meal budget.

—*Cassie Dion, South Burlington, Vermont*

  3/4 pound uncooked turkey breast
    2 tablespoons butter
    2 garlic cloves, minced
1-1/4 cups heavy whipping cream
    2 tablespoons minced fresh basil *or*
       2 teaspoons dried basil
  1/4 cup grated Parmesan cheese
Dash pepper
    3 to 4 cups hot cooked pasta

---

1. Cut turkey into 2-in. x 1/4-in. pieces. In a large skillet, saute turkey in butter until turkey is browned and no longer pink, about 6 minutes. Add garlic; cook 1 minute longer.

2. Add cream, basil, cheese and pepper; bring to a boil. Reduce heat; simmer for 3 minutes, stirring frequently.

3. Stir in pasta and toss to coat.

[2007]

SPANISH RICE TURKEY CASSEROLE

yield: 8 servings ∞ prep: 30 min.
bake: 20 min.

Everyone in my family loves this casserole, even my eighty-year-old grandparents who aren't big fans of Mexican food. Mild green chilies, tender cubes of turkey, tomatoes and lots of cheese make a mouthwatering filling.

—Ann Herren, Pulaski, Tennessee

2 packages (6.8 ounces each) Spanish rice and pasta mix
1/4 cup butter, cubed
4 cups water
1 can (14-1/2 ounces) diced tomatoes, undrained
1 can (10 ounces) diced tomatoes and green chilies, undrained
3 cups cubed cooked turkey *or* chicken
1 can (11 ounces) whole kernel corn, drained
1/2 cup sour cream
1 cup (4 ounces) shredded Mexican cheese blend, *divided*

1. In a large skillet, saute the rice and vermicelli in butter until golden brown. Gradually stir in the water, tomatoes and the contents of the rice seasoning packets. Bring to a boil. Reduce heat; cover and simmer for 15-20 minutes or until rice is tender.

2. Meanwhile, in a large bowl, combine turkey, corn, sour cream and 1/2 cup cheese. Stir in rice mixture.

3. Transfer to a greased 3-qt. baking dish. Sprinkle with the remaining cheese (dish will be full). Bake, uncovered, at 375° for 20-25 minutes or until heated through.

[2004]

TURKEY TACO BAKE

yield: 4 servings ∞ prep: 15 min.
bake: 20 min.

This satisfying casserole is loaded with popular south-of-the border ingredients, including corn chips, salsa, Monterey Jack cheese and refried beans. It's a guaranteed family-pleaser.

—Trudie Hagen, Roggen, Colorado

2 cups coarsely crushed corn chips
1 can (16 ounces) refried beans
2 cups (8 ounces) shredded Monterey Jack cheese, *divided*
1 cup salsa
2 cups shredded cooked turkey
1 teaspoon taco seasoning
1 green onion, sliced
1 medium tomato, chopped

1. Place corn chips in a greased shallow 2-1/2-qt. baking dish. Place the refried beans in a small saucepan; cook and stir over medium heat until beans are heated through. Remove from the heat; stir in 1 cup cheese and salsa. Spread over chips.

2. In a large bowl, combine the turkey and taco seasoning; sprinkle over bean mixture. Top with the remaining cheese. Sprinkle with onion.

3. Bake, uncovered, at 400° for 20-25 minutes or until cheese is melted. Sprinkle with tomato.

TURKEY TACO BAKE

"Easy and very good! I made this a while ago with Thanksgiving leftovers. This is the perfect recipe when you have turkey left and you are tired of the gravy-, mashed-potato and stuffing-type leftovers and want something a little spicy—yum! I added olives and cilantro and topped it with taco sauce and sour cream!"
—badkitty

TURKEY TETRAZZINI

[1994]

TURKEY TETRAZZINI

yield: 6-8 servings ∞ prep: 15 min.
bake: 40 min.

This recipe comes from a cookbook our church compiled. It's convenient because it can be made ahead and frozen. After the holidays, we use leftover turkey to prepare a meal for university students. They clean their plates!

—Gladys Waldrop, Calvert City, Kentucky

- 1 package (7 ounces) spaghetti, broken into 2-inch pieces
- 2 cups cubed cooked turkey
- 1 cup (4 ounces) shredded cheddar cheese
- 1 can (10-3/4 ounces) condensed cream of mushroom soup, undiluted
- 1 medium onion, chopped
- 2 cans (4 ounces each) sliced mushrooms, drained
- 1/3 cup 2% milk
- 1/4 cup chopped green pepper
- 1 jar (2 ounces) chopped pimientos, drained
- 1/4 teaspoon salt
- 1/8 teaspoon pepper

Additional shredded cheddar cheese, optional

1. Cook spaghetti according to package directions; drain. Transfer to a large bowl; add the next 10 ingredients.

2. Spoon mixture into a greased 2-1/2-qt. casserole; sprinkle with the cheese if desired. Bake, uncovered, at 375° for 40-45 minutes or until heated through.

[2008]

TURKEY ENCHILADAS

yield: 8 servings ∞ prep: 40 min.
bake: 40 min.

(Pictured on page 718)

My family likes these enchiladas so much that they request a turkey dinner several times a year just so I'll make this dish with the leftovers. I usually double it because I feed three growing boys.

—Beverly Matthews, Pasco, Washington

- 3 cups cubed cooked turkey
- 1 cup chicken broth
- 1 cup cooked long grain rice
- 2 plum tomatoes, chopped
- 1 medium onion, chopped
- 1/2 cup canned chopped green chilies
- 1/2 cup sour cream
- 1/4 cup sliced ripe *or* green olives with pimientos
- 1/4 cup minced fresh cilantro
- 1 teaspoon ground cumin
- 8 flour tortillas (10 inches)
- 1 can (28 ounces) green enchilada sauce, *divided*
- 2 cups (8 ounces) shredded Mexican cheese blend, *divided*

1. In a large saucepan, combine the first 10 ingredients. Bring to a boil. Reduce heat; simmer, uncovered, for 20 minutes. Remove from the heat.

2. Place 1/2 cup of the turkey mixture down the center of each tortilla; top each with 1 teaspoon enchilada sauce and 1 tablespoon cheese. Roll up and place seam side down in a greased 13-in. x 9-in. baking dish. Pour the remaining enchilada sauce over top; sprinkle with remaining cheese.

3. Cover and bake at 350° for 30 minutes. Uncover; bake 8-10 minutes longer or until bubbly.

[2008]

TURKEY POTPIES

yield: 2 pies (6 servings each) ✎ prep: 40 min.
bake: 40 min. + standing

With golden brown crust and scrumptious filling, these comforting potpies will warm you down to your toes. Because it makes two, you can eat one now and freeze the other for later. They bake and cut beautifully.

—Laurie Jensen, Cadillac, Michigan

2 medium potatoes, peeled and cut into 1-inch pieces
3 medium carrots, cut into 1-inch slices
1 medium onion, chopped
1 celery rib, diced
2 tablespoons butter
1 tablespoon olive oil
6 tablespoons all-purpose flour
3 cups chicken broth
4 cups cubed cooked turkey
2/3 cup frozen peas
1/2 cup plus 1 tablespoon heavy whipping cream, *divided*
1 tablespoon minced fresh parsley
1 teaspoon garlic salt
1/4 teaspoon pepper
1 package (15 ounces) refrigerated pie pastry
1 egg

1. In a Dutch oven, saute the potatoes, carrots, onion and celery in butter and oil until tender. Stir in flour until blended; gradually add broth. Bring to a boil; cook and stir for 2 minutes or until thickened. Stir in the turkey, peas, 1/2 cup cream, parsley, garlic salt and pepper.

2. Spoon into two ungreased 9-in. pie plates. Roll out the pastry to fit top of each pie; place over filling. Trim, seal and flute edges. Cut out a decorative center or cut slits in pastry. In a small bowl, whisk egg and remaining cream; brush over pastry.

3. Cover and freeze one potpie for up to 3 months. Bake the remaining turkey potpie at 375° for 40-45 minutes or until golden brown. Let potpie stand for 10 minutes before cutting.

4. To use frozen potpie: Remove from the freezer 30 minutes before baking. Cover edges of crust loosely with foil; place on a baking sheet. Bake at 425° for 30 minutes. Reduce heat to 350°; remove foil. Bake 55-60 minutes longer or until golden brown.

[2009]

TURKEY WITH CURRIED CREAM SAUCE

yield: 3 servings ✎ prep/total time: 30 min.

(*Pictured on page 717*)

For a different turkey dish, try this delicious curry version. It comes together quickly and disappears fast.

—Lori Lockrey, Scarborough, Ontario

2 tablespoons butter
2 tablespoons all-purpose flour
1/2 teaspoon curry powder
1 cup chicken broth
1/4 cup 2% milk
1 small yellow summer squash, sliced
1 small zucchini, sliced
1/2 small onion, thinly sliced
2 teaspoons canola oil
2 cups cubed cooked turkey breast
1/2 teaspoon grated lemon peel
Hot cooked rice
3 tablespoons chopped cashews

1. In a small saucepan, melt butter; stir in flour and curry until smooth. Gradually add broth and milk. Bring to a boil; cook and stir for 1-2 minutes or until thickened. Remove from the heat; set aside.

2. In a large skillet, saute the squash, zucchini and onion in oil until tender. Add the turkey, lemon peel and reserved sauce; heat through. Serve with rice. Sprinkle each serving with cashews.

❧ SALADS ❧

[2005]
CHEESY BEEF TACO SALAD

yield: 6 servings ❧ prep/total time: 30 min.

My family gobbles up this spicy salad. So I often double the recipe to have leftovers for lunch the next day.

—*Arlene Ghent, St Joseph, Missouri*

1-1/2 pounds ground beef
1-1/2 cups chopped onion
   1 cup diced celery
   1 cup diced green pepper
   2 garlic cloves, minced
   1 pound process cheese (Velveeta), cubed
   1 can (10 ounces) diced tomatoes and green chilies, undrained
   2 teaspoons chili powder
   2 teaspoons ground cumin
1-1/2 cups crushed corn chips
Shredded lettuce
Chopped green onions
   2 large tomatoes, cut into wedges

---

1. In a large skillet, cook the beef, onion, celery and green pepper over medium heat until meat is no longer pink. Add the garlic; cook 1 minute longer. Drain. Stir in cheese, tomatoes, chili powder and cumin. Cook and stir over low heat until cheese is melted. Stir in corn chips.

2. Line six salad plates with the lettuce; sprinkle with green onions. Top each with 1 cup beef mixture. Garnish with tomato wedges.

[1997]
CHICKEN AND BLACK BEAN SALAD

yield: 6 servings ❧ prep/total time: 20 min.

(*Pictured on page 759*)

Here in California, we cook out year-round. I grill extra chicken specifically for this quick meal. It's so colorful and fresh-tasting that even our kids love it.

—*Cindie Ekstrand, Duarte, California*

1/3 cup olive oil
  2 tablespoons lime juice
  2 tablespoons chopped fresh cilantro
1-1/2 teaspoons sugar
  1 garlic clove, minced
1/2 teaspoon chili powder
1/2 teaspoon salt, optional
1/4 teaspoon pepper
  1 can (15 ounces) black beans, rinsed and drained
  1 can (11 ounces) Mexicorn, drained
  1 medium sweet red pepper, julienned
1/3 cup sliced green onions
  6 cups torn romaine
1-1/2 cups cooked chicken strips
Additional cilantro, optional

---

1. In a small bowl, whisk the first eight ingredients; set aside.

2. In a large bowl, toss the beans, corn, red pepper and onions; set aside.

3. Arrange romaine on individual plates; top with bean mixture and chicken. Drizzle with dressing; garnish with cilantro if desired.

[2010]

SOUTHWEST CHICKEN SALAD

yield: 6 cups ∞ **prep/total time: 30 min.**

My husband loves salads, and this flavorful chicken recipe is easy, nutritious and very tasty. Serve it over greens, tucked in a pita or rolled up in a tortilla.

—*Sara Hobbs, Quinlan, Texas*

- 4 cups cubed rotisserie chicken
- 2 cups frozen corn, thawed
- 1 cup chopped roasted sweet red peppers
- 1 cup chopped red *or* sweet onion
- 1 cup minced fresh cilantro

DRESSING:
- 3 tablespoons lime juice
- 3 tablespoons olive oil
- 4 teaspoons honey
- 2 teaspoons ground cumin
- 1 teaspoon salt
- 1 teaspoon chili powder
- 1/2 teaspoon coarsely ground pepper

SALADS:
Torn mixed salad greens and sliced almonds
PITAS:
Whole wheat pita pocket halves and lettuce leaves
WRAPS:
Whole wheat tortillas and sliced ripe avocado

1. In a large bowl, combine the first five ingredients. In a small bowl, whisk the dressing ingredients; pour over chicken mixture and toss to coat. Refrigerate until serving. Serve as desired.

2. Salads: Top salad greens with chicken salad; sprinkle with almonds.

3. Pitas: Line pita halves with lettuce leaves; fill with chicken salad.

4. Wraps: Place chicken salad off-center on tortillas; top with avocado. Roll up.

[2002]

SALMON CAESAR SALAD

yield: 6 servings ∞ **prep: 20 min. grill: 20 min. + cooling**

(Pictured on page 758)

Flaky grilled salmon and Caesar-style dressing, seasoned with lemon juice and grated Parmesan cheese, make this elegant salad.

—*Clara Barrett, Madison, Florida*

- 2 salmon fillets (1 pound *each*)
- 3 cups cubed French bread
- 1 tablespoon olive oil
- 1/4 teaspoon garlic powder
- 1 bunch romaine, torn
- 2 cups small cherry tomatoes

DRESSING:
- 3 tablespoons olive oil
- 2 tablespoons lemon juice
- 4-1/2 teaspoons mayonnaise
- 2-1/4 teaspoons sugar
- 2 garlic cloves, minced
- 1/2 teaspoon salt
- 1/8 teaspoon pepper
- 1 tablespoon grated Parmesan cheese

1. Using long-handled tongs, moisten a paper towel with cooking oil and lightly coat the grill rack. Place salmon skin side down on grill. Grill, covered, over medium-hot heat or broil 4 in. from the heat for 15-20 minutes or until fish flakes easily with a fork. Cool.

2. For croutons, toss the bread cubes, olive oil and garlic powder in a large bowl. In a nonstick skillet, saute bread cubes for 5-6 minutes or until golden brown, stirring occasionally. Remove from the heat; set aside.

3. Flake salmon into chunks. In a large bowl, combine romaine and tomatoes. In a small bowl, whisk the oil, lemon juice, mayonnaise, sugar, garlic, salt and pepper. Pour over salad and toss to coat. Add the salmon, croutons and cheese; toss gently.

SALMON CAESAR SALAD

"My kids hate salmon but they love this dish!! Super easy and super tasty!!"
—*tommuraski*

POPPY SEED CHICKEN SALAD

[2010]

POPPY SEED CHICKEN SALAD

yield: 4 servings plus 1 cup leftover dressing
prep: 30 min. + marinating
cook: 15 min.

Juicy berries, crisp sugar snap peas and crunchy pecans complement the lime-marinated chicken in this pretty salad. The homemade sweet-sour dressing is simply delicious.

—*Rebekah Radewahn*
Wauwatosa, Wisconsin

- 3 tablespoons thawed limeade concentrate
- 1/4 teaspoon pepper
- 3/4 pound boneless skinless chicken breasts, cut into thin strips
- 1 tablespoon canola oil

DRESSING:
- 1/2 cup white vinegar
- 1/3 cup sugar
- 1 teaspoon dried minced onion
- 1 teaspoon ground mustard
- 1/2 teaspoon salt
- 1 cup canola oil
- 1 tablespoon poppy seeds

SALAD:
- 1 package (6 ounces) fresh baby spinach
- 2 cups sliced fresh strawberries
- 1 cup fresh sugar snap peas, trimmed
- 1 small red onion, chopped
- 1/2 cup pecan halves, toasted

---

1. In a large resealable plastic bag, combine limeade concentrate and pepper; add the chicken. Seal bag and turn to coat. Refrigerate for 2 hours.

2. Drain and discard marinade. In a large skillet, saute the chicken in oil until no longer pink.

3. Meanwhile, in a blender, combine the vinegar, sugar, onion, mustard and salt.

While processing, gradually add oil in a steady stream. Stir in poppy seeds.

4. Divide spinach among four salad plates; top with strawberries, peas, onion and chicken. Drizzle each serving with 2 tablespoons dressing; sprinkle with pecans. Refrigerate leftover dressing.

[1993]

SMOKED TURKEY AND APPLE SALAD

yield: 8 servings ∞ **prep/total time: 20 min.**
(Pictured on page 753)

An eye-catching dish, this refreshing salad is a great main course for a summer lunch or light dinner. The dressing's Dijon flavor goes nicely with the turkey, and the apples add crunch.

—*Carolyn Nace, Winter Haven, Florida*
Former Field Editor

DRESSING:
- 5 tablespoons olive oil
- 2 tablespoons cider vinegar
- 1 tablespoon Dijon mustard
- 1 teaspoon lemon-pepper seasoning
- 1/2 teaspoon salt, optional

SALAD:
- 1 bunch watercress *or* romaine, torn into bite-size pieces
- 1 medium carrot, julienned
- 10 cherry tomatoes, halved
- 8 ounces smoked turkey, julienned
- 4 unpeeled apples, sliced
- 1/3 cup chopped walnuts, toasted

---

1. Whisk together dressing ingredients; set aside.

2. Just before serving, arrange salad greens on a platter or individual plates. Top with carrot, tomatoes, turkey and apples. Drizzle dressing over salad; toss to coat. Sprinkle with walnuts.

[2010]
LAYERED TACO SALAD
yield: 12 servings (1 cup each)
prep/total time: 30 min.

My colorful and attractive salad looks very appealing when layered in a trifle dish. It can be used as a main dish or side. I've even served it at potlucks.

—**Elissa Dougherty, Babylon, New York**

- 1 pound ground beef
- 2/3 cup water
- 1 envelope taco seasoning
- 2 medium ripe avocados, peeled and pitted
- 2 tablespoons finely chopped red onion
- 3 garlic cloves, minced
- 1 teaspoon lemon juice
- 4 cups shredded lettuce
- 1 can (2-1/4 ounces) sliced ripe olives, drained
- 2 medium tomatoes, chopped
- 1 small cucumber, peeled and chopped
- 5 green onions, chopped
- 2 cups (8 ounces) shredded cheddar cheese
- 1 cup salsa
- 2 cups (16 ounces) sour cream
- Tortilla chips

1. In a small skillet, cook the beef over medium heat until no longer pink; drain. Stir in the water and taco seasoning. Bring to a boil; cook and stir for 2 minutes. Cool slightly.

2. In a small bowl, mash avocados with onion, garlic and lemon juice. In a 3-qt. glass bowl, layer the beef, avocado mixture, lettuce, olives, tomatoes, cucumber, green onions, cheese, salsa and sour cream. Serve immediately with chips.

[2009]
ITALIAN GARDEN SALAD
yield: 8 servings ◈ **prep: 35 min. + chilling**

This is a great way to use the vegetables my husband grows, and it's always well received. Spaghetti and chunks of chicken make the salad filling.

—**Lori Daniels**
Beverly, West Virginia, Field Editor

- 8 ounces uncooked spaghetti
- 1 cup cut fresh green beans
DRESSING:
- 6 tablespoons canola oil
- 3 tablespoons sugar
- 2 tablespoons white wine vinegar
- 1 garlic clove, minced
- 1 teaspoon salt
- 1 teaspoon dried parsley flakes
- 1 teaspoon dried basil
- 1/2 teaspoon dried oregano
- 1/4 teaspoon onion powder
SALAD:
- 2 cups cubed cooked chicken
- 1 medium green pepper, julienned
- 4 ounces Colby-Monterey Jack cheese, cubed
- 1 medium zucchini, sliced
- 1 small yellow summer squash, sliced
- 8 cherry tomatoes, halved
- 1 small red onion, halved and sliced
- Shredded Parmesan cheese, optional

1. Cook spaghetti according to package directions, adding the green beans during the last 4 minutes of cooking.

2. Meanwhile, in a large bowl, combine the dressing ingredients. Add chicken, pepper, Colby-Monterey Jack cheese, zucchini, squash, tomatoes and onion.

3. Drain the spaghetti and beans; rinse in cold water. Add to other ingredients and toss to coat. Refrigerate until chilled. Sprinkle with Parmesan cheese if desired.

ITALIAN GARDEN SALAD

❝This is just plain delicious and easy to do. I'm just a husband and even I can do it!❞
—*dmalarkey*

CURRIED CHICKEN SALAD

"Delicious! Even better the next day after it sits so the flavors can meld."
—DRitchie747

[2004]

GRILLED CHICKEN CAESAR SALAD
yield: 6 servings
prep: 15 min. + marinating   grill: 15 min.
(Pictured on page 756)

Whenever we're invited to potlucks, I'm always asked to bring a salad because people know it's one of my specialties. This dish is especially good on summer days when it's too hot to cook on the stove.

—*Deb Weisberger, Mullett Lake, Michigan*

- 1/2 cup red wine vinegar
- 1/2 cup reduced-sodium soy sauce
- 1/2 cup olive oil
- 1 tablespoon dried parsley flakes
- 1 teaspoon dried basil
- 1 teaspoon dried oregano
- 1/2 teaspoon garlic powder
- 1/2 teaspoon pepper
- 6 boneless skinless chicken breast halves (4 ounces each)
- 1 large bunch romaine, torn (12 cups)
- 1-1/2 cups Caesar salad croutons
- 1 cup halved cherry tomatoes
- 2/3 cup creamy Caesar salad dressing

1. In a large resealable plastic bag, combine the first eight ingredients; add the chicken. Seal bag and turn to coat; refrigerate for at least 4 hours.

2. Drain and discard marinade. Grill chicken, uncovered, over medium-low heat for 6-8 minutes on each side or until a meat thermometer reads 170°.

3. Meanwhile, in a large bowl, combine the romaine, croutons and tomatoes; add dressing and toss to coat. Divide among six salad plates. Slice chicken; arrange on salads.

[2010]

CURRIED CHICKEN SALAD
yield: 4 servings   prep/total time: 15 min.
(Pictured on page 754)

Curry and mustard complement the sweet fruit and crunchy nuts in this guilt-free salad. I like it on a bed of greens or whole wheat toast, or scooped up with apple slices. Instead of chicken breast, try store-bought rotisserie chicken.

—*Joanna Perdomo, Miami, Florida*

- 3 cups cubed cooked chicken breast
- 1 medium apple, finely chopped
- 1/4 cup slivered almonds, toasted
- 2 tablespoons golden raisins
- 2 tablespoons dried cranberries
- 1/2 cup fat-free plain Greek yogurt
- 1/4 cup apricot preserves
- 2 tablespoons curry powder
- 1 tablespoon Dijon mustard
- 1/2 teaspoon salt
- 1/4 to 1/2 teaspoon pepper

Lettuce leaves

1. In a small bowl, combine the first five ingredients. In a small bowl, whisk the yogurt, preserves, curry, mustard, salt and pepper; pour over the chicken mixture and toss to coat. Serve on lettuce leaves.

Editor's Note: If Greek yogurt is not available in your area, line a strainer with a coffee filter and place over a bowl. Place 1 cup fat-free yogurt in prepared strainer; refrigerate overnight. Discard liquid from bowl; proceed as directed.

[2009]

GRILLED STEAK BRUSCHETTA SALAD

yield: 6 servings ∽ **prep/total time: 30 min.**

You'll want to fire up the grill just to make this impressive entree. The steaks cook quickly, and the salad prep takes almost no time at all.

Devon Delaney, Princeton, New Jersey

1-1/2 pounds beef tenderloin steaks (1 inch thick)
1/2 teaspoon salt
1/4 teaspoon pepper
6 slices Italian bread (1/2 inch thick)
3 cups fresh arugula *or* baby spinach
3/4 cup prepared bruschetta topping *or* vegetable salad of your choice
Crumbled blue cheese, optional
3/4 cup blue cheese salad dressing

1. Sprinkle steaks with salt and pepper. Grill, covered, over medium heat for 6-8 minutes on each side or until meat reaches desired doneness (for medium-rare, a thermometer should read 145°; medium, 160°; well-done, 170°). Let stand for 5 minutes.

2. Grill bread, covered, for 1-2 minutes on each side or until toasted; place on salad plates.

3. Thinly slice steak; arrange over toast. Top with the arugula and bruschetta topping; sprinkle with the cheese if desired. Drizzle with dressing.

Editor's Note: Look for bruschetta topping in the pasta aisle or your grocer's deli case.

[1995]

TARRAGON PASTA SALAD

yield: 4-6 servings ∽ **prep: 15 min. + chilling**

The refreshing tuna salad with pasta and a savory tarragon dressing makes a colorful and flavorful addition to any summer lunch or picnic menu. The recipe can be easily doubled if you need to feed a hungry crowd.

—Toni Churchin, Irvine, California

8 ounces bow tie pasta, cooked and drained
1 can (9 ounces) tuna in water, drained and flaked
1/3 cup chopped sweet red pepper
1/4 cup sliced green onions
3/4 cup Miracle Whip
4 teaspoons minced fresh tarragon *or* 1 teaspoon dried tarragon
2 teaspoons lemon juice
1/2 teaspoon salt
1/4 teaspoon pepper

1. In a large bowl, combine pasta, tuna, red pepper and onions. In a small bowl, whisk remaining ingredients. Pour over salad and toss gently. Chill for 1 hour.

TO RINSE OR NOT TO RINSE PASTA

When pasta is to be served with a sauce or combined in a baked dish, we recommend not to rinse it. Rinsing can wash away starch that may help to slightly thicken the pasta sauce. However, when served cold, as for pasta salads, it can be rinsed in a colander.

—Taste of Home Cooking Experts

GRILLED STEAK BRUSCHETTA SALAD

❝To cut the cost a little, I used a flank steak in place of the beef tenderloin and it was delicious!! I told my hubby this is a recipe for when we have guests!❞

—mamasquish

[2010]

FAST & FABULOUS THAI CHICKEN SALAD

yield: 6 servings ∞ prep/total time: 20 min.

This healthy recipe looks time-consuming, but it's as simple as can be. Aside from mixing, the only prep work is chopping a red pepper. It's a real crowd-pleaser.

—*Elinor Ives, Fiskdale, Massachusetts*

- 1 package (14 ounces) coleslaw mix
- 1/3 cup sesame ginger salad dressing
- 2 cups cubed cooked chicken
- 1/2 cup Thai peanut sauce
- 1 medium sweet red pepper, julienned
- 1/2 cup chow mein noodles
- 2 green onions, chopped

1. In a large bowl, combine coleslaw mix and salad dressing. Transfer to a serving platter. Combine chicken and peanut sauce; place over coleslaw mixture. Top with red pepper, noodles and onions.

[2007]

BERRY TOSSED SALAD

yield: 8 servings ∞ prep/total time: 30 min.

(*Pictured on page 755*)

Kiwi and feta add interest to this delightful salad that's sweet, tangy, creamy and tart all at once. It pairs perfectly with the grilled ribs in my mom's menu; she got the recipe from a good friend.

—*Krista Smith Kliebenstein
Broomfield, Colorado*

- 1 package (10 ounces) ready-to-serve salad greens
- 1 cup sliced fresh strawberries
- 1 kiwifruit, peeled and sliced
- 1/4 cup chopped red onion
- 1/4 cup crumbled feta cheese
- 2 tablespoons slivered almonds

CREAMY RASPBERRY DRESSING:

- 1/2 cup mayonnaise
- 2 tablespoons plus 2 teaspoons sugar
- 1 tablespoon raspberry vinegar
- 1 tablespoon 2% milk
- 2-1/2 teaspoons poppy seeds
- 2-1/2 teaspoons seedless raspberry jam

1. In a large salad bowl, combine the greens, strawberries, kiwi, onion, feta cheese and almonds.

2. In a small bowl, whisk the dressing ingredients. Drizzle desired amount over salad and toss to coat. Refrigerate any leftover dressing.

[2005]

APPLE-WALNUT TOSSED SALAD

yield: 8 servings ∞ prep/total time: 25 min.

(*Pictured on page 754*)

The pretty, flavorful cranberry dressing for this fall salad is also good for gift-giving.

—*Mary LaJoie, Glenoma, Washington*

- 1/4 cup red wine vinegar
- 1/4 cup fresh cranberries
- 2 tablespoons honey
- 1 tablespoon sugar
- 1 tablespoon chopped red onion
- 1/4 teaspoon salt
- 1/4 teaspoon pepper
- 3/4 cup canola oil
- 2 packages (5 ounces *each*) spring mix salad greens
- 3 medium Red Delicious apples, thinly sliced
- 1 cup chopped walnuts, toasted

1. For cranberry vinaigrette, combine first seven ingredients in a blender; cover and process until blended. While processing, gradually add oil in a steady stream.

2. Transfer to a serving dish. In a large bowl, toss the salad greens, apples and walnuts. Serve with vinaigrette.

FAST & FABULOUS THAI CHICKEN SALAD

"I made this last night and my husband told me to make it again tomorrow for when company comes, as it's good enough to serve to others! And it's sooooooo easy!!"
—*rosebud 1962*

[2009]

TASTE-OF-FALL SALAD

yield: 6 servings ∞ **prep/total time: 25 min.**

My parents stayed with me at a friend's beautiful ranch for the holidays and I made them this great salad. It turned into every night's first course.

—*Kristin Kossak, Bozeman, Montana*

- 2/3 cup pecan halves
- 1/4 cup balsamic vinegar, *divided*

Dash cayenne pepper

Dash ground cinnamon

- 3 tablespoons sugar, *divided*
- 1 package (5 ounces) spring mix salad greens
- 1/4 cup olive oil
- 1 teaspoon Dijon mustard
- 1/8 teaspoon salt
- 1 medium pear, thinly sliced
- 1/4 cup shredded Parmesan cheese

1. In a large heavy skillet, cook the pecans, 2 tablespoons vinegar, cayenne and cinnamon over medium heat until nuts are toasted, about 4 minutes. Sprinkle with 1 tablespoon sugar. Cook and stir for 2-4 minutes or until sugar is melted. Spread on foil to cool; break apart.

2. Place salad greens in a large bowl. In a small bowl, whisk the oil, mustard, salt and remaining vinegar and sugar; drizzle over greens and toss to coat. Arrange the greens, pear slices and pecans on six salad plates. Sprinkle with cheese.

[2003]

CHERRY BRIE TOSSED SALAD

yield: 10 servings ∞ **prep/total time: 20 min.**

(*Pictured on page 755*)

Draped in a light vinaigrette and sprinkled with almonds, this pretty salad is a variation of a recipe that's been passed around at school events, church functions and even birthday parties. Everyone wants the recipe. You can also try different cheeses.

—*Toni Borden, Wellington, Florida*

DRESSING:
- 1 cup cider vinegar
- 1/2 cup sugar
- 1/4 cup olive oil

- 1 teaspoon ground mustard
- 1-1/2 teaspoons poppy seeds

SALAD:
- 2 tablespoons butter
- 3/4 cup sliced almonds
- 3 tablespoons sugar
- 8 cups torn romaine
- 1 round (8 ounces) Brie *or* Camembert cheese, rind removed and cubed
- 1 package (6 ounces) dried cherries

1. In a small bowl, whisk the dressing ingredients; set aside.

2. For salad, in a heavy skillet, melt butter over medium heat. Add almonds and cook and stir until nuts are toasted, about 4 minutes. Sprinkle with sugar; cook and stir until sugar is melted, about 3 minutes. Spread on foil to cool; break apart.

3. In a large salad bowl, combine the romaine, cheese and cherries. Whisk dressing; drizzle over salad. Sprinkle with sugared almonds and toss to coat.

Editor's Note: Swiss cheese can be used in place of the Brie or Camembert.

[2006]

SPECIAL SPINACH SALAD

yield: 4 servings ∞ **prep/total time: 15 min.**

I always get compliments when I serve this refreshing salad during the holidays. The creamy dressing is perfect with the colorful cranberries and crunchy nuts.

—*Laurene Hunsicker, Canton, Pennsylvania*

- 1/3 cup olive oil
- 3 tablespoons sugar
- 2 tablespoons white wine vinegar
- 2 tablespoons sour cream
- 1/2 teaspoon ground mustard
- 1 package (6 ounces) fresh baby spinach
- 1/2 cup chopped walnuts, toasted
- 1/2 cup dried cranberries

1. In a small bowl, whisk the oil, sugar, vinegar, sour cream and mustard. Divide spinach among four salad plates; drizzle with dressing. Sprinkle with walnuts and cranberries.

STRAWBERRY-BACON SPINACH SALAD

"I have served this several times and it is always a HIT! Blueberries work well in it and pecans rather than walnuts, too!"

—ndmattern

[2007]

STRAWBERRY-BACON SPINACH SALAD

yield: 6-8 servings
prep/total time: 15 min.

This colorful Strawberry-Bacon Salad is sweet and crunchy with a tangy dressing. I made it for our prayer group, and everyone enjoyed it.

—*Ruth Hayward, Lake Charles, Louisiana*

1 package (6 ounces) fresh baby spinach
1 pint fresh strawberries, sliced
8 bacon strips, cooked and crumbled
1/4 cup chopped red onion
1/4 cup chopped walnuts
1 cup mayonnaise
1/2 cup sugar
1/4 cup raspberry vinegar

1. In a salad bowl, combine the spinach, strawberries, bacon, onion and nuts. In a small bowl, combine the mayonnaise, sugar and vinegar. Serve with salad.

[1995]

CAESAR SALAD

yield: 6-8 servings
prep/total time: 10 min.

This crunchy, refreshing salad has a zippy, zesty dressing that provides a burst of flavor with each bite. It's a great salad to perk up any spring or summer meal.

—*Schelby Thompson
Camden Wyoming, Delaware*

1 large bunch romaine, torn
3/4 cup olive oil
3 tablespoons red wine vinegar
1 teaspoon Worcestershire sauce
1/2 teaspoon salt
1/4 teaspoon ground mustard
1 large garlic clove, minced

1/2 fresh lemon
Dash pepper
1/4 to 1/2 cup shredded Parmesan cheese
Caesar-flavored *or* garlic croutons

1. Place lettuce in a large salad bowl. Combine the next six ingredients in a blender; process until smooth. Pour over lettuce and toss to coat.

2. Juice the lemon by squeezing over the lettuce. Sprinkle with pepper, cheese and croutons.

[2003]

HOT SPINACH APPLE SALAD

yield: 8-10 servings
prep/total time: 20 min.

This salad is just lightly coated in a sweet-tangy dressing so the spinach doesn't wilt and the apples retain their crunch.

—*Denise Albers
Freeburg, Illinois, Field Editor*

6 bacon strips, diced
1/4 cup cider vinegar
3 tablespoons brown sugar
9 cups fresh baby spinach
2 large red apples, thinly sliced
3/4 cup chopped red onion

1. In a large skillet, cook the bacon over medium heat until crisp. Using a slotted spoon, remove to paper towels. Drain, reserving 2 tablespoons drippings.

2. In the same skillet, combine the vinegar, brown sugar and reserved drippings. Bring to a boil; cook and stir until sugar is dissolved. Cool slightly.

3. In a large bowl, combine spinach, apples, onion and bacon. Drizzle with warm dressing; toss to coat. Serve immediately.

[2001]

SUNNY LAYERED SALAD

yield: 10-12 servings
prep: 20 min. + chilling

I top the colorful layers of this appealing salad with mandarin oranges. Presented in a glass bowl, it looks beautiful on a buffet.

—*Susan West, North Grafton, Massachusetts*

- 1/4 cup sliced almonds
- 2 tablespoons sugar
- 6 cups shredded lettuce
- 1 can (8 ounces) sliced water chestnuts, drained
- 1 cup frozen peas, thawed and well drained
- 1/2 medium cucumber, sliced
- 2 medium tomatoes, cut into thin wedges
- 2 cups (8 ounces) shredded part-skim mozzarella cheese
- 1 can (15 ounces) mandarin oranges, drained

DRESSING:

- 1/4 cup canola oil
- 2 tablespoons sugar
- 2 tablespoons cider vinegar
- 1/4 teaspoon salt
- 1/4 teaspoon pepper

1. In a large skillet, cook and stir almonds and sugar over low heat until sugar is dissolved and almonds are coated. Spread almonds on waxed paper and set aside.

2. In a large salad bowl, layer the lettuce, water chestnuts, peas, cucumber, tomatoes, cheese and oranges. Sprinkle with sugared almonds. Cover and refrigerate for at least 2 hours.

3. In a small bowl, whisk the dressing ingredients. Pour over salad.

[2010]

EASY GARDEN TOMATOES

yield: 6 servings **prep/total time: 15 min.**

(Pictured on page 756)

Simple as it is, this is one of my favorite dishes, and my family loves it. I made three batches the first time, and a few stray olive slices were the only thing left on the platter.

—*Heather Ahrens, Columbus, Ohio*

- 3 large tomatoes, thinly sliced
- 1 large red onion, thinly sliced
- 1/3 cup olive oil
- 1/4 cup red wine vinegar
- 2 garlic cloves, minced
- 1 tablespoon minced fresh basil *or* 1 teaspoon dried basil
- 1-1/2 teaspoons minced fresh oregano *or* 1/2 teaspoon dried oregano
- 3/4 cup crumbled feta cheese
- 1 can (2-1/4 ounces) sliced ripe olives, drained

1. Arrange tomatoes and onion on a serving platter. In a small bowl, whisk the oil, vinegar, garlic, basil and oregano; drizzle over salad. Top with cheese and olives. Chill until serving.

SUNNY LAYERED SALAD

"My family always wants me to make a traditional seven-layered salad, and this healthier alternative was a huge hit!"
—*debbschaefer*

CORING LETTUCE

1. Hold the head with both hands and firmly hit the head, core side down, against your countertop. Then twist the core and it should come right out.

2. To clean the lettuce, run water into the area where the core was removed. Invert the lettuce and allow the water to drain out before using.

[2004]

ROASTED POTATO SALAD

yield: 9 servings ∾ prep: 15 min.
bake: 1 hour + cooling

(Pictured on page 759)

I pack this delicious potato salad in a cooler to dish up cold at picnics or transfer it to a slow cooker to serve it warm for church potlucks.

—*Terri Adams, Kansas City, Kansas*

- 6 cups water
- 1/2 pound fresh green beans, cut into 1-1/2-inch pieces
- 1 large whole garlic bulb
- 2 pounds small red potatoes, quartered
- 1/4 cup chicken broth
- 2 medium sweet red peppers, cut into large chunks
- 2 green onions, sliced
- 1/4 cup balsamic vinegar
- 2 tablespoons olive oil
- 2 teaspoons sugar
- 1 teaspoon minced fresh rosemary *or* 1/4 teaspoon dried rosemary, crushed
- 1/2 teaspoon salt

---

1. In a large saucepan, bring 6 cups water to a boil. Add beans; bring to a boil. Cover and cook for 3 minutes. Drain and immediately place beans in ice water; drain and pat dry.

2. Remove papery outer skin from garlic (do not peel or separate cloves). Cut top off garlic bulb. Place cut side up in a greased 15-in. x 10-in. x 1-in. baking pan. Add potatoes; drizzle with broth. Bake, uncovered, at 400° for 30-40 minutes or until garlic is softened.

3. Remove garlic; set aside. Add the red peppers, onions and reserved beans to the pan. Bake 30-35 minutes longer or until tender. Cool for 10-15 minutes.

4. Squeeze softened garlic into a large bowl. Stir in the vinegar, oil, sugar, rosemary and salt. Add vegetables; toss to coat. Serve warm or cold.

[1995]

CREAMY COLESLAW

yield: 6-8 servings ∾ prep: 10 min. + chilling

(Pictured on page 755)

Cabbage, carrots and green pepper are blended with a tasty dressing that gets its zest from a hint of mustard in this special recipe my mom shared with me. When we set this slaw on the table, it disappears fast.

—*Dianne Esposite, New Middletown, Ohio*

- 3 to 4 cups shredded cabbage
- 1 cup shredded carrots
- 1 cup thinly sliced green pepper
- 1/2 cup mayonnaise
- 1/4 cup lemon juice
- 1 to 2 tablespoons sugar
- 1 tablespoon prepared mustard
- 1 teaspoon celery seed
- 1 teaspoon salt

---

1. In a large salad bowl, toss the cabbage, carrots and green pepper. In a small bowl, whisk the remaining ingredients. Pour over cabbage mixture and toss to coat. Chill for at least 2-3 hours.

SHREDDING CABBAGE

To shred cabbage by hand, cut cabbage into wedges. Place cut side down on a cutting board. With a large sharp knife, cut into thin slices.

[1993]

CARROT RAISIN SALAD

yield: 8 servings prep/total time: 10 min.

(Pictured on page 758)

This traditional salad is one of my mother-in-law's favorites. It's fun to eat because of its crunchy texture, and the raisins give it a slightly sweet flavor. Plus, it's easy to prepare.

—**Denise Baumert, Dalhart, Texas, Field Editor**

4 cups shredded carrots (about 4 large)
3/4 to 1-1/2 cups raisins
1/4 cup mayonnaise
2 tablespoons sugar
2 to 3 tablespoons 2% milk

1. Place carrots and raisins in a large bowl. In a small bowl, combine the mayonnaise, sugar and enough milk to achieve dressing consistency. Pour over carrot mixture; toss to coat.

[1994]

MARINATED MUSHROOM SALAD

yield: 6-8 servings prep: 25 min. + chilling

(Pictured on page 758)

Packed with mushrooms and loads of crunchy, colorful ingredients, this salad is perfect at picnics and parties. It keeps so well in the refrigerator you can make it ahead of time.

—**Sandra Johnson**
Tioga, Pennsylvania, Field Editor

2-1/2 quarts water
3 tablespoons lemon juice
3 pounds small fresh mushrooms
2 medium carrots, sliced
2 celery ribs, sliced
1/2 medium green pepper, chopped
1 small onion, chopped
1 tablespoon minced fresh parsley
1/2 cup sliced pimiento-stuffed olives
1 can (2-1/4 ounces) sliced ripe olives, drained
DRESSING:
1/2 cup prepared Italian salad dressing
1/2 cup red *or* white wine vinegar
1 garlic clove, minced

1/2 teaspoon salt
1/2 teaspoon dried oregano

1. In a large saucepan, bring water and lemon juice to a boil. Add mushrooms and cook for 3 minutes, stirring occasionally. Drain; cool.

2. Place mushrooms in a large bowl with carrots, celery, green pepper, onion, parsley and olives. In a small bowl, whisk dressing ingredients. Pour over salad. Cover and refrigerate overnight.

[2008]

TOMATO-CUCUMBER MOZZARELLA SALAD

yield: 8 servings prep: 20 min. + chilling

I used fresh mozzarella for the first time last year and loved it. I wanted to incorporate it into as many dishes as possible and came up with this salad. It has become a mainstay at my house.

—**Jennifer Klann, Corbett, Oregon**

3 medium tomatoes, chopped
1 English cucumber, quartered and cut into 1/4-inch slices
1 small green pepper, chopped
1/4 cup thinly sliced onions
12 pitted Greek olives, sliced
2 tablespoons minced fresh parsley
1 tablespoon minced fresh basil
1/3 cup olive oil
2 tablespoons red wine vinegar
2 tablespoons balsamic vinegar
1 teaspoon sugar
1/2 teaspoon salt
1/2 teaspoon dried oregano
1/4 teaspoon pepper
4 ounces fresh mozzarella cheese, cubed

1. In a large bowl, combine the tomatoes, cucumber, green pepper, onions, olives, parsley and basil.

2. For dressing, in a small bowl whisk the oil, vinegars, sugar, salt, oregano and pepper. Pour over salad; toss to coat.

3. Cover and refrigerate for at least 15 minutes. Just before serving, stir in cheese. Serve with a slotted spoon.

MIXED BEAN SALAD

"Even though I don't care for canned vegetables, this was very good. The celery adds a nice crunch, and you can add in other fresh vegetables if you like—zucchini, pepper, cucumbers. If I make it again, I would cut the oil in half to cut some of the fat from an otherwise healthy salad. If you like pickled dishes, you'll like this!"

—*BrendainPa*

[1995]

SOUTHWESTERN BEAN SALAD

yield: 10 servings ∞ prep: 10 min. + chilling

I've used this zippy salad many times and have received compliments. When it comes to bean salad, most people think of the sweet three-bean variety, so this recipe is a nice surprise.

—*Lila Jean Allen, Portland, Oregon*

1 can (16 ounces) kidney beans, rinsed and drained
1 can (16 ounces) black beans, rinsed and drained
1 can (15 ounces) garbanzo beans *or* chickpeas, rinsed and drained
2 celery ribs, sliced
1 medium red onion, diced
1 medium tomato, diced
1 cup frozen corn, thawed

DRESSING:
3/4 cup thick and chunky salsa
1/4 cup canola oil
1/4 cup lime juice
1-1/2 teaspoons chili powder
1 teaspoon salt
1/2 teaspoon ground cumin

1. In a large bowl, combine the beans, celery, onion, tomato and corn. In a small bowl, combine the salsa, oil, lime juice, chili powder, salt and cumin. Pour dressing over the bean mixture; toss to coat. Cover salad and chill for at least 2 hours.

[2008]

MIXED BEAN SALAD

yield: 8 servings ∞ prep: 15 min. + chilling

Making this colorful salad a day ahead gives it time to marinate. We love its flavorful, tangy-sweet dressing.

—*Merle Dyck*
Elkford, British Columbia, Field Editor

1/2 cup sugar
1/3 cup cider vinegar
1/3 cup canola oil
1/2 teaspoon salt
1/8 teaspoon pepper
1 can (16 ounces) kidney beans, rinsed and drained
1 can (14-1/2 ounces) cut wax beans, drained
1 can (14-1/2 ounces) cut green beans, drained
3 celery ribs, sliced
1/2 medium green pepper, chopped
1/4 cup chopped onion

1. In a small saucepan, combine the sugar, vinegar, oil, salt and pepper. Cook and stir over medium heat until sugar is dissolved. Remove from the heat; cool slightly.

2. In a large salad bowl, combine the remaining ingredients. Drizzle with dressing; toss to coat. Cover and refrigerate overnight. Serve with a slotted spoon.

MIX 'N' MATCH BEAN SALADS

Cold bean salads are such a versatile dish. If you don't have all the canned beans listed in the recipe, just use an interesting mix of beans from your pantry. You can also add your own touches, like radishes, shredded carrots or corn. It's hard to make a bad bean salad.

—*Taste of Home Cooking Experts*

SMOKED TURKEY AND APPLE SALAD, page 742

ANTIPASTO SALAD, page 771

CURRIED CHICKEN SALAD, page 744

APPLE-WALNUT TOSSED SALAD, page 746

CHERRY BRIE TOSSED SALAD, page 747

FABULOUS FRUIT SALAD, page 762

BERRY TOSSED SALAD, page 746

CREAMY COLESLAW, page 750

EASY GARDEN TOMATOES, page 749

GRILLED CHICKEN CAESAR SALAD, page 744

TROPICAL FUSION SALAD WITH SPICY TORTILLA RIBBONS, page 762

MIMI'S LENTIL MEDLEY, page 767

CARROT RAISIN SALAD, page 751

SALMON CAESAR SALAD, page 741

MARINATED MUSHROOM SALAD, page 751

FESTIVE FRUIT AND PECAN SALAD, page 761

CHICKEN AND BLACK BEAN SALAD, page 740

ROASTED POTATO SALAD, page 750

CHERRY RIBBON SALAD, page 764

CANDY BAR APPLE SALAD, page 763

[2004]

MOSTACCIOLI VEGGIE SALAD

yield: 10 servings ∞ prep: 20 min. + chilling

I first sampled this refreshing salad at a church potluck several years ago. The mix of pasta, zucchini, summer squash, cucumber, sweet peppers and black olives is coated with a light vinaigrette. Any pasta can be substituted for the mostaccioli.

—Julie Sterchi
Jackson, Missouri, Field Editor

- 3 cups uncooked mostaccioli
- 1 medium cucumber, thinly sliced
- 1 small yellow summer squash, quartered and sliced
- 1 small zucchini, halved and sliced
- 1/2 cup diced sweet red pepper
- 1/2 cup diced green pepper
- 1/2 cup sliced ripe olives
- 3 to 4 green onions, chopped

DRESSING:
- 1/3 cup sugar
- 1/3 cup white wine vinegar
- 1/3 cup canola oil
- 1-1/2 teaspoons prepared mustard
- 3/4 teaspoon dried minced onion
- 3/4 teaspoon garlic powder
- 1/2 teaspoon salt
- 1/2 teaspoon pepper

---

1. Cook pasta according to the package directions. Drain and rinse in cold water. Place in a large bowl; add the cucumbers, summer squash, zucchini, peppers, olives and onions.

2. In a small bowl, whisk the dressing ingredients. Pour over pasta mixture; toss to coat. Cover and refrigerate for 8 hours or overnight. Toss again before serving. Serve with a slotted spoon.

[1994]

FESTIVE FRUIT AND PECAN SALAD

yield: 12-16 servings
prep: 25 min. + chilling

(Pictured on page 758)

This fruit salad disappears fast down to the last spoonful. The light dressing doesn't hide the refreshing flavors of the fruit. Pecans add crunch and the rich flavor of the harvest season.

—Julianne Johnson
Grove City, Minnesota, Field Editor

- 1 can (20 ounces) pineapple chunks
- 1/2 cup sugar
- 3 tablespoons all-purpose flour
- 1 egg, lightly beaten
- 2 cans (11 ounces *each*) mandarin oranges, drained
- 1 can (20 ounces) pears, drained and chopped
- 3 kiwifruit, peeled and sliced
- 2 large unpeeled apples, chopped
- 1 cup pecan halves

---

1. Drain pineapple, reserving juice. Set pineapple aside. In a small saucepan, combine the sugar and flour; stir in reserved pineapple juice until smooth. Bring to a boil. Remove from the heat. Stir a small amount of hot mixture into the egg; return all to the pan, stirring constantly. Bring to a gentle boil; cook and stir for 1 minute or until mixture is thickened. Remove from the heat; cool for 15 minutes. Cover and refrigerate.

2. In a large serving bowl, combine the oranges, pears, kiwi, apples, pecans and reserved pineapple. Drizzle with dressing; toss to coat. Cover and chill for 1 hour.

FESTIVE FRUIT AND PECAN SALAD

"While I was pregnant with my first child, my nesting instincts were in full force and I first made this recipe. It has been enthusiastically requested every fall since. I love this recipe!!"
—*purpleiris1982*

TROPICAL FUSION SALAD WITH SPICY TORTILLA RIBBONS

TROPICAL FUSION SALAD WITH SPICY TORTILLA RIBBONS

"This salad was easy to make and tasted excellent. I didn't buy enough fresh papaya, so I used some from a can in light syrup, which actually worked out really well. And leftover tortilla strips make a good snack anytime!"

—ashleyva90

[2010]

TROPICAL FUSION SALAD WITH SPICY TORTILLA RIBBONS

yield: 4 servings ∞ **prep/total time: 30 min.**

(Pictured on page 756)

The fresh taste of this colorful salad makes it a perfect choice for a spring or summer meal. Served with spicy tortilla strips, it's special enough for company.

—Jennifer Fisher, Austin, Texas

2	cups cubed peeled papaya
1	can (15 ounces) black beans, rinsed and drained
1	medium ripe avocado, peeled and cubed
1	cup frozen corn, thawed
1/2	cup golden raisins
2	serrano peppers, seeded and chopped
1/4	cup minced fresh cilantro
1/4	cup orange juice
2	tablespoons lime juice
1	tablespoon cider vinegar
2	garlic cloves, minced
2	teaspoons ground ancho chili pepper, *divided*
1/4	teaspoon sugar
1/4	teaspoon salt
2	corn tortillas (6 inches), cut into 1/4-inch strips

1. In a large bowl, combine papaya, beans, avocado, corn, raisins, peppers, cilantro, orange juice, lime juice, vinegar, garlic, 1/2 teaspoon chili pepper, sugar and salt.

2. Place tortilla strips on a baking sheet coated with cooking spray; sprinkle with remaining chili pepper. Bake at 350° for 8-10 minutes or until crisp. Serve with salad.

Editor's Note: Wear disposable gloves when cutting hot peppers; the oils can burn skin. Avoid touching your face.

[2009]

FABULOUS FRUIT SALAD

yield: 20 servings (3/4 cup each)
prep: 45 min. + chilling

(Pictured on page 755)

I first made this for a reunion, and now it's always requested for our family gatherings. The sweet and tangy lemonade-pudding coating goes well with any fruit, so feel free to substitute your favorites.

—Rhonda Eads, Jasper, Indiana

1	medium honeydew, peeled, seeded and cubed
1	medium cantaloupe, peeled, seeded and cubed
2	cups cubed seedless watermelon
2	medium peaches, peeled and sliced
2	medium nectarines, sliced
1	cup seedless red grapes
1	cup halved fresh strawberries
1	can (11 ounces) mandarin oranges, drained
2	medium kiwifruit, peeled, halved and sliced
2	medium firm bananas, sliced
1	large Granny Smith apple, cubed
1	can (12 ounces) frozen lemonade concentrate, thawed
1	package (3.4 ounces) instant vanilla pudding mix

1. In a large bowl, combine the first nine ingredients. Cover and refrigerate for at least 1 hour.

2. Just before serving, stir in bananas and apple. Combine lemonade concentrate and dry pudding mix; pour over fruit and toss to coat.

[2008]
CANDY BAR APPLE SALAD
yield: 12 servings (3/4 cup each)
prep/total time: 15 min.
(Pictured on page 760)

This creamy, sweet salad with crisp apple crunch is a real people-pleaser. It makes a lot, which is good, because it will go fast!

—*Cyndi Fynaardt, Oskaloosa, Iowa*

1-1/2 cups cold 2% milk
  1 package (3.4 ounces) instant vanilla pudding mix
  1 carton (8 ounces) frozen whipped topping, thawed
  4 large apples, chopped (about 6 cups)
  4 Snickers candy bars (2.07 ounces *each*), cut into 1/2-inch pieces

---

1. In a large bowl, whisk the milk and pudding mix for 2 minutes. Let stand for 2 minutes or until soft-set. Fold in whipped topping. Fold in apples and candy bars. Refrigerate until serving.

[2000]
FRUIT SALAD WITH APRICOT DRESSING
yield: 26 servings (1 cup each)
prep/total time: 30 min.

When I serve this lovely, refreshing salad for picnics and holidays, the bowl empties fast.

—*Carol Lambert, El Dorado, Arkansas*

---

  1 cup sugar
  1 tablespoon cornstarch
  2 cans (5-1/2 ounces *each*) apricot nectar
  1 teaspoon vanilla extract
  6 large red apples, coarsely chopped
  8 medium firm bananas, sliced
  1 medium fresh pineapple, peeled and cut into chunks (about 5 cups)
  1 quart fresh strawberries, quartered
  2 cups green grapes

1. In a microwave-safe bowl, stir the sugar, cornstarch and apricot nectar until smooth. Microwave, uncovered, on high for 4-6 minutes or until slightly thickened, stirring every 2 minutes. Stir in the vanilla. Refrigerate.

2. In a large bowl, combine fruit. Drizzle with dressing; gently toss to coat. Cover and refrigerate until serving.

Editor's Note: This recipe was tested in a 1,100-watt microwave.

[1994]
AMBROSIA WALDORF SALAD
yield: 12-14 servings
prep: 10 min. + chilling

A light, lovely pink salad, this recipe puts a different spin on traditional Waldorf salad. It is super served with roast turkey or baked ham. People always go back for seconds. My family didn't think they liked cranberries until they tried this sweet, crunchy salad.

—*Janet Smith, Smithton, Missouri*

---

  2 cups fresh *or* frozen cranberry halves
1/2 cup sugar
  3 cups miniature marshmallows
  2 cups diced unpeeled apples
  1 cup seedless green grape halves
3/4 cup chopped pecans
  1 can (20 ounces) pineapple tidbits, drained
  1 cup heavy whipping cream, whipped
Shredded *or* flaked coconut

---

1. In a small bowl, combine cranberries and sugar. In a large bowl, combine the marshmallows, apples, grapes, pecans and pineapple. Add cranberries and mix well. Fold in whipped cream. Cover and refrigerate. Sprinkle with coconut before serving.

CANDY BAR APPLE SALAD

❝Excellent recipe! I've made it a few times. Added sliced bananas and grapes once and that was good too. Easy to make and a crowd-pleaser!❞
—*JillGingras*

[2006]

CHERRY RIBBON SALAD

yield: 12 servings ∞ **prep: 10 min. + chilling**

(Pictured on page 759)

*Filled with pineapple, pecans and cherry pie
filling, this colorful salad mold adds fun fruity
flavor to any potluck menu.*

—*Virginia Luke, Red Level, Alabama*

---

  1 **package (3 ounces) cherry gelatin**
2-1/4 **cups boiling water,** *divided*
  1 **can (21 ounces) cherry pie filling**
  1 **package (3 ounces) orange gelatin**
  1 **can (8 ounces) crushed pineapple,
    undrained**
  1 **cup whipped topping**
1/3 **cup mayonnaise**
1/4 **cup chopped pecans, optional**

---

1. In a large bowl, dissolve cherry gelatin
   in 1-1/4 cups boiling water. Stir in the
   pie filling. Pour into a 7-cup ring mold
   coated with cooking spray; refrigerate
   for about 1 hour or until thickened
   but not set.

2. In a large bowl, dissolve orange gelatin
   in the remaining boiling water. Stir in
   the pineapple. Chill for about 1 hour
   or until thickened but not set.

3. Combine whipped topping, mayonnaise
   and pecans if desired; fold into orange
   mixture. Spoon over cherry layer.

Refrigerate for at least 1 hour or until
firm. Unmold onto a serving plate.

[2008]

CREAMY ORANGE GELATIN

yield: 12 servings ∞ **Prep: 20 min. + chilling**

*After serving this gelatin mold for two
graduation celebrations in less than a year,
it was clear that this recipe was definitely
everyone's favorite.*

—*Sue Gronholz
Beaver Dam, Wisconsin, Field Editor*

---

  4 **packages (3 ounces** *each***) orange
    gelatin**
  4 **cups boiling water**
  1 **quart vanilla ice cream, softened**
1-1/2 **cups orange juice**
  2 **cans (11 ounces** *each***) mandarin
    oranges, drained**

---

1. In a large bowl, dissolve the gelatin in
   boiling water. Stir in the ice cream and
   orange juice until blended. Chill until
   partially set.

2. Fold in oranges. Pour into two 6-cup
   ring molds coated with cooking spray.
   Refrigerate overnight or until firm.
   Unmold onto a serving plate.

UNMOLDING A GELATIN MOLD

1. Loosen the gelatin from the top edge of mold by gently
pulling the gelatin away from edge with a moistened finger.
Then dip the mold up to its rim in a sink or large pan of warm
water for a few seconds or until the edges begin to release
from the side of the mold.

2. Place a plate over the mold and invert. Carefully lift the mold
from the salad.

[2002]

FROSTED ORANGE SALAD
yield: 12 servings ∞ **prep: 35 min. + chilling**

Pineapple, bananas and marshmallows are folded into orange gelatin in this refreshing salad. Frosted with a creamy topping, pecans and coconut, this yummy dish is a favorite. I've been making it for years.

—**Anna Jean Key, Muskogee, Oklahoma**

- 3 packages (3 ounces each) orange gelatin
- 3 cups boiling water
- 1 can (20 ounces) crushed pineapple
- 3 cups cold water
- 4 medium firm bananas, sliced
- 2-1/2 cups miniature marshmallows
- 1/2 cup sugar
- 1 tablespoon all-purpose flour
- 1 egg, lightly beaten
- 1 package (8 ounces) cream cheese, softened
- 1 cup heavy whipping cream, whipped
- 3/4 cup chopped pecans, toasted
- 1/2 cup flaked coconut, toasted

1. In a large bowl, dissolve the gelatin in boiling water. Drain the pineapple, reserving juice. Stir the cold water, bananas, marshmallows and pineapple into gelatin.

2. Pour gelatin mixture into a 13-in. x 9-in. dish coated with cooking spray; refrigerate until firm.

3. Meanwhile, in a large saucepan, combine the sugar and flour. Stir in the reserved pineapple juice until smooth. Bring to a boil over medium heat; cook and stir for 2 minutes or until thickened and bubbly. Reduce heat; cook and stir 2 minutes longer.

4. Remove from the heat. Stir a small amount of hot filling into egg; return all to the pan, stirring constantly. Bring to a gentle boil; cook and stir 2 minutes longer. Cool.

5. In a large bowl, beat the cream cheese until smooth. Beat in the cooled filling. Fold in whipped cream. Spread over gelatin (dish will be full). Sprinkle with nuts and coconut.

[2004]

SWEET MACARONI SALAD
yield: 14 servings ∞ **prep: 20 min. + chilling**

A sweet, out-of-the-ordinary dressing makes this macaroni salad special. My aunt gave me the recipe, and it's so good, it has a star by it. I'll leave out the green pepper if I know that people don't like it—and it still tastes great.

—**Idalee Scholz, Cocoa Beach, Florida**

- 1 package (16 ounces) elbow macaroni
- 4 medium carrots, shredded
- 1 large green pepper, chopped
- 1 medium red onion, chopped
- 2 cups mayonnaise
- 1 can (14 ounces) sweetened condensed milk
- 1 cup sugar
- 1 cup cider vinegar
- 1 teaspoon salt
- 1/2 teaspoon pepper

1. Cook macaroni according to package directions; drain and rinse in cold water. In a large serving bowl, combine the macaroni, carrots, green pepper and onion.

2. In a small bowl, whisk the mayonnaise, milk, sugar, vinegar, salt and pepper until smooth. Pour over macaroni mixture and toss to coat. Cover and refrigerate overnight.

FROSTED ORANGE SALAD

"Delicious! But I mix all (except topping) ingredients in a deep bowl; let set 1-2 hours, then pour into the 13-in. x 9-in. dish. Dish is VERY full and usually spills!"
—*BrendainPa*

[2003]

CORN BREAD CONFETTI SALAD

yield: 20-22 servings ∾ **prep: 15 min.**
bake: 15 min. + cooling

*This colorful and tasty salad is always well
received at picnics and potlucks. Corn bread
salads have long been popular in the South
but may be new to people in other regions.
No matter where you live, I think you'll like
this one!*

—*Jennifer Horst*
Goose Creek, South Carolina

- 1 package (8-1/2 ounces) corn bread/muffin mix
- 2 cans (15-1/2 ounces each) whole kernel corn, drained
- 2 cans (15 ounces each) pinto beans, rinsed and drained
- 1 can (15 ounces) black beans, rinsed and drained
- 3 small tomatoes, chopped
- 1 medium green pepper, chopped
- 1 medium sweet red pepper, chopped
- 1/2 cup chopped green onions
- 10 bacon strips, cooked and crumbled
- 2 cups (8 ounces) shredded cheddar cheese

DRESSING:

- 1 cup (8 ounces) sour cream
- 1 cup mayonnaise
- 1 envelope ranch salad dressing mix

1. Prepare the corn bread mix according to the package directions. Cool completely; crumble.

2. In a large bowl, combine corn, beans, tomatoes, peppers, onions, bacon, cheese and crumbled corn bread.

3. In a small bowl, whisk the dressing ingredients. Just before serving, pour dressing over salad and toss to coat.

[2003]

DELI-STYLE PASTA SALAD

yield: 12 servings ∾ **prep: 15 min. + chilling**

*When I'm having weekend guests, I make this
salad the day before they arrive. The flavors
blend wonderfully when it is chilled overnight,
and it keeps well for several days. It's also a
great dish to take along to a picnic or potluck.*

—*Jill Evely*
Wilmore, Kentucky, Field Editor

- 1 package (16 ounces) tricolor spiral pasta
- 2 medium plum tomatoes, seeded and julienned
- 8 ounces sliced salami, julienned
- 8 ounces provolone cheese, julienned
- 1 small red onion, thinly sliced and separated into rings
- 1 jar (5-3/4 ounces) pimiento-stuffed olives, drained
- 1 can (2-1/4 ounces) sliced ripe olives, drained
- 1/4 cup grated Parmesan cheese
- 1 bottle (8 ounces) Italian salad dressing

1. Cook pasta according to package directions; drain and rinse in cold water.

2. In a large bowl, combine the pasta, tomatoes, salami, provolone cheese, onion, olives and Parmesan. Add the dressing; toss to coat. Cover and refrigerate for several hours or overnight. Serve with a slotted spoon.

QUICKLY JULIENNE DELI MEATS

Ask the deli person to slice the
meat to the desired thickness
when you order it. At home, stack
the meat and cut into strips.

—*Taste of Home Cooking Experts*

[2000]

SWEET-SOUR PASTA SALAD

yield: 16 servings ∞ **prep: 30 min. + chilling**

Fresh garden vegetables add color and crunch to this attractive salad. Its pleasant vinaigrette-type dressing is sparked with ground mustard and garlic. I like the look of the tricolor spirals, but you can substitute other pasta shapes or use what you have on hand.

—*Launa Shoemaker*
Landrum, South Carolina

- 1 **package (16 ounces) tricolor spiral pasta**
- 1 **medium red onion, chopped**
- 1 **medium tomato, chopped**
- 1 **medium cucumber, peeled, seeded and chopped**
- 1 **medium green pepper, chopped**
- 2 **tablespoons minced fresh parsley**

DRESSING:
- 1-1/2 **cups sugar**
- 1/2 **cup white vinegar**
- 1 **tablespoon ground mustard**
- 1 **teaspoon salt, optional**
- 1 **teaspoon garlic powder**

1. Cook the pasta according to package directions; drain and rinse with cold water. Place in a large serving bowl. Stir in the onion, tomato, cucumber, green pepper and parsley; set aside.

2. In a small saucepan, combine the dressing ingredients. Cook over medium-low heat for 10 minutes or until sugar is dissolved. Pour over salad and toss to coat. Cover and refrigerate for 2 hours. Serve with a slotted spoon.

[2011]

MIMI'S LENTIL MEDLEY

yield: 8 servings ∞ **prep: 40 min.**

(Pictured on page 757)

I made this one summer evening by putting together what I had on hand. It earned my husband Ken's top rating by saying, "You can make this again soon." It is fresh-tasting and attractive.

—*Mary Ann Hazen*
Rochester Hills, Michigan

- 1 **cup dried lentils, rinsed**
- 2 **cups water**
- 2 **cups sliced fresh mushrooms**
- 1 **medium cucumber, cubed**
- 1 **medium zucchini, cubed**
- 1 **small red onion, chopped**
- 1/2 **cup chopped sun-dried tomatoes (not packed in oil)**
- 1/2 **cup rice vinegar**
- 1/4 **cup minced fresh mint**
- 3 **tablespoons olive oil**
- 2 **teaspoons honey**
- 1 **teaspoon dried basil**
- 1 **teaspoon dried oregano**
- 4 **cups fresh baby spinach, chopped**
- 1 **cup (4 ounces) crumbled feta cheese**
- 4 **bacon strips, cooked and crumbled**

1. In a small saucepan, bring lentils and water to a boil. Reduce heat; cover and simmer for 20-25 minutes or until tender. Drain and rinse in cold water.

2. Transfer to a large bowl. Add mushrooms, cucumber, zucchini, onion and tomatoes. In a small bowl, whisk the vinegar, mint, oil, honey, basil and oregano. Drizzle over lentil mixture; toss to coat. Add the spinach, cheese and bacon; toss to combine.

SWEET-SOUR PASTA SALAD

❝Absolute favorite in my family. My daughter will eat the leftovers for breakfast!❞
—*wunsagin*

[2002]

BLT MACARONI SALAD

yield: 12 servings ∽ prep: 20 min. + chilling

This pleasing pasta salad is like eating a BLT in a bowl. Chock-full of crispy crumbled bacon, chopped tomato, celery and green onion, the sensational salad is draped in a tangy dressing.

—Norene Wright
  Manilla, Indiana, Field Editor

  2   cups uncooked elbow macaroni
  5   green onions, finely chopped
  1   large tomato, diced
1-1/4 cups diced celery
1-1/4 cups mayonnaise
  5   teaspoons white vinegar
1/4   teaspoon salt
1/8   to 1/4 teaspoon pepper
  1   pound sliced bacon, cooked and crumbled

1. Cook the macaroni according to the package directions; drain and rinse in cold water. In a large bowl, combine the macaroni, green onions, tomato and celery.

2. In a small bowl, whisk mayonnaise, vinegar, salt and pepper. Pour over macaroni mixture and toss to coat. Cover and refrigerate for at least 2 hours. Just before serving, add bacon.

[2010]

BEAN & BARLEY SALAD

yield: 12 servings (3/4 cup each)
prep/total time: 30 min.

This hearty salad lasts for days in the fridge. We like to spoon it onto pita chips. It's fantastic!

—Janelle Lee
  Appleton, Wisconsin, Field Editor

3/4   cup quick-cooking barley
  1   can (16 ounces) kidney beans, rinsed and drained

  1   can (15 ounces) black beans, rinsed and drained
  1   can (11 ounces) whole kernel corn, drained
  1   large sweet red pepper, finely chopped
  6   green onions, chopped
1/3   cup minced fresh cilantro
DRESSING:
3/4   cup olive oil
1/3   cup red wine vinegar
  2   garlic cloves, minced
1-1/2 teaspoons chili powder
3/4   teaspoon salt
3/4   teaspoon ground cumin
1/4   to 1/2 teaspoon crushed red pepper flakes
1/4   teaspoon pepper

1. Prepare barley according to package directions. Transfer to a large bowl; stir in the beans, corn, red pepper, onions and cilantro.

2. In a small bowl, whisk the dressing ingredients. Pour over salad; toss to coat. Chill until serving.

[1997]

COOL CUCUMBER PASTA

yield: 8-10 servings
prep: 20 min. + chilling

People say this salad is crispy, sweet and refreshingly different.

—Jeanette Fuehring
  Concordia, Missouri, Former Field Editor

  8   ounces uncooked penne pasta
  1   tablespoon canola oil
  2   medium cucumbers, thinly sliced
  1   medium onion, thinly sliced
1-1/2 cups sugar
  1   cup water
3/4   cup white vinegar
  1   tablespoon prepared mustard
  1   tablespoon dried parsley flakes
  1   teaspoon salt

COOL CUCUMBER PASTA

"This is delicious! Whole family loved it! Reminiscent of the old cucumber and onions mixed with vinegar and sugar we used to have for supper in the '60s on a warm night."
—dllano

1 teaspoon pepper
1/2 teaspoon garlic salt

1. Cook pasta according to package directions; drain and rinse in cold water. Place pasta in a large bowl; stir in the oil, cucumbers and onion.

2. In a small bowl, whisk the remaining ingredients. Pour over salad; toss to coat. Cover and chill for 4 hours, stirring occasionally. Serve with a slotted spoon. Refrigerate leftovers.

[2004]

SUMMER GARDEN PASTA
yield: 9 servings ∞ prep: 25 min.
cook: 10 min.

This fresh-tasting side dish pairs pasta with an array of nutritious veggies, including zucchini, bell peppers and a juicy tomato. Our four boys are all grown and out of the house, but I still grow a large garden every summer and give away everything we can't eat.

—*April Johnson, Tonasket, Washington*

1 package (1 pound) small tube pasta
1 cup sliced yellow summer squash
1 cup sliced zucchini
1 cup julienned sweet red pepper
1 cup julienned green pepper
1 cup sliced green onions
1/4 cup butter, cubed
6 garlic cloves, peeled and thinly sliced
1-1/2 cups reduced-sodium chicken broth
1 small tomato, chopped
1/2 cup grated Parmesan cheese
1 tablespoon minced fresh parsley
2 teaspoons garlic pepper
1 teaspoon salt

1. Cook pasta according to the package directions. Meanwhile, in a large skillet, saute the yellow squash, zucchini, peppers and onions in butter until crisp-tender. Add garlic; cook 1 minute longer. Stir in broth and tomato; bring to a boil. Cook and stir until liquid is reduced by half.

2. Drain pasta; stir into vegetable mixture. Cook 1 minute longer or until heated through.

3. Transfer to a large bowl. Sprinkle with the cheese, parsley, garlic pepper and salt; toss to coat.

[2012]

SOBA SALAD WITH GINGERED-SESAME DRESSING
yield: 8 servings ∞ prep/total time: 30 min.

This is a fantastic dish to spice up any meatless menu! If you prefer, you can add grilled shrimp or chicken for a protein-packed main dish as well.

—*Mandy Rivers, Lexington, South Carolina*

1/2 cup reduced-sodium soy sauce
1/4 cup packed brown sugar
2 tablespoons rice vinegar
2 tablespoons canola oil
2 tablespoons orange juice
1 tablespoon minced fresh gingerroot
1 teaspoon sesame oil
1 garlic clove, minced
1 teaspoon Sriracha Asian hot chili sauce *or* 1/2 teaspoon hot pepper sauce
SALAD:
2 cups frozen shelled edamame, thawed
1/2 pound uncooked Japanese soba noodles *or* whole wheat linguini
1 package (14 ounces) coleslaw mix
1 cup shredded carrots
1 cup thinly sliced green onions
3 tablespoons sesame seeds, toasted

1. In a small bowl, whisk the first nine ingredients; set aside. Cook edamame and soba noodles according to the package directions; drain and rinse in cold water.

2. Just before serving, combine the coleslaw mix, carrots, green onions, noodles and edamame in a large bowl. Add dressing; toss to coat. Garnish with sesame seeds.

SOUTHWESTERN RICE SALAD

[2006]

SOUTHWESTERN RICE SALAD

yield: 12 servings ∾ prep/total time: 30 min.

The recipe for this delicious, colorful salad has been in my family for years. My mother used to bring it to many different functions, and I'm carrying on her tradition.

—*Ruth Bianchi, Apple Valley, Minnesota*

1-1/3	cups water
2/3	cup uncooked long grain rice
3/4	cup chopped green pepper
1/2	cup chopped red onion
1	medium carrot, chopped
1	tablespoon canola oil
3	garlic cloves, minced
1	package (16 ounces) frozen corn, thawed
1	can (15 ounces) black beans, rinsed and drained
2	medium plum tomatoes, chopped
1	cup salted peanuts
1/3	cup minced fresh cilantro
2/3	cup olive oil
1/3	cup lemon juice
1/2 to 1-1/2	teaspoons cayenne pepper
1/2	teaspoon ground cumin

1. In a large saucepan, bring water and rice to a boil. Reduce heat; cover and simmer for 15 minutes. Remove from the heat. Let stand for 5 minutes or until rice is tender. Rinse rice with cold water and drain. Place the rice in a large bowl.

2. In a small skillet, saute green pepper, onion and carrot in oil until crisp-tender. Add the garlic; cook 1 minute longer. Add to rice. Stir in the corn, beans, tomatoes, peanuts and cilantro.

3. In a small bowl, combine the oil, lemon juice, cayenne and cumin. Pour over rice mixture; stir to coat. Cover and refrigerate until serving.

[2009]

WILD RICE SALAD

yield: 4 servings
prep: 1-1/4 hours + chilling

I modified a recipe I received years ago and came up with this versatile salad. It's refreshing served cold on a hot day, but it's equally tasty at room temperature or warmed in the microwave.

—*Robin Thompson, Roseville, California*

3	cups water
1	cup uncooked wild rice
2	chicken bouillon cubes
4-1/2	teaspoons butter
1	cup cut fresh green beans
1	cup cubed cooked chicken breast
1	medium tomato, chopped
1	bunch green onions, sliced
1/4	cup rice vinegar
1	tablespoon sesame oil
1	garlic clove, minced
1/2	teaspoon dried tarragon
1/4	teaspoon pepper

1. In a large saucepan, bring the water, rice, bouillon and butter to a boil. Reduce heat; cover and simmer for 45-60 minutes or until rice is tender. Drain if necessary; transfer to a large bowl and cool completely.

2. Place green beans in a steamer basket; place in a small saucepan over 1 in. of water. Bring to a boil; cover and steam for 8-10 minutes or until crisp-tender.

3. Add the chicken, tomato, onions and green beans to the rice; stir until blended. Combine the remaining ingredients; drizzle over mixture and toss to coat. Refrigerate until chilled.

[1996]

ANTIPASTO SALAD
yield: 12-16 servings
prep: 15 min. + chilling

(Pictured on page 754)

I take this fresh-tasting, colorful salad to potluck dinners throughout the year, since everyone who tries it loves it. The pasta, garbanzo beans and pepperoni make it a nice hearty dish.

—*Agnes Bulkley, Hicksville, New York*

  1 package (16 ounces) spiral pasta
  1 can (15 ounces) garbanzo beans *or* chickpeas, rinsed and drained
  1 package (3-1/2 ounces) sliced pepperoni, halved
  1 can (2-1/4 ounces) sliced ripe olives, drained
1/2 cup diced sweet red pepper
1/2 cup diced green pepper
  4 medium fresh mushrooms, sliced
  2 garlic cloves, minced
  2 tablespoons minced fresh basil *or* 2 teaspoons dried basil
  2 teaspoons salt
1-1/2 teaspoons minced fresh oregano *or* 1/2 teaspoon dried oregano
1/2 teaspoon pepper
1/4 teaspoon cayenne pepper
  1 cup olive oil
2/3 cup lemon juice

1. Cook the pasta according to package directions; drain and rinse in cold water. Place in a large salad bowl. Stir in the next 12 ingredients.

2. In a small bowl, whisk oil and lemon juice. Pour over salad and toss to coat. Cover and refrigerate 6 hours or overnight. Stir before serving.

[2004]

WARM ASPARAGUS SPINACH SALAD
yield: 14-16 servings
prep/total time: 30 min.

Spinach, cashews and pasta are mixed with roasted asparagus in this delightful spring salad. The mixture is topped with a light vinaigrette, seasoned with soy sauce and sprinkled with Parmesan cheese. I've used this recipe many times.

—*Kathleen Lucas, Trumbull, Connecticut*

1-1/2 pounds fresh asparagus, trimmed and cut into 1-inch pieces
  2 tablespoons plus 1/2 cup olive oil, *divided*
1/4 teaspoon salt
1-1/2 pounds uncooked penne pasta
3/4 cup chopped green onions
  6 tablespoons white wine vinegar
  2 tablespoons reduced-sodium soy sauce
  1 package (6 ounces) fresh baby spinach
  1 cup coarsely chopped cashews
1/2 cup shredded Parmesan cheese

1. Place the asparagus in a 13-in. x 9-in. baking dish. Drizzle with 2 tablespoons oil; sprinkle with salt. Bake, uncovered, at 400° for 20-25 minutes or until crisp-tender, stirring every 10 minutes. Meanwhile, cook the pasta according to package directions; drain.

2. In a blender, combine onions, vinegar and soy sauce; cover and process until smooth. While processing, gradually add remaining oil in a steady stream.

3. In a large salad bowl, combine the pasta, spinach and asparagus. Drizzle with dressing; toss to coat. Sprinkle with cashews and cheese.

WARM ASPARAGUS SPINACH SALAD

"I loved the combination of spinach and pasta. Great flavor!"
—*Hannah0418*

[2006]

STRAWBERRY VINAIGRETTE

yield: 2-1/2 cups ∞ prep/total time: 10 min.

I enjoy using strawberries in a variety of ways, including featuring them in this pretty, sweet and tart dressing.

—*Carolyn McMunn, San Angelo, Texas*

    1 package (16 ounces) frozen
      unsweetened strawberries, thawed
    6 tablespoons lemon juice
  1/4 cup sugar
    2 tablespoons cider vinegar
    2 tablespoons olive oil
  1/8 teaspoon poppy seeds

1. Place the strawberries in a blender; cover and process until pureed. Add the lemon juice and sugar; cover and process until blended. While processing, gradually add the vinegar and oil in a steady stream, process until thickened. Stir in the poppy seeds. Transfer to a large bowl or jar; cover and store in the refrigerator.

[2002]

CREAMY FRENCH DRESSING

yield: 2-1/2 cups ∞ prep/total time: 10 min.

This dressing is an excellent salad topper that is thick and well-seasoned. It goes great with a variety of salad greens.

—*Ruth Ann Stelfox*
Raymond, Alberta, Field Editor

  1/2 cup mayonnaise
  1/2 cup ketchup
  1/4 cup white vinegar
  1/2 cup sugar
    1 small onion, cut into wedges
  1/2 teaspoon salt
  1/4 teaspoon pepper
    1 cup canola oil
Salad greens, tomato wedges and cucumber slices *or* vegetables of your choice

1. In a blender, combine the mayonnaise, ketchup, vinegar, sugar, onion, salt and pepper; cover and process until smooth. While processing, gradually add oil in a steady stream. Serve with salad. Refrigerate leftover dressing.

[2007]

CRACKED PEPPER SALAD DRESSING

yield: 2-1/2 cups ∞ prep: 15 min. + chilling

The pepper is bold but not too sharp in this creamy dressing that will complement your favorite salad ingredients. It's easy to mix up and great to have on hand.

—*Millie Vickery, Lena, Illinois, Field Editor*

    2 cups mayonnaise
  1/4 cup water
  1/4 cup 2% milk
  1/4 cup buttermilk
    2 tablespoons grated Parmesan cheese
    1 tablespoon coarsely ground pepper
    2 teaspoons finely chopped green onion
    1 teaspoon lemon juice
  1/2 teaspoon garlic salt
  1/2 teaspoon garlic powder

1. In a small bowl, whisk the ingredients. Cover and chill for at least 1 hour. Dressing may be stored in the refrigerator for up to 2 weeks.

STRAWBERRY VINAIGRETTE

" An intense strawberry flavor. We loved it. I did not put in the poppy seeds. I wonder how raspberries or peaches would be in this recipe? "
— *SaraM15*

[2000]

POPPY SEED DRESSING

yield: 2-3/4 cups ∽ **prep/total time: 15 min.**

It's fabulous over any fruit salad and spinach salads.

—Andra Kunkle, Lenoir, North Carolina

- 2 cups sugar
- 3/4 teaspoon salt
- 3/4 teaspoon onion powder
- 3/4 teaspoon ground mustard
- 3/4 cup white vinegar
- 1 cup canola oil
- 3/4 teaspoon poppy seeds

1. In a small bowl, combine the sugar, salt, onion powder and mustard. With a mixer, beat in vinegar for 4 minutes. Gradually beat in oil; continue beating for 5 minutes. Stir in poppy seeds.

[1997]

SUPER EASY THOUSAND ISLAND DRESSING

yield: 2-1/2 cups ∽ **prep/total time: 5 min.**

It's almost unbelievable that a dressing so easy to fix can be so good.

—Darlis Wilfer
West Bend, Wisconsin, Field Editor

- 2 cups mayonnaise
- 1/4 cup chili sauce
- 1/4 cup pickle relish

1. In a small bowl, combine all the ingredients. Cover and refrigerate.

[2006]

BLUE CHEESE BACON DRESSING

yield: 2 cups ∽ **prep/total time: 10 min.**

This dressing is absolutely fantastic. I've made it again and again. It has just about everything we like in it.

—Marion Karlin
Waterloo, Iowa, Field Editor

- 1 cup mayonnaise
- 1/2 cup sour cream
- 5 to 6 tablespoons 2% milk
- 1 tablespoon white wine vinegar
- 1/2 teaspoon sugar
- 1/4 teaspoon salt
- 1/4 teaspoon garlic powder
- 1/4 teaspoon white pepper
- 1 cup (4 ounces) crumbled blue cheese
- 1/4 cup crumbled cooked bacon
- 1/4 cup minced chives

1. In a small bowl, whisk the mayonnaise, sour cream, milk, vinegar, sugar, salt, garlic powder and pepper until blended. Stir in blue cheese, bacon and chives. Cover and store in the refrigerator.

USING THE PERFECT AMOUNT OF SALAD DRESSING

Many of us enjoy salad dressing on our salads, and sometimes we are overly generous with it. To keep the amount of dressing in check, use a tablespoon measuring spoon, a shot glass or a clean plastic measuring cup for medicine.

—Taste of Home Cooking Experts

BLUE CHEESE BACON DRESSING

"Very yummy dressing. I did half the amount of blue cheese since I really prefer a milder taste and also didn't use chives as I didn't have any. I served it over a simple spring and romaine lettuce mix, along with fresh grape tomatoes from our garden."

—grannygourmet

~ SANDWICHES & PIZZA ~

ULTIMATE PANINI

❝The taste was fabulous! Loved it. It's a little messy to make, but my philosophy is: the messier, the better!❞

—*Dawnielleleland*

[2011]

ULTIMATE PANINI

yield: 4 servings ∞ **prep: 40 min.**
cook: 5 min./batch

The aroma of onions cooking at country fairs and street vendor carts makes me crave caramelized onions. I wanted to pair them with something special, and this sandwich is just that.

—*Charlene Brogan, Falmouth, Maine*

- 2 large onions, sliced
- 2 tablespoons canola oil
- 4 slices provolone cheese
- 1/2 pound thinly sliced deli ham
- 1 large tomato, sliced
- 8 garlic-flavored sandwich pickle slices
- 8 slices Italian bread (1/2 inch thick)
- 2 tablespoons butter, softened

1. In a large skillet, saute the onions in oil until onions are softened. Reduce the heat to medium-low; cook, stirring occasionally, for 30 minutes or until deep golden brown.

2. Layer the cheese, ham, tomato, pickles and caramelized onions on four bread slices; top with the remaining bread. Spread outsides of the sandwiches with butter.

3. Cook on a panini maker or indoor grill for 3-4 minutes or until bread is browned and cheese is melted.

[2009]

CHEDDAR FRENCH DIP SANDWICHES

yield: 4 servings ∞ **prep/total time: 20 min.**

(*Pictured on page 811*)

With leftover roast beef or deli beef, it takes almost no time at all to fix these satisfying hot sandwiches. They're perfect for those hectic days.

—*Holly Szwej, Bridgeport, New York*

- 1/4 cup butter, cubed
- 2 garlic cloves, minced
- 4 ciabatta rolls, split
- 1 cup (4 ounces) shredded cheddar cheese
- 1 pound thinly sliced roast beef
- 1 can (14-1/2 ounces) beef broth

1. In a small skillet, melt butter. Add the garlic; saute for 1 minute. Place rolls on a baking sheet; brush cut sides with garlic butter. Sprinkle with the cheese. Broil 3-4 in. from the heat for 2-3 minutes or until cheese is melted.

2. In a large saucepan, combine the beef and broth; heat through. Using tongs or a slotted spoon, place beef on rolls. Serve the sandwiches with remaining broth for dipping.

[2011]

JALAPENO POPPER BURGERS

yield: 4 servings ∾ **prep: 30 min.** ∾ **grill: 15 min.**

What do you get when you combine a jalapeno popper and a great burger? This fantastic recipe! It takes the classic components of a popper and encases them in a juicy patty for a burst of flavor in every bite.

—*Jo Davison, Naples, Florida*

- 3 jalapeno peppers, halved lengthwise and seeded
- 1 teaspoon olive oil
- 6 bacon strips, cooked and crumbled
- 1 package (3 ounces) cream cheese, softened
- 2 garlic cloves, minced
- 1 teaspoon salt
- 1 teaspoon lemon-pepper seasoning
- 1/2 teaspoon pepper
- 1/4 teaspoon paprika
- 2 pounds ground beef
- 4 slices pepper Jack cheese
- 4 hamburger buns, split
- 4 lettuce leaves
- 1 large tomato, sliced
- 3/4 cup guacamole

1. Brush jalapenos with oil. Grill, covered, over medium heat for 3-5 minutes or until tender, turning occasionally. When cool enough to handle, finely chop. In a small bowl, combine the bacon, cream cheese and jalapeno until blended.

2. In a large bowl, combine the garlic, salt, lemon-pepper, pepper and paprika. Crumble beef over mixture and mix well. Shape into eight thin patties. Spoon bacon mixture onto center of four patties; top with remaining patties and press edges firmly to seal.

3. Grill burgers, covered, over medium heat or broil 4 in. from heat for 6-7 minutes on each side or until a thermometer reads 160° and juices run clear. Top with pepper jack cheese. Cover and cook 1-2 minutes longer or until pepper jack cheese is melted.

4. Grill buns, cut side down, over medium heat for 30-60 seconds or until toasted. Serve burgers on buns with lettuce, tomato and guacamole.

Editor's Note: Wear disposable gloves when cutting hot peppers; the oils can burn skin. Avoid touching your face.

[2010]

SPICY CHICKEN LETTUCE WRAPS

yield: 4 servings ∾ **prep/total time: 30 min.**

This is one of my go-to meals when I want a fun and easy dinner. I love the spicy Asian flavors against the cool lettuce and the added crunch of peanuts and water chestnuts.

—*Brittany Allyn, Nashville, Tennessee*

- 1 pound chicken tenderloins, cut into 1/2-inch pieces
- 1/8 teaspoon pepper
- 2 tablespoons canola oil, *divided*
- 1 medium onion, finely chopped
- 1 small green pepper, finely chopped
- 1 small sweet red pepper, finely chopped
- 1 can (8 ounces) sliced water chestnuts, drained and finely chopped
- 1 can (4 ounces) mushroom stems and pieces, drained and finely chopped
- 2 garlic cloves, minced
- 1/3 cup stir-fry sauce
- 1 teaspoon reduced-sodium soy sauce
- 8 Bibb *or* Boston lettuce leaves
- 1/4 cup salted peanuts
- 2 teaspoons minced fresh cilantro

1. Sprinkle chicken with pepper. In a large skillet or wok, stir-fry chicken in 1 tablespoon oil until no longer pink. Remove and set aside.

2. Stir-fry the onion and peppers in remaining oil for 5 minutes. Add the water chestnuts, mushrooms and garlic; stir-fry 2-3 minutes longer or until vegetables are crisp-tender. Add stir-fry sauce and soy sauce. Stir in chicken; heat through.

3. Place 1/2 cup chicken mixture on each lettuce leaf; sprinkle each with 1-1/2 teaspoons peanuts and 1/4 teaspoon cilantro. Fold lettuce over filling.

[2003]

CHEESY HAM BRAID

yield: 6-8 servings ∞ **prep: 25 min. + rising
bake: 25 min. + standing**

*Our congregation is full of wonderful cooks, so
we enjoy many potluck meals throughout the
year. I like to share this chewy and cheesy braid
I got from a family friend.*

—Becky Houston
Grand Junction, Tennessee

1 package (16 ounces) hot roll mix
1 cup warm water (120° to 130°)
1 egg, lightly beaten
2 tablespoons butter, softened, *divided*
1/2 cup chopped onion
1/2 cup chopped green pepper
2 cups chopped fully cooked ham
1-1/2 cups (6 ounces) shredded
cheddar cheese
1 cup (8 ounces) ricotta cheese
1 tablespoon minced fresh parsley
1 egg white
1 tablespoon cold water

1. In a large bowl, combine contents of
the roll mix and yeast packets. Stir in
the warm water, egg and 1 tablespoon
butter. Turn onto a floured surface;
knead until smooth and elastic, about
6-8 minutes; set aside.

2. In a large skillet, saute the onion and
green pepper in remaining butter until
tender. Remove from the heat; stir in
the ham, cheeses and parsley.

3. On a greased baking sheet, roll dough
into a 15-in. x 10-in. rectangle. Spoon
the ham mixture lengthwise down the
center of dough. On each long side,
cut 1-in.-wide strips about 2 in. into
the center. Starting at one end, fold
alternating strips at an angle across the
filling. Pinch ends to seal. Cover and
let rise in a warm place for 15 minutes
or until almost doubled.

4. In a small bowl, beat the egg white and
cold water; brush over the dough. Bake
at 375° for 25-30 minutes or until
bread is golden brown. Let stand for
10 minutes before slicing. Serve warm.
Refrigerate leftovers.

[1997]

HONEY-MUSTARD
CHICKEN SANDWICHES

yield: 4 servings ∞ **prep/total time: 20 min.**

(Pictured on page 811)

*My chicken sandwiches are homemade fast
food that's more delicious than the kind you go
out to pick up.*

—Christina Levrant, Henderson, Nevada

1/4 cup Dijon mustard
2 tablespoons honey
1 teaspoon dried oregano
1 teaspoon water
1/4 teaspoon garlic powder
1/8 to 1/4 teaspoon cayenne pepper
4 boneless skinless chicken breast
halves (4 ounces *each*)
4 sandwich buns, split
1 cup shredded lettuce
8 thin tomato slices

1. In a small bowl, combine the first six
ingredients. Broil chicken 4 in. from
the heat for 4-7 minutes on each side
or until a thermometer reads 170°,
brushing occasionally with mustard
mixture. Serve on buns with lettuce
and tomato.

[1996]
ALOHA BURGERS
yield: 4 servings ∞ **prep/total time: 30 min.**
(Pictured on page 814)

I love hamburgers and pineapple, so it just seemed natural for me to combine them. My family frequently requests these unique sandwiches. It's a nice change of pace from the same old boring burger.

—Joi McKim-Jones, Waikoloa, Hawaii

- 1 can (8 ounces) sliced pineapple
- 3/4 cup reduced-sodium teriyaki sauce
- 1 pound ground beef
- 1 large sweet onion, sliced
- 1 tablespoon butter
- 4 lettuce leaves
- 4 sesame seed *or* onion buns, split and toasted
- 4 slices Swiss cheese
- 4 bacon strips, cooked

1. Drain the pineapple juice into a small bowl; add the teriyaki sauce. Place 3 tablespoons in a resealable plastic bag. Add pineapple; toss to coat and set aside. Shape beef into four patties; place in an 8-in. square baking dish. Pour remaining teriyaki sauce mixture over patties; marinate for 5-10 minutes, turning once.

2. Drain and discard teriyaki marinade. Grill, covered, over medium heat or broil 4 in. from the heat for 6-9 minutes on each side or until a thermometer reads 160° and juices run clear. Meanwhile, in a small skillet, saute the onion in butter until tender, about 5 minutes; set aside.

3. Drain and discard pineapple marinade. Place the pineapple on grill or under broiler to heat through. Layer with the lettuce and onion on bottom of buns. Top with burgers, cheese, pineapple and bacon. Replace tops.

[2006]
PIZZA MEATBALL SUBS
yield: 6-7 servings ∞ **prep: 30 min.**
bake: 25 min.

I made these sandwiches one evening for my family, and they were a huge hit with everyone, including the picky eaters. There's plenty of sauce and cheese to complement the baked meatballs.

—Heather Begin, Athens, Maine

- 1 egg, lightly beaten
- 1/3 cup steak sauce
- 1 cup crushed saltines
- 1 teaspoon onion powder
- 1/4 teaspoon seasoned salt
- 1/8 teaspoon pepper
- 1-1/2 pounds ground beef
- 6 to 7 tablespoons mayonnaise
- 6 to 7 submarine buns, split
- 9 to 11 slices process American cheese, cut into strips
- 1 jar (14 ounces) pizza sauce
- 2 cups (8 ounces) shredded part-skim mozzarella cheese

1. In a large bowl, combine the egg, steak sauce, saltines, onion powder, salt and pepper. Crumble beef over mixture and mix well. Shape into 1-1/2-in. balls.

2. Place meatballs on a greased rack in a shallow baking pan. Bake at 375° for 20-25 minutes or until no longer pink. Drain on paper towels.

3. Spread the mayonnaise over the bun bottoms; top each with American cheese, 1 tablespoon pizza sauce, meatballs and remaining pizza sauce. Sprinkle with mozzarella cheese. Place on a baking sheet. Bake for 5-10 minutes or until cheese is melted.

ALOHA BURGERS
"What a clever combination! A few days after I made this, my fiance was already asking when I would serve it again. We loved it."
—ashleyOHiO

BUFFALO CHICKEN WRAPS

[2005]

BUFFALO CHICKEN WRAPS

yield: 4 servings ∽ **prep/total time: 25 min.**

Blue cheese dressing and hot pepper sauce enhance these yummy tortilla wraps. Filled with chicken, cheese, lettuce and tomatoes, they're colorful, fun to eat...and tote-able, too!

—Athena Russell, Florence, South Carolina

1	cup all-purpose flour
1	teaspoon salt
1/4	teaspoon pepper
1/2	cup buttermilk
4	boneless skinless chicken breast halves (4 ounces *each*)
1	cup canola oil
1/2	cup hot pepper sauce
1/4	cup butter, melted
4	spinach tortillas (10 inches)
1	cup shredded lettuce
1	cup (4 ounces) shredded cheddar cheese
2/3	cup chopped tomatoes
1/2	cup blue cheese salad dressing

1. In a shallow bowl, combine the flour, salt and pepper. Place buttermilk in another shallow bowl. Dip chicken in buttermilk, then roll in flour mixture.

2. In a large skillet, cook chicken in oil for 4-5 minutes on each side or until a meat thermometer reads 170°. Drain on paper towels; cut into strips.

3. In a small bowl, combine hot pepper sauce and butter. Dip chicken strips into mixture, coating both sides. Place chicken in the center of each tortilla. Layer with the lettuce, cheese and tomatoes; drizzle with salad dressing. Fold ends of each tortilla over filling; secure with toothpicks if desired.

[1996]

DOUBLE-DECKER CHEESE MELT

yield: 6 servings ∽ **prep/total time: 25 min.**

This is a recipe that's easy to make and deliciously different. Whenever I serve these tasty sandwiches, my family looks for more.

—Leslie Eisenbraun, Columbiana, Ohio

1	cup (4 ounces) shredded cheddar cheese
1/4	cup butter, softened
1	egg
1/2	teaspoon garlic salt
1/2	teaspoon onion salt
6	slices white bread

Paprika, optional

1. In a food processor, blend the cheese and butter. Add the egg, garlic salt and onion salt; process for 1 minute or until creamy. Spread 2 tablespoons on each slice of bread. Stack two slices of the bread, cheese side up, for each sandwich; sprinkle with the paprika if desired. Cut each sandwich in half diagonally.

2. Place on an ungreased baking sheet. Bake at 400° for 12-15 minutes or until golden and bubbly.

CHEESE MELTS

Cheese sandwiches are comfort food. Adults enjoy them as much as kids. Add an adult spin on the sandwich above by substituting half of the cheddar cheese for Swiss, provolone, pepper jack, Brie or mozzarella.

—Taste of Home Cooking Experts

[2010]

GRILLED VEGETABLE SANDWICHES

yield: 12 servings ∽ **prep: 30 min. grill: 20 min.**

Use some of your fresh garden bounty to build these hearty, unique subs. Basil-lemon mayo adds terrific flavor.

—*Kathy Hewitt, Cranston, Rhode Island*

3 large sweet red peppers
3 medium red onions
3 large zucchini
1/4 cup olive oil
3/4 teaspoon salt
3/4 teaspoon coarsely ground pepper
3/4 cup reduced-fat mayonnaise
1/3 cup minced fresh basil
2 tablespoons lemon juice
6 garlic cloves, minced
12 submarine buns, split
24 slices cheddar cheese
3 medium tomatoes, sliced
3/4 cup hummus

1. Cut the red peppers into eighths; cut onions and zucchini into 1/2-in. slices. Brush vegetables with oil; sprinkle with salt and pepper. Grill vegetables in batches, covered, over medium heat or broil 4 in. from the heat for 4-5 minutes on each side or until crisp-tender. Cool.

2. Combine the mayonnaise, basil, lemon juice and garlic; spread over the bun bottoms. Layer with cheese, grilled vegetables and tomatoes. Spread the hummus over bun tops; replace tops.

[2006]

FIRECRACKER BURGERS

yield: 4 servings ∽ **prep: 20 min. grill: 15 min.**

These tasty stuffed burgers are perfect fare for gatherings throughout the year. They're great with a cool, creamy macaroni salad and an icy cold drink.

—*Kelly Williams*
Morganville, New Jersey, Field Editor

1 pound lean ground beef (90% lean)
1/4 cup chunky salsa
4 frozen breaded cheddar cheese jalapeno peppers, thawed
1/4 cup guacamole
4 hamburger buns, split and toasted
4 lettuce leaves
1/4 cup salsa con queso dip
1/4 cup sliced plum tomatoes
2 tablespoons sliced ripe olives
4 thin slices sweet onion

1. In a large bowl, combine the beef and salsa. Shape into four patties. Place a jalapeno in the center of each; wrap beef around jalapeno, forming a ball. Reshape into patties, about 3-1/2 to 4 in. in diameter and 1 in. thick.

2. Grill, covered, over medium-hot heat for 7-8 minutes on each side or until meat is no longer pink and a thermometer reads 160°.

3. Spread the guacamole over toasted side of bun tops. On each bun bottom, layer with the lettuce, a burger, con queso dip, tomatoes, olives and onion; replace tops.

FIRECRACKER BURGERS

"I must warn you...this burger is very messy to eat, but it's so worth it! I love it. I make my own nacho sauce, instead of the store-bought, which I like better. I think these are definitely worth trying."
—*kristinscotth*

ITALIAN SAUSAGE SANDWICHES

"It is a very good meal, and I have made it several times."
—Blazn H

[2007]

MARINATED BEEF ON BUNS

yield: 12 servings
prep: 15 min. + marinating
bake: 2 hours + standing

I've modified this recipe over the years, increasing the amount of dipping sauce and adding fresh garlic. I cooked triple the amount for a huge family reunion, and all of my in-laws asked for the recipe!

—*Nancy Yarlett, Thornhill, Ontario*

3-1/2 cups ketchup
    2 medium onions, finely chopped
1-1/2 cups packed brown sugar
    1 cup reduced-sodium soy sauce
  1/2 cup white vinegar
  1/2 cup canola oil
    4 garlic cloves, minced
  1/4 teaspoon ground ginger
    1 beef eye round roast (3 pounds)
  3/4 cup water
   12 sandwich buns, split

1. In a large bowl, combine the first eight ingredients. Pour half of the marinade into a large resealable plastic bag; add the roast. Seal the bag and turn to coat; refrigerate overnight. Cover and refrigerate the remaining marinade.

2. Drain and discard marinade from the meat. Place the roast in a large roasting pan. Combine the water and reserved marinade; pour over roast. Cover and bake at 350° for 2 hours or until the meat is tender. Let stand for 15 minutes before slicing. Serve on buns. Skim fat from pan juices; serve with sandwiches.

[1995]

ITALIAN SAUSAGE SANDWICHES

yield: 20 servings   **prep: 30 min.**
cook: 30 min.

When my wife and I have friends over, we love to serve these sandwiches. This is a convenient recipe, since it can be prepared the day before and reheated.

—*Mike Yaeger, Brookings, South Dakota*

   20 Italian sausages
    4 large green peppers, thinly sliced
  1/2 cup chopped onion
    1 can (12 ounces) tomato paste
    1 can (15 ounces) tomato sauce
    1 cup water
    1 tablespoon sugar
    4 garlic cloves, minced
    2 teaspoons dried basil
    1 teaspoon dried oregano
    1 teaspoon salt
   20 sandwich buns
Shredded mozzarella cheese, optional

1. In a large Dutch oven, brown the sausages a few at a time; discard all but 2 tablespoons drippings. Saute peppers and onion in drippings until crisp-tender; drain.

2. In the same pan, combine the tomato paste, tomato sauce, water, sugar, garlic, basil, oregano and salt. Add the sausages; bring to a boil. Reduce heat; cover and simmer for 30 minutes or until heated through. Serve on buns. Top with cheese if desired.

[2001]

GRILLED BEEF GYROS

yield: 8-10 servings ∞ **prep: 20 min. + marinating** ∞ **grill: 20 min.**

A spicy marinade adds zip to these grilled beef slices tucked inside pita bread. Friends from Greece gave us their recipe for the cucumber sauce, which provides a cool contrast to the hot beef.

—Lee Rademaker, Hayfork, California

1 medium onion, cut into chunks
2 garlic cloves
2 tablespoons sugar
1 tablespoon ground mustard
1/2 teaspoon ground ginger
1-1/2 teaspoons pepper
1/2 teaspoon cayenne pepper
1/2 cup reduced-sodium soy sauce
1/4 cup water
1 beef sirloin tip roast (2 to 3 pounds), cut into 1/4-inch-thick slices

CUCUMBER SAUCE:

1 medium cucumber, peeled, seeded and cut into chunks
4 garlic cloves
1/2 teaspoon salt
1/3 cup cider vinegar
1/3 cup olive oil
2 cups (16 ounces) sour cream
8 to 10 pita breads, warmed and halved

Thinly sliced onion
Chopped tomato

1. In a blender, combine the onion, garlic, sugar, mustard, ginger, pepper and cayenne; cover and process until onion is finely chopped. Add soy sauce and water; process until blended.

2. Place the beef in a large resealable plastic bag. Add marinade. Seal bag and turn to coat; refrigerate for 1-2 hours.

3. For sauce, combine the cucumber, garlic and salt in a blender; cover and process until cucumber is chopped. Add vinegar and oil; process until blended. Transfer to a large bowl; stir in sour cream. Refrigerate until serving.

4. Drain and discard marinade. Grill beef, covered, over medium-hot heat until meat reaches desired doneness (for medium-rare, a thermometer should read 145°; medium, 160°; well-done, 170°). Place beef in pita halves. Top with cucumber sauce, sliced onion and chopped tomato. Refrigerate any remaining sauce.

GRILLED BEEF GYROS

"This has been a family favorite for years! I recall my mom marinating and my dad grilling this over the summers! It is also GREAT for entertaining."
—driv0656

[1995]

BAKED LASAGNA IN A BUN
yield: 8 servings ∽ prep: 20 min.
bake: 25 min.

(Pictured on page 815)

This fun-for-kids recipe tucks classic lasagna ingredients into hollowed-out sandwich buns. I find they're a hit with adults, too.

—Cindy Morelock, Afton, Tennessee

- 8 submarine *or* hoagie buns (8 inches)
- 1 pound ground beef
- 1 cup spaghetti sauce
- 1 tablespoon garlic powder
- 1 tablespoon Italian seasoning
- 1 cup ricotta cheese
- 1/4 cup grated Parmesan cheese
- 1 cup (4 ounces) shredded cheddar cheese, *divided*
- 1 cup (4 ounces) shredded part-skim mozzarella cheese, *divided*

TOP 100 RECIPE

1. Make a 2-in.-wide V-shaped cut in the center of each bun to within 1 inch of the bottom. Remove cut portion and save for another use; set aside.

2. In a large skillet, cook the beef over medium heat until no longer pink; drain. Add the spaghetti sauce, garlic powder and Italian seasoning. Cook 4-5 minutes or until heated through.

3. Meanwhile, in a bowl, combine ricotta, Parmesan cheese and half of cheddar and mozzarella cheeses. Spoon meat sauce into buns; top with the cheese mixture. Place on a baking sheet. Cover loosely with foil.

4. Bake at 350° for 20-25 minutes. Uncover; sprinkle with the remaining cheddar and mozzarella. Return to the oven for 2-3 minutes or until the cheese is melted.

BAKED LASAGNA IN A BUN

"Great hot sandwich! Tastes just like lasagna without the fuss."
—misspooches

[1999]

SPECIAL EGGPLANT SUBS
yield: 4 servings ∽ prep: 15 min.
bake: 30 min. + cooling

The idea for this unique sandwich was inspired by a light eggplant dish I made for hot summer evenings. I decided to use the golden eggplant slices as a base for sandwiches. My family goes wild for the delicious combination of toppings.

—Marie Maffucci, New Rochelle, New York

- 2 eggs
- 1 cup dry bread crumbs
- 1 medium eggplant, peeled and sliced 1/4 inch thick
- 4 submarine sandwich buns (10 inches), split
- Leaf lettuce
- 1 jar (7-1/4 ounces) roasted red peppers, drained and sliced
- 8 slices part-skim mozzarella cheese
- 2 medium tomatoes, thinly sliced
- 1 can (4-1/4 ounces) chopped ripe olives, drained
- Italian *or* vinaigrette salad dressing

1. In a shallow bowl, beat the eggs. Place the bread crumbs in another bowl. Dip the eggplant slices into egg, then coat with the crumbs. Place on a greased baking sheet.

2. Bake at 350° for 30 minutes or until crispy. Cool. On the bottom of each bun, layer with lettuce, eggplant, red peppers, cheese, tomatoes and olives. Drizzle with salad dressing; replace bun tops.

[1996]

FRENCH DIP

yield: 8 servings ∞ prep: 15 min.
cook: 5 hours

For a sandwich with more pizzazz than the traditional French dip, give this recipe a try. The seasonings give the broth a wonderful flavor, and the meat cooks up tender and juicy. This new version will soon be a favorite at your house, too.

—*Margaret McNeil*
Germantown, Tennessee, Field Editor

- 1 beef chuck roast (3 pounds), trimmed
- 2 cups water
- 1/2 cup reduced-sodium soy sauce
- 1 teaspoon dried rosemary, crushed
- 1 teaspoon dried thyme
- 1 teaspoon garlic powder
- 1 bay leaf
- 3 to 4 whole peppercorns
- 8 French rolls, split

1. Place roast in a 5-qt. slow cooker. Add the water, soy sauce and seasonings. Cover and cook on high for 5-6 hours or until beef is tender.

2. Remove meat from broth; shred with two forks and keep warm. Strain broth; skim off fat. Pour the broth into small cups for dipping. Serve beef on rolls.

[2007]

FAMILY-PLEASING SLOPPY JOES

yield: 8 servings ∞ prep: 10 min.
cook: 45 min.

My grandchildren love these sandwiches. I like this recipe because it can be made ahead of time and can also be put in the slow cooker. I've found it freezes well, too.

—*Patricia Ringle, Edgar, Wisconsin*

- 2 pounds ground beef
- 1 large onion, chopped
- 1-1/4 cups ketchup
- 1/2 cup water
- 1 tablespoon brown sugar
- 1 tablespoon white vinegar
- 1/2 teaspoon salt
- 1/2 teaspoon ground mustard
- 1/2 teaspoon chili powder
- 1/4 teaspoon ground allspice
- 8 sandwich buns, split

1. In a Dutch oven, cook beef and onion over medium heat until the meat is no longer pink; drain. Stir in the ketchup, water, brown sugar, vinegar, salt, mustard, chili powder and allspice. Bring to a boil. Reduce heat; simmer, uncovered, for 35-40 minutes or until heated through.

2. Spoon about 1/2 cup meat mixture onto each bun.

FAMILY-PLEASING SLOPPY JOES

"My family absolutely loves this recipe. I make it at least once a month. It is great on hot dogs, too!"
—*chevy4482*

SHREDDING MEAT

Remove cooked meat from pan with a slotted spoon if necessary. Reserve cooking liquid if called for. Place meat in a shallow pan. With two forks, pull meat into thin shreds. Return shredded meat to the pan to warm or use as recipe directs.

MILE HIGH SHREDDED BEEF

"We love this recipe!! Oftentimes we just eat it on our plate, skipping the bun. I have also used this recipe for pork. Excellent. Surprisingly, you can use pork loin, which is lean, and still have delicious results."
—plugginalong

[2002]

MILE HIGH SHREDDED BEEF

yield: 12-15 servings ∞ **prep: 35 min.**
cook: 3 hours

This tender beef has become a tasty tradition when I cook for our harvest crews and for neighboring ranchers who come to help us sort our cattle. Those hungry folks have been a good testing ground for recipes. They let me know if a new one I try is a keeper.

—Betty Kay Sitzman
Wray, Colorado, Field Editor

- 1 boneless beef chuck roast (3 pounds)
- 1 can (14-1/2 ounces) beef broth
- 1 medium onion, chopped
- 1 celery rib, chopped
- 3/4 cup ketchup
- 1/4 cup packed brown sugar
- 2 tablespoons white vinegar
- 1 teaspoon salt
- 1 teaspoon ground mustard
- 1 teaspoon Worcestershire sauce
- 1 garlic clove, minced
- 1 bay leaf
- 1/4 teaspoon garlic powder
- 1/4 teaspoon paprika
- 3 drops hot pepper sauce
- 12 to 15 hoagie buns

1. Place the roast in a Dutch oven; add broth, onion and celery. Bring to a boil. Reduce heat; cover and simmer for 2-1/2 to 3 hours or until the meat is tender.

2. Remove roast and cool slightly; shred meat with two forks. Strain vegetables and set aside. Skim fat from cooking liquid and reserve 1-1/2 cups. Return the meat, vegetables and reserved cooking liquid to the pan.

3. Stir in ketchup, brown sugar, vinegar, salt, mustard, Worcestershire sauce, garlic, bay leaf, garlic powder, paprika and hot pepper sauce. Bring to a boil. Reduce heat; cover and simmer for 30 minutes or until heated through. Discard bay leaf. Serve beef on buns.

[2010]

PHILLY CHEESE FAKES

yield: 4 servings ∞ **prep: 30 min.**
broil: 5 min.

Mushrooms are the key to this twist on popular Philly steak sandwiches. They're a nice meatless meal option that's tangy and tasty.

—Veronica Vichit-Vadakan
Portland, Oregon

- 1/4 cup lemon juice
- 3 garlic cloves, minced
- 1 tablespoon olive oil
- 1/2 teaspoon smoked paprika
- 1/4 teaspoon salt
- 1/4 teaspoon pepper
- 1 pound sliced fresh shiitake mushrooms
- 2 medium green peppers, sliced
- 1 small onion, thinly sliced
- 4 hoagie buns, split
- 4 slices reduced-fat provolone cheese

1. In a small bowl, whisk the first six ingredients. In a large bowl, combine the mushrooms, green peppers and onion. Pour dressing over vegetables; toss to coat.

2. Transfer to two 15-in. x 10-in. x 1-in. baking pans coated with cooking spray. Bake at 450° for 15-20 minutes or until crisp-tender, stirring once.

3. Divide mushroom mixture among the buns and top with cheese. Broil 3-4 in. from the heat for 2-3 minutes or until cheese is melted.

[2003]

SHRIMP PO' BOYS

yield: 8 servings ∞ **prep: 30 min.**
cook: 15 min.

*These sandwiches will star on the table and add
a Louisiana flair. You can adjust the cayenne
pepper to suit your tastes.*

—*Betty Jean Jordan, Monticello, Georgia*

1/2	cup mayonnaise
1/2	cup finely chopped onion
1/2	cup chopped dill pickles
1-1/3	cups all-purpose flour
1	teaspoon salt
4	eggs, *separated*
1-1/3	cups 2% milk
2	tablespoons canola oil
8	French sandwich rolls, split

Additional oil for deep-fat frying

2	pounds uncooked large shrimp, peeled and deveined

Cayenne pepper to taste

4	cups shredded lettuce
16	tomato slices

---

1. In a small bowl, combine mayonnaise, onion and pickles; set aside. For batter, combine the flour and salt in a bowl. Add the egg yolks, milk and oil; beat until smooth.

2. In a small bowl and with clean beaters, beat egg whites until stiff peaks form; fold in batter.

3. Wrap the sandwich rolls in foil. Bake at 350° for 10 minutes or until rolls are warmed. Meanwhile, in a large skillet or deep-fat fryer, heat 1/2 in. of oil to 375°. Dip shrimp in batter; fry for 2-3 minutes on each side or until golden brown. Drain on paper towels; sprinkle with cayenne.

4. Spread mayonnaise mixture over the rolls; top with lettuce, tomato slices and shrimp.

[2010]

HERB & CHEESE-STUFFED BURGERS

yield: 4 servings ∞ **prep/total time: 30 min.**

*Tired of the same old ground beef burgers?
This quick-fix alternative, with its creamy
cheese filling, will wake up your taste buds.*

—*Sherri Cox, Lucasville, Ohio*

1/4	cup shredded cheddar cheese
2	tablespoons cream cheese, softened
2	tablespoons minced fresh parsley
3	teaspoons Dijon mustard, *divided*
2	green onions, thinly sliced
3	tablespoons dry bread crumbs
2	tablespoons ketchup
1/2	teaspoon salt
1/2	teaspoon dried rosemary, crushed
1/4	teaspoon dried sage leaves
1	pound lean ground beef (90% lean)
4	hard rolls, split

Lettuce leaves and tomato slices, optional

---

1. In a small bowl, combine the cheddar cheese, cream cheese, parsley and 1 teaspoon mustard; set aside.

2. In another bowl, combine the onions, bread crumbs, ketchup, salt, rosemary, sage and remaining mustard. Crumble beef over mixture and mix well.

3. Shape into eight thin patties. Spoon the cheese mixture onto center of four patties; top with remaining patties and press edges firmly to seal.

4. Grill burgers, covered, over medium heat or broil 4 in. from heat for 5-7 minutes on each side or until a thermometer reads 160° and juices run clear. Serve on rolls with lettuce and tomato if desired.

HERB & CHEESE-STUFFED BURGERS

"My boyfriend and I made these burgers tonight, and they were amazing. I love burgers but don't eat them at fast-food or dine-in restaurants. I was amazed at the great flavor the herbs gave the burgers and loved the cheesy surprise inside. They were very easy to make with quick cleanup. Even with a long list of ingredients, they're made with things most everyone should have in the house already. I will definitely make these again and recommend them to anyone who loves burgers!"

—*foodeater*

[1994]

CHICKEN SALAD PUFFS

yield: 6 servings ∽ prep: 25 min.
bake: 30 min. + cooling

For a unique way to serve chicken salad, these puffs can't be beat! The tasty filling gets color and crunch from the olives and celery. Guests have told me they are delicious and satisfying.

—*Marlys Benning, Ackley, Iowa*

CREAM PUFFS:
- 1/2 cup water
- 1/4 cup butter, cubed
- Dash salt
- 1/2 cup all-purpose flour
- 2 eggs

FILLING:
- 2 cups diced cooked chicken
- 3/4 cup chopped celery
- 1 can (2-1/4 ounces) sliced ripe olives, drained
- 1/3 cup mayonnaise
- 1 tablespoon lemon juice
- 1 teaspoon grated onion
- 1/4 teaspoon Worcestershire sauce
- 1/8 teaspoon pepper
- Salt to taste

1. In a large saucepan, bring water, butter and salt to a boil. Add the flour all at once and stir until a smooth ball forms. Remove from the heat; let stand for 5 minutes. Add the eggs, one at a time, beating well after each addition. Continue beating until mixture is smooth and shiny.

2. Drop by six rounded tablespoonfuls 3 in. apart onto a greased baking sheet. Bake at 400° for 30-35 minutes or until golden brown.

3. Remove to a wire rack. Immediately split puffs open; remove tops and set aside. Discard soft dough from inside. Cool puffs.

4. For filling, in a large bowl, combine the chicken, celery and olives. In a small bowl, combine remaining ingredients; stir into chicken mixture. Fill puffs just before serving.

[2012]

TURKEY CAPRESE SANDWICHES

yield: 12 servings ∽ prep/total time: 30 min.

I went to a friend's party and had a bruschetta with caprese salad on top. I loved the taste and started serving it at my parties. Once I had no bread, only bagels, and added turkey and a few other items. My young daughter thought it was great. I started making the sandwiches for parties and everyone loved them!

—*Maria Higginson, Bountiful, Utah*

- 6 garlic cloves, peeled and halved
- 12 Asiago cheese bagels, cut in half and toasted
- 1/4 cup mayonnaise
- 36 slices deli turkey
- 24 slices fresh mozzarella cheese
- 6 plum tomatoes, thinly sliced
- 1 large red onion, thinly sliced
- 12 fresh basil leaves, thinly sliced
- 1 teaspoon salt
- 1 teaspoon olive oil

1. Rub the garlic cloves over cut sides of bagels.

2. For each sandwich, spread 1 teaspoon mayonnaise over the bagel bottom. Layer with three turkey slices, two cheese slices, two tomato slices, four onion slices and one sliced basil leaf. Sprinkle with salt; drizzle with olive oil. Replace tops.

[2007]

SHRIMP SALAD CROISSANTS

yield: 8 servings ∽ **prep: 15 min. + chilling**

I've had this recipe for years and get raves whenever I make it. It can be served on a bed of lettuce or atop a flaky croissant. Either way, it's perfect for a quick, delicious lunch.

—Molly Seidel, Edgewood, New Mexico, Field Editor

- 1 pound cooked small shrimp
- 2 celery ribs, diced
- 2 small carrots, shredded
- 1 cup mayonnaise
- 1/3 cup finely chopped onion

Dash salt and pepper

- 2 packages (2-1/4 ounces *each*) sliced almonds
- 8 croissants, split

1. In a large bowl, combine the shrimp, celery and carrots. In a small bowl, combine the mayonnaise, onion, salt and pepper. Pour over shrimp mixture and toss to coat.

2. Cover and refrigerate for at least 2 hours. Just before serving, stir in almonds. Serve on croissants.

[2012]

EASY SOUTHWESTERN VEGGIE WRAPS

yield: 6 servings ∽ **prep/total time: 20 min.**

My daughter is a vegetarian, so when fresh produce was abundant, I developed this recipe. The fresh ingredients create a bright-tasting filling in these wonderful wraps. You can add diced cooked chicken for those who want meat in their sandwich.

—Cindy Beberman, Orland Park, Illinois

- 2 large tomatoes, seeded and diced
- 1 can (15 ounces) black beans, rinsed and drained
- 1 cup frozen corn, thawed
- 1 cup cooked brown rice, cooled
- 2 shallots, chopped
- 1 jalapeno pepper, seeded and chopped
- 1/3 cup fat-free sour cream
- 1/4 cup minced fresh cilantro
- 2 tablespoons lime juice
- 1/2 teaspoon ground cumin

- 1/2 teaspoon chili powder
- 1/2 teaspoon salt
- 6 romaine leaves
- 6 whole wheat tortillas (8 inches), at room temperature

1. In a large bowl, combine the first six ingredients. In a small bowl, combine the sour cream, cilantro, lime juice and seasonings. Gently stir into tomato mixture.

2. Place romaine on tortillas; top with filling. Roll up and secure with toothpicks. Cut each in half.

Editor's Note: Wear disposable gloves when cutting hot peppers; the oils can burn skin. Avoid touching your face.

[1994]

ZESTY HAM SANDWICH

yield: 1 serving ∽ **prep/total time: 15 min.**

I learned that in Rome and other parts of Italy, pizza simply started out as bread with oil and herbs on it. In some locales, cheese, tomato and grilled meat were added. With the basic original pizza ingredients surrounding me, I was inspired to make a modern version of an ancient food and this recipe was born.

—Mara Mcauley, Hinsdale, New York

- 1 submarine roll (6 to 7 inches)
- 2 to 3 thin slices fully cooked ham
- 3 to 4 slices part-skim mozzarella cheese
- 1 small tomato, thinly sliced
- 4 sprigs fresh parsley, chopped
- 4 fresh basil leaves, chopped *or* 1/2 teaspoon dried basil
- 1 tablespoon prepared Italian salad dressing *or* reduced-fat Caesar vinaigrette

1. Split the roll enough to open (don't cut all the way through); place open-faced on a baking sheet. Layer the remaining ingredients in order listed over roll. Bake at 350° for 10 minutes or until the cheese is melted and sandwich is warm. Fold top of roll over and serve immediately.

[2000]

LAYERED PICNIC LOAVES

yield: 2 loaves (12 servings each)
prep: 15 min. + chilling

This big sandwich is inspired by one I tried at a New York deli. Made ahead of time, it's easily carted to any gathering.

—Marion Lowery, Medford, Oregon
Former Field Editor

2	**unsliced loaves (1 pound each) Italian bread**
1/4	**cup olive oil**
3	**garlic cloves, minced**
2	**teaspoons Italian seasoning,** *divided*
1/2	**pound deli roast beef**
12	**slices part-skim mozzarella cheese (1 ounce each)**
16	**fresh basil leaves**
3	**medium tomatoes, thinly sliced**
1/4	**pound thinly sliced salami**
1	**jar (6-1/2 ounces) marinated artichoke hearts, drained and sliced**
1	**package (10 ounces) ready-to-serve salad greens**
8	**ounces thinly sliced deli chicken**
1	**medium onion, thinly sliced**
1/4	**teaspoon salt**
1/8	**teaspoon pepper**

1. Cut loaves in half horizontally; hollow out tops and bottoms, leaving 1/2-in. shells (discard removed bread or save for another use).

2. Combine the oil and garlic; brush the inside bread shells. Sprinkle with 1 teaspoon Italian seasoning. Layer the bottom of each loaf with a fourth of roast beef, mozzarella, basil, tomatoes, salami, artichokes, salad greens, chicken and onion. Repeat the layers. Season with salt, pepper and the remaining Italian seasoning.

3. Drizzle with remaining oil mixture if desired. Replace bread tops; wrap tightly in plastic wrap. Refrigerate for at least 1 hour before slicing.

[2004]

VEGGIE CHICKEN WRAPS

yield: 4 servings   ∞   **prep/total time: 15 min.**

I got the idea for these wraps from one I tried at a cafe. During warmer months, I make them for picnics in the park. I also like to prepare a large batch, cut them into slices and serve on a platter. They disappear every time!

—Jolene Britten, Mesa, Arizona

1	**carton (8 ounces) spreadable garden vegetable cream cheese**
4	**flour tortillas (8 inches)**
2	**cups shredded romaine**
2	**small tomatoes, thinly sliced**
8	**slices provolone cheese**
1	**small red onion, thinly sliced**
2	**cups diced cooked chicken**

1. Spread cream cheese evenly over each tortilla. Layer with romaine, tomatoes, cheese, onion and chicken. Roll up tightly. Cut wraps in half to serve.

LAYERED PICNIC LOAVES

"This is great recipe to bring to a potluck! Delicious and easy to transport!"
—*aquinn3*

PERSONALIZE YOUR SANDWICH

Veggie Chicken Wrap is an ideal sandwich to customize. Many flavors of spreadable cheese (such as Garlic-Herb) will go with it. Use fresh vegetables like sliced zucchini, cucumbers or radishes, and add your favorite cheese.

—*Taste of Home Cooking Experts*

[2009]

CASHEW TURKEY SALAD SANDWICHES

yield: 4 servings   prep/total time: 15 min.

One bite and you're sure to be hooked on this sweet and savory sandwich. It's protein-packed, so you can feel good about it while you munch.

—*Mary Wilhelm, Sparta, Wisconsin*

- 1-1/2 cups cubed cooked turkey breast
- 1/4 cup thinly sliced celery
- 2 tablespoons chopped dried apricots
- 2 tablespoons chopped unsalted cashews
- 1 green onion, chopped
- 1/4 cup reduced-fat mayonnaise
- 2 tablespoons reduced-fat plain yogurt
- 1/4 teaspoon salt
- 1/4 teaspoon pepper
- 4 lettuce leaves
- 8 slices pumpernickel bread

1. In a small bowl, combine the turkey, celery, apricots, cashews and onion. Combine the mayonnaise, yogurt, salt and pepper; add to turkey mixture and stir to coat. Place a lettuce leaf on half of the bread slices; top each with 1/2 cup turkey salad and remaining bread.

[1993]

CURRIED EGG SALAD

yield: 6 servings   prep/total time: 15 min.

The curry and ginger add an interesting flavor option to egg salad. I like to serve it as an open-faced sandwich.

—*Joyce McDowell, West Union, Ohio*

- 1/2 cup mayonnaise
- 1/2 teaspoon honey
- 1/2 teaspoon ground curry
- Dash ground ginger
- 6 hard-cooked eggs, coarsely chopped
- 3 green onions, sliced
- 6 slices whole wheat bread
- Sliced tomato, optional

1. In a bowl, combine mayonnaise, honey, curry and ginger. Stir in eggs and green onions. Divide among bread slices. Top with a tomato slice if desired.

[2006]

SALSA RANCH CHICKEN WRAPS

yield: 4 servings   prep/total time: 25 min.

I came up with this easy wrap while working at a deli during college. The combination of salsa and ranch adds a unique twist.

—*Amanda Rasner, Ellis, Kansas*

- 4 tablespoons salsa
- 4 tablespoons prepared ranch salad dressing
- 4 tomato basil tortillas (10 inches), warmed
- 2 boneless skinless chicken breast halves (4 ounces *each*), grilled and cut into strips
- 12 slices cucumber
- 8 slices tomato
- 1/2 cup julienned green pepper
- 6 slices Swiss cheese
- 2 tablespoons butter, *divided*

1. Spread 1 tablespoon of salsa and 1 tablespoon of ranch dressing over each tortilla. Place chicken, cucumber, tomato and green pepper down each center; top with 1-1/2 slices of cheese. Fold ends of each tortilla over filling.

2. In a large skillet, melt 1 tablespoon butter. Place two wraps folded side down in skillet. Cook over medium heat for 3-4 minutes on each side or until lightly browned and cheese is melted. Repeat with the remaining wraps and butter.

CASHEW TURKEY SALAD SANDWICHES

"Nice sandwich. I used multigrain bread. I think I will add extra nuts and apricots next time, as the bites with that combo in it were the best."
—*TheChristmasLady*

[2008]

TURKEY MUFFULETTA

yield: 6 servings ∞ **prep: 30 min. + chilling**

(Pictured on page 810)

You have to resist the temptation to eat this impressive, multi-layered sandwich immediately! It needs to "rest" at least 30 minutes in the refrigerator to allow the flavors to meld. But it's worth the wait.

—*Gilda Lester, Millsboro, Delaware*

- 1 loaf (1 pound) Italian bread
- 1/3 cup olive oil
- 3 tablespoons balsamic vinegar
- 1 tablespoon minced fresh basil *or* 1 teaspoon dried basil
- 1 garlic clove, minced
- 1/2 teaspoon salt
- 1/4 teaspoon crushed red pepper flakes
- 3/4 pound sliced deli turkey
- 6 ounces provolone cheese, thinly sliced
- 1 jar (7 ounces) roasted sweet red peppers, drained and sliced
- 1/2 cup sliced pimiento-stuffed olives
- 1 large tomato, sliced
- 3 tablespoons shredded Romano cheese
- 1 tablespoon minced fresh oregano *or* 1 teaspoon dried oregano
- 1/4 teaspoon pepper

1. Cut bread in half lengthwise; carefully hollow out top and bottom, leaving a 1-in. shell (discard removed bread or save for another use).

2. In a small bowl, combine the oil, vinegar, basil, garlic, salt and pepper flakes; brush over cut sides of bread.

3. In the bottom bread shell, layer the turkey, provolone cheese, red peppers, olives and tomato. Sprinkle with Romano cheese, oregano and pepper. Replace the bread top.

4. Wrap in plastic wrap; refrigerate for 30 minutes. Cut into slices.

[1998]

AVOCADO BACON SANDWICHES

yield: 8 sandwiches ∞ **prep/total time: 30 min.**

Since we grow avocados, I slice or cube them and toss them into whatever I'm cooking. These open-faced sandwiches are one of our favorite light meals or snacks.

—*Alva Snider, Fallbrook, California*

- 1 pound bacon strips
- 2 medium ripe avocados, sliced
- Salt and pepper to taste
- 1/3 cup mayonnaise
- 1 tablespoon lemon juice
- 8 slices whole wheat bread, toasted

1. In a large skillet, cook bacon over medium heat until crisp; drain on paper towels and set aside. Gently toss avocados with salt and pepper. Combine mayonnaise and lemon juice; spread over toast. Top with avocado and bacon.

[2007]

ZESTY VEGETARIAN WRAPS

yield: 2 servings ∞ **prep/total time: 10 min.**

Beautiful in color and very flavorful, the vegetarian wrap is filled with crisp veggies, pepper jack cheese and a zesty sauce.

—*Cori Lehman, Jackson, Tennessee*

- 2 tablespoons fat-free mayonnaise
- 1 teaspoon lime juice
- 2 to 4 drops Louisiana-style hot sauce
- 2 spinach tortillas *or* flour tortillas of your choice (8 inches), room temperature
- 2 lettuce leaves
- 1/2 medium green pepper, julienned
- 2 slices pepper jack cheese

1. In a small bowl, combine the mayonnaise, lime juice and hot sauce. Spread over tortillas. Top with lettuce, green pepper and cheese; roll up tightly.

[2009]

BRUSCHETTA PIZZA

yield: 8 slices ∞ **prep: 25 min.**
bake: 10 min.

(Pictured on page 815)

Loaded with Italian flavor and plenty of fresh tomatoes, this is bound to become a family favorite. It's even better with a homemade, whole wheat crust.

—Debra Keil, Owasso, Oklahoma

- 1/2 pound reduced-fat bulk pork sausage
- 1 prebaked 12-inch pizza crust
- 1 package (6 ounces) sliced turkey pepperoni
- 2 cups (8 ounces) shredded part-skim mozzarella cheese
- 1-1/2 cups chopped plum tomatoes
- 1/2 cup fresh basil leaves, thinly sliced
- 1 tablespoon olive oil
- 2 garlic cloves, minced
- 1/2 teaspoon minced fresh thyme *or* 1/8 teaspoon dried thyme
- 1/2 teaspoon balsamic vinegar
- 1/4 teaspoon salt
- 1/8 teaspoon pepper

Additional fresh basil leaves, optional

1. In a small skillet, cook the sausage over medium heat until no longer pink; drain. Place the crust on an ungreased baking sheet. Top with the pepperoni, sausage and cheese. Bake at 450° for 10-12 minutes or until cheese is melted.

2. In a small bowl, combine the tomatoes, sliced basil, oil, garlic, thyme, vinegar, salt and pepper. Spoon over the pizza. Garnish with the additional basil if desired.

[1999]

BACON CHEESEBURGER PIZZA

yield: 8 slices
prep/total time: 20 min.

Kids of all ages love cheeseburgers and pizza, and this recipe combines them both for delicious results. My grandchildren usually request pizza for supper when they visit me. They like to help me assemble this version, and they especially enjoy eating it!

—Cherie Ackerman, Lakeland, Minnesota

- 1/2 pound ground beef
- 1 small onion, chopped
- 1 prebaked 12-inch pizza crust
- 1 can (8 ounces) pizza sauce
- 6 bacon strips, cooked and crumbled
- 20 dill pickle coin slices
- 2 cups (8 ounces) shredded part-skim mozzarella cheese
- 2 cups (8 ounces) shredded cheddar cheese
- 1 teaspoon pizza *or* Italian seasoning

1. In a large skillet, cook beef and onion over medium heat until meat is no longer pink; drain and set aside.

2. Place crust on an ungreased 12-in. pizza pan. Spread with the pizza sauce. Top with beef mixture, bacon, pickles and cheeses. Sprinkle with the pizza seasoning. Bake pizza at 450° for 8-10 minutes or until cheese is melted.

BRUSCHETTA PIZZA

"Very good. I loved the fresh tomato taste. Paired it with a green salad, and it made a wonderful, light summer meal. It was so tasty I will definitely make it again."
—momto4girls

CHICKEN CORDON BLEU PIZZA

❝This was great right out of the oven, and heated up, it's even better. I have never said that about any pizza, but I heated a leftover slice in the skillet to keep it crisp and it was great. The only problem is this is not the type of pizza where you're likely to have leftovers! It's just too good!❞
—*rainytown81*

[2011]

BLACK-AND-BLUE PIZZAS

yield: 2 pizzas (12 pieces each)
prep: 40 min. ∾ **bake: 15 min.**

(Pictured on page 814)

Gooey with cheese and loaded with flavorful toppings, these pizzas are rich and filling. Add a mixed green salad to make the meal complete.

—*Michelle Huelskamp*
Marion, North Carolina

2	loaves (1 pound *each*) frozen bread dough, thawed
8	bacon strips, chopped
1	pound boneless skinless chicken breasts, cut into strips
5	teaspoons blackened seasoning
3	shallots, finely chopped
2	garlic cloves, minced
1	jar (15 ounces) Alfredo sauce
2-1/2	cups sliced fresh shiitake mushrooms
1	can (3.8 ounces) sliced ripe olives, drained
1/2	cup finely chopped sun-dried tomatoes (not packed in oil)
1-1/4	cups (5 ounces) crumbled blue cheese
3	tablespoons minced fresh basil *or* 3 teaspoons dried basil
2	tablespoons minced fresh thyme *or* 2 teaspoons dried thyme
12	slices provolone cheese
3	ounces Parmesan cheese, shaved into strips *or* 3/4 cup grated Parmesan cheese

1. Roll the dough into two 16-in. x 10-in. rectangles; transfer to ungreased baking sheets. Build up the edges slightly.

2. In a large skillet, cook the bacon over medium heat until crisp. Using a slotted spoon, remove to paper towels. Drain, reserving 2 tablespoons drippings. Sprinkle the chicken with blackened seasoning; cook chicken in drippings until no longer pink. Add shallots and garlic; cook 1 minute longer. Set aside.

3. Spread sauce over crusts; top with the chicken mixture, bacon, mushrooms, olives and tomatoes. Sprinkle with the blue cheese, basil and thyme; top with provolone and Parmesan cheeses.

4. Bake at 450° for 14-18 minutes or until bubbly and cheese is melted.

[2010]

CHICKEN CORDON BLEU PIZZA

yield: 6 pieces ∾ **prep/total time: 30 min.**

This recipe is a combination of my two favorite foods: pizza and Chicken Cordon Bleu. I have made this for my family and also the teachers at my school. Now my teachers ask me to make it for them for lunch!

—*Justin Rippel, Colgate, Wisconsin*

1	tube (13.8 ounces) refrigerated pizza crust
1/2	cup Alfredo sauce
1/4	teaspoon garlic salt
1	cup (4 ounces) shredded Swiss cheese
1-1/2	cups cubed fully cooked ham
10	breaded chicken nuggets, thawed and cut into 1/2-inch pieces
1	cup (4 ounces) shredded part-skim mozzarella cheese

1. Unroll dough into a greased 15-in. x 10-in. x 1-in. baking pan; flatten dough and build up edges slightly. Bake at 425° for 8-10 minutes or until edges are lightly browned.

2. Spread with Alfredo sauce; sprinkle with garlic salt and Swiss cheese. Top with the ham, chicken nuggets and mozzarella cheese. Bake for 8-10 minutes or until crust is golden brown and cheese is melted.

[1998]

PIZZA FROM SCRATCH
yield: 2 pizzas (8 servings each, 2 slices per serving) ∞ prep: 40 min. ∞ bake: 35 min.

You can make this tasty pizza yourself with hardly any fuss. My sister shared the recipe with me years ago. It's now a staple in our home. Have everyone pitch in when assembling the pizza...it's a nice way to get the family together.

—Audra Dee Collins, Hobbs, New Mexico

1	package (1/4 ounce) active dry yeast
1	cup warm water (110° to 115°)
2	tablespoons canola oil
1	teaspoon salt
1	teaspoon sugar
2-3/4	to 3-1/4 cups all-purpose flour

SAUCE:

1	can (15 ounces) tomato sauce
1/2	cup chopped onion
3/4	teaspoon Italian seasoning
1/4	teaspoon garlic powder
1/4	teaspoon salt
1/8	teaspoon pepper

TOPPING:

1/2	pound bulk Italian sausage, cooked and drained
1	can (4 ounces) mushroom stems and pieces, drained
1	medium green pepper, sliced
1-1/2	cups (6 ounces) shredded part-skim mozzarella cheese

---

1. In a large bowl, dissolve yeast in water. Add the oil, salt, sugar and 2 cups flour. Beat on medium speed for 3 minutes. Stir in enough remaining flour to form a soft dough.

2. Turn dough onto a floured surface; knead until smooth and elastic, about 6-8 minutes. Place in a greased bowl, turning once to grease top. Cover and let rest in a warm place for 10 minutes.

3. Meanwhile, combine sauce ingredients; set aside. Divide dough in half. On a floured surface, roll each portion into a 13-in. circle. Transfer to greased 12-in. pizza pans; build up edges slightly. Prick dough thoroughly with a fork.

4. Bake at 375° for 15 minutes or until lightly browned. Spread sauce over hot crusts to within 2-in. of edges; top with sausage, mushrooms, green pepper and cheese. Bake for 20 minutes longer or until cheese is melted.

PIZZA FROM SCRATCH

"When I made this for my in-laws, they loved it! It is easy and delicious. The sauce is the best part. I make it often at my husband's request."
—*MoniMoni*

[2000]

WHOLE WHEAT VEGGIE PIZZA

yield: 2 pizzas (6 slices each) ∞ **prep: 50 min. + rising bake: 15 min.**

A wonderful crust layered with herbed tomato sauce and toppings encourages my family of six to dig right in to this low-fat main course.

—Denise Warner, Red Lodge, Montana

2-1/2 cups all-purpose flour
1/2 cup whole wheat flour
2 packages (1/4 ounce each) quick-rise yeast
1 teaspoon garlic powder
1/2 teaspoon salt
1 cup warm water (120° to 130°)
2 tablespoons olive oil
SAUCE:
1 can (14-1/2 ounces) diced tomatoes, undrained
1 tablespoon minced fresh parsley
1-1/2 teaspoons sugar
1-1/2 teaspoons Italian seasoning
1-1/2 teaspoons dried basil
1/2 teaspoon garlic powder
1/4 teaspoon pepper
TOPPINGS:
1 cup chopped zucchini
1 cup sliced fresh mushrooms
1/4 cup each chopped onion, green and sweet red pepper
1 teaspoon olive oil
1-1/4 cups shredded part-skim mozzarella cheese

1. In a large bowl, combine the first five ingredients. Add water and oil; beat until smooth. Turn dough onto a floured surface; knead until smooth and elastic, about 5 minutes. Place in a greased bowl, turning once to grease the top. Cover and let rise in a warm place until doubled, about 30 minutes.

2. Meanwhile, in a small saucepan, bring the sauce ingredients to a boil. Reduce heat; simmer, uncovered, for 15-18 minutes or until slightly thickened, stirring occasionally. Remove from the heat; set aside.

3. Punch dough down. Divide in half; roll each portion into a 13-in. circle. Transfer to greased 12-in. pizza pans; build up edges slightly. Bake at 400° for 8-10 minutes or until lightly browned.

4. In a small skillet, saute vegetables in oil until tender. Spread pizzas with sauce; sprinkle with the vegetables and cheese. Bake for 12-15 minutes or until the cheese is melted.

[2004]

CHICKEN PESTO PIZZA

yield: 6 slices ∞ **prep/total time: 30 min.**

My wife and I love this pizza! The crisp crust, made from frozen bread dough, is topped with a tasty mixture of sauteed onion, sweet pepper and chicken as well as tomato slices and mozzarella cheese.

—Paul Piantek, Middletown, Connecticut

1 loaf (1 pound) frozen bread dough, thawed
1 egg, lightly beaten
1/2 pound boneless skinless chicken breasts, cut into 1/2-inch pieces
1 small onion, sliced
1 small sweet yellow pepper, julienned
1/4 teaspoon lemon-pepper seasoning
1 tablespoon olive oil
1/4 cup prepared pesto
3 plum tomatoes, thinly sliced
1 cup (4 ounces) shredded part-skim mozzarella cheese

1. Spread dough into an ungreased 12-in. pizza pan. Prick dough with a fork. Brush with egg. Bake at 400° for 12-15 minutes or until lightly browned.

2. In a large skillet, saute the chicken, onion, yellow pepper and lemon pepper in oil until chicken is no longer pink; drain.

3. Spread the pesto sauce over the crust. Top with chicken mixture, tomatoes and cheese. Bake for 12-15 minutes or until lightly browned.

[2006]

CHICAGO-STYLE STUFFED PIZZA

yield: 8 slices ∞ **prep: 30 min. + rising** ∞ **bake: 30 min.**

(Pictured on page 812)

"Excellent" is the rating I give this hearty double-crust pizza. Favorite fillings are tucked inside, and tasty tomato sauce tops the pie.

—*Edie DeSpain, Logan, Utah, Field Editor*

1	teaspoon active dry yeast
1	cup warm water (110° to 115°)
2	teaspoons sugar
2	tablespoons canola oil
1-1/2	teaspoons salt
2-1/2	to 3 cups all-purpose flour
1/2	cup yellow cornmeal
1/2	pound bulk Italian sausage
1	small green pepper, diced
1	small onion, diced
3	garlic cloves, peeled and sliced
2	cups (8 ounces) shredded part-skim mozzarella cheese
1/3	cup chopped pepperoni
1/4	cup grated Parmesan cheese
1	teaspoon dried oregano
1/4	cup tomato sauce

---

1. In a large bowl, dissolve yeast in warm water. Add sugar; let stand for 5 minutes. Add oil and salt. Add 1-1/2 cups flour and cornmeal; beat until smooth. Stir in enough remaining flour to form a soft dough.

2. Turn onto a floured surface; knead until smooth and elastic, about 4-5 minutes. Place in a greased bowl; turn once to grease top. Cover and let rise in a warm place until doubled, about 1 hour.

3. Punch dough down; let rest for 5 minutes. Divide into two portions, one slightly larger than the other. On a lightly floured surface, roll out larger portion to a 12-in. circle. Press onto the bottom and up the sides of a greased 10-in. ovenproof skillet.

4. In a large skillet, cook the sausage, green pepper and onion over medium heat until meat is no longer pink. Add garlic; cook 1 minute longer. Drain. Stir in the mozzarella cheese, pepperoni, Parmesan cheese and oregano. Spread over crust.

5. On a lightly floured surface, roll remaining dough into an 11-in. circle. Place over pizza; seal edges. Cut four slits in top. Bake at 375° for 30-35 minutes or until crust is golden brown. Spread with tomato sauce.

CHICAGO-STYLE STUFFED PIZZA

❝I made two thin-crust pizzas and another deep dish, and it came out almost as good as the Chicago pizza I grew up with. Way better than anything else I have had in Texas.❞

—*chefjoe08*

[2011]

FRENCH ONION PIZZA AU GRATIN

**yield: 8 slices   prep: 30 min.
bake: 10 min.**

I love a hot bowl of French onion soup and am also a fan of pizza after busy workdays. This recipe combines classic onion soup ingredients with everyday pizza staples.

—*Bonnie Long, Lakewood, Ohio*

1   large onion, sliced
2   tablespoons brown sugar
2   tablespoons olive oil, *divided*
3   tablespoons balsamic vinegar
3   garlic cloves, minced
1   tablespoon bourbon, optional
1   cup sliced fresh mushrooms
1/4   pound thickly sliced deli roast beef, coarsely chopped
1   prebaked 12-inch pizza crust
3/4   cup French onion dip
3/4   cup shredded part-skim mozzarella cheese
1   medium sweet red pepper, chopped
3/4   cup shredded Gruyere *or* Swiss cheese
1   teaspoon minced fresh rosemary

1. In a large skillet, saute onion with brown sugar in 1 tablespoon oil until softened. Reduce heat to medium-low; cook, stirring occasionally, for 30 minutes or until deep golden brown. Stir in vinegar and garlic. Remove from the heat; add bourbon if desired. Continue cooking until liquid is nearly evaporated.

2. In another skillet, saute mushrooms in remaining oil until tender; add roast beef and heat through.

3. Place the crust on a pizza pan; spread with the French onion dip. Layer with the mozzarella cheese, onion mixture, red pepper, mushroom mixture and Gruyere cheese.

4. Bake pizza at 425° for 10-15 minutes or until the cheese is melted. Sprinkle with rosemary.

[2006]

STUFFED-CRUST PIZZA

yield: 6-8 slices   prep: 25 min.   bake: 25 min.

String cheese is the secret to success for this popular stuffed-crust pizza. Prebaking the crust before you add the toppings assures that the cheese inside will be completely melted.

—*Terri Gonzalez, Roswell, New Mexico, Field Editor*

2   to 2-1/2 cups all-purpose flour
1   package (1/4 ounce) quick-rise yeast
1   teaspoon salt
1   cup water
2   tablespoons canola oil
8   pieces string cheese
1/2   pound bulk Italian sausage
1   medium green pepper, diced
1   cup tomato sauce
1   teaspoon dried oregano
1/4   teaspoon pepper
1/8   teaspoon garlic powder
1   jar (4-1/2 ounces) sliced mushrooms, drained
1-1/2   cups (6 ounces) shredded part-skim mozzarella cheese

1. In a large bowl, combine 2 cups flour, yeast and salt. In a saucepan, heat water and oil to 120°-130°. Add to dry ingredients; beat just until moistened. Stir in enough remaining flour to form a soft dough. Let rest for 5 minutes.

2. On a lightly floured surface, roll dough into a 14-in. circle. Transfer to a greased 12-in. pizza pan, letting dough drape 2 in. over the edge.

3. Place string cheese around edge of pan; fold dough over cheese and pinch to seal. Prick dough thoroughly with a fork. Bake at 425° for 10 minutes.

4. Meanwhile, in a large skillet, cook the sausage and green pepper over medium heat until the meat is no longer pink; drain. In a small bowl, combine tomato sauce, oregano, pepper and garlic powder; spread over the crust. Sprinkle with the meat mixture, mushrooms and mozzarella.

5. Bake for 15-20 minutes or until cheese is melted and crust is golden brown.

[1999]

PEPPERONI PAN PIZZA

yield: 2 pizzas (9 slices each)
prep: 30 min. ∞ **bake: 10 min.**

I've spent years trying to come up with the perfect pizza crust and sauce, and they're paired up in this recipe. I fix this crispy, savory pizza for my family often; it really satisfies my husband and three sons.

—*Susan Lindahl, Alford, Florida*

2-3/4 to 3 cups all-purpose flour
  1 package (1/4 ounce) active dry yeast
1/4 teaspoon salt
  1 cup warm water (120° to 130°)
  1 tablespoon canola oil
SAUCE:
  1 can (14-1/2 ounces) diced tomatoes, undrained
  1 can (6 ounces) tomato paste
  1 tablespoon canola oil
  1 teaspoon salt
1/2 teaspoon *each* dried basil, oregano, marjoram and thyme
1/4 teaspoon garlic powder
1/4 teaspoon pepper
  1 package (3-1/2 ounces) sliced pepperoni
  5 cups (20 ounces) shredded part-skim mozzarella cheese
1/4 cup grated Parmesan cheese
1/4 cup grated Romano cheese

1. In a large bowl, combine 2 cups flour, yeast and salt. Add water and oil; beat until smooth. Stir in enough remaining flour to form a soft dough.

2. Turn dough onto a floured surface; knead until smooth and elastic, about 5-7 minutes. Cover and let stand for 10 minutes.

3. Meanwhile, in a small bowl, combine the tomatoes, tomato paste, oil and seasonings. Divide dough in half; press each portion into a 15-in. x 10-in. x 1-in. baking pan coated with cooking spray. Prick dough generously with a fork.

4. Bake pizza at 425° for 12-16 minutes or until crust is lightly browned.

5. Spread sauce over each crust; top with pepperoni and cheeses. Bake 8-10 minutes longer or until cheese is melted. Cut into squares.

[2009]

PHILLY CHEESESTEAK PIZZA

yield: 6 slices ∞ **prep: 30 min.**
bake: 10 min.

Sometimes my family likes their pizza crust extra crispy, so I prebake the crust for 5 minutes before adding the toppings. There are never leftovers.

—*Laura McDowell, Lake Villa, Illinois*

  1 small green pepper, julienned
  1 small sweet red pepper, julienned
1-3/4 cups sliced fresh mushrooms
  1 small onion, halved and sliced
1-1/2 teaspoons canola oil
  4 garlic cloves, minced
  1 prebaked 12-inch pizza crust
1/2 cup pizza sauce
  2 ounces cream cheese, cubed
  2 cups (8 ounces) shredded provolone cheese, *divided*
  1 cup shredded *or* julienned cooked roast beef
1/3 cup pickled pepper rings
1/4 cup grated Parmesan cheese
1/2 teaspoon dried oregano

1. In a large skillet, saute peppers, mushrooms and onion in oil until tender. Add garlic; cook 1 minute longer.

2. Place crust on an ungreased 12-in. pizza pan. Spread pizza sauce over crust and dot with cream cheese. Sprinkle with 1 cup provolone cheese. Top with the pepper mixture, beef, pepper rings and remaining provolone cheese. Sprinkle with the Parmesan cheese and oregano.

3. Bake at 450° for 10-12 minutes or until the cheese is melted.

❧ SEAFOOD ❧

CRAB-TOPPED FISH FILLETS

❝Loved this recipe! I used orange roughy and followed the recipe exactly. Quick and easy, will make again for sure.❞
—katlaydee3

[2009]

BROWN SUGAR GLAZED SALMON

yield: 8 servings ∞ prep: 15 min.
bake: 20 min.

I was not a salmon lover until I tried this recipe. Now it is one of my favorite dishes to serve friends.

—*Rachel Garcia*
Arlington, Virginia, Field Editor

- 1 tablespoon brown sugar
- 2 teaspoons butter
- 1 teaspoon honey
- 1 tablespoon olive oil
- 1 tablespoon Dijon mustard
- 1 tablespoon reduced-sodium soy sauce
- 1/2 to 3/4 teaspoon salt
- 1/4 teaspoon pepper
- 1 salmon fillet (2-1/2 pounds)

1. In a small saucepan over medium heat, cook and stir the brown sugar, butter and honey until melted. Remove from the heat; whisk in the oil, mustard, soy sauce, salt and pepper. Cool for 5 minutes.

2. Place the salmon in a large foil-lined baking pan; spoon the brown sugar mixture over salmon. Bake, uncovered, at 350° for 20-25 minutes or until fish flakes easily with a fork.

[2001]

CRAB-TOPPED FISH FILLETS

yield: 4 servings ∞ prep/total time: 30 min.

(*Pictured on page 811*)

Elegant but truly no bother, this recipe is perfect for company. Toasting the almonds gives them a little more crunch, which is a delightful way to top the fish fillets.

—*Mary Tuthill, Fort Myers Beach, Florida*

- 4 sole *or* cod fillets *or* fish fillet of your choice (6 ounces *each*)
- 1 can (6 ounces) crabmeat, drained, flaked and cartilage removed *or* 1 cup imitation crabmeat, chopped
- 1/2 cup grated Parmesan cheese
- 1/2 cup mayonnaise
- 1 teaspoon lemon juice
- 1/3 cup slivered almonds, toasted

Paprika, optional

1. Place fillets in a greased 13-in. x 9-in. baking dish. Bake, uncovered, at 350° for 18-22 minutes or until fish flakes easily with a fork. Meanwhile, in a large bowl, combine crab, cheese, mayonnaise and lemon juice.

2. Drain cooking juices from baking dish; spoon the crab mixture over the fillets. Broil the fish 4-5 in. from the heat for 5 minutes or until topping is lightly browned. Sprinkle with almonds and paprika if desired.

[2004]

SALMON WITH CREAMY DILL SAUCE

yield: 6 servings ∞ **prep/total time: 30 min.**

(Pictured on page 809)

There's nothing like fresh salmon, and my mom bakes it just right. It nearly melts in your mouth! The sour cream sauce is subtly seasoned with dill and horseradish so that it doesn't overpower the delicate fish flavor.

—*Susan Emery, Everett, Washington*

1	salmon fillet (about 2 pounds)
1	to 1-1/2 teaspoons lemon-pepper seasoning
1	teaspoon onion salt
1	small onion, sliced and separated into rings
6	lemon slices
1/4	cup butter, cubed

DILL SAUCE:

1/3	cup sour cream
1/3	cup mayonnaise
1	tablespoon finely chopped onion
1	teaspoon lemon juice
1	teaspoon prepared horseradish
3/4	teaspoon dill weed
1/4	teaspoon garlic salt

Pepper to taste

1. Line a 15-in. x 10-in. x 1-in. baking pan with heavy-duty foil; grease lightly. Place salmon skin side down on foil. Sprinkle with lemon-pepper and onion salt. Top with onion and lemon. Dot with butter. Fold foil around salmon; seal tightly,

2. Bake at 350° for 20 minutes. Open foil carefully, allowing steam to escape. Broil 4-6 in. from the heat for 8-12 minutes or until the fish flakes easily with a fork.

3. Combine the sauce ingredients until smooth. Serve with salmon.

[1993]

CATFISH CAKES

yield: 8 servings

prep: 10 min. + chilling ∞ **cook: 20 min.**

These cakes are crispy on the outside and moist and flavorful on the inside—a real treat. I like to serve them with hush puppies and coleslaw. I developed the recipe to put to good use all the catfish we catch at our lake cabin.

—*Jan Campbell, Hattiesburg, Mississippi*

1-1/2	pounds catfish fillets
2	eggs, lightly beaten
1	large potato, peeled, cooked and mashed
1	large onion, finely chopped
1	to 2 tablespoons minced fresh parsley
2	to 3 drops hot pepper sauce
1	garlic clove, minced
1	teaspoon salt
1/2	teaspoon pepper
1/2	teaspoon dried basil
2	cups finely crushed butter-flavored crackers

Canola oil

Tartar sauce, optional

1. Poach or bake catfish fillets until fish flakes easily with a fork. Drain and refrigerate. Flake cooled fish into a large bowl. Add the eggs, potato, onion, parsley, pepper sauce, garlic, salt, pepper and basil and mix well. Shape into eight patties.

2. Place cracker crumbs in a shallow bowl. Coat patties in cracker crumbs. In a large skillet over medium heat, cook catfish cakes in oil in batches on each side or until golden brown. Serve with tartar sauce if desired.

SALMON WITH CREAMY DILL SAUCE

❝I've been looking for a good salmon and dill recipe for quite a while, and this is it. The fish is moist and delicious since it's steamed in a foil pouch. The sauce is just right!❞

—*10sChick*

TUNA MUSHROOM CASEROLE

"This is comfort food at its best. So reminded me of the flavors I remember a long time ago. My husband does not care for casseroles, so I made this for me. Surprisingly, he loved it! I did add peas as I remember back in the day I had it like that. I also topped the casserole with the Durkee fried onions instead of saltines."

—linsvin

[1994]

STUFFED SOLE

yield: 8 servings ∽ prep: 20 min.
bake: 35 min.

Seafood was a staple for my large family when I was growing up. Inspired by my mother's delicious meals, I developed this recipe. The fish is moist and flavorful, and the sauce is so good over rice. As I do when serving this dish, you'll get many compliments and recipe requests.

—Winnie Higgins, Salisbury, Maryland

- 1 cup chopped onion
- 2 cans (6 ounces *each*) small shrimp, rinsed and drained
- 1 jar (4-1/2 ounces) sliced mushrooms, drained
- 2 tablespoons butter
- 1/2 pound fresh cooked *or* canned crabmeat, drained and cartilage removed
- 8 sole *or* flounder fillets (2 to 2-1/2 pounds)
- 1/2 teaspoon salt
- 1/4 teaspoon pepper
- 1/4 teaspoon paprika
- 2 cans (10-3/4 ounces *each*) condensed cream of mushroom soup, undiluted
- 1/3 cup chicken broth
- 2 tablespoons water
- 2/3 cup shredded cheddar cheese
- 2 tablespoons minced fresh parsley

Cooked wild, brown *or* white rice *or* a mixture, optional

1. In a large saucepan, saute the onion, shrimp and mushrooms in butter until onion is tender. Add crabmeat; heat through. Sprinkle fillets with salt, pepper and paprika. Spoon crabmeat mixture on fillets; roll up and fasten with a toothpick.

2. Place in a greased 13-in. x 9-in. baking dish. Combine the soup, broth and water; blend until smooth. Pour over fillets. Sprinkle with cheese.

3. Cover and bake at 400° for 30 minutes. Sprinkle with the parsley; return to the oven, uncovered, for 5 minutes or until the fish flakes easily with a fork. Serve with rice if desired.

[1997]

TUNA MUSHROOM CASSEROLE

yield: 6 servings ∽ prep: 20 min.
bake: 35 min.

This casserole is a rich-tasting main dish. I usually serve it when I'm short on time and we need something hearty and comforting.

—Connie Moore, Medway, Ohio

- 1 package (12 ounces) wide egg noodles, cooked and drained
- 1 can (12 ounces) light water-packed tuna, drained and flaked
- 1 can (4 ounces) mushroom stems and pieces, drained
- 1 can (10-3/4 ounces) condensed cream of mushroom soup, undiluted
- 1-1/3 cups 2% milk
- 1/2 teaspoon salt
- 1/4 teaspoon pepper
- 1/2 cup crushed saltines
- 3 tablespoons butter, melted

1. In a large bowl, combine the noodles, tuna and mushrooms. In another bowl, combine the soup, milk, salt and pepper; pour over noodle mixture and mix well.

2. Pour into a greased 2-1/2-qt. baking dish. Combine the saltines and butter; sprinkle over noodles. Bake, uncovered, at 350° for 35-45 minutes or until heated through.

[2011]

HEAVENLY GREEK TACOS

yield: 6 servings ∽ **prep: 30 min. + marinating** ∽ **grill: 10 min.**

The first time I made these, my fiance and I were in heaven! I don't think I've ever said "Mmm" so many times. They're sure to satisfy!

—*Meagan Jensen, Reno, Nevada*

1/3 cup lemon juice
2 tablespoons olive oil
4 teaspoons grated lemon peel
3 garlic cloves, minced, *divided*
1 teaspoon dried oregano
1/4 teaspoon salt
1/4 teaspoon pepper
2 pounds mahi mahi
1-1/2 cups shredded red cabbage
1/2 medium red onion, thinly sliced
1/2 medium sweet red pepper, julienned
1/2 cup crumbled feta cheese
6 tablespoons chopped pitted Greek olives, *divided*
1/4 cup minced fresh parsley
1-1/2 cups plain Greek yogurt
1/2 medium English cucumber, cut into 1-inch pieces
1 teaspoon dill weed
1/2 teaspoon ground coriander
12 whole wheat tortillas (8 inches), warmed

---

1. In a large resealable plastic bag, combine the lemon juice, oil, lemon peel, 2 garlic cloves, oregano, salt and pepper. Add the mahi mahi; seal bag and turn to coat. Refrigerate for up to 30 minutes.

2. In a large bowl, combine the cabbage, onion, red pepper, cheese, 3 tablespoons olives and parsley; set aside.

3. Place the yogurt, cucumber, dill, coriander and remaining garlic and olives in a food processor; cover and process until blended.

4. Drain fish and discard marinade. Moisten a paper towel with cooking oil; using long-handled tongs, lightly coat the grill rack. Grill mahi mahi, covered, over medium heat or broil 4 in. from the heat for 3-4 minutes on each side or until fish flakes easily with a fork.

5. Place a portion of fish on each tortilla; top with cabbage mixture and sauce.

HEAVENLY GREEK TACOS

❝Delicious! The marinade on the mahi mahi is especially fabulous.❞
— *trishmccaff*

[2008]

SALMON WITH POLENTA

yield: 6 servings
prep: 20 min. + simmering ∽ **cook: 25 min.**

(Pictured on page 816)

My husband was of Italian-Swiss descent, and one of his favorite dishes was salmon or bass with tomato sauce served over polenta. I still prepare this recipe for my son and his family.

—*Rena Pilotti, Ripon, California*

2	celery ribs, chopped
1	medium onion, chopped
2	tablespoons olive oil, *divided*
1	can (28 ounces) diced tomatoes, undrained
1	can (8 ounces) tomato sauce
1/4	cup minced fresh parsley
1-1/2	teaspoons salt, *divided*
1	teaspoon Italian seasoning
1/2	teaspoon dried thyme
1/2	teaspoon dried basil
1/2	teaspoon pepper
6	cups water
2	cups cornmeal
1/4	cup all-purpose flour
6	salmon fillets (6 ounces *each*)

1. In a Dutch oven, saute the celery and onion in 1 tablespoon oil until tender. Add the tomatoes, tomato sauce, parsley, 1/2 teaspoon salt, Italian seasoning, thyme, basil and pepper. Cover the sauce and simmer for 1 hour, stirring occasionally.

2. In a large heavy saucepan, bring water and remaining salt to a boil. Reduce heat to a gentle boil; slowly whisk in the cornmeal. Cook and stir with a wooden spoon for 15-20 minutes or until polenta is thickened and pulls away cleanly from the sides of the pan.

3. Place flour in a large shallow bowl; coat salmon on both sides. In a large skillet, brown salmon in remaining oil. Transfer salmon to tomato mixture; cook, uncovered, for 3-5 minutes or until fish flakes easily with a fork. Serve salmon and sauce with polenta.

[2002]

HALIBUT STEAKS

yield: 4 servings ∽ **prep/total time: 20 min.**

Each year we travel to Alaska to visit friends and catch our limit of halibut. We especially enjoy it prepared this way.

—*Donna Goutermont, Jackson, Wyoming*

1/2	cup reduced-sodium soy sauce
1/4	cup packed brown sugar
2	garlic cloves, minced
1/8	teaspoon pepper
Dash hot pepper sauce	
Pinch dried oregano	
Pinch dried basil	
4	halibut steaks (6 ounces *each*)
1/2	cup chopped onion
4	lemon slices
4	teaspoons butter

1. In a small bowl, combine first seven ingredients. Place each halibut steak on a double thickness of heavy-duty foil (about 18 in. x 12 in.); top with the soy sauce mixture, onion, lemon and butter. Fold foil around the fish and seal tightly.

2. Grill, covered, over medium heat for 10-14 minutes or until fish flakes easily with a fork.

SALMON WITH POLENTA

❝ Excellent recipe. My children even loved it. The balance of flavors was great. ❞
—*admiller*

[1999]

SAUCY SKILLET FISH
yield: 6-8 servings
prep/total time: 20 min.

The main industry here on Kodiak Island is fishing, so I'm always on the lookout for new seafood recipes. This is my favorite way to fix halibut since it's quick and tasty. I often get recipe requests when I serve this to guests.

—*Merle Powell, Kodiak, Alaska*

1/2   cup all-purpose flour
1-1/4 teaspoons salt
1   teaspoon paprika
1/8   teaspoon pepper
2   pounds halibut, haddock *or* salmon fillets *or* steaks
1   medium onion, sliced
1/3   cup butter, cubed
1-1/2 cups (12 ounces) sour cream
1   teaspoon dried basil
1   tablespoon minced fresh parsley

1. In a large resealable plastic bag, combine the flour, salt, paprika and pepper. Add fish and shake to coat (if using fillets, cut into serving-size pieces first).

2. In a large skillet, saute onion in butter until tender; remove and set aside. Add fish to the skillet, cook over medium heat for 3-5 minutes on each side or until the fish flakes easily with a fork. Remove fish to a serving plate and keep warm.

3. Add the sour cream, basil and onion to the skillet; heat through (do not boil). Serve with fish. Garnish with parsley.

[2009]

GRILLED TILAPIA WITH PINEAPPLE SALSA
yield: 8 servings (2 cups salsa)
prep/total time: 25 min.

I found this recipe in a seafood cookbook years ago, and it's been one of my favorites. The refreshing, slightly spicy salsa is a delightful complement to the fish.

—*Beth Fleming, Downers Grove, Illinois*

2   cups cubed fresh pineapple
2   green onions, chopped
1/4   cup finely chopped green pepper
1/4   cup minced fresh cilantro
4   teaspoons plus 2 tablespoons lime juice, *divided*
1/8   teaspoon plus 1/4 teaspoon salt, *divided*
Dash cayenne pepper
1   tablespoon canola oil
8   tilapia fillets (4 ounces *each*)
1/8   teaspoon pepper

1. In a small bowl, combine pineapple, onions, green pepper, cilantro, 4 teaspoons lime juice, 1/8 teaspoon salt and cayenne. Chill until serving.

2. Combine oil and remaining lime juice; drizzle over fillets. Sprinkle with the pepper and remaining salt.

3. Using long-handled tongs, moisten a paper towel with cooking oil and lightly coat the grill rack. Grill fish, covered, over medium heat or broil 4 in. from the heat for 3-4 minutes on each side or until fish flakes easily with a fork. Serve with salsa.

SAUCY SKILLET FISH

"I'm not big on fish, but I try to have it during Lent for my husband. We both liked this recipe. I used halibut and cut the recipe in half, and it worked very well. I also liked that it was so quick."
—*Sprowl*

[2012]

TUNA LOUIE BURGERS

yield: 4 servings
prep: 30 min. ∞ **grill: 10 min.**

My father and brother are avid fishermen who keep me supplied with fresh fish from the Pacific. I came up with this recipe that blends Louie sauce with grilled tuna to make a very yummy sandwich.

—*Cleo Gonske, Redding, California*

- 4   tuna steaks (6 ounces each)
- 1/4   cup Italian salad dressing
- 1   teaspoon lemon-pepper seasoning

LOUIE SAUCE:
- 1/4   cup mayonnaise
- 1   tablespoon sweet pickle relish
- 1   tablespoon ketchup
- 1   tablespoon chili sauce
- 1-1/2   teaspoons finely chopped onion
- 1   teaspoon capers, drained
- 1/2   teaspoon grated horseradish
- 1/4   teaspoon Worcestershire sauce

BURGERS:
- 4   lemon wedges
- 4   hard rolls, split
- 2   tablespoons butter, softened
- 1   large tomato, sliced
- 4   lettuce leaves

1. Brush tuna steaks with salad dressing; sprinkle with lemon-pepper seasoning. Let stand at room temperature for 15 minutes. Meanwhile, in a small bowl, combine sauce ingredients; set aside.

2. Using long-handled tongs, moisten a paper towel with cooking oil and lightly coat the grill rack. Grill tuna, covered, over high heat or broil 3-4 in. from the heat for 3-4 minutes on each side for medium-rare or until slightly pink in the center. Squeeze lemon over tuna.

3. Spread rolls with butter. Grill, covered, over high heat for 2-3 minutes or until toasted. Serve tuna on rolls with Louie sauce, tomato and lettuce.

[1994]

SOLE IN HERBED BUTTER

yield: 6 servings ∞ **prep/total time: 25 min.**

I often rely on seafood recipes for quick meals. This flavorful fish is easy to make and is ready in just a few minutes. I know your family will request this often throughout the year!

—*Marilyn Paradis*
Woodburn, Oregon, Field Editor

- 4   tablespoons butter, softened
- 1   teaspoon dill weed
- 1/2   teaspoon onion powder
- 1/2   teaspoon garlic powder
- 1/2   teaspoon salt, optional
- 1/4   teaspoon white pepper
- 2   pounds sole fillets

Fresh dill and lemon wedges, optional

1. In a small bowl, combine the butter, dill, onion powder, garlic powder, salt if desired and pepper.

2. Transfer to a large skillet; heat on medium heat until melted. Add the sole and cook several minutes on each side or until the fish flakes easily with a fork. Garnish with dill and lemon if desired.

[2010]
COCONUT-MANGO MAHI MAHI
yield: 6 servings (1-1/2 cups sauce)
prep/total time: 30 min.
(Pictured on page 810)

Take a tropical taste trip in minutes with this special recipe. Whipping a bit of candied ginger into the sauce enhances its unique and delicious flavor.

—*Don Thompson, Houston, Ohio*

1/2	cup all-purpose flour
2	eggs, lightly beaten
1	cup dry bread crumbs
1	cup flaked coconut
6	mahi mahi fillets (5 ounces each)
2	tablespoons peanut *or* canola oil
2	medium mangoes, peeled and cubed
1/4	cup white wine *or* chicken broth
2	tablespoons brown sugar
1	garlic clove, halved
1	teaspoon finely chopped crystallized ginger
1	teaspoon reduced-sodium soy sauce
1/8	teaspoon pepper
2	tablespoons minced fresh basil

---

1. Place flour and eggs in separate shallow bowls. In another shallow bowl, combine bread crumbs and coconut. Dip fillets in flour, eggs, then bread crumb mixture.

2. In a large skillet over medium heat, cook fish in oil for 4-5 minutes on each side or until golden brown on the outside and fish just turns opaque in the center.

3. Meanwhile, in a food processor, combine the mangoes, wine, brown sugar, garlic, ginger, soy sauce and pepper; cover and process until blended. Stir in basil. Serve with fish.

[1996]
TUNA PASTA SALAD
yield: 4 servings   **prep: 15 min. + chilling**

Mustard and dill really add wonderful flair to the flavor of this simple salad. It's really very inexpensive to serve.

—*Pat Kordas, Nutley, New Jersey*

1	package (7 ounces) small pasta shells, cooked and drained
1	can (6 ounces) tuna, drained and flaked
1	large carrot, shredded
1/4	cup chopped onion
3/4	cup mayonnaise
1/4	cup 2% milk
1	tablespoon lemon juice
2	teaspoons prepared mustard
1	teaspoon dill weed
1/2	teaspoon salt
1/8	teaspoon pepper

---

1. In a large salad bowl, combine the pasta, tuna, carrot and onion. Combine the remaining ingredients; whisk until smooth. Pour over the pasta mixture; toss to coat. Cover and refrigerate for 1-2 hours.

TUNA PASTA SALAD

"This is one of my favorite take-to-work salads. I sometimes substitute peas for carrots and add some Italian dressing."
—*mythyagain*

TESTING FILLETS FOR DONENESS

For fish fillets, check for doneness by inserting a fork at an angle into the thickest portion of the fish and gently parting the meat. When it is opaque and flakes into sections, it is cooked completely.

[2012]

LEMON-LIME SALMON WITH VEGGIE SAUTE

yield: 6 servings ∾ **prep/total time: 30 min.**

Whether you serve my salmon recipe for a healthy weeknight meal or on the weekend to company, family and friends will just be thrilled with it. The assortment of veggies adds a splash of color and awesome flavor to this entree.

—*Brian Hill, West Hollywood, California*

6	salmon fillets (4 ounces *each*)
1/2	cup lemon juice
1/2	cup lime juice
1	teaspoon seafood seasoning
1/4	teaspoon salt
2	medium sweet red peppers, sliced
2	medium sweet yellow peppers, sliced
1	large red onion, halved and sliced
2	teaspoons olive oil
1	package (10 ounces) frozen corn, thawed
2	cups baby portobello mushrooms, halved
2	cups cut fresh asparagus (1-inch pieces)
2	tablespoons minced fresh tarragon *or* 2 teaspoons dried tarragon

1. Place salmon in a 13-in. x 9-in. baking dish; add the lemon and lime juices. Sprinkle with seafood seasoning and salt. Bake, uncovered, at 425° for 10-15 minutes or until fish flakes easily with a fork.

2. Meanwhile, in a large nonstick skillet coated with cooking spray, saute the peppers and onion in oil for 3 minutes. Add corn, mushrooms and asparagus; cook and stir 3-4 minutes longer or just until vegetables reach desired doneness. Stir in tarragon. Serve with the salmon.

[1999]

PIERSIDE SALMON PATTIES

yield: 6 servings ∾ **prep: 15 min.**
bake: 30 min.

(*Pictured on page 812*)

Dill adds flavor to the tasty sauce that tops these moist salmon patties. Baking them all at once makes this recipe a breeze to prepare!

—*Martha Conaway, Pataskala, Ohio*

2	eggs, lightly beaten
1	cup 2% milk
2	tablespoons lemon juice
3	cups coarsely crushed saltines (about 66 crackers)
2	teaspoons finely chopped onion
1/4	teaspoon salt
1/4	teaspoon pepper
2	cans (14-3/4 ounces *each*) salmon, drained, bones and skin removed

DILL SAUCE:

2	tablespoons butter
2	tablespoons all-purpose flour
1	teaspoon snipped fresh dill *or* 1/2 teaspoon dill weed
1/4	teaspoon salt
Dash	pepper
Dash	nutmeg
1-1/2	cups 2% milk

1. In a large bowl, combine the eggs, milk, lemon juice, saltines, onion, salt and pepper. Stir in salmon. Shape into twelve 3-in. patties.

2. Place in a greased 15-in. x 10-in. x 1-in. baking pan. Bake at 350° for 30-35 minutes or until lightly browned.

3. In a small saucepan, melt butter. Stir in the flour, dill, salt, pepper and nutmeg until blended. Gradually stir in the milk. Bring to a boil; cook and stir for 2 minutes or until thickened. Serve with salmon patties.

[2002]

BAKED PARMESAN FISH
yield: 4 servings ∽ prep: 10 min.
bake: 25 min.

Here's an easy way to work an elegant fish dish into your menu. I sometimes sprinkle the golden fillets with slivered or sliced almonds before baking. My husband, daughter and I love this tasty way to eat fish.

—Carolyn Brinkmeyer, Aurora, Colorado

1/3 cup grated Parmesan cheese
2 tablespoons all-purpose flour
1/2 teaspoon paprika
1/4 teaspoon salt
1/8 teaspoon pepper
1 egg
2 tablespoons milk
4 orange roughy *or* catfish fillets
    (4 ounces *each*)

1. In a shallow bowl, combine the cheese, flour, paprika, salt and pepper. In another shallow bowl, beat egg and milk. Dip fish fillets into egg mixture, then coat with the cheese mixture.

2. Arrange in a greased 13-in. x 9-in. baking dish. Bake, uncovered, at 350° for 25-30 minutes or until fish flakes easily with a fork.

[1993]

GREEK GRILLED CATFISH
yield: 6 servings ∽ prep/total time: 30 min.

Temperatures here on the Gulf Coast are moderate year-round, so we grill out a lot. My husband, Larry, came up with this recipe by experimenting. Our whole family likes the unique taste of this dish.

—Rita Futral
  Starkville, Mississippi, Field Editor

6 catfish fillets (8 ounces *each*)
Greek seasoning to taste
4 ounces feta cheese, crumbled

1 tablespoon dried mint
2 tablespoons olive oil

1. Sprinkle both sides of fillets with Greek seasoning. Sprinkle each fillet with 1 rounded tablespoon feta cheese and 1/2 teaspoon mint. Drizzle 1 teaspoon oil over each. Roll up fillets and secure with toothpicks.

2. Grill over medium heat for 20-25 minutes or until fish flakes easily with a fork. Or, place fillets in a greased baking dish and bake at 350° for 30-35 minutes or until fish flakes easily with fork.

[2007]

BUSY-DAY BAKED FISH
yield: 6-8 servings
prep/total time: 30 min.

An onion soup and sour cream mixture really adds zip to this recipe. Your family would never guess that it's so quick and easy to prepare.

—Beverly Krueger, Yamhill, Oregon

1 cup (8 ounces) sour cream
2 tablespoons onion soup mix
1-1/2 cups seasoned bread crumbs
2-1/2 pounds fish fillets
1/4 cup butter, melted
1/3 cup shredded Parmesan cheese

1. In a shallow bowl, combine sour cream and soup mix. Place bread crumbs in another shallow bowl. Cut fish into serving-size pieces; coat with sour cream mixture, then roll in crumbs.

2. Place the fish in two greased 13-in. x 9-in. baking dishes. Drizzle with the butter. Bake, uncovered, at 425° for 12 minutes. Sprinkle with cheese; bake 2-6 minutes longer or until fish flakes easily with a fork.

GREEK GRILLED CATFISH

"I grilled them exactly the way the recipe said, and they were really good. The more cheese, the yummier. In addition, they were moist and not too fishy. "
—Francisca3032

[2005]

MOM'S FRIED FISH

yield: 6 servings ∞ **prep/total time: 30 min.**

Our family has an annual fish fry that centers around my mom's recipe. I think she makes the finest fried fish around. It's flaky and flavorful with a golden cracker-crumb coating.

—*Julie Jahnke, Green Lake, Wisconsin*

---

 2 eggs, lightly beaten
1-1/2 cups crushed saltines
 (about 45 crackers)
 2 pounds whitefish fillets, cut in
 half lengthwise
Oil for frying
TARTAR SAUCE:
 1 cup mayonnaise
 2 tablespoons sweet pickle relish
 1 tablespoon finely chopped onion

---

1. Place the eggs and cracker crumbs in separate shallow bowls. Dip fillets into eggs, then coat with crumbs. Let stand for 5 minutes.

2. In an electric skillet or deep-fat fryer, heat oil to 375°. Fry fillets, a few at a time, for 2 minutes on each side or until fish is golden brown and flakes easily with a fork. Drain on paper towels.

3. In a small bowl, combine the tartar sauce ingredients. Serve with fish.

[2008]

CAESAR ORANGE ROUGHY

yield: 8 servings ∞ **prep/total time: 25 min.**

Sprinkled with buttery cracker crumbs, these tender fish fillets are nicely seasoned with Caesar salad dressing and cheddar cheese..

—*Mary Lou Boyce, Wilmington, Delaware*

---

 2 pounds orange roughy fillets
 1 cup creamy Caesar salad dressing
 2 cups crushed butter-flavored crackers
 (about 50 crackers)
 1 cup (4 ounces) shredded cheddar
 cheese

BARBECUED TROUT

"I just tried it tonight. I ended up marinating it overnight instead of for one hour, and it turned out great. My husband said, 'We have to make this again...how about tomorrow night?'"
—*jieastcott*

1. Place the fillets in an ungreased 13-in. x 9-in. baking dish. Drizzle with salad dressing; sprinkle with cracker crumbs.

2. Bake the fish, uncovered, at 400° for 10 minutes. Sprinkle with cheese. Bake 3-5 minutes longer or until fish flakes easily with a fork and cheese is melted.

[1994]

BARBECUED TROUT

yield: 6 servings ∞ **prep/total time: 20 min.**

This delicious recipe came from a friend. The sauce really gives the fish a wonderful flavor. Even those who aren't that fond of fish will like it prepared this way.

—*Vivian Wolfram
Mountain Home, Arkansas*

 2/3 cup reduced-sodium soy sauce
 1/2 cup ketchup
 2 tablespoons lemon juice
 2 tablespoons canola oil
 1 teaspoon dried rosemary, crushed
 6 pan-dressed trout
Lemon wedges, optional

---

1. Combine the soy sauce, ketchup, lemon juice, oil and rosemary; pour two-thirds of marinade into a large resealable plastic bag; add fish. Seal bag and turn to coat; refrigerate bag for 1 hour, turning once. Cover and refrigerate the remaining marinade for basting.

2. Drain and discard the marinade. Place fish in a single layer in a well-greased hinged wire grill basket. Grill, covered, over medium heat for 8-10 minutes or until fish is browned on the bottom. Turn and baste with the reserved marinade; grill 5-7 minutes longer or until fish flakes easily with a fork. Serve with the lemon if desired.

SALMON WITH CREAMY DILL SAUCE, page 799

SEAFOOD CASSEROLE, page 819

TURKEY MUFFULETTA, page 790

COCONUT-MANGO MAHI MAHI, page 805

CRAB-TOPPED FISH FILLETS, page 798

HONEY-MUSTARD CHICKEN SANDWICHES, page 776

CHEDDAR FRENCH DIP SANDWICHES, page 774

CREAMY SEAFOOD-STUFFED SHELLS, page 817

CHICAGO-STYLE STUFFED PIZZA, page 795

PIERSIDE SALMON PATTIES, page 806

SHRIMP PAD THAI, page 824

BLACK-AND-BLUE-PIZZAS, page 792

BACON-WRAPPED SEAFOOD SKEWERS, page 818

ALOHA BURGERS, page 777

SEAFOOD TORTILLA LASAGNA, page 823

SEAFOOD AU GRATIN, page 820

BRUSCHETTA PIZZA, page 791

BAKED LASAGNA IN A BUN, page 782

SALMON WITH POLENTA, page 802

ROASTED SEA SCALLOPS, page 823

[2008]

CREAMY SEAFOOD-STUFFED SHELLS

yield: 8 servings ∞ prep: 40 min. ∞ bake: 30 min.

(Pictured on page 811)

Inspired by my love of lasagna, pasta shells and seafood, I created this recipe that's easy to make but special enough to serve company. I serve it with garlic bread and a salad for a complete meal.

—Katie Sloan, Charlotte, North Carolina, Field Editor

---

24 uncooked jumbo pasta shells
 1 tablespoon finely chopped green pepper
 1 tablespoon chopped red onion
 1 teaspoon plus 1/4 cup butter, *divided*
 2 cans (6 ounces *each*) lump crabmeat, drained
 1 package (5 ounces) frozen cooked salad shrimp, thawed
 1 egg, lightly beaten
1/2 cup shredded part-skim mozzarella cheese
1/4 cup mayonnaise
 2 tablespoons plus 4 cups milk, *divided*
1-1/2 teaspoons seafood seasoning, *divided*
1/4 teaspoon pepper
1/4 cup all-purpose flour
1/4 teaspoon coarsely ground pepper
1-1/2 cups grated Parmesan cheese

---

1. Cook pasta according to package directions. Meanwhile, in a small skillet, saute green pepper and onion in 1 teaspoon butter until tender; set aside.

2. In a large bowl, combine the crab, shrimp, egg, mozzarella cheese, mayonnaise, 2 tablespoons milk, 1 teaspoon seafood seasoning, pepper and green pepper mixture.

3. Drain and rinse pasta; stuff each shell with 1 rounded tablespoon of seafood mixture. Place in a greased 13-in. x 9-in. baking dish.

4. In a small saucepan, melt remaining butter over medium heat. Whisk in flour and coarsely ground pepper; gradually whisk in remaining milk. Bring to a boil; cook and stir for 2 minutes or until thickened. Stir in Parmesan cheese.

5. Pour over stuffed shells. Sprinkle with remaining seafood seasoning. Bake, uncovered, at 350° for 30-35 minutes or until bubbly.

CREAMY SEAFOOD-STUFFED SHELLS

"My whole family loved this recipe. It's easy to make and warms up well in the microwave."
—leeken

BAKED SEAFOOD AVOCADOS

“ This is a really wonderful recipe. I had something similar when I was in Spain. It was served chilled with the crab and a delicate seafood sauce. The dish was not oven prepared. ”
—cooks_alot

[2008]

BACON-WRAPPED SEAFOOD SKEWERS

yield: 3 servings ∾ prep/total time: 30 min.

(Pictured on page 814)

With a little kick from cayenne, these scrumptious kabobs will be the hit of your next barbecue. The crunchy bacon wraps create moist, tender shrimp and scallops.

—Audrey Hagerty
Saylorsburg, Pennsylvania

    2 tablespoons lemon juice
  1/2 teaspoon cayenne pepper
  1/8 teaspoon garlic powder
   12 uncooked jumbo shrimp, peeled and deveined
    6 large sea scallops, halved widthwise
   12 bacon strips, halved
    1 medium lemon, cut into wedges

1. In a large resealable plastic bag, combine the lemon juice, cayenne and garlic powder; add shrimp and scallops. Seal bag and turn to coat; let stand for 10 minutes.

2. Meanwhile, in a large skillet, cook bacon over medium heat until partially cooked but not crisp. Drain on paper towels. Drain and discard marinade. Wrap one bacon piece around each shrimp and scallop half.

3. On six metal or soaked wooden skewers, alternately thread the shrimp, scallops and lemon wedges. Grill the kabobs, covered, over medium heat for 8-12 minutes or until shrimp turn pink and scallops are opaque, turning occasionally. Remove from skewers; squeeze lemon wedges over seafood.

[2000]

BAKED SEAFOOD AVOCADOS

yield: 8 servings ∾ prep: 15 min.
bake: 25 min.

Everyone who tastes this wonderful luncheon dish is surprised that the avocados are baked.

—Marian Platt
Sequim, Washington, Field Editor

    1 cup mayonnaise
  3/4 cup chopped celery
  1/2 cup thinly sliced green onions
  1/8 teaspoon salt, optional
  1/8 teaspoon pepper
    1 can (4-1/2 ounces) crabmeat, drained, flaked and cartilage removed
    1 can (4 ounces) medium shrimp, rinsed and drained
    4 large ripe avocados, halved and pitted
    1 to 2 tablespoons lemon juice
  1/4 cup crushed potato chips, optional

1. In a large bowl, combine mayonnaise, celery, green onions, salt if desired and pepper. Add crab and shrimp; mix well. Peel avocados if desired. Sprinkle the avocados with lemon juice; fill with seafood mixture. Sprinkle with potato chips if desired.

2. Place in an ungreased 13-in. x 9-in. baking dish. Bake, uncovered, at 350° for 25-30 minutes or until bubbly.

[2007]

SEAFOOD CASSEROLE

yield: 6 servings ⚬ **prep: 20 min.**
bake: 40 min.

(Pictured on page 810)

A family favorite, this rice casserole is stuffed with plenty of seafood and veggies. It's hearty, homey and so easy to make!

—Nancy Billups, Princeton, Iowa

- 1 package (6 ounces) long grain and wild rice
- 1 pound frozen crabmeat, thawed *or* 2-1/2 cups canned lump crabmeat, drained
- 1 pound cooked medium shrimp, peeled, deveined and cut into 1/2-inch pieces
- 2 celery ribs, chopped
- 1 medium onion, finely chopped
- 1/2 cup finely chopped green pepper
- 1 can (4 ounces) mushroom stems and pieces, drained
- 1 jar (2 ounces) diced pimientos, drained
- 1 cup mayonnaise
- 1 cup 2% milk
- 1/2 teaspoon pepper
- Dash Worcestershire sauce
- 1/4 cup dry bread crumbs

1. Cook the rice according to package directions. Meanwhile, in a large bowl, combine the crab, shrimp, celery, onion, green pepper, mushrooms and pimientos.

2. In a small bowl, whisk mayonnaise, milk, pepper and Worcestershire sauce; stir into the seafood mixture. Stir in rice.

3. Transfer to a greased 13-in. x 9-in. baking dish. Sprinkle with bread crumbs. Bake, uncovered, at 375° for 40-50 minutes or until bubbly.

[2004]

LINGUINE IN CLAM SAUCE

yield: 4-6 servings ⚬ **prep: 20 min.**
cook: 15 min.

I make this quite often for family celebrations. It sure is a favorite. The zucchini adds such a nice touch to this traditional dish.

—Ken Vouk, Willowick, Ohio

- 1 package (1 pound) linguine
- 1 large onion, finely chopped
- 2 tablespoons olive oil
- 1 medium zucchini, diced
- 1 garlic clove, minced
- 3 cans (6-1/2 ounces *each*) chopped clams
- 1/2 pound sliced fresh mushrooms
- 2 teaspoons chicken bouillon granules
- 1 teaspoon minced fresh basil
- 1/8 teaspoon pepper
- Shredded Parmesan cheese

1. Cook linguine according to package directions. Meanwhile, in a large skillet, saute onion in oil until tender. Add zucchini; cook for 2 minutes or until crisp-tender. Stir in garlic; cook 1 minute longer.

2. Drain clams, reserving 1/2 cup juice. Add the clams, mushrooms, bouillon, basil, pepper and reserved juice to the skillet. Bring to a boil. Reduce heat; simmer, uncovered, for 5 minutes or until vegetables are tender. Drain linguine; top with clam mixture. Sprinkle with cheese.

LINGUINE IN CLAM SAUCE

❝I made this and we loved it. Will make often as it makes my usual recipe seem too bland. I also added some chopped red pepper—delicious!❞
—viesy777

[2007]

SEAFOOD AU GRATIN

yield: 6 servings ∞ prep: 30 min.
bake: 15 min.

(Pictured on page 815)

A seafood casserole is a "must" for a bountiful buffet. My father was a fisherman, so we ate fish almost every day. Over the years, I've tasted many seafood dishes but none better than this one.

—Hazel McMullin, Amherst, Nova Scotia

4	tablespoons butter, *divided*
2	tablespoons all-purpose flour
1/8	teaspoon pepper
1	cup chicken broth
1/2	cup 2% milk
1/2	cup grated Parmesan cheese, *divided*
1/2	pound sea scallops
1	pound haddock *or* cod fillets, cut into six pieces
1-1/2	cups sliced fresh mushrooms
1/2	cup shredded part-skim mozzarella cheese
1/2	cup shredded cheddar cheese

1. In a large saucepan, melt 2 tablespoons butter. Stir in the flour and pepper until smooth; gradually add broth and milk. Bring to a boil; cook and stir for 2 minutes or until thickened. Stir in 1/4 cup Parmesan cheese; set aside.

2. Place the scallops in another saucepan; cover with water. Simmer, uncovered, for 4-5 minutes or until scallops are firm and opaque. Meanwhile, place fillets in a shallow 2-qt. microwave-safe dish. Cover and microwave on high for 2-4 minutes or until fish flakes easily with a fork. Drain the scallops. Arrange fish and scallops in a greased 11-in. x 7-in. baking dish.

3. In a small skillet, saute mushrooms in remaining butter until tender; stir into cheese sauce. Spoon over the seafood. Sprinkle with mozzarella, cheddar and remaining Parmesan cheese.

4. Cover and bake at 350° for 15-20 minutes or until bubbly and cheese is melted.

Editor's Note: This recipe was tested in a 1,100-watt microwave.

[2011]

EASTERN SHORE CRAB CAKES

yield: 3 servings ∞ prep/total time: 25 min.

In Delaware, we're surrounded by an abundance of fresh seafood, particularly terrific crab. The secret to great crab cakes is fresh crab meat, not too much filler and not breaking up the crab too much. This recipe does all that.

—Cynthia Bent
Newark, Delaware, Field Editor

1	egg, lightly beaten
1/2	cup dry bread crumbs
1/2	cup mayonnaise
3/4	teaspoon seafood seasoning
1/2	teaspoon lemon juice
1/2	teaspoon Worcestershire sauce
1/8	teaspoon white pepper
1	pound fresh lump crabmeat
2	tablespoons canola oil

1. In a large bowl, combine the egg, bread crumbs, mayonnaise, seafood seasoning, lemon juice, Worcestershire sauce and pepper. Fold in crab. Shape into six patties.

2. In a large skillet, cook the crab cakes in oil for 4-5 minutes on each side or until browned.

SEAFOOD AU GRATIN

"One of the best seafood dishes we have ever eaten. Friends requested the recipe."
—Aula

[2011]

SHRIMP & TORTELLINI IN TOMATO CREAM

yield: 4 servings ∞ **prep: 20 min.**
cook: 30 min.

This shrimp and pasta combination is one of my husband's favorites. It's healthy, and he doesn't even know it. It's also easy to halve the recipe for two.

—*Mary Kay LaBrie, Clermont, Florida*

- 1 package (9 ounces) refrigerated cheese tortellini
- 1 pound uncooked medium shrimp, peeled and deveined
- 1 tablespoon olive oil, *divided*
- 2 teaspoons grated lemon peel
- 1/4 teaspoon pepper, *divided*
- Dash crushed red pepper flakes
- 2 shallots, chopped
- 2 garlic cloves, minced
- 2 cans (14-1/2 ounces *each*) no-salt-added diced tomatoes, undrained
- 1 bottle (8 ounces) clam juice
- 1/2 cup white wine
- 2 tablespoons balsamic vinegar
- 4 fresh thyme sprigs
- 1/4 cup grated Parmesan and Romano cheese blend
- 1/4 cup half-and-half cream
- 10 fresh basil leaves, thinly sliced
- 2 tablespoons minced chives
- Shredded Parmesan cheese and minced fresh parsley, optional

1. Cook tortellini according to package directions. Meanwhile, in a large nonstick skillet, cook the shrimp in 2 teaspoons oil until shrimp turn pink. Stir in the lemon peel, 1/8 teaspoon pepper and pepper flakes. Remove and keep warm.

2. In the same skillet, cook shallots in remaining oil over low heat for 10-15 minutes or until golden brown, stirring occasionally. Add the garlic and cook 1 minute longer.

3. Add the tomatoes, clam juice, wine, vinegar, thyme and remaining pepper. Bring to a boil; cook until liquid is reduced by half, about 10 minutes. Remove from the heat; discard thyme sprigs. Stir in the cheese, cream, basil, chives and shrimp.

4. Drain tortellini; stir into shrimp mixture. Sprinkle with shredded cheese and parsley if desired.

[2005]

LOUISIANA SHRIMP

yield: 10 servings ∞ **prep: 40 min.**
bake: 20 min.

This is a Lenten favorite at our home. I serve it right out of the roaster with corn on the cob and boiled potatoes.

—*Sundra Hauck*
  Bogalusa, Louisiana, Field Editor

- 1 pound butter, cubed
- 3 medium lemons, sliced
- 2 tablespoons plus 1-1/2 teaspoons coarsely ground pepper
- 2 tablespoons Worcestershire sauce
- 2 garlic cloves, minced
- 1/2 teaspoon salt
- 1/2 teaspoon hot pepper sauce
- 2-1/2 pounds uncooked shell-on medium shrimp

1. In a large saucepan, combine the first seven ingredients. Bring to a boil. Reduce heat; cover and simmer for 30 minutes, stirring occasionally.

2. Place shrimp in a large roasting pan; pour butter mixture over top. Bake, uncovered, at 375° for 20-25 minutes or until shrimp turn pink. Serve warm with a slotted spoon.

SHRIMP & TORTELLINI IN TOMATO CREAM

"This recipe is reminiscent of a five-star Italian restaurant and is a fine meal to impress any discriminating palate."
—*bettyboop1963*

[2005]

PESTO SHRIMP PASTA

yield: 4 servings ✺ **prep/total time: 30 min.**

A dash of red pepper puts zip in this lively entree. It's one of our favorite dishes!

—Gloria Jones Grenga, Newnan, Georgia

8	ounces uncooked spaghetti
3	tablespoons olive oil, *divided*
1	cup loosely packed fresh basil leaves
1/4	cup lemon juice
2	garlic cloves, peeled
1/2	teaspoon salt
1	pound fresh asparagus, trimmed and cut into 2-inch pieces
3/4	pound uncooked medium shrimp, peeled and deveined
1/8	teaspoon crushed red pepper flakes

1. Cook spaghetti according to package directions. Meanwhile, in a blender, combine 1 tablespoon oil, basil, lemon juice, garlic and salt; cover and process until smooth.

2. In a large skillet, saute asparagus in remaining oil until crisp-tender. Add shrimp and pepper flakes. Cook and stir until shrimp turn pink.

3. Drain spaghetti; place in a large bowl. Add basil mixture; toss to coat. Add shrimp mixture and mix well.

PESTO SHRIMP PASTA

❝A great way to use my fresh basil. Even my girls, who were picky eaters, liked this dish.❞

—pettymama

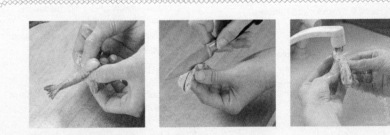

PEELING & DEVEINING SHRIMP

1. Start on the underside by the head area to remove shell from shrimp. Pull legs and first section of shell to one side. Continue pulling shell up around the top and to the other side. Pull off shell by tail if desired.

2. Remove the black vein running down the back of shrimp by making a shallow slit with a paring knife along the back from head area to tail.

3. Rinse shrimp under cold water to remove the vein.

[2000]

SEAFOOD TORTILLA LASAGNA

yield: 12 servings ∞ **prep: 40 min.**
bake: 30 min. + standing

(Pictured on page 815)

My husband and I enjoy lasagna, seafood and Mexican fare. One evening, I combined all three into this deliciously different entree. It certainly is a tempting, memorable change of pace from traditional Italian-style lasagnas.

—*Sharon Sawicki, Carol Stream, Illinois*

1	jar (20 ounces) picante sauce
1-1/2	pounds uncooked medium shrimp, peeled and deveined
1/8	teaspoon cayenne pepper
1	tablespoon olive oil
4	to 6 garlic cloves, minced
1/3	cup butter, cubed
1/3	cup all-purpose flour
1	can (14-1/2 ounces) chicken broth
1/2	cup heavy whipping cream
15	corn tortillas (6 inches), warmed
1	package (16 ounces) imitation crabmeat, flaked
3	cups (12 ounces) shredded Colby-Monterey Jack cheese

Sour cream and minced fresh
cilantro, optional

1. Place picante sauce in a blender; cover and process until smooth. Set aside. In a large skillet cook shrimp and cayenne in oil for about 3 minutes or until the shrimp turn pink. Add the garlic; cook 1 minute longer. Remove and set aside.

2. In the same skillet, melt butter. Stir in flour until smooth. Gradually add the broth. Bring to a boil; cook and stir for 2 minutes or until thickened. Reduce heat. Stir in cream and picante sauce; heat through.

3. Spread 1/2 cup of sauce in a greased 13-in. x 9-in. baking dish. Layer with six tortillas, half of the shrimp, crab and sauce and 1-1/4 cups cheese. Repeat layers. Tear or cut remaining tortillas; arrange over cheese. Sprinkle with remaining cheese.

4. Bake, uncovered, at 375° for 30-35 minutes or until bubbly. Let stand for 15 minutes before cutting. Garnish with sour cream and minced cilantro if desired.

[2007]

ROASTED SEA SCALLOPS

yield: 4 servings ∞ **prep: 10 min.**
bake: 25 min.

(Pictured on page 816)

We like scallops because of their availability here year-round, and they're affordable compared to some seafood. These scallops are delicately seasoned with roasted tomatoes and can be served over rice or toasted garlic bread.

—*Marguerite Shaeffer, Sewell, New Jersey*

1	large tomato, chopped
1	medium onion, chopped
1	tablespoon minced fresh parsley
1	tablespoon olive oil
1-1/2	teaspoons paprika
1/2	teaspoon salt
1/4	teaspoon pepper
12	sea scallops (2 ounces *each*)

Hot cooked rice, optional

1. In an ungreased 3-qt. baking dish, combine first seven ingredients. Bake, uncovered, at 400° for 10 minutes or until bubbly.

2. Stir in scallops. Bake 15 minutes longer or until scallops are firm and opaque. Serve with rice if desired.

Zippy Roasted Scallops: Add 1 chopped seeded jalapeno pepper to the tomato mixture.

ROASTED SEA SCALLOPS

"My whole family will eat it, which is a miracle with three picky kids."
—*lynzileel*

SHRIMP PAD THAI

It was great! Tasted very authentic and I have made a version with 30+ ingredients before. This saved time and money and was truly good. I made pot stickers and chicken satay to go with it. Since my hubby does not like onions, I grated the onion instead of chopping it.
—mlaveway

[2010]

SHRIMP PAD THAI

yield: 4 servings ∞ **prep/total time: 30 min.**

(Pictured on page 813)

You can make this yummy Thai classic in no time. Find fish sauce and chili garlic sauce in the Asian foods aisle of your grocery store.

—*Elise Ray, Shawnee, Kansas*

4	ounces uncooked thick rice noodles
1/2	pound uncooked small shrimp, peeled and deveined
2	teaspoons canola oil
1	large onion, chopped
1	garlic clove, minced
1	egg, lightly beaten
3	cups coleslaw mix
4	green onions, thinly sliced
1/3	cup rice vinegar
1/4	cup sugar
3	tablespoons reduced-sodium soy sauce
2	tablespoons fish sauce *or* additional reduced-sodium soy sauce
2	to 3 teaspoons chili garlic sauce
2	tablespoons chopped salted peanuts

Chopped fresh cilantro leaves

---

1. Cook the noodles according to package directions.

2. In a large nonstick skillet or wok, stir-fry shrimp in oil until shrimp turn pink; remove and set aside. Add onion and garlic to the pan. Make a well in the center of the onion mixture; add egg. Stir-fry for 2-3 minutes or until egg is completely set. Add the coleslaw mix, green onions, vinegar, sugar, soy sauce, fish sauce, chili garlic sauce and peanuts; heat through. Return shrimp to pan; heat through. Drain noodles; toss with the shrimp mixture. Garnish with cilantro.

[2002]

SPICY ISLAND SHRIMP

yield: 6 servings ∞ **prep: 20 min. cook: 20 min.**

My husband got this recipe while he was living on St. Croix Island. We've served the zippy shrimp dish on several holiday occasions. I'm amazed at how even those who claim not to care for shrimp come out of their shells and devour the shrimp when they're prepared this way!

—*Teresa Methe, Minden, Nebraska*

1	large green pepper, chopped
1	large onion, chopped
1/2	cup butter cubed
2-1/4	pounds uncooked large shrimp, peeled and deveined
2	cans (8 ounces *each*) tomato sauce
3	tablespoons chopped green onions
1	tablespoon minced fresh parsley
1	teaspoon salt
1	teaspoon pepper
1	teaspoon paprika
1/2	teaspoon garlic powder
1/2	teaspoon dried oregano
1/2	teaspoon dried thyme
1/4	to 1/2 teaspoon white pepper
1/4	to 1/2 teaspoon cayenne pepper

Hot cooked rice

---

1. In a large skillet, saute green pepper and onion in butter until tender. Reduce heat; add the shrimp. Cook for 5 minutes or until shrimp turn pink.

2. Stir in the tomato sauce, green onions, parsley and seasonings. Bring to a boil. Reduce heat; simmer, uncovered, for 20 minutes or until slightly thickened. Serve with rice.

[2001]

LOUISIANA JAMBALAYA

**yield: 10-12 servings ∞ prep: 10 min.
cook: 30 min.**

*My husband helped add a little spice to my life.
He grew up on Cajun cooking, while I ate
mostly meat-and-potatoes meals.*

—*Sandra Pichon*
Memphis, Tennessee, Field Editor

- 1/2 **pound smoked sausage, halved and sliced**
- 2 **cups cubed fully cooked ham**
- 1/4 **cup canola oil**
- 2 **celery ribs, chopped**
- 1 **large onion, chopped**
- 1 **medium green pepper, chopped**
- 5 **green onions, thinly sliced**
- 2 **garlic cloves, minced**
- 1 **can (14-1/2 ounces) diced tomatoes, undrained**
- 1 **teaspoon dried thyme**
- 1 **teaspoon salt**
- 1/2 **teaspoon pepper**
- 1/4 **teaspoon cayenne pepper**
- 2 **cans (14-1/2 ounces *each*) chicken broth**
- 1 **cup uncooked long grain rice**
- 1/3 **cup water**
- 4-1/2 **teaspoons Worcestershire sauce**
- 2 **pounds cooked shrimp, peeled and deveined**

1. In a Dutch oven, saute sausage and ham in oil until lightly browned. Remove and keep warm. In drippings, saute the celery, onion, green pepper and green onions until tender. Add garlic; cook 1 minute longer. Stir in the tomatoes, thyme, salt, pepper and cayenne; cook 5 minutes longer.

2. Stir in the broth, rice, water and Worcestershire sauce. Bring to a boil. Reduce heat; cover and simmer for 20 minutes or until rice is tender. Stir in the sausage mixture and shrimp; heat through.

[2011]

MEDITERRANEAN SHRIMP SKILLET

yield: 4 servings ∞ prep/total time: 30 min.

*Tender shrimp, fresh spinach and minced basil
combine with tangy lemon and feta cheese to
give this wonderful pasta toss a unique flavor.*

—*Heidi Farnworth, Riverton, Utah*

- 8 **ounces uncooked angel hair pasta**
- 1-1/2 **pounds uncooked medium shrimp, peeled and deveined**
- 1-1/2 **teaspoons olive oil**
- 3 **garlic cloves, minced**
- 1/4 **teaspoon salt**
- 1/4 **teaspoon pepper**
- 1-1/2 **cups chicken broth, *divided***
- 2 **tablespoons lemon juice**
- 1/2 **teaspoon dried basil**
- 2 **teaspoons cornstarch**
- 4 **cups chopped fresh spinach**
- 1/2 **cup crumbled feta cheese**
- 1/4 **cup minced fresh basil**

1. Cook the pasta according to package directions. Meanwhile, in a large skillet, saute the shrimp in oil until shrimp turn pink. Add the garlic, salt and pepper; cook 1 minute longer. Remove and set aside.

2. In the same skillet, heat 1 cup broth, lemon juice and dried basil. In a small bowl, combine cornstarch and the remaining broth until smooth; stir into the pan. Bring to a boil; cook and stir for 2 minutes or until thickened. Stir in the spinach and shrimp; cook until the spinach is wilted.

3. Drain the pasta; serve with shrimp mixture. Sprinkle with cheese and fresh basil.

LOUISIANA JAMBALAYA

"I discovered this little gem years ago, and it quickly became my go-to recipe for not only jambalaya but for good 'company' food. It's quick and easy to make, doubles nicely for a crowd, has the perfect amount of spice and seems fussy and fancy. Serve it with cornbread and sit back as the compliments come pouring in."
—*Missionary*

❦ SIDES ❦

[1997]

BROCCOLI CHEDDAR CASSEROLE

yield: 12-16 servings ❦ **prep: 15 min.**
bake: 45 min. + standing

We're lucky to have fresh fruits and vegetables year-round. I put bountiful Arizona broccoli to great use in this rich side dish. Even those who don't care for broccoli finish off big helpings.

—*Carol Strickland, Yuma, Arizona*

8	cups chopped fresh broccoli
1	cup finely chopped onion
3/4	cup butter, cubed
12	eggs, lightly beaten
2	cups heavy whipping cream
2	cups (8 ounces) shredded cheddar cheese, *divided*
2	teaspoons salt
1	teaspoon pepper

1. In a large skillet over medium heat, saute broccoli and onion in butter until crisp-tender; set aside. In a large bowl, whisk eggs, cream and 1-3/4 cups of cheese. Stir in the broccoli mixture, salt and pepper. Pour into a greased 3-qt. baking dish; set in a large pan. Place 1 in. of hot water in large pan.

2. Bake, uncovered, at 350° for 45-50 minutes or until a knife inserted near the center comes out clean. Sprinkle with remaining cheese. Let stand for 10 minutes before serving.

[2006]

PECAN SWEET POTATO BAKE

yield: 6-8 servings ❦ **prep: 20 min.**
bake: 30 min.

The recipe for this luscious souffle was handed down through my husband's family, and it's become a tradition for me to serve it during the holidays. Everyone loves it!

—*Nanci Keatley, Salem, Oregon*

3	cups mashed sweet potatoes
2	eggs
1/2	cup sugar
1/4	cup half-and-half cream
1/4	cup butter, softened
2	teaspoons vanilla extract
1/8	teaspoon salt
TOPPING:	
1/2	cup packed brown sugar
2	tablespoons all-purpose flour
1/4	cup cold butter, cubed
1/2	cup chopped pecans

1. In a large bowl, combine the first seven ingredients; beat until light and fluffy. Transfer to a greased 11-in. x 7-in. baking dish.

2. For topping, combine the brown sugar and flour in a small bowl; cut in butter until crumbly. Stir in pecans. Sprinkle over sweet potato mixture.

3. Bake, uncovered, at 350° for 30-35 minutes or until a thermometer reads 160°.

[2009]

COUNTRY-STYLE TOMATOES

yield: 8 servings ∾ prep: 25 min.
cook: 10 min./batch

This is an excellent vegetable course when your garden is bursting with tomatoes, and it always gets lots of attention on a buffet table. For a special treat, I'll use beefsteak tomatoes.

—Cathy Dwyer, Freedom, New Hampshire

- 4 large tomatoes
- 1 package (8 ounces) cream cheese, softened
- 1/4 cup minced fresh parsley
- 1-1/2 teaspoons minced fresh basil *or* 1/2 teaspoon dried basil
- 1 garlic clove, minced
- 1/4 teaspoon salt
- 1/4 cup all-purpose flour
- 1 cup panko (Japanese) bread crumbs
- 1 egg
- 1 tablespoon 2% milk
- 3 tablespoons butter
- 3 tablespoons olive oil

1. Cut each tomato into four thick slices; place slices on paper towels to drain. Meanwhile, in a small bowl, beat the cream cheese, parsley, basil, garlic and salt until blended. Spread cream cheese mixture over eight tomato slices; top with the remaining tomato slices.

2. Place the flour and bread crumbs in separate shallow bowls. In another bowl, whisk egg and milk. Coat the top and bottom of each sandwich with flour, dip into egg mixture, then coat with the crumbs.

3. In a large skillet, heat butter and oil over medium-hot heat. Fry tomato sandwiches in batches for 3-4 minutes on each side or until golden brown. Drain on paper towels.

[2008]

CREAMED PEAS AND CARROTS

yield: 4 servings ∾ prep/total time: 25 min.

(*Pictured on page 854*)

This comforting dish features a simply seasoned cream sauce, which nicely complements the peas and carrots.

—Gayleen Grote, Battleview, North Dakota

- 4 medium carrots, sliced
- 2 cups frozen peas
- 1 tablespoon cornstarch
- 1/4 teaspoon salt
- 1/8 teaspoon pepper
- 1/2 cup heavy whipping cream

1. Place carrots in a large saucepan; add 1 in. of water. Bring to a boil. Reduce heat; cover and simmer for 5-8 minutes or until crisp-tender.

2. Add the peas; return to a boil. Reduce heat; cover and simmer 5-10 minutes longer or until vegetables are tender. Drain, reserving 1/2 cup cooking liquid. Return vegetables and reserved liquid to the pan.

3. In a small bowl, combine cornstarch, salt, pepper and cream until smooth. Stir into the vegetables. Bring to a boil; cook and stir for 1-2 minutes or until thickened.

CREAMED PEAS AND CARROTS

"OMG, I could sit and eat the entire pot of this. It is absolutely delicious. I added a bit of ground cloves."
—mollyque

[2002]

ITALIAN GREEN BEANS

yield: 10 servings   prep: 20 min.
cook: 45 min.

When I was first married, I wasn't a great cook. Twenty years later, I have many dishes I'm proud of, including this family favorite. Basil, oregano and Romano cheese give these beans their Italian accent. I serve them with broiled steak, pork roast, lamb chops or pork chops.

—*Andrea Ibzag, Gordon, Wisconsin*

1	small onion, chopped
2	tablespoons olive oil
2	to 3 garlic cloves, minced
1	can (14-1/2 ounces) stewed tomatoes, coarsely mashed
1/2	cup water
3	tablespoons minced fresh oregano *or* 1 tablespoon dried oregano
4-1/2	teaspoons minced fresh basil *or* 1-1/2 teaspoons dried basil
1	teaspoon sugar
1	teaspoon salt
1/4	to 1/2 teaspoon coarsely ground pepper
2	pounds fresh green beans, cut into 1-inch pieces
2	tablespoons grated Romano cheese

1. In a small saucepan, saute onion in oil until tender. Add garlic; saute 1 minute longer. Add tomatoes, water, oregano, basil, sugar, salt and pepper. Bring to a boil. Reduce heat; simmer, uncovered, for 40 minutes.

2. Meanwhile, place the beans in a large saucepan and cover with water; bring to a boil. Cook, uncovered, for 8-10 minutes or until crisp-tender; drain. Add tomato mixture and cheese; cook for 5 minutes or until heated through.

[2007]

MAPLE-GINGERROOT VEGETABLES

yield: 24 servings   prep: 35 min.
bake: 45 min.

My family loves this recipe because it brings out the lovely flavors of the vegetables. Even my children enjoy it...they love the drizzle of maple syrup! It's a tasty way to introduce kids to turnips, rutabaga and parsnips, too.

—*Kelli Ritz, Innisfail, Alberta*

5	medium parsnips, peeled and sliced
5	small carrots, sliced
3	medium turnips, peeled and cubed
1	large sweet potato, peeled and cubed
1	small rutabaga, peeled and cubed
1	large sweet onion, cut into wedges
1	small red onion, cut into wedges
2	tablespoons olive oil
1	tablespoon minced fresh gingerroot
1	teaspoon salt
1/2	teaspoon pepper
1	cup maple syrup

1. Place the first seven ingredients in a large resealable plastic bag; add the oil, ginger, salt and pepper. Seal bag and shake to coat. Arrange vegetables in a single layer in two 15-in. x 10-in. x 1-in. baking pans coated with cooking spray.

2. Bake vegetables, uncovered, at 425° for 25 minutes, stirring once. Drizzle with the maple syrup. Bake 20-25 minutes longer or until vegetables are tender, stirring once.

[1996]

ITALIAN ZUCCHINI CASSEROLE

yield: 6-8 servings ✿ **prep: 35 min.**
bake: 30 min.

(Pictured on page 849)

Compliments crop up as fast as zucchini vines when folks sample this casserole. Even those who generally don't like zucchini find they enjoy it in this savory side dish.

—*Kimberly Speta, Kennedy, New York*

3 medium zucchini, sliced (about 6-1/2 cups)
3 tablespoons olive oil, *divided*
1 medium onion, sliced
1 garlic clove, minced
1 can (28 ounces) diced tomatoes, undrained
1 tablespoon minced fresh basil *or* 1 teaspoon dried basil
1-1/2 teaspoons minced fresh oregano *or* 1/2 teaspoon dried oregano
1/2 teaspoon garlic salt
1/4 teaspoon pepper
1-1/2 cups stuffing mix
1/2 cup grated Parmesan cheese
3/4 cup shredded part-skim mozzarella cheese

1. In a large skillet, cook zucchini in 1 tablespoon oil 5-6 minutes or until tender; drain and set aside. In the same skillet, saute the onion and garlic in remaining oil for 1 minute. Add the tomatoes, basil, oregano, garlic salt and pepper; simmer, uncovered, for 10 minutes. Remove from the heat; gently stir in zucchini.

2. Place in an greased 13-in. x 9-in. baking dish. Top with stuffing mix; sprinkle with Parmesan cheese. Cover and bake at 350° for 20 minutes. Sprinkle with mozzarella cheese. Bake, uncovered, 10 minutes longer or until cheese is melted.

[2005]

PARTY CARROTS

yield: 8 servings ✿ **prep: 15 min.**
bake: 20 min.

People who don't like carrots often change their minds after tasting this easy-to-fix dish. It's nice for potlucks because you can prepare it ahead of time.

—*Bertha Johnson*
Indianapolis, Indiana, Former Field Editor

2 pounds carrots, sliced
2 teaspoons chicken bouillon granules
8 ounces process cheese (Velveeta), cubed
2 tablespoons butter
1 package (8 ounces) cream cheese, cubed
4 green onions, sliced
1/4 teaspoon salt
1/4 teaspoon pepper

1. Place 1 in. of water in a large saucepan; add carrots and bouillon. Bring to a boil. Reduce heat. Cover and simmer for 7-9 minutes or until crisp-tender.

2. Meanwhile, in another large saucepan, combine the process cheese and butter. Cook and stir over low heat until melted. Add the cream cheese, onions, salt and pepper. Cook and stir until cream cheese is melted.

3. Drain carrots; stir into cheese sauce. Transfer to a greased shallow 2-qt. baking dish. Cover and bake at 350° for 20-25 minutes or until bubbly.

ITALIAN ZUCCHINI CASSEROLE

❝This is a great casserole. I made it for my mom, and she went back for three helpings. She said she was so full she couldn't even touch the chicken I made to accompany it!!❞
—*ProblemChild*

SPAGHETTI SQUASH SUPREME

❝I substituted cheddar for Swiss and also added Parmesan cheese as I didn't find the cheddar to be enough. I also omitted the brown sugar as I didn't care for the sweetness the first time I made it. There are tons of things you can do with this recipe; it's fast and so easy.**❞**
—cmatuse

[1993]

SCALLOPED PINEAPPLE CASSEROLE

yield: 6 servings ∞ prep: 15 min.
bake: 40 min.

My family can't get enough of this sweet and satisfying side dish. This casserole disappears quickly whenever I prepare it.

—*Judy Howle, Columbus, Mississippi*

3/4	cup butter, softened
1-1/4	cups sugar
3	eggs
1	can (20 ounces) crushed pineapple, well drained
1-1/2	teaspoons lemon juice
4	cups firmly packed cubed white bread (crusts removed)

1. In a large bowl, cream butter and sugar until light and fluffy. Add eggs, one at a time, beating well after each addition. Stir in the pineapple and lemon juice. Gently fold in bread cubes.

2. Spoon into a greased 2-qt. baking dish. Bake, uncovered, at 350° for 40 to 45 minutes or until top is lightly golden. Serve warm.

[2005]

SPAGHETTI SQUASH SUPREME

yield: 4 servings ∞ prep/total time: 30 min.

(Pictured on page 856)

I often use the empty squash shells as serving dishes for this unique side dish. The bacon complements the squash and Swiss cheese combination nicely. It's attractive and fun to eat!

—*Jean Williams, Stillwater, Oklahoma*

1	large spaghetti squash (3-1/2 pounds)
4	bacon strips, diced
3	tablespoons butter
1	tablespoon brown sugar
1/2	teaspoon salt
1/4	teaspoon pepper
1/2	cup shredded Swiss cheese

1. Cut squash in half lengthwise; discard the seeds. Place one squash half cut side down on a microwave-safe plate. Cover and microwave on high for 8 minutes or until easily pierced with a fork, turning once. Repeat with the second squash half. When cool enough to handle, scoop out squash, separating strands with a fork; set aside.

2. In a large skillet, cook the bacon over medium heat until crisp. Using a slotted spoon, remove to paper towels; drain, reserving drippings. Add butter, brown sugar, salt and pepper to the drippings. Stir in squash and bacon; heat through. Remove from the heat; stir in cheese just until blended.

[2004]

STEAMED BROCCOLI FLORETS

yield: 6 servings ∞ prep/total time: 15 min.

This delightful, fast-to-fix side dish has a tart mustard vinaigrette that is sure to please. My Aunt Marion was a wonderful cook who gave me many recipes, including this one.

—*Peggy Van Arsdale*
Crosswicks, New Jersey
Former Field Editor

1/4	cup sugar
3	tablespoons cider vinegar
2	tablespoons canola oil
2	tablespoons water
1/2	teaspoon prepared mustard
Dash *each* salt, pepper and ground mustard
1	pound fresh broccoli florets

1. In a small bowl, whisk sugar, vinegar, oil, water, prepared mustard, salt, pepper and ground mustard. Set aside.

2. Place the broccoli in a steamer basket. Place in a saucepan over 1 in. of water; bring to a boil. Cover and steam for 5-8 minutes or until crisp-tender. Place in a serving bowl. Whisk the dressing; drizzle over broccoli and toss to coat.

[2008]

SLOW-COOKED BEAN MEDLEY

yield: 12 servings ∞ **prep: 25 min.** ∞ **cook: 5 hours**

(Pictured on page 856)

I often change the variety of beans in this classic recipe, using whatever I have on hand to total five 15- to 16-ounce cans. The sauce makes any combination delicious! It's a gluten-free side dish that's popular with everyone.

—*Peggy Gwillim, Strasbourg, Saskatchewan, Field Editor*

1-1/2 cups ketchup
2 celery ribs, chopped
1 medium onion, chopped
1 medium green pepper, chopped
1 medium sweet red pepper, chopped
1/2 cup packed brown sugar
1/2 cup water
1/2 cup Italian salad dressing
2 bay leaves
1 tablespoon cider vinegar
1 teaspoon ground mustard
1/8 teaspoon pepper
1 can (16 ounces) kidney beans, rinsed and drained
1 can (15-1/2 ounces) black-eyed peas, rinsed and drained
1 can (15-1/2 ounces) great northern beans, rinsed and drained
1 can (15-1/4 ounces) whole kernel corn, drained
1 can (15-1/4 ounces) lima beans, rinsed and drained
1 can (15 ounces) black beans, rinsed and drained

1. In a 5-qt. slow cooker, combine the first 12 ingredients. Stir in remaining ingredients. Cover and cook on low for 5-6 hours or until the onion and peppers are tender. Discard bay leaves.

Editor's Note: Read all ingredient labels for possible gluten content prior to use. If you're concerned that your brand may contain gluten, contact the company.

[2003]

SOUTHWESTERN ONION RINGS

yield: 8 servings ∞ **prep: 10 min. + soaking**
cook: 10 min.

These light, crispy onion rings are sliced thin and spiced just right with garlic powder, cayenne pepper, chili powder and cumin. My family likes them alongside grilled burgers.

—*Tamra Kriedeman, Enderlin, North Dakota*

2 large sweet onions
2-1/2 cups buttermilk
2 eggs
3 tablespoons water
1-3/4 cups all-purpose flour
2 teaspoons salt
2 teaspoons chili powder
1 to 2 teaspoons cayenne pepper
1 teaspoon sugar
1 teaspoon garlic powder
1 teaspoon ground cumin
Oil for deep-fat frying

1. Cut onions into 1/4-in. slices; separate into rings. Place the slices in a large bowl; cover with buttermilk and soak for 30 minutes, stirring twice.

2. In a shallow dish, beat eggs and water. In another shallow bowl, combine the flour, salt, chili powder, cayenne, sugar, garlic powder and cumin. Drain onion rings; dip in egg mixture, then roll in flour mixture.

3. In an electric skillet or deep-fat fryer, heat 1 in. of oil to 375°. Fry onion rings, a few at a time, for 1 to 1-1/2 minutes on each side or until golden brown. Drain on paper towels.

[2008]
BACON 'N' CHEESE STUFFED POTATOES

yield: 8 servings ∽ prep: 1-1/4 hours ∽ bake: 30 min.

Here's my creamy and rich version of twice-baked potatoes. Always a treat, I used them for my holiday dinners.

—*Merle Dyck, Elkford, British Columbia, Field Editor*

 4   medium baking potatoes
1/4 cup butter, cubed
 1   cup (8 ounces) sour cream
 1   cup (4 ounces) shredded cheddar cheese
 4   bacon strips, cooked and crumbled
 3   to 4 green onions, sliced

1. Bake potatoes at 400° for 1 hour or until tender. Cool slightly. Reduce heat to 350°.

2. Cut each potato in half lengthwise. Scoop out pulp, leaving a thin shell. In a large bowl, mash the pulp with butter. Stir in the sour cream, cheese, bacon and onions. Spoon or pipe into potato shells.

3. Place on a baking sheet. Bake for 30-35 minutes or until heated through.

[1995]
UNSTUFFING SIDE DISH

yield: 8 servings ∽ prep: 15 min. ∽ bake: 40 min.

(Pictured on page 853)

With sausage, mushrooms, celery and the perfect blend of seasonings, this moist dressing is irresistible. I like to call it "Unstuffing" since it bakes separately from the turkey, which I do on the grill.

—*Ken Churches, Kailua-Kona, Hawaii, Field Editor*

1/2 pound bulk Italian sausage
1/4 cup butter
1/2 pound fresh mushrooms, sliced
3/4 cup chopped celery
 1   medium onion, chopped
 1   teaspoon poultry seasoning
1/2 teaspoon salt
1/4 teaspoon pepper

 6   cups unseasoned stuffing croutons
     or dry bread cubes
2-1/2 to 3 cups chicken broth

1. In a large skillet, brown sausage until no longer pink; drain. Add the butter, mushrooms, celery and onion; saute 2-3 minutes or until onion is tender. Stir in the poultry seasoning, salt and pepper. Transfer to a large bowl; add croutons and enough broth to moisten.

2. Place in a greased 2-qt. baking dish. Cover and bake at 350° for 30 minutes. Uncover and bake 10 minutes longer or until browned.

[2001]
COLORFUL VEGGIE COINS

yield: 12-15 servings ∽ prep: 10 min. ∽ bake: 50 min.

(Pictured on page 853)

The "doubloons" in this bright side dish are actually garden treasures! It was a hit on the buffet at our pirate theme party. Once you try the fresh-tasting medley, I predict you'll serve it time and again.

—*Sharon Hanson, Franklin, Tennessee*

 3   medium carrots, thinly sliced
 2   medium yellow summer squash, sliced
 2   medium zucchini, sliced
 1   small head cauliflower, broken
     into florets
 2   garlic cloves, minced
 4   tablespoons butter, *divided*
 1   cup chicken broth
 1   teaspoon salt
1/2 teaspoon white pepper

1. Place carrots, squash and cauliflower in a shallow 3-qt. baking dish; set aside. In a small saucepan, saute the garlic in 2 tablespoons butter for 1 minute. Stir in the broth, salt and pepper. Pour over vegetables; dot with remaining butter.

2. Cover and bake at 350° for 50 minutes or until vegetables are tender.

[2006]

STUFFED GRILLED ZUCCHINI

yield: 4 servings ∞ **prep: 25 min.**
grill: 10 min.

(*Pictured on page 850*)

These zucchini boats taste great with the grilled chops on my favorite menu. I've served them with fish and with other grilled meats. I've also made them in the oven on occasion.

—*Nancy Zimmerman*
Cape May Court House, New Jersey
Field Editor

- 4 medium zucchini
- 5 teaspoons olive oil, *divided*
- 2 tablespoons finely chopped red onion
- 1/4 teaspoon minced garlic
- 1/2 cup dry bread crumbs
- 1/2 cup shredded part-skim mozzarella cheese
- 1 tablespoon minced fresh mint
- 1/2 teaspoon salt
- 3 tablespoons grated Parmesan cheese

1. Cut the zucchini in half lengthwise; scoop out pulp, leaving 1/4-in. shells. Brush with 2 teaspoons oil; set aside. Chop pulp.

2. In a large skillet, saute pulp and onion in remaining oil. Add the garlic; cook 1 minute longer. Add bread crumbs; cook and stir for 2 minutes or until golden brown.

3. Remove from the heat. Stir in the mozzarella cheese, mint and salt. Spoon into the zucchini shells. Sprinkle with Parmesan cheese.

4. Grill, covered, over medium heat for 8-10 minutes or until the zucchini is tender.

[2000]

SPECIAL SQUASH CASSEROLE

yield: 8-10 servings ∞ **prep: 50 min.**
bake: 1 hour

Squash has traditionally been a food our family passes up, but this luscious casserole is an exception to the rule. You won't find it among our Thanksgiving leftovers.

—*Kathleen Cox, Wyoming, Michigan*

- 3 pounds butternut squash, peeled, seeded and cubed
- 3/4 cup 2% milk
- 6 tablespoons butter, melted
- 3 eggs, lightly beaten
- 1/2 teaspoon vanilla extract
- 3/4 cup sugar
- 3 tablespoons all-purpose flour
- 1/2 teaspoon ground cinnamon
- 1/8 teaspoon ground cloves
- 1/8 teaspoon ground nutmeg

TOPPING:
- 1/2 cup crushed vanilla wafers (about 15 wafers)
- 1/4 cup packed brown sugar
- 2 tablespoons butter, melted

1. Place squash in a Dutch oven; cover with water. Bring to a boil; cover and cook for 25-30 minutes or until tender. Drain and place in a large bowl; beat just until smooth.

2. Beat in the milk, butter, eggs and vanilla. Combine the dry ingredients; gradually add to squash mixture and mix well.

3. Transfer to a greased 2-qt. baking dish. Cover and bake at 350° for 45 minutes.

4. Meanwhile, in a small bowl, combine topping ingredients until crumbly; sprinkle over squash. Bake, uncovered, for 12-15 minutes longer or until heated through.

STUFFED GRILLED ZUCCHINI

❝My party guests were apprehensive, but one bite and it was raves and compliments on how delicious this was. My cookouts will now be having a healthy veggie.❞
—*edmondsonsha*

FRUIT-STUFFED ACORN SQUASH

"I loved acorn squash as a child but could not figure out how to cook it as an adult. I found this recipe and tried it. Now my husband loves it, too, and we have it every holiday. The sweet and sour filling adds so much flavor."

—Turtle68

[2006]

WHITE CHEDDAR SCALLOPED POTATOES

yield: 6-8 servings ∽ **prep: 40 min.**
bake: 70 min.

This recipe has evolved over the past eight years. After I added the thyme, ham and sour cream, my husband declared, "This is it!" It can be served as a side or entree. For an entree, I round out the meal with homemade French bread and a salad.

—Hope Toole, Muscle Shoals, Alabama

- 1 medium onion, finely chopped
- 1/4 cup butter, cubed
- 1/4 cup all-purpose flour
- 1 teaspoon dried parsley flakes
- 1 teaspoon salt
- 1/2 teaspoon pepper
- 1/2 teaspoon dried thyme
- 3 cups 2% milk
- 1 can (10-3/4 ounces) condensed cream of mushroom soup, undiluted
- 1 cup (8 ounces) sour cream
- 8 cups thinly sliced peeled potatoes
- 3-1/2 cups cubed fully cooked ham
- 2 cups (8 ounces) shredded white cheddar cheese

1. In a large saucepan, saute onion in butter until tender. Stir in the flour, parsley, salt, pepper and thyme until blended. Gradually add the milk. Bring to a boil; cook and stir for 2 minutes or until thickened. Stir in soup. Remove from the heat; stir in the sour cream until blended.

2. In a large bowl, combine the potatoes and ham. In a greased 13-in. x 9-in. baking dish, layer with half of the potato mixture, cheese and white sauce. Repeat layers.

3. Cover and bake at 375° for 30 minutes. Uncover; bake 40-50 minutes longer or until potatoes are tender.

[2002]

FRUIT-STUFFED ACORN SQUASH

yield: 4 servings ∽ **prep: 15 min.**
bake: 70 min.

(Pictured on page 856)

Holiday meals are even more festive when I serve colorful acorn squash with a fruity filling tucked inside each half. This recipe combines the delightful flavor of winter squash with the season's finest apples and cranberries.

—Peggy West
Georgetown, Delaware, Field Editor

- 2 medium acorn squash
- 1/4 teaspoon salt
- 2 cups chopped tart apples
- 3/4 cup fresh *or* frozen cranberries
- 1/4 cup packed brown sugar
- 2 tablespoons butter, melted
- 1/4 teaspoon ground cinnamon
- 1/8 teaspoon ground nutmeg

1. Cut squash in half; discard seeds. Place squash cut side down in an ungreased 13-in. x 9-in. baking dish. Add 1 in. of hot water to the pan. Bake, uncovered, at 350° for 30 minutes.

2. Drain water from pan; turn squash cut side up. Sprinkle with salt. Combine the remaining ingredients; spoon into squash. Bake 40-50 minutes longer or until squash is tender.

[1994]

FOURTH OF JULY BEAN CASSEROLE

yield: 12 servings ∾ **prep: 20 min.**
bake: 1 hour

The outstanding barbecue taste of these beans makes them a favorite for cookouts all summer and into the fall. It's a popular dish with everyone.

—Donna Fancher, Lawrence, Indiana

1/2	pound bacon strips, diced
1/2	pound ground beef
1	cup chopped onion
1	can (28 ounces) pork and beans
1	can (16 ounces) kidney beans, rinsed and drained
1	can (15-1/4 ounces) lima beans
1/2	cup barbecue sauce
1/2	cup ketchup
1/2	cup sugar
1/2	cup packed brown sugar
2	tablespoons prepared mustard
2	tablespoons molasses
1	teaspoon salt
1/2	teaspoon chili powder

1. In a large skillet, cook the bacon, beef and onion until the meat is no longer pink; drain.

2. Transfer to a greased 2-1/2-qt. baking dish; add all of the beans and mix well. In a small bowl, combine the remaining ingredients; stir into beef and bean mixture.

3. Cover and bake at 350° for 45 minutes. Uncover; bake 15 minutes longer.

[1998]

GREEN BEANS AMANDINE

yield: 6 servings ∾ **prep/total time: 20 min.**
(Pictured on page 849)

It's hard to improve on the taste Mother Nature gives to fresh green beans, but Mom has for years using this recipe. I have always thought the crunchy almonds were a super addition.

—Brenda DuFresne, Midland, Michigan

1	pound fresh *or* frozen green beans, cut into 2-inch pieces
1/2	cup water
1/4	cup slivered almonds
2	tablespoons butter
1	teaspoon lemon juice
1/4	teaspoon seasoned salt, optional

1. Place the beans in a large saucepan and cover with water. Bring to a boil. Cover and cook for 10-15 minutes or until crisp-tender; drain and set aside.

2. In a large skillet, cook the almonds in butter over low heat. Stir in the lemon juice and seasoned salt if desired. Add beans and heat through.

GREEN BEANS AMANDINE

❝A nice change of pace from plain green beans.❞
—plschmitz

HOW TO CHOP AN ONION

1. To quickly chop an onion, peel and cut in half from the root to the top. Leaving root attached, place flat side down on work surface. Cut vertically through the onion, leaving the root end uncut.

2. Cut across the onion, discarding root end. The closer the cuts, the finer the onion will be chopped. This method can also be used for shallots.

EGGPLANT PARMIGIANA

[2007]

EGGPLANT PARMIGIANA

yield: 10-12 servings ∽ **prep: 1-1/4 hours**
bake: 35 min.

This delicious eggplant casserole from my mom makes a wonderful meatless meal or a fabulous side to an Italian menu. It's a resourceful way to use up the eggplant in your garden, and the homemade marinara sauce tastes so good.

—*Valerie Belley, St. Louis, Missouri*

2	medium eggplant, peeled and cut into 1/2-inch slices
2	teaspoons salt
2	large onions, chopped
2	tablespoons minced fresh basil *or* 2 teaspoons dried basil
2	bay leaves
1	tablespoon minced fresh oregano *or* 1 teaspoon dried oregano
1	tablespoon minced fresh thyme *or* 1 teaspoon dried thyme
3	tablespoons olive oil
1	can (14-1/2 ounces) diced tomatoes, undrained
1	can (12 ounces) tomato paste
1	tablespoon honey
1-1/2	teaspoons lemon-pepper seasoning
4	garlic cloves, minced
2	eggs, lightly beaten
1/2	teaspoon pepper
1-1/2	cups dry bread crumbs
1/4	cup butter, *divided*
8	cups (32 ounces) shredded part-skim mozzarella cheese
1	cup grated Parmesan cheese

1. Place eggplant in a colander; sprinkle with salt. Let stand for 30 minutes. Meanwhile, in a large skillet, saute the onions, basil, bay leaves, oregano and thyme in oil until onions are tender.

2. Add the tomatoes, tomato paste, honey and lemon pepper. Bring to a boil. Reduce heat; cover and simmer for 30 minutes. Add the garlic; simmer 10 minutes longer. Discard bay leaves.

3. Rinse the eggplant slices; pat dry with paper towels. In a shallow bowl, combine eggs and pepper; place bread crumbs in another shallow bowl. Dip eggplant into the eggs, then coat with crumbs. Let stand for 5 minutes.

4. In a large skillet, cook half of the eggplant in 2 tablespoons butter for 3 minutes on each side or until lightly browned. Repeat with the remaining eggplant and butter.

5. In each of two greased 11-in. x 7-in. baking dishes, layer half of each of the eggplant, tomato sauce and mozzarella. Repeat layers. Top with Parmesan. Bake, uncovered, at 375° for 35 minutes or until a thermometer reads 160°.

[2011]

HERBED VEGGIE MIX-UP

yield: 5 servings ∽ **prep/total time: 25 min.**
(Pictured on page 853)

A simple treatment of mixed herbs and seasonings brings out the best in this colorful medley of vegetables.

—*Marie Forte*
Raritan, New Jersey, Field Editor

1/2	pound fresh green beans, cut into 1-inch pieces
2	medium carrots, julienned
1/4	cup butter, cubed
1/2	pound sliced fresh mushrooms
1	medium onion, sliced
2	tablespoons minced fresh parsley
1/2	teaspoon salt
1/2	teaspoon dried oregano
1/2	teaspoon dried basil
1/8	teaspoon white pepper

1. Place beans and carrots in a steamer basket; place in a large saucepan over 1 in. of water. Bring to a boil; cover and steam vegetables for 7-10 minutes or until crisp-tender.

2. Meanwhile, in a large skillet, melt the butter. Add mushrooms and onion; saute until tender. Stir in the parsley, salt, oregano, basil, pepper, green beans and carrots; heat through.

[2004]

GRILLED ASPARAGUS MEDLEY

yield: 8 servings ∞ **prep/total time: 25 min.**

This colorful veggie recipe happened by accident. One evening, I didn't have room on the grill for all the things I wanted to prepare, so I threw two of the dishes together and came up with this medley. It goes great with any grilled meat.

—*Pam Gaspers, Hastings, Nebraska*

- 1 **pound fresh asparagus, trimmed**
- 1 *each* **sweet red, yellow and green pepper, julienned**
- 1 **cup sliced fresh mushrooms**
- 1 **medium tomato, chopped**
- 1 **medium onion, sliced**
- 1 **can (2-1/4 ounces) sliced ripe olives, drained**
- 2 **garlic cloves, minced**
- 2 **tablespoons olive oil**
- 1 **teaspoon minced fresh parsley**
- 1/2 **teaspoon salt**
- 1/2 **teaspoon pepper**
- 1/4 **teaspoon lemon-pepper seasoning**
- 1/4 **teaspoon dill weed**

1. In a disposable foil pan, combine the vegetables, olives and garlic; drizzle with oil and toss to coat. Sprinkle with parsley, salt, pepper, lemon pepper and dill; toss to coat.

2. Grill vegetables, covered, over indirect medium heat for 20-25 minutes or until the vegetables are crisp-tender, stirring occasionally.

[2001]

SWEET-SOUR RED CABBAGE

yield: 8-10 servings ∞ **prep: 15 min. cook: 40 min.**

(Pictured on page 852)

This crunchy, eye-catching cooked cabbage dish is seasoned with a flavorful blend of vinegar, spices and bacon. Even when my mom fixes a big batch, the bowl gets emptied quickly.

—*Cathy Eland, Hightstown, New Jersey*

- 1/2 **cup cider vinegar**
- 1/4 **cup sugar**
- 1/4 **cup packed brown sugar**
- 1 **medium head red cabbage, shredded (10 cups)**
- 2 **bacon strips, diced**
- 1 **medium tart apple, peeled and chopped**
- 1/2 **cup chopped onion**
- 1/4 **cup water**
- 2 **tablespoons white wine vinegar**
- 1/2 **teaspoon salt**
- 1/4 **teaspoon pepper**
- 1/8 **teaspoon ground cloves**

1. In a large bowl, stir the cider vinegar and sugars until sugars are dissolved. Add cabbage; toss to coat. Let stand for 5-10 minutes. Meanwhile, in a large skillet, cook bacon over medium heat until crisp. Using a slotted spoon, remove to paper towels to drain.

2. In the drippings, saute apple and onion until tender. Stir in water and cabbage mixture. Bring to a boil. Reduce heat; cover and simmer for 30-35 minutes.

3. Stir in the remaining ingredients. Simmer, uncovered, for 5 minutes or until tender. Sprinkle with reserved bacon just before serving.

GRILLED ASPARAGUS MEDLEY

❝This is absolutely wonderful!! The second time I've made it. I used green pepper and red onion because that is what I had on hand.❞

—*mldicus*

CRUMB-TOPPED BRUSSELS SPROUTS

"I made this recipe on Christmas Day to go with our turkey dinner. I used fresh Brussels sprouts and cut them in half since they were so large. We all agreed that these were the best Brussels sprouts we'd ever had."

—jmkasprak

[1997]

CRUMB-TOPPED BRUSSELS SPROUTS

yield: 4-6 servings prep: 15 min. bake: 20 min.

This recipe makes a flavorful side dish sure to dress up any meal.

—*Ruth Peterson*
Jenison, Michigan, Former Field Editor

1-1/2 | pounds fresh *or* frozen Brussels sprouts
3 | tablespoons butter, melted, *divided*
1/4 | cup Italian-seasoned dry bread crumbs
2 | tablespoons grated Parmesan cheese

---

1. Trim the Brussels sprouts and cut an X in the core of each. Place 1/2 inch water in a large saucepan; add sprouts. Bring to a boil. Reduce heat, cover and simmer for 8-10 minutes or until crisp-tender; drain.

2. Place in an ungreased shallow 1-1/2-qt. baking dish. Drizzle with 2 tablespoons butter. Combine bread crumbs, cheese and remaining butter; sprinkle over Brussels sprouts.

3. Cover and bake at 325° for 10 minutes. Uncover and bake 10 minutes longer.

[1998]

FLAVORFUL SUGAR SNAP PEAS

yield: 8 servings prep/total time: 10 min.

Our family enjoys the first peas from our garden stir-fried for this crisp treat.

—*Connie Moore, Medway, Ohio*

---

1 | pound fresh sugar snap *or* snow peas
1 | tablespoon canola oil
1/2 | cup finely chopped fully cooked ham
1 | garlic clove, minced
1/2 | teaspoon dried thyme
1/8 | teaspoon salt
1/8 | teaspoon pepper

---

1. In a small saucepan, bring 1 in. of water and peas to a boil. Reduce heat; cover and simmer for 3-4 minutes or until crisp-tender.

2. Meanwhile, heat oil in a large skillet; add ham, garlic and thyme. Cook and stir for 2 minutes. Drain peas; add to skillet and saute for 2 minutes or until tender. Season with salt and pepper.

PREPARING BRUSSELS SPROUTS

Remove any loose or yellowed outer leaves; trim stem end. Rinse sprouts. When cooking Brussels sprouts whole, cut an X in the core end with a sharp knife.

[2004]

OVERNIGHT ASPARAGUS STRATA

yield: 6-8 servings ∽ **prep: 15 min. + chilling
bake: 40 min. + standing**

*I've made this tasty egg dish for breakfast,
brunch and even as a Christmas dinner side
dish. With its English muffin crust, this is not
your run-of-the-mill strata. Friends always ask
for the recipe.*

—Lynn Licata, Sylvania, Ohio

1	pound fresh asparagus, trimmed and cut into 1-inch pieces
4	English muffins, split and toasted
2	cups (8 ounces) shredded Colby-Monterey Jack cheese, *divided*
1	cup cubed fully cooked ham
1/2	cup chopped sweet red pepper
8	eggs, lightly beaten
2	cups 2% milk
1	teaspoon salt
1	teaspoon ground mustard
1/4	teaspoon pepper

1. In a large saucepan, bring 8 cups water to a boil. Add the asparagus; cover and cook for 3 minutes. Drain; immediately place asparagus in ice water. Drain and pat dry.

2. Arrange six English muffin halves, cut side up, in a greased 13-in. x 9-in. baking dish. Fill in the spaces with the remaining muffin halves. Layer with 1 cup cheese, asparagus, ham and red pepper.

3. In a small bowl, whisk eggs, milk, salt, mustard and pepper; pour over muffins. Cover and refrigerate overnight.

4. Remove strata from the refrigerator 30 minutes before baking. Sprinkle with the remaining cheese.

5. Bake, uncovered, at 375° for 40-45 minutes or until a knife inserted near the center comes out clean. Let stand for 5 minutes before cutting.

[1994]

OVEN PARMESAN CHIPS

**yield: 4-6 servings
prep/total time: 25 min.**

(Pictured on page 852)

*My husband and I avoid fried foods, but
potatoes are part of our menu almost every
day. These delectable sliced potatoes get nice
and crispy, and give our meals a likable lift.*

—Mary Lou Kelly, Scottdale, Pennsylvania

4	medium baking potatoes
1/4	cup butter, melted
1	tablespoon finely chopped onion
1/2	teaspoon salt
1/8	teaspoon pepper
Dash paprika	
2	tablespoons grated Parmesan cheese

1. Cut the potatoes into 1/4-in. slices; place on a greased baking sheet in a single layer. Combine butter, onion, salt, pepper and paprika; brush on one side of potatoes, then turn and brush other side.

2. Bake, uncovered, at 425° for 15-20 minutes or until potatoes are tender and golden. Sprinkle with cheese.

OVEN PARMESAN CHIPS

"I make this recipe often. However, I put the butter, onion and spices in my food processor and then toss the potatoes in the mixure—faster than brushing!"
—JillandLea

[2009]

EVERYTHING STUFFING

yield: 9 servings ∞ **prep: 30 min.**
cook: 3 hours

My husband and father go crazy for this stuffing! It also freezes well so we can enjoy it even after Thanksgiving.

—*Bette Votral, Bethlehem, Pennsylvania*

1/2	pound bulk Italian sausage
4	cups seasoned stuffing cubes
1-1/2	cups crushed corn bread stuffing
1/2	cup chopped toasted chestnuts *or* pecans
1/2	cup minced fresh parsley
1	tablespoon minced fresh sage *or* 1 teaspoon rubbed sage
1/8	teaspoon salt
1/8	teaspoon pepper
1-3/4	cups sliced baby portobello mushrooms
1	package (5 ounces) sliced fresh shiitake mushrooms
1	large onion, chopped
1	medium apple, peeled and chopped
1	celery rib, chopped
3	tablespoons butter
1	can (14-1/2 ounces) chicken broth

1. In a large skillet, cook the sausage over medium heat until no longer pink; drain. Transfer to a large bowl. Stir in the stuffing cubes, corn bread stuffing, chestnuts, parsley, sage, salt and pepper.

2. In the same skillet, saute mushrooms, onion, apple and celery in butter until tender. Stir into the stuffing mixture. Add enough broth to reach desired moistness. Transfer to a 5-qt. slow cooker. Cover and cook on low for 3 hours, stirring once.

[2008]

SMOKY GRILLED CORN

yield: 6 servings ∞ **prep: 25 min.**
grill: 10 min.

(*Pictured on page 854*)

A friend and I cooked up this corn one evening when getting ready to grill. The buttery corn, with its sweet-spicy seasoning, won top honors over our steaks.

—*Linda Landers, Kalispell, Montana*

2	tablespoons plus 1-1/2 teaspoons butter
1/2	cup honey
2	large garlic cloves, minced
2	tablespoons hot pepper sauce
1/2	teaspoon salt
1/4	teaspoon pepper
1/4	teaspoon paprika
6	medium ears sweet corn, husks removed

1. In a small saucepan, melt the butter. Stir in the honey, garlic, pepper sauce and seasonings until blended; heat through. Brush over corn.

2. Moisten a paper towel with cooking oil; using long-handled tongs, lightly coat the grill rack.

3. Grill the corn, covered, over medium heat for 10-12 minutes or until the corn is tender, turning and basting occasionally with the butter mixture. Serve the corn with any remaining butter mixture.

[1997]

CHEESY POTATO BAKE

yield: 6-8 servings ∞ **prep: 15 min.**
bake: 1 hour

(Pictured on page 852)

This saucy side dish satisfies even hearty appetites. It's easy to fix since there's no need to peel the potatoes. The mild, comforting flavor goes nicely with any meat.

—*Michelle Beran, Claflin, Kansas*

---

4 large unpeeled baking potatoes
1/4 cup butter, cubed
1 tablespoon grated onion
1 teaspoon salt
1/2 teaspoon dried thyme
1/8 teaspoon pepper
1 cup (4 ounces) shredded cheddar cheese
1 tablespoon chopped fresh parsley

---

1. Thinly slice the potatoes and place in a greased shallow 2-qt. baking dish. In a small skillet, melt the butter; stir in the onion, salt, thyme and pepper until onion is coated with butter.

2. Spoon over potatoes. Cover and bake at 425° for 45 minutes or until potatoes are tender. Sprinkle with cheese and parsley. Bake, uncovered, 15 minutes longer or until cheese is melted.

[2000]

CREAMY SPINACH BAKE

yield: 10 servings ∞ **prep: 20 min.**
bake: 30 min.

When my brother, sisters and I were growing up, our mom knew how to get us to eat our spinach. This casserole has a rich creamy sauce, french-fried onions and a cracker crumb topping. Who can resist?

—*Debra Falkiner, St. Charles, Missouri*

---

2 packages (8 ounces *each*) cream cheese, softened
2 cans (10-3/4 ounces *each*) condensed cream of mushroom soup, undiluted
4 packages (10 ounces *each*) frozen chopped spinach, thawed and well drained
2 cans (2.8 ounces *each*) french-fried onions
2/3 cup crushed saltines (about 16 crackers)
1/4 cup butter, melted

---

1. In a large bowl, beat the cream cheese until smooth. Beat in the soup. Stir in spinach and onions.

2. Transfer to a greased 2-1/2-qt. baking dish. Combine cracker crumbs and butter; sprinkle over spinach mixture. Bake, uncovered, at 325° for 30-35 minutes or until heated through.

CREAMY SPINACH BAKE

❝I love spinach, and this is one of my favorite spinach dishes. It's very rich.❞
—*NDGirl77*

SQUEEZING SPINACH DRY

Drain spinach in a colander. If spinach was cooked, allow to cool. With clean hands, squeeze the water out of the spinach.

[1995]

MOM'S PICKLED BEETS

yield: 6 servings ∽ prep: 5 min. ∽ cook: 10 min. + chilling

Zesty and fresh-tasting, these bright, beautiful beet slices add spark to any meal. My mouth still begins to water when I think of how wonderful they tasted when my mother prepared them.

—Mildred Sherrer, Fort Worth, Texas, Former Field Editor

- 3/4 cup sugar
- 3/4 cup white vinegar
- 3/4 cup water
- 1-1/2 teaspoons salt
- 3/4 to 1 teaspoon pepper
- 1 large onion, thinly sliced
- 2 cans (13-1/4 ounces *each*) sliced beets, undrained

Sliced green onions, optional

1. In a large saucepan, combine the first six ingredients; bring to a boil. Reduce heat; cover and simmer for 5 minutes. Remove from the heat; add beets. let stand at room temperature for 1 hour. Transfer to a large bowl.

2. Cover and chill 6 hours or overnight. Garnish with green onions if desired.

[1993]

CRUNCHY SWEET POTATO CASSEROLE

yield: 6 servings ∽ prep: 15 min. ∽ bake: 25 min.

(Pictured on page 851)

Some tasty seasonings, such as cinnamon and nutmeg, and a crunchy cornflake and walnut topping make it easy for even kids to eat their nutritious sweet potatoes. This is a terrific Thanksgiving side dish.

—Virginia Slater
West Sunbury, Pennsylvania, Former Field Editor

- 2 cups mashed sweet potatoes
- 1/2 cup butter, melted
- 1/4 cup sugar
- 1/4 cup packed brown sugar
- 2 eggs, lightly beaten

- 1/2 cup 2% milk
- 1 teaspoon ground cinnamon
- 1/2 teaspoon ground nutmeg

TOPPING:

- 1 cup crushed cornflakes
- 1/2 cup chopped walnuts
- 1/4 cup packed brown sugar
- 1/4 cup butter, cubed

1. In a large bowl, combine the first eight ingredients. Spoon into a greased 1-1/2-qt. baking dish. Bake, uncovered, at 375° for 20 minutes or until a thermometer reads 160°.

2. Combine the topping ingredients; sprinkle over potatoes. Bake 5-10 minutes longer or until the topping is lightly browned.

[2006]

SWEET 'N' TANGY CARROTS

yield: 6-8 servings ∽ prep/total time: 20 min.

(Pictured on page 851)

I dress up carrots with a brown sugar and mustard sauce as a side dish for my New Year's meal. Garnished with a little bright green parsley, the carrots add color to the dinner plate.

—Paula Zsiray, Logan, Utah, Field Editor

- 2 pounds carrots, sliced
- 1/4 teaspoon salt
- 1/2 cup packed brown sugar
- 3 tablespoons butter
- 2 tablespoons Dijon mustard
- 1/4 teaspoon white pepper
- 2 tablespoons minced fresh parsley

1. Place 1 in. of water, carrots and salt in a large saucepan; bring to a boil. Reduce heat; cover and simmer for 15-20 minutes or until tender. Drain.

2. Return the carrots to pan; add the brown sugar, butter, mustard and pepper. Cook and stir over low heat until well coated. Sprinkle with the parsley. Serve with a slotted spoon.

[2005]

TRIPLE-CHEESE BROCCOLI PUFF

**yield: 6-8 servings ∞ prep: 15 min.
bake: 50 min. + standing**

This rich-tasting side is a must for our Christmas morning menu. Like any puffy souffle, it will settle a bit after you remove the dish from the oven, but the pretty golden top is very attractive. I often toss in some cubed ham.

—*Maryellen Hays
Wolcottville, Indiana
Former Field Editor*

---

  1 **cup sliced fresh mushrooms**
  1 **tablespoon butter**
  1 **package (3 ounces) cream cheese, softened**
  6 **eggs**
  1 **cup 2% milk**
3/4 **cup biscuit/baking mix**
  3 **cups frozen chopped broccoli, thawed**
  2 **cups (8 ounces) shredded Monterey Jack cheese**
  1 **cup (8 ounces) 4% cottage cheese**
1/4 **teaspoon salt**

---

1. In a small skillet, saute mushrooms in butter until tender; set aside. In a large bowl, beat cream cheese, eggs, milk and biscuit mix just until combined. Stir in broccoli, cheeses, salt and mushrooms.

2. Pour into a greased round 2-1/2-qt. baking dish. Bake the puff, uncovered, at 350° for 50-60 minutes or until a thermometer reads 160°. Let stand for 10 minutes before serving.

[2003]

HERBED NEW POTATOES

**yield: 2 servings ∞ prep: 15 min.
cook: 20 min.**

I make these potatoes often for my husband and me. They're easy to prepare and have a nice dill flavor. We eagerly await the start of farmers market season to get garden-fresh new potatoes.

—*Vi Neiding, South Milwaukee, Wisconsin*

3/4 **pound small red potatoes**
  1 **tablespoon butter, softened**
  1 **tablespoon sour cream**
  2 **teaspoons snipped fresh dill** *or* **1/2 teaspoon dill weed**
  2 **teaspoons minced chives**
1/4 **teaspoon salt**
1/8 **teaspoon pepper**
Dash lemon juice

---

1. Remove a strip of peel from the middle of each potato. Place the potatoes in a saucepan and cover with water. Bring to a boil over medium heat. Reduce the heat; cover and simmer for 15-20 minutes or until tender.

2. In a small bowl, combine remaining ingredients. Drain potatoes; add butter mixture and toss gently.

TRIPLE-CHEESE BROCCOLI PUFF

"This is a delicious, easy, make-ahead recipe. I will definitely make it again."
—*JudithRN3*

SNIPPING DILL & CHIVES

To easily snip the dill and chives, use a kitchen shears instead of a knife and cutting board.

—*Test Kitchen Cooking Experts*

[1997]

TWICE-BAKED NEW POTATOES

yield: about 2 dozen ∞ prep: 70 min.
broil: 10 min.

I've used these rich potatoes as both an appetizer and side dish. Guests seem to enjoy the distinctive taste of Monterey Jack cheese and basil. These satisfying mouthfuls are perfect for a late-afternoon or evening get-together when something a little heartier is needed.

—*Susan Herbert, Aurora, Illinois*

1-1/2 pound small red potatoes
   2 to 3 tablespoons canola oil
   1 cup (4 ounces) shredded Monterey Jack cheese
  1/2 cup sour cream
   1 package (3 ounces) cream cheese, softened
  1/3 cup finely chopped green onions
   1 teaspoon dried basil
   1 garlic clove, minced
  1/2 teaspoon salt
  1/4 to 1/2 teaspoon pepper
  1/2 pound sliced bacon, cooked and crumbled

---

1. Pierce the potatoes; rub skins with oil. Place in a baking pan. Bake, uncovered, at 400° for 50 minutes or until potatoes are tender. Cool.

2. In a large bowl, combine the Monterey Jack cheese, sour cream, cream cheese, onions, basil, garlic, salt and pepper.

3. Cut potatoes in half; carefully scoop out pulp, leaving thin shells. Add the pulp to the cheese mixture and mash; stir in the bacon. Spoon or pipe into potato shells.

4. Place on a baking sheet. Broil 4-6 in. from the heat for 7-8 minutes or until heated through.

TWICE-BAKED NEW POTATOES

"I was eating it out of the bowl, it was so good."
—*laaalaala_13*

[2008]

ONION YORKSHIRE PUDDINGS

yield: 8 servings ∞ prep: 20 min.
bake: 30 min.

(*Pictured on page 849*)

A cross between traditional Yorksire pudding and popovers, this easy recipe makes a great complement to prime rib. We also like it with beef stew and steak. Make more than you need because everyone loves them.

—*Emily Chaney*
Blue Hill, Maine, Field Editor

  1/2 pound yellow onions, thinly sliced
   1 teaspoon salt, *divided*
  1/4 teaspoon pepper
   2 tablespoons butter
  3/4 cup plus 2 tablespoons all-purpose flour
   2 eggs
  3/4 cup water
  3/4 cup 2% milk

---

1. In a large skillet, saute the onions, 1/2 teaspoon salt and pepper in butter until tender but not browned. Divide among eight 6-oz. ramekins or custard cups. Place on a baking sheet.

2. In a large bowl, combine the flour and remaining salt. Whisk the eggs, water and milk; whisk into the flour mixture just until blended. Pour 1/4 cup into each ramekin.

3. Bake at 400° for 30-35 minutes or until pudding is puffed and golden brown. Serve immediately.

[2003]

SUNDAY DINNER MASHED POTATOES

yield: 8 servings ∞ **prep: 35 min.** ∞
bake: 20 min.

Sour cream and cream cheese add delicious dairy flavors to these potatoes. They're special enough to serve guests and can be prepared in advance. Since I'm a busy mother, that's a convenience I appreciate.

—Melody Mellinger
Myerstown, Pennsylvania, Field Editor

---

5 pounds potatoes, peeled and cubed
1 cup (8 ounces) sour cream
2 packages (3 ounces *each*) cream
   cheese, softened
3 tablespoons butter, *divided*
1 teaspoon salt
1 teaspoon onion salt
1/4 teaspoon pepper

---

1. Place potatoes in a Dutch oven; cover with water. Cover and bring to a boil. Cook for 20-25 minutes or until very tender; drain well.

2. In a large bowl, mash the potatoes. Add the sour cream, cream cheese, 2 tablespoons butter, salt, onion salt and pepper; beat until fluffy.

3. Transfer to a greased 2-qt. baking dish. Dot with the remaining butter. Bake, uncovered, at 350° for 20-25 minutes or until heated through.

[2008]

CREAMED CORN WITH BACON

yield: 6 servings ∞ **prep/total time: 25 min.**

My family is addicted to this yummy, crunchy side. I like to make it in the summer with farm-fresh corn!

—Tina Repak Mirilovich
Johnstown, Pennsylvania, Field Editor

---

1 small onion, finely chopped
1 tablespoon butter
4 cups fresh *or* frozen corn, thawed
1 cup heavy whipping cream
1/4 cup chicken broth
4 bacon strips, cooked and crumbled
1/4 teaspoon pepper
1/4 cup grated Parmesan cheese
2 tablespoons minced fresh parsley

---

1. In a large skillet, saute onion in butter for 3 minutes. Add the corn; saute 1-2 minutes longer or until onion and corn are tender.

2. Stir in the cream, broth, bacon and pepper. Cook and stir for 5-7 minutes or until slightly thickened. Stir in the cheese and parsley.

SUNDAY DINNER MASHED POTATOES

"Wow, these are great! If you're going to go through the trouble of making real mashed potatoes (as opposed to instant), then use this recipe! It's so creamy and not too salty. I used reduced-fat sour cream and reduced-fat cream cheese, and these turned out perfect."
—kdhcooks

CUTTING KERNELS FROM FRESH CORN

Stand one end of the cob on a cutting board. Starting at the top, run a sharp knife down the cob, cutting deeply to remove whole kernels. One medium cob yields 1/3 to 1/2 cup kernels.

[2009]

CURRIED SWEET
POTATO LATKES

yield: 24 latkes ∞ **prep: 20 min.**
cook: 10 min./batch

*I first tasted these at a Hanukkah party in
Pueblo, Colorado. The first bite got me hooked.
I love this unusual take on potato latkes.*

—*Rachel Garcia*
Arlington, Virginia, Field Editor

1/2 **cup all-purpose flour**
  2 **teaspoons sugar**
  2 **teaspoons curry powder**
  1 **teaspoon baking powder**
  1 **teaspoon brown sugar**
  1 **teaspoon ground cumin**
3/4 **teaspoon salt**
1/2 **teaspoon cayenne pepper**
1/4 **teaspoon pepper**
  2 **eggs, lightly beaten**
1/2 **cup 2% milk**
  4 **cups grated peeled sweet potatoes**
Oil for frying

---

1. In a small bowl, combine the first nine
   ingredients. Stir in the eggs and milk
   until blended. Add the sweet potatoes;
   toss to coat.

2. Heat oil in a large nonstick skillet over
   medium heat. Drop batter by heaping
   tablespoonfuls into oil; press lightly to

flatten. Fry for 3-5 minutes on each
side or until golden brown, adding oil
as needed. Drain on paper towels.

[1994]

SUGARED ASPARAGUS

yield: 4-6 servings
prep/total time: 30 min.

*When my husband and I moved from
Oklahoma to Rio Grande Valley in Texas
years ago, I gained an appreciation for a
variety of fresh vegetables. This tasty recipe is a
simple way to dress up one of our favorites.*

—*Billie Moss*
Walnut Creek, California, Field Editor

---

  3 **tablespoons butter**
  2 **tablespoons brown sugar**
  2 **pounds fresh asparagus, cut into
     2-inch pieces (about 4 cups)**
  1 **cup chicken broth**

---

1. In a large skillet over medium-high,
   heat butter and brown sugar until
   sugar is dissolved. Add asparagus;
   saute for 2 minutes. Stir in chicken
   broth; bring to a boil. Reduce heat;
   cover and simmer for 8-10 minutes or
   until asparagus is crisp-tender.

2. Remove the asparagus to a serving
   dish and keep warm. Cook sauce,
   uncovered, until reduced by half. Pour
   over the asparagus.

CLEANING ASPARAGUS

To prepare asparagus, rinse stalks well in cold water. Snap
off the stalk ends as far down as they will easily break
when gently bent, or cut off the tough white portion. If
stalks are large, use a vegetable peeler to gently peel the
tough area of the stalk from the end to just below the tip.
If tips are large, scrape off scales with a knife.

[2003]

CARROT BROCCOLI CASSEROLE

yield: 6-8 servings ∾ prep: 25 min.
bake: 35 min.

This colorful side dish feels right at home with any entree. The veggies are coated in a buttery cheese sauce, then layered with cracker crumbs. Even kids who turn up their noses at broccoli will eat this up.

—*Nancy Horsburgh*
Everett, Ontario, Field Editor

---

  1   package (16 ounces) baby carrots
1-1/2 pounds fresh broccoli, chopped *or* 6 cups frozen chopped broccoli, thawed
  8   ounces process cheese (Velveeta), cubed
3/4 cup butter, *divided*
1-3/4 cups crushed butter-flavored crackers (about 40 crackers)

---

1. Place 1 in. of water in a saucepan; add carrots. Bring to a boil. Reduce heat; cover and simmer for 5-8 minutes or until crisp-tender. Add the broccoli; cover and simmer 6-8 minutes longer or until vegetables are crisp-tender. Drain and set aside.

2. In a small saucepan, cook and stir the cheese and 1/4 cup butter until smooth. Stir in broccoli and carrots until combined.

3. Melt the remaining butter; toss with cracker crumbs. Sprinkle a third of the mixture in a greased 2-1/2-qt. baking dish. Top with half of the vegetable mixture. Repeat layers. Sprinkle with remaining crumb mixture.

4. Bake, uncovered, at 350° for 35-40 minutes or until heated through.

[2008]

SWEET & SOUR BRUSSELS SPROUTS

yield: 16 servings ∾ prep: 10 min.
cook: 25 min.

(*Pictured on page 851*)

This side dish has a nice sweet-and-sour balance, and bacon adds a tasty accent. Sprout lovers will definitely approve of this flavorful treatment.

—*Barbara McCalley*
Allison Park, Pennsylvania, Field Editor

1/2 pound sliced bacon, diced
  4   packages (16 ounces *each*) frozen Brussels sprouts, thawed
  1   medium onion, finely chopped
1/3 cup cider vinegar
  3   tablespoons sugar
1-1/2 teaspoons salt
1/2 teaspoon ground mustard
1/8 teaspoon pepper

---

1. In a Dutch oven, cook the bacon over medium heat until crisp. Using a slotted spoon, remove the bacon to paper towels to drain.

2. In the drippings, saute Brussels sprouts and onion until crisp-tender. Add the vinegar, sugar, salt, mustard and pepper. Bring to a boil. Reduce heat; cover and simmer for 4-5 minutes or until sprouts are tender. Stir in bacon.

CARROT BROCCOLI CASSEROLE

❝This is wonderful! I take it to every holiday, and the kids (and adults) love it. It's super easy to make.❞
—*WendiLynne*

[1995]

GARDEN CASSEROLE
yield: 12 servings
prep: 25 min. + standing ∞ **bake: 20 min.**

*This delicious cheesy casserole uses lots of
veggies and herbs from my garden. The dish
includes a sunny medley of eggplant, zucchini
and tomatoes.*

—*Phyllis Hickey*
Bedford, New Hampshire
Former Field Editor

---

  2 **pounds eggplant, peeled**
  5 **teaspoons salt,** *divided*
1/4 **cup olive oil**
  2 **medium onions, finely chopped**
  2 **medium zucchini, sliced 1/2 inch thick**
  2 **garlic cloves, minced**
  5 **medium tomatoes, peeled
and chopped**
  2 **celery ribs, sliced**
1/4 **cup minced fresh parsley**
1/4 **cup minced fresh basil** *or*
    1 tablespoon dried basil
1/2 **teaspoon pepper**
1/2 **cup grated Romano cheese**
  1 **cup seasoned bread crumbs**
  2 **tablespoons butter, melted**
  1 **cup (4 ounces) shredded part-skim
mozzarella cheese**

---

1. Cut eggplant into 1/2-in. thick slices;
sprinkle both sides with 3 teaspoons
salt. Place in a deep dish; cover and let
stand for 30 minutes. Rinse with cold
water; drain and dry on paper towels.

2. Cut the eggplant into 1/2-in. cubes.
Transfer to a large skillet; saute in oil
until lightly browned. Add the onions
and zucchini; cook 3 minutes. Add the
garlic; cook 1 minute longer. Add the
tomatoes, celery, parsley, basil, pepper
and remaining salt; bring to boil.
Reduce heat; cover and simmer for 10
minutes. Remove from the heat; stir in
Romano cheese.

3. Pour vegetable mixture into a greased
13-in. x 9-in. baking dish. Combine the
crumbs and butter; sprinkle on top.
Bake, uncovered, at 375° for 15 minutes.
Sprinkle with mozzarella cheese. Bake
5 minutes longer or until the cheese
is melted.

[2003]

MARINATED MUSHROOMS
yield: 4 cups ∞ **prep: 15 min. + marinating**

*This is a nice way to serve mushrooms as an
appetizer, and it also makes a great side dish
for any type of meat. Sometimes I add these
tangy mushrooms to salads for extra flavor.*

—*Brenda Snyder, Hesston, Pennsylvania*

---

  2 **pounds fresh mushrooms**
  1 **envelope (.7 ounce) Italian salad
dressing mix**
  1 **cup water**
1/2 **cup olive oil**
1/3 **cup cider vinegar**
  2 **tablespoons lemon juice**
  1 **tablespoon sugar**
  1 **tablespoon minced fresh parsley**
  1 **tablespoon reduced-sodium soy sauce**
  2 **teaspoons crushed red pepper flakes**
  3 **garlic cloves, minced**
1/2 **teaspoon salt**
1/8 **teaspoon pepper**

---

1. Remove mushroom stems (discard or
save for another use). Place caps in a
large saucepan and cover with water.
Bring to a boil. Reduce heat; cook for
3 minutes, stirring occasionally. Drain
and cool.

2. In a small bowl, whisk salad dressing
mix, water, oil, vinegar, lemon juice,
sugar and seasonings.

3. Place mushrooms in a large bowl; add
dressing and stir to coat. Cover and
refrigerate for 8 hours or overnight.

ITALIAN ZUCCHINI CASSEROLE, page 829

ONION YORKSHIRE PUDDINGS, page 844

GREEN BEANS AMANDINE, page 835

STUFFED GRILLED ZUCCHINI, page 833

SWEET & SOUR BRUSSELS SPROUTS, page 847

SWEET 'N' TANGY CARROTS, page 842

CRUNCHY SWEET POTATO CASSEROLE, page 842

SWEET-SOUR RED CABBAGE, page 837

OVEN PARMESAN CHIPS, page 839

CHEESY POTATO BAKE, page 841

COLORFUL VEGGIE COINS, page 832

UNSTUFFING SIDE DISH, page 832

COLORFUL VEGGIE BAKE, page 859

HERBED VEGGIE MIX-UP, page 836

CREAMED PEAS AND CARROTS, page 827

SMOKY GRILLED CORN, page 840

CHERRY TOMATO MOZZARELLA SAUTE, page 857

FRUIT-STUFFED ACORN SQUASH, page 834

SPAGHETTI SQUASH SUPREME, page 830

SLOW-COOKED BEAN MEDLEY, page 831

[1994]

BLACK-EYED PEAS WITH BACON

yield: 6-8 servings   prep: 10 min. + standing
cook: 35 min.

*A real Southern favorite, black-eyed peas are traditionally
served on New Year's Day to bring good luck. My mother's recipe
with bacon, garlic and thyme makes them extra special.*

—*Ruby Williams, Bogalusa, Louisiana, Former Field Editor*

- 1   pound dried black-eyed peas, rinsed and sorted
- 1/2 pound bacon, cooked and crumbled
- 1   large onion, chopped
- 1   tablespoon butter
- 1   garlic clove, minced
- 1/2 teaspoon dried thyme

Salt to taste
Additional crumbled bacon, optional

1. In a large Dutch oven, place peas, bacon and enough
   water to cover; bring to a boil. Boil for 2 minutes.
   Remove from the heat; cover and let stand for 1 hour.
   Do not drain.

2. In a small skillet, saute onion in butter until tender.
   Add garlic; cook 1 minute longer. Stir in thyme and
   salt; add to pea mixture. Return to the heat; simmer,
   covered, for 30 minutes or until peas are soft. Top
   with crumbled bacon if desired.

[2012]

THAI VEGETABLES

yield: 8 servings   prep: 25 min.   cook: 10 min.

*Add some zip to a meal with this spicy dish—a contrast of crispy
and tender vegetables in a spicy sauce over rich and creamy
coconut rice. You won't believe it's low in calories!*

—*Melody Savage, Lawrence, Kansas*

- 2   cups cut fresh green beans
- 2   cups fresh asparagus, trimmed
- 1   cup sliced fresh mushrooms
- 1   medium sweet red pepper, julienned
- 1   medium carrot, julienned
- 1   tablespoon sesame oil

- 3   green onions, chopped
- 2   garlic cloves, minced
- 1-1/2 teaspoons minced fresh gingerroot
- 1/4 teaspoon crushed red pepper flakes
- 1/4 cup roasted peanuts, chopped

1. In a large saucepan, bring 5 cups water to a boil. Add
   beans and asparagus; cover and cook for 2 minutes.
   Drain and immediately place vegetables in ice water.
   Drain and pat dry.

2. In a large skillet or wok, stir-fry mushrooms, pepper
   and carrot in oil for 4 minutes. Add the onions, garlic,
   ginger and pepper flakes; cook until vegetables are
   crisp-tender.

3. Add the beans and asparagus; heat through. Sprinkle
   with peanuts.

[2007]

CHERRY TOMATO MOZZARELLA SAUTE

yield: 4 servings   prep/total time: 25 min.

(Pictured on page 855)

*Fast to fix and full of flavor, this warm, refreshing side dish
makes the most of cherry tomatoes, pairing them with fresh
mozarella cubes and seasoning with thyme.*

—*Summer Jones, Pleasant Grove, Utah*

- 1/4 cup chopped shallots
- 1   teaspoon minced fresh thyme
- 2   teaspoons olive oil
- 1   garlic clove, minced
- 2-1/2 cups cherry tomatoes, halved
- 1/4 teaspoon salt
- 1/4 teaspoon pepper
- 4   ounces fresh mozzarella cheese, cut into 1/2-inch cubes

1. In a large skillet, saute the shallots and thyme in oil
   until tender. Add garlic; cook 1 minute longer. Add
   tomatoes, salt and pepper; heat through. Remove from
   the heat; stir in the cheese.

BAKED BROCCOLINI

❝This was SO delicious. My neighborhood grocery doesn't have Broccolini, so I used broccoli florets for this. I wanted to eat the entire pan! I will make this again and will probably try it with cauliflower.❞

—lizardstew1

[2001]

BREADED EGGPLANT SLICES

yield: 4 servings 〜 prep/total time: 25 min.

These crisp golden rounds are a fun and different way to serve eggplant. Even folks who aren't fond of eggplant like it fixed this way."

—*Phyllis Schmalz, Kansas City, Kansas*

- 1 medium eggplant (about 1 pound)
- 1/2 cup dry bread crumbs
- 1/4 cup grated Parmesan cheese
- 1 bottle (8 ounces) fat-free Italian salad dressing

1. Cut eggplant into 1/2-in. slices. In a shallow bowl, combine bread crumbs and cheese. Place the salad dressing in another bowl. Dip the eggplant into salad dressing, then coat with the crumb mixture.

2. Arrange in a single layer on baking sheets coated with cooking spray. Bake at 450° for 6-8 minutes on each side or until golden brown.

[2009]

MAKEOVER FANCY BEAN CASSEROLE

yield: 6 servings 〜 prep: 15 min.
bake: 35 min.

My daughter gave me this wonderful recipe, and I've since shared it with many of my friends. This lightened-up version retains all its crunchy, creamy goodness.

—*Venola Sharpe, Campbellsville, Kentucky*

- 3 cups frozen French-style green beans, thawed
- 1 can (10-3/4 ounces) reduced-fat reduced-sodium condensed cream of chicken soup, undiluted
- 1-1/2 cups frozen corn, thawed
- 1 can (8 ounces) sliced water chestnuts, drained

- 1 medium onion, chopped
- 1/2 cup reduced-fat sour cream
- 1/4 cup cubed reduced-fat process cheese (Velveeta)
- 5 teaspoons reduced-fat butter
- 1/3 cup crushed butter-flavored crackers
- 2 tablespoons slivered almonds

1. In a large bowl, combine the first seven ingredients. Transfer to an 11-in. x 7-in. baking dish coated with cooking spray.

2. In a small skillet, melt butter. Add the cracker crumbs and almonds; cook and stir until lightly browned. Sprinkle over the top.

3. Bake, uncovered, at 350° for 35-40 minutes or until heated through and topping is golden brown.

Editor's Note: This recipe was tested with Land O'Lakes light stick butter.

[2010]

BAKED BROCCOLINI

yield: 4 servings 〜 prep/total time: 15 min.

Broccoli is my favorite vegetable, but I heard about Broccolini and wanted to try it out. This is really tasty, and I think kids will love it.

—*Katie Helliwell, Hinsdale, Illinois*

- 3/4 pound Broccolini *or* broccoli spears
- 2 tablespoons lemon juice
- 2 tablespoons olive oil
- 1/2 teaspoon salt
- 1/8 teaspoon pepper

1. Place the Broccolini in a greased 15-in. x 10-in. x 1-in. baking pan. Combine the lemon juice, oil, salt and pepper; drizzle over the Broccolini and toss to coat.

2. Bake the Broccolini, uncovered, at 425° for 10-15 minutes or until tender, stirring occasionally.

[2008]

RUSTIC ROASTED VEGETABLE TART

yield: 8 servings ∞ **prep: 45 min.**
bake: 20 min.

No one will miss the meat in this appealing tart. The flaky, rustic-style crust holds an assortment of flavorful veggies simply seasoned with garlic and olive oil. It's guaranteed to make an impression.

—Marie Rizzio, Interlochen, Michigan

- 1 small eggplant, cut into 1-inch pieces
- 1 large zucchini, cut into 1/4-inch slices
- 4 plum tomatoes, chopped
- 1 medium sweet red pepper, cut into 1-inch pieces
- 4 tablespoons olive oil, *divided*
- 4 garlic cloves, minced
- 1/2 teaspoon salt
- 1/8 teaspoon pepper
- 1 sheet refrigerated pie pastry
- 1 tablespoon cornmeal
- 2 tablespoons shredded Parmesan cheese

Minced fresh basil, optional

1. In a large bowl, combine vegetables, 3 tablespoons oil, garlic, salt and pepper. Transfer to an ungreased 15-in. x 10-in. x 1-in. baking pan. Bake at 450° for 25-30 minutes or until vegetables are tender and moisture has evaporated, stirring every 10 minutes.

2. On a lightly floured surface, roll pastry into a 13-in. circle. Sprinkle cornmeal over a greased 14-in. pizza pan; place pastry on the prepared pan. Spoon the vegetable mixture over pastry to within 1-1/2 in. of edges. Fold up edges of pastry over filling, leaving center uncovered. Brush pastry with the remaining oil.

3. Bake at 450° for 20-25 minutes or until crust is golden brown. Sprinkle with cheese. Cut into wedges. Garnish with basil if desired.

[2002]

COLORFUL VEGGIE BAKE

yield: 8-10 servings ∞ **prep: 25 min.**
bake: 20 min.

(Pictured on page 853)

It's impossible to resist this cheesy casserole with a golden crumb topping sprinkled over colorful vegetables. Mom has relied on this versatile side (that goes with any meat) to round out many family meals. For a taste twist, try varying the veggies.

—Lisa Radelet, Boulder, Colorado

- 2 packages (16 ounces each) frozen California-blend vegetables
- 8 ounces process cheese (Velveeta), cubed
- 6 tablespoons butter, *divided*
- 1/2 cup crushed butter-flavored crackers (about 13 crackers)

1. Prepare vegetables according to the package directions; drain. Place half in an ungreased 11-in. x 7-in. baking dish. In a small saucepan, combine cheese and 4 tablespoons butter; cook and stir over low heat until melted. Pour half over vegetables. Repeat layers.

2. Melt the remaining butter; toss with cracker crumbs. Sprinkle over the top. Bake, uncovered, at 325° for 20-25 minutes or until golden brown.

RUSTIC ROASTED VEGETABLE TART

"This was very good. It looked great and tasted wonderful. It's not difficult to make but looks impressive. Be sure to roast lots of veggies. I did not use all that it said because I feared it would be too much, but they really cooked down and I barely had enough. I would use more veggies next time. The combination of vegetables was very tasty, and I would not change a thing."
—Canadian Gal

❧ SOUPS ❧

HEARTY SPLIT PEA SOUP

❝It was awesome. My son dropped by for an unexpected visit, and he loved it, too. ❞
—*majelline*

[2008]

BLACK BEAN 'N' PUMPKIN CHILI

yield: 10 servings (2-1/2 quarts)
prep: 20 min. ∽ cook: 4 hours

Our family loves this slow-cooked recipe, especially on cold days. It's a wonderful variation on standard chili that freezes well and tastes even better as leftovers.

—*Deborah Vliet, Holland, Michigan*

 1 medium onion, chopped
 1 medium sweet yellow pepper, chopped
 2 tablespoons olive oil
 3 garlic cloves, minced
 3 cups chicken broth
 2 cans (15 ounces e*a*ch) black beans, rinsed and drained
2-1/2 cups cubed cooked turkey
 1 can (15 ounces) solid-pack pumpkin
 1 can (14-1/2 ounces) diced tomatoes, undrained
 2 teaspoons dried parsley flakes
 2 teaspoons chili powder
1-1/2 teaspoons dried oregano
1-1/2 teaspoons ground cumin
 1/2 teaspoon salt

1. In a large skillet, saute the onion and yellow pepper in oil until tender. Add garlic; cook 1 minute longer. Transfer to a 5-qt. slow cooker; stir in the remaining ingredients. Cover and cook on low for 4-5 hours or until heated through.

[1996]

HEARTY SPLIT PEA SOUP

yield: 12 servings (3 quarts)
prep: 15 min. ∽ cook: 1-1/2 hours

(Pictured on page 876)

For a different spin on traditional split pea soup, try this recipe. The flavor is peppery rather than smoky, and the corned beef is an unexpected yet tasty change of pace.

—*Barbara Link
Rancho Cucamonga, California*

 1 package (16 ounces) dried split peas
 8 cups water
 2 medium potatoes, peeled and cubed
 2 large onions, chopped
 2 medium carrots, chopped
 2 cups cubed cooked corned beef *or* ham
 1/2 cup chopped celery
 5 teaspoons chicken bouillon granules
 1 teaspoon dried marjoram
 1 teaspoon poultry seasoning
 1 teaspoon rubbed sage
 1/2 to 1 teaspoon pepper
 1/2 teaspoon dried basil
 1/2 teaspoon salt, optional

1. In a Dutch oven, combine all the ingredients; bring to a boil. Reduce heat; cover and simmer for 1-1/4 to 1-1/2 hours or until the peas and vegetables are tender.

[1993]

CAJUN CORN SOUP

yield: 12-14 servings ∞ **prep: 20 min.**
cook: 1 hour 20 min.

(Pictured on page 878)

I found this recipe years ago and substituted Cajun stewed tomatoes for a bolder taste. Now I prepare this dish for out-of-state guests who want to taste some Cajun food. Everyone who tries it gives it high marks.

—Sue Fontenot, Kinder, Louisiana

- 1 cup chopped onion
- 1 cup chopped green pepper
- 6 green onions, sliced
- 1/2 cup canola oil
- 1/2 cup all-purpose flour
- 3 cups water
- 2 packages (16 ounces *each*) frozen corn
- 1-1/2 pounds smoked sausage, cut into 1/4-inch pieces
- 3 cups cubed fully cooked ham
- 1 can (14-1/2 ounces) Cajun-style stewed tomatoes
- 2 cups chopped peeled tomatoes
- 1 can (6 ounces) tomato paste
- 1/8 teaspoon cayenne pepper *or* to taste
- Salt to taste
- Hot pepper sauce to taste

1. In a Dutch oven, saute the onion, green pepper and green onions in oil for 5-6 minutes or until tender. Stir in flour and cook until bubbly. Gradually add water; bring to a boil. Add the corn, sausage, ham, tomatoes, tomato paste, cayenne, salt and pepper sauce.

2. Reduce heat; simmer, uncovered, for 1 hour, stirring occasionally.

[2007]

CREAMY BACON MUSHROOM SOUP

yield: 8 servings (2 quarts)
prep/total time: 30 min.

(Pictured on page 875)

I've always enjoyed cooking and recently created this rich soup. It's always a hit. You can also garnish it with chopped green onion tops or shredded Swiss cheese. For a creamier, smoother consistency, try pouring the soup through a strainer.

—Toby Mercer, Inman, South Carolina

- 10 bacon strips, diced
- 1 pound sliced fresh mushrooms
- 1 medium onion, chopped
- 3 garlic cloves, minced
- 1 quart heavy whipping cream
- 1 can (14-1/2 ounces) chicken broth
- 1-1/4 cups shredded Swiss cheese
- 3 tablespoons cornstarch
- 1/2 teaspoon salt
- 1/2 teaspoon pepper
- 3 tablespoons water

1. In a large saucepan, cook the bacon over medium heat until crisp. Using a slotted spoon, remove to paper towels; drain, reserving 2 tablespoons of the drippings. In the drippings, saute the mushrooms, onion and garlic. Stir in the cream and broth. Gradually stir in cheese until melted.

2. In a small bowl, combine cornstarch, salt, pepper and water until smooth. Stir into soup. Bring to a boil; cook and stir for 2 minutes or until thickened. Garnish with bacon.

CREAMY BACON MUSHROOM SOUP

"We really liked this savory mushroom dish. It has such a nice smell!"
—Kate147258

[2006]

ITALIAN WEDDING SOUP
yield: 10 servings (2-1/2 quarts)
prep: 30 min. ∞ **cook: 45 min.**

(*Pictured on page 874*)

I enjoyed a similar soup for lunch at work one day and decided to re-create it in my kitchen. I love the combination of meatballs, vegetables and pasta.

—*Noelle Myers, Grand Forks, North Dakota*

2	eggs, lightly beaten
1/2	cup seasoned bread crumbs
1	pound ground beef
1	pound bulk Italian sausage
3	medium carrots, sliced
3	celery ribs, diced
1	large onion, chopped
4-1/2	teaspoons olive oil
3	garlic cloves, minced
4	cans (14-1/2 ounces *each*) reduced-sodium chicken broth
2	cans (14-1/2 ounces *each*) beef broth
1	package (10 ounces) frozen chopped spinach, thawed and squeezed dry
1/4	cup minced fresh basil
1	envelope onion soup mix
4-1/2	teaspoons ketchup
1/2	teaspoon dried thyme
3	bay leaves
1-1/2	cups uncooked penne pasta

1. In a large bowl, combine the eggs and bread crumbs. Crumble the beef and sausage over mixture and mix well. Shape into 3/4-in. balls.

2. Place meatballs on a greased rack in a foil-lined 15-in. x 10-in. x 1-in. baking pan. Bake at 350° for 15-18 minutes or until no longer pink.

3. Meanwhile, in a Dutch oven, saute the carrots, celery and onion in oil until tender. Add the garlic; cook 1 minute longer. Stir in broth, spinach, basil, soup mix, ketchup, thyme and bay leaves.

4. Drain the meatballs on paper towels. Bring soup to a boil; add the meatballs. Reduce heat; simmer, uncovered, for 30 minutes. Add the pasta; cook 13-15 minutes longer or until the pasta is tender, stirring occasionally. Discard bay leaves.

[2001]

CREAMY WHITE CHILI
yield: 7 servings ∞ **prep: 10 min.**
cook: 40 min.

I got this wonderful recipe from my sister-in-law, who made a big batch and served a crowd one night. It was a hit. Plus, it's easy and quick, which is helpful since I'm a college student. In all my years of 4-H cooking, I've never had another dish get so many compliments.

—*Laura Brewer, Lafayette, Indiana*

1	pound boneless skinless chicken breasts, cut into 1/2-inch cubes
1	medium onion, chopped
1-1/2	teaspoons garlic powder
1	tablespoon canola oil
2	cans (15-1/2 ounces *each*) great northern beans, rinsed and drained
1	can (14-1/2 ounces) chicken broth
2	cans (4 ounces *each*) chopped green chilies
1	teaspoon salt
1	teaspoon ground cumin
1	teaspoon dried oregano
1/2	teaspoon pepper
1/4	teaspoon cayenne pepper
1	cup (8 ounces) sour cream
1/2	cup heavy whipping cream

1. In a large saucepan, saute the chicken, onion and garlic powder in oil until the chicken is no longer pink. Add the beans, broth, chilies and seasonings. Bring to a boil. Reduce heat; simmer, uncovered, for 30 minutes.

2. Remove from the heat; stir in the sour cream and cream.

[2010]

GNOCCHI CHICKEN MINESTRONE

yield: 8 servings (2-3/4 quarts)
prep: 30 min. ∾ **cook: 30 min.**

My Italian heritage and my mother, who was an excellent soup maker, inspired my take on minestrone. Using frozen gnocchi saves time and adds extra heartiness to this chunky soup.

—*Barbara Estabrook*
Rhinelander, Wisconsin

- 1-1/4 pounds chicken tenderloins, cut into 1/2-inch pieces
- 3/4 teaspoon dried oregano
- 1/4 teaspoon salt
- 1/4 teaspoon pepper
- 2 tablespoons olive oil, *divided*
- 1 *each* small green, sweet red and yellow peppers, finely chopped
- 1 medium zucchini, finely chopped
- 1 cup chopped fresh baby portobello mushrooms
- 1/3 cup chopped red onion
- 1/3 cup chopped prosciutto *or* deli ham
- 4 garlic cloves, minced
- 2 cans (14-1/2 ounces *each*) chicken broth
- 1 can (14-1/2 ounces) Italian diced tomatoes, undrained
- 3/4 cup canned white kidney *or* cannellini beans, rinsed and drained
- 1/2 cup frozen peas
- 3 tablespoons tomato paste
- 1 package (16 ounces) potato gnocchi
- 1/2 cup shredded Asiago cheese
- 8 fresh basil leaves, thinly sliced

1. Sprinkle chicken with oregano, salt and pepper. In a Dutch oven, cook chicken in 1 tablespoon oil until no longer pink. Remove from the pan and set aside.

2. In the same pan, cook the peppers, zucchini, mushrooms and onion in remaining oil until tender. Add the prosciutto and garlic; cook 1 minute longer. Add the broth, tomatoes, beans, peas, tomato paste and chicken. Bring to a boil. Reduce the heat; simmer, uncovered, for 20 minutes, stirring occasionally.

3. Meanwhile, cook gnocchi according to package directions. Drain pasta; stir into soup. Garnish each serving with cheese and basil.

Editor's Note: Look for potato gnocchi in the pasta or frozen foods section.

[2009]

CHUNKY CHIPOTLE PORK CHILI

yield: 4 servings ∾ **prep: 15 min.**
cook: 20 min.

Perfect for using leftover pork roast, this tasty, easy recipe can be made ahead and reheated.

—*Peter Halferty, Corpus Christi, Texas*

- 1 medium green pepper, chopped
- 1 small onion, chopped
- 1 chipotle pepper in adobo sauce, finely chopped
- 1 tablespoon canola oil
- 3 garlic cloves, minced
- 1 can (16 ounces) red beans, rinsed and drained
- 1 cup beef broth
- 1/2 cup salsa
- 2 teaspoons ground cumin
- 2 teaspoons chili powder
- 2 cups cubed cooked pork
- 1/4 cup sour cream

1. In a large saucepan, saute the green pepper, onion and chipotle pepper in oil until tender. Add the garlic; cook 1 minute longer.

2. Add beans, broth, salsa, cumin and chili powder. Bring to a boil. Reduce heat; simmer, uncovered, for 10 minutes or until thickened. Add pork; heat through. Serve with sour cream.

GNOCCHI CHICKEN MINESTRONE

"This is my husband's favorite new soup. I used less chicken (about 1/2 pound) and used bell peppers finely chopped instead of sweet peppers, as I had those on hand. When I served the leftovers, I added another can of broth and it was still good."
—*Zinderella58*

[2005]

CORN AND SQUASH SOUP

yield: 8 servings (2-1/2 quarts)
prep/total time: 25 min.

(Pictured on page 877)

This hearty soup pairs squash and cream-style corn for a pleasant taste. My family says this is their favorite squash recipe, and friends also comment on its wonderful flavor.

—Janice Zook
White River Junction, Vermont

12 bacon strips, diced
1 medium onion, chopped
1 celery rib, chopped
2 tablespoons all-purpose flour
1 can (14-1/2 ounces) chicken broth
6 cups mashed cooked butternut squash
2 cans (8-3/4 ounces each) cream-style corn
2 cups half-and-half cream
1 tablespoon minced fresh parsley
1-1/2 teaspoons salt
1/2 teaspoon pepper
Sour cream, optional

1. In a large saucepan, cook the bacon over medium heat until crisp. Using a slotted spoon, remove to paper towels. Drain; reserve 2 tablespoons drippings.

2. In the drippings, saute the onion and celery until tender. Stir in flour until blended. Gradually stir in broth. Bring to a boil; cook and stir for 2 minutes or until slightly thickened.

3. Reduce heat to medium. Stir in the squash, corn, cream, parsley, salt, pepper and bacon. Cook and stir until heated through. Garnish with sour cream if desired.

[2008]

BEEF BARLEY SOUP

yield: 8 servings (about 2 quarts)
prep: 20 min.   cook: 1 hour

(Pictured on page 879)

Once a year, I invite my relatives —about 25 people in all—for soup day to honor my late husband's birthday. I make three soups, including comforting Beef Barley Soup. It's loaded with chunks of beef and chopped veggies.

—Louise Laplante, Hanmer, Ontario

2 pounds beef stew meat, cut into 1-inch pieces
1 tablespoon canola oil
5 cups water
4 medium carrots, chopped
4 celery ribs, chopped
1 large onion, chopped
1 can (14-1/2 ounces) diced tomatoes, undrained
2 tablespoons tomato paste
4 teaspoons beef bouillon granules
1 teaspoon *each* dried oregano, thyme, basil and parsley flakes
1/2 teaspoon salt
1/4 teaspoon pepper
1 cup quick-cooking barley

1. In a Dutch oven, brown meat in oil on all sides; drain. Add the water, carrots, celery, onion, tomatoes, tomato paste, bouillon and seasonings. Bring to a boil. Reduce heat; cover and simmer for 50 minutes or until meat is tender.

2. Stir in the barley; cover and simmer 10-15 minutes longer or until barley is tender.

[2007]

GOLDEN SEAFOOD CHOWDER

yield: 4 servings ∞ **prep: 25 min.**
cook: 25 min.

Flavored with crab, shrimp and cheddar cheese, this chowder is so good that I make it weekly. Sometimes I substitute chicken or ham for the seafood and leave out the juice. Either way, this pretty soup is a winner.

—*Ami Paton, Waconia, Minnesota*

1/2	cup finely chopped onion
1/4	cup butter, cubed
1	can (14-1/2 ounces) chicken broth
1	cup cubed peeled potato
2	celery ribs, chopped
2	medium carrots, chopped
1/4	cup Clamato juice
1/4	teaspoon lemon-pepper seasoning
1/4	cup all-purpose flour
2	cups 2% milk
2	cups (8 ounces) shredded sharp cheddar cheese
1	can (6 ounces) crabmeat, drained, flaked and cartilage removed
1	cup cooked medium shrimp, peeled and deveined

1. In a large saucepan, saute onion in butter until tender. Stir in the broth, potato, celery, carrots, Clamato juice and lemon pepper. Bring to a boil. Reduce heat; cover and simmer for 15-20 minutes or until vegetables are tender.

2. In a small bowl, whisk flour and milk until smooth; add to soup. Bring to a boil; cook and stir for 2 minutes or until thickened. Reduce heat. Add the cheese, crab and shrimp; cook and stir until cheese is melted.

[1996]

HARVEST TURKEY SOUP

yield: 22 servings (5-1/2 quarts)
prep: 35 min. ∞ **cook: 2-1/2 hours + cooling**

The recipe for this super soup evolved over several years. The herbs and spices make it taste terrific!

—*Linda Sand, Winsted, Connecticut*

1	leftover turkey carcass (from a 12-pound turkey)
5	quarts water
2	large carrots, shredded
1	cup chopped celery
1	large onion, chopped
4	chicken bouillon cubes
1	can (28 ounces) stewed tomatoes
3/4	cup fresh *or* frozen peas
3/4	cup uncooked long grain rice
1	package (10 ounces) frozen chopped spinach
1	tablespoon salt, optional
3/4	teaspoon pepper
1/2	teaspoon dried marjoram
1/2	teaspoon dried thyme

1. Place the turkey carcass and water in a Dutch oven or large stockpot; bring to a boil. Reduce the heat; cover and simmer for 1-1/2 hours. Remove the carcass; allow to cool. Remove turkey from bones and cut into bite-size pieces; set aside.

2. Strain broth. Add carrots, celery, onion and bouillon; bring to a boil. Reduce heat; cover and simmer for 30 minutes. Add tomatoes, peas, rice, spinach, salt if desired, pepper, marjoram, thyme and reserved turkey. Return to a boil; cook, uncovered, for 20 minutes or until rice is tender.

HARVEST TURKEY SOUP

"This soup is amazing. My kids called it 'magic soup,' because they said they felt better after they ate it when they were sick. It always turns out delicious and full of flavor. I substitute barley for rice sometimes!!"
—*debihunt*

HEARTY POTATO SOUP

[1996]

GOLDEN SQUASH SOUP

yield: 12-14 servings (3-1/2 quarts)
prep: 35 min. ∞ cook: 30 min. + cooling

This special recipe from my mother-in-law is one that I enjoy making for our fall meals. The soup is so pretty that is dresses up the table. We especially enjoy it on crisp evenings.

—Mary Ann Klein
Washington Township, New Jersey

3	leeks (white portion only), sliced
4	medium carrots, chopped
5	tablespoons butter
3	pounds butternut squash, peeled and cubed
6	cups chicken broth
3	medium zucchini, peeled and sliced
2	teaspoons salt
1/2	teaspoon dried thyme
1/4	teaspoon white pepper
1	cup half-and-half cream
1/2	cup 2% milk

Grated Parmesan cheese and chives, optional

1. In a Dutch oven, saute the leeks and carrots in butter for 5 minutes, stirring occasionally. Add the squash, broth, zucchini, salt, thyme and pepper; bring to a boil. Reduce the heat; cover and simmer for 30-35 minutes or until the vegetables are tender. Cool slightly.

2. In a blender, puree the soup in small batches until smooth; return to pan. Stir in cream and milk; heat through (do not boil). Sprinkle with cheese and chives if desired.

[1993]

HEARTY POTATO SOUP

yield: 8-10 servings (about 2-1/2 quarts)
prep: 10 min. ∞ cook: 30 min.

Having grown up on a dairy farm in Holland, I love our country life here in Idaho's potato country. My favorite potato soup originally called for heavy cream and bacon fat, but I've trimmed down the recipe.

—Gladys De Boer
Castleford, Idaho, Former Field Editor

6	medium potatoes, peeled and sliced
2	carrots, chopped
6	celery ribs, chopped
8	cups water
1	onion, chopped
6	tablespoons butter, cubed
6	tablespoons all-purpose flour
1	teaspoon salt
1/2	teaspoon pepper
1-1/2	cups 2% milk

1. In a Dutch oven, cook the potatoes, carrots and celery in water until tender, about 15-20 minutes. Drain, reserving liquid and set aside vegetables.

2. In the same pan, saute onion in butter until tender. Stir in the flour, salt and pepper; gradually add milk. Bring to a boil, cook and stir for 2 minutes or until thickened. Gently stir in cooked vegetables. Add 1 cup or more of reserved cooking liquid until soup is desired consistency.

STORING WINTER SQUASH

Unwashed winter squash, such as acorn, butternut or spaghetti, can be stored in a dry, cool, well-ventilated place for up to 1 month.

—Taste of Home Cooking Experts

[2009]
HOLIDAY TORTELLINI SOUP
yield: 8 servings (2-1/2 quarts)
prep: 15 min.   cook: 35 min.

(Pictured on page 878)

Hearty and full of flavor, this Italian-style soup freezes well if you want to make it ahead or have leftovers to save for another day.

—Michelle Goggins, Cedarburg, Wisconsin

- 2 tablespoons olive oil
- 2 ounces pancetta *or* bacon, finely diced
- 1 medium onion, finely chopped
- 3 garlic cloves, minced
- 1 can (49-1/2 ounces) chicken broth
- 2 teaspoons Italian seasoning
- 1 package (9 ounces) refrigerated cheese tortellini
- 1 can (28 ounces) crushed tomatoes in puree
- 8 ounces fresh spinach, rinsed and chopped

Salt and pepper to taste
- 1 cup freshly shredded Parmesan cheese

1. Heat the oil in a Dutch oven over medium heat. Add pancetta. Cook until crisp. Add onion; cook 3-4 minutes or until tender. Add garlic; cook 1 minute longer. Add the broth and Italian seasoning; bring to a boil and simmer for 5 minutes.

2. Meanwhile, cook tortellini according to the package directions; drain. Add the cooked tortellini to soup mixture. Stir in crushed tomatoes and simmer 5 minutes. Add the spinach and cook just until wilted. Season with salt and pepper. Garnish with the cheese.

[1994]
PEASANT SOUP
yield: 12 servings (3 quarts)
prep: 30 min. + standing
cook: 1-3/4 hours

(Pictured on page 878)

Don't let the name fool you! This soup is anything but meager. The hearty vegetable broth really satisfies.

—Bertha McClung
Summersville, West Virginia

- 1 pound dried great northern beans
- 6 cups water
- 3 carrots, sliced
- 3 celery ribs, sliced
- 2 medium onions, chopped
- 2 garlic cloves, minced
- 2 bay leaves
- 1 can (14-1/2 ounces) diced tomatoes, undrained
- 1 teaspoon dried basil
- 1/2 teaspoon pepper
- 2 tablespoons olive oil

1. Rinse and sort beans. Place beans in a Dutch oven; add water to cover by 2 in. Bring to a boil; boil for 2 minutes. Remove from the heat; cover and let stand for 1 to 4 hours or until beans are softened.

2. Drain and rinse, discarding liquid. Return to Dutch oven. Add 6 cups water, carrots, celery, onions, garlic, bay leaves, tomatoes, basil and pepper; bring to a boil. Reduce heat; cover and simmer 1-1/2 hours or until the beans are tender.

3. Discard the bay leaves. Add oil and heat through.

PEASANT SOUP

"Very good meatless, but if you want meat, it's easy to add diced ham or sliced smoked sausage. The beans can be varied, too. I really like versatile recipes like this one."
—*Trilby Yost*

[2007]

MINESTRONE WITH ITALIAN SAUSAGE

yield: 11 servings (about 3 quarts)   ∞   prep: 25 min.   ∞   cook: 1 hour

(Pictured on page 879)

I make this zippy, satisfying soup all the time, and it's my dad's favorite. The recipe makes a lot, and I have found that it freezes well and tastes just as great reheated.

—Linda Reis, Salem, Oregon

MINESTRONE WITH ITALIAN SAUSAGE

"If this doesn't warm you up, nothing ever will. I've used both hot and mild Italian sausage and both are equally welcome on our table."
—*Southernmama*

- 1   pound bulk Italian sausage
- 1   large onion, chopped
- 2   large carrots, chopped
- 2   celery ribs, chopped
- 1   medium leek (white portion only), chopped
- 1   medium zucchini, cut into 1/2-inch pieces
- 1/4   pound fresh green beans, trimmed and cut into 1/2-inch pieces
- 3   garlic cloves, minced
- 6   cups beef broth
- 2   cans (14-1/2 ounces *each*) diced tomatoes with basil, oregano and garlic
- 3   cups shredded cabbage
- 1   teaspoon dried basil
- 1   teaspoon dried oregano
- 1/4   teaspoon pepper
- 1   can (15 ounces) garbanzo beans *or* chickpeas, rinsed and drained
- 1/2   cup uncooked small pasta shells
- 3   tablespoons minced fresh parsley
- 1/3   cup grated Parmesan cheese

1. In a Dutch oven, cook sausage and onion over medium heat until meat is no longer pink; drain. Stir in the carrots, celery and leek; cook for 3 minutes. Add the zucchini, green beans and garlic; cook 1 minute longer.

2. Stir in the broth, tomatoes, cabbage, basil, oregano and pepper. Bring to a boil. Reduce heat; cover and simmer for 45 minutes.

3. Return to a boil. Stir in the garbanzo beans, pasta and parsley. Cook for 6-9 minutes or until pasta is tender. Serve with cheese.

HOW TO CLEAN LEEKS

Leeks often contain sand between their many layers. Cut the leeks lengthwise in half. Rinse under cold running water, gently separating the leaves to allow the water to flush out any trapped sand or dirt.

[2012]

CHILI CON CHORIZO

yield: 4 servings ∞ **prep/total time: 30 min.**

We love to eat chili, whether it's vegetarian or with some kind of meat. This recipe was created because a friend of mine gave me some chorizo and I decided to try it in my chili recipe. Most supermarkets carry chorizo, but if it's not available, I found that kielbasa is a good substitution.

—Debbie Limas
North Andover, Massachusetts

1/2	pound uncooked chorizo
1	medium green pepper, chopped
1	medium sweet red pepper, chopped
1	small onion, chopped
2	garlic cloves, minced
1	can (16 ounces) kidney beans, rinsed and drained
1	can (8 ounces) tomato sauce
2	tablespoons dry red wine *or* beef broth
1-1/2	teaspoons chili powder
1	teaspoon ground coriander
1	teaspoon ground cumin
1/4	teaspoon salt
1/4	teaspoon pepper

Hot cooked rice and minced fresh cilantro, optional

---

1. Crumble the chorizo into a large saucepan; add the peppers, onion and garlic. Cook over medium heat for 6-8 minutes or until the sausage is fully cooked; drain.

2. Stir in the beans, tomato sauce, wine, chili powder, coriander, cumin, salt and pepper. Bring to a boil. Reduce heat; simmer, uncovered, for 15 minutes or until heated through. Serve over rice and garnish with cilantro if desired.

[1997]

SLOW COOKER VEGETABLE SOUP

yield: 8-10 servings (about 2-1/2 quarts)
prep: 15 min. ∞ **cook: 8 hours**

(Pictured on page 874)

What a treat to come home from work and have this savory soup ready to eat. It's a nice traditional beef soup with old-fashioned goodness. We pair it with crusty rolls topped with melted mozzarella cheese.

—Heather Thurmeier
Pense, Saskatchewan

1	pound beef top round steak, cut into 1/2-inch cubes
1	can (14-1/2 ounces) diced tomatoes, undrained
2	medium potatoes, peeled and cubed
2	medium onions, diced
3	celery ribs, sliced
2	carrots, sliced
3	beef bouillon cubes
1/2	teaspoon salt
1/2	teaspoon dried basil
1/2	teaspoon dried oregano
1/4	teaspoon pepper
3	cups water
1-1/2	cups frozen mixed vegetables

---

1. In a 3-qt. slow cooker, combine the first 12 ingredients. Cover and cook on high for 6-8 hours. Add the mixed vegetables; cover and cook 2 hours longer or until meat and vegetables are tender.

SLOW COOKER VEGETABLE SOUP

"The recipe this magazine came in is tattered and worn from making this soup so many times. Our family of seven loves it. I usually double it (or more) so we can have some leftovers for lunch. One of the best! Very forgiving recipe, too. You can add whatever you have on hand and it tastes delicious, made in the slow cooker or on top of the stove."
—*ShelleyinNYC*

[2008]

SOUTHWESTERN TURKEY SOUP

yield: 7 servings ∞ **prep: 20 min.**
cook: 30 min.

(Pictured on page 877)

This spicy soup is loaded with turkey, beans, corn and tomatoes. We like it really hot, so we tend to use all three tablespoons of jalapenos... and then some. It's so good on a wintry Midwestern day.

—*Brenda Kruse, Ames, Iowa*

1 medium onion, chopped
1 tablespoon olive oil
1 can (14-1/2 ounces) chicken broth
2 to 3 tablespoons diced jalapeno pepper
3 teaspoons ground cumin
1-1/2 teaspoons chili powder
1/4 teaspoon salt
1/4 teaspoon cayenne pepper
3 cups cubed cooked turkey
1 can (15 ounces) black beans, rinsed and drained
1 can (10 ounces) diced tomatoes and green chilies, undrained
1-1/2 cups frozen corn
Sour cream, coarsely crushed tortilla chips, shredded cheddar cheese and sliced ripe olives, optional

1. In a large saucepan, saute onion in oil until tender. Stir in the broth, jalapeno, cumin, chili powder, salt and cayenne. Add turkey, beans, tomatoes and corn.

2. Bring to a boil. Reduce the heat; cover and simmer for 20-30 minutes to allow the flavors to blend. Garnish with the sour cream, chips, cheese and olives if desired.

Editor's Note: Wear disposable gloves when cutting hot peppers; the oils can burn skin. Avoid touching your face.

TEXICAN CHILI

"I think this chili is so delicious, and kids like it too! I love the addition of carrots. I add garlic and reserve some of the cooked bacon to sprinkle on top of each bowl for a crunchy topping."
—*badkitty*

[1998]

TEXICAN CHILI

yield: 16-18 servings ∞ **prep: 25 min.**
cook: 9 hours

(Pictured on page 876)

This flavorful, meaty chili is my favorite...and it's so easy to prepare in the slow cooker. It's a great way to serve a crowd without worrying about last-minute preparation.

—*Stacy Law, Cornish, Utah*

8 bacon strips, diced
2-1/2 pounds beef stew meat, cut into 1/2-inch cubes
2 cans (one 28 ounces, one 14-1/2 ounces) stewed tomatoes, undrained
2 cans (8 ounces each) tomato sauce
1 can (16 ounces) kidney beans, rinsed and drained
2 cups sliced carrots
1 cup chopped celery
3/4 cup chopped onion
1/2 cup chopped green pepper
1/4 cup minced fresh parsley
1 tablespoon chili powder
1 teaspoon salt, optional
1/2 teaspoon ground cumin
1/4 teaspoon pepper

1. In a large skillet, cook the bacon until crisp. Using a slotted spoon, remove to paper towels to drain. Brown beef in the drippings over medium heat; drain.

2. Transfer to a 5-qt. slow cooker; add the bacon and remaining ingredients. Cover and cook on low for 8-10 hours or until meat is tender; stir occasionally.

[1996]

ZESTY VEGETABLE BEEF SOUP

yield: 12-14 servings (3-3/4 quarts) ∾ **prep: 35 min. + cooling** ∾ **cook: 3-3/4 hours**

(*Pictured on page 873*)

My family loves to come to the table for hot homemade biscuits and a bowl of this flavorful, filling soup. They rave over how good it tastes. A friend shared the recipe with me.

—*Brenda Wood, Portage la Prairie, Manitoba*

BROTH:

- 8 cups water
- 3 pounds bone-in beef short ribs
- 1 large onion, quartered
- 2 medium carrots, quartered
- 2 celery ribs, quartered
- 8 whole allspice
- 2 bay leaves
- 1 tablespoon salt
- 1/2 teaspoon pepper

SOUP:

- 4 cups V8 juice
- 3 celery ribs, sliced
- 2 medium potatoes, peeled and cubed
- 2 medium carrots, sliced
- 1 medium onion, diced
- 2 teaspoons Worcestershire sauce
- 1/2 teaspoon hot pepper sauce
- 1/2 teaspoon dried oregano
- 1/2 teaspoon dried basil
- 1/4 teaspoon chili powder
- 1 cup uncooked noodles

1. In a Dutch oven or stockpot, slowly bring broth ingredients to a boil. Reduce heat; cover and simmer for 2 hours or until meat is tender.

2. Remove ribs; allow to cool. Skim fat and strain broth; discard vegetables and seasonings. Remove meat from bones and cut into bite-size pieces; return to broth. Add the first 10 soup ingredients; bring to a boil. Reduce heat; cover and simmer for 1 hour or until vegetables are tender.

3. Stir in noodles. Return to a boil; cook, uncovered, for 15 minutes or until the noodles are tender. Discard bay leaves.

ZESTY VEGETABLE BEEF SOUP

"This has to be the best soup I've ever made."
—*pferry56*

[2010]

SPICY BLACK BEAN SOUP

yield: 12 servings (3/4 cup each)
prep: 25 min. ∞ **cook: 40 min.**

(*Pictured on page 879*)

A splash of sherry enhances this hearty, easy-to-make soup. For a milder flavor, remove the ribs and seeds from the jalapeno before dicing.

—*Tia Musser, Hudson, Indiana*

1	large red onion, chopped
1	medium sweet red pepper, chopped
1	jalapeno pepper, seeded and minced
2	tablespoons olive oil
3	garlic cloves, minced
3	cans (15 ounces each) black beans, rinsed and drained
3-1/2	cups vegetable broth
1	can (14-1/2 ounces) diced tomatoes with mild green chilies, undrained
1	can (4 ounces) chopped green chilies
1/3	cup sherry *or* additional vegetable broth
2	tablespoons minced fresh cilantro
1/2	cup fat-free sour cream
1/4	cup shredded cheddar cheese

---

1. In a Dutch oven, saute the onion and peppers in oil until tender. Add garlic; cook 1 minute longer.

2. Stir in the beans, broth, tomatoes and chopped green chilies. Bring to a boil. Reduce heat; simmer, uncovered, for 25 minutes. Add sherry and cilantro; cook 5 minutes longer.

3. Remove from the heat; cool slightly. Place half of soup in a blender; cover and process until pureed. Return to the pan and heat through. Top each serving with 2 teaspoons sour cream and 1 teaspoon cheese.

Editor's Note: Wear disposable gloves when cutting hot peppers; the oils can burn skin. Avoid touching your face.

[1994]

OLD-FASHIONED CREAM OF TOMATO SOUP

yield: 8 servings ∞ **prep: 10 min.**
cook: 1 hour

This is an original recipe of my father's that has been a favorite on our menu since the early days. We're always flattered when we receive requests for our tomato soup recipe, and we're proud to share it with others.

—*Susan Henderson, Missoula, Montana*

1	can (28 ounces) diced tomatoes, undrained
1	cup chicken broth
1/4	cup butter, cubed
2	tablespoons sugar
1	tablespoon chopped onion
1/8	teaspoon baking soda
2	cups heavy whipping cream

---

1. In a large saucepan, combine the first six ingredients. Cover and simmer for 1 hour.

2. In the top of a double boiler or metal bowl, heat cream over simmering water; add to tomato mixture just before serving.

SPICY BLACK BEAN SOUP

❝I love, love, love this recipe! So easy to make, and I enjoy it for lunch for several days. Delicious, hearty, healthy and just plain yummy!!❞
—*beckyjayne17*

TRIMMING CILANTRO

To easily trim cilantro (or flat-leaf parsley) from its stems, hold the bunch, then angle the blade of a chef's knife almost parallel with the stems. With short, downward strokes, shave off the leaves where they meet the stems.

ZESTY VEGETABLE BEEF SOUP, page 871

WHITE BEAN CHICKEN CHILI, page 888

SLOW COOKER VEGETABLE SOUP, page 869

PANFISH CHOWDER, page 883

ITALIAN WEDDING SOUP, page 862

CREAMY BACON MUSHROOM SOUP, page 861

TEXICAN CHILI, page 870

HEARTY SPLIT PEA SOUP, page 860

CHICKEN CHILI WITH BLACK BEANS, page 883

SOUTHWESTERN TURKEY SOUP, page 870

CORN AND SQUASH SOUP, page 864

CHICKEN SOUP WITH SPAETZLE, page 884

PEASANT SOUP, page 867

HOLIDAY TORTELLINI SOUP, page 867

CAJUN CORN SOUP, page 861

BEEF BARLEY SOUP, page 864

MINESTRONE WITH ITALIAN SAUSAGE, page 868

LENTIL SPINACH SOUP, page 881

SPICY BLACK BEAN SOUP, page 872

BEST BROCCOLI SOUP, page 882

[1996]

MUSHROOM BARLEY SOUP

yield: about 11 servings (2-3/4 quarts)
prep: 25 min. ∽ **cook: 1-3/4 hours**

A friend at work shared the recipe for this wonderful soup. With beef, barley and vegetables, it's hearty enough to be a meal. A big steaming bowl is so satisfying on a cold day.

—Lynn Thomas, London, Ontario

1-1/2   pounds boneless beef chuck, cut into 3/4-inch cubes
1   tablespoon canola oil
2   cups finely chopped onions
1   cup diced carrots
1/2   cup sliced celery
1   pound fresh mushrooms, sliced
2   garlic cloves, minced
1/2   teaspoon dried thyme
1   can (14-1/2 ounces) beef broth
1   can (14-1/2 ounces) chicken broth
2   cups water
1/2   cup medium pearl barley
1   teaspoon salt, optional
1/2   teaspoon pepper
3   tablespoons chopped fresh parsley

---

1. In a Dutch oven or stockpot, cook the meat in oil over medium heat until no longer pink. Remove meat with a slotted spoon; keep warm and set aside.

2. Saute onions, carrots and celery in drippings over medium heat until tender, about 5 minutes. Add the mushrooms, garlic and thyme; cook and stir for 3 minutes. Stir in broths, water, barley, salt if desired and pepper.

3. Return meat to pan; bring to a boil. Reduce heat; cover and simmer for 1-1/2 to 2 hours or until barley and meat are tender. Add parsley.

[2002]

LENTIL SPINACH SOUP

yield: 5 servings ∽ **prep: 15 min.**
cook: 30 min.

(Pictured on page 879)

Packed with protein, lentils are an easy change of pace from beans in soup.

—Margaret Wilson, Sun City, California

1/2   pound bulk Italian turkey sausage
1   small onion, chopped
4   cups water
1/2   cup dried lentils, rinsed
2   teaspoons chicken bouillon granules
1/8   teaspoon crushed red pepper flakes
1   package (10 ounces) fresh spinach, coarsely chopped
2   tablespoons shredded Parmesan cheese

---

1. In a large saucepan, cook sausage and onion until meat is no longer pink; drain. Stir in the water, lentils, bouillon and red pepper flakes. Bring to a boil. Reduce the heat; cover and simmer for 25-30 minutes or until the lentils are tender. Stir in the spinach, cook 3-5 minutes longer or until the spinach is tender. Sprinkle with cheese.

LENTIL SPINACH SOUP

"Great soup! I double the recipe but still only use one bag of spinach. Everyone eats seconds. It was even better warmed up the next day for lunch."
—Phill

CHEESEBURGER PARADISE SOUP

"Even better than I expected. Not heavy. I'm glad I made the whole recipe so we will get several meals throughout the fall."
—AdeleDegnan

[2007]

CHEESEBURGER PARADISE SOUP

yield: 14 servings (about 3-1/2 quarts)
prep: 30 min. ∞ cook: 25 min.

This creamy soup is hearty enough to serve as a main course with your favorite bread or rolls.

—*Nadina Iadimarco, Burton, Ohio*

- 6 medium potatoes, peeled and cubed
- 1 small carrot, grated
- 1 small onion, chopped
- 1/2 cup chopped green pepper
- 2 tablespoons chopped seeded jalapeno pepper
- 3 cups water
- 2 tablespoons plus 2 teaspoons beef bouillon granules
- 2 garlic cloves, minced
- 1/8 teaspoon pepper
- 2 pounds ground beef
- 1/2 pound sliced fresh mushrooms
- 2 tablespoons butter
- 5 cups 2% milk, *divided*
- 6 tablespoons all-purpose flour
- 1 package (16 ounces) process cheese (Velveeta), cubed

Crumbled cooked bacon

1. In a Dutch oven, combine first nine ingredients; bring to a boil. Reduce heat; cover and simmer for 10-15 minutes or until the potatoes are tender.

2. Meanwhile, in a large skillet, cook the beef and mushrooms in butter over medium heat until meat is no longer pink; drain. Add to soup. Stir in 4 cups milk; heat through.

3. In a small bowl, combine the flour and remaining milk until smooth; gradually stir into soup. Bring to a boil; cook and stir for 2 minutes or until thickened. Reduce heat; add the cheese, stirring until melted. Garnish with bacon.

Editor's Note: Wear disposable gloves when cutting hot peppers; the oils can burn skin. Avoid touching your face.

[1995]

BEST BROCCOLI SOUP

yield: 6-8 servings (2 quarts)
prep: 20 min. ∞ cook: 30 min.

(*Pictured on page 880*)

Broccoli stars in this creamy, comforting soup..

—*Carolyn Weinberg*
Hardin, Montana, Field Editor

- 2 cups water
- 4 cups chopped fresh broccoli (about 1-1/2 pounds)
- 1 cup chopped celery
- 1 cup chopped carrots
- 1/2 cup chopped onion
- 6 tablespoons butter, cubed
- 6 tablespoons all-purpose flour
- 3 cups chicken broth
- 2 cups 2% milk
- 1 tablespoon minced fresh parsley
- 1 teaspoon onion salt
- 1/2 teaspoon garlic powder
- 1/2 teaspoon salt

1. In a Dutch oven, bring water to boil. Add the broccoli, celery and carrots; boil 2-3 minutes or until crisp-tender. Drain; set vegetables aside.

2. In the same pot, saute the onion in butter until tender. Stir in the flour to form a smooth paste. Gradually stir in broth and milk until smooth. Bring to a boil; cook and stir for 1 minute or until thickened.

3. Stir in the reserved vegetables and remaining ingredients. Reduce the heat; cook, for 15 minutes or until the vegetables are tender, stirring occasionally, for 15 minutes or until vegetables are tender.

[1995]

PANFISH CHOWDER
yield: 4-6 servings ∞ prep: 20 min.
cook: 40 min.

(Pictured on page 874)

With my husband being an avid hunter and fisherman, I can never have enough new fish and wild game recipes. We especially enjoy this rich chowder. It's a hearty dish with big chunks of fish, potatoes and bacon in a tempting creamy broth.

—Cyndi Fliss, Bevent, Wisconsin

  6 bacon strips, cut into 1-inch pieces
2/3 cup chopped onion
1/2 cup chopped celery
  3 medium potatoes, peeled and cubed
  2 cups water
1/2 cup chopped carrots
  2 tablespoons minced fresh parsley
  1 tablespoon lemon juice
1/2 teaspoon dill weed
1/4 teaspoon garlic salt
1/8 teaspoon pepper
  1 pound panfish fillets (perch, sunfish *or* crappie), cut into 1-inch chunks
  1 cup half-and-half cream

1. In a 3-qt. saucepan, cook the bacon over medium heat until crisp. Using a slotted spoon, remove bacon to paper towels; drain, reserving 2 tablespoons drippings. Saute the onion and celery in reserved drippings until tender.

2. Add potatoes, water, carrots, parsley, lemon juice and seasonings. Bring to a boil. Reduce heat; simmer, uncovered, until the vegetables are tender, about 30 minutes. Add the fish and bacon; simmer for 5 minutes or just until fish flakes with a fork. Add the cream and heat through.

[1993]

CHICKEN CHILI WITH BLACK BEANS
yield: 10 servings (3 quarts)
prep: 10 min. ∞ cook: 25 min.

(Pictured on page 876)

Because it looks different than traditional chili, my family was a little hesitant to try this dish at first. But thanks to full, hearty flavor, it has become a real favorite.

—Jeanette Urbom
Louisburg, Kansas, Field Editor

  3 whole boneless skinless chicken breasts (1-3/4 pounds), cubed
  2 medium sweet red peppers, chopped
  1 large onion, chopped
  3 tablespoons olive oil
  1 can (4 ounces) chopped green chilies
  4 garlic cloves, minced
  2 tablespoons chili powder
  2 teaspoons ground cumin
  1 teaspoon ground coriander
  2 cans (15 ounces *each*) black beans, rinsed and drained
  1 can (28 ounces) Italian stewed tomatoes, cut up
  1 cup chicken broth *or* beer

1. In a Dutch oven, saute the chicken, red peppers and onion in oil for 5 minutes or until chicken is no longer pink. Add the green chilies, garlic, chili powder, cumin and coriander; cook 1 minute longer. Stir in the beans, tomatoes and broth or beer; bring to a boil. Reduce the heat and simmer, uncovered, for 15 minutes, stirring often.

CHICKEN CHILI WITH BLACK BEANS

"Amazing! I prefer it with ground chicken breast and in a slow cooker, so I skip the oil but it is still the best I've ever had and it's nothing but healthy." — *Luvorlando*

[1994]

CHICKEN SOUP WITH SPAETZLE

yield: 8-10 servings (2 1/2 quarts)
prep: 20 min. + cooling
cook: 2-1/2 hours + cooling

(Pictured on page 877)

*Here's a new and interesting twist to
traditional chicken soup. Everyone who
samples it can't resist the delicious soup
paired with homemade spaetzle.*

—*Elaine Lange, Grand Rapids, Michigan*

1	broiler/fryer chicken (2 to 3 pounds), cut into pieces
2	tablespoons canola oil
8	cups chicken broth
2	bay leaves
1/2	teaspoon dried thyme
1/4	teaspoon pepper
1	cup sliced carrots
1	cup sliced celery
3/4	cup chopped onion
1	garlic clove, minced
1/3	cup medium pearl barley
2	cups sliced fresh mushrooms

SPAETZLE:

1-1/4	cups all-purpose flour
1/8	teaspoon baking powder
1/8	teaspoon salt
1	egg, lightly beaten
1/4	cup water
1/4	cup 2% milk

1. In a Dutch oven or stockpot, brown chicken pieces in oil. Add the broth, bay leaves, thyme and pepper. Bring to a boil; skim foam. Reduce heat; cover and simmer for 45-60 minutes or until chicken is tender. Remove the chicken and set aside until cool enough to handle. Remove meat from bones; discard bones and skin and cut chicken into bite size pieces. Cool broth and skim off fat.

2. Return the chicken to broth along with the carrots, celery, onion, garlic and barley. Bring to a boil. Reduce heat; cover and simmer for 35 minutes. Add mushrooms and simmer 8-10 minutes longer. Remove bay leaves.

3. In a small bowl, combine the first three spaetzle ingredients. Stir in the egg, water and milk; blend well. Drop batter by 1/2 teaspoonfuls into simmering soup. Cook for 10 minutes.

[2007]

ALL-DAY SOUP

yield: 8 servings ∞ **prep: 25 min.**
cook: 8 hours

*I start this soup in the morning, and by
evening, dinner's ready to go! My family loves
all of the hearty vegetable and steak pieces, all
smothered in a zesty tomato broth.*

—*Cathy Logan, Sparks, Nevada*

1	beef flank steak (1-1/2 pounds), cut into 1/2-inch cubes
1	medium onion, chopped
1	tablespoon olive oil
5	medium carrots, thinly sliced
4	cups shredded cabbage
4	medium red potatoes, diced
2	celery ribs, diced
2	cans (14-1/2 ounces each) diced tomatoes, undrained
2	cans (14-1/2 ounces each) beef broth
1	can (10-3/4 ounces) condensed tomato soup, undiluted
1	tablespoon sugar
2	teaspoons Italian seasoning
1	teaspoon dried parsley flakes

1. In a large skillet, brown the steak and onion in oil; drain. Transfer to a 5-qt. slow cooker. Stir in the remaining ingredients. Cover and cook on low for 8-10 hours or until meat is tender.

ALL-DAY SOUP

"This is a fantastic beef soup recipe. I make it many times every winter. Great on a snow day!"
—*Mellerfly*

[2011]

CHICKEN CHORIZO POSOLE

yield: 9 servings   prep: 40 min.
cook: 40 min.

I first tasted posole while visiting a friend in Santa Fe. It was a revelation! I have since been experimenting with many versions, and this one has become a much-loved tradition for my family. The leftovers are fantastic!

—*Jennifer Beckman, Falls Church, Virginia*

- 1 pound tomatillos, husks removed, cut in half
- 1 large onion, quartered
- 2 jalapeno peppers, halved and seeded
- 4 garlic cloves, peeled
- 4 cups water
- 1 cup reduced-sodium chicken broth
- 1 whole garlic bulb, loose paper removed, cut in half
- 5 whole cloves
- 2 bay leaves
- 2 boneless skinless chicken breast halves (6 ounces *each*)
- 1 pound uncooked chorizo *or* bulk spicy pork sausage
- 2 cans (15 ounces *each*) hominy, rinsed and drained
- 3 teaspoons lime juice, *divided*
- 1 teaspoon dried oregano
- 1 teaspoon ground cumin
- 1/2 teaspoon salt, *divided*

SALSA:

- 1 cup minced fresh cilantro, *divided*
- 1 medium mango, peeled and cubed
- 1 medium ripe avocado, peeled and cubed
- 5 radishes, chopped

GARNISH:

- 6 cups tortilla chips

1. Place the tomatillos, onion, jalapenos and garlic cloves on a greased baking sheet. Bake at 425° for 25-30 minutes or until tomatillos are tender. Cool slightly. Transfer to a food processor; cover and process until blended.

2. In a Dutch oven, bring water, broth, garlic bulb, cloves and bay leaves to a boil. Reduce heat; add the chicken breasts and poach, uncovered, for 15-20 minutes or until no longer pink.

3. Remove chicken from broth and shred. Strain broth, discarding seasonings. Crumble chorizo into Dutch oven; cook over medium heat for 6-8 minutes or until fully cooked. Drain. Return broth to Dutch oven. Stir in the hominy, 2 teaspoons lime juice, oregano, cumin, 1/4 teaspoon salt, tomatillo mixture and shredded chicken; heat through. Stir in the 1/2 cup cilantro.

4. For salsa, in a small bowl, combine mango, avocado, radishes and remaining cilantro, lime juice and salt. Serve with soup. Garnish with chips.

Editor's Note: Wear disposable gloves when cutting hot peppers; the oils can burn skin. Avoid touching your face.

WHAT IS POSOLE?

Posole (also spelled Pozole) is a hearty Mexican soup. It usually features pork or chicken, chilies, hominy, onion and garlic. The soup is popular in New Mexico and Texas.

—*Taste of Home Cooking Experts*

CHICKEN CHORIZO POSOLE

"Oh, wow! This is the best posole I have ever had in my life. It was so good. My husband and I took homemade flour tortillas and put the posole, mango salsa and crushed tortilla chips in them and ate it that way...it was delicious. I can't even describe how wonderful the flavors are in this recipe."

—*Meigan31*

[2006]

CLASSIC HAM AND BEAN SOUP

yield: 15 servings (3-3/4 quarts)
prep: 30 min. + soaking ✄ **cook: 1-3/4 hours**

I learned to make this soup when we lived in Pennsylvania near several Amish families. It's a great way to use up ham and mashed potatoes. It freezes well, too.

—*Amanda Reed, Milford, Delaware*

- 1 **pound dried navy beans**
- 2 **medium onions, chopped**
- 2 **teaspoons canola oil**
- 2 **celery ribs, chopped**
- 10 **cups water**
- 4 **cups cubed fully cooked ham**
- 1 **cup mashed potatoes (without added milk and butter)**
- 1/2 **cup shredded carrot**
- 2 **tablespoons Worcestershire sauce**
- 1 **teaspoon salt**
- 1/2 **teaspoon dried thyme**
- 1/2 **teaspoon pepper**
- 2 **bay leaves**
- 1 **meaty ham bone** *or* **2 smoked ham hocks**
- 1/4 **cup minced fresh parsley**

---

1. Place beans in a Dutch oven; add water to cover by 2 in. Bring to a boil; boil for 2 minutes. Remove from the heat; cover and let stand for 1 to 4 hours or until beans are softened. Drain and rinse beans, discarding liquid.

2. In the same pan, saute onions in oil for 2 minutes. Add the celery; cook until tender. Stir in the beans, water, ham, potatoes, carrot, Worcestershire sauce, salt, thyme, pepper and bay leaves. Add ham bone. Bring to a boil. Reduce heat; cover and simmer for 1-1/4 to 1-1/2 hours or until beans are tender.

3. Discard bay leaves. Remove ham bone; and set aside until cool enough to handle. Remove ham from bone and cut into cubes. Discard bone. Return ham to soup; heat through. Garnish soup with parsley.

[2001]

FRENCH ONION SOUP

yield: 8 servings (2 quarts)
prep: 30 min. ✄ **cook: 30 min.**

I like to stir up steaming bowlfuls of this all-time favorite. Not only is this version a bit lighter than traditional French onion soup, but it has a slightly sweet flavor that makes it unique.

—*Lise Thomson*
Magrath, Alberta, Field Editor

- 6 **cups thinly sliced onions**
- 1 **tablespoon sugar**
- 1/2 **teaspoon pepper**
- 1/3 **cup canola oil**
- 6 **cups beef broth**
- 8 **slices French bread (3/4 inch thick), toasted**
- 1/2 **cup shredded Parmesan** *or* **Swiss cheese**

---

1. In a Dutch oven, saute onions, sugar and pepper in oil until the onions are softened. Reduce heat to medium-low; cook for 30 minutes or until onions are a deep golden brown, stirring occasionally. Add the broth; bring to a boil. Reduce heat; cover and simmer for 30 minutes.

2. Ladle the soup into ovenproof bowls. Top each with a slice of French bread; sprinkle with the cheese. Broil 4-6 in. from heat until the cheese is melted. Serve immediately.

[1996]

CHEESEBURGER SOUP

yield: 8 servings (2-1/4 quarts)
prep: 45 min. ∽ **cook: 10 min.**

A local restaurant serves a similar soup but wouldn't share their recipe with me. So I created my own, modifying a recipe I had for potato soup. I was so pleased with how good this "all-American" soup turned out.

—*Joanie Shawhan, Madison, Wisconsin*

- 1/2 pound ground beef
- 3/4 cup chopped onion
- 3/4 cup shredded carrots
- 3/4 cup diced celery
- 1 teaspoon dried basil
- 1 teaspoon dried parsley flakes
- 4 tablespoons butter, *divided*
- 3 cups chicken broth
- 4 cups diced peeled potatoes (1-3/4 pounds)
- 1/4 cup all-purpose flour
- 2 cups (8 ounces) process cheese (Velveeta), cubed
- 1-1/2 cups milk
- 3/4 teaspoon salt
- 1/4 to 1/2 teaspoon pepper
- 1/4 cup sour cream

1. In a 3-qt. saucepan, brown the beef; drain and set aside. In same saucepan, saute the onion, carrots, celery, basil and parsley in 1 tablespoon butter until vegetables are tender, about 10 minutes. Add the broth, potatoes and beef; bring to a boil. Reduce heat; cover and simmer for 10-12 minutes or until potatoes are tender.

2. Meanwhile, in a small skillet, melt the remaining butter. Add the flour; cook and stir for 3-5 minutes or until bubbly. Add to the soup; bring to a boil. Cook and stir for 2 minutes. Reduce heat to low. Stir in the cheese, milk, salt and pepper; cook and stir until the cheese is melted. Remove from the heat; blend in sour cream.

[2004]

CREAMY RED PEPPER SOUP

yield: 12 servings (3 quarts)
prep: 15 min. ∽ **cook: 30 min. + cooling**

Everyone loves this soup's taste, but no one guesses that pears are the secret ingredient.

—*Connie Summers, Augusta, Michigan*

- 2 large onions, chopped
- 1/4 cup butter, cubed
- 4 garlic cloves, minced
- 2 large potatoes, peeled and diced
- 2 jars (7 ounces *each*) roasted red peppers, drained, patted dry and chopped
- 5 cups chicken broth
- 2 cans (15 ounces *each*) pears in juice
- 1/8 teaspoon cayenne pepper
- 1/8 teaspoon black pepper

1. In a Dutch oven, saute onions in butter until tender. Add garlic; cook 1 minute longer. Add the potatoes, red peppers and broth. Bring to a boil. Reduce heat; cover and simmer for 15-20 minutes or until vegetables are tender. Remove from the heat. Add pears; let cool.

2. In a blender, cover and puree pear mixture in batches. Return to the pan. Stir in cayenne and black pepper. Cook until heated through.

BLENDING HOT LIQUID

Always let hot liquids cool slightly before processing in a blender. If the liquid is too hot when processing, steam could build, forcing the top to pop off and allowing the hot liquid to splash.

—*Taste of Home Cooking Expert*

CREAMY RED PEPPER SOUP

"This is a fabulous recipe, and has become a Christmas tradition for our family. Bursting with good wholesome flavor. The pears balance out the onion and garlic nicely."

—*msege*

WHITE BEAN CHICKEN CHILI

yield: 6 servings ∾ **prep: 35 min.**
cook: 3 hours

(Pictured on page 874)

My sister shared this chili recipe with me. I usually double it and add one extra can of beans, then serve with cheddar biscuits or warmed tortillas. The jalapeno adds just enough heat to notice but not too much for my children.

—*Kristine Bowles, Rio Rancho, New Mexico*

3/4 **pound boneless skinless chicken breasts, cubed**
1/2 **teaspoon salt**
1/4 **teaspoon pepper**
1 **medium onion, chopped**
1 **jalapeno pepper, seeded and chopped**
2 **teaspoons dried oregano**
1 **teaspoon ground cumin**
2 **tablespoons olive oil**
4 **garlic cloves, minced**
2 **cans (15 ounces *each*) white kidney *or* cannellini beans, rinsed and drained, *divided***
3 **cups chicken broth, *divided***
1-1/2 **cups (6 ounces) shredded cheddar cheese**
Sour cream and minced fresh cilantro, optional

1. Sprinkle chicken with salt and pepper. In a large skillet over medium heat, cook chicken, onion, jalapeno, oregano and cumin in oil for 3-4 minutes or until chicken is browned and vegetables are crisp-tender. Add the garlic; cook 1 minute longer.

2. Transfer to a 3-qt. slow cooker. In a small bowl, mash 1 cup of beans; add 1/2 cup broth and stir until blended. Add to the slow cooker with remaining beans and broth. Cover and cook on low for 3 to 3-1/2 hours or until chili is heated through.

3. Stir chili before serving. Sprinkle with cheese. Garnish with sour cream and cilantro if desired.

Editor's Note: Wear disposable gloves when cutting hot peppers; the oils can burn skin. Avoid touching your face.

CHEESY CORN CHOWDER

yield: 15 servings (3-3/4 quarts)
prep: 30 min. ∾ **cook: 30 min.**

I've had this chowder recipe for over 30 years, and the whole family really enjoys its cheesy corn taste. It makes a big pot.

—*Lola Comer, Marysville, Washington*

6 **bacon strips, chopped**
3/4 **cup chopped sweet onion**
2-1/2 **cups water**
2-1/2 **cups cubed peeled potatoes**
2 **cups sliced fresh carrots**
2 **teaspoons chicken bouillon granules**
3 **cans (11 ounces *each*) gold and white corn, drained**
1/2 **teaspoon pepper**
7 **tablespoons all-purpose flour**
5 **cups 2% milk**
3 **cups (12 ounces) shredded cheddar cheese**
1 **cup cubed process cheese (Velveeta)**

1. In a Dutch oven, cook the bacon and onion over medium heat until onion is tender. Add water, potatoes, carrots and bouillon; bring to a boil. Reduce heat; cover and simmer for 15-20 minutes or until potatoes are tender.

2. Stir in corn and pepper. In a large bowl, whisk the flour and milk until smooth; add to the soup. Bring to a boil; cook and stir for 2 minutes or until thickened. Reduce heat. Add the cheeses; cook and stir until melted.

WHITE BEAN CHICKEN CHILI

❝This was very good. It was devoured by our fellowship.❞
—*mother of 3*

[1995]

SAVORY CHEESE SOUP

yield: 4 servings ∾ **prep/total time: 25 min.**

This delicious soup recipe was shared by a friend and instantly became a hit with my husband. Its big cheese flavor blends wonderfully with the flavor of the vegetables. I first served this creamy soup as part of a holiday meal, but now we enjoy it throughout the year.

—*Dee Falk*
Stromsburg, Nebraska, Field Editor

- 1/4 cup chopped onion
- 3 tablespoons butter
- 1/4 cup all-purpose flour
- 1/4 teaspoon salt
- 1/8 teaspoon garlic powder
- 1/8 teaspoon pepper
- 2 cups 2% milk
- 1 can (14-1/2 ounces) chicken *or* vegetable broth
- 1/2 cup shredded carrot
- 1/2 cup finely chopped celery
- 1-1/2 cups (6 ounces) shredded cheddar cheese
- 3/4 cup shredded part-skim mozzarella cheese
- Minced chives, optional

1. In a large saucepan, saute the onion in butter until tender. Add the flour, salt, garlic powder and pepper; stir until smooth. Gradually add milk; cook and stir over medium heat until thickened and bubbly.

2. Meanwhile, in a small saucepan, bring broth to a boil. Add carrot and celery; simmer for 5 minutes or until vegetables are tender. Add to milk mixture and stir until blended. Add cheeses. Cook and stir until melted (do not boil). Garnish with chives if desired.

[2010]

GOLDEN CLAM CHOWDER

yield: 7 servings ∾ **prep: 20 min.**
cook: 20 min.

Comfort food at its best! Yes, you can have a warm, homemade bowl of clam chowder for dinner tonight. This soup is expertly seasoned, and the thyme adds a great dimension of flavor.

—*Amanda Bowyer, Caldwell, Idaho*

- 2 celery ribs
- 2 medium carrots
- 1 medium onion
- 2 teaspoons olive oil
- 4 garlic cloves, minced
- 4 medium potatoes, peeled and diced
- 2 cans (6-1/2 ounces *each*) minced clams, undrained
- 1 bottle (8 ounces) clam juice
- 1 cup plus 1 tablespoon water, *divided*
- 1 teaspoon dried thyme
- 1/2 teaspoon salt
- 1/2 teaspoon pepper
- 1 can (12 ounces) evaporated milk
- 2 teaspoons cornstarch
- 2 bacon strips, cooked and crumbled

1. Finely chop the celery, carrots and onion. In a Dutch oven, saute the vegetables in oil until tender. Add the garlic; cook 1 minute longer. Stir in the potatoes, clams, clam juice, 1 cup water, thyme, salt and pepper. Bring to a boil. Reduce the heat; cover and simmer for 12-15 minutes or until the potatoes are tender.

2. Gradually stir in milk; heat through. Combine cornstarch and remaining water until smooth; stir into chowder. Bring to a boil; cook and stir for 2 minutes or until chowder is thickened. Stir in bacon.

SAVORY CHEESE SOUP

"This recipe was extremely successful! Took just about 25 minutes from start to finish as described. It has a delicate and very cheesy flavor. It got rave reviews at my dinner table, and I was asked to keep this one on top of my recipe pile! Would not change a thing. LOVE, LOVE, LOVE. If you are looking for something delicate, cheesy and that you will want to have bowl after bowl of, this is the recipe for you! I was sad to see the bottom of my soup bowl, so I even licked the pot that I cooked it in as well."
—*catmom2011*

Taste of Home *Best Loved Recipes*